Goldmine

Price Guide to
Rock 'n' Roll
Memorabilia

Mark Allen Baker

Published by

700 E. State Street • Iola, WI 54990-0001
Telephone: 715/445-2214

Please call or write for our free catalog of music publications.
Our toll-free number to place an order or obtain a free catalog is 800-258-0929
or please use our regular business telephone 715-445-2214
for editorial comment and further information.

Library of Congress Catalog Number: 97-073040
ISBN: 0-87341-490-X
Printed in the United States of America

ROCK & ROLL MEMORABILIA

ACKNOWLEDGMENTS

First and foremost I would like to thank everyone at Krause Publications for their continued confidence in my work, especially Deborah Faupel, Melissa Warden, Amy Tincher-Durik, Patsy Morrison, Greg Loescher, Pat Klug, Bob Lemke, and the entire staff of *Goldmine* for giving me a chance to sneak into their world, which I found fascinating.

To all the collectors I have had a chance to meet and work with, especially Thomas Grosh from *Very English and Rolling Stone*, Douglas Leftwitch, Hank Thompson, Keystone Record Collectors, and Curt Reichwein. Also thanks to Creative Image Photography and Dr. Dennis Hickey.

To all the numerous companies and their representatives who provided everything from survey data to publicity photographs, I extend my sincerest appreciation. Special thanks to Arista Records, Jive Records, Hollywood Records, Warner Brothers Records Inc., Reprise Records, Giant/Revolution Records, Virgin Records (especially David Blinn), Mercury Records, Capitol Records, Polydor / Atlas Records, MCA Records, Sony Music - Columbia Records, American Recordings Inc. (Stacy Lew), Epic Records, The Rosebud Agency (Eric Hanson), Perri, T-Bird, OTTO, Fender, Dunlop, Ernie Ball, Christie's, Sotheby's, Startifacts, Executive Collectibles Gallery, Inc., Butterfield & Butterfield, and Phillips Son & Neale.

To the Hard Rock Cafe, especially the staff in the "Conch Republic." Thank you for your hospitality!

From 1975-1979 I was given the chance to work on more than forty concert productions in Upstate New York with some terrific people, from Queen, Genesis, Billy Joel, Bob Seger, and Peter Gabriel, to Hot Tuna, the Outlaws, Charlie Daniels, and Art Garfunkel. A tremendous amount of memories flooded back while doing this book and I even managed to sneak a few pictures from the past into the pages.

To my best friend Jim "Bloody" Bird, way down yonder in Charlotte, who skipped an occasional class with me to go up to Syracuse University and rummage through record bins. Your car stereo legacy precedes you, and if I lose my hearing before you do "Blood," I'm going to blame it on you and Eddie Van Halen.

To my Parents, Mr. and Mrs. Ford W. Baker, and especially my dad, who coined the phrase "Turn that goddamn music down!"

To my sister Tracey, who spent months working on a very useful database for this book, my heartfelt appreciation, although I'm still mad you cashed the check.

To my brother Jeff Baker, "a real Elvis fan," and my brother Matt, "a real R.E.M. fan." I miss you both dearly!

To Aaron A. Baker, my son, a Nirvana fan (It's payback time! Grandpa told me this would happen) and forever my best buddy!

To Elizabeth M. Baker, "Sweetness," an R.E.M. fan and forever my best pal!

To Rebecca J. Baker, "RJ," a Danny Elfman fan - "What's this?" - I love you with my whole heart!

To Alison M. Long, who I am a fan of, I love you!

DEDICATION

To Tracey Elizabeth Baker Rachid
My sister, who in recent years has shown me just how special it is to be a big brother!
I Love You Sis!

In memory of Robert and Hazel Baker

1

INTRODUCTION TO COLLECTING ROCK 'N' ROLL MEMORABILIA

Rock 'n' roll is an extension of music, which has been defined as any rhythmic sequence of pleasing sound. Time has proven, however, that the word "pleasing" is far too subjective to take seriously. Music is a volatile form of art and communication and, as such, is often expressive of its time.

Rock 'n' roll is a label we have placed on popular music for decades. It is a designation we have subdivided, redivided, restricted, and expanded where necessary (although no one can ever agree which bands belong in which category). From "Tacky Glitter," "Quality Glitter," "Pub Rock" and "Disco," to "New Wave," "Punk," "Funk" and "New Age"—the more types of music we found, the more we were compelled to add labels. In retrospect, music just evolved faster than we did.

Some would claim that music is the most vital and unpredictable force in our culture. Tough to dispute, as music has often seemed boundless in its keen ability to capture our emotions despite our particular stage of life. It is crafted by artisans, some of whom we understand, some whom we can hardly stand, and others who can barely stand at all. Typically, in its most radical form it has been rebellious in spirit and youthful in presentation. More times than not it has been a product of its time, cherished for its ability to send us deep into the past with just a few simple notes.

Reminders of "the good times" are welcome in our lives, and we often save such artifacts as old prom photographs, nostalgic 45 rpm singles, concert ticket stubs, or programs. Their preservation is always dedicated to keeping a memory and seldom, if ever, to realizing a profit. But like baseball cards, postcards, coins, and postage stamps, they have taken on more than an intrinsic value over the years. Many of these artifacts have proved to be very valuable.

Granted, while you were sitting at a table in the Las Vegas Hilton ordering dinner from your Elvis Presley souvenir menu, you probably had little thought of the item as a collectible. Had you had Elvis sign that menu and saved it until now, it might fetch about $500.

This book is about the type of nonrecorded memorabilia associated with rock 'n' roll (you know—the stuff you threw out that came with your Rolling Stones album). This book won't make you rich, but it might invoke a few good memories or even save you a few bucks along the way. You might even find yourself going through your old high school scrapbook asking yourself, "Why in the world did I glue these concert programs into this thing?" When you were young you bought baseball cards for the gum and threw away the cards; when you went to a concert, you bought a ticket to attend the show, not to save the stub.

In 1981 the famous auction house Sotheby's of London held the first auction of rock 'n' roll collect-

Non-recorded rock 'n' roll memorabilia is getting increased exposure at area record shows.

♪ 7

Paper-based products are increasingly gaining interest.

From magazine covers to ticket proofs, you never know what you may find at a local record show.

ibles. The sale legitimized the market for these forms of relics. As time has passed more and more collectors have entered the market, some for profit, others simply for fun. Less than two decades old, much of the material in demand has still not found its way to market, and even a greater amount hasn't even been documented. Like any market in this state, confusion abounds as new, uneducated collectors chase both trash and treasure with little knowledge as to which is which.

Collectors often purchase an item when they are seeing it for the very first time and have very little regard for the item's markings, characteristics, or provenance. This is a common characteristic of a hungry market and it won't dissipate until both the buyer and ethical seller become better educated. Until that time: "Caveat emptor"—"Let the buyer beware!"

USING THIS BOOK

This is not the first book on rock 'n' roll memorabilia, and certainly not the last, but hopefully it will make many of you "face the music." Education is the key: Read everything you possibly can about this market and your subject. For example, if you are going to collect Led Zeppelin memorabilia, start by purchasing the following books (in no particular order): *A Visual Documentary* by Paul Kendall, *Hammer of the Gods* by Stephen Davis, *A Celebration* and *The Complete Guide to the Music of Led Zeppelin* by David Lewis, *Led Zeppelin* by William Ruhlmann, *Led Zeppelin - Definitive Biography* by Ritchie York, *Led Zeppelin* by Chris Welch, all of Robert Godwin's Zeppelin Guides, and *The Complete Guide to Led Zeppelin Tour Programs* by Alain Blais. This is by no means a complete resource listing, but it will certainly get you started. By the way, rock 'n' roll books are also collectible!

If you collect rock 'n' roll memorabilia of a particular form rather than group-specific or musician-specific items, find resources on your subject. For example, if you want to start collecting "Family Dog" or "Bill Graham Presents" posters, begin by purchasing the following books: *The Collector's Guide to Psychedelic Rock Concert Posters, Postcards and Handbills* by Eric King and *The Art of Rock - Posters from Presley to Punk* by Paul D. Grushkin, followed by *The Official Identification and Price Guide to Rock and Roll* by David K. Henkel and *The 1996 Rock Poster Price Guide* by Fred Williams. All are superb resources and useful in different ways.

Although this book covers many subjects and references many items, it is far from complete. Its goal is to provide an initial resource for collecting nonrecorded rock 'n' roll memorabilia. Remember, it is a guide—a source for basic instruction. If the information you are looking for is not in this book, hopefully this book will lead you to it. Entire books have been written on very specific subjects, catering to limited yet important niches of the market.

Rather than showing you specific examples, such as the difference between an authentic FD-14 (Family Dog) poster and a pirated variation, or a reprinted Beatles program versus an original, I would rather train you about printing technology and the various anomalies associated with the task. Hopefully this global perspective will better lend itself to your overall collecting needs.

Where I have had the opportunity to cover new ground, I have tried to do so. Hopefully it meets your satisfaction. Should you feel that I have (or have not) done so, your comments are certainly welcome and appreciated. You may contact me through the publisher. If I forgot to list a book, your Ramones shoehorn, or your Billy Fury comb, my sincerest apologies. Hopefully future editions will be able to fill the gaps that I have left.

In Section II, the "Rock 'n' Roll Directory," I chose to use the format shown below because I felt it would best suit collectors' needs. For the bands listed (obviously I couldn't include everybody) I gave a brief career overview—in some cases very brief. Some entries may contain additional charts or information that I felt might be particularly useful. Naturally, I have tried to focus on highly collected artists or those who are currently of particular interest. In some areas, such as Beatles buttons, I made no attempt to differentiate between styles, choosing instead to give a price range. Although distinguishing specific items is indeed important, there are other resources available that are far more comprehensive, and supplying such detailed information was not the mission for this book. I have tried to price items appropriately, and in some cases where no accurate price could be given, I felt mentioning the item would at least be beneficial.

AUTOGRAPHS

Not all artists' autographing habits are known, therefore greater research in this area needs to be done. Since authentication of a signature is highly subjective, I have tried to include samples where I have felt they would be useful.

Group:
A CD, LP, magazine cover, ad, photo, or card signed by the artist or group

Individual:
A list of individual band members' signatures

A value range is provided here, the low end reflecting a simple signature(s) on a card, while the high end would be for an item such as an album. Some unique or commonly offered items may also be listed here or in other chapters. In many cases the values are line-up dependent (for example, a Jimi Hendrix signature on an Isley Brothers album would no doubt add tremendous value to the item).

This is an extremely popular area of collecting, requiring a specific knowledge base and a significant commitment by collectors to educate themselves. Forgeries are common and authentic signature samples for comparison are difficult to find.

Author's Comment: Undervalued for vintage performers, overvalued for current stars. Bring your wallet!

TOUR BOOKS/PROGRAMS/PASSES

Tour Programs:
Some knowledge of printing and reproduction will be helpful in this area. Not all artists produce programs, while many overproduce. Print runs are often speculative, causing some concern for collectors, but in general this area is typically overlooked with the exception of vintage items. You may run across some authorized reproductions, reprints, or counterfeits, but in general it is a good starting point for beginning collectors.

Author's Comment: Undervalued, resource poor, and of moderate interest!

Tour programs may be the most undervalued and overlooked segment of the hobby.

An overlooked treasure or a market rip-off, backstage passes can often take center stage at local shows.

Backstage Passes:

Some knowledge of current printing technology is needed, as counterfeits abound, especially laminates! Numerous industry rumors exist regarding manufacturers selling overruns. On the other hand, it could be a highly overlooked area.

Author's Comment: Bring a magnifying glass with you when you buy! Caveat Emptor!

POSTERS/PRESS KITS

Promotional Posters:

Some dealers are now specializing in this form; however, collectors have concerns about production runs. Unlike concert posters, there is minimal counterfeiting risk. As a collector you can anticipate dramatic price variations.

Author's Comment: Undervalued, resource poor, and of moderate interest!

Press Kits:

There are now dealers specializing in this often overlooked form of rock 'n' roll memorabilia. One major deterrent to collecting this form is that press kits can be easily reproduced. Many photographs that are typically included inside these kits have been reproduced and can be found on the market.

Author's Comment: Roll the dice!

USED CLOTHING/EQUIPMENT

Guitar Picks:

Commanding interest with many new collectors; however, authentication is the key. Since they are produced for pennies, sold to customers for nickels, yet may command dollars in an aftermarket, you better watch your step!

Author's Comment: Fun to collect, easy to store, beats a lock of hair!

Drum Sticks:

Some interest, but difficult to authenticate. Picks command a greater interest!

Author's Comment: Don't get caught on the short end....

More and more record companies are moving to special packaging, which often includes non-recorded memorabilia.

OFTEN OVERLOOKED MEMORABILIA

The buck often stops here in this market. Value is based on condition and all items must include original packaging. While I prefer to collect authorized promotional items only, I am far from the majority. What most chose to collect are items that are licensed by the performer or an affiliated source. Videotapes of key performances, such as an appearance on the *Ed Sullivan Show,* are now commanding greater interest by collectors. Don't forget about the memorabilia generated from these appearances—items such as tickets, handbills, and programs. Paper-based memorabilia such as fanzines, newsletters, counter displays, album flats, and personality posters, has also enjoyed significant interest and substantial appreciation.

Many collectors are artist specific, rather than era conscious. Some bands, such as the Beatles, Led Zeppelin, and the Rolling Stones, will require specific reference guides.

Author's Comment: Uncharted water in many areas, bring your wallet!

Tell the tour driver to save his shirts and jackets, which now command top dollar at local shows.

REFERENCES/BOOKS

A very overlooked area in my opinion, with some titles becoming extremely difficult to find. Don't overlook used bookstores, flea markets, garage sales, and so on for many titles.

Author's Comment: If you're going to collect memorabilia there will never be enough!

Some areas I initially planned to cover, such as tickets and concert specific posters, I traded off in favor of hotter item such as presentation discs and awards, and auction related items. Hopefully in future editions I can touch on these developing areas.

Lot Percentage of Rock 'n' Roll Groups Represented in Major Auctions over the Past Decade

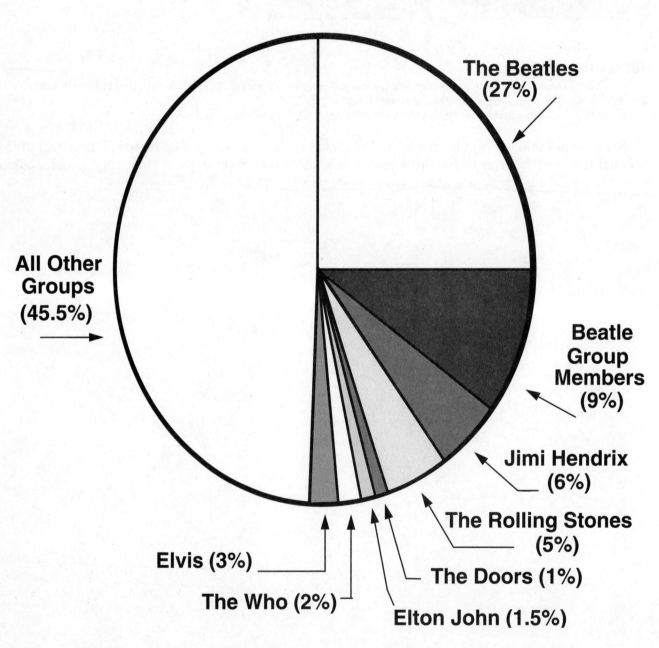

The Beatles (27%)

All Other Groups (45.5%)

Beatle Group Members (9%)

Jimi Hendrix (6%)

The Rolling Stones (5%)

The Doors (1%)

Elton John (1.5%)

Elvis (3%)

The Who (2%)

Source: Author data base - sold lots only!

2

REPRODUCTIONS, COUNTERFEITS, REPRINTS AND FORGERIES

Having collected just about everything imaginable, from postage stamps to sports trading cards, I can say that one thing is certain: "If an object is worth money, it will be counterfeited."

Much publicity has centered around the illegal production of recorded rock 'n' roll memorabilia, but to my knowledge little attention has been given to the counterfeiting of nonrecorded artifacts like tickets (post-show), backstage passes, programs, autographs, and posters. Upon detailed examination, I can honestly state that I encountered more fraudulent rock 'n' roll memorabilia than any other type of memorabilia I have ever collected. In comparison to other markets, including sports memorabilia, the fraud exceeded my wildest imagination.

If this statement scares you, it should! Whether I was walking around a local show or visiting a music shop in another town, it wasn't tough to find counterfeit memorabilia. From guitar picks to passes, from buttons to tour books, nearly every form has been attacked by unethical individuals. Not only the collectors are unaware of this phenomenon; so are many of the dealers.

Education is the best way to be less susceptible to counterfeiters. The most logical place to begin is with printing technology, which affects almost every form of nonrecorded rock 'n' roll memorabilia. The more you know and understand, the better chance you have of unmasking a counterfeit artifact. To say that it could save you hundreds of dollars could be an understatement!

Most of the information provided below deals with paper-based printing, as this is currently where the majority of the problems exist. Counterfeit backstage passes and concert posters have reached epidemic proportions, followed by programs, handbills, mailers/postcards, tickets, and some press kit items. Although other types of unauthorized and nonlicensed merchandise exist, such as toys and souvenirs, they aren't nearly as rampant as paper-based items.

PRINTING TECHNOLOGY

UNDERSTANDING BLACK & WHITE HALFTONE REPRODUCTION

Knowledge about density values, halftone screens, and laser scanning can help you determine an item's authenticity. Paper-based rock 'n' roll memorabilia often includes the reproduction of photographs, either full (four) color or black and white. Before the advent of the sophisticated four-color process (cyan, magenta, yellow, and black inks) and color separations was black and white photographic reproduction—often referred to as halftone reproduction. Halftone reproduction requires an understanding of photography, inks, paper, the printing process, and even chemistry.

A halftone reproduction is made of small, controlled dots appearing in a predesignated grid pattern. Using simple magnification you will notice these dots on any printed photograph, but the human eye translates them into a smooth image. Controlling the dot patterns and their characteristics (spacing, size, etc.) is the key to

15

fine halftone reproduction with good contrast between the different shades of gray that make up the photograph. Small dots spaced further apart are characteristic of highlights, while shadowed areas are made up of larger dots that are so dense that they overlap.

THE ORIGINAL

Often an original paper-based piece of rock 'n' roll memorabilia, such as a poster or a program, includes a photograph. Typically this photograph is of good quality, which means its contrast strength offers excellent details, textures, depth, and so on.

When counterfeiting an item that includes a photograph, it is difficult to reproduce the wide spectrum of contrast in the original. Sophisticated methods can compensate on one end of the scale (such as a dark areas) but this will invariably mean a sacrifice on the other end. Comparing the densities of shadow areas and highlight areas between an original and an unknown example can help determine a counterfeit.

Tonal variations are very important to the reproduction process. A device called a densitometer is often used by printers, color separators, and forgers to measure the optical density or tonal values of photographs. Typically these values are on a scale of 0.0 (pure white) to 2.0 (solid black) in .5 increments. The more increments, the greater the degree of accuracy. Monitoring these readings throughout the printing process, which includes a variety of mediums, can insure the finest possible reproduction.

THE HALFTONE SCREEN

Halftones can be produced through the aid of halftone screens. Often they are made of a material such as mylar, but glass is also used. Many of these screens come in direct contact with the film or negative paper. The screen, which contains a grid of vignetted dots at predetermined amounts, is measured in dots to the inch. The term "100 line halftone" simply means 100 dots to the inch (measured at a 45 degree angle).

So if your Rolling Stone poster has a coarse "65 line halftone" in the center, but the known original poster contains a "120 line halftone" photograph, guess what? It's time to return your poster for that money back guarantee you always see advertised. You may think that you wouldn't be able to tell the difference, but a significant line variation is easy to see with the human eye (the eye can recognize a dot pattern at 120-133 lines or less). Using the above example, the dark shaded areas on Mick Jagger's hat would be gray in the counterfeit, while in the original they would be nearly black. This is an area where considerable counterfeiters make mistakes.

SHAPE OF DOTS

The dots I have been mentioning also come in various shapes. These shapes typically vary by the type of printing press being used to put the ink on the material. Examining the dot formation of the item you are trying to authenticate may uncover a variance against a known original, therefore making the item questionable.

THREE COMMON DOT SHAPES

Dot	Type of Printing Press	Benefit
Round	High-speed, web offset printing	Extends midtones, minimizes dot gain
Square	Letterpresses, sheet-fed and web-fed offset	Most popular, flexible
Elliptical*	Various	Offers smooth gradation of midtones

*Also referred to as chain dots, good for portraits.

LINE SCREENS

The line screen used to print your Beatles program was primarily determined by two factors: the paper and the type of printing press used to produce the item. Cheap paper-based items are often on rough, uncoated paper stock such as newsprint. This stock is typically very absorbent, causing the dot to spread and resulting in tremendous density variations. "Big dots" are referred to in the printing world as "dot gain." Smoother grades of paper, such as coated stock, have better "ink holdout." Simply stated, they reproduce the dot better.

The quality and characteristics of the paper are key factors in reproduction quality and they must be compared in determining the authenticity of an item. In addition to thickness, type, and color, the reflective characteristics of paper also aid in determining an original item. If a counterfeiter uses a different type of paper, contrast variations will be fairly obvious to the eye.

An item that contains varying degrees of halftones will impact the type of press that must be used in order to guarantee a quality end product. Many presses can easily counterfeit cheaper rock 'n' roll items using less than 120 line screens, but a more sophisticated device will be necessary for finer images. Larger screens and more sophisticated imagery offer greater challenges to the counterfeiter while producing more comparison points for the authenticator. Why do you think counterfeiters in this market opt for simply designed posters of minimal color, block letters, and cheap cardboard stock?

LASER SCANNING

Separate, or stand-alone, black-and-white scanners exist in the marketplace to fill the growing demand for laser scanned halftones. A high beam laser scans the image, bypassing the need for screens and their associated problems.

These units became fairly prevalent during the early 1980s when scanning technology was in its infancy. The need was enormous to have scanners as input units to a pagination typesetting station in order to create a complete electronic image (both type and halftones). The improved quality over conventional methods was immediately evident. The laser scanners could significantly increase the subdivisions in a halftone with much greater flexibility. Image control, such as enlarging or reducing a picture's axis (horizontally/vertically), could now be controlled independently. Additional controls included copy sharpening, background controls, and even special screen selections.

Understanding the difference between the conventional technology and laser scanning can help determine the authenticity of your paper-based piece of rock 'n' roll memorabilia. For example, I recently ran across a classic rock 'n' roll poster of Elvis Presley. Upon careful examination I could determine that the photograph used in the poster was a laser-created halftone rather than a conventional example. The latter would have been the only technology available at the time of the original printing of the poster.

Since laser scanners scan images line by line (raster by raster), they alleviate a common problem known as "flaring"—or the "halo" that occurs when a dark area is directly adjacent to a light area. The conventional copy camera will see a gray "halo" over the darker area that the laser will not.

Most counterfeiters will lean toward laser scanning because of the availability of the technology and its capabilities to mask some other problems, such as image sharpness. Developing a trained eye and complementing it with a strong understanding of additional areas will enable you to unmask many good counterfeits.

BASIC COLOR SEPARATION METHODS

Photographic color separation and electronic scanning both put images on four (cyan, magenta, yellow, and black) separation halftone negatives; however, the process differs for each method. Both systems offer a quality product, but the options available to users will depend upon their initial choice. Most of the counterfeits you will encounter will be electronic because that method can compensate for some flaws indicative of not possessing the original art.

Before counterfeiters take on projects they review the same considerations a legitimate user would face: cost (electronic is less expensive), quality, size (if an image such as a poster exceeds 20x28 inches, very few expensive scanners can handle it, so the choice will be conventional), surfaces, and multiple subjects (scanning is practical when more than one image exists on a page, such as is often the case with a tour program).

PHOTOGRAPHIC COLOR SEPARATION

In photographic color separation the operator converts the full-color art to four black-and-white films, each consisting of one-third of the color spectrum (plus black). The operator then converts these continuous-tone films to positive films that will be opposite in value and formed with hundreds of varying dots. Complicating this task is a series of "masks" which are used to arrive at the four halftone negatives used to make the printing plates. The operator carefully monitors the quality at each step of the procedure as to guarantee an accurate end result. This method contains many more variables, versus an electronic system, that can affect the end product.

The photographic color separation system has two primary methods: direct and indirect. Both methods, like that of the electronic system, have the same result—cyan, yellow, magenta, and black halftone negatives. The benefit of electronic scanning is that the computer does all the work instead of the operator.

ELECTRONIC COLOR SEPARATION

Considerable subjectivity exists in the photographic color separation method, but such is not the case with electronic scanning. The computer uses sophisticated programs to compensate accurately for any anticipated color or contrast problem with the artwork. Nearly every new scanner since 1980 has had the ability to directly expose halftone dots to a film without a screen. This has been accomplished primarily through laser technology.

Electronic scanners come in all shapes, sizes, and price ranges. Models capable of scanning a wider variety of originals and having more features naturally cost more. But like most new technologies, capabilities and features have increased over the years as price has decreased.

The input end of a scanner consists of variable-sized transparent plastic drums, by which the original is wrapped. The drums move around an exposing light source. Scan rates are determined by the degree to which the original artwork is enlarged. The operator uses a control panel at the front of the scanner to alter or set variables such as color corrections, enhancements, screen ruling, dot shape, and numerous other factors.

The output end of the device has another drum on which the final film is mounted. When the operator begins the procedure, the scanning light source penetrates the transparency or reflects from a reflective copy such as original artwork. The beams go through an optical system that separates it into the three primary color signals. It is then up to the computer to manipulate the data before converting the output signals to laser beams which are focused to the final film. When all four colors have been scanned and separated, the films are removed and developed just like any conventional film.

The advent of low-cost flatbed scanners has replaced some of the need for high-end drum scanners; however, all the anomalies of the printing process still remain.

ADDITIONAL EQUIPMENT

The entire printing process (like the one it has taken to make this book) involves many steps and many individuals. Although many are specialized in certain areas, all share the goal of producing the finest product possible. Technology has brought these individuals together by producing workstations that streamline the entire process. Combining the finest text available with superior illustrations in the quickest and most flexible environment possible has been the goal for everyone developing devices for this market.

Because many corporations have succeeded in attaining this goal, yesterday's technology has been slowly working itself down to a more personal and inexpensive market. What it took some computer-based workstations to do on microcomputers fifteen years ago can now be done on personal computers at home, more efficiently and with far less cost. While this transition serves the needs of the legitimate user, it also has increased the ease of forgery.

COLOR COPIERS

This leads us to the biggest nemesis you will face in this market, especially those of you who wish to collect backstage passes, handbills, tickets, and occasionally programs. Color copiers are not only becoming more cost-effective to own, but nearly every corner copy store has one that can make copies for under $1.00. "But what about the quality?" you ask. Guess what? It's good—really good. So good that in my opinion there are more counterfeit backstage passes in the market than real ones!

This is perhaps a tough statement to support, but unfortunately I think I can do just that, so give me an opportunity to prove my case.

Having produced over fifty major concerts in the late 1970s, I was smart enough to hold on to the original copies of contracts, passes, tickets, and programs. I also made it a point to have each act autograph a few items for me (in person) before the show. A quarter of a decade later, I'm happy that I took the time to do this—not only do I have numerous artifacts that have priceless memories attached to them, but I know without a doubt that they are authentic.

I spent the entire summer of 1996 traveling along the East Coast buying concert programs, tickets, backstage passes, books, music autographs, and any and all items I felt would be a benefit to this book. Some items that I purchased I knew were counterfeits, some I had a feeling that they might be, and some that I thought might be authentic proved to be bogus. When I initially started my hunt I was actually delighted that I could find some bogus items because I wanted to be able to compare them to actual known authentic pieces. Ironically, finding authentic items became the problem.

Many times when I was buying questionable pieces I was stunned that the dealer made no attempt to warn me, even though some knew that I was writing this book. These were not run-of-the-mill dealers, these were individuals who often ran full-page advertisements in periodicals dedicated to this field. This led me to believe that they, too, did not realize what they were selling. This hypothesis was supported in later research.

Rather than briefly touching on every form (handbills, programs, tickets, etc.), I have opted to tackle the most prominent problem: backstage passes. Many of the techniques I will reference here can be applied to other paper-based areas. While I realize there are counterfeit Rolling Stones programs, Beatles programs, Family Dog posters, and Bill Graham presents postcards, you are less likely to encounter them than a bogus backstage pass, and much of the information already provided here on printing should be able to assist you in unmasking these frauds.

BACKSTAGE PASSES

Backstage passes or "entertainment passes" evolved from professional sporting events. Boxing was the originator of the complex nature of such artifacts. The advent of the "rock star" necessitated a more diverse approach to "rock concerts," which were being conducted in large facilities like stadiums rather than in small halls or auditoriums. Originally intended for those directly connected with a music event—artist, promoter, crew, etc.—a single style of pass normally sufficed. In the mid-1970s this was often just a stock design (printed in various colors) in a simple format that allowed a promoter to label the pass with the date, event, and even name of the holder.

Passes come in every shape, design, and color imaginable. (Passes printed by OTTO) (OTTO is a registered trademark of OTTO Printing & Entertainment Graphics)

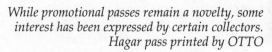

While promotional passes remain a novelty, some interest has been expressed by certain collectors. Hagar pass printed by OTTO

AUTHENTICATION MARKS FOR OTTO BACKSTAGE PASSES

Year	Comments
1982	The company used "OtTtO" logo with a large center "T" with rectangular border; "COLOR ON CLOTH" motto appears vertically next to logo. Address: 1127 Vine Street, Cincinnati, Ohio 45210; phone: 513-621-9779.
1983	Logo change to "OTTO" inside with elliptical border (1-5/16" x 8/16"); address appears inside border with phone number. "THE #1 ENTERTAINMENT PRINTER"; above border reads "PRINTED IN USA BY," below reads "DIVISION OF JACK OTTO & SONS INC."
1987	Numerous back changes including "SAY NO TO DRUGS" backing, also "Specialist In Total Tour Printing." "IMC OTTO US/OTTO UK" added below on some stock.
1988	Logo change to reverse type in "OTTO"; same format as before but new address: 200 CLARK STREET, DAYTON, KY 41074. The "#1" inside border reduced in size to match text. The phrase "DO NOT LITTER" alternates with "PRINTED IN THE U.S.A." at top. New wording between trademarks reads "The Finest in Tour Security, Promotional & Print Materials" as well as, "Do Not Apply to Leather, Suede, Velvet, Corduroy, Metal or Plastic." Fax number is added below border as "FAX: 606-291-7795."
1992	Shift in design, smaller "OTTO" logo moved to top (inside) of border and includes small ® to bottom right. The fax number moves inside design and "THE #1 ENTERTAINMENT PRINTER" moves outside design. New wording between trademarks reads "OTTO is a registered trademark of Otto Printing & Entertainment Graphics," "Artwork protected by copyrights laws. Criminal penalties for infringement." and "Do not apply to leather, Suede, Velvet, Corduroy, Metal, or Plastic." Also appearing is "The finest in tour & event pass security systems."
1996	Alternate design appears and replaces address, phone, and fax (inside border) with the following: "73611.251 @ compuserve.com" and "http://www.ottoprint.com." This new design alternates with logo above on pass backing.

An assortment of Prince tour used passes often given away to fans. (Printed by OTTO)

As acts grew in stature and popularity, their concerts became big events, especially while playing in large venues like stadiums. Size alone necessitated additional personnel that had to be accounted for both by the promoter and the performing act. To guarantee the security of an act while maximizing the publicity generated around the concert, access had to be regulated to various parts of the facility during different times. The answer was logical: Use a variety of passes to control such an event.

Since availability to such passes is normally restricted by the promoter or the act, chances of obtaining one for someone not directly involved in the event are slim, especially prior to the event. The function of a pass is to identify individuals, allow access for the person to perform his or her function, and to secure the facility. As the passes themselves have evolved based on these needs, they have become more elaborate in their production. Passes now come in all shapes, sizes, designs, formats, and colors, but are typically made from either fabric "stain" or paper-based, adhesive-backed stock.

FIVE REASONS WHY YOU WILL PURCHASE A COUNTERFEIT BACKSTAGE PASS

You will be unfamiliar with the format, style, design, and type of the particular pass you encounter.

You will be sold a story by the dealer selling the pass, who in many cases knows less about the pass than you do.

You will not pay attention to the detailed craftsmanship of the pass itself.

You will cost justify the purchase price, saying, "It's only ten bucks for a laminated Nirvana pass!" "Even if it's bogus, ten bucks isn't gonna kill me."

You just don't want to accept that the pass can be counterfeited at the level of quality you have found.

BACKSTAGE PASS BUYING CHECKLIST

[   ] The pass reflects the time period and the group it represents.
[   ] The printing quality makes even the finest detail readable. Images are crisp, not out of focus.
[   ] The back of the pass is correctly labeled with paper stock reflective of the pass manufacturer.
[   ] There are no irregularly cut edges on the pass or its backing.
[   ] There are no stray or unexplainable artifacts: solid lines that are only partially solid, misspelled words, lines around a design that do not register, text that is inconsistent in thickness, etc.
[   ] If the pass is laminated, the material used is very stiff, not flexible enough to bend 45 degrees or more on the top or bottom.
[   ] The hole at the top of the pass, if laminated, is punched cleanly with no stray pieces of laminate.

Passes used during the 1970s were typically printed on the front in one, or occasionally two, colors of ink on either a paper or a stain adhesive stock. Most were very simple in design and flexible in format, with space for event-specific data to be written in. The 1979 Kinks tour used a single-color pass on an adhesive-backed paper stock (tak tik), and was designed in a format flexible enough to be modified for specific dates.

Are passes easy to come by? If so, try finding one of these '70s relics.

Some artists still believe simple is better.

Many promoters during this era, including the Don Law Agency and Concerts East, also printed stock backstage passes in a variety of colors. These passes had a designated area on the front where the event's promoter could write in pertinent information. The backs were typically blank or covered by a repetitive stock manufacturer's pattern, such as "Fasson," "CRACK'N PEEL Plus," "FABRIC AD-HESIVE." Most backstage pass printers during this period used inexpensive over-the-counter stock that was also accessible to the public for uses such as the "Hello My Name is…" labels used at meetings and conferences. During an era that didn't have low-cost color printing services, this method was both practical and cost-effective.

Think of the money you can save with flexibly designed stage passes. (Passes printed by OTTO - Dylan unknown)

For certain highly visible and popular acts, a promoter with enough lead time would have custom passes printed, but they were similar in format to the stock passes. Authentic laminated passes ("laminates," used primarily for tour crew members) from this era are scarce. Laminates typically involved a more custom design, some even challenging forgers by including intricate patterns that could not be produced by low-cost copiers of the time.

Most of the counterfeit 1970s passes I have seen center around the superior designs and key acts of the era. One of the most popular counterfeits on the East Coast is the "KISS JAPAN TOUR 78" laminate. I purchased the same counterfeit at a show in Lancaster, Pennsylvania, and at a record shop in Tampa, Florida. A close examination of the front will immediately indicate to someone knowledgeable in printing technology that it was produced by a color printer not available during the period. Even more obvious is the backing, which includes an OTTO logo not used during the decade (see chart) and printing that was not halftoned (it was not made up of little dots).

 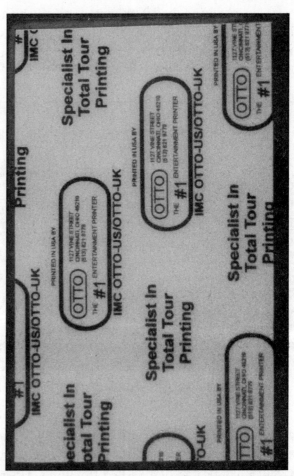

One of the most popular fake passes on the East Coast, with just two small problems: Both front and back were created on a color copier, with the counterfeiter even using the wrong Otto backing material! (OTTO is a registered trademark of OTTO Printing & Entertainment Graphics)

All counterfeiters make mistakes—it's up to you to find them. While some elements can be glaringly obvious, others can be more obscure. Exaggerated dot patterns, lack of detail, misregistration, wrong shape, wrong size, and wrong stock for front or back are all typical mistakes made by counterfeiters. A majority of the counterfeit passes you will encounter will have been printed from a color copier and are laminated. These are easily spotted, particularly if a halftone procedure was used as an original, as the copier is unable to reproduce the halftone dot pattern. For example, I purchased a counterfeit two-color (orange/black) U2 "Zoo TV Tour, aftershow" pass that was incredibly good, although the orange was a bit too red. This adjustment (color correcting) can be made on many color copiers and could fool 90% of perspective buyers. The deception

All laminated passes should be cautiously approached, as more are bad than good.

Easy to tell which one is real. Go ahead, here's your chance! (Original passes printed by OTTO)

was unmasked when I saw that the OTTO backing pattern was not made up of "little dots," but solid color instead.

During the 1980s and '90s backstage passes evolved into an art form, reflective of both their subject and their era. Some are viewed as classics, such as Metallica's "THE CAP'NS OF KRUNCH" and Queen's "the magic tour '86." There is also greater competition in the market, which now includes OTTO, Perri, T-Bird, and a few others. These outstanding manufacturers are showing greater interest in employing counterfeiting deterrents such as holograms, foil, and ultraviolet ink. In fact, if you're a new collector you might be better off concentrating on newer passes such as the "Jimmy Page and Robert Plant, WORLD TOUR 1995" passes, as their "All Area Access" passes employ numerous counterfeit deterrents including holograms and various screening and printing techniques.

Pass manufacturers have differing opinions as to whether their jobs are done once events are complete. When I told the representative of one pass manufacturer that I had run across numerous counterfeits of her company's products, and even sheets of its backing stock, she stated, "We are not interested in the post-event market for our passes." Yet after a lengthy conversation with two other manufacturers, they expressed an interest in exploring the aftermarket for their work.

Generally speaking, most passes (especially laminates) are not easily found. When I asked a representative from one pass manufacturer what his typical printing run was, he answered, "5,000 satins and 150

From paper passes to generic show passes, hologram laminates are the new rage in passes! (Rolling Stones pass printed by PERRI)

Nice laminate—too bad it's not real. Probably ran between $10-$20 for this fake created from color copier output!

laminates" (although there have always been stories about promoters running out of passes and having to photocopy originals). When I asked manufacturers if unclaimed passes, mistakes, printers proofs, and overruns were sold, the answer was often a vehement "never."

If you are going to collect backstage passes and want to do further research, I recommend Roger Pavey's article "Detecting BOGUS Backstage Passes," which appeared in the *Goldmine 1996 Annual.* As mentioned above, another invaluable resource would be to familiarize yourself with color reproduction and obtain various color copier output samples that you can use as reference material.

Will the real "Boss" please step forward—only one real pass here!

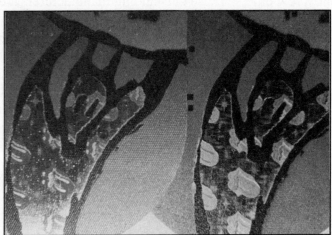

Yeah, but they'll never fake a hologram pass—says who? (Original pass printed by PERRI Entertainment Services, Inc.

Forget about tickets, they're easier to counterfeit than passes. Which one is real? (Original ticket printed by QUIK-TIK)

3
COLLECTING PERSONALLY OWNED ITEMS

CLOTHING

Entertainers are often associated with particular clothing items. If this chapter began with a picture of a black satin bustier trimmed in gold and featuring distinctive padded cups and tassels, it wouldn't take you long to associate the item with Madonna. The more distinctive the item (such as the spectacles worn by John Lennon or Buddy Holly) the more collectible it tends to be. Many items have come to represent certain performers and are designed (often by the world's finest designers) with them specifically in mind. Madonna often turns to Jean Paul Gaultier, one of Europe's most innovative and distinctive designers.

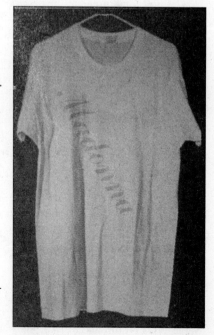

Rock stars have long been linked with flamboyant garments and distinctive attire, from the days of Little Richard and James Brown (whose fifties look was often referred to as "cutting edge") to the Seattle "grunge" look exhibited by groups such as Soundgarden and Nirvana. The logic behind the emphasis, or lack thereof, has always been clear: Music is a competitive market and a distinctive appearance will often have a memorable effect on your audience.

Pop stars can also be trendsetters; take the impact of the Beatles for instance. From their Pierre Cardin-inspired, round-necked, collarless jackets and Chelsea boots of 1963 to their psychedelic garments of the late '60s, their style was mimicked as it evolved. Such trendsetting clothes become desirable (and thus often costly) acquisitions.

Similar to game-worn sports uniforms, authenticity is a key concern. Many entertainers have their clothing specially tagged, making authentication considerably simpler; however, most do not do this. Often photographs are used as references, or accounts of individuals associated with the pop star. Sometimes the star who donates the item may include their own letter of authenticity. Whatever the situation may be, venturing into this area of collectibles requires some research.

Iggy Pop worn stage jacket, handsomely altered. Photo courtesy Executive Collectibles Gallery, Inc.

Like all collectibles, condition is also important. Alterations, stains, or noticeable damage to most items can drastically affect value unless the entertainer is associated with items in less than pristine condition. Modifications are also important to note, as tags can be removed and sewn into another item—a common forgery characteristic in sports uniforms. Sizes are also worth noting. A Madonna size 18 bustier should certainly be an indication that something's up: "The Material Girl" is not noted for using more material, but less.

Accessories are also worth noting. Jimi Hendrix typically adorned hats with scarves and jewelry, and if you collect an artist with a similar flair, looking through books, tour programs, newspaper clippings, videos, and so on will help you identify particular traits and hallmarks. Making notes of these anomalies can help you in your future purchases.

Provenance (the origin and source of the item) is particularly important. If a John Lennon robe was part of a collection sold by his former wife, Cynthia Lennon, then its provenance is far better than if it was found it in the trash at Apple Records by a friend of a friend's cousin. Items bearing no ostensible characteristics that automatically link it to the performer must bear a comprehensive provenance.

Many stars will autograph an item prior to donating it to a charity auction. Some artists, such as Stevie Nicks, Michael Jackson, and Madonna, are notorious for this practice, so

Madonna owned and worn T-shirt. Photo courtesy Executive Collectibles Gallery, Inc.

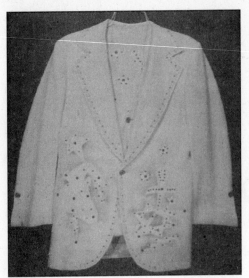
This Spinners worn jacket landed over $400. Photo courtesy Executive Collectibles Gallery, Inc.

even though an autograph on an item can give you an authentication point to observe, it is by no means a guarantee that the item was actually worn by the performer.

Clothing used in promotional videos and film has garnered significant interest over the last few years. Items easily identified with such particular events typically demand premium prices. A jacket worn by glam-rocker Marc Bolan in the movie *Born to Boogie* (1972) will meet a higher demand than a simple stage-worn shirt.

Some entertainers, such as David Bowie and Prince, have undergone dramatic image transformations during their careers. Key items from peak periods during these performers' careers can command significant value. Either a "Ziggy" costume or a significant autographed white fedora can be intriguing to a Bowie fan. Similarly, all items related to the name "Purple Rain" can command a premium price because the movie, soundtrack, and tour bearing the name were highly acclaimed and forever linked with Prince.

Collector interest is also peaked by items associated with particular eras, and many stars are naturally linked to certain time periods (Bill Haley and Buddy Holly are reminiscent of the '50s; the Beatles and Jimi Hendrix, the '60s; and Elton John, the '70s). A prescription pair of glasses worn by Buddy Holly later in his career sold for $45,000 at an auction in New York in 1990, breaking the record for a single piece of rock 'n' roll clothing. This item was both era related and image linked.

Much of the rock 'n' roll clothing that has found its way into the market was purchased through major auction houses. Catalogs from these auctions are instant resources for collectors, and I suggest you monitor all items sold via this method if you're going to collect this form of rock 'n' roll memorabilia. Auction catalogs are not cheap, but mistakes can be far more costly.

For this book a unique database was created from all rock 'n' roll lots sold at major auction houses during the last decade. Sotheby's, Christie's, and numerous smaller galleries were included. Although the prices realized for these lots may vary due to currency fluctuations, they will at least provide readers with a guideline. Just remember that the price an item can command at a highly publicized and prestigious auction may vary significantly from what it would bring at a local show.

Rock 'n' roll clothing accounts for 8% of the lots sold through major auctions. Based on my database, these lots typically range in price from $50 to $40,000, with a mean price of $2,535.46.

ROCK 'N' ROLL CLOTHING: FACTS AND FASCINATIONS

- Some of the Beatles' psychedelic attire was designed by The Fool, who produced numerous pieces for their London Apple Shop.
- It's not unusual to find dresses from the Supremes embroidered with the initial of the specific star.
- Although Buddy Holly was born and raised in Texas, he had a fascination with Italian-made clothing.
- Elton John turned to the designer Bob Mackie for his famous Dodger Stadium suit of October 1975.
- Much of Elton John's elaborate footwear was designed by Ferradini.
- Some of Michael Jackson's "Bad"/bondage clothing bears the label "Western Costume Co., Hollywood" and also includes the artist's name.
- Many of Michael Jackson's fedoras, which were often tossed into the audience, were made by the Golden Gate Hat company in Los Angeles. In addition to having his name stamped inside the hat, they often bear Michael's signature on the brim.

SIZING UP ROCK 'N' ROLL CLOTHING

Jimi Hendrix	Hat Size: 7.5
John Lennon	Foot Size: 8
	Hat Size: 7
Madonna	Shoe Size: 38 (European)
Rod Stewart	Waist Size: 30 (1971)

STAGE-WORN AND PROMOTIONAL APPAREL

Prices realized include premium—in most cases 10%.
Based on author's database.

Abdul, Paula
Stage-WORN shirt and 8x10 promo signed photo, as well as a backstage concert tour pass. $175.

Aerosmith
Signed *Permanent Vacation* Tour Jacket 1978-88. Size medium. All members signed. $150.

Bay City Rollers
Stage suit of sky blue wool, plus two press cuttings. $576.

The Beatles
White suit with letter of authenticity signed by the Beatles' tailor at the time. Photo of Lennon included. $2,750.
Moroccan leather wallet signed by Lennon with letter of authenticity. $330.
Brown suede jacket that fastens with brass poppers, ALLEGEDLY WORN in 1964. Possibly made for the film *HELP!* $2,145.
Suit made for Harrison for the film *HELP!*, 1965, label inscribed "George Beatle." Given by George to his friend Arthur Kelly in the '60s. $2,760.

Benatar, Pat
Black leather jacket with embroidery of "Pat Benatar Wide Awake in Dreamland"; one of three made for her. $363.

Bolan, Marc
One-piece flared, sleeveless jumpsuit, sequins spell "Marc." Back of leg: "Easy Action." POSSIBLY WORN, 1972, in Apple film *Born to Boogie*. $495.

Bowie, David
Limited edition watch with Bowie's portrait on face, inscribed facsimile signature, strap signed/inscribed by Bowie. $1,403.
Limited edition watch with Bowie's portrait and facsimile signature. Thought to be limited to 100 copies. $264.
Limited edition watch with Bowie's portrait and facsimile signature in Perspex box, 9-1/2 inches long. $215.
Short-sleeved khaki crew shirt for *Let's Dance*. Pocket signed, accompanied by a picture disc. $495.

Brown, James
Rare stage outfit of scarlet velvet, gilt wood, and metal encrusted with costume jewelry. WORN, mid-1960s. $9,900.
Two-piece stage suit (rare) of gold satin, with photo of Brown WEARING the suit at Apollo Theatre, 1964. $8,250.
Three-quarter-length stage coat of purple velvet trimmed with sequins and cotton-lined. WORN, 1967. Also the album *The James Brown Show* featuring photo. $3,960.
Flamboyant jacket of gold celluloid simulated fur, WORN onstage, 1968. Also copy of *James Brown Sings Out of Sight*, showing Brown wearing the jacket. $8,580.
Rare stage coat, WORN at the Apollo, 1967, with the album *James Brown Live at the Apollo*, featuring Brown in jacket. $8,250.

Cher
Imitation brown leather bomber jacket, signed/inscribed, 1978. Promo CD: *Love Hurts* with album credits and lyrics printed on 13 tarot cards, signed. $429.

A Cher owned and worn bustier usually commands in the $250 range. Photo courtesy Executive Collectibles Gallery, Inc.

Clapton, Eric
Pair of turquoise leather stage shoes, signed inside the right shoe by Clapton. $1,650.

Collins, Phil
Men's Ex-O-Fit 500 white leather high-top Reeboks. Decorated and signed by the artist. Size 7-1/2. $330.
Autographed cream-colored, double-breasted stage suit worn during the Hello I Must Be Going Tour. Signed with caricature of a drummer. Size 38. $880.

Cooper, Alice
WORN devil's costume with matching scarlet, horned, plush helmet. $2,145.

Costello, Elvis
Shimmering stage jacket of turquoise Lurex, SP's (2) signed by Costello, and a plectrum. $908.

The Cure
Short-sleeved shirt signed with a letter stating that the shirt was WORN by Smith during The Cure's Kissing Tour, 1987. $495.

Duran Duran and The Style Council
Signed Simon Le Bon white silk shirt and a pair of Paul Weller's cotton trousers and bomber jacket. $165.

Eurythmics
Bobber-style jacket embossed with "Eurythmics" on right sleeve. $264.

Fat Boys
Signed men's Ex-O-Fit white leather high-top Reebok sneakers. Decorated. Size 12. $220.

Gabriel, Peter
Sleeveless jacket of white cotton. Signed/inscribed. $330.

Gaye, Marvin
Brown velvet stage jacket with a copy of *Black Stars* magazine, January 1975, featuring Gaye with a copy of magazine showing Gaye WEARING jacket. Plus more. $990.

Brooch, WORN onstage by Gaye, leather wallet made for Gaye, printed handbill, two tour jackets, pair of Gaye-used glass goblets. $594.

Gibson, Debbie
Denim jacket worn by the artist in the video "Only In My Dreams," signed on sleeve. $880.

Hall and Oates
Two pair men's Ex-O-Fit 500 white leather high-top Reeboks. Both decorated and signed. Both size 10. $385.

Harrison, George
Pair of promo sunglasses with red/white/blue plastic frames decorated with "Thirty Three & 1/3" in white lettering. Mounted with album cover, framed. $99.

Hendrix, Jimi
Brown suede boots, Indian style with blue embroidery and multicolored fur lining. $2,750.

Love belt, circa 1968, 38 inches. Brown leather belt with chimes. WORE THROUGHOUT CAREER. $2,200.

A Jimi Hendrix vest proudly displayed at the Hard Rock Cafe in Key West, Florida.

Indian headband, circa 1968, WORN during several live performances. $2,200.

Psychedelic scarf, WORN during various live performances. $1,760.

Near Eastern pendant and guitar picks. Medallion worn during the late 1960s by Hendrix. $1,980.

Green suede fringed pouch with two layers of decorative fringe and shoulder belt. One of Hendrix's favorite possessions. WORN continuously. $2,750.

Cowboy love belt, circa 1968, leather belt with decorative trim and 10 copper cowbells attached with copper eyelet. WORN throughout career. $3,025.

Red velvet stage vest with gray wool lining, WORN during various live performances. $1,980.

Mandarin-style jacket that Hendrix gave to a vendor on the first night of his British tour, 1967. $1,238.

Black felt hat trimmed with an American Indian-style band of leather. WORN onstage. With matching belt. $7,425.

Two printed rayon bandannas and photo of Hendrix wearing similar scarves. $1,650.

Fringed green suede shoulder bag, allegedly one of his favorites. $1,980.

Ornate Eastern bangle with applied beadwork clusters. $150.

Velvet stage pants, purple, visible heavy wear, with photo of Jimi WEARING pants. $1,600.

Holly, Buddy
Buddy Holly stage suit: two-piece, midnight blue tuxedo with black satin lapels. Label reads "N0. 133, Date 1958, Buddy Holly British Tour." Size 40. $5,225.

Pair of slate gray suede shoes, WORN during the late 1960s. $693.

Silk handkerchief WORN by Holly in the '50s. Plus promotional postcard signed by Holly, Joe Mauldin, and Jerry Allison. Common mount, framed. $1,403.

Tooled/painted leather belt with Buddy's name in floral pattern. ALLEGEDLY WORN/MADE by Holly. $2,145.

A rolled-gold Speidel watch bracelet engraved "Buddy Holly," enclosing photo of the star. $660.

A pair of dark brown leather shoes, size 8-1/2. $1,073.

Isley Brothers
Two suits WORN by the Isley Brothers. Six total pieces of clothing. $908.

Jackson, Michael
Rhinestone stage glove thought to be worn at the 1984 Grammys. Most recognizable piece of rock 'n' roll costume of the '80s. $24,750.

WORN black felt trilby, stamped with gilt lettering on inside, reads "Michael Jackson." $1,320.

Black felt trilby hat, and a 1988 baseball-style jacket (BAD, Michael Jackson World Tour). $693.

Military-style stage jacket of navy and scarlet twill, with four machine-print photos showing Jackson wearing the jacket. $5,280.

Exotic stage jacket of black sequins, WORN in the Pepsi Cola commercial and on tour, 1984. $13,200.

Signed Michael Jackson King of Pop T-shirt, mounted in gold display case with a plaque and the *Dangerous* CD. $897.
Leather jacket from the "Thriller" video, 1983. Size 38. $4,830.

Jacksons
Ankle boot of brown imitation leather signed by Michael, Tito, and Randy, given to a fan during the Victory Tour 1984. $281.

Jagger, Mick
Black silk tie, WORN by Jagger and given to him by Marianne Faithful, 1969. $198.

Jam
Signed stage jacket and a copy of the single "Going Underground," with a picture of Buckler wearing the jacket on sleeve/signed. $363.
Two two-piece stage suits, two pairs of stage shoes. All signed and WORN. $908.
Two two-piece stage suits WORN/inscribed/signed by Foxton. $792.
A Union Jack jacket WORN for promo purposes by Buckler. ALS relating to the jacket's authenticity. $693.
Two-piece stage suit with ALS by Buckler regarding the suit's authenticity. WORN. $528.

John, Elton
Hand-knitted jumper with ELT the J on the front and Hercules on the back. $495.
Naval cap of white simulated leather with black patent peak, WORN during American tour in 1982. $231.
Citrus yellow, satin, western-style shirt WORN on the cover of the single "Rocket Man." $495.
White long-sleeved cotton shirt (allegedly WORN) to promote *Goodbye Yellow Brick Road.* $132.
Symmetrically designed spectacles with pale blue prescription lenses. $363.
Pair of shaded spectacles with dark gray prescription lenses. $627.
WORN flamboyant fantasy stage uniform. $4,950.
Black leather loafer-style shoes (pair), printed proof for the album *Elton John Greatest Hits,* and promo color poster. $495.
Loose-fitting raccoon coat WORN during Elton's 1984 World Tour. $4,950.
Statue of Liberty stage costume with photo of Elton wearing the costume in 1977. $3,300.
Straw boater decorated with a black hat band, WORN, 1975, and an in-house disc for *Rock of the Westies,* framed. Plus two chart listings. $660.
Pair of snakeskin platform shoes, each tongue labeled in unidentifiable hand. $693.
Button-down tuxedo shirt WORN for the production of Disney's *Totally Minnie,* includes photocopied pictures of Elton in the shirt. $775.

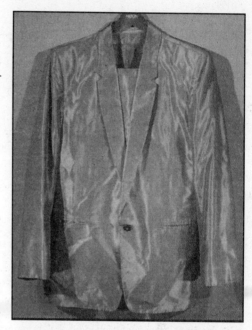

Elton John owned and stage-worn suit estimated at a value of $2,000-$3,000. Photo courtesy Executive Collectibles Gallery, Inc.

Judas Priest
Men's Ex-O-Fit 500 white leather high-top Reeboks, decorated with monogram. Signed. Size 9. $50.

Kinks
Frock coat of bottle greenwool, lined in saffron silk. WORN 1964 onstage. Also a photo of Davies wearing the coat. $2,805.

Kiss
"Smashes Trashes and Hits, 15th anniversary 1974-1989" tour jacket. Size large. $220.
Four super-hero-style costumes WORN by Kiss in their first film, *Meet the Phantom,* 1978. With four corresponding wax-portrait heads exhibited at a wax museum. $31,350.

Led Zeppelin
Red/blue souvenir tour jacket with appliquéd lettering, reads "Swan Song." $215.

Lennon, John
Stage suit, two-piece, dark blue wool with velvet collar and three black satin buttons. Made for *Hard Day's Night.* $3,575.
Black leather jacket, WORN onstage and part of personal wardrobe, 1960-1962. Plus a copy of the album *Rock N Roll with Lennon* wearing jacket. Plus photo. $36,300.
Pair of Chelsea black leather boots, size 8, WORN, 1964. Given to him by his interior designer. Letter of authenticity explaining provenance. $4,620.
Pair of Lennon's sunglasses, photo of him wearing similar glasses at the Hilton Tokyo.1966. $2,933.
Lennon's Homburg, 1960s, in black felt with wide matching band, size 7. $1,208.
1960s, cashmere polo-neck sweaters; a winkle-pinkle-style, knee-length, zip-up boot, size 8, marked "JOHN"; and a ladies' white bathrobe. $1,380.

Little Richard
Exotic stage jacket of scarlet watered silk with matching cape. $2,970.

Madonna
Black lace bustier worn in Madonna's banned Pepsi Cola TV commercial. Praying hands stickpin between the cups. $4,125.

Crucifix pendant with chain, Virgin Tour brochure, three photos of Madonna wearing the crucifix and a letter from the person to whom Madonna gave the crucifix. $6,270.

Black wool beret, signed/WORN, in common mount with photo of Madonna wearing beret. $3,630.

Black satin bustier, signed by Madonna. Plus Who's That Girl Tour brochure with four photos of artist wearing bra, two additional publicity stills. $12,870.

Brief one-piece outfit of supple black leather comprising backless bra. Signed on the crotch. Plus a copy of *Madonna: Sex,* where she is wearing similar outfit. $6,600.

MC Hammer
1991 baseball-style jacket Pepsi Tour '91, Please Hammer Don't Hurt 'Em Tour. $248.

McCartney, Paul and John Lennon
Multicolored striped, knitted sleeveless jumper, with a LS by Denny Laine stating that the vest was OWNED BY BOTH PAUL/JOHN. WORN BY BOTH. $1,568.

Michael, George
Black leather biker's jacket used in the video " Freedom," WORN by the artist. Jacket was later set on fire but was saved due to flame retardant. $2,640.

Mitchell, Joni
Ladies' white leather high-top Freestyle Reeboks. Decorated, signed. Size 8-1/2. $275.

Moon, Keith
Yellow cotton trousers with five copies of press clippings of Moon wearing an identical pair during the shooting of a promo video. $825.

New Kids on the Block
Multicolored souvenir tour jacket, New Kids on the Block Hangin' Tough Tour, U.K. & Europe 1990, with signed photo. $83.

Nicks, Stevie
Signed stage boots WORN during the 1988-89 Fleetwood Mac Tango in the Night Tour. $1,320.

Pair of tan leather boots, top of right boot signed. Also signed/inscribed tambourine USED with Fleetwood Mac Tour 1975. $908.

Black felt top hat, signed/inscribed and annotated. Plus tambourine signed/inscribed by Nicks. $792.

Black velvet stage coat draped off the shoulders, signed/inscribed, WORN onstage during the Wild Heart Tour 1983. Plus diamond ring given to crew members. $1,403.

Stage-worn butterfly top (sequined). WORN during Fleetwood Mac Tour for Tusk. With card signed by Nicks. $500.

Orbison, Roy
Western-style cream suit, leather trimmed with fringe. Made for and WORN by Orbison. $1,238.

Osmond, Donny
Ornate one-piece flared outfit of ivory cotton. $297.

Plant, Robert
Men's white Ex-O-Fit white leather high-top Reeboks. Decorated and signed by the artist. Size 10. $165.

Presley, Elvis
Aviator sunglasses, 14k gold, WORN at the Los Vegas Hilton and broken during July 22, 1974 performance. Comes in three pieces! $4,675.

Stage cape, circa 1972, cream color with brass studs and amber glass jewels mounted in brass bezels, lined with synthetic tiger skin. Authenticity letter. $8,800.

White button-front dress shirt with red and black monograms on various areas of shirt, framed with plaque and authenticity letter. $1,870.

Casual slacks of brown mixed fiber with black woven cotton belt with brass buckle. $281.

Custom-made pendant with monogram TCB (Taking Care of Business) and a cloth concert banner for Las Vegas summer tour. TCB necklaces given to entourage. $792.

Madonna owned and worn bustier. Photo courtesy Executive Collectibles Gallery, Inc.

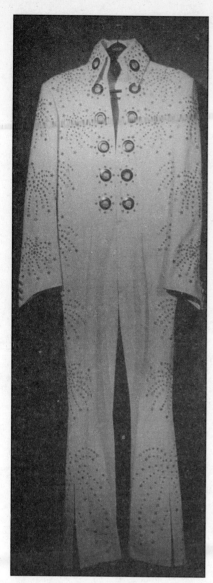

Elvis stage-worn jumpsuit estimated at a value of $60,000-$80,000. Photo courtesy Executive Collectibles Gallery, Inc.

Brass belt buckle in the form of a Sun Record Company label, inscribed "Good Rockin' Tonight, ELVIS PRESLEY." $462.

Blue rayon scarf (36x36 inches) and a black leather belt, both ALLEGEDLY OWNED by Elvis. $825.

Custom-made (rare) karate outfit, WORN. Plus photos of Elvis in outfit, and various other items to prove provenance. $18,150.

Brown/white striped shirt and a red/white/black silk tie WORN by Elvis. $1,070.

Prince

Reebok Men's Ex-O-Fit 500 white leather high-tops. Decorated and signed. Prince tote included with sale. Shoe size: 6-1/2. $935.

Complete stage outfit worn during 1984 Purple Rain Tour. Includes floor-length coat, high-waisted trousers, handkerchief, matching high-heeled ankle boot. $18,150.

A rare complete stage outfit from the Purple Rain Tour, 1984. Ornate-full-length coat, pair of ankle boots, and crucifix/cross chain. WORN. $13,530.

Black trilby of pure wool with letter from Appolonia Kotero stating that Prince gave the hat to her during the filming of *Purple Rain.* $792.

Custom-made Perspex cane filled with translucent fluid and a myriad of purple. USED onstage during Purple Rain World Tour 1984-85. $1,820.

Black matador-style jacket with letter from vendor stating that Prince wore the jacket during Parade Tour and threw it into the crowd while performing "Kiss." $ 2,310.

Pair of long evening gloves of scarlet machine lace, and matching handkerchief, pair of white gloves, white velvet headband, and rhinestone necklace/bracelet. $1,155.

Queen

Black/white printed silk scarf, black/white crepe cummerbund, pair of white cotton gloves (WORN in the video "I'm Going Slightly Mad"). $156.

A kettle hat, cotton, breast pocket handkerchief (WORN in the video "I'm Going Slightly Mad"). $215.

Jesters hat and oversized black/white tie (WORN in the video "I'm going Slightly Mad"). $248.

Penguin waistcoat. WORN in the video "I'm Going Slightly Mad." $248.

Black wet-look, two-piece stage suit, official Queen Fan Club magazine, giving details of the suit, photo of Mercury WEARING the suit. $3,960.

Richards, Keith

Beige felt fedora with matching silk hat band. WORN in late '60s. $1,650.

Ring shaped as a skull, inscribed on inside (Take It Hard). Thought to be one of the limited edition rings used to promote Richards's *Talk Is Cheap* solo album. $462.

Rolling Stones

Tour Jacket with Rolling Stones appliqué and tongue logo, made in Korea. Size large. (Cotton promotional baseball jacket with leather sleeves). $264.

Single-breasted, three-button jacket. WORN by Jagger. $1,733.

Three striped waistcoats. WORN, 1967 by Jagger. $1,238.

Single-breasted, three-button jacket. WORN by Jagger, 1967. $660.

Single-breasted, two-button jacket. WORN by Jagger, 1967. $908.

A suit of tan twill WORN by Jagger in 1969. $990.

Royal blue satin trousers, WORN by Jagger. $413.

Suit of dark salmon twill, WORN by Jagger. $990.

Black leather belt with silver buckle, secret zip compartment. WORN in the early 1970s. $743.

Promo watch, WORN 1969-70, made by the Rolling Stones Merchandising Co. $330.

Gray plush velvet hipsters and pair of black plush velvet hipsters. WORN 1969-73. $1,073.

Single-breasted suit of purple plush velvet. WORN 1972 by Richards. $1,155.

Long-sleeved, black jersey T-shirt with tongue logo worked in pastes and diamonds. Fastens with a zip at the rear. $413.

Souvenir tuxedo-style tour jacket for The Stones, Rich Stadium, Fourth of July, 1978, SIGNED by Jagger with SP: Jagger and tour program for Stones '65. $330.

Promo tuxedo-style jacket produced for the Fourth of July concert 1978, Stones logo. $100.

Ross, Diana/Supremes

Three sleeveless sheath dresses of black silk crepe, embroidered inside with artist's initial: D, M & F, respectively. Back cover photo from *Funny Girl*. $1,815.

Three caftans of bubblegum pink with rainbow-colored batwing sleeves, one marked Mary, the other Diane. Copy of *Funny Girl*, showing them WEARING the garments on the cover. $1,650.

Seger, Bob and The Silver Bullet Band

Men's Ex-O-Fit 500 white leather high-top Reeboks. Signed, decorated. Size 11-1/2. $715.

Sex Pistols

Pale pink cotton sleeveless T-shirt (2). 1976. $863.

Shakespeare's Sister

Costume WORN, 1992, throughout the Harmoniously Yours marketing campaign, as well as in the "Stay" video. $1,466.

Stewart, Rod

Daily WORN red silk tie, with 8x10 promo photo of Rod, signed. $110.

Tom Tom Club

Ladies' white high-top freestyle Reeboks. Decorated and signed. Size 7-1/2. $165.

Tuiti Fruiti

Black leather two-piece suit WORN by Roeves along with selection of lyrics. Plus semi-acoustic guitar with case (nameplate). $1,238.

U2

Stage jacket, signed "Bono 85/ the Unforgettable Fire Tour." Size 40. $1,320.

Clothing signed by U2 members (not Bono) and advertising handbill for *Rattle and Hum,* signed by U2 (not Bono). $231.

Wilson, Jackie

Black cashmere Crombie overcoat and five patterned ties. $297.

4
COLLECTING AUTOGRAPHS

Collecting rock 'n' roll autographs can be an extremely rewarding hobby. Like with collecting other forms of memorabilia, it is best to begin with a goal that will act as a framework for determining how you will acquire autographed items.

ACQUIRING AUTOGRAPHS

Acquiring rock 'n' roll autographs often necessitates a combination of direct and indirect methods consisting of six major techniques:

Direct Method:
1. In-person request

Indirect Methods:
2. Correspondence with the individual, usually by mail
3. Acquiring through a friend, relative, or associated personnel
4. Purchasing items from dealers, promoters, memorabilia outlets, catalogs, shopping networks, etc.
5. Purchasing at an auction
6. Trading

IN-PERSON REQUEST

The preferred (and most enjoyable) way to acquire rock 'n' roll autographs is in person. Not only do collectors have the opportunity to meet celebrities, but they also receive visual confirmation of the signatures' authenticity. Timing is usually the critical factor for success in acquiring signatures in person. Being "at the right place at the right time" is still a great formula for success; however, most collectors don't know where that place is or when to get there.

For years I made it a point to track down the celebrity entertainment that appeared at the New York State Fair in Syracuse, New York. Syracuse, with a population near 160,000, is very accessible and easy to navigate. I have found that celebrities are easy to track down in cities with a population under 200,000 because there is usually only a handful of quality hotels, restaurants, limousine services, theaters, and auditoriums. Cities of this size also have small airports and limited charter jet service.

Tour buses used by Bon Jovi.

The first two things to find out are how the group is traveling and where they are staying. Typically I answer both of these questions in less than two hours. Smaller musical acts, such as Bon Jovi or Dolly Parton, charter custom tour buses that are very difficult to hide, so look for them outside the hotels. The group typically stays where the road crew stays, unless the band is of the caliber of The Rolling Stones. Always start by visiting the five best hotels in town, looking for charter deluxe tour buses and active limousine services outside, and road crew, unusual security, and blocked floor access inside.

Here are just a few of the celebrities I have received autographs from using this method (and then simply waiting patiently in a hotel lobby): Linda Ronstadt, Wayne Newton, Genesis, Waylon Jennings, The Beach Boys, Bon Jovi, Cheap Trick, Amy Grant, Adam Ant, The Doobie Brothers, Bob Dylan, Kris Kristofferson, Heart, Boston, Van Halen, The Rolling Stones, Peabo Bryson, Sting, REO Speedwagon, Greg Lake, The Who, Charlie Daniels, and Jefferson Starship.

A common mistake among novice rock 'n' roll autograph collectors is thinking that the only chance to obtain a signature is at the beginning or end of an event. This, in fact, is probably the worst approach to take. Most successful celebrity autograph collectors never even buy a ticket. They opt instead to become totally familiar with daily routines of their subjects, and choose specific times and places for their autograph requests. This may mean showing up at a hotel hours before an event and waiting in the lobby, or waiting until after an event and stopping by a premier gourmet restaurant known to be frequented by celebrities. It's ridiculous to wait for hours, pushing and shoving outside an arena, when you'll have far greater success at an airport, hotel, or restaurant.

Rock 'n' roll tour itineraries, given to both crew and band members, are particularly useful to autograph hunters and are even considered collectible. Typically offered for sale at between $20 and $35, more and more are finding their way into the market. Despite many being dated, the information inside can prove useful in determining how to plot out your celebrity search. A band's schedule and travel details are contained within these often photocopied and simply bound books.

ROCK 'N' ROLL ITINERARY

U2 "The Joshua Tour" USA, Spring 1987

Contents:
- Overview of tour by day (April 1-May 17): lists arenas, days off, travel days
- Group and Management: includes baggage tag number *
- Crew Personnel: includes baggage tag number **
- Group flight times and video location: 23rd to 28th March ***
- Individual Day Sheets: includes group travel, group hotel, video information, crew travel, crew hotel (different), venue information, concert timetable, and notes. ****

* (4) band members, (8) management, (3) security, (1) merchandising
** (13) crew, (6) sound techs, (5) lighting techs, (2) riggers, (5) truck drivers, (3) coach drivers, (3) plane crew, (2) merchandising
*** Details video shoot in Los Angeles, personnel, flight info, group travel, group hotel, etc.
**** Sample concert timetable:

Get In	8:00 a.m.
Sound Check	4:00 p.m.
Doors Open:	6:00 p.m.
Guests On Stage	7:30 p.m.
Interval	8:15 to 8:45 p.m.
U2 On Stage	8:45 p.m.

If you are a serious rock 'n' roll autograph collector, you should spend one afternoon outside the major concert facilities in your city of choice, especially when there is an event scheduled for that evening. The first two areas you should locate are the "performer entrances" and "designated event parking areas." Public access to both of these areas, especially if they are unguarded, allows for direct contact. Familiarize yourself with the band's transportation and the time they usually arrive at a facility. Knowing the band's form of transportation often allows you to determine who has already arrived and who has not. Since most band members stay at the same hotel, they usually arrive at an arena or stadium as a group, making it hectic to stop each member individually. The best approach in this situation is to team up with three other collectors and predetermine which collector is going to stop which member. A group of four collectors, each stopping a different member, is particularly useful for members arriving in limousines or tour buses.

Inside a facility, familiarize yourself with areas that could offer the greatest opportunity for direct member contact. Although acquiring autographs inside a facility before a concert is nearly impossible, I have seen it happen. If you finally find the right autographing position inside the a facility, don't be conspicuous; act like you belong there.

It is not unusual for artists, particularly newer acts, to make appearances at local record stores or radio stations. If you know Don Henley is appearing at a local bookstore, make every effort to get there and take advantage of a free autograph. Depending on building access, you may even have better luck catching the celebrity arriving at a book signing than you would waiting in line inside the store. Attending a book signing is not a typical function of most rock stars, but providing radio interviews (often conducted in the sponsoring station) is common, so familiarize yourself with the radio and television studios in your town. If you are unaware of any local celebrity appearances, consult your local newspaper—the advertisements in the entertainment sections are a great place to start.

The most overlooked in-person sources for acquiring celebrity autographs are local businesses, especially restaurants, nightclubs, and shopping malls. Some performers, such as Prince and Eric Clapton, are notorious for late night after-show gigs at local blues clubs or nightclubs. It is often difficult to predict where band members will head after a performance, but more times than not they will return first to their hotel.

Most rock stars are more than happy to autograph items for their fans, especially away from the chaos of an event, as long as the requests are made congenially and not while the celebrity is in the middle of eating a meal. Nothing upsets celebrities more than autograph collectors who completely disrespect their right to privacy.

CORRESPONDENCE WITH THE INDIVIDUAL, USUALLY BY MAIL

Many collectors choose to send autograph requests to the celebrity through the mail or other international postal services. This method of obtaining a signature has an unpredictable success rate: typically 25-35%. Not only do many requests go unanswered, but often they are lost or even misplaced. The increased popularity of collecting rock 'n' roll autographs has inundated many entertainment figures with mail requests for their signatures. Because collecting celebrity autographs has become a business in the eyes of many, some musicians are skeptical of the sincerity associated with a mail request. There are certain individuals who do respond to mail requests, particularly if they are perceived as sincere and brief in length, and include a self-addressed stamped envelope.

ACQUIRING THROUGH A FRIEND, RELATIVE, OR ASSOCIATED PERSONNEL

This method of adding signatures to your collection is usually very successful. The greater your access to the subject, the increased chance of adding his or her autograph to your collection. As a collector you should make a sincere effort to get to know anyone affiliated with major hotels, local professional sports teams (their offices can be inside a concert facility), limousine services, charter airlines, event promoters, and restaurant owners. From ushers to waitresses, knowing personnel that may have access to a celebrity will only serve to increase your autograph success rate. Additionally, don't forget about the media, especially newspaper reporters. They have tremendous access to celebrities and are usually very willing to discuss their subjects.

PURCHASING ITEMS FROM DEALERS, PROMOTERS, MEMORABILIA OUTLETS, CATALOGS, SHOPPING NETWORKS, ETC.

An entire book could be written on this subject alone, but simply stated, "Let the buyer beware." Purchasing items from an established dealer with a good reputation for quality, service, price, and availability is paramount. An established dealer will often offer a wide variety of autographed material at a fair market price. When you are purchasing autographed celebrity memorabilia of any kind, each item should carry an unconditional guarantee of authenticity. This type of guarantee is not based solely on a printed certificate of authenticity, but also upon the dealer's willingness to accept a returned item due to authenticity concerns.

An established dealer should provide a reasonable return policy, typically fourteen days from time of purchase. If you are unsatisfied with an item you have purchased from a dealer, promptly return it in the same condition. If the item you are purchasing for your collection is extremely unique or costly, don't hesitate to ask the dealer about its origin (or provenance).

Acoustic guitar signed by Peter, Paul & Mary, displayed at the Hard Rock Cafe in Key West, Florida.

Another benefit of established dealers is their knowledge base, not only in authenticating a specific item, but in acquiring certain autographed collectibles. Developing a good relationship with a variety of established dealers will only add to your collecting satisfaction. Once dealers learn of your commitment to your collecting goal, they may help by providing you access to some of their purchasing sources. As a serious collector, always have a comprehensive "want list" of desired items. The list should indicate price range, condition, and time frame for acquisition. Many quality autographed celebrity items never reach dealer advertisements; they are acquired by known collectors who specialize in a certain field.

Always request to be added to a dealer's mailing list for future catalogs or sale notifications. Most dealers will comply, but catalogs can be very expensive to produce and distribute, so staying on a dealer's mailing list will probably require either a purchase or a catalog fee. On average, a good collector receives between three and five catalogs a week. They are excellent sources of comparison shopping, and they provide collectors with new insights into the hobby, knowledge of recent acquisitions, and an understanding of each dealer's specialties. Periodic contact with established dealers is necessary to avoid missing a key acquisition, as catalogs only represent a small amount of available inventory. It won't take long for a collector to realize that dealer prices for similar or identical items can vary significantly. Dealers price their items based primarily on local appeal or demand, and availability.

Purchasing from satellite shopping networks and gift catalogs has its benefits and drawbacks: they offer every collector instant access to a wide variety of autographed celebrity memorabilia, but they do so at what most collectors consider to be extravagant price levels. There are significant costs involved in printing catalogs and renting satellite time, which is partially responsible for the large price tags. It is not impossible to find an outstanding limited edition celebrity collectible at a great price, though. Just be realistic in your purchases and keep your collecting goal in mind. In my opinion, this method of acquiring autographed rock 'n' roll collectibles will eventually prove to be very worthwhile to collectors.

PURCHASING AT AN AUCTION

As the hobby has matured, many major auction houses have increased their level of participation. These auctions have become platforms for the sale of some the hobby's finest examples of rock 'n' roll autographs. From record contracts signed by John Lennon to handwritten song lyrics from Jimi Hendrix, these major auction houses are unearthing some of the finest pieces available

This acoustic guitar signed by Garth Brooks, Willie Nelson, and Waylon Jennings brought $1,150 at a recent auction. Photo courtesy Executive Collectibles Gallery, Inc.

in the market, while attracting some very prominent buyers. In addition to the discovery of key collectibles, these auction houses are also gauging market demand and keeping collectors current on what is attracting buyers.

Although shrewd buyers may find bargains, the excitement of the event usually leads to overpriced acquisitions. Many agree that the greatest advantage auction houses bring to the average collector is their catalogs, most of which provide detailed descriptions and photographs and are generally available for public purchase weeks before the event. Serious collectors who cannot attend the auctions should still purchase the catalogs for the research value they offer and consider submitting mail bid forms on items that interest them most. Collectors who wish to acquire autographed material this way should be aware of all the terms and conditions of sale.

Prince/Jesse Johnson owned and used Fender-Stratocaster guitar landed over $600 at a recent auction. Photo courtesy Executive Collectibles Gallery, Inc.

TRADING

Trading with fellow collectors is another option available to the collector of rock 'n' roll autographs. Many veteran collectors have built a wonderful network of individuals to trade with. This method of acquiring celebrity autographs is particularly gratifying because you often receive items to fill your needs while helping other collectors toward their hobby goals. Choose trading partners in the same manner that you choose dealers. Try to find someone who specializes in the same type of material that you collect. Before you make or approve any trade be sure that all items involved in the transaction are clearly identified, especially with regard to condition. Should you receive any material in a trade that does not meet your level of satisfaction, immediately return it. Collectors vary in their interpretation of the condition of an item, as well as in their knowledge level of signature variations. Do not be surprised if a collector rejects a trade item because of either factor, and don't take it personally. The returned items are strictly based on one collector's interpretation.

Finding someone to trade with is simply a matter of contacting individuals whose names appear in many of the advertisements in trade periodicals such as *Autograph Collector, Autograph Times,* and *Goldmine.* Many collectors also offer autographed celebrity memorabilia for sale on the Internet.

AUTOGRAPHED ALBUMS - AUCTION LOTS PRICES REALIZED

Rock 'n' roll autographed albums, album covers, and album sleeves account for 9% of the lots sold at major auctions.
Source: Author's database.

Abbreviation Key
AA: Autographed Album (the album itself)
AAC: Autographed Album Cover
AAS: Autographed Album Sleeve

Prices include 10% buyer's premium.

The Beach Boys
AAC: *15 Big Ones,* 1976, signed by all members. $165.
AAC: *Endless Summer,* 1974, signed by all members. $396.

The Beatles
AAC: *Meet The Beatles* album cover signed by all members of the band. Matted and framed. $2,475.
AAC: Original copy of *Meet The Beatles* signed by all the members (inscribed to Ann) matted/framed with plaque. $3,575.
AAC: *Double Fantasy* album cover signed by Lennon/Ono, matted/framed. Along with original Beatles 45 picture sleeve for "Yesterday" (Paul M. signed). $1,430.
AAC: *A Hard Day's Night,* signed by all four members. $908.

AAC: *Revolver,* 1966, signed by all the members, inscribed to Sheila. $2,310.

AA: *Twist and Shout* EP, 1963, signed on back cover by all four members. $792.

AAC: *All My Loving* EP cover, signed by all four members. $2,063.

AA: *Please Please Me,* 1963, Paul, George and Ringo signed. $578.

AA: "Love Me Do"/"P.S. I Love You" single, 1962, Parlophone, signed by all four Beatles. $825.

AA: *Please Please Me,* 1963, signed by all four members/inscribed. $1,650.

AAC: *All My Loving,* signed/inscribed by all four members. $660.

AA: *A Hard Day's Night,* 1964, signed by all four members. $1,403.

AAC: *Revolver,* 1965, signed twice by Paul. $198.

AA: *Please Please Me,* signed by all four Beatles and inscribed by Lennon. $1,073.

AA: Australian *Please Please Me,* signed by all four members, piece of paper signed/inscribed by Starr. $1,815.

AAC: *The Beatles Million Sellers,* 1964, Parlophone, signed by all four Beatles and inscribed/signed by Lennon. $1,238.

AAC: *Beatles For Sale,* 1964, Parlophone, signed by all four members. $743.

AAC: *Abbey Road,* 1969, signed by McCartney and Starr. $495.

AAS: *She Loves You,* 1963, signed by all four Beatles plus inscribed by an unidentified hand. $990.

AAS: *Sgt. Peppers Lonely Heart Club Band* signed and inscribed by McCartney and Peter Blake (sleeve designer). $363.

AAC: (2) *Sgt. Peppers Lonely Hearts Club Band,* one signed by Lennon/Ono, the other signed/inscribed by Paul and Linda Mc-Cartney/Harrison/Starr/George Martin/Peter Blake. $2,475.

AAC: *Meet The Beatles,* American, 1964. $2,415.

AAC: *A Hard Day's Night,* signed by all of the Beatles. $1,001.

AA: *The White Album* and *The Magical Mystery Tour,* both signed/inscribed by Starr. $165.

Bowie, David

AA: *Labyrinth,* SP "Luv on ya! Bowie/76," and promotional mirror for *Let's Dance.* $385.

AA: Double-sided acetate, "Prettiest Star"/"Conversation Piece," EMI disc, white label, inscribed by artist. $215.

AA: *Alladin Sane,* RCA Records, 1973, signed in blue by Bowie and his band members at that time (Ronson, Woodmansey, and Bolder). $297.

Chapman, Tracy

AA: Platinum album and cassette award for *Tracy Chapman,* framed. Signed on the front of the glass. $990.

The Clash

AA: *Give Em Enough Rope* and *The Clash,* both with concert tickets. Signed by the group. $74.

Cream

AAS: "Crossroads"/"Passing The Time," signed by Clapton, Ginger Baker, and Jack Bruce. $363.

The Doors

AA: Autographed gold award album for *The Doors 13,* signed by all members except Jim Morrison, matted and framed. $1,320.

AA: Autographed platinum album award for *Waiting For The Sun,* matted and framed. (Jim Morrison did not sign.) $1,000.

AA: Gold award album for *Morrison Hotel,* matted and framed, $990.

AAC: *Morrison Hotel,* 1970, signed by all members and further inscribed by Morrison and Kreiger. $2,150.

Dylan, Bob

AAC: *The Times They Are A Changin',* 1963, signed. $396.

AAC: *Planet Waves,* 1974, Asylum Records, signed/inscribed by Dylan and additionally signed by his band members. $281.

AAC: *Empire Burlesque,* signed. $281.

AAC: *Planet Waves,* 1974, Asylum Records, signed/inscribed by Dylan and four members of the band. $281.

AAC: *Bringing It All Back Home,* signed and framed. $297.

AAC: *Good As I Been To You,* 1992, signed. $528.

AAC: *Bringing It All Back Home,* 1965, signed/inscribed. $495.

AAC: *Planet Waves,* signed/inscribed. $828.

Ferry, Bryan

AA: Swedish gold award for *Another Time Another Place,* mounted/framed/plaque. Signed on the reverse by artist, $281.

Fleetwood Mac

AAC: Color reproduction artwork for *Mirage* album cover, signed by McVie, Nicks, and Mick Fleetwood. $297.

AAS: *Little Lies,* 1987, signed/inscribed by the band. $462.

AA: Presentation gold single disc award for "Dreams," RIAA, framed. Signed/inscribed by Nicks. $743.

Foreigner

AAC: *Head Games,* 1979, signed by the members in common mount with the inside sleeve, framed. $182.

Genesis/Peter Gabriel

AA: Four albums signed by all the artists, along with a signed single and photo. $149.

Grateful Dead

AAC: *Built To Last,* signed by all six of the most current members. $518.

Harrison, George

AAS: Swedish gold album for *Cloud Nine* and autographed album slick, both framed. $770.

AA: Three albums: *Beatles For Sale, A Hard Day's Night, and Rubber Soul* signed by Harrison. One additionally signed by Pattie Boyd and Cynthia Lennon. $495.

AAC: *George Harrison,* Dark Horse Records, 1979, signed/inscribed. Also publicity photo signed by Harrison. $330.

AAC: *Cloud Nine,* signed by George, framed. $165.

AAC: *Cloud Nine,* 1987, signed. $248.

AA: Signed copy of the box set *All Things Must Pass* and other signed material to include signed note, wedding table place card, bl/wh photo, and more. $483.

Hendrix, Jimi

AA: Singles "Purple Haze" (signed on sleeve) and "Hey Joe" (signed on record label). "Purple Haze" sleeve is faded. $1,403.

Hendrix, Jimi & The Experience

AAC: *Axis Bold As Love* signed by Hendrix and The Experience. $1,035.

Holly, Buddy And The Crickets

AA: Piece of paper signed by Holly in common mount with *Rave On* EP signed by Mauldin/Allison. $578.

AAC: *The Chirping Crickets* by Buddy Holly and The Crickets. Signed by three of the Crickets and Holly. $863.

Jackson Five

AA: Promo album: *Maybe Tomorrow,* 1971. With a song sheet in common mount for *Never Can Say Goodbye,* framed. $462.

Jackson, Michael

AA: *Thriller,* 1982, signed on inside of gatefold sleeve. $396.

AAC: *Dangerous,* 1991, signed/inscribed. $363.

Jackson, Michael and Janet

AAC: *Bad,* signed by Michael, publicity card signed by Michael and *Rhythm Nation,* signed/inscribed by Janet. $231.

AA: *Thriller,* signed/inscribed by Michael; multi-platinum award album for *Control* by Janet Jackson, mounted/framed with plaque; Jackson 5 Action Game in original sealed box; and more. $314.

A collection of album covers signed by Michael Jackson. Photo courtesy Phillips Son & Neale.

Jagger, Mick
AAS: "Brown Sugar" and "She Was Hot" picture disc singles, signed. $198.

Jagger, Mick/Keith Richards
AA: "It's All Over Now" single, 1964, Decca, signed on slip-sleeve by Richards/Jagger, with a typescript letter signed from Eric Easton to Brian Jones. $363.

Jam
AAC: *In The City,* signed by all members of The Jam. Plus two illustrated souvenir programs for The Jam's 1981 and '82 Japanese Tours. $330.
AAS: Seven singles, each signed on sleeve by all members of the group. $281.

John, Elton
AAC: *Captain Fantastic And The Brown Dirt Cowboy,* signed by Elton and Bernie Taupin, $327.

Joplin, Janis
AAC: *Big Brother* LP, matted/framed with nameplate. $880.

Led Zeppelin
AAC: *Led Zeppelin,* signed/inscribed by: Plant, Page, Jones, and Bonham. $1,073.
AAC: *Led Zeppelin,* signed by all four members. $636.

Lennon, John
AAS: Zapple *Unfinished Music #2: Life With The Lions* album/cover, with caricature drawings of John and Yoko, matted and framed. $1,540.
AAS: *Live Peace in Toronto,* The Plastic Ono Band, 1970. Annotated/caricature, inscribed/signed by Lennon. $627.
AA: "I Am The Walrus" single signed by Lennon, 1967, signed/inscribed/annotated with a line drawn through McCartney's name on the song credit (only me really wrote, John). $815.
AAC: *Imagine,* Apple Records, 1971, signed/annotated by Lennon with self portrait caricature. $1,073.
AAS: *Walls and Bridges,* signed, 1974, with caricatures. $776.

Lennon, John/Yoko Ono
AAS: "Instant Karma" single, Apple Records, 1970, signed/inscribed by John and Yoko. $528.

Madness
AAC: *One Step Beyond,* signed by all members. $429.

Madonna
AA: *True Blue* and 12-inch single "Holiday," signed and inscribed. Plus two crew passes for her Virgin Tour 85/86. $330.
AAC: *I'm Breathless,* signed. $182.

McCartney, Paul
AA: *Venus and Mars, London Town, Wings Over America,* and *Flowers In The Dirt.* $660.
AA: *McCartney, McCartney II,* and *The McCartney Interview.* $578.
AAC: *Choba B CCCP* album, 1989, signed/inscribed; *Off The Ground* promo box set, 1993; "Spies Like Us" promo single; and three publicity photos. $576.
AAC: *Flowers In The Dirt* signed by Paul/Linda, and another with machine-print photo of Paul,1965, signed by Paul. $396.
AAC: *Tug Of War,* 1982, signed by Paul and annotated with a caricature of a smiling face. $528.

McCartney, Paul and Wings
AA: *Paul McCartney -Wings on the Road* bootleg signed by Paul, Linda, and Denny Love, along with Paul's autograph mounted and framed. $550.

Metallica
AA: Platinum album and cassette award for *And Justice For All,* framed and signed by all band members. $715.

Michael, George
AA: Signed silver album for *Faith,* mounted/framed. Plaque. $693.

Miller, Steve
AA: *I Wanna Be Loved,* blue vinyl signed with yellow paint pen. $100.

Miscellaneous
AA's and band cover slicks, 29 items. $1,870.
AA: Cream's *Disraeli Gears.* Also autographed paper: Yardbirds with Clapton, matted and framed. $1,430.
AA: Group including 18 separate bands and signatures. $2,090.
AA: *Venus and Mars* album signed by the McCartneys and Laine. Plus photo of Paul signed and seven other signed photos (The Who). $297.
AAC (6) and signed photos (4): Includes Alice Cooper, Phil Collins, Peter Gabriel, Billy Idol, Ted Nugent, Def Leppard, and Meat Loaf. $182.

Mountain
AA: Autographed gold album and cassette award for *Climbing* signed by Laing. $550.

Nelson, Willie
AAC with a WORN bandanna and signed promo poster, all displayed together in western-style frame. $225.

Nicks, Stevie
AAC: *Rumours,* signed/inscribed, 1977, and a tambourine, signed/inscribed. $363.

Pearl Jam
AA: *10* picture disc from the UK, signed by all members. $350.

Pink Floyd
AAS: *The Wall,* signed by Waters, Gilmour, Mason, and Wright. $264.
AAC: *The Wall,* signed by all members. $380.

Pink Floyd/Yes
AAC: Signed by the members of Yes, and a color poster signed by the members of Pink Floyd. $314.

Presley, Elvis
AA: *Elvis Sails,* RCA, signed by Presley on the original cover. $627.
AAS: "Surrender" single, signed/inscribed (1976). $297.
AAS: "Love Letters" single, signed/inscribed (1966). $528.
AAS: *Strictly Elvis,* 1959, signed/inscribed. $693.
AAS: *Love Me Tender,*1960, signed/inscribed. $1,155.
AA: *Elvis Is Back,* Single-sided acetate under the RCA Victor White Label, signed/inscribed. $182.
AAC: *Speedway.* $327.
AAC: *Elvis Volume II.* $414.
AAC: *It Happened At The World's Fair.* $414.
AAC: *Elvis Golden Records, Vol. III.* $449.
AAC: *Elvis Good Times.* $449.
AAC: *Elvis Volume I.* $449.

Prince
AAC: *Around The World The World In A Day,* signed by Prince and the Revolution. $264.
AAC: *Batdance,* signed/inscribed. $264.
AAC: *Around The World In A Day,*1985, signed/inscribed. $297.

Prince and The Revolution
AAC: *Lovesexy,*1988, signed on the front by Prince and the Revolution, and a VIP pass for the same tour, framed in common mount. $330.
AAC: *Parade,* 1986, signed by Prince and The Revolution. $396.

Queen
AAS: *The Works* and *A Kind of Magic,* each signed by all members of Queen. Plus gold presentation single for "We Are The Champions," framed/plaque. $396.
AAS: *The Game,* signed by Mercury, May, and Taylor. $231.
AA: Gold album award for "We Are The Champions" single, mounted/framed with plaque. BPI signed by Peter Brown. $908.
AAC: *Sheer Heart Attack,* 1974, signed by the members of Queen. $363.
AAC: *A Night At The Opera,* 1975, signed by all members, in common mount with inside sleeve. $908.
AAC: *A Night At The Opera,* signed by all members. $258.
AAC: *Barcelona* CD signed by Mercury and Montserrat Caballe. Plus two recording sheets signed with dedication by Mercury. $690.
AAC: Thirteen record albums signed by the members of Queen. $3,278.
AAC: *A Night At The Opera,* signed by all members of Queen. $449.

Redding, Otis
AAC: *Otis Redding Sings Soul Ballads,* 1965, signed/inscribed. $396.
AAC: *The Soul Album,* 1966, signed by Redding. $363.

Richards, Keith
AAC: *Take It So Hard,* signed in common mount with a concert guest pass, framed with corresponding record/inner sleeve. $248.

The Rolling Stones
AA: Rolling Stones album with all members' signatures, including Brian Jones. Mounted in a two-sided frame. $770.
AA: Limited edition promo album of *The Rolling Stones,* signed by Mick, Keith, Bill, Charlie, and Mick Taylor. Plus another album. $627.
AAS: *Sticky Fingers* signed by all five members (with Taylor),1971. $264.
AAC: Signed by all five members plus Andrew Loog Oldham, annotated. $578.
AA: Ed. radio promo album: *The Rolling Stones,* Decca, 1969, signed/inscribed. Plus album insert poster for *Sticky Fingers.* $495.

AAC: *The Rolling Stones,* 1964, signed by all five members. $528.

AAC: *Sticky Fingers,* signed by the members. $825.

AA: *Beggar's Banquet,* 1968, signed by all five members. $743.

AAC: Three signed albums, 1964: *The Rolling Stones* (album) *The Rolling Stones* (EP) and *Five By Five.* Signed by all five Stones. $1,121.

AA: *Five by Five,* signed by all five members. $575.

The Rolling Stones/Beatles

AAC: *Between The Buttons,* signed by the Stones (including Brian Jones). Plus autographed portrait of the Beatles, matted/framed. $1,760.

Springsteen, Bruce

AAC: *War,* signed, in common mount with promo key ring in the shape of a concert ticket, unused ticket, promo T-shirt. $297.

AAC: *Lucky Town,* 1992, signed. $198.

Springsteen, Bruce & E Street Band

AA: *Folkways,* plus platinum display album for *Born in the USA,* and a 1975-1985 denim tour jacket. $3,025.

AA: *Born to Run,* signed by Bruce and all the E Street Band members, 1984. $578.

Valens, Richie/Rick Nelson

AA: Richie Valens 45 rpm record and *Richie Valens* album, Rick Nelson one-sided 45 rpm record "Give 'Em My Number," cover mechanicals (4). $1,100.

Vaughn, Stevie Ray

AAC: *Couldn't Stand The Weather,* signed/inscribed, 1989. $578.

T-Rex

AAS: *The Warlock of Love,* 1969, signed and inscribed on fly. $149.

AAS: *The Warlock of Love,* 1969, signed and inscribed on the fly leaf by Bolan. $116.

Talking Heads

AAC: *Talking In Tongues,* signed by David Byrne. $70.

Ten Thousand Maniacs

AA: Gold album and cassette award for *In My Tribe,* framed. Signed on the glass. $880.

Thin Lizzy

AA: *Live and Dangerous* double album, signed by all members including Phil Lynott. $693.

Traveling Willburys

AA: *The Traveling Willburys,* matted and framed. 16 in. by 20 in. $5,500.

U2

AA: Three albums signed by all band members. Plus War Tour program signed by all band members. Also includes two signed stills of Bono/The Edge. $264.

AAC: *Rattle and Hum* reproduction album cover, signed. $116.

AAC: *Boy,* 1980, and *October,* 1981, both signed by all four members. $297.

AAC: *Under A Blood Red Sky,* 1983, and *The Unforgettable Fire,* 1984, both signed by all four members. $660.

AAS: "With Or Without You" single sleeve, signed by all four band members. $132.

AA: *October,* signed on vinyl by all members of the band. $210.

The Who

AAC: *Tommy,* signed by Daltrey, Townshend, and Entwisle. Paper signed by Moon. Plus signed photo of Daltrey and signed letter from Townshend dated 6/15/68. $495.

AAC: *Face Dances,* signed by Townshend, Daltrey, Entwistle, and Jones. $107.

Wings

AA: *Flowers In The Dirt* promotional LP, signed by Paul and Linda McCartney and all band members. $578.

The Yardbirds

AA: *Over Under Sideways Down,* 1966, signed by all members of the Yardbirds. $627.

AAS: Signed by all members of The Yardbirds. $743.

AAC: *Over Under Sideways Down,* 1966, signed by all the members of the band. $627.

AUTOGRAPHED INSTRUMENTS

Rock 'n' roll autographed instruments sold through major auctions typically account for 2.6% of the lots sold. The mean price for an autographed instrument lot is $1,350.

AC/DC

Remo Weather King bass drum skin decorated with hand-painted letters and AC/DC logo, signed by Young. $297.

The Beatles
Drumsticks with gold embossing, RINGO STARR, Made in England. Signed by Ringo in black marker. $1,320.

Bon Jovi
Kalamazoo Oriole acoustic guitar, body signed by Jon Bon Jovi, in case. $627.
Kramer Baretta custom guitar, incorporating design on *New Jersey* album cover, signed. $2,475.

Buchanan, Roy
Fender Telecaster #E1005778 electric guitar, signed by the artist, with letter of authenticity. $2,090.

Clapton, Eric
Fender Stereocaster solidbody guitar, signed and inscribed by Clapton. $1,733.
Signed Signature series Fender Stratocaster electric guitar, in soft-Fender case. $2,243.

Collins, Albert
1991 Fender Squier Telecaster solidbody electric guitar, with hardshell case. Guitar signed by Collins. $594.

Collins, Phil
Drum skin signed with self portrait caricature by Collins. $429.
Drumstick pair signed/inscribed along with two promo photos signed by Collins. $264.
Drum skin signed/inscribed and annotated with self portrait caricature. $248.

Collins, Phil and Elton John
Signed Premiere Everplay Extra plus drum skin signed by Collins, publicity photo signed by Elton John. $330.

Costello, Elvis
Fender Stratocaster guitar, signed on black pick guard. $410.

Crash Test Dummies
Signed guitar, plus two photos of the band signing guitar. $500.

Cream
Psychedelic guitar with portraits of Cream members, signed by Nemethy only. $462.

The Doors
Autographed synthesizer with "Riders on the Storm" stored in memory bank, copy of photo of artist signing this instrument. $1,300.

Everly Brothers and Others
Hofner acoustic guitar, signed, in plush lined, shaped case. $1,035.

Fleetwood Mac
REMO Weather King drum skin, signed by the band, obtained during 1987-1988 tour. $396.

Genesis
KORG 01/W Workstation synthesizer keyboard, with three strips of black tape signed by Collins, Rutherford, and Banks. $2,228.

Hendrix, Jimi
Fender guitar string packet, signed, 1967. Also inscribed by Hendrix. $1,121.

Iggy Pop
Gibson Marauder electric guitar signed by the artist along with photograph of the signing. $792.

Iron Maiden
Fender Stratocaster Serial #417101, signed by Dave Murray, with original carrying case. 39 inches. $1,650.

Jam
1978 Rickenbacker bass guitar signed by Foxton, with an signed letter stating the guitar was USED by the artist. $2,640.
Snare drum signed/inscribed by Buckler, with signed letter regarding the drum's authenticity and that he USED the drum. $825.

John, Elton and Phil Collins
Tambourine signed/inscribed by Phil Collins and allegedly used during 1985 Live Aid concert. Plus *Greatest Hits* album by Elton John, signed/inscribed. $627.

A signed guitar by Spencer Davis on display at the Hard Rock Cafe in Key West, Florida.

A signed guitar by Mike Pinera (Iron Butterfly) on display at the Hard Rock Cafe in Key West, Florida.

Kiss
1980 Kramer Axe electric guitar, signed by Simmons and numbered 118/1000, with case. $4,950.
1980 Kramer Axe electric guitar, limited edition #55/1000, signed/inscribed by Simmons, 1981, in hardshell case. $2,310.

Led Zeppelin
Yamaha acoustic guitar signed on the body by Page. Original carrying case and picks. THIS ITEM WAS STOLEN FROM JIMMY PAGE, USED ON ZEPPELIN'S 1975 world tour. $4,675.

Nicks, Stevie
Tambourine signed/inscribed by Nicks, signed backstage pass for the Rock Little Tour, and signed/inscribed album cover. $582.

Page, Jimmy
Mortello amp, inscribed, with letter stating that the amp is believed to have been used as a practice/tune-up amp in the early 1970s. Obtained by roadie Carter in 1974. $825.
Gibson Les Paul, signed/inscribed by Page, case and letter of provenance, signed in June 1991. $2,673.

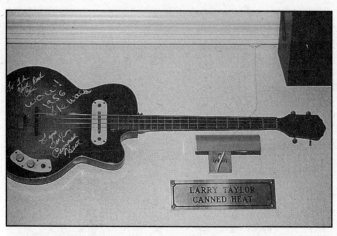

A signed guitar by Larry Taylor (Canned Heat) on display at the Hard Rock Cafe in Key West, Florida.

Paul, Les
Autographed electric guitar: Gibson Les Paul Custom #130056, along with Paul Stanley's original amp autographed by Les Paul (circa 1957). $1,760.

Police
Roland G-707 synth guitar signed by artist (Summers) across the front of the instrument. With case. $550.

Prince
Fender Squier Telecaster electric guitar, signed/inscribed. $3,630.

Queen
Pair of drumsticks, with printed lettering, "ROGER TAYLOR," each signed, with letter of authenticity by Taylor. $330.

Rea, Chris
Signed/used Fender Squier Stratocaster, inscribed: "Key Colour Guitar AUBERGE VIDEO, to the lucky winner Chris Rea May 1993." $1,073.

Reed, Lou
Custom electric guitar with custom designed wooden body, also used by Al Kooper and Steve Martin. $3,850.

Richards, Keith
1978 Fender Telecaster solidbody electric guitar. Signed on the front by Wood and on the back by Richards. Facsimile Clapton signature on front. $1,815.

Ringo Starr's All Starr Band
Les Paul Model (GIBSON) Epiphone electric guitar signed by the band members, with concert program, ticket stubs, guitar case. Signatures obtained August 1992. $1,293.

A signed guitar by Craig Chaquico (Jefferson Starship) on display at the Hard Rock Cafe in Key West, Florida.

Rolling Stones
1974 Fender Telecaster electric guitar, signed/inscribed, with hardshell case. $1,650.

Satriani, Joe
Signed 1991 Fender Stratocaster Plus Deluxe electric guitar. $908.

Shadows
Signed/used 1982 Fender Squier Precision Bass Guitar, with letter from Jones stating it was USED on various albums. $1,403.

T-Rex
Tambourine signed by Bolan with applied T-Rex sticker. $528.
Tambourine signed by Bolan with Marc Bolan and T-Rex lettering. $116.

Townshend, Pete
Takamine acoustic/electric guitar signed by the artist in 1985. USED at 1985 Brixton Academy performance. $1,760.

Van Halen
Signed Kramer electric guitar, includes hardshell case. $1,403.

Winter, Johnny
Autographed electric guitar: The Kramer "Duke" #CO301, signed across front of instrument. $1,320.
Signed 1982 Fender Squier Stratocaster electric guitar. $1,238.

Young Rascals
Instruments/memorabilia: Vina and sarod played by Felix Cavaliere (both signed), brown suede leisure suit worn by Felix, signed photo of Eddie Brigati. $660.

ZZ Top
Signed Gibson Explorere reissue 1986, eccentric shaped body signed, with corresponding case. $1,230.
Guitar, formally OWNED, NOT PLAYED by Steve Vai. Signed twice. Comes with case. $1,200.

Three guitars from left to right: Grateful Dead signed Ibanez acoustic guitar, Eagles signed Goya acoustic guitar, and a Conway Twitty played Martin guitar. Photo © Butterfield & Butterfield, Auctioneers Corp., 1997.

5

PRESENTATION DISCS AND AWARDS

A growing segment of the rock 'n' roll memorabilia market is the collecting of presentation discs and awards. These items, which are typically awarded by record industries in recognition of sales levels for singles and albums, vary from country to country, but the three levels of certification remain consistent: silver, gold, platinum. These attractive display pieces are enticing to collectors because of their minimal distribution, association, and historical and market value.

The rising popularity of presentation discs and awards has led to escalating prices, especially for key awards. As such, this segment of rock 'n' roll memorabilia is prone to fraud, deception, and even broad-based abuse of the system.

More and more interest is being taken in the pursuit of presentation discs and awards. This is a white-matte RIAA award for the Beatles' Something New, valued at $12,000. From the Doug Leftwitch Collection.

A nice approach to a presentation may include autographed CDs. Photo courtesy Executive Collectibles Gallery, Inc.

ORGANIZATION

In January of 1958 the Recording Industry Association of America (RIAA) began formally presenting awards; the British Pop Industry (BPI) followed in 1976. [The tradition can be traced well into the 1940s, however, when on certain occasions, artists received discs for the sale of one million copies (as did Glen Miller for "Chattanooga Choo Choo").] The awards were originally given to pop stars in recognition of the number of records sold, but branched out to include a hierarchy of sorts, moving from the artist to those associated with production, to the artist's record company, and even to key figures involved, such as radio stations. The practice of giving awards has blossomed since its inception: In 1964 only 35 awards were presented for albums and singles; a decade later that number had grown to 127.

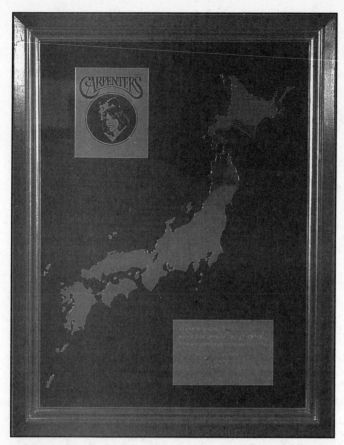

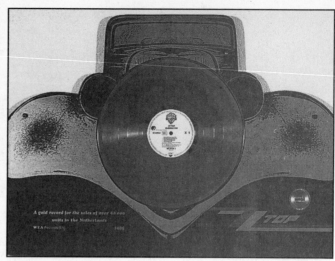

A ZZ Top Eliminator *custom gold record from the Netherlands, valued at $700, 1985. From the Doug Leftwitch Collection.*

A 1976 Carpenters award from Japan, valued at $800. From the Doug Leftwitch Collection.

Many collectors prefer only RIAA discs awarded prior to 1975, because they are far limited in distribution compared to those awarded today. Although many awards from a variety of artists are sought, the Beatles are the most collectible and most expensive, but as the number of vintage Beatles discs has dwindled and prices have risen, some collectors have turned their interest toward other landmark acts such as the Rolling Stones or Eric Clapton. Currently, British and American awards are the most collectible, as they represent the largest markets for recordings, followed by Japan, Canada, Australia, and Northern Europe.

AMERICAN PRESENTATION DISCS

1958-1963		
	Disc:	Gold-plated metal disc
	Background:	Green felt-like material
	Frame:	Unpainted wood frame
	Plate:	Engraved metal plate, inscribed "RIAA"

Collector's Note:

Presentation discs of this era did not follow an acknowledged standard. Discs were typically gold-plated and identified by the term "stampers" or "mothers."

Common formats:
Gold disc mounted on wood with presentation plate mounted underneath. The RIAA logo was a round "coin" and mounted separately, typically to the right.
Gold disc mounted on green felt with presentation plate and RIAA "coin" mounted to the right of disc, framed in wood with gold leaf paint.
Anomalies do exist, one of which was a Lucite table-top display mounted on a wooden base. It featured a gold mini-disc with the RIAA logo acid-etched in the center. Underneath the disc was a photographic miniature of the LP cover. A presentation plate was also attached to the award. (The example cited here was for the Vaughan Meader *First Family* LP.)

"White Matte Era"* (1963-1975)		
	Disc:	Gold-plated metal disc
	Background:	Off-white linen material (turns reddish-brown with age)
	Frame:	Stained brown frame with gold inner trim
	Plate:	Metal plate with "RIAA" logo placed to right (dedication engraved, seal typically etched)
	Details:	Albums include miniature cover of LP in lower left-hand corner (mounted separately)

*Manufactured exclusively by New York Picture & Frame Company

A 1965 Rolling Stones white-matte award for December's Children, *valued at $7,500. From the Doug Leftwitch Collection.*

"Floater Era" (1975-1981)	Disc:	Gold-plated record
	Background:	Dark
	Frame:	Wood frame painted gold or white
	Plate:	"Presented To" and RIAA logo are silk-screened
	Details:	Albums include miniature cover of LP, mounted separately from plate

This is an RIAA gold "floater" award for the Beatles' Rock 'n' Roll Music, *valued at $2,500, 1976. From the Doug Leftwitch Collection.*

"Strip Plate Era" (1982-1984)	Disc:	Gold-plated record
	Background:	Dark
	Frame:	Varies
	Plate:	RIAA logo, engraving and miniature LP cover are all on the same strip of metal inside the frame
	Details:	First format that could include gold or silver plated cassette

A 1965 Rolling Stones white-matte award for December's Children, *valued at $7,500. From the Doug Leftwitch Collection.*

"Hologram Era" (1985-1989)	Disc:	Gold-plated record, always includes cassette
	Background:	Dark
	Frame:	Dark
	Plate:	RIAA logo hologram, dedication and cover on same strip
	Details:	Beginning in August 1989 the RIAA logo was ltered and the seal dropped, some may include gold or silver compact disc

This is a "hologram era" award for the Monkees' Then and Now, *valued at $300, 1986. From the Doug Leftwitch Collection.*

"R-Hologram Era"	Disc:	Disc; disc and cassette; or disc, cassette, and CD
(1989-Present)	Background:	Varies, may include custom backgrounds and colored mattes
	Frame:	Varies, but often dark
	Plate:	RIAA logo changed to "R" hologram pattern
	Details:	Relaxed size and style restrictions

This early example (1984) of a multi-platinum award was for Fleetwood Mac's Rumours, which sold 12,000,000 units. Valued at $700. From the Doug Leftwitch Collection.

SALES REQUIREMENTS

1958-1974

Gold Discs	Albums:	$1,000,000 wholesale net
	Singles:	1,000,000 unit sales
	EP:	500, 000 unit sales

1975-1988

Platinum Discs	Albums:	1,000,000 unit sales
(begin in 1976)	Singles:	2,000,000 unit sales
	EP:	1,000,000 unit sales

Gold Discs	Albums:	500,000 unit sales
	Singles:	1,000,000 unit sales
	EP:	500,000 unit sales

1989-Present

Platinum Discs	Albums:	1,000,000 unit sales
	Singles:	1,000,000 unit sales
	EP:	500,000 unit sales

Gold Discs	Albums:	500,000 unit sales
	Singles:	500,000 unit sales
	EP:	250,000 unit sales

This gold 45 award for Styx's "Babe," 1979, valued at $100, was made by DeJay Products. From the Doug Leftwitch Collection.

BRITISH PRESENTATION DISCS

1976-1988

Singles	Platinum:	1,000,000 unit sales
	Gold:	500,000 unit sales
	Silver:	250,000 unit sales

1989-Present

Singles	Platinum:	600,000 unit sales
	Gold:	400, 000 unit sales
	Silver:	200,000 unit sales

Albums	Platinum:	300,000 unit sales
	Gold:	100,000 unit sales
	Silver:	60,000 unit sales

Note: The lack of the initials "BPI" is an indication of a second pressing or internal award, rather than an original.

This British BPI certified multi-platinum award was presented to Davey Johnstone, Elton John's guitarist, for The Very Best of Elton John, 1991, valued at $1,000. From the Doug Leftwitch Collection.

The Eagles compilation *Greatest Hits 1971-1975* was the first album certified platinum (February 1976), and "Disco Lady" by Johnny Taylor was the first single to claim such a distinction. By 1983 nearly five hundred platinum certifications had been granted, prompting the recording industry to "up the bar" a bit and offer a multiplatinum distinction (1984). Additional platinum awards were then granted for every subsequent $2 million in sales. With sales in excess of twenty million units, Michael Jackson's *Thriller* became one of the first albums with multiplatinum distinction.

Unlike American presentation discs, British awards have changed little in style over the years. The basic design has remained fairly consist, with the incorporation of the BPI seal in the upper left-hand corner of the plate and a British "Union Jack" included in the upper left-hand corner of the enclosed area. The BPI awards do not use reduced-size album replicas in their designs, opting instead for a cassette insert.

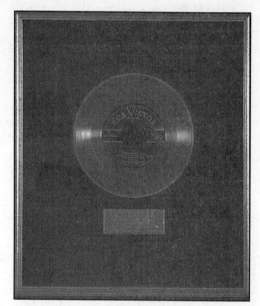

The advent of the compact disc as a recording medium has changed the style of both countries' awards. This will no doubt impact the value of vinyl awards in the future. Vinyl gold certification fell from seventy in 1983 to only three in 1987, prompting the medium to be reclassified by RIAA.

This is a British BPI Certified gold 45 for John Lennon's "(Just Like) Starting Over," valued at $1,500, 1981. From the Doug Leftwitch Collection.

An in-house gold 45 for Perry Como's "Dig You Later," valued at $1,000, 1945. The million-seller mark was achieved innn 1952. From the Doug Leftwitch Collection.

Not every artist who has qualified for an RIAA award has received one. Record companies choose which records to recognize and apply to the RIAA for certification. Not until certification is granted will the record companies be able to buy the official award plaques from a licensed RIAA plaque manufacturer. It has never been a requirement for a record company to join the RIAA, or to allow open access to its financial records, so many artists have never had their discs certified, most notably the early Motown artists.

"In-house" or "internal" awards can also be found in the market. They are easily distinguished from recording industry awards by the lack of an official seal. This type of award, often presented by record companies or the artists themselves, is currently less desirable to the collector and commands far less than recording industry discs. The exception, however, would be unique items from companies such as Motown, where no RIAA awards were issued. Such internal awards would be the only awards relating to the artist, making them extremely valuable.

AWARD RECIPIENTS

As presentation discs and awards have migrated to various levels of the industry, so has their appeal expanded among collectors. Most hobbyists prefer to purchase awards in the following descending order: artist, record company, related key individual or organization, production company, radio station or record company executive.

The broader-based levels of receipt have led to multiple orders, be it duplicates of previous awards or new awards based on higher sales levels. "Extras" can typically equate to profit for the recipient, be it a producer, executive, or even radio station manager. Adding to the confusion of the process is the "ordering" of presentation discs and awards from anyone other than the proper record company executives. Keep in mind that the record company is considered the sole legal distributor of the award. The RIAA is aware of these practices and has been taking steps to reduce illegitimate orders, including the addition of serial numbers for tracking purposes. RIAA-licensed manufacturers are now also required to keep records of how many designated awards they have made, and an additional fee is paid by the manufacturer for each award using the RIAA logo. As producers of these prestigious industry awards, manufacturers' tags are placed on the back of the items. Lack of such a tag, or a variation of the process, should immediately incite concern of the award's authenticity by a would-be purchaser. Please remember, however, that the tag alone is by no means proof that the item is indeed legitimate.

Although one might infer that the hierarchy of presentation disc recipients should affect an award's value, such has not always been the case. There are too many variables in the market to draw such a conclusion—variables such as economic climate, recording significance, recording media, supply, authentication concerns, provenance, auction house variations/expertise, and so on.

The next wave in presentation awards is this momento that fetched just over $2,500. Photo courtesy Executive Collectibles Gallery, Inc.

AWARD CONDITION

The condition of an item is of utmost importance to collectors, and seldom is lesser than mint condition acceptable. Although most agree with this position, there are isolated occasions when mint-condition items are just not realistic and some level of restoration is necessary. So be it said that mint is a must, but rarity has its tendency to yield an exception. Keep in mind that restoration is acceptable ONLY in an isolated circumstance and by a qualified individual. To most potential buyers, an alteration to an award will send up an immediate flag concerning its authenticity.

A white-matte award presented to the Beatles for Sgt. Pepper's Lonely Hearts Club Band *in 1967, valued at $25,000. From the Doug Leftwitch Collection.*

FOCUSING ON THE "WHITE MATTE ERA"

Presentation discs from 1963 to 1968 featured a white-linen matte board that was hand cut, producing a beveled edge. The manufacturer of the matte board (Bainbridge) was so deluged by orders that in 1969 it opted to produce a die-cut version. The first batch of these die-cut mattes had been cut backwards, making the rectangle for the RIAA plate to the left, and the square for the LP mini to the right. Disc experts have noted that the batch was indeed used until the supply ran out (est. September 1969). Examples of this phenomenon include Led Zeppelin, "Led Zeppelin"; Herman's Hermits, "There's a Kind of Hush"; Fifth Dimension, "The Age of Aquarius"; Wes Montgomery, "A Day in the Life"; and Simon and Garfunkel, "Wednesday Morning, 3AM." By 1971 the New York Picture & Frame Company began using matte board manufactured by Miller, which continued for the rest of the "white-matte" era.

The frame that housed the award was made of wood that was stained brown (some variations due to the process). The inner beading was actually hand-painted gold leaf. This "legal document" frame was used for both LPs and single awards.

Plates during this era also underwent transformations:

LP Plates

1963-Early 1967	Satin-like finish
Mid-1967-Mid-1973	Shiny finish
Mid-1973-Early 1974	Satin-like finish (light colored)
Early 1974-End of era	Satin-like finish (darker)

Singles

During this period single plates differed from LP plates by using a light-colored satin finish. All the information presented on the plate was machine engraved, while the RIAA logo was a "coin" similar to those used in earlier awards. These acid-etched coins (darker in surface) were adhered to the right side of the engraved information on the plate. By mid-1964, single plates followed suit with LP plates.

The text on single plates also varied from "FOR THE POP SINGLE RECORD" (late-1963-mid-1973) to simply, "FOR THE SINGLE RECORD."

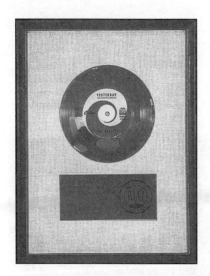

This white-matte 45 award was presented to the Beatles for the 45 "Yesterday" in 1965, valued at $20,000. From the Doug Leftwitch Collection.

"WHITE-MATTE ERA" COUNTERFEITS

What to look for:

• The plates were acid-etched using artwork supplied by RIAA. This would be hard, but not impossible, to reproduce, so carefully examine the artwork.

• Removing a label from a record without destroying it in the process is a task beyond most counterfeiters' abilities, but having one reproduced on a color copier is not. Some anomalies regarding color printing versus screening are covered in Chapter 2 of this book. Read UP!

• The framing material used for "white-matte era" presentation discs is no longer manufactured, so familiarizing yourself with the material and what is offered today is a must.

Also:

• The "stamper" and "mother" discs used in authentic awards are not easily found these days.

"Floater Era" Awards

- The background consists of black cardboard with pebble finish and is essentially similar in design to its predecessor. The image of the LP was reduced to 3" x 3" from the 3-1/8" x 3-1/8" found on white-matte era awards. Components were mounted with 1/4" spacers, creating the appearance that they were floating.

- The frame used for this award was painted gold with a black painted wood spacer.

- Although the RIAA criteria was changed effective January 1, 1975, some certifications were done in a white-matte format during the first four months. Examples include Led Zeppelin, "Physical Graffiti"; Johnny Rivers, "Johnny Rivers Golden Hits" and "A Touch of Gold"; Todd Rundgren, "Something/Anything"; and Bob Dylan, "Blood on the Tracks." (Some of these examples have appeared as "floaters" as well.)

- In late 1975 a company called Creative Glassics received a license from the RIAA to create presentation discs and became the first competitor to the New York Frame and Picture Company. Creative Glassics chose to mount components flush on the background rather than utilizing spacers.

- Platinum designations had silver painted frames.

- All original awards use mother stampers or mothers and are easily distinguished from counterfeits, which often include plated vinyl discs. Exceptions were awards (mostly country titles) produced by Al's Frame Shop.

- During the late '70s and early '80s, DeJay Products out of Burbank, California, began producing RIAA awards, although they were not licensed until the mid-80s. For albums the company used black painted wood frames, plated vinyl discs, and presentation plates with all the text photo engraved. The album jacket "mini" was affixed to the left, and a record company or band logo adorned the right. When the RIAA caught wind that the words "Certified by the Record Industry of America" were being used, the company was notified to cease production or apply for a license.

An RIAA gold 45 "floater" for Queen's "Bohemian Rhapsody," 1975, valued at $800. From the Doug Leftwitch Collection.

This gold white-matte award for Bob Dylan's Blood on the Tracks, *1975, was one of the very last white-mattes. Valued at $2,000. From the Doug Leftwitch Collection.*

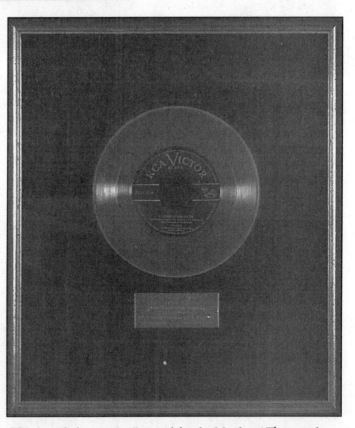

This is a "hologram era" award for the Monkees' Then and Now, *valued at $300, 1986. From the Doug Leftwitch Collection.*

VALUE

Most dealers were unhappy when I told them I was including prices realized at major auctions for presentation disc and awards. The reason: although auctions are common, they are affected by numerous elements not typical to the majority of common transactions. There is currently no price guide for presentation discs, however, so auction prices can be useful to spot trends.

The market for presentation discs and awards is growing much faster than anticipated and quicker than various other elements in the rock 'n' roll market. In 1997, presentation discs and awards make up 9.6% of all rock 'n' roll auction lots sold at major sales. The average price paid for a presentation disc at major auctions conducted over the past decade was $1157.18. Although presentation discs are popular, my research would indicate that no single disc will land in the "Top Ten Overall Selling Items" during the next decade.

PRESENTATION DISCS AND AWARDS

Assorted Selected Entries - Prices realized including premium (10%). Source: Author's database

AC/DC
Presentation Platinum Disc for "Back in Black," RIAA, framed. $363.

Aerosmith
Gold Album Award for *Pump,* mounted/framed with plaque, RIAA. $297.
Gold Presentation Award for *Aerosmith,* American, RIAA. $431.
Gold Album Award for *Aerosmith,* 1975, RIAA. $385.

Average White Band
Platinum Album Award for *Soul Searching,* mounted/framed with plaque, RIAA. $495.
Gold Album Award for *Cut The Cake,* mounted/framed with plaque, RIAA. $528.
Platinum Album Award for *Average White Band,* mounted/framed with plaque plus two other awards. $215.

Bad Company
Presentation Gold Disc Award for *Run with the Pack,* RIAA, framed. $297.

Beach Boys
Gold Album Award for *I Get Around,* mounted/framed with plaque, RIAA. $1,238.
Presentation Gold Disc Award for *Endless Summer,* framed, RIAA. $1,155.

Beatles
Gold Album for *Rubber Soul,* hung at Beatles' Headquarters until the early 1970s, presented December 1965. $3,850.
Gold Record Award for *Help!,* presented to the Beatles. $2,750.
Gold Album for *Reed Music* and cover slicks, matted and framed together. $2,750.
Gold 45 rpm Record Award for "All You need Is Love." $2,475.
Gold Album Award for *Meet The Beatles,* RIAA, mounted/framed, with plaque. $3,465.
Gold Record Award for "Get Back," mounted/framed with plaque, RIAA. $2,805.
Platinum Album Award for *Sgt. Peppers Lonely Hearts Club Band,* RIAA, mounted/framed. $3,960.
Gold Album Award for *Yellow Submarine,* mounted/framed with plaque, RIAA. $3,135.
Gold Album Award for "The Ballad of John and Yoko," mounted/framed with plaque, RIAA. $2,805.
Gold Album Award for the single "Long and Winding Road," mounted/framed with plaque, RIAA. $1,485.
Gold Album Award for the single "Let It Be," mounted/framed with plaque, RIAA. $1,485.
Gold Album Award for *Meet The Beatles,* mounted/framed with plaque. $792.
Gold Album Award for *Beatles 65,* mounted/framed with plaque, RIAA. $858.
Gold Album Award for *Rubber Soul,* mounted/framed with plaque, RIAA. $2,150.

Gold Album Award for *Abbey Road,* mounted/framed with plaque. $2,310.
Gold Album Award for *The Beatles,* mounted/framed with plaque, RIAA. $660.
Gold Album Award for the single "Another Day," mounted/framed with plaque, RIAA. $1,238.
Gold Album Award for the single "Penny Lane," mounted/framed with plaque, RIAA. $1,238.
Gold Album Award for *The Early Beatles,* mounted/framed with plaque, RIAA. $908.
Gold Album Award for *Sgt. Peppers Lonely Hearts Club Band,* mounted/framed with plaque, RIAA. $3,300.
Gold Album Award for *Magical Mystery Tour,* mounted/framed with plaque, RIAA. $1,073.
Gold Album Award for *Revolver,* mounted/framed with plaque, RIAA. $2,145.
Gold Album Award for *Abbey Road,* mounted/framed with plaque, RIAA. $2,145.
Platinum Album Award for the single "Let It Be," mounted/framed with plaque. $1,238.
Presentation Gold Disc for "Let It Be," from KGFJ Radio Station, mounted/framed with plaque. $660.
Presentation Gold Disc for the single "I Want to Hold Your Hand," RIAA, framed. $1,485.
Presentation Gold Disc for the single "Can't Buy Me Love," RIAA. $2,640.
Presentation In-House Platinum Disc for *Beatles 65,* framed. $495.
Presentation In-House Gold Award for *Rubber Soul,* framed. $1,485.
Presentation In-House Platinum Disc for *Sgt. Pepper's Lonely Hearts Club Band,* framed. $1,238.
Presentation Gold Disc for *Sgt. Pepper's Lonely Hearts Club Band,* framed, RIAA. $2,145.
Presentation Platinum Award for *The Beatles at the Hollywood Bowl,* American, RIAA. $1,121.
Gold Presentation Award for *Abbey Road,* American, RIAA. $1,725.
Gold Award for *Sgt. Pepper's Lonely Hearts Club Band,* American. $1,035.
Gold Award for *Rubber Soul,* American, RIAA. $948.
Platinum Album Award for *Sgt. Pepper's Lonely Hearts Club Band,* RIAA. $700.

Black Crows
Platinum Album Award for *Shake Your Money Maker,* RIAA. $300.

Blondie
Gold Album Award for *Auto America,* mounted/framed, with plaque, RIAA. $248.

Bon Jovi

Presentation Platinum Disc Award for *New Jersey,* BPI, framed, $594.

Presentation Gold Disc Award for *New Jersey,* BPI, framed, $462.

Bowie, David

Gold Album Award for *Alladin Sane,* matted and framed, 20" by 17". $1,320.

Gold 45 rpm Record Award for "Fame" (presented to John Lennon), framed, 16-1/2" by 12-1/2". $4,125.

Gold Album Award for *Young Americans,* mounted/framed with plaque, RIAA. $693.

Gold Album Award for *The Rise and Fall of Ziggy Stardust and the Spiders from Mars,* mounted/framed with plaque. $1,403.

Campbell, Glen

Presentation Gold Disc for the single "Rhinestone Cowboy," mounted with plaque, framed. $330.

Clapton, Eric

Platinum Album Award for *Journeyman,* mounted/framed with plaque. $495.

Presentation Platinum Disc Award for *Slowhand,* framed, RIAA. $2,145.

Clash

Gold Album Award for *London Calling,* mounted/framed with plaque, BPI. $1,073.

Collins, Phil

Platinum Album Award for *Face Value,* mounted in blue perspex. $281.

Culture Club

Platinum Album Award for the 1983 single, "Karma Chameleon," framed. $627.

Cure

Gold Album and Cassette Award for *Standing on a Beach,* framed. $330.

Dire Straits

Presentation Canadian Platinum Disc Award for *Brothers In Arms,* CRIA, framed. $792.

Doobie Brothers

Gold Award Album for *Takin' It to the Streets,* matted and framed, 20" by 16-1/2". $660.

Doors

Gold Album and Cassette Award for *Alive She Cried,* framed, signed by all members (excluding Morrison). $1,320.

Presentation Gold Disc Award for "L.A. Woman," framed, RIAA. $2,145.

Dylan, Bob

Platinum Album and Cassette Award for *Highway 61 Revisited,* 20-1/2" by 16-1/2". $880.

Gold Award Album for *Slow Train Coming,* mounted and framed, $825.

Platinum Award for *Highway 61 Revisited,* RIAA. $600.

Earth Wind And Fire

Silver Album Award for *Faces,* mounted/framed with plaque, BPI. $231.

Platinum Album for *Gratitude,* and Grammy Nomination Plaque for 1976. Album framed. $495.

Easton, Sheena

Presentation Gold Disc Award for "Morning Train," RIAA, framed. $231.

Electric Light Orchestra

Platinum Award Album for *A New World's Record,* matted and framed along with ELO presentation plaque presented to Les Garland. $935.

Gold 45 rpm Record for "Telephone Line" and Citation of Achievement Award 1977, framed. $715.

Fleetwood Mac

Presentation Disc for *Fleetwood Mac,* mounted/framed with plaque. Signed/inscribed by Nicks. $1,320.

Presentation Gold Disc Award for *Tusk,* framed, RIAA. Signed by Stevie Nicks. $1,155.

Flying Pickets

Presentation Gold Disc for the single "Only You," framed. $182.

Frankie Goes To Hollywood

Gold Disc Award for British Disco Awards 1984, framed. Also similar World Disco Award, framed,1984. $528.

Presentation Canadian Gold Double Single Award for "Relax" and "Two Tribes," framed. $297.

Presentation Canadian Gold Double and Platinum Disc for *Welcome To The Pleasuredome,* framed. $363.

Hendrix, Jimi

Gold album for *Rainbow Bridge* (soundtrack recordings from the film *Rainbow Bridge*), framed, 20-1/2" by 16-1/2". $1,430.

Platinum Album for *Jimi Hendrix* (soundtrack from the documentary film *Jimi Hendrix*), framed. $1,100.

Gold Album Award for *Electric Ladyland,* mounted/framed/with plaque. $908.

Gold Album Award for *Radio One,* mounted/framed with plaque, BPI. $990.

Presentation Gold Disc for *Are You Experienced?,* RIAA, framed. $1,485.

Gold Award for *Electric Ladyland,* mounted/framed with plaque, RIAA. $6,900.

With Otis Redding: Platinum Album Award for *Historic Performances at the Monterey Pop Festival,* matted and framed. $1,210.

Presentation Gold Disc Award for *Are You Experienced?,* RIAA, framed. $1,403.

Gold RIAA award for the 1968 double LP *Electric Ladyland.* $1,550.

Hollies

Presentation Gold Disc Award for "Long Cool Woman," mounted, framed with plaque, RIAA. $908.

Holly, Buddy

Presentation Gold Disc for *20 Golden Greats,* framed, RIAA. $908.

Houston, Thelma

Gold Award Album for the single "Don't Leave Me This Way," mounted/framed with plaque. $83.

Jackson Five

Platinum Album and Cassette Award for *Triumph,* framed with a plaque. $660.

Jackson, Michael

Platinum Album and Cassette Award for *Thriller,* 20-1/2" by 16-1/2". $660.

Platinum Album and Cassette Award and stand-up display for *Bad.* $880.

Presentation Platinum Disc Award for the single "Beat It," RIAA. $908.

Presentation Gold Disc Award for *Off the Wall,* RIAA, framed. $908.

Gold Award for the single "She's Out of My Life," American, RIAA. $345.

Jethro Tull

Silver Award Album for *Live-Bursting Out,* mounted/framed with plaque. $215.

John, Elton

Gold Album Award for *Goodbye Yellow Brick Road,* mounted/framed with plaque. $990.

Gold Album Award for *Photograph: Elton John,* mounted/framed with plaque, RIAA. $1,238.

Presentation In-House Album Award for *Elton John,* Ltd. Ed. record: *Sasson Presents Elton John,* and three backstage passes for various shows. $264.

Gold Award for *Greatest Hits by Elton John,* American, RIAA. $1,242.

Gold Award for *The Single Man,* American, $690.

Gold Award for *Breaking Hearts,* British, $518.

Kiss

Platinum Album for *Animalize,* framed, 20-1/2" by 16-1/2". $330.

Led Zeppelin

Gold Album Award for *Physical Graffiti,* matted and framed, 20" by 16-1/2". $1,650.

Gold Album Award for *Presence,* matted and framed, 20" by 16-1/2". $1,760.

Gold Album Award for *Led Zeppelin,* mounted/framed with plaque, RIAA, and artwork for a concert poster. $594.

Presentation Gold Disc for *Houses of the Holy,* framed, RIAA. $2,475.

Gold Award for the album and cassette for *Led Zeppelin VI,* RIAA hologram logo. $690.

Lennon, John

Gold Award album for *John Lennon Live In New York City,* matted and framed. $2,475.

Gold Album Award for *Rock 'n' Roll,* mounted/framed with plaque, RIAA. $2,640.

Gold Album Award for the single "Just Like Starting Over," mounted/framed with plaque, RIAA. $1,155.

Gold Album Award for "Woman," mounted/framed with plaque, RIAA. $1,155.

Presentation Gold Disc Award for *Imagine,* mounted/framed with plaque, RIAA. $3,960.

Presentation Gold Disc Award for *Imagine,* framed, RIAA. With a rare press pack for Lennon's first version of the film *Imagine* (1971). $660.

Gold Album Award for *Imagine,* mounted/framed, with plaque. RIAA. $4,290.

Gold CD/Album/Cassette Award for *Imagine,* American, RIAA. $1466.

Silver Award for the album *Rock 'n' Roll,* 1975, British, BPI logo. $1,380.

Platinum Award Album for the single "Woman," American, RIAA. $1,208.

Lennon, John/Phil Spector

Presentation Gold Disc Award for *Imagine,* presented to Phil Spector, framed, RIAA. $3,135.

Lennon, John/Yoko Ono

Presentation Gold Disc Award for *Double Fantasy,* RIAA, framed. $1,485.

Platinum Album Award for *Double Fantasy,* American, RIAA. $1,121.

M.C. Hammer

Platinum Album Award for *Please Hammer Don't Hurt 'Em,* mounted/framed with plaque, RIAA. $495.

Madness

Platinum Album Award for *Absolutely,* 1981, framed, plaque. $182.

McCartney, Paul

Platinum Album and Cassette Award for *Press to Play.* $550.

Meatloaf

Platinum Display Award for *Bat Out of Hell* and Presentation Plaque with picture disk. $825.

Miscellaneous/ Woodstock Performers

Gold Record Award for *Woodstock,* matted and framed, 22" by 17", presented to Ed Denson. $660.

Gold Album Award for *Woodstock,* presented to Joe (Country Joe and Fish) McDonald, matted and framed, 22" by 17". $1,760.

Monkees

Gold Album Award for *The Monkees,* and Gold 45rpm Record Award for "Valleri ," framed. $990.

Gold Album Award for *The Monkees' Headquarters,* and Gold Single Award for "A Little Bit Me, A Little Bit You" (both framed). $880.

Nicks, Stevie

Platinum Album Award for *Bella Donna,* mounted/framed with plaque, RIAA. $743.

Platinum Award for the single "Dreams," American, RIAA logo. $828.

Pink Floyd

Gold Album Award for *The Final Cut,* mounted/framed with plaque, RIAA. $627.

Presentation Platinum Disc for *The Final Cut,* framed, RIAA. $792.

Presentation Gold Disc for *Dark Side of the Moon,* framed, RIAA. $1,815.

Pogues

Silver Album Award for *The Best of the Pogues,* mounted/framed with plaque, BPI. $297.

Gold Album Award for *If I Should Fall from Grace with God,* mounted/framed with plaque, BPI. $363.

Presley, Elvis

Gold Album for *Promised Land,* framed, 20-1/2" by 16-1/2". $990.

Gold "Presley Gold 16 Number One's" single, mounted/framed with plaque. $908.

Gold Album Award for the single "Good Luck Charm," mounted/framed with plaque. $792.

Gold Album Award for *In Concert,* mounted/framed with plaque. $627.

Gold Album Award for *Stuck On You,* mounted/framed with plaque. $908.

Gold Album Award for *Elvis' Golden Records,* mounted/framed with plaque, RIAA. $1,160.

Presentation 93-KHJ Music award for "Heartbreak Hotel," mounted. Four concert tickets for canceled dates and cardboard cut-out of Elvis. $693.

Pretenders

Platinum Award for *Pretenders,* American, RIAA. $380.

Prince

Presentation Gold Disc for *Prince,* RIAA, framed. $4,290.

Presentation Platinum Disc for "When Doves Cry," RIAA, framed $743.

Queen

Silver Album Award for the single "Radio Ga Ga," mounted/framed with plaque, BPI. $908.

Gold Album Award for the single "Another One Bites The Dust," mounted/framed with plaque, RIAA. $1,320.

Presentation Platinum Single Disc Award for "Another One Bites The Dust," framed, RIAA. $1,568.

Gold Award for *Jazz,* American, 1978, RIAA logo, along with a Record World Singles Chart dated 1/21/78 with Queen's "We Are The Champions" at #1. $518.

Gold Award for *The Works,* Japanese. $311.

Queensryche
Gold Sales Award for *Operation Mindcrime*. $200.

Richard, Cliff
Presentation Silver Award for the single "Power to All Our Friends," colored disc mounted on purple above a card with presentation details. $431.

Rogers, Kenny
Presentation Gold Disc for sales in New Zealand: *Monumental*, mounted within hinged glass-fronted mahogany case. $264.

Rolling Stones
Platinum Album for *Some Girls* (autographed by Ahmet Ertegun). $1,320.
Gold Album Award for *Goat's Head Soup*, mounted/framed with plaque, RIAA. $1,320.
Platinum Award Album for *Black and Blue*, mounted/framed with plaque, RIAA. $1,238.
Presentation Platinum Disc for *Some Girls*, framed, RIAA. $2,310.
Silver Presentation Award by *Disc* magazine for the single "It's All Over Now." $2,328.
Gold Award for *Between the Buttons*, mounted/framed with plaque, RIAA. Presented to Charlie Watts. $4,830.
Platinum Award for the single "Miss You." Presented to Keith Richards, mounted/framed with plaque, RIAA. $1,070.

Roxy Music
Presentation Gold Disc Award for *Flesh & Blood*, BPI, framed. $908

Sade
Presentation Platinum disc for *Promise*, BPI certified, framed. $413.

Shadows
Silver Album Award for *Change of Address*, mounted/framed with plaque. BPI. $330.

Sly and the Family Stone
Gold Album Award for *Fresh*, matted and framed, 20" by 16-1/2". $880.

Somerville, Jimmy
Gold Award for the CD *The Singles Collection*, Swiss, 1991. $276.

Spandau Ballet
Gold and Platinum Awards for *Parade*, British, 1984, BPI logo. $414.

Status Quo
Gold Album Award for Status Quo's *Ain't Complaining*, mounted/framed with plaque, BPI. $363.
Presentation Dutch Disc Award for *Whatever You Want*, NVPI certified, framed. $990.
Presentation Gold Disc for *Blue For You*, BPI certified, framed. $165.
Presentation French Gold Disc Award for *Hello*, CIDD certified, framed. $462.

Steve Miller Band
Gold Album and promotional light-box for *Book of Dreams*, along with plaque. $550.

Sting
Platinum Award for *The Soul Cages* mounted above a CD, framed with plaque, BPI. $743.

Talking Heads
Platinum Album for *Talking Heads 77*, matted and framed, 20" by 16-1/2". $605.

Ten CC
Gold Album Award for *Deceptive Bends*, mounted, framed with plaque, BPI. $330.
Gold Album Award for the single "Dreadlock Holiday," mounted/framed with plaque. $198.
Silver Album Award for *Deceptive Bends*, mounted/framed with plaque, BPI. $107.
Silver Album Award for "The Things We Do for Love," mounted/framed with plaque, BPI. $156.

Thin Lizzy
Gold Album Award for *Bad Reputation*, 1977, BPI, mounted. $603.

Ultravox
Gold Album Award for *The Collection*, mounted/framed with plaque. $107.

Vaughn, Stevie Ray
Gold Award for *Texas Flood* album, CD, and cassette, American, RIAA. $569.
Presentation Gold Disc Award for *Couldn't Stand the Weather*, framed, RIAA. $2,640.
Gold Award for *Live Alive* album, CD, and cassette, American, RIAA. $603

Who
Gold Album for *Who's Next*, framed 20-1/2" by 16-1/2". $1,430.
Gold Album Award for *Tommy*, matted and framed, 20" by 17". $2,310.
Gold Album Award for *Odds and Sods*, mounted/framed with plaque, RIAA. $462.
Gold Album Award for *It's Hard*, mounted/framed with plaque, RIAA. $660.
Gold Award for *The Kids Are Alright*, mounted/framed with plaque, RIAA, together with an In-House Gold Award for John Parr. $690.

Will To Power
Presentation Gold Single for "Baby I Love Your Way"/"Freebird Melody," RIAA, framed. $149.

Wings
Presentation Platinum Disc Award for *Wings Over America*, RIAA, presented to Denny Laine, framed. $1,155.
Presentation Gold Disc for *Wings Greatest*, RIAA, framed. $908.

Wonder, Stevie
Presentation Gold Single Disc Award for "Tell Me Something Good," framed Ticket Sales Award for Stevie Wonder In Concert, and black tour jacket. $627.

Young, Paul
Silver Album Award for the single "Wherever I Lay My Hat," mounted and framed with plaque. $215.
Platinum Award for *The Secret of Association*. $173.

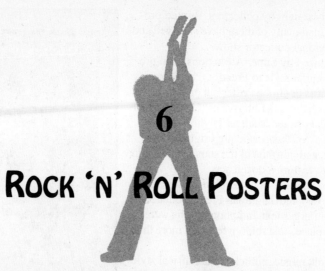

6

ROCK 'N' ROLL POSTERS

Posters are relatively easy to create using inexpensive materials, and thus are a popular form of advertising. Since their inception, posters have evolved with their time periods both in the graphics that adorn them and the technology used to create them. Experienced poster collectors often have considerable success in dating a poster simply upon examining the technology and materials used to create it.

Until the birth of rock 'n' roll, the leading edge in poster designs in the United States centered around those created for the circus or major amusements such as fairs and boxing matches. These generic designs were often simple, emphasizing "key words," and employed little if any graphics. As improvements in halftone screening became more cost effective, black and white photographs or graphics were added.

The renaissance in rock 'n' roll poster art came during the psychedelic era of the mid and late 1960s, even extending into the early 1970s. It began in Los Angeles and San Francisco, and was heavily influenced by the bands it represented—groups such as the Grateful Dead, the Byrds, the Doors, the Charlatans and Country Joe and the Fish, Jefferson Airplane, and Big Brother and the Holding Company. Since the music was vivid, imaginative, and hallucinogenic, it inspired the artists who would contribute so greatly to the posters of this period. The works were in stark contrast to their predecessors—colorful, intricate, bold—and were printed in enormous quantities when compared to earlier pieces.

THE BIRTH OF ROCK 'N' ROLL (1955-1965)

Early rock posters, particularly those featuring Elvis Presley, are extremely valuable and highly sought by collectors. Early advertisements (1955) were printed on thick white cardboard stock with primarily block letters, and seldom featured graphics or more than three colors of ink. A popular poster of this era is "The Elvis Presley Show, Jordanaires Show" from the Florida Theatre in Jacksonville, Florida, 1956. It features an outstanding single-color screen cut-out of "The King" to the right center of the poster. The red text between his legs reads "RCA Victor Recording Star/ HEAR HIM SING/ HEARTBREAK HOTEL/ HOUND DOG/ AND HIS OTHER GREAT/ RECORDING HITS." The poster has been heavily counterfeited over the years, and collectors should exercise extreme caution when making such a purchase. Consult an expert before buying!

Disc jockey Alan Freed, who is credited with coining the name "rock 'n' roll," began producing regular shows in 1955, first at the St. Nicholas Arena, followed by the Brooklyn Paramount. The success of these shows led the music-industry pioneer to create touring "cavalcades," for which he printed colorful stock posters. The tops of the white stock posters were left blank so that show details could be added at a later time, often as a separate print run.

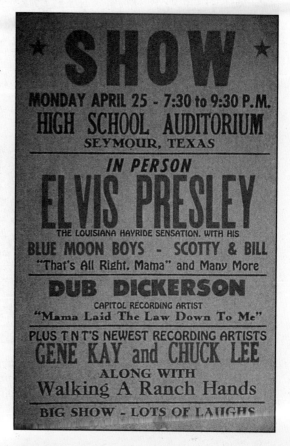

This 1955 Elvis poster is probably one of the rarest concert posters in existence. Any Elvis poster is incredibly collectible, but one from a high school in a tiny Texas town is especially desireable. This is the only poster known to have survived from this event. It is valued at $10,000. From the collection of Dr. Dennis Hickey.

These posters are scarce and highly sought by collectors. Printed programs were also sold at the shows, and many of these have survived and can be picked up at auctions or regional collector shows.

Other tours, such as those produced by Super Attractions, also produced posters and programs in a similar style to Freed's. The company typically utilized the printing services of Globe Poster out of Baltimore, Maryland. Other promoters such as Schwartz Enterprises (Oakland, California) utilized the services of local printers such as Tilghman Press (Oakland, California). Characteristic of this period are bright-colored posters featuring single-color screened portraits of the stars next to bold text. It's not unusual for a poster to feature a dozen acts.

The blues circuit also produced its share of collectible posters. Both Fred Marshall Press (Houston, Texas) and Tilghman Press produced many outstanding advertisements. Larger text and photographs were featured on these simply designed pieces that seldom featured more than three colors of ink.

Posters promoting American folk music mimicked the musical style and were rooted in simplicity. Early folk posters, often one-color or two-color, were simple in design, with the majority featuring words or a graphic rather than a photograph. Only when the more dominate manufacturers, such as Tilghman, crossed into the market did folk-style posters resemble those for other forms of music.

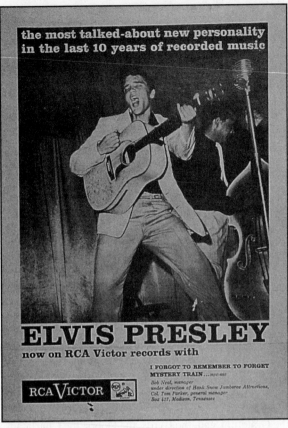

A 1955 Elvis promo poster. This was his first promo poster for RCA (after he left Sun records). This 11x14" poster is valued at $1,000 to $1,500. From the collection of Hank Thompson.

This February 24, 1957 "Biggest Show of Stars" poster featured a show in Topeka, Kansas. Globe Poster of Baltimore printed this 17x22" poster. It is one of three known. From the collection of Hank Thompson.

A predecessor to the '60s psychedelic movement, the Berkeley Folk Festival began in 1958. Founded by Barry Olivier, it contributed its fair share to the American music scene through its images, both visual and artistic. The first poster they produced for the festival clearly exhibited academic undertones, but by 1963 and 1964 their images were more striking and dramatic. Like all folk posters, with the exception of those made by the crossover presses, the emphasis was always the music and its mission. Seldom were individual performers singled out before 1965, and then only the revered, such as Bill Monroe.

By 1965 America had two new heroes, Joan Baez and Bob Dylan. Both showed equal promise and were highlighted on one of the most important folk posters of the era: Eric Von Schmidt's Toulouse-Lautrec homage, "East Coast Tour, In Concert, Joan Baez and Bob Dylan." While Dylan's image remained more rustic on West Coast graphics, his East Coast posters featured him more as a rebel.

Also making waves in the music scene during this era was, of course, the British Invasion. The Beatles adorned one of the most popular posters of the era (which is still sold today): The Beatles, "Royal Command Performance," London Palladium, 1963. The image of the four inside the doorway, with facsimile signatures to their sides, is one of the first posters to make exceptional use of color photography.

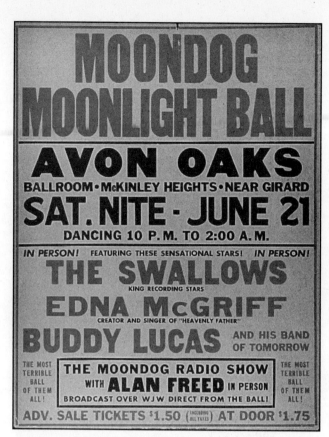

This June 21, 1952, poster for the Moondog Moonlight Ball, McKinley Heights, Ohio, is from the third show ever promoted by Alan Freed. This 22x28" poster was printed by Smith and Setron, Cleveland, Ohio, and is valued at $4,000. From the collection of Hank Thompson.

Globe Poster of Baltimore printd this 22x28" poster for the "Biggest Show of Stars" in Topeka, Kansas on April 26, 1961. It is valued at $2,500. From the collection of Hank Thompson.

THE PSYCHEDELIC ERA (1965-1971)

America answered the British Invasion with the San Francisco sound, ignited by the Charlatans, Big Brother, the free-form "Acid Tests," "Grateful Dead," and "Jefferson Airplane," and commemorated in two landmark posters series.

The "Family Dog" series (February 1966-November 1968) consists of 147 pieces, with 13 additional "Denver Family Dog" items. The first several Family Dog posters were printed in black and white, and may even include colored portions done by hand.

Running parallel to the Family Dog was the "Bill Graham Presents" series (1966-1971), representing 287 images, with a possible 8-12 additional works as candidates for inclusion.

These two sets fueled the "psychedelic era," while having a profound effect on poster art. While many prominent psychedelic artists, such as Peter Max, would surface in other mediums

This Vulcan Gas Company poster afvertises a 1968 performance by the 13th Floor Elevators. It is an extremely important piece because of its stunning art, the fact that the Elevators are considered to be America's first truly psychedlic band, and because it was an Austin performance. It is valued between $400 and $700. From the collection of Dr. Dennis Hickey.

and quickly become household names, the artists from the two historical sets were building an equally impressive legacy on the West Coast. Although Rick Griffin and Stanley Mouse might not be household names, if you lived during this era, there was no escaping their work and its impact on American pop culture. Other prominent artists of the era were "Hapshash and The Coloured Coat" (Martin Sharp, Nigel Weymouth, and Michael English, from the U.K.) and "The Fool" (Simon Posthuma, Josje Leeger, and Marijke Koger, from the Netherlands).

The "Family Dog" (FD) and "Bill Graham Presents" (BGP) series have become the foundation for collecting poster art. They are popular with collectors and investors because of the extensive documentation that now exists about the images, the relatively tight controls that evolved during their production, and the willingness of certain people to protect and defend their associated copyright. Many other poster manufacturers did not perform similar functions, which detracts from a collector's willingness to pursue their images. Other posters manufactured before and during this period are indeed valuable, but far less is publicly known about the size of print runs, reprints, distribution, copyright protection, and so on.

The Art of Rock: Posters from Presley to Punk by Paul D. Grushkin is not only a must purchase for any poster collector, but proof of just how expansive this topic can be. As such, I am going to restrict my coverage to only BGP and FD concert posters. Additional recommended purchases for collectors are *The Collector's Guide to Psychedelic Rock Concert Posters, Postcards and Handbills, 1965-1973* by Eric King, *The Great Poster Trip: Art Eureka* by Coyne and Blanchard, and *The 1996 Rock Poster Price Guide* by Fred Williams. Also handy are the numerous books about the subject of rock 'n' roll memorabilia, many of which are referenced throughout this book.

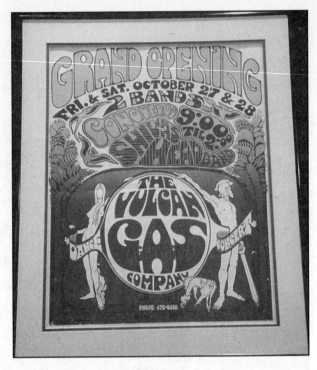

The Grand Opening poster from the Vulcan Gas Company—Austin's first psychedlic nightclub—was printed in 1967. It is valued at about $500. From the collection of Dr. Dennis Hickey.

Subscribing to or purchasing auction catalogs is a must for all poster collectors. Posters are primarily grouped in large lots for inclusion in major auctions and will not always specifically relate to each other. Therefore, don't be surprised to see a poster for the Woodstock Festival in Bethel, New York (1969) paired with a Rolling Stones European tour (1970) poster. (This lot sold for $2,673.) One of the most expensive poster lots sold during the last decade was a collection of 34 Peter Max posters, which also included a couple of other unrelated posters. The lot brought over $30,000. Based on my data, anticipate spending an average of $1,710.86 per poster lot.

Poster lots typically account for less than 1% of the total items sold at recent rock 'n' roll auctions.

BILL GRAHAM PRESENTS SERIES

The assigned poster numbers are generally accepted by the public as proper identification.

Pricing reflects poster in Near Mint condition: modest handling, very slight roundings of corners, obviously no stains, folds, tears, water damage, holes, etc. More than one value (i.e. $250, $125) indicates pricing for subsequent printings

Prices are based on auction results, advertisements in *Goldmine,* and various dealer catalogs.

(Auction Item) = Pricing for this poster is volatile
UA = Unable to accurately assess value

A format such as this indicates three printings (descending order), Poster: (Auction Item; 1st printing), (Auction Item; 2nd printing), $60 (3rd printing)

Item	Performer(s), Venue and Date(s)
BG1	Jefferson Airplane, Fillmore Auditorium 2/4-6/66, Peter Bailey Poster: (Auction Item), (Auction Item), $60 Handbill: (Auction Item) Postcard: $15
BG2	"Batman," Mystery Trend:QMS (Quicksilver Messenger Service), Fillmore Auditorium (FA) 3/18-20/66, Wes Wilson Poster: (Auction Item), (Auction Item), (Auction Item) Handbill: UA Postcard: $120
BG3	"Blues Rock Bash," Paul Butterfield Blues Band, JA (Jefferson Airplane), Fillmore Auditorium (FA) 4/15,17/66, Harmon Gymnasium, UC Berkeley 4/16/6, Wes Wilson Poster: (Auction Item) Handbill: $225 Postcard: $10
BG0	"Grass Roots, QMS," FA 4/22-23/66, Bonnie MacLean Poster: $250

Collector's Note:
An address worth remembering -
Bill Graham Presents (BGP)
* Fillmore Auditorium, 1805 Geary Blvd., San Francisco, California

Item	Performer(s), Venue and Date(s)
BG4	"JA, QMS," FA 4/29-30/66, Wes Wilson Poster: (Auction Item) Handbill: $135
BG5	"JA, Jay Walkers," FA 5/6-7/66, Wes Wilson Poster: (Auction Item) Handbill: $110 Postcard: $15
BG6	"New Generation, Jay Walkers," FA 5/13-14/66, Wes Wilson Poster: (Auction Item), $200 Handbill: $215 Postcard: $15

Item	Performer(s), Venue and Date(s)
BG7	"QMS, Final Solution," FA 5/20-21/66, Wes Wilson Poster: (Auction Item), $250 Handbill: UA Postcard: $10
BG8	"Pop-Up Rock," Andy Warhol and His Plastic Inevitable, VU (Velvet Underground), FA 5/27-29/66 Wes Wilson Poster: (Auction Item) Handbill: UA Postcard: $40
BG9	"QMS, GD (Grateful Dead)," FA 6/3-4/66, Wes Wilson Poster: (Auction Item), (Auction Item) Handbill: (Auction Item) Postcard: $10

Collector's Note

Many printing estimates, with regard to these earlier posters, have been made at under 1,000 copies. Stark in comparison to later posters which may exceed this amount by over three fold.

Item	Performer(s), Venue and Date(s)
BG10	"JA, Great Society," FA 6/10-11/66, Wes Wilson Poster: $400, $45 Handbill: (Auction Item) Postcard: $10
BG11	"Wailers, QMS," FA 6/17-18/66, Wes Wilson Poster: (Auction Item), UA, UA Handbill: (Auction Item) Postcard: $10
BG12	"Them, New Tweedy Brothers," FA 6/23/66, Wes Wilson Poster: (Auction Item), $50 Handbill: (Auction Item) Postcard: $10
BG13	"Lenny Bruce, Mothers," FA 6/24-25/66, Wes Wilson Poster: (Auction Item), (Auction Item), UA, $100 Handbill: (Auction Item) Postcard: (Auction Item), $10

Item	Performer(s), Venue and Date(s)
BG14	"Independence Ball" QMS, Love, FA 7/1-3/66, Wes Wilson Poster: $425 Handbill: $225
BG15	Turtles, Oxford Circle, FA 7/6/66, Wes Wilson Poster: (Auction Item),UA, $75 Handbill: $200 Postcard: $20
BG16	Mindbenders, Chocolate Watchband, FA 7/8-9/66, Wes Wilson Poster: $500, $75, $50 Handbill: $200 Postcard: $10
BG17	JA, GD, FA 7/15-17/66, Wes Wilson Poster: (Auction Item), $65 Handbill: (Auction Item)
BG18	Association, QMS, FA 7/22-23/66, Wes Wilson Poster: $425, $80 Handbill: (Auction Item) Postcard:$10

Collector's Note

It's common knowledge among many who collect, that numerous, often minor variations exist in the initial runs of the posters, all of which are still considered first printings.

Item	Performer(s), Venue and Date(s)
BG19	The American Theater performing "The Beard" by Michael McClure, FA 7/24/66, Wes Wilson Poster: (Auction Item), UA Handbill: $225
BG20	Them, Sons of Champlin, FA 7/29-30/66, Wes Wilson Poster: (Auction Item), $45 Handbill: UA Postcard: $10
BG21	Love, Everpresent Fullness, FA 8/5-6/66, Wes Wilson Poster: (Auction Item), $40 Handbill: (Auction Item)
BG22	Sam the Sham and the Pharoahs, The Sit-Ins, FA 8/10/66, Wes Wilson Poster: $300, $65 Handbill: $130 Postcard: $5 - $8
BG23	JA, GD, FA 8/12-13/66, Wes Wilson, photo. Herb Greene Poster: $425, $200, $35 Handbill: $250 Postcard: $5 - $10
BG24	Young Rascals, QMS, FA 8/19-20/66, Wes Wilson Poster: $400, $50, $40 Handbill: $65 Postcard: $5 - $10

Item	Performer(s), Venue and Date(s)
BG25	13th Floor Elevators, Great Society, FA 8/26-27/66, Wes Wilson, photo. Herb Greene Poster: $425, $350 Handbill: $175 Postcard: $15
BG26	JA, GD, FA 9/2-5/66, Wes Wilson Poster: $400, $65 Handbill: 4225 Postcard; $10
BG27	The Mothers, Oxford Circle, FA 9/9/66, Scottish Rites Temple 9/10/66, John H. Myers Poster: $375, UA, $65 Handbill: $75 Postcard: $10
BG28	Byrds, Wildflower, FA 9/16-17/66, Wes Wilson Poster: $375, $150, $50 Handbill: $50 Postcard: $8
BG29	"The Sound," JA, Butterfield Blues Band, Winterland 9/23-24,30/66, FA 9/25, 10/2/66, Wes Wilson Poster: $225, $75, $50 Handbill: $60 Postcard: $8

Collector's Note

Numerous printings, and thus variations, exist of this poster, for further detail refer to Eric King's "The Collector's Guide to Psychedelic Rock Concert Posters, Postcards and Handbills, 1965 - 1973).

Item	Performer(s), Venue and Date(s)
BG30	Butterfield Blues Band, JA, Winterland 10/7-8/66, Wes Wilson Poster: $190, $85 Handbill: (Auction Item) Postcard: $8
BG31	Butterfield Blues Band, JA, FA 10/14-16/66, Wes Wilson Poster: $150, $25, (Auction Item) Handbill: $60 Postcard: $8 - $6
BG32	GD, Lightning Hopkins, FA 10/21-23/66, Wes Wilson Poster: $300 (lg.), $100 (sm.) Handbill: $25 Postcard: $10
BG33	Yardbirds, Country Joe and the Fish, FA 10/23/66, John H. Myers Poster: $450, $135, $60 Handbill: $50 Postcard: $10
BG34	Captain Beefheart and His Magic Band, Chocolate Watchband, FA 10/28-30/66, Wes Wilson Poster: (Auction Item), $60 Handbill: $45 Postcard: $8

Item	Performer(s), Venue and Date(s)
BG35	Muddy Waters Blues Band, QMS, FA 11/4-6/66, Wes Wilson Poster: $325, $65, (Auction Item) Handbill: (Auction Item) Postcard. $10
BG36	Bola Sete, Country Joe and the Fish, FA 11/11-13/66, Wes Wilson Poster: (Auction Item), (Auction Item) Handbill: (Auction Item) Postcard: $8
BG37	"New Year Bash," JA, GD, FA 12/30-31/66, Wes Wilson Poster: (Auction Item), $200 Handbill: (Auction Item) Postcard: $10
BG38	GD, James Cotton Chicago Blues Band, Lothar and Hand People, FA 11/18-20/66, Wes Wilson Poster: (Auction Item), $65, $40 Handbill: (Auction Item) Postcard: $10

Collector's Note

Some reprints during this era are nearly impossible to distinguish from an original without the assistance of an expert.

Item	Performer(s), Venue and Date(s)
BG39	JA, James Cotton Chicago Blues Band, FA 11/25-27/66, Wes Wilson Poster: $300, $80 Handbill: $60 Postcard: $8
BG40	Love, Moby Grape, Lee Michaels, FA 12/2-4/66, Wes Wilson Poster: $325, $100, $50 Handbill: $25 Postcard: $10
BG41	GD, Big Mama Mae Thornton, Tim Rose, FA 12/9-11/66, Wes Wilson Poster: $100, $55 Handbill: $55 Postcard: $10
BG42	JA, Junior Wells Chicago Blues Band, Tim Rose, FA 12/16-18/66, Wes Wilson, photo. Herb Greene" Poster: $150, $60 Handbill: $40 Postcard: $10
BG43	Otis Redding and His Orchestra, GD, FA 12/20-22/66, Wes Wilson Poster: $100 Handbill: $200 Postcard: $30

Item	Performer(s), Venue and Date(s)
BG44	Young Rascals, Sopwith Camel, FA 1/6-8/67, Wes Wilson Poster: $85, UA, UA Handbill: $75 Postcard: $10
BG45	GD, Junior Wells Chicago Blues Band, FA 1/13-15/67, Wes Wilson Poster: $400, UA, UA Handbill: $50 Postcard: $8
BG46	Butterfield Blues Band, Charles Lloyd Quartet, FA 1/20-22/67, Wes Wilson Poster: $65 Handbill: U/A Postcard: $7
BG47	Butterfield Blues Band, Charles Lloyd Quartet, FA 1/27-29/67, Wes Wilson Poster: $60 Handbill: UA Postcard: $10
BG48	JA, QMS, FA 2/3-5/67, Wes Wilson Poster: $400, $75 Handbill: UA Postcard: $10
BG49	Blues Project, Jimmy Reed, FA 2/10-12/67, John H. Myers Poster: $50 Postcard: $5
BG50	Blues Project, Mothers, FA 2/17-19/67, Wes Wilson Poster: $75, $50 Postcard: $8

Collector's Note

During this period "Post Cards" were printed on the identintical stock to the "Poster."

Item	Performer(s), Venue and Date(s)
BG51	Otis Rush and His Chicago Blues Band, GD, FA 2/24-26/67, Wes Wilson Poster: $150, $85 Postcard: $12
BG52	B.B. King, Moby Grape, FA 2/26/67, John H. Myers Poster: $50, UA Postcard: $7
BG53	Otis Rush and His Chicago Blues Band, Mothers, FA 3/3-5/67, Wes Wilson Poster: $300, 50 Postcard: $20
BG54	JA, Jimmy Reed, Winterland 3/10-11/67, FA 3/12/67, Wes Wilson Poster: $100, $55 Postcard: UA

Item	Performer(s), Venue and Date(s)	Item	Performer(s), Venue and Date(s)
BG55	Chuck Berry, GD, Winterland 3/17-18/67, FA 3/19/67, Wes Wilson Poster: $175, $50 Postcard: $10	BG70	Chuck Berry, Eric Burdon and the Animals, FA 6/27-7/2/67, Greg Irons Poster: UA Postcard: $30
BG56	Moby Grape, Chambers Brothers, Winterland 3/24-25/67, FA 3/26/67, Wes Wilson Poster: $50 Postcard: $10	BG71	Bo Diddley, Big Brother and the Holding Company, FA 7/4-9/67, Bonnie MacLean Poster: $40 Postcard: $10
BG57	Byrds, Moby Grape, Winterland 3/31-4/1/67, FA 4/2/67, Wes Wilson Poster: $60 Postcard: $7	BG72	Butterfield Blues Band, Roland Kirk Quartet, FA 7/11-16/67, Bonnie MacLean Poster: $35 Postcard: $10
BG58	Chambers Brothers, QMS, FA 4/7-9/67, Wes Wilson Poster: $60 Postcard: $18	BG73	Sam and Dave, James Cotton Blues Band, FA 7/18-23/67, Bonnie MacLean Poster: $35 Postcard: $7
BG59	Howlin' Wolf, Country Joe and the Fish, FA 4/14-16/67, Peter Bailey Poster: $40 Postcard: $22	BG74	"The San Francisco Scene in Toronto" "JA, GD," "O'Keefe Center, Toronto, 7/31-8/5/67" James H. Gardner, photo. Herb Greene Poster: (Auction Item) Postcard: UA
BG60	Howlin' Wolf, Big Brother and the Holding Company, FA 4/21-23/67, Wes Wilson Poster: $40 Postcard: $10	BG75	Yardbirds, Doors, FA 7/25-30/67, Bonnie MacLean Poster: $100, $50 Postcard: $10
BG61	Buffalo Springfield, Steve Miller Blues Band, FA 4/28-30/67, Wes Wilson Poster: $45, 30 Postcard: $12	BG76	Muddy Waters, Buffalo Springfield, FA 8/1-6/67, Bonnie MacLean Poster: $35 Postcard: $6
BG62	GD, Paupers, FA 5/5-6/67, Wes Wilson Poster: $300, $60 Postcard: $35	BG77	Electric Flag American Music Band, Moby Grape, FA 8/8-13/67, Bonnie MacLean Poster: $40 Postcard: $15
BG63	JA, Paupers, FA 5/12-14/67, Bonnie MacLean, photo. Herb Greene Poster: $60 Postcard: $20	BG78	Count Basie, Chuck Berry, FA 8/15-21/67, Jim Blashfield Poster: $40 Postcard: $10
BG64	Martha and the Vandellas, Paupers, FA 5/19-20/67, Bonnie MacLean Poster: $40 Postcard: $7	BG79	Paul Butterfield Blues Band, Cream, FA 8/22-27/67, Bonnie MacLean Poster: $85 Postcard: $10
BG65	Big Brother and the Holding Company, Steve Miller Blues Band, FA 5/26-27/67, Bonnie MacLean Poster: $50 Postcard: $7	BG80	Cream, Electric Flag American Music Band, FA 8/29-9/3/67, Jim Blashfield Poster: $130, $60 Postcard: $10
BG66	Jim Kweskin Jug Band, Peanut Butter Conspiracy, FA 6/2-3/67, Bonnie MacLean Poster: $60, $30 Postcard: $6	BG81	"The San Francisco Scene in Los Angeles" JA, GD, Hollywood Bowl 9/15/67 "Jim Blashfield, photo. Herb Greene" Poster: $100 Postcard: $10
BG67	Doors, Jim Kweskin Jug Band, FA 6/9-10/67, Bonnie MacLean Poster: $170 Postcard: $25	BG82	Byrds, Loading Zone, FA 9/7-9/67, Jim Blashfield Poster: $60 Postcard: $15
BG68	Who, Loading Zone, FA 6/16-17/67, Bonnie MacLean Poster: $325 Postcard: $20	BG83	Electric Flag American Music Band, Mother Earth, FA 9/14-16/67, Jim Blashfield Poster: $40 Postcard: $8
BG69	"Opening of the Summer Series," JA, Jimi Hendrix, FA 6/20-25/67, Clifford Charles Seeley Poster: (Auction Item) Postcard: $12	BG84	Blue Cheer, Vanilla Fudge, FA 9/21,23/67, Cow Palace 9/22/67, Bonnie MacLean Poster: $40 Postcard: $22

Item	Performer(s), Venue and Date(s)	Item	Performer(s), Venue and Date(s)

BG85   JA, Mother Earth, FA 9/28/67, Winterland
9/29-30/67, Greg Irons
Poster: $50
Postcard: $10

BG86   Donovan, Cow Palace 9/22/67, Bonnie MacLean
Poster: $40
Postcard: $10

BG87   QMS, Grass Roots, FA 10/5-7/67,
Bonnie MacLean
Poster: $50, $25
Postcard: $10

BG88   JA, Charlatans, FA 10/11-12/67, Winterland
10/13-14/67, Bonnie MacLean, photo.
Herb Greene
Poster: $60
Postcard: $10

BG89   Eric Burdon and the Animals, Mother Earth,
FA 10/19-21/67, Bonnie MacLean
Poster: $45
Postcard: $10

BG90   Pink Floyd, Lee Michaels, FA 10/26-28/67,
Bonnie MacLean
Poster: $200
Postcard: $30

BG91   Big Brother and the Holding Company, Pink Floyd,
FA 11/2/67, Winterland 11/3-4/67 Bonnie
MacLean
Poster: $200
Postcard: $20

BG92   Procol Harum, Pink Floyd, FA 11/9/67, Winterland
11/10-11/67, Nicholas Kouninos
Poster: $200
Postcard: $30

BG93   Doors, Procol Harum, FA 11/16/67,
Winterland 11/17-18/67, Jim Blashfield
Poster: $150
Postcard: $10

BG94   Donovan, H.P. Lovecraft, FA 11/23/67, Winterland
11/24-25/67, Nicholas Kouninos
Poster: $50
Postcard: $7

BG95   Nitty Gritty Dirt Band, Clear Light,
FA 11/20-12/2/67, Bonnie MacLean
Poster: $40
Postcard: $10

BG96   Byrds, Electric Flag American Music Band, FA
12/7/67, Winterland 12/8-9/67, Bonnie MacLean
Poster: $65
Postcard: $10

BG97   Mothers of Invention, Tim Buckley, FA 12/14/67,
Winterland 12/15-16/67, Stanley Mouse
Poster: $200
Postcard: $25

BG98   Buffalo Springfield, Collectors, FA 12/21-23/67,
Alton Kelley, Stanley Mouse
Poster: $80, $40
Postcard: $12

BG99   "Six Days of Sound Doors," Chuck Berry,
Winterland 12/26-31/67, Bonnie MacLean
Poster: $200
Postcard: $18

BG100   "New Year's Eve," JA, Big Brother and the Holding
Company," Winterland 12/31/67Bonnie MacLean
Poster: $125
Postcard: $10

BG100A   Lee Michaels, Taj Mahal, Youngbloods, Love,
Olympic Auditorium, LA, CA 12/31/69
Poster: $300
Postcard: UA

BG101   Vanilla Fudge, Steve Miller Band, FA 1/4/68,
Winterland 1/5-6/68, Lee Conklin
Poster: $350, UA
Postcard: $12

BG102   Chambers Brothers, Sunshine Company,
FA 1/11-13/68, Bonnie MacLean
Poster: $60, $30
Postcard: $15

BG103   Butterfield Blues Band, Charles Lloyd Quintet, FA
1/18-20/68, Jack Hatfield, photo. Louis Sozzi
Poster: $50
Postcard: $6

BG104   Big Brother and the Holding Company, FA
1/25/68, Winterland 1/26-27/68, Jack Hatfield
Poster: $40
Postcard: $15

BG105   "Flying Eyeball" Jimi Hendrix Experience, John
Mayall and the Blues Breakers, FA 2/1,4/68,
Winterland 2/2-3/68, Rick Griffin
Poster: (Auction Item), (Auction Item)
Postcard: $100

BG106   John Mayall and the Blues Breakers, Arlo Guthrie,
FA 2/8-10/68, Stanley Mouse
Poster: $100
Postcard: $6

BG107   Butterfield Blues Band, James Cotton Blues Band,
FA 2/15/68, Winterland 2/16-17/68 Lee Conklin
Poster: $70, $25
Postcard: $5

BG108   Who, Cannonball Adderly, FA 2/22/68, Winterland
2/23-24/68, Lee Conklin
Poster: (Auction Item), $100
Postcard: $20

BG109   Cream, Big Black, FA 3/3/68, Winterland
2/29-3/2/68, Lee Conklin
Poster: $500, $150
Postcard: $25

BG110   Cream, James Cotton Blues Band, FA 3/7/68,
Winterland 3/8-10/68, Stanley Mouse
Poster: $525, $200
Postcard: $25

BG111   Traffic, H.P. Lovecraft, FA 3/14/68, Winterland
3/15-16/68, Stanley Mouse, Alton Kelley, photo.
Bob Seidemann
Poster: $70, $35
Postcard: $6

BG112   Moby Grape, Traffic, FA 3/21/68, Winterland
3/22-23/68, Lee Conklin
Poster: $80, $40
Postcard: $5

BG113   Country Joe and the Fish, Steppenwolf, FA
3/28-30/68, Dana W. Johnson
Poster: $60
Postcard: $6

Item	Performer(s), Venue and Date(s)	Item	Performer(s), Venue and Date(s)

BG114 Eric Burdon and the Animals, QMS, FA 4/4/68, Winterland 4/5-6/68, Dana W. Johnson
Poster: UA
Postcard: $10

BG115 Big Brother and the Holding Company, Iron Butterfly, FA 4/11/68, Winterland 4/12-13/68, Patrick Lofthouse, photo. Thomas Weir
Poster: $60
Postcard: $10

BG116 Love, Staple Singers, FA 1/18/68, Winterland 4/19-20/68, Patrick Lofthouse
Poster: $40
Postcard: $6

BG117 Albert King, Electric Flag American Music Band, FA 4/25/68, Winterland 4/26-27/68, Mari Tepper
Poster: $35
Postcard: $7

BG118 Moby Grape, Hour Glass, FA 5/2-4/68, Mari Tepper
Poster: $35
Postcard: $10

BG119 Loading Zone, Crome Syrcus, FA 5/9-11/68, Weisser
Poster: $30
Postcard: $7

BG120 Country Joe and the Fish, Incredible String Band, FA 5/16-18/68, Weisser
Poster: $40
Postcard: $8

BG121 Yardbirds, Cecil Taylor, FA 5/23-25/68, Lee Conklin
Poster: $60
Postcard: $10

BG122 Buffalo Springfield, Chambers Brothers, FA 5/29-30/68, Winterland 5/31-6/1/68, Lee Conklin
Poster: $70
Postcard: $6

BG123 Mothers of Invention, B.B. King, FA 6/6/68, Winterland 6/7-8/68, Bob Fried
Poster: $50
Postcard: $15

BG124 Big Brother and the Holding Company, Crazy World of Arthur Brown, FA 6/13/68, Winterland 6/14-15/68, Bob Fried, photo. Jonathan Julian
Poster: $50
Postcard: $10

BG125 Chambers Brothers, QMS, FA 6/18-23/68, Lee Conklin
Poster: $50
Postcard: $7

BG126 Albert King, Ten Years After, FA 6/25-30/68, Lee Conklin
Poster: $40
Postcard: $10

BG127 Creedence Clearwater Revival, Butterfield Blues Band, FA 7/2-7/68, Lee Conklin
Poster: $45
Postcard: $10

BG128 "Blues Bash," Electric Flag, Blue Cheer, FA 7/9-14/68, Lee Conklin
Poster: $40
Postcard: $8

BG129 Big Brother and the Holding Company, Sly and the Family Stone, Fillmore-Carousel 7/16-21/68 (future Fillmore-West), Lee Conklin
Poster: $70
Postcard: $10

BG130 Moby Grape, Jeff Beck Group, Fillmore-Carousel 7/23-28/68, Lee Conklin
Poster: $40
Postcard: $8

BG131 Butterfield Blues Band, Santana, FW 7/30-8/4/68, Lee Conklin
Poster: $65
Postcard: $12

BG132 Chambers Brothers, Eric Burdon and the Animals, FW 9/6-11/68, Lee Conklin
Poster: $50
Postcard: $8

BG133 Who, Creedence Clearwater Revival, FW 8/13-25/68, Alton Kelley, Rick Griffin
Poster: $400
Postcard: $30

BG134 Steppenwolf, GD, FW 8/27-9/1/68, Lee Conklin
Poster: (Auction Item), $50
Postcard: $35

BG135 Chuck Berry, Steve Miller Band, FW 9/5-7/68, Lee Conklin
Poster: $50
Postcard: $7

BG136 "Heart and Torch," Big Brother and the Holding Company, Santana, FW 9/12-14/68, Rick Griffin
Poster: $250
Postcard: $25

BG137 "Bull's Eye" Albert King, CCR, FW 9/19-21/68, Rick Griffin
Poster: $70
Postcard: UA

BG138 "Super Session (Mike Bloomfield, Al Kooper, and Friends), It's a Beautiful Day," FW 9/26-28/68 Lee Conklin
Poster: $25
Postcard: $6

BG139 Canned Heat, Gordon Lightfoot, FW 10/3-5/68, Lee Conklin
Poster: $40
Postcard: $20

BG140 Jimi Hendrix Experience, Buddy Miles Express, Winterland 10/10-12/68, "Rick Griffin, Victor Moscoso"
Poster: (Auction Item), $100
Postcard: $20

BG140A Buck Owens and His Buckaroos, FW 10/11-12/68, Pat Hanks
Poster: $60
Postcard: $35

Item	Performer(s), Venue and Date(s)	Item	Performer(s), Venue and Date(s)

BG141   Iron Butterfly, Sir Douglas Quintet,
FW 10/17-19/68, "Rick Griffin, Victor Moscoso
Poster: $110
Postcard: $10

BG142   JA, Ballet Afro Haiti, FW 10/24-26/68,
Lee Conklin
Poster: $65
Postcard: $10

BG143   Procol Harum, Santana, FW 10/31-11/2/68,
Lee Conklin
Poster: $35
Postcard: $10

BG144   QMS, GD, FW 11/7/68, Lee Conklin
Poster: $120, $60
Postcard: $10

BG145   Ten Years After, Country Weather,
FW 11/14-11/17/68, Lee Conklin
Poster: $50
Postcard: $8

BG146   Moody Blues, Chicago Transit Authority,
FW 10/21-24/68, Rick Griffin, Alton Kelley
Poster: $65
Postcard: $15

BG147   "It's A Beautiful Day, Deep Purple,"
FW 11/28-12/1/68, Alton Kelley, Rick Griffin
Poster: $40
Postcard: $10

BG148   Jeff Beck Group, Spirit, FW 12/5-8/68,
Lee Conklin
Poster: $40
Postcard: $10

BG149   Country Joe and the Fish, Sea Train,
FW 12/12-15/68, Lee Conklin
Poster: $45
Postcard: $6

BG150   Santana, Grass Roots, FW 12/19-22/68,
Wes Wilson
Poster: $25
Postcard: $10

BG151   Steve Miller Band, Sly and the Family Stone, FW
12/26-29/68, Wes Wilson
Poster: $25
Postcard: $7

BG152   "New Year's Eve" GD, QMS, Winterland 12/31/68,
Lee Conklin
Poster: UA

BG153   "New Year's Eve" Vanilla Fudge, Youngbloods,
FW 12/31/68, Lee Conklin
Poster: $175

BG154   GD, Blood, Sweat and Tears, FW 1/2-4/69,
Randy Tuten
Poster: $50
Postcard: $10

BG155   Country Joe and the Fish, Led Zeppelin,
FW 1/9-11/69, Randy Tuten, D.Bread, photo.
P. Pynchon
Poster: $325
Postcard: $20

BG156   CCR, Fleetwood Mac, FW 1/16-19/69,
Lee Conklin
Poster: $40
Postcard: $9

BG157   Iron Butterfly, James Cotton Blues Band,
FW 1/23-26/69, Lee Conklin
Poster: $40
Postcard: $8

BG158   Chuck Berry, Jam (Mike Bloomfield, Nick
Gravenites, Mark Naftalin and Friends),
FW 1/30-2/2/69 Randy Tuten
Poster: $35
Postcard: $6

BG159   Mike Bloomfield and Friends - Nick Gravenites
and Mark Naftalin (Jam), Byrds, FW 2/6-9/69
Randy Tuten
Poster: $30
Postcard: $9

BG160   Santana, Melanie, FW 2/14-16/69, Greg Irons
Poster: $40
Postcard: $10

BG161   Move, Cold Blood, FW 2/20-23/69, Greg Irons
Poster: $35
Postcard: $8

BG162   GD, Pentangle, FW 2/27-3/2/69, Lee Conklin,
photo. Herb Greene
Poster: $110, $45
Postcard: $12

BG163   Spirit, Ten Years After, FW 3/6-9/69, Lee Conklin
Poster: $30
Postcard: $6

BG164   CCR, Jethro Tull, FW 3/13-16/69, Randy Tuten
Poster: $50
Postcard: $12

BG165   Janis Joplin and Her Band, Savoy Brown,
Winterland 3/20-22/69, FW 3/23/69, Randy Tuten,
D. Bread
Poster: $200, $50
Postcard: $10

BG166   Butterfield Blues Band, Michael Bloomfield and
Friends, FA 3/27-30/69, Greg Irons
Poster: $40
Postcard: $8

BG167   Procol Harum, Buddy Miles Express, FW 4/3-6/69,
Greg Irons
Poster: $50
Postcard: $10

BG168   Jeff Beck Group, Aynsley Dunbar Retaliation,
FW 4/10-13/69, Randy Tuten
Poster: $50
Postcard: $10

BG169   The Band, Sons of Champlin, Winterland
4/17-19/69, Randy Tuten
Poster: $80, $40
Postcard: $10

BG170   Led Zeppelin, Julie Driscol, Brian Auger and
Trinity, FA 4/24,27/69, Winterland 4/25-26/69
Randy Tuten, photo. P. Pynchon
Poster: $150
Postcard: $15

BG171   JA, GD, FA 5/1,4/69, Winterland 5/2-3/69,
Randy Tuten
Poster: $100, $50
Postcard: $15

Item	Performer(s), Venue and Date(s)	Item	Performer(s), Venue and Date(s)
BG172	Albert King, It's a Beautiful Day, FW 5/8-11/69, Lee Conklin Poster: $30 Postcard: $8	BG187	Chuck Berry, Chicago Transit Authority, FW 8/12-17/69, David Singer Poster: $50 Postcard: $10
BG173	Santana, Youngbloods, FW 5/15-18/69, Lee Conklin Poster: $30 Postcard: $4	BG188	John Mayall, Mother Earth, FW 8/19-21/69, Golden Gate Park 8/22-24/69, David Singer Poster: $125 Postcard: $10
BG174	CCR, Northern California State Youth Choir with Dorothy Morrison, FW 5/22,25/69, Winterland 5/23-24/69, Randy Tuten Poster: $50 Postcard: UA	BG189	Ten Years After, Spirit, FW 9/26-31/69, David Singer Poster: $50 Postcard: $10
BG175	Steve Miller Band, Chicago, FW 5/29-6/1/69, Randy Tuten Poster: $35 Postcard: UA	BG190	Santana, Sea Train, FW 9/4-7/69, David Singer Poster: $45 Postcard: $10
BG176	GD, Junior Walker and the All Stars, FW 6/5-6/8/69, Randy Tuten Poster: $100, $35 Postcard: $20	BG191	Steve Miller Band, James Cotton Blues Band, FW 9/11-14/69, Randy Tuten Poster: $30 Postcard: $20
BG177	Byrds, Joe Cocker and the Grease Band, FW 6/12-15/69, Randy Tuten Poster: $50 Postcard: $10	BG192	Taj Mahal, Buddy Guy, FW 8/18-21/69, Randy Tuten, photo. Jim Marshall Poster: $30 Postcard: $20
BG178	Who, Woody Herman and His Orchestra, FW 6/17-22/69, David Singer Poster: $85 Postcard: $15	BG193	Chuck Berry, Aum, FW 9/25-28/69, Greg Irons Poster: $70 Postcard: $20
BG179	Iron Butterfly, Spirit, FW 6/24-29/69, David Singer Poster: $50 Postcard: $8	BG194	Crosby, Stills, Nash and Young, Blues Image, FW 10/2/69, Winterland 10/3-4/69, Greg Irons Poster: $200 Postcard: $15
BG180	Johnny Winter, Eric Burdon and the Animals, FW 7/1-4/69, David Singer Poster: $60 Postcard: $6	BG195	Country Joe and the Fish, Albert King, FW 10/9-12/69, Randy Tuten Poster: $40 Postcard: $8
BG181	B.B. King, Santana, FW 7/9-13/69, David Singer Poster: $45 Postcard: $10	BG196	Joe Cocker and the Grease Band, Little Richard, FW 10/16-19/69, David Singer, Randy Tuten Poster: $80 Postcard: $12
BG182	B.B. King, Country Joe and the Fish, FW 7/15-20/69, David Singer Poster: $40 Postcard: $8	BG197	JA, GD, Winterland 10/24-25/69, Bonnie MacLean Graham Poster: $55 Postcard: $10
BG183	Ten Years After, Steve Miller Band, FW 7/22-27/69, David Singer Poster: $40 Postcard: $10	BG198	It's a Beautiful Day, Ike and Tina Turner, FW 10/30-11/2/69, Bonnie MacLean Graham Poster: $70 Postcard: $10
BG184	Canned Heat, Everly Brothers, FW 7/29-8/3/69, David Singer Poster: $50 Postcard: $25	BG199	Led Zeppelin, Bonzo Dog Band, Winterland 11/6-8/69, Oakland Coliseum 11/9/69, Randy Tuten Poster: $700, UA Postcard: $45
BG185	Fleetwood Mac, Junior Walker and the All Stars, FW 8/5-10/69, David Singer Poster: $50 Postcard: $20	BG200	Crosby, Stills, Nash and Young, Cold Blood, Winterland 11/13-16/69, Randy Tuten Poster: $200 Postcard: $15
BG186	Doors, Lonnie Mack, Cow Palace 7/25/69, Randy Tuten Poster: $400, $120 Postcard: $30		

Item	Performer(s), Venue and Date(s)

BG201 Rolling Stones, Oakland Coliseum 11/9/69, Randy Tuten, photo. Ran Raffaelli (misspelled Rafaelli)
Poster: $250, $125
Postcard: $20

BG202 Rolling Stones, San Diego International Sports Arena 11/10-11/69, Randy Tuten, photo. Ran Raffaelli (misspelled Rafaelli)
Poster: (Auction Item)
Postcard: $125

BG203 Jethro Tull, MC5, Fillmore West 11/20-23/69, Randy Tuten
Poster: $50
Postcard: $10

BG204 Kinks, Taj Mahal, Fillmore West 11/27-30/69, Randy Tuten
Poster: $40
Postcard: $15

BG205 Grateful Dead, Flock, Fillmore West 12/4-7/69, David Singer
Poster: $80
Postcard: UA

BG206 Chambers Brothers, Nice, Fillmore West 12/11-14/69, David Singer
Poster: $50
Postcard: $10

BG207 Santana, Grand Funk Railroad, Winterland 12/18-21/69, David Singer
Poster: $40
Postcard: $10

BG208 Sly and the Family Stone, Spirit, Winterland 12/26-28/69, David Singer
Poster: $70
Postcard: $15

BG209 Santana, Jefferson Airplane, Fillmore West 12/31/69, Winterland 12/31/69, Bonnie MacLean Graham
Poster: $150
Postcard: $15

BG210 Byrds, Fleetwood Mac, Fillmore West 1/2-4/70, David Singer
Poster: $45
Postcard: UA

BG211 Chicago, Guess Who, Fillmore West 1/8-11/70, David Singer
Poster: $45
Postcard: $7

BG212 B.B. King, Buddy Guy, Fillmore West 1/15-18/70, David Singer
Poster: $50
Postcard: $20

BG213 Albert King, Savoy Brown, Fillmore West 1/22-25/70, David Singer
Poster: $55
Postcard: $20

BG214 Steve Miller, Sha Na Na, Fillmore West 1/29-2/1/70, Steve Miller
Poster: $40
Postcard: $15

BG215 Laura Nyro, The Band, Berkeley Community Theater 1/24 & 1/31/70, Bonnie MacLean Graham, Pat Hanks
Poster: $225
Postcard: $100

Collector's Note

Shows that occurred midweek are believed to have had lower print runs than those during weekends

BG215A Moody Blues, Richie Havens, Berkeley Community Theater 4/2 & 4/11/70, Bonnie MacLean Graham, Pat Hanks
Poster: $275
Postcard: $25

BG216 Grateful Dead, Taj Mahal, Fillmore West 2/5-8/70, David Singer
Poster: $200, $100
Postcard: UA

BG217 Country Joe and the Fish, Sons, Fillmore West 2/12-15/70, David Singer
Poster: $35
Postcard: $15

BG218 Delaney and Bonnie and Friends with Eric Clapton, New York Rock and Roll Ensemble, Fillmore West 2/19-22/70, David Singer
Poster: $70
Postcard: $15

BG219 Doors, Cold Blood, Winterland 2/5-6/70, Randy Tuten
Poster: (Auction Item)
Postcard: $40

BG220 Jack Bruce and Friends, Johnny Winter, Fillmore West 2/26/70, 3/1/70, Winterland 2/27-28/70, Randy Tuten
Poster: $40
Postcard: $20

BG221 Butterfield Blues Band, Savoy Brown, Fillmore West 3/5-8/70, David Singer
Poster: $25
Postcard: $10

BG222 Jefferson Airplane, Quicksilver Messenger Service, Winterland 2/23/70, David Singer*
Poster: (Auction Item)
Postcard: $50
*A gray signed print run of the poster exists, as does a gray postcard.

BG223 Ten Years After, Buddy Rich and His Orchestra, Fillmore West 3/12-15/70, David Singer
Poster: $20
Postcard: UA

BG224 It's a Beautiful Day, Chuck Berry, Fillmore West 3/19-22/70, David Singer
Poster: $40
Postcard: $6

Item	Performer(s), Venue and Date(s)	Item	Performer(s), Venue and Date(s)
BG225	Chicago, James Cotton Blues Band, Fillmore West 3/26 & 3/29/70, Winterland 3/27-28/70, David Singer Poster: $45 Postcard: $25	BG239	Quicksilver Messenger Service, Don Ellis and His Orchestra, Fillmore West 6/18-21/70, David Singer Poster: $40 Postcard: $15
BG226	Jethro Tull, Manfred Mann, Fillmore West 4/2-5/70, David Singer Poster: $425 Postcard: $50	BG240	Sha Na Na, Pacific Gas and Electric, Fillmore West 6/25-28/70, David Singer Poster: $50 Postcard: $12
BG227	Grateful Dead, Miles Davis Quintet, Fillmore West 4/9-12/70, David Singer Poster: $250, $100 Postcard: $80	BG241	Traffic with Steve Winwood, Chris Wood and Jim Capaldi, John Hammond, Fillmore West 6/30-7/2/70, David Singer Poster: $30 Postcard: $20
BG228	John Mayall, Larry Coryell, Fillmore West 4/16-19/70, David Singer Poster: $45 Postcard: $15	BG242	Quicksilver Messenger Service, Mott the Hoople, Fillmore West 7/9-12/70, David Singer Poster: $40 Postcard: $25
BG229	Joe Cocker, Van Morrison, Fillmore West 4/23 & 4/26/70, Winterland 4/24-25/70, David Singer Poster: $50 Postcard: $15	BG243	Steve Miller Band, Bo Diddley, Fillmore West 7/16-19/70, David Singer Poster: $50 Postcard: $25
BG230	Pink Floyd, Fillmore West 4/29/70, Pat Hanks (David Singer listed in error) Poster: (Auction Item) Postcard: UA	BG244	Lee Michaels, Cold Blood, Bretheren, Fillmore West 7/23-26/70, 7/28-30/70, Wilfred Satty, David Singer Poster: $35 Postcard: $15
BG230-A	Pink Floyd, Fillmore West 10/21/70, Pat Hanks Poster: (Auction Item) Postcard: UA	BG245	Ten Years After, Fleetwood Mac, Fillmore West 7/28-8/9/70, David Singer Poster: $200 Postcard: UA
BG231	Jethro Tull, Fairport Convention, Fillmore West 4/20-5/3/70, David Singer Poster: $120 Postcard: UA	BG246	Byrds, Led Zeppelin, Fillmore West 8/13-16 & 8/20-26/70, Berkeley Community Theater 8/30/70, David Singer Poster: $350 Postcard: $35
BG232A	Lee Michaels, Small Faces with Rod Stewart, Fillmore West 5/7-10/70, David Singer Poster: $60 Postcard: $15	BG247	Iron Butterfly with Pinera and Rhino, John Mayall, Fillmore West 8/24-9/1/70, 8/3-6/70, Alton Kelley Poster: $110 Postcard: $30
BG232A	Incredible String Band, Fillmore West 5/11,13/70, Pat Hanks Poster: $175 Postcard: UA	BG247A	Jefferson Airplane, Fillmore West 9/14-15/70, Pat Hanks Postcard: $100
BG233	Spirit, Poco, Fillmore West 5/14-17/70, David Singer Poster: $40 Postcard: $20	BG248	Santana, Dr. John, Fillmore West 9/10-13/70, Norman Orr Poster: $45 Postcard: $15
BG234	No poster bears this marking	BG249	Quicksilver Messenger Service, Buddy Miles, Fillmore West 9/17-20/70, Norman Orr Poster: $70 Postcard: UA
BG235	B.B. King, Albert King, Fillmore West 5/21-24/70, David Singer, Wilfred Satty Poster: $75 Postcard: $15	BG250	Chuck Berry, Eric Burdon and War, Fillmore West 9/24-27, 10/1-4/70, David Singer Poster: UA Postcard: $25
BG236	Country Joe and the Fish, Blues Image, Fillmore West 5/28-31/70, David Singer Poster: $50 Postcard: $10	BG251	Van Morrison, Captain Beefheart and His Magic Band, Fillmore West 10/8-11/70, Norman Orr Poster: $40 Postcard: $25
BG237	Grateful Dead, New Riders of the Purple Sage, Fillmore West 6/4-7/70, David Singer Poster: $70 Postcard: $30	BG252	Leon Russell, Miles Davis, Fillmore West 10/15-18/70, Norman Orr Poster: $30 Postcard: $12
BG238	John Sebastian, Buddy Miles, Fillmore West 6/11-14/70, David Singer Poster: $40 Postcard: $15		

Item	Performer(s), Venue and Date(s)	Item	Performer(s), Venue and Date(s)
BG253	Bo Diddley, Lightning Hopkins, Fillmore West 10/21-25 & 10/28/70, David Singer Poster: $50 Postcard: $20	BG270	Fleetwood Mac, Steppenwolf, Fillmore West 2/11-14 & 2/18-21/71, Winterland 2/12-13/71, Pierre Poster: $120 Postcard: $15
BG254	Procol Harum, Poco, Fillmore West 10/28-11/1/70, David Singer Poster: $50 Postcard: $20	BG271	New Riders of the Purple Sage, Boz Scaggs, Fillmore West 2/25-28/71, David Singer Poster: $35 Postcard: $6
BG255	Frank Zappa, Boz Scaggs, Fillmore West 11/6-8/70, David Singer Poster: $55 Postcard: $25	BG272	Aretha Franklin, King Curtis and the Kingpins, Fillmore West 3/5-7/71, David Singer Poster: $45 Postcard: $10
BG256	Kinks, Elton John, Fillmore West 11/12-15/70, David Singer Poster: $40 Postcard: $20	BG 273/274	Poco, Siegal Schwall, Sons of Champlin, Mark Almond, Fillmore West 3/11-14 & 3/18-21/71, Norman Orr Poster: $75 Postcard: $25
BG 257/258	Love with Arthur Lee, James Gang, Sha Na Na, Elvin Bishop, Fillmore West 11/19-22 & 11/26-29/70, Norman Orr Poster: $120 Postcard: $20	BG275	Eric Burdon and War, Santana, Fillmore West 3/25-28 & 4/1-4/71, Winterland 3/26-27/71, David Singer Poster: $100 Postcard: $10
BG259	Savoy Brown, Ry Cooder, Fillmore West 12/3-6/70, David Singer Poster: $45 Postcard: $15	BG276A	John Mayall, Johnny Winter, Fillmore West 4/8-11 & 4/15-18/71, Winterland 8/9-10 & 8/18/71, Willyum Rowe Poster: $110 Postcard: $15
BG260	Lee Michaels, Albert King, Fillmore West 12/10-13/70, David Singer Poster: $32 Postcard: $15	BG276B	Same as 276A except Dave Mason replaced with Van Morrison Poster: $100 Postcard: UA
BG261	Butterfield Blues Band, Ravi Shankar, Fillmore West 12/14 & 12/16-20/70, Norman Orr Poster: $30 Postcard: $15	BG277	Taj Mahal, Stoneground, Fillmore West 4/22-25/71, Winterland 4/30-5/1/71, Randy Tuten, D. Bread Poster: $30 Postcard: $10
BG262	Delaney and Bonnie and Friends, Voices of East Harlem, Fillmore West 12/26-29/70, Norman Orr Poster: $30 Postcard: $15	BG278	Mike Bloomfield with Chicago Slim, Bola Sete and Mike Finnigan, Ten Years After, Fillmore West 4/29-5/2/71, Winterland 4/20-5/1/71, Randy Tuten, D. Bread Poster: $40 Postcard: $12
BG263	Cold Blood, Grateful Dead, Fillmore West 12/31/70, Winterland 12/31/70, David Singer Poster: $80 Postcard: $15	BG279	Miles Davis, Elvin Bishop Group, Fillmore West 5/6-9/71, David Singer Poster: $35 Postcard: UA
BG264	Cold Blood, Boz Scaggs, Fillmore West 12/31/70-1/3/71, Norman Orr Poster: $45 Postcard: $15	BG280	Humble Pie, Swamp Bogg, Fillmore West 5/13-16/71, David Singer Poster: $40 Postcard: $15
BG265	Spirit, Elvin Bishop Group, Fillmore West 1/7-10/71, Norman Orr Poster: $30 Postcard: $15	BG281	Rascals, Grootna, Fillmore West 5/20-23/71, Randy Tuten Poster: $35 Postcard: $15
BG 266/267	Free, Bloodrock, Spencer Davis, Taj Mahal, Fillmore West 1/14-17 & 1/21-24/71, David Singer Poster: $125 Postcard: $20	BG282	Cold Blood, Grateful Dead, Fillmore West 5/27-30/71, Winterland 5/28-29/71, Randy Tuten Poster: $40 Postcard: $15
BG268	Hot Tuna, Allman Brothers, Fillmore West 1/28-31/71, Norman Orr Poster: $85 Postcard: $20		
BG269	B.B. King, Ballin' Jack, Fillmore West 2/4-7/71, Norman Orr Poster: $100 Postcard: $20		

Item	Performer(s), Venue and Date(s)	Item	Performer(s), Venue and Date(s)

BG283   Albert King, Mott the Hoople, Fillmore West 6/3-6/71, Willyum Rowe
Poster: $35
Postcard: $12

BG284   Cactus, Flamin' Groovies, Fillmore West 6/10-13/71, Willyum Rowe
Poster: $35
Postcard: $15

BG285   Boz Scaggs, Tower of Power, Fillmore West 6/17-20/71, David Singer
Poster: $35
Postcard: $15

BG286   Moby Grape, Spencer Davis and Peter Jameson, Fillmore West 6/24-27/71, David Singer
Poster: $45
Postcard: $15

BG287   Boz Scaggs, Grateful Dead, Fillmore West 6/30-7/4/71, David Singer
Poster: $700

BG288   Grateful Dead, Nassau Coliseum, Uniondale, Long Island, NY 3/15-16/73, David Byrd
Poster: $500

BG289   Rolling Stones, Winterland Auditorium 6/6 & 6/8/72, David Singer
Poster: $375, $125

FAMILY DOG SERIES

FD-1   Tribal Stomp, 2/19/66
Jefferson Airplane, Big Brother & The Holding Company
Poster: (Auction Item), $50
Handbill: UA

Collector's Hint
Handbills on their own can be an enigma. Some, such as FD-1, were printed on three different colors of paper.

FD-2   King Kong (Memorial Dance), 2/26/66
Great Society, Big Brother & The Holding Company, Grass Roots, Quicksilver Messenger Service
Poster: (Auction Item), $25
Handbill: UA

FD-3   Paul Butterfield, 3/25-27/66
Paul Butterfield Blues Band, Quicksilver Messenger Service
Poster: (Auction Item), $100, $35
Handbill: (Auction Item)

Collector's Hint
Many early Family Dog reprints add "© Family Dog Productions, 1725 Washington St., San Francisco" in a lower corner. Additional text, such as franchise distributor info, may also be found.

FD-4   Love Dancers, 4/8-9/66
Love, Sons of Adam, Charlatans
Poster: (Auction Item), $175, $35
Handbill: (Auction Item)

FD-5   Baby Jesus/Blues Project, 11/22-23/66
Blues Project, Great Society
Poster: $550, UA, $35, 5b -UA
Handbill: (Auction Item)

FD-6   Sin Dance, 4/29-30/66
Grass Roots, Sons of Adam, Big Brother & The Holding Company
Poster: $600
Handbill: $125

FD-7   Euphoria, 5/6-7/66
Daily Flash, Rising Sons, Big Brother & The Holding Company, 5/6, Charlatans, 5/7
Poster: (Auction Item), $65, $30
Handbill: UA

FD-8   Laugh Cure, 5/13-14/66
Blues Project, Sons of Adam, Quicksilver Messenger Service
Poster: $650, $65, $35
Handbill: UA

FD-9   Hupmobile 8, 5/20-22/66
Love, Captain Beefheart & His Magic Band, Big Brother & The Holding Company
Poster: (Auction Item), $50, $35
Handbill: UA

FD-10   Hayfever, 5/27-28/66
Leaves, Grass Roots, Grateful Dead, 5/28
Poster: (Auction Item), $35
Handbill: UA

Item	Performer(s), Venue and Date(s)

FD-11   Stone Facade, 6/3-4/66
Grass Roots, Big Brother & The Holding
Company, Buddha From Muir Beach
Poster: (Auction Item), $35
Handbill: UA

FD-12   The Quick and the Dead, 6/10-11/66
Grateful Dead, Quicksilver Messenger Service,
New Tweedy Brothers
Poster: (Auction Item), $35
Handbill: UA

Collector's Note:

With some slight exceptions, Wes Wilson was the
artist behind all of Bill Graham's work until May
1967, while also creating eleven of the first dozen
Family Dog pieces. The Fillmore Auditorium was a
regular venue for rock dances, which began in February 1966. Graham took over the lease in late
March 1966, and began creating the Fillmore legacy. The Fillmore would serve as Graham's showcase for two and a half years, when he then opted
for the Carousel Ballroom ("Fillmore-Carousel" or
"Fillmore West") (6/68).

FD-13   Red Bull, 6/17-18/66
Captain Beefheart & His Magic Band, Oxford
Circle
Poster: UA, $30
Handbill: UA

FD-14   Zig-Zag, 6/24-25/66
Big Brother & The Holding Company, Quicksilver
Messenger Service
Poster: (Auction Item), $175, $40
Handbill: $425

FD-15   Wonderland, 7/1-3/66
Grass Roots, Daily Flash, Sopwith Camel
Poster: $400, $30
Handbill: $150

FD-16   Keep California Green, 7/8-10/66
Sir Douglas Quintet, Everpresent Fullness
Poster: (Auction Item), $30
Handbill: $375

Collector's Hint

The numbering system used in this chart is now
widely accepted despite the discrepancies in it, including no BG-234 or FD-D-16 or FD-D-17.

Item	Performer(s), Venue and Date(s)

FD-17A   Odd One, 7/15-16/66
Love, Big Brother & The Holding Company
Poster: $300
Handbill: $75

Collector's Hint

FD-17A: Since this concert was canceled, opinions
differ as to whether a complete set should include
these items.

FD-17   Snake Lady, 7/22-23/66
Jefferson Airplane, Great Society
Poster: (Auction Item), $125, $65
Handbill: $200

FD-18   Voice of Music, 7/28-30/66
Bo Diddley, Quicksilver Messenger Service
Poster: $500, $40
Handbill: $225

FD-19   Dollar Bill, 8/5-6/66
Bo Diddley, Sons of Adam, Big Brother & The
Holding Company, Oxford Circle
Poster: UA, $30
Handbill: $150

FD-20   Men in a Rowboat, 8/5-7/66
Bo Diddley, Sons of Adam, Little Walter
Poster: $1,500
Handbill: $225

Collector's Hint

Although sources may differ, estimated print runs
were as follows: 1,000-2,000 for posters; 10,000-
15,000 for handbills. On some occasions an additional 1,000 copies of a poster may have been printed.

FD-21   Earthquake, 8/12-13/66
Bo Diddley, Big Brother & The Holding Company
Poster: (Auction Item), $35
Handbill: $200

FD-22   Grateful Dead, 8/19-20/66
Grateful Dead, Sopwith Camel
Poster: $300, $45, $35
Handbill: $175

FD-23   Merry Old Souls, 8/26-27/66
Captain Beefheart & His Magic Band, Charlatans
Poster: $275, $35, $25
Handbill: $200

Item	Performer(s), Venue and Date(s)	Item	Performer(s), Venue and Date(s)

FD-24 Barnyard, 9/2-3/66
13th Floor Elevators, Sir Douglas Quintet
Poster: $200, $35
Handbill: $200

FD-25 Indian, 9/9-10/66
Quicksilver Messenger Service, Great Society
Poster: $200, $50, $25
Handbill: $225

FD-26 Skeleton and Roses, 9/16-17/66
Grateful Dead, Oxford Circle
Poster: (Auction Item), (Auction Item), $225
Handbill: (Auction Item)

FD-27 Wolf, 9/23-24/66
Howlin' Wolf, Big Brother & The Holding
Company
Poster: $700, $225
Handbill: UA

FD-28 Space Man, 9/30/66-10/1/66
13th Floor Elevators, Quicksilver Messenger
Service
Poster: $250, UA, $25
Handbill: $125

FD-29 Girl with Green Hair, 10/7-8/66
Jim Kweskin, Big Brother & The Holding
Company, Electric Train
Poster: $600, $125, $40
Handbill: $200

FD-30 One Year Anniversary, 10/15-16/66
Big Brother & the Holding Company, Sir Douglas
Quintet
Poster: $350, $350, $35
Handbill: $200

FD-31 Edgar Allan Poe
Daily Flash, Country Joe & the Fish
Poster: $175, $200 (wrong date), $35 (third)
Handbill: $75, $150 (wrong date)

FD-32 Roostercycle
Quicksilver Messenger Service, Blackburn &
Snow, Sons of Champlin
Poster: $300
Handbill: UA

Collector's Hint

Some handbills have been counterfeited, with most
documented in Eric King's book, *The Collector's
Guide to Psychedelic Rock Concert Posters, Postcards and Handbills, 1965-1973*. Those of you serious about collecting paper-based products should
read the Printing Technology section of Chapter
Two to assist you in unmasking a forgery.

FD-33 Family Dog Logo
Grateful Dead, Oxford Circle
Poster: $300, $300, $75
Handbill: $150

FD-34 Pyramid
13th Floor Elevators, Moby Grape
Poster: $225, $225, $30
Handbill: $175

FD-35 Hot Air Balloon
Daily Flash, Quicksilver Messenger Service,
Country Joe & the Fish
Poster: $60, $60, $20
Handbill: $50

FD-36 Sunflowers
Quicksilver Messenger Service, Big Brother & The
Holding Company, Country Joe & the Fish
Poster: $75, $75, $30
Handbill: $100

FD-37 Cake
Buffalo Springfield, Daily Flash, Congress of
Wonders
Poster: $65, $30
Handbill: $125

FD-38 Indian Eyes
Big Brother & the Holding Company, Oxford
Circle, Lee Michaels
Poster: $225, $225, $30, UA
Handbill: $80

FD-39 Redskin, 12/16-17/66
Youngbloods, Sparrow, Sons of Champlin
Poster: $150, $30
Handbill: $80

FD-40 Santa Claus, 12/23-24/66
Grateful Dead, Steve Miller Blues Band, Moby
Grape
Poster: $175
Handbill: $100

FD-41 Ship, 12/30-31/66
Country Joe & the Fish, Moby Grape, Lee Michaels
Poster: $200, $30
Handbill: UA

FD-42 Dancing Lady, 1/6-7/67
Quicksilver Messenger Service, Steve Miller Blues
Band, Other Half
Poster: $300
Postcard: $125

FD-43 Movie Star, 1/13-14/67
Moby Grape, Sparrow, Charlatans
Poster: $250, $40
Postcard: $125

Item	Performer(s), Venue and Date(s)	Item	Performer(s), Venue and Date(s)

FD-44   Pouring, 1/20-21/67
Steve Miller Blues Band, Lee Michaels, Congress of Wonders
Poster: $25
Postcard: $10

FD-45   Girl with Long Swirling Hair, 1/20-21/67
Grateful Dead, Quicksilver Messenger Service
Poster: $300, $150
Postcard: UA

FD-46   Dance of the Five Moons, 2/3-4/67
Country Joe & the Fish, Sparrow, Kaleidoscope
Poster: $35, UA, UA
Postcard: $8

FD-47   Sphinx Dance, 2/10-11/67
Steve Miller Blues Band, Lee Michaels, Peanut Butter Conspiracy
Poster: $80, $40
Postcard: $150

FD-48   Tribal Stomp #2, 2/17-18/67
Big Brother & The Holding Company, Quicksilver Messenger Service, Oxford Circle
Poster: $30, $20
Postcard: $5

FD-49   Neptune's Notion, 2/24-25/67
Moby Grape, Charlatans
Poster: $30
Postcard: $5

FD-50   Break On Through, 3/3-4/67
Country Joe & the Fish, Sparrow, The Doors
Poster: $225, $75, $35
Postcard: $10

Collector's Hint

Handbill forgeries typically fall short when they fail to pick up very fine screens that often appear in brighter areas such as white.

FD-51   Peacock Ball, 3/10-11/67
Quicksilver Messenger Service, Steve Miller Blues Band, Daily Fresh
Poster: $45 (white logo), $25 (magenta)
Postcard: $10

FD-52   Contact, 3/17-18/67
Big Brother & The Holding Company, Charles Lloyd, Sir Douglas Quintet
Poster: $70, $35
Postcard: $10

FD-53   Plains of Quicksilver, 3/22-23/67
Quicksilver Messenger Service, John Lee Hooker, Steve Miller Blues Band
Poster: UA, $35
Postcard: $5

FD-54   Three Indian Dudes, 3/24-26/67
Grateful Dead, Quicksilver Messenger Service, John Hammond & His Screaming Nighthawks, Robert Baker
Poster: $30, $10
Postcard: $80

FD-55   Eye, 3/31-4/1/67
Big Brother & The Holding Company, Charlatans, Blue Cheer
Poster: $30
Postcard: $10

FD-56   Front Porch, 4/7-8/67
Charlatans, Sparrow, Canned Heat
Poster: $35, $20
Postcard: $10

FD-57   Psychedelic Swirl, 4/14-15/67
The Doors, Steve Miller Blues Band, Haji Baba
Poster: $225, $125
Postcard: $50

FD-58   Pot, 4/21-22/67
Quicksilver Messenger Service, John Hammond & His Screaming Nighthawks, Charles Lloyd
Poster: $40, $25
Postcard: $10

FD-59   Bobbsey Twins, 4/28-29/67
Chambers Brothers, Iron Butterfly
Poster: $20
Postcard: $5

FD-60   Motherload, 5/5-7/67
Big Brother & The Holding Company, Sir Douglas Quintet, Orkustra
Poster: $40
Postcard: $15

FD-61   Butterfly Lady, 5/12-13/67
The Doors, Sparrow
Poster: $65
Postcard: $25

FD-62   Sutters Mill, 5/19-21/67
Quicksilver Messenger Service, Country Joe & the Fish
Poster: $35
Postcard: $10

FD-63   CHA, 5/26-28/67
Charlatans, Salvation Army Banned, Blue Cheer
Poster: $70, $45
Postcard: $20

FD-64   Pink Panther, 6/1-4/67
Steve Miller Blues Band, Daily Flash, The Doors
Poster: UA, $50
Postcard: $20

Item	Performer(s), Venue and Date(s)
FD-65	Magic Show, 6/8-11/67 Big Brother & The Holding Company, Canned Heat Blues Band Poster: $250, $40 Postcard: $10

Collector's Hint

Postcard variations do exist, such as inclusion or exclusion of a bulk rate permit on verso, as well as the mode used to address the item. Please refer to Eric King's book *The Collector's Guide to Psychedelic Rock Concert Posters, Postcards and Handbills, 1965-1973* for details.

Item	Performer(s), Venue and Date(s)
FD-66	Strongman, 6/15-18/67 Youngbloods, Siegal Schwall Band Poster: $35 Postcard: $15
FD-67	RLAT, 6/22-25/67 Charlatans, 13th Floor Elevators Poster: $70, $40 Postcard: $10
FD-68	Horns of Plenty, 6/29-7/267 Quicksilver Messenger Service, Mount Rushmore, Big Brother & The Holding Company Poster: $40, $35 Postcard: $10
FD-69	Independence, 7/4/67 Quicksilver Messenger Service, Siegal Schwall, Phoenix Poster: $40, $10 Postcard: $10
FD-70	Chicago Fire, 7/6-9/67 Steve Miller Blues Band, Siegal Schwall Band Poster: $30 Postcard: $5
FD-71	TANS, 7/13-16/67 Charlatans, Youngbloods, Other Half Poster: $45, $45 Postcard: $10
FD-72	Family Portrait, 7/20-23/67 Big Brother & The Holding Company, Mount Rushmore, Canned Heat, Mother Earth Poster: $25 Postcard: $10
FD-73	Smiling Hun, 7/27-30/67 Blue Cheer, Captain Beefheart & His Magic Band, Youngbloods Poster: $30, $10 Postcard: $10

Item	Performer(s), Venue and Date(s)
FD-74	Taj Mahal, 8/3-6/67 Charles Lloyd Quartet, West Coast Natural Gas Co, Tripping West to East Poster: $50, $25 Postcard: $12
FD-75	Three Little Bares, 8/10-13/67 Moby Grape, Canned Heat, Vanilla Fudge Poster: $20 Postcard: $10
FD-76	High Yo Silver Quicksilver Messenger Service, Other Half, Melvin Q Poster: $25 Postcard: $10
FD-77	War and Peace, 8/24-27/67 Big Brother & The Holding Company, Bo Diddley, Bukka White, Salvation Army Banned Poster: $50, $30 Postcard: $10
FD-78	Angel, 9/1-3/67 Steve Miller Blues Band, Mother Earth, Bukka White Poster: $60, $30 Postcard: $10
FD-79-D1	Denver Opening Big Brother & The Holding Company, Blue Cheer, Eighth Penny Matter Poster: $375 (lg), $35 (sm) Postcard: $30
FD-80	Tea Party, 9/8-10/67 South Side Sound System, Phoenix, Freedom Highway Poster: $30 Postcard: $10
FD-D2	Denver, 9/15-16/67 Haw Haw, Quicksilver Messenger Service, Charlatans Poster: $35 Postcard: $10
FD-81	Mist Dance, 9/15-17/67 Youngbloods, Other Half, Mad River Poster: $35, $20 Postcard: $10
FD-82-D3	The Head, 9/22-23/67 Grateful Dead, Mother Earth Poster: $45, UA Postcard: $30
FD-83	Sky Web, 9/22-24/67 Charlatans, Buddy Guy Poster: $30 Postcard: $10

Item	Performer(s), Venue and Date(s)
FD-84-D4	Flash, 9/29-30/67 Lothar Hand People, The Doors, Captain Beefheart & His Magic Band Poster: $100 Postcard: $25
FD-85-D4	Dian, 9/29-10/1/67 Vanilla Fudge, Charles Lloyd Quartet Poster: $100 Postcard: $25
FD-D5	Kitty, 10/6-7/67 Buffalo Springfield, Eighth Penny Matter Poster: $30 Postcard: $10
FD-86	Flower Pot, 10/6-8/67 Blue Cheer, Lee Michaels, Clifton Chenier Poster: $60, $30 Postcard: $10
FD-D6	Apache, 10/13-14/67 Van Morrison, Daily Flash Poster: $45 Postcard: $10
FD-87	King of Spades, 10/13-15/67 Buddy Guy, Captain Beefheart & His Magic Band, Blue Cheer Poster: $25 Postcard: $10
FD-D7	Celestial Moonchild, 10/20-21/67 Canned Heat, Allman Joy Poster: $35, $20 Postcard: $10
FD-88	Burning, 10/20-22/67 Van Morrison, Daily Flash, Hair Poster: $35 Postcard: $10

Collector's Hint

An area often overlooked by counterfeiters is paper stock, and with over 1,500 classifications of paper it's easy to understand why mistakes are typically made. Besides whiteness and brightness, the smoothness of the printing surface influences the appearance of ink placed on it. Typically when someone is having an item such as a poster printed, they will specify the grade, weight, and finish of the desired paper. Most posters printed today are done on a text grade paper, which comes in a standard size (25 x 38) at various weights (90, 100, 120, 140, 160, 180). Many of the counterfeit posters you will encounter can be identified by a variance in one of these parameters. Refer to Eric King's book *The Collector's Guide to Psychedelic Rock Concert Posters, Postcards and Handbills, 1965-1973* for specifics on stock thickness variances.

Item	Performer(s), Venue and Date(s)
FD-89	Morning Paper, 10/27-29/67 Quicksilver Messenger Service, Sons of Champlin Poster: $50 Postcard: 25
FD-D8	Incidental Inca, 10/27-28/67 Allman Joy, Lothar and Hand People Poster: $35 Postcard: $10
FD-D10	Washday Detergent, 11/3-4/67 Blue Cheer, Superfine Dandelion Poster: $30 Postcard: $10
FD-90	Super Ball, 11/3-5/67 Canned Heat, Lothar and Hand People Poster: $20 Postcard: $10
FD-D9	Fan Fare, 11/7-8/67 Jefferson Airplane, Other Half Poster: $35 Postcard: $10
FD-D11	Expansion, 11/10-11/67 Other Half, Sons of Champlin Poster: $30 Postcard: $10
FD-91	Sunny Side, 11/10-12/67 Youngbloods, Mad River Poster: $30 Postcard: $7
FD-92	Squiggly Trinity, 11/17-19/67 Bo Diddley, Lee Michaels Poster: $25 Postcard: $7
FD-D12	Chaotic License, 11/17-18/67 Chuck Berry, Sons of Champlin Poster: $25 Postcard: $8
FD-93	Optical Occlusion, 11/23-25/67 Big Brother & The Holding Company, Mount Rushmore Poster: $35 Postcard: $15
FD-94	Nashville Katz, 11/30-12/2/67 Flatt & Scruggs, Lewis & Clarke Expedition Poster: $25 Postcard: $10
FD-D13	Denver Splash, 12/1-2/67 Jim Kweskin and His Jug Band, Solid Muldoon Poster: $35 Postcard: $7

Item	Performer(s), Venue and Date(s)	Item	Performer(s), Venue and Date(s)

FD-D14   Fireball, 12/8-9/67
Canned Heat, Siegal Schwall
Poster: $35
Postcard: $7

FD-95   Avalon Splash, 12/8-10/67
Jim Kweskin Jug Band, Sons of Champlin
Poster: $25
Postcard: $10

FD-D15   Truth, 12/15-16/67
Soul Survivors, Box Tops
Poster: $30
Postcard: $5

FD-96   Dance, Dance, 12/15-17/67
Quicksilver Messenger Service, Charlatans,
Congress of Wonders
Poster: $30
Postcard: $10

FD-97   Collage, 12/21-23/67
Siegal Schwall, Blue Cheer, Soul Survivors
Poster: $25
Postcard: $8

FD-98   Tree Frog, 12/28-30/67
Jim Kweskin & His Jug Band, Lee Michaels, Blue
Cheer
Poster: $35
Postcard: $8

FD-D18   Pay Attention, 12/29-31/67
Doors, Allman Joy
Poster: $275, $75
Postcard: $15

FD-99   Sitting Pretty, 12/21/67
Blue Cheer, Jim Kweskin & His Jug Band, Lee
Michaels, Flamin' Groovies, Mad River, Mount
Rushmore
Poster: $35, UA
Postcard: $7

FD-100   Rocking Cloud, 1/5-7/68
Youngbloods, Ace of Cups, John Bauer's Rocking
Cloud
Poster: $30
Postcard: $8

FD-101   Eternal Reservoir, 1/12-14/68
Quicksilver Messenger Service, Kaleidoscope,
Charley Musselwhite
Poster: $60
Postcard: $20

FD-102   Rocking Chair, 1/19-21/68
Genesis, Siegal Schwall, Mother Earth
Poster: $30
Postcard: $8

FD-103   Heavy, 1/26-28/68
Country Joe & the Fish, Charlatans, Dan Hicks &
The Hot Licks
Poster: $35
Postcard: $10

FD-104   The Finger, 2/2-4/68
Electric Flag, Mad River, Fugs, 13th Floor
Elevators
Poster: $30
Postcard: $14

FD-105   Dinosaur, 2/9-11/68
Siegal Schwall, Buddy Guy, Hour Glass, Mance
Lipscomb
Poster: $30
Postcard: $8

FD-106   One Hundred Six, 2/16-18/68
Youngbloods, Mount Rushmore, Phoenix
Poster: $25
Postcard: $8

FD-107   The Circus Is Coming, 2/23-25/68
Quicksilver Messenger Service, Buddy Guy, Jon
House
Poster: $25
Postcard: $10

FD-108   Peyote Bird, 3/1-3/68
Blues Project, Genesis, Taj Mahal, Blue Flames
Poster: $30
Postcard: $10

FD-109   Love Lady, 3/8-10/68
Love, Congress of Wonders, Sons of Champlin
Poster: $45, $30
Postcard: $10

FD-110   Liberty, 3/15-17/68
Blood, Sweat & Tears, John Handy, Son House
Poster: $25
Postcard: $10

FD-111   Charlie Chaplin, 3/22-24/68
Siegal Schwall, Kaleidoscope, Savage
Resurrection
Poster: $25
Postcard: $5

FD-112   Triplets, 3/29-31/68
Jerry Steig & Styrs, Sons of Champlin, 4th Way,
Alexander's Timeless Bloozband
Poster: $20
Postcard: $5

FD-113   Rorschach Test, 4/5-7/68
Blues Project, It's a Beautiful Day, Nazz Are Blues
Band
Poster: $25
Postcard: $5

Item	Performer(s), Venue and Date(s)
FD-114	Flip Flop, 4/12-14/68 Fugs, Aces of Cups, Allman Joy Poster: $25 Postcard: $10
FD-115	The Sorcerer, 4/19-21/68 Steppenwolf, Charley Musselwhite, 4th Way, Indian Head Band Poster: $30 Postcard: $8
FD-116	It's a Gas, 4/26-28/68 Quicksilver Messenger Service, Charlatans, It's a Beautiful Day Poster: $30 Postcard: $10
FD-117	Giddyap, 5/3-5/68 Junior Wells, Canned Heat, Crome Syrcus, Clover Poster: $30 Postcard: $15
Fd-118	Dancing Bear, 5/10-12/68 Quicksilver Messenger Service, Ace of Cups Poster: $25 Postcard: $7
FD-119	245765, 5/17-19/68 Junior Wells, Santana Poster: $30 Postcard: $7
FD-120	Spaghetti Hair Lady, 5/24-26/68 Youngbloods, Kaleidoscope Poster: $25 Postcard: $15
FD-121	Mechanico Mandala, 5/31-6/2/68 Taj Mahal, Creedence Clearwater Revival Poster: $25 Postcard: $15
FD-122	Iron Butterfly, 6/7-9/68 Iron Butterfly, Velvet Underground Poster: $40 Postcard: $15
FD-123	Rorschach II, 6/14-16/68 Frumius Bandersnatch, Clear Light Poster: $30 Postcard: $20
FD-124	Pop-Up Poster, 6/21-23/68 Mother Earth, Kaleidoscope Poster: $25 Postcard: $10
FD-125	Alice Jaundice Youngbloods, It's a Beautiful Day Poster: $30 Postcard: UA
FD-126	Alice Griffin, 7/4-7/68 Iron Butterfly, Indian Head Nickel Poster: $40 Postcard: $15
FD-127	Forest, 7/12-14/68 Steve Miller Band, Howlin' Wolf Poster: $25 Postcard: $15
FD-128	In a Woodpile, 7/19-21/68 Tim Buckley, Velvet Underground Poster: $40 Postcard: $15
FD-129	Rosebud, 7/23-25/68 Country Joe & the Fish, Dan Hicks and His Hot Licks Poster: $25 Postcard: $8
FD-130	Black and White Indian, 7/26-28/68 Quicksilver Messenger Service, Dan Hicks and His Hot Licks Poster: $25 Postcard: $8
FD-131	Cosmos, 8/2-4/68 Holy Modal Rockers, Pink Floyd Poster: $45 Postcard: $15
FD-132	Aurora, 8/9-11/68 Steppenwolf, Siegal Schwall Poster: $22 Postcard: $10
FD-133	Tom Donohue, 8/9-11/68 Bill Haley and the Comets, Drifters Poster: $45 Postcard: $20
FD-134	Reach, 8/23-25/68 Spirit, Sir Douglas Quintet Plus 2 Poster: $40 Postcard: $15
FD-135	Alligator Bush, 8/29-31/68 Youngbloods, It's a Beautiful Day Poster: $25 Postcard: $10
FD-136	Garden of Eden, 9/6-8/68 James Cotton Blues Band, Sir Douglas Quintet Plus 2 Poster: $35 Postcard: $15

Item	Performer(s), Venue and Date(s)	Item	Performer(s), Venue and Date(s)
FD-137	Train Trip, 9/13-15/68 John Myall, Big Mama Thornton and the Hound Dog Band Featuring Harmonica George Poster: $60 Postcard: $15	FD-142	Velvet Underground, Charles Musselwhite, 10/18-20/68 Poster: $50 Postcard: $15
FD-138	Distortion, 9/20-22/68 Steve Miller Band, Muddy Waters Poster: $25 Postcard: $15	FD-143	Buddy Miles Express, Dino Valenti, 10/25-27/68 Poster: $22 Postcard: $7
FD-139	Flatt and Scruggs, Jack Elliott, 9/27-29/68 Poster: $40 Postcard: $10	FD-144	Byrds, Taj Mahal, 11/1-3/68 Poster: $25 Postcard: $12
FD-140	Quicksilver Messenger Service, Black Pearl, 10/4-6/68 Poster: $30 Postcard: $12	FD-145	Mother Earth, Kaleidoscope, 11/8-10/68 Poster: $30 Postcard: $15
FD-141	Grateful Dead, Lee Michaels, 10/11-13/68 Poster: $40 Postcard: $12	FD-146	Love, Lee Michaels, 11/15-17/68 Poster: $30 Postcard: $10
		FD-147	Quicksilver Messenger Service, Sons of Champlin, 11/28-30/68 Poster: $20 Postcard: $8

7
A PLETHORA OF PLECTRUMS:
COLLECTING GUITAR PICKS

Would you pay $150 for a guitar pick used by Eric Clapton? I did, and I am not alone. Picks, like baseball card wrappers (which are worth money!), often go unnoticed, but they are essential elements to guitarists and their modes of playing. A pick for a guitarist can be like a certain bat for a baseball player, and some guitarists have been known to be a bit stingy with their plectrums.

Picks come in all shapes and sizes and can be made of ebony and ivory and even stone and silver. They can have a dull finish or a sparkling shine, and can be opaque or translucent. They can include initials, a caricature, a band's logo, a facsimile of a signature, or even a creative quotation. Take your pick!

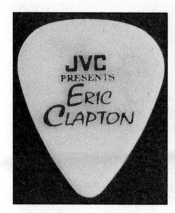  

A stage used Eric Clapton versus a promotional pick: the difference is about $140.

A guitar pick used by Garth Brooks. His picks are typically valued between $20 and $35.

A nice selection of Cheap Trick guitar picks. Rick Nielsen picks usually fetch between $10 and $30.

PICK POPULARITY

The most ubiquitous of all plectra is the No. 351 medium Fender pick. Typically made of celluloid, this one-inch triangular pick is often .71 millimeters thick. Celluloid was one of the first commercial plastics and, although picks can be found of other materials, this substance has clearly dominated pick production.

Celluloid has been popular primarily because of its durability and flexibility, but rising costs began inhibiting its practicality during the early 1990s, so many manufacturers were forced to turn to alternative materials. Fender Musical Instruments Company announced during the summer of 1993 that it would be phasing out its celluloid pick production. D'Andrea, one of the world's largest pick manufacturers, has also seen the migration to other forms of materials, and has also noted the decrease in pick shapes. Half a century ago the company was offering dozens of styles and shapes; now it offers dramatically fewer.

The search for new pick materials has seen everything from coconut and ebony to brass and steel. In combining new material with the search for the perfect pick grip, any combination is conceivable. Pick innovators have tried a "KORK-GRIP," unique notching, and even a variety of resins, all in search of the perfect pick.

Why all the fuss? Simply put, more than 57 million adults in the U.S. play at least one instrument and half of them play two or more. The number of guitar players (over 19 million) is second only to the number of piano players (over 21 million). If they all buy at least one pick per year, that's about a five million dollar market.

ORIGINS

A plectrum, or pick, is a thin piece of material for plucking the strings of a guitar or similar stringed instrument. When and where the pick originated is only conjecture. Feather quills were used for centuries to pluck stringed instruments, so they may indeed be the first plectra.

By the late 1800s birds were out and turtles were in, specifically the Atlantic hawksbill sea turtle, whose shell (when crafted properly) yielded the perfect pick. The tonal qualities and flexibility of tortoise shell picks could not be matched. Although the first pick ever patented in the United States came from John Farris of Hartford, Connecticut, in 1885, most plectrums at that time were imported from Europe. Because imports were taxed and sea turtles were not as plentiful as one might think, tortoise shell picks were not cheap. After a thorough analysis of nearly every type of material conceivable, the quest for a tortoise shell substitute yielded a synthetic substance: celluloid.

CELLULOID

The first synthetic plastic material, celluloid was first produced by Alexander Parkes in 1856, but it wasn't until 1869 that John Wesley Hyatt developed it into a commercial product. Celluloid is made from a mix of cellulose nitrate and camphor. Because of its strength, toughness, luster, coloribility, and cost effectiveness, it made an outstanding substitute for ivory and other materials in such items as billiard balls, collar stays, dentures, brushes, combs, photographic film, and plectrums.

The drawback of the material is that, chemically, cellulose nitrate is closely related to the explosive material nitrocellulose. Celluloid burns furiously when ignited, as many early movie theater owners found out. It was eventually replaced as a photo film base by cellulose acetate, but is still commonly used in ping pong balls and drafting triangles.

Celluloid offered greater flexibility than tortoise shell picks at a dramatically reduced cost. The material also proved durable and had a high tensile strength, commonly referred to as "memory," or its ability to return to its original shape after being bent. This element is critical to a plectrum, as musical notes are often just a split second apart.

Celluloid mandolin picks were available through the Sears & Roebuck catalog at the turn of the century, but celluloid's nemesis was always combustibility, and many manufacturers began to move away from the material in the 1940s. The alternative, although not a great one, was composite plastics.

PIONEERS OF PLECTRA

The most revered guitar pick is the (Luigi) D'Andrea No. 351 shape. The shape itself has not changed in six decades, and has been around since the late 1920s. In the '20s, flat picks were strictly for mandolins or banjos, and even though manufacturers were making steel guitars, they were often plucked with a distinct finger-picking style.

Before Tiny Tim sang "Tiptoe Thru the Tulips," it was a hit by Nick Lucas in the 1929 film *Gold Diggers*. Lucas, playing a steel-string guitar with a flat pick, popularized the practice that soon had many musicians casting away their mandolins. The result was Gibson's highly marketed Nick Lucas Guitar that came with "The Pick with the Crooning Tune"—an original Nick Lucas pick manufactured by D'Andrea. The exclusive design even bore his name, the first guitar pick to do so. The shape of the pick was No. 351, eventually known as the "Nick Lucas shape."

The pick eventually evolved into the Fender Medium guitar pick, or "Fender Pick," during the late 1950s. The "sideman pick" or "The Famous No. 351" was soon instantly recognizable by guitar players all across the nation.

A plethora of plectra pioneers soon permeated the market, in search of the perfect pick, new and improved, with greater flexibility and firmer grip.

PICK PIONEERS, PATENTS AND PROBLEM SOLVERS

David W. Barnes: celluloid and leather plectrum
Charles F.W. Seidel: multipoint plectrum, similar to a pocket knife in operation
Frederick Wahl: a pair of concave rubber discs attached to a thumb ring
Wurlitzer: the Vacuum Pick, an improvement on above design
Carolyn Cockrane: a shank that could wedge a pick
Louis Knackstedt: oblong plectrum with rubber plugs
Aaron Burdise: wire loop pick
Carpenter & Towner: Kork Grip pick
Peter Rudestyle: nonslip pick
Luigi D'Andrea: creator of No. 351
Joseph Moshay: pick with holes, nylon picks
Herco: nylon picks, Flex 50 , Flex 75, and Fleylon line
Bob Clifton: Tu-Way pick, diamond shaped
Gretsch: "Non--Skid," laminated with hard rubber edges
D'Andrea: "Cuhin-Grip" pick
Herco: 720 line

LUIGI D'ANDREA

Originally from Lamis, Foggia, Italy, Luigi D'Andrea immigrated to this country in 1902, while still a teenager. He loved music, good food, and a good cigar. He began the world's largest pick company as a one-room operation at 395 W. Broadway in New York City. Within ten years he had dozens of shapes and styles, made of both celluloid and tortoise shell. His heart-shaped pick eventually evolved and closed at the top, first dubbed No.44, and later No. 351 the most famous of them all.

Gibson, Martin, Fender, and Gretsch all turned to D'Andrea for their picks. The company was always on the edge of innovation, establishing the pick imprint industry and new guidelines for pick thicknesses, and being the only American manufacturer of authentic tortoise shell plectrums—notoriety that would last until the turtle landed on the endangered species list.

D'Andrea essentially dominated the industry into the 1960s, when a few other vendors emerged primarily armed with nylon picks.

PICK PRODUCTION

Hand-cast picks, created via mallet and die, went through a sanding process, although unsanded variations were sold at discounted prices. Eventually the die-casting procedure became automated, with edges smoothed through a tumbling procedure. Picks created during this automated era typically came in three gauges: light (.02"), medium (.03") and heavy (.04").

Gibson, Gretsch, and Martin eventually emerged to market instrument accessories. Gibson was one of the first to include celebrity imprint plectrums—Harry Reser and Eddie Lang, a noted jazz guitarist. Little did they know what a business would be derived in later years from celebrity imprint plectrums. By the 1940s, numerous celebrities had their own line of picks, including Nick Lucas, George Barnes, and Les Paul.

Mosaic picks also became popular, primarily due to the unique chemical properties that make up celluloid. An advantage for manufacturers is that they could fuse leftover scraps or irregular production pieces back into the celluloid to create new multicolored pieces (perhaps this was a prelude to the psychedelic era that was to follow).

ROCK 'N' ROLL

Rock 'n' roll thrust the six-string guitar (electric and acoustic) into the spotlight, and with it the pick. Other companies emerged to try to grab a share of the D'Andrea-dominated market. The Hershman Musical Instrument Company (New York) chose to market nylon picks, primarily because of the low cost and ease of production.

D'Andrea reacted by phasing out many older lines—banjo, mandolin, etc.—and restandardizing its thickness gauges to .018" (.46mm), .028" (.71mm), and .038" (.96mm). In the 1970s the company added three new celluloid gauges: .58mm, .84mm, and 1.21mm.

In Japan, Shoji Nakano began pick production in 1961, and a decade later was creating hundreds of thousands of Pick Boy picks. The company eventually became one of the top three pick manufacturers in the world. Jim Dunlop also saw opportunities in the small pieces of celluloid, and he built a company that rivaled both D'Andrea and Pick Boy.

COLLECTING PICKS AS ROCK 'N' ROLL ARTIFACTS

When I tell people that I collect guitar picks, they are sometimes surprised that I would even make an effort, yet alone spend money, collecting these little pieces of plastic that most musicians discard at will. I then remind them that most people in the 1950s and 1960s bought sports trading cards just for the gum.

A theory that I have quoted to numerous dealers, especially those looking to make money in collectibles, is that often, people throw things away that may be valuable without realizing it. If they can be dated, someone will end up collecting them and someone else will make money selling them. Another piece of advice while I'm at it: By the time the general public realizes that some item is worth collecting—because they may have heard it was worth money—it's probably too late to begin a cost-effective collection.

Guitar picks are fun to collect and a bit addicting, not unlike other areas of rock 'n' roll memorabilia. In general they are inexpensive, durable, easy to store, often unique in design, and part of rock 'n' roll history. Ever since the name Nick Lucas appeared on a pick, the little pieces of celluloid have taken on a whole new meaning.

Pick collecting can take a number of different forms. Collecting pick display cards is one option. These counter displays have been used as a direct marketing method since the 1930s and '40s. A variety of picks can be easily displayed and stored on these specially made displays. Many also include pictures of famous guitarists endorsing the product. Other areas of collecting include historical and vintage picks of all shapes, forms, and sizes; and pick advertisements from magazines or newspapers. I have seen collectors who choose to collect only the guitar picks of a certain musician or group, while others may choose only odd-shaped picks, tortoise shell picks, or promotional picks.

I remember reading an article in the July 1975 issue of *Guitar Player* magazine. In it the guitar pick was examined as a logical rock 'n' roll artifact, which it indeed is. If you ever have wondered what it would be like to own an actual piece of memorabilia once used by John Lennon, Elvis Presley, or Jimi Hendrix, maybe guitar pick collecting is for you.

Who is Mr. Meat Science? (Mills' picks are valued at $15 to $25.)

If you're going to collect guitar picks, your first step should be going to a music store and familiarizing yourself with the different forms of picks made by the various manufacturers. Next, get a subscription to an industry periodical such as *Goldmine* and scan the advertisements for pick ads, both buying and selling. Then familiarize yourself with the types of picks used by celebrities: gauge, style, and any unique imprinting that is indicative of that guitarist. This might take a little time, but it is well worth it. For example, if you're going to collect the bass picks of Michael Edward Mills of R.E.M., you may want to learn some of his preferences. Many R.E.M. guitar pick collectors are familiar with the fact that the bassist often uses a Fender (heavy) tortoise shell pick, often personalized with a quote, such as "MR. MEAT SCIENCE." Contacting other collectors and resources can be extremely useful.

KEITH RICHARDS - A SELECTION OF PERSONALIZED GUITAR PICKS

FRONT/BACK	COLORS
At the Voodoo Lounge/Open 24 Hours	Black on White
Blame-Hound/Blank	Gold on Tortoise
C.D. on G.P./Room No.	Black on Blue
Crushed Pearl/Blank	White on Red
Five String King/Keef Riffhard	Black on White
Keef Riff Hard/Blank	White on Red
Lord Richards/Thru And Thru	Black on White, White on Red
Main Offender/Keef Riff Hard	White on Red
Main Offender/The X-Pensive Winos	White on Red
Mr. Keith Richards/Sparks Will Fly	White on Red
Mr. Keith Richards/Voodoo Lounge	Black on White
Keith Richards/Main Offender	White on Red
Keith Richards/Midnight Rambler	Black on White
Keith Richards/The Worst	White on Red
Rated XXX/Blank	Black on White, White on Red
Room No./Bay 7	Black on Pink
Talk Is Cheap/Touring Ain't	White on Red
Talk Is Cheap/Touring Ape	White on Red
The Biff Hitler Trio/Blank	Black on White, White on Red
The Glimmer Twins/Blank	White on Tortoise
The Rebel Smells/Blank	Gold on White, White on Red
The Rolling Stones/Blank	Black on Blue, Black on Yellow
The Rolling Stones/(Tongue Logo)	Black on White
Trail of Terror/Blank	White on Red

Note: As you can see by the pick quotes, both the roadies and techs have had their share of fun with the guitarist. You can also see just how indicative these are of the person who uses them. Sorry Keef!

Guitar picks used by the Rolling Stones. Keith's picks can cost anywhere from $50 to $75, while picks from Ron Woods and Darryl Jones are valued at $50 to $60 and $25 to $30, respectively.

EDWARD VAN HALEN - A SELECTION OF PERSONALIZED GUITAR PICKS

*facsimile signature

FRONT/BACK	COLORS
Ou812/*5150	Gold on White
5150/Blank	Black on White
Balance 1995/(Logo)*	Gold on Yellow
Balance Tour 1995/Blank	Gold on Yellow
For Unlawful...(Logo/Ring)/*	Gold on Black, Gold on Tortoise
For Unlawful...(Logo/Ring)*/You Wanker	Gold on White, White on Black
For Unlawful...(Logo/Ring)*/But Of Course	Gold on Tortoise
For Unlawful...(Logo/Ring)*/Uh Guh Guh Guh Guhh!	Gold on Black
Friday Viernes/(Logo)*	Gold on Yellow
(Logo)/Edward Van Halen	Black on Red, White on Black
(Logo)*/I Just Can't Stop Loving You (Japanese)	Black on Yellow
(Logo/Ring)/Blank	Red on White
(Logo/Ring) You Have A Nice Day/* See Ya Next Time	White (Raised)
(Logo/Ring)/*	Black on Yellow, Gold on Yellow
(Logo/Ring)/*	Gold on Black (Japanese Tour Only)
(Logo/Ring)/*	Gold on Red (Japanese Tour Only)
(Logo/Ring)/*	Gold on Clear Blue
Monday Lunes/(Logo)*	Gold on Yellow
Ou812/5150*	Gold on White, Silver on White
Peavey Evh 5150/*	Black & White on Red
Peavey, Evh Wolfgang/I Saw It!	Yellow on Purple
Saturday Sabado/(Logo)*	Gold on Yellow
Sunday Domingo/(Logo)*	Gold on Yellow
Thursday Jueves/(Logo)*	Gold on Yellow
Tuesday Martes/Blank	Gold on Yellow
Tuesday Martes/(Logo)*	Gold on Yellow

Note: This is just a very small selection of the numerous forms of picks the guitarist uses. Add to it the number of color variations, many of which are not included on this list, and you can realize the effort involved in documenting all of these pieces.

The greatest obstacle facing the collector of guitar picks today is authenticity. It's extremely hard to authenticate a pick, and even harder to prove it was actually used by the particular guitarist it represents. This is where knowing the provenance (history) of an item is particularly handy. Knowing where the pick originated and some of the details about the piece can be helpful in determining the likelihood of its authenticity. It all boils down to purchasing items from reliable and trustworthy sources.

PICK CARE

The first rule all pick collectors need to learn is DO NOT STORE CELLULOID PICKS NEAR HEAT! The second thing to learn is how to tell a celluloid pick from a tortoise shell pick. Usually the sound is a good way: celluloid picks emit a dull sound when striking a surface, while tortoise shells emit a sharp sound and even bounce a bit more. The surface of a tortoise shell pick is also variable, not a smooth matte finish like celluloid.

Most pick collectors know where the nearest coin shop is because they use half dollar holders to store their guitar picks. They display nicely through the clear opening and are protected by the cardboard surrounding the pick. The holders also conveniently slip into specially designed three-hole punched plastic storage sheets. If you use these sheets, it is best to use archival (inert polypropylene or polyethylene), as other types may damage the picks. The cardboard surface of the holder is also easy to write on for identification purposes. When these sheets are slipped into a convenient three-ring binder and stored in a cool (not cold), dry, dark place, your picks should be safe.

PICK POTENTIAL: VALUES

How much would you pay for an authentic guitar pick from Jimi Hendrix, Duane Allman, or Stevie Ray Vaughan ? I ask the question because if you're going to collect picks, then you are also going to contribute to the market price for the item. An authentic Edward Van Halen pick will run between $40 and $250, depending upon scarcity and style. Hey Eddie, now you know why the roadies and techs are ordering so many of your guitar picks! (OUGOT12?)

Unless you have connections inside a band or work at the pick factory, some of these pieces could cost you some money. (I'd personally rather pay the money than risk my life in a mosh pit trying to grab a Trent Reznor pick.) Like any market, dealer prices vary, so shop around. For example, at a collectors' show I paid $30 for a Mike Mills bass pick from one dealer and $4 for the identical pick from another dealer, all because I failed to check prices and merchandise before buying.

Remember, for years the standard personalized pick consisted of about ten to twelve block letters, die-printed. Many of rock's legendary guitarists never had personalized picks, only "freebies" or samples. It's common knowledge that Hendrix used "Manny's" picks, from a music store in New York City. Typically picks are ordered and sold in large lots, with the smallest orders now about 100 items.

Since cheap picks are common, so are forgeries. I have seen numerous collectors purchase a style of pick never used by the associated artist. Again, deal only with reputable sources and research before you buy. Networking is the key: Know the top collectors in certain areas and don't be afraid to ask questions.

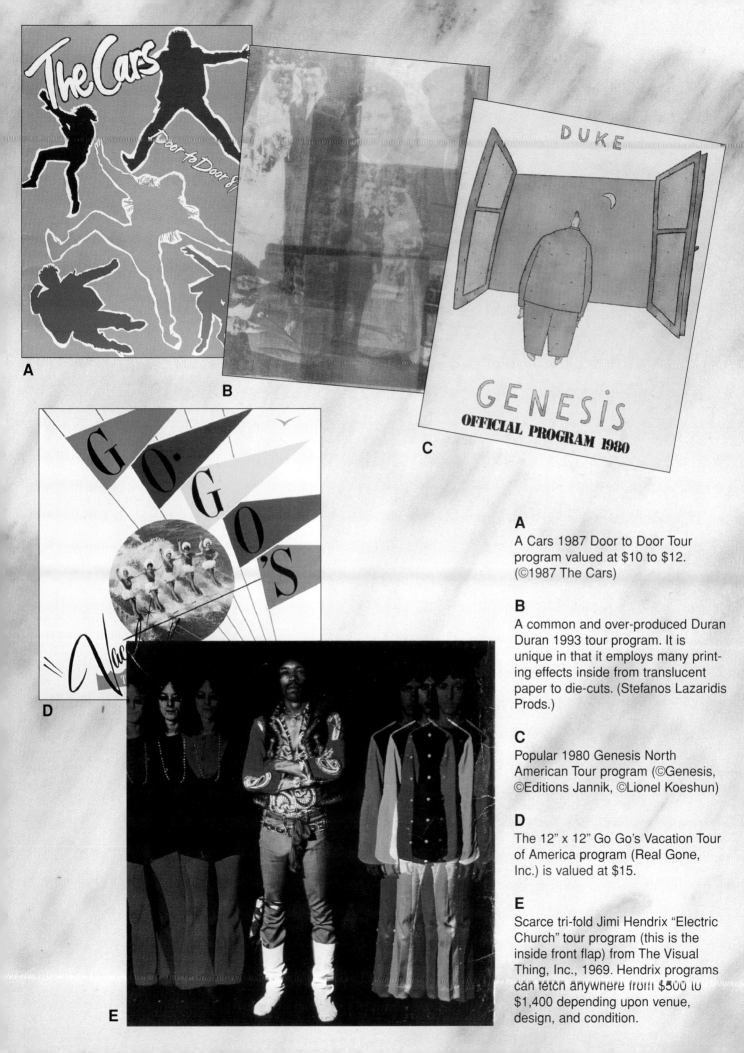

A

A Cars 1987 Door to Door Tour program valued at $10 to $12. (©1987 The Cars)

B

A common and over-produced Duran Duran 1993 tour program. It is unique in that it employs many printing effects inside from translucent paper to die-cuts. (Stefanos Lazaridis Prods.)

C

Popular 1980 Genesis North American Tour program (©Genesis, ©Editions Jannik, ©Lionel Koeshun)

D

The 12" x 12" Go Go's Vacation Tour of America program (Real Gone, Inc.) is valued at $15.

E

Scarce tri-fold Jimi Hendrix "Electric Church" tour program (this is the inside front flap) from The Visual Thing, Inc., 1969. Hendrix programs can fetch anywhere from $500 to $1,400 depending upon venue, design, and condition.

F

A classic 1987 Pink Floyd tour program (Prom Productions, Inc.) valued at $15 to $17.

G

This 12" x 12" Rolling Stones 1973 Tour in Hawaii program (Oblin Printing Co. Inc., 1973) is worth $30 to $35.

H

Common Supertramp 1983 concert program worth $10. (©1983 Supertramp; cover design by Norman Moore)

I

Popular Van Halen 5150 Tour program (Yessup Merch, 1986) worth $18 to $20.

J

This ZZ Top tour program (1981 Gold Knight Dist.) is valued at $20 to $23. This program is noted for its use of a thick paper stock.

K

Buddy Guy's legendary guitar pick is valued at $35 to $50.

L

Guitar picks from George Harrison and Paul McCartney. Harrison guitar picks can fetch $150 while McCartney picks are typically valued at $150 to $200, but because this is a promo pick, it is only valued at $5 to $10.

M

Picks from Eddie Van Halen can range in value from $35 to $200.

N

An Eric Clapton guitar pick can command a price of $100 to $150.

O

Reba McEntire guitar picks are valued between $10 and $15.

P

A nice assortment of typical Stevie Nicks backstage passes.
(Green passes printed by Otto)

Q

Backstage passes from the Monkees range in value from $8 to $10 for cloth
and $10 to $12 for laminated (post 1990). The pass pictured here is a
common counterfeit. Always exercise caution when buying foreign laminates.

R

A backstage pass from the Jacksons' Victory Tour. (Printed by Otto)

S

A 1988 Guns 'N' Roses counterfeit backstage pass. Authentic passes from
the band generally are valued at $8 to $12 for cloth and $15 for laminated.
The lack of image sharpness is an immediate cause of concern.

T

Backstage passes from the Judds are valued at $10 to $15 for cloth and $15
to $25 for laminated. (Printed by Otto—a premier printer of backstage
passes)

U

INXS "Dirty Honeymoon" V.I.P. passes from Otto. Passes from the band range
in value from $10 to $12 for cloth and $15 for laminated. Color variations in
the passes differentiate individual events.

V

This poster for the Motown Revue in Detroit, Michigan, is one of only two Motortown Revue posters known. Globe Poster of Baltimore printed this colorful 22" x 23" Christmas poster. From the collection of Hank Thompson.

W

Direct from Youngstown, Ohio, comes the "Biggest Show of Stars." This 17" x 22" poster was printed by Globe Poster of Baltimore. It is valued at $2,500. From the collection of Hank Thompson.

X

This September 2, 1968, poster features, among others, Mary Wells, and is valued at $1,500. Globe Poster of Baltimore printed this 22" x 32" poster. From the collection of Hank Thompson.

Y

This Rick Nelson concert poster from 1971 is valued at $1,000. From the Doug Leftwitch Collection.

Z

A very rare poster from the "Surf Fair," 1962, which features the Beach Boys in concert. This poster is valued at $3,000. From the Doug Leftwitch Collection.

AA

BB

CC

EE

FF

DD

AA

An RIAA certified Hologram gold 45 for Dionne Warwick and Friends for "That's What Friends Are For," 1985, valued at $250. From the Doug Leftwitch Collection.

BB

This early white-matte gold 45 for the Beatles' "A Hard Days Night" features an RIAA coin. Due to its scarcity, this award from 1964 is valued at $20,000. From the Doug Leftwitch Collection.

CC

Cream earned a gold white-matte award for *Disraeli Gears* in 1968. It is valued at $3,500. From the Doug Leftwitch Collection.

DD

This gold BPI award was presented to David Bowie for *Let's Dance* in 1983. It is valued at $1,500. From the Doug Leftwitch Collection.

EE

"(I Can't Get No) Satisfaction" earned the Rolling Stones this white-matte award in 1965. It is valued at $7,000. From the Doug Leftwitch Collection.

FF

A very rare 8-track award—this gold 8-track award went to Kiss for the *Destroyer* album, 1976. It is valued at $800. From the Doug Leftwitch Collection.

GG

Valued at $500, this attractive custom platinum award from Australia was for *Xanadu* featuring Olivia Newton John. From the Doug Leftwitch Collection.

GG

HH

David Bowie stage-worn suit from 1991. Its estimated value is between $800 and $1,200. Courtesy Christie's Images.

II

Madonna stage-worn shorts from the 1993 Girlie Tour. She can be seen wearing the shorts on the 1993 *Girlie Tour Down Under* video. The shorts have an estimated value between $4,000 and $6,000. Courtesy Christie's Images.

JJ

This blue denim work shirt was worn by John Lennon, c. 1974, while recording "Whatever Gets You Through the Night," his first solo record. Its estimated value is between $4,000 and $6,000. Courtesy Christie's Images.

KK

This Dolce & Gabbana bustier is from Madonna's Like a Virgin Tour. She is seen wearing the bustier in the Like a Virgin video. The estimated value for this item is between $6,000 and $8,000. ©Butterfield & Butterfield, Auctioneers Corp., 1997.

HH

II

JJ

KK

ABBA

Formed 1971

Benny Andersson, Born: December 16, 1946, Bjorn Ulvaeus, Born: April 25, 1945; Agnetha "Anna" Fältskog, Born: April 5, 1950; Anni-Frid "Frida" Synni-Lyngstad-Fredriksson-Andersson, Born: November 15, 1945

It was pop entrepreneur Stig (Stikkan) Anderson who persuaded Bjorn (Hootenanny Singers), whom he already had as a client, and Benny (The Hep Cats) to leave their prospective groups and pool their resources. Following the release of *Lycka* by the duo Benny and Bjorn, the group started to evolve out of the members' personal relationships. Benny and Anna-Frid were living together, and Bjorn and Agnetha were married in July 1971. Both women had already contributed some backing vocals to the duo's recordings and even joined them onstage. The platform they chose to catapult them to success was the Eurovision song contest. Since each member had been successful as solo artists, the name ABBA (an acronym of their first initials) was an appropriate group name. They finally won the contest in 1974 with "Waterloo," having lost the previous year singing "Ring Ring." Although winning the event doesn't guarantee success, the 500 million viewers who saw the contest helped push "Waterloo" to the top of the charts in most European countries. The song even went to #6 in the United States (1974), where most of the public was unfamiliar with Eurovision.

The group's successful song recipe led to other hit singles including "Fernando," "Money, Money, Money," "Knowing Me, Knowing You," "Dancing Queen" (#1, 1977) and "Take a Chance on Me" (#3, 1978). The group was far less successful with their personal lives, as both couples eventually divorced. The group did manage to remain harmonious long enough to sell over 100 million records worldwide.

The group members eventually pursued their own directions. Phil Collins produced Frida's solo debut *Something's Going On* in 1982. The self-titled single from the album became a Top Twenty hit. Anna also released solo albums with some minor hits including "Can't Shake Loose" (#29, 1983). Benny and Bjorn teamed up with noted lyricist Tim Rice to write the successful musical *Chess*. "One Night in Bangkok"(#3, 1985), a song from the musical, was a single for Murray Head.

Through the years, the group's appeal has endured, with numerous groups making successful covers of ABBA hits. Bjorn and Benny even joined U2 onstage in Stockholm to perform "Dancing Queen."

AUTOGRAPHS

Group:

A CD, LP, magazine cover, ad, photo, or card signed by the entire band: $50-$100*

*High end reflects vintage signed memorabilia

Individual:

Benny Andersson: $20-$30
Bjorn Ulvaeus: $20-$30
Anna Fältskog: $10-$20
Frida Synni-Lyngstad-Fredriksson-Andersson: $15-$25

TOUR BOOKS/PROGRAMS/PASSES

Tour Programs:

ABBA: The Movie Program (Japan): $25
1979 World Tour: $30

Backstage Passes:

Laminated: 1979 U.S. & European Tour: $35-$40
(first American tour) 1980 Japan '80 Tour: $35
Cloth: 1980 Japan Tour: $30-$35

POSTERS/PRESS KITS

Promotional Posters: $15-$45

USED CLOTHING/EQUIPMENT

Guitar Picks: Bjorn Ulvaeus: $20-$40

OFTEN OVERLOOKED MEMORABILIA

Super Trouper, Epic ABBOX-1, 1980, box set with book and poster; *The Singles, The First Ten Years,* Epic ABBOX-2, 1983, double picture disc box set with book; *The Album,* die-cut pop-up display, 1977 - $105; book cover - $10; dolls (set of 4), Matchbox 9-inch, each - $60; copies of *ABBA News;* copies of *ABBA* magazine (No. 1-24); any 1974 Eurovision artifacts—a scarce artifact is the specially designed publicity folders distributed with "Waterloo" (Europe); movie memorabilia from *ABBA: The Movie* (1977); videotapes of the group's numerous worldwide television appearances; bottles of Anna and Frida cologne

REFERENCES/BOOKS

ABBA by Rasmussen: $10; *The Name of the Game,* by Andrew Oldham; other resources exist dating back to 1977; no dedicated collector books

ABC

Formed 1980

Original Lineup: Martin Fry, Mark White, Mark Lickley, David Robinson, Stephen Singleton*

*Lickley and Robinson departed in 1980, David Palmer was added. Singleton and Palmer left in 1983 and David Yarritu joined the band.

Martin Fry was interviewing the band Vice Versa for his own music fanzine *Modern Drugs* when, as fate would have it, he was asked to join. The band changed its name to ABC and (under Fry's direction) its musical sound. *Tears Are Not Enough* (#19, U.K.) was the band's first effort on their own Neutron Records. Their success led to a signing with Mercury Records, where they were teamed with Trevor Horn for the production of *The Lexicon of Love* (#24, 1982). The album yielded three hit singles, "Poison Arrow" (#6, U.K., 1982), "The Look Of Love" (#19, 1982), and "All Of My Heart" (#5, U.K., 1982).

The group's appeal in America flourished with well-made videos suited for the MTV generation. Critics took shots at the band, calling them "overpro duced" due to their clever sound and Fry's powerful vocals. What ground they gained with *The Lexicon of Love,* they lost with *Beauty Stab* (#69, 1983). Their harder-rock approach was unexpected and far too harsh for a sophomore effort. It did yield one single in "That Was Then This Is Now" (#89, 1984). *How to be a ... Zillionaire* (#30, 1985) picked up some ground—the singles "Be Near Me" (#9, 1985) and "(How to be a) Millionaire" (#20, 1986) helped push sales. Two new members added a different touch to the band's image, but added nothing musically (neither sang or played instruments).

ABC was out of the music scene until 1987, a result of Fry being diagnosed with Hodgkin's disease. The band returned with *Alphabet City* (#48, 1987), which featured the single "When Smokey Sings" (#5, 1987). The song, which was a tribute to Motown legend Smokey Robinson, was the group's biggest single to date. The band signed on with Parlophone in 1991, releasing *Abracadabra* (#50, U.K., 1991), which failed to yield a Top Forty single.

AUTOGRAPHS
Group:
A CD, LP, magazine cover, ad, photo, or card signed by the entire band: $15-$25*
*High end reflects vintage signed memorabilia
Individual:
Martin Fry: $5-$15

TOUR BOOKS/PROGRAMS/PASSES
Backstage Passes: $5-$8

POSTERS/PRESS KITS
Promotional Posters: $10-$12
Press Kits: $10

USED CLOTHING/EQUIPMENT
Guitar Picks: Mark White: $5

OFTEN OVERLOOKED MEMORABILIA
Issues of *Modern Drugs* magazine - $6; *Man Trap,* an hourlong documentary filmed as the group toured Britain in 1982; promotional pin - $20; World Tour 1982/83 scarf - $25

Abdul, Paula

Born: June 19, 1962

With little musical experience, Paula Abdul used her rich talent in choreography, combined with a newly accepted medium (MTV) to enhance sales of her first record *Forever Your Girl*. Her gifted dance techniques had already proved successful for the other artists she had worked with, and the simplicity of her look—an often quoted "girl-next-door" charm—worked well with her upbeat rhythms and bubblegum arrangements.

Paula Abdul. Photo by Walter Chin. Courtesy of Virgin Records.

A born dancer, Abdul won a scholarship to study tap and jazz dancing at the young age of ten. Cheerleading would take her to another level, first with her high school, then at California State college, and finally with the Los Angeles Lakers squad. As a Laker girl she was spotted by Jackie Jackson, who asked Abdul to choreograph the Jacksons' "Torture" video. She then moved on to work with other groups, including the Pointer Sisters, Janet Jackson, ZZ Top, Dolly Parton, and Duran Duran.

Abdul was signed to a recording contract with Virgin America, and in 1988 released "Knocked Out" (#41), an outstanding dance cut complemented by a streamlined promotional video. Quickly following the single's release came her debut album *Forever Your Girl* (#1, 1988), which spun off four number one singles: "Straight Up," "Forever Your Girl," "Cold Hearted" and "Opposites Attract." It was the first time a debut effort accomplished such a feat.

Shut Up And Dance (The Dance Mixes) (#7, 1990) was a reshuffled and remixed version of her debut album. It was followed by *Spellbound* (#1, 1991), another successful album that spawned a series of hit

singles, including "Rush, Rush" (#1, 1991), "The Promise of a New Day" (#1, 1991), "Blowing Kisses in the Wind" (#6, 1991), "Vibeology" (#16, 1992) and "Will You Marry Me" (#19, 1992). With this album, Abdul became the first act of the '90s to have two chart-topping albums.

On April 20, 1992, Abdul married actor Emilio Estevez, but the relationship faltered in the spring of 1994, and the couple separated. *Head Over Heels* (#18, 1995) followed *Spellbound,* and although successful, it couldn't match the achievements of its predecessors.

As a subject for collecting, Abdul is intriguing. Her achievements in both music and dance have led to speculation of a film career. Her multimedia appeal bodes well as a marketing spokesperson. Abdul, who has already inked lucrative sponsorship deals with Diet Coke and Reebok, will no doubt continue such ventures. Much will depend on her ability to sustain a certain level of success in the fields she chooses to participate in.

AUTOGRAPHS

A CD, LP, magazine cover, ad, photo, or card signed by the artist: $30-$40

The signature of Paula Abdul

TOUR BOOKS/ PROGRAMS/PASSES

Tour Programs:
Under My Spell: $15
Backstage Passes:
Cloth: $10-$12;
Laminated: $15-$20

POSTERS/PRESS KITS

Promotional Posters:
$10-$25
Spellbound - On Tour (18" x 24"): $20
Under My Spell Tour - stock (23" x 35"): $10
Press Kits:
Forever Your Girl: $25
Shut Up and Dance: $18-$20
Spellbound: $20
Head over Heels: $15-$20

A gorgeous large tour book produced by John Coulter Design—it is a must for Paula fans (John Coulter Design).

USED CLOTHING/EQUIPMENT

Nothing to date has really hit the market. Since she has been active in charity work it is only a matter of time before some costumes come out of the closets.

OFTEN OVERLOOKED MEMORABILIA

Los Angeles Laker cheerleading memorabilia, posters, photographs, etc.; promotional videotapes of her choreographed work; animation cels from her "Opposites Attract" video; July 1990 issue of Vanity Fair (features shots of Abdul with dancer Gene Kelly); memorabilia from the Disney album *For Our Children* (1991) [Abdul contributes "Good Night My Love (Pleasant Dreams)"]; posters, etc.; MTV-related projects; performances at Video Music Award shows; *Club MTV Party To Go, Volume One* release; rubbing from her star on the Hollywood Walk of Fame; bubble gum folder - $3; bubble gum pack - $5; bubble gum tin box - $5; earrings - $10; jigsaw puzzle (Milton Bradley), 500 pcs. - $10; school folder - $3

REFERENCES/BOOKS

The Paula Abdul Story by W.B. Williams: $12; *Paula Abdul: Forever Yours* by Grace Catalano; a few other resources exist; no dedicated collector books

AC/DC

Formed 1973

Angus Young, Born: March 31, 1955; Malcolm Young, Born: January 6, 1953; Bon Scott (Ronald Belford), Born: July 9, 1946, Died: February 19, 1980; Phillip Rudd (1974), Born: May 19, 1946; Mark Evans*

*Evans left in 1977 and Cliff Williams replaced him on bass. Brian Johnson was added in 1980 following Scott's death. Rudd left in 1983 and Simon Wright was added to the band. Wright departed in 1989 and Chris Slade was added on drums.

Australia's premier metal band is known for their raucous image and simple "party down" approach to rock and roll. The band features the hyperactive, knickers-clad guitarist Angus Young, who races around stage as if he's just downed 26 pots of coffee. Their raw approach to music is both juvenile and habit forming, exhibited on classic songs like "Big Balls" and "The Jack."

They have been a consistent live draw and record seller for decades now, having really broken through with "Highway to Hell" (#17, 1979). Within months after their success, Bon Scott died and was replaced by Brian Johnson. *Back in Black* (#4, 1980) scored with hit extract "You Shook Me All Night Long" and was followed by the reissued *Dirty Deeds Done Dirt Cheap* (#3, 1981). *For Those About to Rock We Salute You* (#1, 1981) became the band's first (and only to date) number one album.

The next two albums didn't fair as well (only selling gold), but the problem was immediately corrected with the multiplatinum *Who Made Who* and *The Razor's Edge* (#2, 1990). The latter contains the group's most successful single, "Moneytalks" (#23, 1991).

AUTOGRAPHS

Group:
A CD, LP, magazine cover, ad, photo, or card signed by the entire band: $125-$300*

*High end reflects vintage signed memorabilia including Scott

Individual:
Angus Young: $35-$45
Malcolm Young: $30-$35
Bon Scott: $125-$150
Phillip Rudd: $30
Mark Evans: $25
Cliff Williams: $10-$15
Brian Johnson: $25
Simon Wright: $10-$15
Chris Slade: $10-$15

TOUR BOOKS/ PROGRAMS/PASSES

Tour Programs:
Blow Up Your Video World Tour 1988: $10-$12
Dirty Deeds Done Dirt Cheap, U.K. 1976: $100-$135
Rockupation, Japan, 1982: $40-$55

Backstage Passes:
Cloth: $8-$15;
Laminated: $15-$25

This awesome 1988 World Tour program was designed by Bill Smith Studio. Its larger scale makes it particularly pleasing to AC/DC fans

POSTERS/PRESS KITS

Promotional Posters: $15-$30
Razor's Edge large promotional (40" x 60"): $25
Who Made Who tour poster: $15
Press Kits: $20-$30

USED CLOTHING/EQUIPMENT

Guitar Picks:
Angus Young: $20-$30
Mark Evans: $15-$20
Malcolm Young: $15-$25
Cliff Williams: $15

A backstage pass for AC/DC's Ballbreaker World Tour (Printed by OTTO Printing & Entertainment Graphics)

An AC/DC guitar pick

Drum Sticks:
Phillip Rudd: $25-$35
Simon Wright: $17-$25
Chris Slade: $15-$20

OFTEN OVERLOOKED MEMORABILIA
Tour patches - $4-$6; "The Razor's Edge" promotional retractable knife key ring - $10-$12; pins - $5-$8; trading cards - $8-$12; dollar bills (Angus and AC/DC) - $3-$5; videotapes from their numerous television appearances,

including "Rock Goes To College" (11/10/78) and "In Concert Halloween Jam at Universal Studios" (1992); movie memorabilia from *Let There Be Rock, Maximum Overdrive* (1986), and *The Last Action Hero* (1993); circular promotional pin (Australian) - $10; European Tour 80/81 promotional scarf (B&W) - $45; "Ballbreaker" Australian Souvenir Box, includes tour book, belt buckle, etc. - $45

REFERENCES/BOOKS
AC/DC: The World's Heaviest Rock by Martin Huxley (1996); *AC/DC Photo Book*: $20; *AC/DC Shock to the System* by Putterford: $18; a few other resources exist; no dedicated collector books

Ace

Formed 1972

Original Lineup: Alan "Bam" King; Phil Harris; Paul Carrack, Born: April 1951; Terry "Tex" Comer; Steve Witherington

One of London's pub rock bands, best known for Paul Carrack-penned "How Long" (#3, 1975). After the band split in 1977, Carrack went on to Squeeze, followed by a stint with Carlene Carter, then Nick Lowe's Noise To Go, and Mike and The Mechanics. He also landed the single "Don't Shed A Tear" in the Top Ten in 1987.

AUTOGRAPHS
A CD, LP, magazine cover, ad, photo, or card signed by the group: $15-$20

POSTERS/PRESS KITS
Promotional Posters: $10-$15
Press Kits: $10-$20

Ackerman, Will

Born: November 1949

Best known as the founder and force behind Windham Hills Records, one of the world's finest new age labels.

AUTOGRAPHS
A CD, LP, magazine cover, ad, photo, or card signed by the artist: $5-$10

Acklin, Barbara

Born: February 28, 1943

A talented R&B singer/songwriter who is best known for the late '60s hit "Love Makes a Woman" (#15, 1968). She also wrote Jackie Wilson's hit "Whispers (Gettin' Louder)" (1966). She was successful duetting with Gene Chandler, including "From the

Teacher to the Preacher" (#57, 1968). She scored with other R&B Top Forty hits and even co-wrote the Chi-Lites hit "Have You Seen Her."

AUTOGRAPHS
A CD, LP, magazine cover, ad, photo, or card signed by the artist: $6-$10

OFTEN OVERLOOKED MEMORABILIA
Memorabilia associated with other musicians' covers of her music

Acuff, Roy

Born: September 15, 1903, Died: November 23, 1992

"The King of Country Music," Roy Acuff could do it all! He spent half a century at the Grand Ole Opry, right up until he died at the age of 83. Ironically, he wanted to be a professional baseball player, but a bout with sunstroke saw him picking up the fiddle instead. He crafted his music and stage presence by traversing through the South in medicine and tent shows.

In 1933 he formed the Tennessee Crackerjacks (re-named the Crazy Tennesseeans in 1934) and began recording, including the country classics "Great Speckled Bird" and "Wabash Cannonball." By 1938 the group was called the Smoky Mountain Boys, regulars on Nashville's *Grand Ole Opry*.

During his career he sold over 25 million records, including the hits "Night Train To Memphis," "Fire Ball Mail," and "Wreck on the Highway." In 1942 he turned his sights to music publishing with Fred Rose, forming the Acuff-Rose Music Publishing Company, eventually one of the biggest country music publishing companies in the world.

In 1962 he became the first living musician elected to the Country Music Hall of Fame. His numerous other honors included a Grammy Lifetime Achievement Award (1987), the National Medal of Art, and the Kennedy Lifetime Achievement Award (both 1991).

AUTOGRAPHS
A CD, LP, magazine cover, ad, photo, or card signed by the artist: $10-$45

REFERENCES/BOOKS
King of Country Music: The Life Story of Roy Acuff by A.C. Dunkleberger; a few other resources exist; no dedicated collector books

Adam and the Ants/Adam Ant

Formed 1977

Prominent Lineup: Adam Ant (Stuart Goddard), Born: November 3, 1954; David Barbe; Matthew Ashman; Andrew Warren*

*Numerous personnel changes

An "ant"ithesis to what was happening in the music scene, this colorful group provided an "ant"idote to other rising forms of the era. Although the group took England by storm, Stateside seemed less appreciative of their English "ant"ics. The band made their debut at the Roxy Club in London on April 29, 1977, on a bill that also included Siouxsie & the Banshees. The following year they made their radio debut on *The John Peel Show* (1/23) and signed a two-single deal with Decca Records on July 29.

The band's first major U.K. tour in 1979 marked the beginning of "antpeople" (fans). The band sold out two shows at London's Electric Ballroom, attracting the attention of many, including svengali Malcolm McLaren, whose work with the Sex Pistols is now legendary. McLaren took the band under his wing as their manager. Their debut album *Dirk Wears White Sox* reached #1 on the U.K. Independent label charts in mid-January of 1980.

The Ants left Adam in January of 1980 to form Bow Wow Wow. Ant then hooked up with guitarist Marco Pirroni to create "antmusic" with a new band and manager. The "Ant Invasion" tour began in May 1980 and played for sellout crowds in the U.K. A new flamboyant image combined with double-drum rhythms and yodeling vocals was unveiled. The band signed to CBS Records in July and released *King of the Wild Frontier*. "Dog Eat Dog" from their new album reached #4 on U.K. charts in November, and was enhanced by the band's first appearance on BBC1-TV *Top of the Pops* (11/8/80).

King of the Wild Frontier made the U.S. Top 50 with little exposure and no released singles. A well-publicized tour did little to garner U.S. attention and the band headed home to release the single "Prince Charming" (U.K., #1) from the identically titled album. "Ant Rap" soon became the band's sixth straight hit produced by Chris Hughes, although Adam dismantled the band with the exception of Pirroni in January 1982. Accolades continued for the Ants, as Adam began work on his first solo release, *Friend or Foe*. The album was well received and spun off the single "Goody Two-Shoes" (U.S., #12).

"Ant" collectors will want to make sure they get a copy of Adam's appearance on MTV in March 1982 as their first ever guest VJ! Less understood, but no less desirable, is his appearance on NBC-TV's Motown 25th anniversary show (5/16/83).

Phil Collins was recruited to produce Adam's next album *Strip* (1983), whose controversial lyrics soon created an uproar. "Puss 'N Boots" (U.K., #5) and "Apollo 9" (U.K., #13) did well on the charts, but Adam showed signs of an "ant"iclimax. *Vive Le Rock* (1985) was his last chart entry for five years as he set his sights on an acting career.

Adam and the Ants represented an interesting phase in musical history. The band ruled Britain's early-80s fantasy rock "movement" (for lack of a bet-

ter term). As such, their memorabilia was collected and in time may resurface as "ant"ique.

AUTOGRAPHS

Adam has always been accommodating to autograph requests.

Group:

A CD, LP, magazine cover, ad, photo, or card signed by the entire band: $30-$40*

*High end reflects vintage signed memorabilia - *King of the Wild Frontier*

Individual:

Adam Ant: $10-$15
Marco Pirroni: $4-$7

TOUR BOOKS/PROGRAMS/PASSES

Backstage Passes:

Cloth: $5-$12; Laminated: $10-25

POSTERS/PRESS KITS

Promotional Posters: $10-$30
Press Kits: $10-$30

USED CLOTHING/EQUIPMENT

Guitar Picks:

Marco Pirroni: $5

OFTEN OVERLOOKED MEMORABILIA

Videotapes of Adam's television and film appearances

REFERENCES/BOOKS

The Official Adam Ant Story by James Maw; other resources exist dating back to 1981, primarily published in the UK; no dedicated collector books

Adams, Bryan

Born: November 5, 1959

Another successful Canadian export, Adams, often clad in a T-shirt and blue jeans, has captured a large audience with his straightforward anthemic rock. When still a teenager he hooked up with songwriter Jim Vallance and delivered tunes to a myriad of artists including Joe Cocker, Bachman-Turner Overdrive and Juice Newton, before inking a deal on his own with A&M Records.

Although his debut album bombed, he returned with *You Want It, You Got It* (#118, 1982), which was heavily supported by extensive touring, gradually building Adams' cult following. *Cuts Like a Knife* (#8, 1983) was his breakthrough record, producing three hits: the title cut (#15, 1983), "Straight from the Heart" (#10, 1983), and "This Time" (#24, 1983). *Reckless* (#1, 1984), his fourth album, produced the hits "Run to You" (#6, 1984), "Somebody" (#11, 1985), "Summer of '69" (#5, 1985), "Heaven" (#1, 1985), and "It's Only Love" (#15, 1985).

Into the Fire continued his series of hit singles with "Heat of the Night" (#6, 1987), "Hearts of Fire" (#26, 1987), and "Victim of Love" (#32, 1987). *Waking Up the Neighbors* (#6, 1992), his seventh album, was pre-

ceded by his smash #1 hit "(Everything I Do) I Do It For You" from the Kevin Costner film *Robin Hood: Prince of Thieves*.

While the compilation *So Far So Good* (#6, 1994) climbed the charts, extract "Please Forgive Me" (#7, 1993) scored again for Adams, who was busy with his next effort *All For Love* (#1, 1994), recorded with Sting and Rod Stewart. "Have You Ever Really Loved A Woman?" (#1, 1995) quickly topped the U.S. singles chart, as Adams dedicated time to his next album *18 Til I Die* (1996).

A prolific and gifted songwriter, Bryan Adams is to music what Tony Gwynn is to major league baseball. Each are quietly building a legacy that few in their field will be able to achieve.

AUTOGRAPHS

A CD, LP, magazine cover, ad, photo, or card signed by the artist: $25-$65

TOUR BOOKS/PROGRAMS/PASSES

Tour Programs:

Waking Up The World Tour (1992): $15-$20
So Far So Good Tour (1994): $15-$17

Backstage Passes:

Cloth: $5-$8; Laminated: $10-$15

A 1992 tour program for Bryan Adams (Reiner Design Consultants, Inc.)   *Backstage pass for Bryan Adams' Waking Up the World Tour (Printed by OTTO)*

POSTERS/PRESS KITS

Promotional Posters: $10-$30
Press Kits: $15-$25

USED CLOTHING/EQUIPMENT

Guitar Picks: $10-$20

OFTEN OVERLOOKED MEMORABILIA

Videotapes of his numerous performances on television, including *Late Night with David Letterman* (1/10/92), *Top of the Pops* (7/9/92), *The Late Show with David Letterman* (3/2/93, 10/10/95, 6/3/96), *Apollo Theatre Hall of Fame* (6/15/93), *Elvis Presley: The Tribute* (10/8/94), *The Today Show* (6/4/96); movie memorabilia from *Robin Hood: Prince of Thieves, The Three Musketeers* (1994), *Don Juan DeMarco* (1995), *The Wall* (1990), *Waking Up The Neighbourhood;* A&M promotional clock, 1991; "Reckless" counter display - $30; "Cuts Like a Knife" letter opener - $30

REFERENCES/BOOKS

Illustrated Biography by Robertson: $11; *Bryan Adams* by Goode: $12; *Bryan Adams, Everything He Does* by Saidman: $12; a few average resources exist, nothing deeply introspective; no dedicated collector books; serious collectors should opt for the fan club: Bad News, #406-68 Water Street, Vancouver, DC 46D 1A4 Canada ($20 per year)

Adams, Faye

(Faye Scruggs)

Powerful R&B singer, in the tradition of Big Maybelle, who scored with the 1953 hit "Shake A Hand" (#22, 1953) and also with "I'll Be True" (#1, R&B, 1953) and "Hurts Me to My Heart" (#1, R&B, 1954).

AUTOGRAPHS

A CD, LP, magazine cover, ad, photo, or card signed by the group: $7-$12

Adams, Johnny

(Lathan Adams) Born: January 5, 1932

"The Tan Canary," this New Orleans based R&B vocalist scored R&B hits with "Release Me" (#34, R&B, 1969), "Reconsider Me" (#28, 1969), "I Can't Be All Bad" (#45, R&B, 1969), and "I Won't Cry" (#41, R&B, 1970).

AUTOGRAPHS

A CD, LP, magazine cover, ad, photo or card signed by the group: $7-$10

Adams, Marie

A talent both as a gospel singer and later as a recorded R&B vocalist, Marie Adams had an R&B Top Ten hit with her first recording, "I'm Gonna Play the Honky Tonks." With the hit came opportunities, and she later ended up with the Johnny Otis Show, where she took part in the Three Tons of Joy, which scored a British hit with "Ma, He's Making Eyes at Me" (#1, U.K., 1957). The following year she duetted with Otis on the Top Twenty hit "Bye Bye Baby."

AUTOGRAPHS

A CD, LP, magazine cover, ad, photo, or card signed by the artist: $7-$12

Adanson, Barry : See Magazine

Ade, King Sunny

(Sunny Francis Adeniyi) Born: September 1, 1946

Juju bandleader King Sunny Ade has been a superstar in his native Nigeria since the late '60s. Although acclaimed for his work in America, his commercial success has never matched that of Bob Marley (whom he is often compared to) although he has substantially opened the door for many Afro-pop artists. His "Challenge Cup" became a national hit with his band the Green Spots, later known as the African Beats.

By the mid-70s he had a half dozen albums under his belt, selling over a million records combined, and was a recognizable star in his homeland and an influence to many other artists worldwide. His exposure was increased in the U.S. when he signed with Island Records and released *Juju Music* (#111, 1983) and *Synchro System* (#91, 1983), but when *Aura* (1984) failed to chart he was dropped from his contract.

AUTOGRAPHS

A CD, LP, magazine cover, ad, photo or card signed by the group: $15-$20

****

"On The Edge"

Adverts

Britpunk band whose stench of the '70s still stains the best ripped T-shirt in my closet. Worth grabbing any artifacts from *Crossing the Red Sea with the Adverts* (1978). As the second group ever signed to Stiff Records, any related promotional items would also be of interest to label collectors. Just remember you have "Gary Gilmore's Eyes"!

****

Aerosmith

Formed 1970

Steven Tyler (Steven Tallarico) Born: March 26, 1948; Joe Perry, Born: September 10, 1950; Brad Whitford, Born: February 23, 1952; Tom Hamilton, Born: December 31, 1951; Joey Kramer, Born: June 21, 1950*

*Perry departed in 1979 and Jimmy Crespo was added. Whitford left in 1980 and Rick Dufay was added. The original lineup returned and both Dufay and Crespo departed in 1984.

The blues-based "bad boys from Boston" were never really welcomed by critics, who opted to classify them more as a poor man's Rolling Stones rather than an evolutionary rock band. They eventually lead the American based rock 'n' roll revival in the mid-70s.

The group formed in 1970, with Tyler playing drums, and eventually added Kramer and Whitford. A heavy New England club schedule eventually landed them at Max's Kansas City in New York where Clive Davis saw them and inked them to a deal with Columbia Records. The band's first record, *Aerosmith* (1973), landed a regional hit "Dream On," which would eventually become an FM classic. Aerosmith artifacts from the pre-1973 days are considered sacred relics and, as such, are difficult to find. Any promotional items relating to the release of "Dream On" are also especially noteworthy.

Heavy touring landed "Dream On" back on the charts (#6) in 1976, with the band beginning to headline performances. *Get Your Wings* and *Toys in the Attic* joined *Aerosmith* at the platinum sales level, while "Walk This Way" reached the Top Ten in 1977. With success beginning to take its toll, the band began unraveling during the late 1970s. Animosity between Tyler and Perry reached its pinnacle in 1979, with Perry leaving to pursue a solo career. Brad Whitford also split in 1980, leaving Aerosmith with Jim Crespo and Rick Dufay to pick up the pieces. The "Train Kept a Rollin'," but the steam was running out. Neither Perry nor Whitford's outside work met with commercial success; however, both exhibited signs of the magic formula that made Aerosmith. Aerosmith pushed *Rock in a Hard Place* to a Top Forty album placement, but collector interest in the group plummeted, no doubt due to the lack of interest in a non-Tyler and Perry project.

In 1984 the band met backstage at an Aerosmith concert and decided to re-form. This was the beginning of one of the most successful comebacks in rock 'n' roll history. *Done with Mirrors,* the band's "comeback" LP, sold moderately but showed promise that

what once was, still could be. Perry and Tyler rapped out "Walk This Way" with Run-D.M.C. and ignited collector interest in the band all over again. *Permanent Vacation* placed a firm cornerstone in music history and introduced the band to a new generation. "Angel," "Dude (Looks Like A Lady)," and "Rag Doll" hit the charts hard, all landing in the Top Twenty.

Pump (1989) vaulted the band back into superstar status: "Love in an Elevator" and "Janie's Got a Gun" found a home in the Top Five. The band's commercial appeal was entrenched by a 1990 Grammy for Best Rock Performance by a Duo or Group. *Pandora's Box* (1991), *Get a Grip* (1993) and *Big Ones; Box of Fire* (1994) regurgitated a bit—the "Same Old Song and Dance" if you'll pardon the pun. It remains to be seen whether the band will "Let the Music Do the Talking" or let record executives determine how the band will finish the end of the century.

AUTOGRAPHS

Aerosmith has always been accessible to their fans, with all of the band members obliging to autograph requests.

Group:

A CD, LP, magazine cover, ad, photo, or card signed by the entire band: $200-$400*

*High end reflects vintage signed memorabilia

Individual:

Stephen Tyler: $25-$40   Joe Perry: $20-$35
Brad Whitford: $20-$30   Tom Hamilton: $20-$25
Joey Kramer: $20-$25

The signature of Aerosmith frontman Steven Tyler

TOUR BOOKS/PROGRAMS/PASSES

Tour Programs:

1979 Japan Tour: $100
Permanent Vacation (Japan):
$40 Permanent Vacation
(U.S.): $27
Get A Grip: $20

Backstage Passes:

(1990-Present)
Cloth/paper: $10-$18;
Laminated: $15-$25

POSTERS/PRESS KITS

Promotional Posters:
$10-$55
Pump: $10; Get A Grip: $8
Press Kits:
$15-$100
Permanent Vacation: $20;
Pump: $15;
Done with Mirrors: $45

Aerosmith signed Greatest Hits *album cover. Its estimated value is between $200 and $400. Photo courtesy Executive Collectibles Gallery, Inc.*

Aerosmith concert photo

A nice example of Aerosmith passes, produced by one of the nation's leading tour pass manufacturers, Otto. The "Boston Garden" passes have been heavily counterfeited, so approach purchases with caution.

USED CLOTHING/EQUIPMENT

Steven Tyler stage-worn vest: $500-$600

Guitar Picks: (1990 - Present)
Whitford: $15-$50
Perry: $30-$50
Hamilton: $20-$25

Drum Sticks:
Kramer:
$20-$25

Aerosmith guitar picks: pick one up and let the music do the talkin'!

OFTEN OVERLOOKED MEMORABILIA

Rock & Roll Comics $3-$5; Pump Tour golf shirt - $50; metallic wings pin - $6; pad of paper, "Soaring Thru SW Tour 1986" - $20; Done With Mirrors Geffen promotional mirror, 1985; Done With Mirrors Geffen promotional playing cards, 1985; Pump Geffen promotional skateboard, 1989; Done With Mirrors promotional bumper sticker - $10; Get A Grip promotional tattoo - $3; Get A Grip promotional shopping bag - $10; videotapes from the group's numerous television appearances including *Saturday Night Live* (2/17/90, 10/9/93), *The Simpsons* (11/21/91), *MTV 10* (11/27/92), and the *Spider Man* cartoon series (1994); movie memorabilia from *Sgt. Pepper's Lonely Hearts Club Band* (1978) and *Mrs. Doubtfire;* autographed copy of *Draw The Line,* signed by Al Hirshfeld - $150-$200; memorabilia from the CompuServe Aerosmith download of Head First (1994); memorabilia from the band's "Cyberspace Tour '94" (1994); associated memorabilia from Mama Kins, a club co-owned by the band; Draw the Line promotional straw, source unknown; Done With Mirrors counter display - $45; Done With Mirrors promotional pin - $20; Rock In A Hard Place promotional pin - $20; Nine Lives bumper sticker - $5; Nine Lives promotional cat food can - $20; Pump 1990-91 World Tour pen - $25; Nine Lives promotional display - $35

REFERENCES/BOOKS

Aerosmith, The Fall and Rise by Mark Putterford: $20; *Aerosmith Live* by Mark Putterford: $10; a few other resources exist, but none do justice to the band in my opinion; no dedicated collector books; serious collectors should opt for the fan club: Aero Force One, Dept. Pick, P.O. Box 882494, San Francisco, CA 94168

****

"On The Edge"

Afghan Whigs

Gentlemen (Elektra, 1993) is a good collectible starting point, as little happened before or after its release. The record has its share of the typical male vs. female tensions, or the Whigs version of "Women Look like Jars, and Men Have a Penis."

****

a-ha

Formed 1982

Morten Harket, Magne "Mags" Furuholmen, and Pal Waaktaar

Music video super heroes who appeared with "Take On Me" (#1, 1985), driven to the top of the U.S. singles chart by a creative video that received heavy MTV rotation. They landed two more singles, "The Sun Always Shines on TV" (#20, 1985) and "Cry Wolf" (#50, 1987), before disappearing into the Norwegian hills.

AUTOGRAPHS

A CD, LP, magazine cover, ad, photo, or card signed by the group: $15-$30*

* Relating to the hit "Take On Me"

POSTERS/PRESS KITS

Promotional Posters: $10
Press Kits: $10

OFTEN OVERLOOKED MEMORABILIA

"Train of Thought," Warner Bros., promotional trainspotters' pack including a whistle, pen, and guide book in a travel bag - $40; "Stay On These Roads," 1988 promotional car kit - $25; promotional cartoon booklet w/ single "Take On Me" - $8

Air Supply

Formed 1976

Graham Russell, Born: June 1, 1950; Russell Hitchcock; Ralph Cooper; David Moyse; David Green; Rex Goh; and Frank Esler-Smith*

*Group disbanded in 1988 and re-formed in 1991 with Hitchcock, Russell, and Cooper

An Australian band centered around the duo of Graham Russell and Russell Hitchcock, Air Supply scored first at home with "Love and Other Bruises" (1976), "Empty Pages" (1977), and "Do What You Do" (1977) before taking the wind out of the U.S. singles chart with "Lost in Love" (#3, 1979), "Every Woman to Me" (#5, 1980), "The One That You Love" (#1, 1981), "Even the Nights are Better" (#6, 1982) and "Making Love Out of Nothing at All" (#2, 1983). The group disbanded in 1988, but re-formed in 1991.

AUTOGRAPHS

A CD, LP, magazine cover, ad, photo or card signed by the group: $15-$20

TOUR BOOKS/PROGRAMS/PASSES

Tour Books:

World Tour 1982: $10
In Motion Tour 1986: $10

Backstage Passes:

Cloth/paper: $5-$7; Laminated: $8-$12

POSTERS/PRESS KITS

Promotional Posters: $10-$20
Press Kits: $10-$15

USED CLOTHING/EQUIPMENT

Guitar Picks: $15

OFTEN OVERLOOKED MEMORABILIA

Scarf (blue), 1983 - $15

Aitken, Laurel

Born: 1928

Aitken is best known as having the first Jamaican record issued in the U.K. with her single "Little Sheila" (1953), and later for her brash and unabashed sexual humor in cult classics such as "Pussy Price" (1968)—as rude of a song as one might imagine!

AUTOGRAPHS

A CD, LP, magazine cover, ad, photo, or card signed by the artist: $8-$20

Alabama

Formed 1969; formerly Young Country

Jeff Cook, Born: August 27, 1949; Randy Owen, Born: December 13, 1949; Teddy Gentry, Born: January 22, 1952*

*Rick Scott was added on drums in 1973, and left in 1979. Mark Herndon was added in 1979.

A landmark band in country music history, Alabama owned the '80s country charts, with 37 C&W chart-toppers following "Tennessee River" (#1, 1980)—their debut RCA single. The band has sold over 50 million records worldwide, and with *In Pictures* (1996), Alabama had its 18th gold RCA album! With the influx of new blood such as the "hat acts," critics have been trying to dethrone the band for years, but "the closer you get" to Alabama, you'll see they're as "close enough to perfect" as a band could be.

AUTOGRAPHS

A CD, LP, magazine cover, ad, photo, or card signed by the entire band $35-$100*

* High end reflects vintage signed memorabilia; responsive to autograph requests.

TOUR BOOKS/PROGRAMS/PASSES

Backstage Passes: $5-$8 (1990 - Present)

POSTERS/PRESS KITS

Promotional Posters: $10-$25
Press Kits: $10-$30

USED CLOTHING/EQUIPMENT

Guitar Picks: $10-$20

REFERENCES/BOOKS

A couple of resources exist, nothing that does justice to the band in my opinion; no dedicated collector books

The Alarm

Formed 1978

Eddie McDonald, Mike Peters, Dave Sharp, and Nigel Twist

This guitar-fused Welsh group relocated to London in 1981, where club exposure led to their signing with I.R.S. The group's third album *Strength* (#39, 1985) was their only Top Forty entry, but they landed minor hits with "Strength" (#61, 1985) and "Rain in the Summertime" (#71, 1987). The band gained considerable attention when they opened for U2's 1983 tour.

AUTOGRAPHS

A CD, LP, magazine cover, ad, photo, or card signed by the group: $5-$10

TOUR BOOKS/PROGRAMS/PASSES

Tour Books:
Spirit of '86: $10

OFTEN OVERLOOKED MEMORABILIA

Spirit of '86 business card dispenser: $10

Al B. Sure

(Albert Brown)

A talented artist who stole what he could from R&B and laced it with sensuous undertones, Al B. Sure signed on with Warner Brothers Records and released an impressive debut *In Effect Mode,* with hit extract "Nite and Day" (#1, R&B; #7, pop, 1988). Unfortunately, since his initial release he has had little commercial success.

AUTOGRAPHS

A CD, LP, magazine cover, ad, photo, or card signed by the artist: $5-$12

Alexander, Arthur

Born: May 10, 1940, Died: June 9, 1993

Country-soul vocalist and songwriter Arthur Alexander is perhaps best known for his 1962 hit "You Better Move On" (#24, 1962), the first hit to emerge out of Rick Hall's Muscle Shoals studios. He suffered when Dot Records tried to market him as a pop artist—an area in which his songs were succeeding. Other musicians' covers of his tunes included The Beatles with "Anna," Bob Dylan with "Sally Sue Brown," and Elvis Presley with "Burning Love." He reentered the charts in the mid-70s with "Every Day I Have to Cry" (#45, 1975), but then quit the business. Having always been popular in England, some of his albums were reissued in the '80s. Just after his first release in two decades, "Lonely Just Like Me," he died of heart failure.

AUTOGRAPHS

A CD, LP, magazine cover, ad, photo or card signed by the group: $20-$35

OFTEN OVERLOOKED MEMORABILIA

Associated memorabilia from other musicians' covers of his songs

Alice in Chains

Formed 1987

Jerry Cantrell, Layne Staley, Sean Kinney, and Mike Starr*

*Starr departed in 1992 and Mike Inez was added

Another alt-metal band spewed from the Seattle grunge scene, Alice in Chains ripped into the typical "DTs" (dysfunctional topics)—death, despair, depression, and drugs. The band was formed by Layne Staley in high school, with an earlier lineup. He hooked up with Cantrell at Seattle's infamous warehouse rehearsal space before adding Kinney and Starr. Columbia Records picked the band up in 1989 and, under an aggressive campaign, drove their five-song promotional EP *We Die Young* and their album *Face Lift* (#42, 1990) into the public spotlight. The single "Man in the Box" picked up a Grammy nomination, and the band toured extensively in support of their efforts.

Dirt (#6, 1992) catapulted the band up the album chart, and they gained significant attention from touring and having a track included in the movie *Singles.* Late in 1983 *Dirt* sold double-platinum, as the band prepared for the release of their acoustic *Jar of Flies* (#1, 1993)—the first EP to ever top the Billboard album chart.

In 1994 Staley formed a parallel ad-hoc group called the Gacy Bunch, later renamed Mad Season. He teamed up with Pearl Jam's Mike McCready, John Baker Saunders, and Screaming Trees' Barrett Martin to release *Above* (1995). Meanwhile, AIC was in a state of flux, with both Cantrell and Kinney upset over Staley's alleged drug problem. The reunited Alice in Chains then released their self-titled album (#1, 1995), which debuted at #1.

AUTOGRAPHS

A CD, LP, magazine cover, ad, photo, or card signed by the entire band: $40-$80

TOUR BOOKS/PROGRAMS/PASSES

Backstage Passes: (1990 - Present)
Cloth: $7-$10; Laminated: $10-$17

POSTERS/PRESS KITS

Promotional Posters: $15-$30
Press Kits: $15-$40

USED CLOTHING/EQUIPMENT

Guitar Picks: $15-$35

OFTEN OVERLOOKED MEMORABILIA

A copy of the film *Live Facelift;* movie memorabilia from the movies *Singles* (1991) and *The Last Action Hero* (1993); videotapes of their television appearances, including *In Concert,* ABC-TV (8/91) and *Top of the Pops* (1/21/93)

REFERENCES/BOOKS

Difficult to find information; serious collectors should opt for the fan club: Alice in Chains Fan Club, P.O. Box 61475, Seattle, WA 98121 ($12 fee)

Allen, Lee

Born: July 2, 1927, Died: October 18, 1994

Extraordinary tenor saxophone session player who played with Fats Domino, Little Richard, and Sam Cooke, Allen also scored a solo single with "Walkin' with Mr. Lee" (#54, 1958).

AUTOGRAPHS

A CD, LP, magazine cover, ad, photo, or card signed by the artist: $10-$20

OFTEN OVERLOOKED MEMORABILIA

Associated memorabilia from his session work

Allen, Peter

(Peter Woolnough) Born: February 10, 1944, Died: June 18, 1992

The ever talented and flamboyant Peter Allen was not only a successful singer/songwriter and pianist, but a brilliant cabaret-style performer. He toured the world with Chris Allen (Bell), and the duo was spotted by Judy Garland, who quickly hired them as her opening act. In 1964 Allen and Garland's daughter, Liza Minelli, were engaged. Three years after their marriage in 1967, the couple split up on the very same day Allen called it quits with his partner Chris Bell.

As a performer and recording artist, Allen's breakthrough came in 1974 when a song he wrote, "I Honestly Love You," topped the singles chart for Olivia Newton-John. Subsequent minor hits, such as "I Go To Rio," also brought him into the spotlight. He was also one of four writers to coauthor the #1 hit "Arthur's Theme (The Best That You Can Do)," from the hit movie *Arthur*. "Don't Cry Out Loud," which he wrote with Carole Bayer Sager, also landed atop the singles chart for Melissa Manchester.

Allen was a legendary live performer (a cross in style between Elton John and Liberace), whose humor was his hallmark.

AUTOGRAPHS

A CD, LP, magazine cover, ad, photo, or card signed by the artist: $35-$125

OFTEN OVERLOOKED MEMORABILIA

Associated memorabilia from other musicians' covers of his songs; movie memorabilia from *Arthur;* videotapes of his numerous television appearances, including *The Tonight Show*

Allison, Luther

Born: August 17, 1939, Died: August 21, 1997

Legendary blues guitarist and a regular on the Chicago R&B scene during the '60s, Allison played with many of the best, including Freddie King. He traveled extensively, playing the Fillmore West in the late '60s before heading east to perform at the Fillmore East and Max's Kansas City. He has delighted audiences all over the world with his music.

AUTOGRAPHS

A CD, LP, magazine cover, ad, photo, or card signed by the artist: $10-$25

OFTEN OVERLOOKED MEMORABILIA

Movie memorabilia from *Cooley High*

Allison, Mose

Born: November 11, 1927

A staple on the jazz circuit for decades, Mose Allison is a gifted musician and a cynical songwriter, who has had his songs covered by the Who, Bonnie Raitt, Van Morrison, and even the Clash. His popular songs have included "A Young Man Blues," "Parchman Farm," and "Look Here." He was fortunate enough to be a part of the New York "cool" jazz scene of the late '50s, working with Al Cohn, Stan Getz, and Zoot Sims. His work is periodically rediscovered, and his legacy enhanced.

AUTOGRAPHS

A CD, LP, magazine cover, ad, photo, or card signed by the artist: $15-$30

OFTEN OVERLOOKED MEMORABILIA

Associated memorabilia from other musicians' covers of his songs

The Allman Brothers

Formed 1968

Duane Allman, Born: November 20, 1946, Died: October 29, 1971; Gregg Allman, Born: December 8, 1947; Berry Oakley, Born: April 4, 1948, Died: November 11, 1972; Dickey Betts, Born: December 12, 1943; Jaimoe a.k.a. Jai Johnny Johanson (John Johnson), Born: July 8, 1944; and Butch Trucks*

*Following the deaths of Duane Allman and Berry Oakley, Chuck Leavell and Lemar Williams (1947-1983) were added. Both Leavell and Williams left in 1978, when Dan Toler and Rook Goldflies were added. Leavell returned in 1982, but then Johanson left and the group disbanded. The group re-formed in 1989, consisting of Allman, Betts, Jaimoe, Trucks, Warren Haynes, Allen Woody, and Johnny Neel. Neel left in 1990.

The Allman Brothers Band has left an indelible mark on rock 'n' roll. They were the first band to truly mix deep Southern-rooted music—blues, country, gospel—and turn it into a magic recipe that would lead a wave of new bands from below the Mason-Dixon line. Nearly from its inception, the band has en-

dured considerable personal tragedy and yet has always remained transfixed upon its music.

Duane and Greg Allman began with a band called the Escorts, which before long was the hottest group in Daytona Beach. The first break the Escorts got was opening an Easter weekend show in 1065 for the Beach Boys. Soon the band evolved into the Allman Joys, but was short lived and broke up by the end of 1966.

The band re-formed and ended up with the name Hour Glass. The band signed with Liberty Records in Los Angeles and cut the self-titled *Hour Glass* (1968) and *Power of Love* (1969). They made their L.A. concert debut opening for The Doors at the Hullaballoo Club. Despite success in Southern California, the band—Duane and Gregg—eventually drifted back to Florida and wound up with a band called the 31st of February. This band recorded some sessions (Bold, 1973) that were eventually released, but the 31st of February came to an end when Gregg headed west and Duane headed to Muscle Shoals to cut some songs with Wilson Pickett.

Hour Glass is a good starting point for Allman enthusiasts to begin a memorabilia collection. Both of the albums have been released on compact disc and might have some associated memorabilia. Because the band made their concert debut with The Doors, it's likely that some material from this period may still be found in the market.

The debut of the Allman Brothers Band, although not billed as such, came on March 29, 1969, when Duane and Gregg Allman, Berry Oakley, Dickey Betts, and the rest of the Second Coming played a concert at the Jacksonville Beach Coliseum. The Boston Tea Party, a small Boston club, ended up being the first gig for the band outside of the South. The band first played the Fillmore East in November 1969, the same month their debut album, *The Allman Brothers Band,* was released. In January 1970 the band headed to the West Coast to play the now legendary Fillmore West. It was the Fillmore East, however, that eventually accommodated the band on March 12 and 13, 1971, while they recorded four concerts for *At Fillmore East* (Capricorn, 1971). Considered a classic, this became one of the greatest live albums in music history. A relic (poster, ticket, program, etc.) from any of these four live shows is a must for rock 'n' roll memorabilia collectors and a mandatory acquisition for collectors of the Allman Brothers Band. Both of the Fillmore theaters eventually closed. The Allman Brothers Band played for the last time at the East on the weekend of June 26 in what many historians deem their best performance ever.

On October 29, 1971, at 8:40 p.m., Howard Duane Allman, twenty-four years of age, was pronounced dead from injuries sustained from a motorcycle accident. His death shattered everyone associated with the great musician and put the Allman Brothers Band into a prolonged tailspin. *Eat a Peach,* the first

post-Duane album, was released in February 1972. The album, viewed by many historians as both a benediction and bridge to the future, became the guiding force for the surviving members. They toured in support of the album (spring to fall, 1972), added Chuck Leavell on keyboards, and began work on what was to become *Brothers and Sisters.* But it wasn't long before tragedy again struck the band.

On November 11, 1972, at 3:40 p.m., Raymond Berry Oakley III was pronounced dead from injuries sustained from a motorcycle accident. The similarities in the deaths of Duane Allman and Berry Oakley were uncanny: both were motorcycle accidents at parallel sites within 1,000 yards of each other; both were at intersections; and in both accidents the victims and drivers of the vehicles involved were all twenty-four years old. Allman and Oakley were both buried in Rose Hill Cemetery.

Just a few days after Oakley's death, *Duane Allman: An Anthology* was released (Capricorn, 1972). It was an amazing package that was one of the first rock albums to include an informative booklet—now a collector's item.

The decision was made to continue the Allman Brothers Band, and Lemar Williams was added. The band played New Year's Eve 1973 at the Warehouse in New Orleans, and on July 28, 1973, they played The Summer Jam at Watkins Glen (NY), which was the largest concert in rock history. *Brothers and Sisters* (Capricorn, 1973) was released just four days after the concert and became a #1 hit by the first of September. The end of the year found the band doing a live radio broadcast from their New Year's Eve concert at the Cow Palace in San Francisco, generating one of the largest radio audiences of all time. The year 1973 was a banner year for the band and thus a year worth concentrating on for Allman Brothers Band memorabilia collectors.

The success of Gregg Allman's solo album *Laid Back* spawned a world tour with his own band, and also gave rise to speculation that the Allman Brothers Band was finished. On the final date of Gregg's solo tour (April 25, 1974, in Cincinnati, Ohio) the Allman Brothers walked onstage during an encore to dismiss all the rumors.

Dickey Betts released a solo album in 1974, called *Highway Call* (Capricorn, 1974), and it became clear that despite what the band was saying publicly, schedules and music directions were beginning to differ between band members. *Win, Lose or Draw* (Capricorn, 1975) charted to number five, but was the first indication of the band's decline.

By 1975 Gregg Allman and Cher were involved in a roller-coaster marriage that transcended all media boundaries. The Allman Brothers Band was soon identified more for the tabloid headlines than their music. The media circus made it easy for fans to dismiss the contributions made by the band. The final straw came when Allman testified against his per-

sonal road manager, Scooter Herring, who was charged with dealing narcotics. The band felt their fraternal loyalty had been violated and the only direction left was for everyone to go their separate ways.

Dickey Betts formed Great Southern and had limited success. Such was also the case with Allman, who released *Playin' Up a Storm* (Capricorn, 1977) following his disastrous duet release with Cher. Leavell, Williams, and Johanson gained some attention with "Sea Level," but it was primarily a "stepping stone" for Leavell. In addition to session work, he toured with the Rolling Stones in 1989 and 1994.

The Allman Brothers regrouped on August 16, 1978, at the Wollman Skating Rink in New York City's Central Park, where Great Southern was playing to a crowd of about 5,000 people. The band (third version) settled back in Florida late in 1978, before recording a comeback album, *Enlightened Rogues* (Capricorn, 1979). *Reach for the Sky* (Arista, 1980) and *Brothers of the Road* (Arista, 1981) did little to bolster the band's reputation; however, a new record company meant new promotional items for collectors. Gregg Allman was in a dire financial state and some of his items were auctioned off to pay bills.

On January 23, 1982, the band played on *Saturday Night Live* in what was their last performance for four years. They performed at the Volunteer Jam in Nashville in 1986, then again at a benefit three months later. The band regrouped in 1989 in conjunction with *Dreams* (Polydor, 1989), a five-record boxed compilation. *Seven Turns* (Epic, 1990) revitalized the band and was followed by other albums, including *Shades of Two Worlds* (Epic, 1991) and *Where It All Begins* (Epic, 1994).

In 1995 the group was inducted into the Rock and Roll Hall of Fame.

AUTOGRAPHS

Autographs from deceased members Duane Allman and Berry Oakley are very difficult to find

Group:

A CD, LP, magazine cover, ad, photo, or card signed by the entire band: $175-$700*

*High end reflects vintage signed memorabilia

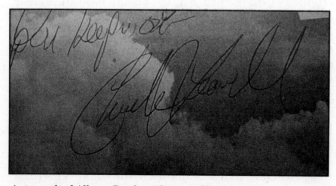

Autograph of Allman Brother Alumnus Chuck Leavell

Individual:

Duane Allman: $400-$500	Gregg Allman: $40
Berry Oakley: $150-$300	Dickey Betts: $25
Jaimoe: $20	Butch Trucks: $20
Chuck Leavell: $5-$15	

TOUR BOOKS/PROGRAMS/PASSES

Tour Programs:

Highly sought are the Fillmore programs—not easy to find, but not impossible either. Anticipate a price range of $75-$100.
American Music Show, 1978 (Betts): $35

Backstage Passes:

Cloth: $10; Laminated: $10-$20 (1990 - Present)
Backstage passes pre-dating 1989 are not easy to find. Passes from the 20th Anniversary Tour 1989 and later can be found for about $10.

Allman Brothers tour passes (L: OTTO, R: Wonder Graphics)

POSTERS/PRESS KITS

Promotional Posters:
Primarily Capricorn are sought by collectors and can be tough to find; price range $20-$100. Fillmore West (Bill Graham Presents) posters (January 15-18, 1970, and January 28-31, 1970) are highly sought by collectors and tough to find. Both are believed to be single printings and have associated postcards.

Press Kits:

$15-$20 (1990s)

USED CLOTHING/EQUIPMENT

Duane Allman used Martin D35 acoustic guitar: $10,000-$14,000

Guitar Picks:

Duane Allman: $400-$500*	Gregg Allman: $30-$40
Berry Oakley: $150-$300*	Dickey Betts: $25-$40
*Difficult to authenticate.	

Drum Sticks:

Jaimoe: $20-$25	Butch Trucks: $20-$25

OFTEN OVERLOOKED MEMORABILIA

Court transcripts and "Cher and Gregg" periodicals; Shades of Two Worlds Epic promotional sunglasses, 1991; Gregg Allman I'm No Angel Epic promotional drinking glass, 1990; I'm No Angel Epic promotional sling shot; videotapes of the group's numerous television appearances, including *The Tonight Show* (10/9/91), *The Dennis Miller Show* (7/25/92), *Late Show with David Letterman* (8/14/94, 2/28/96), and *Win, Lose or Draw;* 1975 promotional playing cards; movie memorabilia from *Rush* (1991); mushroom pewter pin or necklace - $35

REFERENCES/BOOKS

Midnight Riders, The Story of The Allman Brothers Band by Scot Freeman: $13; *The Allman Brothers Band: A Biography in Words and Pictures* by Tom Nolan; no dedicated collector books; serious collectors should opt for the fan club: GABBA, Georgia Allman Brothers Band Association, P.O. Box 870, Macon, GA 31202 ($15 fee)

Almond, Marc: See Soft Cell

Alpert, Herb

Born: March 31, 1935

"The King of Ameriachi" in the mid-60s, Herb Alpert is a musical force who has sold more instrumental records than anyone in history. He was also the co-founder and vice-chairman of A&M records, which he and partner Jerry Moss sold in 1990 to PolyGram.

In his early years he wrote with Lou Adler and Sam Cooke, producing such classics as "Only Sixteen" and "Wonderful World." He and Adler were notorious for recording tunes under various pseudonyms. In 1962 he and Moss started A&M Records out of Alpert's garage, largely on the royalties of Herb Alpert's Tijuana Brass, which scored numerous hits including "The Lonely Bull" (#6, 1961), "A Taste of Honey" (#7, 1965), and "The Mexican Shuffle" (#85, 1964). The group was such a force in modern music that it had five albums in the Top Twenty during 1965 alone.

A&M Records signings included Carole King and The Carpenters. Alpert returned to the charts in 1979 with "Rise," which became his second #1 hit.

AUTOGRAPHS

A CD, LP, magazine cover, ad, photo, or card signed by the artist: $10-$25

Autograph of Herb Alpert

TOUR BOOKS/PROGRAMS/PASSES

1984 World Tour: $15

OFTEN OVERLOOKED MEMORABILIA

Associated memorabilia from other musicians' covers of his songs; a bottle of "Listen" and associated memorabilia;

videotapes of *The Dating Game;* movie memorabilia from *Casino Royale* (1967) and *The Happening* (1967); episodes of *General Hospital* that feature "Rise"; memorabilia from Super Bowl XXII (Alpert performed the national anthem); "Rise" unused display - $35

Alvin, Dave and Alvin, Phil: See the Blasters

Amazing Rhythm Aces

Formed 1974

Russell Smith, Butch McDade, Jeff Davis, Billy Earhart, James Hooker, and Barry "Byrd" Burton*

*Burton left in 1979 and was replaced with Duncan Cameron

This country-rock group was headed by Russell Smith, and scored one hit, "Third Rate Romance" (#14, 1975).

AUTOGRAPHS

A CD, LP, magazine cover, ad, photo, or card signed by the group: $7-$15

Ambitious Lovers: See DNA/Arto Lindsay

Amboy Dukes: See Ted Nugent

Ambrosia

Formed 1971

David Pack, Joe Puerta, Burleigh Drummond, and Christopher North

A talented group of four musicians who could play more than 70 instruments, Ambrosia is best known for its '70s hit singles "Holdin' On to Yesterday" (#17, 1975), "How Much I Feel" (#3, 1978), "Biggest Part of Me" (#3, 1980), and "You're the Only Woman (You & I)" (#13, 1980)—all pop singles with just a touch of classical flavor.

AUTOGRAPHS

A CD, LP, magazine cover, ad, photo, or card signed by the group: $15-$25

OFTEN OVERLOOKED MEMORABILIA

Associated memorabilia from other musicians' covers of their songs; album mobiles: $25-$30

Amen Corner/Andy Fairweather-Low

Formed 1966

Andy Fairweather-Low, Neil Jones, Blue Weaver, Clive Taylor, Dennis Byrn, Allen Jones, and Mike Smith

This British mod band led by Andy Fairweather-Low scored with hits "Gin House," "(If Paradise Is) Half As Nice" (#1, 1969), and "Hello Suzie." Unfortunately, their label folded at the height of the band's popularity. They did manage to grab a Top Five single in 1970 with "Natural Sinner."

AUTOGRAPHS

A CD, LP, magazine cover, ad, photo, or card signed by the group: $5-$10

OFTEN OVERLOOKED MEMORABILIA

Movie memorabilia from *Scream and Scream Again* (1969) and *The Wall* (1990)

America

Formed 1969

Dewey Bunnell, Born: January 19, 1952; Dan Peek, Born: November 1, 1950; Gerry Beckley, Born: September 12, 1952*

*Peek left in 1977

America, one of the premier bands of the early 1970s, impressed fans with their smooth vocal harmonies, simple composition, and crisp technical production. At a time when folk-rock groups seemed to draw considerable attention, America shot straight to number one with "A Horse with No Name" in March of 1972. Equally as impressive as their rise to stardom was the string of successful hits that followed for the next three years: " I Need You," "Ventura Highway," "Tin Man," "Lonely People," and "Sister Golden Hair." (Famed Beatles producer George Martin took the knobs on *Holiday* in 1974, and it was this album and the new collaboration that brought them "Tin Man" and the hits that followed.)

Dan Peek's departure in 1977 forced the band to continue as duo, which they did, but with far less success. Peek ended up grabbing a Grammy nomination with "All Things Are Possible" (a religious recording), and Buckley and Bunnell stumbled through a controversial South African tour. *View from the Ground* was released in 1982 and yielded a Top Ten hit, "You Can Do Magic." Unfortunately for America, the domestic music scene was moving faster than they were and subsequent album releases were met with far less commercial success.

America continued to tour, drawing new interest in their earlier catalog, and Peek also joined them in 1993. Beckley and Bunnell returned to the studio af-

ter a decade of absence to record *Hourglass*, but interest in the band had faded considerably.

AUTOGRAPHS

America has always been fairly accessible to their fans.
Group:
A CD, LP, magazine cover, ad, photo, or card signed by the entire band: $50-$65*
* High end reflects vintage signed memorabilia
Individual:
Gerry Beckley: $10-$15
Dewey Bunnell: $10-$15
Dan Peek: $15-$20

TOUR BOOKS/ PROGRAMS/PASSES

Tour Programs:
1977 Tour: $15-$17
Backstage Passes:
$8-$15

POSTERS/PRESS KITS

Promotional Posters:
Primarily pre-1975 posters are sought by America collectors. Although not particularly easy to find, they are also not usually expensive upon discovery: $8-$15.
Press Kits:
$10-$40

Typical '70s-style America program, printed on thin stock, designed by Phil Hartmann in association with Winterland Productions.

USED CLOTHING/ EQUIPMENT

Guitar Picks:
Beckley: $8
Bunnell: $8
Drum Sticks:
Peek: $10

OFTEN OVERLOOKED MEMORABILIA

Album inserts, stickers, etc.; movie memorabilia from *California Dreaming* (1979) and *The Last Unicorn* (1984); videotapes of the group's numerous television performances, including *The Old Grey Whistle Test* (9/21/71) and *Lonely People;* 6-inch metal loving cup - $40

The American Breed

Formed 1966

Al Ciner, Gary Loizzo, Lee Graziano, Charles Colbert, and Kevin Murphy

One of Chicago's top pop bands, The American Breed is best remembered for a short string of singles that included "Step Out of Your Mind" (#24, 1967), "Green Light" (#39, 1968), and "Bend Me Shape Me" (#1, 1968). When the band disintegrated, Murphy and Andre Fischer (a later member, married to Natalie Cole) hooked up with Chaka Khan to form Rufus in 1972.

AUTOGRAPHS

A CD, LP, magazine cover, ad, photo, or card signed by the group: $10-$25

OFTEN OVERLOOKED MEMORABILIA

Associated memorabilia from other musicians' covers of their songs

American Flyer: See Eric Kaz

American Music Club

Formed 1983

Mark Eitzel, Mark Pankler, Dan Pearson, Brad Johnson, and Matt Norelli*

*Johnson left in 1987; Tom Mallon and Dave Scheff were added. Scheff departed in 1988, and Mallon left the following year. Mike Simms and Bruce Kaplan were added. Simms left in 1993 and Tim Mooney joined the band.

An important underground band of the '80s that developed a cult following based on such depression-ary classics as "Gary's Song," "Nightwatchman," and "Outside This Bar," American Music Club (AMC) nearly broke through at the turn of the decade, but it wasn't until *Everclear* finally surfaced on indie label Alias in 1991 that the band received their well deserved acclaim, even from *Rolling Stone*. Unfortunately, negligible sales did little to bolster the critical accolades.

AUTOGRAPHS

A CD, LP, magazine cover, ad, photo, or card signed by the group: $12-$30

Amos, Tori

(Myra Amos) Born: August 22, 1963

Proficient at piano at an early age, Amos attended the Peabody Conservatory (John Hopkins) in Baltimore, Maryland, under a music scholarship. Amos was playing by ear at age eleven, and playing bars around "the beltway" in her late teens. She (Myra Ellen Amos) and brother Michael recorded "Baltimore" on her own MEA label (7-inch, 5290) in 1980, and the following year she established a residency at the Hilton Hotel in Myrtle Beach, South Carolina, where she crafted her art and sent demo tapes all around the recording industry. Although there was some initial interest, nothing seemed to pan out for the young Myra Ellen Amos.

Amos relocated to Los Angeles in 1984, changed her first name to Tori, and by 1987 had a recording contract with Atlantic Records. *Y Kant Tori Read*

[featuring a packaged Amos, along with Matt Sorum (Guns N' Roses) and Steve Ferris (Mr. Mister)], was released by Atlantic in 1988 and included the singles "The Big Picture" (89086, 1988) and "Cool On Your Island" (89021, 1988). When both the album and singles were virtually ignored, she guested on Al Stewart's *Last Days of the Century* (Enigma, 73316, 1988) before moving to London in February 1991.

The strategy in London was to develop a strong club following, leading to good press coverage and hopefully a breaking record in a smaller market. She quickly overwhelmed the U.K. press, who fell in love with the cute but frail, five-foot-two-inch redhead. She then released a four-track EP, *Me and a Gun* (East West, YZ618), in October 1991. It featured the autobiographical ballad "Silent All These Years" (#51, U.K., 1991), a traumatic reflection of rape by gunpoint, that garnered immediate attention and U.K. airplay.

On January 25, 1992, *Little Earthquakes* (#14, U.K., 1992), what many refer to as her bona fide debut album effort, established her as a talented songwriter. The single "China" (#51, U.K., 1992) gained some airplay before "Winter" (#25, U.K., 1992), also from the album, was released on March 28, 1992. The *Winter* EP also featured covers of "Smells Like Teen Spirit," "Angie," and "Thank You." In May she headed back to Los Angeles with a new image and her album *Little Earthquakes* at #54 on the U.S. album charts.

On July 4, 1992, "Crucify" (#15, U.K., 1992), another extracted single from *Little Earthquakes*, climbed the charts. She was voted Best New Female Artist in *Rolling Stone*'s 1992 annual readers' poll, and decided to spend the following year concentrating on her sophomore album.

On February 12, 1994, *Under the Pink* (#1, U.K., 1994), entered atop the U.K. charts, while debuting at #12 on U.S. album charts. Extracted singles "God" (#72, 1994) and "Past the Mission" (#31, U.K., 1994) were released as the Under the Pink Tour prepared to begin its aggressive 181 worldwide dates. During the year she duetted with Tom Jones on his album *The Lead and How to Swing It,* and contributed a song to the Atlantic Records' Christmas promotional CD, *Little Drummer Boy*.

In 1995 she contributed to *Encomium: A Tribute to Led Zeppelin* [which included her duet with Robert Plant on "Down by the Seaside" (#17, 1995)], and *Tower of Song: The Songs of Leonard Cohen*. She released her third album, *Boys For Pele* (#2, 1996), before beginning the Dew Drop Inn Tour '96, which featured numerous tour legs including a 40-city U.S. trek.

With each passing year Tori Amos seems to grow exponentially in popularity. Her memorabilia is already heavily collected, with some items already commanding significant prices. Popular items include the "Baltimore" single, *Y Kant Tori Read* items,

the "Crucify" limited edition CD box with four miniature art prints, and the "Under the Pink" promo CD, gatefold digipak w/unapproved cover photo (versions eventually destroyed).

TORI ON THE TELI

Selected Television Appearances by Tori Amos

January 29, 1992	*Wogan*, BBC-1TV
April 23, 1992	*Late Night with David Letterman*, NBC-TV
June 24, 1992	*Summer Scene*, BBC1-TV
June 25, 1992	*Top of the Pops*
December 10, 1992	*Later*, BBC2-TV
February 1, 1994	*The Beat*, ITV
February 11, 1994	*The Tonight Show*, NBC-TV
March 16, 1994	*The Big Breakfast*, C4-TV
March 28, 1994	*Late Show with David Letterman*, CBS-TV
June 15, 1994	*Naked City*, C4-TV
August 25, 1994	*Later with Greg Kinnear*, NBC-TV
February 24, 1995	*The Tonight Show*, NBC-TV
March 1, 1995	*37th annual Grammy Awards*, presented an award
April 8, 1996	*Late Show with David Letterman*, CBS-TV

AUTOGRAPHS
A CD, LP, magazine cover, ad, photo, or card signed by the artist: $40-$60

TOUR BOOKS/PROGRAMS/PASSES
Backstage Passes:
Cloth: $10-$15; Laminated: $15-$30

POSTERS/PRESS KITS
Promotional Posters: $10-$35
Cornflake Girl (U.K.) (24" x 24"): $15; Under the Pink (U.K., stock) (25" x 36"): $15
Press Kits: $15-$25
Music Books: $18-$25*
*Note: Little Earthquakes: $40; gatefold bio scarce!

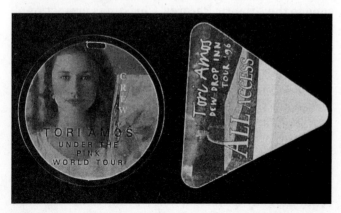

Two examples of Tori Amos backstage passes. Left-watch for counterfeits, right-printed by OTTO.

OFTEN OVERLOOKED MEMORABILIA
Movie memorabilia from *Toys* and *Higher Learning*, Cornflake Girl Atlantic promotional CD in a Kellogg's variety-sized Corn Flakes box - $35; magazines: *Spin*, October 1994, *Q*, May 1994, *Creem*, March 1994 - $5-$8; Under the Pink/Fall Tour '94 Itinerary - $25-$35; Marbury House flyers - $10-$15; At The Door flyers - $15-$20

REFERENCES/BOOKS:
All These Years by Kalen Rogers (two versions): $20; Limited edition CD-sized book, 120 pp.: $18; a few other resources exist; no dedicated collector books

---

Anderson, Eric

Born: February 14, 1943

Another artifact from the burgeoning New York City folk scene of the '60s, Anderson established himself as both a singer and songwriter while playing the normal haunts—Gerede's Folk City and the Gaslight Cafe. Although he never had a hit, his "Blue River" and "Ghosts upon the Road" are considered landmark pieces for their era. His more memorable compositions include "Thirsty Boots," "Be True to You," "Violets Are Dawn," and "Is It Really Love at All."

AUTOGRAPHS
A CD, LP, magazine cover, ad, photo, or card signed by the artist: $5-$15

OFTEN OVERLOOKED MEMORABILIA
Associated memorabilia from other musicians' covers of his songs

---

Anderson, John

Born: December 13, 1954

A gifted songwriter often compared to Lefty Frizzell, Anderson turned his sights from rock to country music after hearing Merle Haggard. George Jones gave the songwriter his first Top Forty hit with "The Girl at the End of the Bar" (#40, C&W, 1978). Anderson followed with five Top Forty hits before Warner Brothers finally released his first album in 1980. One of the first "new traditionalist" stars, he enjoyed more than 20 Top Forty C&W hits during a five-year span in the '80s. With "Swingin'" (#43) from his album *Wild & Blue* (#58), he successfully crossed into the pop market.

Just when it seemed his momentum had been diffused by label problems and changes, Mark Knopfler (Dire Straits) helped Anderson with a comeback. *Seminole Wind* (#35, 1992), with extract "When It Comes To You" (#2, C&W, 1991), brought him quickly back into the spotlight and gained him a whole new audience.

AUTOGRAPHS

A CD, LP, magazine cover, ad, photo, or card signed by the artist: $7-$12

OFTEN OVERLOOKED MEMORABILIA

Associated memorabilia from other musicians' covers of his songs

Anderson, Jon: See Yes

Anderson, Laurie

Born: June 5, 1947

An avant-garde multimediast, Anderson's artistic work—based on words and their oratory—takes on many forms. Best known perhaps for her unusual 1981 recording "O Superman" (#2, U.K.), her work is often presented in a creative arts environment, such as a museum. Although her work has had some success in the U.S., it has been better accepted in Europe.

AUTOGRAPHS

A CD, LP, magazine cover, ad, photo, or card signed by the artist: $20-$35

REFERENCES/BOOKS

Notebook (1977), *Empty Places* (1991) and others by Anderson

Angel

Formed 1975

Frank DiMino, Gregg Giuffria, Punky Meadows, Mickey Jones, and Barry Brandt*

*Jones left in 1977 and Felix Robinson was added

Like Starz, another Casablanca concept band, Angel was all show and no go. Given every opportunity to succeed, from tours with Kiss, to enough finances to build an elaborate stage show, nothing seemed to get the act off the ground. With Angel's wings clipped, Gregg Giuffria started his own self-titled band and landed a Top Forty hit with "Call to the Heart" in 1985, before moving on to the House of Lords.

AUTOGRAPHS

A CD, LP, magazine cover, ad, photo, or card signed by the group: $5-$10

OFTEN OVERLOOKED MEMORABILIA

All Casablanca promotional displays, posters, and other associated memorabilia are highly sought by Angel collectors

Angel City/Angels

Formed 1973

Doc Neeson, John Brewster, Rick Brewster, Graham Bidstrup, and Chris Bailey

Australian hard rockers who have found success in their native land with outstanding albums such as *Face to Face* and other platinum offerings. They have generated little interest in the U.S.

AUTOGRAPHS

A CD, LP, magazine cover, ad, photo, or card signed by the group: $15-$30

The Angels

Formed 1961

Barbara Allbut, Phyllis Allbut Meister, and Linda Jansen*

*Jansen left in 1962 and Peggy McCannon was added

One of the most successful '60s girl groups, The Angels are best known for "My Boyfriend's Back" (#1, 1963). The group scored other hits with "Cry Baby Cry" (#38, 1962), "I Adore Him" (#25, 1963), and "Wow Wow Wee (He's the Boy For Me)" (#41, 1964), before eventually fading from the spotlight.

AUTOGRAPHS

A CD, LP, magazine cover, ad, photo, or card signed by the group: $25-$40

****

"On the Edge"

Angry Samoans

A sludge-rock metal band whose wired power chords spatter refuse like a 300-pound gorilla doing squat thrusts in a mud puddle. Garbage rock connoisseurs will leave with their palette cleansed for the next course. Begin your collection with *Back from Samoa* (1982, Triple X) and *31 Garage Pit Hits* (PVC, 1987), then sharpen your "Steak Knife" and go look for the guy who was laughing when he sold the records to you!

****

The Animals

Formed 1962

Original Lineup: Alan Price, Born: April 19, 1942; Eric Burdon, Born: May 11, 1941; Bryan "Chas" Chandler, Born: December 18, 1938, Died: July 17, 1996; John Steel, Born: February 4, 1941; Hilton Valentine, Born; May 21, 1943*

*Additional personnel included Dave Rowberry, Barry Jenkins, Johnny Weedier, Vic Briggs, Danny McCulloch, Zoot Money, and Andrew Somers (Summers)

One of the original British Invasion bands (best known for the classic "House of the Rising Son" [#1, 1964], their second single), The Animals were heavily influenced by the roots of American R&B. After they had three hits with "Don't Let Me Be Misunderstood" (#15, 1965), "We Gotta Get Out of This Place" (#13, 1965), and "It's My Life" (#23, 1965), Price left the band. John Steel left after the band scored with "Inside-Looking Out" (#34, 1966). "Don't Bring Me Down" (#12, 1966) and "See See Rider" (#10, 1966) continued their string of hits, but were followed by the departure of Valentine.

Billed as Eric Burdon and the Animals, "San Franciscan Nights" (#9, 1967), "Monterey" (#15, 1968), and "Sky Pilot" (#14, 1968) all struck gold in that rich California soil before the group fell apart. Efforts to resurrect the band failed, even with new members such as future Police guitarist Andy Summers, although the group had a number of one-off gigs and recordings in the years that followed.

The Animals were inducted into the Rock and Roll Hall of Fame in 1994.

AUTOGRAPHS
Group:
A CD, LP, magazine cover, ad, photo, or card signed by the entire band: $65-$175*
*High end reflects vintage signed memorabilia
Individual:
Eric Burdon: $20-$35

OFTEN OVERLOOKED MEMORABILIA
Videotapes of their numerous television appearances including *The Ed Sullivan Show* (5/30/65); movie memorabilia from *Pop Gear* (1965) and *Stranger in the House* (1967); Before We Were Interrupted mobile - $75

REFERENCES/BOOKS
I Used to Be an Animal, But I'm Alright Now, by Eric Burdon (1986); no dedicated collector books; serious collectors should opt for the fan club: The Eric Burdon Connection Newsletter, Phil Metzger, 448 Silver Lane, Oceanside, NY 11572

Anka, Paul

Born: July 30, 1941

A late '50s teen idol, talented singer, and gifted songwriter, Paul Anka, scored with numerous hits, including "Diana" (#1, 1958), "You Are My Destiny" (#7, 1958), "Crazy Love" (#15, 1958), "Lonely Boy" (#1, 1959), "Hello Young Lovers" (#23, 1960), "Put Your Head on My Shoulder" (#2, 1959), and "Puppy Love" (#2, 1960). When the hits slowed in 1962 he continued to write and record in numerous other languages, while also trying his luck at acting. He rebounded in 1974 with his hit "(You're) Having My Baby" (#1, 1974), followed by his last Top Forty hit, "Hold Me 'Til the Mornin' Comes" (1983).

"It Doesn't Matter Anymore" (Buddy Holly), "My Way" (Frank Sinatra), "It's Really Love" (The Tonight Show Theme), and "Times of Your Life" are just a few of his 400-plus compositions that have been recorded.

AUTOGRAPHS
A CD, LP, magazine cover, ad, photo, or card signed by the artist: $5-$20

TOUR BOOKS/PROGRAMS/PASSES
Anka appeared on "The Biggest Show of Stars for 1957" and other package tours with acts such as Buddy Holly & the Crickets, Chuck Berry, and so on; therefore, memorabilia from these appearances is not only highly sought, but expensive.

OFTEN OVERLOOKED MEMORABILIA
Movie memorabilia from *Girls Town* (1959), *Look in Any Window* (1961), *The Longest Day* (1962) and others, videotapes of his numerous television appearances, including *The Ed Sullivan Show* (5/17/64); a videotape from the very first *Tonight Show* (10/2/62), which used Anka's theme; videotapes of the Kodak television commercials featuring Anka's "Times of Your Life"; Ottawa Senator memorabilia (Anka is part owner); The Painter light up display - $95

Annette: See Annette Funicello

Anthrax

Formed 1981

Scott Ian, Born: December 31, 1963; Dan Spitz, Born: January 28, 1963; Dan Lilker, Born: October 18, 1964; Charles Benante, Born: November 27, 1962; and Neil Turbin*

*Turbin and Lilker departed in 1984, and Joey Belladonna and Frank Bello were added. Belladonna left in 1992 and John Bush joined the band

Critically acclaimed metal band Anthrax (similar to Metallica and Megadeth) has exhibited proven staying power by delivering solid and consistent output. Combining speed and intensity with vivid emotion, Anthrax redefined the metal genre of the '80s.

Scott Ian formed the band, spawned from New York City's postpunk metal scene. *Fistful of Metal,* their debut album, was released on Megaforce in February 1984. The band underwent a series of personnel changes, and following the release of *Armed and Dangerous* (1985), a five track mini-album, they had impressed Island Records executives enough to land a recording contract.

Spreading the Disease (#113, 1986), with extract "Madhouse," was supported by extensive touring, including the group's U.K. debut (6/86). "I Am the Law" (#32, U.K., 1987), an extract from their next album, became the group's first placement on the U.K. singles chart. *Among the Living* (#62, 1987) was praised by critics who watched the album climb up the U.S. and U.K. charts. The band capitalized on their strong live performance by issuing the EP *I'm the Man,* which was welcomed by a growing fan base.

State of Euphoria (#30, 1988) made it onto the U.S. Top Forty album chart, while earning gold certification. *Persistence of Time* (#24, 1990) solidified the band's breakthrough with its chart success, enhanced by a Grammy Award nomination for Best Metal Performance. *Attack of the Killer B's* (#27, 1991) followed as the band kicked off its unique thrash/rap Bring the Noise Tour with Public Enemy.

Following a multimillion dollar deal with Elektra, Belladonna departed and was replaced by John Bush. *Sound of White Noise* (#7, 1993), was the band's first studio recording in three years, and the first to feature Bush. Spitz was next to depart, prior to the band's *Stomp 442* (#47, 1995).

AUTOGRAPHS

A CD, LP, magazine cover, ad, photo, or card signed by the entire band: $40-$60
Individual member signatures run about $10 each

TOUR BOOKS/PROGRAMS/PASSES

Backstage Passes: (1990 - Present) Cloth: $8; Laminated: $8-$15

POSTERS/PRESS KITS

Promotional Posters: $10-$30
Press Kits: $10-$20
Live, The Island Years: $20; Persistence of Time: $12

USED CLOTHING/EQUIPMENT

Guitar Picks: $ 8-$10*

Two examples of Anthrax guitar picks

*Frank's custom quote picks are a favorite with collectors—"That's the Flavor," "Can I Say This?" etc.
Drum Sticks: $15-$25
Personalized sticks ("Charlie's Stick"): $15;
Tour sticks: $25

OFTEN OVERLOOKED MEMORABILIA

Any indie label Caroline/Megaforce promotional items; State of Euphoria promotional license plate - $17; Killer B's promotional jar of honey - $25; movie memorabilia from *The Last Action Hero* (1993); videotapes of the group's television show appearances, including *Newsradio* (11/28/95)

REFERENCES/BOOKS

Serious collectors should opt for the fan club: NFC: The Official Anthrax Fan Club, P.O. Box 254, Kulpsville, PA 19443 ($10 fee)

****

"On The Edge"

Aphex Twin

Drop two hits, then start spinning to this "armchair techno" electronica. Begin with *Selected Ambient Works 85-92* (R&S, 1992), a prepubescent salute to Brian Eno with just enough craft to work! Aphex artifacts are far easier to find on the Sire/Warner Bros. label, but are far less worthy.

****

April Wine

Formed 1969
David Henman, Ritchie Henman, Jimmy Henman, and Myles Goodwyn, Born: June 23, 1948*

*J. Henman departed in 1970 and Jimmy Clench was added. David Henman and Ritchie Henman left in 1971 and Gary Moffet and Jerry Mercer were added. Clench left in 1975 and Steve Lang was added. Brian Greenway joined the band in 1977. Additional changes followed as the group disbanded and re-formed.

During the 1970s, April Wine was one of Canada's top heavy metal acts. Their hard-rock following was developed through extensive touring and strong album sales. The group even became one of the few Canadian groups to have an album shipped platinum *(The Whole World's Going Crazy)*. The group struck gold in the United States with *The Nature of the Beast* (#26, 1981). The record, composed of all Goodwyn tunes, spun off the single "Just Between You and Me" (#21, 1981). Goodwyn attempted a solo career in 1984, but was unsuccessful.

Any items worth putting away should relate to *The Nature of the Beast* or *The Whole World's Going Cra-*

zy. Early Big Tree Record related memorabilia won't be easy to find; an autographed copy of the group's debut self-titled album would be worthy of a Canadian time capsule.

AUTOGRAPHS

A CD, LP, magazine cover, ad, photo, or card signed by the group: $15-$20

Arc Angels: See Charlie Sexton

Arcadia : See Duran Duran

The Archies

Formed 1968

An "artificial band" based on the comic book, The Archies captured the hearts of children with their mid-60s cartoon series of the same name. Ellie Greenwich, Jeff Barry, and Andy Kim overlooked their songwriting, penning hits such as "Sugar, Sugar" (#1, 1969), "Bang-Shang-a-Lang" (#2, 1968), "Jingle, Jangle" (#10, 1969), and "Who's Your Baby" (#40, 1970).

Meanwhile, the singing Archies were led by Ron Dante, who later produced a number of acts and commercials before becoming editor of the literary magazine *Paris Review*. Andy Kim went on to a successful pop career with hits "Baby I Love You" (#9, 1969) and "Rock Me Gently" (#1, 1974).

OFTEN OVERLOOKED MEMORABILIA

Videotapes of the cartoon series; Archies kit (50th Anniversary, pen note pad, button & membership card) - $25; beanie (Jughead, cereal promo) - $10; bubble funnies - $7; button making set - $100; carry case (Marx) - $60; McDonald's premium cars, set of 6 -$20, Burger King premium cars, set of 4 - $10; coloring book (Whitman) - $12; Marx 8" dolls, set of 4 - $50; Mattel 8" dolls, set of 5 - $40; Presents 18" dolls, set of 4 - $35; Jesco 6" dolls, mail-in, set of 5 - $20; drum (Emenfe) - $15; face puppet (foam rubber) - $14; fuzzy face (toy and candy) - $4; game (Jaru Fuzzy Face)- $5; Hasbro Archie Fun game - $80; Whitman Archie game - $40; hair dryer - $5; Halloween costume - $40; Marx 12" jalopy - $80; LJN metal jalopy- $45; jelly glasses (Welch's, set of 6, 1971, 1973) - $60; junior shaver kit (Jughead) - $5; loonies (bubbles/straw) - $6; Aladdin steel lunch box- $95; Merro Kane lunch box - $50; model kit (jalopy) - $135; money set - $5; pchinko game - $5; Whitman paper dolls - $20; Whitman boxed paper dolls - $40; pencil by numbers - $20; phone set - $5; pocket puzzle - $20; poppers (3"), set of 3 - $30; puffy stickers - $6; purse - $12; Whitman boxed set of 4 puzzles - $100; Jaymar puzzle, 1969 - $40; Jaymar puzzle, 1988 - $10; record cut-outs (cereal box) - $7; skin rub-ons (cereal premium) - $15; slide viewer (Kenner) - $15; squirt pen - $8; stationery - $50; stencil set - $7; stickers (set of 180) - $30; sticker album - $10; tattoos (Topps, set of 16) - $30; thermos (Aladdin) $25; trading cards (Topps, set of 120) - $15; transfer book - $22; trace and color - $6; watch (Cheval LED) - $35; View-Master - $32

REFERENCES/BOOKS

Comic books

Argent

Formed 1969

Rod Argent, Jim Rodford, Robert Henrit, and Russ Ballard*

*Ballard departed in 1974 and was replaced with John Grimaldi and John Verity

Keyboardist Rod Argent started his own band when the Zombies died in 1967, capitalizing on their hit "Time of the Season" (#3, 1969) and landing his own with "Hold Your Head Up" (#5, 1972). The band folded in mid-1976 after leaving a series of FM staples, but no more hit singles. Ballard went on to a successful songwriting and production career. Argent has always remained active in the business, primarily as a pianist. Rodford joined the Kinks and was followed by Henrit.

AUTOGRAPHS

A CD, LP, magazine cover, ad, photo, or card signed by the group: $30-$45

OFTEN OVERLOOKED MEMORABILIA

Individual members' solo efforts; covers of the musicians' songs; bin divider - $20

Armatrading, Joan

Born: December 9, 1950

A master of blending musical sounds, from reggae to soul, and an excellent lyricist, Joan Armatrading is best known in the U.S. for songs such as "Me, Myself, I" (#28, 1980), "The Key" (#32, 1980), and "Drop the Pilot" (#78, 1983). In Britain, however, she is a major star who has placed many albums in the U.K. Top Ten.

AUTOGRAPHS

A CD, LP, magazine cover, ad, photo, or card signed by the artist: $7-$18

OFTEN OVERLOOKED MEMORABILIA

Copies of criticism over her writing and performing the theme for *The Wild Geese* (1978); a videotape from her appearance on NBC-TV's *The Tonight Show* (1992)

Arrested Development

Formed 1988

Speech (Todd Thomas), Headliner (Tim Barnwell), Rasa Don (Donald Jones), Aerle Taree, Monbtsho Eshe, Baba Oje

One of rap's most successful crossover acts, Arrested Development has managed to blend many ingredients into their sound, from hip-hop to gospel-tinged lyrics. "Tennessee" (#6, 1992), their debut single, helped drive their first album into the Top Twenty. Their politically and philosophically charged songs acknowledge the history of their culture and have provided inspiration to many of their listeners. The group placed two other singles into the Top Ten from their debut, "People Everyday" (#8,1992) and "Mr. Wendal" (#6, 1992). *Unplugged* (#38, R&B, 1993), from their MTV performance, followed, as the band took part in the third annual Lollapalooza tour. *Zingalamaduni* (1994) was the group's next album offering.

AUTOGRAPHS
A CD, LP, magazine cover, ad, photo, or card signed by the group: $10-$25

OFTEN OVERLOOKED MEMORABILIA
Copies of the *Milwaukee Community Journal;* D.L.R. (Disciples of a Lyrical Rebellion) and Secret Society artifacts; videotapes of the group appearing on MTV's *Unplugged* (12/92), *MTV Drops the Ball '93* (12/31/92), *Top Of The Pops* - BBC-TV (4/1/93) and the *Late Show With David Letterman* - CBS-TV (7/23/94); movie memorabilia from *Malcolm X* (1993); Woodstock II, Lollapalooza '93, and WOMAD memorabilia

Arrow

(Alphonsus Cassel) Born: November 16, 1954

A purveyor of a Trinidad-based blend of soul and calypso called soca, Arrow is best known in the U.S. for having penned "Hot, Hot, Hot" (1983).

AUTOGRAPHS
A CD, LP, magazine cover, ad, photo or card signed by the artist: $5-$10

Art Ensemble of Chicago

Formed 1969

Roscoe Mitchell, Lester Bowie, Malachi Favors (Magoustous), Joseph Jarman

An innovative jazz group that emerged in the '70s, Art Ensemble of Chicago has been noted for their ro-bust use of a variety of world sounds and extensive instrumentation. Their use of conceptual theater as part of their show also garnered accolades for the band. In 1969 the group moved to Paris, where they recorded numerous albums and produced three film scores. Each member has been successful as a solo artist, and brings an additive creative element to the band.

AUTOGRAPHS
A CD, LP, magazine cover, ad, photo or card signed by the group: $12-$32*
*Original members

OFTEN OVERLOOKED MEMORABILIA
The group's film scores

The Art of Noise

Formed 1983

Anne Dudley, Jonathan "J.J." Jeczalik, and Gary Langan

An eclectic spinoff from Trevor Horn's innovative production team, Art of Noise focused on creating state-of-the-art dance instrumentals. They recruited Duane Eddy to update his 1960 smash hit "Peter Gunn" (#50, 1986) before moving on to "Paranoimia" (#34, 1986), which included a guest video appearance from computer-generated television character Max Headroom. They even revived Tom Jones for the Prince remake "Kiss" (#31, 1988).

AUTOGRAPHS
A CD, LP, magazine cover, ad, photo, or card signed by the group: $6-$10

OFTEN OVERLOOKED MEMORABILIA
Associated artifacts from the group's advertising work, including Revlon, Swatch, etc.; movie memorabilia from *Dragnet* (1987)

Asher, Peter: See Peter and Gordon

Ashford and Simpson

Nickolas Ashford, Born: May 4, 1943; Valerie Simpson, Born: August 26, 1948

Ashford & Simpson emerged from the late '60s to write and produce some of Motown's greatest hits. Since the early '70s (having turned their attention to performing) they have scored with such hits as "Found a Cure," "Solid"(#12, 1985), "Outta the World" (#4, 1985), and "Count Your Blessings" (#4, 1986).

Their influence on romantic Motown duets, best exhibited by "Ain't No Mountain High Enough," "You're All I Need to Get By," and "Reach Out and Touch (Somebody's Hand)," is particularly worth noting, as is their independent writing and production work. With clients such as Whitney Houston, Diana Ross, Gladys Knight and the Pips, need we say more!

AUTOGRAPHS
A CD, LP, magazine cover, ad, photo, or card signed by the group: $15-$45

TOUR BOOKS/PROGRAMS/PASSES
Backstage Passes:
Cloth: $6-$10; Laminated: $10-$15

POSTERS/PRESS KITS
Promotional Posters: $12-$28
Press Kits: $15-$25

OFTEN OVERLOOKED MEMORABILIA
Memorabilia associated with their Motown days; movie memorabilia from *The Bodyguard* (1993); memorabilia associated with other musicians' covers of their work

Asia

Formed 1981

Carl Palmer, Born: March 20, 1947; John Wetton, Born: July 12, 1949; Steve Howe, Born: April 8, 1947; and Geoffrey Downes*

*Wetton departed in 1983 and was replaced with Greg Lake. Howe left in 1985 and was replaced with Mandy Meyer. Laje departed in 1985 and Wetton returned. Group disbanded in 1986 and re-formed in 1990. Numerous personnel changes followed.

Another "sweighties"—"second-wave eighties"—band that scored with their can't-miss debut album *Asia* (#1, 1982), which included the hits "Heat of the Moment" (#4, 1982) and "Only Time Will Tell" (#17, 1982). Follow-up album *Alpha,* with hit extract "Don't Cry" (#10, 1983), also sold well, but band members began to change—an indication of problems. Their third album, *Astra,* had fans confused as to who left and who returned, and the record failed to sell to expectations. The group disbanded in 1986, then sporadically re-formed to little notice.

AUTOGRAPHS
A CD, LP, magazine cover, ad, photo or card signed by the group: $18-$50

TOUR BOOKS/PROGRAMS/PASSES
Tour Programs:
Aqua World Tour 1992: $15
Backstage Passes:
Cloth: $10; Laminated: $10-$15

POSTERS/PRESS KITS
Promotional Posters: $15-$22
Press Kits: $15-$32

USED CLOTHING/EQUIPMENT
Guitar Picks:
John Wetton: $60   Steve Howe: $30-$55

OFTEN OVERLOOKED MEMORABILIA
Memorabilia associated with their "Asia in Asia" live TV concert from Japan (12/6/83)

Asleep at the Wheel

Formed 1970

Original lineup: Ray Benson (Seifert), Leroy Preston, Lucky Oceans (Reuben Gosfield)*

* Numerous personnel changes

For more than two decades this group has dedicated itself to resurrecting the western swing sound pioneered by Bob Willis, while picking up a few Grammy awards in categories such as Best Country Instrumental Performances and Best Country Performances by a Duo or Group with Vocal. Their continued success is not built through album or singles sales, but through the band's outstanding live performances.

AUTOGRAPHS
A CD, LP, magazine cover, ad, photo, or card signed by the group: $10-$25*
*On Grammy Award associated piece

POSTERS/PRESS KITS
Promotional Posters: $10-$15
Press Kits: $10

The Association

Formed 1965

Jules Alexander, Terry Kirkman, Brian Cole (1942-1972), Ted Bluechel Jr., Jim Yester, and Russ Giguere*

*Alexander departed in 1967 and was replaced by Larry Ramos. Alexander returned in 1969. Giguere left in 1970 and Richard Thompson joined the band.

Best remembered for their soft romantic ballads, this outstanding vocal band sold over 15 million records in the '60s alone, driven by such hits as "Cherish" (#1, 1966), "Windy" (#1, 1967), "Never My Love" (#2, 1967), and "Everything That Touches You" (#10, 1968).

AUTOGRAPHS
A CD, LP, magazine cover, ad, photo, or card signed by the group: $20-$50*
*Original lineup

OFTEN OVERLOOKED MEMORABILIA
Movie memorabilia from *Goodbye Columbus* (1969); videotapes of the group's numerous television appearances, including *The Smothers Brothers Comedy Hour* (5/28/67) and *Top of the Pops* (5/2/68)

Atkins, Chet

Born: June 20, 1924

The "Country Gentleman," Chet Atkins is nothing short of a living legend, having sold well over 35 million records with his unique finger-picking style, and being the recipient of the Grammy Lifetime Achievement Award. He has been pivotal in the development of the guitar as a musical instrument and has even designed his own signature series. At the age of 49 he became the youngest inductee into the Country Music Hall of Fame in 1973.

As a producer and record executive, he was a key player in the "Nashville Sound" of the '60s and '70s, while working with some of the best in the business, including Elvis Presley, Eddy Arnold, Perry Como, and Roy Orbison. While others balked, Atkins would bite the bullet and follow his heart, giving performers such as Charlie Pride, Waylon Jennings, and Willie Nelson opportunities to pursue their musical directions.

Incredibly insightful, gifted, and intuitive, Atkins let his actions speak for themselves. As country music has evolved, there have been many opportunities for him to say, " I told you so," but the ever-refined gentleman would never stoop to that.

Chet Atkins. Photo by Deborah Feingold. Courtesy of Columbia.

The signature of Chet Atkins

AUTOGRAPHS

A CD, LP, magazine cover, ad, photo, or card signed by the group: $10-$25

REFERENCES/BOOKS

His book *Country Gentleman* (1974)

Atlanta Rhythm Section/ARS

Formed 1971

Barry Bailey, Rodney Justo, Paul Goddard, Robert Nix, J.R. Cobb, Dean Daughtry*

*Justo departed in 1972 and was replaced by Ronnie Hammond. Numerous changes followed.

This gifted group of sessionmen, despite their lack of a distinctive frontman or identity, scored a series of hits in the late '70s with such songs as "So in to You" (#7, 1977), "Imaginary Lover" (#7, 1978), "I'm Not Gonna Let It Bother Me Tonight" (#14, 1978), "Do It or Die" (#19, 1979), and even a cover of "Spooky" (#17, 1979). "Alien" (#29, 1981) was their last chart success before the band faded away.

AUTOGRAPHS

A CD, LP, magazine cover, ad, photo, or card signed by the group: $10-$20

POSTERS/PRESS KITS

Promotional Posters: $10-$20
Press Kits: $10-$25

OFTEN OVERLOOKED MEMORABILIA

Champagne Jam mobile - $85; radio promotional pinback button - $10

Atlantic Starr

Formed 1976

Sharon Bryant, Wayne Lewis, David Lewis, Jonathan Lewis, William Sudderth, Koran Daniels, Clifford Archer, Porter Carroll, and Joseph Phillips

Led by the Lewis brothers, Atlantic Starr's deep, rich ballad duo found a home on the R&B chart during the late '70s and through the '80s. The band delivered 20 chart singles (13 in the Top Twenty) during this period. "Secret Lovers" (#3, 1985), "Always" (#1, 1987), and "Masterpiece" (#3, 1992) crossed over and were huge hits for the band.

AUTOGRAPHS

A CD, LP, magazine cover, ad, photo, or card signed by the group: $12-$30

Auger, Brian

Born: July 18, 1939

Auger was an influential British keyboardist who planted the seeds for fusion with his jazz-rock varieties in the '60s and '70s, playing with numerous bands including Steampacket and Trinity.

AUTOGRAPHS

A CD, LP, magazine cover, ad, photo, or card signed by the artist: $5-$12

OFTEN OVERLOOKED MEMORABILIA

Oblivion Express mobile: $40

Avalon, Frankie

(Francis Avallone)
Born: September 18, 1939

This teen idol struck pay dirt with such '50s classics as "Ginger Bread" (#9, 1958), "Bobby Sock to Stockings" (#8, 1959), "A Boy Without a Girl" (#10, 1959), "Just Ask Your Heart" (#7, 1959), "Venus" (#1, 1959), and "Why" (#1, 1960) before the British Invasion struck.

His second home became Dick Clark's *American Bandstand,* while he also planted his feet in the sand with Annette Funicello in "those damn beach movies." Although his acting couldn't hold a surfboard to his singing, he nevertheless appeared on assorted television shows, such as *Love, American Style.* During the '70s he was also a regular on the Western lounge lizard and resort circuit. He later appeared with Bobby Rydell and Fabian on the "Boys of the Bandstand" tour, also dubbed "Look at all the grease in this comb" tour.

AUTOGRAPHS

A CD, LP, magazine cover, ad, photo, or card signed by the group: $10-$25

OFTEN OVERLOOKED MEMORABILIA

Movie memorabilia from *Beach Blanket Bingo* (1965), *Disc Jockey Jamboree* (1957), *Guns of the Timberland* (1960), *The Carpetbaggers* (1962), and *Back to the Beach* (1987); videotapes of his numerous television appearances, including *American Bandstand, Pee Wee's Playhouse,* and *Love, American Style;* pillow - $60

Average White Band

Formed 1972

Alan Gorrie, Onnie McIntyre, Roger Ball, Malcolm "Molly" Duncan, Robbie McIntosh (1950 - 1974), and Hamish Stuart*

*McIntosh departed in 1974 and Steve Ferrone was added. Group re-formed in 1989.

AWB is best remembered as helping usher in the era of disco in the U.S. with their hit "Pick Up the Pieces" (#1, 1975), even though the band was not from this country. That hit was followed by the successful single "Cut the Cake" (#10, 1975), which was their last Top Ten entry.

AUTOGRAPHS

A CD, LP, magazine cover, ad, photo, or card signed by the group: $10-$20

Axton, Hoyt

Born: March 25, 1938

Hoyt Axton, son of songwriter/singer Mae Axton ("Heartbreak Hotel"), is himself a gifted songwriter/singer and actor. Best known for his songs "Joy to the World," "Greenback Dollar," "The Pusher," and the "No No Song" (all successful covers for other artists), Axton eventually slowed his own touring schedule to make more time for his acting, having landed roles in *The Black Stallion, E.T.,* and *Gremlins.*

AUTOGRAPHS

A CD, LP, magazine cover, ad, photo, or card signed by the artist: $5-$15

OFTEN OVERLOOKED MEMORABILIA

Movie memorabilia from *The Black Stallion, E.T., Gremlins,* and *We're No Angels;* videotapes of his numerous television appearances, including *Bonanza*

Ayers, Kevin

Born: August 16, 1945

Ayers is an eccentric musician who has been active in British progressive rock for decades, while playing in numerous sessions and bands such as Soft Machine.

AUTOGRAPHS

A CD, LP, magazine cover, ad, photo, or card signed by the artist: $5-$10

Ayers, Roy

Born: September 10, 1940

This noted vibraphonist has crossed many musical lines, playing with some of R&B's greats (including

Herbie Mann) before beginning a solo career. He has successfully placed numerous singles on the R&B chart over the years, including "Running Away" (1977) and "Hot" (1986). During the '90s he has been involved in the acid-jazz scene in Britain, while working with many artists.

AUTOGRAPHS

A CD, LP, magazine cover, ad, photo, or card signed by the group: $5-$10

****

"On The Edge"

Albert Ayler

A jazz innovator reminiscent of the freedom sought by Ornette Coleman, Ayler used melodies as creative springboards to tear open the moment with his powerful

tenor sax. Start with "Spiritual Unity" (1964, ESP)—it will take little time for the spirit to move you further.

****

Aztec Camera

Formed 1980

Roddy Frame, Born: January 29, 1964

A one-man, folky pop-style vehicle, Aztec Camera scored well in the U.K., but gained little attention here. Frame's clever assemblage of melodies with assorted word plays has always bode well with the music press.

AUTOGRAPHS

A CD, LP, magazine cover, ad, photo, or card signed by the group: $5-$10

OFTEN OVERLOOKED MEMORABILIA

Green Jacket Grey postcard, 1981, withdrawn - $20; Knife promotional micro camera with film, 1985 - $30

Babes in Toyland

Formed 1987

Michelle Leon, Katherine "Kat" Bjelland, Lori Barbero*

*Maureen Herman replaced Leon in 1992

One of the breakthrough female bands leading the grunge movement of the 1990s, Babes in Toyland is typically compared in the same breath with Hole or Bikini Kill. The band formed after Bjelland, sensing that Minneapolis would be the next indie-rock hotbed, left San Francisco in 1987 for the Midwest. She had already established herself somewhat with an act called Sugar Baby Doll, which included Hole's Courtney Love and L7's Jennifer Finch.

Bjelland's voice added a crisp edge to the group's sound and although *Spanking Machine* (Twin/Tone, 1990) and *To Mother* (Twin/Tone, 1991) helped create a cult following and credibility in Europe, it took *Fontanelle* (Reprise, 1992) to bring them into perspective in the U.S. Extensive live performances, including a tour with Sonic Youth and a spot at the Reading Festival, landed "To Mother" on top of the U.K. indie charts and was also a factor in the group's overseas success. Youth's Lee Renaldo even produced *Fontanelle*.

The group was the only female-led band on the 1993 summer Lollapalooza tour. This, along with a

video pitch by MTV's Beavis and Butt-head for "Bruised Violet" off of *Painkillers* (Reprise, 1993), helped draw much needed U.S. attention to the band. If Bjelland can succeed in creating greater interest in her stage tantrums, while developing a more intriguing persona , the Babes' media attention may improve and Toyland might be a more interesting destination.

AUTOGRAPHS

Group:
A CD, LP, magazine cover, ad, photo, or card signed by the entire band: $15-$25*

Individual:
Michelle Leon: $5-$10   Katherine "Kat" Bjelland: $10-$15
Lori Barbero: $5   Maureen Herman: $5

TOUR BOOKS/PROGRAMS/PASSES

Backstage Passes:
Cloth: $3-$5; Laminated: $6-$10

POSTERS/PRESS KITS

Promotional Posters: $5-$10
Press Kits: $10

USED CLOTHING/EQUIPMENT

Guitar Picks:
Michelle Leon: $3-$5 Kat Bjelland: $5-$10 Maureen Herman: $3-$5

REFERENCES/BOOKS

Babes in Toyland: The Making of a Rock and Roll Band, by Neal Karlen; no dedicated collector books

The Babys/John Waite/Bad English

Formed 1976

John Waite, Born: July 4, 1955; Wally Stocker; Mike Corby; Tony Brock*

*Corby left in 1977, and both Jonathan Cain and Ricky Phillips were added in 1978. Cain left in 1981.

Bad English was formed in 1988. Waite, Cain, and Phillips were joined by Neal Schon, Born: February 27, 1954; and Dean Castronovo. The latter two left in 1991.

A '70s pop-rock group geared toward FM airplay, The Babys scored hit singles with "Isn't It Time" (#13, 1977), "Back on My Feet Again" (#33,1980), and "Turn and Walk Away" (#42, 1980). Cain went on to join Journey.

When the group disbanded, Waite concentrated on his solo career. "Change" (from his solo album Ignition [1982]) nearly sold into the Top Forty. His breakthrough was his sophomore effort *No Brakes,* which sold into the Top Ten on the strength of the singles "Missing You" (#1, 1984) and "Every Step of the Way" (#25, 1985). When his fourth album stalled, he turned to a "sweighties" — "second-wave eighties" — band, Bad English. The group's impressive debut album included two hit singles, "When I See You Smile" (#1, 1989) and "Price of Love" (#5, 1989), but personnel changes led to their demise.

AUTOGRAPHS
Group:
A CD, LP, magazine cover, ad, photo, or card signed by the entire band (The Babys): $15-$25
A CD, LP, magazine cover, ad, photo, or card signed by the entire band (Bad English): $25-$45

TOUR BOOKS/PROGRAMS/PASSES
Backstage Passes:
Cloth: $5-$8; Laminated: $10-$15

POSTERS/PRESS KITS
Promotional Posters: $10-$20
Press Kits: $15-$20

Bachman-Turner Overdrive/BTO

Formed 1972

Randy Bachman, Born: September 27, 1943; Tim Bachman; Robbie Bachman; and Fred Turner*

*Blair Thornton replaced Tim Bachman in 1973. Randy Bachman left in 1977 and Jim Clench was added.

"BTO" is pure blue-collar rock 'n' roll — music you just want to build a bridge to. Extensive touring and a well-established Canadian foundation with the Guess Who enabled Randy Bachman to cross the border and pound BTO into the hearts of a newly developed legion of fans.

Randy Bachman and Chad Allan founded the Guess Who, but both departed before 1970. In a line-up that also included Robbie Bachman, the two re-united as Brave Belt for just two non-charting albums before Randy replaced Allan with Tim Bachman and Fred Turner. The result was Bachman-Turner Overdrive, a logical name with an eighteen-wheel twist (taken from a trucker magazine).

Mercury Records finally took a chance with the band and released their self-titled debut (#70, 1973). The band drove the record up the chart with extensive touring, and their first single, "Blue Collar" (#68, 1973), grabbed some attention.

Bachman-Turner Overdrive - II (#4, 1974) spun off two hits, "Let It Ride" (#23, 1974) and "Takin' Care of Business" (#12, 1974), giving the band enough horsepower to send them to their next level. On November 9, 1974, "You Ain't Seen Nothing Yet" landed on top of the singles chart, while *Not Fragile,* the band's third major effort, coasted to the top of the album chart. Interest in the band found Reprise Records digging into the archives to reissue a Brave Belt offering, making #180 in the U.S.

The band followed with *Four-Wheel Drive* (#5, 1975) and *Head On* (#23, 1976), neither of which toted a smash single. "Lookin' Out for #1" (#65,1976) was just one of the singles that critics felt turned the band back down Guess Who Boulevard. Touring (always the magic recipe) managed to turn the band around briefly, and *The Best of BTO (So Far)* (#19, 1976) peaked in the fall of 1976.

By spring 1977 Randy Bachman was ready for a change and embarked on a solo tour. Jim Clench replaced the Canadian rock legend, but couldn't drive *Freeways* (#70, 1977) as far as the band was hoping. *Street Action* (#130, 1978) generated little action, and Randy Bachman's solo effort failed to even chart.

Unsure of what to do, BTO released *Rock 'n' Roll Nights* (#165, 1979), pushing it on only one spark plug, "Heartaches" (#60, 1979). Meanwhile, Bachman pulled out of the garage with *Ironhorse* (#153, 1979). An extracted single, "Sweet Lui-Louise" (#36, 1979), pushed the album as far as it could. The memorable *Everything Is Grey* (#89, 1980) followed, but it was increasingly clear that nobody was taking the train anymore. Bachman toyed with further pet projects with little success.

The band re-formed in 1984, and continues to be a nostalgic live draw in both the U.S. and Canada. Bachman also toured with a re-formed Guess Who, laughing a little slower these days.

AUTOGRAPHS
Group:
A CD, LP, magazine cover, ad, photo, or card signed by the entire band: $40-$50*
*Original lineup
Individual:

Randy Bachman: $10-$25	Tim Bachman: $10-$12
Robbie Bachman: $10-$12	Fred Turner: $10
Blair Thornton: $5	Jim Clench: $5

TOUR BOOKS/PROGRAMS/PASSES

Backstage Passes:
Cloth: $3-$10; Laminated: $8-$25

POSTERS/PRESS KITS

Promotional Posters: $10-$90
"Four Wheel Drive" die-cut promo: $45
Press Kits: $10-$40

Bad Brains

Formed 1979

(Paul Hudson) H.R., (Gary Miller) Dr. Know, Darryl Jenifer, Earl Hudson*

*Numerous personnel changes after 1990

These pioneers of punk's hardcore (like Black Flag and Dead Kennedys) combined numerous musical elements from jazz-rock fusion to reggae, to produce classic works such as single "Pay to Cum"—a tough to find relic of the early 1980s.

Plagued by numerous personnel changes over the years, the band's releases have been erratic and fragmented. The band's early years have been undocumented both on and off record, making collecting their memorabilia a bit complex. Any items pre-1990 would be well worth grabbing, especially if one of the members manages to break out on his own.

AUTOGRAPHS

Group:
A CD, LP, magazine cover, ad, photo, or card signed by the entire band: $10-$15

Bad Company

Formed 1973

Original Lineup: Paul Rodgers, Born: December 12, 1949; Mick Ralphs, Born: March 31, 1948; Simon Kirke, Born: July 28, 1949; and Boz Burrell (Raymond Burrell), Born: 1946

Rock veterans Paul Rodgers and Simon Kirke joined forces with former Mott The Hoople guitarist Mick Ralphs and drummer Boz Burrell to form Bad Company (the name taken from a film title). The band made its live debut on March 9, 1974, at City Hall (Newcastle-upon-Tyne). The band then inked a record deal with Island Records (U.K.) and Swan Song (U.S.), and stepped into Ronnie Lane's mobile studio. Ten days later they emerged with their self-titled debut album *Bad Company* (#1, 1974). The record spun off the hit singles "Can't Get Enough" (#5, 1974) and "Movin' On" (#19, 1975). Peter Grant's (Led Zeppelin) management and Led Zeppelin's Swan Song Label certainly didn't hurt the band's chances for success; however, the group's fundamen-

tal sound and Rodger's vocals built a solid foundation on their own.

Straight Shooter (#3, 1975), led by extracted single "Feel Like Makin' Love" (#10, 1975), was the band's strong sophomore effort. *Run with the Pack* (#5, 1976), the group's third album, contained the hit Coasters' cover "Young Blood" (#20, 1976), and (not unlike its predecessors) was a no-frills approach to rock 'n' roll.

Burnin' Sky (#15, 1977), although certified gold, was a bit of a disappointment. The band's follow-up was *Desolation Angels* (#3, 1979), with extracted single "Rock 'n' Roll Fantasy" (#13, 1979), and was a step back on track despite the added synthesizers and strings. Just when the band began to re-energize itself, Bad Company disappeared from sight for three years.

In 1982 the group emerged with *Rough Diamonds* (#26, 1982)—rough indeed, but most definitely not diamonds. The failure of the album wasn't a surprise, but Paul Rodgers's departure in the fall of 1982 (Confirmed 7/83) was, despite rumors during *Desolation Angels* that the band was going to split.

Rodgers released a solo album in 1983, before forming another supergroup, the Firm. Ralphs toured with David Gilmour before releasing his solo effort *Take This*. Burrell and Kirke went on to individual efforts with far less success. In November 1986 Bad Company—minus Rodgers—re-formed and released *Fame and Fortune* (#106, 1986), followed by *Dangerous Age* (#58, 1988), *Holy Water* (#35, 1990), and *Here Comes Trouble* (#40, 1992).* The latter album contained the hit single "How About That" (#38, 1992).

By *Company of Strangers* (#159, 1995), Bad Company consisted of Kirke, Ralphs, Robert Hart, David Colwell, and Rick Wills, and even with extensive touring, they couldn't push the album into the Top One Hundred Fifty on the U.S. album charts.

*Numerous personnel changes/alterations.

AUTOGRAPHS

Group:
A CD, LP, magazine cover, ad, photo, or card signed by the entire band: $45-$70*
*Original lineup

Individual:
Paul Rodgers: $20-$30
Mick Ralphs: $15-$25
Simon Kirke: $10-$15
Boz Burrell: $10-$15
Brain Howe: $5-$10
Rick Wills: $10-$15
Dave Colwell: $5-$10

TOUR BOOKS/ PROGRAMS/PASSES

Tour Books:
USA Tour 1979: $20-$25

1979 Bad Company tour program (Swan Song)

Bad Company backstage pass from the Here Comes Trouble Tour 1992-93 (Printed by T-bird Entertainment)

Backstage Passes:
Cloth: $10-$15; Laminated: $15-$20 (1979 tour)
Cloth: $ 5-$8; Laminated: $8-$10 (post 1980)

POSTERS/PRESS KITS
Promotional Posters:
$10-$50*
*Swan Song promotional posters only!
Press Kits: $10-$40

USED CLOTHING/ EQUIPMENT
Guitar Picks:
Mick Ralphs: $10-$20
Boz Burrell: $10
Rick Wills: $5-$10
Dave Colwell: $5-$8

Guitar pick from Mick Ralphs

Paul Rodgers and Company backstage passes (Printed by OTTO)

OFTEN OVERLOOKED MEMORABILIA
Copy of 1990 Levi's television commercial featuring "Can't Get Enough"

Badfinger

Formed 1968

Peter Ham, Born: April 27, 1947, Died: April 23, 1975; Tom Evans, Born: June 5, 1947; Mike Gibbins, Born: March 12, 1949; and Ron Griffiths. Joey Molland, Born: June 21, 1947, replaced Griffiths in 1968.*

*Bob Jackson replaced Molland in 1974. Group disbanded in 1975 following Ham's death. The group re-formed in 1978.

In 1968 Paul McCartney signed a band called the Iveys to an Apple Records recording contract, after listening to a demo tape given to him by Mal Evans. The Iveys' debut effort, "Maybe Tomorrow"

(#67,1969), was released in November, but plans for an album stalled. Griffiths, who was having trouble getting along with Evans, was asked to leave and was replaced by Molland. For Badfinger collectors, as well as Apple collectors, the single (SAPCO-8) and its related memorabilia are considered the most difficult items to find.

During a recording session in September 1969, McCartney penned "Come and Get It" (#7, 1970) while producing a session for the upcoming film *The Magic Christian* (#55, 1970). The band (renamed Badfinger) cut the song, which spun off the soundtrack as a successful hit single. Following an eight-week tour of the U.S., the band's second effort *No Dice* (#28, 1970) peaked, as the single "No Matter What" (#8, 1970) dropped into the Top Ten.

In 1971 the band performed at George Harrison's benefit concert for Bangladesh (8/1), while preparing for the release of their next album, *Straight Up* (#31, 1972). In a bit of irony, the first single from the album, "Day After Day" (#4, 1972), reached the Top Five, but couldn't displace the single in front of it, "Without You" (#1, 1972) sung by Harry Nilsson, but penned by Ham and Evans. "Baby Blue" (#14, 1972), also off *Straight Up,* charted well in the U.S. while its parent album struggled for success in the U.K.

In 1973 the group recorded their final Apple product, *Ass* (#122, 1973), which was a major disappointment. The group then jumped to Warner Brothers Records for a reported $3 million advance. *Badfinger* (#161, 1974) followed in the hooves of its predecessor, while Warner Brothers withdrew copies when a substantial advance payment was discovered missing from the group's escrow account. A frustrated Pete Ham, reluctant to tour, quit for a few days and was replaced by Bob Jackson. *Wish You Were Here* (#148, 1974) was released during the tour amid significant disappointment felt by band members. Molland left following the U.K. leg of the tour.

In January 1975 the group began work on their next album, which was tentatively called *Head First.* As the band's problems persisted, Pete Ham was found hanging in his London garage on April 23, the result of a suicide. With the death of

This white-matte award, valued at $2,500, was given to Badfinger for "Day After Day" in 1972. From the Doug Leftwitch collection.

their main songwriter, the band essentially collapsed. The other members went on to separate ventures, although Evans and Molland reunited in 1978 to record *Airwaves* (#125, 1979) on Elektra Records while trying to resurrect the group. Following *Say No More* (#155, 1981), the band once again split up. Evans, continually frustrated by business problems created by the band and the industry, committed suicide in identical fashion to Ham in 1983.

Molland and Gibbons still tour as Badfinger, having now recovered some of the royalties from the group's days with Apple.

AUTOGRAPHS
Group:
A CD, LP, magazine cover, ad, photo, or card signed by the entire band: $125-$175*
*Original lineup
Individual:

Peter Ham: $25-$50	Tom Evans: $20-$30
Mike Gibbons: $10-$15	Ron Griffiths: $5-$10
Joey Molland: $10-$20	Bob Jackson: $5-$10

TOUR BOOKS/PROGRAMS/PASSES
Backstage Passes:
Cloth: $8; Laminated: $10-$12*
*Re-formed group only!

USED CLOTHING/EQUIPMENT
Guitar Picks:

Peter Ham: $30-$50	Tom Evans: $20-$35
Ron Griffiths: $8-$10	Joey Molland: $8-$10
Mike Gibbons: $10-$12	

OFTEN OVERLOOKED MEMORABILIA
Promotional balloon issued by Private Stock in conjunction with "Natural Gas"

Baez, Joan

Born: January 9, 1941

Baez attended Boston University in the mid-50s, but the purity of her voice first captured the hearts of many at the 1959 Newport Folk Festival. She signed on with Vanguard Records in 1960, where she released her album debut *Joan Baez* (#15, 1962), made up primarily of traditional folk songs and Scottish ballads.

In April 1961 she met Bob Dylan for the first time at Gerdes Folk City in Greenwich Village, New York. The two became both musically and romantically involved, while making numerous appearances together including the first Monterey Folk Festival (5/17/63). From 1963 to 1965 the pair were almost inseparable, sharing their music and fighting for the same causes. Baez later became a voice of the early '60s civil rights movement, often marching to her now associated theme song "We Shall Overcome."

By the mid-60s politics seemed to overshadow Baez's pursuit of a musical career. Instead of lining her own pockets, she began to fight for those causes that became so true to her—the Institute for the Study of Nonviolence, Humanitas International Human Rights Committee, and numerous others.

In 1968 she married activist David Harris, and upon his being jailed for draft evasion, Baez' antiwar fervor was at a peak. Both *David's Album* (#36, 1969) and *One Day at a Time* (#80, 1970) quickly became reflections of the growing dissatisfaction developing within America's youth. Her antiwar protest continued on *Where Are You Now, My Son?* (#138, 1973), which included one side dedicated to the sound of U.S. bombing in Vietnam. The period is not without commercial success, as Baez took "The Night They Drove Old Dixie Down" (#3, 1971) and "Diamonds and Rust" (#35, 1975) into the U.S. Top Forty.

Baez remains politically active and has toured on behalf of Amnesty International, war-torn Bosnia relief efforts, and AIDS research, and has appeared at Sound Action (1992) and Live Aid (1985). Where there has been a worthy cause, there has been Joan Baez. As a musician she has contributed significantly to her field, but as a humanitarian she has given to all people.

AUTOGRAPHS
A CD, LP, magazine cover, ad, photo, or card signed by the artist: $15-$25

POSTERS/PRESS KITS
Promotional Posters: $10-$50
Press Kits: $10-$50

USED CLOTHING/EQUIPMENT
Guitar Picks: $10-$20

OFTEN OVERLOOKED MEMORABILIA
Memorabilia from the many causes she has fought for, including brochures, flyers, etc.; stand-up of Joan (circa 1970s) - $80; Blowin' Away mobile - $40; various pinback buttons - $15

REFERENCES/BOOKS
Daybreak by Joan Baez, 1968: $10-$15; *And a Voice to Sing With* by Joan Baez, 1987; *Diamonds & Rust: A Bibliography and Discography* by Joan Swanekamp—a dated, but must reference for Baez collectors; other resources exist dating back to 1968

Baker, Anita

Born: December 20, 1957

In 1976 Baker replaced Carolyn Crawford in the Detroit-based group Chapter 8. The soul outfit, formed by Michael Powell in 1971, was a nice fit for Baker's ability, and she stayed there until quitting the lineup in 1980. She departed to pursue a solo ca-

reer and soon signed with indie R&B-based label Beverly Glen. Her debut release, "No More Tears" (#49, R&B, 1983), was a catchy ballad that was strong enough to land her in the Top Fifty U.S. R&B chart. "Angel," her next single, was even stronger, landing in the Top Five (R&B).

The Songstress (#139, 1983), her debut album, was well received and driven up the charts by the success of single "You're the Best Thing Yet" (#28, R&B, 1984). In 1985 Baker resolved a contract dispute with Beverly Glen, before signing with Elektra Records. There she was reunited with Michael Powell, who produced her first Elektra offering.

Rapture (#11, U.S., 1986) was released in 1986, and entered the U.K. album chart at #13, while topping the R&B chart and nearly reaching the U.S. Top Ten. Extracted single "Sweet Love" (#8, 1986) was nothing short of perfect, showcasing the artist's vocal dexterity, superb songwriting, and capable crossover ability. "Caught Up in the Rapture" (#37, 1987) landed on the singles chart next, and provided the artist enough time to concentrate on her next offering. Meanwhile *Rapture* began racking up awards, including Best R&B Vocal Performance (Female) at the 29th Annual Grammy Awards.

Giving You the Best That I Got (#3, 1988), Baker's next album, was a sensation and was driven by the title track single (#3, 1988), which brought her to the attention of a much larger fan base. *Compositions* (#5, 1990) was a departure for the artist, who chose to record much of the jazz-flavored album live without overdubs. Despite the lack of an extracted hit single, the release became Baker's third multiplatinum album.

Rhythm of Love (#3, 1994) continued the successful album sales trend, this time including a hit single, "Body and Soul" (#36, 1994). Meanwhile Baker continued to immerse herself in a number of projects, including a contribution to Frank Sinatra's *Duets* album and even gave a seminar at the 15th Annual Black Radio Exclusive Conference.

This enormously talented and extremely popular artist is a worthy collecting subject. She too collects artifacts: in 1992 she purchased Alex Hailey's manuscript of *The Autobiography of Malcolm X* for $100,000 at auction.

AUTOGRAPHS

A CD, LP, magazine cover, ad, photo, or card signed by the artist: $30-$40

TOUR BOOKS/PROGRAMS/PASSES

Tour Books:
Rhythm of Love, 1994: $10
World Tour, 1990: $15
Backstage Passes:
Cloth: $5-$8; Laminated: $8-$12

POSTERS/PRESS KITS

Promotional Posters: $10-$15
Press Kits: $10-$15

OFTEN OVERLOOKED MEMORABILIA

All Chapter 8 memorabilia (1976-1980); videotapes from her numerous television appearances

Baker, LaVern

Born: November 11, 1929

A major presence in R&B during the '50s, Baker's Atlantic years were fruitful and included songs such as "Jim Dandy," "Jim Dandy Got Married," "Tweedle Dee," and "Voodoo Voodoo." She was born in Chicago, where she began her career as a gospel singer. She then moved to Detroit and garnered fame under the name Little Miss Sharecropper. Her only pop hits were "I Cried a Tear" (#6, 1959) and "I Waited Too Long" (#33, 1959), although she did land minor hits into the '60s. She was inducted into the Rock and Roll Hall of Fame in 1990.

AUTOGRAPHS

A CD, LP, magazine cover, ad, photo, or card signed by the artist: $10-$45

TOUR BOOKS/PROGRAMS/PASSES

Tour Books: Atlantic Records 40th Anniversary (5/14/88): $10-$15

OFTEN OVERLOOKED MEMORABILIA

Memorabilia associated with her work on Broadway in *Black and Blue*

Baldry, Long John

Born: January 12, 1941

"Long John" (a nickname attributed to his lanky six-foot-seven frame) played a significant role in the blues influence of many future British superstars. He began by singing in London clubs and coffee bars. His first public appearance was at the World Turned Upside Down club in London. He then ventured into other bands before finally finding a good home with Alexis Korner's Blues Incorporated. He stayed there until 1962, when he toured Germany with a jazz band before returning home to join Cyril Davies R&B All-Stars. When Davies died of leukemia in January 1964, Baldry recruited other members to join his band the Hoochie Coochie Men, which also included Rod Stewart.

Long John's Blues, the group's debut album, was released in December 1964. The band toured extensively in support of the album, including a package tour with Chuck Berry and the Moody Blues in 1965. By fall 1965, the band split apart, with Baldry joining Rod Stewart, Brian Auger, and Julie Driscoll in Steampacket. When this band fell apart in September 1966, Baldry joined Bluesology. The band, which

included piano player Reg Dwight (Elton John), released "Cuckoo"—its sixth United Artist single—in May 1967, just prior to Baldry quitting to pursue a solo career.

Baldry signed to Pye Records and released the ballad single "Let the Heartaches Begin" (#88, 1968), which topped the U.K. charts in 1967. "Mexico" (#15, 1968), a Latin-style theme to the BBC-TV's coverage of the Mexico Olympics, soon followed and successfully climbed the charts. *It Ain't Easy* (#83, 1971), a blues and rock album approach, was produced by Rod Stewart and Elton John, and was released as Long John Baldry readied for his first U.S. tour in 1971.

Baldry's Out, his first album since spending a couple months in a mental institution in 1976, included the Righteous Brothers cover "You've Lost That Lovin' Feeling" (#89, 1979), his final chart success.

Now living in Vancouver, Baldry occasionally tours and records. He also works on television commercials and is even the voice of Captain Robotnick, enemy of cartoon hero Sonic the Hedgehog.

AUTOGRAPHS
A CD, LP, magazine cover, ad, photo, or card signed by the artist: $30-$40

TOUR BOOKS/PROGRAMS/PASSES
Backstage Passes:
Cloth: $5-$8; Laminated: $8-$15 (1980 - Present)

POSTERS/PRESS KITS
Promotional Posters: $10-$25
Press Kits: $10-$20

OFTEN OVERLOOKED MEMORABILIA
Videotapes of commercials and cartoons he has worked on

Ballard, Hank

Born: November 18, 1936

A pioneer of rock music, he is best remembered for his risqué lyrics over gospel infused rhythms. He and the Midnighters had three Top Ten R&B hits in the early '50s with their "Annie" trilogy—"Work with Me Annie," "Annie Had a Baby," and "Annie's Aunt Fanny." His next major hit was in 1958 with "Teardrops on My Letter," also noted for its Ballard-penned flip side, "The Twist." The Midnighters also scored with "Finger Poppin' Time" (#7, 1960) and "Let's Go, Let's Go, Let's Go" (#6, 1960), before Ballard went solo in 1963. He was inducted into the Rock and Roll Hall of Fame in 1990.

AUTOGRAPHS
A CD, LP, magazine cover, ad, photo, or card signed by the artist: $10-$30

OFTEN OVERLOOKED MEMORABILIA
Memorabilia associated with "The Twist"

Bambaataa, Afrika

(Kevin Donovan) Born: April 10, 1960

A pioneer in rap best known for "Planet Rock" (#48, 1982), which influenced an entire school of electro-boogie rap and dance music. "The Master of Records" was also a very successful DJ in the South Bronx rap scene and an influence to similar artists who followed.

AUTOGRAPHS
A CD, LP, magazine cover, ad, photo, or card signed by the artist: $7-$15

OFTEN OVERLOOKED MEMORABILIA
Movie memorabilia from *Beat Street* (1984)

Bananarama/Shakespear's Sister

Formed 1981

Sarah Dallin, Born: December 17, 1960; Keren Woodward, Born: April 2, 1961; and Siobhan Fahey, Born: September 10, 1960*

*Jacqui O'Sullivan replaced Fahey in 1988. Fahey and Marcella Detroit (Marcella Levy) formed Shakespear's Sister.

Bananarama is one of Britain's most successful girl groups, despite their reluctance to tour and inability to play instruments. The group scored hits with "Cruel Summer" (#9, 1984), "Venus" (#1, 1986), and "I Heard A Rumour" (#4, 1987) before being affected by personnel changes. Fahey, who cowrote "Lay Down Sally" with Eric Clapton, married Eurythmics' Dave Stewart, left the band, and started Shakespear's Sister, who later scored a hit single with "Stay" (#4, 1992).

AUTOGRAPHS
A CD, LP, magazine cover, ad, photo, or card signed by the artist: $20-$45*
*Original lineup

TOUR BOOKS/PROGRAMS/PASSES
Tour Books:
The 1989 World Tour: $10-$12
Backstage Passes:
Cloth: $5-$8; Laminated: $10

POSTERS/PRESS KITS
Promotional Posters: $10-$15
Press Kits: $15

Brockum-distributed Bananarama 1989 tour program

OFTEN OVERLOOKED MEMORABILIA
Movie memorabilia from *Disorderlies;* Cruel Summer banana-shaped pouch jacket $55

The Band

Formed 1967

James Robbie Robertson, Born: July 5, 1944; Richard Manuel, Born: April 3, 1945, Died: March 4, 1986; Garth Hudson, Born: August 2, 1943; Levon Helm, Born: May 26, 1940; Rick Danko, Born: December 9, 1943

Mark Levon Helm (the Jungle Bush Beaters) joined Ronnie Hawkins & the Hawks and settled in Toronto. Local favorite Jamie Robertson (Robbie & the Robots, Thumper & the Trombones, Little Cesar & the Consuls) soon joined the band on bass, and Rick Danko, who had opened in the past for Hawkins, was also added. Garth Hudson (Paul London & the Capers) was added just prior to Christmas 1961 (when the band was called the Levon Helm Sextet—later Levon Helm & the Hawks, followed by the Canadian Squires).

The band toured extensively through the college and bar circuit and recorded their first single, "Leave Me Alone," as the Canadian Squires on the Toronto label Ware. In March of 1965, "The Stones I Throw" (penned by Robertson) was released by the Atlantic Records subsidiary Atco. Acting on a suggestion by his secretary, Albert Grossman suggested them as a support band for Bob Dylan, who agreed after hearing them play.

On April 30, 1965, Bob Dylan's Don't Look Back Tour began in England. Following the tour (1967—after Dylan's 1966 motorcycle accident), which saw Helm quit unhappy with the nightly booing during the electric portion of the show, Dylan moved to Woodstock, New York. There he worked with band members to edit a documentary of the tour. Danko moved into a pink house nearby in West Saugerties, New York, while Helm was asked to rejoin the group, which was writing and rehearsing new material. The new material became the famed *Great White Wonder* bootleg, eventually released as *The Basement Tapes* by CBS in 1975.

Grossman helped ink a deal with the group on Capitol Records, as the Crackers. *Music From Big Pink* (#30, 1968) became the Band's debut album. Recorded in the basement studio of Danko's pink house, the music had a lasting impact on the face of rock and roll music. It included the now classic "The Weight." *The Band* (#9, 1969) followed and was the group's commercial breakthrough. The album includes "The Night They Drove Old Dixie Down"—a Joan Baez cover hit—and "Up on Cripple Creek" (#25, 1970). The group undertook their first headlining tour in support of the album.

"Rag Mama Rag" (#57, 1970) exhibited Robertson's flair for songwriting, the majority of which was handled by him for the Band. *Stage Fright* (#5, 1970) documented the perils of the road, while *Cahoots* (#21, 1971) was a reflection of values and also included a track cut in collaboration with Van Morrison. The double-live album *Rock of Ages* (#6, 1972) was followed in 1973 by *Moondog Matinee*—a tribute to radio DJ Alan Freed. Following the December 1971 concert at New York Academy of Music (Rock of Ages show), the band made no appearances until the Watkins Glen Festival on July 28, 1973.

Before The Flood (#3, 1974) was a testament to the live work with Dylan during the 1974 tour. The Band had provided all back-up work on his *Planet Waves* album and would not reappear with new material until *Northern Lights - Southern Cross* (#26, 1976). Unfortunately, the long-awaited album of new material didn't receive the expected adulation. *The Best of the Band* (#51, 1976) was released among rumors that the band was splitting up, which it eventually did, but not without stating that it intended to hold one final show, "The Last Waltz" (#16, 1978), on November 25, 1976.

"The Last Waltz," held at San Francisco's Winterland, was a triumph: star-studded and filled with priceless moments. Filmed by famed director Martin Scorsese, "The Last Waltz" became a concert celluloid classic and a fitting end to the Band.

Jericho (#166, 1993), the first new band material in 16 years, was released in the fall of 1993. The group consisted of Danko, Helm, Hudson, James Weider, Richard Bell, and Randy Ciarlante. Other miscellaneous projects followed to keep the Band in the limelight, but the group finally emerged in March 1996, promoting the new studio set *(High On The Hog)* on CBS-TV's *Late Show With David Letterman*.

AUTOGRAPHS

Group:
A CD, LP, magazine cover, ad, photo, or card signed by the entire band: $175-$225*

*Vintage memorabilia item

Individual:
James Robbie Robertson: $30-$45   Richard Manuel: $30-$50
Garth Hudson: $20-$25   Levon Helm: $30-$50
Rick Danko: $20-$25

TOUR BOOKS/PROGRAMS/PASSES

Backstage Passes:
Cloth: $25-$35; Laminated: $30-$45

POSTERS/PRESS KITS

Promotional Posters: $25-TBD*
*Many earlier Capitol posters are extremely scarce and considered auction-type items
Press Kits: $25-$75

USED CLOTHING/EQUIPMENT

Guitar Picks:
James Robbie Robertson: $30-$45
Rick Danko: $20-$25

Drum Sticks:
Levon Helm: $25-$30

OFTEN OVERLOOKED MEMORABILIA

Movie memorabilia from *The Last Waltz, Coal Miners Daughter* (Helm), *Carny* (Robertson), *The King Of Comedy, Raging Bull,* and *The Color Of Money;* television

documentary *The Native Americans* with Robertson composed soundtrack; memorabilia from Roger Waters' performance of "the Wall" (1990) - the band minus Robertson took part; *Rolling Stone*'s September issue of fall fashions (1991) - features Robertson; the famed pink house in Saugerties, NY - $150,000-$170,000

REFERENCES/BOOKS

The Wheel's On Fire by Levon Helm; no dedicated collector books

The Bangles

Formed 1981

Susanna Hoffs, Born: January 17, 1957; Debbi Peterson, Born: August 22, 1961; Vicki Peterson, Born: January 11, 1958; Annette Zilinskas, Born: November 6, 1964*

*Michael Steele, Born: June 2, 1954 replaces Zilinskas in 1984

A California all-girls group first known as the Colours, followed by the Bangs, and finally the Bangles. They were first labeled part of the "paisley underground" scene in L.A. and signed to I.R.S. before landing with Columbia. They released their debut album, *All Over the Place,* which drew attention to the band with classic cuts such as "Hero Take A Fall" and "Going Down to Liverpool." "Hero" impressed Prince enough for him to give the band his song "Manic Monday" (#2, 1986). The single preceded their next album *Different Light* (#2, 1986), which included extracts "Walk Like An Egyptian" (#1, 1986), "If She Knew What She Wants" (#29, 1986) and "Walking Down Your Street" (#11, 1987). Their next hit came off the soundtrack to *Less Than Zero*—the Paul Simon penned "Hazy Shade of Winter" (#1).

Everything (#15, 1988) would be the group's final studio album due to personality conflicts. It yielded "In Your Room" (#5, 1988) and "Eternal Flame" (#1, 1989). The focus of the band had shifted to Susanna Hoffs, who was also doing some acting at the time. The group went their separate ways in 1989.

AUTOGRAPHS

A CD, LP, magazine cover, ad, photo, or card signed by the group: $30-$70

OFTEN OVERLOOKED MEMORABILIA

Movie memorabilia from *Less Than Zero* and *The Allnighter* (1987)

The Barbarians

Formed 1965

Jerry Causi, Jeff Morris, Bruce Benson, Moulty (Victor Moulton)

A typical mid-60s protopunk assemblage that had a minor hit with "Are You a Boy or Are You a Girl?" (#55, 1965), followed by "Moulty" (#90, 1966), about the band's drummer.

AUTOGRAPHS

A CD, LP, magazine cover, ad, photo, or card signed by the artist: $7-$15

OFTEN OVERLOOKED MEMORABILIA

A copy of the documentary *The T.A.M.I. Show*

Barclay James Harvest

Formed 1967

Stewart "Woolly" Wolstenholme, Born: April 15, 1947; Melvyn Pritchard; John Lees; Les Holroyd

An English art-rock band with a considerable cult following, that never was able to achieve commercial success despite its consistency in both music and personnel. Often labeled a "poor man's Moody Blues."

AUTOGRAPHS

A CD, LP, magazine cover, ad, photo, or card signed by the artist: $15-$25

OFTEN OVERLOOKED MEMORABILIA

Movie memorabilia from *Beat Street* (1984)

The Bar-Kays

Formed Mid-1960s

Jimmy King*, Ron Caldwell*, Phalin Jones*, Carl Cunningham*, Ben Cauley, and James Alexander

*Died in a plane crash on December 10, 1967. Also killed was Otis Redding.

One of soul's premier backing bands, which survived adversity when group members were tragically killed in the same plane crash that killed Otis Redding. They first achieved success with "Soul Finger" (#17, 1967), followed by "Shake Your Rump To The Funk" (#23, 1976) and numerous R&B hits that took the group well into the '80s.

OFTEN OVERLOOKED MEMORABILIA

Movie memorabilia from *Shaft* (1971) and *Breakin'* (1984)

Basia

(Basia Trzetrzelewska) Born: September 30, 1956.

An international pop singer whose music has become a fixture on jazz stations around the world. She performed with the band Alibabki in 1975, before

heading to Chicago, then on to London to sing in the jazz-funk group Bronze.

Her solo album *Time and Tide* (#36, 1988) included two successful extracts, "Time and Tide" (#26, 1988) and "New Day For You" (#53, 1989). Her sophomore effort *London Warsaw New York* (#20, 1990) included the single "Cruising for Bruising" (#29, 1990).

AUTOGRAPHS

A CD, LP, magazine cover, ad, photo, or card signed by the artist: $5-$15

Bauhaus/Peter Murphy/ Love and Rockets

Formed 1979

Peter Murphy, Born: July 11, 1957; Daniel Ash, Born: July 31, 1957; David J. (Dave Haskins), Born: April 24, 1957 ; and Kevin Haskins

This gothic rock assemblage came to the attention of record company executives following an appearance on the BBC radio DJ John Peel's show. The band developed a quick British cult following inspired by "Kick in the Eye" (#59, 1981) and *Mask* (#30, 1981), before releasing *The Sky's Gone Out*—their American debut. The group broke up shortly after this point, with Murphy first joining Dali's Car, before going solo in 1988. His Bowie-esque vocals landed him a minor hit with "Cuts You Up" (#55, 1990) from the album *Deep* (#44, 1990).

The other members of the band reunited, after faltering solo attempts, as Love and Rockets, releasing their self-titled breakthrough album (#14, 1989), which included the Top Ten hit "So Alive" (#3, 1989).

AUTOGRAPHS

A CD, LP, magazine cover, ad, photo, or card signed by the group: $12-$20*
*Original lineup

Love and Rockets. Photo courtesy American Recordings.

REFERENCES/BOOKS
Dark Entries: Bauhaus and Beyond, by Ian Shirley; no dedicated collector books

The Bay City Rollers

Formed 1970

Alan Longmuir, Eric Faulkner, Derek Longmuir, Leslie McKeown, and Stuart "Woody" Wood*

*Ian Mitchell replaces A. Longmuir in 1976, then Pat McGlynn replaces Mitchell. McGlynn leaves in 1977. McKeown leaves in 1978, and Duncan Faure is added.

Another second coming of the Beatles that, although profitable for a period, lacked the genius and talent to sustain the long and winding road. Aggressively marketed at teenagers, the Scottish group scored their first English hit in 1971. While "Rollermania" hit the U.S. briefly in early 1976, fueled by the success of chart-topping single "Saturday Night" (#1), "the knickerclad and plaid" bunch was having difficulty coping with stardom. In the wake of personnel issues and a *Greatest Hits* (#77, 1978) package that couldn't even climb into the U.S. Top Seventy-Five albums, the Rollers opted for the comfort of smaller venues. A decade later, the band (in various forms) was riding the bar circuit.

AUTOGRAPHS

A CD, LP, magazine cover, ad, photo, or card signed by the entire band: $15-$25*
*Original members on vintage memorabilia only!

POSTERS/PRESS KITS

Promotional Posters: $10-$40
Press Kits: $10-$35

USED CLOTHING/EQUIPMENT

Guitar Picks: $10-$25

OFTEN OVERLOOKED MEMORABILIA

Videotapes of the *Shang-A-Lang* television series - ITV (4/1/75 - 8/17/77); newspaper clippings of "Rollermania" incidents; a videotape of the band's performance on Howard Cosell's *Saturday Night Variety Show* - ABC-TV (9/20/75); an empty bottle of valium; a copy of Faulkner's Skol commercial (1991); trading cards, set of 66 - $50-$70

REFERENCES/BOOKS

A few mediocre resources exist; no dedicated collector books

The Beach Boys

Brian Wilson, Born: June 20, 1942; Dennis Wilson, Born: December 4, 1944, Died: December 28, 1983; Carl Wilson, Born: December 21, 1946; Mike Love, Born: March 15, 1941; Al Jardine, Born: September 3, 1942

*Personnel also included David Marks; Bruce Johnston, Born: June 24, 1944; Blondie Chaplin; and Ricky Fataar

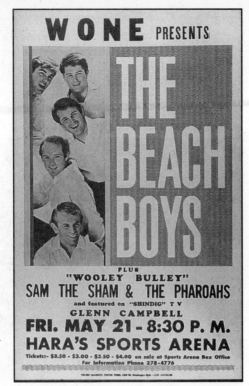

This poster printed by Majestic Poster Press, Hollywood, CA, for the Beach Boys' May 21, 1965 performance in Dayton, Ohio. From the collection of Hank Thompson.

From 1965, this Beach Boys concert poster is valued at $2,500. From the Doug Leftwitch collection.

The sun, surf, sand, and summer have all become synonymous with the Beach Boys. During the '60s they epitomized the life of most southern California teenagers, and were one of the few American bands to successfully tackle the British invasion. Their crisp vocal harmonies and clean guitar transitions accompanied their teenage topics for a recipe that would prove successful for the decades that followed.

Growing up in Hawthorne, California, was like a dream come true for the three Wilson brothers, who, combined with cousin Mike Love and friend Al Jardine, formed first the Pendletones, then Kenny and the Cadets, followed by Carl and the Passions, and finally the Beach Boys.

With a little prompting from Dennis, Brian and Mike wrote "Surfin'," which quickly became a local hit on the then Candix label by late 1961. Through the efforts of their father, Murry Wilson, the Wilsons and the band landed a record deal with Capitol. Although only Dennis surfed

This white-matte award was presented to the Beach Boys in 1964 for their LP All Summer Long. It is valued at $5,000. From the Doug Leftwitch collection.

regularly, the rest of the band had no problem riding the crest of the "surf music" they helped create with songs such as "Surfin' Safari" (#14, 1962), "Surfin' U.S.A." (#3, 1963), and "Surfer Girl" (#7, 1963).

"I Get Around" (#1, 1964), "Fun, Fun, Fun"(#5, 1964), "Help Me, Rhonda" (#1, 1965), and "California Girls" (#3, 1965) sustained their pop sound, which would occasionally be supplemented by successful ballads such as "In My Room" (#23, 1963) and "Don't Worry, Baby" (#24, 1964). By the mid-60s, however, the musical scene was putting pressure on the band to stay at the top, and Brian eventually suffered a nervous breakdown. It was during this period that one of rock music's most monumental efforts emerged—*Pet Sounds*. Although sales were far from staggering, the album was reflective of an emerging age driven by studio technology. "Wouldn't It Be Nice" and "God Only Knows" predated rival songs from The Beatles, with the Beach Boys pinnacle of creativity coming with "Good Vibrations" (#1, 1966). Brian Wilson, who no longer toured, found solace in the studio working with collaborators such as Van Dyke Parks on *Smile* in late 1966. Unfortunately, a mysterious fire claimed most of the precious *Smile* tapes, although several songs such as "Heroes and Villains" (#12, 1967) and "Surf's Up" did later emerge.

The period put an end to the momentum the Beach Boys had gathered, and an end to Brian's reign as the group's producer. Accompanied by a myriad of touring musicians including Bruce Johnston, Glen Campbell, Daryl

Valued at $5,000, this RIAA white-matte gold 45 "Good Vibrations" award was presented to the Beach Boys in 1966. From the Doug Leftwitch collection.

Valued at $6,000, these extremely rare 1966 cover "slicks" from the Beach Boys' Smile LP consist of two front covers, one back cover, and a B&W proof. From the Doug Leftwitch collection.

Dragon, Blondi Chaplin, and Ricky Fataar, the other members now shared in the responsibilities of songwriting and production. Now on custom label Brothers Records with Reprise, the group continued to release material, although their live repertoire was still packed with their vintage '60s material. "Sail On Sailor" (#79, 1973) returned them briefly to the charts, while numerous efforts to lure Brian back onto the road failed.

Finally in 1976, during a very publicized campaign, Brian emerged in support of *15 Big Ones,* with extracts "Rock and Roll Music" (#5, 1976) and "It's O.K." (#29). Personality clashes and management conflicts soon followed, nearly leading to the end of the band. "Come Go with Me" put them back in the Top Twenty in 1982. The decade would be challenging for the band and although Brian returned to the stage in 1983, his brother Dennis drowned while swimming off his boat in Marina Del Rey. Dennis had a passion for pushing life to the maximum. Often a center of controversy, he had been linked to everyone from Charles Manson (whom he only befriended briefly) and romantically to Christine McVie.

In 1988 the Beach Boys put "Kokomo," their fourth #1 hit, extracted from the soundtrack to *Cocktail,* on top of the charts. While Brian's "on again, off again" participant role in the band continued, he released a long-awaited solo album, which garnered critical acclaim, but little commercial interest. Mike Love

and Brian battled over a myriad of legal issues, but later patched things up, albeit possibly for the benefit of the media. To date, the Beach Boys endure.

The group was inducted into the Rock and Roll Hall of Fame in 1988.

Attractive signatures of all Beach Boys band members

AUTOGRAPHS

Group:

A CD, LP, magazine cover, ad, photo, or card signed by the artist: $200-$475*

*Original lineup

Individual:

Brian Wilson: $50-$125*	Dennis Wilson: $45-$150*
Carl Wilson: $20-$40	Mike Love: $20-$40
Al Jardine: $15-$25	Bruce Johnston: $8-$12
Blondie Chaplin: $5	Ricky Fataar: $5

*Price has varied significantly over the years.

The signature of Beach Boys drummer Dennis Wilson

TOUR BOOKS/PROGRAMS/PASSES

Tour Books:
1966/67 Tour: $65
1976 Tour: $15
1977 Tour: $15

Backstage Passes:
Cloth: $10; Laminated:
$10-$15 (1990 - Present)

1976 tour program-"15 Big Ones"
©American Productions

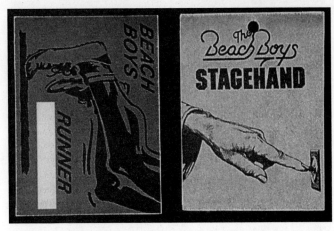

A couple examples of simple Beach Boys backstage passes

POSTERS/PRESS KITS

Promotional Posters:
1975-1980: $35-$60
1981-1990: $20-$35
1991-Present: $20-$70

USED CLOTHING/EQUIPMENT

Guitar Picks: $10-$25

Several Beach Boys' guitar picks

OFTEN OVERLOOKED MEMORABILIA

Promotional only postcard, 1972, "So Tough/Pet Sounds"; 1973 promotional booklet (12 pages) - $35; "Runaway" promotional beach ball from Sunkist (Beach Boy Logo) and a pair of boxer shorts; mail-order Coppertone suntan lotion offer, 1983 "Fourteen All-Time Greats"; *The Capitol Years*, Japanese Capitol promotion five-track sampler with fan and promotional T-shirt in resealable bag; "25th Anniversary" embroidered tour shorts - $12; "15 Big Ones" promotional frisbee - $45; "Made in USA" promotional postcard - $1;

"30th Anniversary" promotional staff satin jacket - $125; "Deuce Coupe" car model kit (sealed) - $50; L.A. postcards (set of 7) - $25

REFERENCES/BOOKS

Surf's Up! The Beach Boys on Record, 1961 - 1981 - handy for collectors! Numerous other resources. Many worldwide fan clubs exist, but start first with The Beach Boys Fan Club, P.O. Box 84282, Los Angeles, CA 90073 ($5 per year).

The Beastie Boys

Formed 1981

MCA (Adam Yauch), Born: August 5, 1965; Mike D. (Michael Diamond), Born: November 20, 1966; John Berry; Kate Schellenbach, Born: January 5, 1966*

*Berry and Schellenbach depart in 1982 and King Ad-Rock (Adam Horovitz), Born: October 31, 1967, is added

The Beastie Boys emerged from New York's hardcore punk underground scene of the early '80s to crossover into the mainstream with their "white rap" on *Licensed to Ill* (#1, 1986), featuring the hit extract "(You Gotta) Fight for Your Right (To Party)" (#7, 1986). The success of the album, Columbia's fastest-selling debut ever, led to their own headlining tour.

Plagued by legal issues, three years passed before the group's next album, *Paul's Boutique* (#14, 1989), which included the extract "Hey Ladies" (#36, 1989). The album was followed by *Check Your Head* (#10, 1992), *Some Old Bullshit* (1994), and finally *Ill Communication* (#1, 1994).

AUTOGRAPHS

A CD, LP, magazine cover, ad, photo, or card signed by the entire band: $25-$50

POSTERS/PRESS KITS

Promotional Posters: $15-$30
Press Kits: $15-$35

OFTEN OVERLOOKED MEMORABILIA

Ill Communication set of 4 window stickers - $15; Check Your Head double-sided banner - $12; Hey Girls cowbell - $50

The Beat/The Nerves

Formed 1979

Paul Collins, Steve Huff, Mike Ruiz, and Larry Whitman The Nerves formed in 1976 Collins; Peter Case, Born: April 5, 1954; and Jack Lee

Part of the early San Francisco new-wave scene, The Beat is best remembered for their penned "Hangin' on the Telephone" (covered by Blondie). The group broke up in 1978.

AUTOGRAPHS

An EP, magazine cover, ad, photo, or card signed by the entire band: $8-$15

POSTERS/PRESS KITS

Promotional Posters: $15-$30
Press Kits: $15-$35

The Beatles

Formed 1959

John Lennon, Born: October 9, 1940, Died: December 8, 1980; Paul McCartney (James Paul McCartney), Born: June 18, 1942; George Harrison, Born: February 25, 1943; Stu Sutcliffe (Stuart), Born: June 23, 1940, Died: April 10, 1962; and Pete Best, who was replaced in 1962 by Ringo Starr (Richard Starkey), Born: July 7, 1940

The Beatles were the most influential music group of their era and one of rock and roll's greatest acts. As a testament to their influence and popularity, they remain the most collected group today, decades after their existence. Beatles memorabilia has typically accounted for between 25 and 30% of all major rock 'n' roll auction lots over the past decade.

The Early Beatles 16x 20" gold LP, awarded in 1974, is valued at $5,000. From the Doug Leftwitch collection.

AUTOGRAPHS

Group:

An album page signed by the entire band: $600-$1,400*
A postcard (datable) signed by the entire band: $1,200-$1,700*
A photograph signed by the entire band: $1,400-$2,500*
A poster signed by the entire band: $1,750-$2,000*
A tour program signed by the entire band: $1,600-$3,000*
An album signed by the entire band: $1,000-$2,500*
*High end reflects vintage signed memorabilia

Individual:	Sig.	Signed Photo	Typed Letter Signed	Written Letter Signed
John Lennon	$700	$1,200	$2,500	$6,000
Paul McCartney	$250	$ 400	$1,250	$4,000
George Harrison	$200	$ 350	$1,100	$3,500
Ringo Starr	$125	$ 250	$1,000	$2,750

Notes on Beatles autographs:

How common are authentic Beatles autographs? "Not very" is the response often given by collectors of their signatures. Some collectors even claim they are the most forged of all autographs. The group's enormous popularity would attest to both the scarcity of their signatures in authentic form and the concern for forgeries.

During the band's rise to celebrity status, they were accessible to their fans (pre-1964, primarily in Europe). The group was seen for the first time on television (taped) in America on NBC-TV's *Jack Paar Show* (1/3/64) and live on CBS-TV's *The Ed Sullivan Show* (2/9/64). The Beatles' U.S. concert debut was in Washington, DC, at the Washington Coliseum on February 11, 1964.

Meet The Beatles! topped the U.S. chart (2/15) the week of their arrival in America, and security for the band was extremely tight. In hotels, the band would take over entire floors with guards covering every possible entryway. The group's road manager at the time was Neil Aspinall, and he is known to have signed literally hundreds of items on behalf of the band. In addition to Aspinall, Mal Evans ("The Fifth

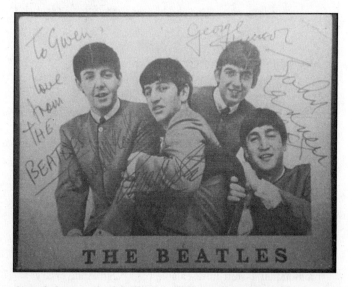

Signed photograph of the Beatles, also personalized by Paul McCartney, which was typical of examples from this era.

Beatle") and numerous fan club secretaries also "ghost-signed" for the band. Little material was actually signed following 1963, and since the band ceased live performances in 1966, they were primarily together as a group only during recording sessions (until August 1969).

In baseball, players have groupies called "Annies"; for the Beatles they were called "Apple Scruffs" (you may remember the song on Harrison's "All Things Must Pass" album). "Scruffs" could often be found lingering about outside of EMI Abbey Road Studios or Apple Headquarters, waiting for a Beatle. The hope was to eventually gather all four members' signatures on a single item such as an al-

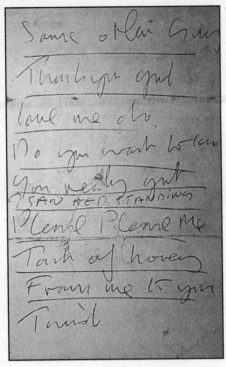

A rare song list written by John Lennon

bum. This task was seldom accomplished.

Items autographed by the entire group after 1963 are difficult to find, and following 1969, extremely scarce. Although it's possible to conceive of someone obtaining the signatures of all four during the solo years, it could be a genuinely difficult and costly task—often requiring someone with access to the musicians or unlimited resources.

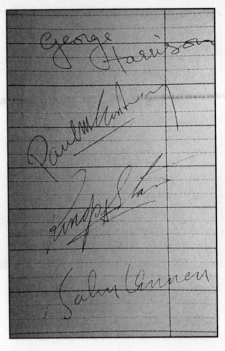

A nice example of the "Fab Four" together on one sheet

Beatles experts believe that there were only three occasions when the group actually sat down for "autograph sessions":

• October 6, 1962 (the day after "Love Me Do" was released) at Dawson's Music Shop, Widnes, Lancashire (15 miles from Liverpool) from 4:00-4:30 pm.

• January 24, 1963, at Brian Epstein's NEMS Record Store (two weeks after the release of *Please, Please Me*)

• December 14, 1963, at the site of "The Beatles London Fan Club Convention." Some 3,000 fans greeted the group, who by now had gained considerable popularity. This would have been the only session in which albums (*Please, Please Me and Meet The Beatles*) could have been signed. Word from those who attended was that most just greeted the band, shaking hands, etc., with only a few requesting autographs.

Key radio stations were issued this very rare Beatles Award, which has a current value of $3,000, from Capitol Records in 1964. From the Doug Leftwitch collection.

Paul McCartney handwritten lyrics for "Good Day Sunshine." Courtesy Butterfield & Butterfield, Auctioneers Corp., 1997.

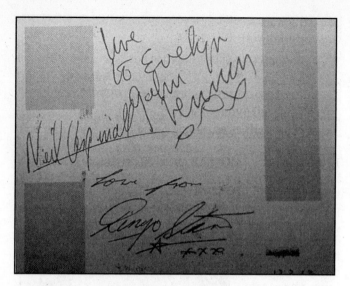

Beatles signatures including that of legendary "ghost signer" Neil Aspinall.

Some common characteristics:

• It is not unusual for Paul McCartney to add an inscription or "Beatles" or "The Beatles" with his signature. He typically found himself fulfilling a promotional role more than the others. His signature has shown less formality with age, often just "Paul-MC" with an ending stroke.

• Of the four members, John Lennon's signature will exhibit the most variation, making it extremely difficult to authenticate. His two-stroke self-portrait beneath his name is as common as his drawings with Yoko. Near the end of his life his signature often looked like a "JiLeuu" formation.

• Ringo Starr's signature has been relatively consistent over time, with a "star" added between both names. Nowadays he typically signs just "Ringo" with a "star."

Paul added the "Beatles" inscription on this example

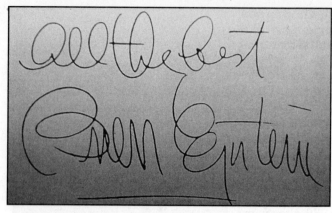

The signature of Beatles manager Brian Epstein

• George Harrison, the most reclusive of all the living members, has shown much variation in his signature over the years. He went through a period where he often added a Sanskrit symbol. Earlier signature examples are much stiffer with an extra stroke or two. Current examples are sloppier with more curvature to the strokes. They also are larger and exhibit less character definition.

If you are determined to collect Beatles autographs, additional study will be required to familiarize yourself with authentic signatures. There are experts in the market and in my opinion you should consult them whenever you intend to purchase an item signed by all four members of the band.

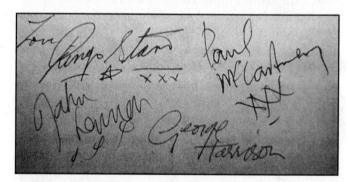

Another example of signatures of the Beatles

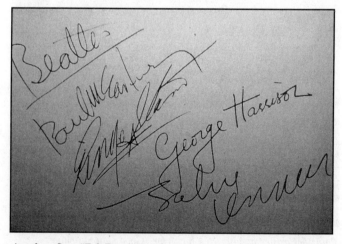

Another fine "Fab Four" sample

TOUR BOOKS/PROGRAMS/PASSES

1961: 1 Program

Albany Cinema, Liverpool - 10/25. The scarcest of all Beatles' programs. This program is seldom found in better than very good condition. Full ink bleeding on the right side of the cover typically enhances chipping along the edge of the program
Price Range: $300-$750

1962: 3 Programs

Tower Ballroom, Brighton - 10/12; Empire Theatre, Liverpool - 10/28; Embassy Cinema, Petersborough - 12/2. All three are tough to find, none are obvious to the novice as Beatles programs.
Price Range: $250-$550

1963: 23 Programs

Helen Shapiro Tour - 2/2-3/3; Royal Hall, Harrogate - 3/8*; Roe/Montez Tour - 3/9-3/31; Royal Albert Hall, London - 4/18; Empire Pool, Wembley - 4/21; Beatles/Roy Orbison Tour - 5/18-6/9**; Odeon Theatre, Romford - 6/16; ABC Cinema, Yarmouth - 6/30; Winter Gardens, Margate - 7/8-7/13; Odeon Theatre, Weston Super-Mare - 7/22-7/27; Urmston Show, Abbotsfield Park, Flixton - 8/5; Odeon Cinema, llandudno - 8/12-8/17; Princess Theatre, Torquay - 8/18; Gaumont Theatre, Bournemouth - 8/19-8/24; Odeon Theatre, Southport - 8/26-8/31; Worcester, Taunton, Luton, and Croydon - 9/4-9/7; ABC Theatre, Blackpool - 9/8; Scottish Tour - 10/5-10/7; Beatles Fall Tour - 11/1-12/13; Prince Of Wales Theatre - 11/4; Empire Theatre, Liverpool - 12/7; Wimbledon Palais, London - 12/14; Astoria Cinema, London - 12/24-1/4/63.
Price Range: $100-$375
Most Sought: 11/4 - $250-$600 ("rattle your jewelry" show)
Least Sought: 11/1-12/13 - $100-$225
*Beatles appeared on the cover of a program for the first time
**There is speculation that two versions of this program may exist, tough to find in VG or better condition. This program, autographed, seems to turn up in the market more than any other in 1963.

1964: 19 Programs

Olympia Theatre, Paris - 1/16-2/4; Carnegie Hall, New York - 2/12; Empire Pool, Wembley - 4/26; Prince of Wales Theatre, London - 5/31; Veilinghal Blokker, Holland - 6/6; Princess Theatre, Holland - 6/9; Australian Tour - 6/12-6/20; New Zealand Tour - 6/22-6/27; Hippodrome Theatre, Brighton - 7/12; Palladium Theatre, London - 7/23; Gaumont Cinema, Bournemouth - 8/2; Futurist Theatre, Scarborough - 8/9; Opera House, Blackpool - 8/16; 1964 North American Tour - 8/19-9/20; Auditorium, Milwaukee - 9/4*; International Amphitheatre, Chicago - 9/5**; Paramount Theatre, New York - 9/20, 1964 British Tour - 10/9-11/10; Odeon Theatre, Hammersmith - 12/24-1/16***. Price Range: $30-$450 Most Sought: 2/12 - $250-$525
Least Sought: 8/19-9/20 - $25-$35 (also available from fan club)
*Program has names beneath John and George switched
**Same as above; however, a corrected version also exists (add $25-$35)
***Examples other than original exist

1965: 5 Programs

Empire Pool, Wembley - 4/11; Plaza de Toros, Madrid - 7/2*; 1965 North American Tour - 8/15-8/31**; White Sox Park, Chicago - 8/20; 1965 British Tour 12/3-12/12.
Price Range: $435-$425
Most Sought: 7/2 - $175-$425
Least Sought: 8/15-8/31 - $20-$35
*Two concerts held in bullfighting stadiums
**This program was also available from fan club

1966: 5 Programs

Empire Pool, Wembley - 5/1*; Budokan Hall, Tokyo - 6/30- 7/2**; Rizal Stadium, Manila - 7/4; 1966 North American Tour - 8/12-8/29***; International Amphitheatre, Chicago - 8/12.
Most Sought: 7/4
Least Sought: 8/12-8/29
*Last British concert
**This program also available from fan club
***Examples other than original exist

In 1966, this white-matte award was presented to the Beatles for the Revolver LP. It is valued at $15,000. From the Doug Leftwitch collection.

This 1964 Record of the Year Grammy plaque was awarded to the Beatles in recognition of the I Want To Hold Your Hand nomination. It is valued at $15,000. From the Doug Leftwitch collection.

THE NATIONAL ACADEMY OF RECORDING ARTS AND SCIENCES presents this certificate to THE BEATLES in recognition of NOMINATION for the RECORD OF THE YEAR "I WANT TO HOLD YOUR HAND" for the awards period 1964

USED CLOTHING/EQUIPMENT

Used Clothing:

John Lennon:
Jackets, not stage-worn (various material and wear, worn during noteworthy appearance): $2,000-$2,500
Jackets, not stage-worn (various material, limited wear, daily wear): $1,000-$1,500
Jacket, stage-worn, velvet: $2,200-$2,600

Jacket, stage-worn, leather, early 1960s:
$45,000-$50,000
Hat, not stage-worn:
$1,500-$1,750
Boots, leather:
$4,250-$5,000
Personal Items:
John Lennon, lock of hair:
$1,000-$1,250

One of John Lennon's jackets. Courtesy Butterfield & Butterfield, Auctioneers Corp., 1997.

THE BEATLES - AN OVERVIEW OF ASSOCIATED COLLECTIBLES

* = Consult a more specific resource

Books and Periodicals:

Books, hardcover:
The Beatles Book. Ed. Edward E. Davis, Cowles Pub., 1968: $35-$75
The Beatles Illustrated Lyrics. Ed. by Alan Aldridge, Delacorte Press, 1969: $20-$30
The Beatles Illustrated Lyrics, Vol 2. Ed. by Alan Aldridge, Delacorte Press, 1971: $22-$35
The Beatles: The Authorized Biography. Hunter Davies, McGraw Hill, 1968: $20-$35
The Beatles: The Authorized Biography, (BCE). Hunter Davies, McGraw Hill, 1968: $10-$20
The Beatles: The Real Story. Julius Fast, Putnam and Sons, 1968: $20-$45
A Cellarful of Noise. Brian Epstein, Doubleday, 1964: $35-$65
Dear Beatles. Comp. by Bill Adler, Laugh, 1966: $10-$15
En Flagrant Delire (In His Own Write En Fran.). John Lennon, Simon & Schuster, 1964: $10-$15
The Girl Who Sang With The Beatles. Robert Hemenway, Alfred A. Knopf, 1970: $20-$35
Grapefruit. Yoko Ono, Simon & Schuster, 1970: $25-$50
Help! Random House, 1965: $25-$50
In His Own Write. Simon & Schuster, 1964, first edition: $50-$150
The Lennon Factor. Paul Young, Stein and Day, 1972: $20-$40
The Lennon Play: In His Own Write. Lennon, Kennedy, Spinetti, S&S, 1968: $20-$55
Lennon Remembers. Jann Wenner, Straight Arrow Books, 1971: $20-$40
The Longest Cocktail Party. Richard DiLello, Playboy Press, 1972: $20-$40
A Spaniard in the Works. John Lennon, Simon & Schuster: $30-$60

Twilight of the Gods. Wilfred Mellers, Viking Press, 1973: $20-$40
We Love You Beatles. Margaret Sutton, Doubleday & Co., 1971: $20-$50
Books, Softcover:
Various; see more specific resource. Prices vary significantly: $5-$50
Magazines:
Various; see more specific resource. Prices vary significantly: $5-$75

Buttons:

Under 2", most gumball. Various slogans and photos: $10-$25
2"-3", most flasher style. Various slogans and photos: $5-$10
3" and up, slogans. Add $10 for "Hate" buttons. Various slogans and photos: $10-$20
3" and up, slogans. Add $10 for "Hate" buttons. Various slogans and photos: $10-$20

Beatles, Wings, and solo career paraphernalia

Clothing & Accessories:

Apron, paper (white). Includes pics, names, song titles: $125-$270
Arm band, radio promotional, 1969, red felt, "Paul Lives Radio WRIT": $40-$100
Barrette Brass, inc. B&W photo (round): $50-$95
Beach hat, 9" diameter, red, white and blue, solid color brim: $50-$95
Belts, numerous styles. High-end pricing only can vary 50% (NM): $50-$160
Boots, Canadian, black leather, 7", 1" heels: $50-$100
Cap, "The Ringo Cap." Various sizes, fabrics and colors: $50-$100
Clutch purses. Various sizes, fabrics, styles and colors: $90-$175

Dresses, many originate in Holland. Various sizes, fabrics, styles and colors: $275-$650

Garter, Leonard Page & Co., Ltd. (U.K.). Various colors with picture: $100-$170

Hair bow, Mfd. by Burlington, "I Love ...." Two styles, no price variation: $150-$325

Hair clip. "Yeh, Yeh, Yeh," brass: $40-$75

Handbags, square w/built-in brass handles. Various designs, some alterations: $180-$380

Handkerchiefs, size and design variations. Add 10% for tagged Sleeted Inc.: $24-$45

Headbands, size and design variations. High end: Burlington, L&C Vincent Ind.: $25-$85, $125-$325*

Nightshirt. Cotton, ankle length: $80-$165

Nylons, type and color variations: $70-$160

Nylons box, "Carefree": $125-$230

Scarves, design variations, min. size variations. High end: Scammonden Wollen Co. Ltd.: $20-$75*, $125-$225

Scarves, design variations, min. size variations. High end: Scammonden Wollen Co. Ltd.: $20-$75*, $125-$225

Shirts: $50-$125

Shoulder bags, style, size and design variations. High end: 14", no ropes or cords: $175-$350, $275-$600

Socks, white crew: $90-$200

Suit, faces and names on jacket lining. No markings on pants: $325-$650

Sunglasses. Mfd. by Solarex, green lens: $40-$80

Sunglasses display card. Bachman Bros. "The Beatles by Solarex": $225-$400

Sweatshirts, design, color and type variations: $50-$100

T-shirt: $40-$65

Tennis shoes, mfd. by Wing Dings. Add 200% for orig. box. High end: Includes poster: $80-$225, $200-$400

Tie, lariat, mfd. by Press-Initial Corp. Add 50% for card, picture varies, 2 styles: $50-$120

Dishes and Glassware:

Ashtray, plastic, B&W photo. Square, white 3.75": $175-$325

Bamboo plate, mfd. by Bamboo Tray Spec. Diameter variances, Beatles in chairs (Hard Day's Night): $50-$75

Bread/biscuit plate, exercise caution! Mfd. by Washington Pottery, 7", U.K.: $50-$80

Bowl, exercise caution! Mfd. by Washington Pottery, 6", U.K.: $50-$75

Candy dishes, set of 4. Mfd. by Washington Pottery, 4.5", U.K.: $180-$400

Coasters, Canada. 2.5", soft drink premium, set price: $35-$70

Corks, decorative. West Germany, 4.5", wooden, set of 4: $600-$1,350

Cup, minor variations, exercise caution!. Mfd. by Washington Pottery, 4", U.K.: $50-$75

Glasses, numerous styles, variations. Minimal price variations: $50-$170

Mugs, plastic and pottery (high end). Plastic mfd. by Burrite Co., exercise caution!: $25-$50, $50-$150

Plate, Washington Pottery, U.K., 7". Exercise caution!: $50-$75

Saucer, Washington Pottery, U.K., 6". Exercise caution!: $50-$75

Trays, metal (low end), glass (high end). Exercise caution with metal trays!: $30-$50, $250-$500*

Tumblers, plastic, exercise caution on all! Burrite (low end), Goodwill Prod. (high end): $35-$65

Wall plate, decorative. Mfd. by Ross of Mayfair, U.K., 5": $100-$225

Fan Club Related Items:

U.S.:

Booklets, 1969-1971. Twenty ('69, '70) to twenty-four pp. ('71). 8.5" x 11": $10-$30

Bulletin/poster (1964-1966). Size, page, and content variations: $10-$30

Christmas records, 1964 -1969 (no 1965). If record is detached from card (-50-75%, '66 & '67): $100-$225 (1964), $35-$110 (others)

Christmas album. 1963-1969, all messages, counterfeit alert!: $50-$250*

Concert booklet, 1964-1966. Souvenir Pubs. ('64/'65), Raydell ('66, add $20): $12-$25

Cube/mailer, 1970. Mailer (5") and envelope: $12-$25

Membership cards. 1964-1971: $7-$14

Photo album, set of 4, June 1965. 8 pp., B&W photos: $10-$22

Photographs, postcards, 1964-1971. "Copyright Beatles ...," "Beatles (USA) Ltd.": $3-$6

Poster, 1971, 21" x 28" montage. By Patti Randall, The Apple Tree: $10-$25

Poster, 1971, 21" x 28" montage. By Patti Randall, The Apple Tree: $10-$25

U.K.:

Christmas records, 1963-1969. Missing sleeve deduct 50%, '67 insert add 10%: $100-$225 (1963), $50-$130 (others)

Christmas album, 1963-1969. Counterfeit alert!: $80-$325*

Membership cards. 1963-1971: $7-$14

Newsletter #2-#8. #2 inside 1963 Christmas record sleeve: $15-$40; Summer 64, 65, Summer 66: $5-$10

Jewelry:

Bracelets. Over 10, various styles & designs. Consult more detailed resource: $10-$95*

Brooches. Over 10, various styles & designs. Consult more detailed resource: $10-$125*

Brooch Display, Cards & Boxes. Consult more detailed resource: $150-$300

Charms. Consult more detailed resource: $10-$60*

Cuff Links. Mfd. by PRESS-Initial Corp., price per pair: $55-$125

Key Chains, two vintage styles. One Mfd. by Randall, unsure other: $40-$80

Lockets, numerous styles, most brass. Most 1-1.25": $25-$50 (leather), $45-$90 (brass)

Necklaces, over 15 varieties. Consult more detailed resource: $30-$100*

Pins, over 10 varieties. Consult more detailed resource: $20-$125*; $20-$60 (mean)

Pins, Display Cards. Consult more detailed source: $150-$375

Rings, various styles and designs. Consult more detailed source: $10-$50

A Yellow Submarine pin. Courtesy Amy Tincher-Durik.

Rings, Display Cards. Saymore Co., A&R.C. Ltd.: $100-$225

Tie Clips, two varieties, photo version +15%. Mfd. by PRESS-Initial Corp., brass, 1": $35-$70

Tie Tacks, three varieties. Mfd. by PRESS-Initial Corp.: $5-$20; $30-$70 (color group picture version)

Watch, + 50% in original box. Mfd. by Smiths, U.K., brooch watch: $125-$275

Movie Related:

Yellow Submarine Alarm Clock. Mfd. by Sheffield Watch, Inc. Add 100% for box: $200-$350

Yellow Submarine Bank, Set of 4. Mfd. by Pride Creations, 8", Add 50% for box: $200-$375

Yellow Submarine Bicycle Seat. Mfd. by Huffy, yellow: $200-$400

Yellow Submarine Binder. Mfd. by Vernon Royal: $125-$225

Yellow Submarine Book, hardcover. Mfd. by World Press: $30-$55

Yellow Submarine Book, softcover. Mfd. by Signet: $10-$15

Yellow Submarine Bookmarks. Mfd. by Unicorn Creations, Inc., set of six: $10-$15

Yellow Submarine Bulletin Board, 7.5" x 23", 4 varieties. Mfd. by Unicorn Creations, Inc. (-50% open): $20-$55

Yellow Submarine Bulletin Board, 24" x 24", 6 varieties. Mfd. by Unicorn Creations, Inc. (sealed): $40-$110

Yellow Submarine Buttons, 6 varieties, 1.75". Mfd. by Yellow Submarine Ent.: $8-$12

Yellow Submarine Buttons, 6 varieties, 2", slogans. Mfd. by A & M Leatherline: $8-$12

Yellow Submarine Button Box. Mfd. by A & M Leatherline: $25-$60

Yellow Submarine Buttons, set of 4. 3" pinbacks: $5-$12

Yellow Submarine Calendar, 1969 (w/envelope +25%). Mfd. by Golden Press, 12" x 12": $5-$12

Yellow Submarine Candle. Mfd. by Concept/Development: $100-$180

Yellow Submarine Coasters, package of 12. Mfd. by K. Cennar Ent. (sealed): $40-$85

Yellow Submarine Coloring Book, 2 varieties. Mfd. by Gold Key Comics: $60-$140; World Dis (add $10)

Yellow Submarine Dimensionals, wall hangings, 6 varieties. Mfd. by Craft Master Paper. Unassembled: $125-$275 (Add $25 for D-1)

Yellow Submarine Figurines, set of 4, porcelain. Mfd. by Goebel, W. Germany: $200-$650

Yellow Submarine Gift book, 60 pages. Mfd. by World Distributors, U.K.: $40-$480

Yellow Submarine Greeting Cards, vary in size and box amount. Mfd. by Sunshine Card Co., 3 varieties: $40-$90 (Add $10 for 5" x 7", box of 20)

Yellow Submarine Halloween Costume, 2 varieties. Mfd. by Collegeville Costumes: $125-$275 (Add $50 for Deluxe-style)

Yellow Submarine Hangers, set of 4 (add 25% for original packaging). Mfd. by Henderson - Haggard, Inc., 16": $45-$90

Yellow Submarine Key Chains, 11 varieties. Mfd. by Pride Creations, round and rectangular: $12-$30 (Beatles); $20-$40 (other)

Yellow Submarine Lunch Box. Mfd. by Thermos, metal, price for lunch box only!: $160-$425

Yellow Submarine Magazine, 2 varieties, 48 pp. and 60 pp. Mfd. by Pyramid Publications: $15-$27

Yellow Submarine Mobile. Mfd. by Sunshine Art Studios, unassembled: $50-$125

Yellow Submarine Model (unassembled). Mfd. by Model Products Corp.: $150-$275

A button manufactured by Yellow Submarine Ent. Courtesy Amy Tincher-Durik.

Yellow Submarine Notebook, 2 varieties. Mfd. by Vernon Royal.: $30-$70 (5" x 7.5"), $80-$165 (9" x 12")

Yellow Submarine Pen Holder, ceramic, brass holder. Mfd. by A&M Leatherline: $150-$325

Yellow Submarine Pencil Holder, cork-lined. Mfd. by A&M Leatherline: $125-$225

Yellow Submarine Pennant, 5" x 7" cloth.: $35-$75

Yellow Submarine Photo Album, 2 sizes. Mfd. by A & M Leatherline: $100-$225 (4.5" x 3.75"); $165-$325 (large)

Yellow Submarine Pop-Out Art Decorations. Mfd. by Western Pubs. Co., 9.5" x 15": $15-$30

Yellow Submarine Postcards, 2 varieties. Mfd. by Personality Posters/Unicorn Creations: $10-$15

Yellow Submarine Posters, 5 varieties. Mfd. by Poster Prints, etc.: $20-$40

Yellow Submarine Poster Put-Ons, over 60 stickers. Mfd. by Craft Master, 21" x 15": $50-$125

Yellow Submarine Press-Out Book. Mfd. by World Distributors, U.K.: $50-$125

Yellow Submarine Puzzles, over 20 varieties, 3 sizes. Mfd. by Jaymar Specialty Co. (650 pcs. lg.): $40-$100 (lg.), $30-$75 (md.), $30-$55 (sm.)

Yellow Submarine Rub-Ons. Cereal premium (sealed): $20-$45

Yellow Submarine Rub-Ons Offer on Cereal Box. Cereal premium (sealed): $175-$375

Yellow Submarine Scrapbook. Mfd. by A & M Leatherline: $175-$350

Yellow Submarine Snow Dome, Hong Kong. Plastic: $165-$325

Yellow Submarine Stationery, 18 different designs. Mfd. by Unicorn Creations, 20 sheets & envelopes: $25-$50

Yellow Submarine Stick-Ons, The Beatles. Mfd. by DAL Man. Corp. "Pop-Stickles": $20-$40

Yellow Submarine Stick-Ons, 3 varieties. Mfd. by DAL Man. Corp. "Pop-Stickles": $20-$40 (The Beatles); $10-$25 (others)

Yellow Submarine Stick-Ons, Store Display. Mfd. by Beemans, 19" x 20": $150-$375

Yellow Submarine Stickers, premiums, 2 sizes. Varied characters: $10-$25

Yellow Submarine Stickers, Display. Mfd. by Laura Scudder's potato chips: $175-$325

Yellow Submarine Stickers, Fun Book. 12 pp. (4 pp. stickers): $65-$165

Yellow Submarine Submarine, add 100% w/packaging. Mfd. by Corgi. Die-cast, 5.25" : $125-$250

Yellow Submarine Switchplate Covers, 5 varieties. Mfd. by DAL Manufacturing Corp.: $15-$30

Yellow Submarine Thermos, pink. Mfd. by Thermos, 6.5": $100-$150

Yellow Submarine Wall Plaque, 6 varieties (Glove - $10). cardboard wall hanging 9" x 21": $20-$45 (Beatles)$40-$80 (Yellow Sub.)

Yellow Submarine Water Color Set, 2 varieties (6" x 8"), (8" x 10"). Mfd. by Craft Master: $45-$90 (sm.), $80-$165 (lg.)

Yellow Submarine Wristwatch, possible reproductions! Mfd. by Sheffield, brass watch, 8" band: $500-$1,000

Musical Instruments:

Banjo, original packaging add 50%. Mfd. by Mastro, 22", 4 strings: $450-$1,100

Bongos, original packaging add 50%. Mfd. by Mastro, two sizes - 5.25" and 6.25": $300-$625

Bongos, original packaging add 50%. Mfd. by Mastro, two sizes - 5.25" and 6.25": $300-$625

Combination Set, New Beat Guitar and Drum. Mfd. by Selcol, U.K., box and both instruments: $650-$1,350

Drums, three styles, original packaging + 60%. Mfd. by Selcol, Mastro: $350-$1,000*

Drum sticks, original packaging +100%. Mfd. by Ludwig, Dallas Arbiter: $80-$160

Guitars, minimum ten varieties. Consult more detailed source: $175-$375, $400-$950*

Guitar String, six dif. strings. Mfd. by Hofner, Selmar, U.K.: $40-$80

Harmonica Box, no markings on instrument. Mfd. by Hohner, Selmar, U.K.: $40-$80

Harmonica Box Display Card, 7" x 11". Mfd. by Hohner, Selmar, U.K., sealed + 300%: $45-$125*

Hummer, 11" tube, cardboard/plastic ends. Mfd. by Louis F. Dow Co.: $50-$80

Hummer Box, die-cut. Mfd. by Louis F. Dow Co.: $100-$200*

Hummer Poster, 20" x 11.25". Mfd. by Louis F. Dow Co. (1 poster per box): $60-$125

Pennants, over 25 varieties. Numerous sizes, shapes and colors (consult more detailed resource): $20-$75; $20-$55 (mean)

Posters, some may have been reproduced. Numerous sizes, shapes and designs (consult more detailed resource): $20-$45 (each)

Poster Coupon. Used for Heinz poster offering: $10-$15

Poster Displays, two styles. Avedon (add $50) and Heinz card display: $150-$350

School Supplies:

Assignment Book, vinyl. Mfd. by Select-O-Pack: $125-$250

Autograph Book, vinyl. Mfd. by Seagull Ent., U.K.: $125-$250

Binder, white cover. Mfd. by N.Y. Looseleaf Corp.: $50-$80

Binders, six color varieties. Mfd. by Standard Plastic Products: $40-$85 (off-white), $60-$140 (others)

Binder Promo Box, holds gum and Standard Plastic Products binder. Mfd. by Fleer Corp. for promo, box only: $100-$225

Book Cover, promo Capitol Records. "Back to Cool!" 8/67: $15-$30

Book Covers, possibly reproduced. Mfd. by Book Covers Inc., set of 7: $25-$50

Brief/Pocket Cover. Mfd. by Select-O-Pak, inc. ID and photo card: $110-$250

Brunch Bag. Mfd. by Aladdin, 8", includes thermos: $200-$500

Cellophane Tape. Mfd. by Starlight, 1/2" tape, 3 yards: $45-$100

Cellophane Tape Display Card. Mfd. by Starlight, holds 12 rolls: $150-$275*

Lunch box, price for lunch box only! Mfd. by Aladdin, embossed, sold w/thermos: $150-$425

Notebook, 3 binding versions. Mfd. by Westab, 8.5" x 11": $20-$40

Notebook, set of 4, each Beatle. Mfd. by Westab, 8.5" x 11": $40-$80

Pen, two manufacturers. Mfd. by PRESS-Initial Corp. (- 25%): $40-$100

Pencil, U.K., 7". No eraser, may have been reproduced: $30-$65

Pencil Cases, at least 4 varieties. Add 40% for German case, 10" x 3.5", vinyl: $50-$100; Standard Plastic Products: $120-$225

Pouch, flat, side zipper. Mfd. by Select-O-Pak: $75-$150

School Bag, outstanding piece! Canada, "THE BEATLES" (on flap): $300-$600*

School Report Cover, 5 hole. Mfd. by Select-O-Pak, "Beatles Approved": $50-$95

Thermos. Mfd. by Aladdin, 7", sold w/lunch & brunch box: $80-$170*

Toys, Costumes, Games, etc.:

Airbed. Mfd. by Li-LO, U.K., 6' x 3': $325-$750

Balls, inflatable, 8", 9", 14" diameter. Add upwards of 50% for packaging: $250-$500

Balloon, "Blow up!...a FAB." Mfd. by United industries, price for unopened: $40-$80

Bank, U.K., 10", "The Beatles Bank." White plastic: $250-$500

Bingo Game. Mfd. by Toy Works, U.K.: $40-$80

Colorforms. Mfd. by Colorforms, 1966, two trays: $300-$550*

Coloring Book. Mfd. by Saalfield, 8.5" x 11": $30-$65

Coloring Book Display, scarce. Mfd. by Saalfield: $25-$500

Dolls, set of 4 (-50% without instruments). Mfd. by Remco, 5", hard and soft bodies: $40-$80 (Add 25% for John)

Doll Box, set of 4, single box. Mfd. by Remco, holds 5", hard and soft bodies: $50-$100

Doll Box, set of 4 box. Mfd. by Remco, holds 5", hard and soft bodies: $100-$225

Doll Poster, 18" x 17". Mfd. by Remco., poster instruments incorrect color: $200-$400

Doll, Bendy, 10", U.K. Mfd. by Newfeld, Ltd., add 75% for packaging: $80-$175

Doll, Mascot, 29". Mfd. by Remco Ind., price w/guitar & tag: $300-$650

Dolls, Bobb'n Head Dolls. Mfd. by Carmascot, 8" set of 4: $350-$700; individual: $50-$100

Dolls, Display, 14", scarce. Mfd. by Carmascot, set of 4: $2,750-$5,500

Dolls, Inflatable, 1966, 13", purple. Set of 4: $50-$120

Dolls, Offer for Inflatable dolls, 1966. Lux Soap Box, 4 different color soaps: $135-$250

Dolls, Offer Motion Display, scarce. Lux Soap Box Display, "Beatle Bargains": $2,000-$3,500

The complete set of the Beatles Bobb'n Head Dolls. Courtesy Phillips Son & Neale.

Dolls, Offer Nestle's "Quik" can. Mfd. by Nestle's, 8": $200-$375

Figurines. Mfd. by Subuteo Ltd. Add 200 % for box: $45-$125

Board Game, "Flip Your Wig." Mfd. by Milton Bradley, complete game: $75-$175

"Watch The Beatles Grow Green Hair." Mfd. by A&B Industries: $150-$275

Halloween Costumes, set of 4. Mfd. by Ben Cooper. Add 100% for original box: $450-$1,000

Hand Puppet, Ringo. Mfd. by World Candies: $150-$325

Magic Slate Game. Mfd. by Merit: $250-$575

Magic Trick. Mfd. by The Supreme Magic Co.: $150-$275

Goodie Bag, "P.S. I Love You." Mfd. by AER Rekab Productions: $100-$300

Magnetic Hairstyle Game. Mfd. by Merit, U.K.: $200-$400

Megaphone, "Beatle Bugle." Mfd. by Yell-a-Phone, 7.25": $200-$400

Models, plastic, unassembled. Mfd. by Revell, John/George. High-end: $120-$225 (PM/RS), $160-$350 (JL/GH)

Model Kit Promotional Poster. Mfd. by Revell, "Build The Beatles": $175-$400*

Paint By Number. Set of 4. Mfd. by Artistic Creations. Priced individually: $200-$500

Pencil by Number. Mfd. by Kitfix, U.K.: $300-$550

Playing Cards, two decks. "Doorway" shot, "Studio" shot in suits: $100-$250

Playing Cards, two decks in same box. Two decks in deluxe box: $200-$400

Puzzle, U.K., four versions, group illustrations. Beatles Jigsaw, 340 pieces: $125-$250

Puzzle, U.K., 1970. "The Beatles Illustrated ... Puzzle, 880 pieces: $100-$225

Skateboard, wooden w/metal wheels. Mfd. by Surf Skater Co.: $275-$625

Spatter Toy. Mfd. by Spatter Toy Co., Twirl with the Beatles: $50-$75

Twig, unique toy: $150-$300 *

Wig, two varieties. Mfd. by Bell Toy Co & Lowell Toy Co.: $175-$400 (Bell), $30-$70 (Lowell)

Trading Cards:

First Series, #1-#60 (B&W). Mfd. by Topps (T.C.G.): $30-$100

Second Series, #61-#115 (B&W). Mfd. by Topps (T.C.G.): $25-$85

Third Series, #116-#165 (B&W). Mfd. by Topps (T.C.G.): $25-$50

Wrapper, First three series, 2 variations. Mfd. by Topps (T.C.G.): $10-$20

First Series Box. Mfd. by Topps (T.C.G.): $100-$175*

New Series Box. Mfd. by Topps (T.C.G.): $100-$150*

Shipping Carton. Mfd. by Topps (T.C.G.): $200-$375*

Color Series, #1-#64. Mfd. by Topps (T.C.G.): $35-$100

Diary Series, #1A-#60A, card #21A variation. Mfd. by Topps (T.C.G.): $30-$100

Color Photos Wrapper. Mfd. by Topps (T.C.G.): $10-$25

Color Photos Box. Mfd. by Topps (T.C.G.): $70-$160

Color Photos Shipping Carton. Mfd. by Topps (T.C.G.): $200-$375*

"A Hard Day's Night" Series, #1-#55. Mfd. by Topps (T.C.G.): $30-$100

"A Hard Day's Night" Wrapper, 2 variations. Mfd. by Topps (T.C.G.): $15-$25

"A Hard Day's Night" Rac Pack. Mfd. by Topps (T.C.G.), sealed: $75-$175*

"A Hard Day's Night" Box. Mfd. by Topps (T.C.G.): $100-$200*

"A Hard Day's Night" Shipping carton. Mfd. by Topps (T.C.G.): $175-$375*

Beatles Plaks Series (Test Market Issue) : $175-$550*

Beatles Plaks Series (Test Market Issue) Wrapper: $75-$175

Beatles Plaks Box: $325-$750*

Series #1-#60. Mfd. by A. & B.C. Chewing Gum Ltd., U.K.: $50-$100

Series #1-#60, Wrapper. Mfd. by A. & B.C. Chewing Gum Ltd., U.K.: $10-$40

Series #1-#60, Box. Mfd. by A. & B.C. Chewing Gum Ltd., U.K.: $150-$275

Series #61-#105. Mfd. by A. & B.C. Chewing Gum Ltd., U.K.: $100-$200

Series #61-#105, Wrapper. Mfd. by A. & B.C. Chewing Gum Ltd., U.K.: $20-$45

Color Series #1-#40. Mfd. by A. & B.C. Chewing Gum Ltd., U.K.: $40-$100

Color Series #1-#40, Wrapper. Mfd. by A. & B.C. Chewing Gum Ltd., U.K.: $20-$40

Yellow Submarine Series, #1-#50. Mfd. by Promrose Confectionary: $75-$145

Yellow Submarine Box. Mfd. by Promrose Confectionary: $50-$125

Yellow Submarine Series, #1-#66. Mfd. by Anglo Confectionary: $225-$675

Yellow Submarine Series, Wrapper. Mfd. by Anglo Confectionary, 4 variations: $65-$150 (each wrapper)

Yellow Submarine Series, Box. Mfd. by Anglo Confectionary, 4 variations: $180-$400*

Yellow Submarine Complete Giant Picture. Mfd. by Anglo Confectionary, premium: $200-$350

Miscellaneous Items:

Arcade/Exhibit Cards. B&W cards, often mass produced in this format: $2-$6

Beach Towel, 35" x 65". Mfd. by Towel Decorators for Cannon: $125-$225

Beat Seat. Mfd. by Unitrend, Ltd., U.K.: $200-$425

Bedsheet Swatches, all 1964. Hotels: Madison (M), Whittier (W), Riviera (R): $20-$40 (M), $25-$70 (W), 450-$100 (R)

Binder. Mfd. by Beat Publications: $100-$150

Birth Certificates, set of 4. Mfd. by Davidson's Authentic Documents: $35-$75

Birthday Cards, 6 different. Mfd. by American Greetings (Hi Brows): $20-$45

Blanket, 62" x 80". Mfd. by Witney, U.K.: $125-$275

Booty Bag, 10" x 15". With paper insert add $20: $25-$50

Bubble Bath, "Personality Bath." Mfd. by Colgate, 1965, Paul & Ringo each: $50-$175

Bubble Bath Display Board, scarce. Mfd. by Colgate, 1965: $100-$350*

Bust, Ringo. Mfd. by Starfans, 6.25": $150-$250

Cake Decorations, numerous styles. Various sizes, designs and variations: $10-$45*

Calendars, numerous styles. Various sizes, designs and variations: $35-$300 (Possible repros & counterfeits!)

Calendar Cards. Mfd. by Louis F. Dow Co. (9/64-6/65): $10-$15

Candy Sticks. Mfd. by World Candies, 6 variations: $50-$100

Candy Sticks Display Box. Mfd. by World Candies, scarce, cello wrapped: $300-$550

Carrying/Storage Case. Mfd. by Air Flite, vinyl: $350-$750

Chocolate Wrapper. Mfd. by Mac Robertson, Australia: $30-$75

Christmas Cards, various styles. Various sizes, designs and manufacturers: $10-$50*

Christmas Seals. Mfd. by Hallmark Merch., 100 color stamps: $20-$40

Cigar Bands. Paper labels, Holland, set of 4: $15-$25

Coin Holder. 2" x 3", watch for repros & counterfeits!: $10-$30

Coin Holder Display, nice, holds 12 items. Displays are generally very scarce: $60-$150

Coin Purses, numerous varieties. Various sizes and outer designs: $40-$125*

Comb, plastic. Mfd. by Lido Toys, various colors: $50-$200*

Compact, U.K.. 3", brass, makeup w/B&W picture: $150-$275

Curtains, Holland. Various colors, watch for swatches cut up!: $275-$750*

Diary, vinyl, 1965. Mfd. by H.B. Langamn Co., Scotland: $20-$30

Diary, Display. Mfd. by H.B. Langamn Co., Scotland: $45-$100*

Gumball Charms. Beatles photo/Capitol logo: $6-$12

Gumball Figures, w/card. 3" rubber figures, gumball issued, set of 4: $40-$80

Gumball stickers. Have seen numerous variations: $2-$15

Hair Brush. Mfd. by Belliston Prod., various colors: $10-$35

Hair Brush Promotional Flyer. Use caution with paper-based items!

Hair Pomade. Mfd. by H.H. Cosmetic Lab, Philippines: $30-$60

Hair Pomade Box, contains 50. Mfd. by H.H. Cosmetic Lab, Philippines: $200-$400

Hair Spray, w/white plastic cap. Mfd. by Bronson Products, 8" can: $400-$700

Hangers, set of 4. Mfd. by Saunders Ent., U.K., 16": $200-$400

Headphones, scarce, w/box. Mfd. by Koss Electronics, earphone stickers: $1,200-$2,100

Ice Cream Wrapper, Foil. Various styles, sizes, etc.: $30-$75

Ice Cream Wrapper, Paper. Mfd. by Hood Ice Cream Co.: $3-$7

Ice Cream Wrapper, Paper, various. Other manufacturers other than Hood: $30-$75

Ice Cream Box. Mfd. by Hood Ice Cream Co.: $225-$450

Kaboodle Kit, various colors. Mfd. by Standard Plastic Prod.: $350-$800*

Lamp, Table & Wall. Various types and varieties: $225-$450

Licorice Record Candy, set of 4. Mfd. by Clevedon Confectionery, U.K.: $200-$400

Licorice Record Candy Box. Mfd. by Clevedon Confectionery, U.K.: $200-$400

Linen. Mfd. by Ulster, 21" x 31": $100-$150

Lollipop Wrappers, waxed paper. One Beatle per wrapper: $15-$40

Napkin. Mfd. by Rolex Paper Co.: $15-$25

Oil Paintings, set of 4, group shots. Mfd. for Beatles Buddies Fan Club: $15-$45*

Overnight Case. Mfd. by Air Flite, 13", red or black vinyl: $300-$600

Patches, various. Numerous manufacturers, styles, etc.: $300-$600

Perfume. Mfd. by Olive Adair, Ltd. "With the Beatles...": $250-$450

Pictures, set of 6, 8" x 10". Mfd. by J.M. Dist.: $30-$65

Pillows, 3 varieties. Mfd. by Nordic House, 12" x 12": $50-$250*

Pin-Up Screamers. Mfd. by Matthews Rotary Press, 9" x 12": $15-$30

Pom-Pom. 3", black with eyes, tough to authenticate: $25-$50

Pom-Pom Display. Cardboard, 28" x 16": $200-$450

Pom-Pom Poster. "We Have Official Beatle Pom-Poms," only 98¢: $250-$450*

Record Boxes, hard to find in good condition. Mfd. by Air Flite, 2 sizes: $150-$375 (sm.), $275-$650 (lg.)

Record Cabinet, U.K. Wood Cabinet, Beatles paper on doors: $650-$1,500*

Record Carriers. Different manufacturers & styles: $100-$300*

Record Case, round, plastic. Mfd. by Charter Indus., 1966: $50-$150, add $50 for tag or banner

Record Case Poster, "Disk-Go-Case." Mfd. by Charter Indus., 1966: $200-$400*

Record Player. Four speed, with serial number in lid: $1,100-$2,200*

Record Rack. Mfd. by Selcol, U.K., holds 40 singles: $175-$325

Ringo Roll. Mfd. by Scotts Bakery, Liverpool, U.K.: $125-$300

Rug. Made in Belgium, 21.5" x 33.5": $150-$325

Rug Sample, Sheraton Hotel in Cleveland. 1" square piece of rug, 1964: $25-$50

Scrapbooks. Mfd. by Whitman, two sizes: $20-$60

Shampoo Box. Mfd. by Bronson Products Co., holds 12: $150-$350*

Stamps, Stamp Displays and Related. Various manufacturers including Hallmark: $10-$50*

Surveys, radio. Various stations, may be easily copied!: $1-$10*

Talcum Powder. Mfd. by Margo of Mayfair, U.K., 7": $250-$500*

Tiles, 2 manufacturers, various designs. Mfd. by Holman and Carter, U.K.: $10-$25 (Holman); $100-$200 (Carter Tiles)

Towel. Made in Holland, 20" x 40": $100-$225

Towel Swatch, Riviera Hotel. Mfd. by Delsner. 2": $20-$65

Transfer. Iron-on: $20-$35

Vinyl Fabric. Used for multiple applications.: $55-$125 (yard)

Wall Hanging. Made in Germany, linen: $150-$325

Wall Plaque, set of 4. Mfd. by Kelsboro Ware, U.K., 5": $400-$1,400 *

Wallets, Various styles, designs, manufacturers. Most are vinyl: $60-$125 (May vary 10-20%)

Wallet Display, scarce. Mfd. by Standard Plastic Products, holds 12: $125-$300*

Wallet Photo Booklet. Mfd. by Dell, 20 B&W fold-out photos: $10-$25

Wallet Photo Booklet Display Box. Mfd. by Dell, 20 B&W fold-out photos: $35-$80

Wallpaper, various styles. Rolls or sheets: $15-$35

THE BEATLES - Selected Ticket Overview with Values

The Beatles performed in the United States on their yearly tour in 1964, 1965, and 1966. Ticket value is for full or unused ticket.

Ticket	Description/Comments	Value*
8/30/64	Atlantic City Convention Hall, nonillustrated, single stub, printed by The National Printing Co., single color, simple design	$150
9/3/64	Indiana State Fair, illustrated (single head shots), single stub, printed by The Arcus Ticket Co. of Chicago, single color	$215
9/5/64	International Amphitheater, nonillustrated, single stub, Printed by The Arcus Ticket Co. of Chicago, single color	$160
9/17/64	Municipal Stadium, nonillustrated, single stub, simple design, "CHARLES O. FINLEY IS PLEASED TO PRESENT..."	$180
8/18/65	Atlanta Stadium, illustrated, single stub, nice design, printed by the Globe Ticket Co., a popular ticket!	$225
8/20/65	White Sox Park, nonillustrated, single stub, simple design, printed by The Arcus Ticket Co. of Chicago, single color	$165
8/30/65	Hollywood Bowl, nonillustrated, single stub, printed by Globe Ticket Co., single color, simple design	$170
8/16/66	John F. Kennedy Stadium, illustrated, single stub, printed by Globe Ticket Co., two color, vertical format, a popular ticket with collectors, great photo!	$235
8/21/66	Busch Memorial Stadium, illustrated, single stub, printed by Globe Ticket Co., two color	$225

The Beatles Anthology NonRecorded Memorabilia

A = Anthology (complete)
A1 = Anthology One
A2 = Anthology Two

A2	Mexico	Promo coffee mug w/Sgt. Pepper log	40.00
A	Mexico	Press Kit	55.00
A	U.S.	Press Kit, laminated folder, 28 pp., bios	80.00
A	U.K.	Screening copy, 3 tapes	400.00
A	U.K.	Electronic Press Kit, Press preview	50.00
A	U.S.	CD-ROM Press Kit, exp. 12/31/95	350.00
A	U.S.	Electronic Press Kit, Press trailer	40.00
A	U.S., U.K.	Promotional Posters	20.00
A	U.S., U.K.	Promotional Postcards, two styles	10.00
A	U.S., U.K.	Promotional, 7.5" bus model	N/A
A	U.K.	Press Kit, embossed white from Nov. L.A. party	50.00
A1	Japan	88-page booklet from A1 album	15.00
A1	U.K.	U.F.O. - photo book, program replica, b.card	40.00
A1	U.K.	Mad Hatter paperweight, 4 prints, T-shirt	55.00
A1	U.S.	Capitol Electronic Press Kit, 18 minutes	30.00
A1	U.S.	Capitol Electronic Press Kit, 28 minutes	40.00
A1	U.K.	Apple Electronic Press Kit	40.00
A1	U.S.	Press Kit - white folder, 2 photos, info	25.00
A1	U.K.	Press Kit - black folder, 1" button "Ask Me About"	40.00
A1	U.K.	Button - 3" "Ask Me About The Beatles" w/b	25.00
A1	U.K.	Press Kit - EMI, w/enamel pin, passes	25.00
A1	U.S.	Posters, flats, window stickers	25.00
A1	U.S.	Stand-ups, counter displays, etc.	40.00
A2	Japanese	Booklet, 76 pp.	15.00
A2	U.S.	CD booklets/J-cards org. song order	75.00
A2	U.S.	Capitol Electronic Press Kit, 9 minutes	40.00
A2	U.S., U.K.	CD-ROM album Press Kit, "Multimedia"	125.00
A2	U.S.	Press Kit, yellow folder, photos, track listing	50.00
A2	U.K.	Press Kit, photos, track listing	35.00
A2	U.S.	Posters, flats	15.00
A2	U.S.	Stand-up, display	35.00
A2	U.S.	Bus model	N/A
AHV	U.S.	Press Kit, gray folder	30.00
A1	U.S.	Set of 14 promotional buttons	35.00
A1	U.S.	Catalog flyer	8.00
A1	U.S.	Catalog flyer	8.00
A1	U.K.	London Weekend television comic book	20.00

The Beau Brummels

Formed 1964

Sal Valentino (Spampinato), Ron Elliott, Declan Mulligan, John Petersen, Ron Meagher*

*Elliott, followed by Petersen departed in 1965. Group disbands in 1968, but reforms in 1975.

One of the first bands to break nationally from the Bay Area, The Beau Brummels scored hits with "Laugh, Laugh" (#15, 1965), followed by "Just A Little" (#8), then a series of minor offerings including, "You Tell Me Why," "Don't Talk To Strangers," "Good Time Music" (1966), and "One Too Many Mornings" (1966). Although the band never regained its commercial sales during their stint with Warner Brothers, *Triangle* (1967), their second offering on the label, met with accolades for its country rock flavor.

AUTOGRAPHS

A CD, LP, magazine cover, ad, photo, or card signed by the entire band: $15-$20

OFTEN OVERLOOKED MEMORABILIA

All Autumn records memorabilia

Beausoleil

Formed 1976

Tommy Alesi, Jimmy Breaux, David Doucet, Michael Doucet, Al Tharp, and Billy (John) Ware

Migrating successfully from their Cajun music roots into rock, jazz and folk, Beausoleil is best known for their soundtrack work and their appearances on the folk festival circuit. They have had a consistent following, while remaining strong enough to open for acts such as the Grateful Dead and Mary Chapin Carpenter during the '90s.

AUTOGRAPHS

A CD, LP, magazine cover, ad, photo, or card signed by the entire band: $15-$20

OFTEN OVERLOOKED MEMORABILIA

Memorabilia from the folk festival circuit makes an interesting collection on the band

Be-Bop Deluxe

Formed 1972

Bill Nelson, Robert Bryan, Nicholas Chatterton-Dew, Ian Parking, and Richard Brown*

*In 1974 the group disbanded, then re-formed: Nelson, Milton Reame-James, Simon Fox, and Paul Jeffreys. Charles Tumahai was added when Reame-James and Jeffreys departed later in the year. Andrew Clark was added on keyboards in 1975.

Led by the talented guitarist Bill Nelson, the group drew its inspiration from David Bowie's Ziggy Stardust phase and, although attaining modest success in Britain, failed to ignite in the U.S.

AUTOGRAPHS

A CD, LP, magazine cover, ad, photo, or card signed by the entire band: $8-$12

OFTEN OVERLOOKED MEMORABILIA

"Modern Music" Harvest promotional black tie, 1976; "Sunburst Finish" Harvest promotional note pad, 1976; "Live In The Air Age" Harvest promotional notepad; promotional pin - $25

Beck

(Beck Hansen)
Born: July 8, 1970

Down home "what you get is what you got" indie rock at its core, Beck drew accolades and considerable sales for his lo-fi satirical ballad "Loser," drawing immediate Dylan comparisons. A child of eclectic

'60s parents—his mother a former member of the band Black Flag and his father a bluegrass musician—Beck opted for a postpunk brand of acoustic country blues.

Beck found himself in New York City during the end of the ill-fated East Village antifolk scene in 1989, before heading back to California. Hitting the artsy coffeehouse circuit, he found solace with other acts such as Ethyl Meatplow and That Dog. Indie released "Loser" (#10, 1994) hit solid on local alt-radio stations, enough to start a record company bidding war for the artist. *Mellow Gold* (#13, 1994) quickly shot up the album charts, while his second single "Beer-can" struggled into the Top Forty.

His later releases have been well received, but with lackluster sales. *Odelay* (#16, 1997), by the way!

AUTOGRAPHS

A CD, LP, magazine cover, ad, photo, or card signed by the artist: $20-$40

POSTERS/PRESS KITS

Promotional Posters: $8-$15*
Press Kits: $10-$20*
Mellow Gold

Beck, Jeff

Born: June 24, 1944

Jeff Beck Group formed in 1967. Its members included Rod Stewart, Born: January 10, 1945; Ron Wood, Born: June 1, 1947; Jeff Beck; and Aynsley Dunbar*

*Dunbar departed in 1967 and was replaced by Mickey Waller. In 1968 Waller left and Nicky Hopkins and Tony Newman were added. A new version formed in 1971: Beck; Cozy Powell, Born: December 29, 1947; Max Middleton; Clive Chaman; and Bobby Tench. In 1972 another new version was formed: Beck, Tim Bogert, and Carmine Appice.

Along with Jimmy Page and Eric Clapton, Beck is often referred to as one of rock music's most influential guitarists. Jeff Beck has been a major contributor to blues, rock, and all of its diverse offshoots. Although his group results have been fragmented, his guitar work has not.

Beck backed Lord Such, replaced Eric Clapton in the Yardbirds, and founded the Jeff Beck Group (with Ron Wood and Rod Stewart, followed by its various roster changes), before finally concentrating on his solo work, which often included other key musicians he had been associated with over the years. Beck's 1985 album *Flash* included the extract "People Get Ready" (#48, 1985) and the Grammy-winning "Escape," written by Jan Hammer.

Jeff Beck's Guitar Shop with Terry Bozio and Tony Hymas (#49, 1989) picked up a Grammy for Best Rock Instrumental Performance. In the decade that followed—a prolific period for the artist—he has con-

centrated on session work with others (including Mick Jagger and Roger Waters), released a couple of modestly acclaimed albums, and toured.

AUTOGRAPHS

A CD, LP, magazine cover, ad, photo, or card signed by the artist: $25-$60

TOUR BOOKS/PROGRAMS/PASSES

Tour Books:
Jeff Beck/Bad English/Steve Lukather, Japan: $100
Backstage Passes:
Cloth: $10-$12; Laminated: $15-$20 (1990-Present)

POSTERS/PRESS KITS

Promotional Posters: $15-$30 (1990-Present)
Press Kits: $10-$30 (1990-Present)

USED CLOTHING/EQUIPMENT

Guitar Picks: $25-$65

OFTEN OVERLOOKED MEMORABILIA

Beckology promotional pick - $10; articles about his enthusiasm for automobiles/car collections

---

The Bee Gees

Formed 1958

Barry Gibb, Born: September 1, 1947; Robin Gibb, Born: December 22, 1949; and Maurice Gibb, Born: December 22, 1949

Barry Gibb and his twin brothers Robin and Maurice emigrated to Australia from the U.K. with their parents in the late 1950s. Their father Hugh had his own orchestra and was under contract with Mecca, while their mother Barbara was a singer. They began performing in the mid-1950s, and by 1960 they were performing as the Rattlesnakes at Brisbane's Speedway Circus, where they met Bill Good. Good introduced them to a friend of his, a DJ named Bill Gates, who aired the Gibb tapes on his radio show. Good coined the name B.G.'s after his own and Gates' initials.

The first Bee Gees concert poster, printed in 1968, is currently valued at $1,500. From the Doug Leftwitch collection.

The band relocates to Sydney in 1962, and performs as the Bee Gees at Sydney Stadium on a Chubby Checker headliner. The group signs with Australia's Festival Records in

1962. Already penning their own music, they release numerous singles and two albums over the next five years.

It wasn't until 1967, when "Spicks and Specks" hit #1 in Australia, that others recognized the trio's ability. On February 24, 1967, they sign a five-year management agreement with Robert Stigwood. Stigwood, who is in partnership with Brian Epstein, lands the Bee Gees a long-term contract with Polydor Records. They expand to a quintet, adding drummer Colin Peterson and bassist Vince Melouney, both Australians. The stage is now set for what would be the first leg of the band's career. "New York Mining Disaster" (#14, 1967) is the first of many successful ballads that spotlight the groups harmonic sound. "To Love Somebody" (#17, 1967), "Holiday" (#16, 1967), "Massachusetts" (#11, 1967), "Words" (#15, 1968), "I've Got To Get A Message To You" (#8, 1968), and "I Started A Joke" (#6, 1969) soon followed.

Although extremely successful, internal strife develops and by March 1969 the group collapses. Both Melouney and Petersen depart, while Robin Gibb pursues a solo career. Barry and Maurice continue as the Bee Gees, while Stigwood sues Robin for leaving the group. Robin's solo debut "Saved by the Bell" (#2, 1969) is well received, while Barry and Maurice film *Cucumber Castle*. The trio does manage to reunite for two more hits, "Lonely Days" (#3, 1970) and "How Can You Mend A Broken Heart" (#1, 1971), before bottoming out until 1975.

The second stage of the group's career begins with Robert Stigwood recruiting producer Arif Marden. The result was *Main Course* (#14, 1976) with its two hit singles "Jive Talkin" (#1, 1975) and "Nights On Broadway" (#7, 1975). The group's new sound, complemented by the advent of disco, gave the Bee Gees their first platinum album.

Children of the World followed, now on Stigwood's RSO label, and yielded the hit singles "You Should Be Dancing" (#1, 1976) and "Love So Right" (#3, 1976). Stigwood, who had produced films such as *Jesus Christ Superstar* and *Tommy,* asked the Bee Gees for songs he could include on the soundtrack to *Saturday Night Fever.* The album, forever associated with the disco sound, would give the Bee Gees three straight chart-toppers. The group also penned the Frankie Valli sung title to the movie *Grease. Spirits Having Flown* (1979) included three number one singles: "Too Much Heaven," "Tragedy," and "Love You Inside Out." This stage of their career would come to a close in 1980 when the group files a multimillion dollar lawsuit against Stigwood for mismanagement, perhaps prompted by the group's appearance in the 1978 movie bomb *Sgt. Pepper's Lonely Hearts Club Band.*

By the summer of 1981, Stigwood and the Bee Gees rectify their lawsuit. *Living Eyes* (#41, 1981) fails to draw the attention of previous releases. In an attempt to regain some of their lost fame, the group composes the soundtrack to the *Saturday Night Fe-*ver sequel, *Stayin' Alive* (#6, 1983). The album spins off the Top Thirty hit "Woman In You"(#24, 1983). By now, however, a backlash against disco was taking place and, unfortunately for the band, they were too closely associated with the phenomenon. Some individual projects thrived, including the Barry-produced and trio-written "Islands in the Stream" (#1, 1983), a duet by Kenny Rogers and Dolly Parton.

In 1987 the group returns to the studio to produce *E.S.P.* (#96, 1987) and although the release did little in the U.S., it had strong sales overseas. The album yields the single "You Win Again" (#75, 1987) which climbs to the top of the charts in the U.K. The Bee Gees now become the only band to top the singles charts in Britain in each of the past three decades (they also repeated the performance in the 1990s). On March 10, 1988, the Bee Gees' youngest brother Andy Gibb dies in a U.K. hospital five days after his 30th birthday. The event shatters the band, who now only performs sporadically at special events.

One (#68, 1989) becomes the group's next effort and spins off a self-titled single (#6, 1989) that falls into the Top Ten. It's followed by another compilation album, then *High Civilization,* which fails to chart in the U.S., but yields the U.K. hit single "Secret Love." *Size Isn't Everything* (#153, 1993) falls far short of expectations as the band enters another dry spell.

The group's diverse interests and individual solo projects make the band a fascinating subject to collect. Their stages of success are also interesting transitions and make for intriguing elements of collecting.

The signature of Bee Gee Barry Gibb

AUTOGRAPHS

Group:
A CD, LP, magazine cover, ad, photo, or card signed by the entire band: $25-$75*
*High end reflects vintage signed memorabilia

Individual:
Barry Gibb: $15-$30
Robin Gibb: $10-$25
Maurice Gibb: $10-$25

TOUR BOOKS/PROGRAMS/PASSES

Tour Books:
Spirits Having Flown, 1979
(11" x 14"): $40-$50
1989 European Tourbook
(9-1/2" x 13-1/2"): $15-$22
One For All, 1989, 12 pp.: $15

Backstage Passes:
Cloth: $5-$8; Laminated: $8-$12 (1985 - Present)

POSTERS/PRESS KITS

Promotional Posters: $15-$100 depending upon scarcity, significance, and size
Press Kits: $10-$75
"E.S.P.," Warner Bros., 1987: $20

USED CLOTHING/EQUIPMENT

Guitar Picks:
Barry Gibb: $20-$35
Maurice Gibb: $20-$35

OFTEN OVERLOOKED MEMORABILIA

Official Sgt. Pepper's Lonely Hearts Club Band scrapbook - $20; magazines with the Bee Gees on cover: *Rolling Stone* $8-$25, *People* $10-$15, *Billboard "Salutes the Bee Gees"* (Sec. 2, September 2, 1978) - $50-$75; sheet music - $15-$25; songbooks - $19-$35; "Saturday Night Fever" Phonograph - $85-$100; Complete set of Sgt. Pepper trading cards - $20; "Saturday Night Fever" book bag/backpack - $40-$50; "Saturday Night Fever" Barry Gibb lunch box with thermos - $50; The Official fan Club photo folder, newsletter and bios, membership certificate, etc. - $20; "Love and Hope Tennis Festival" invitation (Barry Gibb) with original envelopes - $40-$50; "I Love The Bee Gees" bumper stickers - $5; promotional postcards - $3-$15; "Spirits Having Fun" RSO Promotional wine, goblet and cassette, 1979; "ESP" Warners Brothers promotional lump of quartz in an embroidered pouch, 1987; belt buckle - $15; doll (Andy Gibb)- $40; glass (logo) - $15; thermos, steel: Barry - $60, Maurice - $50, Robin - $50; thermos, plastic: Bee Gees - $25; toy guitar, 24" - $125; microphone and amplifier - $50; phonograph - $60; puzzles - $30; radio - $35; "Main Course" mobile - $65; "Children of the World" cube mobile - $75

REFERENCES/BOOKS

A few resources exist, nothing that does justice to the band in my opinion; no dedicated collector books; serious collectors should opt for fan club: Bee Gees Quarterly, Attention: Renee Schreiber, P.O. Box 2429, Miami Beach, FL 33140

Bees Make Honey

Formed 1972

Ruan O' Lochlainn, Deke O'Brien, Bob Cee Benberg, Barry Richardson, and Mick Molloy*

*O'Lochlainn, Benberg and O'Brien leave in 1973 and are replaced by Malcolm Morley, Fran Byrne and Rod Demick. Numerous changes follow.

The pub-rock group is best remembered as a stopping ground for drummers Bob Cee Benberg (Supertramp) and Fran Byrne (Ace).

AUTOGRAPHS

A CD, LP, magazine cover, ad, photo, or card signed by the entire band: $8-$12

Belew, Adrian

(Robert Steven Belew)
Born: December 23, 1949

A highly recruited instrumentalist, guitarist, and producer who has played with some of the best in the business, including Frank Zappa, David Bowie, King Crimson, Nine Inch Nails, and the Talking Heads. His art-rock sound, constantly in an evolving state, is indicative of Belew's passion for cutting-edge technology. Forever versatile, he is as happy producing Jars of Clay as he is touring with David Bowie, as long as he has access to a path of creativity. His lack of success as a solo artist should not overshadow this very talented musician.

AUTOGRAPHS

Group:
A CD, LP, magazine cover, ad, photo, or card signed by the artist: $10-$15

USED CLOTHING/EQUIPMENT

Guitar Picks: $10-$20

OFTEN OVERLOOKED MEMORABILIA

His contributions to other artists' work

Bell, Archie and the Drells

Formed mid-1960s

Archie Bell, Born: September 1, 1944; Huey "Billy" Butler; Joe Cross; and James Wise*

*Both Butler and Cross depart in 1969 and are replaced by Willie Parnell and Lee Bell

Best remembered for "Tighten Up" (#1, 1968), "I Can't Stop Dancing," "There's Gonna Be A Showdown," and "Wrap It Up" (#33, R&B, 1970).

AUTOGRAPHS

An LP, magazine cover, ad, photo, or card signed by the entire band: $12-$20

Bell, William

(William Yarborough)
Born: July 16, 1939

A player in the Memphis Sound, William Bell is a versatile soul singer who emerged in the mid-60s with numerous R&B hits including "Everybody Loves a Winner," "A Tribute to a King," and "I Forgot to Be Your Lover," along with duets with Judy Clay, "Private Number" and "My Baby Specializes." In 1976 he also hit the top of the R&B charts with "Trying To Love Two." He has always been a low-profile artist of considerable talent.

AUTOGRAPHS

A CD, LP, magazine cover, ad, photo, or card signed by the artist: $8-$12

Bell Biv DeVoe

Formed 1988

Michael Bivins, Ricky Bell, and Ronnie DeVoe

As members of New Edition, the sensational teen-age vocal group, Michael Bivins, Ricky Bell, and Ronnie DeVoe left the limelight to Ralph Tresvant and Bobby Brown and later Johnny Gill. They emerged (through prodding by Jimmy Jam and Terry Lewis) as Bell Biv DeVoe, ushering in a more provocative sound for the trio. Their debut album *Poison* (#5, 1990), which contained hits "Poison" (#3, 1990), "Do Me!" (#3, 1990), "B.B.D. (I Thought It Was Me)" (#1, R&B, 1990) and "When Will I See You Smile Again" (#3, R&B, 1990), was a smash success.

"She's Dope" (#9, R&B, 1991) and "Gangsta" (#21, 1993) maintained the band's chart success before the release of their third album *Hootie Mack* (#19, 1993) with extract "Something In Your Eyes" (#38, 1993).

AUTOGRAPHS

A CD, LP, magazine cover, ad, photo, or card signed by the entire band: $20-$40

TOUR BOOKS/PROGRAMS/PASSES

Tour Books: 1991 Tour: $15

OFTEN OVERLOOKED MEMORABILIA

Videotapes of the group's appearances on *Dick Clark's New Year's Rockin' Eve* - ABC-TV (12/31/90), *James Brown - Living in America* - pay-per-view (6/10/91) and *Dick Clark's New Year's Rockin' Eve '93* - ABC-TV; artifacts from Biv 10 Entertainment

Belle, Regina

Born: July 15, 1963

A talented vocalist with roots in gospel and jazz, Belle is commonly associated with her 1992 duet with Peabo Bryson on "A Whole New World (Aladdin's Theme)" (#1, 1992). Her debut, *All By Myself*, received accolades and spun off the hit single "Show Me The Way" (32, R&B, 1987). Belle followed up with *Stay With Me* (#1, R&B, 1989), which included two R&B chart toppers, "Baby Come To Me" and "Make It Like It Was." The same year she also scored with her duet with "J.T." Taylor on "All I Want Is Forever" (#2, R&B, 1989).

AUTOGRAPHS

A CD, LP, magazine cover, ad, photo, or card signed by the artist: $10-$20

POSTERS/PRESS KITS

Promotional Posters: $10-$15
Press Kits: $10-$15

OFTEN OVERLOOKED MEMORABILIA

Movie memorabilia from *Taps* (1989), *Aladdin* (1992)

Belvin, Jesse

Born: December 15, 1933, Died: February 6, 1960

An extremely talented individual who assisted many vocal "doo-wop" acts of the '50s in getting recorded. He scored his first Top Ten R&B hit in 1953 with "Dream Girl." His talent extended to songwriting, best exhibited in "Earth Angel," the smash hit for the Penguins in 1956.

AUTOGRAPHS

A CD, LP, magazine cover, ad, photo, or card signed by the artist: $15-$35

Benatar, Pat

(Patricia Andrzejewski)
Born: January 10, 1953

The most successful female rocker of the '80s, Benatar scored with her debut album and never looked back. Her '80s hits included "Heartbreaker" (#23), "Hit Me With Your Best Shot" (#9, 1980), "Treat Me Right" (#18, 1981), "Promise in the Dark" (#38, 1981), "Fire and Ice" (#17, 1981), "Shadows of the Night" (#13, 1982), "Little Too Late" (#20, 1983), "Love Is a Battlefield" (#5, 1983), and "We Belong" (#5, 1984), before she took some time off to start a family. When she returned to the business, so did the hits, including "Invincible" (#10, 1985), "Sex as a Weapon" (#28, 1985), and "All Fired Up" (#19, 1988).

"Tell Me Why" (#31, 1991), was her first charting single of the '90s—a decade that saw the performer's success tail off a bit. Time will tell if her 1997 release, *Innamorata,* will be her comeback.

AUTOGRAPHS

A CD, LP, magazine cover, ad, photo, or card signed by the artist: $20-$50

POSTERS/PRESS KITS

Promotional Posters: $10-$30
Press Kits: $12-$35

OFTEN OVERLOOKED MEMORABILIA

Movie memorabilia from *Legend of Billie Jean* (1985); "7 The Hard Way" store display - $50; promotional guitar pin - $8; "Get Nervous" promotional notebook - $45

Bennett, Tony

(Anthony Benedetto)
Born: August 13, 1926

Crooner extraordinaire, Tony Bennett has survived more dry spells than the Sahara Desert. Now

four decades into his recording career, he can still sell out venues in many cities in the U.S. Brilliantly marketed in recent years, he has won an entirely new legion of fans with releases such as *Perfectly Frank* (1992), *Steppin' Out* (1993), *Forty Years: The Artistry of Tony Bennett* (1991), and *Tony Bennett - MTV Unplugged* (1994).

Over the years his hits have included "Because Of You" (#1, 1951), "Cold, Cold Heart," "Rags to Riches" (#1, 1953), "Stranger in Paradise" (#2, 1953), and "There'll Be No Teardrops Tonight" (#7, 1954). His partnership with Ralph Sharon, his lifelong collaborator, began in 1956, during a period that saw Bennett sell out Carnegie hall and record his trademark, "I Left My Heart in San Francisco" (#19, 1962).

Although he didn't record from 1978 to 1985, he stayed active performing concerts while working on his other interest, painting. With no apparent end in sight to this extraordinary performer's career, don't be surprised to see him land a few more Grammy awards before he's through.

AUTOGRAPHS

A CD, LP, magazine cover, ad, photo, or card signed by the artist: $7-$35*

*Vintage memorabilia

OFTEN OVERLOOKED MEMORABILIA

How about an original painting from Bennett?

Benson, George

Born: March 22, 1943

A talented jazz guitarist and vocalist, Benson was catapulted into the public eye with his multiple Grammy Award-winning 1975 album *Breezin'*, which featured the hit extract "This Masquerade"—the first song in history to top the jazz, R&B, and pop charts. His Warner Brothers years remained fruitful as he landed hits with "On Broadway" (#7, 1978), "Give Me The Night" (#4, 1980) and "Turn Your Love Around" (#5, 1981), while consistently selling albums gold.

AUTOGRAPHS

A CD, LP, magazine cover, ad, photo, or card signed by the entire band: $15-$35

TOUR BOOKS/PROGRAMS/PASSES

Tour Books:
Livin' Inside Your Love: $22

POSTERS/PRESS KITS

Promotional Posters: $15-$35
Press Kits: $15-$50

USED CLOTHING/EQUIPMENT

Guitar Picks: $30-$50

Benton, Brook

(Benjamin Peay)
Born: September 19, 1931, Died: April 9, 1988

A gifted singer and songwriter, Benton tallied 16 Top Twenty hits over his long career, including "A Million Miles From Nowhere" (1958), before forming a lucrative trio with Clyde Otis and Belford Hendrick, which struck hits for Nat "King" Cole and Clyde McPhatter, and also produced "It's Just A Matter of Time" (#3), "Endlessly" (#12), "Thank You Pretty Baby" (#16) and "So Many Ways" (#6).

The '60s saw the artist land with duets "Baby (You've Got What It Takes)" (#5, 1960) and "A Rockin' Good Way" (#7, 1960), before "The Boll Weevil Song" (#2, 1961), "Frankie and Johnny" (#20, 1961), "Think Twice" (#11, 1961), "Revenge" (#15, 1961), "Lie to Me" (#13, 1962), "Shadrack" (319, 1962), and "Hotel Happiness" (#3, 1963). His final hit came in 1970 with "Rainy Night in Georgia" (#4, 1970), sung by Tony Joe White on Cotillion.

AUTOGRAPHS

A CD, LP, magazine cover, ad, photo, or card signed by the artist: $20-$45

Berlin

Formed 1979
John Crawford, Rob Brill, and Terri Nunn

"Take My Breathe Away" (#1, 1986) is Berlin's claim to fame, as is teen actress Terri Nunn, who also worked in television (*Lou Grant*).

AUTOGRAPHS

A CD, LP, magazine cover, ad, photo, or card signed by the entire band: $8-$15

Berry, Chuck

Born: October 18, 1926

A talented guitarist, performer, and songwriter, Berry opted to go against the current of modern music. Berry melded rhythm & blues with country and added just enough defiance to make it interesting, while Alan Freed called what he was doing "rock 'n' roll" music.

Having met Muddy Waters in Chicago in May 1955, it was through the musician that Berry got hooked up with Leonard Chess. Chess liked Berry's demo tape, especially the song "Ida Red," which was renamed and mailed to DJ Alan Freed, and the artist quickly had his first Top Ten hit, "Maybelline." The

A very early 1955 fall Tour Blank for the "Chuck Berry Trio" valued at $1500-$2,000. From the collection of Hank Thompson.

hits just kept a rollin': "School Days" (#3, 1957), "Rock & Roll Music" (#8, 1957), "Sweet Little Sixteen" (#2, 1958), "and "Johnny B. Goode" (#8, 1958) just to name a few.

Berry played and filled nearly every concert hall in America during the '50s and his trademark "duck-walk" seemed more popular than the president at the time. Berry then met his first obstacle, "the Mann Act." Following an unfortunate incident, he was convicted and sent to federal prison for a couple years. Upon his release, the British Invasion was in full swing and the public actually preferred Beatles and Rolling Stones covers of his songs over his own versions. His last Number One was "My Ding-a-Ling" (#1, 1972).

He was inducted into the Rock and Roll Hall of Fame in January 1986.

AUTOGRAPHS

A CD, LP, magazine cover, ad, photo, or card signed by the artist: $45-$150

TOUR BOOKS/PROGRAMS/PASSES

Tour Books: 1964 (UK): $75-$100

OFTEN OVERLOOKED MEMORABILIA

Movie memorabilia from *Rock, Rock, Rock* (1956), *Mister Rock and Roll* (1957), *Go, Johnny, Go* (1959), *American Hot Wax* (1979) and *Hail! Hail! Rock 'n' Roll* (1987); all artifacts from Irving Feld's "Greatest Show of 1957," "Alan

Freed's Christmas Rock & Roll Spectacular" (1958), "The Biggest Show of Stars For 1957" and his first U.K. caravan (1964) package tours; videotapes from his television appearances on *The Big Beat* - ABC-TV (7/57), *Thank Your Lucky Stars* - ITV (5/64), *Aspel* - ITV (1988), "Apollo Theater Hall Of Fame" concert (9/94 air date) and *Late Show With David Letterman* - CBS-TV (9/16/94); a copy of the documentaries *Jazz On A Summer's Day* and *Gather No Moss* (1966); artifacts from Berryland Amusement Park; a rubbing from his star on the Hollywood Walk of Fame; any artifacts relating to his appearance on the Voyager Interstellar Record (1989); newspaper clippings from his various bouts with law enforcement officials

REFERENCES/BOOKS

Chuck Berry: The Autobiography (1987); *Chuck Berry: Rock 'n' Roll Music* by Howard DeWitt—a must for Berry collectors; a few other resources exist

The B-52's

Formed 1976

Cindy Wilson, Born: February 28, 1957; Keith Strickland, Born: October 26, 1953; Fred Schneider III, Born: July 1, 1956; Ricky Wilson, Born: March 19, 1953, Died: October 12, 1985; Kate Pierson, Born: April 27, 1948*

*C. Wilson departed in 1990

The B-52's made their debut at an Athens, Georgia, Valentine's Day party in 1977. The band specialized in nostalgic "glee-rock," dressed in vintage '50s and '60s attire, they poked fun at the past with just enough edge to make their efforts interesting. They quickly developed a cult following, especially in cities like New York, where they could manage their image on the club circuit. Warner Brothers signed the band in 1979; however, it wasn't until their sophomore effort, *Wild Planet* (#18, 1980), that sales picked up. *Whammy* sold into the Top Thirty album charts, thanks to two extracts, "Legal Tender" and "Song for a Future Generation."

Cosmic Thing (1989) would be a breakthrough album for the band, driven by the hit singles "Love Shack" (#3, 1990), "Roam" (#3, 1990), and "Deadbeat Club" (#30, 1990). Although Cindy Wilson would retire from the band shortly after this point, the group would continue on as a trio, releasing *Good Stuff* (#16, 1992)*.

*Wilson would make occasional on-off appearances with the group

AUTOGRAPHS

A CD, LP, magazine cover, ad, photo, or card signed by the entire band: $20-$50*
*Original band members

TOUR BOOKS/ PROGRAMS/PASSES

Backstage Passes:
Cloth: $8-$15;
Laminated: $15-$25

Backstage pass from the B-52's Interdimensional Tourgasm (Printed by OTTO)

POSTERS/PRESS KITS
Promotional Posters: $10-$20
Press Kits: $12-$25

OFTEN OVERLOOKED MEMORABILIA
Movie memorabilia from *Meet the Flintstones* (1994); plastic clamshell form their "Meet The Flintstones" promo CD, 1994; plastic bag from Island Records promo CDs $5; promotional pins $5-$8

REFERENCES/BOOKS
A few mediocre resources exist; no dedicated collector books

Big Audio Dynamite/B.A.D. II/Big Audio

Formed 1984

Mick Jones, Born: June 26, 1955; Don Letts; Leo Williams; Greg Roberts; and Dan Donovan

These bands were creative outlets for Mick Jones, who mixed a variety of sounds together to form his own form of fusion, even opting for sampling—one of the first British bands to experiment with the technique. Notable bursts of creative elegance came on "C'mon Every Beatbox" and "Just Play Music," while B.A.D. II landed the single "Rush" (#32, 1991).

AUTOGRAPHS
A CD, LP, magazine cover, ad, photo, or card signed by the entire band: $15-$20

OFTEN OVERLOOKED MEMORABILIA
Number Ten Upping Street, Columbia promo cassette, 1986, packaged in cardboard tube similar to dynamite stick

The Big Bopper

(Jiles Perry "J.P." Richardson)
Born: October 24, 1930, Died: February 3, 1959

Richardson had been working as a disc jockey at KTRM in Beaumont, Texas, since high school and returned home from a stint in the army to pick up where he left off at the station. He had been working on writing songs while in the service and in 1957 was able to get a copy of his demo tape into the Mercury Records office. Richardson cut two country & western singles under his real name and a novelty record under his radio name the "Big Bopper." The novelty single included "The Purple People Eater Meets the Witch-Doctor" on the A side, and the 1958 international smash hit "Chantilly Lace" on the flip side.

"The Big Bopper" followed his hit with two minor singles, "Little Red Riding Hood" and "The Big Bopper's Wedding," and posthumously with his penned "Running Bear" sung by Johnny Preston. On February 3, 1959, he died in the same plane crash that killed Buddy Holly and Ritchie Valens.

AUTOGRAPHS
A CD, LP, magazine cover, ad, photo, or card signed by the artist: $275-$450

Big Brother and the Holding Company

Formed 1965

Peter Albin, Sam Andrew, James Gurley, David Getz, and Janis Joplin, Born: January 19, 1943, Died: October 4, 1970*

*Joplin and Andrew depart in 1968. David Shallock and Nick Gravenites join briefly in 1970, but depart the same year. Gurley also leaves in 1970. Michael Pendergrass, Kathy McDonald, and Mike Finnigan are added, while Andrew returns.

Led by Peter Albin, the band is best known as the career launching pad for Janis Joplin. "Pearl" joined the group in June of 1966 and departed at the end of 1968. The band had established itself in the Bay Area, and even became the house band at the Avalon Ballroom. The band was thrust into the national spotlight with the combination of Janis, their appearance at the Monterey Pop Festival in June 1967, and their strong debut record *Cheap Thrills* (#1, 1968), with its extract "Piece of My Heart" (#12, 1968).

When Joplin and Sam Andrew departed late in 1968, the band tried numerous unsuccessful attempts to recover their success (even with Andrew back). They officially disbanded in 1972.

AUTOGRAPHS
Peter Albin: $10-$25	Sam Andrew: $6-$12
James Gurley: $5-$10	David Getz: $5-$10
Janis Joplin: $600-$1,000	

OFTEN OVERLOOKED MEMORABILIA
Any and all items associated with Janis Joplin

Big Country

Formed 1982

Stuart Adamson, Mark Brzezicki, Tony Butler, and Bruce Watson

An early '80s Scottish band whose Celtic charm and flavored arrangements scored with its first and largest hit "In a Big Country" (#17, 1983). The band's releases continue to draw acceptance in the U.K., but have failed commercially in the U.S.

AUTOGRAPHS
A CD, LP, magazine cover, ad, photo, or card signed by the entire band: $10-$15*
*Original band members

OFTEN OVERLOOKED MEMORABILIA
Republican Party reptile; vertigo promotional bag and single; sticker; Big Country birthday card and a tag, 1991;

promotional pin - $8; "Peace In Our Time" 1988 Reprise flag - $35; Big Country, Mercury promo box set, 1984, first two albums plus six 12" singles, all autographed

REFERENCES/BOOKS

Serious collectors should opt for fan club: All of Us, Attention: James Birch, 201 Gay Street #4, Denton, MD 21629 ($12 per year)

Big Daddy Kane

(Antonio M. Hardy)
Born: September 10, 1968

One of rap's first sex symbols. Having written material for Juice Crew and Curtis Blow, by 1988 he had landed covers with Biz Markie ("Vapors" and "Pickin' Boogers") and Roxanne Shante ("Have a Nice Day" and " Go On Girl"). Since his solo debut, Kane has received consistent acclaim, yet has created some controversy over his handling of certain subjects. He has also pursued a career in acting.

AUTOGRAPHS

A CD, LP, magazine cover, ad, photo, or card signed by the artist: $10-$20*

*Something provocative

OFTEN OVERLOOKED MEMORABILIA

Movie memorabilia from *Posse* and *Meteor Man;* issues of *Playgirl* magazine (June 1991); a copy of Madonna's 1992 book *Sex,* in which Big Daddy Kane appears

Big Star/Alex Chilton

Alex Chilton, Born: December 28, 1950; Chris Bell (1951-1978); Andy Hummel; and Jody Stephens*

*Bell departs in 1973, with Hummel leaving the following year. Jonathan Auer and Ken Stringfellow are added in 1993.

Although the pop group lasted less than four years, they have taken on a mythical status through such enduring tracks as "September Gurls" and the solo work of Alex Chilton. The band, formed in Memphis by Chris Bell, garnered much attention with their first two releases, *#1 Record* and *Radio City,* but no commercial success. Bell died in an automobile accident in 1978. Afterwards Chilton moved to New York, where he ventured into numerous bands and projects before slipping into obscurity. He has, however, occasionally resurfaced and even played!

AUTOGRAPHS

A CD, LP, magazine cover, ad, photo, or card signed by the entire band: $20-$45*

*Original band members

Big Youth

(Manley Buchanan)
Born: 1949

One of Jamaica's most popular "toasters" in the '70s, Big Youth has influenced the rap culture that followed. "Ace 90 Skank" was his first hit, laying the foundation for much of the work that followed. He couldn't resist singing about the heavyweight championship that took place in Kingston in 1973 between "Big George" Foreman and "Smokin'" Joe Frazier, so he took the airways with his commemorative fight songs. Later in his career (now a Rastafarian) his songs took on a heavier meaning, such as in "House of Dreadlocks" and "Natural Cultural Dread."

AUTOGRAPHS

A CD, LP, magazine cover, ad, photo, or card signed by the artist: $8-$15

OFTEN OVERLOOKED MEMORABILIA

Associated memorabilia from the annual Reggae Sunsplash Festival

Bikini Kill

Formed 1990

Tobi Vail, Kathleen Hanna (-Dando), Billy Boredom (Karren), and Kathi Wilcox

"Revolution Girl Style Now," the bands anthemic chant, has guided Bikini Kill since their inception in the early '90s. They took the punk underground by storm, confronting a variety of feminist issues with their music and live performances. It was the feisty Hanna, a former stripper, who spray painted "Smells Like Teen Spirit" on Kurt Cobain's house. The band tackles sexual expectations like football linebacker Junior Seau locking his sights on an opposition fullback. The band refuses to work with major labels, opting instead for Olympia indie-label Kill Rock Stars. They worked with Joan Jett on their single "Rebel Girl" and even toured with her the following year.

AUTOGRAPHS

A CD, LP, magazine cover, ad, photo, or card signed by the entire band: $10-$25*

*Original band members

OFTEN OVERLOOKED MEMORABILIA

An autographed copy of *Smells Like Teen Spirit* (EP) signed by Hanna - $20; one of Hanna's discarded stage-worn pieces of clothing

The Birthday Party/Nick Cave and the Bad Seeds

Formed 1977

Nick Cave, Born: September 22, 1957; Rowland Howard; Mick Harvey; Tracy Pew; and Phil Calvert

Furious, overdriven gothic guitar ignited by despondent and morose chants, the Birthday Party has been Nick Cave's godson since 1977. Personnel changes are as common as guitar picks, with Cave's steady diet of violent and sacrilegious song subject matter (such as "Big-Jesus-Trash-Can") doing its very best to piss everybody off. The group calmed a bit during the '80s, with Cave even going through his Elvis stage before turning his attention to writing and even acting.

AUTOGRAPHS

A CD, LP, magazine cover, ad, photo, or card signed by the entire band: $10-$30*

*Original band members

OFTEN OVERLOOKED MEMORABILIA

Movie memorabilia from *Wings of Desire* (1988), *Johnny Suede* (1991), *Ghosts ... of the Civil Dead*, *Until the End of the World* (1990), and *Faraway, So Close* (1993)

REFERENCES/BOOKS

King Ink by Nick Cave (1988); *And the Ass Saw the Angel* by Nick Cave (1989)

Bishop, Elvin

Born: October 21, 1942

Ex-Paul Butterfield guitarist whose breakthrough came with his album *Struttin' My Stuff*, with its hit extract "Fooled Around and Fell in Love" (#3, 1976).

AUTOGRAPHS

A CD, LP, magazine cover, ad, photo, or card signed by the artist: $8-$10

USED CLOTHING/EQUIPMENT

Guitar Picks: $15-$20

Biz Markie

(Marcel Hall)
Born: April 8, 1964

One of rap's jesters, whose debut album *Goin' Off* (#90, 1988) included such rap slaps as "Vapors" (#80, 1988), "Make the Music with Your Mouth, Biz" and "Pickin' Boogers." His sophomore effort, *The Biz Nev-*

er Sleeps (#66, 1989), proved more fruitful and included the hit extract "Just a Friend" (#9, 1990). He also holds the dubious distinction of losing the first rap-sampling lawsuit for his "Alone Again" cut on his third album, *I Need a Haircut* (1991)—making any items associated with this release highly collectible, as Warner Brothers Records ordered to remove all copies.

AUTOGRAPHS

A CD, LP, magazine cover, ad, photo, or card signed by the artist: $10-$15

OFTEN OVERLOOKED MEMORABILIA

All memorabilia associated with his *I Need a Haircut* album (1991)

Bill Black Combo

Formed 1959

Bill Black, Born: September 17, 1926, Died: October 21, 1965; Carl McAvoy; Martin Wills; Reggie Young; and Jerry Arnold*

*Bobby Emmons and Bob Tucker are added around 1961. Black departs in 1962.

A neighbor of guitarist Scotty Moore, Black happened upon a chance meeting between himself, Moore, and a truck driver named Elvis Presley in 1954. The trio recorded "That's All Right," Presley's first hit, under the watchful eye of Sam Phillips, founder of Sun Records. Black then went out on tour with Elvis until 1959, when he opted to form his own instrumental group, the Bill Black Combo. The group went on to score hits with "Smokie (Part 2)" (1959), "Josephine," "White Silver Sands," and "Don't Be Cruel" (1960). Black retired from the band in 1962 and died of a brain tumor three years later.

AUTOGRAPHS

Group:

A CD, LP, magazine cover, ad, photo, or card signed by the entire band: $25-$50*

*Original band members

OFTEN OVERLOOKED MEMORABILIA

All Elvis Presley related artifacts

Black, Clint

Born: February 4, 1962

Clint Black scored a dozen singles on the top of the C&W charts from 1989 to 1994. His debut album, *Killin' Time* (#31, 1989) included the country chart toppers "A Better Man," "Killin' Time" (1989), "Nobody's Home" (1989), and "Walkin' Away" (1990).

Put Yourself in My Shoes (#18, 1990), his sophomore effort, also scored high marks and spun off two Number One's, "Where Are You Now" (1991) and "Loving Blind" (1991).

Through his turbulent marriage to actress Lisa Hartman, Black released *The Hard Way*, a slightly more melancholy release than expected, but it still sold well.

No Time To Kill followed in 1993, and included the extracted hit duet "A Bad Goodbye" (#2, C&W, 1993) sung with Wynonna Judd. The hits kept coming with "A Good Run of Bad Luck" (#1, C&W, 1994), lifted from Black's *One Emotion* (1994). *The Greatest Hits* (1996) sold to the #26 spot on the yearly album chart.

AUTOGRAPHS

A CD, LP, magazine cover, ad, photo, or card signed by the artist: $15-$45

TOUR BOOKS/PROGRAMS/PASSES

Backstage Passes:
Cloth: $6-$8; Laminated: $10-$12

POSTERS/PRESS KITS

Promotional Posters: $10-$30
Press Kits: $15-$25

USED CLOTHING/EQUIPMENT

Guitar Picks: $10-$20

The Black Crowes

Formed 1988

Chris Robinson, Born: December 20, 1966; Rich Robinson; Jeff Cease; Johnny Colt; and Steve Gorman*

*Cease departs in 1990 and Mark Ford is added. Eddie Harsch is added in 1994.

The Black Crowes, who physically resemble a '70s biker group more than a band, hit solid in 1990 with *Shake Your Moneymaker* (#4, 1990), which sold well on the album charts, was praised by critics, and even scored three minor hits—"Jealous Again " (#75, 1990), "She Talks to Angels" (#30, 1991), and "Hard to Handle" (#26, 1991).

Band members are far from bashful, and not ashamed to mix it up. Their behavior has led to some conflicts with the law, conflicts with other bands, and even conflicts among themselves. The group's second album, *The Southern Harmony and Musical Companion,* entered the Billboard pop album chart at #1 and, similar to its predecessor, included a couple of minor hits—"Remedy " (#48, 1992) and "Thorn in My Pride" (#80, 1992).

Amorica (#11, 1994) quickly sold gold, but yielded no singles. In 1995 the group toured in support of the Rolling Stones "Voodoo Lounge Tour" and contributed a song to *HEMPilation,* a compilation album for the National Organization for the Reform of Marijuana Laws. The band, known for its incessant touring, is always worth monitoring, as conflict follows Chris Robinson like flies outside a butcher shop.

AUTOGRAPHS

A CD, LP, magazine cover, ad, photo, or card signed by the entire band: $25-$45*
*Original band members

TOUR BOOKS/PROGRAMS/PASSES

Backstage Passes:
Cloth: $5-$7; Laminated: $8-$10

POSTERS/PRESS KITS

Promotional Posters: $10-$20
Press Kits: $15-$25

USED CLOTHING/EQUIPMENT

Guitar Picks: $10-$25

OFTEN OVERLOOKED MEMORABILIA

Videotapes of the band's television appearances, including *Late Night With David Letterman* (10/9/90), *Saturday Night Live* (3/16/91), *The Tonight Show* (5/27/92), and *Halloween Jam at Universal Studios* (10/31/92); a printout of Robinson's cyberlink chat on America On-Line (12/12/94); an autographed "Slurpee" cup from a Denver, CO, 7-Eleven signed by Elizabeth Juergens - $5; Remedy promotional double-sided display - $10; Remedy promotional pack with Aching Heart medicine, Broken Heart bandage and Remedy thermometer, 1992; Shake Your Money Maker promotional playing cards, dice, poker chips in a velvet pouch; black cloth cap with logo - $20

REFERENCES/BOOKS

The Southern Harmony and Musical Companion: $30

Black Flag/Henry Rollins/Greg Ginn

Original lineup: Greg Ginn, Charles Dukowski, Keith Morris and Brian Migdol*

*Numerous personnel changes. Additional musicians have included: Chavo Pederast; Robo; Dez Cadena; Henry Rollins (Garfield), Born: February 13, 1961; Bill Stevenson; Dale Nixon; Kira Roessler; and Anthony Martinez.

In the early '80s Black Flag emerged as a premier hardcore punk group, driving rhythms like nails into a piece of balsa wood. The band was founded by Greg Ginn in 1977 and has faced numerous personnel changes during its existence. Their most prolific period was between 1984 and 1986, just prior to the group's split. Henry Rollins emerged from the ashes with his own Rollins Band, who attracted significant attention after the 1991 Lollapalooza tour.

AUTOGRAPHS

Group:
A CD, LP, magazine cover, ad, photo, or card signed by the entire band: $15-$25*
*Original band members

Blackfoot

Formed mid-1970s

Rick Medlocke, Jakson Spires, Greg Walker, and Charlie Hargrett

Another band who traveled the Florida bar circuit, Blackfoot followed their predecessors, The Allman Brothers and Lynyrd Skynyrd, and adapted their own variation of the British modified heavy guitar sound. Ironically, both Medlocke and Walker would go on to join Skynyrd following the band's tragic plane crash. A year later Medlocke returned to re-unite the band and release their platinum album *Strikes* (1979) with its hit extracts "Highway Song" and "Train, Train."

AUTOGRAPHS

A CD, LP, magazine cover, ad, photo, or card signed by the entire band: $15-$25*

*Original band members

POSTERS/PRESS KITS

Promotional Posters: $10-$12
Press Kits: $10

Blackmore, Ritchie/Rainbow

Formed 1975

Ritchie Blackmore, Born: April 14, 1945; Ronnie James Dio; Gary Driscoll; Craig Gruber; Mickey Lee Soule*

*Numerous personnel changes. Additional musicians have included: Cozy Powell, Born: December 29, 1947; Tony Carey; Jim Bain; Bob Daisley; David Stone; Roger Glover, Born: November 30, 1945; Don Airey; Graham Bonnet; Joe Lynn Turner; Bob Rondinelli; and David Rosethal.

Blackmore cofounded Deep Purple in 1968, where he and bandmates enjoyed considerable success. Blackmore quickly developed a reputation for being difficult and left the band in 1975. He then founded his own band based around the upstate New York (Cortland) group Elf. The band landed a Top Forty hit with "Stone Cold" in 1982, but personnel changes plagued the band. By the mid-80s the band had dissolved, with Blackmore and Glover returning to Deep Purple.

AUTOGRAPHS

A CD, LP, magazine cover, ad, photo, or card signed by the entire band: $15-$30*

*Original band members

OFTEN OVERLOOKED MEMORABILIA

Early Elf memorabilia

Black Oak Arkansas

Formed 1975

Jim Dandy Mangram, Born: March 30, 1948; Ricky Reynolds; Jimmy Henderson; Stan Knight; Pat Daugherty; and Wayne Evans*

*Numerous personnel changes

Seventies raunch and roll bar band fronted by mountain man Jim "Dandy" Mangrum, whose incessant touring finally led to a cult following strong enough to sell their single "Jim Dandy" (#25) into the Top Forty. The group sustained an acceptable level of popularity during the decade, but personnel changes saw to it that by 1977, Mangrum was the only original member left in the band.

AUTOGRAPHS

A CD, LP, magazine cover, ad, photo, or card signed by the entire band: $10-$15*

*Original band members

OFTEN OVERLOOKED MEMORABILIA

Ain't Life Grand standup: $50

Black Sabbath

Formed 1967

Ozzy Osbourne, Born: December 3, 1948; Terry "Geezer" Butler, Born: July 17, 1949; Tony Iommi, Born: February 19, 1948; and Bill Ward, Born: May 5, 1948

*Numerous personnel changes. Musicians have included Ronnie James Dio; Vinnie Appice; Dave Donato; Ian Gillian, Born: August 19, 1945; Glenn Hughes; Geoff Nichols; Dave Spitz; Eric Singer; Bob Daisley; Tony Martin; Bev Bevan, Born: November 25,1946; Cozy Powell, Born: December 29, 1947; Lawrence Cottle; Neil Murray; and Bob Rondinelli.

The heavy metal scene of the '70s belonged to Black Sabbath. There were simply no peers to the band, whose eardrum crushing volume and black magic pronouncements found little sympathy among members of the media. Those who saw the band live took one look at lead singer Ozzy Osbourne and knew "the apocalypse was indeed upon us."

The band's debut effort landed in the Top Ten on the U.K. album chart, while also pushing its way almost to the Top Twenty in the U.S. Their breakthrough occurred with their sophomore effort, *Paranoid,* whose title track became the group's only Top Twenty hit. The band toured the U.S. relentlessly during the '70s, establishing a solid base of fans that helped sell their albums in the millions of copies.

The band seemed to have an insatiable appetite for the topics of death and destruction, complemented by a fascination for the occult. The image entranced their fans, while Black Sabbath's shows looked more

like exorcisms than concerts. As album sales began to slide in the latter half of the decade, so did band members, whose substance and alcohol abuse was beginning to take a toll. Osbourne, who had sporadically left the band, finally departed for good in 1979, and was replaced by Ronnie James Dio, formerly of Ritchie Blackmore's Rainbow.

Personnel changes would take a considerable toll on the band during the '80s, as album sales continued to falter. By 1986 only Iommi remained from the original lineup. Osbourne had gone on to considerable success and was even joined by Butler for a period. Despite the personality conflicts between Iommi and Osbourne, the band did manage to reunite for the 1985 Live Aid and again in 1992.

AUTOGRAPHS

A CD, LP, magazine cover, ad, photo, or card signed by the entire band: $45-$175*
*Vintage item, all original members

TOUR BOOKS/PROGRAMS/PASSES

Tour Books:
Born Again World Tour '83-'84: $20
Mob Rules World Tour: $20

Backstage Passes:
Cloth: $10; Laminated: $12-$15 (1990-Present)

POSTERS/PRESS KITS

Promotional Posters:
$15-$75

Press Kits:
$35-$75 (1970-1979)
$20-$25 (1980-1989)
$15-$25 (1990-Present)

A Black Sabbath backstage pass (Printed by OTTO)

USED CLOTHING/EQUIPMENT

Guitar Picks:
Terry "Geezer" Butler: $40-$60
Tony Iommi: $15-$35

Drum Sticks:
Bill Ward: $30-$45

OFTEN OVERLOOKED MEMORABILIA

All artifacts relating to the group's vintage performances at the Star-Club (Hamburg, Germany); the novels of Dennis Wheatley; all Paranoid-related items; promotional pieces for *The Black Sabbath Story Volume1: 1970-1978* video collection

Black Sheep

Formed 1983

Dres (Andres Titus) and Mista Lawnge (William McLean)

Best known for their debut record, *A Wolf in Sheep's Clothing* (1991), with creative extract "Flavor of the Month."

AUTOGRAPHS

A CD, LP, magazine cover, ad, photo, or card signed by the entire band: $6-$10

Black Uhuru

Formed 1974

Original lineup: Don Carlos (Euvin Spencer), Rudolph "Garth" Dennis, and Derrick "Duckie" Simpson*

*Numerous personnel changes. Additional members have included Errol Nelson, Michael Rose, Sandra "Puma" Jones, Delroy "Junior" Reid, and Olafunke (Janet Reid).

An enduring act who has remained steadfast in its commitment to Rastafarian politics with its music. Most fruitful from 1977 to 1985, when the group attracted its nation's premier instrumentalists and released their most powerful reggae music.

AUTOGRAPHS

A CD, LP, magazine cover, ad, photo, or card signed by the entire band: $15-$25*
*Original band members

Blades, Ruben

Born: July 16, 1948

Panamanian singer, actor, and activist, Ruben Blades is a multitalented individual who has focused on salsa music, adding his own personal touches, resulting in more widespread appeal. A graduate of Harvard with a master's degree in international law, he began acting before turning to politics and forming a political party in Panama dedicated to social justice. He ran for the presidency of Panama in 1994, but lost.

AUTOGRAPHS

A CD, LP, magazine cover, ad, photo, or card signed by the artist: $10-$20

OFTEN OVERLOOKED MEMORABILIA

Movie memorabilia associated with *Critical Condition, Fatal Beauty, Waiting for Salazar, The Milagro Beanfield War, Mo' Better Blues, The Two Jakes, Mountains Tremble, Caminos Verdes* and *Q&A;* political memorabilia surrounding his Panamanian presidential run in 1994

Bland, Bobby "Blue"

Born: January 27, 1930

Classic blues vocalist and soul singer whose grainy voice has endured over three decades, while drawing from his deep roots in both gospel and blues. A former member of the Beale Streeters, his first successful single, "It's My Life, Baby," was released in 1955. Since his success with "Farther Up the Road" (#5, R&B, 1957), he has over 30 R&B Top Twenty singles,

including "I'll Take Care of You" (#2, 1959), "I Pity the Fool" (#1, 1961), "Don't Cry No More" (#2, 1961), "Turn On Your Love Light" (#2, 1961), and "That's The Way Love Is" (#1, 1963). He was inducted into the Rock and Roll Hall of Fame in 1992.

AUTOGRAPHS

A CD, LP, magazine cover, ad, photo, or card signed by the artist: $15-$50*

*Vintage material

The Blasters

Formed 1979

Phil Alvin, Dave Alvin, John Bazz, Bill Bateman, and Gene Taylor

Los Angeles-based group formed by brothers Phil and Dave Alvin, who have been on the verge of success since their inception in 1979.

AUTOGRAPHS

A CD, LP, magazine cover, ad, photo, or card signed by the entire band: $15-$20*

*Original band members

Bley, Carla

(Carla Borg)
Born: May 11, 1938

Experimental musician and composer, Bley has crossed numerous sects in music, integrating sophisticated elements to complete an often bittersweet parody. A keyboardist and sax player, Bley also both arranges and conducts.

AUTOGRAPHS

A CD, LP, magazine cover, ad, photo, or card signed by the artist: $5-$10

Blige, Mary J.

Born: January 11, 1971

A little bit of pop crossed with classical soul, and then melded with hip-hop has landed Blige on the charts with songs such as "You Remind Me" (#29, 1992), "Real Love" (#7, 1992) and "Sweet Thing" (#28, 1993). In 1994 her album *My Life* (#7, 1994) scored well and was aided by the sales of extract "Be Happy" (#7, 1994).

AUTOGRAPHS

A CD, LP, magazine cover, ad, photo, or card signed by the artist: $10-$15

Blind Faith

Formed 1969

Steve Winwood, Born: May 12, 1948; Eric Clapton, Born: March 30, 1945; Ginger Baker, Born: August 19, 1939; Rick Grech, Born: November 1, 1946, Died: March 17, 1990

The first rock and roll supergroup proved to be a one-album, one-tour, and one-off gig for its established members. The band debuted in London's Hyde Park on June 7, 1969,* before undertaking a sold-out U.S. tour, after which they split. The band's album, with its controversial prepubescent nude girl cover, does contain two landmark cuts—"Can't Find My Way Back Home" and "Presence of the Lord."

The album cover, photographed by Bob Seidemann, is eventually replaced with a photograph of the band (U.S.), thereby creating an instant collector's item. The group's first record was actually a studio instrumental issued by Island Records (estimated at 500) to inform clients of their change of address. (Eric Clapton - Rarities on Compact Disc, Vol. II, Westwood One - promotional.)

*The concert was filmed, with a segment appearing on a Bee Gees television special called *Cucumber Castle*. Unfortunately "Well All Right" was overdubbed with the studio version.

BLIND FAITH - THE TOUR

Normal Set:

"Had to Cry Today," "Can't Find My Way Home," "Sleeping in the Ground," "Well All Right," "In the Presence of the Lord," "Means to an End," "Do What You Like," "Crossroads," and "Sunshine of Your Love." (Est. length: 60-70 minutes)

July: 7 Dates

7/12 - Madison Square Garden, NY; 7/13 - Kennedy Center, Bridgeport; 7/16 - The Spectrum, Philadelphia; 7/18 - Varsity Stadium, Toronto; 7/20 - Civic Center, Baltimore; 7/26 - County Stadium, Milwaukee; 7/27 - International Amphitheater, Chicago

August: 13 Dates

8/1 - Olympia Stadium, Detroit; 8/3 - Kiel Stadium, St. Louis; 8/8 - Seattle Center Stadium, Seattle; 8/9 - PNE Coliseum, Vancouver; 8/10 - Memorial Coliseum, Portland; 8/14 - Alameda County Coliseum, Oakland; 8/15 - The Forum, Los Angeles; 8/16 - Arena, Santa Barbara; 8/19 - Sam Houston Coliseum, Houston; 8/20 - Hemisfair Arena, San Antonio; 8/22 - Salt Palace, Salt Lake City; 8/23 - Memorial Coliseum, Phoenix; 8/24 - HIC Arena, Honolulu

AUTOGRAPHS

A CD, LP, magazine cover, ad, photo, or card signed by the entire band: $50-$200

OFTEN OVERLOOKED MEMORABILIA

Newspaper clippings and accounts of the violence encountered during the band's tour

Blind Melon

Formed 1990

Shannon Hoon, Rogers Stevens, Christopher Thorn, Brad Smith, Glen Graham

Folk rock influenced band Blind Melon garnered accolades for their self-titled debut (#3, 1992). The video for its second single "No Rain" (receiving heavy airplay on MTV) helped it top the AOR, modern rock, and metal charts. Lead singer Shannon Hoon died of a drug overdose in October 1995.

AUTOGRAPHS
A CD, LP, magazine cover, ad, photo, or card signed by the entire band: $15-$25

POSTERS/PRESS KITS
Promotional Posters: $10-$15
Press Kits: $12-$17

USED CLOTHING/EQUIPMENT
Guitar Picks: $25

Blodwyn Pig

Formed 1968

Original lineup: Mick Abrahams, Born: April 7, 1943; Jack Lancaster; Andy Pyle; and Ron Berg*

*The band was resurrected in 1993: Abrahams, Dave Lennox, Graham Walker, and Mike Summerland

A rock, blues, and jazz oriented late-60s band best known for its members than for its work. It was formed by Mick Abrahams after his departure from Jethro Tull, in hopes of creating a more blues-based group.

AUTOGRAPHS
A CD, LP, magazine cover, ad, photo, or card signed by the entire band: $20-$30*
*Original band members

Blondie

Formed 1975

Deborah Harry, Born: July 1, 1945; Chris Stein, Born: January 5, 1950; Clem Burke, Born: November 24, 1955; Gary Valentine; and Jimmy Destri, Born: April 13, 1954*

*Valentine leaves in 1976 and is replaced by Frank Infante. Nigel Harrison is added in 1977.

One of the few successful survivors of the New York punk scene, Blondie opted for the more melodic side of punk captured in their platinum albums, *Parallel Lines* (1978), *Eat to the Beat* (1979), and *Autoamerican* (1980). The bulk of the band's repertoire was penned by Harry and then boyfriend Chris Stein, who played together in the Stilettos, later Angel, followed by Snakes and finally Blondie.

Like many who broke from the New York club scene, they became regulars at CBGB, one of the homes of the burgeoning punk underground. Private Stock released the band's first single "X Offender" and their debut self-titled LP late in 1976. Needing to expand their following, the group headed to Los Angeles, played L.A.'s Whiskey-a-Go-Go (1977), and landed a spot opening for a national Iggy Pop tour. In July of 1977, Valentine departs and is replaced by Frank Infante, while the band is fighting legal battles over the release of their next record.

Plastic Letters (1977) was the group's Chrysalis Records album debut, after which Infante moves to rhythm guitar and bassist Nigel Harrison is added. The following two years will see the band's breakthrough, first with their debut charting single "Denise" (#2, U.K., 1978), followed by *Parallel Lines*' ascension up many worldwide album charts, and finally the success of their single "Heart of Glass" (#1, 1979). The band scored again with "Call Me" (#1, 1980), "The Tide Is High" (#1, 1980), and "Rapture" (#1, 1981). The diverse range of the group's material was making it difficult for other record companies to counter the band's chart success.

The following year will see the band self-destruct, beginning first with legal action presented by Infante, followed by the disappointing album *The Hunter* (#33, 1982) with minor hit extract "Island of Lost Souls" (#37, 1982)—the group's final U.S. chart single, a canceled U.K. tour due to poor ticket sales, and finally the dissolution of the band. Band members now move to solo projects and session work, while Stein launches his own label and Harry turns toward her acting career.

AUTOGRAPHS
Group:
A CD, LP, magazine cover, ad, photo, or card signed by the entire band: $30-$75
Individual:
Deborah Harry: $10-$30

TOUR BOOKS/PROGRAMS/PASSES
Tour Books:
Parallel Lines, 1979: $25-$28

POSTERS/PRESS KITS
Promotional Posters:
1976-1981: $15-$40
1981-Present: $10-$15
Press Kits:
1976-1981: $25-$60
1981-Present: $15-$25

USED CLOTHING/EQUIPMENT
Guitar Picks: $10-$25

OFTEN OVERLOOKED MEMORABILIA
Movie memorabilia from *The Foreigner, Blank Generation, Union City, American Gigolo, Roadie, Videodrome, Hairspray, Scarface, Krush Groove, and The Kilbillies;*

videotapes from their numerous television appearances including *The Old Grey Whistle Test* (12/31/79), *Wiseguy* (3/89), *Mother Goose Rock 'n' Rhyme* (7/12/89), *Intimate Stranger* (1991), *Satisfaction* - ITV (4/8/93), and *Tribeca* (4/27/93); all memorabilia associated with Harry's failed theater appearance: *Teaneck Tanzi: The Venus Flytrap*; promotional license plate (yellow & black) - $25; "I Can See Clearly" promotional static window sticker - $10; key chain - $10; buttons - $10-$15; bumper stickers - $10; fan club newsletters - $12 each; promotional pins - $10-$15; fan club poster - $15; patches - $10-$15; set of fan club postcards - $30

REFERENCES/BOOKS

Blondie by Ann Bardach; *Making Tracks: The Rise of Blondie* by Stein and Harry; *Blondie* by Lester Bangs: $7; no dedicated collector books

Bloodstone

Formed 1962

Willis Draffen Jr., Charles Love, Charles McCormick, Harry Williams Jr., and Roger Durham*

*McCormick leaves in 1981 and is replaced by Ron Wilson. Ronald Bell is also added in 1981.

Known for their pop sound blended with a bit of soul and funk, Bloodstone is best remembered for their single, "Natural High" (#10, 1973), along with R&B hits, "Never Let You Go" (#7, R&B, 1973), "Outside Woman" (#34, 1974), "That's Not How it Goes" (#22, R&B, 1974), "My Little Lady" (#4, R&B, 1975), "Give Me Your Heart" (#18, R&B, 1975), and "Do You Wanna Do A Thing" (#19, R&B, 1976).

AUTOGRAPHS

A CD, LP, magazine cover, ad, photo, or card signed by the entire band: $10-$20*
*Original band members

OFTEN OVERLOOKED MEMORABILIA

Movie memorabilia from *Train Ride to Hollywood*

Blood, Sweat and Tears

Formed 1967

Al Kooper, Born: February 5, 1944; Steven Katz, Born: May 9, 1945; Fred Lipsius; Jim Fielder; Bobby Colomby; Dick Halligan; Randy Brecker; Jerry Weiss*

*Numerous personnel changes. Additional members have included Chuck Winfield, Lew Soloff, Jerry Hyman, David Clayton-Thomas, Born: September 3, 1941, Dave Bargeron, Bobby Doyle, Lou Marini Jr., Georg Wadenius, Larry Willis, Jerry Fisher, Tom Malone, Ron McClure, Tony Klatka, Bill Tillman, Jerry LaCroix, Joe Giogianni, Danny Trifan, Mike Stern, Forrest Buchtell, Don Alias, and Roy McCurdy. Additional changes followed beyond 1980.

Founded by Al Kooper, who ironically was forced out after the band's debut album, the band estab-

lished an easy listening R&B sound mixed with rock and complemented by a brass section. The band opened the door for many groups who would follow, most notably of which would be Chicago. Since the band's inception it was plagued with personnel changes, but finally found a somewhat stable and successful formula in the late '60s, when the band was fronted by David-Clayton Thomas.

Blood, Sweat & Tears (#1, 1969) smashed through the U.S. album charts and spent seven weeks at the top. The album was driven in sales by three hit extracts, all of which managed to climb to #2 in 1969: "You've Made Me So Very Happy," "Spinning Wheel," and "And When I Die." Their follow-up album, *Blood, Sweat & Tears 3* (#1, 1970) was nearly as popular as its predecessor and contained two hit extracts, "Hi-De-Ho" and "Lucretia MacEvil."

By *B, S & T; 4*, interest in the group was beginning to wane, some attributing it to their poor original material. The group's last single was "Go Down Gamblin'" in 1971. Thomas left for a solo career in 1972, while the band (in a variety of formats) became regulars in Las Vegas.

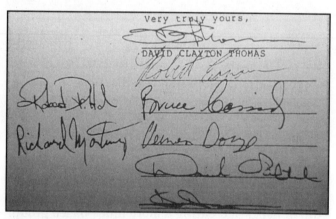

A contract signed by Blood, Sweat and Tears

AUTOGRAPHS

A CD, LP, magazine cover, ad, photo, or card signed by the entire band: $30-$85*
*Original band members from 1969 lineup

Bloomfield, Michael

Born: July 28, 1944, Died: February 15, 1981

A talented guitarist who drew inspiration from his folk and blues roots, having developed his musicianship in Chicago clubs during the early '60s. It was there he attracted the attention of Paul Butterfield, whose band he joined in 1965. His now legendary guitar work can be heard on such classics as Dylan's *Highway 61 Revisited* and *Super Session* with Al Kooper. Bloomfield formed the Electric Flag with Nick Gravenites, but departed after their debut effort, while a similar scenario also occurred when he

was part of KGB in 1975. The artist later turned to movie soundtracks and releasing solo albums, up until his death from an accidental drug overdose in 1981.

AUTOGRAPHS

A CD, LP, magazine cover, ad, photo, or card signed by the artist: $15-$30

OFTEN OVERLOOKED MEMORABILIA

Movie memorabilia from *Medium Cool, Steelyard Blues* and *Andy Warhol's Bad*

REFERENCES/BOOKS

Michael Bloomfield: The Rise and Fall of an American Guitar Hero by Ed Ward; no dedicated collector books

Blow, Kurtis

(Kurt Walker)
Born: August 9, 1959

Best known as a pioneer of rap and for his pivotal song "The Breaks" (#87, 1980), Blow helped push the genre outside of the New York metropolitan area. By the '90s his sound was passé, so he began promoting and performing at classic rap shows.

AUTOGRAPHS

A CD, LP, magazine cover, ad, photo, or card signed by the artist: $10-$15

OFTEN OVERLOOKED MEMORABILIA

All memorabilia associated with the release of "The Breaks" (1980)

Blue, David

(S. David Cohen)
Born: February 18, 1941, Died: December 2, 1982

Best known as part of Greenwich Village folk scene of the early '60s, Blue/Cohen (along with Dylan, Phil Ochs, Fred Neil, and Eric Anderson) forged the New York City folk movement. A better songwriter than musician, his work has been covered by numerous artists including the Eagles, who put "Outlaw Man" on their *Desperado* album. He joined Dylan on his Rolling Thunder Revue and appeared in *Renaldo and Clara* (1978), the film that documented the event. He later died while jogging in New York City.

AUTOGRAPHS

Group:
A CD, LP, magazine cover, ad, photo, or card signed by the artist: $15-$20

OFTEN OVERLOOKED MEMORABILIA

Movie memorabilia from *Renaldo and Clara;* associated memorabilia from other musicians' covers of his work

Blue Cheer

Formed 1967

Dickie Peterson, Paul Whaley, and Bruce Stevens*

*Numerous personnel changes

Best remembered for their heavy-metal approach to Eddie Cochran's "Summertime Blues" (#14, 1968)—one of rock's first metal records—the powerhouse trio of Blue Cheer released a stellar debut album, *Vincebus Eruptom* (#11, 1968). Unfortunately, their future releases drew little attention.

AUTOGRAPHS

A CD, LP, magazine cover, ad, photo, or card signed by the group: $10-$25*
*Original members

OFTEN OVERLOOKED MEMORABILIA

Movie memorabilia from *Medium Cool, Steelyard Blues,* and *Andy Warhol's Bad*

Blue öyster Cult

Formed 1969

Eric Bloom, Albert Bouchard, Joe Bouchard, Allen Lanier, and Donald "Buck Dharma" Roeser*

*A. Bouchard departs in 1981 and is replaced by drummer Rick Downey. Downey leaves in 1985 and is replaced by Jimmy Wilcox. Numerous changes follow.

The band formed in 1969, first as Soft White Underbelly, then Oaxaca, followed by the Stalk-Forrest Group and finally Blue öyster Cult. They became a major draw on the heavy-metal circuit, which also included Black Sabbath and Alice Cooper (both of which the band played with). Extensive touring with a flashy stage act helped build the band a loyal following, which was drawn on for years until the release of *Agents of Fortune*. Their fifth album for Columbia broke, thanks to extract "Don't Fear the Reaper" (#12, 1976), a Buck Dharma composition that is now considered a rock classic in many circles.

Fire Of Unknown Origins (#24, 1981) would be the group's final gold record, driven by the extract "Burnin' for You" (#40, 1981). The group's commercial status slowly diminished during the '80s, although the '90s have seen an increased appreciation of their work.

AUTOGRAPHS

A CD, LP, magazine cover, ad, photo, or card signed by the entire band: $20-$35*
*Original members on *Agents of Fortune* or related material

TOUR BOOKS/PROGRAMS/PASSES

Backstage Passes:
Cloth: $5-$10; Laminated: $10-$12

POSTERS/PRESS KITS
Promotional Posters: $15-$25
Press Kits: $15-$20

USED CLOTHING/EQUIPMENT
Guitar Picks: $10-$25
Drum Sticks:
Rick Downey: $15

OFTEN OVERLOOKED MEMORABILIA
Movie memorabilia from *Bad Channels;* a stack of fantasy novels from Michael Moorcock; promotional bumper sticker, 1984 - $10; "Mirrors" stand-up display - $45; logo pin - $25

REFERENCES/BOOKS
Serious collectors should opt for fan club: Blue öyster Cult International Fan Club, P.O. Box 931324, Los Angeles, CA 90093; no dedicated collector books

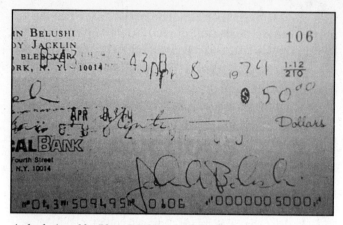

A check signed by Blues Brother John Belushi

REFERENCES/BOOKS
Samurai Widow by Judith Jacklin Belushi; few other resources exist

---

The Blues Brothers

Formed 1977

Jake Blues (John Belushi, Born: January 24, 1949, Died: March 5, 1982) and Elwood Blues (Dan Aykroyd, Born: July 1, 1952)

Essentially starting as a satire to warm up audiences on the television show *Saturday Night Live,* The Blues Brothers became a hit attraction. During the fall of 1977, Belushi and Aykroyd donned '50s-style suits, complete with ties, fedoras and Ray-Ban sunglasses, to front a band made up of talented musicians, including Steve Cropper, and Donald "Duck" Dunn. The group toured to promote their upcoming film, *The Blues Brothers* (1980) and scored hits with "Soul Man" (#14, 1979), "Rubber Biscuit" (#37, 1979), "Gimmie Some Lovin'" (#18, 1980), and "Whose Making Love" (#39, 1980).

Following Belushi's death from an accidental drug overdose, the band split. Their backing band began touring again in 1988 and even released an album in 1992. The Blues Brothers (now with some new personnel, including Belushi's brother Jim) would later perform as part of the half-time show at Super Bowl XXXI (1997).

AUTOGRAPHS
Group:
A CD, LP, magazine cover, ad, photo, or card signed by the group: $400-$1,200*
Individual:
John Belushi: $250-$800
Dan Aykroyd: $15-$30
*Original members

OFTEN OVERLOOKED MEMORABILIA
Movie memorabilia from *The Blues Brothers* (1980); videotape copies of their appearances on *Saturday Night Live;* record bag - $15; "Briefcase of Blues" mobile - $100

Blues Image

Formed 1966

Malcolm Jones, Mike Pinera, Joe Lala, and Manuel Bertematti*
*Frank "Skip" Konte is added in 1968

One of the first acts to add Latin-flavored rock to their repertoire, Blues Image was perhaps best known for their hit "Ride Captain Ride" (#4, 1970)— their lone hit! The Tampa-based group split two years later, with Mike Pinera finally landing in Iron Butterfly, and Lala going on to session work.

AUTOGRAPHS
A CD, LP, magazine cover, ad, photo, or card signed by the group: $10-$20*
*Original members

Blues Magoos

Formed 1964

Ralph Scala, Ronnie Gilbert, Peppy Castro (Emil Thielhelm), Geoff Daking, and Mike Esposito*
*Group disbands in 1968. Group re-forms in 1969: Castro, Eric Kaz, Roger Eaton, and Richie Dickon. Numerous changes follow.

A popular psychedelia band, the Blues Magoos are best remembered for their debut album *Psychedelic Lollipop* (#21, 1966) with extract "(We Ain't Got) Nothin' Yet" (#5, 1967). The band played many prestigious gigs (Fillmores) and tours (Herman's Hermits and the Who), which drives up the cost of the associated memorabilia.

AUTOGRAPHS
A CD, LP, magazine cover, ad, photo, or card signed by the group: $10-$25*
*Original members

The Blues Project

Formed 1965

Danny Kalb, Roy Blumenfeld, Andy Kulberg, Steve Katz, Tommy Flanders, and Al Kooper*

*Flanders departs in 1966. Group re-forms in 1971: Kalb, Blumenfeld, and Don Kretmar. David Cohen and Bill Lussenden join in 1972, while Flanders returns. The group later disbands. The group re-forms once again in 1973.

Key in the development of the blues revival of the late '60s, The Blues Project is probably known best for who played in the band rather than the group's output. They began in the summer of 1965 playing the Greenwich Village scene, before touring extensively and releasing their debut album in 1966. Their sophomore effort yielded two FM standbys ("I Can't Keep from Crying" and "Flute Thing," an instrumental), but the project had trouble projecting beyond the New York metropolitan area and some select minor markets. Personnel changes plagued the band, but numerous members have gone on to other successful endeavors.

AUTOGRAPHS

A CD, LP, magazine cover, ad, photo, or card signed by the group: $15-$45*
*Original members

OFTEN OVERLOOKED MEMORABILIA

Individual members' solo or collaborative work

The Bobbettes

Formed 1956

Helen Gathers, Laura Webb, Reather Dixon, Emma Pought, and Janice Pought*

*Gathers departs in 1961

The Bobbettes were the first female vocal group to have a #1 R&B hit and a Top Ten pop hit with their song "Mr. Lee" (#6, 1957). Several other of their songs became minor hits, such as "Have Mercy, Baby" (1960) and "Dance with Me Georgie" (1960). The band also backed up Johnny Thunders' "Loop De Loop" (#4, 1962) and "Love That Bomb" for the movie *Dr. Strangelove*.

AUTOGRAPHS

Group:
A CD, LP, magazine cover, ad, photo, or card signed by the group: $10-$30*
*Original members

OFTEN OVERLOOKED MEMORABILIA

Movie memorabilia from *Dr. Strangelove*

The BoDeans

Formed 1985

Guy Hoffman, Sam Llanas, and Kurt Neumann*

*Bob Griffin is added in 1986. Hoffman leaves in 1988, while Michael Ramos is added in 1989. Rafael "Danny" Gayol joins in 1991, but departs in 1993.

Often viewed as a cross between the Rolling Stones and the Ramones, the group has done their best to cultivate a loyal following and amass critical acclaim, without having to deal with the stress of commercial success.

AUTOGRAPHS

A CD, LP, magazine cover, ad, photo, or card signed by the group: $8-$10*
*Original members

Bolin, Tommy

(1951-1976)

Gifted guitarist/songwriter who is best known for his work in Deep Purple and the James Gang, although he could play more than rock, as evidenced in Billy Cobham's album *Spectrum* (1973). He died of a drug overdose following Deep Purple's split, just after his solo album *Private Eyes* was released.

AUTOGRAPHS

A CD, LP, magazine cover, ad, photo, or card signed by the artist: $10-$30

Bolton, Michael

(Michael Bolotin)
Born: February 26, 1953

Heartthrob Michael Bolton, who has had record deals since the age of 15, watches Laura Branigan take his song "How Am I Supposed to Live Without You" (#12, 1983) nearly into the pop Top Ten. The result ignites Bolton's career, as stars flock to his doorstep to record his material. His eponymous debut solo record (#89, 1983) gets another look by Columbia, after *The Hunger* (#46, 1987) spins off "That's What Love Is All About" (#19, 1987) and "(Sittin' on) The Dock of the Bay" (#11, 1988).

Soul Provider (#3, 1989), his third Columbia offering, becomes his breakthrough as the album's title cut (#17, 1989), "How Am I Supposed to Live Without You" (#12, 1990), "How Can We Be Lovers" (#3, 1990), and "When I'm Back On My Feet Again" (#7, 1990) all score high on the singles charts. Bolton fol lows up with another successful album, *Time, Love, and Tenderness* (#1, 1991), that includes the title track (#7, 1991), "When a Man Loves a Woman" (#1, 1991), and "Love is a Wonderful Thing" (4, 1991). The latter creates a legal controversy between Bolton and the Isley Brothers, surrounding copyright issues.

Timeless (The Classics) is Bolton's next album and next Number One, driven by extract "To Love Somebody" (#11, 1992). *The One Thing* (#3, 1993) another successful Bolton album, yields "Said I Loved You ... But I Lied" (#6, 1993). The artist's *The Greatest Hits 1985-1995* (#5, 1995) is released and contains twelve hits plus five new cuts, including "I Found Someone," which Cher scored with in 1987.

AUTOGRAPHS

A CD, LP, magazine cover, ad, photo, or card signed by the artist: $100-$150

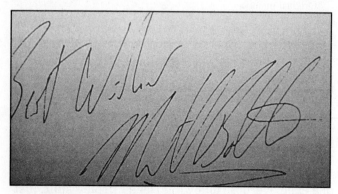

The signature of Michael Bolton

TOUR BOOKS/PROGRAMS/PASSES

Tour Books:
The One Thing, 1994: $15

POSTERS/PRESS KITS

Promotional Posters: $15-$25
Press Kits: $20-$30

USED CLOTHING/EQUIPMENT

Guitar Picks: $10-$15

REFERENCES/BOOKS

A couple resources exist, but nothing that does the subject justice. Serious collectors should opt for these fan clubs: Bolton Behind the Scenes/The Gold Club/The Michael Bolton Official International Fan Club, P.O. Box 679, Branford, CT 06405 ($22 fee/$50 fee/$22 fee). No dedicated collector books.

Bond, Graham

Born: October 28, 1937, Died: May 8, 1974

A pioneer of British R&B, Graham Bond is best remembered for the Graham Bond Organization (GBO), which also included drummer Ginger Baker and bassist Jack Bruce, who formed Cream just

months after leaving the GBO. Bond, like so many others of his era, also played with Alexis Korner's R&B band, Blues Incorporated.

AUTOGRAPHS

A CD, LP, magazine cover, ad, photo, or card signed by the artist: $20-$40

OFTEN OVERLOOKED MEMORABILIA

Periodical clippings referencing his fascination with the occult and his mysterious death

Bonds, Gary "U.S."

(Gary Anderson)
Born: June 6, 1939

Early-60s artist who scored hits with "New Orleans," "School Is Out" (#5, 1961), "Dear Lady Twist" (#9, 1962), "Twist, Twist Señora" (#9, 1962), "Copy Cat" (1962), and "Quarter to Three" (#1, 1961). He is probably best known for the latter, inspired pop star Bruce Springsteen who would later urge the former star to come out of retirement, which he did brilliantly with *Dedication* (1981). Bonds even landed a single with the Springsteen-penned "This Little Girl" (#11, 1981)—his first hit in nearly two decades—and later with "Out of Work" (#21, 1982).

AUTOGRAPHS

A CD, LP, magazine cover, ad, photo, or card signed by the artist: $10-$25

POSTERS/PRESS KITS

Promotional Posters: $10-$15 (1981-Present)
Press Kits: $20 -$25 (1981-Present)

OFTEN OVERLOOKED MEMORABILIA

All items relating to Springsteen are highly sought by "Boss" collectors, thus memorabilia associated with Bonds' comeback may command a few more bucks than you may have anticipated

The Bongos

Formed 1980

Richard Barone, Frank Giannini, and Rob Norris*

*James Mastro (Mastrodimus) is added in 1984

The Hoboken sound of the Bongos ignited a brief flame in the early '80s, primarily as a result of a 1982 tour with the B-52's. Although the tour garnered them a record deal with RCA, their releases put the flame out!

AUTOGRAPHS

A CD, LP, magazine cover, ad, photo, or card signed by the artist: $10-$15

Bon Jovi

Individual:

Jon Bon Jovi: $15-$40   Richie Sambora: $10-$30
David Bryan: $5-$15   Alec Such: $5-$10
Tico (Hector) Torres: $5-$15

Formed 1983

Jon Bon Jovi (John Bongiovi Jr.), Born: March 2, 1962; Richie Sambora, Born: July 11, 1959; David Bryan (David Rashbaum), Born: February 7, 1962; Alec Such, Born: November 14, 1956; and Tico (Hector) Torres, Born: October 7, 1953

A mainstream "rock till you drop" sound, Bon Jovi packaged their act with a New York City shine, then planted it firmly in the rich soil of the Garden State. The band's self-titled debut yielded hits with "Runaway" (#39, 1984)—a previous local hit—and "She Don't Know Me" (#48, 1984). The group followed it up with *7800 Fahrenheit* (#37, 1985), but the album only yielded two minor hits, "Only Lonely" (#54, 1985) and "In and Out of Love" (#69, 1985).

Disappointed by the response, the band opted to remarket themselves and enlisted the help of noted song guru Desmond Child, who pushed them "back to their roots" with their songwriting. The band's next release, *Slippery When Wet* (#1, 1986), played off of the band's good looks and star appeal, and with polished promotional videos, the album went straight to the top of the charts. The album's hit extracts included "You Give Love A Bad Name" (#1, 1986), "Livin' on a Prayer" (#1, 1986), and "Wanted Dead or Alive" (#7, 1987).

The recipe kept working with *New Jersey* (#1, 1988), as the album spun off "Bad Medicine" (#1, 1988), "Born to Be My Baby" (#3, 1988), "I'll Be There for You" (#1, 1989), "Lay Your Hands on Me" (#7, 1989), and "Living in Sin" (#9, 1989). Extensive touring began to take a toll on the band, who took some time off to contemplate their next direction. Jon Bon Jovi released his solo *Blaze of Glory* (#3, 1990) as a movie soundtrack. The record's title cut (#1, 1990) topped the U.S. singles chart, while extract "Miracle" (#12, 1990) also sold well. Amid breakup rumors the band recorded *Keep the Faith* (#5, 1992), which spun off the title track (#27, 1993) and "Bed of Roses" (#10, 1993).

Cross Road: 14 Classic Grooves (#8, 1994), the band's 1994 anthology, yielded "Always" (#4, 1994). During this period Such left the band and Richie Sambora married actress Heather Locklear. *These Days* (#9, 1995) was the band's first studio album in nearly three years, and was supported with some dates on the Rolling Stones tour. Meanwhile, "This Ain't a Love Song" (#14, 1995) became the band's only hit single from their latest release, as Jon Bon Jovi turned his sights more toward acting.

AUTOGRAPHS

Group:

A CD, LP, magazine cover, ad, photo, or card signed by the entire band: $55-$175

Individual:

Jon Bon Jovi: $15-$40   Richie Sambora: $10-$30
David Bryan: $5-$15   Alec Such: $5-$10
Tico (Hector) Torres: $5-$15

The signature of Jon Bon Jovi

TOUR BOOKS/ PROGRAMS/PASSES

Tour Books:
1986 (Japan): $50
Backstage Passes:
Cloth: $8-$15;
Laminated: $20

POSTERS/PRESS KITS

Promotional Posters:
$10-$50
Press Kits: $20-$35

USED CLOTHING/ EQUIPMENT

Jon Bon Jovi, custom pair of J. Chisholm cowboy boots, autographed: $300
Bon Jovi, 1987 Australian Tour shirt owned and worn by Cher (Richie's ex): $150
Guitar Picks:
Jon Bon Jovi: $25-$40
Richie Sambora: $25-$40
Alec Such: $15-$30
Drum Sticks:
Tico (Hector) Torres: $15-$25

Guitar pick used during Bon Jovi "Slippery When Wet" tour

Guitar pick used by Richie Sambora

OFTEN OVERLOOKED MEMORABILIA

Movie memorabilia from *Moonlight And Valentino, The Leading Man, Young Guns II, The Adventures of Ford Fairlane*, and *Netherworld;* videotapes from the group's numerous television appearances including *Late Night With David Letterman* (12/18/91), *Unplugged* (10/29/92), *Saturday Night Live* (1/9/93, 2/18/95), and *Late Show With David Letterman* (12/31/93, 10/28/94); promotional lighter, 3rd LP - $12; copies of fan club newsletters - $8-$12; "New Jersey" map shaped plastic key chain- $35; "New Jersey" mercury promotional map, 1989 - $20-$30; any and all items associated with the controversial original wet T-shirt cover from *Slippery When Wet* - 1986; logo necklace - $15

REFERENCES/BOOKS

Bon Jovi by Bateman, 120 pp.: $8; *All Night Long: The True Story of Bon Jovi* by Mick Wall - $15; *These Days* (large Japanese-only hardcover w/2 CDs) - $125; *Complete Guide to the Music of Bon Jovi* by Dome & Wall - $8; *Bon Jovi*, Ltd. Edition CD-sized book - $18; no dedicated collector books

Bonoff, Karla

Born: December 27, 1952

Closely associated with Linda Ronstadt, who has included many of Bonoff's compositions on her albums, including "Someone To Lay Down Beside Me" and "All My Life." A Grammy award winner, she has established herself as an outstanding songwriter. During the '60s Bonoff was part of a short-lived band that included Andrew Gold and Wendy Waldman, called Bryndle. Her third album, *Wild Heart of the Young,* spun off the hit "Personally" (#19, 1982). "Tell Me Why" was a Bonoff tune that topped the country chart for Wynonna.

AUTOGRAPHS

A CD, LP, magazine cover, ad, photo, or card signed by the artist: $10-$25

TOUR BOOKS/PROGRAMS/PASSES

Backstage Passes:
Cloth: $5; Laminated: $8-$10

POSTERS/PRESS KITS

Promotional Posters: $15-$20
Press Kits: $10-$20

OFTEN OVERLOOKED MEMORABILIA

Movie memorabilia from *8 Seconds*

The Bonzo Dog Band

Formed 1965

Roger Spear, Rodney Slater, Vivian Stanshall, Neil Innes, Vernon Bohay-Nowell, "Legs" Larry Smith, Sam Spoons*

*Bohay-Nowell and Spoons depart in 1968 and Dennis Cowan is added. Group disbands in 1970, but re-forms in 1971.

The Bonzo Dog Band was an eclectic mix of misdirected personalities who desperately needed an outlet for their creativity. The band's performances were more like shows, kind of a cross between Benny Hill and Captain Beefheart with just a touch of Mr. Wizard. "I'm an Urban Spaceman" was a Top Five British hit and was even produced by Paul McCartney—who either fancied the boys or just plain felt sorry for the chaps! Nevertheless, the group appeared in *Magical Mystery Tour* singing "Death Cab for Cutie."

Vivian Stanshall and Neil Innes went on to accomplish bigger and brighter things, the latter teaming up with Eric Idle on projects like *The Rutles,* while the former would take advantage of his narration skills, before dying in an apartment fire in 1995.

AUTOGRAPHS

A CD, LP, magazine cover, ad, photo, or card signed by the group: $15-$35*

*Original members

Boogie Down Productions/KRS-One

Formed 1986

KRS-One (Lawrence "Kris" Parker) and Scott LaRock (Scott Sterling, deceased)

Someone is going to make a movie about Kris Parker's life and I want to be in it. He is a fascinating soul who has picked himself up from his boot straps more than once, survived the death of his close friend Scott LaRock, lived on the streets, pioneered gangsta rap while professing anti-violence, lectured, and even assaulted humanitarian issues with "H.E.A.L. (Human Education Against Lies): Civilization vs. Technology." All while making a little noise along the way on such albums as *Ghetto Music* (#36, 1989) and *Edutainment* (#32, 1990).

AUTOGRAPHS

A CD, LP, magazine cover, ad, photo, or card signed by the artist: $10-$20

Booker, James

Born: December 17, 1939, Died: November 8, 1983

Gifted keyboard artist and session man James Booker was New Orleans' first notable musician to play the organ. He scored a single hit with "Gonzo" (#3, R&B, 1960)—long before Ted Nugent—and worked with some of the best in the business including B.B. King, Little Richard, and Wilson Pickett.

AUTOGRAPHS

A CD, LP, magazine cover, ad, photo, or card signed by the artist: $15-$30

OFTEN OVERLOOKED MEMORABILIA

Other artists' covers of his songs, such as The Clash with their version of "Junco Partner"

Booker T. and the MG's

Formed 1961

Booker T. Jones, Born: November 12, 1944; Lewis Steinberg, Born: September 13, 1933; Al Jackson, Born: November 27, 1935, Died: October 1, 1975; and Steve Cropper*

*Steinberg departs in 1963 and Donald "Duck" Dunn, Born: November 24, 1941, is added. Jackson leaves in 1975 and is replaced by Willie Hall in 1976. A new lineup is formed in 1992: Dunn, Cropper, Jones, and Steve Jordan. Additional changes follow.

An outstanding and gifted act that was essentially the rhythm section of the Stax Records house band, Booker T. and the MG's are commonly associated with their 1962 gold single "Green Onions" (#3) and numerous minor singles including "Hip Hug-Her" (#37, 1967), "Soul-Limbo" (#17, 1968) and a variety of soundtracks including *Hang 'Em High* (#9, 1969). More monumental is their support work heard on recordings of Otis Redding, Sam and Dave, Wilson Pickett, Albert King, Eddie Floyd, and Rufus.

Perhaps the most notable lineup remains: Jones, Cropper, Jackson, and Dunn. Cropper alone holds writing credits on Pickett's "In the Midnight Hour," Floyd's "Knock On Wood," Sam and Dave's "Soul Man," and Redding's "(Sittin' on) The Dock of the Bay," along with numerous MG's works. In 1975 the MG's disbanded, with their members heading in various directions and surfacing on numerous key musical pieces over the decades that followed.

The group was inducted into the Rock and Roll Hall of Fame in 1992.

AUTOGRAPHS

A CD, LP, magazine cover, ad, photo, or card signed by the group: $25-$75*

*Jones, Cropper, Jackson and Dunn

OFTEN OVERLOOKED MEMORABILIA

Associated memorabilia from the numerous sessions the group has participated on

The Boomtown Rats

Formed 1975

Bob Geldof, Born: October 5, 1954; Johnny Fingers; Pete Briquette; Simon Crowe; Gerry Cott; and Garry Roberts*

*Cott departs in 1981

A top Irish new-wave pop act of the late '70s, The Boomtown Rats by 1981 had landed nine consecutive Top Fifteen singles on the U.K. chart, including "Rat Trap" (1978) and "I Don't Like Mondays" (1979), but had minimal success here in the U.S. By the mid-80s the group was overshadowed by the humanitarian efforts of their lead singer Bob Geldof, who even managed a Noble Peace Prize nomination.

AUTOGRAPHS

A CD, LP, magazine cover, ad, photo, or card signed by the group: $25-$75

OFTEN OVERLOOKED MEMORABILIA

Movie memorabilia from *The Wall* (1982); periodical clippings from Geldof's humanitarian efforts; a Monday morning paper autographed by Brenda "I Don't Like Mondays" Spencer - $25; all adverse media attention surrounding the release of "I Don't Like Mondays"; memorabilia from "Do They Know It's Christmas" (#1, U.K., 1984); "Live Aid" memorabilia; videotapes from *The Big Breakfast* U.K. television show; pins - $10-$15

REFERENCES/BOOKS

Geldof's autobiography, *Is That It?*

Boone, Debby

Born: September 22, 1956

Debby Boone, one of four of singer Pat Boone's daughters, is best known for her movie theme song "You Light Up My Life" (#1, 1977), which captured an Oscar for Best Song. She retired from her music career to start a family, but returned to performing in 1982 briefly in a Broadway play and later in a revival of *The Sound of Music*.

AUTOGRAPHS

A CD, LP, magazine cover, ad, photo, or card signed by the artist: $5-$15

OFTEN OVERLOOKED MEMORABILIA

Movie memorabilia from *You Light Up My Life;* playbills or handbills from her theater performances; videotapes of her television performances; doll (Mattel) - $55

REFERENCES/BOOKS

Her autobiography, *Debby Boone ... So Far;* numerous resources exist

Boone, Pat

(Charles Boone)
Born: June 1, 1934

Fifties teen idol Pat Boone was one of the most commercially successful performers of his era. His wholesome image allowed him to capitalize on racy songs by producing cleaned-up cover versions, such as "Tutti-Frutti" (#12, 1956), "Long Tall Sally" (#8, 1956), and "I Lost My Mind" (#1, 1956). He landed on the chart 54 times during a seven-year period, scoring numerous hits including "Don't Forbid Me" (#1, 1957), "April Love" (#1, 1957), and "Love Letters

in the Sand" (#1, 1957). During the same period he also worked on his film career, which would include over a dozen films, including *April Love* and *State Fair*.

His talent also crossed into television. From 1957 to 1960 he hosted his own show, *The Pat Boone - Chevy Showroom* on ABC-TV. Like many teen idols of the era, he could not compete against the British invasion, and failed to land a Top Forty single beyond 1962. From this point on he concentrated on his family and even performed with his four daughters. He has hosted a successful Christian radio show since 1983 and even returned to the stage in 1994, appearing in a production of *The Will Rogers Follies*.

As a '50s teen idol, his image adorned numerous items including many magazines. He was highly collected during his productive years.

AUTOGRAPHS

A CD, LP, magazine cover, ad, photo, or card signed by the artist: $5-$10

TOUR BOOKS/PROGRAMS/PASSES

Tour Books:

1957 Tour Book: $50-$60

OFTEN OVERLOOKED MEMORABILIA

Copies of videotapes from *The Pat Boone - Chevy Showroom* television series (October 3, 1957-June 23, 1960); associated movie memorabilia from his over a dozen films including *Bernadine* (1960) and *State Fair* (1962), Cooga Mooga Inc. souvenirs, including charm bracelet - $80-$135, jewel box - $135, necklace - $100, nylons - $125, phonograph - $500, radio - $150, record tote - $150, socks - $50, sunglasses - $100, wallet - $175, beach towel - $110, lamp - $275; paper dolls (Whitman) - $75; party cups - $50; writing tablet - $20; LIFE magazine (2/59) - $10

REFERENCES/BOOKS

Twist Twelve and Twenty, Between You, Me and the Gatepost by Pat Boone; *The Care and Feeding of Parents* by Pat Boone; *Pray to Win* by Pat Boone; serious collectors should opt for fan club: National Pat Boone Fan Club, Ms. Chris Bujnovsky, 1025 Park Road, Leesport, PA 19533

Bostic, Earl

Born: April 25, 1913, Died: October 28, 1965

Famous alto saxophonist who starred in Lionel Hampton's big band in the late '40s before forming his own nine-piece band that landed hits with "Flamingo" (#1, R&B, 1951) and "Sleep" (#9, R&B, 1951).

AUTOGRAPHS

An LP, magazine cover, ad, photo, or card signed by the artist: $15-$45

OFTEN OVERLOOKED MEMORABILIA

Memorabilia from his years with Hampton

Boston

Formed 1976

Tom Scholz, Born: March 10, 1947; Brad Delp, Born: June 12, 1951; Barry Goudreau, Born: November 29, 1951; Fran Sheehan, Born: March 26, 1949; and Sib Hashian, Born: August 17, 1949*

*Goudreau, Sheehan, and Hashian depart in the early 1980s. Gary Phil and Jim Masdea are added in 1986. Group disbands in 1986.

Boston was formed in 1976 by high-tech guru Tom Scholz. A graduate of Massachusetts Institute of Technology with a master's degree in mechanical engineering, Scholz often dabbled with rock music during his spare time. He sophisticates his new rock sound from the basement recording studio he has built, and his demos impress Epic records executives enough to sign him to a recording contract. Recruiting local musicians, he forms the band Boston, named appropriately after their hometown.

Boston (#3, 1976), the group's first effort, becomes the fastest selling debut in U.S. rock history. The band's sound is deeply entrenched with Scholz's guitar work and complemented masterfully by the vocals of Brad Delp. The album spins off three hit singles, "More Than a Feeling" (#5, 1976), "Long Time" (#22, 1977), and "Peace of Mind" (#38, 1977).

Don't Look Back (#1, 1978), the band's sophomore effort, takes only three weeks to top the U.S. charts. Despite the two years elapsed between releases, the band's unique sound has remained intact, primarily due the perfectionist Scholz. During the first week of November 1978, the band makes its major concert debut, playing large arenas and selected smaller venues. The album spins off three successful singles, "Don't Look Back" (#4, 1978), "A Man I'll Never Be" (#31, 1979), and "Feelin' Satisfied" (#46, 1979).

In 1980 guitarist Barry Goudreau records a self-titled solo effort that charts to #88. Frustrated by the prolonged periods between releases, he quits Boston to form Orion The Hunter. The internal strife is accompanied by contractual disagreements between Scholz and Epic Records. In 1986 Boston resurfaces with *Third Stage* (#1, 1986) on an MCA label after a seven-year market absence. The new album includes the group's first Number One single "Amanda," along with "We're Ready" (#9, 1987) and "Can'tcha Say (You Believe In Me)/Still in Love" (#20, 1987).

The group remains hampered by legal problems, as Goudreau brings legal action against Scholz in 1989 (the suit settles out of court). Following a seven-year legal battle, CBS finally loses its $20 million lawsuit against Scholz in 1990. Meanwhile, the strife does little to enhance creativity. Scholz continues to labor over the band's fourth album. Both Delp and

Goudreau form RTZ (Return To Zero). The group's self-titled debut album charts at #169.

Walk On (#7) is released in 1994 and includes only Scholz from the original lineup. In May of the following year Boston decides to tour again, and in the midst of the event MCA terminates their contract. In 1997, the release of the band's greatest hits, which includes three new tracks, finds Boston back on tour.

AUTOGRAPHS

Group:
A CD, LP, magazine cover, ad, photo, or card signed by the entire band: $60-$100*
*High end reflects vintage signed memorabilia from original lineup

Individual:
Tom Scholz: $25- $30   Brad Delp: $15-$25
Barry Goudreau: $10-$15   Fran Sheehan: $10
Sib Hashian: $10

TOUR BOOKS/ PROGRAMS/PASSES

Tour Books:
1978 Tour Book (U.S.): $40-$50 (scarce)

Backstage Passes:
Cloth: $10-$15; Laminated: $12-$25

POSTERS/PRESS KITS

Promotional Posters:
$15-$50 depending upon scarcity, significance, and size
Press Kits: $20-$30

Boston tour program with paper guest pass, used during "Don't Look Back" tour (Boston World Tour, Inc.)

USED CLOTHING/EQUIPMENT

Guitar Picks:
Tom Scholz: $25-$40
Barry Goudreau: $10
Fran Sheehan: $5

Drum Sticks:
Sib Hashian: $10-$20

OFTEN OVERLOOKED MEMORABILIA

Copies of one of Tom Scholz's patents - $20-$25; Feelin' Satisfied promotional Epic T-shirt - $40

Bowie, David

(David Jones)
Born: January 8, 1947

"The Chameleon" has endured for decades with his artistic prowess and ability to transform himself into whatever image is most desirable at the time. He began his career during the '60s and evolved from folk singer to alien, alien to soul man, soul man to pop star, pop star to artist, artist to contributor, and numerous other variations. His eccentric behavior and selected collaborations (most notably with Brian Eno) allowed him to be accepted as "cutting edge" rather than another rock and roll fossil.

Early Bowie Artifacts

Early Bowie bands included the Konrads, David Jones and the Buzz, the King Bees, the Manish Boys (w/Jimmy Page), and David Jones and the Lower Third. Of these, the latter three each recorded a single. Following his name change in 1966 (to avoid confusion with Monkees' Davy Jones) he recorded three singles for Pye Records before going on to Deram for his self-titled debut album. Any associated items, posters, handbills, advertisements, etc. from these recordings are highly sought by Bowie collectors. During this period he was also performing "The Bowie Showboat" (Fall 1966) on Sunday afternoons at the Marquee, and it was broadcast by Radio London. In December 1967 he also appeared in "Pierrot In Turquoise," a mime production in Oxford. Memorabilia (posters and advertisements) from these two events are scarce.

During the summer of 1968, he briefly appeared in a band called Feathers that played clubs and col-

David Bowie. Photo by Enrique Badulescu. Courtesy of Virgin Records

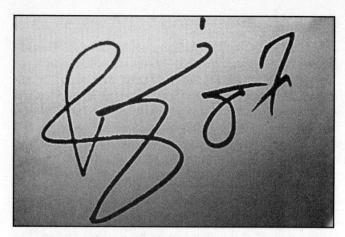
The typically illegible signature of David Bowie

leges before splitting up within six months. In May of 1969 he co-founds the Beckenham Arts Lab, a performance club that occupies the back of a local pub. The following month he will meet Angela Barnett at a King Crimson reception at the Speakeasy Club in London. By the end of August he will have won two song festivals, in Malta and in Italy. All of these events had associated advertisements, forms, and invitations, all of which are collectible. Videotape collectors will want to grab a copy of the BBC-TV astronomy programs that feature "Space Oddity" (9/69) as their theme. During the fall of 1969 Bowie toured the U.K. as an acoustic solo act opening for Humble Pie. Artifacts from this period of the artist's career are extremely scarce and difficult to find.

Changesonebowie - The Seventies Harvest of Collectibles (1970-1979)

Most Bowie collections have a bulk of artifacts from this fruitful period for the artist. The period includes Bowie's first visit to the U.S. on January 23, 1971. This visit did not include performances; it was strictly scheduled as a public relations event only! During the same year controversy erupted over the (U.K.) sleeve variations for *The Man Who Sold The World,* thus any associated items picturing Bowie in a dress are highly sought by collectors. This era saw the artist host his first television special (11/16/73), score his first Number One hit—"Fame" (9/75), and perform the following key tours: 1972 - U.S. & U.K.; 1973 - Japanese Tour Leg & U.K. Tour; 1974 - "Diamond Dogs" North American Tour; 1976 - World Tour; and 1978 - World Tour.

Fame and Fashion - The Eighties (1980-1989)

The decade begins with Bowie press over his divorce from Angela (1980). It will be a decade where he will concentrate on other media, including theater and film. Some controversy will erupt over his promotional video for "Day In, Day Out" (1987), which creates some related collectibles. The year 1988 will

be the first year since 1971 that Bowie will see no chart activity! He will perform at Live Aid during a decade that will see two major tours for the artist: Serious Moonlight '83 World Tour and Glass Spider '87 World Tour. The decade will finish with Bowie's latest project, Tin Machine (1989).

Black Tie White Noise - The Nineties (1990-Present)

During the '90s Bowie marries supermodel Iman (1992), becomes the first human to appear on the cover of Architectural Digest (9/92), and chats on America On-Line (1994), creating some great Bowie collectibles. As for performing, thus far two major tours have happened: the 1990 Sound and Vision World Tour and the 1995 Outside Tour World Tour. On January 17, 1996, David Bowie was inducted into the Rock and Roll Hall of Fame by David Byrne.

AUTOGRAPHS

A CD, LP, magazine cover, ad, photo, or card signed by the artist: $100-$180*
*High end reflects vintage signed memorabilia from original lineup

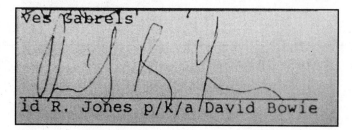
A contract signature from David R. Jones, a.k.a. David Bowie

TOUR BOOKS/PROGRAMS/PASSES

Tour Books:
Isolar 2 Tour '78: $30-$40 (newspaper style)
Glass Spider: $15-$17
Serious Moonlight (European): $20-$22
Sound & Vision Tour: $15
Outside Tour '95 (U.K.): $15-$17

Backstage Passes:
Cloth: $10-$25; Laminated: $15-$40 (1990-Present)

POSTERS/PRESS KITS

Promotional Posters:
$10-$40
depending upon scarcity, significance, and size
Press Kits: $15-$50
Fame (1990): $18-$20

USED CLOTHING/EQUIPMENT

Stage-worn cap and shirt: $1,200-$1,400
Stage-worn jacket: $1,500-$2,500
Guitar Picks: $75-$125

David Bowie backstage pass from The Glass Spider Tour (Printed by T-Bird)

David Bowie backstage pass from The Glass Spider Tour

DAVID BOWIE - SELECTED TELEVISION APPEARANCES

Date	Show
5/20/68	*The Pistol Shot* - BBC2-TV
10/18/73	*The Midnight Special* - U.S. TV
11/16/73	His first U.S. television special - NBC-TV
1/26/75	*Omnibus* - BBC1-TV, airs documentary about Bowie "Cracked Actor"
11/4/75	*Soul Train* - U.S. TV
11/8/75	Conducts satellite interview LA to U.K. with Russell Harty - U.K. TV
4/5/77	*The Dinah Shore Show* - U.S. TV
9/9/77	*Marc* - ITV show with Marc Bolan
9/11/77	*Bing Crosby's Merrie Olde Christmas*
12/31/79	*The Kenny Everett New Year TV Show*
3/2/82	*Baal* - BBC-TV (play)
10/24/84	*The Tube* - C4 U.K.
7/7/91	*Dream On* - HBO-TV
8/14/91	*Wogan* (Tin Machine)
9/6/91	*In Concert* - ABC-TV (Tin Machine)
11/23/91	*Saturday Night Live* - NBC-TV (Tin Machine)
5/12/93	*Late Night With David Letterman* - NBC-TV
12/2/95	*Later With Jools Holland* - BBC2-TV
12/31/95	*The White Room New Year Special* - C4-TV

Note: Bowie also composed television soundtrack to *Buddha of Suburbia*

OFTEN OVERLOOKED MEMORABILIA

Tonight pin (blue & white) - $3; EMI 5" x 8" Let's Dance promotional pad of paper - $10; Serious Moonlight (1983) sweatshirt - $15; khaki button-down promotional Let's Dance shirt - $75; set of three Let's Dance buttons - $4; sheet of 36 scary monster stamps - $2; Sound & Vision white embroidered cap - $10; Sound & Vision tour fanny pack - $5; Labyrinth paper napkins - $1; Diamond Dogs promotional dog tag with chain - $75; Fame '90 EMI-USA promotional tennis shoes; Let's Dance EMI-USA promotional mirror (1983); Sound & Vision Ryko promotional notepad with logo (1989); Labyrinth promotional crystal ball (1986); Serious Moonlight nearly lifesize stand-up with LP bins - $100; Serious Moonlight CD bin display - $40; Stage 3-D die-cut counter display - $50; Tonight 3-D display, die-cut - $40; Tonight die-cut LP & tape bin display - $30; sticker trading cards, Smash Hits, 1985 (U.K.) - $10-$12; *Architectural Digest* (9/92) - $15-$20; *Time* magazine (7/12/83); Tonight 3-D stand-up - $125; Ziggy Stardust necklace - $35; Ziggy Stardust shopping bag - $25; Station to Station ashtray - $120

Singles:

"Alabama Song"/"Space Oddity." RCA pink vinyl with poster BOW-5, 1980 (U.K.)

"Ashes To Ashes"/"Move On." RCA BOW-6, 1980, three different sleeves with four different sets of stamps inside (U.K.)

"Modern Love." Studio (long)/live. EMI-U.S. 12" 12EAS-158, 1983, Rare poster issue (U.K.)

"Tonight"/"Tumble And Twirl." EMI-U.S. promo PB-8246, 1984, with poster (U.S.)

Albums:

Lifetimes. RCA promo LIFETIMES-1, 1983, compilation, numbered on cover with booklet (U.K.)

Sound And Vision. Ryko triple CD plus bow set, 1989, limited edition wooden box with certificate signed by David Bowie (U.S.)

Rock n' Roll Now. RCA promo SPLD-1052, includes Japanese Tour program (Japan)

REFERENCES/BOOKS

David Bowie Out of the Cool by Phillip Kamin and Peter Goddard -$10; *David Bowie Serious Moonlight, The World Tour* - $17; *David Bowie, Glass Idol* by Currie - $15; *The Complete Guide to the Music of David Bowie* by Buckley - $8; *Alias David Bowie: A Biography* by Peter Gillman and Leni Gillman; numerous other resources exist, including some that offer collectibles references, but none have yet to hit the nail on the head; serious collectors should opt for fan club: Best of Bowie, P.O. Box 9103, 1006 AC Amsterdam, Holland ($27 per year)

DAVID BOWIE - SELECTED CINEMA RELATED OFFERINGS

The Man Who Fell To Earth - (1976, British Lion) One Sheet: $17-$35
Just A Gigolo
Christiana F - (German)
The Hunger - (1983, MGM-UA) One Sheet: $15-$22
Cat People - provided the theme
The Falcon and the Snowman - provided the theme
Into the Night - (1985)
Absolute Beginners - (1986, Virgin) One Sheet: $10-$22
Labyrinth - (1986, Tri-Star) One Sheet: $6-$15
When The Wind Blows - provided the theme
The Last Temptation Of Christ - (1988, Universal) One Sheet: $20-$32
Pretty Woman - song included on soundtrack
Cool World - song included on soundtrack
Twin Peaks: Fire Walk With Me - (1992, New Line) One Sheet: $8-$16
The Linguini Incident (1992)
Basquiat

Bow Wow Wow

Formed 1980

Annabella Lwin (Myant Aye), Matthew Ashman, Dave Barbarossa, and Leigh Gorman

Best known as Malcolm McLaren's next project after the Sex Pistols, the group, which also included members of Adam and the Ants, centered around the sexy Annabella Lwin. As is typical with all McLaren acts, controversy was inevitable, this time centered around unpromoted releases and even a nude photo of Annabella. The neatest collector's item was the band's *Your Cassette Pet,* a 20-minute cassette-only release that was shaped like a pack of Marlboro cigarettes. It became the first tape to place on the British singles chart. The band is best known in the

States for their 1982 EP, containing the minor hit "I Want Candy," which also included the photograph of Annabella as the nude woman of Manet's painting "Dejeuner sur l'Herbe" on its jacket.

AUTOGRAPHS

An LP, magazine cover, ad, photo, or card signed by the band: $10-$25*

*Original members

The Box Tops

Formed 1967

Alex Chilton, Bill Cunningham, Gary Talley, John Evans, and Danny Smythe*

*Numerous personnel changes

Memphis soul group that landed hits in the late '60s with "The Letter" (#1, 1967) and "Cry Like A Baby" (#2, 1968). Fronted by the graveled voice of Alex Chilton, the band made few public appearances and scored their last minor hit—"Sweet Cream Ladies" (#28, 1969)—just months before their breakup in 1970.

AUTOGRAPHS

An LP, magazine cover, ad, photo, or card signed by the band: $15-$40*

*Original members

Boyce, Tommy and Bobby Hart

Formed 1964

Tommy Boyce (1939-1994) and Bobby Hart, Born: February 18, 1939

An outstanding songwriting team of the '60s that is credited with over 300 compositions, including most of the material used for the Monkees television show—"Last Train to Clarksville" and "Valerie," and other songs such as "Come a Little Bit Closer" and "I Wonder What She's Doing Tonite." Hart also penned the songs "Over You" (Lane Brody), "My Secret" (New Edition), and "Dominoes" (Robbie Nevil).

AUTOGRAPHS

An LP, magazine cover, ad, photo, or card signed by the duo: $25-$50*

*On a vintage Monkees item

OFTEN OVERLOOKED MEMORABILIA

Memorabilia associated with other artists' covers of their songs; all associated Monkees memorabilia; movie memorabilia from *Tender Mercies* (1982)

Boyd, Eddie

(1914-1994)

Singer, guitarist, and songwriter Eddie Boyd is best remembered for "Five Long Years" (#1, R&B, 1952) and his famous relatives, Memphis Slim and Muddy Waters. During his time with Chess Records he scored R&B hits with "24 Hours" (1953) and "Third Degree" (1953).

AUTOGRAPHS

An LP, magazine cover, ad, photo, or card signed by the artist: $15-$25

OFTEN OVERLOOKED MEMORABILIA

Memorabilia from his years with the Dixie Rhythm Boys and contributions to other artists' records

Boyz II Men

Formed 1988

Wayna "Squirt" Morris, Born: July 29, 1974; Michael "Bass" McCary, Born: December 16, 1972; Shawn "Slim" Stockman, Born: September 26, 1973; Nathan "Alex Vanderpool" Morris, Born: June 18, 1972

A hip-hop quartet that took the country by storm with their debut release *Cooleyhighharmony* (#3, 1991), Boyz II Men's distinctive, sweet harmonies melded the nostalgic sounds of their predecessors with an up-to-date feel on hit extracts "It's So Hard To Say Goodbye to Yesterday" (#2, 1991) and "Uhh Ahh" (#16, 1991). The band's sophomore effort *II* (#1, 1994) also smashed through album charts on the way to the top, yielding hit extracts "I'll Make Love To You" (#1, 1994) and "On Bended Knee" (#1, 1994). Other hits followed, including "Thank You" (#21, 1995), "The Water Runs Dry" (#2, 1995), and "One Sweet Day"—a duet with Mariah Carey (#1, 1995).

With no end in sight for this talented group, collectors should buy now!

AUTOGRAPHS

An LP, magazine cover, ad, photo, or card signed by the group: $75-$150

TOUR BOOKS/PROGRAMS/PASSES

Tour Books: 1995 Tour: $15

POSTERS/PRESS KITS

Promotional Posters: $20-$45
Press Kits: $25-$45

OFTEN OVERLOOKED MEMORABILIA

Movie memorabilia from *White Men Can't Jump* (1992), *Boomerang* (1992), and *Mr. Holland's Opus* (1996); videotapes from their numerous television appearances including *Super Bowl Saturday Night* (1/25/92), *Bob Hope's America Red, White & Beautiful - The Swimsuit*

Edition (5/16/92), *Out All Night* (10/17/92), *Keep Christmas With You* (12/18/92), *The Jacksons* (1/1993), *The Tonight Show* (2/23/93), *The John Larroquette Show* (11/8/94), *Bootleg* (10/21/95), and BBC-TV appearances on *Going Live!, Dance Energy House Party, Top Of The Pops,* and *The O Zone* (all 1992); memorabilia from the first expansion NFL Jacksonville Jaguar football game, 9/3/95 (the group sings the national anthem)

REFERENCES/BOOKS

Boyz II Men Success Story: Defying the Odds by Rita E. Henderson; a few other resources exist; no dedicated collector books; serious collectors should opt for fan club: Boyz II Men International Fan Club, P.O. Box 884448, San Francisco, CA 94188

Bragg, Billy

(Steven Bragg)
Born: December 20, 1957

A creative and witty singer/songwriter whose anthems appeal to the working class, Bragg tackles such issues as political power and poor working conditions with his music. He's best known in the U.K. for songs such as "A New England," "Levi Stubbs Tears," and "She's Leaving Home."

AUTOGRAPHS

A CD LP, magazine cover, ad, photo, or card signed by the artist: $5-$10

Brand Nubian/Grand Puba

Formed 1990

Lord Jamar (Lorenzo DeChalus), Sadat X (Derek Murphy), Grand Puba (Maxwell Dixon), and DJ Alamo

Outspoken advocates of the Five Percent Nation, an Islamic branch, this hip-hop group of the '90s scored with the minor singles "Wake Up" (#92, 1991) and "Slow Down" (#63, 1991) and later with "Punks Jump Up to Get Beat Down" (#42, R&B, 1992).

AUTOGRAPHS

An LP, magazine cover, ad, photo, or card signed by the artist: $5-$10

POSTERS/PRESS KITS

Promotional Posters: $10
Press Kits: $10

Branigan, Laura

Born: July 3, 1957

Eighties disco and pop diva who scored big with her hit "Gloria" (#2, 1982), Branigan also landed hit singles with "Solitaire" (#7, 1983) and Michael Bol-

ton-penned "How Am I Supposed to Live Without You" (#12, 1983) and "Self-Control" (#4, 1984).

AUTOGRAPHS

An LP, magazine cover, ad, photo, or card signed by the artist: $5-$15

POSTERS/PRESS KITS

Promotional Posters: $10
Press Kits: $10

Bread

Formed 1969

David Gates, Born: December 11, 1940; James Griffin; and Robb Royer*

*Mike Botts is added in 1969. Royer departs in 1971 and is replaced with Larry Knechtel.

Be it "adult contemporary," "soft rock" or "breath mint rock," Bread, led by guitarist and songwriter David Gates, dominated this order of music from 1970-1972, with hits such as "Make It With You" (#1, 1970), "It Don't Matter to Me" (#10, 1970), "If" (#4, 1971), "Baby, I'm A Want You" (#3, 1971), "Everything I Own" (#5, 1972), and "Guitar Man" (#11, 1972). The group split up in 1973, with Gates later scoring hits with "Never Let Her Go" (#29, 1975), and "Goodbye Girl" (#15, 1978). The band regrouped in late 1976 and landed another successful single with "Lost Without Your Love" (#9, 1977).

AUTOGRAPHS

An LP, magazine cover, ad, photo, or card signed by the group: $20-$80

OFTEN OVERLOOKED MEMORABILIA

A loaf of Wonder Bread; movie memorabilia from *Lovers and Other Strangers* and *Goodbye Girl*

Brewer and Shipley

Formed 1968

Mike Brewer and Tom Shipley

L.A. folk rockers of the late '60s best known for their hit "One Toke Over the Line" (#10, 1971).

AUTOGRAPHS

An LP, magazine cover, ad, photo, or card signed by the artists: $5-$10

Brickell, Edie and New Bohemians

Formed 1985

Edie Brickell, Kenny Withrow, Brad Houser, Wes Burt-Martin, Matt Chamberlain, and John Bush

Improvisational and impromptu band that is best remembered for their single "What I Am" (#7, 1988) and lead singer Edie Brickell, who would later become Mrs. Paul Simon.

AUTOGRAPHS

An LP, magazine cover, ad, photo, or card signed by the group: $10-$22

OFTEN OVERLOOKED MEMORABILIA

Brickell's solo work, often influenced by Paul Simon

Brinsley Schwartz

Formed 1970

Brinsley Schwartz, Nick Lowe, Billy Rankin, and Bob Andrews*

*Ian Gomm added in 1970

Better known for its members individual output than that of the band, Brinsley Schwartz contributed Nick Lowe to Rockpile for "Cruel to Be Kind" (#12, 1979), written by bandmate Ian Gomm, who himself scored with "Hold On" (#18, 1979), while Bob Andrews and Brinsley Schwartz went on to the Rumour.

AUTOGRAPHS

An LP, magazine cover, ad, photo, or card signed by the artist: $20-$45

OFTEN OVERLOOKED MEMORABILIA

Memorabilia from the group members' individual efforts

Bromberg, David

Born: September 19, 1945

Bromberg, a collector and dealer of stringed instruments, was spawned from the mid-60s Greenwich Village folk scene. He developed a cult following

The signature of David Bromburg

through extensive touring, particularly on the college circuit, while contributing to nearly 100 albums, including for such legends as Bob Dylan, Ringo Starr, and Carly Simon.

AUTOGRAPHS

An LP, magazine cover, ad, photo, or card signed by the artist: $10-$20

OFTEN OVERLOOKED MEMORABILIA

Items associated with his collection of stringed instruments

The Brooklyn Bridge

Formed 1968

Johnny Maestro (Mastrangelo), Fred Ferrara, Mike Gregorio, Les Cauchi, Tom Sullivan, Carolyn Woods, Jim Rosica, Jim Macicoe, Artie Cantanzarita, Shelly Davis, and Joe Ruvio

Best remembered for their hit single "Worst That Could Happen" (#3, 1969) and other hits including "Blessed Is the Rain," "Your Husband - My Wife," and "Welcome Me Love" (all in 1969).

AUTOGRAPHS

An LP, magazine cover, ad, photo, or card signed by the group: $20-$45

Brooks, Garth

(Troyal Garth Brooks)
Born: February 7, 1962

Garth Brooks has blended rock and country successfully by drawing from his often surprising inspirations, from Kiss to George Jones. After spotting him in Nashville, Capitol Records signed him and released his eponymous debut album (#2, C&W, 1989) that skyrocketed up the charts driven by the help of four Top Ten country singles, "Much Too Young (to Feel This Damn Old)," "If Tomorrow Never Comes" (#1, C&W, 1989), "Not Counting You," and "The Dance" (#1, C&W, 1990). He built a quick and large following as a result of his extensive and intensive touring, which was a far cry from what many Grand Ole Opry followers were used to. Inspired by the theatrical groups of the '80s (such as Queen), Brooks was determined to put on a show that his audience would not soon forget.

No Fences (#1, 1990) outperformed his debut album with four #1 country hits: "Friends In Low Places" (1990), "Unanswered Prayers" (1990), "Two of a Kind, Workin' on a Full House" (1991), and "The Thunder Rolls" (1991). His next effort, *Ropin' the Wind* (#1, 1991), became the first album in history to enter both Billboard's pop and country album charts at #1. It also spun off three #1 country hits,

"Shameless" (1991), "What's She Doing Now" (1992), and "The River" (1992), as well as "Rodeo" (#3, C&W, 1991) and "Papa Loved Mama" (#3, C&W, 1992).

In 1992 Brooks released the seasonal album *Beyond the Season* (#2, 1992) before releasing *The Chase*, with hit extracts "We Shall Be Free" (#12, C&W, 1992), "Somewhere Other Than the Night" (#1, C&W, 1992), "Learning to Live Again" (#4, C&W, 1993), and "That Summer" (#1, C&W, 1993).

In Pieces (#1, 1993) also topped both charts and yielded two #1 country singles, "Ain't Going Down (Til the Sun Comes Up)" (1993) and "American Honky-Tonk Bar Association" (1993). Just in case no one recognized his extraordinary commercial sales abilities, he decide to release *The Hits,* which repeated his previous album's chart accomplishments and even spun off the two hit singles "Standing Outside the Fire" (#3, C&W, 1994) and "One Night a Day" (#7, C&W, 1994).

AUTOGRAPHS

A CD, LP, magazine cover, ad, photo, or card signed by the artist: $20-$65

POSTERS/PRESS KITS

Promotional Posters: $15-$40
Press Kits: $25-$50

USED CLOTHING/EQUIPMENT

Guitar Picks: $20-$35

REFERENCES/BOOKS

A few resources exist, nothing that does justice to the singer in my opinion; no dedicated collector books; serious collectors should opt for *the believer* magazine, P.O. Box 507, Goodlettsville, TN 37070

The Brothers Johnson

George Johnson and Louis Johnson

A talented R&B band that successfully crossed into the pop market with songs such as "I'll Be Good To You" (1976), "Get the Funk Out Ma Face" (#30, 1976), "Strawberry Letter 23" (#5, 1977), "Q" (1977 Grammy award winner), "Stomp" (#7, 1980), and "The Real Thing" (#11, R&B, 1981). The Brothers Johnson began their career working with Billy Preston's the God Squad before hooking up with A&M Records and Quincy Jones, who produced their first four albums.

AUTOGRAPHS

An LP, magazine cover, ad, photo, or card signed by the artists: $10-$25

OFTEN OVERLOOKED MEMORABILIA

Their work with Billy Preston's the God Squad, where they contributed "Struttin'" (#22, 1974) to their hit repertoire

Brown, Arthur

Born: June 24, 1942

Best remembered for his band the "Crazy World of Arthur Brown" [which included Carl Palmer (ELP)], his one U.S. hit "Fire" (#2, 1968), and his pyromaniac stage show that included lighting his locks ablaze!

AUTOGRAPHS

An LP, magazine cover, ad, photo, or card signed by the artist: $5-$10

OFTEN OVERLOOKED MEMORABILIA

Movie memorabilia from *Tommy* (1975)

Brown, Bobby

Born: February 5, 1969

The bad boy of New Jack Swing, sex symbol, and former member of the popular New Edition, Bobby Brown scored on his solo debut with "Girlfriend" (#1, R&B, 1986). After linking up with "L.A." and "Babyface," his next album *Don't Be Cruel* (#1, 1988) yielded the extract "My Prerogative" (#1, 1988) along with the hits "Don't Be Cruel" (#8, 1988), "Roni" (#3, 1989), "Every Little Step" (#3, 1989), "On Our Own" (#2, 1989), and "Rock Wit'cha" (#7, 1989).

"She Ain't Worth It" (#1, 1990), a duet with Glenn Medeiros, also added to his string of successful singles, while Brown seemed to be constantly in the media tabloids for a variety of allegations, many of which ceased upon his 1992 marriage to pop singer Whitney Houston. "Humpin' Around" (#3, 1992) and "Good Enough" (#7, 1992) were extracted from his album *Bobby* (#2, 1992), while the artist enjoyed a new addition to his family, a baby girl named Bobbi born in 1993.

AUTOGRAPHS

A CD, LP, magazine cover, ad, photo, or card signed by the artist: $20-$45

POSTERS/PRESS KITS

Promotional Posters: $10-$20
Press Kits: $15-$30

OFTEN OVERLOOKED MEMORABILIA

His previous work with New Edition; copies of the numerous tabloids featuring him and his wife

Brown, Charles

Born: 1922

The master of "ballad blues," Charles Brown's wistful R&B hits of the late '40s and '50s would later become classics, like "Trouble Blues" (#1, 1949), "Black Night" (#1, 1951), "Seven Long Days" (#2, 1951), and "Hard Times" (#7, 1952), along with seasonal favorites "Merry Christmas Baby," and "Please Come Home For Christmas." His material has been covered by numerous musicians, including B.B. King, Sam Cooke, Fats Domino, and Bruce Springsteen.

AUTOGRAPHS

An LP, magazine cover, ad, photo, or card signed by the artist: $15-$40

OFTEN OVERLOOKED MEMORABILIA

Items associated with other artists' covers of his material

Brown, Clarence "Gatemouth"

Born: April 18, 1924

Blues singer, guitarist, and songwriter who has built himself a legendary reputation based on such classic songs as "Mary Is Fine," "You Got Money," "Pale Dry Boogie," and "Okie Dokie Stomp." He has led numerous bands and, as such, has been able to cross over into a variety of musical forms while always going home to his roots. *Alright Again!* won a Best Blues Grammy in 1982.

AUTOGRAPHS

An LP, magazine cover, ad, photo, or card signed by the artist: $15-$35

Brown, James

Born: May 3, 1933

The "Godfather of Soul," James Brown is simply one of rock 'n' roll's authentic disciples. Original, brash, energetic, and talented, this entertainer has influenced nearly every act that has followed. Pure Dynamite!

AUTOGRAPHS

A CD, LP, magazine cover, ad, photo, or card signed by the artist: $35-$75

OFTEN OVERLOOKED MEMORABILIA

Two Spot Nightclub artifacts (Brown lived above the club); Lawson Motor Company artifacts (Brown worked days at the company); Artifacts from the Three Swanees, the Swanee Quintet, and the Swanees, who evolved into the Famous Flames; All memorabilia associated with his album *Live At The Apollo*; Artifacts from his first package tour, "The Biggest Show of Stars" (1963); Artifacts from his second package tour, "The Summer Shower of Stars" (1964); Movie memorabilia from *Ski Party* (1964); Artifacts from the Arthur Smith Studios in Charlotte, North

Globe Poster of Baltimore, MD, printed this poster for a Dec. 10, 1961, James Brown appearance in Olympia, WA. The value is $2,500. From the collection of Hank Thompson.

Carolina; A videotape of ITV's *Ready Steady, Go!* (March 1966); A videotape of CBS-TV's *The Ed Sullivan Show* (May 1966, October 1966); A picture of his first Lear jet; "Don't Be a Drop Out" (Stay in School) campaign flyers (Brown worked on its behalf); Radio station artifacts from stations WJBE (Knoxville, Tennessee), WEBB (Baltimore, Maryland), and WRDW (Augusta, Georgia) - Brown owned these stations by 1968; A videotape of his national TV appeal on April 5, 1968, from the Boston Garden, Boston, Massachusetts (Brown urged restraint and nonviolence following Martin Luther King assassination); Newspaper clippings surrounding his White House dinner appearance (5/8/68); Media artifacts from his Nixon inaugural performance (1/69); Artifacts from his numerous festival appearances including Newport Jazz Festival (7/3/69) and Montreaux Jazz Festival (11/81); An autographed bag of popcorn, or pair of hot pants; Newspaper clippings concerning his misunderstanding in Knoxville, Tennessee on 12/11/72; Movie memorabilia from *Black Caesar* (1973) and *Slaughter's Big Rip-Off* (1973); Media artifacts documenting his battles with the IRS; Movie memorabilia from *The Blues Brothers* (1981) and *Rocky IV* (1986); All artifacts concerning his induction into the Rock and Roll Hall of Fame (1986); Media artifacts surrounding his 1988 troubled marriage and conflicts with the law; Artifacts surrounding his six-year jail term (1988); A videotape of the U.S. cable TV special *James Brown - Living in America* (6/10/91); also CBS-TV's *Party For Richard Pryor* (9/7/91 - recorded); A copy of the Kenneth Cole shoe manufacturer advertisement referring to Brown; A videotape of his

appearance on NBC-TV's *Late Night With David Letterman* (2/27/92, 3/18/93) and CBS-TV's *Late Show With David Letterman* (2/20/96); Copies of his numerous lawsuits against a variety of companies alleging illegal use of his work or likeness; Artifacts, such as tickets and programs, from the numerous award shows featuring or honoring the performer; A James Brown Boulevard street sign; A piece of the bicycle that accompanied a cyclist struck by Brown on 8/28/94; Memorabilia from the 1996 Centennial Olympic Games (7/19/96)

REFERENCES/BOOKS

A few resources exist, nothing that does justice to the singer in my opinion; no dedicated collector books

Brown, Roy

Born: September 10, 1925, Died: May 25, 1981

Jump-blues guru who wrote and recorded such R&B and rock classics as "Good Rockin' Tonight" (#13, R&B, 1948), "Long About Midnight" (#1, 1948), "Boogie at Midnight" (#3, 1949), "Cadillac Baby" (#6, 1950) and "Hard Luck Blues" (#1, 1950). Brown was inspiration to many performers who followed, including B.B. King, Bobby "Blue" Bland, and Fats Domino.

AUTOGRAPHS

An LP, magazine cover, ad, photo, or card signed by the artist: $25-$75

OFTEN OVERLOOKED MEMORABILIA

Associated memorabilia from other musicians who covered his music

Brown, Ruth

Born: January 30, 1928

After Yankee Stadium was named "the house that Ruth Built," the moniker was picked up by Atlantic records, where Ruth Brown stepped into the batter's box and delivered more than 80 songs with plenty of RBI for the label before 1962. In this case, RBI means rhythm and blues included, as Brown released such classics as "Lucky Lips" (#25, 1957), "This Little Girl's Gone Rockin'" (#24, 1958) and "Don't Deceive Me."

AUTOGRAPHS

An LP, magazine cover, ad, photo, or card signed by the artist: $20-$50

OFTEN OVERLOOKED MEMORABILIA

Memorabilia from the off-Broadway musical *Staggerlee* (1986) and Broadway's *Black and Blue* (1989), for which Brown won a Tony Award; movie memorabilia from *Hairspray* (1988)

Browne, Jackson

Born: October 9, 1948

Bohemian singer/songwriter who arrived late to the Greenwich Village folk scene (where he backed Tim Buckley and Nico) but nonetheless began having his songs recorded by musicians of similar style, including Linda Ronstadt and the Byrds. He gained a wider exposure by opening tours for Laura Nyro and Joni Mitchell before releasing his solo self-titled debut, which included the hit "Doctor My Eyes" (#8, 1972). The album, along with the Eagles covering his song "Take It Easy," brought him into the forefront of the Southern California folk-rock movement of the '70s.

The Pretender became his first platinum album, *Running On Empty* scored a hit with its title track and a remake of "Stay" (#20, 1978), and *Hold Out* (#1, 1980) topped the chart during its first week of release. Browne then shifted gears to more sociopolitical themes. In 1993 he seemed to come back to his roots with *I'm Alive,* while continuing to devote considerable time to his numerous humanitarian interests, including Amnesty International, MUSE, and the Christic Institute.

AUTOGRAPHS

A CD, LP, magazine cover, ad, photo, or card signed by the artist: $15-$45

TOUR BOOKS/PROGRAMS/PASSES

Backstage Passes:
Cloth: $8-$10;
Laminated: $12-$15

POSTERS/PRESS KITS

Promotional Posters:
$12-$40
Press Kits: $15-$30

USED CLOTHING/EQUIPMENT

Guitar Picks: $10-$25

A Jackson Browne backstage pass (Printed by OTTO)

OFTEN OVERLOOKED MEMORABILIA

Memorabilia associated with other musicians' covers of his songs; propaganda from the numerous humanitarian causes Browne has been fighting for; "The Pretender" mobile - $45

REFERENCES/BOOKS

A few resources exist, but nothing that does justice to the singer in my opinion; no dedicated collector books

Brownsville Station

Formed 1969

(Michael) Cub Koda, Michael Lutz, T. J. Cronley, and Tony Driggins

Saloon rockers whose combustible live act drew them a cult following during the early '70s, Brownsville Station is best remembered for their rowdy 1973 hit, "Smokin' in the Boys' Room" (#3, 1974).

AUTOGRAPHS

An LP, magazine cover, ad, photo, or card signed by the group: $7-$15

OFTEN OVERLOOKED MEMORABILIA

Copies of Koda's *Goldmine* articles; associated memorabilia from other musicians' covers of their work

Bruford, Bill

Born: May 17, 1949

Bohemian drummer/composer who, like Aynsley Dunbar, seemed to find more satisfaction surfing the "Help Wanted" ads than laying down a foundation with a band. When Bruford has had more than a spot of tea with an act, his extraordinary abilities have shown through, most notably with Yes.

AUTOGRAPHS

Group:
A CD, LP, magazine cover, ad, photo, or card signed by the artist: $10-$30

OFTEN OVERLOOKED MEMORABILIA

His numerous contributions to other bands' and musicians' work

Bryson, Peabo

Born: April 13, 1951

Gifted R&B and pop singer who had his first hit—"Do It With Feeling" (1976)—with Michael Zager's Moon band, and has gone on to tremendous commercial success with hits such as "Tonight, I Celebrate My Love" (#16, 1983), a duet with Roberta Flack; "If Ever You're In My Arms Again" (#6, 1994); "Beauty and the Beast" (#9, 1992) with Celine Dion; and "A Whole New World (Aladdin's Theme)" (#1, 1993), the latter two each earning Oscars for best song.

AUTOGRAPHS

A CD, LP, magazine cover, ad, photo, or card signed by the artist: $15-$30

POSTERS/PRESS KITS

Promotional Posters: $10-$30
Press Kits: $10-$30

OFTEN OVERLOOKED MEMORABILIA

All Disney-related memorabilia is highly sought by collectors

Buchanan, Roy

Born: September 23, 1939, Died: August 14, 1988

Blues guitarist who learned his craft under the watchful eye of Dale Hawkins before working with Ronnie Hawkins and establishing himself as a noteworthy session man. Roy Buchanan was brought into the limelight by an article in a 1971 *Rolling Stone* and a PBS documentary called *The Best Unknown Guitarist in the World*. He played regularly along the East Coast and built a considerable cult following before taking his own life in a Virginia jail cell.

AUTOGRAPHS

An LP, magazine cover, ad, photo, or card signed by the artist: $15-$45

POSTERS/PRESS KITS

Promotional Posters: $10-$20
Press Kits: $15-$25

OFTEN OVERLOOKED MEMORABILIA

The 1971 *Rolling Stone* issue that helped the artist achieve recognition; a copy of the PBS documentary *The Best Unknown Guitarist in the World;* associated memorabilia from his session work

The Buckinghams

Formed 1965

Carl Giammarese, Dennis Tufano, Nick Fortune (Fortuna), Jon-Jon Poulos, and Dennis Miccolis*

*Numerous personnel changes

The middle-class sound of The Buckinghams dominated radio airwaves in 1967 with hits such as "Kind of a Drag" (#1, 1967), "Don't You Care" (#6, 1967), "Mercy, Mercy, Mercy" (#5, 1967), "Hey Baby (They're Playing Our Song)" (#12, 1967), and "Susan" (#11, 1967), before the group slipped into obscurity almost as fast as they arrived.

AUTOGRAPHS

An LP, magazine cover, ad, photo, or card signed by the group: $20-$40*
*Original members on a hit-related item

Buckley, Tim

Born: February 14, 1947, Died: June 29, 1975

Transient singer/songwriter who garnered some level of respect through his performing and affiliations, enough at least to land a record deal with Elektra. He recorded fairly consistently through 1974, but commercial success eluded him, possibly due to

the inconsistent nature of his recordings. He died of a drug overdose in 1975.

AUTOGRAPHS
An LP, magazine cover, ad, photo, or card signed by the artist: $10-$15

Buckwheat Zydeco

(Stanley Dural, Jr.)
Born: November 14, 1947

An apostle of Zydeco, this bayou-born keyboard slinger played with master Clifton Chenier before forming Ils Sont Partis and releasing a series of indie spins that were embraced by critics, including "On a Night Like This." So respected that he has opened shows for U2 and Robert Cray, and even toured with Eric Clapton.

AUTOGRAPHS
A CD, LP, magazine cover, ad, photo, or card signed by the artist: $5-$15

OFTEN OVERLOOKED MEMORABILIA
Movie memorabilia from *The Big Easy* and *Casual Sex?*

Buffalo Springfield

Formed 1966

Neil Young, Stephen Stills, Ritchie Furay, Dewey Martin, and Bruce Palmer*

*Palmer departs in 1967, Ken Koblun is added only briefly before being replaced by Jim Fielder. Young departs in 1967 and Doug Hastings is added. Palmer, Fielder and Hastings then leave, while Young returns and Jim Messina joins the group (1967).

Short-lived, late-60s California pop act best remembered for its members (most of whom would go on to bigger and better things) rather than the group's music. Buffalo Springfield is perhaps best remembered for the song "For What It's Worth" (#7, 1967). See entries for Crosby, Stills, Nash & Young, Loggins and Messina, and Poco for additional details.

Buffet, Jimmy

Born: December 25, 1946

Author, "Master of the Margaritaville Empire," songwriter, "King Parrot Head," singer, performer, and seafaring philosopher extraordinaire, Jimmy Buffet's philosophical and satirical look at life has been encapsulated in songs such as "My Head Hurts, My Feet Stink and I Don't Love Jesus," "Growing Older But Not Up," and "Why Don't We Get Drunk."

Despite other barroom classics, he is still best known for "Margaritaville" (#8, 1977), around which he has built an empire including a record label, and store and cafe outlets in both Key West and New Orleans.

He remains extremely popular and can often be found crusading on behalf of Florida's endangered manatees.

AUTOGRAPHS
A CD, LP, magazine cover, ad, photo, or card signed by the artist: $30-$35

TOUR BOOKS/PROGRAMS/PASSES
Backstage Passes:
Cloth: $8-$10; Laminated: $10-$15

POSTERS/PRESS KITS
Promotional Posters: $15-$40
Press Kits: $15-$50

USED CLOTHING/EQUIPMENT
Guitar Picks: $20-$35

OFTEN OVERLOOKED MEMORABILIA
Movie memorabilia from *Rancho Deluxe* (1974), *FM* (1977), and *The Firm* (1993); copies of his official fanzine *Coconut Telegraph* (First Issue February 1985); a piece of sponge cake - $3; a piece from the original Henry Flagler East Coast Railroad bridge; a relic from 704 Waddell Street in Key West; a piece from Buffet's 1953 Chevy pickup he bought from the Monroe County Glass & Mirror Co.; a relic from the Old Anchor Inn (closed in the early '70s); a cocktail napkin from the Pier House (Key West); Buffet-related periodicals like *Rolling Stone* (10/4/79), *Florida Trend* (5/91), and *Esquire Sportsman* (Autumn 1992); a pack of matches from the Full Moon Saloon (Key West); any and all associated items from Margaritaville (500 Duval Street, Key West); memorabilia from the Miami Miracles baseball team; Corona Beer advertisements relating to Buffet, a cocktail napkin from Capt. Tony's Saloon - the original Sloppy Joes, located at 428 Greene St., Key West, Florida

REFERENCES/BOOKS
Tales From Margaritaville by Jimmy Buffet (1989); *Where is Joe Merchant?* by Jimmy Buffet (1992); children's books *The Jolly Mon* (1988) and *Trouble Dolls* (1991) by Buffet and his daughter Savanah Jane; *The Jimmy Buffet Scrap Book* by Mark Humphrey with Harris Lewine - $20

The Buggles

Formed 1979

Trevor Horn and Geoffrey Downes

Best known for "Video Killed the Radio Star," the first video ever aired by MTV, this electro-pop duo biggest surprise hit was joining the band Yes.

AUTOGRAPHS
A CD, LP, magazine cover, ad, photo, or card signed by the group: $8-$25*
*Videotape autographed from "VKTRS"

OFTEN OVERLOOKED MEMORABILIA
All associated memorabilia from Yes and Asia

Burdon, Eric

Born: May 11, 1941

The frontman of the Animals who became a major player in the British Invasion, Eric Burdon went on to declare War following his stint with the Animals, but after a second album with the group, he was just too damn tired to continue, so War went on without him. The group did manage to "Spill the Wine" (#3, 1970) however, before Burdon's departure.

Burdon lived through the '70s and '80s, trying his luck at acting with mixed attempts at reuniting the Animals. So far he has also lived through the '90s, still forming bands by resurrecting '60s rock fossils, in hopes of, well, living through the '90s.

AUTOGRAPHS
A CD, LP, magazine cover, ad, photo, or card signed by the artist: $5-$25

Autograph of Animal Eric Burden

OFTEN OVERLOOKED MEMORABILIA
Movie memorabilia from his many European movies, including *Come Back* (German); videotapes of his television appearances, such as *China Beach* (1990)

REFERENCES/BOOKS
I Used to Be An Animal, But I'm All Right Now, Burdon's autobiography

Burke, Solomon

Born: 1936

Talented pioneer of soul music with gospel roots, Solomon Burke scored with R&B crossover hits in the early '60s, such as "Cry To Me" (#44, 1962), "If You Need Me" (#49, 1963), "You're Good For Me" (#49, 1963), "Got to Get You Off My Mind" (#22, 1965), and "Tonight's the Night" (#28, 1965). He continued to land hits on the R&B charts, but realizing his powerful voice lends itself beautifully to gospel music, he released *Take Me, Shake Me,* which was critically acclaimed and a recipient of a 1981 Grammy nomination.

AUTOGRAPHS
A CD, LP, magazine cover, ad, photo, or card signed by the artist: $5-$15

OFTEN OVERLOOKED MEMORABILIA
Movie memorabilia from *The Big Easy* (1987)

Burnett, T Bone

John Burnett, Born: January 14, 1948

Singer and songwriter who has eclipsed his previous recording efforts with his talented production work for such artists as Elvis Costello, Los Lobos, and Counting Crows. Former guitarist in Dylan's Rolling Thunder Revue, Burnett's songwriting has also won praise from many including Pete Townshend and Mark Knopfler.

AUTOGRAPHS
A CD, LP, magazine cover, ad, photo, or card signed by the artist: $5-$25

OFTEN OVERLOOKED MEMORABILIA
Memorabilia from his numerous productions; artifacts from the Rolling Thunder Revue

Burnette, Billy

Born: May 8, 1953

Dorsey Burnette's son, and child prodigy, Billy made his singing debut at age seven and quickly found a home in the music business. He sang with Delaney Bramlett in the '70s; watched numerous musicians cover his songs, including Loretta Lynn, Conway Twitty, and Ray Charles; released a few albums; and in 1987 joined Fleetwood Mac, replacing Lindsey Buckingham.

AUTOGRAPHS
A CD, LP, magazine cover, ad, photo, or card signed by the artist: $5-$15

OFTEN OVERLOOKED MEMORABILIA
Associated memorabilia from other musicians' covers of his songs; promotional pin die-cut & logo - $15

Burnette, Dorsey

Born: December 28, 1932, Died: August 19, 1979

Member of brother Johnny's Rock 'n' Roll Trio. See listing below.

AUTOGRAPHS
A CD, LP, magazine cover, ad, photo, or card signed by the artist: $10-$20

OFTEN OVERLOOKED MEMORABILIA
Associated memorabilia from other musicians' covers of his songs

Burnette, Johnny

Born: March 25, 1934, Died: August 1, 1964

Founder of the Rock 'n' Roll Trio, who after scoring brief fame in 1955-56, went on to write successful songs for Rick Nelson, while recording hits such as "Tall Oak Tree" (#23, 1960) and "Hey Little One." He played the teen idol role during 1960, and scored a hit with "You're Sixteen."

AUTOGRAPHS
A CD, LP, magazine cover, ad, photo, or card signed by the artist: $25-$110

OFTEN OVERLOOKED MEMORABILIA
Associated memorabilia from other musicians' covers of his songs

Burnette, Rocky

Born: June 12, 1953

Son of Johnny Burnette, Rocky is best remembered for his hit "Tired of Toein' the Line" (#8, 1980).

AUTOGRAPHS
An LP, magazine cover, ad, photo, or card signed by the artist: $5-$10

OFTEN OVERLOOKED MEMORABILIA
Associated memorabilia from other musicians' covers of his songs

Burning Spear

(Winston Rodney)
Born: March 1, 1945

One of reggae's bona fide mystic men, Burning Spear is best known for his Jamaican hit "Marcus Garvey" (1974) along with a handful of minor hits.

AUTOGRAPHS
An LP, magazine cover, ad, photo, or card signed by the artist: $5-$10

OFTEN OVERLOOKED MEMORABILIA
Movie memorabilia from *Rockers* (1980); a videotape of the documentary *Reggae Sunsplash* (1980)

Bush, Kate

Born: July 30, 1958

British singer/songwriter whose gifted four-octave range has lent itself nicely to numerous hits including "Wuthering Heights" (#1, U.K.), "Running Up That Hill" (#30, 1985), "The Man With The Child in His Eyes" (#85, 1987), "Wow," and "Cloudbusting." Bush has yet to achieve the broad-based popularity in the U.S. that she has so gallantly earned in the U.K., Western Europe, and Australia. So talented that she has often been referred to as an inspiration for both Sinead O'Connor and Tori Amos, Bush has expanded her abilities to include the studio, as evidenced by the album *Hounds of Love* (#30, 1985). She draws significant inspiration from literature, which has attracted more and more fans to her work. Because her exposure has been relatively limited in the U.S., many of her collectibles can be found at a relatively inexpensive price. Well worth keeping an eye on!

AUTOGRAPHS
A CD, LP, magazine cover, ad, photo, or card signed by the artist: $25-$75

TOUR BOOKS/PROGRAMS/PASSES
Backstage Passes:
Cloth: $6-$10; Laminated: $10-$15

POSTERS/PRESS KITS
Promotional Posters: $10-$30
Press Kits: $15-$25

OFTEN OVERLOOKED MEMORABILIA
Associated memorabilia from other musicians' covers of her songs, also from her collaborations; three unique U.K. album packages can be found:
Hounds of Love EMI promotional box set, 1985, includes album, glossies (3), biography, and autographed cover, placed in a carry bag and tied up with a pink ribbon
The Sensual World EMI promotional box set, 1989, includes CD, cassette, biography, and lyric book
The Red Shoes EMI promotional CD and video box set, 1993, includes red fountain pen and two parchment-type scrolls tied with a red ribbon

REFERENCES/BOOKS
The Illustrated Collector's Guide to Kate Bush by Robert Goodwin—a good place to begin! Serious collectors should opt for fan club: American Kate Bush Society, Ernest Heramia, 167 Central Avenue, E. Providence, RI 02914 ($10 fee); also Homeground: The International Kate Bush Fanzine, P.O. Box 176, Orpington, Kent BR5 3NA, England.

The Bush Tetras

Formed 1979
Pat Place, Laura Kennedy, Dee Pop, and Cynthia Sley*
*Kennedy and Dee Pop leave in 1983

"New wave" remnant best remembered for their club anthem "Too Many Creeps" before fizzling out in the mid-80s.

AUTOGRAPHS
A CD, LP, magazine cover, ad, photo, or card signed by the artist: $5-$10

Butler, Jerry

Born: December 8, 1939

Talented soul singer who, along with Curtis Mayfield, defined the musical boundaries of Chicago as members of the Impressions. Butler has landed hits with "For Your Precious Love" (#11, 1958) and "He Will Break Your Heart" (#7, 1960). He later teamed up with Gamble and Huff for "The Iceman Cometh" and "Ice on Ice," both of which became '60s soul hallmarks. "Never Give Up" (#20, 1968), "Hey, Western Union Man" (#16, 1968) and "Only the Strong Survive" (#4, 1969) rounded out the rest of his decade hits.

The Impressions were inducted into the Rock and Roll Hall of Fame in 1991.

AUTOGRAPHS

An LP, magazine cover, ad, photo, or card signed by the artist: $10-$25

OFTEN OVERLOOKED MEMORABILIA

Associated memorabilia from other musicians' covers of his songs

Paul Butterfield Blues Band/ Paul Butterfield

Formed 1963

Paul Butterfield (1942-1987), James Arnold, Sam Lay, Elvin Bishop, Mark Naftalin, and Mike Bloomfield (1944 - 1981)*

*Numerous personnel changes

Singer and harmonica player who apprenticed in Chicago's South Side clubs with many blues legends such as Howlin' Wolf, Buddy Guy, and Otis Rush, Paul Butterfield was a catalyst of the '60s American blues revival. He played as a part of the Salt and Pepper Shakers, the South Side Olympic Blues Team, and finally in 1963 as the Paul Butterfield Blues Band. He backed Dylan at the 1965 Newport Folk Festival during his controversial "plug-in." By the late '60s and early '70s he was shifting more toward R&B, while contributing to numerous efforts including Muddy Waters' 1969 album *Father and Sons*.

The '70s saw him making appearances with The Band at "The Last Waltz" (1976) and even touring with Levon Helm's RCO All Stars and the Danko-Butterfield Band. During the '80s he was stricken by an illness that led to numerous operations and finally his death in 1987.

AUTOGRAPHS

An LP, magazine cover, ad, photo, or card signed by the group: $45-$125*
*Original band members

OFTEN OVERLOOKED MEMORABILIA

All associated memorabilia from his numerous collaborations and contributions; movie memorabilia from *The Last Waltz* (1976)

Butthole Surfers

Formed 1981

Gibby Haynes and Paul Leary*

*King Coffey and Theresa Nervosa are added in 1983, while Jeff Pinkus is added in 1986. Nervosa departs in 1989.

Gastrointestinal, avant-garde late '70s no wave metal maulers who delight in turning the stomachs of their followers through the hyperbole and misgivings of singer Gibby Haynes. Marching to their anthem "The Shah Sleeps in Lee Harvey's Grave," one can only wonder what members of their Deadhead-like following do during daylight hours. The group gained some recognition through their appearance on the first Lollapalooza Tour in 1991, at least enough to convince Capitol to sign the band. *Independent Worm Saloon* was their major label debut, and was produced by Zeppelin bassist John Paul Jones, who allegedly changed his name to "Pope John Paul is really Jonesin'" following the whole experience.

AUTOGRAPHS

A CD, LP, magazine cover, ad, photo, or card signed by the group: $15-$35*
*Original band members

POSTERS/PRESS KITS

Promotional Posters: $10-$15
Press Kits: $15

The Buzzcocks

Formed 1975

Howard Devoto (Trafford), Steve Diggle, John Maher, and Pete Shelley (McNeish)*

*Numerous personnel changes

Late-70s new wave singles band whose energetic tempos and aggressive guitar riffs landed them an impressive cult following on the London club scene. Best known for their *Spiral Scratch* four-song EP (credited as Britain's first indie punk recording) and as an inspiration for many who followed, including Kurt Cobain. In 1993 the band re-formed and released the well-received album *Trade Test Transmissions*.

AUTOGRAPHS

A CD, LP, magazine cover, ad, photo, or card signed by the group: $15-$30*
*Original band members

OFTEN OVERLOOKED MEMORABILIA

Outer plastic carrier bag from *A Different Kind of Tension*, 1980: $12

The Byrds

Formed 1964

(James) Roger McGuinn, Born: July 13, 1942; Chris Hillman, Born: December 4, 1942; (Harold) Gene Clark (1941-1991); David Crosby (Van Cortland), Born: August 14, 1941; Michael Clarke (1944-1993)*

*Clark departs in 1966, while Clarke and Crosby both leave in 1967. Kevin Kelley and Gram Parsons are added. Numerous personnel changes follow.

Folk rock pioneers whose hallmark harmonies, guitar hooks, and screaming Rickenbacker riffs have inspired many rock bands for generations. The Byrds are best remembered for songs such as "Mr. Tambourine Man" (#1, 1965), "Turn!, Turn! Turn!" and "Eight Miles High" (#14, 1966). Formed in 1964, by the summer of 1966 Gene Clark had left, Crosby followed in 1967, and by October 1968, McGuinn remained as the only original member and kept the band alive until 1973. The band did enjoy modest success during their latter existence and an occasional noteworthy tune such as "Chestnut Mare." The band re-grouped in 1973 for a one-off album, while the closest thing to a reunion that followed was the group McGuinn, Clark, and Hillman (1979) that had one minor hit, "Don't You Write Her Off" (#33, 1979).

In January 1991 The Byrds were inducted into the Rock and Roll Hall of Fame. The original members constantly battled over the legal rights to the name, which ended up in the hands of McGuinn, Hillman, and Crosby. Gene Clark died in 1991 and Michael Clarke passed away in 1993.

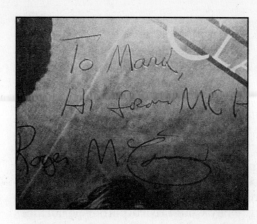

The signature of Byrd Roger McGuinn (1979)

OFTEN OVERLOOKED MEMORABILIA

All associated memorabilia from band members' numerous collaborations and contributions; nightclub artifacts from Ciro's (Los Angeles); videotapes from the group's numerous television appearances, including *Hullabaloo* (5/11/65), *Shindig* (9/16/65), *TNT Award Show* (12/65), *Inside Pop: The Rock Revolution* (4/25/67) and *The Smothers Brothers Comedy Hour* (10/22/67); any controversial periodical clippings referencing the song "Eight Miles High"; Monterey International Pop Festival (1967) and Newport Pop Festival (1968, 1969) artifacts; movie memorabilia from *Don't Make Waves* (1967), *Easy Rider* (1969) and *Candy* (1969); all memorabilia from the group's final live appearance on February 24, 1973 at the Capitol Theatre in Passaic, New Jersey; artifacts from Bob Dylan's "Rolling Thunder Revue" - includes McGuinn, and all McGuinn, Clark & Hillman memorabilia

AUTOGRAPHS

A CD, LP, magazine cover, ad, photo, or card signed by the group: $50-$160*
*Original band members

Early Contract signed by the Byrds

The signature of Byrd Gene Clark (1979)

The signature of Byrd Roger McGuinn (1979)

Byrne, David

Born: May 14, 1952

A highly creative, eclectic, multimedia artist whose first work outside the Talking Heads was the critically acclaimed *My Life in the Bush of Ghosts*, produced by Brian Eno. He has since gone on to theatrical collaborations, movie soundtracks, and numerous collaborations. "Rock's Renaissance Man" has also contributed his production skills to numerous efforts including the B-52's, and has had his photographs published and exhibited worldwide.

AUTOGRAPHS

A CD, LP, magazine cover, ad, photo, or card signed by the artist: $15-$40

POSTERS/PRESS KITS

Promotional Posters: $15-$30
Press Kits: $20-$45

OFTEN OVERLOOKED MEMORABILIA

Memorabilia from the theatrical production *The Catherine Wheel* (1981); movie memorabilia from *True Stories* (1986), *Married to the Mob* (1988), and *The Last Emperor* (1988)—won an Oscar Award; a copy of the film documentary *Ile Aiye (The House of Life)* (1989); the issue of *Time* magazine featuring Byrne on the cover

C C Music Factory

Formed 1990

Robert Clivillés, David Cole (1962-1995), Zelma Davis, and Freedom Williams

One of the premier producer/songwriter teams to emerge during the early '90s, Robert Clivillés and David Cole set their sights on making original recordings using keyboards and a computer to handle the arranging. They would recruit other performers to lay down vocal tracks, their breakthrough happening when they landed the trio Seduction. The group's debut effort, *Gonna Make You Sweat* (#2, 1991), spun off a chart-topping title track (#1), along with the single "Here We Go" (#3, 1991). Unfortunately for the group, a staged video and the lack of appropriate album liner notes (not fully recognizing the efforts of Martha Wash, Deborah Cooper, and rapper Freedom Williams) landed the band in hot water. While legal battles ensued, "Things That Make You Go Hmmm..." (#4, 1992) was extracted off the group's *Greatest Remixes Vol. 1* (#87, 1992).

Clivillés and Cole later went on to win a Grammy for their work on Whitney Houston's soundtrack to *The Bodyguard*. On January 24, 1995, Cole died of complications from spinal meningitis.

AUTOGRAPHS

A CD, LP, magazine cover, ad, photo, or card signed by the group: $30-$50

POSTERS/PRESS KITS

Promotional Posters: $10-$20
Press Kits: $15-$20

OFTEN OVERLOOKED MEMORABILIA

Movie memorabilia from *The Bodyguard*

C, Roy

(Roy Hammond)
Born: 1943

Roy C's first professional music success came as lead singer of the Genies, who in 1959 had the minor R&B hit "Who's That Knockin." He had joined the Long Island -based band in 1956 and was with them when they split up in 1960.

"Shotgun Wedding" (#14, R&B, 1965) started C's solo career off on the right foot. He formed his own record company, Alaga, and landed on the charts in 1972 with "Got To Get Enough." "Honey I Still Love You," penned and produced by C for the Mark IV in 1972, reinforced Mercury Records' decision to sign the artist. The company repackaged his early singles and released them in album form.

"Don't Blame The Man" (1973), "Loneliness Had Got A Hold of Me" (1974), and "Love Me Till Tomorrow Comes" (1975) were just a few of his trademark classics released during the early '70s.

AUTOGRAPHS

An LP, magazine cover, ad, photo, or card signed by the artist: $5-$10

Cabaret Voltaire

Formed 1973

Stephen Mallinder, Richard Kirk, Christopher Watson

Cabaret Voltaire was one of the premier bands driving the electronic-industrial dance movement in the late '80s and early '90s. Originating out of the blue-collar city of Sheffield and inspired by the work of Brian Eno, they blended everyday sounds with a variety of musical textures. Their name evolved out of the dadaist club formed in 1917 by Hugo Ball, but their attitude was purely modern.

A very prolific group, they peaked artistically with 1982's *2 x 45*. Of the original trio, Christopher Watson departed in 1981 and later turned up in the avant-garde Hafler Trio, while Stephen Mallinder cut a few solo discs, and Richard Kirk teamed up with Peter Hope for a 1987 release. Although the group never had a major hit, they had a strong cult following.

AUTOGRAPHS

A CD, LP, magazine cover, ad, photo, or card signed by the group: $5-$15

The Cadets

Formed 1954

Original Lineup: Ted Taylor, William "Dub" Jones, Aaron Collins, Willie Davis

This band was known both as the Jacks and the Cadets. As the Jacks they released "Why Don't You Write Me" (#4, R&B, 1955) and as the Cadets they charted with "Stranded in the Jungle" (#15, 1956). The original lineup broke up in the late '50s, and Taylor went on to a successful solo career before he and his wife were killed in an automobile accident. Jones went on to join the Coasters, while both Collins and Davis continued with a new lineup.

AUTOGRAPHS

An LP, magazine cover, ad, photo, or card signed by the group: $17-$40

The Cadillacs

Formed 1953

Prominent Lineup: Earl Carroll, Born: November 2, 1937; Robert Phillips; LaVerne Drake; Johnny "Gus" Willingham; James "Poppa" Clark

Originally the Carnations, the group often gathered informally in Harlem to sing together. The Cadillacs formed in 1953 and soon hooked up with manager Esther Navaroo, who convinced them to record a song she had penned called "Gloria." They quickly established not only a reputation for their outstanding sound, but also for their stage appeal. Tightly choreographed numbers, in flamboyant costumes, soon became their hallmark and a precursor of the Motown sound that would follow.

"Speedo" (#17, 1956), a very uptempo number accompanied by scat harmonies, was the first of a handful of singles the group would enjoy. "Peek-a-Boo (#28, 1959), and "What You Bet" (#30, R&B, 1961), were later followed by "Zoom," "Woe Is Me," and "Rudolph the Red-Nosed Reindeer" (1956).

In 1957 the band split into two different groups with the same name, the Cadillacs. They continued to record and release singles, but by 1963 interest in the band had dwindled. In 1961 Earl Carroll went on to the Coasters. The band continued into the '60s before splitting up. They re-formed briefly in the early '80s in a lineup that also included Carroll and Phillips.

AUTOGRAPHS

A CD, LP, magazine cover, ad, photo, or card signed by the group: $25-$60

Cale, J.J.

(Jean Jacques Cale)
Born: December 5, 1938

Cale took up the guitar at a very early age and performed with numerous bands in high school. In the late '50s he quits the U.S. Air Force and heads west with his friend Leon Russell to seal their fame and fortune in the music business. He goes to Nashville to try his luck as a country singer, but returns to Los Angeles and again teams up with Russell and some friends, playing the local circuit while also arranging and producing.

In 1967 he releases *A Trip Down Sunset Strip* (a psychedelic reflection album) under the name the Leathercoated Minds. A year later he decides to head home to Oklahoma to build his own home studio.

Cale then signs to the fledgling Shelter Records, established by buddy Russell and producer Denny Cordell. In 1970 he begins recording his first solo album, *Naturally* (#51, 1972), which contains the hit "Crazy Mama" (#22, 1972). Just prior to the album's release, Eric Clapton takes the Cale-penned "After Midnight" (#18, 1970) into the Top Twenty on the U.S. singles chart.

Really (#92, 1973), and *Ohio* (#128, 1974) are his second and third albums, but it's *Troubadour* (#84, 1976) that garners more attention, partially due to the Cale penned-song "Cocaine," later covered by Eric Clapton (#30, 1980). Criticized for his shyness, Cale refrains from extensive touring or promotion in support of his albums.

5 (#136, 1979), *Shades* (#110, 1981), *Grasshopper* (#149,1982, Mercury), and *8* (#47, U.K., 1983) are his album contributions for the '80s. Disappointed by the sales of the latter two albums, he requests a release from his record contract, then spends the next six years living in a mobile home, moving at will but not willfully moving.

During the '90s, Cale has released *Travelog* (#131, 1990), *Number 10* (1992) and *Closer To You* (1994) and even did a short tour to promote the latter.

AUTOGRAPHS

A CD, LP, magazine cover, ad, photo, or card signed by the artist: $20-$30

POSTERS/PRESS KITS

Press Kits: $15 (1990-Present)

USED CLOTHING/EQUIPMENT

Guitar Picks: $20-$35

OFTEN OVERLOOKED MEMORABILIA

Movie memorabilia from *La Femme De Mon Pote* (1984) and *50/50* (1986, German); all memorabilia associated with his songs covered by other musicians

Cale, John

Born: March 9, 1942

A musical prodigy, Cale studies classical piano as a child and eventually lands in NY's Eastman Conservatory on a scholarship from the Leonard Bernstein Foundation. After meeting Lou Reed at a party, he decides to join him in a new band, the Velvet Underground, in which he plays the bass, viola, and keyboards.

Cale is fired from the band in March 1968 after recording two albums. Personality conflicts between he and Reed could not be resolved and he is replaced by Doug Yule.

Cale then signs to CBS/Columbia in 1970, both as a producer and recording artist, and releases his solo debut *Vintage Violence,* followed by Church of Anthrax (1971), *Academy In Peril* (1972) and the eloquent *Paris 1919* (1973). In 1974 he moves on to Island Records and in similar capacity, produces Nico's *The End,* and releases his next album, *Fear,*

which features Roxy Music members Phil Manzanera and Eno.

Slow Dazzle (1975) and *Helen Of Troy* (1975) are his next solo albums, in a year that would also seem him produce Patti Smith's debut album *Horses.* The following year will see him release his album *Guts,* appropriate perhaps, as the performer feels compelled to decapitate a live chicken onstage. The incident causes his band to walk out in protest, but inspires the artist to release the subsequent 12-inch EP *Animal Justice.*

During the next decade, *Sabotage Live* (1980), *Honi Soit* (#154, 1981), *Music For A New Society* (1982), *Caribbean Sunset* (1983), *John Cale Comes Alive* (1983) and *Artificial Intelligence* are his album releases, all varying considerably in style, composition, and collaboration. The end of the decade also finds him linking back up with Lou Reed for a few projects, including a Velvet Underground reunion in June 1990.

Fragments Of A Rainy Season is released in 1993, and the artist promotes the album through numerous live appearances, including *The Tonight Show.* While commercial success continues to elude him, his contributions to numerous other musicians' work is astounding—from Iggy Pop to Patti Smith, he has been influential on many of rock's most noted albums.

AUTOGRAPHS
A CD, LP, magazine cover, ad, photo, or card signed by the artist: $20-$25

POSTERS/PRESS KITS
Press Kits: $20-$25 (1990-Present)
And His Collaborations: $20

USED CLOTHING/EQUIPMENT
Guitar Picks: $20-$40

OFTEN OVERLOOKED MEMORABILIA
Movie memorabilia from Andy Warhol's *Heat,* Roger Corman's *Caged Heat,* and Jonathan Demme's *Something Wild;* copies of his television appearances on *The Late Show: Later* - BBC2-TV (1992) and *The Tonight Show* (1/19/93); his projects and contributions with other musicians

Cameo

Formed 1974

Larry Blackmon, Tomi Jenkins, Nathan Leftenant

Originally the New York City Players, by the early '70s Larry Blackmon, who was now the leader of the group, changed the name to Cameo. The band became closely affiliated with Funkadelic, having opened numerous times for the band and sharing the same record label. In the late '70s the band charted with "I Just Want To Be" (#3, R&B, 1979), "Sparkle"(#10, R&B, 1979), and "Shake Your Pants"(#8, R&B, 1980).

Blackmon then moved his operation south to start his Atlanta Artists label. When his early albums were unsuccessful, he was forced to reduce the band to the trio of Blackmon, Tomi Jenkins, and Nathan Leftenant. This version of the band became successful with songs such as "She's Strange"(#1, R&B, 1984), "Word Up" (#1, R&B, 1986), "Candy" (#1, R&B, 1986) and "Back and Forth" (#3, R&B, 1987).

Blackmon's flamboyance and elaborate stage costuming created a striking visual impression of the band. From outfits designed by Jean-Paul Gaultier to geometric haircuts, Cameo was a major attraction. While the band was collaborating with some of the industry's finest talent, Blackmon was also crafting his art as a producer, even lending his talents to Bobby Brown's debut. He released *In the Face of Funk* in 1994, following a stint as vice president of A&R at Warner-Reprise Records.

AUTOGRAPHS
Group:
A CD, LP, magazine cover, ad, photo, or card signed by the group: $20-$30
Individual:
Larry Blackmon: $10-$15

TOUR BOOKS/PROGRAMS/PASSES
Backstage Passes:
Cloth: $5-$7; Laminated: $7-$10

POSTERS/PRESS KITS
Promotional Posters: $7-$10
Press Kits: $10-$15

OFTEN OVERLOOKED MEMORABILIA
Videotapes of their performance on *Rock Around The Clock* - BBC2-TV (9/20/81, 9/20/86)

Campbell, Glen

Born: April 22, 1936

After signing with Capitol Records in 1962, Campbell has sparse success until his 1965 cover of Donovan's "Universal Soldier" (#39, 1967) lands in the Top Forty. "Gentle On My Mind" (#39, 1967), accompanied by his regular stints on the Smothers Brothers' variety program, quickly drew attention to the rising star. Campbell then hooked up with Jimmy Webb and scored hits with "By The Time I Get To Phoenix" (#11, 1967), "Wichita Lineman" (#3, 1968), and "Galveston" (#4, 1969).

He hosted his own variety show *(The Glen Campbell Goodtime Hour)* from January 1969 to June 1972, tried his hand at acting, and spun out an occasional hit or two, including "Rhinestone Cowboy" (#1, 1975), "Southern Nights" (#1, 1977), and "Country Boy (You Got Your Feet in L.A.)" (#11, 1976).

He returned to country music and gospel in the '80s, while doing his own syndicated television show. The following decade saw him take *The Glen Camp-*

bell Music Show on the road; undertake a 25th Anniversary tour of the U.K. and Ireland; host a month-long stint in Branson, Missouri; and publish his autobiography.

GLEN CAMPBELL - SELECTED TELEVISION APPEARANCES

12/15/61	*American Bandstand*
1965	A regular on *Shindig* music show - ABC-TV
1/21/68	*The Smothers Brothers Comedy Hour* - CBS-TV
1968	*The Summer Brothers Smothers Show* - June 23-September 8, 1968
1969-1972	*The Glen Campbell Goodtime Hour* - CBS-TV - January 29, 1969 - June 13, 1972
5/5/70	U.S. TV Special with the Fifth Dimension
1973	Narrates *The Incredible Flight of the Snow Goose* - NBC-TV
1975	*The Tonight Show* (2) *The Mike Douglas Show* *Glen Campbell Music Shows* (6)
1976	*Salute By Satellite* *Hi, I'm Glen Campbell* - NBC-TV *Glen Campbell Down Home, Down Under* - CBS-TV *All Star Tribute to John Wayne* - ABC-TV
1982-1983	*The Glen Campbell Music Show*
10/1/93	*A Day in the Life of Country Music*

The signature of Glen Campbell

AUTOGRAPHS

A CD, LP, magazine cover, ad, photo, or card signed by the artist: $10-$25

TOUR BOOKS/PROGRAMS/PASSES

Backstage Passes:
Cloth: $5; (1980-Present) Laminated: $5-$10

POSTERS/PRESS KITS

Promotional Posters: $10-$45
Press Kits: $10 (1980-Present)

USED CLOTHING/EQUIPMENT

Guitar Picks: $20-$35

OFTEN OVERLOOKED MEMORABILIA

Movie memorabilia from *True Grit* (1969), *Norwood* (1970), and *Rock-a-Doodle* (1992); all associated memorabilia from his 1965 eight-month stint with the Beach Boys

REFERENCES/BOOKS

Rhinestone Cowboy, Campbell's autobiography

Camper Van Beethoven/Cracker

Formed 1984

David Lowery, Born: September 10, 1960; Victor Krummenacher; Chris Molla; Jonathan Segal; and Greg Lisher*

*Chris Pedersen is added in 1986 when Molla departs. Segal leaves in 1989 and Morgan Fichter is added. Cracker is formed in 1992.

An eclectic, humorous, avant-garde post punk band of the mid-80s, Camper Van Beethoven is perhaps best known for Dave Lowery's pre-Cracker barrel days and the song "Take The Skinheads Bowling"—a college cult classic. When the band split in 1989, Lowery took the pop drift of the band to Cracker, who scored with their sophomore effort *Kerosene Hat* (#59, 1993), which included "Low."

AUTOGRAPHS

Group:
A CD, LP, magazine cover, ad, photo, or card signed by the group: $15-$25
Individual:
David Lowery: $10-$20

Canned Heat

Formed 1966

Original lineup: Bob Hite, Born: February 26, 1945, Died: April 5, 1981; Alan Wilson (1943-1970); Henry Vestine; Frank Cook; and Larry Taylor*

*Numerous personnel changes

Canned Heat emerged during the late '60s and scored hits with "On The Road Again" and "Going Up To The Country" (#11, 1969), while playing some of the era's premier gigs, such as Woodstock and the Isle of Wight Festival. Tragically, Wilson died of a drug overdose in late 1970, and the band never fully recovered. Personnel changes ensued and although they went on to back some of the greatest bluesmen, such as John Lee Hooker, Memphis Slim and Clarence "Gatemouth" Brown, they never reclaimed their previous success. Following Hite's death in 1981, the members drifted apart.

AUTOGRAPHS

A CD, LP, magazine cover, ad, photo, or card signed by the group: $22-$60

Cannon, Freddie

(Frederick Picariello)
Born: December 4, 1939

A talented singer/songwriter and guitarist who is perhaps best remembered for three songs: "Tallahassee Lassie" (#6, 1959), an updated "Way Down Yonder In New Orleans" (#3, 1960), and "Palisades Park" (#3, 1962)—penned by Chuck Barris. His album *The Explosive Freddie Cannon* became the first American LP to hit #1 in England.

AUTOGRAPHS

A CD, LP, magazine cover, ad, photo, or card signed by the artist: $12-$32

Captain and Tennille

Formed Mid-1970s

Daryl Dragon (a.k.a. "Captain"), Born: August 27, 1942; and Toni (Catheryn)Tennille, Born: May 8, 1943

The talented husband and wife team hit the pop charts hard with the Sedaka-penned "Love Will Keep Us Together" (#1, 1975), then with the re-release of a regional hit, "The Way I Want To Touch You" (#4, 1975). This was followed by a string of hits that led into the late '70s, including "Lonely Night (Angel Face)" (#3, 1976), "Muskrat Love" (#4, 1976), "Shop Around" (#4, 1976)—the classic Smokey Robinson song, "Can't Stop Dancin" (#13, 1977), "You Never Done It Like That" (#10, 1978), and "Do That To Me One More Time" (#1, 1979).

The band's upbeat sound and popularity even led to a short-lived television show in 1976.

AUTOGRAPHS

A CD, LP, magazine cover, ad, photo, or card signed by the artists: $10-$20

POSTERS/PRESS KITS

Promotional Posters: $10-$30

Press Kits: $15-$35

OFTEN OVERLOOKED MEMORABILIA

Videotapes of their television musical variety show (9/20/76 - 3/14/77); memorabilia associated with Dragon's work with other musicians including the Beach Boys, the Byrds and Natalie Cole; Toni Tennille doll (Mego, 1977) - $60; Daryl Dragon doll (Mego, 1977) - $65

Captain Beefheart and the Magic Band

Formed 1964

Original lineup: Don Van Vliet a.k.a. "Captain Beefheart," Born: January 15, 1941; Alex St. Clair; Doug Moon; Jerry Handley; and Paul Blakely*

*Numerous personnel changes

With a nondescript form of twentieth century music, Captain Beefheart and the Magic Band are perhaps best remembered because of their affiliation with Frank Zappa. *Trout Mask Replica* and *Lick My Decals Off, Baby,* captured enough attention to at least pursue a national tour. Despite the extensive exposure, their next offerings catered to the depths of the U.S. album chart. Beefheart's 1980 American and European tours captured an audience strong enough to land them on *Saturday Night Live* (11/80). Van Vliet has since left the music business to paint in the Mojave Desert. His abstract and primitive paintings, which have been exhibited throughout the U.S. and Europe, can command a significant price.

AUTOGRAPHS

A CD, LP, magazine cover, ad, photo, or card signed by the group: $15-$40

OFTEN OVERLOOKED MEMORABILIA

Videotapes of the group's television appearances including *Saturday Night Live* (11/80); a Van Vliet original artwork - up to $25,000; a trout mask replica

Carey, Mariah

Born: March 27, 1970

Weaned by her opera-singing mother on the music of Aretha Franklin, Minnie Ripperton, and Stevie Wonder, Mariah—named after the song "They Call The Wind Mariah" from the Lerner and Lowe musical *Paint Your Wagon*—wins an audition to be backup singer for Brenda K. Starr. It will be Starr who passes Carey's demo tape on to record executive Tommy Mottola, who signs Carey (his future wife) to CBS/Columbia Records. Carey then spends most of 1989 commuting between coasts recording her debut album.

Mariah Carey (#1, 1991) was a smash debut, spinning off five #1 singles: "Vision Of Love" (1990), "Love Takes Time" (1990), "Someday" (1991), and "I Don't Wanna Cry" (1991). The album also brought her two 1991 Grammy Awards for Best New Artist and Best Female Vocalist. *Emotions* (#1, 1991), her second album, picked up where her debut left off, yielding the hit singles "Can't Let Go" (#2, 1991), "Make It Happen" (#5, 1992), and "Emotions" (#1, 1990).

Carey's appearance on the popular MTV *Unplugged* series yielded an EP that included a hit cover

of the Jackson 5's "I'll Be There" (#1, 1992). In 1993 Carey released her third studio album, *Music Box* (#1, 1993), which promptly secured two chart toppers ("Dreamlover" and "Hero") while being supported by her first tour. In March, "Without You/Never Forget You" (#3, 1994) peaks as she appears on CBS TV's *Late Show With David Letterman* (3/19/94). "Anytime You Need A Friend" (#12, 1994) and "Endless Love" (#2, 1994) sustain her presence on the single charts as she prepares her album *Merry Christmas* (#3, 1994), which includes her hit single "All I Want For Christmas Is You" (#2, U.K., 1994).

Daydream (#1, 1995), her next album, debuts at #1, while hit single "Fantasy" (#1, 1995) bows in at #1, setting U.S. chart history as the first single by a female to complete such a task. "One Sweet Day" (#1, 1995), a duet with Boyz II Men, also debuts at #1 and stays there for a record 16 weeks. The song will also become Carey's tenth U.S. #1 single in five years.

"Open Arms" (#2) and "Always Be My Baby" (#1) highlight her singles releases for 1996, as the performer continues to pick up just about every recording award conceivable. Go, "Honey" (#1, 1997).

AUTOGRAPHS

A CD, LP, magazine cover, ad, photo, or card signed by the artist: $35-$50

TOUR BOOKS/PROGRAMS/PASSES

Backstage Passes:
Cloth: $10-$15; Laminated: $15-$20

POSTERS/PRESS KITS

Promotional Posters: $15-$40
Press Kits: $15-$45

OFTEN OVERLOOKED MEMORABILIA

An invitation to her gala Columbia Records launch in New York City (April, 1990) - $15-$25; videotapes of her appearances on *The Tonight Show* (4/90, 11/20/90), *The Arsenio Hall Show* (4/90), *Saturday Night Live* (10/27/90, 11/16/91), *MTV Music Awards Ceremony* (9/5/91), *Entertainers '91* (12/26/91), *Top Of The Pops* (1/23/92), *Wogan* (4/27/92), MTV's *Unplugged* (5/20/92), *NBC-TV Special* (7/14/93- date held), and *Des O'Conner Tonight* (2/9/94, 2/7/96), along with numerous award shows that she has attended; a videotape of Mariah singing the national anthem before the first game of the 1990 NBA finals; "Merry Christmas" 10" promo counter standup - $20; videotapes: *Mariah Carey: The First Vision* and *Here Is Mariah Carey*

REFERENCES/BOOKS

Mariah Carey: Her Story by Chris Nickson; no dedicated collector books; serious collectors should opt for fan club: Mariah Carey Official International Fan Club, P.O. Box 679, Bramford, CT 06405 ($22 per year)

A child star, he first became known as "Little Carl Carlton" and released "Competition Ain't Nuthin" (#36, R&B, 1968) and "46 Drums, 1 Guitar" (a Top Twenty R&B hit) in 1968. As his voice matured the hits still followed: "Drop By My Place" (#12, R&B, 1970), "Everlasting Love" (#6, 1974), "Smokin' Room" (#13, R&B, 1975), and "She's a Bad Mama Jama (She's Built, She's Stacked)" (#22, 1981).

AUTOGRAPHS

A CD, LP, magazine cover, ad, photo, or card signed by the artist: $10-$20

Carnes, Kim

Born: July 20, 1945

Seventies and eighties singer/songwriter Kim Carnes paid her dues by playing the Los Angeles club circuit before landing a job with the New Christy Minstrels. She composed with her husband Dave Ellingson on occasion, but stuck primarily with ballads in her earlier years. Her first real big break came when Kenny Rogers, who had recorded her material for his 1980 album *Gideon,* asked her to duet with him on "Don't Fall In Love With A Dreamer."

She finally signed with EMI in 1978, and turned more toward rock-oriented material, scoring first in 1980 with a Smokey Robinson cover, "More Love," which sold into the Top Ten. Although album sales were still slow, she remained optimistic, and when *Mistaken Identity* (1981) was released, she had her breakthrough album. Extract "Betty Davis Eyes" (#1, 1981), quickly topped the singles chart and later won the artist a Grammy for Record of the Year. Her later hits have included "Draw of the Cards" (#28, 1991), "Voyeur" (#29, 1982), "What About Me?" (sung with Kenny Rogers and James Ingram), and "Crazy in the Night (Barking at Airplanes)" (#15, 1985).

She redirected her career more toward a country-oriented audience in 1988, having then signed with MCA Records. She tours extensively and has contributed to numerous projects including film soundtracks and musicals.

AUTOGRAPHS

A CD, LP, magazine cover, ad, photo, or card signed by the artist: $5-$20

OFTEN OVERLOOKED MEMORABILIA

Videotapes of the CBS-TV series *Sunday Dinner* - a Carnes theme; movie memorabilia from *Flashdance* (198), *That's Dancing* (1985), and *Impulse* (1991)

Carlton, Carl

Born: 1952

Carpenter, Mary Chapin

Born: February 21, 1958

AUTOGRAPHS

A CD, LP, magazine cover, ad, photo, or card signed by the artist: $15-$25

TOUR BOOKS/PROGRAMS/PASSES

Backstage Passes:

Cloth: $5-$8; Laminated: $8-$15

POSTERS/PRESS KITS

Promotional Posters: $10-$20
Press Kits: $12

OFTEN OVERLOOKED MEMORABILIA

Videotapes from her television appearances: *The Tonight Show* (11/10/94), *Later With Jools Holland* (12/10/94), *Late Show With David Letterman* (1/30/95), *In The Spotlight* (7/26/95), and *Tony Bennett: Here's To The Ladies* (12/1/95); movie memorabilia from *Dead Man Walking* (1996)

The Carpenters

Formed 1960s

Richard Carpenter, Born: October 15, 1946; and Karen Carpenter, Born: March 2, 1950, Died: February 4, 1983

Karen and Richard, having performed together numerous times as they were growing up, hook up with Wes Jacobs to form a trio. While playing at the County of Los Angeles Department of Parks and Recreation annual "Battle Of The Bands," they are spotted by an RCA Records executive who signs them as the Richard Carpenter Trio (9/66). They record eleven tracks, but are soon dropped by the label. Jacobs then moves on to study at Juillard in New York, before eventually playing in the Detroit Symphony Orchestra.

Richard and Karen then find themselves in another band, the Summerchimes, which changes their name to Spectrum. This group manages to play some key one-off gigs at venues such as the Troubadour and Whiskey A-Go-Go before folding in mid-1968. Karen and Richard then decide to pursue the matter on their own, and begin shopping a demo tape through their manager. The tapes finally come to the attention of A&M Records founder Herb Alpert, who signs them to the label in April 1969.

Offering (1969) is their debut album, and their first single is Beatles cover "Ticket To Ride" (#54, 1970). By this time the band has also met songwriter Burt Bacharach, who will become a close personal friend. *Close To You* (#2, 1970), the group's sophomore offering, includes the hit "(They Long To Be) Close To You" (#1, 1970)—a Bacharach/Hal David composition. From this point on, the duo would record a string of hits that would rival the best in the business: "We've Only Just Begun" (#2, 1970), "For All We Know" (#3, 1971, Song Of The Year), "Rainy Days and Mondays" (#2, 1971), "Superstar" (#2, 1971), "It's Going To Take Some Time" (#12, 1972), "Hurting Each Other" (#2, 1972), "Goodbye To Love" (#7, 1972), "Sing" (#3, 1973), "Yesterday Once More"

Having lived in a variety of places as a child, including Tokyo, Japan, Carpenter's family settles in the Washington, DC, area in 1974. She goes on to attend Brown University and graduates with a degree in American Civilization. Having played the Washington bar and club circuit, she establishes a solid reputation. She enters the studio in 1986 to record a demo tape with guitarist friend and producer John Jennings. The tape finds its way to Columbia Records, who signs her. Her debut album *Hometown Girl* is well received by critics and features self-written folk and country-sounding numbers, one of which is a cover version of Tom Waits' "Downtown Train."

State Of The Heart (#183, 1990), with "Never Had It So Good" and "Quittin Time," *Shooting Straight In The Dark* (#70, 1992) with "Down At The Twist And Shout" and "Come On Come On" (#31, 1992), are her next album offerings, with the latter including the country hit "The Bug" (penned by Mark Knopfler) and a total of seven hit singles. Her production earns her numerous awards including three Grammys for 1992-94 Best Country Vocal Performance, Female for "Down At The Twist And Shout," "I Feel Lucky," and "Passionate Kisses."

Stones In The Road (#10, 1994) featured numerous guest musicians and continued her Grammy streak in "her category"—Best Country Vocal Performance, Female—for "Shut Up and Kiss Me."

(#2, 1973), "Top of the World" (#1, 1973), "I Won't Last A Day Without You" (#11, 1974), "Please Mr. Postman" (#1, 1975), "Only Yesterday" (#4, 1975), and "Solitaire"(#17, 1975).

After five years of nonstop touring and recording, Karen Carpenter, now only weighing 90 pounds, is forced to take some time off to recuperate. "There's A Kind Of Hush (All Over The World)" (#12, 1976), "I Need To Be In Love" (#25, 1976), and "Goofus" (#56, 1976) are the duo's next singles, the latter being the release that would break a run of 17 consecutive Top 30 hits.

In 1979 Richard checks into the Menninger Clinic, suffering from substance abuse. He decides to take a year off, while sister Karen embarks on some solo work. Before she is able to finish work on a solo record, she rejoins Richard for work on a new album titled *Made In America*. The group then returns to the Top Twenty in 1981 with "Touch Me When We're Dancing" (#16, 1981), while album *Made In America* (#52, 1981) lands in the U.K. at #12.

"Those Good Old Dreams" (#63, 1982) and "Beachwood 4-5789" (#74, 1982) are the group's last two entries on the singles chart. On December 17, 1982, Karen makes her final singing appearance at Buckley School in Sherman Oaks, California. On February 4, 1983, Karen Carpenter dies at the young age of 32, of cardiac arrest brought about by a chemical imbalance associated with anorexia nervosa.

Three-time Grammy winners, hosts of their own television series, and guests of President Nixon at the White House, there was little the Carpenters failed to accomplish. As time has passed, their work has become more respected and their achievements more grand.

AUTOGRAPHS
Group:
A CD, LP, magazine cover, ad, photo, or card signed by the group: $500-$525
Individual:
Karen Carpenter: $150-$250   Richard Carpenter: $15-$20

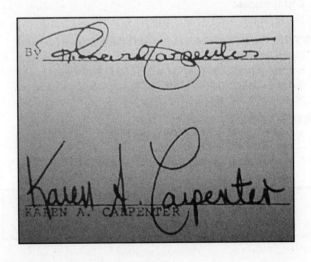

Contract signed by the Carpenters

TOUR BOOKS/PROGRAMS/PASSES
Tour Books:
1972 Tour program: $35-$40
Backstage Passes:
Cloth: $10-$20; Laminated: $15-$30

POSTERS/PRESS KITS
Promotional Posters: $15-$50
Press Kits: $15-$50

OFTEN OVERLOOKED MEMORABILIA
"Passages" A&M promotional plastic mug, 1977; "Made In America" A&M promotional money cube, 1981 - $55; A&M Record Cube Display "A Song For You" - $65

REFERENCES/BOOKS
The Carpenters: The Untold Story by Ray Coleman; no dedicated collector books

Carrasco, Joe "King" and the Crowns

Formed 1979

(Joe Teutsch) a.k.a. Joe "King" Carrasco

Carrasco has won critical acclaim over the years for his musical offerings he calls "nuevo wavo," a form of Tex-Mex-effects, mixed with chicano polkas, with just a touch of thrash. He has managed to sustain a small but loyal cult audience, but has never achieved widespread popularity.

AUTOGRAPHS
A CD, LP, magazine cover, ad, photo, or card signed by the artist: $5-$10

Carroll, Jim

Born: 1950

Jim Carroll accidentally fell on rock 'n' roll with the almost charting single "People Who Died" from his Atco debut record *Catholic Boy* (1980). A poet and novelist, Carroll's friendship with Patti Smith led him into the studio, and his realization brought him back out. When his second and third albums failed to reach their full commercial potential, he turned back toward writing.

Carroll returned to the studio in the '90s, first with *Praying Mathis* (1991), followed by *A World Without Gravity* (1993). He remains a gifted writer and although it's not often you can catch him singing, he does appear in public to read his work and is well worth listening to over a cup of Swiss Mocha.

AUTOGRAPHS
A CD, LP, magazine cover, ad, photo, or card signed by the artist: $10-$20

OFTEN OVERLOOKED MEMORABILIA
Movie memorabilia from *The Basketball Diaries* (1995); back issues of the *Paris Review* that include his work

REFERENCES/BOOKS
The Book of Nods (1986), *Forced Entries, The Downtown Diaries 1971-1973* (1987), *Fear of Dreaming,* and *The Selected Poems of Jim Carroll* (1993)

The Cars

Formed 1986

Ric Ocasek (Otcasek), Born: March 23, 1949; Ben Orr (Orzechowski); Elliot Easton (Steinberg); Greg Hawkes; and David Robinson

Ric Ocasek and Ben Orr, having been musical partners for nearly a decade, form the Cars in early 1976, along with Greg Hawkes (formerly with Ocasek and Orr in Milkwood), Elliot Easton, and David Robinson (ex-Modern Lovers and DMZ). The band make their live debut at Pease Air Force Base in Portsmouth, New Hampshire, on New Year's Eve 1976. The band records a demo tape that lands "Just What I Needed" as the most requested song on two local Boston radio stations. The group signs with Elektra Records in November 1977.

The group's debut single, "Just What I Needed" (#27, 1978), is released in 1978. A late 1978 mini-tour of Europe helps send a picture-disc single of "My Best Friend's Girl" (#35, 1978) to #3 in the U.K. Recorded in just two weeks, *The Cars* yields three hits singles: the two previously mentioned and "Good Times Roll" (#41, 1979). *Candy-O* (#3, 1979) is the group's sophomore release and features a sleeve designed by pin-up artist Alberto Vargas. The album spins off singles "Let's Go" (#14, 1979) and "It's All I Can Do" (#41, 1979). Ocasek's vocals and the band's new wave edge have by now landed them a recognizable sound. The release of *Panorama* (#5, 1980) would slightly alter their style, but not their success. The album includes the single "Touch and Go" (#37, 1980).

The group's commercial success allows them to purchase the Intermedia Studio in Boston (renaming it Synchro Sound) to produce future albums and help launch other local bands. *Shake It Up* (#9, 1982) follows with a self-titled single (#4, 1982) and "Since You're Gone" (#41, 1982). The same year the band also performs at the "US Festival" in San Bernadino, California. In March 1983, Ocasek releases his first solo album, *Beatitude* (#28, 1983), yielding the single "Something To Grab For" (#47, 1983).

Heartbeat City (#3, 1984), the Cars long-awaited fifth album, is finally released in 1984 and yields singles "You Might Think" (#7, 1984), "Magic" (#12, 1984), "Drive" (#3, 1984) and "Hello Again" (#20, 1984). "You Might Think" wins Video Of The Year at the inaugural MTV Video Music awards. The band also appears on *Saturday Night Live* NBC-TV on May 12, 1984.

The group's final Top Twenty hits—"Tonight She Comes" (#7, 1985) and "You Are The Girl" (#17, 1987)—come off of *Door To Door* (#26, 1987). Person-al conflicts, some fueled by solo efforts, now begin taking a toll on the band. On February 1, 1988, the band dissolves after six studio albums.

The band's members return to other projects. Ocasek marries model Paulina Porizkova, releases *Quick Change World* (his fourth solo album) in 1993, and produces Weezer's self-titled album (#16, 1994). The band, minus Orr, did meet for a rehearsal in May 1994, but despite rumors of reconciliation, nothing happened.

AUTOGRAPHS
Group:
A CD, LP, magazine cover, ad, photo, or card signed by the entire band: $40-$55

Individual:
Ric Ocasek: $15-$25   Ben Orr: $10-$20
Elliot Easton: $10-$15   Greg Hawkes: $5-$7
David Robinson: $5-$7

TOUR BOOKS/ PROGRAMS/PASSES
Tour Books:
'79 Tour Guide: $15-$17
Door To Door (1987): $10-$12
Tour '84: $15

Backstage Passes:
Cloth/paper: $10-$12;
Laminated: $12-$30

POSTERS/PRESS KITS
Promotional Posters:
$10-$50
Recent promotional posters run about $7-$20 depending upon size, stock, and scarcity
Press Kits: $20-$65

The Cars' Shake It Up '82 backstage pass (Printed by OTTO)

USED CLOTHING/EQUIPMENT
Guitar Picks:
Ric Ocasek: $10-$15
Ben Orr: $10
Elliot Easton: $10
Drum Sticks:
David Robinson: $20-$25

OFTEN OVERLOOKED MEMORABILIA
Candy-O wallet calendar (1979-80) - $5-$6; Candy-O enamel promotional pin on card - $8-$10; "Shake It Up" die-cut counter display (girl & shaker) - $15; Checkered promotional racing (B&W) flag - $35

REFERENCES/BOOKS
A couple resources exist, but none that put the pedal to the metal; no dedicated collector books

Carter, Carlene

(Rebecca Smith)
Born: September 26, 1955

Part of the third generation of Country's Royal Family, Carlene Carter is the daughter of June Carter Cash and '50s crooner Carl Smith. Somewhat misguided at the start of her career in the late '70s, she has struck country gold in the '90s with songs like "I Fell In Love" (#3, C&W, 1990), "Come On Back" (#3, C&W, 1990), "The Sweetest Thing" (#25, C&W, 1991), and "One Love" (#33, C&W, 1993).

AUTOGRAPHS

A CD, LP, magazine cover, ad, photo, or card signed by the artist: $5-$20

POSTERS/PRESS KITS

Promotional Posters: $10-$12 (1990-Present)
Press Kits: $10

OFTEN OVERLOOKED MEMORABILIA

Memorabilia associated with her first five albums (1978-1983) on Warner Brothers and Epic

Carter, Clarence

Born: January 14, 1936

"Slip Away" (#6, 1968) and "Patches" (#4, 1970) are two songs that quickly come to mind when you think about the blind singer/guitarist Clarence Carter, although he has scored with numerous R&B hits.

AUTOGRAPHS

An LP, magazine cover, ad, photo, or card signed by the artist: $10-$20

OFTEN OVERLOOKED MEMORABILIA

His early work with the Mellow Men, backing such legends as Otis Redding

The Carter Family

Formed 1926

Alvin Carter (1891-1960), Sara Dougherty Carter (1898-1979), and Maybelle Carter (1909-1978)

The pioneer family of country music, the Carter's were America's most popular band from 1926 until they disbanded in 1943. They set folk songs to string-band backup on popular favorites such as "Wildwood Flower," "Wabash Cannonball," "I'm Thinking Tonight of My Blue Eyes," "Will The Circle Be Unbroken," and "Keep On The Sunny Side."

AUTOGRAPHS

Group:
A magazine cover, ad, photo, or card signed by the group: $150-$475*
Individual:
Alvin Carter: $70-$210
Sara Dougherty Carter: $40-$75
Maybelle Carter: $40-$85

OFTEN OVERLOOKED MEMORABILIA

All items associated with the 1967 Newport Folk Festival, where Maybelle and Sara reunited; memorabilia associated with other musicians' covers of their songs

REFERENCES/BOOKS

The Carter Family by John Atkins—a must for collectors; no dedicated collector books

Case, Peter

Born: April 5, 1954

Singer/songwriter and folk-rock transient who has performed with the Nerves with Paul Collins, followed by the Plimsouls ("A Million Miles Away") and later as a solo artist.

AUTOGRAPHS

An LP, magazine cover, ad, photo, or card signed by the artist: $5-$10

Cash, Johnny

Born: February 26, 1942

An apostle of country music, Johnny Cash (the "Man in Black") helped bridge the gap between country and rock and roll with songs such as "I Walk The

Johnny Cash. Photo by Andy Earl. Courtesy of American Recordings.

Line" (#17, 1956) and "Ring of Fire" (#1, 1963). He began recording with Sam Phillips's Sun Records in 1955, scoring country hits with "Cry, Cry, Cry" (#14, C&W, 1955) and "Folsom Prison Blues" (#5, C&W, 1956).

His next productivity phase came when he met June Carter, who helped change his self-destructive ways and married him in 1968. They had numerous hit duets, including "Jackson" (#2, C&W, 1967), "Long-Legged Guitar Pickin' Man" (#6, C&W, 1967), "It Ain't Me, Babe" (#58, 1964), and "If I Were A Carpenter" (#36, 1970).

Well into the '70s the hits continued, including "A Boy Named Sue" (#2, 1969), "A Thing Called Love" (#2, C&W, 1972), and "One Piece At A Time" (#1, C&W, 1976). In the mid-80s he hooked up with Kris Kristofferson, Waylon Jennings, and Willie Nelson to form the Highwaymen, releasing a few well-received albums (1985, 1990, 1995) while occasionally touring.

Cash is a member of the Nashville Songwriter's Hall of Fame, Country Music Hall of Fame, and the Rock and Roll Hall of Fame (1992).

AUTOGRAPHS

An LP, magazine cover, ad, photo, or card signed by the artist: $10-$20

USED CLOTHING/ EQUIPMENT

Guitar Picks: $30-$50*
*Like all picks, price will vary due to significance, style, and use.

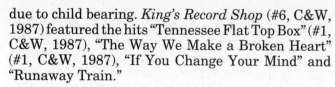

A guitar pick from the legendary Johnny Cash

OFTEN OVERLOOKED MEMORABILIA

Videotapes of his numerous television appearances

REFERENCES/BOOKS

The Johnny Cash Discography (three-volume series) by John L. Smith—a must for all Cash collectors!

Cash, Rosanne

Born: May 24, 1955

The oldest daughter of country legend Johnny Cash, she toured with her father's show, traveled, and attended Vanderbilt University in Nashville. In 1978 Cash recorded a demo tape with producer Rodney Crowell (her first husband) that landed her a German recording deal, and eventually a deal in the U.S. Her Columbia Records debut was *Right or Wrong* (1980) and was followed by *Seven Year Ache* (1981), which included three C&W chart toppers. This would mark the beginning of a series of hits for the performer, including "I Don't Know Why You Don't Want Me" (#1, C&W, 1985) and "Never Be You" (#1, C&W, 1985), during a time of minimal touring

due to child bearing. *King's Record Shop* (#6, C&W, 1987) featured the hits "Tennessee Flat Top Box" (#1, C&W, 1987), "The Way We Make a Broken Heart" (#1, C&W, 1987), "If You Change Your Mind" and "Runaway Train."

She began producing her own records in the '90s, and although the country hits stopped, the music was still intriguing for its honesty and clean style. Her marriage to Crowell ended in divorce (1992) and she later moved to New York City where she worked with her next husband, John Leventhal (Shawn Colvin).

AUTOGRAPHS

An LP, magazine cover, ad, photo, or card signed by the artist: $5-$20

Cassidy, David

Born: April 12, 1950

Teen heartthrob forever linked to his television character Keith Partridge on the popular series *The Partridge Family,* David Cassidy has endured successfully considering everyone's attempts to only link him with his teen idol image. The son of actor Jack Cassidy and actress Evelyn Ward, his role with Shirley Jones (his real-life stepmother and TV mother in *The Partridge Family*) launched his acting and musical career. He made a fortune alone off the television show's related memorabilia (see individual listing), not to mention his parallel music career.

The Partridge Family ran from September 25, 1970, to August 31, 1974, while an often forgotten animated series, *The Partridge Family, 2200,* ran on ABC from September 1974 to September 1975. Cassidy then signed an agreement with RCA, which failed to reach his target market here in the U.S. but scored in the U.K., where he placed 10 Top Twenty singles on the charts from 1972-1985. Cassidy later returned to his television and theater ventures, while not ignoring his musical career and even landing in the Top Thirty with "Lyin' To Myself" (#27, 1990).

AUTOGRAPHS

A CD, LP, magazine cover, ad, photo, or card signed by the artist: $5-$20

OFTEN OVERLOOKED MEMORABILIA

Videotapes of his numerous television appearances, including *Bonanza, Marcus Welby, The Partridge Family* series, and *David Cassidy - Man Undercover* (1978-79); associated memorabilia from his theater roles in *Joseph and the Amazing Technicolor Dreamcoat, Time* (U.K.), *Blood Brothers,* etc.

REFERENCES/BOOKS

Come On, Get Happy by David Cassidy (1994)

Cassidy, Shaun

Born: September 27, 1959

Similar to his half brother David Cassidy, Shaun was a teen idol, only later in the decade ('70s). He's best known for his songs "Da Doo Run Run" (#1, 1977), "That's Rock 'n' Roll," and "Hey Deanie" (#7, 1978), the latter two penned by Eric Carmen. Like his brother, when his records cooled on the charts he tried to make a transition to heavier sound, but failed. Cassidy later turned his interest to acting.

AUTOGRAPHS

A CD, LP, magazine cover, ad, photo, or card signed by the artist: $10-$30

The signature of Shaun Cassidy

POSTERS/PRESS KITS

Promotional Posters: $10-$20
Press Kits: $15-$25

OFTEN OVERLOOKED MEMORABILIA

Videotapes of his numerous television appearances, including *Like Normal People* (1979), *Breaking Away* (1980), and *General Hospital;* Broadway memorabilia from *Blood Brothers* (1993); doll (12", Kenner) - $40; guitar (Carnival Toys) - $50; Halloween costume - $25; jigsaw puzzle - $15

Castor, Jimmy

Born: June 22, 1943

Saxophonist, singer, and songwriter best remembered for his novelty singles "Troglodyte" (#6, 1972), "Hey, Leroy, Your Mama's Callin' You" (#31, 1967) and "The Bertha Butt Boogie" (#16, 1975).

AUTOGRAPHS

A CD, LP, magazine cover, ad, photo, or card signed by the artist: $5-$12

OFTEN OVERLOOKED MEMORABILIA

Associated memorabilia from his session work

Chad and Jeremy

Formed 1963

Chad Stuart, Born: December 10, 1943; and Jeremy Clyde, Born: March 22, 1944

One of the most popular mid-60s folk-rock duos, Chad and Jeremy are best remembered for their hits "Yesterday's Gone" (#21, 1964), "A Summer Song" (#7, 1964) and "Distant Shores" (#30, 1966). The duo broke up in late 1966.

AUTOGRAPHS

A CD, LP, magazine cover, ad, photo, or card signed by the group: $10-$20

OFTEN OVERLOOKED MEMORABILIA

Videotapes of the duo's numerous television appearances, including *Hullabaloo* and *The Hollywood Palace;* memorabilia from London stage productions and movies

Chairman of the Board

Formed 1969

Original lineup: General Norman Johnson, Danny Woods, Harrison Kennedy, and Eddie Curtis

Songwriter General Norman Johnson and his soul act of the '70s is best known for their debut hit "Give Me Just A Little More Time" (#3, 1970), followed by the minor hit "Pay to the Piper" (#13, 1970). Johnson tunes scored hits as covers for other acts—songs like "Want Ads," "Stick Up," and "Patches" just to name a few.

AUTOGRAPHS

A CD, LP, magazine cover, ad, photo, or card signed by the group: $12-$25

OFTEN OVERLOOKED MEMORABILIA

Associated memorabilia from Johnson's songs covered by other artists

The Chambers Brothers

Formed early 1960s

George E. Chambers, Willie Chambers, Lester Chambers, and Joe Chambers*

*Brian Keenan is added in 1965

Talented psychedelic regulars inspired by their soul, gospel and funk roots, The Chambers Brothers are best remembered for their hits "Time Has Come Today" (#11, 1968) and "I Can't Turn You Loose" (#37, 1968).

AUTOGRAPHS

An LP, magazine cover, ad, photo, or card signed by the group: $10-$25

OFTEN OVERLOOKED MEMORABILIA

Copies of the numerous commercials the band has worked on or has had their music appear in (Levi Strauss, for example)

The Champs

Formed 1957

Original lineup: Dave Burgess, Dale Norris, Chuck Rio, Gen Alden, and Bobby Morris

Drinking has never been the same since The Champs scored with their #1 hit "Tequila" in 1958. These West Coast session musicians also had minor hits with "Too Much Tequila" (#30, 1960), "Limbo Rock" (#40, 1962), and "Tequila Twist" (#99, 1962). The group also became a home for many other well-known musicians, including Delaney Bramlett, Jimmy Seals, and Dash Crofts.

AUTOGRAPHS

A CD, LP, magazine cover, ad, photo, or card signed by the group: $20-$40*

*"Tequila" related

Chandler, Gene

(Eugene Dixon)
Born: July 6, 1937

A veteran of the Chicago soul scene for over three decades, Chandler, who began on the street as a doo-wop singer, is best remembered for hits such as "Duke of Earl" (#1, 1962), "Just Be True" (#19, 1964), "You Can't Hurt Me No More" (#92, 1965), "Nothing Can Stop Me" (#18, 1965) and "What Now" (#40, 1965). He also scored later singing with Barbara Acklin on "Groovy Situation" (#12, 1970) and with the disco hit "Get Down" (#53, 1979).

AUTOGRAPHS

A CD, LP, magazine cover, ad, photo, or card signed by the artist: $8-$20

The Chantels

Formed 1956

Arlene Smith, Lois Harris, Sonia Goring, Jackie Landry, and Rene Minus*

*Arlene Smith and Lois Harris depart in 1959 and Annette Smith is added

Very popular girl act of the late '50s who are best remembered for their hit "Maybe" (#15, 1958) along with "Look in My Eyes" (#14, 1961) and "Well, I Told You" (#29, 1961), before disbanding in 1970.

AUTOGRAPHS

A CD, LP, magazine cover, ad, photo, or card signed by the group $15-$25

Chapin, Harry

Born: December 7, 1942, Died: July 16, 1981

Harry Chapin came from a musical family and learned to play the trumpet by the age of seven. He studied architecture and philosophy at Cornell University, following a period at the Air Force Academy. He pursued a career in making films, primarily documentaries, before extending himself into music. Although he was very successful in film, having been nominated for an Academy Award for *Legendary Champions,* his love for music was a passion. Harry quickly attracted attention performing in the New York City area, and in December 1971, signed a lucrative nine-album deal with Elektra Records.

In June 1972 his debut album *Heads and Tails* (#60, 1972) successfully enters the charts and spins off the lengthy hit single "Taxi" (#24). *Sniper and Other Love Songs* (#160, 1972) and *Short Stories* (#61, 1974) soon follow, with the latter yielding the single "W-O-L-D" (#34, U.K.), but it is *Verities and Balderdash* (#4, 1975), with its hit single "Cat's in the Cradle" (#1, 1974), that catapults Chapin into the limelight.

Chapin wrote a musical, *The Night That Made America Famous,* which garnered two Tony nominations and 75 Broadway performances. He then went on to win an Emmy Award in 1975 for his music to the ABC-TV children's series *Make A Wish,* which was hosted by his brother Tom.

In 1975 Chapin co-founded WHY (World Hunger Year) to combat the world's famine. His involvement becomes a tireless pursuit—from acting as a delegate to the Democratic Convention to presidential briefings on world hunger, his mission seems undaunted. His subsequent albums sold respectably through the '70s, a decade that found him performing almost constantly—often not for himself, but for his causes. On January 9, 1981, he plays his 200th performance at New York's famous Bottom Line.

On July 16, 1981, Chapin was driving his car on the Long Island Expressway near Jericho, New York, when a tractor-trailer ran into the back of his vehicle. The crash ruptured the car's gas tank, causing an explosion that killed the performer. Chapin is remembered as a performer and humanitarian whose unselfishness was not only exhibited through his work, but also through his heart.

On December 7, 1987, "The Gold Medal Celebration" memorial concert was held at Carnegie Hall in New York. At the ceremony, Harry's widow Sandy received a Special Congressional Medal, an honor bestowed on only 114 citizens and only four

songwriters. Harry Chapin now shares an award with only George & Ira Gershwin, George M. Cohan, and Irving Berlin!

AUTOGRAPHS

Harry Chapin loved not only his fans, but people in general. His warm smile drew people to him and when asked for an autograph, I never saw him refuse

A CD, LP, magazine cover, ad, photo, or card signed by the artist: $150-$225

An in-person example of Harry Chapin's signature

TOUR BOOKS/ PROGRAMS/PASSES

Tour Books:
"On The Road" 1976: $15-$25

Backstage Passes:
Cloth: $10-$25;
Laminated: $13-$40

POSTERS/PRESS KITS

Promotional Posters:
Promotional posters run about $20-$40 depending upon size, stock, and scarcity

Press Kits: $20-$45

A not so easy to find program from Harry Chapin, autographed inside, which was typical of Chapin following his shows.

USED CLOTHING/ EQUIPMENT

Guitar Picks: $100-$175

OFTEN OVERLOOKED MEMORABILIA

Items surrounding his film documentaries, especially *Legendary Champions;* promotional items concerning the numerous causes he represented

REFERENCES/BOOKS

Taxi: The Harry Chapin Story by Peter Coan; no dedicated collector books

Chapman, Marshall

Born: January 7, 1949

Singer/songwriter and guitarist who is best known for having her songs covered by other musicians, including Olivia Newton-John, Emmylou Harris, Conway Twitty, and Jimmy Buffet. Despite other artists' success with her material, her own records have sold poorly.

AUTOGRAPHS

A CD, LP, magazine cover, ad, photo, or card signed by the artist: $5-$10

OFTEN OVERLOOKED MEMORABILIA

Memorabilia associated with other musicians' covers of her material

Chapman, Tracy

Born: March 20, 1964

Tracy Chapman's folk-rock influenced, self-titled debut album landed a hit extract with "Fast Car" (#6, 1988) and earned her four Grammys, including Best New Artist. She returned with *Crossroads* (#9, 1989) a more forthright album that failed to spin off a single but still sold relatively well. She then withdrew for a few years in her typical reluctance to deal with the media before returning with *Matters of the Heart* (#53, 1992), which also failed to live up to commercial expectations. Chapman resurfaced in 1995 with *New Beginning,* and like its title foresaw, it was an improvement over her last effort, even yielding the hit "Give Me One Reason."

AUTOGRAPHS

Chapman is not a very public person and can be evasive to autograph requests

A CD, LP, magazine cover, ad, photo, or card signed by the artist: $15-$35

TOUR BOOKS/PROGRAMS/PASSES

Backstage Passes:
Cloth: $5-$8; Laminated: $8-$10

POSTERS/PRESS KITS

Promotional Posters: $10-$20
Press Kits: $10-$20

USED CLOTHING/EQUIPMENT

Guitar Picks: $10-$20

The Charlatans

Formed 1964

George Hunter, Mike Wilhelm, Richard Olson, Michael Ferguson, Sam Linde*

*Linde departs and is replaced by Dan Hicks. Ferguson leaves in 1967 and Patrick Gogerty and Terry Wilson are added. Additional changes follow in 1968.

Haight-Ashbury band who shared billing with many of the local favorites (The Warlocks, Jefferson Airplane, etc.) at the Fillmore, Avalon and other Bay Area haunts, The Charlatans are best known by collectors as the band that ended up adorning a lot of expensive rock posters. The group had no hits and released their first album just before disbanding.

AUTOGRAPHS

A CD, LP, magazine cover, ad, photo, or card signed by the group: $15-$30

Charles, Bobby

(Robert Guidry)
Born: February 21, 1938

Louisiana swamp musician and well-known songwriter who penned such classics as "See You Later Alligator," "I Don't Know Why I Love You But I Do," and "Walkin' to New Orleans," Bobby Charles toured with rock's best, including Chuck Berry, the Platters, and Little Richard. The early '70s found him in Woodstock where Albert Grossman took Charles under his wing and signed him to Bearsville Records. He managed to spin out some great tunes, including "Small Town Talk," but he just couldn't generate enough commercial sales.

AUTOGRAPHS

A CD, LP, magazine cover, ad, photo, or card signed by the artist: $10-$40

OFTEN OVERLOOKED MEMORABILIA

Memorabilia from the Band's *Last Waltz* concert, where Charles made a rare live appearance in 1976

Charles, Ray

(Ray Robinson)
Born: September 23, 1930

Ray Charles put the heart in soul music and synthesized more flavors of music than any entertainer in rock 'n' roll. "Baby Let Me Hold Your Hand" became his first R&B Top Ten in 1951, and was only a prelude to what was to follow. "I've Got a Woman" became his national hit (#2, R&B, 1955) and was followed by "Georgia on My Mind" (#1, 1960), "Hit the Road, Jack" (#1, 1961), "I Can't Stop Loving You" (#1, 1962), and "Let's Go Get Stoned" (#31, 1966).

From the late '60s on, Charles moved more toward a jazz vein, watched as his version of "Georgia on My Mind" became the state's official song (1979), and even appeared in television and film. He pitched a Pepsi with "You Got The Right One, Baby, Uh-huh!" in 1990, the same year that pitched him his tenth performance Grammy, not including his 1987 Lifetime Achievement Award. He also found himself among the first inductees in the Rock and Roll Hall of Fame in 1986, and a recipient of the Kennedy Center Honors. There just seems no end to the genius in the "Genius!"

AUTOGRAPHS

A CD, LP, magazine cover, ad, photo, or card signed by the artist: $50-$150

OFTEN OVERLOOKED MEMORABILIA

Movie memorabilia from *Ballad in Blue* (1964), *Light Out Of Darkness* (1964), *In The Heat Of The Night* (1967), *The Blues Brothers* (1980) and *Any Which Way You Can* (1980); videotapes from his numerous television show appearances, including *It's What's Happening Baby* (1965), *Carol Burnett Show* (1972), *Three's Company* (sings theme song), *Saturday Night Live* (11/12/77), *The Second Barry Manilow Special* (2/24/78), "American Presidential Inaugural Gala" (1/19/85), *Moonlighting* (1987), *St. Elsewhere* (1987), *Who's The Boss* (1987), *The Tonight Show* (11/21/90, 4/16/92), *Designing Women* (uses his song for its theme), *Ray Charles 50 Years in Music* (10/6/91), *The Genius Of Ray Charles* (1/3/92), *Willie Nelson The Big Six-O* (5/22/93), *Apollo Theatre Hall of Fame* (6/15/93) and *Ray Alexander: A Taste For Justice* (5/13/94); artifacts from his numerous performances at jazz and soul festivals; memorabilia from the "We Are The World" fundraising single; all items from his salute at the annual Kennedy Center Honors ceremony in Washington, DC (12/26/86); audio and videotapes from his numerous advertising campaigns, such as American Express, Kentucky Fried Chicken, and Pepsi Cola; sidewalk rubbings from his various concrete salutes

REFERENCES/BOOKS

Brother Ray, his autobiography with David Ritz (1978); a few other resources exist; no dedicated collector books

Chase

Formed 1970

Original lineup: Bill Chase, Alan Ware, Jerry Van Blair, Ted Piercefield, Jay Burrid, Terry Richards, Angel South, and Dennis Johnson*

*Numerous personnel changes

Jazz rock group who scored with their debut album and hit extract "Get It On" (#24, 1971), before releasing two more albums and calling it quits. Bill Chase later reorganized nearly an entirely new group and was on a comeback tour when the small plane the band was traveling in crashed near Jackson, Minnesota, killing him and three other band members.

AUTOGRAPHS

A CD, LP, magazine cover, ad, photo, or card signed by the group: $20-$40*

*Original band on debut album

Cheap Trick

Formed 1974

Robin Zander, Born: January 23, 1953; Tom Petersson (Peterson), Born: May 9, 1950; Rick Nielsen, Born: December 22, 1946; and Bun E. Carlos (Brad Carlson), Born: June 12, 1951*

*Petersson leaves in 1980 and is replaced with Pete Comita. Comita leaves and is replaced by Jon Brant in 1981. Brant departs and Petersson returns in 1986.

In 1968 veteran rocker Rick Nielsen (Phaetons, Boyz and the Grim Reapers) is teamed with Tom Petersson and Bun E. Carlos (Bo Diddley, Del Shannon, Freddy Cannon, and others) to release *Fuse*, a self-titled record for Epic. Personnel changes infused the group, until the final successful combination of Nielsen, Carlos, Petersson, and vocalist Robin Zander formed Cheap Trick.

In January 1977 their debut self-titled album is released. It sells moderately well in the U.S. (although uncharted), but it earns a gold disc in Japan. The group's second album, *In Color* (#73, 1977), fairs better in the States and goes gold in Japan. Capitalizing on their Far East success, the group heads to Tokyo in February 1978. "Trickmania" is rampant, and the group records a live album at the Budokan Arena.

In July 1978 Cheap Trick releases their third album, *Heaven Tonight* (#48), which yields the single "Surrender" (#62). *Cheap Trick At Budokan* is released on February 24, 1979. The album, with its single "I Want You To Want Me" (#7, 1979), ignites the band's career and propels them into stardom. "Ain't That A Shame" (#35, 1979) is also taken as a single from the album, just prior to the release of *Dream Police* (#6, 1979).

By know the band was headlining arenas and stadiums, with the group's members well-established and visually trademarked. Nielsen, capped and bow-tied, had struck a nerve with his outrageous guitars and his playing antics, while frontman Zander had become Japan's latest heartthrob. *Found All The Parts* (10" EP) (#39, 1980) is released prior to the departure of band member Petersson in the summer of 1980. Pete Comita, followed by Jon Brandt, fill in for Petersson, just prior to the recording of *All Shook Up* (#24, 1980). Although the album is produced by George Martin, its lack of singles labels it a disappointment.

The next decade would be quite different for the band. Epic rejects an album in 1981 and the band returns to the studio to record *One on One* (#39, 1982). The album spins off two singles, "If You Want My Love" (#39) and "She's Tight" (#65). *Next Position Please* (#61, 1983) and *Standing On The Edge* (#35, 1985) fall well below everyone's expectations and Cheap Trick's fortunes sag while record executives contemplate alternatives.

In 1988 the band decides to utilize outside writers for their next album, *Lap Of Luxury* (##16, 1988). This, combined with Petersson's return, finds the band back in the commercial spotlight. "The Flame" (#1, 1988) tops the U.S. charts and fuels album sales. In October the release of Elvis Presley cover "Don't Be Cruel" (#4, 1988) puts the band back once again in the Top Ten.

The group's next release, *Busted* (#48, 1990), did exactly what its title projected, even though "Can't Stop Falling Into Love" (#12, 1990) reached the Top Twenty. The event spins the group into mediocrity. Even *The Greatest Hits* (#174, 1991) barely charts. Solo projects are the focus of members' attention until the release of *Woke Up With A Monster* (#123, 1994, Warner Brothers Records).

The band continues to tour, and although their future remains somewhat clouded, watching "The Trick" perform still remains a treat!

AUTOGRAPHS

Cheap Trick, with the exception of the Japanese Tours, has always been accessible and obliging to autograph requests.

Group:

A CD, LP, magazine cover, ad, photo, or card signed by the entire band: $30-$45

Individual:

Robin Zander: $10-$20   Rick Nielsen: $15-$25
Tom Petersson: $5-$10   Bun E. Carlos: $5-$10
Pete Comita: $5   John Brandt: $5
Band-used song list signed
by Rick Nielsen: $75

TOUR BOOKS/ PROGRAMS/PASSES

Tour Books:

1979 - In Concert: $20-$25
Japan Tour - Dream Police: $15-$20
1989 Tour: $15

Backstage Passes:

Cloth: $8-$15;
Laminated: $10-$25

POSTERS/PRESS KITS

Promotional Posters:
$10-$35
Press Kits: $15-$45

USED CLOTHING/ EQUIPMENT

Guitar Picks:

Tom Petersson: $8-$10
Rick Nielsen: $10-$30*
Robin Zander: $10-$25

*Rick Nielsen is notorious for his drawing (self-portrait) that he often adds to his signature. The popularity also spread to his guitar picks, and true Cheap Trick collectors will want his guitar pick variation that includes the drawing.

Drum Sticks:

Bun E. Carlos: $20

Cheap Trick 1979 tour program (KAM, 1979)

A Cheap Trick guitar pick

OFTEN OVERLOOKED MEMORABILIA

Logo patch (3"), black & white - $4; satin silver tour jacket (1979) - $250; bow ties - $15-$20; key chains - $4-$6; belt buckles - $15-$20; buttons - $5-$8; tank tops - $20; shorts - $15-$20; Dream Police badge - $15; Heaven Tonite mobile - $50; At Budokan mobile - $45; pins (2"x 2", mirrored) - $15

Checker, Chubby

(Ernest Evans)
Born: October 3, 1941

He may not have written the song, but "The Twist" (#1, 1960) was the breakthrough he was looking for and it catapulted Checker into stardom, while hooking him on the dance craze bandwagon. He followed the hit with "Ponty Time" (#1, 1961), "Let's Twist Again" (#8, 1961), "The Fly" (#7, 1961), "Slow Twistin'" (#3, 1962), "Limbo Rock" (#2, 1962), and "Popeye the Hitchhiker" (#10, 1962). Although his hits stopped in 1965, he certainly didn't, as Checker began an endless journey on the nightclub circuit.

In 1988 a rap version of "The Twist" featuring the Fat Boys landed him in the Top Forty for the first time in 25 years. Checker is still a regular on rock 'n' roll revival shows.

AUTOGRAPHS

A CD, LP, magazine cover, ad, photo, or card signed by the artist: $10-$30

OFTEN OVERLOOKED MEMORABILIA

Movie memorabilia from *Let The Good Times Roll;* videotapes from his numerous television appearances

Chenier, Clifton

Born: June 25, 1925, Died: December 12, 1987

The king of zydeco (a form of Creole party music rooted in Cajun blues and traditional French folk) and a talented keyboardist and harmonica player, he is best remembered for his hits "Ay 'Tit Fille" and "Boppin' the Rock." Chenier even garnered a Grammy Award for his 1983 album *I'm Here* before passing away in 1987.

AUTOGRAPHS

A CD, LP, magazine cover, ad, photo, or card signed by the group: $20-$35

OFTEN OVERLOOKED MEMORABILIA

A videotape from the 1974 documentary *Hot Pepper*

Cher

(Cherilyn Sarkasian LaPier)
Born: May 20, 1946

Having moved to fast-paced Los Angeles, Cher attends acting classes before meeting and subsequently marrying Sonny Bono in Tijuana, Mexico. Through Bono, Cher begins singing back-up vocals for Phil Spector and even finds herself recording "Ringo I Love You" on Spector's minor label, Annette, as Bonnie Jo Mason.

In March 1965, "Dream Baby," Cher's first solo single is released, under her full name Cherilyn. With "I Got You Babe" (#1, 1965) topping the singles chart, Cher releases her cover of Dylan's "All I Really Want To Do" (#15, 1965), which will also be the name of her solo album debut (#16, 1965). "Where Do You Go" (#25, 1965) and "Bang Bang (My Baby Shot Me Down)" (#2, 1966) soon follow, with the latter becoming her first solo million seller. "Alfie" (#32, 1966) and "You Better Sit Down Kids" (#9, 1967) are her last two singles on Imperial before she signs on with Atco, who already enjoys her services as part of the duo. Her first big hit for the label comes with "Gypsies, Tramps And Thieves" (#1, 1971) from the album of the same name. "The Way Of Love" (#7, 1972), also extracted from the album, makes it into the Top Ten.

Half Breed (#28, 1973), with self-titled extract (#1, 1973), establishes her immediately on her new MCA label. "Dark Lady" (#1, 1974) quickly tops the U.S. singles chart, prior to the finalization of her divorce from Bono. "Train Of Thought" (#27, 1974) and "I Saw A Man And He Danced With His Wife" (#42, 1974) were her last two singles of the year. Cher then moved on to Warner Brothers Records, signing a lucrative deal in December 1974.

Stars (#153, 1975) would be her only album to chart for Warner Brothers under her new contract. On June 30, 1975, she weds Gregg Allman of the Allman Brothers. Both "Brothers"—Allman and Warner—will become a problem for the artist, who severs ties with the pair in 1979. The Allmans will later record *Allman And Woman: Two The Hard Way* (1977) and support it with much of their own money and a European tour, but to little success.

"Take Me Home" (#8, 1979), the title track from her first Casablanca label release, lands in the Top Ten, while Cher is now romantically linked with Kiss bassist and "God Of Thunder" Gene Simmons. It is followed by singles "Wasn't It Good" (#49, 1979) and "Hell On Wheels" (#59, 1979), the latter being her last chart entry for nine years. She then engages in a brief stint with the band Black Rose before turning her attention back to acting.

In 1984 she is nominated for an Oscar for Best Supporting actress in the movie *Silkwood*. Her emphasis now on acting, she will star in numerous projects and collect an Academy Award as best actress for her work in *Moonstruck*. Meanwhile, "I Found Someone" (#10, 1988) puts her back on the singles chart, extracted from the Geffen Records album *Cher* (#32, 1988). *Heart Of Stone,* her next album offering, also does well and is preceded by her duet with Peter Cet-

era, "After All" (#6, 1989), from the movie *Chances Are.*

"If I Could Turn Back Time" (#3, 1989) and "Just Like Jesse James" (#8, 1989) sustain her presence in the entertainment spotlight, as do performances such as that given at the sixth annual MTV Video Music Awards. A risqué Cher, clad in little more than a black leather coat, turns more than her fair share of heads while singing "If I Could Turn Back Time." "Heart Of Stone" (#20, 1990), extracted from the eponymous album, is followed by "The Shoop Shoop Song (It's In His Kiss)" (#33, 1991), which was featured in the movie *Mermaids.* "Love And Understanding" (#17, 1991), "Save Up All Your Tears" (#37, 1992), "I Got You Babe" (#35, 1994, with Beavis and Butt-Head), and "Walking In Memphis" (#11, 1995) add to her hit catalog.

Cher, with her diverse skills, is a fascinating subject to collect. Her achievements in both music and film offer collectors a wide range of material to choose from. Her unpredictability also intrigues collectors, who often find her turning up unannounced at a variety of events. Her memorabilia is strong at auctions and can command a fair dollar. She is also no stranger to charity work, putting her support behind numerous important causes, especially the Children's Craniofacial Association.

AUTOGRAPHS

A CD, LP, magazine cover, ad, photo, or card signed by the artist: $25-$65

TOUR BOOKS/ PROGRAMS/PASSES

Tour Books:
Love Hurts Tour: $10
Backstage Passes:
Cloth: $8-$10;
Laminated: $10-$15

POSTERS/PRESS KITS

Promotional Posters:
$10-$20
Love Hurts (24" x 32"): $10;
It's A Man's World
(24" x 35"); Cher with
snake and apple: $10
Press Kits: $15-$20
(1990-Present)

An outstanding Cher tour program, rich with photos and many classic shots

USED CLOTHING/EQUIPMENT

A black leather coin purse: $500
Heart Of Stone Tour bathrobe, 1990: $700-$725
Guitar Picks: $15-$20

OFTEN OVERLOOKED MEMORABILIA

Videotapes from her television appearances: *The Sonny and Cher Comedy Hour, Cher* - CBS-TV (February 16, 1975-January 4, 1976), *Late Night With David Letterman* (5/22/86, 11/13/87 [Sonny & Cher sing "I Got You Babe"], 11/91), *The Late Show Starring Joan Rivers* (10/9/86), *Cher at the Mirage* (2/4/91), *Backstage Pass To Summer* (6/1/691), *The Tonight Show* (7/30/91, 11/91), *Sally Jesse Raphael* (11/91), *Dame Edna's Hollywood* (11/30/91), *Maury*

Povich Show (2/10/92), *Larry King Show* (10/26/92), *Elvis Aaron Presley: The Tribute* (10/8/94), *Christmas With Cher* (12/24/95) - ITV, *National Lottery Live Program* (1/6/96) - BBC1-TV; movie memorabilia from *Alfie* (1966), *Good Times* (1967), *Chastity* (1969), *Silkwood* (1984), *Mask* (1985), *The Witches of Eastwick* (1987), *Moonstruck* (1987), *Suspect* (1987), *Chances Are* (1989), *Mermaids* (1989), and *Faithful* (1996); a handbill from her Broadway debut in *Come Back To The Five And Dime, Jimmy Dean, Jimmy Dean* (1982); released videotapes including *Cher's Video Canteen* (1991); all associated references to Cher from Mr. Blackwell's worst-dressed woman list; copies of commercials for Lonely Hearts costume jewelry and Equal sugar substitute; a copy of her gothic mail order catalog "Sanctuary" available at 1-800-726-2882; If I Could Turn Back Time, Geffen, promotional watch, 1989

REFERENCES/BOOKS

A few resources exist, nothing that does justice to the singer in my opinion; no dedicated collector books

Cherry, Neneh

(Neneh Karlsson)
Born: March 10, 1964

Rough-edged, late-80s, post-rap dance pop artist who briefly performed with the Slits before singing and playing percussion with Rip Rap + Panic. Her debut record on the Virgin label, *Raw Like Sushi* (#40, 1989), cited by some critics as one of the first alternative rap albums, included the hits "Buffalo Stance" (#3, 1989) and "Kisses on the Wind" (#8, 1989). It was

Neneh Cherry. Photo by Eddie Monsoon. Courtesy of Virgin Records.

followed by *Homebrew,* a more toned down and less commercial effort that was well received by alt and college radio stations.

AUTOGRAPHS

A CD, LP, magazine cover, ad, photo, or card signed by the artist: $8-$15

POSTERS/PRESS KITS

Promotional Posters: $10-$12
Press Kits: $10-$12

OFTEN OVERLOOKED MEMORABILIA

Videotapes from her television performances

Chic/Nile Rodgers/Bernard Edwards

Formed 1976

Bernard Edwards, Born: October 31, 1952, Died: April 18, 1996; Nile Rodgers, Born: September 19, 1952; Norma Jean Wright; Tony Thompson; and Alfa Anderson*

*Numerous personnel changes

Late-70s and early-80s disco group who scored with a series of hits, including "Le Freak" (#1), "Dance, Dance, Dance" (#1, 1977), "I Want Your Love" (#7, 1979), and "Good Times" (#1, 1979), before disbanding in 1983. Chic is now probably best known for two of its former members who evolved into the industry's leading producers, Nile Rodgers and Bernard Edwards. Rodgers produced over 50 records in a dozen years, while Edwards has worked with Rod Stewart, Kenny Loggins, Gladys Knight, and with Robert Palmer on "Riptide."

AUTOGRAPHS

A CD, LP, magazine cover, ad, photo, or card signed by the group: $20-$35

POSTERS/PRESS KITS

Promotional Posters: $15-$30
Press Kits: $15-$25

OFTEN OVERLOOKED MEMORABILIA

Memorabilia associated with Rodgers' and Edwards' production work

Chicago

Formed 1967

Terry Kath, Born: January 31, 1946, Died: January 28, 1978; Peter Cetera, Born: September 13, 1944; Robert Lamm, Born: October 13, 1944; Walter Parazaider, Born: March 14, 1945; Danny Seraphine, Born: August 28, 1948; James Pankow, Born: August 20, 1947; and Lee Loughnane, Born: October 21, 1946*

*Laudir De Oliveira is added in 1974. Kath dies and Donnie Dacus is added in 1978. Dacus leaves the following year and Chris Pinnick is added. Pinnick departs in 1981 and Bill Champlin joins the band. Cetera leaves in 1984 and Jason Scheff joins the band. DeWayne Bailey is added in 1988 at

guitar. Seraphine leaves in 1989 and Tris Imboden joins the band.

CHICAGO I - 1967-1981

While Blood, Sweat and Tears and The Electric Flag opened the door for brass-laden rock bands, Chicago drove through it by establishing themselves as the premier group in that genre. Formed by Terry Kath and Walter Parazaider, they were first known as the Big Thing, then Chicago Transit Authority, and later simply Chicago. The group put together an impressive series of hits in the early '70s, including "Does Anybody Really Know What Time it Is?" (#7, 1970), "Colour My World" (#75, 1971), "Saturday in the Park" (#3, 1972), "Feeling Stronger Everyday" (#10, 1973), "Wishing You Were Here" (#11, 1974) and many others.

They became a force on radio airwaves and sold millions of records before sales started tailing off in the later half of the decade. The group then decided to split with producer James Guercio (who later started Caribou studio) in 1977, just a year before Kath would die of an accidental self-inflicted gunshot wound. Donnie Dacus then replaced the founder, as Columbia Records dropped the group from their roster (1981).

CHICAGO II - 1982-PRESENT

The band then moved over to Warner Brothers Records, who believed that Chicago still had a few hits left in them. What an understatement that turned out to be: the band scored with "Hard to Say I'm Sorry" (#1, 1982), "Hard Habit To Break" (#3, 1984), "You're the Inspiration" (#3, 1984), "Will You Still Love Me" (#3, 1986), "I Don't Wanna Live Without Your Love" (#3, 1988), "Look Away" (#1, 1988), "You're Not Alone" (#10, 1989), and "What Kind of Man Would I Be" (#5, 1989).

During this period Peter Cetera left the band (1985) to pursue a solo career and scored with the hits "Glory of Love" (#1, 1986), "The Next Time I Fall" (#1, 1986, a duet with Amy Grant), "One Good Woman" (#4, 1988), and "After All" (#6, 1989, a duet with Cher).

AUTOGRAPHS

A CD, LP, magazine cover, ad, photo, or card signed by the group: $35-$100*
*Add $50-$75 for Kath on a group item

TOUR BOOKS/PROGRAMS/PASSES

Tour Books:
1973 (Japan) Tour Program: $150
1977 Tour Program: $50

Backstage Passes:
Cloth/paper: $10-$25; Laminated: $20-$40 (1967-1981)
Cloth: $8-$10; Laminated: $10-$20 (1981-Present)

POSTERS/PRESS KITS

Promotional Posters:
1967-1981: $15-$60
1981-Present: $10-$25

Press Kits:
1967-1981: $20-$65
1981-Present: $15-$25

USED CLOTHING/EQUIPMENT
Guitar Picks: $10-$25

OFTEN OVERLOOKED MEMORABILIA
"Hot Streets" pop-out mobile - $85; promotional pin w/logo - $15-$20; 1975 canvas promotional calendar - $100; Chicago X songbook - $25; promotional buttons - $20-$25

Chicken Shack

Formed 1967

Stan Webb; Andy Sylvester; Christine Perfect, Born: July 12, 1943; and Dave Bidwell*

*Perfect leaves in 1969 and Paul Raymond is added. Numerous changes follow.

British blues revival band of the late '60s who scored hits with "I'd Rather Go Blind" (1969) and "Tears in the Wind," but is best remembered for pianist/singer Christine Perfect, who later was better known as Christine McVie of Fleetwood Mac.

AUTOGRAPHS
A CD, LP, magazine cover, ad, photo, or card signed by the group: $32-$55

OFTEN OVERLOOKED MEMORABILIA
Memorabilia associated with Fleetwood Mac

The Chieftains

Formed 1963

Original lineup: Paddy Moloney, Sean Potts, Michael Tubridy, Martin Fay, and David Fallon*

*Numerous changes follow

Exporters of traditional Irish folk music, these multiple Grammy Award winners became a full-time act in 1975 and, under the watchful eye of Paddy Moloney, are recognized worldwide for their musical accomplishments. Talk about a tough opening act— the Chieftains played before 1.3 million people at an outdoor mass in Dublin supporting Pope John Paul II in 1979. Their albums have spanned a wide variety of music, from folk rock to American country music, and have had such guest contributors as Elvis Costello, Roger Daltry, Willie Nelson, Sting, and the Rolling Stones.

AUTOGRAPHS
A CD, LP, magazine cover, ad, photo, or card signed by the group: $25-$50

POSTERS/PRESS KITS
Promotional Posters: $15-$30
Press Kits: $15-$25

OFTEN OVERLOOKED MEMORABILIA
Movie memorabilia from *Barry Lyndon*, their Grammy Award-winning soundtrack; videotapes from their numerous television performances, as the band typically plays NBC's *Today* on St. Patrick's Day; all items associated with their opening stint for Pope John Paul II

The Chiffons

Formed 1960

Barbara Lee, Patricia Bennett, and Judy Craig*

*Sylvia Peterson is added in 1962

Distinctive vocal group of the early '60s, The Chiffons are best remembered for their hits "He's So Fine" (#1, 1963), "One Fine Day" (#5, 1963), "Nobody Knows What's Going On" (#49, 1965), and "Sweet Talkin' Guy" (#10, 1966).

AUTOGRAPHS
A CD, LP, magazine cover, ad, photo, or card signed by the group: $25-$60

POSTERS/PRESS KITS
Promotional Posters: $15-$30
Press Kits: $15-$25

The Chi-Lites

Formed 1960

Original lineup: Marshall Thompson, Creadel Jones, Robert Lester, Eugene Record, and Clarence Johnson*

*Numerous personnel changes

A soul vocal group of the early '70s, The Chi-Lites are best remembered for their hits "Have You Seen Her" (#3, 1971) and "Oh Girl" (#1, 1972), although they also had eleven Top Twenty R&B hits between 1969 and 1974.

AUTOGRAPHS
A CD, LP, magazine cover, ad, photo, or card signed by the group: $15-$30*
*Item relating to their two most prominent hits

The Chipmunks

Formed mid-1950s

Alvin, Simon and Theodore Chipmunk

Brainstorm of creator Ross Bagdasarian (a.k.a. David Seville), who was also responsible for putting "Witch Doctor" atop the singles chart in 1958, The Chipmunks were born out of synchronized tracks recorded at different speeds. "The Chipmunk Song"

(#1, 1958) sold nearly four million copies during its first month of release (on its way to seven million) while collecting three Grammy Awards. "Alvin's Harmonica" (#3, 1959), "Ragtime Cowboy Joe" (#16, 1959), "Alvin's Orchestra" (#33, 1960), "Rudolph the Red-Nosed Reindeer" (#21, 1960), and "The Alvin Twist" (#40, 1962) all followed.

The Alvin Show premiered on CBS prime time television during the 1961-62 season beginning on October 4, 1961, and ending on September 5, 1962 (26 episodes). When Bagdasarian died in 1972, his son—a chip off the old block—followed in his footsteps, releasing "Chipmunk Punk" (1980), which created "Chipmunkmania" all over again. By 1983 they were back on television, this time in a Saturday morning series, and now were even backed by the "Chipettes." *Chipmunks in Low Places* (#21, 1992) even featured country stars Billy Ray Cyrus, Tammy Wynette, and Waylon Jennings, while picking a Grammy nomination.

OFTEN OVERLOOKED MEMORABILIA

Alarm clock - $15; Alvin tattoos (Fleer), two sizes - $5-$10; bandages - $5; bank - $10; books: Little Golden Book - $20, Whitman - $25, Wonder Book - $20; bowl - $40; card game - $15; coloring books - $35-$45; comics: First Issue, 1962 - $20, all others - $5; cup dispenser (paper cups) - $20; curtain call theater (Ideal) - $45; dolls: (Knickerbocker, 14", set of 3) - $50 each, (CBS, 12", set of 3) - $10 each, (Ideal, 10", set of 3) - $15, (Ideal, 18" talking, set of 3) - $30, (Burger King, 7", set of 3) - $7 each, (Ideal, wind-ups 4") - $10, (Ideal, paint and play figures) - $7, (Ideal, poseable play pals 4") - $5, (Ideal, play pals 2-1/2", set of 19) - $5 each, (Ideal, play pals, 2-1/2", 4 themes) - $12 each, (Timely Toys, 3 styles) - $70; Easy-show movies - $35; flashlight - $20; foot stool - $60; games: Hasbro Acron Hunt - $75, Hasbro Big Record - $50, Hasbro Cross Country - $60, Ideal Go Hollywood - $20; glasses (numerous) - $6; greeting cards - $12; hand puppets: Dayton Hudson - $5, Knickerbocker - $30; Halloween costume - $125; harmonica - $65; jigsaw puzzle: APC, 125 pcs. - $8, Burger King - $5; kite - $55; loot box (storage box) - $50; lunch boxes - $400 (scarce), thermos (plastic) - $15, (plastic, 1984) - $7, (metal) - $70; magic drawing slate - $25; marionette - $75; mugs - $35; outfits (ideal, 10") - $7; paint & crayon set (Hasbro) - $100 (scarce); picnic buggy - $20; plate - $70 (scarce); pocket book - $70; premium (Colgate, record sendaway) - $50; press-out book (Whitman) - $40; purse - $45; radio - $25; record player - $80; slide tray puzzle - $50; slippers - $10; soakies (Palmolive, 10") - $20 each; soap - $15; song tote - $100; fork & spoon set - $10; squeeze toy - $40; sticker fun (Whitman) - $40; tablecloth (Hallmark) - $10; telephone - $40; toothbrush (battery operated) - $40; toothbrush holder - $40; tote bag (Hallmark) - $5; treat mobile - $20; tumbler (plastic) - $5; van (Ideal, complete & boxed) - $80; walkie talkie set - $30; wallet (1959) - $40; watch (premium) - $20; yo-yo (premium) - $20; Christmas stocking - $35; buttons - $7; bumper sticker - $10; videotapes of their 26 original episodes

Christian, Charlie

Born: 1919, Died: March 2, 1942

Innovator and talented musician who played in Benny Goodman's sextet and orchestra, where he revolutionized jazz guitar with his single-string picking and his ability to handle the instrument as a solo voice.

AUTOGRAPHS

A CD, LP, magazine cover, ad, photo, or card signed by the artist: $70-$200

OFTEN OVERLOOKED MEMORABILIA

His related work with Benny Goodman

Christie, Lou

(Lou Sacco)
Born: February 19, 1943

Sixties quavering, falsetto-style singer Lou Christie is best remembered for his songs "The Gypsy Cried" (#24, 1963), "Two Faces Have I" (#6, 1963), "Lightnin' Strikes" (#1, 1966), "Rhapsody in the Rain" (#16, 1966), and "I'm Gonna Make You Mine" (#10, 1969).

AUTOGRAPHS

A CD, LP, magazine cover, ad, photo, or card signed by the artist: $7-$15

Cinderella

Formed 1983

Eric Brittingham, Tom Keifer, Jeff LeBar, and Tony Destra*

*Destra leaves in 1986 and Jody Cortez is added briefly before he is replaced by Fred Coury. Coury leaves in 1990.

Leather and lace with each hair in its place, late-80s thunder metal gurus Cinderella made the shoe fit with singles such as "Nobody's Fool" (#13, 1986), "Don't Know What You Got (Till It's Gone)" (#12, 1988), "Coming Home" (#20, 1989), and "Shelter Me" (#38, 1990). When *Still Climbing* (1994) stopped, so did the band. Rumor has it that a reunion is in the works, so keep your shoes on and get home by midnight!

AUTOGRAPHS

A CD, LP, magazine cover, ad, photo, or card signed by the group: $17-$35

TOUR BOOKS/PROGRAMS/PASSES

Backstage Passes:
Cloth: $5-$8; Laminated: $10-$15

POSTERS/PRESS KITS

Promotional Posters:
$10-$20
Press Kits: $10-$25

USED CLOTHING/ EQUIPMENT

Guitar Picks. $10-$15

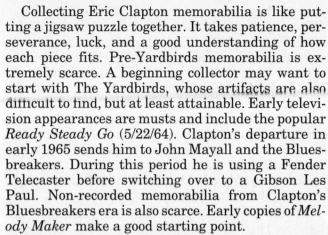

A Cinderella guitar pick

The Circle Jerks

Formed 1980

Keith Morris, Greg Hetson, Roger Rogerson, and Lucky Lehrer*

*Lehrer leaves in 1982 and is replaced with John Ingram. In 1983 both Ingram and Rogerson leave and the band adds Zander Schloss and Keith Clark.

A "back to basics," hardcore, "slammin' and jammin'" skateboard junkie band, The Circle Jerks are led by ex-Black Flag frontman Keith Morris. The band has developed an extensive cult following through playing the L.A. club circuit, but to date has undersold commercial expectations.

AUTOGRAPHS

A CD, LP, magazine cover, ad, photo, or card signed by the group: $10-$20

USED CLOTHING/EQUIPMENT

Guitar Picks: $10

OFTEN OVERLOOKED MEMORABILIA

A copy of the L.A. punk documentary *Decline of Western Civilization* (1981)

Clapton, Eric

(Eric Clapp)
Born: March 30, 1945

Eric Clapton is a rock 'n' roll disciple and a blues god. As he has evolved, so has the music he so dearly respects. Constantly evoking his rhythm and blues roots, he has managed to stay in the forefront of the music industry through his endless touring, guest appearances, and session work. The bands he has played with are now legendary—Blind Faith, Cream, The Yardbirds, Derek and the Dominos—as are the musicians he has played with—Muddy Waters, Buddy Guy, Jeff Beck, Jimmy Page, Duane Allman. In a career that has spanned decades, there is little he has failed to accomplish. By most accounts he is one of the greatest musicians ever to pick up a guitar.

Collecting Eric Clapton memorabilia is like putting a jigsaw puzzle together. It takes patience, perseverance, luck, and a good understanding of how each piece fits. Pre-Yardbirds memorabilia is extremely scarce. A beginning collector may want to start with The Yardbirds, whose artifacts are also difficult to find, but at least attainable. Early television appearances are musts and include the popular *Ready Steady Go* (5/22/64). Clapton's departure in early 1965 sends him to John Mayall and the Bluesbreakers. During this period he is using a Fender Telecaster before switching over to a Gibson Les Paul. Non-recorded memorabilia from Clapton's Bluesbreakers era is also scarce. Early copies of *Melody Maker* make a good starting point.

Cream debuted in Manchester at the Twisted Wheel on July 29, 1966. Any items associated with Cream's appearance on October 1, 1966, at the Regent Polytechnic are highly sought, as Jimi Hendrix joined the band for a version of "Killing Floor." Videotape collectors will want to get a hold of a copy of the band's appearance on *Ready Steady Go* (11/4/66), *Simon Dee Show* (4/6/67), *Our World* (6/25/67), *Twice a Fortnight* (11/26/67), and *Smothers Brothers Comedy Hour* (5/20/68). Cream's first American tour began in August 1967 with dates at the Fillmore Auditorium in San Francisco. The band's farewell was on November 26, 1968—a live show at Royal Albert Hall, London.

The key Blind Faith piece of memorabilia is a package sent out by Island Records to inform clients of their change of address. It includes Blind Faith's first record release and was limited to 500 copies. The instrumental never had a general release, but surfaced in 1992 on a Westwood One radio-only release titled *Eric Clapton Rarities on Compact Disc, Vol. II*. The group's first live appearance was in Hyde Park on June 7, 1969, and was filmed. The band's first tour of America was filled with violence between fans and police. Naturally, all memorabilia from this tour is highly sought by Clapton collectors. The band's first and only album caused a controversy because it featured a nude eleven-year-old girl holding a spaceship. Atco issued an alternate sleeve, thereby creating more collectibles.

Clapton hits the road with Delaney and Bonnie at the end of 1969 for a short tour of the U.K., then the U.S. The band appears on the *Dick Cavett Show* (2/5/70), performing three songs. All memorabilia from both Fillmore gigs (2/6-7, 2/19-22) is highly sought by collectors.

On June 14, 1970, Derek and the Dominos perform their debut gig at "Dr. Spock's Civil Liberties Legal Defense Fund" in London. Dave Mason also appears with the band before pursuing his solo career. The band opens their first tour in August 1970, and later that month they would find themselves in Miami, Florida, to record with Tom Dowd. It's Dowd who arranges Eric Clapton's meeting with Duane Allman. The chemistry is instantaneous, as *Layla and Other*

Assorted Love Songs is recorded. The band tours the U.S. in October 1970. Clapton ends up on the *Johnny Cash TV Show* (11/5/70) and even jams with Cash and Carl Perkins. The band's last gig is on December 6, 1970, at Suffolk Community College in Selden, New York. Key collectibles include tickets, posters, and handbills from all of the band's gigs, particularly those at Curtis Hixon Hall in Tampa, Florida (12/1) and at the War Memorial in Syracuse, New York (12/2), as those gigs included Duane Allman. The band dissolves during the recording session for their second album in May 1971. Afterwards, Clapton slips out of sight to cater to a heroin problem.

Clapton emerges on January 13, 1973, at "The Rainbow Theatre Concert" in London. The concert is recorded and eventually released. Clapton again slips out of sight, but later returns to appear in the film *Tommy*. Following the recording of *461 Ocean Boulevard* in Miami, Clapton prepares his band for an upcoming tour. Interesting memorabilia from the release includes pins and even a license plate. The record is the first in three years for Clapton and he follows it up with *There's One in Every Crowd*. Clapton, who is a tax exile, finally returns to England in May 1975. During the visit he suffers a near fatal crash when his Ferrari collides with a truck near his home. A picture of the demolished car appears inside the *Slowhand* album. In June 1975 he undertakes an extensive U.S. tour. While performing in the Civic Center in New Haven (6/25), Clapton performs "Sunshine of Your Love" for the first time since Cream disbanded. The tour provides Clapton's numerous friends—Carlos Santana, Keith Moon, and Joe Cocker—with a chance to jam with him when he visits their hometown. In September his live album *EC Was Here* is released.

A Japanese tour begins in October 1975, followed by a British tour in 1976. On August 5, 1976, while in Birmingham, he makes a controversial political speech during the gig. The statement forces Clapton to send a letter to *Sounds,* which publishes it in their September 11, 1976 issue—now a collectors item! A short U.S. tour begins in November 1976. During the tour Clapton attends The Band's farewell concert (The Last Waltz) at the Winterland in San Francisco (11/26). On February 14, 1977, Clapton plays an unpublicized Valentine's Day dance at Cranleigh Village Hall in Surrey. The posters for the event advertise the band as "Eddie and the Earth Tremors." On February 26, 1977, the band is filmed for *The Old Grey Whistle Test* television program.

Slowhand is released in November 1977. On April 19, 1978, he takes part in Alexis Korner's fiftieth birthday party celebration, which is later released on videotape and record. The touring continues as *Backless* is released in December 1978. While at Budokan, Tokyo, on December 2 and 3, Clapton records live for *Just One Night,* his next double album release (5/80). This is soon followed by *Another Ticket* (2/81) and

supported by an extensive tour that eventually grinds to halt on March 14, 1981, when Clapton enters a hospital for ulcers. The illness forces Clapton to cancel 47 shows and he is not seen publicly again until September.

Money and Cigarettes is released in February 1983, and the tour that follows is appropriately sponsored by Camel cigarettes, which produces promotional trinkets for the tour. In October 1984, Clapton undertakes an Australian tour and releases a duet with Phil Collins, "You Don't Know Like I Know," which hasn't been released elsewhere. On January 2, 1985, Clapton films his first video ("Forever Man"). *Behind the Sun* is released in March 1985. Clapton appears on *Late Night With David Letterman* on May 8, 1985, and performs "White Room" for the first time since Cream. He also makes an appearance at the historic "Live Aid" show in Philadelphia on July 13, 1985.

On June 20, 1986, Clapton appears at the "Prince's Trust" tenth birthday party concert at Wembley Arena. The all-star show is filmed for later release. In August he films his video for "Tearing Us Apart" at a club in London's Soho. On November 8, he jams with Robert Cray in London, producing "Phone Booth," which is released as a free flexi-disc with the May issue of *Guitar Player* magazine. With the end of the month comes the release of *August*.

The following year is filled with extensive touring, much of which is recorded. Major gigs include "Prince's Trust" and the "Free Nelson Mandela" concert in Wembley Stadium. The *Crossroads* retrospective (six sides of numerous Clapton classics as well as unreleased gems) is released in April.

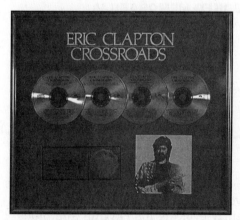

The early RIAA certified CD award for Eric Clapton's Crossroads boxed set from 1988. Valued at $750. From the Doug Leftwitch collection.

Journeyman is released in November 1989. Extensive touring includes a 1990 U.K. Tour, Scandinavian Tour, European Tour, and American Tour. The American Tour would prove tragic: Following the band's gig at Alpine Valley Music Theater, the helicopter carrying members of his entourage and Stevie Ray Vaughan crashed, leaving no survivors. Although extremely difficult, the decision was made to continue the tour.

On March 20, 1991, Clapton's four-and-a half-year-old son, Connor, died after falling from a Manhattan apartment. The devastating event would change his life forever and cause the artist to enter a period of seclusion. His next project would be music for the film *Rush,* a story about drug addiction. In March 1992 he taped a segment for MTV's *Unplugged* series. In addition to a classic remake of "Layla" (#12, 1993), Clapton performed "Tears in Heaven" (#2, 1993), which he had written for his son. He was later nominated for nine Grammy awards, taking home six. At their Rock 'n' Roll Hall of Fame induction, Clapton reunited with Cream cohorts Jack Bruce and Ginger Baker for three songs on January 12, 1993.

In 1994 he won a Grammy for Best Traditional Blues Album for *From The Cradle.* Accolades for the artist continue as he receives an OBE in H.R.H. Queen Elizabeth II's New Year's Honours List, as well as a Silver Clef Award. On November 15, 1995, he pays $17,000 for an autographed Gibson "Lucille" guitar signed by blues legend B.B. King.

The Royal Albert Hall celebrates its tenth anniversary as host to Eric Clapton and his extended stay. Memorabilia from this annual event continues to draw collector interest and will probably prove to be a worthy investment.

Whether you collect obscure Clapton memorabilia or relics from his now traditional Royal Albert Hall stay, you have the added benefit of collecting a legend. As a prolific artist who is prone to extensive touring, session work, and even film soundtracks, he generates a significant amount of related artifacts. Although often overlooked, his role in film is worth acknowledgment and is a fascinating area for Clapton collectors to explore.

ERIC CLAPTON - FILM WORK

(Selected entries)

December 1967	*Wonderwall* - a George Harrison project	June 20, 1986	*Prince's Trust* tenth birthday party
February 1968	*On a Saturday Night* - a short Danish film	September 1986	*Color Of Money* - contributes two songs for soundtrack****
November 26, 1968	*Farewell Cream* - shot for broadcast by BBC Television, eventually released on videotape	December 1986	*Lethal Weapon* soundtrack**
December 10, 11, 1968	*Rock and Roll Circus* - a Rolling Stones film	October 19, 1987	*Hearts Of Fire* soundtrack released; Clapton plays on three tracks*****
March 18, 1969	*Supershow* at Staines television studio	March 25, 1988	*Buster* - records "The Robbery" for the soundtrack*****
June 7, 1969	Blind Faith debut, partially shown on *Cucumber Castle,* a Bee Gees TV special	April 1988	*Homeboy* soundtrack
September 13, 1969	Plastic Ono Band - the gig was filmed and later released	February 7, 1989	*License To Kill* - records title music, which faces legal problems for release
December 12, 1969	Delaney and Bonnie - Falkoner Theatre, Copenhagen	March 1989	*Lethal Weapon II* soundtrack****
August 1, 1971	*The Concert For Bangladesh* - Madison Square Garden, NY*	December 1989	*Communion* soundtrack*****
March 1974	*Tommy* - the Who rock opera**	January 1992	*Rush* soundtrack*****
September 14, 1975	*Circasia* - a 37 minute film	April 1992	*Lethal Weapon III* soundtrack
November 26, 1976	*The Last Waltz* - The Band's farewell concert***	1996	*Phenomenon* soundtrack
May 1985	*Water* - appears in film and on soundtrack; also records his first soundtrack for the BBC drama *Edge Of Darkness*****		

Values for One Sheets:
*$15-25
**$15-$30
***$20-$40
****$10-$20
*****$5-$10

ERIC CLAPTON - A ROCK 'N' ROLL CHRONOLOGY 1963-1990

Year	Band/Group	Members/Contributors
1/63-8/63	Roosters	Brennan, Mason, Palmer, McGuinnes (Played The Marquee!)
9/63	Casey Jones & The Engineers	Jones, Stock, McGuinnes (Played only 7 gigs!)
10/63-3/65	Yardbirds	Dreja, McCarty, Relf, Samwell-Smith (Replaced by Jeff Beck!)
4/65-8/65	John Mayall's Bluesbreakers	Mayall, Flint, McVie
8/65-10/65	Greek Loon Band	Palmer, Bailey, Ray, Milton, Greenwood (Played in Greece during summer!)
11/65-7/66	John Mayall's Bluesbreakers	Mayall, Flint, McVie
7/66-11/68	Cream	Ginger Baker, Jack Bruce (7 real albums)
2/69-1/70	Blind Faith	Ginger Baker, Ric Grech, Steve Winwood (Only one album!)
1/70-3/70	Delaney & Bonnie & Friends	Bramlett, Bramlett, Price, Coolidge, Keys, Radle, Whitlock, Gordon, Harrison, Mason
5/70-4/71	Derek and the Dominos	Radle, Whitlock, Gordon, Mason, Allman
8/1/71	Bangladesh Concert Group	Harrison, Starr, Voorman, Russell, Keltner, Preston, Davies, Radle, and others (Clapton made numerous session appearances)
1/13/73	Rainbow Concert	Townshend, Wood, Karstein, Winwood, Capaldi, Grech, and Bop
4/74-6/77	Eric Clapton and his band	Radle, Oldmaker, Simms, Levy, Terry, Elliman, Pastora
6/77-8/78	Eric Clapton and his band	Radle, Oldmaker, Simms, Levy, Terry
8/78-1/79	Eric Clapton and his band	Radle, Oldmaker, Simms
1/79-3/79	Eric Clapton and his band	Radle, Oldmaker, Simms, Lee
3/79-5/80	Eric Clapton and his band	Lee, Stainton, Markee, Spinetti (47 city tour of U.S.A. begins 3/28/79)
5/80	Eric Clapton and his band	Lee, Stainton, Markee, Spinetti, Brooker (13 date U.K. tour begins 5/2, followed by Scandinavian tour)
9/12/81	The Secret Policeman's Other Ball	Jeff Beck, Sting, Phil Collins, and others
2/83-2/15/83	Eric Clapton and his band	Lee, Stainton, Dunn, Hawkins
2/15/83-6/84	Eric Clapton and his band	Lee, Stainton, Dunn, Oldaker
3/17/83	"Prince's Trust Rock Gala"	Appice, Beck, Fairweather-Low, Lane, Page, Wyman (An ARMS benefit concert, additional shows follow on 9/20 and 12/8)
6/84-7/84	The Roger Waters Band	Clapton, Waters, Renwick, Kamen, Newmark, Collins, Chanter, Kissoon, Stainton
11/84-2/85	Eric Clapton and his band	Stainton, Oldaker, Dunn, Levy, Murphy, Robinson
2/85-12/85	Eric Clapton and his band	Stainton, Oldaker, Dunn, Levy, Murphy, Renwick
12/85	The Pier Head Restoration Band	Clapton, Gary Brooker, and others (Played two gigs in Surrey)
6/86-1/87	Eric Clapton and his band	Collins, East , Phillinganes
1/87-4/87	Eric Clapton and his band	Knopfler, Phillinganes, East, Ferrone
4/87-10/87	Eric Clapton and his band	Collins, Phillinganes, East
10/87-1/88	Eric Clapton and his band	Clark, East, Ferrone
1/88-8/88	Eric Clapton and his band	Knopfler, Clark, East, Ferrone, Cooper, Kissoon, Niles (Clark and Cooper are replaced at "Prince's Trust" show with Elton John and Phil Collins)
8/88-12/88	Eric Clapton and his band	Knopfler, Clark, East, Ferrone, Linscott, Kissoon, Niles
8/88-12/88	Eric Clapton and his band	Knopfler, Clark, East, Ferrone, Linscott, Kissoon, Niles, Cooper, John
1/89-2/89	Eric Clapton and his band	Collins, East, Phillinganes
2/89-6/89	Eric Clapton and his band	Knopfler, Clark, East, Ferrone, Linscott, Kissoon, Niles, Cooper, Phillinganes
6/89-1/90	Eric Clapton and his band	Palmer, Clark, East, Ferrone, Cooper, Kissoon, Niles

Not intended to be comprehensive, as benefit bands, jam sessions and various single-day or two-day projects have been omitted.

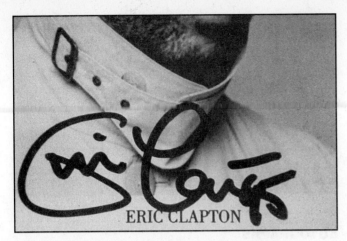

ERIC CLAPTON

A recent signature of the legendary guitarist Eric Clapton

AUTOGRAPHS

Group:
A CD, LP, magazine cover, ad, photo, or card signed by the members of Cream: $500-$600

Individual:
Eric Clapton: $50-$60
Signed handwritten letter: $750-$1,200
Signed self-portrait: $1,100-$1,200
Signed baseball: $600-$700

TOUR BOOKS/PROGRAMS/PASSES

Tour Books:
1974 Japan Tour: $100-$165 (scarce)
1975 Japan Tour: $120-$150
From the Cradle: $20
1978 Japan Tour: $50
1985 Tour: $25
1992 U.K. Tour: $20
1981 Canceled Tour: $10-$15
1981 Japan Tour: $40
1994 Royal Albert Hall: $15-$20
1989 Tour Programme: $25-$30
1988 "25" Programme: $30

One of the many collectible programs from Clapton's annual appearance at the Royal Albert Hall. The whole series is highly sought after by "EC" collectors. (Winterland Productions, Ltd.).

Backstage Passes:
Cloth: $10-$25;
Laminated: $15-$60

Promotional Posters:
Recent promotional posters run about $10-$20 depending upon size, stock, and scarcity

Tour Posters:
Derek and the Dominos (1970): $400-$500
Early posters are scarce and relatively expensive. Highly sought are Fillmore and Winterland posters, along with their associated handbills and tickets. Of the numbered "Bill Graham Presents" series, Cream is featured on BG: 79, 80*, 109*, and 110*. BG: 79 appears to be the most difficult to find. "Delaney & Bonnie & Friends" appear on BG: 218 and 262. Both are tough to find and believed to have been printed only once. Associated postcards are also used for promotional purposes. "The Yardbirds" appear on BG: 33, 75, and 121—all created after Eric Clapton had left the band.
*Indicates reprinting/second printing

USED CLOTHING/EQUIPMENT

Autographed Fender Stratocaster (Not used): $3,500
Stage-worn shoes: $1,000-$2,000
Acoustic guitar, extensive use both on and off stage, with case: $10,000-$12,000
Promotional Guitar Picks: $30 (1992)
Guitar Picks: $100-$150*
Creative guitar pick quotes include "E.C. IS HERE/ E.C. WAS THERE," "E.C. AND HIS BAND/NO PROBLEMO," and "E.C./ THE GREAT PRODDING NO GLO"

OFTEN OVERLOOKED MEMORABILIA

Copies of newspapers surrounding his 1968 drug bust; session work promos, such as The Beatles *White Album*, where he plays on "While My Guitar Gently Weeps"; invitations to various special events that he attended - $30-$40; buttons - $3-$10; metal guitar pin with "Eric Clapton" - $8; "No Reason To Cry" 3-D mobile - $100; "24 Nights" counter display of video cover - $15; "From The Cradle" giant display of E.C. in suit & sweater (36 x 56) - $50; "From The Cradle" banner (3 dogs) - $15-$18; all associated movie memorabilia

REFERENCES/BOOKS

Eric Clapton: The Complete Recording Sessions 1963-1992 by Marc Roberty and *Eric Clapton: The Man, the Music and the Memorabilia* by Marc Roberty—both essential to Clapton collectors! Numerous resources exist; serious collectors should opt for fan club: Slowhand: The Quarterly Magazine for Eric Clapton Fans, P.O. Box 488, Pelham, N.Y. 10803

The Dave Clark Five

Formed 1961

Dave Clark, Born: December 15, 1942; Mike Smith, Born: December 6, 1943; Rick Huxley, Born: August 5, 1942; Lenny Davidson, Born: May 30, 1944; and Denis Payton, Born: August 11, 1943

A June 10, 1964, poster from the Westchester, NY, appearance by the Dave Clark Five. New York City's Murray Poster Printing Co. printed the 14" x 22" poster, which is valued at $1,000. From the collection of Hank Thompson.

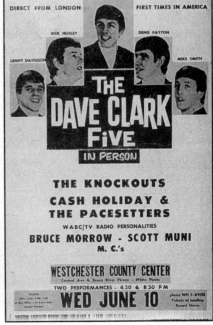

Part of the British Invasion, The Dave Clark Five was led by producer, manager, songwriter, and sex symbol Dave Clark. The band actually appeared on the *Ed Sullivan Show* more times than either the Beatles or the Rolling Stones, and had 17 Top Forty hits over a three-year period, including "Glad All Over" (#6, 1964), "Bits and Pieces" (#4, 1964), "Can't You See That She's Mine" (#4, 1964), "Because" (#3, 1964), "I Like It Like That" (#7, 1965), "Catch Us If You Can" (#4, 1965), "Over and Over" (#1, 1965), and "You Got What It Takes" (#7, 1967). When the hits stopped, the band eventually split up, although it had some later success in the U.K.

AUTOGRAPHS

A CD, LP, magazine cover, ad, photo, or card signed by the group: $30-$120

OFTEN OVERLOOKED MEMORABILIA

Movie memorabilia from *Get Yourself a College Girl* (1964) and *Having a Wild Weekend* (1965); videotapes of the group's 18 appearances on the *Ed Sullivan Show;* mail-order card and associated memorabilia from Ponds' Fresh Start Cold cream

Clark, Petula

Born: November 15, 1932

Child prodigy, singer, actress, and thespian, Petula Clark is best known in the United States for her hits "Downtown" (#1, 1964), "I Know a Place" (#3, 1965), "My Love" (#1, 1966), "I Couldn't Live Without Your Love" (#9, 1966), "Don't Sleep in the Subway" (#5, 1967), "The Other Man's Grass Is Always Greener" (#31, 1967) and "Kiss Me Goodbye" (#15, 1968). In the U.K. she is also remembered for "The Little Shoemaker" (#12, U.K.), "Majorca," "Sailor" (#1, U.K., 1961) and "Romeo" (#3, U.K., 1961). At the age of twelve, Clark made her film debut in *A Medal for the General* and by the '50s she had appeared in over twenty films. She later turned her sights on the theater, including Broadway.

AUTOGRAPHS

A CD, LP, magazine cover, ad, photo, or card signed by the artist: $10-$30

OFTEN OVERLOOKED MEMORABILIA

Movie memorabilia from her numerous films, including *A Medal for the General, Goodbye, Mr. Chips,* and *Finian's Rainbow;* theater memorabilia from her appearances in *The Sound of Music* (1981), *Candida, Someone Like You* (1990) and *Blood Brothers* (1993).

Clarke, Stanley

Born: June 30, 1951

A bassist whose acoustic precision and electric plunking have become his trademarks, Stanley Clarke has played with jazz greats Art Blakey, Gil Evans, Thad Jones-Mel Lewis Orchestra, Stan Getz, and Chick Corea, to whom he is often linked. Clarke has also crossed over into rock as a member of the New Barbarians, joining Rolling Stones Ron Wood and Keith Richards. He had a hit with the ballad "Sweet Baby" in 1981, before joining Corea, White, and DiMeola on a Return to Forever reunion tour in 1983. He joined Paul McCartney on *Tug of War* (1982) before turning his attention to composing for television and motion pictures.

AUTOGRAPHS

A CD, LP, magazine cover, ad, photo, or card signed by the artist: $10-$25

OFTEN OVERLOOKED MEMORABILIA

His compositions for television and film, including *What's Love Got to Do with It, Boyz N the Hood,* and *Poetic Justice;* all associated memorabilia from his numerous groups and one-off performances

The Clash

Formed 1976

Mick Jones, Born: June 26, 1955; Paul Simonon, Born: December 15, 1955; Tory Crimes (Chimes); and Joe Strummer (John Mellor)*

*Crimes leaves in 1977 and is replaced with Nicky "Topper" Headon. Crimes returns in 1982 and Headon departs. Jones and Crimes both leave in 1985 and Vince White and Pete Howard are added.

When everything was said and done with British punk, they tallied up the scores and found out that the real winner of this movement was The Clash. Visionaries, protesters, and rebels, their anti-everything attitude was exemplified in everything they did both on and off the stage. Unfortunately, they were self-destructing just as they were breaking through in America.

Managed by British punk emperor Malcolm McLaren (which means you immediately knew this band would not be boring), the band hit America in February 1979, during their Pearl Harbour Tour, and in conjunction with the release of their first album in the States. They toured again in the fall of 1979, before *London Calling* (#27, 1980) became their commercial breakthrough. Extract "Train in Vain (Stand By Me)" (#23, 1980) helped push the album, as did the band's pop style.

Their triple album *Sandinista!* (#24, 1981) actually sold more copies in America than the U.K., partly due to the band's insistence that the effort be sold at a reduced price. The band then began disintegrating: Headon was arrested for heroin possession, Strummer just up and disappeared for a period of time, then Headon left the band. Ironically, the Headon-penned

"Rock the Casbah" (#8, 1982) then hit the charts and became the group's biggest hit.

Combat Rock (#7, 1982) followed and sold platinum, aided by the hit "Should I Stay or Should I Go" and a fall tour with The Who. Not long after Simonon and Strummer kicked Jones out of the band, and added two new guitarists. The move proved fatal, as the band quickly fell out of favor and later disbanded. "Should I Stay or Should I Go" was re-released after being featured in the now infamous Levi's commercial and shot to #1 in the U.K.

HISTORIC CLASHES WITH THE CLASH

(Selected Confrontations Worthy of Periodical Clipping)

6/10/77	Strummer and Headon are fined for spray-painting "Clash" on a wall
7/11-12/77	Strummer and Headon are detained overnight in prison, having failed to appear before magistrates to answer charges relating to the theft of a hotel pillowcase
10/8/77	The Clash spend an afternoon in a German jail after a dispute over a hotel bill
3/30/78	Strummer and Headon are arrested in London after shooting down racing pigeons with air rifles from the top of a recording studio
7/8/78	Strummer and Simonon are arrested and fined for being drunk and disorderly after a show
5/24/80	Strummer is arrested in West Germany after smashing his guitar over the head of an aggressive audience member
7/2/82	Headon is charged with stealing a bus stop! An old Hollies trick!

AUTOGRAPHS

A CD, LP, magazine cover, ad, photo, or card signed by the group: $40-$120

OFTEN OVERLOOKED MEMORABILIA

"Give 'Em Enough Rope" CBS promotional album with poster showing the nations currently in conflict; "Give "Em Enough Rope" Epic promotional jigsaw and box, 1978; "Combat Rock" Epic promotional notepad, 1982; Strummer's film soundtrack work, including *Sid & Nancy, Straight to Hell, Walker, Permanent Record,* and *Mystery Train;* movie memorabilia from *Rude Boy;* any and all items from their first announced gig opening for the Sex Pistols in the summer of 1976; videotape of the Levi's commercial that helped them score their #1 U.K. hit

REFERENCES/BOOKS

Numerous resources exist; no dedicated collector books

The Classics IV

Formed mid 1960s

J.R. Cobb, Dennis Yost, Kim Venable, Joe Wilson, and Wally Eaton*

*Wilson is replaced by Dean Daughtry

Soft rock act best known for hits "Spooky" (#3, 1968), "Stormy" (#5, 1968) and "Traces" (#2, 1969), The Classics IV had their fifteen minutes of fame in rock and roll. Dean Daughtry later formed the Atlanta Rhythm Section in 1974.

AUTOGRAPHS

A CD, LP, magazine cover, ad, photo, or card signed by the group: $10-$30

Cleveland, The Reverend James

Born: December 23, 1932, Died: February 9, 1991

A major force in gospel music, especially through his work with the Gospel Music Workshop Convention (GMWC), "Gospel's Louis Armstrong" is responsible for such staples as "Peace Be Still," "Lord Remember Me," "Father, I Stretch My Hands to Thee," and "The Love of God." His 1972 album with Aretha Franklin, *Amazing Grace,* sold double-platinum and has become a recognized classic.

AUTOGRAPHS

A CD, LP, magazine cover, ad, photo, or card signed by the artist: $10-$45

OFTEN OVERLOOKED MEMORABILIA

Any and all items associated with the GMWC

Cliff, Jimmy

(James Chambers)
Born: April 1, 1948

One of the few reggae stars to gain international recognition, Cliff is best known as star of the film *The Harder They Come,* and for his hits "Under the Sun, Moon and Stars," Struggling Man," "House of Exile," "Many Rivers to Cross," "Waterfall," "Wonderful World, Beautiful People," and "Give and Take." His album *Cliff Hanger* earned him a Grammy for Best Reggae Recording in 1985.

AUTOGRAPHS

A CD, LP, magazine cover, ad, photo, or card signed by the artist: $15-$30

OFTEN OVERLOOKED MEMORABILIA

Movie memorabilia from *The Harder They Come, Bongo Man, Club Paradise,* and *Images*

Climax Blues Band

Formed 1968

Original lineup: Colin Cooper, Peter Haycock, Arthur Wood, Derek Holt, and George Newsome

Derivative blues band that evolved into an FM staple, the band is best known for its hits "Couldn't Get It Right" (#3, 1977) and the tender ballad "I Love You" (#12, 1981).

AUTOGRAPHS

A CD, LP, magazine cover, ad, photo, or card signed by the group: $10-$15

Cline, Patsy

(Virginia Hensley)
Born: September 8, 1932, Died: March 5, 1963

She made an appearance on Arthur Godfrey's *Talent Scout* and was spotted by Owen Bradley of Decca Records, who signed her. "Walkin' After Midnight" (#3, 1957) was her first record, her first pop Top Fifteen, and first country Top Five. As a result she quickly became one of country music's big stars with songs such as "I Fall to Pieces" (#12, 1961), "Crazy" (#9, 1961), and "She's Got You" (#14, 1962).

On March 5, 1963, the single-engine plane she was traveling in, piloted by her manager, crashed. She was killed at the young age of 30, just as her career was hitting a full head of steam. She became the first woman solo artist elected to the Country Music Hall of Fame.

AUTOGRAPHS

An LP, magazine cover, ad, photo, or card signed by the artist: $500-$1,500

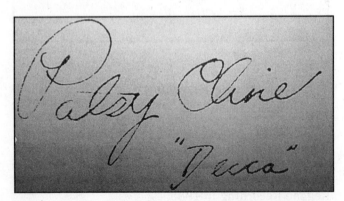

A rare signature of the legendary country singer Patsy Cline

REFERENCES/BOOKS

I Fall to Pieces: The Music and Life of Patsy Cline by Mark Bego; numerous resources exist; no dedicated collector books

Clinton, George/Parliament/Funkadelic

Born: July 22, 1940

"Dr. Funkenstein" and "The Mothership Connection" are best known for such instant booty shakers as "(I Wanna) Testify" (#20, 1967), "Up for the Down Stroke" (#63, 1974), "Tear the Roof Off the Sucker" (#15, 1976), "Flashlight" (#16, 1977), "One Nation Under Groove" (#28, 1978) and "Atomic Dog" (#1, R&B, 1982). Forever diverse, he has played at both President Clinton's Youth Inaugural Ball and on the 1994 Lollapalooza tour. His approach to recording was a dichotomy of sorts, as Parliament was the more commercial Clinton and Funkadelic more experimental, although it was sometimes tough to tell the two apart.

AUTOGRAPHS

A CD, LP, magazine cover, ad, photo, or card signed by the artist: $15-$40

The Clovers

Original lineup: John Bailey, Matthew McQuater, Harold Lucas Jr., Harold Winley, and Bill Harris*

*Bailey leaves in 1953 and is replaced by Charles White. White leaves the following year and is replaced by Billy Mitchell.

Pivotal R&B vocal group of the '50s who injected their music with big-beat and gospel-like vocals, The Clovers are best remembered for songs such as "Don't You Know I Love You," "Fool, Fool, Fool," "One Mint Julep," "Ting-A-Ling," "Hey Miss Fannie," "Crawlin'," "Good Lovin'" (1953), "Lovey Dovey," "I've Got My Eyes on You," "Your Cash Ain't Nothing but Trash" (1954), "Blue Velvet," "Devil or Angel," "From the Bottom of My Heart," and "Love Potion No. 9" (#23, R&B, 1959). The group disbanded in 1961.

AUTOGRAPHS

A CD, LP, magazine cover, ad, photo, or card signed by the group: $20-$60

OFTEN OVERLOOKED MEMORABILIA

Memorabilia associated with other musicians' covers of their songs

The Coasters/The Robins

Formed 1955

Original lineup: Carl Gardner, Leon Hughes, Billy Guy, and Bobby Nunn*

*Additional personnel included Will Jones, Cornell Gunter, Earl "Speedoo" Carroll, Ronnie Bright, and Jimmy Norman

Creative doo-wop act of the late '50s that was taken under the wing of Jerry Leiber and Mike Stoller, The Coasters successfully crossed into rock and roll with a series of well-known hits, including "Yakety Yak" (#1, 1958), "Charlie Brown" (#2, 1959), "Along Came Jones" (#9, 1959) and "Poison Ivy" (#7, 1959). Both Nunn and Gardner had left The Robins, who had scored with R&B hits like "Double Crossing Blues," "Framed," "The Hatchet Man" and "Smokey Joe's Cafe." The Coasters landed early on the R&B charts with "Down in Mexico" (1956), followed by "Searchin" b/w "Young Blood" (#3, 1957)—the first of four gold records for the band. The group was inducted into the Rock and Roll Hal of Fame in 1987.

AUTOGRAPHS

A CD, LP, magazine cover, ad, photo, or card signed by the group: $50-$150

OFTEN OVERLOOKED MEMORABILIA

Memorabilia associated with other musicians' covers of their songs

REFERENCES/BOOKS

The Coasters by Bill Millar; few resources exist; no dedicated collector books

Cobham, Billy

Born: May 16, 1944

Innovator, drummer, and important figure in the evolution of jazz-rock fusion for three decades, Billy Cobham is often associated with the Miles Davis Band, where he appeared on eight albums, and the Mahavishnu Orchestra, with his friend and peer John McLaughlin. The journeyman also has spent time as part of the Billy Cobham-George Duke Band, Jack Bruce's band, Bob Weir's Midnites, along with numerous sessions for many key musicians.

AUTOGRAPHS

A CD, LP, magazine cover, ad, photo, or card signed by the artist: $10-$25

OFTEN OVERLOOKED MEMORABILIA

Memorabilia associated with the many sessions he has contributed to, including work with George Benson, James Brown, Quincy Jones, Carlos Santana, and many others; also drum clinic posters featuring Cobham

Cochran, Eddie

Born: October 3, 1938, Died: April 17, 1960

Energetic stage performer, talented guitarist, and studio jock, Eddie Cochran made a considerable impression in a very short amount of time, with songs such as "Summertime Blues" (1958), "Sittin' in the Balcony" (1957), "C'mon Everybody" (1958), "Some-

thin' Else" (1959) and "Three Steps to Heaven" (1960). He was killed in an auto accident en route to the London airport; also in the car was his fiancee Sharon Sheeley and Gene Vincent, who both survived.

Eddie Cochran was inducted into the Rock and Roll Hall of Fame in 1987.

AUTOGRAPHS

An LP, magazine cover, ad, photo, or card signed by the artist: $300-$1,000

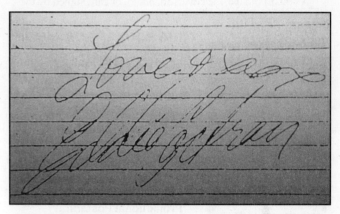

The signature of Eddie Cochran

TOUR BOOKS/PROGRAMS/PASSES

Tour Books:
Christmas Jubilee (Alan Freed, 1958): $200

OFTEN OVERLOOKED MEMORABILIA

Movie memorabilia from *The Girl Can't Help It*

Cockburn, Bruce

Born: May 27, 1945

Canadian singer, songwriter, and guitarist who is best known in the U.S. for his songs "Wondering Where the Lions Are" (#21, 1980) and the satirical "If I Had a Rocket Launcher" (#88, 1984). Cockburn has won numerous Juno awards and has been a mainstay in his homeland for nearly three decades.

AUTOGRAPHS

A CD, LP, magazine cover, ad, photo, or card signed by the artist: $5-$10

Cocker, Joe

(John Cocker)
Born: May 20, 1944

One of rock music's most distinctive voices, this British soul singer is best known in the U.S. for hits such as "The Letter" (#7, 1970), "Cry Me a River" (#11, 1970), "You Are So Beautiful" (#5, 1975), "Up

Where We Belong" (#1) and "When the Night Comes" (#11, 1990). He delivered one of Woodstock's most memorable performances singing "With a Little Help from My Friends" (#1, U.K., 1968) while trademarking his habit of wildly flailing his arms. Although substance abuse took a toll on the singer during the '70s, by the '80s he had cleaned up his act enough to begin a second career, mainly contributing songs to motion pictures.

AUTOGRAPHS
A CD, LP, magazine cover, ad, photo, or card signed by the artist: $20-$35

Joe Cocker backstage pass from the One Night of Sin tour (Printed by OTTO)

TOUR BOOKS/PROGRAMS/PASSES
Tour Books:
Power & The Passion (1990): $10
Backstage Passes:
Cloth/paper: $10-$20; Laminated: $20-$50 (1969-1981)
Cloth: $8-$10; Laminated: $10-$20 (1982-Present)

POSTERS/PRESS KITS
Promotional Posters:
1969-1981: $15-$60
1982-Present: $10-$30
Press Kits:
1969-1981: $25-$75
1982-Present: $15-$30

OFTEN OVERLOOKED MEMORABILIA
Movie memorabilia from *Woodstock, An Officer and a Gentleman, 9-1/2 Weeks* (1986), *An Innocent Man* (1990), *Carlito's Way* (1993), and *Mad Dogs and Englishmen;* videotapes of his numerous television appearances; an early stand-up from A&M records (1970s) - $75; "With a Little Help from My Friends" counter display - $50

REFERENCES/BOOKS
Joe Cocker: With a Little Help from My Friends by J.P. Bean; few resources exist; no dedicated collector books

Cocteau Twins

Formed 1981
Robin Guthrie, Elizabeth Fraser, and Will Heggie*
*Heggie leaves in 1983 and is replaced with Simon Raymonde

Peculiar U.K. trio that has managed to maintain a strong cult following, particularly in their homeland, despite their lack of a hit single. The group does typically adorn the indie charts and, as such, has developed an eclectic appeal with their dreamy transcendental sound. Elizabeth and Robin share a daughter together, born in 1989.

AUTOGRAPHS
A CD, LP, magazine cover, ad, photo, or card signed by the group: $10-$20

POSTERS/PRESS KITS
Promotional Posters: $10-$15
Press Kits: $10-$15

USED CLOTHING/EQUIPMENT
Guitar Picks: $10

OFTEN OVERLOOKED MEMORABILIA
A videotape of their appearance on *The Tonight Show With Jay Leno* (1994)

Coe, David Allan

Born: September 6, 1939
Outlaw, singer, and songwriter, Coe is best known for the latter as evidenced by hits like "Take This Job and Shove It," "Would You Lay with Me (in a Field of Stone)," "The Ride" (#1, C&W, 1983), and "Mona Lisa Lost Her Smile." He lived through a rough childhood, but was encouraged by fellow inmate Screamin' Jay Hawkins to pursue a music career upon his release from prison.

AUTOGRAPHS
A CD, LP, magazine cover, ad, photo, or card signed by the group: $10-$15

OFTEN OVERLOOKED MEMORABILIA
Memorabilia from other musicians' covers of his songs; a copy of the PBS documentary *The Mysterious Rhinestone Cowboy* (1976); movie memorabilia from the films he has appeared in, including *The Last Days of Frank and Jesse James*

Cohen, Leonard

Born: September 21, 1934
Poet, author, singer, and songwriter, Cohen has had his work covered by Judy Collins and Aaron Neville, among others. He began his interest in the form by reciting poetry over a jazz backup in 1957, a la beat-style. He performed at the 1967 Newport Folk Festival and in 1970 at the Isle of Wight Festival. He is best known for his songs "Suzanne," "Famous Blue Raincoat," and "Bird on a Wire."

AUTOGRAPHS
A CD, LP, magazine cover, ad, photo, or card signed by the artist: $10-$25

OFTEN OVERLOOKED MEMORABILIA
Memorabilia from other musicians' covers of his songs; movie memorabilia from *McCabe and Mrs. Miller*

REFERENCES/BOOKS
Cohen's books alone make a nice collection: *The Favorite Game* (1963), *Beautiful Losers* (1966), *Let Us Compare Mythologies* (1956), *The Spice-Box of Earth* (1961), *Flowers For Hitler* (1964), *Selected Poems, 1956 - 1968* (1968), *The Energy of Slaves* (1972), and *Stranger Music*

(1993), to name just some of his work. Also *Leonard Cohen: Prophet of the Heart* by L.S. Dorman and C.L. Rawlins. Numerous other resources exist; no dedicated collector books.

Cohn, Marc

Born: July 5, 1959

Singer and songwriter whose self-titled debut album earned him a 1991 Grammy for Best New Artist and a hit extract with "Walking in Memphis" (#13, 1991).

AUTOGRAPHS
A CD, LP, magazine cover, ad, photo, or card signed by the artist: $10-$15

POSTERS/PRESS KITS
Promotional Posters: $10
Press Kits: $10

OFTEN OVERLOOKED MEMORABILIA
Memorabilia from other musicians' covers of his songs

Cole, Natalie

Born: February 6, 1950

Singer, performer, and Grammy collector who just happens to be the second of Nat "King" Cole's five children, Natalie Cole is best known for her hits "This Will Be" (#6, 1975), "I've Got Love on My Mind" (#5, 1977), "Our Love" (#10, 1978), "Jump Start" (#13, 1987), "Pink Cadillac" (#5, 1988), and "Miss You Like Crazy" (#7, 1989). She garnered considerable accolades for her debut album *Inseparable,* and followed it by releasing a top-selling album every year for the remainder of the decade.

Her successful duets have included "Gimme Some Time" and "What You Won't Do For Love" with Peabo Bryson, "I Don't Think a Man Should Sleep Alone" and "Over You" with Ray Parker, Jr., and of course the work on *Unforgettable with Love* with her father.

She has looked toward acting in the '90s and continues to release intriguing and often award-winning work.

AUTOGRAPHS
A CD, LP, magazine cover, ad, photo, or card signed by the artist: $15-$35

POSTERS/PRESS KITS
Promotional Posters: $10-$25
Press Kits: $20-$30

OFTEN OVERLOOKED MEMORABILIA
Videotapes of her numerous television appearances, including *The Natalie Cole Special* (1978) and her acting debut on *I'll Fly Away* (1993); all associated Grammy memorabilia: posters, programs, etc

Coleman, Ornette

Born: March 19, 1930

Creative, talented, and innovative, Ornette Coleman transformed jazz in the '60s with the concept of "free jazz"— no player has the lead, while ignoring regular harmonies and rhythm. By the '70s he was laying down the foundation for harmolodics, in which harmonies, rhythms, and melodies function independently. The vehicle for his principles became the group Prime Time, which would fuse any form of music it could import. During his career he has played with everyone from Pat Metheny to Jerry Garcia, influencing many while forging a legacy.

AUTOGRAPHS
A CD, LP, magazine cover, ad, photo, or card signed by the group: $10-$35

POSTERS/PRESS KITS
Promotional Posters: $10-$30
Press Kits: $15-$25

OFTEN OVERLOOKED MEMORABILIA
Memorabilia from the numerous jazz festivals he has participated in, such as 1972's Newport in New York festival

Collins, Albert

Born: October 1, 1932, Died: November 24, 1993

Legendary guitarist, singer, and songwriter who recorded with everyone from Johnny "Guitar" Watson, Little Richard, and Willie Mae Thornton to John Lee Hooker, David Bowie, and Branford Marsalis. "The Master of the Telecaster" introduced his "cool sound" in 1958 with the instrumental "The Freeze," which was followed by more instrumentals, including "Defrost," "Thaw-Out," "Sno-Cone," "Hot 'n' Cold" and "Frosty." His lone R&B charter was "Get Your Business Straight" (#46, 1972). Nominated for nu-

The signature of blues guitarist Albert Collins

merous Grammy awards, he won in 1986 for best Traditional Blues Recording.

AUTOGRAPHS

A CD, LP, magazine cover, ad, photo, or card signed by the group: $10-$35

OFTEN OVERLOOKED MEMORABILIA

Memorabilia associated with his numerous musical contributions, a copy of his wine cooler advertisement with actor Bruce Willis; Live Aid memorabilia (1985)

Collins, Bootsy

(William Collins)
Born: October 26, 1951

Supersonic mystery funk bassist spawned from P-Funk, Bootsy Collins is best remembered for his numerous R&B hits, including "The Pinocchio Theory" (#6, 1977), "Hollywood Squares" (#17, 1978) and "Body Slam" (#12, 1982), and also for his outlandish wardrobe. He faded into obscurity for six years until resurfacing in 1988 with his album *What's Bootsy Doin'?* Proving that this is one boot that's still kicking, he released three Bootsy albums in 1994.

AUTOGRAPHS

A CD, LP, magazine cover, ad, photo, or card signed by the group: $10-$20

POSTERS/PRESS KITS

Promotional Posters: $10-$20
Press Kits: $10-$25

OFTEN OVERLOOKED MEMORABILIA

Memorabilia from his P-Funk contributions; copies of the videotapes he has appeared in such as Ice-Cube's video for "Bop Gun"

Collins, Judy

Born: May 1, 1939

Sixties folk rock singer responsible for bringing the work of many unknown songwriters into the spotlight, including Joni Mitchell and Randy Newman, and best known for her hits "Both Sides Now" (#8, 1968) and "Send in the Clowns" (#36, 1975; #18, 1977). She has also been involved in theater, codirected the Academy Award-nominated documentary *Antonia: A Portrait of the Woman,* and published the novel *Shameless* (1995).

AUTOGRAPHS

A CD, LP, magazine cover, ad, photo, or card signed by the artist: $10-$25

POSTERS/PRESS KITS

Promotional Posters: $10-$40
Press Kits: $10-$40

USED CLOTHING/EQUIPMENT

Guitar Picks: $10-$25

OFTEN OVERLOOKED MEMORABILIA

Memorabilia associated with the CS&N song "Suite: Judy Blues Eyes," inspired by Collins; a videotape of her documentary *Antonia: A Portrait of the Woman;* artifacts from her theater work; clippings of President Clinton stating that Collins' song "Chelsea Morning" was the inspiration for his daughter's name

REFERENCES/BOOKS

Amazing Grace by Judy Collins; *Trust Your Heart* (1987), her autobiography; *Shameless* by Judy Collins (1995); *Voices* by Judy Collins—a must! Numerous resources exist; no dedicated collector books.

Color Me Badd

Formed 1987

Bryan Abrams, Mark Calderon, Sam Watters, and Kevin "KT" Thornton

Early-90s R&B revival act best known for the their hits "I Wanna Sex You Up" (#2, 1991), "I Adore Mi Amor" (#1, 1991) and "All 4 One" (#1, 1991). Color Me Badd, along with Boyz II Men and En Vogue, brought back some of the rich sounds of the past with an updated hip-hop harmonic pop.

AUTOGRAPHS

A CD, LP, magazine cover, ad, photo, or card signed by the group: $15-$45

POSTERS/PRESS KITS

Promotional Posters: $10-$20
Press Kits: $20-$25

Colter, Jesse

(Miriam Johnson)
Born: May 25, 1947

Country-pop singer, songwriter, and former wife of Duane Eddy (later married to Waylon Jennings), Colter is often associated with her pop hit "I'm Not Lisa" (#4, 1975). She turned her attention to writing songs for children in the '90s, while also touring with her husband.

AUTOGRAPHS

A CD, LP, magazine cover, ad, photo, or card signed by the artist: $6-$18

POSTERS/PRESS KITS

Promotional Posters: $10
Press Kits: $10

OFTEN OVERLOOKED MEMORABILIA

Memorabilia from other musicians' covers of her songs

Colvin, Shawn

(Shanna Colvin)
Born: January 10, 1958

Folk-pop artist of the Joni Mitchell mold who won a Grammy for her debut album as Best Contemporary Folk Recording, despite that commercial success has eluded her.

AUTOGRAPHS

A CD, LP, magazine cover, ad, photo, or card signed by the artist: $5-$10

POSTERS/PRESS KITS

Promotional Posters: $8-$10
Press Kits: $10

USED CLOTHING/EQUIPMENT

Guitar Picks: $10

OFTEN OVERLOOKED MEMORABILIA

Memorabilia from her contributions to other artists' records

Commander Cody and His Lost Planet Airmen

Formed 1967

Commander Cody (George Frayne), Joe Tichy, Andy Stein, Billy Farlow, Rick Higginbotham, Stan Davis, and Bill Kirchen*

*Lance Dickerson and Bruce Barlow are added in 1971

Honky tonk, beer drinkin', boogie-woogie band best known for their "party down" saloon attitude and songs such as "Hot Rod Lincoln" (#9, 1972), "Smoke, Smoke, Smoke," and "Don't Let Go." Led by the dynamic George Frayne (the band's only constant throughout their decades of touring), the group remains active.

AUTOGRAPHS

A CD, LP, magazine cover, ad, photo, or card signed by the group: $10-$20

OFTEN OVERLOOKED MEMORABILIA

A George Frayne original painting

The Commodores/Lionel Ritchie

Formed 1968

Lionel Ritchie, Milan Williams, Ronald LaPread, Walter "Clyde" Orange, William King Jr., and Thomas McClary*

*Ritchie leaves in 1982. "J.D." Nicholas is added in 1983, while McClary departs. LaPread leaves in 1986 and Williams leaves in 1988.

Meeting at Tuskegee Institute, the six original members performed first as the Mystics before changing their name to the Commodores. They signed first with Atlantic Records, releasing one non-charting single before moving over to Motown, where the group spent two years opening shows for the Jackson 5. Their debut album, featuring their funk-oriented sound, wasn't released until 1974. "Machine Gun" (#22, 1974), "I Feel Sanctified" (#75, 1974), "Slippery When Wet" (#19, 1975) and "Fancy Dancer" (#39, 1977) were the group's early hits, before the tender ballads of Lionel Ritchie took the forefront—songs such as "Just to Be Close to You," "Sweet Love," and "Easy."

By the late '70s the group had successfully crossed over into pop, beginning their chart domination with songs like "Three Times a Lady" (#1, 1978), and later with Top Ten ballads such as "Sail On" and "Still" (both 1979). During this period, Ritchie also started branching out into other projects, putting "Lady" atop the singles chart, producing records, and even dueting with Diana Ross on his movie theme "Endless Love" (#1). His self-titled solo debut (#3) was released in 1982 and contained the hit extract "Truly." Prior to its release it was becoming increasingly apparent that Ritchie was destined to go his own way, which he did, as did Thomas McClary. The band then added James "J.D." Nicholas to the band and two years later scored a Grammy and a hit with "Nightshift" (#3). By the time the band moved to the Polydor label in 1986, only Orange, King, and Nicholas remained.

Lionel Ritchie, meanwhile, was building nothing short of a spectacular career for himself. His sophomore solo effort won the 1984 Grammy for Album of the Year and included the hit extracts "All Night Long (All Night)" (#1, 1983), "Running with the Night" (#7, 1983), "Hello" (#1, 1984), "Stuck on You" (#3, 1984) and "Penny Lover" (#8, 1984). From here, the hits just kept coming: "We Are the World" (cowrote with Michael Jackson), "Say You, Say Me" (an Oscar winner), "Dancing on the Ceiling" (#2, 1986), "Love Will Conquer All" (#9, 1986), "Ballerina Girl" (#7, 1987) and "Se La" (#20, 1987), before Ritchie took some time off. In 1992 he returned with *Back to Front*, which included the hit extracts "Do It To Me" (#1, 1992) and "My Destiny" (#56, 1992).

AUTOGRAPHS

Group:
A CD, LP, magazine cover, ad, photo, or card signed by the group: $25-$75
Individual:
Lionel Ritchie: $15-$45

TOUR BOOKS/PROGRAMS/PASSES

Backstage Passes:
Cloth/paper: $10-$15; Laminated: $15-$30 (1974-1982)
Cloth: $8-$10; Laminated: $10-$20 (1982-Present)

POSTERS/PRESS KITS

Promotional Posters:
1974-1982: $15-$40
1982-Present: $10-$20

Press Kits:
1974-1982: $20-$40
1982-Present: $15-$20

OFTEN OVERLOOKED MEMORABILIA

Movie memorabilia from *Thank God It's Friday* (1978), *Endless Love,* and *White Nights;* associated memorabilia from USA for Africa

REFERENCES/BOOKS

A few resources exist, but none do justice to Ritchie in my opinion. There are no dedicated collector books.

Concrete Blonde

Formed 1981

Johnette Napolitano, Jim Mankey, and Harry Rushakoff*

*Rushakoff leaves in 1989, while Paul Thompson and Alan Bloch are added. The latter leave over the following couple years and Rushakoff returns. Thompson returns in 1993.

Enduring L.A. club circuit band of the early '80s known best for their songs "Joey" (1990) and "Heal It Up" (1993).

AUTOGRAPHS

A CD, LP, magazine cover, ad, photo, or card signed by the group: $10-$25

Con Funk Shun

Formed 1968

Michael Cooper, Karl Fuller, Paul Harrell, Cedric Martin, Louis McCall, Felton Pilate, and Danny Thomas

Successful Memphis soul band of the late '70s and early '80s who landed numerous hits on the R&B charts, including "Fun" (#1, 1977), "Shake and Dance with Me" (#5, 1978), "Chase Me" (#4, 1979), "Got to Be Enough" (#8, 1980), "Too Tight" (#8, 1980), "Baby I'm Hooked (Right into Your Love)" (#5, 1983), "Electric Lady" (#4, 1985) and "Burnin' Love" (#8, 1986). The group disbanded in 1987.

AUTOGRAPHS

A CD, LP, magazine cover, ad, photo, or card signed by the group: $8-$20

POSTERS/PRESS KITS

Promotional Posters: $10
Press Kits: $10

Conley, Arthur

Born: April 1, 1946

Best known as Otis Redding's protégé, this soul singer landed hits with "Sweet Soul Music" (#2,

1967), "Shake, Rattle and Roll" (#31, 1967), and "Funky Street" (#14, 1968) before fading into obscurity.

AUTOGRAPHS

An LP, magazine cover, ad, photo, or card signed by the group: $5-$10

Connick, Harry Jr.

Born: September 11, 1967

Successful jazz pianist and Tin Pan Alley retro crooner, Connick proved that you can look back to get ahead. Often identified as a young Sinatra for his off-the-cuff delivery, his recordings have been extremely successful and his pure image has also fit him nicely, especially as a live drawing card. During the '90s he has tried his luck at acting while maintaining a consistent recording schedule.

AUTOGRAPHS

A CD, LP, magazine cover, ad, photo, or card signed by the artist: $25-$50

TOUR BOOKS/PROGRAMS/PASSES

Backstage Passes:
Cloth: $10; Laminated: $10-$15

POSTERS/PRESS KITS

Promotional Posters: $10-$20
Press Kits: $15-$25

OFTEN OVERLOOKED MEMORABILIA

Movie memorabilia from *When Harry Met Sally* (1989), *Memphis Belle,* and *Little Man Tate*

The Contours

Formed 1958

Billy Gordon, Billy Hoggs, Joe Billingslea, Sylvester Potts, Huey Davis, and Hubert Johnson

Mid-60s R&B dance band best known for their pop song "Do You Love Me?" (#3, 1962) and their R&B charting songs "Shake Sherry" (#21, 1963), Can You Jerk Like Me" (#15, 1965), "The Day When She Needed Me" (#37, 1965), "First I Look at the Purse" (#12, 1965), "Just a Little Misunderstanding" (#18, 1966) and "So Hard Being a Loser" (#35, 1967). Also noteworthy is that later member Dennis Edwards went on to join the Temptations.

AUTOGRAPHS

A CD, LP, magazine cover, ad, photo, or card signed by the group: $10-$40

Cooder, Ry

Born: March 15, 1947

String virtuoso, composer, and experimentalist, Cooder has established himself as a pivotal session-man, playing with a variety of musicians including the Rolling Stones, Randy Newman, and Arlo Guthrie. His album *Talking Timbuktu* was #1 on the world music chart for a record 25 weeks and earned him and guitarist Ali Farka Touré 1994's Best World Music Grammy.

His work for film soundtracks has included *Candy* (1980), *Performance* (1970), *Blue Collar* (1979), *The Long Riders* (1980), *Southern Comfort* (1981), *The Border* (1981), *Paris, Texas* (1984), *Streets of Fire* (1984), *Cocktail* (1988), *Steel Magnolias* (1989) and *Geronimo* (1993).

AUTOGRAPHS
A CD, LP, magazine cover, ad, photo, or card signed by the artist: $10-$20

POSTERS/PRESS KITS
Promotional Posters: $10-$20
Press Kits: $10-$20

USED CLOTHING/EQUIPMENT
Guitar Picks: $10-$20

OFTEN OVERLOOKED MEMORABILIA
Movie memorabilia from the films listed above; memorabilia from his contributions to other artists' musical efforts

Cooke, Sam

Born: January 22, 1935, Died: December 11, 1964

A foundation for soul music whose gospel roots and crisp vocals would be an inspiration for decades, Sam Cooke, grew up in Chicago and was a top gospel artist by 1951. He spent six productive years with the Soul Stirrers before releasing his pop debut "Loveable" (1956). The following year he struck gold with "You Send Me" (#1, 1957), followed by a series of classics, including "Only Sixteen" (#28, 1959), "Chain Gang" (#2, 1960), "Wonderful World" (#12, 1960), "Twistin' the Night Away" (#9, 1962), "Another Saturday Night" (#10, 1963) and "Shake" (#7, 1965).

On December 11, 1964, Cooke was shot and killed in what was ruled as a justifiable homicide. Decades later mystery still surrounds the controversial death of the performer, who was inducted into the Rock and Roll Hall of Fame in 1986 and again three years later as a member of the Soul Stirrers.

AUTOGRAPHS
An LP, magazine cover, ad, photo, or card signed by the artist: $300-$550

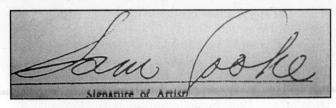

A nice example of a Sam Cooke signature on a contract

OFTEN OVERLOOKED MEMORABILIA
Any artifacts from his record label (SAR/Derby) or his music publishing enterprise (Kags Music)

REFERENCES/BOOKS
You Send Me: The Life and Times of Sam Cooke by Daniel Wolff with S.R. Crain, Clifton White and David Tenenbaum—a must for Cooke fans! A few resources exist; no dedicated collector books.

Coolidge, Rita

Born: May 1, 1944

Late-70s and early-80s soloist who had been part of Delaney and Bonnie and Friends and a successful backup singer, Rita Coolidge is commonly associated with her hit singles "Higher and Higher" (#2, 1977), "We're All Alone" (#7, 1977), "The Way You Do the Things You Do" (#20, 1978) and "All Time High" (a James Bond movie theme). Coolidge was married to Kris Kristofferson from 1973 to 1980, picking up Grammys for Best Country Duo along the way. She later appeared as one of the original veejays on the video music channel VH-1.

AUTOGRAPHS
A CD, LP, magazine cover, ad, photo, or card signed by the artist: $10-$25

POSTERS/PRESS KITS
Promotional Posters: $10-$20
Press Kits: $10-$20

OFTEN OVERLOOKED MEMORABILIA
Movie memorabilia from *Pat Garrett and Billy the Kid, Convoy,* and *A Star Is Born*

Cooper, Alice

(Vincent Furnier)
Born: February 4, 1948

Group formed mid-1960s: Glen Buxton, Michael Bruce, Dennis Dunaway, and Neal Smith

Shock-rock pioneers who established themselves on the Southern California bar circuit with a bizarre stage show and strange antics, Alice Cooper is best known for their hits singles "Eighteen" (#21, 1971), "School's Out" (#7, 1972), "Elected" (#26, 1972), "Hello, Hooray" (#35, 1973) and "No More Mr. Nice Guy"

(#25, 1973). He later landed with softer hits including "Only Women "Bleed" (#12, 1975), "I Never Cry" (#12, 1976) and "You and Me" (#9, 1977).

Following a 1978 visit to a psychiatric hospital for alcoholism, Cooper returned with the song "How You Gonna See Me Now" (#12, 1978) before taking some time off. In 1989 he scored a hit with "Poison" (#7, 1989), his first in over a decade.

AUTOGRAPHS
A CD, LP, magazine cover, ad, photo, or card signed by the group: $20-$75

Rather large Alice Cooper "After Show Pass" (unsure of manufacturer)

TOUR BOOKS/ PROGRAMS/PASSES
Tour Books:
Killer 1971 Tour Program (w/ cutout 45): $100
Raise Your Fist and Yell Tour, 1987: $20
Backstage Passes:
Cloth: $8-$10; Laminated: $15-$20 (1980-Present)

POSTERS/PRESS KITS
Promotional Posters:
1969-1978: $20-$60
1980-Present: $10-$20

Press Kits:
1969-1978: $25-$75
1980-Present: $20-$30

USED CLOTHING/EQUIPMENT
Guitar Picks: $10-$20

OFTEN OVERLOOKED MEMORABILIA
A videotape of his numerous television appearances including *Alice Cooper - The Nightmare* (4/1975) and *The Hollywood Squares;* movie memorabilia from *Prince of Darkness* (1988), *Freddy's Dead: The Final Nightmare* (1991) and *Wayne's World* (1992); *Rolling Stone* scrapbook (1975) w/poster - $40; "Hey Stoopid" promo stickers - $4; "Trash" promotional stickers - $3; Christmas '90 promotional postcard - $3; "House of Fire" promotional stickers - $3; "Last Temptation" promotional slide -$10; "Trash" promotional cups and napkins (one set) - $30; "Welcome to My Nightmare" promotional jigsaw puzzle, 1974; "Schools Out" free paper panties (3 colors); "School's Out" promotional report card

REFERENCES/BOOKS
Dell Special 1756 (All Alice Cooper): $75; numerous resources exist; no dedicated collector books

Cope, Julian/The Teardrop Explodes

Born: October 21, 1957
The Teardrop Explodes formed in 1978; original lineup: Julian Cope, Michael Finkler, Paul Simpson, and Gary Dwyer

Eccentric and unpredictable lead singer Julian Cope has built a cult following based primarily on his bizarre behavior and the single "World Shut Your Mouth" (#84, 1987), extracted from his well-received album *Saint Julian* (#105, 1987).

AUTOGRAPHS
A CD, LP, magazine cover, ad, photo, or card signed by the artist: $5-$10

POSTERS/PRESS KITS
Promotional Posters: $10-$15
Press Kits: $10-$15

REFERENCES/BOOKS
Head On, Cope's memoir (1994)

Corea, Chick

(Armando Corea)
Born: June 12, 1941
Influential jazz keyboardist who spent three years working with Miles Davis before moving on to the creative rock fusion act Return to Forever. With Davis, he appeared on the landmark jazz-rock albums *In a Silent Way* and *Bitches Brew,* while Return to Forever enjoyed substantial popularity on the rock circuit during the mid-70s.

AUTOGRAPHS
A CD, LP, magazine cover, ad, photo, or card signed by the artist: $10-$30

POSTERS/PRESS KITS
Promotional Posters: $10-$15 (1990-Present)
Press Kits: $15-$20 (1990-Present)

The Cornelius Brothers and Sister Rose

Formed circa 1970
Eddie Cornelius, Carter Cornelius (1948-1991), and Rose Cornelius

Gospel-rooted pop act best known for their hits "Treat Her Like a Lady" and "Too Late to Turn Back Now" (#2, 1972) before quickly fading from sight.

AUTOGRAPHS
An LP, magazine cover, ad, photo, or card signed by the group: $7-$15

Coryell, Larry

Born: April 2, 1943
Jazz rock guitarist who has appeared in numerous bands and recorded with numerous key figures in rock and jazz, including Chick Corea, Billy Cobham, and John McLaughlin.

AUTOGRAPHS
A CD, LP, magazine cover, ad, photo, or card signed by the artist: $10-$15

POSTERS/PRESS KITS
Promotional Posters: $10
Press Kits: $10-$15

USED CLOTHING/EQUIPMENT
Guitar Picks: $10-$20

OFTEN OVERLOOKED MEMORABILIA
Memorabilia associated with his many musical contributions

Elvis Costello. Photo by Tim Kent. Courtesy of Warner Bros. Records Inc.

Costello, Elvis

(Declan McManus)
Born: August 25, 1954

The son of a successful big-band singer, Costello was working as a computer operator for in London during the '70s, while also writing, recording demos, and occasionally performing under the name D.C. Costello (his mother's maiden name).

He quit his job to become a roadie for the band Brinsley Schwarz, where he befriended their bass player, Nick Lowe. It was Lowe who would guide Costello to Stiff Records, where he was signed to a recording contract. One of the label's owners, Jake Riviera, modified the D.C. Costello to Elvis Costello. For Costello collectors, "The Stiff Years" are where you want to concentrate your initial collecting. Memorabilia from this period is scarce and highly sought.

Costello's impressive debut album, *My Aim Is True* (#32, 1977), thrust him into a growing alternative audience who welcomed his distinctive sound and stage antics. *This Year's Model* (#30, 1978) continued where the first album left off, but added harder riffs complemented by greater depth in sound produced by a permanent backing group, The Attractions.

Armed Forces (#10, 1979) was supported by his "Armed Funk" U.S. Tour in the Spring of 1979. Unfortunately, the tour was marred by a highly-publicized conflict with Bonnie Bramlett and Stephen Stills, regarding alleged racist remarks. The controversy turned much of the press against Costello, who was forced to reduce his exposure to the music scene for a period of time. *Taking Liberties* followed, but consisted of previously released material and studio outtakes.

With *Trust* (#28, 1981), a new and politer Costello emerged and was welcomed by the press. He went on tour with Squeeze, for whom he had coproduced an album (*East Side Story*, 1981), as his skills in the studio continued to develop. Costello found himself in a stage of transformation during the '80s, as diverse album releases ranged from country & western covers, as exemplified with the album *Almost Blue* (1981),

to the McCartney-Costello collaboration "Veronica" (#19, 1989). His appetite for a variety of songs also carried over to his musicians, as Costello utilized the services of the Attractions, the Confederates, or simply performed acoustically by himself. Many critics blamed the lack of consistency on Costello's troubled personal life, which included a divorce in 1985, followed by an additional marriage a year later to Pogues' bassist Caitlin O'Riordan.

As diverse as the '80s were for the artist, his flair for variety, or perhaps just pure boredom, also led him down many paths in the '90s. Working with the Attractions on albums such as *Mighty Like a Rose* (#55, 1991) and *Brutal Youth* (1994) seemed to temporarily satisfy the artist's needs, but he couldn't help to feed his insatiable appetite for alternative directions. *The Juliet Letters* (1993), performed with England's Brodsky Quartet, broke new ground for Costello and garnered critical praise, but baffled his fan base. It was as if he used the Attractions to pay the bills or pacify his followers, just long enough to complete his current alternative project.

The mid-90s find Costello working with Burt Bacharach, Brian Eno, the Fairfield Four and of course, the Attractions. Costello makes for a fascinating subject to collect, with his diverse directions only fueling the market for his memorabilia.

AUTOGRAPHS
Elvis Costello has been very obliging to autograph requests both in-person and via mail
Group:
A CD, LP, magazine cover, ad, photo, or card signed by the artist: $15-$35

TOUR BOOKS/PROGRAMS/PASSES
Backstage Passes:
Cloth: $8-$12; Laminated: $10-$25 (Post-1980)*
*Pre-1980 add $5 for each
Promotional Posters:
Recent promotional posters run about $10-$50 depending upon size, stock, and scarcity
Stock giant (40" x 60"), first LP, hunched hands together: $50
"The Very Best" (24" x 36"), black & white face shot: $10

Press Kits: $10-$25
The Juliet Letters: $10; Brutal Youth: $12; All This Useless
Beauty: $15

USED CLOTHING/EQUIPMENT
Stage-worn jacket: $750-$1,000
Guitar Picks: $25-$50

ELVIS COSTELLO - KEY LIVE DATES
(Selected Dates)

Date	Comments
5/27/77	He makes his live debut as Elvis Costello at the Nashville, London
7/14/77	Elvis Costello and the Attractions' first gig together, at the Garden, Penzance, Cornwall
10/3/77	"Stiffs Live" label package tour of the U.K.
11/15//77	First U.S. tour begins at the Old Waldorf, San Francisco
12/17/77	Plays NBC-TV's *Saturday Night Live*
1/78-3/78	Begins three-month tour of North America
4/1/78	Begins 14-date U.K. tour
12/78	Plays seven sold-out nights at London's Dominion Theatre
4/1/79	Plays three sets at three different clubs during his "Armed Funk" U.S. tour: The Great Gildersleeves, The Lone Star Cafe and the Bottom Line!
12/22/79	Plays first of four benefit concerts at London's Hammersmith Odeon
8/17/80	"Edinburgh Rock Festival"
8/23/80	"Heatwave Festival," Toronto, Ontario, Canada
11/30/80	"Benefit concert for the family of boxer Johnny Owen," Swansea, South Wales
2/81	In the midst of a U.S. headlining tour
12/31/81	Plays the Palladium in New York during current U.S. tour
1/82	Plays at London's Royal Albert Hall with the Royal Philharmonic Orchestra
7/13/85	"Live Aid," Wembley Stadium, Wembley, Middlesex, U.K.
6/19-21/87	"Glastonbury Festival," Glastonbury, Somerset
5/14/89	Plays the first of four dates, "A Month Of Sundays," London Palladium, U.K.
7/89	Embarks on major U.S. tour
10/28/89	"Montreux Jazz Festival," Montreux, Switzerland
10/26/90	"Fourth Annual Bridge School Benefit," Mountain View, California
5/18/91	Guests on NBC-TV's *Saturday Night Live*
5/25/91	Begins U.S. tour in Santa Barbara, California
6/22/91	Madison Square Garden, New York City
7/1/91	Plays first of six nights at London's Hammersmith Odeon, U.K.
8/3/91	"Feile '91 Festival," Eire
2/22/93	Performs "The Juliet Letters" at London's Theatre Royal with the Brodsky Quartet
4/1/94	*Late Show With David Letterman* - CBS-TV, with the Attractions
6/1/94	*MTV Unplugged* - duets with crooner Tony Bennett
3/26/95	Embarks on a 13-date U.K. tour
5/16/95	*Late Show With David Letterman* - CBS-TV, from London with Little Richard and Chuck Berry
5/17/95	Live simulcast performance at London's Shepard's bush empire
6/23- 7/1/95	"Southbank Meltdown Festival" at London's Royal Festival Hall
8/2/95	Begins five-night stay at New York's Beacon Theatre

OFTEN OVERLOOKED MEMORABILIA

Items associated with his collaborations, such as those with Paul McCartney; a cocktail napkin from the Holiday Inn in Columbus, OH - $3; a Hoover vacuum cleaner manufactured at a site on the A40 highway outside London; items from the movies *Party, Party* (soundtrack by Costello), *No Surrender* (Costello's acting debut), *The Courier* (soundtrack by Costello), and *Until The End Of The World* (contributes a song); a videotape of Alan Bleasdale's *Scully* (ITV) in which Costello appears (he also pens the theme, *Turning The Town Red*); a copy of the Bruce Thomas book *The Big Wheel* (1990); memorabilia from *Songs in the Key of X*, music inspired by *The X-Files* - FOX-TV (Costello contributes track with Brian Eno); "Armed Forces" Columbia-issued green and white promotional whistles, 1979; "Almost Blue" Columbia/Hitline promotional belt buckle, 1981; "Mighty Like A Rose" Warner Brothers promotional red chocolate rose, 1991 - $20-$25; "Blood & Chocolate" U.K. limited cassette in "chocolate bar" pack - $35; "Mighty Like A Rose" baseball cap - $15; "It's Time" promotional standee - $16; "Almost Blue" promotional sticker -$8-$10; "Useless Beauty" four-foot standee - $50-$60.

REFERENCES/BOOKS

A few resources exist; no dedicated collector books; serious collectors should opt for fan club: Elvis Costello Information Service, Primulastraat 46, 1441 hc, Pumerend, Netherlands ($17, 6 issues)

Cotton, James

Born: July 1, 1935

Legendary blues harmonica player honed under the watchful eye of Sonny Boy Williamson before joining Muddy Waters for a dozen years and contributing to numerous artists' work, including Janis Joplin and Steve Miller. He also recorded with Howlin' Wolf, Otis Spann, and Big Mama Thornton.

AUTOGRAPHS

A CD, LP, magazine cover, ad, photo, or card signed by the artist: $12-$35

The Count Five

Formed 1965

Ken Ellner, John Michalski, Sean Byrne, Roy Chaney, and Craig Atkinson

California "clean air and good livin'" garage band best remembered for their one major hit, "Psychotic Reaction" (#5, 1966), before folding up their bell-bottom pants and closing the drawer.

AUTOGRAPHS

An LP, magazine cover, ad, photo, or card signed by the group: $5-$10

Counting Crows

Formed 1991

Adam Duritz, David Bryson, Dan Vickrey, Matt Malley, Charlie Gillingham, and Steve Bowman*

*Bowman leaves in 1994 and is replaced with Ben Mize

Early-90s alt band with a folk-based sound, the Counting Crows debut album *August and Everything After* (#4, 1994) sold well over five million copies despite its lack of a hit single. A heavy rotation on MTV of both "Mr. Jones" and "Round Here" contributed greatly to the album's success.

AUTOGRAPHS

A CD, LP, magazine cover, ad, photo, or card signed by the group: $15-$50

TOUR BOOKS/PROGRAMS/PASSES

Backstage Passes:
Cloth: $5-$8; Laminated: $10-$25

POSTERS/PRESS KITS

Promotional Posters: $10-$25
Press Kits: $15

USED CLOTHING/EQUIPMENT

Guitar Picks: $10

Country Joe and the Fish

Formed 1965

Country Joe McDonald, Born: January 1, 1942; Chicken Hirsch; Bruce Barthol; Barry Melton; and David Cohen

The overtly political, late-60s Bay Area band Country Joe and the Fish are best remembered for their "F-U-C-K" cheer (Gimme an F!...) and their appearance at both Woodstock and Monterey. The fish remained fresh until about 1969, when they started getting less bookings, and finally disbanded in 1970.

AUTOGRAPHS

A CD, LP, magazine cover, ad, photo, or card signed by the artist: $20-$30

OFTEN OVERLOOKED MEMORABILIA

Movie memorabilia from *Zachariah* (1971), *Quiet Days in Clinchy* (Dutch) and *Que Hacer* (Chile)—which should keep you busy for awhile; videotapes of their classic performances at Woodstock and Monterey; artifacts from the FTA Revue, a non-USO effort.

County, Wayne/Jayne

Before RuPaul, there was Jayne County, rock's most famous transsexual, who haunted Max's Kan-

sas City in New York during the latter half of the '70s, playing in bands such as Queen Elizabeth and the Electric Chairs.

AUTOGRAPHS

A CD, LP, magazine cover, ad, photo, or card signed by the artist: $10-$20

REFERENCES/BOOKS

Man Enough to Be a Woman, County's autobiography (1995)

Covay, Don

Born 1938

Sixties and seventies soul singer who landed a handful of R&B and pop hits including "Mercy, Mercy" (#35, 1964) and "I Was Checkin' Out, She Was Checkin' In" (#26, 1973). Convay is better known for his songwriting, which has included Aretha Franklin's "See Saw" and "Chain of Fools."

AUTOGRAPHS

A CD, LP, magazine cover, ad, photo, or card signed by the artist: $8-$15

OFTEN OVERLOOKED MEMORABILIA

Memorabilia associated with other artists' covers of his work

Cowboy Junkies

Formed 1985

Michael Timmins, Alan Anton (Alizojvodic), Margo Timmins, and Peter Timmins

Toronto-based country blues band with a strong enough local following to land them a deal with RCA, the Cowboy Junkies have become a popular college radio station band, although commercial success still eludes these cattle drivers.

AUTOGRAPHS

A CD, LP, magazine cover, ad, photo, or card signed by the group: $10-$15

The Cowsills

Formed mid-1960s

Barbara (1929-1985), William "Bud," Bob, Dick, Paul, Barry, John, and Susan Cowsill

Mid-60s New England family and inspiration for the television series *The Partridge Family*, the Cowsills performed regularly in New York City before landing a recording contract with MGM. "The Rain, the Park, and Other Things (#2, 1968) and "Hair" (#2,

1969) are two hits that they are often associated with. The group disbanded in 1970.

AUTOGRAPHS

An LP, magazine cover, ad, photo, or card signed by the group: $15-$30

REFERENCES/BOOKS

A few resources exist; no dedicated collector books; serious collectors should opt for fan club: Cowsills Fan Club, P.O. Box 83, Lexington, MS 39095

Coyne, Kevin

Born: January 21, 1944

Seventies British songwriter who has attracted a cult following over the years, but no commercial success. Coyne is probably known best today as having Andy Summers in his backup band before the guitarist joined The Police.

AUTOGRAPHS

A CD, LP, magazine cover, ad, photo, or card signed by the artist: $10

OFTEN OVERLOOKED MEMORABILIA

Memorabilia from the theater productions he has appeared in; a piece of his artwork

Cramer, Floyd

Born: November 27, 1933

"Slip note" piano playing session veteran, Floyd Cramer has backed virtually every country legend during his lifetime, from Elvis Presley to Patsy Cline and Roy Orbison. "Last Date" (#2, 1960), "On the Rebound" (#4, 1961), "San Antonio Rose" (#8, 1961) and "Chattanooga Choo Choo" (#36, 1962) are some of the numerous songs that made him famous.

AUTOGRAPHS

A CD, LP, magazine cover, ad, photo, or card signed by the artist: $15-$40

OFTEN OVERLOOKED MEMORABILIA

Memorabilia associated with the numerous sessions he has contributed to

The Cranberries

Formed 1990

Dolores O'Riordan, Born: September 6, 1971; Noel Hogan, Born: December 25, 1971; Mike Hogan, Born: April 29, 1973; and Fergal Lawler, Born: March 4, 1971

Irish pop band whose debut album was extremely well received (#18, 1993) and aided in sales by extract

"Linger" (#8, 1993) and an appearance at Woodstock. Their follow-up *No Need to Argue* (#6, 1995) included extracts "Zombie" and "Ode to My Family." The group's increased exposure through television appearances, including *Saturday Night Live* (2/25/95), and complemented by additional releases on movie soundtracks, continues to elevate their popularity. The year 1995 finds the band touring excessively, with O'Riordan even performing the song Ave Maria with Luciano Pavarotti at a benefit concert. The band also delights as "Zombie" is named Best Song at the second annual MTV Europe Music Awards held in Paris, France. In 1996, Island releases *To The Faithful Departed,* the group's third album, which spins off the singles "Free to Decide" and "Salvation." As the appetite for the Cranberries seems insatiable, the time to begin your collection is NOW!

AUTOGRAPHS

A CD, LP, magazine cover, ad, photo, or card signed by the artist: $15-$40

TOUR BOOKS/PROGRAMS/PASSES

Backstage Passes:
Cloth: $5-$8; Laminated: $10-$15

POSTERS/PRESS KITS

Promotional Posters: $10-$15
Press Kits: $10-$15

USED CLOTHING/EQUIPMENT

Guitar Picks: $10

OFTEN OVERLOOKED MEMORABILIA

All Woodstock '94 memorabilia; "Boys on the Side" promotional photo - $5; CD-ROM EPK promo - $10; "No Need to Argue" promotional T-shirt - $20

REFERENCES/BOOKS

A few resources exist; no dedicated collector books; serious collectors should opt for fan club: The Cranberries Official International Fan Club, P.O. Box 679, Branford, CT 06405

Cray, Robert

Born: August 1, 1953

Singer, songwriter, and blues guitarist, Robert Cray helped resurrect the blues during the '80s with albums such as *False Accusations* (1985) and *Strong Persuader* (1986), the latter of which climbed into the Top Twenty and earned the artist a Grammy. Cray is so well respected that he has had his songs covered by a variety of artists including Eric Clapton.

AUTOGRAPHS

A CD, LP, magazine cover, ad, photo, or card signed by the artist: $10-$25

POSTERS/PRESS KITS

Promotional Posters: $10-$20
Press Kits: $10-$20

USED CLOTHING/EQUIPMENT

Guitar Picks: $15-$25

OFTEN OVERLOOKED MEMORABILIA

Movie memorabilia from *Animal House* (he appears as a band member) and *Hail!, Hail! Rock 'n' Roll*

Cream

Formed 1966

Eric Clapton, Born: March 30, 1945; Jack Bruce, Born: May 14, 1943; and Ginger Baker, Born: August 19, 1939

Cream scored in the U.S. with "Sunshine of Your Love" (#5, 1968), "White Room" (#6, 1968) and "Crossroads" (#28, 1969). Their live debut was on July 29, 1966, at the Twisted Wheel in Manchester, and their farewell concert took place on November 26, 1968, in London at the Royal Albert Hall.

The group was inducted into the Rock and Roll Hall of Fame in 1993.

AUTOGRAPHS

A CD, LP, magazine cover, ad, photo, or card signed by the group: $150-$500

REFERENCES/BOOKS

Limited resources exist; no dedicated collector books

CREAM COLLECTOR DATA

First single: "Wrapping Paper"/"Cat's Squirrel" (10/66)
First historic gig with a guest: October 1, 1966, Jimi Hendrix joins Cream on "Killing Floor" at London's Regent Polytechnic
First television appearance: *Ready Steady Go,* November 4, 1966
First live radio session: BBC Studios, November 9, 1966
Second single: "I Feel Free"/"NSU" (12/66)
Second live radio session: BBC Studios, December 9, 1966
Live appearances in 1966: Est. 56 venues
First American gig: RKO 58th Street Theater, New York, March 25-31, 1967
Third single: "Strange Brew"/"Tales of Brave Ulysses" (6/67)
First gigs at the Fillmore, San Francisco: August 22-September 3, 1967
First gig at an American college or university: September 9, 1967, Brandeis University, Waltham, Massachusetts
First film as a band: *On a Saturday Night* (Danish) (2/68)
Fourth single: "Anyone for Tennis"/"Pressed Rat and Warthog" (5/68)
First U.S. television appearance: *The Smothers Brothers Comedy Hour,* mime to "Anyone for Tennis," also perform "Sunshine of Your Love" live!
Fifth single: "Sunshine of Your Love"/"Swlabr" (9/68)
Last U.S. show: November 4, 1968, Rhode Island Auditorium, Providence, Rhode Island
Guitars used by Eric Clapton during final show: Gibson Firebird (first), Gibson ES335 (second)
Sixth single: "White Room"/"Those Were the Days" (1/69) - after the band's split

Creedence Clearwater Revival/ John Fogerty/Tom Fogerty

Formed 1959

John Fogerty, Born: May 28, 1945; Tom Fogerty, Born: November 9, 1941, Died: September 6, 1990; Stu Cook, Born: April 25, 1945; and Doug "Cosmo" Clifford, Born: April 24, 1945*

*Tom Fogerty departs in 1971

Dominant rock act of the late '60s and early '70s, John Fogerty's unique and powerful vocals mixed with classic slick guitar riffs helped send CCR's singles up the chart, including "Proud Mary" (#2, 1969), "Bad Moon Rising" (#2, 1969), "Green River" (#2, 1969), "Fortunate Son" (#14, 1969), "Down on the Corner" (#3, 1969), "Travelin' Band" (#2, 1970), "Up Around the Bend" (#4, 1970) and "Lookin Out My Back Door" (#2, 1970). Originally billed as Tommy Fogerty and the Blue Velvets, followed by the Golliwogs and later Creedence Clearwater Revival, the band originally signed with Fantasy records (San Francisco) and released a few singles including "Brown-Eyed Girl." Any and all items associated with this period are highly sought by CCR collectors.

The group seemed to peak at *Cosmo's Factory* (1970), while Tom Fogerty would leave shortly after (1971), primarily due to John Fogerty's dominant role. The group continued as a trio, with John slowly relinquishing his hold on things such as songwriting, only to find that the result would be less commercially successful. *Mardi Gras* (1972), which equalized the trio's responsibilities, was the first album not to sell platinum.

The group disbanded in 1972, with John Fogerty enjoying the greatest success as a solo artist. He re-leased two albums before getting fed up with the industry and retreating into the Oregon hillside. In 1985 he emerged and, as if he had been caught in a time warp, released *Centerfield* (#1, 1985), which sounded like it was written just after *Cosmo's*. The album yielded three hits: "The Old Man Down The Road" (#10, 1985), "Rock and Roll Girls" (#20, 1985) and "Centerfield" (#44, 1985). The album caused a legal battle between Fogerty and Fantasy Records, which the former finally won and retreated once again. He emerged from the forest twelve years later to deliver *Blue Moon Swamp* (1997).

In 1993 CCR was inducted into the Rock and Roll Hall of Fame.

AUTOGRAPHS

A CD, LP, magazine cover, ad, photo, or card signed by the artist: $60-$175

OFTEN OVERLOOKED MEMORABILIA

Any Golliwogs artifacts; all festival artifacts, including Woodstock (1969) memorabilia; any items relating to the 1981 Fantasy release of *The Royal Albert Hall Concert* (actually recorded at the Oakland-Alameda County Coliseum); promotional cardboard mobile (26" x 28") - $195

REFERENCES/BOOKS

Creedence Clearwater Revival by John Hallowell; few resources exist; no dedicated collector books

---

Crenshaw, Marshall

Born: November 11, 1953

Guitarist, singer, and songwriter best known for his single "Someday Someway" (#36, 1982) from his debut record, along with his theater and movie roles.

AUTOGRAPHS

A CD, LP, magazine cover, ad, photo, or card signed by the artist: $5-$10

POSTERS/PRESS KITS

Promotional Posters: $10
Press Kits: $10

USED CLOTHING/EQUIPMENT

Guitar Picks: $10

OFTEN OVERLOOKED MEMORABILIA

Movie memorabilia from *La Bamba* (1987) and *Peggy Sue Got Married;* "Beatlemania" memorabilia from his stint as John Lennon; memorabilia associated with other artists' covers of his material

REFERENCES/BOOKS

Hollywood Rock: A Guide to Rock 'n' Roll in the Movies (1994) - Crenshaw collaborated on the work

---

The Crests

Formed 1956

Johnny Maestro (Mastrangelo), Tommy Gough, Jay Carter, Harold Torres, and Patricia Vandross

This 14" x 22" poster for a Golliwogs concert in Fairfax, CA, is valued at $1,000. The Golliwogs was a pre-CCR band for John Fogerty (far right in picture). From the collection of Hank Thompson.

Late-50s doo-wop group best remembered for their songs "16 Candles" (#2, 1959) and "Step by Step" (#14, 1960).

AUTOGRAPHS

A CD, LP, magazine cover, ad, photo, or card signed by the artist: $15 $30

The Critters

Formed 1960s

Don Ciccone, James Ryan, Kenneth Gorka, Christopher Daraway, and Jack Decker

Soft-rock act that scored three minor hits in 1966: "Younger Girl," "Mr. Dieingly Sad," and "Don't Let the Rain Fall Down on Me."

AUTOGRAPHS

A CD, LP, magazine cover, ad, photo, or card signed by the group: $10

Croce, Jim

Born: January 10, 1943, Died: September 20, 1973

Talented early-70s singer and songwriter who scored hits with "Operator" (#17, 1972), "You Don't Mess Around with Jim" (#8, 1972) and "Bad, Bad Leroy Brown" (#1, 1973) before being killed in a Louisiana plane crash on September 20, 1973. His album *I Got a Name* (1973, completed before his death) scored hits with the title track (#10, 1973) and "Time in a Bottle" (#1, 1973).

AUTOGRAPHS

A CD, LP, magazine cover, ad, photo, or card signed by the artist: $100-$300

OFTEN OVERLOOKED MEMORABILIA

Memorabilia from the San Diego club Croce's, owned by his widow

REFERENCES/BOOKS

Jim Croce: The Feeling Lives by Linda Jacobs; few resources exist; no dedicated collector books

Crosby, Stills, Nash and Young

Formed 1968

David Crosby (David Van Cortland), Born: August 14, 1941; Stephen Stills, Born: January 3, 1945; Graham Nash, Born: February 2, 1942; and Neil Young, Born: November 12, 1945

Volatile '60s, '70s, and '80s band whose high harmonic sound put to largely acoustic-based songs became their hallmark. Crosby, Stills, Nash and Young

are best associated with hits such as "Marrakesh Express" (#28, 1969), "Suite: Judy Blue Eyes" (#21, 1969), "Woodstock" (#11, 1970), "Teach Your Children" (#16, 1970), "Our House" (#30, 1970) and "Ohio" (#14, 1970).

AUTOGRAPHS

Group:

A CD, LP, magazine cover, ad, photo, or card signed by the group: $50-$175

Individual:

David Crosby: $15-$30   Stephen Stills: $40-$75
Graham Nash: $10-$25   Neil Young: $20-$50

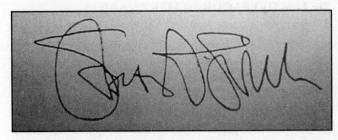

Signature of Stephen Stills

USED CLOTHING/EQUIPMENT

Guitar Picks:

David Crosby: $25   Stephen Stills: $25-$35
Graham Nash: $25   Neil Young: $30-$45

Take your pick! Crosby, Stills & Nash

OFTEN OVERLOOKED MEMORABILIA

Memorabilia from both Woodstock festivals

REFERENCES/BOOKS

Crosby, Stills, Nash & Young: The Visual Documentary by Johnny Rogan—a must for collectors! Numerous resources exist; no dedicated collector books.

Cross, Christopher

(Christopher Geppert)
Born: 1951

Singer and songwriter who came out of the hills of Austin to land with Warner Brothers Records in 1978, where he became an overnight sensation with his self-titled debut album that yielded four Top twenty hits: "Sailing" (#1, 1980), "Ride Like the

Wind" (#2, 1980), "Never Be the Same" (#15, 1980) and "Say You'll Be Mine" (#20, 1980). The release earned five Grammy Awards including Record of the Year, Album of the Year, and Song of the Year.

"Arthur's Theme (The Best That You Can Do)," from the hit movie, was also a huge smash for the artist, but his follow-up albums were not. Slowly decreasing sales have drawn allegations that Cross will "Never Be the Same."

AUTOGRAPHS

A CD, LP, magazine cover, ad, photo, or card signed by the artist: $5-$10

OFTEN OVERLOOKED MEMORABILIA

Movie memorabilia from *Arthur*

Crow, Sheryl

Born: February 11, 1962

Crow's first big break was as a backup singer for Michael Jackson's Bad tour (1987-88), before assuming the same role with other musicians. Her debut album *Tuesday Night Music Club* (#3, 1994) spun off the single "All I Wanna Do" (#2, 1994), which earned her a Grammy Award as 1994's Record of the Year.

AUTOGRAPHS

A CD, LP, magazine cover, ad, photo, or card signed by the artist: $15-$50

POSTERS/PRESS KITS

Promotional Posters: $15-$20
Press Kits: $20

OFTEN OVERLOOKED MEMORABILIA

Memorabilia from Woodstock '94

Crowded House

Formed 1985

Neil Finn, Paul Hester, and Nick Seymour*

*Tim Finn is added in 1991, but departs in 1993. Mark Hart is added in 1993.

The boys from "down unda" landed a well-respected self-titled debut album that spun off two Top Ten hits, "Don't Dream It's Over" (#2, 1987) and "Something So Strong" (#7, 1987), but follow-up efforts have proved less fruitful for Crowded House.

AUTOGRAPHS

A CD, LP, magazine cover, ad, photo, or card signed by the group: $15-$35

POSTERS/PRESS KITS

Promotional Posters: $10
Press Kits: $10

REFERENCES/BOOKS

Crowded House: Private Universe by Kerry Doole and Chris Twomey; few resources exist; no dedicated collector books

Crowell, Rodney

Born: August 7, 1950

Country/rock singer and songwriter who is probably better known for the latter, as musicians from Willie Nelson to Bob Seger have covered his songs. He was a member of Emmylou Harris' Hot Band, joining in 1975 and leaving in 1978. In 1979 he began producing Roseanne Cash, whom he later married. "Ashes by Now" landed in the Top Forty for him in 1980, a prelude to what would eventually follow. *Diamonds & Dirt,* released in 1988, included five #1 C&W singles, all penned by Crowell, who was the first C&W artist to accomplish such a feat. In 1992 the couple's marriage fell apart—no surprise to the many who had seen the clues in their music.

AUTOGRAPHS

A CD, LP, magazine cover, ad, photo, or card signed by the artist: $10-$25

OFTEN OVERLOOKED MEMORABILIA

Memorabilia associated with the numerous artists who have covered his material; artifacts from his production efforts

The Crows

Formed 1951

Daniel "Sonny" Norton, William Davis, Harold Major, Gerald Hamilton, Jerry Wittick*

*Wittick departs in 1952 and is replaced by Mark Jackson

The Crows are best remembered for their one and only hit, "Gee" (#14, 1954).

AUTOGRAPHS

A magazine cover, ad, photo, or card signed by the group: $10-$20

Crudup, Arthur "Big Boy"

(1905-1974)

Early bluesman best remembered for his classics "That's All Right Mama" (Elvis Presley's first hit), "My Baby Left Me" and "Rock Me Mama." Crudup, who also recorded under the name Elmore Jones or Percy Crudup (his son's name), did so up into the mid-50s before leaving the business. He returned in the late '60s and toured the U.S. and Europe.

AUTOGRAPHS

A CD, LP, magazine cover, ad, photo, or card signed by the artist: $40-$120

Cruise, Julee

Born: December 1, 1956

Singer, hornist, and actress commonly associated with her ethereal vocals to the film *Blue Velvet* (1986). She has appeared in television and radio ads and even sung off-Broadway before replacing Cindy Wilson on the B-52's 1992 tour.

AUTOGRAPHS

A CD, LP, magazine cover, ad, photo, or card signed by the artist: $10-$15

OFTEN OVERLOOKED MEMORABILIA

Artifacts associated with her theater career; copies of her advertising work; movie memorabilia from *Blue Velvet* (1989)

The Crusaders/Joe Sample

Formed 1954

Wilton Felder, Joe Sample, Nesbert "Stix" Hooper, Wayne Henderson*

*Numerous personnel changes

One of the most well known and prolific instrumental bands in the '70s, The Crusaders placed numerous songs on the R&B charts during the dance decade, such as "Put It Where You Want It" (39, 1972), "Don't Let It Get You Down" (#31, 1973), "Keep That Same Old Feeling" (#21, 1976) and "Street Life" (#17, 1979). In 1975 they even opened for the Rolling Stones. As session players they have appeared on hundreds of recordings.

AUTOGRAPHS

A CD, LP, magazine cover, ad, photo, or card signed by the artist: $20-$35

OFTEN OVERLOOKED MEMORABILIA

Associated artifacts from their numerous sessions

The Crystals

Formed 1961

Original lineup: Dee Dee Kennibrew (Delores Henry), Dolores "La La" Brooks, Mary Thomas, Barbara Alston, and Patricia Wright

Commonly associated with Phil Spector, as they were one of his first acts to appear on Philles Records, they are best remembered for hits such as "There's No Other (Like My Baby)" (#20, 1961), "Uptown" (#13, 1962), "Da Doo Ron Ron" (#3, 1962) and "Then He Kissed Me" (#6, 1963).

AUTOGRAPHS

A CD, LP, magazine cover, ad, photo, or card signed by the artist: $15-$45

The Cult

Formed 1983

Ian Astbury (Lindsay), Billy Duffy, Jamie Stewart, and Les Warner*

*Stewart and Warner leave in 1989, and Scott Garrett and Craig Adams are added in 1991

Indie-label metal merchants whose major label debut *Love* spawned two successful U.K. singles, "She Sells Sanctuary" and "Rain," while follow-ups *Electric* (#38, 1987) and *Sonic Temple* (#10, 1989) also sold well, the latter of which featured cult single "Edie (Ciao Baby)" (#93, 1989, a tribute to Edie Sedgwick) and "Fire Woman" (#46, 1989). They drifted on *Ceremony* (#25, 1991) and by the time they returned in 1994 with *The Cult* (#69, 1994) they had to remind their following of who they were, if they could find them.

AUTOGRAPHS

A CD, LP, magazine cover, ad, photo, or card signed by the artist: $25-$40

TOUR BOOKS/ PROGRAMS/PASSES

Backstage Passes:
Cloth: $5-$10;
Laminated: $10-$20

POSTERS/PRESS KITS

Promotional Posters: $10-$20
Press Kits: $15

USED CLOTHING/ EQUIPMENT

Guitar Picks: $10-$20

A guitar pick from the Cult

OFTEN OVERLOOKED MEMORABILIA

"Electric" Beggars Banquet, 1987 promotional can of non-alcoholic beer - $35; "Pre Cult" Sire 1993 promotional box set, included 4 CD singles, a backstage pass, video and T-shirt

Culture Club

Formed 1981

Boy George (George O'Dowd), Born: June 14, 1961; Roy Hay; Mikey Craig; and Jon Moss

London postpunk, early-80s, New Romantic club scene pop group led by the eccentric Boy George. Cul-

ture Club's sensual rhythms and habit-forming hooks landed hit singles with "Do You Really Want To Hurt Me" (#2, 1982), "Time (Clock of the Heart)" (#2, 1983), "I'll Tumble 4 Ya" (#9, 1983), "Church of the Poison Mind" (#10, 1983), "Karma Chameleon" (#1, 1983), "Miss Me Blind" (#5, 1984) and "It's a Miracle" (#13, 1984). In 1983 the group took home the Grammy for Best New Artist, before the bottom dropped out.

Their third album was a commercial failure, as drug allegations abounded about George, who later went public with his problem in 1986. Following a possession charge and the death of two of his friends, one of which contained implication charges against George, the singer entered a rehabilitation program. Cleared of the charges and making attempts to get his house in order, George went about a solo career that failed to do much in the U.S., although he did score dance hits in Europe. In 1992 he sang "The Crying Game" (#15,1992), which was featured in the film of the same name, and it took him back up the U.S. singles chart.

AUTOGRAPHS
Group:
A CD, LP, magazine cover, ad, photo, or card signed by the group: $20-$50
Individual:
Boy George: $15-$40

TOUR BOOKS/PROGRAMS/PASSES
Backstage Passes:
Cloth: $8-$10; Laminated: $10-$15

POSTERS/PRESS KITS
Promotional Posters: $15-$25
Press Kits: $15-$25

USED CLOTHING/EQUIPMENT
Guitar Picks: $10-$15

OFTEN OVERLOOKED MEMORABILIA
Books: *Boy George and Culture Club* - $25, and *In His Own Words* - $15; dolls: cloth - $100, LJN, 12-inch - $125; mirror - $10; figurine - $45; stickers - $10; mug - $15; buttons - $5; pin (enamel) - $5; movie memorabilia from *The Crying Game* (1992)

REFERENCES/BOOKS
Take It Like a Man, George's autobiography; numerous resources exist; no dedicated collector books

The Cure

Formed 1976

Robert Smith, Michael Dempsey, and Laurence "Lol" Tolhurst*

*Numerous personnel changes.

Obscure British late-70s punk scene survivor and cult favorite, The Cure is one of the better-selling indie acts of the era. The group took off in the U.S. after they moved to Elektra and had minor hits with "Why Can't I Be You" (#54, 1987), "Just Like Heaven" (#40, 1987) and "Hot Hot Hot!" (#65, 1988). "Love Song" (#2, 1989) became one of their biggest hits and was followed by extract "Friday I'm in Love" (#18, 1992) from their album *Wish* (#2, 1992).

AUTOGRAPHS
A CD, LP, magazine cover, ad, photo, or card signed by the group: $40-$80

POSTERS/PRESS KITS
Promotional Posters: $10-$35
Press Kits: $15-$30

USED CLOTHING/EQUIPMENT
Guitar Picks: $10-$25

OFTEN OVERLOOKED MEMORABILIA
"The Top" promotional U.K. album, includes top and snake; "Kiss Me, Kiss Me, Kiss Me" Elektra U.S. promotional box set, 1987, includes album, CD, cassette, biographies, glossies, package of Red Hots candy packaged in a first aid kit, scarce (only 100)

REFERENCES/BOOKS
The Cure on Record by Daren Butler; numerous resources exist; no dedicated collector books

Curved Air

Formed 1970

Sonja Kristina, Darryl Way, Florian Pilkington-Miksa, Ian Eyre, and Francis Monkman*

*Numerous personnel changes

Early-70s British act that garnered attention through their female lead singer Sonja Kristina, an elaborate marketing job by Warner Brothers Records, and U.K. single "Back Street Luv." The group broke up when Eddie Jobson jumped to replace Brian Eno in Roxy Music—if there is such a thing!

AUTOGRAPHS
A CD, LP, magazine cover, ad, photo, or card signed by the group: $10-$20

Cymbal, Johnny

Born: February 3, 1945

Songwriter and producer who is best remembered for his two hits, "Hey Mr. Bassman" (#16, 1963) and "Cinnamon" (#11, 1969), the first as Johnny Cymbal and the Latter as Derek.

AUTOGRAPHS
A CD, LP, magazine cover, ad, photo, or card signed by the artist: $10-$15

Cypress Hill

Formed 1988

B-Real (Louis Freese), Sen Dog (Senen Reyes), and DJ Muggs (Lawrence Muggerud)

Successful L.A. Latino trio who rapped favoring blunts, on a nasty debut hunch that broke the Top Forty bunch, garnering attention over a controversial single "How Could I Just Kill a Man" (#77, 1992).

Posed to follow, *Black Sunday* (#1, 1993) maxed the U.S. album charts fueled by the extract "Insane in the Brain" (#19, 1993).

AUTOGRAPHS
A CD, LP, magazine cover, ad, photo, or card signed by the artist: $20-$35

POSTERS/PRESS KITS
Promotional Posters: $10-$20
Press Kits: $10-$15

Dale, Dick

(Richard Monsour)
Born: May 4, 1937

Dale grew up in Quincy, MA, and migrated to Southern California with his family during his teenage years. He soon formed the Del-Tones and established residency at the Rinky Dink Ice Cream Parlor and then the Rendezvous Ballroom. The group's rockabilly sound was augmented by Dale's quick riffs and heavily-reverberated staccato slide. His love for music was overshadowed by only one thing—surfing. If it were possible to ride a wave with a Fender Stratocaster, Dick Dale would have done it.

He formed his own locally-distributed Deltone label in 1960, and when his vocal release failed to sell, he turned to his instrumental material. Dale's unique style was labeled "Surf Guitar," and spawned an entire rock movement based in Southern California—Surf Music.

In January 1962, "Let's Go Trippin" (#60, 1962) climbed the U.S. singles chart as more kids were setting down their sun block and dancing to the very first surf record ever. The song quickly became a must cover for every new surf act. When *Surfer's Choice* (#59, 1963) climbed the album chart the following year, the big record companies begin anchoring off the coast of Balboa, CA. The following month, Dale inked a lucrative and lengthy contract with Capitol Records, who also purchased his Deltone label.

King of the Surfer Guitar (1963) was released in June, along with eponymous title track, and while it sold well in Southern California, it failed to impress the rest of the country, where there are more cows per square foot that coast line. A guitar instrumental single, "The Scavenger" (#98, 1963) climbed into the Top One Hundred while Dale focused on the logical next direction for the band—hot rods.

In December 1963, "Checkered Flag" (#106, 1963) was released, with Dale now waxing his car instead of his surfboard. It was followed by "Summer Surf" (1964) and the abysmal "Rock Out With Dick Dale: Live At Ciro's" (1964), both of which create a ripple in the market. The following year Dale fell very ill, and required surgery. The setback forced him to retire from performing. Following a lengthy recuperation, he opened a nightclub in 1969. The new venture provided the perfect opportunity to form a new Del-Tones and establish residency.

In the years that followed, he would play on a few scattered projects, but generally remained out of the mainstream. In 1987, he recorded a duet with Stevie Ray Vaughan, "Pipeline," which appeared on the movie soundtrack to *Back To The Beach* and also earned a Grammy nomination.

Then in 1992 he began to record his first album of original material in twenty-seven years. What emerged from the tide was *Tribal Thunder*, an album that won't catapult him to the top of the charts, but made strong enough waves to at least allow him to sell out a few gigs. The album was followed by *Unknown Territory* in 1994. What's next for the "King of the Surf Guitar," that old southpaw slider of upside-down guitar playing? Well, rumor has it that before you can finish a box of saltwater taffy, he might just have another album out.

AUTOGRAPHS
A CD, LP, magazine cover, ad, photo, or card signed by the artist: $20-$30

POSTERS/PRESS KITS
Promotional Posters: $10 (1984-Present)
Press Kits: $10-$15 (1984-Present)

USED CLOTHING/EQUIPMENT
Guitar Picks: $25

OFTEN OVERLOOKED MEMORABILIA
Movie memorabilia from *Beach Party* (1963), *A Swingin' Affair* (1963), *Muscle Beach Party* (1964), *Back To The Beach* (1987), and *Pulp Fiction* (1994), which includes the classic "Misirlou"; a videotape from the *Ed Sullivan Show* (1963), *The Late Show With David Letterman* (11/4/94), or *Jools Hootenanny* BBC2-TV; any advertising or promotional items associated with his work for the Fender company; a copy of his MTV video "Nitro"

The Damned/Captain Sensible

Formed 1976

Brian James (Brian Robertson); Captain Sensible (Ray Burns), Born: April 23, 1955; Rat Scabies (Chris Miller); and Dave Vanian (Dave Letts)

The band's history can be traced to 1975, and with the Burns brothers in particular, all the way back to 1970 (Black Witch Climax Blues Band). The band's first performance was at the 100 in July 6, 1976, in support of the Sex Pistols. In September the group signed to Stiff Records and released the debut single "New Rose/Help" (Lennon/McCartney). The record, produced by Nick Lowe, is commonly regarded as the first-ever punk release. Although the record failed to chart, it would go on to be the record company's biggest seller. In December the group briefly supported the Sex Pistols' "Anarchy in the U.K." tour, but was later fired. All memorabilia from this tour is scarce and highly sought after by collectors. Of the nineteen dates scheduled, only three dates—Leeds, Manchester, and Plymouth—actually included both bands. Keep that in mind, poster and ticket collectors!

On April 8, 1977, The Damned open at CBGB's in New York and was the first punk group to play the U.S., while the group's debut album *Damned, Damned, Damned* (#34, U.K., 1977) climbed into the U.K. Top Forty. When it return home, the group began a U.K. tour, supported by the Adverts. The poster from this tour is a classic and highly prized by collectors. It reads, "The Damned can play three chords, the Adverts can play one. Hear all four at...." In June, The Damned's gigs began to turn a bit violent; band member Vanian was even attacked in the dressing room.

Just prior to the recording of the group's next album, James insisted upon adding a second guitarist and Robert "Lu" Edmonds joined. There was a heightened tension between band members, most attributable to the firing of a producer during recording "Problem Child," which was released as a single. The following month Scabies left during a European tour and was replaced by Jon Moss (later of Culture Club). *Music For Pleasure* was released in November and supported by a U.K. tour with the U.S. band the Dead Boys. The following month the band would leave Stiff, after the release of "Don't Cry Wolf."

On February 28, 1978, the band split. James formed his own band, Tanz Der Youth, followed by Brian James' Brains & the Hellions and the Lords of the New Church. Sensible joined the Softies, followed by King. Vanian joined the Doctors of Madness, while Scabie moved to the White Cats. Moss and Edmunds went on to the Edge. On April 8, 1978, The Damned re-formed for a final gig at London's Rainbow Theatre. In September, Vanian, Scabies,

and Sensible decided to resurrect the band, and added bassist Alistair Ward (Saints). Before securing the name from James, the outfit played as The Doomed. The group then quickly signed to Chiswick Records.

Ironically, the group's new records were the most popular of its four years. "Love Song" (#20, U.K., 1979), "Smash It Up" (#35 , U.K., 1979) and "I Just Can't Be Happy Today" (#46, U.K., 1979) gave them a series of three consecutive hit singles, while the group continually drew a larger audience. The following year (1980) Ward left and was replaced by Paul Gray (Eddie and the Hot Rods). In November the band released *The Black Album* (#29, U.K.), which included the seasonal favorite "There Ain't No Sanity Caluse."

In 1982 Captain Sensible released a solo effort in the U.K., *Women and Captains First*, which included the hit extract "Wot" (#26, U.K., 1982). On October 23, 1982, The Damned released *Strawberries*, with a collectable strawberry smelling lyric sheet, that peaked at #15 in the U.K. Roman Jugg now joined and replaced Tosh, who had joined a year earlier.

In 1984 Captain Sensible left the band and was replaced by Bryn Merrick. The band then continued its Top Forty U.K. success with "Grimly Fiendish," "The Shadow of Love," "Is It a Dream," "Eloise" (#3, 1986), "Anything," "Gigilo," and "Alone Again Or." During the late '80s and into the '90s, the band regrouped on certain occasions like its "20th Anniversary Special" in 1996.

AUTOGRAPHS
Group:
A CD, LP, magazine cover, ad, photo, or card signed by the group: $50-$75
Individual:
Brian James (Brian Robertson): $15-$20
Captain Sensible (Ray Burns): $10-$15
Rat Scabies (Chris Miller): $10-$15
Dave Vanian (Dave Letts): $10-$15

USED CLOTHING/EQUIPMENT
Guitar Picks: $25

OFTEN OVERLOOKED MEMORABILIA
Handbills and newspaper clippings

REFERENCES/BOOKS
The History of The Damned (Part One), scrapbook format, supposedly limited to 2,500 copies: $20

Damn Yankees

Formed 1989

Ted Nugent, Born: December 13, 1948; Jack Blades, Born: April 24, 1954; Tommy Shaw, Born: September 11, 1953; and Michael Cartellone, Born: June 7, 1962

Damn Yankees, like the Firm and Bad English, was one of many "sweighties" (second-wave '80s)

bands constructed of pre-geriatric rock superstars. In 1988 Nugent and Shaw (Styx) met at a record-label convention. A series of casual jamming sessions led to some composing, and then the addition of bassist Blades. Ironically, rumors that record executives had paired the musicians was in stark contrast to the truth of the situation. The new group actually had some problems enticing a label to take a shot at the act, but finally convinced Warner Brothers.

The band's powerful debut album, eponymously titled (#13, 1990), scored well with the aging baby boomers audience. Sales were also driven by both the extracted single "High Enough" (#3, 1990) and extensive tour support. *Don't Tread* (#22, 1992), the band's sophomore album effort, also landed a hit single with "Where You Goin' Now" (#20, 1992). This record was also well publicized; of course it didn't hurt that the never lost-for-words "Motor City Madman" Ted Nugent was going through one of his "I hate animal activists" periods. Verbal attacks on other musicians were as routine to Nugent as bowhunting.

AUTOGRAPHS

Group:
A CD, LP, magazine cover, ad, photo, or card signed by the group: $35-$50

Individual:
Ted Nugent: $20-$25   Jack Blades: $10-$15
Tommy Shaw: $20-$25   Michael Cartellone: $10

POSTERS/PRESS KITS
Promotional Posters: $10-$20
Press Kits: $15

USED CLOTHING/EQUIPMENT

Guitar Picks:
Ted Nugent: $10-$20   Jack Blades: $15-$20
Tommy Shaw: $10-$15

The Charlie Daniels Band

Charlie Daniels, Born: 1937

Charlie Daniels grew up in the woods of North Carolina and was the son of a lumberman. At 21, he formed the Jaguars and spent nearly the entire next five years on the road. Playing the southern circuit, he crafted his musical skills and a strong taste for road living. His first real claim to fame was an association with "The King," Elvis Presley, who recorded the Daniels co-penned tune "It Hurts Me," which would become the flip side to his hit single "Kissin' Cousins" (1964). In 1967 Daniels disbanded the Jaguars to set up residence in Nashville as a session musician. There he would add guitar, fiddle, bass, or banjo to albums by numerous musicians including Bob Dylan, Ringo Starr, and Pete Seeger.

As he became comfortable in the studio, he was learning more and more about production and writing. He produced many of the Youngbloods albums during this period and even had a couple of his songs covered by other musicians. Destined for a change, he formed the Charlie Daniels Band in 1971. Patterned after the now traditional and successful Allman Brothers band structure, it featured two drummers and two lead guitars. *Honey in the Rock* was the band's first full effort and included the novelty single "Uneasy Rider" (1973) which climbed into the Top Ten on the singles chart.

The group's extensive touring schedule, a characteristic that it would become known for, built a very loyal following in the South and West that slowly migrated northward. *Nightrider* (1975), the band's fourth effort, included the Dixie anthem and single "The South's Gonna Do It" (#29, 1975). By now, Daniels had established his annual concert event known as the Volunteer Jam (Est.1974), of which many had found their way to vinyl over the years.

In 1975 Daniels also moved to Epic Records and signed a very lucrative contract that began with the release of *Saddle Tramp*. This record, like most of Daniel's releases, was heavily supported by touring in a band that now found a richer sound with the addition of three new members. During this period Daniels also aligned himself politically with Former Georgia Governor Jimmy Carter, whom he later enlightened with a performance at the Presidential inaugural ball.

Million Mile Reflections was a breakthrough album for the band, which yielded hit extraction "The Devil Went Down To Georgia" (#3, 1979) and a Grammy Award for Best Country Vocal. By now the band was a foundation on the college circuit and was even drawing heavily in many cross over markets. Despite the success, Daniels always made it clear where his origins were Mt. Juliet, Tennessee, not Nashville. "You see," he often says, "those few miles east make all the difference in understanding where we're coming from." The foundation of the CDB band in the late '70s was made up of Tommy Crain, Charlie Heyward, Joel "Taz" DiGregorio, Don Murray, and Fred Edwards.

The years that followed saw Daniels sharpen his political edge with hit singles such as "In America" (#11, 1980), which drew on the Iranian hostage crisis and "Still In Saigon," which empathized with the traumas of Vietnam veterans. In 1993, after switching to Liberty Records, he released the politically charged "America, I Believe In You," followed by his first gospel album *The Door* (Sorrow, 1994). Always a favorite, "The Godfather of Country Rock" never fails to strike a nerve in his followers, of which there have been many in the past few decades.

"Ain't it good to be alive and to be in TENNESSEE!"

AUTOGRAPHS
Charlie Daniels and his band are outstanding to their fans and seldom, if ever, avoid an autograph request!

An in-person signature of Charlie Daniels

Group:
A CD, LP, magazine cover, ad, photo, or card signed by the group: $20-$35

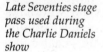

Late Seventies stage pass used during the Charlie Daniels show

Individual:
Charlie Daniels: $10-$20
Joel "Taz" DiGregorio: $5

TOUR BOOKS/PROGRAMS/PASSES
Tour Books:
The Charlie Daniels Band (1977/78): $15-$20
Backstage Passes:
Cloth: $8-$10; Laminated: $10-$12 (1990-Present)
Cloth: $10; Laminated: $12-$15 (1980-1989)
Cloth: $12-15; Laminated: $15 (Pre-1980)

POSTERS/PRESS KITS
Promotional Posters: $10-$25
Press Kits: $10-$20

USED CLOTHING/EQUIPMENT
Guitar Picks:
Charlie Daniels: $15-$25

OFTEN OVERLOOKED MEMORABILIA
Volunteer Jam posters and promotional items; official "CDB" belt buckles: $7-$10

REFERENCES/BOOKS
The Devil Went Down to Georgia by Charlie Daniels; no dedicated collector books

Danny and the Juniors

Formed 1957

Danny Rapp, Born: May 10, 1941, Died: April 5, 1983, Joe Terranova, Born: January 30, 1941, Frank Maffei, and Dave White (Dave Tricker)

The group got together as the Juvenairs while attending high school in 1955. Upon graduation they were introduced to Artie Singer, a music entrepreneur who offered to manage them. Singer, White, and mutual friend Johnny Medora wrote "Do The Bop," later changed and recorded as "At The Hop."

The song, recorded on Singer's Philadelphia-based label, was a local smash and was quickly picked up for national distribution by ABC-Paramount Records. By January 11, 1958, the record topped the U.S. singles chart, driven primarily by the group's appearance on Dick Clark's *American Bandstand* TV showcase in 1957. While the record also stayed near the top of the U.K. charts, the group released the follow-ups "Rock And Roll Is Here To Stay" (#19, 1958) and "Dottie" (#39, 1958).

Its hit production slowed the following year, but the group still remained a popular live draw. Bill Carlucci replaced a departed White, and the group signed to Swan Records. The group's first single release for the label was "Twistin' USA" (#37, 1960). The following year the group released "Pony Express" (#60, 1961) and "Back To The Hop" (#80, 1961); both were far less successful than their predecessors. Unfortunately, the chart slide continued with both "Twistin' All Night Long" (#68, 1962) and "Doin' the Continental Walk" (#93, 1962), their final two singles for Swan.

Their final hit was "Oo-La-La-Limbo" (#99, 1963) for Guyden Records. Meanwhile, White went on to some solo success—he cowrote Len Barry's 1965 U.S. hit "1-2-3" (#2, 1965). Since the group's fall from grace, it has been a regular feature on the oldies circuit, now led by Terranova (Rapp committed suicide in 1983).

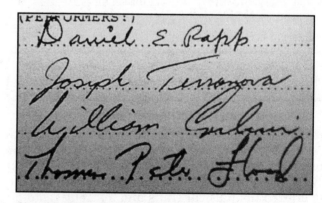

Signed contract - Danny & the Juniors

AUTOGRAPHS
Group:
A CD, LP, magazine cover, ad, photo, or card signed by the group: $10-$25*
*Original members
Individual:
David White: $5-$7

OFTEN OVERLOOKED MEMORABILIA
Movie memorabilia from *American Graffiti*

Dante and the Evergreens

Formed Late 1950s

Dante Drowty, Tony Moon, Frank Rosenthal, and Bill Young

Another novelty act of the '60s, the group scored a hit with "Alley Oop" (#13, 1960). Speculation still surrounds the origins of the band. Herb Alpert, who produced the group's demo tape, actually claimed years later that the band was made up of himself and fellow producer Lou Adler. If this is indeed the case, the group's collectibility would center around Alpert and no doubt make associated items of greater value.

Danzig

Formed 1986

Glenn Danzig, Born: June 23, 1955, John Christ, Eerie Von, and Chuck Biscuits

Danzig, led by former Misfit Glenn Danzig, is primarily a "cult" band that features music heavily tainted in satanic and "anti-everything" themes. While the Misfits were part of a late-70s punk scene that actually influenced some metal bands, we have yet to be treated to the influences of Danzig.

Glenn Danzig and Eerie Von hooked up in 1982 with the band Samhain. The quartet was completed with the addition of Biscuits and Christ—not some type of meal. While stardom still miraculously eluded the band, despite the strong album showing from *Danzig III: How the Gods Kill* (#24, 1992), the band endured. *Danzig 4* (#29, 1994) was a solid sales release, which followed the Beavis and Butthead thumbs-up album *Thralldemonsweatlive's*—my answer to an exploding appendix.

In 1995, Glenn Danzig began Verotik, a comic book publisher catering to mature readers. The company recruited some industry heavyweights including Frank Frazetta, Simon Bisley, and Hart Fisher, just to name a few. The company's first issue "Satanika," part of *The New Covenant*, was both impressive and offensive at the same time, a recipe that typically translates into success. For Danzig die-hards, the comics are a must. Glenn Danzig has also supported the effort with numerous comic book signings often held at major comic book stores in cities he performs in.

AUTOGRAPHS
Group:
A CD, LP, magazine cover, ad, photo, or card signed by the group: $20-$30
Individual:
Glenn Danzig: $10-$20

TOUR BOOKS/PROGRAMS/PASSES
Backstage Passes:
Cloth: $5-$7; Laminated: $7-$10

POSTERS/PRESS KITS
Promotional Posters: $10-$20
Press Kits: $15-$25
Thrall: $15

USED CLOTHING/EQUIPMENT
Guitar Picks: $10-$20

D'Arby, Terence Trent

Born: March 15, 1962

D'Arby, the son of a Pentecostal preacher, was a regional Golden Gloves boxing champ before he studied journalism at the University of Central Florida. During a stint in the U.S. Army, that found him in Germany performing with the nine-piece funk outfit Touch, D'Arby met Klaus Pieter Schleinitz (K.P.). After being officially discharged from the army in 1983, D'Arby left Touch and he, along with K.P.—D'Arby's now full-time manager—headed for London.

On the strength of his demo tape, the artist signed to CBS/Columbia Records in June 1986. At that time, he was residing in London and released "If You Let Me Stay" (#7, U.K., 1987), which was well-received by the R&B audience. In addition to numerous successful public performances, the artist developed a relationship with the press that was reminiscent of a young Cassius Clay, although the phrase "I'm pretty" is not uttered.

His debut album, *Introducing The Hardline According To Terence Trent D'Arby* (#4, 1988), was preceded by the single "Wishing Well" (#4, U.K., 1987). He promoted the album through his own brief U.K. tour and dates supporting David Bowie. D'Arby returned to the U.S. in September and made his live debut at the Roxy in Los Angeles on September 30. Meanwhile, single "Dance Little Sister" (#20, U.K., 1987) climbed the U.K. charts, prior to the release of U.S. single "If You Let Me Stay" (#68, 1987).

In January 1988, "Sign Your Name" (#2, 1988) nearly hit the top of the U.K. singles chart, as a D'Arby U.S. assault was planned by management. In March the artist embarked on an aggressive U.S. Tour. Sales of his debut album soared and the single "Wishing Well" (#1, 1988) topped the R&B listing, followed by the U.S. pop chart. "Sign Your Name" (#4, 1988), which climbed the singles chart. The artist was also featured on Brian Wilson's solo debut album.

Neither Fish Nor Flesh (#61, 1989), his controversial sophomore album effort, was released in fall 1989, the same year he captured a Grammy award for Best R&B Vocal Performance. Although his second album received some critical praise, it was a com-

mercial disaster and yielded no hit singles. Four years elapsed before *Symphony or Damn* (#119, 1993) was released. Similar to its predecessors, it too failed, but did manage one U.S. single, "Delicate" (#74, 1993).

In February 1995, D'Arby bounced back to the charts with the single "Supermodel Sandwich" (#29, 1995) from the *Pret-A-Porter* soundtrack. *Terrence Trent D'Arby's Vibrator* (#11, U.K., 1995) was his fourth album release and while it sold well in Britain, it charted for only a one week in the U.S. D'Arby has supported numerous humanitarian efforts including AIDS research.

AUTOGRAPHS
A CD, LP, magazine cover, ad, photo, or card signed by the artist: $15-$25

POSTERS/PRESS KITS
Press Kits: $15-$30

USED CLOTHING/EQUIPMENT
Guitar Picks: $20-$25

OFTEN OVERLOOKED MEMORABILIA
All copies of the New Musical Express quoting the artist; his Easter 1988 controversial publicity photograph; a copy of the June 1988 issue of *Rolling Stone* with D'Arby interview; movie memorabilia from *Pret-A-Porter* (1995); television soundtrack to *Promised Land* (1995); a copy of his television appearances on *The Late Show With David Letterman* (5/8/95) and *The Tonight Show* (2/28/94 and 8/17/95)

Darin, Bobby

(Walden Robert Cassotto)
Born: May 14, 1936, Died: December 20, 1973

Darin attend Hunter College on a scholarship, but quit after just one term to pursue a career in acting, recording, or songwriting in conjunction with manager Don Kirshner. He signed with an Atlantic Records subsidiary in May 1957. His initial releases met with little success until "Split Splash" (#3, 1958), a song he wrote in 12 minutes, became a smash hit. The song ignited his career, and he followed with a string of other hits including "Queen of the Hop" (#9, 1958), "Dream Lover" (#2, #1 - U.K., 1959), and "Mack the Knife" (#15, 1959).

That's All (#7, 1959) was Darin's debut album and it climbed the chart, driven by extract "Mack The Knife" (#1, U.K., 1959). The single earned Record of the Year and Darin took home the Best New Artist of 1959 at the second annual Grammy Awards.

"Beyond The Sea" (#6, 1960) became the first of many songs that featured the Darin trademark of a brass rich swing arrangement that was more like a traditional big-band sound than rock and roll. This remake of a 1945 French hit would earn him his fifth U.S. gold disc. At that time, he hit the night club/cab-

aret circuit of both Las Vegas and New York. The year also saw him drop three other singles into the Top Fifty, including "Clementine," "Won't You Come Home Bill Bailey," and "Artificial Flowers."

"Christmas Auld Lang Syne" (#51, 1961), "Lazy River" (#14, 1961), "Nature Boy" (#40, 1961), "You Must Have Been a Beautiful Baby" (#5, 1961), and "Come September" (#50, U.K., 1961) all added to the list of successful singles for the brash and outspoken singer. Darin also released two albums in 1961, *The Bobby Darin Story* (#18, 1961) and *Love Swings* (#92, 1961), and he appeared in a few films.

The following year was also productive for the artist as "Irresistible You" (#15, 1961), "Multiplication" (#30, 1962), "What'd I Say" (#24, 1962), "Things" (#3, 1962), "Baby Face" (#42, 1962), "If a Man Answers" (#32, 1962), and "I Found A New Baby" (#90, 1962) hit the singles chart. Darin also released four albums—*Twist With Bobby Darin* (#48, 1962), *Bobby Darin Sings Ray Charles* (#96, 1962), *Things And Other Things* (#45, 1962), and *Oh! Look At Me Now* (#100, 1962)—while continuing his film appearances.

You're The Reason I'm Living (#43, 1963), with the self-titled hit extract (#3, 1963), was a bit of a twist for the artist, who found himself briefly embracing more of a country audience. He also started his new publishing and recording venture, TM Music Inc., with the single release "Heart! (I Hear You Beating)" penned by Wayne Newton. The singles "18 Yellow Roses" (#10, 1963), "Treat My Baby Good" (#43, 1963), and "Be Mad Little Girl" (#64, 1963) concluded his singles releases for the year, while his film role in *Captain Newman MD* earned him an Oscar nomination for Best Supporting Actor.

In the mid-60s, the British invasion became the focal point for the youth market that Darin once catered to, and although his recording success diminished, his live act continued to sustain his popularity. During the next two years, his highest charting single reached only #45—a version of the Edith Piaf classic "Milord." He then turned to more contemporary material and released "If I Were A Carpenter" (#8, 1966), which landed him back in the Top Ten, followed by "Lovin' You" (#32, 1967).

In 1968, Darin turned his attention to politics and the presidential campaign for Robert F. Kennedy, who became a close friend of the artist. When Kennedy was assassinated, Darin claimed he was overcome by a mysterious religious experience that urged him to sell his possessions and retreat to a mobile home in Big Sur, California.

When he emerged, he started his own short-lived label, Direction Records, but failed to ignite any significant interest in his recorded work. In 1971, Darin underwent successful heart surgery and recuperated for the remainder of the year. In 1972 he turned his efforts to television and scored a hit with *The Bobby Darin Show*, while the following year he appeared in

his last film, *Happy Mother's Day*, with Patricia Neal.

On December 20, 1973, Darin died following surgery to repair a heart valve. Plagued by heart problems throughout his life, he had commented numerous times that he wouldn't reach the age of 30. In 1990, Bobby Darin was inducted into the Rock and Roll Hall of Fame during its fifth annual dinner in New York.

AUTOGRAPHS

An LP, magazine cover, ad, photo, or card signed by the artist: $150 (signed photo), $50 (sig.)

OFTEN OVERLOOKED MEMORABILIA

Movie memorabilia from *Pepe* (1960), *Heller in Pink Tights* (1960), *Come September* (1961), *State Fair* (1961), *Too Late Blues* (1961), *Pressure Point* (1962), *Hell Is for Heroes* (1962), *If A Man Answers* (1962), *Captain Newman MD* (1963), *That Funny Feeling* (1965), *Gunfight in Abilene* (1967), *Cop Out* (1967), *The Happy Ending* (1969), *Happy Mother's Day* (1973); any associated Robert Kennedy campaign items; videotapes of *The Bobby Darin Show* (1972/73); all Direction records associated memorabilia

REFERENCES/BOOKS

Dream Lovers, by Dodd Darin (1994); *That's All: Bobby Darin on Record, Stage & Screen* by Jeff Bleiel—a must for Darin collectors! A few resources exist.

Das Fürlines

Formed 1985

Wendy Wild, Holly Hemlock, Liz Luv, Deb O'Nair, and Rachel Schnitzel

The band relocated from Germany to New York and became a part of the East Village postpunk music scene. The sensually alluring fivesome quickly developed a reputation for its elaborate costumes and high-energized performances. From chicken polka dancing contests to storytelling segments, the group pioneered the punk-polka genre.

Das Fürlines Go Wild (1985), and *Lost in the Translation* (1986) were the first two albums released by the group. Neither captured the live spirit of the band, or generated a whole lot of additional interest. *Das Fürlines Live at Paddles* (1987), an expected breakthrough release, also did little commercially. *The Angry Years*, a concept album, became almost too biographical and following a tour in support of the release, the band split up.

Davies, Cyril

Born: 1932, Died: January 7, 1964

Davies laid a foundation for the early-60s British R&B scene. Although he began his career as a "stringsmith" in a traditional jazz band, he would migrate to other forms of music including skiffle, blues, and R&B by the late '50s. By this period in time, singing and playing the harmonica became his focus. He then hooked up with Alexis Korner and opened up a series of blues clubs in London's Soho district. It was there that the finest blues performers of the world found a home, as well as a few extra colleagues one could jam with. From Memphis Slim to Muddy Waters, Davies jammed with them all, while he influenced an entire new generation of British youths.

By the early '60s Korner and Davies "plugged in" and formed Blues Incorporated. The band would quickly become a spawning ground for new talent, many of whom would go on to ignite the British invasion of the '60s. Mick Jagger, Brian Jones, Jack Bruce, and Ginger Baker all paid their dues with Blues Inc. The band became a favorite at London's Marquee Club by the end of 1962, but Davies was itching to get out on his own, and he did by starting the Cyril Davies All-Stars. It too became a breeding ground for talent—with the likes of both Jeff Beck and Nicky Hopkins—and quickly developed a strong cult following.

When Davies died in 1964, many of his band members went on to Baldry's Hoochie Coochie Men.

AUTOGRAPHS

A photo or card signed by the artist: $20-$35

Davis, The Reverend Gary

Born: April 30, 1896, Died: May 5, 1972

Ry Cooder, Taj Mahal, and Jorma Kaukonen all patterned their skills after the percussive finger-picking guitar style of Reverend Gary Davis. Totally blind by the age of thirty and partially blind as a youth, he had spent much of his earlier years jamming with blues greats around the Carolinas. But by the end of the Roaring '20s, Davis decided the blues was the "devil's music" and instead turned to God. In 1933 he was ordained at the Free Baptist Connection Church in North Carolina. He quickly became a popular gospel singer and eventually recorded a few religious songs for New York's Perfect Records.

For the next three decades Davis lived as a street singer in Harlem, treated himself to an occasional studio session, and subsisted through life's daily challenges, often by passing a plate in front of a passing congregation. He did make an appearance at the 1959 Newport Folk Festival before touring America. He died in Hammonton, New Jersey, on May 5, 1972.

Davis, Mac

Born: January 21, 1942

Davis was a regional sales manager for Vee Jay Records in the '60s. At the same time, he crafted his skills as a songwriter. He went on to Liberty Records, where he moved to the music publishing division in Hollywood. It was there that he sold many of his songs including "In the Ghetto," "Memories," and "Don't Cry Daddy" (recorded by Elvis Presley), to major artists.

By the early '70s, his reputation was well established as a songwriter, and it was time for him to begin his career as a performer. He quickly delivered a series of hit singles including "I Believe In Music," "Baby Don't Get Hooked On Me," "Rock and Roll (I Gave You the Best Years of My Life)" (#15, 1975), "One Hell of a Woman" (#11, 1974), and "Stop and Smell the Roses" (#9, 1974). His career was so solid that he landed his own television variety program, *The Mac Davis Show*.

When his later recordings became less successful, he turned to acting and made his film debut in *North Dallas Forty* (1979). He then went on to Las Vegas to play a stint at the MGM Grand Hotel in 1981 before he nearly made a career out of appearing on numerous television talk shows. He made his Broadway debut as the title character in *The Will Rogers Follies* in 1992. Many musicians still continued to cover his music.

In 1994, the ever versatile Davis inked a deal with Columbia Nashville and released "Will Write Songs For Food." If the title ends up being any indication of his ability, there will be plenty of food for everybody.

AUTOGRAPHS

A CD, LP, magazine cover, ad, photo, or card signed by the artist: $10-$20

Davis, Miles

Born: May 25, 1926, Died: September 28, 1991

Miles Davis played a role in every major jazz development from the '40s until his death in 1991. He dropped out of New York's Julliard School to become the protégé of his then roommate Charlie Parker and played in his quintet during the 1945 Savoy sessions, the hallmark recording of the bebop movement. He also played with Benny Carter, Billy Eckstine, and Charles Mingus during a time when he was relying more on his ear for sound, than his gift for producing it.

He slowly became more introspective, and his work with Gil Evans on the *Birth of Cool* sessions in 1949 and early 1950 set a new course for the artist. It was also a challenging time for Davis who was fighting substance abuse, a curse that would impact his work until he cleaned up in the mid-50s. The Miles Davis quintet was then formed, with interchanging personnel right through the end of the decade. During this period his work became more complex, slowly maturing, and then reevaluated and streamlined.

Kind of Blue (1959) threw all the rules out the window, along with chords as the basis for improvisation. Then in 1963 he struck gold with his quintet that included bassist Ron Carter, pianist Herbie Hancock, drummer Tony Williams, and sax player George Coleman, who was replaced by Wayne Shorter in 1965. The group stayed together until 1968 and became the crystal ball for the jazz that followed. Davis worked hard on his material, especially with Shorter, whom he wrote the majority of original material with.

With *Miles in the Sky* (1968) the Davis quintet fused jazz with rock, while introducing electric instruments. With this sound came more rock influence and a prelude to a monumental piece, *Bitches Brew* (1969). With no rehearsals or instructions, Wayne Shorter, John McLaughlin, Dave Holland, Chick Corea, and Joe Zawinul, along with Larry Young, Harvey Brooks, Benny Maupin, Jack DeJohnette, Lenny White, Charles Alias, and Jim Riley all played. The jam, a double LP set, sold over 400,000 copies.

Bitches Brew put Davis is a whole new class of his own and made jazz-rock fusion a dominant new form of music. Seizing the opportunity was not only left to Davis, but also to his protégés and their spin-offs including Weather Report and the Mahavishnu Orchestra. In 1972, Davis was sidelined with two broken legs following an automobile accident, which resulted in an increased behavior toward reclusion. *Agharta* (1976), a live album recorded in Japan, would be his last album of new material for half a decade.

Prompted by his new wife, actress Cicely Tyson, Davis reemerged with *The Man with the Horn*, a more commercial departure than anticipated, it nonetheless served the needed inspiration for the artist. Critics, failing to realize the artist's evolutionary process, didn't like Davis' more commercial efforts. He surrounded himself with younger musicians and planted seeds that would be sewn years later. The artist was still painting, but the audience couldn't see the picture.

He experimented with albums such as *Tutu* (1986), on which he used his horn as the only live instrument. Tragedy again struck Davis, when his marriage to Tyson ended in 1988 and he lost his dear

friend Gil Evans. The events moved him toward television and film. If it was greater recognition he sought, it was achieved now through television commercials and even appearances on *Miami Vice*. It was if he once again knew something no one else did.

Davis became introspective, published an autobiography, and became a subject for a 1986 public television special. In the summer before his death, he participated in a career retrospective—something he had always traditionally avoided. In 1990 he received the Grammy Award for Lifetime Achievement, and the following year, he died.

AUTOGRAPHS

A CD, LP, magazine cover, ad, photo, or card signed by the artist: $200-$450

OFTEN OVERLOOKED MEMORABILIA

Movie memorabilia from *Siesta*, *The Hot Spot*, *Scrooged*, and *Dingo*; videotapes of his television appearances including *Miami Vice*, the *Amnesty International Concert*, and the 1986 public television show devoted to Davis

The Spencer Davis Group

Formed 1963

Original Lineup: Spencer Davis, Born: July 17, 1942; Pete York, Born: August 15, 1942; Steve Winwood, Born: May 12, 1948; and Muff Winwood, (Mervyn Winwood), Born: June 14, 1943

This mid-60s R&B influenced rock band is best remembered for the hits "Gimmie Some Lovin" (#7, 1967) and "I'm a Man" (#10, 1967) and as a temporary stop for a young and talented musician, Steve Winwood.

Nice wall display featuring an article autographed by the Spencer Davis Group. This artifact is from the Hard Rock Cafe in Key West, Florida.

AUTOGRAPHS

A CD, LP, magazine cover, ad, photo, or card signed by the group: $30-$100

OFTEN OVERLOOKED MEMORABILIA

All artifacts from the groups September 1965 U.K. tour with the Rolling Stones and the group's April, 1966 U.K. tour with the Who; movie memorabilia from *The Ghost Goes Gear* (1966) and *Here We Go Round the Mulberry Bush* (1967)

Davis, Tyrone

Born: May 4, 1938

Tyrone Davis, a talented R&B and soul singer from the '70s, is best remembered for the songs "Can I Change My Mind" (#5, 1969) and "Turn Back the Hands of Time" (#3, 1970), along with numerous R&B hits.

AUTOGRAPHS

A CD, LP, magazine cover, ad, photo, or card signed by the artist: $8-$15

Day, Bobby

(Robert Byrd)
Born: July 1, 1930

Singer Bobby Day is best remembered for his hit "Rockin' Robin" (#2, 1958).

AUTOGRAPHS

An LP, magazine cover, ad, photo, or card signed by the artist: $10-$20

Dayne, Taylor

(Leslie Wunderman)
Born: March 7, 1963

This Long Island disco pop diva, who couldn't garner any attention under the name "Leslee," changed it to Taylor Dayne, and released her Arista debut *Tell It to My Heart* (#21, 1988) that spun off the hit title track (#7, 1987) and three others: "Prove Your Love" (#7, 1988), "I'll Always Love You" (#3, 1988), and "Don't Rush Me" (#2, 1988).

Her sophomore effort, *Can't Fight Fate* (#25, 1989), contained four hit extracts: "With Every Beat of My Heart" (#5, 1989), "Love Will Lead You Back" (#1, 1990), "I'll Be Your Shelter" (#4, 1990), and "Heart of Stone" (#12, 1990).

AUTOGRAPHS

A CD, LP, magazine cover, ad, photo, or card signed by the artist: $8-$15

POSTERS/PRESS KITS

Promotional Posters: $10
Press Kits: $10

The dB's

Formed 1978

Will Rigby, Born: March 17, 1956; Peter Holsapple, Born: February 19, 1956; Gene Holder, Born: July 10, 1954; and Chris Stamey, Born: December 6, 1954

The dB's, the '80s indie rockers and favorites of the New York club scene, garnered most of its exposure when it opened for R.E.M. on its 1984 and 1987 U.S. tours before the group finally signed to the I.R.S. label. *The Sound of Music* (#171, 1987) was greeted with moderate accolades, but not enough to sustain long term commercial success.

The dB's now deceased Holsapple moved on to play keyboards and guitar on the R.E.M. Green tour and guested on *Out of Time*, before he joined the Continental Drifters and married Susan Cowsill. Stamey went solo and toured. Rigby followed similar suit, but also played sessions. Holder went on to production work.

AUTOGRAPHS

A CD, LP, magazine cover, ad, photo, or card signed by the group: $15-$35

POSTERS/PRESS KITS

Promotional Posters: $10-$20
Press Kits: $10-$15

The Dead Boys

Formed 1976

Cheetah Chrome (Gene Connor), Stiv Bators (Stiven Bator, 1949-1990), Jimmy Zero, Jeff Magnum, and Johnny Blitz

Migrants to the happening New York Bowery music scene, The Dead Boys were punk to the core, raw unabated energy, and anti-everything—the group quickly found a home. CBGB owner Hilly Crystal managed the group that was long on image and short on talent; in retrospect the group lasted considerably longer than it should have. The analogy quickly draws comparisons to the U.K.'s The Damned.

AUTOGRAPHS

A CD, LP, magazine cover, ad, photo, or card signed by the group: $15-$20

The Dead Kennedys

Formed 1978

Jello Biafra (Eric Boucher), East Bay Ray, Klaus Flouride, and J.H. Pelligro

These late-70s hard core punk pioneers from San Francisco may have been America's closest link to the Sex Pistols. The Dead Kennedys had an enormous cult following fueled by songs such as "Drug Me" and "California Uber Alles." Led by singer Jello Biafra, whose distaste for the Moral Majority and middle class mediocrity made him an instant attraction, the band even landed in the Top Five in the U.K. with the airplay banned "Too Drunk to Fuck." Proving he was no pudding in a cloud, Jello also ran for mayor of San Francisco in 1979, but lost.

Alternative Tentacles, the band's own record label, made history with the group's release of *Frankenchrist* (1985), which led to Biafra and others being charged with distributing pornography to minors under the country's revised obscenity laws. A hung jury eventually ended the case just before the group split up.

AUTOGRAPHS

A CD, LP, magazine cover, ad, photo, or card signed by the group: $20-$40

OFTEN OVERLOOKED MEMORABILIA

All press clippings from the band's controversial antics, especially the *Frankenchrist* issue

DeBarge/El DeBarge

Formed 1978

Bunny DeBarge, Born: March 15, 1955; El (Eldra) DeBarge, Born: June 4, 1961; Marty (Mark) DeBarge, Born: June 19, 1959; and Randy DeBarge, Born: August 6, 1958*

*James DeBarge joined in 1982. El and Bunny departed in 1988. Chico (Jonathan) DeBarge appeared on the scene in 1986.

This mid-80s pop-soul family act may be best remembered for what didn't happen versus what did. Destined to be the next Jackson 5, El, with his outstanding singing and dancing skills, was even compared to Michael Jackson; the closest he would get, however, would be marrying Janet. The marriage led to an annulment within seven months.

Rhythm of the Night, which yielded the successful title track (#3, 1985) and "Who's Holding Donna Now" (#6, 1985), was perhaps the band's finest hour. El left shortly thereafter and scored with "Who's Johnny" (#3, 1986) from the *Short Circuit* soundtrack, while Chico also hit with "Talk to Me" (#21, 1986).

AUTOGRAPHS

A CD, LP, magazine cover, ad, photo, or card signed by the group: $15-$30

OFTEN OVERLOOKED MEMORABILIA

Movie memorabilia from *Short Circuit*; periodical clippings from some of the band members more forgettable moments, like their arrests etc.

Joey Dee and the Starliters

Formed 1958

Joey Dee (Joseph DiNicola), Born: June 11, 1940; Carlton Latimor; Willie Davis; Larry Vernieri; and David Brigati

A great answer to numerous rock trivia questions, Joey Dee and the Starlighters are best remembered for adding flavor to Chubby Checker's "The Twist," "Peppermint Twist" (#1, 1961), along with "Hey Let's Twist," "Shout," and "What Kind of Love Is This," before slipping back into the lounge lizard circuit.

Now, your trivia questions:

Q. By 1963, which three Starliters would go onto to greater stardom together in their next band?

A. Young Rascals' Felix Cavaliere, Gene Cornish, and Eddie Brigati!

Q. What famous '60s guitarist was a Starliter in 1966?

A. Jimi Hendrix

AUTOGRAPHS

A CD, LP, magazine cover, ad, photo, or card signed by the artist: $15-$25*

*Original band members

OFTEN OVERLOOKED MEMORABILIA

Movie memorabilia from *Hey Let's Twist* and *Two Tickets to Paris*

Deee-Lite

Formed 1986

Lady Miss Kier (Kier Kirby), Super DJ Dmitry (Dmitry Brill), and Jungle DJ Towa Towa (Towa Tei)

These fashion-glam rockers of the '90s built up a solid underground following in the New York club scene before landing such hits as "Groove Is in the Heart" (#4, 1990) and "Power of Love" (#47, 1990). Deee-Lite is truly a delight to watch because of the artists' outrageous visual flair and enormous sex appeal.

AUTOGRAPHS

A CD, LP, magazine cover, ad, photo, or card signed by the group: $15-$30

OFTEN OVERLOOKED MEMORABILIA

A stage-thrown flower: $5

Deep Purple

Formed 1968

Rod Evans, Nick Simper, Jon Lord, Ritchie Blackmore, and Ian Paice*

*Ian Gillan replaced Evans in 1969, and Roger Glover replaced Simper. In 1973 Glenn Hughes replaced Glover

and David Coverdale replaced Gillan. Tommy Bolin replaced Blackmore in 1975.

*In 1984 the group re-formed: Blackmore, Gillan, Glover, Lord, and Paice. Joe Lynn Turner replaced Gillan in 1989, however, Gillan returned in 1993.

The group initially formed as the Roundabout in February 1968 with band members Lord, Blackmore, Chris Curtis, Dave Curtis, and Bobby Woodman. When it became clear that certain members weren't going to work out, the lineup was altered. Paice, Evans, and Simper were added, and the band debuted in Tastrup, Denmark (4/20/68), under a new name, Deep Purple.

The group played the Sunbury Festival, its first major venue on August 10, 1968. "Hush" (#4, 1968), a revival of an old Joe South number, was the group's debut single and its first hit. It was followed by another cover, Neil Diamond's "Kentucky Woman" (#38, 1968). With interest in the band growing, the debut album *Shades Of Deep Purple* (#24, 1968) made a very respectable chart showing, and was followed by *The Book of Taliesyn* (#54, 1969) which included the single extract "River Deep, Mountain High" (#53, 1969).

During the summer of 1969, the band encountered a few challenges because members Evans and Simper both left, and while the album *Deep Purple* (#162, 1969) peaked in sales, the group's label folded. Glover and Gillian were added; both were playing in a band called Episode Six prior to accepting the new opportunity. The band's next release was *Concerto For Group and Orchestra* (#149, 1970, Warner Bros.), composed by Lord with the Royal Philharmonic Orchestra. The record became the group's U.K. chart debut. The group continued to tour extensively, first with a short U.K. tour in February (1970) and then a summer European tour.

Deep Purple In Rock (#143, 1970), the group's next album, included the U.K. hit single "Black Night" (#2, 1970). "Strange Kind Of Woman" (#8, U.K., 1971) was the band's first 1971 single release. The group toured the U.S. with the Faces in July. *Fireball* (#32, 1971), the group's only album that year, contained its title cut that climbed to #15 on the U.K. singles chart.

In 1972, the band spent the majority of the year on the road—44 out of 52 weeks—in support primarily of its new album *Machine Head* (#35, U.K., 1972). In August the band toured Japan where numerous concerts were recorded for a future album release. Gillian left the group following its tour commitments.

The following year began with a double dose of Deep Purple, first with the double-disc *Made In Japan* (#16, U.K., 1973), released in January, and then followed by the studio album *Who Do We Think We Are* (#15, 1973). Gillian's services ended in June, and the group also discovered Glover would be departing in July both were reportedly leaving due to differ-

ences with Blackmore. Meanwhile, "Smoke On The Water" climbed the U.S. singles chart and finally reached #4. The single earned the band its first gold disc.

David Coverdale and Glenn Hughes were added to fill the vacancies, while single "Woman From Tokyo" peaked at #60. The group's first album with the new lineup, *Burn* (#9, 1974), was followed later in the year by *Stormbringer* (#20, 1974). The following year Blackmore announced that he was leaving to form his own band, Rainbow, with members of Ronnie James Dio's Elf. Deep Purple then added former James Gang guitarist Tommy Bolin, and toured with Rainbow supporting the new lineup.

Come Taste The Band (#43, 1976) featuring Bolin, climbed into the U.K. Top Twenty album chart, while the band began a world tour. On July 19, 1976, following the tour, the band split. Members went their separate ways; Coverdale formed Whitesnake, Lord and Paice stuck together in their own band, and Hughes rejoined Trapeze. Bolin returned to the U.S. to form his own band and died of a heroin overdose on December 4, 1976. Various incarnations of the band would surface, disappear, and resurface over the decades that followed.

In 1984, Deep Purple reunited for the its first new album since 1976, *Perfect Strangers* (#17, 1984). The album sold well and included extract "Knocking at Your Back Door"(#61, 1985), but personnel problems continued and Gillian left again in 1989. He did, however, return briefly for the album *The Battle Rages On* (#192, 1993).

OFTEN OVERLOOKED MEMORABILIA

Memorabilia surrounding Ian Gillian's role of Jesus in *Jesus Christ Superstar* (1970); copy *of The Guinness Book of Records* listing Deep Purple as "world's loudest" (1975/76); *Perfect Strangers* stand-up display - $45

REFERENCES/BOOKS

A few resources exist; no dedicated collector books

Def Leppard

Formed 1977

Joe Elliott, Born: August 1, 1959; Pete Willis, Born: February 16, 1960; Rick Savage, Born: December 2, 1960; Rick Allen, Born: November 1, 1963; and Steve Clark, Born: April 23, 1960, Died: January 8, 1991*

*Phil Collen replaced Willis in 1982. Vivian Campbell, born August 25, 1962, was added in 1992.

Pete Willis and Elliott left the band Jump to join Atomic Mass led by Savage. The group then changed its name to Def Leppard and added Clark as a second guitarist. The group's live debut came in July 1978 at the Westfield School in Sheffield. At the time, the band was still searching for a permanent drummer.

The band recorded a three-track EP, *Getcha Rocks Off* with a stand-in drummer before recruiting Allen.

The success of the group's EP led to a prestigious session for BBC Radio's John Peel show. Phonogram Records took notice and signed the band to its Vertigo label, where the group cut its debut album, *On Through The Night* (#15, U.K., #51, U.S., 1980). The group supported the release with an appearance at "Reading Rock "80" in the U.K. before it embarked on a U.S. tour opening for Ted Nugent.

High 'n' Dry (#38, 1981), the group's next album, was supported by an extensive touring schedule. An exhausted Def Leppard then decided to take some time off. The following year the group entered the studio and when it became clear that Willis' services were conflicting with the band, he was fired and Collen replaced him.

Pyromania (#2, 1983) was the group's breakthrough album; it spent a 92-week run on the U.S. album chart, driven by extracted single "Photograph" (#12, 1983). In May, the band began a comprehensive world tour in support of the release, and spun off two more singles: "Rock of Ages" (#16, 1983) and "Foolin'"(#28, 1983).

The following year the band took eight months off to recover from the previous tour before re-entering the studio. In December the recording was halted for a holiday break and producer Jim Steinman was fired. On December 13, 1984, while racing his Corvette Stingray, Allen crashed and severed his left arm. Surgeons tried, but were unsuccessful at, reattaching his arm. In January, Allen affirmed his desire to return despite the extraordinary circumstances. Encouraged by the news, the band returned to its recording duties. The sessions, however, were scrapped while the band awaited the services of producer John Lange.

In 1986, the band eased into live performances to allow Allen to acclimate to his new situation. "Animal"(#6, U.K., 1987) was the first extract from the group's new album *Hysteria* (#1, 1988). Three years in the making, the new album also spun off five other Top Twenty hits: "Love Bites" (#1, 1988), "Pour Some

Def Leppard. Photo by Cynthia Levine. Courtesy of Mercury Records.

Sugar On Me" (#2, 1988), "Hysteria" (#10, 1988), "Armageddon It" (#3, 1988), and "Rocket" (#12, 1989). The album eventually sold more than 14 million copies, and the band was thrust into the spotlight. Unfortunately, tragedy again reared its ugly head—Steve Clark died of a fatal dose of drugs and alcohol on January 8, 1991. His replacement, Vivian Campbell, was formerly with Ronnie James Dio and Whitesnake. The new guitarist joined shortly after the release of *Adrenalize* (#1, 1992), which like its predecessor, yielded a plethora of hits including "Have You Ever Needed Someone So Bad" (#12, 1992), "Let's Get Rocked" (#15, 1992), "Make Love Like a Man" (#36, 1992), and "Stand Up (Kick Love Into Motion)" (#34, 1992).

A compilation of flip sides, rarities, and covers, *Retro Active* (#9, 1993), the band's next full release, included extracted singles "Two Steps Behind" (#32, 1994) and "Miss You In A Heartbeat" (#39, 1994). On October 23, 1995, the band played three concerts in three continents on the same day—an impressive feat to say the least. During the same year, the group pushed off a studio release in favor of *Vault: Greatest Hits 1980 to 1995* (#15, 1995). In May 1996, the band released *Slang*, a more experimental album than anticipated, and began planning a thirtieth anniversary tour for 1997.

AUTOGRAPHS
Group:
A LP, magazine cover, ad, photo, or card signed by the group: $75-$175*
*Elliott, Savage, Allen, Clark, and Collen
Individual:

Joe Elliott: $20-$30	Pete Willis: $5-$10
Rick Savage: $12-$20	Rick Allen: $20-$25
Phil Collen: $15-$20	Steve Clark: $30-$40
Vivian Campbell: $12-$15	

TOUR BOOKS/PROGRAMS/PASSES
Tour Books:
1984 Japan Tour: $60-$75
Backstage Passes:
Cloth: $8-$10; Laminated: $10-$15 (1990-Present)

POSTERS/PRESS KITS
Promotional Posters: $10-$65
Retro Active, U.K. (40" x 60"): $25
Press Kits: $20-$50

USED CLOTHING/EQUIPMENT
Guitar Picks:

Rick Savage: $20-$40	Phil Collen: $25-$80
Steve Clark: $40-$65	Vivian Campbell: $15-$20

Drum Sticks:
Rick Allen: $35-$40

OFTEN OVERLOOKED MEMORABILIA
Movie memorabilia from *The Last Action Hero* (1994); "Pyromania" Mercury promotional lighter, 1983; promotional pins - $8-$10; logo necklace - $15; Promotional British flag shorts - $40

REFERENCES/BOOKS
Def Leppard by Jason Rich: $10; *Def Leppard, An Illustrated Biography* by Welch : $15; *Def Leppard* by Willy McGilly: $15; a few resources exist, nothing that does justice to the band in my opinion; no dedicated collector books

The DeFranco Family

Formed 1973
Benny, Nino, Marisa, Merlina, and Tony DeFranco

The Canadian-spawned wholesome family act, backed and managed by Laufer Publications (*Tiger Beat*), is best remembered for the songs "Heartbeat - It's a Lovebeat" (#1, 1973), "Abra-Ca-Dabre" (#32, 1974), and "Save the Last Dance for Me" (#18, 1974), before it disappeared from sight.

AUTOGRAPHS
An LP, magazine cover, ad, photo, or card signed by the group: $10-$15

OFTEN OVERLOOKED MEMORABILIA
Numerous DeFranco related memorabilia appeared in *Tiger Beat* and *Fave* magazines, fan-club material, etc.

Dekker, Desmond

(Desmond Dacres)
Born: July 16, 1941

The "King of the Bluebeat," the pioneer of reggae, Desmond Dekker is best known for such Caribbean classics as "Honour Thy Father and Mother" (#1, Jamaica), "007 (Shanty Town)," "The Israelites" (#9, 1969), "It Miek" (#7, U.K., 1969), and "You Can Get It If You Really Want" (#2, 1970).

AUTOGRAPHS
A CD, LP, magazine cover, ad, photo, or card signed by the artist: $10-$15

OFTEN OVERLOOKED MEMORABILIA
Movie memorabilia from *The Harder They Come* (1972); a videotape of his British television ad for Maxell Tapes that features "The Israelites"

Delaney and Bonnie

Bonnie Bramlett, Born: November 8, 1944; and Delaney Bramlett, Born: July 1, 1939

This duo, whose hit songs included "Never Ending Song of Love" (#13, 1971) and "Only You Know and I Know" (#20, 1971), is best remembered in rock's archives as a stop along the path for Eric Clapton. The couple's relationship with Clapton was fueled when the duo became the opening act for Blind Faith on

its 1969 tour. When the supergroup disbanded, Clapton opted for a low-key role, if there is such a thing for him, in the duo's band. As is typically the case with someone of Clapton's stature, wherever he went, his friends followed (like George Harrison, Dave Mason, and Leon Russell). Much of the relationship was captured on the duo's *On Tour with Eric Clapton* (#29, 1970). In 1972, the married couple made its last album together before the two divorced.

AUTOGRAPHS
A CD, LP, magazine cover, ad, photo or card signed by the artists: $15-$40

OFTEN OVERLOOKED MEMORABILIA
Videotapes of Bonnie's appearance on *Roseanne;* clippings regarding Bonnie's famous punch thrown at Elvis Costello while she was on tour with Stephen Stills in 1979

De La Soul

Formed 1985

Posdnous (Kelvin Mercer), Born: August 17, 1969; Trugoy The Dove (David Jolicoeur), Born: September 21, 1968; and P.A. Pasemaster Mase (Vincent Mason), Born: March 24, 1970

The nice-and-easy, go-with-the-flow, '90s "alternative rap" group that went against the grain of the current in-your-face attitude of hip-hop and set a well-received course down easy street with hits such as "Me Myself and I" (#34, 1989) and "Ring Ring Ring (Ha Ha Hey)" (#22, R&B, 1991).

AUTOGRAPHS
A CD, LP, magazine cover, ad, photo, or card signed by the group: $15-$30

POSTERS/PRESS KITS
Promotional Posters: $10
Press Kits: $10

The Delfonics

Formed 1964

Original lineup: William Hart, Wilbert Hart, Ricky Johnson, and Richard Daniels

The smooth, elegant, late-60s Philadelphia soul act which scored numerous hits is probably best remembered for "La La Means I Love You" (#4, 1968) and "Didn't I (Blow Your Mind This Time)," the latter of which hit the Top Ten in 1970. Veteran R&B artist Major Harris, known for his hit "One Monkey Don't Stop No Show" landed with the group in 1973, but departed the following year.

AUTOGRAPHS
A CD, LP, magazine cover, ad, photo, or card signed by the group: $20-$45*
*Original band members

The Dells

Formed 1953

Marvin Junior, Michael "Mickey" McGill, Johnny Funches, Chuck Barksdale, and Vern Allison*

*Funches left in 1959 and Johnny Carter replaced him.

The Dells, a Chicago rooted R&B soul act that has survived for over four decades by a gradual evolution and membership change, have carved out a unique niche in rock's rich history. From an a cappella streetcorner doo-wop group to a contemporary soul group during the '60s, the band scored hits such as "There Is" (#20, 1968), "Always Together" (#18, 1968), "Stay in My Corner" (#10, 1968), and later "Oh What a Night"—a Top Ten remake in 1969. The hit songs tailed off in the '70s after the group had already landed thirty Top Forty tunes on the R&B chart.

The group was the inspiration for Robert Townshend's film *The Five Heartbeats,* and suitably so because the group's career had indeed endured. "The Heart Is the house of Love" (#13, R&B, 1991) was included on the film's soundtrack.

AUTOGRAPHS
A CD, LP, magazine cover, ad, photo, or card signed by the group: $20-$65*
*Lineup from 1968

OFTEN OVERLOOKED MEMORABILIA
Movie memorabilia from *The Five Heartbeats* (1991)

The Del-Vikings/Dell Vikings

Formed 1956

Clarence Quick, Dave Lerchey, Norman Wright, Don Jackson, and Corinthian "Kripp" Johnson*

*Jackson departed in 1957 and was replaced by Donald "Gus" Backus. Numerous personnel changes followed.

This vocal quintet of the late '50s is best remembered for the Top Ten hits, "Come Go With Me" (#5, 1957) and "Whispering Bells" (#9, 1957).

AUTOGRAPHS
A CD, LP, magazine cover, ad, photo, or card signed by the group: $15-$20

Denny, Sandy

Born: January 6, 1947, Died: April 21, 1978

Denny, the Popular British singer/songwriter of the early '70s, is primarily known for her work with the group Fairport Convention and for authoring the tune "Who Knows Where the Time Goes," which Judy

Collins covered. She also contributed vocals to Led Zeppelin's "The Battle of Evermore."

AUTOGRAPHS

A CD, LP, magazine cover, ad, photo, or card signed by the artist: $20-$45

Denver, John

(John Deutschendorf)
Born: December 31, 1943

Working as a draftsman in Los Angeles, CA, Denver supplemented his income by playing the folk scene at night, a situation that eventually led to a position in the Chad Mitchell Trio. He stayed in the group, while he developed his songwriting skills and perfected his on stage demeanor, until he signed as a solo artist with RCA Records in 1968. *Rhymes And Reasons* (#148, 1969) features his composition "Leaving On A Jet Plane," which trio Peter, Paul, and Mary took to the top of the charts.

Take Me Tomorrow (#197, 1970) was followed by *Poems, Prayers and Promises* (#15, 1971) with the hit extract "Take Me Home, Country Roads" (#2, 1971), his debut chart single and first hit. *Rocky Mountain High* (#4, 1972), with extracted title track (#9, 1973) became his next hit album and thrusted the artist even further into the limelight.

John Denver's Greatest Hits (#1, 1974), his next major release and his first Number One album, featured the singles "Sunshine On My Shoulders"(#1, 1974) and "Annie's Song" (#1, 1974), which became the artist's first two consecutive chart toppers. *Back Home Again* (#1, 1974), driven by the extracted title track (#5, 1974), gave Denver his second consecutive Number One album. Now at the top of his craft, opportunities and accolades were thrusted upon Denver on a daily basis.

In 1975, Denver released three albums: *An Evening With John Denver* (#2, 1975), *Windsong* (#1, 1975), and *Rocky Mountain Christmas* (#14, 1975). "Thank God I'm A Country Boy" (#1, 1975), "I'm Sorry" (#1, 1975), and "Calypso" (#2, 1975) added to his series of hit singles in 1975, a year that also saw him guest on the premiere edition of ABC-TV's *Saturday Night Live With Howard Cosell* (9/20/75).

"Fly Away" (#13, 1976), "Looking For Space" (#29, 1976), "It Makes Me Giggle" (#60, 1976), and "Like A Sad Song" (#36, 1976) were Denver's 1976 singles releases, which complimented his albums *The John Denver Gift Pack* (#138, 1976), *Live In London* (#2, U.K. only, 1976), and *Spirit* (#7, 1976). In July 1976, humanitarian Denver plays for one week in Los Angeles, and donates the proceeds to thirty different charities.

From 1977 until the end of the decade, Denver will see only one single land in the Top Forty, "My Sweet

Lady" (#32, 1977). Although *John Denver's Greatest Hits, Volume 2* (#6, 1977), and *I Want To Live* (#45, 1978) climbed the album charts, the artist concentrated on acting and made his debut in *Oh, God* (1977).

The '80s saw Denver albums *A Christmas Together* (#26, 1980), *Autograph* (#39, 1980), *Some Days Are Diamonds* (#32, 1981), *Perhaps Love* (#17, U.K., 1982), *Seasons of the Heart* (#39, 1982), *It's About Time* (#61, 1983), *Dreamland Express* (#90, 1984), *One World* (#91, U.K., 1986), and *Higher Ground* (1988). His Top Forty singles included "Some Days Are Diamonds" (#36, 1981) and "Shanghai Breezes" (#31, 1982). Most of his time was then spent educating the public on critical issues, such as endangered species and conservation concerns. In 1987 Denver was presented with the Presidential World Without Hunger Award by Ronald Reagan, and although prestigious, it was just one of many humanitarian awards he won during his lifetime.

In 1990, Denver released the album *The Flower That Shattered The Stone* (#185), which to-date has been his highest charting of the decade. While the artist continues to speak on behalf of numerous causes, much of the media attention is negative publicity surrounding the artist's bouts with alcohol. Despite the adversity, John Denver continues to forge onward, thankfully never allowing the trivial things in life to interfere with the many major causes he has fought for. He remains one of our country's finest spokesman for environmental concerns.

AUTOGRAPHS

A CD, LP, magazine cover, ad, photo, or card signed by the artist: $10-$25

TOUR BOOKS/PROGRAMS/PASSES

Backstage Passes:
Cloth: $8-$12; Laminated: $12-$20 (1969-1978)
Cloth: $5-$7; Laminated: $7-$10 (1978-Present)

POSTERS/PRESS KITS

Promotional Posters:
1969-1978: $12-$35
1978-Present: $8-$10

Press Kits:
1969-1978: $20-$45
1978-Present: $10-$15

USED CLOTHING/EQUIPMENT

Guitar Picks: $25

OFTEN OVERLOOKED MEMORABILIA

Videotapes of episodes of the weekly BBC2-TV special *The John Denver Show* (1973); movie memorabilia from *The Bears And I* (1975), includes hit "Sweet Surrender" (#13, 1975); *Oh, God* (1977); a videotape of *John Denver And Friends* (3/29/76); a copy of *Newsweek* magazine (12/76) proclaiming Denver as "the most popular singer in America"; a videotape from *Muppets Christmas Special* (1979); a copy of his co-produced television special "The Higher We Fly" (1980); associated memorabilia from the 1984 Winter Olympics of which Denver penned "The Gold

and Beyond" theme song; program and exhibit poster from his photographic exhibition held at Manhattan's Hammer Galleries in New York (1984); videotapes from his numerous 1987 Christmas shows; a copy of documentaries: *Rocky Mountain Reunion* (1987) (award winning) *John Denver's Alaska: The America Child* (1987); a copy of the August 1988 issue of *Aviation Week & Space Technology* which includes Denver references; a videotape of *In Performance At The White House* - NBC-TV (1989); copies of *Christmas In Washington* - NBC-TV (1990); *John Denver's Montana Christmas Skies* - CBS-TV (1991); associated memorabilia from his press conference with the Dalai Lama at the Earth Summit in 1992

REFERENCES/BOOKS

Take Me Home: An Autobiography, by John Denver (1994); numerous resources exist, nothing that does justice to the artist in my opinion; no dedicated collector books; serious collectors should opt for fan club: Hearts in Harmony: World Family of John Denver, Attention: Carol Blevinsm, 1213 River Rd., Quarryville, PA 17566 ($24 fee)

Depeche Mode

Formed 1980

Vince Clarke, Born: July 3, 1960; Andrew Fletcher, Born: July 8, 1961; Dave Gahan, Born: May 9, 1962; and Martin Gore, Born: July 23, 1961*

*Clarke departed in 1981and Alan Wilder was added the following year. Wilder departed in 1995.

A heavy foundation of synthesizers and drum machines was just as much out of convenience as it was for desire for this group which originated in 1980 from the working-class London suburb Basildon. Singles "Dreaming Of Me" (#57, U.K., 1981), "New

Depeche Mode. Photo by Anton Corbijn. Courtesy of Reprise Records.

Life" (#11, U.K., 1981), and "Just Can't Get Enough" (#8, U.K., 1981) all preceded the group's debut album *Speak and Spell* (#10, U.K., 1981). The album peaked in the Top Ten on the album charts as the band ended its first U.K. tour. The group was labeled a force in the New Romantic scene. Songwriter Clarke, reluctant to touring, announced in December that he was leaving to form Yazoo, and Gore was left as the primary songwriter.

Alan Wilder replaced Clarke in January 1982 and immediately joined the band's first U.S. trip and debut at the Ritz Club in New York. Meanwhile, "See You" (#6, U.K., 1982) peaked in the British singles chart and was followed later by "The Meaning Of Love" (#12, U.K., 1982) and "Leave In Silence" (#18, U.K., 1982). The band's next album effort was the Gore-penned *A Broken Frame* (#8, U.K., #177, U.S., 1982).

The band's breakthrough album came with *Some Great Reward* (#5, U.K., 1984) which included the hit extract "People Are People" (#13, 1985). Despite its U.S. singles chart debut and solid live performances, however, the band was still considered an alternative act, and was not taken seriously in America. The situation was much different in the U.K. where the band had posted more than twenty Top Ten hit singles.

U.S. single success eluded the band until 1990, when "Personal Jesus" (#28, 1990), extracted from *Violator* (#7, 1990), preceded the group's first Top Ten single "Enjoy The Silence" (#8, 1990). Now extremely popular on both sides of the Atlantic, *Songs of Faith and Devotion* (#1, 1993) entered the U.S. chart at Number One.

The band then suffered a series of setbacks in 1995. Alan Wider, who had already released a pair of solo records, decided to leave the band in June. A few months later Gahan was found in critical condition in his Los Angeles home after a suicide attempt. Thankfully he survived and the band resumed work on its next album in December 1995.

AUTOGRAPHS

Group:
An LP, magazine cover, ad, photo, or card signed by the group: $40-$65

Individual:
Vince Clarke: $10-$15
Andrew Fletcher: $10
Dave Gahan: $10-$15
Martin Gore: $15-$20
Alan Wilder: $10-$12

TOUR BOOKS/ PROGRAMS/PASSES

Tour Books:
USA 94 Tour: $10*
Devotional Tour 93/94: $10-$12
*Large quantities of this program have been sold to certain book retailers who drastically reduced prices.

Common Depeche Mode program with nice slipcase (Anton Corbijn)

Backstage Passes:
Cloth: $8-$10; Laminated: $10-$15

POSTERS/PRESS KITS
Promotional Posters: $10-$50
Violator (20" x 36"): $10;
Songs of Faith, U.K. (40" x 60"): $40
Press Kits: $20-$25
Songs of Faith and Devotion: $20; all prior $25 minimum

USED CLOTHING/EQUIPMENT
Guitar Picks: Scarce*
*Used a guitar for the first time on a single in 1986, "Stripped" (#15, U.K.)

OFTEN OVERLOOKED MEMORABILIA
A copy of the *Melody Maker* ad (1/82) that recruited Wilder; Songs of Faith and Devotion incense urn; 1993, World Violator Tour scarf - $10; "Music For The Masses" hanging mobile - $45; "Songs of Faith and Devotion" promotional sticker - $5

REFERENCES/BOOKS
Strangers by Corbijn: $20; a few resources exist; no dedicated collector books

Derringer, Rick

(Rick Zehringer)
Born: August 5, 1947

Zehringer formed the McCoys before he was even old enough to drive. By mid-1965, "Hang On Sloopy" (#1, 1965) had topped the charts. Although it would be the band's only #1 hit, it did manage to put "Fever" (#7, 1965) into the Top Ten. Only minor hits followed and by 1969 the group was essentially a club band.

Zehringer met Johnny Winter through the owner of the club the group was playing at. He switched his name to Derringer and went on to both produce and play on several Winter albums. When Winter quit touring in 1971, Derringer hooked up with his brother Edgar Winter and his band White Trash. After touring with the band, he produced Edgar's *They Only Come Out At Night*, an album that included the smash extract and chart topper "Frankenstein."

The public now had developed considerable respect for his proficient guitar playing ability, which was showcased on tour. In 1973 he cut his first solo album *All American Boy* (#25, 1973), driven in sales by his reputation and his now trademark single "Rock and Roll Hoochie Coo"(#15, 1973). He continued his production work which included Johnny Winter's *Still Alive And Well* and played on numerous sessions throughout the decade.

When sales of his second album, *Spring Fever*, fell short of commercial expectations, he shifted his efforts toward the formation of a band. His new band, Derringer, released four albums and toured extensively on the club and college circuit, but was able to muster only moderate success. The '80s found him

continuing his production, while still offering a lick or two on various projects. In 1993, a decade after his last album, he released *Back To The Blues*.

AUTOGRAPHS
An LP, magazine cover, ad, photo, or card signed by the artist: $20-$25

TOUR BOOKS/PROGRAMS/PASSES
Backstage Passes: $5-$10 (cloth/paper)

POSTERS/PRESS KITS
Promotional Posters: $20-$40
Press Kits: $20-$35

USED CLOTHING/EQUIPMENT
Guitar Picks: $15-$30

OFTEN OVERLOOKED MEMORABILIA
His production efforts and contributions to other artists

DeShannon, Jackie

Born: August 21, 1944

DeShannon, a gifted singer and songwriter, is best known for her hit compositions "Dum Dum" (#4, 1961), covered by Brenda Lee, "When You Walk Into the Room" (#35, 1964), covered by the Searchers, and "Bette Davis Eyes," which she cowrote and earned a Grammy for Song of the Year. As a performer, she opened for the Beatles during their first American tour in 1964 and also scored hits with the Bacharach-penned "What the World Needs Now Is Love" (#7, 1965) and later with "Put a Little Love in Your Heart" (#4, 1969).

AUTOGRAPHS
A CD, LP, magazine cover, ad, photo, or card signed by the artist: $15-$25

OFTEN OVERLOOKED MEMORABILIA
Memorabilia associated with other performers' covers of her songs

Devo

Formed 1972

Jerry Casale, Mark Mothersbaugh, Bob Mothersbaugh, Bob Casale, and Alan Myers*

*Myers departed in 1984 and was replaced by Dave Kendrick

Mark Mothersbaugh and Jerry Casale met while attending Kent State University and decided to form a deliberately anonymous four-piece band. Both recruited their brothers and drummer Alan Myers and produced a ten minute video clip entitled *The Truth About De-Evolution*, which won a prize at the 1975 annual Ann Arbor Film Festival. After shortening

the name to Devo, the group released the debut single "Jocko Homo/Mongoloid" (#51, U.K., Stiff, 1978) on its own label Booji Boy Records (12/1976). The name Booji is taken from the group's robot mascot who made periodic appearances at concerts and in videos.

"(I Can't Get Me No) Satisfaction" (#41, U.K., 1978), a fragmented and augmented version of the Rolling Stones' classic, was the group's next single. Shortly after its release, the band made its New York debut at Max's Kansas City; David Bowie introduced the band. The appearance attracted both cult followers and record company personnel.

The bands non-conformist, anonymous style, presented in robotic fashion, enticed the media. Dressed in matching one-piece yellow attendant suits with flower pot hats, the group's style was labeled "industrial rock" or "industrial new-wave," but in traditional New York fashion, everything must be labeled something even if it's incorrect.

Are We Not Men? We Are Devo! (#12, U.K., 1978), the band's album debt, was produced by knob-turner extraordinaire Brain Eno. The albums *Duty Now For The Future* (#49, U.K., 1979) and *Freedom of Choice* (#47, U.K., 1980) followed. The latter contained the hit extract "Whip It" (#14, 1980), the group's first U.S. chart entry and best-selling single.

New Traditionalists (#24, 1981) sold well despite the lack of hit singles. In 1982, the group toured Australia where the mini-album *Devo Live* (#49, 1981) topped the chart. *Oh No, It's Devo* (#47, 1982) also failed to extract a single, but the band finally scored a minor hit—its last—with the theme from *Dr. Detroit* (#59, 1983). The band then lost its contract with Warner Brothers and disappeared for a few years. Mark Mothersbaugh went on to a successful career writing music for television, primarily for children's shows. The band successfully reunited, after previous failed attempts, in 1991, for a European tour and later even recorded a new tune for the soundtrack of *Mighty Morphin Power Rangers* (1995).

AUTOGRAPHS
Group:
An LP, magazine cover, ad, photo, or card signed by the group: $30-$75
Individual:
Mark Mothersbaugh: $8-$12

TOUR BOOKS/PROGRAMS/PASSES
Backstage Passes
Cloth: $10-$15; Laminated: $15-$45

POSTERS/PRESS KITS
Promotional Posters: $10-$40
Press Kits: $15-$40

USED CLOTHING/EQUIPMENT
Guitar Picks: $10-$20
Drum Sticks: $15-$20

OFTEN OVERLOOKED MEMORABILIA
A copy of the band's *In The Beginning Was The End* (16mm film); a copy of the band's appearance on the television show *The Old Grey Whistle Test* (3/78); movie memorabilia from *Rust Never Sleeps* (1979), *Dr. Detroit*, and *Mighty Morphin Power Rangers*; videotapes of Mark Mothersbaugh television work

Diamond, Neil

Born: January 24, 1941

Neil Diamond, while attending New York University on a fencing scholarship, dropped out of his pre-med program in favor of an apprenticeship as a songwriter at Sunbeam Music. Diamond, who has always been interested in music, attended high school with Barbara Streisand. Following high school graduation, he hooked up with friend Jack Parker and formed the duo Neil & Jack. The duo recorded two non-charting singles—"What Will I Do" (1960) and "I'm Afraid" (1961)—for a small New York label called Duel Records.

In 1965, he set up his own songwriting office. During this time he also released the one-off solo single "Clown Town" for CBS/Columbia Records while performing in Greenwich Village coffee houses. It was during one of these live gigs that Jeff Barry and Ellie Greenwich spotted him and signed him to their publishing organization.

With numerous musicians now recording his music, royalties began to flow to Diamond from songs like "Sunday And Me" (Jay & the Americans), and "Just Another Guy" (Cliff Richard). His success by this point was not difficult to recognize and when he was given an opportunity to sign with Bang Records, he did so.

"Solitary Man" (#55, 1966), his impressive debut single release, was followed a few months later by "Cherry Cherry" (#6, 1966), his first major hit. During the year he also released his debut solo album *The Feel Of Neil Diamond* (#137, 1966). His final single of the year, "I Got The Feelin (Oh No No)" (#6, 1966), generated less interest than another one of his tunes that occupied the top of the charts on the very first day of release, the last day of the year, "I'm A Believer" (#1, 1966) by the Monkees.

The following year was also filled with successful Diamond-penned singles including "You Got To Me" (#18, 1967), "Girl, You'll Be a Woman Soon" (#10, 1967), "Thank The Lord For The night Time" (#13, 1967), and "Kentucky Woman" (#22, 1967). Meanwhile, other artists competed against him with his own music including "A Little Bit You, A Little Bit Me" (#2, 1967) by the Monkees and "The Boat That I Row" (#6, U.K., 1967) by Lulu. His only album release of the year, *Just For You* (#80, 1967), was a sales improvement over its predecessor.

His first single release of 1968, "New Orleans" (#51, 1968), penned by Gary "U.S." Bonds, was also his first non-original single. It was followed by "Red Red Wine" (#62, 1968) before Diamond left Bang Records, due primarily over a fall out over his single releases. *Velvet Gloves and Spit*, his first Uni album release, featured the single "Brooklyn Roads" (#58, 1968). "Two-Bit Manchild" (#66, 1968) and "Sunday Sun" (#68, 1968) were his final single releases for the year. The compilation album *Greatest Hits* (#100, 1968) peaked and fell on the album chart.

Brother Love's Traveling Salvation Show (#82, 1969), with the self-titled extract (#22, 1969), was his only album of 1969. That same year Diamond released two consecutive hit singles, "Sweet Caroline" (#4, 1969)—his first million plus seller—and "Holly Holly" (#6, 1969).

Touching You, Touching Me (#30, 1970) was his first album release of the new decade and included the extracted single "Until It's Time For You To Go" (#53, 1970), a song that unfortunately had to compete with the Bang disputed and now released single "Shilo" (#24, 1970). Diamond, who now had to contend with the release of his older material, countered with the single "Soolaimon" (#30, 1970), while Bang then fired back with a re-issue of "Solitary Man" (#21, 1970). Diamond then released the single "Cracklin' Rosie" (#1, 1970), followed by the live album *Gold* (#10, 1970). Bang then issued "Shilo" (#52, 1970), a compilation of earlier material, and Diamond countered with the *Tap Root Manuscript* (#13, 1970), an experimental album that included "African Trilogy." Bang had the last word of the year with the release of the single "Do It" (#36, 1970). While the battle waged on, Diamond's image as a songwriter gained considerable respect—a factor that contributed greatly to his success in the following years.

"I Am... I Said" (#4, 1971) and "Stones" (#14, 1971) contribute to his series of hit singles, while the latter eponymous album (#11, 1971) also sold very well. The following year, his album releases *Moods* (#5, 1972) and *Hot August Night* (#5, 1973), both catapulted him into super stardom, as the singles "Song Sung Blue" (#1, 1972), "Play Me" (#11, 1972), and "Walk On Water" (#11, 1972), drove sales. The single "Cherry Cherry" (#31, 1973), taken from *Hot August Night*, would be his last for MCA/Uni, because Diamond signed a lucrative deal with CBS/Columbia Records. "Be" (#34, 1973), his first CBS single, was extracted from the soundtrack album to *Jonathan Livingston Seagull* (#2, 1973), which earned the artist both a Grammy and a Golden Globe. MCA then released *His 12 Greatest Hits* (#29, 1974), a compilation album, before Diamond's next album *Serenade* (#3, 1974), which included the hit extract "Longfellow Serenade" (#5, 1974)—his first Top Ten single in over two years!

The singles "I've Been This Way Before" (#34, 1975), "If You Know What I Mean" (#11, 1976), "De-siree" (#16, 1978), "You Don't Bring Me Flowers" (#1, 1978), and "Forever In Blue Jeans" (#20, 1979) finished the decade for the artist, who now turned to acting; he received the largest salary ever paid for a debut film role for *The Jazz Singer*. Diamond's albums *Beautiful Noise* (#4, 1970), *Love at the Greek* (#8, 1977), *I'm Glad You're Here With Me Tonight* (#6, 1978), and *You Don't Bring Me Flowers* (#4, 1979) sustained Diamond's reputation as a songwriter, while they enhanced his image as a live performer—perhaps the best of the decade!

Diamond still shone brightly during the '80s, as *The Jazz Singer* soundtrack yielded three Top Ten singles in "Love on the Rocks," Hello Again," and "America," the latter of which became Diamond's most played and requested song. The album *Heartlight* (#9, 1982) followed. The extracted title track (#5, 1982) was written by the famous Bacharach and Sager combo. *Primitive* (#35, 1984), *Headed For The Future* (#20, 1986), *Hot August Night II* (#59, 1987), and *The Best Years of Our Lives* (#46, 1989) all went gold as the artist's audience grew more toward the "adult-contemporary" market. The decade also found Diamond inducted into the Songwriters Hall of Fame at an annual ceremony in New York (1984).

Well into his career during the '90s, Neil Diamond continued to be one of the most popular live performers of all time. He opened the decade with the Award of Merit presented to him at the 17th American Music awards show (1990). His album releases for the decade have included *Lovescape* (#44, 1991), *The Christmas Album* (#8, 1992), *Up on the Roof—Songs from the Brill Building* (#28, 1993), *Live in America* (#93, 1994), *The Christmas Album Volume II* (#51, 1994), and *Tennessee Moon* (#14, 1996). The latter album was a commercially successful, refreshing departure, and even featured a duet with country star Waylon Jennings. Diamond's significant contribution to music is nearly unparalleled, and as we approach the end of the millennium, he certainly could be a candidate for entertainer of the century.

AUTOGRAPHS

An LP, CD, magazine cover, ad, photo, or card signed by the artist: $30-$80

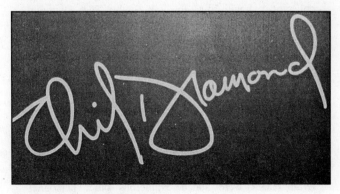

Facsimile signature of Neil Diamond

TOUR BOOKS/PROGRAMS/PASSES

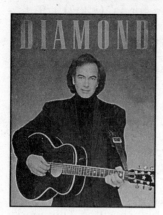

Tour Books:
Diamond (1988): $15-$20

Backstage Passes:
Cloth: $10-$20;
Laminated: $15-$35
(1970-1979)
Cloth: $8-$10; Laminated:
$10-$25 (1980-1989)
Cloth: $6-$8; Laminated:
$8-$15 (1990-Present)

An always informative program from Neil Diamond

POSTERS/PRESS KITS
Promotional Posters:
$10-$30 (1980-Present)
Live in America (24" x 36"): $10; Heartlight (36" x 36"): $20
Press Kits:
1970-1979: $30-$65
1980-1989: $20-$30
1990-Present: $15-$20

USED CLOTHING/EQUIPMENT
Guitar Picks: $50-$75

OFTEN OVERLOOKED MEMORABILIA
A copy of his appearance on the television show *Mannix* - CBS-TV (1968); a copy of his appearance on *American Bandstand 20th Anniversary* - ABC-TV (6/20/73); movie memorabilia from *Jonathan Livingston Seagull* (1973) and *The Last Waltz* (1976); a videotape of the NBC-TV television concert taped in September 1976 at the Greek Theatre; a videotape from the 22nd annual Grammy Awards ceremony (2/27/80) which includes Diamond/Streisand duet; a copy of Super Bowl XXI at which Diamond sang the National Anthem (1987); copies from both of his 1992 Christmas specials *Neil Diamond's Christmas Special* (HBO) and *Christmas in Washington* (NBC); a copy of his appearances on *The Late Show With David Letterman* (9/27/93, 2/14/96); videotapes from his appearances on *The Tonight Show* (12/20/93, 12/2/94); *The Jazz Singer* (1980) Capitol promotional soap on a rope - $20-$25; Songbooks: *Early Classics* (1978) - $25, *Hot August* Night (1973) - $45-$50, and *I'm Glad You're Here With Me Tonight* (1978) - $40

REFERENCES/BOOKS
Numerous resources exist, nothing that does justice to the artist in my opinion; no dedicated collector books; serious collectors should opt for fan club: The Diamond Connection, P.O. Box 2764, Witham, Essex CM8 2SF England ($25 fee)

The Diamonds

Formed 1954

Stan Fischer, Ted Kowalski, Phil Leavitt, and Bill Reed*

*Kowalski and Reed departed in 1958 and John Felton and Evan Fisher were added. Numerous other personnel changes followed.

This popular late-50s vocal group, which landed 16 hits over a five-year period, did covers of songs recorded by black R&B artists. The group's popular hits included "Why Do Fools Fall in Love?," "Little Darlin," and "The Stroll."

AUTOGRAPHS
An LP, magazine cover, ad, photo, or card signed by the group: $20-$35

OFTEN OVERLOOKED MEMORABILIA
Videotapes of the group's numerous appearances on television variety shows

Dibango, Manu

Born: February 10, 1934

Dibango is best known for his "Soul Makossa," one of the first African pop songs to land on American charts.

AUTOGRAPHS
An LP, magazine cover, ad, photo, or card signed by the artist: $12-$30

REFERENCES/BOOKS
Trios Kilos de Café, his autobiography

Dick and DeeDee

Formed 1961

Dick St. John Gosting and Deedee Sperling

This clean-cut, popular duo of the '60s appealed to middle-class America with song such as "I Want Someone/"The Mountain's High" (#2, 1961), "Young and in Love" (#17, 1963), "Turn Around" (#27, 1963), and "Thou Shalt Not Steal" (#13, 1964).

AUTOGRAPHS
An LP, magazine cover, ad, photo, or card signed by the group: $10-$15

REFERENCES/BOOKS
Rock & Roll Cookbook by Dick and Sandy St. John

The Dickies

Formed 1977

Chuck Wagon, Stan Lee, Billy Club, Leonard Graves Phillips, Karlos Kabellero, John Melvoin, Enoch Hain, Charlie Alexander, Lorenzo Buhne, and Cliff Martinez

This late-70s L.A. punk band—a sort of a six pots of coffee version of the Ramones—is best known for its "fast forward" cover versions of songs such as "Nights in White Satin," "Paranoid," and "Hair." Not to be remiss of its creative element, the Dickies also

penned such cult classics as "(I'm Stuck in a Pagoda) with Tricia Toyota" and "Rondo (The Midget's Revenge)"—the type of songs that would make E.B. White roll over in his grave.

AUTOGRAPHS

A LP, magazine cover, ad, photo, or card signed by the group: $8-$15

OFTEN OVERLOOKED MEMORABILIA

Movie memorabilia from *Killer Klowns from Outer Space* (1988)

The Dictators

Handsome Dick Manitoba (Richard Blum), Ross The Boss Funicello, Scott "Top Ten" Kempner, Adny (Andy) Shernoff, and Stu Boy King*

*King departed in 1975 and Ritchie Teeter and Mark Mendoza were added. Frank Funaro joined a new lineup in 1994.

Early '70s metal/punk refuse from the CBGB scene, The Dictators, fronted by roadie-turned-lead singer Handsome Dick Manitoba, were kings without a kingdom. The group's slapstick amateurish punk was more abrasive than persuasive, leading many to just simply ignore them. Ironically, Manitoba is better remembered for nearly getting killed when he heckled transvestite Wayne/Jayne County at CBGB— County hammered him with a microphone stand. The band broke up in 1978, but still does occasional reunion shows.

AUTOGRAPHS

An LP, magazine cover, ad, photo, or card signed by the group: $6-$10

OFTEN OVERLOOKED MEMORABILIA

Newspaper accounts of the Manitoba vs. County confrontation

Diddley, Bo

(Ellas Bates)
Born: December 30, 1928

The Mississippi master of the syncopated "hambone" beat, Bo Diddley is best known for the now classic rock and roll songs "Who Do You Love," "Mona," "Bo Diddley," and "I'm a Man." He has, at one time or another, affected every rocker who has followed him, including The Who and Bruce Springsteen. He became a regular on Chicago's South Side in 1951, and by 1955, Leonard Chess had found him and recorded his first single, "Bo Diddley" (#1, R&B). Diddley's biggest pop success came in 1959 with the song "Say Man" which entered the top twenty, as he maintained his steady diet of touring.

Florence, Alabama's April 27, 1960, "Biggest Show of Stars," two shows—one for "whites" and one for "colored." Printed by Globe Poster, Baltimore, MD, this "Segregation Issue" poster measures 22" x 28" and is valued at $5,000+. From the collection of Hank Thompson.

His place in rock's history was enhanced during the '60s British Invasion, when groups such as the Rolling Stones and Yardbirds successfully recorded his songs. He took advantage of the increased exposure by touring and sporadically recording records, the latter of which typically found him experimenting with a variety of off-shoots from surfing music to traditional blues. Diddley even opened for the Clash on its 1979 U.S. tour. I guess you just "Can't Judge a Book by the Cover"!

AUTOGRAPHS

An LP, magazine cover, ad, photo, or card signed by the artist: $25-$50

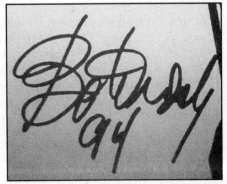

*The signature of
Bo Diddley*

OFTEN OVERLOOKED MEMORABILIA

Any and all artifacts from his mid-50s appearances at the Apollo Theatre; videotapes of his numerous television appearances including *The Ed Sullivan Show* - CBS-TV (11/20/55) and *Thank Your Lucky Stars* - ITV (1963); memorabilia from his appearances in package tours such as Alan Freed's Christmas Rock & Roll Spectacular (1958); artifacts from the numerous Rock & Roll Revival Concerts he has attended; all Checker label artifacts are highly sought by collectors; movie memorabilia from *Let the Good Times Roll*, *Keep On Rockin'*, *Trading Places*, *Book of Love*, and *La Bamba*; a casting from his handprints adorning Sunset Boulevard's Rock walk; a videotape of the 1989 Nike commercial featuring Bo Jackson and Bo Diddley; opening night artifacts from Fleetwood's blues club, Santa Monica, CA (2/14/91); all KFC Musical Fest contest artifacts (1992)

REFERENCES/BOOKS

The Complete Bo Diddley Sessions by George R. White—a MUST for collectors! Few resources exist.

Digable Planets

Formed 1989

Original lineup: Butterfly (Ishmael Butler), Ladybug (Katrina Lust), and Squibble the Termite (Michael Gabredikan). Second lineup: Butler, Doodlebug (Craig Irving) and Ladybug (Mary Ann Vieira)

Early '90s "jazz-rap" movers whose impressive debut album *Reachin'* (#15, 1993) included the hit extract "Rebirth of Slick (Cool Like Dat)" (#15, 1993).

AUTOGRAPHS

An LP, magazine cover, ad, photo, or card signed by the artist: $10-$20

POSTERS/PRESS KITS

Promotional Posters: $10
Press Kits: $10

Digital Underground

Formed 1988

Shock-G (Greg Jacobs), Humpty Hump (Edward Humphrey), Money B. (Ronald Brooks), and DJ Fuze (David Scott)

Rap's P-Funk clones, led by digital mastermind Shock-G, who takes the looks with his clever hooks, are a variety of egos all wrapped up into one package. Utilizing a core of Bay Area players and a revolving cast of musicians is DU's master recipe. *Sex Packers* (#24, 1990) was the group's impressive debut and included the hit extract "Humpty Dance" (#11, 1990).

AUTOGRAPHS

An LP, magazine cover, ad, photo, or card signed by the artist: $10-$20

The Dillards

Formed 1962

Rodney Dillard, Born: May 18, 1942; Doug Dillard, Born: March 6, 1937; Mitchell Jayne; and Dean Webb*

*Byron Berline was added in 1964. Doug Dillard left in 1965 and Herb Pederson was added. Paul York joined the band in 1970. Pederson left in 1972 and Billy Ray Latham was added. Jayne left in1974 and Jeff Gilkinson joined on bass. Rodney Dillard left in 1990 and the group disbanded, only to later re-form.

The Dillards, an Ozark mountain bluegrass band that "plugged in" and garnered a record contract after being cast on *The Andy Griffith Show* as the hillbilly band, the Darling Family, were the forerunners of country rock, the bluegrass revival, and even newgrass. The group impressed many with the debut album *Back Porch Bluegrass* (1963) which included "Duelin' Banjos," later popularized by Eric Weissberg (1972). The band toured with The Byrds in 1965 with a lineup that then included fiddling champion Byron Berline.

Doug Dillard left in 1965 and later hooked up with Gene Clark in the Dillard-Clark Expedition, which also included future Eagle Bernie Leadon. When the group split up in 1969, Dillard went on to solo work, while The Dillards were busy working with neighbor John Hartford. By 1987, Rodney was the only original member of the band who remained.

AUTOGRAPHS

An LP, magazine cover, ad, photo, or card signed by the group: $25-$60

OFTEN OVERLOOKED MEMORABILIA

Videotapes of their appearances on *The Andy Griffith Show*; a copy of the home video *A Night in the Ozarks*

Dino, Desi and Billy

Formed c. 1964

Dino Martin Jr., Born: November 17, 1953, Died: March 21, 1987; Desi Arnaz Jr., Born: January 19, 1953; and Billy Hinsche, Born: June 29, 1953

Nepotism at work—this teenybopper trio landed a recording contract when "Ole Blue Eyes" heard them playing at Dino Sr.'s and recommended the group to Reprise. The trio hit the charts in 1965 with "I'm a Fool" (#17, 1965) and "Not the Lovin' Kind" (#25, 1965) before psychedelia pushed them aside.

Hinsche later drummed with the Beach Boys, Arnez pursued acting, and Martin, a member of the California Air National Guard, crashed his F-4C Phantom jet into the San Bernardino mountainside.

AUTOGRAPHS

An LP, magazine cover, ad, photo, or card signed by the group: $25-$60

Dinosaur Jr.

Formed 1984

Original lineup: J Mascis (Joseph Mascis), Lou Barlow, and Murph (Emmett Murphy)*

*Various personnel changes

This late-80s, early-90s postpunk combo, led by introspective grunge guitarist J Mascis, Dinosaur Jr. is best known for its cult single "Freak Scene" and for putting out quality albums, despite numerous personnel changes. Both *Where You Been* (#50, 1993) and *Without a Sound* (#44, 1994) have been applauded by critics.

AUTOGRAPHS

An LP, magazine cover, ad, photo, or card signed by the group: $15-$40*

*Mascis is notorious for just signing his name "J"

POSTERS/PRESS KITS

Promotional Posters: $10-$15
Press Kits: $10-$15

USED CLOTHING/EQUIPMENT

Guitar Picks: $15

Dion, Celine

Born: March 30, 1968

Dion, the youngest of fourteen children, and blessed with a golden voice, gave her first public performance by age five. Before she even became a teenager, she had already recorded a demo tape. Her international recognition began when she captured the Golf Medal at the 1982 Yamaha World Song Festival in Tokyo, Japan. The following year she became the first Canadian to receive a gold disc in France for the sale of her "D'Amour Ou D'Amite" (1983).

Her next platform became the prestigious Eurovision Song Contest, held in Ireland, where she won with "Ne Partez Pas Sans Moi." She went on to record a number of platinum selling Canadian albums before the end of the decade.

"Where Does My Heart Beat Now" (#4, 1991), her first English-speaking release, sold extremely well partly due to her new contract with Epic Records. *Unison* (#74, 1991), her English-speaking album debut, garnered significant attention including a Juno for Album of the Year (1991). "(If There Was) Any Other Way" (#35, 1991) was be her last Top Forty single of the year.

In 1992, Dion gained significant attention when she duetted with Peabo Bryson for the Disney movie theme song to "Beauty and the Beast" (#9, 1992). The song went on to win an Academy Award for Best Song Written for a Motion Picture, on the same night Dion received another Juno, this time for Female Vocalist of the Year. Her duet with Bryson also won a Grammy the following year for Best Pop Performance, Duo or Group with Vocal. During the summer, she went on her first U.S. tour, opening for Michael Bolton, while her album *Celine Dion* (#34, 1992) peaked on the U.S. chart. "Nothing Broken But My Heart" (#29, 1992) climbed into the Top Forty during the fall.

"Love Can Move Mountains" (#36, 1993) was her first Top Forty single of 1993 and was followed by "When I Fall in Love" (#23, 1993), a duet remake of the Nat King Cole classic. The following year, "The Power Of Love" (#1, 1994) topped the charts just prior to the album release of *The Colour of My Love* (#4, 1994). In June, "Misled" (#23, 1994) climbed the U.S. singles chart; it was her last Top Forty hit of the year.

The following year she topped the U.K. charts with the single "Think Twice" (#1, U.K., 1995) and her album *The Colour of My Love* (#1, U.K., 1995). The album stayed at the top of the charts for five consecutive weeks—Dion was the first artist, since the Beatles, to accomplish this feat. Her worldwide accolades continued, and it seemed like hardly a music award show was held that Dion didn't receive an honor. In December, "To Love You More" (#1, Japan, 1995) became the first non-Japanese language song to top the charts since 1983. *Falling Into You* (#2, 1996) climbed high up the album charts, driven by hit extract "Because You Loved Me" (#1, 1996). "It's All Coming Back To Me Now" finished the year as the 18th top single of 1996.

Celine Dion has really made a mark for herself in the last few years, and judging by her track record thus far, it is well worth a collector's time to put away memorabilia associated with her career.

AUTOGRAPHS

An LP, magazine cover, ad, photo, or card signed by the artist: $30-$45

TOUR BOOKS/PROGRAMS/PASSES

Backstage Passes:
Cloth: $10-$12; Laminated: $12-$15

POSTERS/PRESS KITS

Promotional Posters:
$10-$15 (U.S. & U.K.), $15-$25 (Canadian)
Falling Into You, U.S. (23" x 35"): $10
Press Kits: $20-$35

OFTEN OVERLOOKED MEMORABILIA

Movie memorabilia from *Beauty and the Beast* (1992), *Sleepless in Seattle* (1993), and *Up Close and Personal* (1996); videotapes of her television performances on *The Arsenio Hall Show* (9/29/92), *The Tonight Show* (12/8/92), *The Late Show With David Letterman* (8/8/94), *Gala For The President* (held - 10/30/94), *The Brian Conley Show* (6/

17/95) - ITV; a videotape of the *22nd Annual Juno Awards* that Dion hosted (3/21/93); a copy of Celine Dion special that aired February 6, 1994, on The Disney Channel; a copy of the *American Music Awards* (1995) during which she performed

Dion and the Belmonts/Dion DiMucci

Formed 1958

Dion (Dion DiMucci), Born: July 18, 1939; Fred Milano, Born: August 22, 1939; Carlo Mastrangelo, Born: October 5, 1938; and Angelo D'Aleo, Born: February 3, 1940

Forever the epitome of cool, Dion DiMucci was one of the late '50s premier teen idols. He swaggered to successful hit classics such as "A Teenager in Love" (#5, 1959), "Runaround Sue" (#1, 1962), "The Wanderer" (#2, 1962), "Lovers Who Wander" (#3, 1962), "Little Diane" (#8, 1962), "Ruby Baby" (#2, 1963), "Drip Drop" (#6, 1963), and "Donna the Prima Donna" (#6, 1963), all before the British Invasion hit . He later scored with the ballad tribute "Abraham, Martin, and John" (#4, 1968), before moving on to the coffee house circuit.

DiMucci's relationship with the Belmonts basically ended in 1959, just after he passed up a ride on a chartered plane that crashed, killing Buddy Holly, Ritchie Valens, and the Big Bopper, during a package tour.

He was inducted into the Rock and Roll Hall of Fame in 1989.

AUTOGRAPHS

A CD, LP, magazine cover, ad, photo, or card signed by the artist: $15-$50

OFTEN OVERLOOKED MEMORABILIA

Videotapes of his numerous television appearances

REFERENCES/BOOKS

The Wanderer: Dion's Story, his autobiography (1988)

Dire Straits

Formed 1977

Mark Knopfler, Born: August 12, 1949; David Knopfler, Born: 1951; John Illsley; and Pick Withers*

*David Knopfler departed in 1980 and Hal Lindes was added. Alan Clarke was added on keyboards in 1982. Withers left in 1982 and Terry Williams and Tommy Mandel joined the group. Mandel then left in 1984 and Guy Fletcher was added. Both Lindes and Clark left in 1985 and the group eventually disbanded in 1988. The group re-formed in 1991.

Dire Straits was one of the most successful mid- to late-80s pop groups. Its Dylanesque minor key sound, creative lyrics, and guitar hooks helped the group score numerous hits such as "Sultans of Swing" (#4, 1979), "Skateaway" (#58, 1980), "Money for Nothing" (#1, 1985), "Walk of Life" (#7, 1985), and "So Far Away" (#19, 1986). The latter three were from the band's massive hit album *Brothers in Arms* (#1, 1985), after which Mark Knopfler found himself engaged in numerous outside projects that eventually led to the dissolution of the band in 1988.

The multi-talented Knopfler produced albums for the likes of Bob Dylan and Aztec Camera, wrote Tina Turner's comeback hit "Private Dancer," appeared on numerous albums, and scored numerous soundtracks including *Princess Bride* (1987) and *Last Exit To Brooklyn* (1989). He also appeared on Grammy Award winning duets with his idol Chet Atkins.

The group re-formed in 1991 for the album *On Every Street* (#12, 1991), which garnered mixed reviews.

AUTOGRAPHS

An LP, magazine cover, ad, photo, or card signed by the group: $30-$80

POSTERS/PRESS KITS

Promotional Posters: $10-$25
Press Kits: $15-$30*
*Brothers in Arms

USED CLOTHING/EQUIPMENT

Guitar Picks: $25-$40
Drum Sticks: $15-$25

OFTEN OVERLOOKED MEMORABILIA

Movie memorabilia from *Local Hero* (1983), *Cal* (1984), *The Princess Bride* (1987), *Comfort and Joy* (1987), and *Last Exit to Brooklyn* (1989); the musicians' numerous contributions to other groups and musicians; copies of Mark Knopfler's rock reviews in the *Yorkshire Evening Post*; Brothers in Arms promotional T-shirt - $25; Brothers in Arms jigsaw puzzle - $35; "Calling Elvis" Vertigo promotional leather-bound address book, 1991

REFERENCES/BOOKS

Numerous resources exist, nothing that does justice to the band in my opinion; no dedicated collector books

Disposable Heroes of HipHoprisy

Formed 1990

Michael Franti and Rono Tse

This politically charged Bay Area rap group, which scored points with its debut record for attacking prejudice, the Disposable Heroes of HipHoprisy has opened for a variety of bands from U2 to Arrested Development. In 1991 the group landed on the first Lollapalooza package tour of alternative rock and rap groups. The band also struck a chord when it appeared with cult author William S. Burroughs on his readings called *Spare Ass Annie and Other Tales*.

AUTOGRAPHS

An LP, magazine cover, ad, photo, or card signed by the group: $10-$25

Divinyls

Formed 1980

Christina Amphlett, Mark McEntee, Bjarre Ohlin, Rick Grossman, and Richard Harvey*

*Ohlin, Grossman, and Harvey depart in 1988

The Divinyls, led by nasal-voiced Amphlett, whose sexy young school girl charm created a cult following down-under, was a crafty, punkish Australian band. Amphlett also tried her luck in acting and costarred in *Monkey Grip*. The band, and/or its members, is best remembered in the U.S. for the minor hit "Pleasure and Pain" before it landed the erotic smash "I Touch Myself" (#4, 1991).

AUTOGRAPHS

An LP, magazine cover, ad, photo, or card signed by the group: $10-$25*
*Item relating to "I Touch Myself"

POSTERS/PRESS KITS

Promotional Posters: $10
Press Kits: $10

OFTEN OVERLOOKED MEMORABILIA

Movie memorabilia from *Monkey Grip*

The Dixie Cups

Formed 1964

Barbara Ann Hawkins, Rosa Lee Hawkins, and Joan Johnson

This mid-60s, Phil Spector-produced vocal act scored big with the smash hit "Chapel of Love," followed by "People Say" (#12, 1964) and "Iko Iko" (#20, 1965).

AUTOGRAPHS

An LP, magazine cover, ad, photo, or card signed by the group: $20-$35*
*"Chapel of Love" related

Dixie Dregs

Formed 1973

Original lineup: Steve Morse, Andy West, Rod Morgenstein, Steve Davidowski, and Allen Slaon*

*Numerous personnel changes

The Dixie Dregs, the Grammy nominated late-70s jazz rock fusion act, led by acclaimed guitarist Steve

Morse, managed to release six critically acclaimed albums. Although the albums sold moderately and the band developed a strong cult following, it was not enough to sustain the group, which split up in 1982. Morse went on to Kansas, West stuck with computer programming, and Morgenstein joined Winger.

AUTOGRAPHS

An LP, magazine cover, ad, photo, or card signed by the group: $12-$25

USED CLOTHING/EQUIPMENT

Guitar Picks: $10-$20

The Dixie Hummingbirds

Formed 1928

Original lineup: James Davis, Barney Gipson, Barney Parks, and J.B. Matterson*

*Others musicians included: Fred Owens, Jimmy Bryant, Ira Tucker, William Bobo, Beachy Thompson, James Walker, Howard Carroll, and Paul Owen

The Dixie Hummingbirds, a talented Southern gospel quartet for half a century, founded by James Davis, has influenced many, especially soul singers such as Clyde McPahtter, Bobby Bland, and Jackie Wilson. The group delivered such gospel classics as "Jesus Walked the Water," "In the Morning," and "I Just Can't Help It." It performed at the Newport Folk Festival in 1966, while evolving into a more contemporary style. The group's cover of Paul Simon's "Love Me Like A Rock" landed it a Grammy for Best Gospel Performance in 1973.

AUTOGRAPHS

An LP, magazine cover, ad, photo, or card signed by the group: $20-$40

Dixon, Willie

Born: July 1, 1915, Died: January 29, 1992

A pivotal Mississippi bluesman who helped define postwar urban blues, Willie Dixon was a gifted and prolific songwriter. He contributed such classics as "You Shook Me," "Little Red Rooster," "Back Door Man," "Bring It Home," "I'm Your Hoochie Coochie Man," "I Just Wanna Make Love to You," and "Wang Dang Doodle." Many of these songs were covered by the key movers in early rock and roll, including the Rolling Stones, Cream, and The Doors.

Dixon played in the house band at Chess Records during the '50s, backing the likes of Chuck Berry, Bo Diddley, and Muddy Waters, while he even did some arranging and production. Dixon toured actively in Europe beginning in 1960 and in the U.S. in 1975 and 1976 with his band the Chicago Blues All-Stars.

He later formed the Blues Heaven Foundation, a preservation society determined to secure copyrights and royalties for other artists, after his involvement in a bitter lawsuit with Led Zeppelin over ownership of the song "Whole Lotta Love."

AUTOGRAPHS

An LP, magazine cover, ad, photo, or card signed by the artist: $60-$120

OFTEN OVERLOOKED MEMORABILIA

All Chess Records artifacts

REFERENCES/BOOKS

I Am the Blues: The Willie Dixon Story by Willie Dixon and Don Snowdon—essential to Dixon collectors!

DNA/Arto Lindsay

Formed 1977

Arto Lindsay, Born: May 28, 1953

One of the pioneers of New York's no wave movement during the late '70s, DNA challenged rock conventions with its turbulent approach on songs such as "Little Ants" and "You and You." The band split in 1981, when the creative and avant-garde Lindsay moved on to other projects including the Kitchen, a New York haven for experimental sound, and the band Arto.

AUTOGRAPHS

An LP, magazine cover, ad, photo, or card signed by the artist: $5-$12

Dr. Feelgood

Formed 1971

Lee Brilleaux (Lee Green, 1953-1994), John B. Sparks, Wilko Johnson (John Wilkinson), and John "The Figure" Martin*

*Additional personnel have included John Mayo, Johnny Guitar, Buzz Barwell, Pat McMullen, Paul Mitchell, Gordon Russell, and others

These dedicated British R&B artists of the mid-70s, who were known for their commitment to a fundamental sound, are best remembered for songs such as "She's a Wind Up," "Milk and Alcohol," and "As Long as the Price is Right." Although its albums sold well in the U.K., the group never caught on in America.

AUTOGRAPHS

An LP, magazine cover, ad, photo, or card signed by the group: $10-$15

OFTEN OVERLOOKED MEMORABILIA

All artifacts from the band's first U.S. tour (1976) with Kiss—the band was dropped from the tour; periodicals featuring the band

Dr. Feelgood and the Interns

Formed 1962

Dr. Feelgood and the Interns was not a group—it was a front for bluesman William Perryman (1912 - 1985), who is best known for two hits "Dr. Feel-Good" and "Right String but the Wrong Yo Yo," the former of which had "Mr. Moonlight" as its flip side (it was later covered by the Beatles).

AUTOGRAPHS

A magazine cover, ad, photo, or card signed by the artist: $20-$40

OFTEN OVERLOOKED MEMORABILIA

Artifacts associated with other musicians' covers of his songs; his work recorded under the alias Piano Red

Dr. Hook (and the Medicine Show)

Formed 1968

Ray Sawyer, Dennis Locorriere, William Francis, George Cummings, and John "Jay" David*

*Roy Elswit and Jance Garfat were added in 1971. David left in 1973 and John Wolters was added. Cummings departed in 1975 and Bob Henke was added in 1976.

This '70s and '80s parody rock group scored hits with "Sylvia's Mother" (#5, 1972), "The Cover of Rolling Stone" (#6, 1973), "Only Sixteen" (#6, 1976), "A Little Bit More" (#11, 1976), "Sharing the Night Together" (#6, 1978), "When You're in Love With a Beautiful Woman" (#6, 1979), "Better Love Next Time" (#12, 1979), "Sexy Eyes" (#5, 1980), and "Baby Makes Her Blue Jeans Talk" (#25, 1982). Dr. Hook was well-known in the U.S., but was also an extremely popular attraction in Australia and Scandinavia before the group broke up in 1985.

AUTOGRAPHS

An LP, magazine cover, ad, photo, or card signed by the artist: $15-$30

OFTEN OVERLOOKED MEMORABILIA

Movie memorabilia from *Who is Harry Kellerman and Why Is He Saying All Those Terrible Things About Me?* (1971)

Dr. John

(Malcolm Rebennack)
Born: November 20, 1942

Dr. John Creaux the Night Tripper, the Funky Bourbon Street bluesman and part time voodoo mystic, lent his enchanting keyboard to numerous mid-60s sessions before unveiling his alter-ego in 1968.

His Cajun roots and creative Creole chants helped him develop a loyal cult following which even included Mick Jagger and Eric Clapton. His album *In The Right Place* (#24, 1973) included his biggest hit "Right Place, Wrong Time" (#9, 1973), followed later by "Such a Night" (#42, 1973).

During the '80s he became more introspective and pleasured in the exploration of his roots with the albums *In a Sentimental Mood*, and *Goin' Back to New Orleans*, both of which won him Grammy Awards, one of which he received for his duet "Makin' Whoppee" with Ricki Lee Jones. His image as a television spokesman, with his easily identifiable gruff voice, has helped maintain his loyal following, while creating interest in his work. The '90s rap craze has even put a few cents in his pocket, from the samplings of his work.

AUTOGRAPHS
An LP, magazine cover, ad, photo, or card signed by the artist: $10-$25

POSTERS/PRESS KITS
Promotional Posters: $10-$20
Press Kits: $10-$15

OFTEN OVERLOOKED MEMORABILIA
Videotapes of television commercials that he has voiced over.

REFERENCES/BOOKS
Under a Hoodoo Moon, by Dr. John and Jack Rummel (1994)

Doggett, Bill

Born: February 6, 1916, Died: November 13, 1996

Doggett, a boogie-woogie keyboardist artist of the '50s, scored hits with "Honky Tonk" (#2, 1956), an instrumental, and "Slow Walk" (1956), along with numerous minor pop and R&B hits.

AUTOGRAPHS
An LP, magazine cover, ad, photo, or card signed by the artist: $10-$15

OFTEN OVERLOOKED MEMORABILIA
A videotape of his appearance on *American Bandstand*

Dolby, Thomas

(Thomas Robertson)
Born: October 14, 1958

This early-80s electronic guru, who is best remembered for his hit "She Blinded Me with Science" and for penning "New Toy" (1981) for Lena Lovich and "Magic's Wand" for Whodini, eventually went on to score films, while he maintained a solo career.

AUTOGRAPHS
An LP, magazine cover, ad, photo, or card signed by the artist: $10-$15

OFTEN OVERLOOKED MEMORABILIA
Movie memorabilia from *Fever Pitch* (1985), *Gothic* (1986), and *Howard the Duck* (1986); a copy of the "Mind's Eye" video game

---

Domino, Fats

(Antoine Domino), Born: May 10, 1929

Domino, a gifted New Orleans singer and piano player, outsold all of his rock and roll peers except Elvis Presley. He mastered the easy rolling left-hand patterns anchored by right hand arpeggios of the local R&B piano style to score hits such as "Goin' Home" (1952), "Going to the River" (1953), "Ain't That a Shame" (1955), "I'm in Love Again" (#3, 1956), "Blueberry Hill" (#2, 1956), "Blue Monday" (#5, 1956), "I'm Walkin'" (#4, 1957), "Whole Lotta Loving" (#6, 1958), and "Walkin to New Orleans" (1960).

This Nov. 5, 1957, "Biggest Show of Stars," for Topeka, KS, poster is from the first national tour for Buddy Holly and the Crickets, and features a great line-up. Globe Poster of Baltimore, MD, printed this 17" x 22" poster of which only two are known to exist. From the collection of Hank Thompson.

Domino continued to tour and perform through the '70s and '80s and even recorded an album, *Christmas Is a Special Day*, in 1993.

AUTOGRAPHS

An LP, magazine cover, ad, photo, or card signed by the artist: $25-$50

OFTEN OVERLOOKED MEMORABILIA

All artifacts from vintage package shows including the Top Ten R&B Show (1955), The Greatest Show of 1957, the Biggest Show of Stars (1957), and The Biggest Show of Stars 1961; videotapes of his numerous television appearances including *The Ed Sullivan Show* - CBS-TV (11/18/56), *The Perry Como Show* (1957), *Late Night With David Letterman* - NBC-TV (11/5/91), and "Elvis Aaron Presley: The Tribute" (pay-per-view, 1994); movie memorabilia from *Shake, Rattle and Roll* (1956), *The Girl Can't Help It* (1957), *Jamboree* (1957), and *Let the Good Times Roll*; all Imperial Records artifacts; artifacts from his appearance at the House of Blues, New Orleans, LA (1995)

Donegan, Lonnie

(Anthony Donegan), Born: April 29, 1931

The late-50s British "King of Skiffle" is best remembered for his hits "Rock Island Line," "Lost John," "Does Your Chewing Gum Lose Its Flavor (on the Bedpost Overnight)," and numerous other hits, most of which charted in the U.K. His chart success was quickly cut short, though, primarily due to Beatlemania. He continued touring and even landed a stint as the opening act for the 1974 Tom Jones U.S. Tour. By the mid-70s there was a renewed interest in his work, which resulted in an all-star reunion album, *Puttin' on the Style*.

AUTOGRAPHS

An LP, magazine cover, ad, photo, or card signed by the artist: $15-$30

Donner, Ral

Born: February 10, 1945, Died: April 6, 1984

Donner, an Elvis Presley imitator of the mid-60s, scored hits with "Girl of My Best Friend," "Please Don't Go," "She's Everything," and his biggest seller "You Don't Know What You've Got."

AUTOGRAPHS

An LP, magazine cover, ad, photo, or card signed by the artist: $12-$25

OFTEN OVERLOOKED MEMORABILIA

Movie memorabilia from the documentary *This Is Elvis*, narrated by Donner

Donovan

(Donovan Leitch)
Born: May 10, 1946

This talented cosmic folk-rock hippie disciple of the late '60s is best remembered for his period-defining work in songs such as "Catch the Wind," "Colours," "Universal Soldier," "Sunshine Superman," "Mellow Yellow," "Epistle to Dippy," "There Is a Mountain," "Wear Your Love Like Heaven," "Jennifer Juniper," "Hurdy Gurdy Man," and "Atlantis." He followed trends, and even created some of his own, and when it was cool to travel to India and study with Maharishi Mahesh Yogi, he went. From flower power, to guitars and sitars, he epitomized the '60s, and when the '70s finally got here, he still epitomized the '60s, thus the lack of attention.

After a period of seclusion, probably to deal with the reality of both success and time, he emerged to work on films. He toured little and recorded less during the decades that followed, but by the '90s, there seemed to be renewed interest in his work.

AUTOGRAPHS

An LP, magazine cover, ad, photo, or card signed by the artist: $15-$35

Donovan. Photo by American Recordings. Courtesy of American Records.

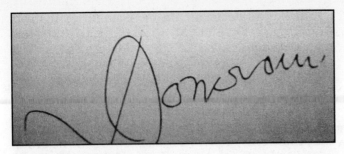

The signature of Donovan

REFERENCES/BOOKS

Dry Songs and Scribbles by Donovan—a book of poetry; few resources exist, nothing that does justice to the singer in my opinion; no dedicated collector books

OFTEN OVERLOOKED MEMORABILIA

Videotapes of his numerous television appearances including Ready Steady Go (1965), *Shindig* (1965), *The Hollywood Palace* (1965), *Top of the Pops* - BBC-TV (1965), "A Boy Called Donovan" - ITV special (1966), *Hogmanay Show* (1967), *It Must Be Dusty* (1968), and *The Smothers Brothers Comedy Hour* (1968); movie memorabilia from *Don't Look Back* (1965), *Poor Cow* (1968), *If It's Tuesday, This Must Be Belgium* (1969), *The Pied Piper* (1971), and *Brother Son, Sister Moon* (1972); newspaper clippings from his attendance at protest marches and similar events; all artifacts associated with the Beatles; festival relics

---

The Doobie Brothers

Formed 1970

Tom Johnston; John Hartman, Born: March 18, 1950; Patrick Simmons, Born: January 23, 1950; and Dave Shogren*

*Shogren left in 1971 and was replaced by Tiran Porter. Michael Hossack was also added. Hossack departed in 1973 and Keith Knudsen, Born: October 18, 1952, joined the band. Jeff "Skunk" Baxter was added in 1974, Born: December 13, 1948. Michael McDonald, Born: February 12, 1952, joined the band in 1975. Johnston left in 1977, followed by Hartman and Baxter in 1979. John McFee, Born: November 18, 1953; Chet McCracken, Born: July 17, 1952; and Cornelius Bumpus, Born: January 13, 1952, were added in 1979. The group disbanded in 1982, only to reform in 1988.

The Doobie Brothers, a highly versatile and extremely successful California-based pop band, first landed with a country-boogie feel before it phased into an intricate jazz-inflected white funk, primarily due to the transition of band members.

PHASE 1: 1970-1977
"THE CAPTAIN'S VICES ARE NOW WHAT?"

Tom Johnston and John Hartman were critical elements to the first country-boogie phase of the Doobies that started when the band jammed on Sundays amidst its biggest fans, the California Hell's Angels motorcycle gang. Ted Templeman then took the group under his wing at Warner Brothers and, although its debut album fell far short of expectations, *Toulouse Street* (1972) immediately corrected the problem by showcasing the band's high harmonies and flair for repetitive one liners in songs such as "Listen to the Music." From this point onward the foundation was built for the hits that followed including "Long Train Runnin'" (#8, 1973), "China Grove" (#15, 1973), and "Black Water" (#1, 1975)—all solidified the band's reputation as a premier act of the decade.

The delicate transformation came as result of two Steely Dan session artists who filled empty slots in the band. Jeff "Skunk" Baxter, who had done session with the band, joined full time, and when Johnston quit touring as a result of stomach problems, Michael McDonald filled in and began to alter the group's sound.

PHASE 2: 1978-1982
"ONE MINUTE CLOSER TO THE FAREWELL TOUR"

Minute by Minute (#1, 1978) became a showcase for McDonald's abilities, which I think were far greater than most had anticipated, including the band. "What a Fool Believes" (#1, 1978), quickly topped the chart, and the band road with the successful recipe, at least for awhile. Baxter left in 1978 for session work and production, while Hartman departed to tend to his investments. The group then added John McFee, Chet McCracken, and Cornelius Bumpus. With much of the earlier roots gone, the band clearly belonged to McDonald. The group disbanded in 1982 after a farewell tour. McDonald was the key benefactor of a solo career.

PHASE 3: 1987-PRESENT?
"A BROTHERHOOD OR JUST ANOTHER VICIOUS CYCLE"

In 1987, much of the band again turned toward Johnston as the group returned with the gold album *Cycles* which included the hit extract "The Doctor." It was just like the old days all over again, but when *Brotherhood* didn't fare as well, the floor got shaky. A version of the group came back in 1994 for a major summer tour and a live album. As for the future, "hey were getting hungry, is that a McDonald we just passed?"

AUTOGRAPHS

Group:

A CD, LP, magazine cover, ad, photo, or card signed by the group: $45-$85

Individual:

Michael McDonald: $15-$30

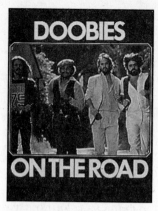

Getting tougher to find are earlier Doobie Brother programs (Dobro Group)

TOUR BOOKS/ PROGRAMS/PASSES

Backstage Passes:
Cloth/paper: $8-$15;
Laminated: $10-$40

Tour Books
On the Road, 1979:
$25-$30
1979 Japan Tour: $50
1981 Japan Tour: $50
1989 Cycles Tour: $20

POSTERS/PRESS KITS

Promotional Posters:
$10-$30

Press Kits: $10-$25
One Step Closer: $15

USED CLOTHING/EQUIPMENT

Guitar Picks: $10-$25
Drum Sticks: $10-$20

OFTEN OVERLOOKED MEMORABILIA

Videotapes of the band's numerous television performances

The Doors

Formed 1965

James Douglas Morrison, Born: December 8, 1943; Died: July 3, 1971, Ray Manzarek, Born: February 12, 1935; Robby Krieger, Born: January 8, 1946; and John Densmore, Born: December 1, 1944

Two months after graduating from UCLA, Jim Morrison and Ray Manzarek met along a Southern California Beach. The two were acquaintances at the school's film department. During this meeting, Morrison recited one of his poems, "Moonlight Drive," to Manzarek. Manzarek, who was playing in a local band (Rick & the Ravens) with his brothers, suggested that they collaborate on songs. Manzarek recruited John Densmore, who eventually suggested Robby Krieger for the band, who was also playing in a local band (Psychedelic Rangers).

The newly formed group recorded a demo tape in September 1965 at World Pacific Studios. It eventually landed into the hands of a CBS/Columbia executive, who signed the band. Morrison chose the group's name after a line in a book (*The Doors of Perception*) by Aldous Huxley. Five months of rehearsing put the group on the stage at the London Fog Club, and eventually the Whisky A-Go-Go, where The Doors became the house band. The exposure at the latter club landed the group with Elektra records (after it was released by Columbia) thanks to a recommendation by Love band member Arthur Lee. The band's time at "the Whiskey" drew to an abrupt close, and finally ended when it was fired following Morrison's dramatic recitations during the song "The End."

The band's debut album included an edited version of Krieger's "Light My Fire" (#1, 1967) and Morrison's Opus "The End." Morrison's almost shamanistic invocations entranced his audiences, while the critics and fans pondered the band's lyrics for some introspective gratification. On September 17, 1967, The Doors appeared on *The Ed Sullivan Show*. Although the show's management demanded that the word "higher" not be used when the group sang an abbreviated live version of "Light My Fire," Morrison simply ignored the request.

Strange Days (#3, 1967) and *Waiting for the Sun* (#1, 1968) followed the debut album and, like their predecessor, they contained hit singles that drove album sales up the charts. Meanwhile, Morrison's persona was enhanced through numerous concert disruptions. His first arrest happened during a performance in New Haven, CT on December 9, 1967. There he was charged with a breach of peace and resisting arrest. Perhaps, it was his mythic alter ego, the Lizard King, that surfaced from the poem printed inside the record jacket of *Waiting for the Sun*, or maybe it was something in the water. No one will ever know.

During this time the band was captured on film numerous times, including a promo for "The Unknown Soldier" (1968), a performance at the Hollywood Bowl (7/5/68), which was eventually released on videotape, *Top of the Pops* (BBC-TV), and a film documentary, *The Doors Are Open*, which was shot during a London gig and broadcast on British television.

The band's musical success was then shrouded by a drug and alcohol infused Morrison, whose overtly sexual behavior often offended the public. On March 1, 1969, Morrison was arrested following a show at the Dinner Key Auditorium in Miami, FL. The lead singer was charged with "lewd and lascivious behavior in public by exposing his private parts...." He was arrested again in Los Angeles on April 3 by the FBI and charged with "interstate flight to avoid prosecution on his Miami charges." Although the alleged incident had no eyewitnesses or photos of Morrison performing the acts, the result, even after the charges were dropped, was devastating to the band. Promoters no longer wanted to take chances on booking the band out of fear of similar circumstances.

The Soft Parade (#6, 1969) met with somewhat mixed emotions due to a sleeker production. It did, though, spin off the hit single "Touch Me" (#3). The Doors did play at the Toronto Rock 'n' Roll Revival Show on September 13, 1969, in Toronto, ON, Canada. But trouble soon followed when Morrison was arrested again on November 11, 1969, and charged with "interfering with the flight of an aircraft, as well as public drunkenness." Although these charges were also dropped, the incident continued to enhance Morrison's image as a troublemaker.

On January 17 and 18, 1970, the band played two nights at New York's Felt Forum. The shows were recorded and eventually became *Absolutely Live* (#8, 1970), a double-album released in September (1970). *Morrison Hotel* (#4, 1970) was the only studio album released during the year. During this period Morrison began to devote more time to his other interests—writing and film. On November 8, 1970, he entered the studio to record his poetry. The session was eventually released as part of *An American Prayer*. On November 12, 1970, The Doors played its last concert with Jim Morrison in New Orleans, LA. The band then moved to the studio and completed the recording of *L.A. Woman* (#9, 1971).

In March 1971, Morrison moved to Paris, France, to concentrate more on his writing. *The Lords and the New Creatures*, after selling 15,000 hardback copies (Simon & Schuster), entered the softcover market. On July 3, 1971, at 5:00 a.m., Morrison was found dead in a bathtub at 17, rue Beautreillis, Paris 4, France. The cause of death was heart failure as certified by Dr. Max Vassille. Morrison was interred in Pere Lachaise Cemetery, 16th Division, Paris, France, on July 7, 1971. The cemetery is also the final resting place of Oscar Wilde, Frederic Chopin, and Honore de Balzac. His headstone reads "Kata ton daimona eay toy," which is Greek for "True to his own spirit." The sight became a graffiti-infested shrine in the years that followed; the headstone was even stolen in 1990.

Speculation, fascination, and perhaps even hype still fuels the mystery surrounding Morrison's death. A mystery was created when Pamela Courson Morrison, his wife, the only one who saw his corpse, died of a heroin overdose on April 25, 1974. In 1980 the Morrison fires were stirred again, when *No One Here Gets Out Alive*, a book by Danny Sugarman and Jerry Hopkins, was released. Oliver Stone's film biography of the band followed in 1991 and, although controversial, it was commercially successful. And even in 1995, we were not spared from his reminder, when *An American Prayer*, which features a new track, "The Ghost Song," was reissued.

AUTOGRAPHS

The Doors were always obliging to autograph requests. Morrison was obviously the key. Seldom sober, his signature can exhibit significant variation. He typically signed "Cheers, J. Morrison." A typical characteristic of his signature is that all the letters are often close, or identical in height, as measured from the baseline. Common signature breaks fall between the "M" and "o," and between the "r" and the "i" in Morrison. The finishing strokes in his name also have a tendency to fall below the baseline, particularly the last stroke.

Group:

A CD, LP, magazine cover, ad, photo, or card signed by the entire band: $1,750-$3,000*

*High end reflects vintage signed memorabilia all on one item, such as publicity photo. Low end would be signatures of each band member individually mounted around an item.

The back of a check endorsed by the Doors' Jim Morrison

Individual:

Jim Morrison: $700-$1,500	Ray Manzarek: $20-$45
Robby Krieger: $20-$40	John Densmore: $20-$35

TOUR BOOKS/PROGRAMS/PASSES

An autographed copy of *An American Prayer* or *The New Creatures*, self-published (1970), signed and inscribed by Jim Morrison: $3,000-$3,750

USED CLOTHING/EQUIPMENT

Guitar Picks:
Robby Krieger: $100-$275

Drum Stick:
John Densmore: $60-$125

OFTEN OVERLOOKED MEMORABILIA

Copy of Jim Morrison's *Last Will and Testament* - $5-$15; Rick & the Ravens memorabilia; Los Angeles Third Street Transcendental Meditation Center memorabilia

REFERENCES/BOOKS

Numerous resources exist, as well as fan clubs; no dedicated collector books

Dorsey, Lee

Born: December 24, 1924, Died: December 1, 1986

This Bourbon Street howler carried Allen Toussaint's songs including "Working in a Coal Mine," "Holy Cow," and "Get Out of My Life Woman" up the charts. Dorsey had scored earlier in his career with "Ya Ya" (#7, 1961), and "Do Re Mi" (#27, 1961) before the collapse of his record company. He had two minor hits in 1967, before he faded from the music scene. He took on a variety of projects over the decades that followed, and he even opened for The Clash during its 1980 U.S. Tour!

AUTOGRAPHS

An LP, magazine cover, ad, photo, or card signed by the artist: $8-$12

Doug E. Fresh

(Douglas Davis), Born: September 17, 1966

A walking mid-80s sound effect record, Davis gained recognition through the his *Get Fresh Crew*, which landed the R&B hit "The Show" (#4, R&B, 1985). His subsequent projects fell short of expectations.

AUTOGRAPHS

An LP, magazine cover, ad, photo, or card signed by the artist: $5-$10

Douglas, Carl

Best known for his hit song "Kung Fu Fighting" (#1, 1974) and his follow-up "Dance the Kung Fu" (#48, 1975), his last chart single, Carl Douglas was on the next bus outta town just as fast as he had arrived.

AUTOGRAPHS

An LP, magazine cover, ad, photo, or card signed by the artist: $5-$10

The Dovells

Formed 1959

Original Lineup: Len Barry, Arnie Satin, Jerry Summers, Mike Dennis, and Danny Brooks

This Philadelphia-based early-60s doo-wop group is best known for its hits "Bristol Stomp" (#2, 1961), "Bristol Twistin Annie" (#27, 1962), "Hully Gully Baby" (#25, 1962), and "You Can't Sit Down" (#3, 1963), along with its frequent attendance on Dick Clark's road revue.

AUTOGRAPHS

An LP, magazine cover, ad, photo, or card signed by the group: $20-$40

Drake, Nick

(1948 - 1974)

Drake, a late-60s British jazz-tinged folk artist, released three albums prior to his death and went on to become a cult idol of sorts.

AUTOGRAPHS

By all accounts, a scarce signature and an elusive character

The Dream Academy

Formed 1983

Gilbert Gabriel, Nick Laird-Clowes, and Kate St. John

The Dream Academy, the mid-80s British retromania group, whose eclectic single "Life in a Northern Town" (#7, 1985) had enough hooks and MTV play to land in the Top Ten, released two more albums, only to find out that we fell asleep to its first.

AUTOGRAPHS

A CD, LP, magazine cover, ad, photo, or card signed by the group: $10

The Dream Syndicate/Steve Wynn

Formed 1981

Original lineup: Steve Wynn, Born: February 21, 1960; Karl Precoda; Kendra Smith; and Dennis Duck

This early-80s L.A. "paisley underground" artifact garnered a cult following plagued by a short attention span. The Dream Syndicate fused, fed-back, threw-back, and cow-punked, before going kerplunk!

AUTOGRAPHS

An LP, magazine cover, ad, photo, or card signed by the group: $10

The Drifters/Clyde McPhatter

Formed 1953

Original lineup: Clyde McPhatter (1931-1972), David Baughan (Died: 1970), William Anderson, David Baldwin, and James Johnson*

*The group disbanded in 1958 and then re-formed. They have had numerous personnel changes. Musicians have included Billy Pinckney, Andrew Thrasher, Gerhart Thrasher, Willie Ferbee, Johnny Moore, Charlie Hughes, Tommy Evans, Bobby Hendricks, Jimmy Millinder, followed by Charlie Thomas, Ben E. King, Doc Green, Elsbeary Hobbs, Johnny Lee Williams, James Pointdexter, Rudy Lewis, William Van Dyke, George Grant, Tommy Evans, Gene Pearson, Johnny Terry, J. Moore, Dan Danbridge, William Brent, and Rick Shepard.

PHASE 1: BEGINNINGS

The Drifters was an institution of creative soul whose breadth of talent spanned decades. The group's music drew deep into its gospel roots to extract key elements, that when combined with emotional essence, provided a magic recipe for success. Its reputation was immediately enhanced by well-known Clyde McPhatter, who hand picked his mates from the Mount Lebanon Singers at the Mount Lebanon Church in Harlem.

The group scored a series of hits right out of the gate with such songs as "Money Honey" (#1, R&B, 1953), "Such a Night" (#2, R&B, 1954),"Honey Love" (#21, 1954), "White Christmas" (#80, 1954), and "Whatcha Gonna Do" (#2, R&B, 1955), before

Valued at $2,000, the Oct. 23, 1955, LaVern Baker/ Drifters poster for a Danville, VA, performance is a "Segregation issue" due to the notation, "Balcony reserved for white spectators." The poster was printed by Globe Poster of Baltimore, MD. From the collection of Hank Thompson.

McPhatter found himself drafted into the army at the end of 1954.

PHASE 2: "MOORE OF THE SAME"

Vocal responsibilities fell briefly to "Little David" Baughan before they fell to Johnny Moore, who tried to anchor the group with singles such as "Hypnotized" and "Fools Fall in Love." Personnel changes persisted, and by 1957, both Moore and Highes were also drafted. George Treadwell, who had rights to the group's name, then fired the entire lineup, and replaced them with a new found treasure, the Crowns (the new Drifters).

PHASE 3: "KING WITH A NEW CASTLE"

The new Drifters then joined producers Mike Leiber and Jerry Stoller, who guided the group which included Ben E. King, to its first release, "There Goes My Baby" (#2, 1959). Other hits quickly followed, including "This Magic Moment" (#16, 1960), "Save the Last Dance for Me" (#1, 1960), and "I Count the Tears" (#17, 1961), before King then left to pursue a solo career.

PHASE 4: "MOORE HITS"

During the next period of the group, the leads were split between Rudy Lewis—"Some Kind of Wonder-ful" (#32, 1961), "Please Stay" (#14, 1961), "Up on the Roof" (#5, 1962), and "On Broadway" (#9, 1963)—Charlie Thomas, "Sweets for My Sweet" (#16, 1961), and Johnny Moore—"I'll Take You Home" (#25, 1963) and "Under the Boardwalk" (#4, 1964). Tragically Lewis died in 1964 and Moore then assumed the key responsibility. The group then scored R&B hits with "I've Got Sand in My Shoes" and "Saturday Night at the Movies," before it was reduced to the club circuit. The Drifters time with Atlantic Records passed in 1972, and the band moved to the U.K. where it scored more Top Ten hits.

McPhatter, of course, went on to a very successful solo career that included such hits as "Treasure of Love" (#16, 1956), "A Lover's Question" (#6, 1958), and "Lover Please" (#7, 1962). He was inducted into the Rock and Roll Hall of Fame in 1987.

AUTOGRAPHS

An LP, magazine cover, ad, photo, or card signed by the group:
Phase 1: $500-$1,000
Phase 2: $60-$160
Phase 3: $50-$150
Phase 4: $30-$75

REFERENCES/BOOKS

Few resources exist, nothing that does justice to the band in my opinion; no dedicated collector books

Ducks Deluxe

Formed 1972

Sean Tyla, Martin Belmont, Nick Garvey, and Tim Roper*

*Andy McMasters was added in 1974. Garvey, McMasters, and Roper left the following year.

These early-70s British pub rockers managed to build a strong cult following. The group released four albums before it split up on July 1, 1975.

AUTOGRAPHS

An LP, magazine cover, ad, photo, or card signed by the group: $8-$15

Duran Duran

Simon Le Bon, Born: October 27, 1958; Andy Taylor, Born: February 16, 1961; Nick Rhodes, Born: June 8, 1962; John Taylor, Born: June 20, 1960; and Roger Taylor, Born: April 26, 1960*

*Roger and Andy Taylor left in 1984. Warren Cuccurullo was added in 1989.

Duran Duran, the highly successful British New Romantic pop band, scored numerous hits during the '80s including "Hungry Like the Wolf" (#3, 1983), "Rio" (#14, 1983), "Is There Something I Should

Duran Duran autographed drum cover from the Hard Rock Café in Key West, Florida

Know" (#4, 1983), "New Moon on Monday" (#10, 1984), "The Reflex" (#1, 1984), "The Wild Boys" (#2, 1984), "Save a Prayer" (#16, 1985), "Notorious" (#2, 1987), "Skin Trade" (#39, 1987), "I Don't Want Your Love" (#4, 1988), and "All She Wants Is" (#22, 1989).

By the '90s, the group, which had undergone some personnel changes, was beginning to slip—most notably with *Liberty* (1990). The group did manage to land two singles off of *Duran Duran (The Wedding Album)* (#7, 1993), the extracts "Ordinary World" (#3,1993) and "Come Undone" (#7, 1993).

In 1984 both Johnny Taylor and Roger Taylor (none of the Taylors were related), joined Robert Palmer and Tony Thompson in the band Power Station. The band scored hits with "Some Like It Hot" (#6, 1985) and "Get It On" (#9, 1985). Meanwhile, Le Bon, Rhodes, and Roger Taylor had formed off-shoot Arcadia, that scored a hit with "Election Day" (#6, 1985). The same year Duran Duran appeared at Live Aid, but didn't release a studio album until *Notorious*. With all the musicians' individual projects, and three original members with the same last name, it got a bit confusing as to whom was where.

AUTOGRAPHS

A CD, LP, magazine cover, ad, photo, or card signed by the group: $45-$135*
*Original members

TOUR BOOKS/PROGRAMS/PASSES

Tour Books: European Tour (opens to poster): $6-$10

Backstage Passes:
Cloth: $10-$25;
Laminated: $15-$40

Duran Duran backstage pass (Printed by OTTO)

POSTERS/PRESS KITS

Promotional Posters: $10-$60
Press Kits: $25-$60
Duran Duran (The Wedding Album): $25

USED CLOTHING/EQUIPMENT

Guitar Picks:
Andy Taylor: $45-$60
John Taylor: $65-$80
Warren Cuccurullo: $55-$65

OFTEN OVERLOOKED MEMORABILIA

Bumper stickers - $5; Liberty counter sales tent - $5; batteries (Toshiba) - $40; game (Milton Bradley) - $50; trading cards (Topps) - $15 (set); mirror - $10; school folder - $10; *Thank You* EP (promo video) - $15; Thank You promotional embossed T-shirt - $15; static window sticker (Italian) - $15; Seven and the Ragged Tiger counter display - $40; all items relating to the groups promotional video for Girls on Film; Live Aid memorabilia

REFERENCES/BOOKS

The ABC of Duran Duran: $15; numerous resources exist, nothing that does justice to the band in my opinion; no dedicated collector books; serious collectors should opt for fan club: The ICON, P.O. Box 158, Allen Park, MI 48101

Dury, Ian

Born: May 12, 1942

This British pop star of the late '70s, best remembered for his songs "What a Waste" (#9, U.K., 1978), "Hit Me with Your Rhythm Stick" (#1, U.K., 1978), and "Reasons to Be Cheerful (Part 3)" (#3, U.K., 1979) had little impact here in America. He later turned to acting and writing material for television.

AUTOGRAPHS

A CD, LP, magazine cover, ad, photo, or card signed by the artist: $10-$15

OFTEN OVERLOOKED MEMORABILIA

Movie memorabilia from *The Cook, The Thief, His Wife, Her Lover* (1989); videotapes of this television work; artifacts from his musical *Apples*; videotapes of his television program *Metro*

Dylan, Bob

(Robert Allen Zimmerman)
Born: May 24, 1941

Upon graduating from Hibbing High School in 1959, Robert Zimmerman said in his yearbook that he was leaving "to follow Little Richard." Could these four simple words have been any more eloquent? Zimmerman lasted briefly at the University of Minnesota before he became employed briefly by Bobby Vee's backing group the Shadows. He then decided to change his name to Bob Dylan, packed for New York City, and set off in search of Woody Guthrie.

On April 11, 1961, he played his first gig in New York City at Gerde's Folk City, 130 West 3rd. St. (at 6th Ave.) in Greenwich Village. Dylan opened for John Lee Hooker and nervously performed his five-song set. The show was the first of a two-week stint and, as fate might have it, he met Joan Baez. It was during this period that he earned extra money playing harmonica on such recordings as Harry Belafon-

te's "Midnight Special." In September 1961, Dylan signed a recording contract with CBS/Columbia Records. John Hammond, Sr., who heard Dylan and was impressed, had also read an impressive review (written by Robert Shelton) of his performance at Gerde's Folk City in the *New York Times*—a must acquisition for any Dylan collection!

Bob Dylan was released in March 1962 and, although it sent a shock through the folk community, the record failed to chart. On December 21, 1962, he made his U.K. debut at the King & Queen Pub at Foley street in London. *The Freewheelin' Bob Dylan* (#22, 1963) followed his debut and carried with it "Blowin' in the Wind" (Popularized by Peter, Paul & Mary), "A Hard Rain's a-Gonna Fall," and "Masters of War." The release positioned him nicely in the popular folk singer/songwriter genre an area that was showing increased interest in protest-type material. That summer Joan Baez invited Dylan to tour with her; the pair created quit a stir in the folk scene. His first performance at Carnegie Hall in New York took place on October 26, 1963.

The Times They Are a-Changin' (#20, 1964) and *Another Side of Bob Dylan* (#43, 1964) were accompanied by intensive touring. The young folk singer began to forge his path to stardom. He met the Beatles, ex-model Shirley Nozinisky (Sara Lowndes), and Jim (Roger) McGuinn in 1964, giving him the later "Mr. Tambourine Man" and the Byrds their first hit. As the Baez-Dylan relationship faltered, Nozinisky entered the picture and became Mrs. Bob Dylan in 1965.

On June 25, 1965, Dylan "plugged-in" at the Newport Folk Festival. *Bringing It All Back Home* (#6, 1965) had been a prelude to what was going to come (half the album was backed by a rock 'n' roll band), but when he walked onstage with the Paul Butterfield Blues band and opted for an electric guitar, he was booed. Whether or not it was the right choice, at the right time, has been debated for generations, but one thing was certain—Bob Dylan had become a controversial focal point.

"Like A Rolling Stone" (#2, 1965) became his first major hit, while his compositions were covered by a myriad of talent, from Cher to the Turtles; most sent songs into the Top Ten. The Byrds hit Number One first with "Mr. Tambourine Man" on June 26, 1965. The song soon became an origination point for a music movement called folk-rock by many historians.

Highway 61 Revisited (#3, 1965) and *Blonde on Blonde* (#9, 1966) catapulted Dylan to a new level: Rock Star/Diety. His every lyric was analyzed and re-analyzed, and his every move was documented. He became a character within a character, an optimistic pessimist, positive that everything that can go wrong, will, and a disciple for a generation that knew it desperately needed something, it just wasn't sure what it was.

On July 25, 1966, while riding his Triumph 55 motorcycle near his home in Woodstock, New York, he suffered a crash that left him with a cracked vertebra. Rumors abounded, as the accident, which was never clearly explained, caused great public confusion. Following the incident he spent nine months in seclusion, convalescing, before he began working with the Band recording *The Basement Tapes* (#7, 1975). On January 20, 1968, he emerged from the incident for the first time publicly, to play with the Band at a memorial concert for Woody Guthrie, who died on September 3, 1967. The show was held at Carnegie Hall.

On May 17, 1967, a documentary—*Don't Look Back*—of his 1965 tour premiered. It was the subject's first film and one that portrayed the musician as one who suffered from all the charms associated with becoming famous. The following year Dylan won his first Grammy, not for a performance, but for an album cover, *Bob Dylan's Greatest Hits* (#10, 1967). *John Wesley Harding* (#2, 1968) became the first post-accident recording, unless of course you can't rule out *Great White Wonder*, a best-selling bootleg.

Nashville Skyline (#3, 1969) brought with it a more soft spoken Dylan, but country infused. It yielded the singles "Lay, Lady, Lay" (#7, 1969) and "Tonight I'll Be Staying Here With You" (#50, 1969). The album also included a duet with Johnny Cash—"Girl from the North Country."

Self Portrait (#4, 1970), a double album, was a collage of old and new material, and even included takes from the 1969 Isle of Wight concert. Despondent over critical reaction to the work, Dylan re-entered the studio to cut *New Morning* (#7, 1970); the record quickly returned him to form. His first protest song in years, "George Jackson" (#33, 1972), about an inmate who was shot during a prison uprising, was released in 1971. Other types of media continued to interest the musician, who released *Tarantula*, a book of mid-60s writings, and traveled to Mexico to star in a Sam Peckinpah film.

Pat Garrett and Billy the Kid (#16, 1973), the soundtrack from the movie he starred in, was released and contained three vocal tracks, one of which was "Knockin' on Heaven's Door" (#12, 1973). The song became his best-selling single since "Lay, Lady, Lay." Dylan's *Writings and Drawings*, a collection of creative material up to *New Morning*, was published in 1973. Dylan headed West amidst rumors that he was splitting from CBS. The news that he would be jumping to Geffen's Asylum Records came in November 1973.

CBS retaliated with *Dylan* (#17, 1973), a series of out-takes from *Self Portrait*, as the artist began a 39-date U.S. Tour, his first in nearly eight years. Asylum counter punched with *Planet Waves* (#1, 1974), which spun off the single "On a Night Like This" (#44, 1974), and then struck again with *Before the Flood*

(#3, 1974), a compilation of live performances recorded during the last tour. Dylan then settled his diferences with CBS, which after long delays, knocked out Asylum with *Blood on the Tracks* (#1, 1975). The album spun off the single "Tangled Up in Blue" (#31, 1975). It was during this period that the legitimate version of *The Basement Tapes* (#7, 1975) was released. In the Fall of 1975, the Rolling Thunder Revue Tour began in Plymouth, MA, and ended in Madison Square Garden at a benefit for convicted boxer Rubin "Hurricane" Carter.

Desire (#1, 1976) topped the charts in 1976, and the singles "Hurricane" (#33, 1976) and "Mozambique" (#54, 1976) also faired well. *Hard Rain* (#17, 1976), recorded at two events during the last tour, followed a rare television special, of the same name, about the artist. The artist attended *The Last Waltz*, held at the Winterland Ballroom in San Francisco, CA.

A divorce and *Renaldo and Clara*, a film, occupied most of the artist's time and finances during 1977. He then embarked on a ten country extensive tour that included Japan, where he recorded *Bob Dylan at Budokan* (#13, 1979). *Slow Train Coming* (#3, 1979) confirmed rumors of Dylan's move toward Christianity, and included the single "Gotta Serve Somebody" (#24, 1979), which netted him his first Grammy. *Saved* (#24, 1980) and *Shot of Love* (#33, 1981) continued his religious convictions and were followed by *Infidels* (#20, 1983).

A varied series of releases left critics a bit perplexed to the artist's musical direction. The releases included *Empire Burlesque* (#33, 1985), a bit different, and backed by Tom Petty and the Heartbreakers; *Biograph* (#33, 1985), a nice retrospective with some unreleased material; *Knocked Out Loaded* (#53, 1986) a bit sloppy, and produced by Dave Stewart; *Down in the Groove* (#61, 1988), which included numerous guest musicians; and finally, *Dylan and the Dead* (#37, 1989), a souvenir from the Dylan/Grateful Dead 1987 Tour. The most noteworthy album of this period was *Traveling Wilburys Volume One*, which met with strong commercial success and mixed Dylan with George "Nelson" Harrison, Tom "Charlie T. Jr." Petty, Roy "Lefty" Orbison, and Jeff "Otis" Lynne. On January 18, 1989, Dylan was inducted into the Rock and Roll Hall of Fame. *Oh Mercy* (#30, 1989) was his last record of the decade.

Dylan entered the 1990s with *Under the Red Sky* (#38, 1990), *The Bootleg Series Volumes 1-3* (#49, 1991), *Good As I Been to You* (#51, 1992), and *World Gone Wrong* (#70, 1993), the latter of which earned a Grammy for Best Traditional Folk Album—it was almost as if the artist had gone full circle. In 1990, Dylan earned France's highest cultural honor (*Commandeur dans l'Ordre des Arts et des Lettres*), and the Grammy Lifetime Achievement Award (1991). He made notable appearances at Woodstock '94, although he snubbed the original event, and in late 1994 he even performed on *MTV Unplugged*, which generated the now customary album (#23, 1995). Dylan was back in the news in 1997 due to health problems, while his son Jakob brought the Wallflowers up the charts.

BOB DYLAN - SELECTED *ROLLING STONE* MAGAZINE ISSUES

Date	Price Range
6/22/68	$30-$35
11/29/69	$25-$30
3/4/71	$18-$20
3/2/72	$15-$20
3/16/72	$15-$20
2/14/74	$12-$15
3/14/74	$12-$15
1/26/78	$8-$10
11/16/78	$8-$10
6/21/84	$6-$8

BOB DYLAN - SELECTED TELEVISION APPEARANCES

January 10, 1971	*Fanfare Show* with Earl Scruggs
September 14, 1976	*Hard Rain* - NBC-TV special
March 22, 1984	*Late Night With David Letterman* - NBC-TV
January 18, 1992	*Late Night With David Letterman* - NBC-TV
February 6, 1993	*A Country Celebration* - CBS-TV
May 22, 1993	*Willie Nelson The Big Six-O* - CBS-TV

BOB DYLAN - SELECTED FILM APPEARANCES

May 17, 1967	*Don't Look Back* - documentary film
February 8, 1971	*Eat The Document* - 1966 U.K. Tour with the Band, scarce.
July 31, 1971	*Concert For Bangla Desh* - Madison Square Garden, NY
December 18, 1972	*Pat Garrett and Billy the Kid* - Dylan arrives on location.
November 25, 1976	*The Last Waltz*
February 1, 1978	*Renaldo and Clara* - a four hour film that includes band footage.
December, 1987	*Hearts of Fire* - released in the U.K.

In-person signature from Bob Dylan

AUTOGRAPHS

Dylan's signature is an extremely difficult one to acquire; the only viable method is an in-person request. It is impossible via mail.

A CD, LP, magazine cover, ad, photo, or card signed by the entire band: $275-$500*

*High end reflects vintage signed memorabilia—key poster or album

Handwritten lyrics, 5-7 lines of a key song: $8,000-$10,000

Handwritten/typed lyrics, minor song: $2,500-$6,500

Drawings, unsigned: $1,500-$3,000

Note: He legally changed his name to Bob Dylan in August of 1962

TOUR BOOKS/ PROGRAMS/PASSES

Tour Books/Programs:*

Nice 1981 Bob Dylan European Concert Tour Program (Arena Merch. Ltd.)

1966 U.K. Tour (scarce): $275-$425**

Hard Rain Tour: $25-$30

U.K. Tour 1978 (oversize): $40-$45

European Concert Tour 1981: 20-$25

Dylan & Petty True Confessions Tour: $15-$17

True Confessions, 1986 (Japan): $100

*Also see Books/References

**Watch out for counterfeits of the 1966 tour program

Backstage Passes:

Cloth: $8-$20; Laminated: $15-$40 (1985-Present)

Cloth/paper: $10-$15; Laminated: $20-$25 (1975-1985)

*Scarce before 1975

POSTERS/PRESS KITS

Promotional Posters:

1962-1974: $100 and up (most considered auction items)*

1975-1979: $70-$110

1980-1990: $15-$50

1990-Present: $10-$25

*Early album promotional posters are considered auction material (scarce). Collectors will also pay more for "Highway 61 Revisited" and "Blonde on Blonde."

Press Kits:

1962-1974: Auction Items*

1975-1979: $80-$125

1980-1990: $30-$60

1990-Present: $25

True Confessions Tour: $25

*Early Press/Promotional Kits are considered auction material (scarce)

USED CLOTHING/EQUIPMENT

Autographed Ibanez acoustic guitar, scarce in this form: $3,500-$5,000

Stage-worn jackets, high-end design work: $10,000-$15,000

Guitar Picks: $175-$300

OFTEN OVERLOOKED MEMORABILIA

Defunct Dylan Fanzines: *Fourth Time Around, Occasionally, Endless Road, Zimmerman Blues, Dylan, Homer the Slut,* and *Look Back* (listed in approximate difficulty in finding, although it can vary considerably); Current Dylan Fanzines: *The Telegraph* (U.K.), *Isis* (U.K.), *On the Tracks* (U.S.)—these three are musts for collectors!; Major magazine covers: *Saturday Evening Post,* July 30, 1966, *Saturday Evening Post,* November 2, 1968, *People,* November 10, 1975, *Rolling Stone,* January 26, 1978, etc.; memorabilia from the Orpheum Theater in Minneapolis, MN, owned by Bob Dylan and his brother, in his childhood home at 2425 W. Seventh St., Hibbing, MN, - $55,000 - $63,500; a videotape of the Coopers & Lybrand ad featuring Ritchie Havens singing "The Times They Are a-Changin'" (the first time a Bob Dylan song was used in advertising)

REFERENCES/BOOKS

Collecting the books written about Bob Dylan's life is a fascinating area of rock 'n' roll memorabilia. He is one of the few personalities who lends himself to such an enterprise. The list below is far from comprehensive, but provides a good starting point for the Dylan collector.

Primary:

Books in this category include many major publishers and easier-to-find books. Those marked with an asterisk may be somewhat more difficult to find.

*Anderson, Dennis. *The Hollow Horn.* Hobo Press, 1981

Bauldie, John. *Bob Dylan and Desire.* Wanted Man, 1984

Bauldie, John. *Wanted Man: In Search of Bob Dylan.* Citadel, 1991

Bauldie, John and Gray, Michael. eds. *All Across the Telegraph.* Sedgwick & Jackson, (U.K.), 1987

Bowden, Betsy. *Performing Literature: Words and Music by Bob Dylan.* IN University Press, 1982

Cable, Paul. *Bob Dylan: His Unreleased Recordings.* Schrimer, 1980

Cott, Jonathan. *Dylan.* Doubleday, 1984

Crowe, Cameron. *Biography.* CBS Records, 1985, Included in boxed set.

Day, Adrian. *Bob Dylan: Escaping on the Run.* Wanted Man, 1984

Day, Adrian. *Jokerman: Reading the Lyrics of Bob Dylan.* Blackwell, 1988

De Somogyi, Nick. *Jokerman & Thieves: Bob Dylan and the Ballad Tradition.* Wanted Man, 1986

Dorman, James E. *Recorded Dylan: A Critical Review and Discography*. Soma Press, 1982

Dowley, Tim, and Barry Dunnage. *Bob Dylan: From A Hard Rain to A Slow Train*. Hippocrene, 1982

Dylan, Bob. *Tarantula*. Macmillan, 1971*

Dylan, Bob. *Writings and Drawings*. Knopf, 1973*

Dylan, Bob. *The Songs of Bob Dylan from 1966 Through 1975*. Knopf, 1976*

Dylan, Bob. *Lyrics 1962 -1985*. Knopf, 1986

Dylan, Bob. *Drawn Blank*. Random House, 1994

Gans, Terry Alexander. *What's Real and What is Not: Bob Dylan Through 1964*. Hobo Press, 1983

Gray, Michael. *Song & Dance Man: The Art of Bob Dylan*. Dutton, 1972 rev. ed. St, Martin's Press, 1981

Gross, Michael. *Bob Dylan: An Illustrated History*. Elm Tree, 1978

Herdman, John. *Voices Without Restraint*. Paul Harris, 1982

Heylin, Clinton. *Bob Dylan Stolen Moments*. Wanted Man, 1988

Heylin, Clinton. *Bob Dylan Behind the Shades*. Summit, 1991

Heylin, Clinton. *Bob Dylan: The Recording Sessions 1960-1994*. St. Martin's Press, 1995

Heylin, Clinton. ed. *Saved! The Gospel Speeches of Bob Dylan*. Hanuman, 1990

Heylin, Clinton. *Bob Dylan : a life in stolen moments : day by day. 1941-1995*. Schirmer Books, 1996

Hinchey, John. *Bob Dylan's Slow Train*. Wanted Man, 1983

Hoggard, Stuart, and Jim Shields. *Bob Dylan: An Illustrated Discography*. Transmedia Express, 1978

Humphries, Patrick, and John Bauldie. *Absolutely Dylan*. Viking Studio, 1992*

Kramer, Daniel. *Bob Dylan*. Citadel, 1967* (About $40 in mint)

Krogsgaard, Michael. *Twenty Years of Recording: The Bob Dylan Ref. Bk.* SSRR, Denmark, 1981, 1988

Krogsgaard, Michael. *Positively Bob Dylan: A 30-Year Discography*. Popular Culture Inc., 1992**

McGregor, Craig. *Bob Dylan: A Retrospective*. William Morrow, 1972, De Capo, 1990

McKeen, William, *Dylan: A Bio-Bibliography*. Greenwood, 1993

Mellers, Wilfred. *A Darker Shade of Pale*. Faber & Faber, 1985 (check date)

Miles, Barry. *Bob Dylan*. Big O, 1978*

Miles, Barry, ed. *Bob Dylan in His Own Words*. Quick Fox, 1978*

Milne, Larry, *Hearts of Fire*. NEL, 1987

Pennebaker, D.A., ed. *Don't Look Back*. Ballantine, 1967*

Pickering, Stephen. *Bob Dylan Approximately: A Por. of the Jewish Poet in Search of God*. McKay, 1975

Ribakove, Sy and Barbara. *Folk Rock: The Bob Dylan Story*. Dell, 1966 *(The first book on Dylan!)

Riley, Tim. *Hard Rain: A Dylan Commentary*. Knopf, 1992

Rinzler, Alan. *Bob Dylan: The Illustrated Record*. Harmony, 1978

Rolling Stone, ed. *Knockin' on Dylan's Door: On the Road in '74*. Pocket Books, 1974

Rolling Stone, ed. *The Rolling Stone Interviews: 1967-1980*. St. Martin's Press, 1981

Rowley, Chris. *Blood on the Tracks*. Proteus, 1984

Sarlin, Bob. *Turn It Up! I Can't Hear The Words*. Simon & Schuster, 1973

Scaduto, Anthony. *Bob Dylan: An Intimate Biography*. Grosset and Dunlap, 1971, 1973

Scobie, Stephen. *Alias Bob Dylan*. Red Deer College Press (Canada), 1971*

Shelton, Robert. *No Direction Home*. Beech Tree, 1986

Shepard, Sam. *Rolling Thunder Logbook*. Viking, 1977

Sloman, Larry. *On the Road with Bob Dylan: Rolling with the Thunder*. Bantam, 1978

Spitz, Bob. *Bob Dylan: A Biography*. McGraw-Hill, 1989

Stein, George. *Bob Dylan: Temples in Flames*. Palmyra, Germany, 1989

Thompson, Toby. *Positively Main Street: An Unorthodox View of Bob Dylan*. Coward-McCann, 1971*

Thomson, Elizabeth M., ed. *Conclusions on the Wall: New Essays on Bob Dylan*. Thin Man, 1980

Thomson, Elizabeth M., and David Gutman. *The Dylan Companion*. Macmillan, (U.K.), 1990

Williams, Chris. *Bob Dylan: In His Own Words, Vol. 2*. Omnibus Press

Williams, Don. *The Man, The Music, The Message*. Revell, 1985

Williams, Paul. *Dylan: What Happened?*. Entwhistle, 1979

Williams, Paul. *Performing Artist: The Music of Bob Dylan Vol.1 (1960-1973)*. Underwood-Miller, 1990

Williams, Paul. *Performing Artist: The Music of Bob Dylan Vol.2 (1974-1986)*. Underwood-Miller, 1992

Williams, Richard. *Dylan: A Man Called Alias*. Bloomsbury

Woliver, Robbie. *Bringing It All Back Home: 25 Years of Amer. Music at Folk City*. Pantheon Books, 1986

Worrell, Denise. *Icons: Intimate Portraits*. Atlantic Monthly Press, 1989

Wraith, John, and Mike Wyvill. *Still on the Road: 1991 Tourbook*. Wanted Man, 1992

Wraith, John, and Mike Wyvill. *Heading for Another Joint: 1992 Tourbook*. Wanted Man, 1993

Wraith, John, and Mike Wyvill. *Down the Highway: 1993 Tourbook*. Wanted Man, 1994

Wraith, John, and Mike Wyvill. *From Town to Town: 1994 Tourbook*. Wanted Man, 1995

Wurlitzer, Rudy. *Pat Garrett & Billy the Kid*. Signet, 1973*

*Published in U.K. as, *Oh No! Not Another Bob Dylan Book*

**A revised edition of *Twenty Years of Recording*

Secondary:

Books in this category include many self-published or private offerings; some are extremely difficult/impossible to find. Quality and condition may vary considerably.

Auschlag, Hermann. *Small Talk* (German)

Bauldie, John. *The Ghost of Electricity* (U.K.)

Bauldie, John. *Positively The Dream & other assorted interviews and tall tales*, (U.K.)

Bergerau, E. *Every Grain of Sand* (Germany)

Bicker, Stewart. *The Red Rose and the Briar: A Commentary on Renaldo and Clara* (U.K.)

Bicker, Stewart, ed. *Friends & Other Strangers: Bob Dylan in Other People's Words* (U.K.)

Bicker, Stewart, ed. *Talkin Bob Dylan 1984 & 1985 (Some Educated Rap)* (U.K.)

Cooper, Chris, and Keith Marsh. *The Circus is in Town: England: 1965* (U.K.)

Dergoth, Jonas. *Renaldo and Clara: A Concise Synopsis* (Scandinavia)

Diddle, Gavin. *Images and Assorted Facts: A Peek Behind the Picture Frame* (U.K.)

Diddle, Gavin, ed. *Talkin' Bob Dylan 1978* (U.K.)

Diddle, Gavin, ed. *Talkin' Bob Dylan 1984* (U.K.)

Dreau, Jean-Louis, and Robert Schlockoff. *Hypnotist Collectors: An Inter. Ill. Discography* (France)

Dundas, Glen. *Tangled Up in Tapes: The Recordings of Bob Dylan* (Canada) Multiple Editions

Dunn, Tim. *I Just Write Em As They Come*

Gant, Sandy. *A Discography of Bob Dylan*

Garrett, B. *My Back Pages* (U.K.)

Gilbert, Joel. *The Acoustic Bob Dylan*

Hansen., Larry. *A Million Faces at My Feet: 1986 True Confessions Tour*

Heylin, Clinton. *The Bob Dylan Interviews: A List*

Heylin, Clinton. *Rain Unraveled Tales (The Nightingale's Code Examined): A Rumourography*

Heylin, Clinton. More *Rain Unravelled Tales (The Nightingale's Code Re-examined): A Rumourography*

Heylin, Clinton. *To Live Outside the Law: A Guide to Bob Dylan Bootlegs*

Jansen, Gerhard, ed. *Slow Train Coming* (Netherlands)

Jansen, Gerhard. *Passing On* (Netherlands)

Jansen, Gerhard. *Shot of Love* (Netherlands)

Karpel, Craig. *The Tarantula in Me: Behind Bob Dylan's Novel*

Lawlan, Val and Brian. *Steppin' Out*

Ledbury, John. *Mysteriously Saved: An Astrological... Fundamentalism*

Liff, Dennis. *Raging Glory*

Lindley, John. *Seven Day*

Michel, Steve. *The Bob Dylan Concordance*

Percival, Dave. *The Dust of Rumour* (U.K.)

Percival, Dave. *This Wasn't Written in Tin Pan Alley* (U.K.)

Percival, Dave. *Just a Personal Tendancy* (U.K.)

Percival, Dave. *Dylan Songs: A Listing* (U.K.)

Percival, Dave. *The Concert Charts* (U.K.)

Percival, Dave. *Love Plus Zero/With Limits* (U.K.)

Pickering, Stephen. *Dylan: A Commemoration*

Pickering, Stephen. *Praxis: One*

Pickering, Stephen. *Tour 1974*

Rawlins, Adrian. *Dylan Through the Looking Glass*

Roberts, John. *Mixed Up Confusion: The Krogsgaard Companion*

Roques, Dominique. *The Great White Answers: The Bob Dylan Bootleg Records* (France)

Russell, Alex. *Flagging Down the "Double E": Dylan and Allusions* (U.K.)

Stone, Lee Anderson. *Temptation?* (Germany)

Stone, Lee Anderson. *Who's Gonna Go to Hell for Anybody* (Germany)

Styche, Geoff. *A Discography of Bob Dylan* (U.K.)

Townshend, Phil. *Strangers and Prophets Vol.1* (U.K.)

Townshend, Phil. *Strangers and Prophets Vol.2* (U.K.)

Van Estrick, Robert. *Concerted Efforts* (Netherlands)

Way, John B. *Hungry as a Raccoon (Bob Dylan Talks to His Fans & Other Strangers)* (U.K.)

Williams, Alan. *Whaaat? The Original Playboy Interview* (U.K.)

Williams, Paul. *Dylan: One Year Later*

Wilson, Keith. *Bob Dylan: A Listing* (Canada)

Wissolik, David. *Bob Dylan: American Poet & Singer - An Annotated Bibliography*

Witting, Robin. *Isiah on Guitar: A Guide to John Wesley Harding* (U.K.)

Witting, Robin. *The Cracked Bells: A Guide to Tarantula* (U.K.)

Witting, Robin. *Orpheus Revisited: A Celebration of Highway 61 Revisited* (U.K.)

Woodward, Ian. *Back of the Tapestry* (U.K.)

Yenne, Bill. *One Foot on the Highway: Bob Dylan on Tour 1974*

Note: As you explore the books on Bob Dylan, you will no doubt run across numerous anonymous publications, reprints, and unauthorized publications. Keep in mind that there are numerous book services that can assist you in your search.

E., Sheila

(Sheila Escovedo)

Born: December 12, 1957

A percussionist and Prince protégée, Sheila E. is the daughter of Pete Escovedo, formerly of Santana and Azteca. Like her brothers, she chose to follow in her father's footsteps and even played with Azteca for a period of time. She is a successful studio musician and has contributed to works by Diana Ross, Lionel Ritchie, and Marvin Gaye.

Sheila E. met Prince in 1978 while she was playing with George Duke. Although their friendship was immediate, they didn't work together until 1984 ("Erotic City," the flip side to "Let's Go Crazy"). It was Prince who convinced her of the potential she had and packaged her as a solo act.

The Glamorous Life (#28, 1984) spun off the self-titled single that climbed into the Top Ten. *Sheila E. in Romance 1600* (#50, 1985) followed and contained the successful duet with Prince "A Love Bizarre" (#11, 1985). *Sheila E.* (#56, 1987), her third album, had only one minor single, "Hold Me" (#68, 1987). The lack of interest in this album caused her to abandon her solo career until 1991. She joined Prince on his world tour (Sign 'O' the Times), which proved to be a welcome change for the artist. After recording *Sex Cymbal* (#146, 1991), she suffered a collapsed lung.

AUTOGRAPHS

A CD, LP, magazine cover, ad, photo, or card signed by the entire band: $15-$25

TOUR BOOKS/PROGRAMS/PASSES

Backstage Passes:

Cloth: $6-$8; Laminated: $10

POSTERS/PRESS KITS

Press Kits: $10

USED CLOTHING/EQUIPMENT

Drum Sticks: $10-$15

OFTEN OVERLOOKED MEMORABILIA

All of her session work—Marvin Gaye, Herbie Hancock, etc.; all of her work with Prince; memorabilia from the movie *Krush Groove* (it contained "A Love Bizarre"); her early work with her father's band Azteca

The Eagles

Formed 1971

Don Henley, Born: July 22, 1947; Glenn Frey, Born: November 6, 1948; Bernie Leadon, Born: July 19, 1947; and Randy Meisner, Born; March 8, 1946*

*Don Felder was added in 1974. Leadon departed in 1976 and Joe Walsh, Born: November 20, 1947, was added. Meisner departed in 1977 and Timothy Schmit, Born: October 30, 1947, joined the group. The Eagles re-formed in 1994.

The four founding members were recruited by Linda Ronstadt in 1971 to perform in her backing band during an upcoming tour. Both Frey (Longbranch Pennywhistle) and Henley (Four Speeds) were currently with a band called Shiloh (Felicity), while Leadon (Scottsville Squirrel Barkers, Hearts & Flowers, Dillard & Clark, Corvettes) and Meisner (Dynamics, Soul Survivors, the Poor, Poco) were with The Flying Burrito Brothers and Rick Nelson's Stone Canyon Band. It was during the summer of 1971 that numerous friends urged them to form their own group. In August, David Geffen visited Jackson Browne's home, where Frey also resided, and, after hearing the band, signed them to a recording contract. The group then honed its skills during a month-long stay at the Gallery Club in Aspen, CO, while it rehearsed numerous self-written compositions.

In March 1972 the group traveled to London to record its self-titled debut. *The Eagles* (#22,1972) gave the group its first hit single with "Take It Easy" (#12, 1972), which was penned by both Frey and Browne. "Witchy Woman" (#9, 1972), followed by "Peaceful Easy Feeling" (#22, 1973), were also extracted from the album. At this point, the band's sound was coined "country rock," much to the dismay of the group's members. In line with expectations, the group released *Desperado* (#41, 1973). Both "Tequila Sunrise" (#64, 1973) and "Outlaw Man" (#59, 1973) were lifted from the album, but failed to break into the Top Forty.

In January 1974, Don Felder (the Continentals, Flow), a friend of Leadon, contributed "Good Day in Hell" to the Eagles' third album. The group, impressed by his skills, invited him to permanently join the band. *On the Border* (#17, 1974) included singles the "Already Gone" (#32, 1974) and "James Dean" (#77, 1974), but it was "Best of My Love" (#1, 1975) that finally landed the Eagles at the top. On July 26, 1975, "One Of These Nights" topped the U.S. album chart, while the self-titled single eventually reached #1. "Lyin' Eyes" (#2, 1975), also extracted from the album, rose quickly up the singles chart, while rumors circulated that the band was having some personnel problems.

On January 15, 1976, the band confirmed during a press conference that Bernie Leadon had left the band over musical differences. His replacement was Joe Walsh (James Gang), a hard-edged barnstormer who had made stage appearances in the past with the band. The group, in an effort to buy some time, released *Eagles: Their Greatest Hits 1971-1975* (#1, 1976), while "Take It To The Limit" (#4, 1976) pushed into the Top Five on the singles chart. Meanwhile, the group entered the studio to carve out its next album under the new lineup.

On January 15, 1977, the long-awaited album *Hotel California* (#1) topped the charts. It was the group's third consecutive #1. The extracted singles included the self-titled "Hotel California" (#1, 1977), "New Kid In Town" (#1, 1977), and "Life In The Fast Lane" (#11, 1977). In September, just after the band's European Tour, Meisner decided to leave the band. In a twist of fate, Timothy B. Schmit, who had replaced Meisner in Poco, replaced him in the Eagles.

Numerous projects and problems ensued over the next two years before the release of *The Long Run* (#1, 1979). Singles from the album included "The Long Run" (#8, 1980), "Heartache Tonight (#1, 1979), and "I Can't Tell You Why" (#8, 1980). The record marked the end of a period for the band—most members went on to pursue solo endeavors. *Live* (#6, 1980) was released amidst rumors that the band no longer existed. "Seven Bridges Road" (#21, 1981), extracted from the album, became what many believe to be the band's final single.

As the Eagles flew, Don Felder faded into obscurity, while Timothy B. Schmit stalled following two low-charting releases. Joe Walsh spun out a six-pack of unsuccessful pieces of vinyl, which left Henley and Frey—the only two members to appear on every Eagles album—to enjoy successful solo careers. Frey charted with singles "The One You Love" (#15, 1982), "Sexy Girl" (#20, 1984), "The Heat Is On" (#2, 1985), "Smuggler's Blues" (#12, 1985), and "You Belong to the City" (#2, 1985). Henley scored with "Dirty Laundry" (#3), "Boys of Summer" (#5, 1984), "All She Wants to Do Is Dance" (#9, 1985), "Sunset Grill" (#22, 1985), "The End of the Innocence" (#8, 1989), "The Last Worthless Evening" (#21, 1989), "The Heart of the Matter" (#21, 1990), and "New York Minute" (#48, 1990) before a contract with Geffen Records kept the bird in the nest for awhile. In 1990 Henley founded the Walden Woods Project, dedicated to the preservation of land around Walden Pond (made famous by Henry David Thoreau) in Concord, Massachusetts. During the '90s, Don Henley has dedicated himself to many humanitarian efforts and has raised millions of dollars for numerous causes including Witness, AIDS, etc..., while he has educated the public on many key issues. Of all who have traveled far from the Eagles, he has flown the greatest distance.

Amid rumors, Henley, Frey, Walsh, Felder, and Schmit appeared in a Travis Tritt video of his "Take It Easy" cover. In November 1994 the band released *Hell Freezes Over* (#1, 1994), which contained live cuts from an MTV appearance, along with four new

songs. The reunited group then toured for 26 months, playing 165 shows to 3.5 million fans. Following 130 shows the group's concert gross had tabulated at around $160 million.

AUTOGRAPHS
Group:
A CD, LP, magazine cover, ad, photo, or card signed by the entire band $150-$250*

*High-end reflects vintage signed memorabilia

Individual:

Don Henley: $40-$50	Glenn Frey: $30-$40
Bernie Leadon: $20-$25	Randy Meisner: $25-$30
Don Felder: $20-$25	Joe Walsh: $40-$50
Timothy B. Schmit: $30	

TOUR BOOKS/ PROGRAMS/PASSES
Programs:
1976 Tour: $25-$40
1980 The Long Run Tour: $25
1994 World Tour program: $20-$25

Backstage Passes:
Cloth: $10-$15;
Laminated: $15-$40

The Eagles 1976 Tour program (Eagles, Ltd.)

POSTERS/PRESS KITS
Promotional Posters:
$10-$40
Press Kits: $20-$50

USED CLOTHING/EQUIPMENT
Guitar Picks:

Glenn Frey: $25-$30	Bernie Leadon: $30
Randy Meisner: $30	Don Felder: $25-$30
Joe Walsh: $30-$40	Timothy B. Schmit: $20-$25
Don Henley: $25-$40	

Drum Sticks:
Don Henley: $25-$35

OFTEN OVERLOOKED MEMORABILIA
Building The Perfect Beast, Don Henley, 1985 promotional sunglasses - $25; Frey's early work with Longbranch Pennywhistle (J.D.

A selection of Eagles' guitar picks

Souther); Henley's early work with Shiloh (Amos label); Hotel California promotional mobile - $75; Hell Freezes Over counter display - $10; Hell Freezes Over mobile - $15; Hell Freezes Over promo static window sticker - $10; Greatest Hits mobile - $65

REFERENCE BOOKS
The Story of The Eagles, The Long Run by Marc Shapiro: $20; a couple resources exist, but nothing that does justice to the band in my opinion; no dedicated collector books

---

Born: January 17, 1955

Earl, the '80s guitarist, singer, songwriter, and vagabond, released his critically acclaimed debut album, *Guitar Town* (1986), at the age of 31.

AUTOGRAPHS
A CD, LP, magazine cover, ad, photo or card signed by the artist: $6-$10

OFTEN OVERLOOKED MEMORABILIA
Artifacts from his appearances for humanitarian causes; newspaper clippings regarding his altercations with the law

---

Earth, Wind and Fire

Formed 1969

Maurice White, Born: December 19, 1941; Verdine White, Born: July 25, 1951; Donald Whitehead; Wade Flemons; Michael Beale; Phillard Williams; Chester Washington; Lesile Dayton; Alex Thomas; and Sherry Scott*

*The group disbanded in 1972, then regrouped with new lineup: M. White, V. White; Phillip Bailey, Born: May 8, 1951; Larry Dunn, Born: June 19, 1953; Jessica Cleaves; Roland Bautista; and Roland Laws. Jessica Cleaves, Roland Bautista, Roland Laws left, and Johnny Graham, Al McKay, Andrew Woolfolk, and Ralph Johnson joined the band. Freddie White was added in 1974 and departed in 1975. McKay left in 1980 and Bautista rejoined group. Bautista left again in 1983 and Sheldon Reynolds was added. Gary Bias, Ray Brown, and Reggie Young were added in 1993.

This extremely popular and successful '70s pop band, which successfully blended a variety of musical forms into its own hallmark funk-rhythms with gospel style harmonies and brass accompaniments, was the brainchild of leader and producer Maurice White. While with the Ramsey Lewis Trio (from 1967-1969), White took up the African thumb piano, kalimba, which eventually grew into one of the band's trademarks.

White moved to L.A. from Chicago and formed his first version of EW&F in late 1969, but after two mediocre-selling albums, he fired everyone but his brother Verdine. As new band personnel kept shifting, the group's second LP, *Head to the Sky* (1973) climbed into the Top Fifteen on the U.S. album chart. The recipe was now set for a string of hit albums and extracts that allowed the band to dominate the charts for the remainder of the decade. "Shining Star" (#1, 1975), "Got to Get You into My Life" (#9, 1978), "Boogie Wonderland" (#6, 1979), and "Fall in Love with Me" (#17, 1983) were just a few of the group's hits, but are reflective of the dynamic range of this talented group.

EW&F member Phillip Bailey, best known for his golden falsetto, like other members, went on to individual projects. "Easy Lover" (#2, 1985), a duet with Phil Collins, helped bring Bailey out to the forefront, and he also became involved in musicals and even landed a Grammy for his gospel LP *Triumph!* (1986).

AUTOGRAPHS

A CD, LP, magazine cover, ad, photo, or card signed by the group: $30-$75*

*Second and successful version

POSTERS/PRESS KITS

Promotional Posters: $10-$45
Press Kits: $25-$50

USED CLOTHING/EQUIPMENT

Drum Sticks: $15-$25

OFTEN OVERLOOKED MEMORABILIA

Movie memorabilia from *Sgt. Pepper's Lonely Hearts Club Band* (1978); White's earlier work as a drummer with Chess Records and later with the Ramsey Lewis Trio; Phillip Bailey's extracurricular projects

REFERENCES/BOOKS

No resources or dedicated collector books

Easton, Sheena

Born: April 27, 1959

Easton, the Scottish pop star who was groomed for success, scored first in the U.K. with her single "Modern Girl," and later broke through the American market with her hit "Morning Train." She then gleaned tremendous exposure through singing the theme for the James Bond film "For Your Eyes Only" (#4, 1981), before she landed the extract "When He Shines" (#30, 1982), from her sophomore album effort. In 1981 Easton captured the Grammy for Best New Artist, and she also captured a second award, three years later, for Best Mexican/American Performance for her duet with Luis Miguel on "Me Gustas Tal Como Eres."

In 1984, feeling cramped by her wholesome image, she opted for a more sensual, yet tougher look and sound, with her album *A Private Heaven* (#15, 1984). The latter produced the hit extracts "Strut" (#7, 1984) and "Sugar Walls" (#9, 1984). Easton also scored with her Prince duet "U Got the Look" (1987). The following decade would find her turning more toward her acting skills in both television and film.

AUTOGRAPHS

A CD, LP, magazine cover, ad, photo, or card signed by the artist: $15-$45

TOUR BOOKS/PROGRAMS/PASSES

Backstage Passes:
Cloth: $6-$8; Laminated: $10

POSTERS/PRESS KITS

Promotional Posters: $10-$20
Press Kits: $20-$25

OFTEN OVERLOOKED MEMORABILIA

Videotapes of her numerous television appearances including *Miami Vice* (1987), *Jack's Place*, *Body Bags*, and *The Highlander*; movie memorabilia from *Indecent Proposal*; body lotion - $50

The Easybeats

Formed 1963

George Young, Gordon Fleet, Dick Diamonde, Harry Vanda (Harry Vandenberg), and Steve Wright

This '60s Australian rock band is now best remembered for launching producers/songwriters Harry Vanda and George Young, although the band did well with the international hit "Friday on My Mind" (#16, 1967). Young is also typically associated with his brothers Angus and Malcolm of AC/DC.

AUTOGRAPHS

A CD, LP, magazine cover, ad, photo, or card signed by the group: $10-$15

OFTEN OVERLOOKED MEMORABILIA

Artifacts from both Young and Vanda's production companies

Echo and the Bunnymen

Formed 1978

Original Lineup: Pete De Freitas; Ian McCulloch, Born: May 5, 1959; Les Pattinson; and Will Sergeant*

*Additional personnel: Blair Cunninham, Noel Burke, and Damon Reece

Liverpool's neopsychedelic and theatrical punk disciples are best known for their U.K. hits "The Back of Love" (#19, 1982), "The Cutter" (#8, 1983), and "The Killing Moon" (#9, 1984), and also for McCulloch's vertical nest of locks.

AUTOGRAPHS

A CD, LP, magazine cover, ad, photo, or card signed by the group: $10-$15*
*Original lineup

POSTERS/PRESS KITS

Promotional Posters: $10-$15
Press Kits: $10-$15

REFERENCES/BOOKS

A couple resources exist, but nothing that does justice to the band in my opinion; no dedicated collector books

Eddy, Duane

Born: April 26, 1938

Eddy, the Late '50s staccato guitarist, is best known for his instrumental hits "Rebel Rouser" (#6, 1958) and "Peter Gunn" (#27, 1960). His other hits included "Ramrod" (#27, 1958), "Cannonball" (#15, 1958), "Forty Miles of Bad Road" (#9, 1959), "Dance with the Guitar Man" (#12, 1962), "The Ballad of Palladin" (#3, 1962), "Play Me Like You Play Your Guitar" (#9, 1975), and "Because They're Young" (#4, 1960). He was an influence to many artists, including George Harrison. Eddy was inducted into the Rock and Roll Hall of Fame in 1994.

AUTOGRAPHS
A CD, LP, magazine cover, ad, photo, or card signed by the artist: $25-$50

OFTEN OVERLOOKED MEMORABILIA
Movie memorabilia from *Because They're Young* (1960)

Edmunds, Dave

Born: April 15, 1944

Edmunds, the Welch guitarist, singer, producer, songwriter, and rockabilly pub-rocker, was the co-founder of Rockpile, best known for its remake of "I Hear You Knockin'" and other numerous minor hits. Edmunds also landed a solo hit with "Slipping Away" from his well-received album *Information* (1983) before he went on to a very successful career as a producer.

AUTOGRAPHS
A CD, LP, magazine cover, ad, photo, or card signed by the artist: $10-$15

POSTERS/PRESS KITS
Promotional Posters: $10-$15
Press Kits: $10-$15

USED CLOTHING/EQUIPMENT
Guitar Picks: $10-$20

OFTEN OVERLOOKED MEMORABILIA
Movie memorabilia from *Stardust* (1975) and *Give My Regards to Broad Street* (1984); associated artifacts from his other productions for artists such as the Fabulous Thunderbirds and k.d. lang

808 State

Formed 1988

Graham Massey, Andrew Barker, Sarren Partington, Martin Price, and Gerald Simpson

This late-80s British techno-rave act, best known for dance club favorites such as "Pacific State" and "Cubik," saw Simpson depart in 1989 and Price in 1999.

AUTOGRAPHS
A CD, LP, magazine cover, ad, photo, or card signed by the group: $15-$30

Einstürzende Neubauten

Formed 1980

Blixa Bargeld, Born: January 12, 1959; N.U. Unruh; Beate Bartel; and Gudrun Gut*

*Additional personnel: F.M. Einheit, Alexander Hacke, and Mark Chung

These '80s German hard-hat Dadaists are best known as the world's first "industrial" band.

AUTOGRAPHS
A CD, LP, magazine cover, ad, photo, or card signed by the group: $10-$15

The Electric Flag

Formed 1967

Michael Bloomfield, Born: July 28, 1944, Died: February 15, 1981; Buddy Miles, Born: September 5, 1946; Barry Goldberg; Nick Gravenites; Harvey Brooks; Peter Strazza; Marcus Doubleday; and Herbie Rich*

*Roger "Jellyroll" Troy was added in 1974

The Electric Flag, the late-60s short-lived Bay Area band, is best remembered for its talented membership. The group acted as a catalyst for the rock-with-brass trend that would follow which included groups such as Blood, Sweat and Tears and Chicago. The band debuted at the Monterey Pop Festival (1967) while its successful debut album made the Top Forty shortly thereafter (1968). As is the case in many a would-be supergroup, it became difficult getting all the egos into one room; eventually the band broke up.

AUTOGRAPHS
A CD, LP, magazine cover, ad, photo, or card signed by the group: $40-$110

OFTEN OVERLOOKED MEMORABILIA
Memorabilia from the Monterey Pop Festival (1967); artifacts from the individual members' numerous other musical efforts

The Electric Light Orchestra

Formed 1971

Original Lineup: Roy Wood, Born: November 8, 1946; Jeff Lynne, Born: December 30, 1947; Bev Bevan, Born: November 25, 1944; and Rick Price

*Numerous personnel changes

This popular British orchestral-rock and pop act, which is best remembered for the hits "Showdown" (#53, 1974), "Can't Get It Out of My Head" (#9, 1975), "Evil Woman" (#10, 1976), "Strange Magic" (#14, 1976), "Don't Bring Me Down" (#15, 1979), "Shine a Little Love" (#15, 1979), and "Hold On Tight" (#10, 1981), quickly became a popular live draw that eventually even included a laser-equipped spaceship as part of its elaborate stage show.

By the beginning of the '80s, ELO began slipping commercially, although it was still landing hit singles. By 1986 only Lynn, Bevan, and Tandy remained. Lynne was testing the waters with side projects, and by this time, he was becoming a sought-after record producer. He joined the Traveling Wilburys in 1988. Bevan, who had gone off briefly to join Black Sabbath, returned in 1991 to resurrect ELO II, which didn't include Lynne.

AUTOGRAPHS

A CD, LP, magazine cover, ad, photo, or card signed by the group: $40-$75

POSTERS/PRESS KITS/TOUR BOOKS

Promotional Posters: $15-$60
Press Kits: $25-$40
Tour Books:
The Big Night (Out of the Blue), 1978: $25-$30

OFTEN OVERLOOKED MEMORABILIA

Movie memorabilia from *Xanadu* (1980); store display sign with original members - $50; ELO moon w/logo mobile - $50; "A New World Record" bin divider - $30; bin display (pop out moon), 3' tall - $75; ELO spaceship necklace - $20; spaceship patch - $25; Out of the Blue poster offer, 1977, metallic paper - $10

REFERENCES/BOOKS

A couple resources exist, but nothing that does justice to the band in my opinion; no dedicated collector books

The Electric Prunes

Formed 1965
James Lowe, Mark Tulin, Ken Williams, Preston Ritter, and Weasel Spagnola

Formed 1967
John Herren, Mark Kincaid, Ron Morgan, Brett Wade, and Richard Whetstone

These are actually two separate groups. The first was a mid-60s psychedelic group that specialized in reverb, which landed a hit with "I Had Too Much to Dream (Last Night)" (#11, 1966), followed by "Get Me to the World on Time" (#27, 1967) before it disappeared from sight. The second version proved little, and accomplished even less.

AUTOGRAPHS

A CD, LP, magazine cover, ad, photo, or card signed by the group: $10-$25*
*First version, formed 1965

Elephant's Memory

Formed 1967
Rick Frank, Born: February 12, 1942; and Stan Bronstein, Born: July 17, 1938*

*Numerous personnel changes

Elephant's Memory, the theatrical jazz and funk flavored '70s street-band, is best known for working on the soundtrack to *Midnight Cowboy*, a minor hit ("Mongoose" (1970)), and a solid New York City East Village following before it became John Lennon's band in 1972. The group worked with Lennon and his wife, Yoko, on *Some Time in New York City* (1972) and *Approximately Infinite Universe* (1973), and it also released an LP on Apple. The group also had the opportunity to back rock legends such as Chuck Berry and Bo Diddley. The group appeared at the One to One benefit concert that resulted in the release of *John Lennon Live in New York City* (1986).

AUTOGRAPHS

A CD, LP, magazine cover, ad, photo, or card signed by the group: $8-$15

OFTEN OVERLOOKED MEMORABILIA

Movie memorabilia from *Midnight Cowboy*; all Apple and Lennon related material; any artifacts from Carly Simon's brief stint with the band

Eleventh Dream Day

Formed 1983
Janet Bean, Born: February 10, 1964; Rick Rizzo, Born: July 4, 1957; and Shu Shubat*

*Shubat left in 1985 and Douglas McCombs and Baird Figi were added. Figi left in 1991 and Matthew "Wink" O'Bannon was added. Bean, Catherine Irwin, and Dave Gay formed Freakwater in 1983.

This enduring '80s and '90s Midwestern alt band is known best for its survival techniques.

AUTOGRAPHS

A CD, LP, magazine cover, ad, photo, or card signed by the group: $5-$10

Elliott, Ramblin' Jack

(Elliott Adnopoz)
Born: August 1, 1931

Elliott, a Brooklyn cowboy and vagabond, wandered the West briefly with Woody Guthrie before he landed in Greenwich Village's Washington Square Park in the early '50s where he helped plant a seed for the following decade's folk-boom. He quickly be-

came known for his flat-picking tributes to Guthrie, and a strong cult following that even included Bob Dylan, who even invited Elliott on his 1975 Rolling Thunder Revue.

Elliot performed at the all-star memorial concert for Guthrie at Carnegie Hall in 1968 and his Vanguard compilation *The Essential Ramblin' Jack Elliott* (1976) is a must for all folk-rock fans.

AUTOGRAPHS

A CD, LP, magazine cover, ad, photo, or card signed by the artist: $10-$20

OFTEN OVERLOOKED MEMORABILIA

All associated artifacts from his early Greenwich Village days

Ellis, Shirley

Born: 1941

This mid-60s novelty soul singer is best remembered for "The Nitty Gritty" (#8, 1964), "The Clapping Song" (#8, 1965), and "The Name Game" (#3, 1965). Ellis also wrote "One Two, I Love You" for the Heartbreakers and married songwriter Lincoln Chase.

AUTOGRAPHS

A CD, LP, magazine cover, ad, photo, or card signed by the artist: $8-$15

Ely, Joe

Born: February 9, 1947

Ely, the late-70s honky-tonk, Tex-Mex, Austin swing guru, garnered a strong cult following in Texas before he joined Merle Haggard on his British tour in 1979 and The Clash during its 1980 romp through the Lone Star State. He is a gifted musician who has played with Jimmie Dale Gilmore, with whom he has collaborated on various projects for decades.

AUTOGRAPHS

A CD, LP, magazine cover, ad, photo, or card signed by the group: $10-$15

OFTEN OVERLOOKED MEMORABILIA

Associated memorabilia from his tour with Merle Haggard (1979) and the Clash (1980)

Emerson, Lake and Palmer

Formed 1970

Keith Emerson, Born: November 1, 1944; Greg Lake, Born: November 10, 1948; Carl Palmer, Born: March 20, 1947*

*1986 Emerson, Lake and Powell (Cozy Powell), Born: December 29, 1947. Palmer returned and left in 1987. Robert Barry was added briefly in 1988. Palmer returned in 1992.

Keith Emerson, formerly of Nice, Greg Lake, formerly with King Crimson, and Carl Palmer, of Atomic Rooster, formed a talented musical trio that forged into the 1970s with a new form of musical showmanship, marked by a form of rock/classical fusion. On August 29, 1970, the group performed alongside The Doors, The Who, and others at the Isle of Wight Festival. The group's self-titled first album (#18), spun off "Lucky Man" (#48, 1971), a successful single in the U.S. *Tarkus* (#9, 1971), a conceptual album, followed the debut before a live classical adaptation of Mussorgsky's *Pictures at an Exhibition* (#10, 1972) was released. ELP's musical prowess was firmly established by the release of its fourth album, *Trilogy* (#5, 1972), which contained the synthesizer-infused single "From the Beginning" and the ballad "Lucky Man" (#51, 1973).

Brain Salad Surgery (#11, 1973), with its elaborate die-cut cover design by H.R. Giger, provided the band with an outstanding array of popular live numbers including "Karn Evil 9." The band enjoyed a growing following due to extensive FM airplay, an elaborate stage setting, and the explosive antics of keyboardist Keith Emerson. The group's tour in support of the record included 36 tons of elaborate equipment (quadraphonic sound, lasers, etc.) and was successfully documented in the group's triple-release *Welcome Back My Friends to the Show That Never Ends* (#4, 1974).

A two-year break followed; in retrospect, it proved to slow the momentum of the group's success. Although solo projects occasionally brought each member back into the spotlight, such as Lake's seasonal classic "Father Christmas," the group didn't emerge again until the release of *Works, vol.1* (#12, 1977). The release was actually a solo spotlight—each member had a designated side, and side four was saved for the group. Emerson's appreciation of Aaron Copland's classical work was evident in his interpretation of "Fanfare for the Common Man," which soon became the band's standard opening live number. Certain dates of the 1977 world tour included a full orchestra and choir. *Works, vol. 2* (#37, 1977) followed, and like its predecessor, was interpreted as another solo sampler.

Love Beach (#55, 1978) was the band's final solo album. The group disbanded, following a farewell world tour, on December 30, 1978. Contractual record obligations were met with subsequent releases *Emerson, Lake and Palmer* (#73, 1979) and *The Best of Emerson, Lake and Palmer* (#108, 1980). The band members went their separate ways—Emerson released a number of film soundtracks including the one for *Nighthawks*, Lake briefly joined Asia, and Palmer formed One P.M. before he became a full-time member of Asia.

The successful reunion of other similar bands, such as Yes, enticed the group to re-form. ELP regrouped in 1985, but minus Palmer—his role was now filled by drummer Cozy Powell (formerly of Rainbow). *Emerson, Lake and Powell* (#23) debuted in 1986, and the group had moderate success with the single "Touch And Go" (#60). The group supported the album with a U.S. tour, but the project soured when Powell decided to pursue other projects.

The group tried to reunite again in 1987, but failed. This led to the release of *The Power of Three* (#97, 1988) on Geffen Records. The third was drummer Robert Berry. A successful reunion was finally made and the band released *Black Moon* (#78) in the summer of 1992. The group toured in support of the album, its first in fifteen years. *Live at Royal Albert Hall* preserved the tour on disc. In November 1993, *Return of the Manticore*, a four-CD/boxed set with a booklet was released as a career anthology in the U.S.

In the Hot Seat was released in the fall of 1994 and included the Lake-penned song "Daddy." The song was inspired by an Upstate New York family's struggle to deal with the loss of a child. Lake contributed $5,000 to the Sara Anne Wood (the missing child) Rescue Center in Litchfield, NY. The little girl was believed to have been murdered by an alleged Massachusetts serial killer. Lake, so moved by the incident, also donated royalties to the song to the center. Lake also attended a sold-out benefit held on December 14, 1994, at the Landmark Theater in Syracuse, NY to benefit the center. The show, hosted by radio station 95X, included a silent auction and donations were given to the family, including a letter and religious medal from Mother Teresa given by this author.

AUTOGRAPHS

The members of Emerson, Lake & Palmer have always been obliging to autograph requests.

Group:

A CD, LP, magazine cover, ad, photo, or card signed by the entire band: $150-$200*

*High-end reflects vintage signed memorabilia

Individual:

Keith Emerson: $30-$45
Greg Lake: $30-$45
Carl Palmer: $30-$40

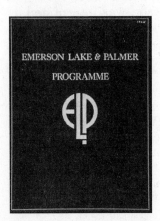

EMERSON LAKE & PALMER
PROGRAMME

TOUR BOOKS/ PROGRAMS/PASSES

Programs:

North American Tour 1977: $20-$30
Backstage Passes:
Cloth: $10-$20;
Laminated: $15-$40

ELP 1977 "Works" program (Brockum Int. Inc.)

Emerson, Lake and Palmer backstage passes (Printed by OTTO)

POSTERS/PRESS KITS

Promotional Posters:
$15-$45
Press Kits: $15-$60
Black Moon: $15

USED CLOTHING/EQUIPMENT

A 1989, 12-string Fender Stratocaster used on tour by Greg Lake: $1,200-$1,500

Guitar Picks:
Greg Lake: $25-$35

Drum Sticks:
Carl Palmer: $30-$40

OFTEN OVERLOOKED MEMORABILIA

Love Beach stand-up (w/band pop out): $50

EMF

Formed 1989

James Atkin, Ian Dench, Derran "Derry" Brownson, Zachary Foley, and Mark Decloedt

EMF, the Gloucester gurus of techno dance pop, erupted with its smash hit "Unbelievable" (#1, 1991) and had a minor hit the same year with "Lies" (#18, 1991).

AUTOGRAPHS

A CD, LP, magazine cover, ad, photo, or card signed by the group: $7-$15

An Emotional Fish

Formed 1988

Gerald Whelan, David Frew, Martin Murphy, and Enda Wyatt

These Irish rockers got their start on U2's Mother Records label, which is dedicated to aspiring performers in need of a recording opportunity. Following the band's success with the single "Celebrate," which went Top Ten in Ireland, the band signed with Atlantic. The band's first two albums garnered mixed reviews and no hit singles, but did catch the interest of college rockers in the U.S.

AUTOGRAPHS

A CD, LP, magazine cover, ad, photo, or card signed by the group: $5-$10

The Emotions

Formed 1968

Wanda Hutchinson, Sheila Hutchinson, and Jeanette Hutchinson*

*Theresa Davis was added in 1970. Jeanette departed in 1977 and returned, while Pamela Hutchinson was added.

The Emotions, a late-70s, Chicago family soul group, commonly associated with the hits "I Don't Wanna Lose Your Love" (#51, 1976), the Grammy winning "Best of My Love" (#1, 1976), "Don't Ask My Neighbors" (#44, 1977), and "Smile" (#6, R&B, 1978), toured with numerous prominent artists including the Jackson 5, B.B. King, and Stevie Wonder. The group gave up recording in the mid-80s following its album *New Affair* (1981).

AUTOGRAPHS

A CD, LP, magazine cover, ad, photo, or card signed by the group: $10-$25*
*Grammy related piece

OFTEN OVERLOOKED MEMORABILIA

Memorabilia from the band before it became the Emotions

The English Beat

Formed 1978

Andy Cox, Born: January 25, 1956; Everett Morton, Born: April 5, 1951; David Steele, Born: September 8, 1960; and Dave Wakeling, Born: February 19, 1956*

*Ranking Roger and Saxa were added in 1979. Wakeling and Roger became General Public.

This late-70s British ska revival band is best remembered as a stopping point for its members who went on to form the Fine Young Cannibals and General Public. The group scored singles with a remake of "Tears of a Clown," followed by "Hands Off... She's Mine," "Mirror in the Bathroom," "Best Friend," "Too Nice to Talk To" (#7, 1981), "Drowning," and "Doors to Your Heart." The group broke up shortly after its first album, *Special Beat Service* (#39, 1982), became its first to sell well in America.

AUTOGRAPHS

A CD, LP, magazine cover, ad, photo, or card signed by the group: $10-$20

POSTERS/PRESS KITS

Promotional Posters: $10-$12
Press Kits: $12

Eno, Brian

Born: May 15, 1948

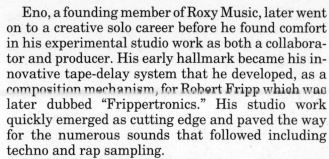

Eno, a founding member of Roxy Music, later went on to a creative solo career before he found comfort in his experimental studio work as both a collaborator and producer. His early hallmark became his innovative tape-delay system that he developed, as a composition mechanism, for Robert Fripp which was later dubbed "Frippertronics." His studio work quickly emerged as cutting edge and paved the way for the numerous sounds that followed including techno and rap sampling.

In 1975 his Obscure Records became a haven for creativity. Eno collaborated on some of the most innovative and promising recordings of the decade including *Evening Star* with Robert Fripp and *Low*, "Heroes" and *Lodger* with David Bowie. He also worked with the Talking Heads, Ultravox, Devo, and even a no-wave compilation.

Another creative outlet for the artist became ambient music albums, such as *Discreet Music* and *Music for Airports*. The end of the decade found his collaborations with Daniel Lanois bearing fruit, especially his work with Eno's brother Roger on *Voices* and later on a project with minimalist Harold Budd. The imaginative results led to a successful repackaging of the group U2 on its albums *The Unforgettable Fire* and *The Joshua Tree*. Eno later directed the band to a heavier, more industrial feel on *Achtung Baby* and *Zooropa*.

In the '90s, Eno remains a significant player in an industry that has relatively few, especially over the long haul. Eno has thought and rethought his creativity, and has simplified the complex while often overriding preparation with spontaneity.

AUTOGRAPHS

A CD, LP, magazine cover, ad, photo, or card signed by the artist: $20-$45

OFTEN OVERLOOKED MEMORABILIA

Associated artifacts from his numerous productions

En Vogue

Formed 1988

Cindy Herron, Born: September 26, 1965; Maxine Jones, Born: January 16, 1966; Terry Ellis, Born: September 5, 1966; and Dawn Robinson, Born: November 28, 1968

En Vogue, the successful early '90s R&B girl group, was hand-picked by Bay Area producers for a specific look, feel, and sound. The group scored with its debut album *Born to Sing* (#21, 1990) that included their smash extract "Hold On" (#2, 1990). The band's exposure was then enhanced through a tour with Freddie Jackson and Hammer and a Grammy Nomination.

Funky Divas (#8, 1992), the band's sophomore effort, yielded two smash extracts, "My Lovin' (You're Never Gonna Get It)" (#2, 1992) and "Free Your

Mind" (#8, 1992). The album solidified En Vogue's essence as visually exciting, sensually stimulating, and formidably chic. The group's ability to share the spotlight has also worked successfully toward its longevity.

AUTOGRAPHS

A CD, LP, magazine cover, ad, photo, or card signed by the group: $25-$50

Enya

(Eithne Ni Bhraonain)
Born: May 17, 1961

Enya is the daughter of showband leader Lee O. Bhraonain. Classically trained in piano at an early age, and inspired by her mother Maira who is a music teacher, she joined her relatives band Clannad in 1980. The experience and the urging of others pushed her to embark on a solo career. The first targeted audience was film producers; lyricist Roma Ryan helped by distributing Enya's work. David Puttnam became the first to use her work in his 1985 feature *The Frog Prince*. Memorabilia from this movie is a good place to begin your collecting.

Her first major work was a 70-minute soundtrack to the BBC television series *The Celts*, which was renamed *Enya* (#69, U.K., Atlantic) and released in the summer of 1987. (This work eventually reverted back to *The Celts* in a 1992 reissue.) Her unique sound blended elements of classical and traditional Irish folk music with her ethereal voice. The result was a New Age sound.

Her second album, *Watermark* (#5, U.K., 1988), spun off the successful singles "Orinoco Flow" (#1, U.K.) and "Evening Falls" (#20, U.K.). The work was well received by the public and was a fine example of the partnership she created with producer Nicky Ryan and lyricist Roma Ryan. *Watermark* (#25, U.S., Geffen) hit the U.S. chart in February 1989, where "Orinoco Flow (Sail Away)" peaked on the singles chart at #24. Music from the album also found its way to the cinema, and appeared in *L.A. Story* and *Green Card*.

On November 16, 1991, her third album, *Shepherd Moons* (#17, 1992, Reprise), debuted at the top of the U.K. chart. "Book of Days," a cut from the album, found its way into the movie *Far and Away*. The album earned her the Best New Age Album category at the 35th annual Grammy Awards.

The Memory of Trees (#5, U.K., 1995, Reprise) picked up where *Shepherd Moons* left off. Enya now has estimated worldwide sales approaching 20 million.

AUTOGRAPHS

A CD, LP, magazine cover, ad, photo, or card signed by the artist: $20-$55

POSTERS/PRESS KITS

Promotional Posters: $10-$40
Press Kits: $15-$30

OFTEN OVERLOOKED MEMORABILIA

Memory of Trees counter display - $20; The Celts banner - $15; Shepherd Moons cover display - $25

EPMD

Formed 1986

Erick Sermon and Parrish Smith

EPMD, the Long Island monetary driven hip-hop act, which landed first on the R&B charts with "You Gots to Chill" (#22, 1988), "Strictly Business" (#25, 1988), "Gold Digger" (#14, 1991), "Rampage" (#30, 1992), and "Crossover" (#42, pop, 1992), became successful in its agenda. The two called it quits in 1993 when they each released solo efforts.

AUTOGRAPHS

A CD, LP, magazine cover, ad, photo, or card signed by the group: $10-$15

Erasure

Formed 1985

Vince Clarke, Born: July 3, 1960; and Andy Bell, Born: April 24, 1964

This late-80s techno-pop British duo is best known for its U.K. chart topping album *The Innocents* (#1, U.K., 1988) and its hit extracts "Chains of Love" (#12, 1988) and "A Little Respect" (#14, 1988), both of which brought the band into the U.S. spotlight. Unfortunately the band couldn't sustain its American presence, but delivered three more successive U.K. chart-topping albums.

AUTOGRAPHS

A CD, LP, magazine cover, ad, photo, or card signed by the group: $10-$20

TOUR BOOKS/PROGRAMS/PASSES

Programs:
Phantasmagorical: $15

POSTERS/PRESS KITS

Promotional Posters: $15-$25
Press Kits: $15

OFTEN OVERLOOKED MEMORABILIA

All of Clarke's Yazoo artifacts; pizza box form Chorus promotional CD, 1991; Wild Mute promotional box set includes LP, CD, Cassette, stickers, postcard, photo, press sheet, and lyric book, 1989; Chorus Software Installation Guide User Manual, Sire promotional hardback book that has a hidden compartment with CD and Cassette, 1991 (also "E" logo dust cover)

Eric B. and Rakim

Formed 1985

Eric. B. (Barrier) and Rakim (William Griffin Jr.)

These acclaimed late-80s New York rappers, best known for their legal conflicts with James Brown over sampling and their numerous R&B hits including "I Ain't No Joke" (#38, R&B, 1987) and "What's on Your Mind?" (#34, R&B, 1991)—the latter was the theme to *House Party 2*—broke up in 1992.

AUTOGRAPHS

A CD, LP, magazine cover, ad, photo, or card signed by the group: $10-$15

OFTEN OVERLOOKED MEMORABILIA

A copy of legal documents associated with their cases involving sampling; movie memorabilia from *House Party 2* (1991)

Erickson, Roky/13th Floor Elevators

(Roger K. Erickson)
Born: July 15, 1947

This mid-60s psychedelic pop group is best remembered for its hit "You're Gonna Miss Me" (#56, 1966) and the erratic singing, songwriting, and performing of cult figure Roky Erickson. Erickson's life is nothing short of a made-for TV movie, complete with ridiculous legal interaction, electroshock therapy, and claims of UFO possession. Through the years Erickson's cult status has grown significantly, enhanced by projects such as the album *Where the Pyramid Meets the Eye: A Tribute to Roky Erickson*, which included contributions from R.E.M., ZZ Top, and the Butthole Surfers. If you've never listened to it, it is well worth checking out from your local public library.

AUTOGRAPHS

A CD, LP, magazine cover, ad, photo, or card signed by the group: $15-$30*
*An intriguing item to a select crowd.

OFTEN OVERLOOKED MEMORABILIA

Any and all artifacts associated with the Elevators; a videotape of his brief performance at the Austin Music Awards in 1993.

REFERENCE BOOKS

Roky, or friends thereof, tell him I want to write his biography!

Esquerita

Esquerita, the pompadoured, pre-Little Richard, pumping pianist performer of the '50s, is best remem-

bered for his songs "Oh, Baby," "Rockin' the Joint," "I Need You," "Batty over Hattie," and "Esquerita Voola." He also penned Jim Lowe's 1956 #1 hit "The Green Door." He died in New York City in 1986.

Essex, David

(David Cook)
Born: July 23, 1947

This mid-70s British pop star and teen idol, who scored numerous U.K. hits including "Lamplight," "Gonna Make You a Star," "Hold Me Close," and "Rock On," the latter of which is best known in America, later turned his attention toward acting in both film and theater.

AUTOGRAPHS

A CD, LP, magazine cover, ad, photo or card signed by the artist: $10-$25

OFTEN OVERLOOKED MEMORABILIA

Movie memorabilia from *That'll be the Day* (1973), *Stardust* (1975), *Silver Dream Machine*, and *Child Byron*; artifacts from the theater productions he was involved in including *Evita* (1978), *Mutiny*, *The Fantastiks*, and *Godspell* (1971)

REFERENCES/BOOKS

A couple resources exist, but nothing that does justice to the singer in my opinion; no dedicated collector books

Estefan, Gloria

(Gloria Fajardo)
Born: September 1, 1957

Miami Sound Machine formed 1975

Estefan, the '80s Hispanic-rooted pop star, gained popularity first in Latin markets in the U.S. with Miami Sound Machine before crossing over to the dance market. *Primitive Love* (#21, 1985) was the band's first all-English album; it went double platinum and yielded the smash extracts "Conga" (#10, 1986), "Bad Boy" (#8, 1986), and "Words Get in the Way" (#5, 1986).

The band then changed its billing to Gloria Estefan and the Miami Sound Machine for *Let It Loose* (#6, 1987), its next album. It spun off four Top Ten hits: "Rhythm Is Gonna Get You" (#5, 1987), "Can't Stay Away from You" (#6, 1988), "Anything for You" (#1, 1988), and "1-2-3" (#3,1988). Estefan then departed for a solo career.

Cuts Both Ways (#8, 1989), her debut solo album, yielded the successful hits "Don't Wanna Lose You" (#1, 1989) and "Here We Are" (#6, 1989). Tragedy struck shortly thereafter when the tour bus she was traveling in was struck by a tractor-trailer (3/20/

90)—one of the singer's vertebrae broke. Fortunately she survived; she returned to her music with the introspective "Coming Out of the Dark" (#1, 1991), and the hits "Can't Forget You" (#43, 1991), and "Live for Loving You" (#22, 1991).

In 1993 she moved more toward her Latin roots with her album *Mi Tierra* (#27, 1993). The following year, *Hold Me, Thrill Me, Kiss Me* yielded the hit "Turn the Beat Around" (#13, 1994).

AUTOGRAPHS
A CD, LP, magazine cover, ad, photo, or card signed by the group: $20-$45

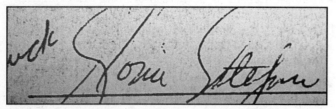

Signature of Gloria Estefan

POSTERS/PRESS KITS
Promotional Posters: $10-$25
Press Kits: $15-$30

OFTEN OVERLOOKED MEMORABILIA
Christmas Through Your Eyes promotional hanging banner: $50

REFERENCES/BOOKS
Numerous resources exist; no dedicated collector books

A Gloria Estefan backstage pass (Printed by Perri)

Estes, Sleepy John

(1903-1977)

This early blues pioneer, who moved to Chicago in the '30s, teamed up with harmonica player Hammie Nixon. The two worked as a street musicians and performed such songs as "Someday Baby" and "Drop, Down, Mama," both of which Estes and Nixon would record on the Bluebird label during the '40s. Estes remained in obscurity until the late '50s when filmmaker Ralph Blumenthal uncovered his abilities. The performer then recorded on Delmark, toured Europe, and even played at the 1964 Newport Folk Festival. Both Mike Bloomfield and Ry Cooder played with "Sleepy" during recording sessions, and the band Joy of Cooking later had a minor hit with "Going to Brownsville" (1971).

AUTOGRAPHS
A CD, LP, magazine cover, ad, photo, or card signed by the artist: $25-$45

OFTEN OVERLOOKED MEMORABILIA
Memorabilia from the 1964 Newport Folk Festival; a copy of the documentary Blumenthal was shooting when he discovered Estes; associated memorabilia from musicians who covered his material

Etheridge, Melissa

Born: May 29, 1961

Etheridge, the raspy-voiced singer/songwriter best known for her hard luck love songs and fervent guitar playing, was spotted in an L.A. club—she was offered a recording contract with Island Records. In 1988 she released her eponymous debut, which yielded two interesting and well-received singles, "Bring Me Some Water" and "Like the Way I Do." Her third album, *Never Enough* (1992), produced the song "Ain't It Heavy," which, although failing to make a major chart appearance, won her a Grammy for Best Rock Vocal Performance Female.

The stage was then set for her next album, *Yes I Am* (#16, 1993), which thrust her into the spotlight with the hit singles "Come to My Window" (#25, 1994), "I'm the Only One" (#11, 1994), and "If I Wanted To" b/w "Like the Way I Do" (#16, 1995). Etheridge has firmly established herself as a leading player in music's future.

AUTOGRAPHS
A CD, LP, magazine cover, ad, photo, or card signed by the artist: $10-$30

TOUR BOOKS/PROGRAMS/PASSES
Tour Books:
Yes I Am, 1995: $15
Your Little Secret: $12
Backstage Passes:
Cloth: $8-$12; Laminated: $15

POSTERS/PRESS KITS
Promotional Posters: $10-$18
Press Kits: $15-$20

USED CLOTHING/EQUIPMENT
Guitar Picks: $15-$25

OFTEN OVERLOOKED MEMORABILIA
Movie memorabilia from *Weeds*

REFERENCES/BOOKS
Few resources exist; no dedicated collector books; serious collectors should opt for fan club: Melissa Etheridge Information Network, P.O. Box 884563, San Francisco, CA 94188 ($19 fee)

Eurythmics

Formed 1980

Annie Lennox, Born: December 25, 1954; and Dave Stewart, Born: September 9, 1952

This premier '80s British synth-pop band, driven by Stewart's powerful studio wizardry combined with Lennox's theatrical imagery and haunting vocals, set a new musical agenda with hits songs such as "Sweet Dreams (Are Made of This)" (#15, 1983), "Here Comes the Rain Again" (#4, 1984), "Sisters Are Doin' It for Themselves" (#18, 1985), a duet with Aretha Franklin, and "Missionary Man" (#14, 1986).

The '90s have found both artists pursuing solo careers and alternative projects such as producing or recording film soundtracks. Lennox's solo records have included *Diva* (#23, 1992) and *Medusa* (#11, 1995), both of which sold well. Stewart, on the other hand, became a Spiritual Cowboy, scored the film *Lily Was Here*, and produced records for Daryl Hall, Mick Jagger, and Bob Dylan. Many critics consider Stewart a leading force in studio craftsmanship and creativity.

AUTOGRAPHS

A CD, LP, magazine cover, ad, photo, or card signed by the group: $50-$100

TOUR BOOKS/ PROGRAMS/PASSES

Programs:
The Revenge Tour (1986): $25
Touch Tour (U.K.): $25
Backstage Passes:
Cloth: $8-$12;
Laminated: $15

POSTERS/PRESS KITS

Promotional Posters: $10-$20
Press Kits: $15-$30

USED CLOTHING/ EQUIPMENT

Guitar Picks: $15-$25

OFTEN OVERLOOKED MEMORABILIA

Movie memorabilia from *Weeds* and *Here Comes The Rain Again*; RCA promotional Umbrella, 1984; Live 83-89 counter display - $15; all memorabilia relating to the Tourists (1979-80) - they produced three albums

REFERENCES/BOOKS

Numerous resources exist; no dedicated collector books

Outstanding Eurythmics "Touch Tour" program (Art & design by Laurence Stevens)

Everett, Betty

Born: November 23, 1939

Everett, the '60s soul/pop diva who landed hits with "The Shoop Shoop Song (It's in His Kiss)" (#6, 1964), "Let It Be Me" (#5, 1964), a duet with Jerry Butler, "You're No Good," "I Can't Hear You," "Getting Mighty Crowded," and "Smile," later moved on to more soul-related material.

AUTOGRAPHS

A CD, LP, magazine cover, ad, photo, or card signed by the artist: $10-$20

Everly Brothers

Don Everly, Born: February 1, 1937; and Phil Everly, Born: January 19, 1939

The Everly Brothers, the most influential duo in rock history, whose expressive country harmonies combined eloquently over a rock beat, inspired all who followed. The two established themselves with "Bye Bye Love" (#2, 1957), and from this point onward, the hits flowed like a mountain stream during a springtime rain. The group's #1 hits included "Wake Up Little Susie," "All I Have to Do Is Dream," "Cathy's Clown," and "Bird Dog." At one point the two were even averaging three Top Ten hits per year. The streak came to a halt in June 1962 with "That's Old Fashioned" (#9, 1962).

The brothers continued to be popular in Europe, while they still landed sporadic hits in America such as "Bowling Green" (#40, 1967) and "On the Wings of a Nightingale" (#50, 1984), which Paul McCartney wrote. The duo was inducted into the Rock and Roll Hall of Fame in 1986.

AUTOGRAPHS

A CD, LP, magazine cover, ad, photo, or card signed by the group: $40-$80

OFTEN OVERLOOKED MEMORABILIA

Memorabilia associated with other musicians covers of their material; videotapes of their summer television show on CBS; any and all memorabilia associated with the duo's gig at the John Wayne Theater in Knott's Berry Farm (Buena Park, CA) on July 14, 1973, in which Phil smashed his guitar and bolted offstage, leaving Don to announce the duo's difficult decision to split; all memorabilia associated with the video documentary *Reunion Concert* (1983); wedding memorabilia (you know, matches and stuff) from Don's daughter's marriage to Axl Rose (Guns 'n' Roses)

Beautiful and historical Everly Brother "Reunion" tour program (Delilah Com., Ltd.)

REFERENCES/BOOKS

Numerous resources exist; no dedicated collector books; serious collectors should opt for fan clubs: Everly Brothers Foundation, P.O. Box 309, Central City, KY 42330 and The Fun Club for Fans of the Everly Brothers, P.O. Box 3933, Seattle, WA 98124 ($15 for six issues)

Everything But the Girl

Formed 1981

Tracey Thorn and Ben Watt

This '80s-crafted pop duo is best known earlier for its cover "I Don't Want to Talk About It" (#3, U.K., 1988) and the popular single "Driving" from *The Language of Life* (#77, 1990) album. Their single "Missing" (#69, 1994, U.K.), later radically remixed (#3, 1995, U.K.), has been the group's hallmark thus far in the '90s.

AUTOGRAPHS
A CD, LP, magazine cover, ad, photo, or card signed by the group: $10-$25

POSTERS/PRESS KITS
Promotional Posters: $8-$20
Press Kits: $10-$20

Exposé

Formed 1986

Jeanette Jurado, Ann Curless, and Gioia Bruno*

*Bruno departed in 1992 and Kelly Moneymaker was added

Exposé, the late-80s strategically crafted marketing group, overseen by masterful Miami music maven Lewis Martinee, has had two distinct lineups, the latter of which was the most successful. The group broke all records with its landmark debut album *Exposure* (#16, 1987), which spun off the four Top Ten singles "Come Go with Me" (#5, 1987), "Point of No Return" (#5, 1987), "Let Me Be the One" (#7, 1987), and "Seasons Change" (#1, 1987).

What You Don't Know (#33, 1989) was the group's successful follow-up and included the hit extracts "What You Don't Know" (#8,1989), "Tell Me Why" (#9, 1989), "When I Looked at Him" (#10, 1989), and "Your Baby Never Looked Good in Blue" (#17, 1990).

For its third album, the group broke from Martinee, replaced Bruno with Kelly Moneymaker—due to throat problems—and linked up with hit maker Diane Warren. The eponymous album yielded the hit "I'll Never Get Over You (Getting Over Me)" (#8, 1993).

AUTOGRAPHS
An LP, magazine cover, ad, photo, or card signed by the group: $25-$60*

*Original lineup on debut album

POSTERS/PRESS KITS
Promotional Posters: $10-$20
Press Kits: $10-$20

Extreme

Formed 1985

Par Badger, Nuno Bettencourt, Gary Cherone, and Paul Geary

These '90s "Beantown" bashers, ironically known more for ballads than blistering Bettencourt guitar compositions, built a strong local following before it landed with A&M Records in 1987. The group's debut stalled, but its second album, *Pornograffitti*, yielded the two hit ballads "More Than Words" (#1, 1991) and "Hole Hearted" (#4, 1991). While both songs thrust the group into the mainstream, it kept its metal juices flowing by touring with ZZ Top.

The group followed with the ambitious albums *III Side* (#10, 1992) and *Waiting for the Punchline*, both of which exhibited the dynamic range of the group. Cherone's name surfaced in 1996 as a possible replacement for Sammy Hagar in Van Halen.

AUTOGRAPHS
A CD, LP, magazine cover, ad, photo, or card signed by the group: $15-$40

TOUR BOOKS/PROGRAMS/PASSES
Programs:
III Sides Tour program: $6-$10
Backstage Passes:
Cloth: $5-$8; Laminated: $10

POSTERS/PRESS KITS
Promotional Posters: $10-$30
Press Kits: $10-$15

USED CLOTHING/EQUIPMENT
Guitar Picks:
Par Badger: $15-$20
Nuno Bettencourt: $15-$50
Drum Sticks:
Paul Geary: $15-$20

OFTEN OVERLOOKED MEMORABILIA
Waiting for the Punchline promotional stickers (6): $10

Fabian

(Fabiano Forte)
Born: February 6, 1943

Fabian, the late-50s Philadelphia teen idol, is best remembered for his hits "Turn Me Loose" (#9, 1959), "Tiger" (#3, 1959), and "Hound Dog Man" (#9,1959).

He then moved on to acting in both film and television, television production, and performing at oldies shows.

AUTOGRAPHS
A CD, LP, magazine cover, ad, photo, or card signed by the artist: $5-$20

OFTEN OVERLOOKED MEMORABILIA
Movie memorabilia from *Hound Dog Man* (1959), *North to Alaska* (1960), and *Fireball 500* (1966); videotapes of his

numerous television appearances including *Laverne and Shirley* and *Blossom*; fanzines and periodicals; volunteer items associated with his work for Governor Jerry Brown (CA); trading cards (Topps) (set of 55) - $100

The Fabulous Thunderbirds

Formed 1974

Jimmie Vaughan, Born: March 20, 1951; Kim Wilson, Born: January 6, 1951; Keith Ferguson, Born: July 23, 1946; and Mike Buck, Born: June 1, 1952

These '80s Austin "no frills" blues mavens, founded by Jimmie Vaughan (Stevie Ray's older brother), built a substantial following through extensive touring, particularly in the South. The T-birds went through numerous personnel changes before the group landed with Columbia Records and scored with the Top Ten hit single "Tuff Enuff." The band also toured with the Rolling Stones and Santana, which bolstered its exposure and helped the album *Hot Number* (#49, 1987) drive up the chart. By the late '80s only Vaughan and Wilson remained; the former then chose to go on and record with his brother.

AUTOGRAPHS

A CD, LP, magazine cover, ad, photo, or card signed by the group: $25-$45

POSTERS/PRESS KITS

Promotional Posters: $15-$40
Press Kits: $25-$30

USED CLOTHING/EQUIPMENT

Guitar Picks:
Jimmie Vaughan: $35-$60

OFTEN OVERLOOKED MEMORABILIA

Any and all items relating to Stevie Ray Vaughan

Fagen, Donald: See Steely Dan

Fairport Convention/Fairport

Formed 1967

Judy Dyble; Richard Thompson, Born: April 3, 1949; Simon Nicol; Ashley "Tyger" Hutchings; Martin Lamble; and Iain Matthews (Ian MacDonald)*

*Numerous personnel changes. Musicians included Sandy Denny, Dave Swarbrick, Dave Mattacks, Dave Pegg, Roger Hill, Tom Farnell, David Rea, Trevor Lucas, Jerry Donahue, Paul Warren, Bruce Rowland, Martin Allcock, and Ric Sanders.

Fairport Convention, the eclectic and electric surviving pioneers of British folk-rock, has also become known for its alumni, many of whom have gone on to more fruitful opportunities.

AUTOGRAPHS

A CD, LP, magazine cover, ad, photo, or card signed by the group: $15-$40*
*Varies depending upon lineup

TOUR BOOKS/PROGRAMS/PASSES

Programs:
1988 Red & Gold Tour: $20

Fairweather-Low, Andy: See Amen Corner

Faith, Adam

(Terry Nelhams)
Born: June 23, 1940

This early-60s British teen idol, best remembered for his U.K. hits "What Do You Want" (#1, 1959), "Poor Me" (#1, 1960), "Someone Else's Baby" (#2, 1960)," and "Lonely Puppy" (#4, 1960), was yet another singer who turned his attention toward acting. He later became the manager and producer for Leo Sayer, who ended up in litigation with Faith over royalties.

AUTOGRAPHS

A CD, LP, magazine cover, ad, photo, or card signed by the artist: $10-$30

OFTEN OVERLOOKED MEMORABILIA

Movie memorabilia from *Beat Girl* (1962); videotapes of his numerous television show appearances including *Drumbeat* (1959) and *Budgie*; periodical clippings relating to his legal battles with Leo Sayer; artifacts from his numerous production opportunities

REFERENCE BOOKS

Poor Me, his autobiography; a couple resources exist but were published in the 1960s; no dedicated collector books

Faith No More

Formed 1982

Chuck Mosely; James "Jim" Martin, Born: July 21, 1961; Roddy Bottum, Born: July 1, 1963; Billy Gould, Born: April 23, 1963; Michael Bordin, Born: November 27, 1962*

*Mosely left in 1988, Michael Patton joined in 1989, Dean Menta replaced Martin in 1994

The late-80s thrash punk-funk and cover band Faith No More is commonly associated with its album *The Real Thing* (#11, 1990) and hit extract "Epic" (#9, 1990).

Faith No More backstage pass from the Summer 1992 Stadium Tour (Printed by OTTO)

AUTOGRAPHS
A CD, LP, magazine cover, ad, photo, or card signed by the group: $10-$15*
*1990 lineup.

POSTERS/PRESS KITS
Promotional Posters: $10-$15
Press Kits: $10

USED CLOTHING/EQUIPMENT
Guitar Picks: $10

OFTEN OVERLOOKED MEMORABILIA
Movie memorabilia from *Bill & Ted's Bogus Journey* and *Four Live from Five Fat Bastards*; Slash promotional CD package that includes rubber fish wrapped in newspaper, 1990

REFERENCES/BOOKS
A couple resources exist, but nothing that does justice to the band in my opinion; no dedicated collector books

Faithfull, Marianne

Born: December 29, 1946

Faithfull, the mid-60s British pop sweetheart, is best remembered for her hits "As Tears Go By" (#22, 1964), "Come and Stay with Me" (#26, 1965), "This Little Bird' (#32, 1965), and "Summer Nights" (#24, 1965) and for being Mick Jagger's girlfriend. She also garnered substantial press over her substance abuse problems. She later turned to acting and the theater.

AUTOGRAPHS
A CD, LP, magazine cover, ad, photo, or card signed by the artist: $5-$15

OFTEN OVERLOOKED MEMORABILIA
Movie memorabilia from *Ned Kelly*, *The Girl on the Motorcycle*, *Turn of the Screw*, and *Shopping*; her theater work in *Three Sisters*, *Hamlet*, *Seven Deadly Sins*, and *Threepenny Opera*; copies of the numerous fanzines and periodicals that have covered her career

REFERENCE BOOKS
Faithfull, her autobiography, written with David Dalton, 1994; *Marianne Faithfull: As Tears Go By* by Mark Hodkinson; no dedicated collector books

Falco

(Johann Holzel)
Born: February 19, 1957

Falco, the late-80s Austrian techno-pop guru is internationally known for two songs: "Der Kommissar" (1983) and "Rock Me Amadeus" (1986).

AUTOGRAPHS
A CD, LP, magazine cover, ad, photo, or card signed by the artist: $5-$10

The Fall

Formed 1977

Mark E. Smith, Born: March 5, 1957; Martin Bramah; Una Baines; Tony Friel; and Karl Burns*

*Numerous personnel changes

This prolific late-70s punk-rock group's common denominator has been Mark E. Smith, a British white rapper of sorts who refuses to be forgotten. The band, well-known for its longevity and large cult following, has given us the anthemic "Totally Wired" and a Kink's cover ("Victoria"). Although these are the two songs most commonly associated with the band, there have been numerous compositions since 1977.

AUTOGRAPHS
A CD, LP, magazine cover, ad, photo, or card signed by the artist: $10-$20

Fame, Georgie

(Clive Powell)
Born: June 26, 1943

Georgie Fame, the late-60s British keyboardist, is best known for his songs "Yeh Yeh" (#1, U.K., 1965), "Get Away" (#1, U.K., 1966), "The Ballad of Bonnie and Clyde" (#7, 1968) and "Rosetta" (#11, U.K., 1971) (with Alan Price). He later wrote for the stage and produced musical tributes.

AUTOGRAPHS
A CD, LP, magazine cover, ad, photo, or card signed by the artist: $5-$10

Family

Formed 1967

Roger Chapman, Born: August 8, 1944; Rob Townsend, Born: July 7, 1947; Rick Grech, Born: November 1, 1946; Jim King; and Charlie Whitney, Born: June 4, 1944*

*Numerous personnel changes

The late-60s British progressive rock group Family is best remembered as a stepping stone for Blind Faith member Rick Grech who quit after two albums, for its (Chapman's) historic fistfight with promoter Bill Graham, and for the U.K. singles "In My Own Time" (#4, 1971) and "Burlesque" (#13, 1972). Despite exposure, including a 1972 tour with Elton John, the band failed to find a U.S. audience.

AUTOGRAPHS

A CD, LP, magazine cover, ad, photo, or card signed by the group: $20-$35*

*Original lineup

OFTEN OVERLOOKED MEMORABILIA

Movie memorabilia from *Stomping Ground*; all items associated with the group's U.S. debut at the Fillmore East that resulted in the fistfight with Graham

Fanny

Formed 1970

June Millington, Alice de Buhr, Addie Clement, and Jean Millington*

*Clement left in 1970 and Nicole Barclay was added. June Millington and de Buhr left in 1974 and Patti Quarto and Brie Brandt-Howard joined the band.

Bona-fide early-70s all-female rock and roll group, the Sveltes were spotted playing L.A.'s Troubadour and signed to Warner Brothers Records as Fanny. The band is best remembered for its songs "Charity Ball" and "Butter Boy" and albums *Fanny Hill* (1972) and *Mother's Pride* (1973). The group also backed Barbra Streisand on her *Stoney End* LP (1970).

AUTOGRAPHS

A CD, LP, magazine cover, ad, photo, or card signed by the group: $10-$15

Farina, Richard and Mimi

Richard Farina and Mimi Farina (Baez)

This mid-60s husband and wife folk act was successful at melding folk with rock rhythms on its Vanguard albums before Richard was tragically killed in a motorcycle accident on April 30, 1966. Mimi, whose sister is Joan Baez, has remained active in humanitarian issues, while making an occasional rare stage appearance.

AUTOGRAPHS

A CD, LP, magazine cover, ad, photo, or card signed by the duo: $15-$20

OFTEN OVERLOOKED MEMORABILIA

Richard Farina's literary works

REFERENCE BOOKS

Been Down So Long It Looks Like Up to Me by Richard Farina

Farlowe, Chris

(John Deighton)
Born: October 13, 1940

Farlowe, the early-60s British R&B singer and guitarist, is best remembered for his cover hit "Out of Time" (#1, 1966) and for the numerous musicians he played with in a variety of bands including Carl Palmer, Albert Lee, Pete Solley, and Dave Greenslade. He later attempted unsuccessful comebacks while owning and operating his Nazi war memorabilia shop in London.

AUTOGRAPHS

A CD, LP, magazine cover, ad, photo, or card signed by the artist: $5-$10

OFTEN OVERLOOKED MEMORABILIA

Adverts from his store; artifacts from his numerous musical contributions on other artists' records

Feathers, Charlie

Born: June 12, 1932

Legendary Mississippi rockabilly pioneer, best remembered for cowriting Elvis Presley's "I Forgot to Remember to Forget" (#1, C&W, 1955) and singles "I've Been Deceived," "Tongue-Tied Jill," and "Get With It," Charlie Feathers was a regular along local roadhouses and even earned a gig at London's Rainbow Theatre in 1977.

AUTOGRAPHS

A CD, LP, magazine cover, ad, photo, or card signed by the artist: $15-$35

The Feelies

Formed 1976

Bill Million (Clayton), Glenn Mercer, John J., and Dave Weckerman*

*Numerous personnel changes

The Feelies, the late-70s New York postpunk band that shunned a commercial recording contract in favor of a sabbatical, returned years later to tackle the indie rock scene.

AUTOGRAPHS

A CD, LP, magazine cover, ad, photo, or card signed by the group: $8-$16

OFTEN OVERLOOKED MEMORABILIA

Movie memorabilia from *Something Wild*

Feliciano, Jose

Born: September 10, 1945

Incredibly talented blind musician, and one of the finest guitarists I have ever had the opportunity to see, Jose Feliciano has won over an international audience through his flamenco-flavored arrangements on such hits as "Light My Fire" (#3, 1968). He also landed minor hits such as "Hi Heel Sneakers" and the theme to "Chico and the Man" (#96, 1974); he even created a controversial rendition of "The Star Spangled Banner" which he played at the 1968 World Series. A multiple Grammy winner, he has made numerous television appearances.

AUTOGRAPHS

A CD, LP, magazine cover, ad, photo, or card signed by the artist: $5-$20

OFTEN OVERLOOKED MEMORABILIA

Movie memorabilia from *MacKenna's Gold*; videotapes of his numerous television appearances including *Kung Fu* and *McMillan and Wife*; 1968 World Series memorabilia from the game at which he performed

REFERENCES/BOOKS

Limited resources; no dedicated collector books

Fender, Freddie

(Baldemar Huerta)
Born: June 4, 1937

This '70s country, conjunto, and Tex-Mex rocker, best known for his songs, "Before the Next Teardrop Falls" (#1, 1975), "Wasted Days and Wasted Nights" (#8, 1975), and "Secret Love" (#20, 1975), took part in more than 100 regional recordings. His music has spanned decades and included the influences of numerous musical forms.

AUTOGRAPHS

A CD, LP, magazine cover, ad, photo, or card signed by the artist: $7-$15

POSTERS/PRESS KITS

Promotional Posters: $10-$15
Press Kits: $12

USED CLOTHING/EQUIPMENT

Guitar Picks: $10-$15

OFTEN OVERLOOKED MEMORABILIA

Movie memorabilia from *Short Eyes* (1977) and *The Milagro Beanfield War* (1987)

Ferguson, Jay: See Spirit

Ferry, Bryan: See Roxy Music

The Fifth Dimension

Formed 1966
LaMonte McLemore, Born: September 17, 1940; Marilyn McCoo, Born: September 30, 1943; Ron Townson, Born: January 20, 1941; Florence LaRue Gordon, Born: February 4, 1944; and Billy Davis Jr., Born: June 26, 1940

One of the premier late-60s and early-70s pop-soul vocal acts, which was responsible for introducing the work of such talented songwriters as Jimmy Webb and Laura Nyro, was the Fifth Dimension. The group produced a series of successful hits that included "Up, Up and Away" (#7, 1967), "Stoned Soul Picnic" (#3, 1969), "Sweet Blindness" (#13, 1969), "Aquarius/Let the Sunshine In" (#1, 1969), a medley from the musical *Hair*, "Wedding Bell Blues" (#1, 1969), and later with "(Last Night) I Didn't Get to Sleep at All" (#8, 1972).

The band's popularity slowly diminished in the early '70s, and by mid-decade, McCoo and Davis, who were married, left the group and later landed on the charts with "You Don't Have to Be a Star" (#1, 1976) before they too split up. McCoo went on to host the television show *Solid Gold* while the remaining members of the band attempted an unsuccessful comeback.

AUTOGRAPHS

A CD, LP, magazine cover, ad, photo, or card signed by the group: $20-$60

POSTERS/PRESS KITS

Promotional Posters: $15-$60
Press Kits: $25-$50

OFTEN OVERLOOKED MEMORABILIA

Memorabilia from members individual projects beyond the group; early artifacts from the Hi-Fi's and the Versatiles

Fin Boy Three: See the Specials

Finn, Tim: See Crowded House

Fine Young Cannibals

Formed 1983
Andy Cox, Born: January 25, 1956; David Steele, Born: September 8, 1960; and Roland Gift, Born: April 28, 1961

This mid-80s British pop band, made up of two former members of the band the English Beat and singer Roland Gift, combined numerous influences to produce its unique sound on hits "Good Thing" (#1, 1989), "She Drives Me Crazy" (#1, 1989), and "Don't

Look Back" (#11, 1989) before the band—primarily Gift—went on to film and theater work.

AUTOGRAPHS

A CD, LP, magazine cover, ad, photo, or card signed by the group: $5-$10

POSTERS/PRESS KITS

Promotional Posters: $10-$20
Press Kits: $15-$20

OFTEN OVERLOOKED MEMORABILIA

Movie memorabilia from *Tin Men*, *Sammy and Rosie Get Laid*, and *Scandal*; artifacts from Gift's numerous theater appearances

REFERENCES/BOOKS

Limited resources; no dedicated collector books

The Fireballs

Formed 1957

Chuck Tharp, Stan Lark, Eric Budd, George Tomsco, and Dan Trammell*

*Trammell left in 1959, while Tharp left in 1960 and was replaced by Jimmy Gilmer. Budd departed in 1962 and was replaced by Doug Roberts.

The Fireballs, an early-60s pop group, first scored with the instrumentals "Torquay" (#39, 1959) and "Bulldog" (#24, 1960), before it added vocalist Jimmy Gilmer and landed the hits "Quite a Party," the smash "Sugar Shack" (#1, 1963), and "Daisy Petal Pickin'" (#15, 1963). Shortly thereafter Gilmer went his own way. The Fireballs charted again in 1968 with "Bottle of Wine" (#9).

An In-House gold award for Jimmy Gilmer and the Fireballs' "Sugar Shack," 1963, valued at $500. From the Doug Leftwitch collection.

AUTOGRAPHS

A LP, magazine cover, ad, photo, or card signed by the group: $10-$30

Firefall

Formed 1974

Rick Roberts, Jock Bartley, Mark Andes, Larry Burnett, and Michael Clarke

Late-70s contemporary soft pop band, whose members provenance included the Byrds, Spirit, and numerous others, Firefall broke on the national scene with the hit "You Are the Woman" (#9, 1976), followed by "Just Remember I Love You" (#11, 1977), "Strange Way" (#11, 1978), "Headed For a Fall" (#35, 1980) and "Staying with It" (#37, 1981) before it faded away.

AUTOGRAPHS

A CD, LP, magazine cover, ad, photo, or card signed by the artist: $20-$45

TOUR BOOKS/PROGRAMS/PASSES

Backstage Passes:
Cloth/paper: $5-$10; Laminated: $10-$12 (Pre-1981)

POSTERS/PRESS KITS

Promotional Posters: $10-$25
Press Kits: $20-$30

Firehose: See Minutemen

The Firm: See Jimmy Page

First Edition: See Kenny Rogers

Fischer, Wild Man

Born: 1945

Vagabond, streetwalker, and former mental patient—Fischer is known most for his association with Frank Zappa, who produced *An Evening with Wild Man Fischer* in 1969. The record created a large cult following for Fischer, who then traveled the land seeking them. He later recorded *Wildmania* (1977) for his friends at Rhino Records, followed by *Pronounced Normal* (1981) and *Nothing Crazy* (1984). Little else is known about Fischer, who occasionally resurfaces during a sighting, similar to Syd Barrett and the Loch Ness Monster.

AUTOGRAPHS

A CD, LP, magazine cover, ad, photo, or card signed by the artist: $5-$20

OFTEN OVERLOOKED MEMORABILIA

Artifacts from his affiliation with Rhino and Zappa

Fishbone

Formed 1980s

John "Norwood" Fisher, Phillip Dwight "Fish" Fisher, Kendall Rey Jones, Angelo Christopher Moore, Christopher Gordon Dowd, and Walter Adam Kibby II*

*John Bigham was added in 1990 and Jones departed in 1993

This late-80s Southern California metal menagerie band is hell-bent on proving a point, except no one is quite sure what it is. Fishbone, formerly Hot Ice, Megatron, and Counterattack, has backed Little Richard, mangled Christmas carols on its *It's a Wonderful Life (Gonna Have a Good Time)* EP, and even backed Annette Funicello in the film *Back to the Beach*.

The group won over a legion of alt-rock fans with the album *The Reality of My Surroundings* (1991) which included favorites such as "Everyday Sunshine" and "Sunless Saturday," the latter complemented by a Spike Lee-directed promotional video.

The band, which surprisingly garners little airplay, relies on its high-energy live shows to build its following. A stint on the main stage at Lollapalooza '93 helped bolster the act's exposure. Later Jones called it a day after denouncing the band as demonic.

AUTOGRAPHS
A CD, LP, magazine cover, ad, photo, or card signed by the group: $10-$25

OFTEN OVERLOOKED MEMORABILIA
Movie memorabilia from *Back to the Beach*; newspaper and periodical clippings concerning Fisher's arrest for trying to kidnap Jones

The "5" Royales

Formed late 1940s

Johnny Tanner, Lowman Pauling (1927-1974), Clarence Pauling (Paul), Otto Jeffries, and William Samuels*

*Additional personnel included Obadiah Carter, Jimmy Moore, Johnny Holmes, and Eugene Tanner

The "5" Royales, the '50s R&B and pop group with deep gospel roots, are best remembered for two #1 R&B hits—"Baby Don't Do It" and "Help Me Somebody"—and later by "Dedicated to the One I Love" (#81, 1961), which was later a Top Five hit for the Shirelles and the Mamas and the Papas.

AUTOGRAPHS
A CD, LP, magazine cover, ad, photo, or card signed by the group: $20-$35

The Five Satins

Formed 1955

Original lineup: Fred Parris, Lou Peebles, Ed Martin, Stanley Dortch, and Jim Freeman*

*Numerous personnel changes

This popular doo-wop lineup of the '50s, which started out as the Scarlets before evolving into the Five Satins, was formed by Freddie Parris, who recorded his classic "In The Still of the Night" in the basement of a church on a two track recorder. The record was released in 1956 and later became a #24 hit and the group's hallmark. Other hits followed including "To the Isle" (#25, 1957), "Shadows," and "I'll Be Seeing You," but none captured the intensity of their predecessor. The band appeared on many of Dick Clark's road revues in the late '50s. The Five Satins later had a Top Forty R&B hit with "Everybody Stand Up and Clap Your Hands" in 1976 under the moniker the Black Satins.

AUTOGRAPHS
A CD, LP, magazine cover, ad, photo, or card signed by the group: $20-$55

OFTEN OVERLOOKED MEMORABILIA
Movie memorabilia from *Let the Good Times Roll* (1973) and *Been Down So Long It Looks Up To Me* (1970); associated memorabilia from the numerous musicians who have covered the group's songs

Flack, Roberta

Born: February 10, 1939

With over twenty-five years in the business, nearly all of which were highly successful, this soul, R&B, and pop singer has lent her golden voice to numerous memorable hits including "You've Gotta Friend" (#29, 1971), "Will You Love Me Tomorrow," "The First Time Ever I Saw Your Face" (#1, 1972), "Where Is the Love" (#5, 1972), "Killing Me Softly with His Song" (#1, 1973), "Feel Like Makin' Love" (#1, 1974), and "The Closer I Get to You" (#2, 1978) before the death of her close friend and duet partner, the talented Donny Hathaway.

In 1980 Flack returned, toured, and recorded with Peabo Bryson. Both later scored with "Tonight, I Celebrate My Love" (#16, 1983). In 1981 she scored her first soundtrack, *Bustin' Loose*, later followed by her hit "Making Love" (#13, 1982). In 1991, after some brief time off the charts, she returned with a duet sung with Maxi Priest: "Set the Night to Music" (#6, 1991).

AUTOGRAPHS
A CD, LP, magazine cover, ad, photo, or card signed by the artist: $15-$40

POSTERS/PRESS KITS
Promotional Posters: $15-$40
Press Kits: $15-$50

OFTEN OVERLOOKED MEMORABILIA
Movie memorabilia from *Play Misty for Me* (1972) and *Bustin' Loose* (1981); all items associated with her duets, particularly those with Donny Hathaway

A couple resources exist, but nothing that does justice to the singer in my opinion; no dedicated collector books

The Flamingos

Formed 1951

Original lineup: Earl Lewis, Zeke Carey, Jake Carey, Johnny Carter, Sollie McElroy (1933-1995), and Paul Wilson (1935-1988)*

*Numerous personnel changes. Group disbanded in 1956 and re-formed in 1957

One of South Side Chicago's premier vocal groups of the late '50s, The Flamingos are best remembered for their crossover hit "I Only Have Eyes for You" (#11. 1959), although the group had numerous minor hits including "I Was Such a Fool," "Nobody Love Me Like You," "Time Was," "Boogaloo Party," and "Buffalo Soldier."

AUTOGRAPHS

A LP, magazine cover, ad, photo, or card signed by the group: $25-$75

OFTEN OVERLOOKED MEMORABILIA

Associated artifacts from other musicians' covers of their work

The Flamin' Groovies

Formed 1965

Cyril Jordan, Roy Loney, George Alexander, and Tim Lynch*

*Numerous personnel changes

This mid-60s Bay Area survival band, which spent decades trying to get someone to notice its efforts, finally did in Europe, Australia, and New Zealand, where the band has remained popular. Commercial success, however, has eluded the group thus far in the U.S.

AUTOGRAPHS

A CD, LP, magazine cover, ad, photo, or card signed by the group: $10-$20

OFTEN OVERLOOKED MEMORABILIA

The Rockfield Session, Australia, 1989, (107 copies) includes Teenage Head comic

Flash and the Pan: See the Easybeats

The Flatlanders: See Joe Ely

Fleetwood Mac

Formed 1967

Original lineup: Peter Green (Greenbaum), Born: October 29, 1946; Mick Fleetwood, Born: June 24, 1947; John McVie, Born: November 26, 1945; and Jeremy Spencer, Born: July 4, 1948*

*Numerous personnel changes—see chart below

Fleetwood Mac has never fought transition. It has instead chosen to let time take its course. As a result, the band has evolved from a traditional blues band to a highly commercial and successful pop group. The only common denominator is the presence of both Mick Fleetwood and John McVie.

Born out of John Mayall's Bluesbreakers, Green and Fleetwood hooked up with both Jeremy Spencer and bassist Bob Brunning. Brunning was essentially sitting in until John McVie made his decision to join the band. The original group made its major debut at the Windsor Jazz & Blues Festival on August 12-13, 1967, where a successful performance netted the group a record contract. On November 3, 1967, the group released its first single, "I Believe My Time Ain't Long," billed as Peter Green's Fleetwood Mac. The group's debut album *Fleetwood Mac* was released in March 1968.

For the next two years the group had hits including "Black Magic Woman" (#37, U.K., 1968), "Need Your Love So Bad" (#31, U.K., 1968), "Albatross" (#1, U.K., 1969) and "Man of the World" (#2, U.K., 1969), but its popularity didn't spread to America. In July

1968 the group undertook its first U.S. tour and even

guested on *The Ed Sullivan Show* on July 13. On December 4, 1968, Fleetwood Mac returned to America to play thirty dates including the Fillmore East, Boston Tea Party, and Miami Pop Festival. The band's next album, *English Rose* (#184, U.S.), was released in 1969 and made the U.S. charts. Another U.S. tour began on July 16, 1969, and included a stop at the Fillmore West. "Pious Bird of Good Omen" (#18, U.K., 1969), "Then Play On" (#109, U.S., 1969), and "Blues Jam at Chess" soon followed. Increasingly erratic behavior was now exhibited by Peter Green, who played his final gig with Fleetwood Mac on May 24, 1970. His departure pulled another "blues root" out of the band. The addition of Danny Kirwan and Christine Perfect brought a more melodic rock sound to the group.

In February 1971, Jeremy Spencer disappeared while supposedly buying newspapers. It was the last time the band saw him for two years. He later turned up as a member of a religious cult called the Children of God. Ironically, it was Green who came to the rescue; he flew to the U.S. to help the group complete its tour. The group then spun into disarray as personnel changes inflicted chaos on the band. From court injunctions to members refusing to appear on stage, Fleetwood Mac's stability was challenged.

Mick Fleetwood then stepped up as the group's leader/manager and moved the band to California in 1974. Bob Welch left in December and formed the group Paris. He eventually found success as a solo artist; his association in Fleetwood Mac was a key element. Fleetwood, meanwhile, in a by-chance meeting, found producer Keith Olsen and singing/songwriting duo Buckingham & Nicks. The duo was invited to join the group, while Olsen, along with the band, produced *Fleetwood Mac* (#1, 1976). The combination proved fruitful—the songwriting flourished, the studio work was embellished, and an onstage focal point was found with Stevie Nicks. Despite many personal problems between band members (breakups, divorce, etc.) *Rumours* (#1, 1977) was finally released in February 1977. Although it clearly reflected the turmoil in the band, it connected with the public who bought it at a record pace. By April it topped the U.S. charts and was on the way to becoming the second-best-selling album of all time. The album yielded the hit singles "Go Your Own Way" (#10), "Dreams" (#1), "Don't Stop" (#3), and "You Make Loving Fun" (#9).

Extensive touring, solo projects, and award ceremonies dominated the next two years before *Tusk* (#4, 1979) was released. A somewhat experimental album, it was criticized for its cost—1 million dollars—and spun off only two singles, "Sara" (#7, 1979) and the self-titled "Tusk" (#8, 1979). The group's support of the album began on November 26, 1979, in Idaho and ended on September 1, 1980, in Los Angeles, CA. Warner Brothers Records released *Fleetwood Mac Live* (#14, 1980) to recoup losses on *Tusk*;

this gave the band members an opportunity to pursue solo efforts. Fleetwood headed to West Africa, while Stevie Nicks worked on her first solo LP *Bella Donna* (#1, 1981). The album netted Nicks three Top Twenty singles: "Stop Draggin' My Heart Around" (duet with Tom Petty) , "Leather and Lace" (duet with Don Henley), and "Edge of Seventeen." Meanwhile, Buckingham released *Law and Order* (#32, 1981), which yielded his Top Ten single "Trouble."

After a three-year studio absence, Fleetwood Mac's *Mirage* (#1, 1982) dominated the charts in the late summer of 1982. The album produced the hit singles "Hold Me" (#4), "Gypsy" (#12), and "Love in Store" (#22). Its less experimental sound was well received and ignited comparisons to *Rumours*. Meanwhile, band members began to focus on other concerns: Nicks with her highly successful solo career, McVie and Buckingham with moderately successful individual efforts, and Fleetwood with financial issues that led to bankruptcy. Stir in a little individual management conflicts, some chemical dependency (Nicks), and studio egos, and it's time for a vacation.

Tango in the Night (#7, 1987) was released in April 1987 and generated three Top Twenty hits: "Little Lies," "Seven Wonders," and "Everywhere." Buckingham, who was unhappy about the idea of touring with fellow band members, told the group that he was quitting. Although he still intended on leaving, he committed himself to a final tour with the group.

Behind the Mask (#18, 1990) was released and supported by a lengthy tour. It was during this time that both McVie and Nicks announced their intentions of leaving upon the tour's completion. Personal issues and personnel changes dominated the years to follow, always with "rumours" of a reconciliation. The re-formed group did perform at President Clinton's inaugural gala on January 19, 1993. *The Dance* (#1, 1997) exhibited the strength of a band whose popularity has diminished little over the years.

AUTOGRAPHS

Group:

A CD, LP, magazine cover, ad, photo, or card signed by the entire band: $175-$300*
*High end reflects a *Rumours* autographed piece

The autograph of Mick Fleetwood

Individual:

Peter Green: $50-$100*
John McVie: $40-$50
Christine McVie: $35-$40
Danny Kirwan: $10-$15
Dave Walker: $5-$10
Stevie Nicks: $40-$50
*inclusive

Mick Fleetwood: $40-$50
Jeremy Spencer: $10-$17
Bob Welch: $20-$25
Bob Weston: $5-$10
Lindsey Buckingham: $45-$55

TOUR BOOKS/PROGRAMS/PASSES

Programs:

Rumours: $50-$55
Behind the Mask: $15-$30
Tango in Europe: $20-$40
Tango in the Night: $10-$15
Tusk: $40-$75
Japan Tour, 1977: $200 (scarce)

Programs (Stevie Nicks):

The Wild Heart, 1983: $75
Rock A Little Tour, 1986: $30
Timespace Tour, 1991: $35
The Other Side of the Mirror: $165 (scarce)

Classic and highly sought Fleetwood Mac program (Penguin Proms. Inc.)

Stevie Nicks Timespace tour program

Backstage pass from the Tusk Tour 1980

Backstage Passes:

Cloth/paper: $8-$20;
Laminated: $15-$45 (1975-Present)

POSTERS/PRESS KITS

Promotional Posters:

1975-Present: $15-$60
Tango in the Night: $15; "Schlitz Presents the Mirage Tour," 1982: $25

Press Kits:

1975-Present: $20-$70

USED CLOTHING/EQUIPMENT

Stevie Nicks stage-worn coat: $1,500-$1,750
Stevie Nicks stage-used tambourine, 1979: $600-$650

Guitar Picks:

Lindsey Buckingham: $20-$40
Billy Burnette: $15
John McVie: $20-$25
Dave Mason: $20-$25

Drum Sticks:

Mick Fleetwood: $25-$30

FLEETWOOD MAC ALUMNI

Date	Members
7/67 9/67	Fleetwood, McVie, Green, Spencer, Bob Brunning*
9/67-8/68	Fleetwood, McVie, Green, Spencer
8/68-5/70	Fleetwood, McVie, Green, Spencer, Danny Kirwan
5/70-8/70	Fleetwood, McVie, Spencer, Kirwan, Christine McVie
8/70-2/71	Fleetwood, McVie, Spencer, Kirwan, McVie, Green**
4/71-8/72	Fleetwood, McVie, Kirwan, McVie, Bob Welch
9/72-6/73	Fleetwood, McVie, McVie, Welch, Bob Weston, Dave Walker
6/73-1/74	Fleetwood, McVie, McVie, Welch, Weston
1/74-12/74	Fleetwood, McVie, McVie, Welch
1/75-8/87	Fleetwood, McVie, McVie, Stevie Nicks, Lindsey Buckingham
8/87-8/88	Fleetwood, McVie, McVie, Nicks, Billy Burnette, and Rick Vito, Buckingham***
8/88-12/90	Fleetwood, McVie, McVie, Nicks, Burnette, Vito
12/90-11/91	Fleetwood, McVie, Burnette, Vito
11/91-1/93	Fleetwood, McVie, Burnette
1/19/93	Fleetwood, McVie, McVie, Nicks, Buckingham
1/93-7/94	Fleetwood, McVie, McVie, Burnette
7/94-present	Fleetwood, McVie, Dave Mason, Bekka Bramlett, Burnette****
1997	Fleetwood, McVie, McVie, Nicks, Buckingham

*Filled in briefly for McVie
**Green joined only temporarily
***Buckingham changed his mind and joined for one final tour
****Burnette was added to U.S. and U.K. performances because C. McVie declined to tour during the summer

A selection of Fleetwood Mac guitar picks

Mick Fleetwood's drum sticks and a clear plastic drum cover with his signature on it. Courtesy Butterfield & Butterfield, Auctioneers Corp., 1997.

OFTEN OVERLOOKED MEMORABILIA

1990 Rumours Fan Club Calendar - $10; Warner Brothers/ Fleetwood Mac penguin brass belt buckle - $25; enamel pin (penguin over Warner Bros. label) - $12-$17; Mirage cardboard album cover stand-up - $30-$45; Warner Brothers promotional Mirage (word appears when hot) coffee mug (1982)- $100-$150; Rhiannon postcard - $20-$30; Rumours postcard - $15; Rumours - stand-up with penguins - $50-$65; Tango in the Night two-sided jigsaw puzzle (1987) - $20; Tango 3-D counter promo - $12; Tusk promotional scarf - $150-$170; Issues of *Rolling Stone* magazine with the group on cover - $5-$10; Tusk video documentary - $40; Heroes are Hard to Find, 1974 mobile - $100; Rumours promotional three-foot inflatable penguin

REFERENCES/BOOKS

Numerous resources exist, but start with Mick Fleetwood's *My Twenty-Five Years in Fleetwood Mac;* no dedicated collector books

The Fleetwoods

Formed 1958

Gary Troxel, Barbara Ellis, and Gretchen Christopher

This late-50s R&B/pop vocal group, originally known as Two Girls and a Guy, is best remembered for the hits, "Come Softly to Me" (#1, 1959), "Tragedy" (#12, 1959), and "Mr. Blue" (#1, 1959). The group broke up following the release of "Goodnight My Love" (#32, 1963).

AUTOGRAPHS

A CD, LP, magazine cover, ad, photo, or card signed by the group: $15-$30

The Fleshtones

Formed 1976

Peter Zaremba, Keith Streng, Jan Pakulski, and Lenny Calderone*

*Numerous personnel changes

A group of '80s alley rockers, which built a substantial following by playing at CBGB and Max's

Kansas City during the post-punk scene, The Fleshtones never grew beyond a cult status band.

AUTOGRAPHS

A CD, LP, magazine cover, ad, photo, or card signed by the group: $7-$15

Flipper

Formed 1979

Will Shatter (Russell Wilkinson, 1956-1987), Bruce Loose (Calderwood), Ted (Laurence) Falconi, and Steve DePace*

*Shatter was replaced by John Dougherty in 1992

Flipper, an early-80s Bay Area post-punk band, whose sound was influential to the grunge scene that followed, gave us the songs "Love Canal," "Life," and the seventeen minute "Sex Bomb." Flipper was led by "Will E" Shatter, whose unpredictable onstage attitude befriended his audience and complimented Bruce "Is the Screw" Loose, who was often found flailing about the floor during his ritualistic Worm dance.

Flipper shattered when Shatter flipped and died of an accidental heroin overdose.

AUTOGRAPHS

A CD, LP, magazine cover, ad, photo, or card signed by the group: $12-$25*

*Original band members

A Flock of Seagulls

Formed 1980

Mike Score, Ali Score, Paul Reynolds, and Frank Maudsley*

*Reynolds departed in 1984 and Gary Steadnin, along with Chris Chryssaphis, were added.

The 80s post-new-wave pop band A Flock of Seagulls is best remembered for Score's "waterfall" haircut, the band's constant MTV play, and hits such as "I Ran (So Far Away)" (#9, 1982), "Space Age Love Song" (#30, 1982), "Wishing" (#26, 1983), and "The More You Live, The More You Love" (#56, 1984), before the hairspray, videotape, and audience ran out!

AUTOGRAPHS

A CD, LP, magazine cover, ad, photo, or card signed by the group: $10-$20

POSTERS/PRESS KITS

Promotional Posters: $12-$15
Press Kits: $12-$15

Floyd, Eddie

Born: June 25, 1935

Floyd, the talented performer, singer, and songwriter, was the cofounder of the Falcons ("You're So Fine," "I Found a Love") before he moved on to both a successful solo and songwriting career. Floyd cowrote "Knock on Wood" with Steve Cropper for Otis Redding, while his own demo version landed in the Top Thirty. He scored with other hits including "Bring It On Home to Me" (#17, 1970), while he watched other artists also take his songs up the charts.

AUTOGRAPHS

A CD, LP, magazine cover, ad, photo, or card signed by the artist: $10-$15

OFTEN OVERLOOKED MEMORABILIA

Artifacts associated with other musicians' covers of his songs

The Flying Burrito Brothers

Formed 1968

Gram Parsons (Ingram Connor III, 1946-1973); Chris Hillman, Born: December 4, 1942; Sneaky Pete Kleinow; and Chris Ethridge*

*Numerous personnel changes. Additional musicians have included Michael Clarke (1944-1993), Bernie Leadon, Born: July 19, 1947, Rick Roberts, Al Perkins, Byron Berline, Roger Bush, Kenny Wertz, Alan Munde, Don Beck, and Erik Dalton. Group re-formed in 1974 with additional personnel changes.

This inspiring, late-60s California incarnated country rock band prompted great interest and a strong local following until the departure of cofounder Gram Parsons in 1970. The band now is most remembered for who played in it, rather than what was played. Numerous ex-Burritos went on to greater success with other acts including the Eagles (Leadon), Firefall (Roberts), and the Desert Rose Band (Hillman). In baseball terms, it was a AAA minor league ball club.

OFTEN OVERLOOKED MEMORABILIA

Often forgotten is that the Burritos played at Altamont

The Flying Lizards

Formed 1978

David Cunningham and Deborah Evans

The Flying Lizards, an '80s Irish conceptual duo, is best known for its dismemberment and rearrangement of classics song with a minimalist approach, which was best exemplified in "Money" (#50, U.S., #5, U.K., 1979).

AUTOGRAPHS

A CD, LP, magazine cover, ad, photo, or card signed by the group: $5-$10

Focus

Thijs Van Leer, Born: March 31, 1948; Martin Dresden; and Hans Cleuver*

*Jan Akkerman was added in 1970. Cleuver departed in 1971 and Pierre Van der Linden was added. Dresden also left in 1971 and was replaced by Cyril Havermanns, who stayed briefly before he was replaced by Bert Ruiter. Numerous other changes occurred in 1973 and beyond— most note worthy is Steve Smith, who went on to Journey.

This early-70s Netherlands progressive-rock band is ironically best remembered in the U.S. for its yodeling novelty hit "Hocus Pocus" (#9, 1973) instead of its depth of talent. Both Van Leer and Akkerman were classically trained and are extremely good musicians. This is evident in the group's later, more complex compositions and their solo work.

AUTOGRAPHS

A CD, LP, magazine cover, ad, photo, or card signed by the group: $15-$40

Fogelberg, Dan

Born: August 31, 1951

Fogelberg, the '70s singer/songwriter, landed a deal with Columbia Records while still in his early twenties. At Columbia, he released his relatively ignored debut album, followed by the successful *Souvenirs* that spun off the hit "Part of the Plan" (#31, 1975). He went from the Midwest to the L.A. music scene and finally settled in Boulder, Colorado, during the middle of the decade, where he put together an impressive series of platinum albums that seemed to hit a crescendo with *The Innocent Age* (1981), which yielded four extracts: "Hard to Say," "Leader of the Band," "Run for the Roses," and "Same Old Lang Syne."

Ironically, his biggest hit was the "Language of Love" (#13, 1984), which was more of rock song for the generally acoustic-minded Fogelberg. He then switched gears by recording bluegrass on *High Country Snows* (1985) and later even began experimenting with world rhythms on *River of Souls* (1993). The result caused a drastic decline in record sales, of

which he has had a difficult time rebounding from even after he reenlisted the help of Tim Weisberg.

AUTOGRAPHS
A CD, LP, magazine cover, ad, photo, or card signed by the artist: $10-$25

TOUR BOOKS/ PROGRAMS/PASSES
Programs: Exiles (1987): $10

POSTERS/PRESS KITS
Promotional Posters: $10-$35
Press Kits: $15-$40

USED CLOTHING/ EQUIPMENT
Guitar Picks: $10-$20

OFTEN OVERLOOKED MEMORABILIA
His contributions to numerous other musicians' efforts

A 1987 Dan Fogelberg Program (Dan Fogelburg)

Foghat

"Lonesome" Dave Peverett, Roger Earl, Rod Price, and Tony Stevens*

*Stevens left in 1974 and was replaced by Nick Jameson. Jameson departed in 1975 and Craig MacGregor was added. Price left in 1980 and Erik Cartwright joined the band.

Popular '70s rock and boogie-blues band, founded out of Savoy Brown by "Lonesome" Dave Peverett, Foghat built an enormous and loyal following that helped the group's albums go gold. Its first hit single came in 1976 with "Slow Ride" (#20, 1976), and was followed by "Stone Blue" (#36, 1978), "Third-Time Lucky" (#23, 1979), and a live version of Foghat favorite, "I Just Want to Make Love to You" (#33, 1977).

AUTOGRAPHS
A CD, LP, magazine cover, ad, photo, or card signed by the group: $25-$45

Two signatures from members of Foghat

POSTERS/PRESS KITS
Promotional Posters: $10-$25
Press Kits: $15-$35

USED CLOTHING/EQUIPMENT
Guitar Picks: $10-$15
Drum Sticks: $15

OFTEN OVERLOOKED MEMORABILIA
Boogie Motel promotional popout motel display - $100; energized promo mobile - $30

Fontana, Wayne and the Mindbenders

Formed 1963

Wayne Fontana (Glynn Ellis), Bob Lang, Eroc Stewart, and Ric Rothwell*

*Fontana departed in 1966 and was replaced by Graham Gouldman.

This '60s British Invasion group is best remembered for "Game of Love" (#1, 1965), "It's Just a Little Bit Too Late" (#45, 1965), "A Groovy Kind of Love" (#2, 1966), and "Ashes to Ashes" before the group broke up in the late '60s.

AUTOGRAPHS
A CD, LP, magazine cover, ad, photo, or card signed by the group: $20-$50

OFTEN OVERLOOKED MEMORABILIA
Movie memorabilia from *To Sir With Love*

Forbert, Steve

Born: 1955

Folk-rock singer/songwriter, best known for his album *Jackrabbit Slim* (#20, 1979), which included the hit extract "Romeo's Tune" (#11, 1979), Steve Forbert has built and established a loyal following over the decades he has performed.

AUTOGRAPHS
A CD, LP, magazine cover, ad, photo, or card signed by the artist: $10-$15

POSTERS/PRESS KITS
Promotional Posters: $10-$15
Press Kits: $10-$15

USED CLOTHING/EQUIPMENT
Guitar Picks: $10

OFTEN OVERLOOKED MEMORABILIA
A copy of Cyndi Lauper's video "Girls Just Wanna Have Fun" (Forbert made a cameo tuxedoed appearance)

Force M.D.'s

Formed 1979

Stevie D. (Lundy), T.C.D. (Antoine Lundy), Jesse Lee Daniels, Trisco Pearson, and Mercury (Charles Nelson)*

*Numerous personnel changes

The Force M.D.'s, a pivotal early R&B/rap group of the '80s, were best known for songs such as "Tears"

(#5, R&B. 1984), "Itchin' for a Scratch" (#13, R&B, 1985), "Tender Love" (#10, 1986), "Love Is a House" (#1, R&B, 1987), and "Touch and Go" (#10, R&B,1987), before the group gradually faded from the music scene.

AUTOGRAPHS

A CD, LP, magazine cover, ad, photo, or card signed by the group: $8-$12

Ford, Emile and the Checkmates

(Emile Sweetman)
Born: October 16, 1937

Sweetman, a late-50s pop singer, became the first West Indian to land on the British pop chart with "What Do You Want To Make Those Eyes at Me For?" in 1959.

AUTOGRAPHS

A LP, magazine cover, ad, photo, or card signed by the group: $10-$15

Ford, Lita

(Rosanna Ford)
Born: September 23, 1959

This '80s hard-rock guitarist and singer, formerly with the Runaways, took her RCA debut *Lita* (#29, 1988) into the Top Thirty on the strength of such songs as "Kiss Me Deadly" (#12, 1988), "Can't Catch Me," and "Close My Eyes Forever" (#8, 1989), a duet with Ozzy Osbourne, before her subsequent albums fell short of expectations.

AUTOGRAPHS

A CD, LP, magazine cover, ad, photo, or card signed by the artist: $10-$15

USED CLOTHING/ EQUIPMENT

Guitar Pick: $10-$15

OFTEN OVERLOOKED MEMORABILIA

Videotapes of her performing in Howie Mandel's house band on *Howie* (1992)

A classic Lita Ford guitar pick

Fordham, Julia

Born: August 10, 1962

Fordham, the late-80s folk-influenced alt-pop singer/songwriter, has managed to attract a strong following through her albums like *Porcelain* that landed at the top of the adult-contemporary chart.

AUTOGRAPHS

A CD, LP, magazine cover, ad, photo, or card signed by the artist: $5-$10

Foreigner

Formed 1976

Mick Jones, Born: December 27, 1944; Ian McDonald, Born: June 25, 1946; Al Greenwood; Lou Graham, Born: May 2, 1950; Ed Gagliardi; and Dennis Elliott*

*Gagliardi departed in 1979 and Rick Wills was added. Both McDonald and Greenwood left in 1980. Gramm departed in 1991 and Johnny Edwards was added. Numerous changes followed.

This late-70s, highly-commercial rock band enjoyed enormous success with hits such as "Feels Like the First Time" (#4, 1977), "Cold as Ice" (#6, 1977), "Long, Long, Way From Home" (#20, 1978), "Hot Blooded" (#3, 1978), "Double Vision" (#2, 1978), "Dirty White Boy" (#12, 1979), and "Head Games" (#14, 1979) before its first round of personnel changes came about. By 1980 only the core of Jones, Gramm, and Elliott remained, but with Rick Wills (Frampton's Camel, Small Faces, and Roxy Music), the quartet still felt strong and looked toward the next decade with anticipation.

Foreigner's next album, *4* (#1, 1981), was a smash and yielded the powerful extracts "Waiting for a Girl Like You" (#2, 1981) and "Urgent" (#4, 1981). Other hits followed including the AOR gospel flavored "I Know What Love Is" (#1, 1984), "That Was Yesterday" (#12, 1984), and "Say You Will" (#6, 1987) before Gramm decided to split. "Midnight Blue" (#6, 1989) and "Just Between You and Me" (#6, 1989) became Gramm's first solo hits, while Jones' solo album garnered little attention before he moved on to production work. Impending resurrections of the band have yet to bear fruit, but with such powerful players, Foreigner has still not been written off!

AUTOGRAPHS

A CD, LP, magazine cover, ad, photo, or card signed by the group: $30-$90

TOUR BOOKS/PROGRAMS/ PASSES

Backstage Passes:
Cloth/paper: $10-$20;
Laminated: $15-$40

POSTERS/PRESS KITS

Promotional Posters: $15-$55

Press Kits: $15-$30
Head Games (1979): $22-$25

Backstage pass from the Can't Stop Rockin' Tour featuring Foreigner, REO Speedwagon, and Peter Frampton

USED CLOTHING/EQUIPMENT

Guitar Picks:
Mick Jones: $20-$25
Drum Sticks: $15-$25

OFTEN OVERLOOKED MEMORABILIA

Promotional Greatest Hits die-cut sign - $25; Double Vision promotional eye chart - $45; 4 promotional pin - $15; Inside Information, Atlantic promotional box set, includes: cassette, single and press kit, 1987

The Foundations

Formed 1967

Peter Macbeth, Alan Warner, Clem Curtis, Eric Dale, Tony Gomez, Pat Burke, Mike Elliot, and Tim Harris*

*Curtis departed in 1968 and Colin Young was added

This mid-60s "feel happy" pop band is best remembered for two hits—"Baby Now That I've Found You" (#11, 1968) and "Build Me Up Buttercup" (#3, 1969)—before it split up in 1970.

AUTOGRAPHS

A CD, LP, magazine cover, ad, photo, or card signed by the group: $20-$35

The Four Seasons

Formed 1956

Original lineup: Frankie Valli (Francis Casteluccio), Born: May 3, 1937; Tommy DeVito; Nick DeVito; and Hank Majewski*

*Numerous personnel changes

Perhaps the most durable and successful of all doo-wop groups, The Four Seasons, led by the three octave range and falsetto voice of Frankie Valli, have transcended generations with priceless hits such as "Sherry" (#1), "Big Girls Don't Cry" (#1), "Walk Like a Man" (#1), "Candy Girl" (#3), "Dawn" (#3), "Let's Hang On" (#3), "Working My Way Back to You" (#9), "I've Got You Under My Skin," "Tell It to the Rain" (#10), and "C'mon Marianne" (#9)—these are just some of fifty hits the group recorded during the '60s.

The group's popularity began tailing off, though, and by 1971, only Valli and Gaudio remained as original members. The first few years of the '70s were extremely tough on the group, which was enduring considerable debt, canceled records, allegations of ties with organized crime, and Valli's ongoing hearing problems.

In 1974, Valli signed a solo contract with Private Stock and released several hits including "My Eyes Adored You" (#1, 1975), "Swearin' to God" (#6, 1975), and "Our Day Will Come" (#11, 1975), all of which ignited interest in his career and the Four Seasons.

The group, which was close to an end, rebounded and landed hits "Who Loves You" (#3, 1975) and "December 1963 (Oh What a Night)" (#1, 1976). The icing on the cake was "Grease" (#1), the theme song to the hit movie that quickly topped the charts; it sold more than 7 million copies.

In 1990 the original members of the group were inducted into the Rock and Roll Hall of Fame.

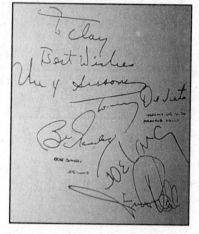

Signature sheet of the Four Seasons

AUTOGRAPHS

Group:
A CD, LP, magazine cover, ad, photo, or card signed by the group: $40-$115

Individual:
Frankie Valli: $20-$40

OFTEN OVERLOOKED MEMORABILIA

Movie memorabilia from *Grease*, *Eternity*, and *Modern Love*; memorabilia from the group's early days as the Variations and the Four Lovers; videotapes of the group's numerous television appearances including *The Ed Sullivan Show* (1956); newspaper and periodical clippings surrounding the group's difficult years (1970-1974); all items relating to the group's product promotional work for clients such as Coke, Beechnut Gum, Sun Tan oils, etc.; The Beatles vs. The Four Seasons, Vee-Jay, 1964, contained valuable inserts, poster, score cards, etc.

The Four Tops

Formed 1954

Levi Stubbs (Stubbles), Renaldo "Obie" Benson, Lawrence Payton, and Abdul "Duke" Fakir

This enormously successful contemporary soul and R&B act has spanned more than four decades and has provided music history with some of its all-time classic hits including "Baby I Need Your Loving" (#11, 1964), "Same Old Song" (#5, 1965), "I Can't Help Myself (Sugar Pie, Honey Bunch)" (#1, 1965), "Reach Out I'll Be There" (#1, 1966), "Standing in the Shadows of Love" (#6, 1967), and "Bernadette" (#4, 1967).

The magic mix of Levi Stubbs' lead vocals, complimented by the other Tops, became the voice for the successful and legendary Motown production and writing team of Holland-Dozier-Holland. In retrospect, this recipe may have been rock and roll's finest collaboration. Anyone would be hard pressed to argue the sheer talent potential possessed by their mix.

When Holland-Dozier-Holland left Motown in 1967, the group was struck a devastating blow and quickly turned to covers such as "Walk Away Renee" (#14, 1968) and other works from members of the Motown staff. Although the group did send numerous singles to the charts, the aggressiveness and impact was far less than its predecessors.

The Four Tops "Still Water (Love)" gold in-house 45 award from 1970 is valued at $500. From the Doug Leftwitch collection.

In 1972, the group jumped to ABC/Dunhill and scored with "Keeper of the Castle" (#10, 1973) and "Ain't No Woman (Like the One I Got)" (#4, 1973), while it continued its tradition of extensive touring and powerful live performances. In 1981, the group moved to Casablanca Records and landed with "When She Was My Girl" (#11, #1, R&B, 1981), but two years later it was back with Motown.

Occasional resurgences followed, including "Sexy Ways" (#21, R&B, 1985), The Four Tops' last Motown hit, and "Indestructible" (#35, 1988, Arista), all as the band remained intact—four decades without a personnel change!

The group was inducted into the Rock and Roll Hall of Fame in 1990.

AUTOGRAPHS
A CD, LP, magazine cover, ad, photo, or card signed by the group: $50-$110

OFTEN OVERLOOKED MEMORABILIA
Movie memorabilia from *Buster* and *Little Shop of Horrors* (Stubb's provided a voice over); videotapes of their numerous television appearances

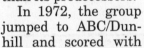

Fowley, Kim

Born: July 21, 1939

A true rock & roll Renaissance man who has contributed to the business in so many diverse ways, from songwriter to consultant, Kim Fowley produced the novelty singles "Popsicles and Icicles" (#3, 1964), "Alley Oop" (31, 1960), "Nutrocker" (#23, 1962), and "Papa-Oom-Mow-Mow" (#48, 1962). He has also written and cowritten songs with numerous artists, including the Beach Boys, the Byrds, and Cat Stevens, and formed the Runaways in the late '70s.

AUTOGRAPHS
A CD, LP, magazine cover, ad, photo, or card signed by the artist: $10-$25*
*A hit-related item

OFTEN OVERLOOKED MEMORABILIA
Artifacts from the works he has written, sessions he has produced, and artists who have covered his work

REFERENCE BOOKS
Fowley has written two poetry books!

Foxx, Inez and Charlie

Inezz Foxx and Charlie Foxx

This early-60s brother-and-sister vocal act is best remembered for the novelty hit "Mockingbird" (#7, 1963), which was later covered by James Taylor and Carly Simon.

AUTOGRAPHS
A LP, magazine cover, ad, photo, or card signed by the duo: $10-$15

Frampton, Peter

Born: April 22, 1950

Frampton, the popular late-60s British guitarist, first received notice in the teen act the Herd ("From the Underworld," "Paradise Lost," etc.) before he left in 1969 to form Humble Pie ("I Don't Need No Doctor") with ex-Small Face Steve Marriott. He was determined to make it as a solo act and left Humble Pie in 1971. What surprised many, including Frampton, was how long it would take and how extensive his popularity would become when he succeeded in getting there.

Following some significant session work, including "All Things Must Pass" for George Harrison, he formed Frampton's Camel (1973). For the next three years he wrote, recorded, released, and toured consistently with a gradual increase in popularity that exploded with *Frampton Comes Alive* (#1, 1976), which at one point was among the ten best-selling albums ever. The album spun off three successful extracts: "Show Me the Way" (#6, 1976), "Baby I Love Your Way," (#12, 1976), and "Do You Feel Like We Do" (#10, 1976). Frampton was then catapulted into the spotlight, and everyone anxiously awaited his follow-up album.

What had been one of rock's all-time greatest success stories quickly became nothing short of a bomb. Although *I'm In You* (#2, 1977) was a commercial success, it was a critical failure and a very big disappointment to the legion of fans who had followed him for years. To add insult to injury, he then opted to star in Robert Stigwood's film *Sgt. Pepper's Lonely Hearts Club Band*—it too was a catastrophe.

By the late '70s, Frampton had returned to small hall touring and he landed one last hit during the decade: "I Can't Stand It No More" (#14, 1979). His four albums during the '80s were virtually ignored, but he did redeem himself somewhat by playing on David Bowie's Glass Spider Tour, a humbling experience that caught the interest of his fans. *Comes Alive II* was an attempt to recapture the fans that he had lost, most of whom were now in their forties. While it caught some interest, it never received the marketing attention that an effort such as this sorely needed.

There is still a good album or two left in Frampton, if he can regain the momentum, dedication, and perseverance he had going into *Comes Alive!*

AUTOGRAPHS

A CD, LP, magazine cover, ad, photo, or card signed by the artist: $15-$45

TOUR BOOKS/PROGRAMS/PASSES

Backstage Passes:
Cloth/paper: $8-$20; Laminated: $15-$40

POSTERS/PRESS KITS

Promotional Posters: $10-$50*
Press Kits: $10-$45*
*Frampton Comes Alive! (1976)

USED CLOTHING/EQUIPMENT

Guitar Picks: $20-$35

OFTEN OVERLOOKED MEMORABILIA

Movie memorabilia from *Sgt. Pepper's Lonely Hearts Club Band* (1978); numerous periodicals relating to Frampton have been available in the market

REFERENCES/BOOKS

A couple resources exist, but nothing that does justice to the singer in my opinion; no dedicated collector books

Francis, Connie

(Concetta Franconero)
Born: December 12, 1938

This major late-50s multilingual international pop star, who during a five year time span landed thirty-five Top Forty hits on the charts including the toppers, "Everybody's Somebody's Fool," "My Heart Has a Mind of Its Own," and "Don't Break the Heart That Loves You," stands, along with Aretha Franklin, as one of the most successful female vocalists in rock history.

Her first big hit was "Who's Sorry Now" (#4, 1958), a remake of a 1928 classic, that began her long series of hits, which finally slowed when the British Invasion took hold. She then turned to acting and even did a Brylcreem commercial—a real collectors item for Francis fans! Respiratory and numerous personal problems then plagued the artist through the '70s. She thankfully maintained her composure despite the odds not being in her favor and eventually returned to the stage.

AUTOGRAPHS

A CD, LP, magazine cover, ad, photo, or card signed by the artist: $5-$15

OFTEN OVERLOOKED MEMORABILIA

Movie memorabilia from *Where the Boys Are, Follow the Boys, Looking for Love,* and *When the Boys Meet the Girls;* videotapes of her numerous television appearances, including *Arthur Godfrey's TV Talent Show,* her first at age 12; commercials and press clippings regarding her career

REFERENCE BOOKS

Who's Sorry Now?, her autobiography; no dedicated collector books

Franke, Christopher: See Tangerine Dream

Frankie Goes to Hollywood

Formed 1980

Holly (William) Johnson, Paul Rutherford, Nasher Nash, Mark O'Toole, and Peter Gill

This controversial British mid-80s techno-dance band, best remembered for its controversial hit "Relax" (#10, 1985) that was banned by the BBC along with the promotional video, was also a media favorite. "Frankiemania" enveloped Liverpool, as did Frankie collectibles, the most sought being the "Frankie Says..." T-shirts. Following the group's debut album, the band faded quickly as subsequent albums fell short of sales expectations. Johnson later became active as an AIDS spokesman after he was diagnosed as HIV-positive.

AUTOGRAPHS

A CD, LP, magazine cover, ad, photo, or card signed by the group: $15-$30

POSTERS/PRESS KITS

Promotional Posters: $15-$20
Press Kits: $15-$20

OFTEN OVERLOOKED MEMORABILIA

"The Power of Love" promotional vibrator, 1984; Relax computer game; Watching the Wildlife promo with condom, 1987; Frankie Goes to Hollywood, ZZT promo pack with T-shirt, sweat bands, pencils, badges, etc.

REFERENCE BOOKS

A Bone in My Flute, Johnson's autobiography; a couple resources exist, but nothing that does justice to the band in my opinion; no dedicated collector books

Franklin, Aretha

Born: March 25, 1942

Aretha Franklin, "Lady Soul," has become an icon in American music. With a career that has spanned decades, she has scored more than a dozen million-selling singles and more than twenty R&B hits, including "I Never Loved a Man (the Way I Love You)" (#9, 1967), "Respect" (#9, 1967), "Baby I Love You" (#4, 1907), "Chain of Fools" (#2, 1968), and "Since You've Been Gone" (#5, 1968). Her relationship with the Muscle Shoals Sound Rhythm Section has become legendary as a result of its successful and prolific output. She also worked extensively with a band led by saxophonist King Curtis.

During the '70s she landed numerous hits including "Spanish Harlem" (#2, 1971), "Rock Steady" (#9, 1971), "Day Dreaming" (#5, 1972), and "Until You Come Back to Me (That's What I'm Gonna Do)" (#3, 1973), all while she handled numerous projects and raised a family.

The '80s were hard on the entertainer who lost her father, sister Carolyn, and brother Cecil, all in a relatively short period of time, amongst other personal problems. She did have numerous musical highlights that included "Hold On, I'm Comin'," which earned her a Grammy, "Jump to It" (#1, R&B, 1982), "Who's Zoomin' Who" (#7, 1985), "Freeway of Love" (#3,1985), "Sisters Are Doin' It For Themselves," "Jimmy Lee" (#2, R&B, 1986), and "I Knew You Were Waiting (for Me)" (#1, 1987), a Grammy winning duet with George Michael. She did this before she ended the decade with another Grammy award garnering project *One Lord, One Faith, One Baptism* (1987), this time a gospel performance.

In 1987, Aretha Franklin became the first woman inducted into the Rock and Roll Hall of Fame.

AUTOGRAPHS

A CD, LP, magazine cover, ad, photo, or card signed by the artist: $15-$40

OFTEN OVERLOOKED MEMORABILIA

Any artifacts relating to her father, the distinguished Reverend C.L. Franklin; any early pieces of memorabilia relating to her work on the Checker label or at Chicago's Trade Winds club; movie memorabilia from *The Blues Brothers* (1980), *Jumpin' Jack Flash* (1986), *White Men Can't Jump* (1992), and *Waiting to Exhale* (1995); videotapes of her numerous television appearances including "Aretha Franklin: The Queen of Soul" - PBS-TV (1988), *Murphy Brown* (11/11/91), "Aretha Franklin: Duets" (1993), and *Saturday Night Live* (1994); a program from the 1968 and 1992 Democratic Party National Conventions where Franklin sang "The Star Spangled Banner"; memorabilia from President Jimmy Carter's Inaugural Eve Gala (1977); festival artifacts; 1993 World Series memorabilia (she sang the national anthem for Game 1); Karenna Gore and Dr. Andrew Schiff wedding artifacts (1997)—Franklin sang "The Way I Love You" for more than 300 guests

REFERENCES/BOOKS

A few resources exist, but start with Mark Bego's *Aretha Franklin: The Queen of Soul;* no dedicated collector books

Franks, Michael

Born: September 18, 1944

This relaxed '70s songwriter is best known for his novelty tune "Popsicle Toes" (#43, 1976) and his songs covered by other artists including Melissa Manchester, the Carpenters, and Manhattan Transfer.

AUTOGRAPHS

A CD, LP, magazine cover, ad, photo, or card signed by the artist: $7-$10

POSTERS/PRESS KITS

Promotional Posters: $8-$10
Press Kits: $10

USED CLOTHING/EQUIPMENT

Guitar Picks: $8

OFTEN OVERLOOKED MEMORABILIA

Movie memorabilia from *Count Your Bullets* and *Zandy's Bride*

Freakwater: See Eleventh Dream Day

Fred, John and his Playboy Band

Formed Late '50s

John Fred, Charlie Spinosa, Ronnie Goodson, Andrew Bernard, James O'Rourke, Harold Cowart, Joe Micelli, and Tommy Dee (DeGeneres)

This late-60s Louisiana rock band, best remembered for the hit "Judy in Disguise (with Glasses)" (#1, 1968), quickly faded back into the bayou.

AUTOGRAPHS

An LP, magazine cover, ad, photo, or card signed by the group: $10-$15

Freddie and the Dreamers

Formed 1960

Freddie Garrity, Derek Quinn, Roy Crewsdon, Pete Birrell, and Bernie Dwyer

Freddie and the Dreamers, the '60s British Invasion act which enjoyed a half a dozen hits in the U.K., is best remembered in the U.S. for "I'm Telling You Now" (#1, 1965) and possibly "Do the Freddie" (#18, 1965), or simply the group's bespectacled ex-milk-man nerd frontman Freddie Garrity.

AUTOGRAPHS

A CD, LP, magazine cover, ad, photo, or card signed by the group: $10-$30

OFTEN OVERLOOKED MEMORABILIA

Movie memorabilia from *Seaside Swingers*, *Just For You*, and *Cuckoo Patrol*; videotapes of the group's numerous television performances including *Shindig!* and *Hulabaloo*; copies of the U.K. kid show *The Little Big Time*; trading cards (Donruss) - $75 (set)

Free

Formed 1968

Paul Rodgers, Born: December 12, 1949; Paul Kosoff (1950 - 1976); Andy Fraser, Born: August 7, 1942; and Simon Kirke, Born: July 28, 1949*

*Group disbanded in 1971, then re-formed in 1972 under new lineup

This British blues-rooted rock band is best remembered for the song "All Right Now" (#4, 1970) and for setting a sound that would heavily influence the '70s hard-rock bands. This is not surprising because the group's members would later move on to other significant bands (i.e. Bad Company).

The band's first two albums stalled in the U.S., but touring with Blind Faith in 1969 increased its exposure and when *Fire and Water* hit, the group was better positioned to score a successful single, which it did with "All Right Now." Just months afterwards the band fell apart.

AUTOGRAPHS

A CD, LP, magazine cover, ad, photo, or card signed by the group: $20-$60

Freeman, Bobby

Born: June 13, 1940

Freeman, the late-50s R&B singer, best remembered for his hit and cover classic "Do You Wanna Dance" (#5, 1958) and numerous minor hits, including "Shimmy Shimmy" (1960) and "The Mess Around" (1961), later scored, during the dance craze era, with the Top Five "C'mon and Swim," before he left the mainstream music scene.

AUTOGRAPHS

A CD, LP, magazine cover, ad, photo, or card signed by the artist: $7-$15

Frey, Glen: See the Eagles

Friedman, Kinky

(Richard Friedman)
Born: October 31, 1944

Kinky Friedman, the Texas songwriter, performer, and band leader, has been releasing albums since 1973. He is commonly associated with saloon classics "High on Jesus," "Asshole from El Paso," and "Get Your Biscuits in the Oven and Your Buns in the Bed," along with numerous others.

He has built a substantial following through the years, no doubt attributed to his dynamic stage shows and extensive touring. Friedman impressed Bob Dylan enough to get invited on the Rolling Thunder Revue, impressed Nashville enough to perform at the Grand Ole Opry, and depressed himself enough to now concentrate on writing novels instead of performing.

AUTOGRAPHS

A CD, LP, magazine cover, ad, photo, or card signed by the artist: $10-$25

OFTEN OVERLOOKED MEMORABILIA

Memorabilia from his 1986 political campaign for Justice of the Peace in Kerrville, Texas

REFERENCE BOOKS

Copies of his numerous mystery novels, such as *A Case of Lone Star* (1987)

The Friends of Distinction

Formed 1967

Harry Elston, Floyd Butler, Jessica Cleaves, and Barbara Love

This late-60s pop vocal group, best remembered for two songs, "Grazin' in the Grass" (#3, 1969) and "Love or Let Me Be Lonely" (#6, 1970), and for being backed by football Hall of Famer Jim Brown.

AUTOGRAPHS

A CD, LP, magazine cover, ad, photo, or card signed by the group: $8-$15

Fripp, Robert

Born: May 16, 1946

Progressive rock pioneer, futurist, composer, metaphysical disciple, guitarist, and producer, Robert Fripp is best acknowledged for his conceptual, yet state-of-the-art approach to his tasks, along with his involvement with Brian Eno (Frippertronics), and his hobby King Crimson.

AUTOGRAPHS

A CD, LP, magazine cover, ad, photo, or card signed by the artist: $15-$25

Frisell, Bill

Born: March 18, 1951

Formally trained, '80s leading experimental guitarist, Bill Frisell has left his mark on more than 50 albums. He played the New York avant-garde scene before he finally settled on the West Coast.

AUTOGRAPHS

A CD, LP, magazine cover, ad, photo, or card signed by the artist: $5-$10

Frith, Fred: See Henry Cow

Frizzell, Lefty

(1928-1975)

Legendary country and western singer and songwriter, whose honky-tonk style influenced many who followed including Merle Haggard and Willie Nelson, Lefty Frizzell had 15 Top Ten country hits over a four year span (1950-54) including "Always Late (with Your Kisses)" (#1, 1951), "Mom and Dad's Waltz (#2, 1951), "I Want to Be with You Always" (#1, 1951), and "Travelin' Blues" (#6, 1951). He turned his back to the business in the late '50s and charted only on occasion. His last major hit to chart was "Saginaw, Michigan" (#1, C&W, 1964).

AUTOGRAPHS

A LP, magazine cover, ad, photo, or card signed by the artist: $25-$75

Froese, Edgar: See Tangerine Dream

Front 242

Formed 1981

Daniel B. (Bressanutti), Patrick Codenys, and Jean-Luc De Meyer

These influential '80s European techno-industrial pioneers, who, although they never charted, were still successful in planting the seed for future bands such as Ministry and Nine Inch Nails, who would later cultivate and nurture the music form. Throughout the '80s they infiltrated the underground dance-club scene through powerful statements such as "Quite Unusual" and the "Headhunter," but didn't garner national exposure until their inclusion in the 1993 summer Lollapalooza Tour.

AUTOGRAPHS

A CD, LP, magazine cover, ad, photo, or card signed by the group: $10-$15

OFTEN OVERLOOKED MEMORABILIA

Lollapalooza '93 artifacts

Fugazi

Formed 1987

Ian MacKaye, Guy Picciotto, Joe Lally, and Brendan Canty

Fugazi, a late-80s hardcore indie punk survivor, turned its backs on mainstream record labels and chose pride in the message rather than the money. As such, the respect for the band and its indie roots has only grown over the years; the band still enjoys the fact that it can fill a large venue. Another reason for its success, similar to the Clash, is its willingness to forgo profit for principle. That's why Fugazi releases and concert tickets for Fugazi shows are still affordable.

If you could bottle the best of hardcore punk rock, it would be Fugazi.

AUTOGRAPHS

A CD, LP, magazine cover, ad, photo, or card signed by the group: $10-$20

The Fugs

Formed 1965

Ed Sanders, Tuli Kupferberg, and Ken Weaver

These late-60s poets and cosmic satirists of the hippie era, who delighted or offended numerous individuals who attended their off-Broadway rock experience in Greenwich Village during the late '60s, were beat musicians who found cynicism in the absurd and often appeared as if they had fallen out of a Diane Arbus photography portfolio. Nonetheless they delighted in their association with beat figures of their time, of which in reality they too could be included. Sanders, despite having published the literary magazine *Fuck You*, now a collectors item, turned out to be a talented writer; he published the best-selling book *The Family* about the Charles Manson case. Kupferberg also got involved in numerous avant-garde projects, while he still developed his writing. The Fugs remain an enigma! Peace!

AUTOGRAPHS

A CD, LP, magazine cover, ad, photo, or card signed by the group: $10-$20

OFTEN OVERLOOKED MEMORABILIA

Any and all 60s artifacts, from Allen Ginsburg poems to old Greenwich Village corn muffins

REFERENCE BOOKS

The Family by Ed Sanders

The Bobby Fuller Four

Formed Mid-60s

Bobby Fuller (1943 - 1966), Randy Fuller, DeWayne Quirico, and Jim Reese

Texas picante sauce sipping varmints of the mid-60s, the Bobby Fuller Four is best remembered for two hits: "I Fought the Law" (#9, 1966) and "Love's Made a Fool of You" (#26, 1966). Tragically, Fuller died under mysterious circumstances in the summer of 1966, the police claimed suicide, and others foul play.

AUTOGRAPHS

An LP, magazine cover, ad, photo, or card signed by the group: $20-$45*

*Original members

Fuller, Jesse "Lone Cat"

Born: March 12, 1896, Died: January 29, 1976

One of rock's original one-man bands, "Lone Cat" was a superb country-bluesman and is known best for his song "San Francisco Bay Blues" (1954).

AUTOGRAPHS

A LP, magazine cover, ad, photo, or card signed by the artist: $20-$40

OFTEN OVERLOOKED MEMORABILIA

Movie memorabilia from *The Thief of Bagdad, East of Suez*; artifacts from the 1959 Monterey Jazz Festival

Fulson, Lowell

Born: March 31, 1921

This talented '60s R&B performer and songwriter wrote the early R&B hits "Three O'Clock Blues," "You Know That I Love You," "Come Back Baby," and later penned "Blue Shadows" (#1, R&B, 1950), "Lonesome Christmas" (#7, R&B, 1950), "Reconsider Baby" (#3, R&B, 1954), and "Tramp" (#5, R&B, 1957), just to name a few. He toured into the '70s and has received a "Handful of Handys" (5 W.C. Handy Awards).

AUTOGRAPHS

A CD, LP, magazine cover, ad, photo, or card signed by the artist: $10-$25

Funicello, Annette

Born: October 22, 1942

Mouseketeer, teen queen, actress, and singer, "Annette" had Disney's help in launching her recording career, which included the classic "milk & cookies" songs "Tall Paul" (#7, 1959), "First Name Initial" (#20, 1959), and "Pineapple Princess" (#11, 1960), before she befriended Paul Anka and ran off to the beach.

AUTOGRAPHS

A CD, LP, magazine cover, ad, photo, or card signed by the artist: $15-$30

OFTEN OVERLOOKED MEMORABILIA

Movie memorabilia from *Babes in Toyland, Monkey's Uncle* (1965), *Beach Party* (1963), *Muscle Beach Party, Bikini Beach*, and *Pajama Party* (all 1964), *Beach Blanket Bingo* (1965), *Head* (1968), and *Back to the Beach* (1987); an autographed jar of Skippy peanut butter - $25; videotapes of *The Mickey Mouse Club* (1955-1959)

REFERENCE BOOKS

A Dream Is a Wish Your Heart Makes: My Story, her autobiography (1994)

*See other books on Disney memorabilia

Funkadelic: See George Clinton

Furay, Richie: See Poco

Fury, Billy

(Ronald Wycherly) Born: April 17, 1941, Died: January 28, 1983

This '60s British pop idol best remembered for his U.K. hits "Maybe Tomorrow" (#18, 1959), "Colette" (#9, 1960), "That's Love" (#19, 1960) and later for "Halfway to Paradise" (#3), "Jealousy" (#2), and "I'd Never Find Another You" (#5), racked up nearly 20 U.K. hits during his brief stardom.

AUTOGRAPHS

An LP, magazine cover, ad, photo, or card signed by the artist: $45-$120

OFTEN OVERLOOKED MEMORABILIA

Movie memorabilia from *That'll Be the Day* (1973)

G, Kenny

(Kenneth Gorelick)
Born: June 5, 1956

Kenny G's contemporary jazz style has made him a crowd favorite and an extremely successful instrumental recording artist. Gorelick took up the saxophone as a child and by the time he was 17 he played in Barry White's Love Unlimited Orchestra. He then landed in a funk band (Cold, Bold, and Together), graduated with honors from college, and played in Jeff Lorber's Fusion Band.

His first three albums on Arista Records did well, but he hit gold with *Duotones* (#6, 1986). The album successfully crossed over markets and yielded the hit "Songbird" (#4, 1986). *Silhouette* (#8, 1988) and *Breathless* (#2, 1992) soon followed with similar success. *Breathless* featured vocals by noted singers Aaron Neville and Peabo Bryson. He has also recorded with the likes of Aretha Franklin, Whitney Houston, and Natalie Cole. His Christmas album, *Miracles: The Holiday Album,* became the first holiday album to hit the U.S. #1 position since 1962.

AUTOGRAPHS

A CD, LP, magazine cover, ad, photo, or card signed by the artist: $20-$40

TOUR BOOKS/PROGRAMS/PASSES

Backstage Passes:
Cloth: $5-$8; Laminated: $8-$15

POSTERS/PRESS KITS

Promotional Posters: $10-$20
Live (17" x 22"): $10
Press Kits: $15-$32

Gabriel, Peter

Born: February 13, 1950

On August 16, 1975, Peter Gabriel confirmed his decision to leave Genesis with a belated press announcement. His first of four eponymously-titled albums, *Peter Gabriel* is released in February 1977. The release coincides with his first solo tour of North America. The album spins off two singles, "Solsbury Hill" (#68, 1977) and "Modern Love," although both do little to draw attention to the singer. His second solo album *Peter Gabriel* (#45) is released in June 1978. The album shoots off the single "D.I.Y.," which does well in the U.K. (#10). Gabriel turns his attention to writing a screenplay for the Genesis epic *The Lamb Lies Down On Broadway,* but the movie never materializes. His third *Peter Gabriel* (#22, 1980) album is released in May 1980 and includes the U.K. hit "Games Without Frontiers." Also recorded in Ger-

man for a separate release, the album also contains a protest song in memory of South African activist Steven Biko. For his fans it's the first indication that Gabriel has not lost his beliefs and his concern for human rights.

Gabriel inaugurates WOMAD, the "World of Music Arts and Dance" Festival on July 16-18, 1982. The event, often personally costly, is another tribute to his convictions. The last of the *Peter Gabriel* (#28) albums is released in September 1982. In the U.S., Geffen Records (Gabriel's new label) slaps stickers on the sleeve that read "Security" ($3-$5) to separate it from earlier albums. The album spins off "Shock The Monkey" (#29, 1983). During this period a documentary feature on Gabriel appears on *The South Bank Show* (ITV). To satisfy Gabriel fans, Geffen releases *Peter Gabriel Plays Live* (#44, 1983), while Gabriel contributes "Walk Through The Fire" to the *Against All Odds* soundtrack. In 1985 Gabriel releases *Birdy,* a soundtrack composed and performed by him.

So (#2) is released in 1986, and becomes Peter Gabriel's biggest-selling album of the decade. It also takes the performer to a new commercial level, transcending the average chart performance of his previous albums. The album's first single, "Sledgehammer" (#1, 1986), tops the chart as Gabriel's innovative claymation promotional videotape becomes an all-time favorite. The album also spawned "Big Time" (#8, 1987), "In Your Eyes" (#26, 1986) and "Don't Give Up" (#72, 1987). Unlike so many other performers, Peter Gabriel's commercial success brought him back to his principles, as the artist dedicated his efforts during the years that followed to Amnesty International. Like performers such as U2, Sting, and Bruce Springsteen, his humanitarian efforts begin to equal his musical accomplishments.

In August 1988 the controversial Martin Scorsese-directed film *The Last Temptation of Christ,* with a

Peter Gabriel

Peter Gabriel score, premieres in the U.K. and U.S. The one sheet for the film can command $15-$35 and is of great interest to Gabriel collectors. On February 21, 1990, he wins a Grammy in the Best New Age Performance Category. In 1991 Geffen issues *Shaking The Tree: Sixteen Golden Greats* (#48), as the artist again focuses on humanitarian causes, raising money for Kurdish refugees during a performance. On September 10, 1991, the soundtrack to *Until The End Of The World*, featuring Gabriel, is released.

Of interest to collectors is the musician's interest in other fields of the arts. On January 21-24, 1993, the "ART 93" exhibition at the Business Design Center, Islington, London, holds an interesting display of the work of worldwide artists asked to interpret a track on Gabriel's most recent album. Memorabilia surrounding this exhibit is a nice complement to a Gabriel collection. For videotape collectors the early 1990s is also rich in artifacts, including *What's That Noise* (BBC1-TV, 10/7/92), *Late Show With David Letterman* (CBS-TV, 8/9/94) and *The Secret World Of Peter Gabriel* (ITV, 8/28/94). In his pursuit of conquering other media, Gabriel releases the "Xplora 1: Peter Gabriel's Secret World" CD-ROM—hopefully the first of many contributions into cyberspace.

Peter Gabriel's unlimited boundaries make him a fascinating subject to collect.

AUTOGRAPHS
Peter Gabriel is very obliging to autograph requests.
A CD, LP, magazine cover, ad, photo, or card signed by the artist: $20-$50

A Peter Gabriel backstage pass

TOUR BOOKS/ PROGRAMS/PASSES
Programs:
1993 U.K. Tour: $15
1986 European Tour Book (So): $12-$18
Backstage Passes:
Cloth: $8-$20; Laminated: $10-$25

POSTERS/PRESS KITS
Promotional Posters:
$10-$40
1987 Italian Concert Poster (27" x 40"): $20
French Tour Poster (50" x 70"): $40
Press Kits: $15-$30

OFTEN OVERLOOKED MEMORABILIA
Contributions to numerous recording compilations, most of which are benefits; any literature or associated items from the various organizations he has been involved with: Witness, Human Rights Youth In Action, WOMAD, etc.; "Us" Real World promotional box set that includes CD, 10 color prints, and press information, 1992; a pair of mirrored contact lenses; the CD ROM *Eve*

REFERENCES/BOOKS
A couple resources exist, but nothing that does justice to the singer in my opinion; no dedicated collector books

****

"On The Edge"

Galas, Diamanda
The Divine Punishment, Saint of the Pit, and *Masque of Red Death Trilogy* are a testament to Galas's powerful multi-octave vocal range. Never without a mission, her appreciation for so many different elements of life often engages her audience. Her seriousness was set aside as she teamed up with former Zeppelin bassist John Paul Jones and former Attractions drummer Pete Thomas for *The Sporting Life* (Mute, 1994). The effort may not have been her best, it certainly brought with it a new dimension and introduced her to a new audience. Pre-1990 memorabilia, most of which is associated with Mute Records Limited, is a good starting point for collectors.

****

Gallagher, Rory

Born: March 2, 1949, Died: June 14, 1995

Irish blues guitarist Rory Gallagher learned the guitar at an early age and took up with groups such as the Fontana Showband, Impact, and finally with the talented trio Taste (Gallagher, Charlie McCracken, and John Wilson). With Taste, Gallagher was able to showcase his guitar prowess, which was rich in hard-rock licks, melded blues, and a slight taste of country. When the band split up in 1971, Gallagher took to the road under his own name to build a fairly successful solo career. His talents landed him on Muddy Waters' *The London Sessions* (1972) and Lonnie Donegan's comeback album in 1978. His 1974 Irish Tour was the subject of a documentary by director Tony Palmer.

On June 14, 1995, he died from complications following a liver transplant.

AUTOGRAPHS
A CD, LP, magazine cover, ad, photo, or card signed by the artist: $15-$35

Gang of Four

Formed 1977

Jon King, Born: June 8, 1955; Hugo Burnham, Born: March 25, 1956; Andy Gill, Born: January 1, 1956; and Dave Allen, Born: December 23, 1955*

*Allen departs in 1981 and Sara Lee is added on bass

Formed in London in the late 1970s, Gang Of Four fused funk, punk, and reggae, with a dash of political

sarcasm. They were successful in the U.K. and also drew well in the U.S. Memorabilia surrounding the band's debut EP on the indie label Fast Product is scarce, but worth searching for, while *Entertainment* artifacts are a must. The band moved to Warner Brothers Records in 1979, which, in hindsight, may have hampered their success by a series of fragmented releases. With little U.S. radio play, the band built a following around club release hits such as "At Home, He's a Tourist," "Damaged Goods" and "I Love a Man in Uniform."

The group disbanded in 1984, with each member going different ways. Dave Allen went on to other bands before founding his own indie label World Domination. Andy Gill went on to showcase his production work with bands such as the Red Hot Chili Peppers. He even teamed up with fellow Four member Jon King to produce the soundtrack for *The Karate Kid* (1984). The band later re-formed for the comeback release *Mall* (Polydor, 1991).

AUTOGRAPHS

Group:

A CD, LP, magazine cover, ad, photo, or card signed by the group: $20-$30

Individual:

Jon King: $5-$10
Andy Gill: $5-$10
Dave Allen: $5-$10

USED CLOTHING/EQUIPMENT

Guitar Picks: $5

OFTEN OVERLOOKED MEMORABILIA

A one sheet from *The Karate Kid*: $8-$16

Gang Starr

Formed 1988

The Guru Keith E. (Keith Elam) and DJ Premeir (Chris Martin)

Director Spike Lee brought the group together with Branford Marsalis to combine efforts on music for *Mo' Better Blues*. It became the big break they were looking for and expanded the exposure of their music. Their first release, *No More Mr. Nice Guy* on Wild Pitch Records (1989), got them off to a good start with numbers such as "Jazz Music" and "Positivity" before they moved up to Chrysalis Records and put out *Step In The Arena* (1991). The Chrysalis release landed them in the Top Twenty on the R&B charts.

Keith Elam later released *Jazzmatazz* (1993), a solo effort that brought him some attention. The album was infused with tastes of jazz, hip-hop, and a tad of rock, and featured guest artists Courtney Pine and Marsalis.

AUTOGRAPHS

A CD, LP, magazine cover, ad, photo, or card signed by the group: $20-$25

The Gap Band

Formed early 1970s

Ronnie Wilson, Charles Wilson, and Robert Wilson

Born into the Pentecostal religion, it wasn't long before the three Wilson brothers were singing in front of their father's sermon. Using the first initials of three local streets, they came up with the name Gap (Greenwood, Archer, Pine). In 1974 they impressed a fellow Oklahoma musician Leon Russell, who signed them to his Shelter Records label. There the band cut their debut, *Magician's Holiday,* and even played in Russell's backup band. The brothers then headed to Los Angeles in hopes of increasing their success. Their self-titled debut release for Tattoo Records (1977) started building a foundation that was well in place when Mercury records signed them.

"Shake," "Steppin'(Out)," and "I Don't Believe You Want To Get Up and Dance" were all R&B Top Ten hits that catapulted the group into the limelight. *The Gap Band III* (#16, 1981) was their springboard and it spun off their first Number One R&B hit: "Burn Rubber (Why You Wanna Hurt Me)" (1980). *Gap Band IV* (#16) followed and packed two #1 R&B singles: "Early in the Morning" and "Outstanding."

With the band firmly planted in the R&B charts by 1983, the hits just kept coming: "All of My Love" (#1, R&B, 1989), "Beep a Freak" (#2, 1984), and "Party Train" (#3 R&B, 1983) just to name a few.

Charles Wilson soon extended his interest in other directions, working with Dave Stewart (Eurythmics) on a variety of projects, including some song collaborations and even a soundtrack *(Rooftops)*.

AUTOGRAPHS

A CD, LP, magazine cover, ad, photo, or card signed by the group: $20-$45

Garfunkel, Art

Born: December 5, 1941

Art Garfunkel's dynamic vocal range and creative arrangements were integral to the success of Simon & Garfunkel. When the two finally separated, it was Garfunkel's interest in film that contributed to the departure. His first film appearance was in *Catch-22* (1969), leading to casting in *Carnal Knowledge* (1971) and *Bad Timing/A Sensual Obsession* (1980).The success of the duo, however, constantly led to regrouping rumors, some even coming true,

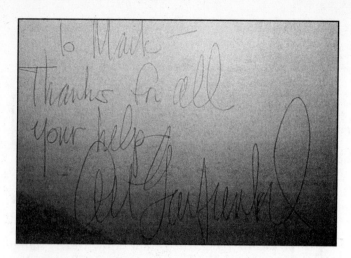

Art Garfunkel's signature

A mid-70s teen idol, Garrett scored first with his own television series, *Three for the Road* (1975). His popularity landed him a debut record contract with Atlantic in 1977 for his self-titled album. He put together a string of moderate cover hits including "Surfin' U.S.A." (#20, 1977), "Runaround Sue" (#13, 1978) and "The Wanderer" (#49, 1978). His 1979 single "I Was Made for Dancin'" went Top Ten in both the U.S. and U.K.

Garrett put together some film credits that included a 1969 role in *Bob and Carol and Ted and Alice* and the *Walking Tall* movies. He later slipped into obscurity only to surface on an occasional music retrospective such as those on VH-1.

AUTOGRAPHS
A CD, LP, magazine cover, ad, photo, or card signed by the artist: $5-$10

---

such as the September 19, 1981, concert in New York's Central Park.

It wasn't until 1973 that Garfunkel decided to resurrect his music career with *Angel Clare* (#5). This album also spun off the single "All I Know" (#9, 1973), his first solo hit single and successful collaboration with songwriter Jimmy Webb. *Breakaway* (#39, 1976) followed and yielded the single "I Only Have Eyes For You" (#18, 1975), "My Little Town" (#9, 1975) and a self-titled track (#39, 1976). *Watermark* (#19, 1978) followed and Garfunkel supported the album with his first U.S. solo tour. A consummate perfectionist, it wasn't unlike him to have two-hour sound checks prior to a show during this 50-city tour. *Fate For Breakfast* (1979), *Scissors Cut* (1981) and *Garfunkel:Lefty* (1988) follow on Columbia Records.

Up 'Til Now (1993) was his first release for Sony, and coincided with his appearance at Carnegie Hall as part of a Paul Simon career retrospective.

AUTOGRAPHS
Garfunkel is a reluctant, but obliging signer of autographs. He is a very quiet and introspective individual who cherishes his privacy.
A CD, LP, magazine cover, ad, photo, or card signed by artist: $20-$45

TOUR BOOKS/PROGRAMS/PASSES
Backstage Passes:
Cloth/paper: $10; Laminated: $12-$20

POSTERS/PRESS KITS
Promotional Posters: $15-$40
Press Kits: $20-$40

OFTEN OVERLOOKED MEMORABILIA
Movie one sheets for *Catch-22* - $17-$35 and *Carnal Knowledge* - $25-$45; "Watermark" circular mobile - $65; "Watermark" 3-D mobile - $50

Garrett, Leif

Born: November 8, 1961

Gaye, Marvin

(Marvin Pentz Gay Jr.)
Born: April 2, 1939, Died: April 1, 1984

For more than two decades, Marvin Gaye's dynamic rich vocal range, put to romantic ballads and gifted compositions, broke the hearts or ignited the souls of pop, soul, and R&B audiences. Considered by many as one of the premier performers of his era, he was tragically struck down just hours before his 45th birthday.

May 23, 1964 poster for Marvin Gaye, who performed at the Hollywood Bowl in New West Minster, British Columbia. Printed by Tilghman Press of Oakland, CA, this 16" x 24" poster is worth more than $2,000. From the collection of Hank Thompson.

With a talent nurtured both in church and on the street corners of Washington DC, Gaye joined the Marquees—later the Moonglows—followed by Harvey & the Moonglows. Transplanted to Detroit via Chicago Gaye worked as both a session drummer and backup vocalist before signing as a solo artist in 1961.

The singles "Stubborn Kind of Fellow," "Pride and Joy" (#10, 1963), "What's the Matter With You Baby" (#17, 1964), "Try It Baby" (#15, 1964), and duets with Mary Wells on "You're a

Wonderful One" and "Once Upon a Time" quickly drew attention to the performer. Meanwhile, teamed with William Stevenson, Gaye penned "Dancing in the Streets," which Martha & the Vandellas sent up the singles chart (#2, 1964).

"How Sweet It Is (to Be Loved By You)" (#6, 1965), "I'll Be Doggone" (#8, 1965, #1 R&B), and "Ain't That Peculiar" (#8, 1965, #1 R&B) quickly solidified Gaye as a force to be contended with on the singles charts. The success allowed the performer a chance to release two albums of a different vein, *A Tribute to the Great Nat "King" Cole* (1965) and *Hello Broadway* (1965). Both albums are a tribute to his influence and a testament to his extraordinary abilities.

Gaye then teamed up with Philadelphia singer Tammi Terrell, taking the duets "Ain't No Mountain High Enough" (#19, 1967), "Your Precious Love" (#5, 1967), "If I Could Build My Whole World Around You" (#10, 1968), "Ain't Nothing Like the Real Thing" (#8, 1968), and "You're All I Need to Get By" (#7, 1968) up the charts. While the duo scored other hits, Terrell battled a brain tumor. Following eight operations in less than two years, she died on March 17, 1970.

Gaye's successful solo efforts "I Heard It Through the Grapevine" (#1, 1968) and "That's The Way Love Is" (#7, 1969) took a backseat to his concern for Terrell. Her death sent him into seclusion. His performance at Super Bowl V marked the end of his isolation period.

During the '70s, Gaye scored with the anthem-like singles "What's Going On" (#2, 1971), "Mercy Mercy Mercy (The Ecology) (#4, 1971), and "Inner City Blues (Make Me Wanna Holler)." The transition to a greater sense of social consciousness in his music was less commercially successful worldwide, however, in the U.S. Gaye scored big with "Let's Get It On" (#2, 1973), "You Are Everything" (#9, 1974) with Diana Ross, "I Want You" (#15, 1976), and "Got to Give It Up" (#1, 1977). The decade was not without tarnish, however, as Gaye battled numerous lawsuits, the IRS, depression, and substance abuse. "Sexual Healing" (1983) captured the artist his first Grammy. With a plethora of personal problems, Gaye, who was living at his parents' home at 2101 S. Grammercy in Los Angeles, was fatally shot by his father during an argument.

AUTOGRAPHS

A CD, LP, magazine cover, ad, photo, or card signed by the artist: $100-$150

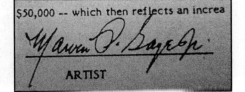

A tough signature to run across— Marvin Gaye

OFTEN OVERLOOKED MEMORABILIA

The Moonglows related artifacts; The Motown Revue and Murray The K's "Rock 'n' Roll Extravaganza" (1964) memorabilia; videotapes of his numerous television appearances including *TAMI Show* (10/28/64), *Scene At 6:30* (1964), *Ready, Steady, Go!* (1964), *Thank Your Lucky Stars* (1964), *Saturday Club* (1964), *It's What's Happening Baby* (6/28/65); his recordings, often as a drummer, with other musicians such as Little Stevie Wonder; memorabilia from the 1968 World Series—Gaye sang the national anthem; movie memorabilia from *Trouble Man* (1973) and *The Big Chill* (1983); Super Bowl V memorabilia; boxing memorabilia from Larry Holmes vs. Ernie Shavers (9/28/79); artifacts from the 1983 NBA All-Star Game; a rubbing from his star on the Hollywood Walk of Fame; a copy of the documentary *Inner City Blues: The Music of Marvin Gaye.*

REFERENCES/BOOKS

A couple resources exist, but start with Sharon Davis's book *I Heard It Through the Grapevine;* no dedicated collector books

---

Gaynor, Gloria

Born: September 7, 1949

Late-70s disco dance diva best remembered for her singles "Honey Bee," "Never Can Say Goodbye" (#9, 1975), the smash dance classic "I Will Survive" (#1) and finally "I Am What I Am" (#13, U.K.).

AUTOGRAPHS

A CD, LP, magazine cover, ad, photo, or card signed by the artist: $5-$10

Geils, J. Band

Formed 1967

Jerome Geils, Born: February 20, 1946; Peter Wolf (Peter Blankfield) Born: March 7, 1946; Magic Dick (Dick Salwitz), Born: May 13, 1945; Danny Klein, Born: May 13, 1946; and Stephen Jo Bladd, Born: July 13, 1942. Seth Justman is added in 1968.*

*Wolf departs in 1983. Bluestime is formed and releases first album in 1994.

Seventies R&B and blues-rooted pop band led by frantic former DJ and "Woofuh Goofuh" frontman Peter Wolf, the J. Geils Band toured constantly in the early 70s, building a strong following especially in New England. Their down-home party reputation and showmanship made them an enticing live act that was cultivated by the hit singles "Looking for a Love" (#39, 1971), "Give It to Me" (#30, 1973) and "Must of Got Lost" (#12, 1974).

Their tenth album, *Sanctuary* (1978), was also their debut record for EMI America and was followed by *Love Stinks* (1980), which introduced a more synthesizer and keyboard-flavored approach. The twist in sound bore fruit with the album *Freeze-Frame* (#1, 1981), which yielded three hit singles: "Centerfold" (#1, 1981), "Freeze-Frame" (#4, 1982) and "Angel in Blue" (#40, 1982).

Tension between Wolf and Justman, both of whom were the band's principle song writers, led to the former's departure in 1983. Wolf's *Lights Out* yielded both the title track (#12, 1984) and "I Need You Tonight" (#36, 1984) as singles. Geils then broke up after one unsuccessful album without Wolf.

AUTOGRAPHS

A CD, LP, magazine cover, ad, photo, or card signed by the group: $20-$40

TOUR BOOKS/PROGRAMS/PASSES

Tour Books:
Freeze Frame Tour: $12-$15

Backstage Passes:
Cloth/paper: $10-$20; Laminated: $15-$30

Geldof, Bob: See Boomtown Rats

Gene Loves Jezebel

Formed 1981

Jay Aston, Michael Aston, Ian Hudson, Peter Rizzo, and Chris Bell*

*Hudson departs in 1985 and is replaced with James Stevenson. M. Aston leaves in 1988. Robert Adam is added in 1990.

Mid-80s New Romantic pop band led by the Aston twins and best remembered for their single "Motion of Love" (#87, 1988), before Michael's departure and the eventual demise of the band.

AUTOGRAPHS

A CD, LP, magazine cover, ad, photo, or card signed by the group: $5-$10

Genesis

Formed 1966

Tony Banks, Born: March 27, 1950; Michael Rutherford, Born: October 2, 1950; Peter Gabriel, Born: February 13, 1950; Anthony Phillips; and Chris Stewart*

*Stewart leaves in 1968 and John Silver joins the band. John Mayhew replaces Silver on drums in 1969. Mayhew and Phillips depart in 1970 and Phil Collins, Born: January 31, 1951, is added on drums, while Steve Hackett, Born: February 12, 1950, replaces Phillips. Peter Gabriel leaves in 1975, Collins assumes vocal role. Hackett leaves in 1977. Phil Collins leaves in 1996, and Ray Nelson is added.

A Genesis concert photo

Rock historians often break down Genesis into two distinct periods, defined simply by the group's lead singers: "The Peter Gabriel Period" followed by "The Phil Collins Period." From inception until the time Peter Gabriel decided to leave the band, they had developed a strong cult following through their period-defined music and a theatrical stage presence. Their music, often defined as "art rock," was given far less credit than it deserved for the period. Although classical undertones were indeed present, the group camouflaged them with complex chord patterns and intricate storylines.

THE PETER GABRIEL PERIOD

The band was formed from two groups: The Anon (Anthony Phillips, Michael Rutherford, Rob Tyrell, Richard MacPhail, and Rivers Job) and Garden Wall (Tony Banks, Peter Gabriel, and Chris Stewart). The band (Rutherford, Phillips, Banks, Gabriel, and Stewart) records a demo tape in December 1966 that catches the ear of Jonathan King, an intuitive businessman who signs Genesis to a contract. The band's first single ("The Silent Sun"/"That's Me") was released on Decca Records on February 22, 1968; their first album (*From Genesis To Revelation*, March 1969) followed. On the first album were Rutherford, Gabriel, Banks, Phillips, and Silver. In April 1970 they sign with Charisma Records and release *Trespass* (October 1970). Group personnel on their second album is identical to their first, minus Silver on drums (he is replaced by John Mayhew).

Nursery Cryme (November 1971), *Foxtrot* (October 1972), *Presenting Genesis* (Compilation, 1973) and *Genesis Live* (August 1973) soon followed, but by this time some changes had taken place in the band. Phil

Collins replaces John Mayhew on drums (9/70) and Steve Hackett replaces guitarist Anthony Phillips (1/71). The group joins a Charisma package tour in January 1971 supporting Lindisfarne and Van Der Graaf Generator. The U.K. tour consists of only nine major halls, making memorabilia from this tour extremely scarce. The band's first foreign concert is in Brussels in January 1972, but it's Italy that greets *Nursery Cryme* with open arms and a strong charting position. The band undertakes a tour there in April 1972, consisting of only seven dates. By the time *Foxtrot* is released, frontman Peter Gabriel is focusing his full attention on the Genesis stage show. His theatrics, while upstaging some songs, certainly add a creative twist to the band and intrigue the press. In December 1972 the band made their first appearance in the U.S., but only for a brief time. The band tops the bill at London's Rainbow Theater during their first headlining U.K. tour in 1973. They return to America in March 1973 to find that outside of New York City, little is known of the band. With *Genesis Live*, the group's U.K. fans had a chance to recall the band's powerful live stage presence.

Selling England By The Pound is released in the fall of 1973, with a brief tour of America in November and December. The tour was a success in the U.S. and the band returned to the U.K. and Europe to sustain their momentum. During the summer of 1974, work begins on the band's epic, *The Lamb Lies Down on Broadway*, which was released in November. It met with mixed reviews, while the band began a six-month world tour to promote the album. It was during this tour that Peter Gabriel determined that he was going to leave the band. Although Gabriel's departure is impending, Genesis continues touring, with the final show at St. Etienne in France in May 1975. When the announcement is given to the press, most become pessimistic that Genesis can continue.

THE PHIL COLLINS PERIOD

Following intense deliberation, it is determined that Gabriel will not be replaced, but Phil Collins will assume the additional role. Collins, who had sung back-up vocals with the band, became a welcome alternative after 400 singers had auditioned. But there was still doubt as to whether he could handle both duties (vocalist and drummer) especially during some of the band's intricate songs. The band released *Trick Of The Tail* to coincide with their first world tour without Gabriel. The band asked drummer Bill Bruford (Yes, King Crimson) to join them on tour to take some of the tension away from Collins. Collins, whose wit and charm soon became an alternative for elaborate stage costumes, succeeded in providing a strong dynamic vocal range. The band combined this with a tour that for the first time included state-of-the-art lighting combined with special effects. *Wind & Wuthering* followed and even spun off a hit single,

"Your Own Special Way" (#62, 1977). Supporting *Wind & Wuthering* was a tour that included nearly 30 tons of equipment. The elaborate lighting included lasers and two rows of 48 Boeing 747 landing lights that flooded down to the stage from overhead lighting trusses. During the tour the band recorded a new double live album, *Seconds Out* (October, 1977), but before its release, Genesis loses another member, Steve Hackett.

Once again the band elects to continue, and recording sessions begin for *And Then There Were Three*. The album takes on a more commercial sound with shorter songs arranged in a more traditional fashion. Live performances are enhanced by drummer Chester Thompson, who had continued where Bruford left off, and guitarist Daryl Stuermer. The album soon sported a Top Forty single, "Follow You, Follow Me" (#23, 1978). *Duke*, a concept album, follows in 1980, with a sound similar to early Genesis, but with a commercial flair. It yields the band's second Top Forty single, "Misunderstanding" (#14, 1980). *Abacab* (#7, 1981) also follows successfully with two singles, "Abacab" (#26, 1981) and "No Reply At All" (#29, 1981). By now the group's enormous popularity and commercial success had begun to entice more solo activity by all three remaining members.

Phil Collins hits "pay dirt" first with his solo album *Face Value* (#7, 1981), although he was not the first member to do a solo project. The album spins off two Top Twenty hits: "I Missed Again" (#19, 1981) and "In The Air Tonight" (#19, 1981). He followed his first venture with *Hello, I Must Be Going!* (1982) and another hit with the Supremes' cover "You Can't Hurry Love" (#10, 1982). During these ventures Genesis remained intact and released *Genesis* (#9, 1983) with its two hits, "That's All" (#6, 1983) and "Illegal Alien" (#44, 1984). Collins's success continued with hits "Easy Lover" (#2, 1984, duet with Philip Bailey), "Against All Odds" (#1, 1984, Grammy winner) and "Separate Lives" (#1, duet with Marilyn Martin). His next solo project, *No Jacket Required* (#1, 1985), pounded the singles charts with "One More Night" (#1, 1985), "Sussudio" (#1, 1985), "Don't Lose My Number" (#4, 1985) and "Take Me Home" (#7, 1986).

Rutherford, who released solo albums of his own, eventually formed Mike + the Mechanics. The group was also successful with hits such as "Silent Running" (#6, 1985), "All I Need Is A Miracle" (#5, 1986) and "The Living Years" (#1, 1988).

Genesis returned in 1986 with *Invisible Touch* (#3), which had a hit title track (#1), "Throwing It All Away" (#4, 1986), "Land Of Confusion" (#4, 1986) and "Tonight, Tonight, Tonight" (#3, 1987). *We Can't Dance* (#4, 1991) pushed Genesis into the next decade and spun off "No Son Of Mine"(#12, 1991), "Hold On My Heart" (#12, 1992) and "I Can't Dance" (#7, 1992). Visions of the old Genesis surfaced in "Driving the Last Spike," but it was becoming increasingly clear

that the interest level, as exhibited by all members, was seriously waning.

AND THEN THERE WERE TWO

The end of "The Phil Collins Period" was on March 28, 1996. Genesis now faced the monumental task of replacing one of the most successful musicians of his era before recording the group's 20th album, *Calling All Stations* (1997).

Because of the sheer amount of memorabilia from both the band and individual members, Genesis can be an interesting band to collect. Collectors will want to pay specific attention to key dates such as the band's U.S. debut at Brandeis University, Waltham, Massachusetts, on December 11, 1972; and the band's last gig with Peter Gabriel as a member of the band at St. Etienne, France, in May 1975. A must is memorabilia from "Six of the Best," a WOMAD benefit concert held on October 2, 1982. During the show Gabriel and Hackett join Genesis for the encore "I Know What I Like." Genesis cartoon buffs can follow the work of Lionel Koechlin, who pens "Albert" on the front of *Duke*. Movie buffs can take solace in Genesis soundtrack contributions, including *The Wicked Lady* (Banks), *On Dangerous Ground* (Mike + The Mechanics) and *Against All Odds* (Collins). Genesis even appeals to beer drinkers, as they are featured in commercials for Michelob, who sponsored their Invisible tour. They move to automobiles in 1992 as Volkswagen sponsors the European leg of their tour. Also, don't forget about product brochures from Cambridge Technology Display—a Banks and Rutherford investment in light-emitting polymers.

AUTOGRAPHS

Genesis has always been very obliging to autograph requests. The entire band typically signs very small, with only Collins exhibiting any flamboyance in his signature.

Group:

Entire band on a photograph, CD, album flat, or poster: $75-$125*

*Collins, Rutherford, Banks

Tony Banks' signature (obtained in-person)

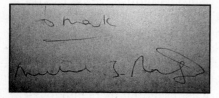

Also obtained in-person—Michael Rutherford's autograph

Phil Collins' signature (obtained in-person)

Individual:

Tony Banks: $15-$35	Peter Gabriel: $20-$50
Michael Rutherford: $15-$40	Phil Collins: $20-$50
Steve Hackett: $20-$30	Anthony Phillips: $15-$20
Chris Stewart: $5-$10	John Silver: $5-$10
John Mayhew: $5-$10	

Autographed Phil Collins drum skin used during early Genesis years: $2,500-$3,000

Alvanez 12-string acoustic guitar signed by Collins, Banks, and Rutherford: $1,500

TOUR BOOKS/PROGRAMS/PASSES

Programs:

Lindisfarne/Genesis - Autumn: $70-$85 (1972)
Genesis Compendium (10/73): $80-$120**
"The Lamb Lies Down...": $40-$55
World Tour 1977: $35
European Tour 1977 (picture book): $35
Poster/Programme (1978): $30-$32
Knebworth (6/24/78): $30-$32
"Summertime Open Air Festival" (1978, English/German): $30
"A Film of a Rock Band and..." (1976, film brochure): $25
Genesis "Tour of Japan" (1978): $25-$27
Duke (1980): $18-$22
Abacab (1981): $18-$22*
European Tour 1982: $18-$20
Genesis "Three Sides Live" (1983): $18-$22
The Mama Tour (America, 1983/84): $17-$20
Invisible Tour (1986): $15-$17
U.K. Tour 1992: $15-$17

*U.K. copies include Abacab album lyrics
**Includes poster, sticker, cardboard cut-out "Genesis" dice, and revolver!

Program from the Invisible Tour (Designed by Reiner Design Consultants, Inc.)

Backstage Passes:

World Tour 1978 (cloth): $25-$30
1983-84 Tour Staff (laminated): $20-$22
"Mama" (cloth, all forms): $12-$15
Tour 1984 (Football Uniforms) (laminated): $20
Tour 1986 Staff (laminated): $15
"Invisible Touch" (cloth, all forms): $10

1987 - Final Leg (cloth, all forms): $10
"We Can't Dance" (cloth, all forms): $10
"We Can't Dance" (laminated, laser foil): $20-$22

POSTERS/PRESS KITS

Promotional Posters:
1992-Present: $10-$15
1991-1976: $15-$40
1974-1969: $40-Utd.*
*Undetermined, many unique auction-type pieces

Press Kits:
1992-Present: $15-$20
1991-1976: $20-$50
1974-1969: $50-Utd.*
*Undetermined

USED CLOTHING/ EQUIPMENT

Guitar Picks:
Michael Rutherford:
$25-$35
Steve Hackett: $20-$30
Anthony Phillips:
$10-$15
Daryl Stuermer:
$15-$20*

Drum Sticks:
Phil Collins: $25-$35
Peter Gabriel: $40
Chris Stewart: $10
John Silver: $10
John Mayhew: $10
Chester Thompson: $15-$17

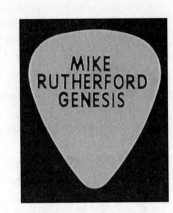

A guitar pick used by Michael Rutherford

OFTEN OVERLOOKED MEMORABILIA

"Abacab" numbered limited edition print (9,800) - $100; Rock N Roll Comics - $3-$4; "Duke" postcard - $5-$7; "World Tour 1978" button - $12; "Illegal Alien" postcard - $4; "Trick of the Tail" button - $15; "Nursery Cryme" button - $25-$30; "Lamb Lies Down on Broadway" button - $20-$25; the band's first tour advertisement in *Melody Maker* (2/28/70), page 28; "Duke" promotional pin - $15; promotional satin scarf (grey & blue) - $50; "Twilight Alehouse," Genesis Information "bag set" package that includes flexi, dice, poster, sticker, etc.; "We Can't Dance" Virgin promo box set, includes CD, (3) prints, 1991; "We Can't Dance" Virgin promo box set, includes cassette, badge, bios, pass and photos; "Selling England by the Pound" promotional Charisma yellow yo-yo, 1973, scarce; "Invisible Touch" handkerchief - $10

REFERENCES/BOOKS

Complete Guide to the Music of Genesis by Welch: $8; *Gabriel, Collins & Beyond* by Kamin & Goddard: $15; numerous resources exist; no dedicated collector books; serious collectors should opt for the numerous fan clubs, including USA Genesis Fan Club, c/o R. Baxter, P.O. Box 562, Mays Landing, NJ 08330

Gentle Giant

Formed 1970

Derek Shulman, Born: February 2, 1947; Ray Schulman; Phil Shulman; Kerry Minnear; Gary Green; Martin Smith; and Malcolm Mortimer

Seventies British progressive rock band Gentle Giant was formed with the remains of a late-60s U.K. pop band called Simon Dupree and the Big Sound ("Kites"). They quickly developed a cult following before finally breaking in America with *The Power and the Glory*. Not a singles band, the group never enjoyed the benefits of overwhelming commercial success, and by the '80s parted ways. Derek Shulman has since enjoyed success as a record executive with a variety of companies.

AUTOGRAPHS

A CD, LP, magazine cover, ad, photo, or card signed by the group: $15-$30

OFTEN OVERLOOKED MEMORABILIA

A blow-up yellow octopus - $100; "Giant for a Day" Capitol promo lollipop, mask ,and trick or treat bag

Gentry, Bobbie

(Roberta Lee Street)
Born: July 27, 1944

Late-60s pop star Bobbie Gentry is best remembered for her ballad "Ode to Billie Joe" (#1, 1967) and her duet with Glen Campbell on the Everly's "All I Have to Do Is Dream" (#27, 1970), before later marrying country singer Jim Stamford and retiring from the business.

AUTOGRAPHS

A CD, LP, magazine cover, ad, photo, or card signed by the artist: $5-$10

OFTEN OVERLOOKED MEMORABILIA

Movie memorabilia from *Ode to Billie Joe;* videotapes of her British television series *The Bobbie Gentry Show*

The Gentrys

Formed 1963

Larry Raspberry, Larry Wall, Jimmy Johnson, Bobby Fisher, Pat Neal, Bruce Bowles, and Jimmy Hart

Mid-60s Memphis band best remembered for their song "Keep on Dancing" (#4, 1965) and a few minor hits, The Gentrys broke up in 1970, then were reformed by Jimmy Hart, landing three more minor hits before calling it a day. Hart would later become familiar to a television viewing audience as a professional wrestling manager, and has even recorded songs with Hulk Hogan.

AUTOGRAPHS

A CD, LP, magazine cover, ad, photo, or card signed by the group: $10-$15

OFTEN OVERLOOKED MEMORABILIA

Videotapes of the group's television performances, including *Ted Mack's Original Amateur Hour* (1964); Bay City Rollers artifacts relating to their cover of *Keep On Dancing;* videotapes of Jimmy Hart's numerous appearances on professional wrestling shows

Georgia Satellites

Formed 1979, Keith and the Satellites

Dan Baird, Born: December 12, 1953; Mauro Megellan; Rick Price; and Rick Richards*

*Group disbands in 1991 and regroups in 1993 with Richards, Price, Joey Huffman, and Billy Pitts

Late-80s Atlanta beer-drinkin' boogie band best remembered for their song "Keep Your Hands to Yourself" (#2, 1986) and their cover version of "Hippy Hippy Shake" that appeared on the soundtrack of *Cocktail.* The Georgia Satellites called it a day in 1991, when interest in their work dissipated.

AUTOGRAPHS

A CD, LP, magazine cover, ad, photo, or card signed by the group: $10-$20

OFTEN OVERLOOKED MEMORABILIA

Movie memorabilia from *Cocktail* (1988)

Gerardo

(Gerardo Mejia III)
Born: April 16, 1965

Early-90s Latino rapper best identified with his sexy image and the song "Rico Suave" (#7, 1991), which was followed by "We Want the Funk" (#16, 1991), before slipping into obscurity.

AUTOGRAPHS

A CD, LP, magazine cover, ad, photo, or card signed by the artist: $5-$10

OFTEN OVERLOOKED MEMORABILIA

Movie memorabilia from *Colors* (1988), in which he played a gang member

Gerry and the Pacemakers

Formed 1959

Gerry Marsden, Born: September 24, 1942; Les Maguire, Born: December 27, 1941; John Chadwick, Born: May 11, 1943; and Freddie Marsden, Born: October 23, 1940

Another mid-60s British Merseybeat band that forged an early path similar to the Beatles and even shared their manager Brian Epstein. Gerry and the Pacemakers are best remembered for songs such as

"How Do You Do It?," (#9, 1964), "I Like It," "You'll Never Walk Alone," "Don't Let the Sun Catch You Crying," and "Ferry Cross the Mersey," after which interest in the band waned.

Marsden then went on to the cabaret circuit, scoring some minor hits; hosted a children's show; and even has the distinction of being the only British artist to ever top the singles chart twice with different renditions of the same song ("You'll Never Walk Alone," which he re-released under the moniker "Crowd" in 1985).

Numerous artifacts from the band, such as programs, posters, and handbills, exist with the band as a supporting act to the Beatles; thus, these items may command a hefty price.

AUTOGRAPHS

A CD, LP, magazine cover, ad, photo, or card signed by the group: $15-$60

TOUR BOOKS/PROGRAMS/PASSES

Tour Books:

Playbill, 1967, Saville Theatre, London : $80

OFTEN OVERLOOKED MEMORABILIA

Videotapes of the band's numerous television appearances; videotapes of Marsden hosting *The Sooty and Sweep Show*; Playbill (1967) Saville Theatre, London : $80

REFERENCES/BOOKS

Begin with Gerry Marsden's autobiography, *I'll Never Walk Alone;* no dedicated collector books

The Geto Boys

Formed 1986

Scarface (Brad Jordan), Born: November 9, 1969; Willie D (Willie Dennis), Born: November 1, 1966; Bushwick Bill (Richard Shaw), Born: December 8, 1966; and Ready Red*

*Willie D departs in 1992 and Big Mike is added

Late-80s gangsta rappers best known for the controversy they created surrounding the release of their first major label product, which was refused distribution on grounds of an extraordinary level of violence, and for the song "Mind Playing Tricks on Me" (#23, 1991). The Geto Boys have each also pursued solo endeavors. Mike Barnett replaced Willie D, who left the group permanently, prior to the release of the group's successful *Till Death Do Us Part* (#1, R&B, 1993).

AUTOGRAPHS

A CD, LP, magazine cover, ad, photo, or card signed by the group: $10-$25

Gibb, Andy

Born: March 5, 1958, Died: March 10, 1988

Late-70s teen idol and pop star who just happened to be the younger brother of the Bee Gees, Andy Gibb scored three chart toppers, "I Just Want to Be Your Everything" (#1, 1977), "(Love Is) Thicker Than Water" (#1, 1977), and "Shadow Dancing" (#1, 1978), and also had hits with "An Everlasting Love" (#5, 1978) and "(Our Love) Don't Throw It All Away." By the '80s his popularity had slowed and his personal life had faced the obstacle of both substance abuse and bankruptcy. While recording a new album under a new contract, he died suddenly of a viral heart inflammation.

AUTOGRAPHS

An LP, magazine cover, ad, photo, or card signed by the artist: $15-$50

POSTERS/PRESS KITS

Promotional Posters: $15-$30
Press Kits: $15-$35

OFTEN OVERLOOKED MEMORABILIA

Videotapes of his host appearances on the syndicated television show *Solid Gold;* associated memorabilia from his appearance on Broadway in *Joseph and the Amazing Technicolor Dreamcoat;* Andy Gibb doll - $40; posters (Donruss, set of 42, 1978) - $45; puzzle (11" x 17") - $30

Gibson, Debbie

Born: August 31, 1970

Late-80s wholesome teen idol, Debby Gibson is typically associated with her hit songs "Only in My Dreams" (#4, 1987), "Shake Your Love" (#4, 1987), "Out of the Blue" (#3, 1987), "Foolish Beat" (#1, 1988), "Electric Youth" (#11, 1989) and "No More Rhyme" (#17, 1989). Although she sold well, by late 1989 people were getting tired of her cutsie bubble-gum image. She then took some time off to appear in the Broadway company of *Les Miserables,* before trying to repackage herself into a sexy diva and releasing *Body Mind Soul* (#109, 1993). The public just didn't buy the transformation (or the record) and she lost her recording contract the following year.

AUTOGRAPHS

A CD, LP, magazine cover, ad, photo, or card signed by the artist: $10-$20

TOUR BOOKS/PROGRAMS/PASSES

Programs:
Electric Youth: $20
Out of the Blue: $20

Jimmie Gilmer and the Fireballs: See the Fireballs

Gilmore, Jimmie Dale

Born: May 6, 1945

Late-70s Texas "western beat" singer/songwriter best known as a member of the Flatliners, and for his critically acclaimed solo work on albums such as *After Awhile* (1991) and *Spinning Around the Sun* (#62, C&W, 1993).

AUTOGRAPHS

A CD, LP, magazine cover, ad, photo, or card signed by the artist: $20-$45

OFTEN OVERLOOKED MEMORABILIA

Associated artifacts from other musicians' covers of his work

Gilmour, David: See Pink Floyd

Ginn, Greg: See Black Flag

Glass, Philip

Born: January 31, 1937

One of America's most gifted postmodernist composers, Phillip Glass has influenced numerous forms of music with his integration of common elements into his innovative yet simplistic compositions. Having played everywhere from Max's Kansas City to the Metropolitan Opera House and Carnegie Hall, his diverse avenues have led to collaborations with a number of musicians, including ex-Doors Ray Manzarek and even poet Allen Ginsberg, while recording the music of David Bowie and David Byrne. He remains the first musician to sign an exclusive composer's contract with CBS Masterworks since the gifted Aaron Copland.

AUTOGRAPHS

A CD, LP, magazine cover, ad, photo, or card signed by the artist: $10-$45

Glitter, Gary

(Paul Gadd)
Born: May 8, 1940

Early-70s British glam-rock and rhinestone king, Gary Glitter racked up thirteen consecutive English hits, but is remembered in America for his classic "Rock and Roll Part II" (1972)—now a staple at

NCCA sporting events. Financial problems would later force him to sell many of his trademark extravagant stage costumes and custom guitars. He has periodically emerged in a number of projects, from late-night television programs to joining the Who during their mid-90s Quadrophenia tour.

AUTOGRAPHS

A CD, LP, magazine cover, ad, photo, or card signed by the artist: $10-$25

OFTEN OVERLOOKED MEMORABILIA

Videotapes of his late-night British television show *Night Network;* artifacts associated with the soundtrack to *Jesus Christ Superstar*

The Go-Betweens

Formed 1977

Robert Forster, Born: June 29, 1957; Grant McLennan, Born: February 12, 1958; and Lindy Morrison, Born: November 2, 1951*

*Robert Vickers is added in 1984 and Amanda Brown joins in 1987. Vickers leaves in 1988 and John Willsteed is added.

Eighties Australian crafty pop-rock group whose longevity and creativity have led to a substantial cult following, but little commercial success in the U.S.

AUTOGRAPHS

A CD, LP, magazine cover, ad, photo, or card signed by the group: $10-$15

The Go-Go's

Formed 1978

Belinda Carlisle, Born: August 17, 1958; Charlotte Caffey, Born: October 21, 1953; Jane Wiedlin, Born: May 20, 1958; Margot Olaverra; and Elissa Bello*

*Bello leaves in 1979 and Gina Schock is added. Olaverra departs in 1980 and Kathy Valentine joins the group. Wiedlin leaves in 1984 and the group disbands. Group reforms in 1990.

Eighties all-girl cutsie pop punk act turned headliner, best known for their upbeat hits "We Got the Beat," "Our Lips Are Sealed," "Vacation" (Top Ten), "Head Over Heels" (#11, 1984) and "Turn to You" (#32, 1984), before Wiedlin's departure and the dissolution of the group.

Belinda Carlisle went on to a successful solo career, landing hits such as "Mad About You" (#3, 1986), "Heaven Is a Place on Earth" (#1, 1987), "I Get Weak" (#2, 1987) and "Circle in the Sand" (#7, 1987), while Wiedlin landed one single, "Rush Hour" (#9, 1988), before both eventually faded from sight. The group reunited briefly for a tour to promote their hits compilation package and later to record new material.

AUTOGRAPHS

Group:
A CD, LP, magazine cover, ad, photo, or card signed by the group: $15-$50
Individual:
Belinda Carlisle: $10-$30

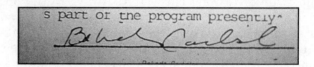

Belinda Carlisle's signature

TOUR BOOKS/PROGRAMS/PASSES

Programs:
Vacation: $15
Backstage Passes:
Cloth: $8-$12; Laminated: $12-$20

POSTERS/PRESS KITS

Promotional Posters: $10-$30
Press Kits: $22-$40

USED CLOTHING/EQUIPMENT

Guitar Picks: $10-$15
Jane Wiedlin: $15-$20
Drum Sticks: $15

OFTEN OVERLOOKED MEMORABILIA

Videotapes of their numerous television appearances

REFERENCES/BOOKS

Limited resources exist; no dedicated collector books; serious collectors should opt for fanzine: *Beatnik Beat: The Go-Go's Fanzine,* 4960 Alamaden Expy #186, San Jose, CA 95118

Godley and Creme: See 10cc

Gold, Andrew

Born: August 2, 1951

Late-70s pop guitarist, singer, songwriter, and arranger who is commonly associated with two of his hits, "Lonely Boy" (#7, 1977) and "Thank You for Being a Friend" (#25, 1978). Andrew Gold is a prolific songwriter who has had numerous musicians cover his work, including Carly Simon, James Taylor, and Art Garfunkel. Gold's association with Linda Ronstadt was instrumental in bringing him to the forefront. She hired both Gold and Kenny Edwards after listening to their demo tape, although she had also worked with Edwards in the Stone Poneys. Gold later teamed up with Graham Gouldman for four albums under the name Wax, which yielded one U.S. hit single: "Right Between the Eyes" (#43, 1986).

AUTOGRAPHS

A CD, LP, magazine cover, ad, photo, or card signed by the artist: $10-$15

The signature of Andrew Gold

POSTERS/PRESS KITS
Promotional Posters: $10-$25
Press Kits: $10-$20

USED CLOTHING/EQUIPMENT
Guitar Picks: $10

Golden Earring

Formed 1961

Prominent lineup: George Kooymans, Rinus Gerritsen, Barry Hay, and Cesar Zuiderwijk

The Netherlands' most successful band, Golden Earring is perhaps best known for their longevity. They have scored numerous hits in their homeland, but are best remembered in America for two songs, "Radar Love" (#13, 1974) and "Twilight Zone" (#10, 1982).

AUTOGRAPHS
A CD, LP, magazine cover, ad, photo, or card signed by the group: $15-$30

OFTEN OVERLOOKED MEMORABILIA
Mechanical robot mobile: $75

The Golden Palominos

Formed 1981

Anton Fier, Born: June 20, 1956

The Golden Palominos are musical assemblies consisting of various musicians all gathered by the former drummer from the Feelies, Pere Ubu, and Lounge Lizards: Anton Fier. The musical experiments have drawn a variety of musicians, including Michael Stipe, Jack Bruce, and John Lydon.

AUTOGRAPHS
A CD, LP, magazine cover, ad, photo, or card signed by the group: $10-$15

Goldsboro, Bobby

Born: January 18, 1941

Late-60s pop singer/songwriter Bobby Goldsboro landed over twenty hits on the charts during just over a decade of consistent recording, including "See the Funny Little Clown" (#9, 1964), "Little Things" (#13, 1965), "Honey" (#1, 1968) and "Watching Scotty Grow" (#11, 1971). He later went on to host his own nationally syndicated television show, form a successful music publishing venture, and write children's stories.

AUTOGRAPHS
A CD, LP, magazine cover, ad, photo, or card signed by the artist: $5-$10

OFTEN OVERLOOKED MEMORABILIA
His early contribution backing Roy Orbison (1962 to 1964); videotapes of *The Bobby Goldsboro Show* (78 episodes, 1972-1975, 39 hours of videotape required!); a Jonathan Rebel hand puppet; a videotape of the animated *Easter Egg Mornin'* (1991)

Goodman, Steve

Born: July 25, 1948

Seventies singer/songwriter best remembered for writing Arlo Guthrie's 1972 hit "The City of New Orleans," Steve Goodman's songs have been covered by numerous artists including John Denver and Joan Baez.

AUTOGRAPHS
A CD, LP, magazine cover, ad, photo, or card signed by the artist: $15-$30

The Good Rats

Formed 1965

Peppi Marchello, Mickey Marchello, Joe Franco, John Gatto, and Lenny Koe

Seventies Long Island saloon band always "on the verge of success" that they never found, The Good Rats endured even if their fans did not. Joe Franco went on to Twisted Sister, successful session and tour work, and even wrote a best-selling book on drumming, while the others slipped into the music store maintenance mode.

AUTOGRAPHS
A CD, LP, magazine cover, ad, photo, or card signed by the group: $10-$15

OFTEN OVERLOOKED MEMORABILIA
Band member independent projects

Gordon, Robert

Born: 1947

Late-70s New York new-wave rockabilly crooner, formerly a member of the Tuff Darts (veterans of the CBGB scene), Gordan's eponymous debut solo album featured guitarist Link Wray and scored a minor hit with "Red Hot" (1977), while his second album included Bruce Springsteen's "Fire," which was written specifically for the singer, only to later become a hit for the Pointer Sisters. In 1981 Gordon had a minor hit with "Someday, Someway," penned by Marshall Crenshaw, before fading from the U.S. music scene.

AUTOGRAPHS
A CD, LP, magazine cover, ad, photo, or card signed by the artist: $5-$10

OFTEN OVERLOOKED MEMORABILIA
Memorabilia from his CBGB days

Gore, Lesley

Born: May 2, 1946

Sixties teen queen and pop hit "weeper-sweeper," Gore is best remembered for her classics "It's My Party" (#1, 1963), "Judy's Turn to Cry," "She's a Fool," and "You Don't Own Me," all charting in the Top Five in 1963. The following year she landed with "That's the Way Boys Are" (#12, 1964) and "Maybe I Know" (#12, 1964), followed by "Sunshine, Lollipops and Rainbows" (#13, 1965) and "California Nights" (#16, 1967). When the hits faded, she tried acting before moving on to other moderately successful projects.

AUTOGRAPHS
A CD, LP, magazine cover, ad, photo, or card signed by the artist: $10-$15

OFTEN OVERLOOKED MEMORABILIA
Movie memorabilia from *Girls on the Beach,* and *Ski Party;* videotapes of her numerous television efforts, including *Batman*

Graham, Larry/Graham Central Station

Born: August 14, 1946

Late-70s progressive funk artist best known as former bassist for Sly and the Family Stone, Graham scored minor hits with "Can You Handle It" and "Feel the Need," before moving on to his successful ballads as a solo artist, including "One in a Million You" (#9, 1980). He scored a few other R&B hits before fading from the scene. He surfaced in 1993 backing comedian Eddie Murphy.

AUTOGRAPHS
A CD, LP, magazine cover, ad, photo, or card signed by the artist: $5-$15

OFTEN OVERLOOKED MEMORABILIA
Memorabilia from his Sly and the Family Stone days

Grand Funk Railroad

Formed 1968

Mark Farner, Born: September 29, 1948; Mel Schacher, Born: April 3, 1951; and Don Brewer, Born: September 3, 1948*

*Craig Frost on keyboards added in 1972

Early-70s blues-rock power trio who became America's most commercially successful band during the first half of the decade, despite lack of critical acclaim and singles production. Through continuous touring, Grand Funk Railroad amassed a monstrous following so big that in 1971 they broke the Beatles ticket sales record at New York's Shea Stadium.

Selling over 20 million records, the group became the benchmark for future power trios to follow, such as Cream and the Jimi Hendrix Experience. Farner wrote and sang most of the early material, with Brewer filling in when necessary, while the band was under the control of manager Terry Knight, who would later (1972) become involved in a bitter litigation battle with the band.

The group's first post-Knight release was *Phoenix* (1972), which saw the addition of keyboardist Craig Frost, followed by the Todd Rundgren produced *We're an American Band,* whose title track yielded the group's first big hit (#1, 1973). Other hits followed, including "The Locomotion" (#1, 1974), "Some Kind of Wonderful" (#3, 1975) and "Bad Time" (#4, 1975), before the group's split in 1976.

AUTOGRAPHS
A CD, LP, magazine cover, ad, photo, or card signed by the group: $30-$100

TOUR BOOKS/PROGRAMS/PASSES
Programs:
1971 Japan Tour: $200
1975 Japan Tour: $75

OFTEN OVERLOOKED MEMORABILIA
"All the Girls Beware" mobile - $50; "Good Singin', Good Playin'" mobile - $50

Grandmaster Flash and the Furious Five

Formed 1977

Grandmaster Flash (Joseph Saddler), Cowboy (Keith Wiggins), Melle Mel (Melvin Glover), Kid Creole (Nathaniel Glover), Mr. Ness (Eddie Morris), and Rahiem (Guy Williams)

Early-80s premier DJ-rap group who pioneered the urban "cutting" (segueing between tracks exactly on the beat) technique and scored hits such as "The Message" (#4, R&B, 1982), Grandmaster Flash and the Furious Five were pivotal in rap's development.

AUTOGRAPHS

A CD, LP, magazine cover, ad, photo, or card signed by the artist: $10-$30

Grant, Amy

Born: November 25, 1960

Late-80s Christian singer/songwriter who would successfully cross over into pop with her numerous hits, including "The Next Time I Fall" (#1, 1986, a duet with Peter Cetera), "Baby Baby" (#1, 1991), "Every Heartbeat" (#2, 1991) and "That's What Love Is For" (#7, 1991).

AUTOGRAPHS

A CD, LP, magazine cover, ad, photo, or card signed by the artist: $10-$20

TOUR BOOKS/PROGRAMS/PASSES

Programs:
House of Love: $20

Backstage Passes:
Cloth: $10; Laminated: $15

POSTERS/PRESS KITS

Promotional Posters: $10-$35
Press Kits: $25-$50

OFTEN OVERLOOKED MEMORABILIA

Videotapes of her television appearances

Grant, Eddy

Born: March 5, 1948

Early-80s pop/funk Rastafarian and shrewd businessman who scored hits with "Living on the Frontline" (#11, U.K., 1979), "Electric Avenue" (#2, 1983), "I Don't Wanna Dance" (#53, 1983) and "Romancing the Stone" (#26, 1984). Earlier in his career he was in the British pop-rock band the Equals, who scored a minor hit with "Baby, Come Back" (#32, 1968).

AUTOGRAPHS

A CD, LP, magazine cover, ad, photo, or card signed by the artist: $5-$10

OFTEN OVERLOOKED MEMORABILIA

Memorabilia from his days in the Equals

The Grass Roots

Formed 1966

Warren Entner, Born: July 7, 1944; Creed Bratton, Born: February 8, 1943; Ricky Coonce, Born: August 1, 1947; and Rob Grill, Born: November 30, 1944*

*Dennis Provisor replaces Bratton in 1969. Reed Kailing, Virgil Webber and Joel Larson replace Coonce and Provisor in 1972. Grill leaves in 1975.

Late-60s and early-70s pivotal American pop band who scored with a series of successful hits singles, including "Midnight Confessions" (#5, 1968), "I'd Wait a Million Years" (#15, 1969), "Temptation Eyes" (#15, 1971), "Sooner or Later" (#9, 1971) and "Two Divided by Love" (#16, 1971), before slipping out of the Top Forty.

AUTOGRAPHS

An LP, magazine cover, ad, photo, or card signed by the artist: $35-$100*
*original line-up

The Grateful Dead

Formed 1965

Jerry Garcia, Born: August 1, 1942, Died: August 9, 1995; Bob Weir, Born: October 16, 1947; Ron "Pigpen" McKernan, Born: September 8, 1945, Died: March 8, 1973; Phil Lesh, Born: March 15, 1940; Bill Kreutzmann (Sommers), Born: April 7, 1946*

*Mickey Hart, Born: 1950, added in 1967. Tom Constanten is added in 1968 and leaves in 1970, as does Hart. Keith Godchaux, Born: July 14, 1948, Died: July 23, 1980, and Donna Godchaux are added in 1971.

Hart returns in 1974. Both Godchaux depart in 1979 and Brent Myland, Born: 1953, Died: July 26, 1990, is added. Vince Welnick is added in 1990.

THE IMMORTAL LIVING CARAVAN: Write to The Grateful Dead Almanac, P.O. Box X, Novato, CA 94948. Dead relics are a book on their own and beyond the scope of this segment. See other sections of this book and don't forget to mail some pictures of your collection for the next edition. TWIRL!

AUTOGRAPHS

Group:
A CD, LP, magazine cover, ad, photo, or card signed by the group: $150-$425

Individual:

Jerry Garcia: $75-$200	Bob Weir: $35-$110
"Pigpen" McKernan: $100-$325	Phil Lesh: $30-$50
Bill Kreutzmann: $20-$40	Mickey Hart: $20-$40
Tom Constanten: $10-$20	Keith Godchaux: $20-$45
Donna Godchaux: $10-$25	Brent Myland: $20-$40
Vince Welnick: $15-$30	

KEY DEAD DATES

Date	Event
5/5/65	Magoo's Pizza Parlor, Menlo Park, CA - The Warlocks' first gig
11/65	Band changes name to Grateful Dead
11/6/65	Opening night at Bill Graham's Fillmore Auditorium in San Francisco, CA Includes: Jefferson Airplane, the Mothers of Invention and the Grateful Dead
1/8/66	Fillmore Acid Test
1/14/66	Mime Troupe Benefit, Fillmore Auditorium - poster refers to band as "formerly the Warlocks"
5/28/66	Avalon Ballroom - first Family Dog production
6/66	The group moves to 710 Ashbury Street in the Haight-Ashbury neighborhood
7/1/66	"Don't Ease Me" (Scorpio Label) is released
7/16/66	Fillmore Auditorium
7/29/66	P.N.E. Garden Auditorium, Vancouver, B.C., Canada - first show outside of U.S., also first show outside California
7/66	"Don't Ease Me In/Stealin" - first single released
8/4/66	First headline gig at the Fillmore Auditorium
8/19-20/66	The Avalon Ballroom, San Francisco, CA
9/16-17/66	The Avalon Ballroom, San Francisco, CA - first use of "skeleton and roses" design
9/66	Band moves to 710 Ashbury Street, San Francisco, CA
12/20/66	The Fillmore Auditorium, sharing the bill with Otis Redding
12/31/66	The Dead's first New Year's Eve Show - Fillmore Auditorium
1/14/67	The first "Human Be-In," Golden Gate Park, San Francisco, CA
2/24-26/67	The Fillmore Auditorium
3/3/67	First show at the Winterland
3/17/67	The release of their debut album, *Grateful Dead*, on Warner Brothers Records. The group begins a three-day stint at the Fillmore West.
6/18/67	Monterey International Pop Festival
5/18/68	Northern California Rock Festival
6/22/68	The Fillmore East - support includes Jeff Beck group (U.S. debut)
6/28/67	First show at Oakland Auditorium Arena
10/1/67	First show at Greek Theatre, UC Berkley, CA
12/13/67	Shrine Auditorium, Los Angeles, CA - first performance of "Dark Star"
12/26/67	First show at Village Theater, NY (Fillmore East)
5/5/68	Central Park, NY
6/14/68	Fillmore East, NY - now under Graham's management
8/4/68	Newport Pop Festival, Costa Mesa, CA
9/2/68	Sky River Rock Festival...Fair, Sultan, WA
12/6/68	Quaker City Rock Festival, Philadelphia, PA
12/28/68	New Orleans Pop Festival, Prairieville, LA
12/6/69	Altamont Speedway, Livermore, CA
12/21/69	Fillmore Auditorium - last performance as the Auditiorium

Date	Event
2/13/70	The Fillmore East
3/17/70	Kleinhans Music Hall, Buffalo, NY - with Buffalo Philharmonic Orchestra
5/24/70	Hollywood Rock Music Festival, Newcastle-Under-Lyme, Staffs., U.K. - first gig outside North America
8/30/70	KQED Studios, San Francisco, CA - TV with FM simulcast (5 songs)
10/4/70	Winterland - TV with FM simulcast of full concert
4/26-29/71	The Fillmore East - group's last appearance
7/4/71	Fillmore West - last appearance
12/31/71	Winterland
4/7-8/72	Empire Pool, Wembley, Middlesex, U.K.
5/7/72	Bickershaw Festival, near Wigan, Lancashire, U.K.
5/26/72	The Strand Lyceum, London
6/17/72	Hollywood Bowl, Los Angeles, CA - McKernan's final show with the Grateful Dead
7/28/73	Watkins Glen Festival, Watkins Glen, NY
9/9-21/73	European Tour starts in London
10/16-20/74	Winterland, San Francisco, CA
3/23/75	Kezar Stadium, San Francisco, CA - benefit
8/13/75	Great American Music Hall, San Francisco, CA
6/3/76	Begin U.S. Tour in Portland, OR
8/7/76	Wembley Stadium, Wembley, U.K.
10/9/76	Oakland-Alameda County Stadium, Oakland, CA
5/8/77	Cornell University, Ithaca, NY
6/1/77	*The Grateful Dead Movie* premieres in New York
7/7/78	First show at Red Rocks Amphitheater, Morrison, CO
9/14-16/78	Sound & Light Amphitheater, (Great Pyramids) Cairo, Egypt
10/17-20/78	Winterland Ballroom, San Francisco, CA
11/11/78	First appearance on *Saturday Night Live*
12/17/78	Loyola University, Chicago, IL - rare acoustic set
12/31/78	Winterland Ballroom, San Francisco, CA - final show
1/2-4/79	Fillmore West
1/7/79	First show at Madison Square Garden, NY
1/13/80	Benefit for "The People of Kampuchea"
3/30/80	Capitol Theatre, Passaic, NJ - John Belushi makes guest appearance
4/5/80	*Saturday Night Live* - NBC-TV
6/5/80	Compton Terrace, Phoenix, AZ - 15th Anniversary
6/12/80	Memorial Coliseum, Portland, OR
6/19-21/80	West High Auditorium, Anchorage, Alaska
7/1/80	Sports Arena, San Diego, CA - attempted drug bust causes riot and prompts arrests
3/20/81	Rainbow Theater, London - beginning of short European tour
5/7/81	"The Tomorrow Show"
9/11/81	Greek Theatre - first show of a traditional run
9/30/81	The Grateful Dead undertake a European tour that ends October 17th

Date	Event
12/31/81	Oakland Auditorium, CA
5/28/82	"Benefit for Vietnam Veterans Project," Moscone Center, San Francisco, CA
9/5/82	U.S. Festival, San Bernadino, CA
10/9/82	First show at Frost Amphitheater, Stanford University
11/25/82	Jamaica World Music Festival, Montego Bay, Jamaica
12/30-31/82	Oakland Auditorium, CA
4/16-17/83	Meadowlands Arena, East Rutherford, NJ
6/1/85	Greek Theater - "Official" 20th Anniversary show
12/31/85	Oakland-Alameda County Coliseum, CA - TV and FM broadcast - "star-lit sky" design with large red rose on ticket.
6/26/86	The band resumes full-time U.S. touring with Bob Dylan and Tom Petty and the Heartbreakers. Band has to withdraw due to Garcia's health problems.
12/15/86	Oakland-Alameda County Coliseum, CA - band begins touring again
12/31/86	Oakland-Alameda County Coliseum, CA - one of the worst designs of all the traditional New Year's Eve tickets
7/13/87	Last show at Red Rocks
8/23/87	"Summer Of Love" - 20th Anniversary celebration concert - marred by shootings
12/31/87	Oakland-Alameda County Coliseum, CA - New Year's Eve Show - nice ticket design, includes skeleton with top hat and cane
9/24/88	Madison Square Garden, NY -close of a nine-concert series that includes benefit
12/4/88	Oakland-Alameda County Coliseum, CA - "Music Festival"
12/31/88	Oakland-Alameda County Coliseum, CA - "UFO" ticket design
5/18/89	AIDS Benefit, Oakland, CA
7/9-10/89	Giants Stadium, East Rutherford, NJ
9/19/89	Last show at Greek Theatre
10/8-9/89	Hampton Coliseum, Hampton, VA - billed as "formerly the Warlocks"
12/10/89	Great Western Forum, Inglewood, CA - show marred by tragedy
12/31/89	Oakland-Alameda County Coliseum, CA - nice foil ticket with balloons
2/25-27/90	Oakland-Alameda County Coliseum, CA - band begins another major U.S. Tour - "skull" design on simple ticket

Date	Event
5/5-6/90	California State University, Carson, CA
7/16/90	Rich Stadium, Buffalo, NY
9/14-20/90	Madison Square Garden, NY - six sellout dates
10/13-11/1/90	European Tour begins in Stockholm
12/27-31/90	Oakland-Alameda County Coliseum, CA - includes 21st New Year's Eve concert. The New Year's Eve ticket is extremely popular with Dead collectors.
3/17-21/91	Capital Center, Landover, MD - four sellout dates
4/3-5/91	Atlanta, GA - major drug busts
4/20/91	Norfolk Naval Air Station, Norfolk, VA
5/3-5/91	Cal Expo Amphitheater, Sacramento, CA - three sellout dates
6/1/91	Los Angeles Coliseum, Los Angeles, CA - sellout crowd
6/22/91	Soldier Field, Chicago, IL
9/20-26/91	Boston Garden, Boston, MA - six shows
10/25/91	Bill Graham dies in a tragic helicopter crash
11/3/91	Golden Gate Park, CA - memorial concert for Bill Graham
12/27-31/91	Oakland-Alameda County Coliseum, CA - four sellout shows
2/22-7/1/92	Oakland-Alameda County Coliseum, CA - 21-city tour begins
12/11-13/92	McNichols Arena, Denver, CO
12/16-17/92	Oakland-Alameda County Coliseum, CA
1/24-26/93	Oakland-Alameda County Coliseum, CA
3/31/93	Nassau Veterans Memorial Coliseum, Uniondale, NY- five sellout shows
9/16-18, 20-22/93	Madison Square Garden, NY - follow summer stadium tour with this stay
1/19/94	The Grateful Dead are inducted into the Rock and Roll Hall of Fame
2/25-27/94	Oakland-Alameda County Coliseum, CA
3/23-25, 27-28/94	Nassau Veterans Memorial Coliseum, Uniondale, NY
6/17-19/94	Autzen Stadium, University of Oregon, Eugene, OR
9/27-29, 10/1-3/94	Boston Garden, Boston, MA - six dates
12/15-16, 12/18-19/94	Los Angeles Sports Arena, Los Angeles, CA
3/19/95	Spectrum, Philadelphia, PA
6/4/95	Shoreline Amphitheater, Mountain View, CA - last bay area gig!
6/15/95	"The Final Tour Begins" - it was marred by a variety of strange events
7/9/95	Soldier Field, Chicago, IL - The final gig!

TOUR BOOKS/ PROGRAMS/PASSES

Tour Books:
Mickey Hart's Planet Dream: $15
1976-1980 15 Year Anniversary (Radio City): $27
1976 - 1980 15 Year Anniversary : $25 - $30
1990 - Twenty Five Years : $15
Mickey Hart's Planet Drum : $15

The Grateful Dead's Twenty Five Years program (© 1990 Grateful Dead Merchandising, Inc.)

Backstage Passes:
An entire book alone on this topic, could and, should be written.

USED CLOTHING/ EQUIPMENT

Guitar Picks:
Jerry Garcia - $125 - $200
Bob Weir - $35 - $50
Phil Lesh - $30 - $40

Drum Sticks:
Bill Kreutzmann - $20 - $40
Mickey Hart - $25

A Grateful Dead guitar pick

REFERENCES/BOOKS

Numerous resources exist. Start with John Scott, Mike Dolgushkin, and Stu Nixon's book *DeadBase IX: The Complete Guide to Grateful Dead Song Lists*. Fan clubs and fanzines are a must for collectors: Dupree's Diamond News: Documenting the Deadhead Experience, P.O. Box 936, Morthampton, MA 01061; Relix: Music for the Mind, Relix Magazine, Inc., P.O. Box 94, Brooklyn, NY 11229; Unbroken Chain, P.O. Box 49019, Austin, TX 78765.

Gray, Dobie

(Leonard Ainsworth)
Born: July 26, 1942

Mid-60s pop turned mid-70s country soul singer, Dobie Gray is best remembered for his hits "The 'In' Crowd" (#13, 1965), "Drift Away" (#5, 1973) and "Loving Arms."

AUTOGRAPHS

An LP, magazine cover, ad, photo, or card signed by the artist: $8-$15

Great White

Formed 1981

Mark Kendall, Born: April 29, 1957; Jack Russell, Born: December 5, 1960; Lorne Black; and Garry Holland*

*Audie Desbrow replaces Holland in 1986. Keyboard player Michael Lardie is added in 1987. Tony Montana replaces Black in 1988. Montana departs in 1992 and Dave Spitz is added briefly before Teddy Cook joins the band.

Short-lived mid-80s raunch blues/metal band, Great White is best remembered for their cover of Ian Hunter's "Once Bitten Twice Shy" (#5, 1989) and their successful selling albums *Once Bitten* (#23, 1987), *Twice Shy* (#9, 1989) and *Hooked* (#18, 1991). The band built a strong and loyal cult following through their extensive touring and high-energy stage shows before both elements eventually took their toll on the group.

AUTOGRAPHS

A CD, LP, magazine cover, ad, photo, or card signed by the group: $20-$50

POSTERS/PRESS KITS

Promotional Posters: $10-$20
Press Kits: $15

USED CLOTHING/EQUIPMENT

Guitar Picks: $10
Drum Sticks: $15

Grebenshikov, Boris

Born: November 27, 1953

Late-80s Russian singer/songwriter best known for his involvement in the band Aquarium, Boris Grebenshikov is commonly associated with the pre-perestroika Soviet musical underground.

AUTOGRAPHS

A CD, LP, magazine cover, ad, photo, or card signed by the artist: $10-$30

Green, Al

Born: April 13, 1946

One of the most popular vocalists in the '70s, Al Green incorporated numerous elements of soul music. He went on to modify his career from R&B and pop sensation to gifted and respected gospel singer. His numerous hits have included "Tired of Being Alone" (#11, 1971), "Let's Stay Together" (#1, 1971), "Look What You've Done for Me" (#4, 1972), "I'm Still in Love with You" (#3, 1972), "You Ought to Be with Me" (#3, 1972), "Call Me (Come Back Home)" (#10, 1973), "Here I Am (Come and Take Me)" (#10, 1973) and "Sha La La (Make Me Happy)" (#7, 1974).

Following a tragic incident in 1974 that left Green with second-degree burns and a former girlfriend dead from a suicide, the artist was inspired to turn to the ministry. He then found himself a church, built himself a studio, and began preaching and producing simultaneously. A multiple Grammy recipient in Gospel, he also performed on Broadway, watched others successfully cover his songs (such as the Talking Heads with "Take Me to the River") and dueted with Annie Lennox on the soundtrack *Scrooged* (1988) and Lyle Lovett on *Funny How Time Slips Away* (1994).

AUTOGRAPHS

A CD, LP, magazine cover, ad, photo, or card signed by the artist: $10-$40

OFTEN OVERLOOKED MEMORABILIA

Movie memorabilia from *Scrooged* (1988); artifacts associated with other musicians' covers of his work

Greenbaum, Norman

Born: November 20, 1942

Early-70s folksinger/songwriter who scored a minor hit with "The Eggplant That Ate Chicago" (#52, 1966) while in Dr. West's Medicine Show and Junk

Band. Greenbaum is primarily remembered for the hit "Spirit in the Sky" (#3, 1970).

AUTOGRAPHS
An LP, magazine cover, ad, photo, or card signed by the artist: $8-$20

OFTEN OVERLOOKED MEMORABILIA
Movie memorabilia from *Apollo 13*

Green Day

Formed 1989

Billie Joe Armstrong, Born: February 17, 1972; Mike Dirnt (Pritchard), Born: May 4, 1972; and Al Sobrante*

*Sobrante leaves in 1990 and John Kiftmeyer is brought in briefly before he is replaced by Tre' Cool (Frank Wright III), Born: December 9, 1972

Nineties punk fragments whose ritual three-minute ax driven tunes, appearances at Woodstock '94 and Lollapalooza, along with a strong MTV rotation, helped send their debut major-label effort, *Dookie* (#2, 1994) up the album chart. The same year they picked up a Grammy for Best Alternative Music Performance.

Green Day. Photo by Alison Dyer. Courtesy Reprise Records.

AUTOGRAPHS
Group:
A CD, LP, magazine cover, ad, photo, or card signed by the group: $40-$50

Individual:
Billie Joe Armstrong: $15-$20
Mike Dirnt: $15-$18
Tre' Cool: $10-$12

TOUR BOOKS/PROGRAMS/PASSES
Backstage Passes:
Unlaminated: $8-$10;
Laminated: $10-$20

POSTERS/PRESS KITS
Promotional Posters: $10-$20
Press Kits: $15

A common counterfeit Green Day backstage pass.

USED CLOTHING/EQUIPMENT
Guitar Picks:
Billie Joe Armstrong: $15
Mike Dirnt: $10
Drum Sticks: $15

REFERENCES/BOOKS
A couple resources exist, but nothing that does justice to the band in my opinion; no dedicated collector books

Griffith, Nanci

Born: July 6, 1953

Eighties Texas "folkabilly" singer/songwriter, Nanci Griffith covers songs from a range of artists, including those in traditional folk and even current country. Despite critical acclaim, a strong fan base, and the admiration of her peers, she has yet to see any substantial level of commercial success.

AUTOGRAPHS
A CD, LP, magazine cover, ad, photo, or card signed by the artist: $5-$10

Grin: See Nils Lofgren

Grossman, Stefan

Born: April 16, 1945

Seventies transient blues guitarist and teacher who was active in the British blues scene in the late '60s before relocating to Italy to work on instructional books and videos on blues guitar techniques.

AUTOGRAPHS
An LP, magazine cover, ad, photo, or card signed by the artist: $7-$10

OFTEN OVERLOOKED MEMORABILIA
Copies of his instructional guides and videos on blues guitar techniques

The Groundhogs

Formed 1963

T.S. "Tony" McPhee, Born: March 22, 1944; Pete Cruikshank; Ken Pustelnik; and Steve Rye*

*Rye departs in 1969. The band re-formed in 1976.

Early-70s British blues turned metal advocates who managed to build a significant following in Britain, but have failed to garner much attention in the U.S.

AUTOGRAPHS
An LP, magazine cover, ad, photo, or card signed by the group: $5-$10

The Guess Who

Formed 1962

Chad Allan (Allan Kobel); Bob Ashley; Randy Bachman, Born: September 27, 1943; Garry Peterson, Born: May 26, 1945; and Jim Kale, Born: August 11, 1943*

*Ashley departs in 1965 and is replaced with Burton Cummings, Born: December 31, 1947. Allan leaves in 1966 and Bruce Dekker is added briefly. Bachman leaves in 1970 and Greg Leskiw and Kurt Winter join the band. Leskiw leaves in 1972 and Don McDougall is added. Bill Wallace also replaces Kale in 1972. Winter and McDougall leave in 1974 and Dominic Troiano joins the band. The Guess Who disband in 1975. Various flavors of the group exist after the group reforms in 1979.

Early-70s Canadian pop-rock band who scored a series of successful singles, beginning with the cover "Shakin' All Over" (#22, 1965) and including "These Eyes" (#6, 1969), "Laughing" (#10, 1969), "Undun" (#22, 1969), "American Woman" (#1, 1970) and "No Time" (#5, 1970), before the departure of guitarist Randy Bachman, who would later find success in Bachman-Turner Overdrive.

The band then replaced Bachman with two guitarists, Greg Leskiw and Kurt Winter, and continued landing hits such as "Share the Land" (#10, 1970), "Hand Me Down World" (#17, 1970), "Rain Dance" (#19, 1971) and "Albert Flasher" (#29, 1971), before becoming sporadic. The group did land in the Top Ten with the novelty tune "Clap for the Wolfman" (a tribute to Wolfman Jack) before disbanding the following year.

Burton Cummings, who had been the focal point for the band as its lead vocalist, went on to a moderately successful solo career, landing a hit single with "Stand Tall" (#10, 1976). Both Cummings and Bachman eventually got back together for an album and video in 1983, and later even toured together.

AUTOGRAPHS

A CD, LP, magazine cover, ad, photo, or card signed by the group: $35-$100

OFTEN OVERLOOKED MEMORABILIA

Videotapes from the band's numerous television appearances, including *Where It's At* (CBS-TV, 1968)

REFERENCES/BOOKS

Limited resources exist; start with John Einarson's book *American Woman: The Story of the Guess Who;* no dedicated collector books

Guitar Slim

(Eddie Jones)
Born: December 10, 1926, Died: February 7, 1959

Legendary bluesman best remembered for his song "Things That I Used to Do" (1954), which bridged the gap between traditional blues and deep-rooted gospel. A fashionable dresser and electric guitar pioneer, when he died of pneumonia at the young age of 33, they buried him with his ax—a gold-top Gibson Les Paul.

AUTOGRAPHS

An LP, magazine cover, ad, photo, or card signed by the artist: $55-$350

Guns 'N' Roses

Formed 1985

Axl Rose (William Bailey), Born: February 6, 1962; Slash (Saul Hudson), Born: July 23, 1965; Duff (Michael) McKagan, Born: February 5, 1964; Steve Adler, Born: 1965; Izzy Stradlin (Jeff Isbell), Born: April 8, 1962*

*Matt Sorum replaces Adler in 1990 and Dizzy (Darren) Reed is added. Stradlin leaves in 1991 and Gilby Clarke replaces him on guitar.

Late-80s hard-rock L.A. bad boys whose take-no-prisoners attitude was shared both on and off stage (the latter typically providing a plethora of unwanted media), Guns 'N' Roses, formed from the L.A. Guns and Hollywood Roses, broke onto the music scene with *Appetite for Destruction* (#1) which became the biggest-selling debut in history. The album included the hit extracts "Sweet Child o' Mine" (#1, 1988) and "Welcome to the Jungle" (#7, 1988).

Their debut was followed by *GN'R Lies,* which included their controversial "Used to Love Her" and "One in a Million," both cited for violence and disparaging lyrics. It was just one of numerous controversies that would dominate the media and continually follow the band, which would eventually be better known for what they did off the stage than on. From audience members being killed in crowd disturbances to their obscenity-laden speech at the 1990 American Music Awards, the band would take one step forward, then two back.

The group continued, playing Farm Aid IV and contributing "Knockin' on Heaven's Door" to the soundtrack of *Days of Thunder,* during a time in which rumors of substance abuse dominated the press—rumors that were somewhat confirmed when Adler was fired for not straightening out. Matt Sorum and Dizzy Reed were then brought into the band in 1990, as they tried desperately to regroup.

"You Could Be Mine" (#29, 1991), extracted from the soundtrack to *Terminator 2* was released as the band began its first headlining tour. Meanwhile Rose split with his wife Erin Everly (daughter of Don Everly) amidst allegations of physical abuse, and even got hit with four misdemeanor counts of assault and one for property damage after allegedly attacking a

fan carrying a camera. For band members it was just another day at the office for GN'R!

Use Your Illusion I and *Use Your Illusion II* were released simultaneously, during a time that saw Stradlin leave, to be replaced by Gilby Clarke, as the band embarked on a 28 month tour. The band later released the punk-rooted *The Spaghetti Incident?*, which even included a tune penned by Charles Manson. Amidst the continual controversy were the incessant rumors of the band's break-up, fueled somewhat by solo efforts by its members.

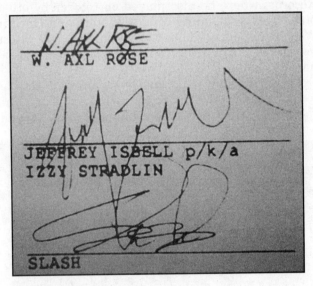
Contract signed by Guns 'N' Roses

AUTOGRAPHS

Group:
A CD, LP, magazine cover, ad, photo, or card signed by the group: $175-$200

Individual:
Axl Rose: $45-$50
Slash: $40-$45
Duff McKagan: $35-$40
Steve Adler: $35-$40
Izzy Stradlin: $35-$40
Matt Sorum: $30
Dizzy Reed: $30-$35
Gilby Clarke: $25-$30

Use Your Illusion tour program (Satori)

Some nice backstage pass examples (Printed by OTTO)

TOUR BOOKS/PROGRAMS/PASSES

Programs:
Use Your Illusion: $15

Backstage Passes:
Unlaminated: $8-$12;
Laminated: $15-$20;
Laser foils: $20-$30;
$30 for very significant gigs

POSTERS/PRESS KITS

Press Kits:
Appetite for Destruction (1987): $50
Use Your Illusion
I & II (1991): $25
Spaghetti
Incident? (1993):
$20

USED CLOTHING/EQUIPMENT

Guitar Picks:
Slash: $20-$60*
Duff: $12-$15
Gilby: $10-$15
Izzy: $15-$40*
*High end includes group named spelled out or tortoise shell

Drum Sticks:
Steve Adler: $15-$20
Matt Sorum: $15

Guitar picks from Guns 'N' Roses

OFTEN OVERLOOKED MEMORABILIA

Guns 'N' Roses/Great White Tour Bag - $75; Spaghetti Incident triangular mobile - $20

REFERENCES/BOOKS

Numerous resources exist, but nothing that does justice to the band in my opinion; no dedicated collector books; the band's fan club is a must: Guns 'N' Roses International Fan Club, P.O. Box 884088, San Francisco, CA 94188 ($19.95 fee)

Guthrie, Arlo

Born: July 10, 1947

Late-60s folk singer and one of several children born to folk singer Woody Guthrie, Arlo Guthrie is typically associated with two songs: "Alice's Restaurant," an 18-minute classic ballad now ritually played every Thanksgiving Day across America; and Steve Goodman's penned "City of New Orleans" (#18, 1972). Guthrie played at Woodstock in August 1969, and often performed and recorded with Pete Seeger during the '70s, while both were active in numerous causes, particularly centering around ecological concerns.

AUTOGRAPHS

An LP, magazine cover, ad, photo, or card signed by the artist: $10-$15

OFTEN OVERLOOKED MEMORABILIA

All related artifacts from "Alice's Restaurant"; videotapes form the television show *Byrds of Paradise,* in which Guthrie appeared as an aging hippie

REFERENCES/BOOKS

Numerous resources exist dating back to 1968; no dedicated collector books

Guthrie, Woody

Born: July 14, 1912, Died: October 3, 1967

Pre-World War II folk icon who learned how to "stir the water" with a good old-fashioned American ballad, Woody Guthrie is typically associated with the songs "This Land Is Your Land," "Pastures of Plenty," and "So Long, It's Been Good to Know You," among the thousands of songs he wrote during his lifetime.

His intriguing life was extremely well documented in his autobiography *Bound for Glory* (1976), which was made into a movie. His legacy has only grown over the years, so revered as a singer that Bob Dylan traveled to New York to visit the singer while he was hospitalized, and to this day sings his idol's praise. In 1988 he was inducted into the Rock and Roll Hall of Fame.

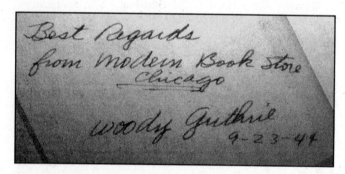

A rare and highly sought after autograph from Woody Guthrie

AUTOGRAPHS

An LP, magazine cover, ad, photo, or card signed by the artist: $300-$1,200

OFTEN OVERLOOKED MEMORABILIA

"This Machine Kills Fascists" sticker - $5; copies of the columns he wrote for the communist newspaper, *The People's Daily World*

REFERENCES/BOOKS

Bound for Glory, his autobiography (1976); *Seeds of Man,* a book of his prose (1976); numerous resources exist; no dedicated collector books

Gutterball: See Dream Syndicate; Long Ryders

Guy, Buddy

(George Guy)
Born: July 30, 1936

Arguably the best guitarist alive, Buddy Guy gained mainstream prominence through his touring with the Rolling Stones in 1970, and his Grammy-winning 1991 album, *Damn Right, I've Got the Blues.* Willie Dixon helped him land a contract at Chess Records, where he also played on records by other blues greats including Muddy Waters and Howlin' Wolf. He later moved to the Vanguard label where he worked on numerous collaborations with the great harmonica player Junior Wells.

Primarily known for his live performances, he tours frequently when not appearing at his two Chicago clubs, The Checkerboard Lounge and Legends.

Buddy Guy. Photo by Brad Hitz. Courtesy Silvertone Records.

AUTOGRAPHS

An LP, magazine cover, ad, photo, or card signed by the artist $15-$40

POSTERS/PRESS KITS

Press Kits: $15-$50

USED CLOTHING/ EQUIPMENT

Guitar Picks: $35-$50

OFTEN OVERLOOKED MEMORABILIA

All artifacts from his Chicago blues clubs

REFERENCES/BOOKS

Limited resources exist. Start with the artist's biography, *Damn Right I've Got the Blues: Buddy Guy and the Roots of Rock and Roll;* no dedicated collector books

---

Guy/Teddy Riley

Formed 1985

Teddy Riley, Born: October 8, 1966; Aaron Hall, Born: August 10, 1964; and Timmy Gatling*

*Gatling departs in 1990 and Damion (Albert) Hall is added

Late-80s pioneer of the New Jack Swing (which fused R&B with soul singing to hip-hop beats), Teddy Riley and Guy are commonly associated with the songs "Groove Me" (#4, 1988), "Mr. Fantasy," "New Jack City," "Do Me Right" (#2, R&B, 1991), "Let's Chill" (#3, R&B, 1991) and "D-O-G Me Out" (#8, R&B, 1991). Riley would later go on to successful production work, while working with numerous artists, including Michael Jackson, before forming Backstreet (1994).

Hagar, Sammy

Born: October 13, 1947

The son of a boxer, Hagar nearly considered the "sweet science" as a viable occupation, but instead opted to become a musician. He rocked the saloons of Southern California for seven long years before catching a break and becoming the lead singer for Montrose in 1973. The band, years ahead of its time, cut two outstanding records for Warner Brothers, both of which showcased Hagar as a powerful front man and a solid songwriter. But in 1975 Sammy Hagar wanted more and left Montrose to pursue a solo career.

Nine on a Ten Scale (1976, Capitol) received some airplay (primarily generated by his former affiliation) but it wasn't until 1977, when joined by three Montrose alumni—Bill Church, Alan Fitzgerald, and Dennis Caramasi—that the recipe started to gel. The Sammy Hagar band toured extensively, opening up for such powerhouse acts as Boston, Kansas, and Kiss, and began creating a whole new legion of fans. While a consistent and respectable seller, Hagar knew it would take a hit single to put him on the map. That finally happened when "Your Love Is Driving Me Crazy," off of *Two Lock Box. VOA* (#32, 1984) landed in the Top Twenty, generating the single "I

AUTOGRAPHS

A CD, LP, magazine cover, ad, photo, or card signed by the artist: $10-$20

GWAR

Formed 1985

Odorus Urungus (David Brockie), Balsac the Jaws of Death (Michael Derks), Flattus Maximus (Peter Lee), Beefcake the Mighty (Michael Bishop), Jizmak the Gusha (Brad Roberts), Slymenstra Hymen (Danyelle Stampe), Sexicutioner (Charles Varga), Sampler Sound-EFX (David Musel), Techno-Destructo (Hunter Jackson), Sleazy P. Martini (Don Drakulich)

Late-80s theatrical shock-rock speed-metal group whose stage shows often resembled an aircraft crash site, GWAR assembled, performed, or recorded; released, retreated, or repeated.

AUTOGRAPHS

A CD, LP, magazine cover, ad, photo, or card signed by the group: $10-$30

OFTEN OVERLOOKED MEMORABILIA

Artificial decapitated limbs or impaled body parts thrown into the audience.

Can't Drive 55" (#26, 1984), an anthem-like protest song, which was now indicative of the Hagar sound. Just when you thought the "red rocker" was going to shove his Trans-Am into overdrive, he decided to replace David Lee Roth in Van Halen (1985).

Many critics, most of which seemed to fancy the swashbuckling Roth, felt Hagar would never cut it in Van Halen. On April 26, 1986, Van Halen's *5150* hit Number One on the album charts and stayed there for four weeks. What little doubt anyone had of Hagar's ability dissipated with this recording and his subsequent first live appearances with the band. His musical depth—he played guitar and Roth didn't—freed up Eddie Van Halen to pursue some alternative directions, which he did. The recipe seemed to work with Van Halen until 1996 when Hagar's work ethic was criticized and he departed from the band. His maintenance of a solo career during the Van Halen years was a smart decision on his part, and one that left him with a logical alternative path.

AUTOGRAPHS

Sammy Hagar has always been fairly responsive to autograph requests, even answering requests via mail

A CD, LP, magazine cover, ad, photo, or card signed by the artist: $30-$40

TOUR BOOKS/PROGRAMS/PASSES

Backstage Passes:

Cloth: $8-$10; Laminated: $10-$20

POSTERS/PRESS KITS
Promotional Posters: $10-$20
Press Kits: $15-$25

USED CLOTHING/EQUIPMENT
Guitar Picks: $25-$50

OFTEN OVERLOOKED MEMORABILIA
His earlier material with Montrose; newspaper clippings regarding his departure from Van Halen

---

Hagen, Nina

Born: March 11, 1955

Nina Hagen, who was born into an artistic German family, is an eccentric artist at heart, never afraid to take on controversy and then try to tame it. She moved to West Berlin in 1976 and signed on with CBS in Germany. While experiencing London first hand in the late '70s and hanging out with the Slits, her first CBS release, *Nina Hagen Band* (EP, 1980), was extremely well received—especially in Europe. She then moved to Holland to hang out with some friends, and appear in the film *Cha Cha* alongside Lena Lovich.

Nunsexmonkrock (Columbia, 1982) was recorded in New York and included "African Reggae" and the Tubes' "White Punks on Dope" from her previous work. While the album was certainly interesting, it failed to garner the accolades her management was expecting. In a completely new twist, which is always the next step with Hagen, her songs seemed to reflect her sighting of a UFO which happened to her while in Malibu in 1981. *Fearless* (1983) followed the previous frenzy and included the club hit "New York New York." It also featured the Red Hot Chili Peppers rapping on "What It Is," my favorite extraterrestrial song next to the television theme to *My Favorite Martian.*

Nina Hagen in Ekstasy (1985) combined just about every sound she could find and even included covers of those classics "My Way" and "Spirit in the Sky." Despite the novelty, no hits emerged and no additional UFOs were sighted, so the artist stopped recording. It was now time for another twist, which happened to be her marriage to a teenage fan. The event sparked the Canadian EP *Punk Wedding* (1988), followed by *Nina Hagen* (1989), which contained a bizarre mix—everything from "Viva Las Vegas" to "Ave Maria." If you like a collecting challenge, Nina Hagen is for you!

AUTOGRAPHS
A CD, LP, magazine cover, ad, photo, or card signed by the artist: $10-$20

TOUR BOOKS/PROGRAMS/PASSES
Backstage Passes:
Cloth: $5; Laminated: $8-$10

POSTERS/PRESS KITS
Promotional posters: $10-$15
Press Kits: $10-$15

Haggard, Merle

Born: April 6, 1937

The working man's singer, Merle Haggard has the ability to squeeze a lifetime into a song. He's the type of entertainer you're not sure whether you want to watch perform or if you would rather just take him to a local saloon and converse over a beer or two. Although he has often shunned notoriety, his gifted and prolific songwriting landed him into the Country Music Hall of Fame in 1994, a place where he can finally call home.

When he was young his family landed in California, via Oklahoma, and lived in a converted boxcar for awhile. His father died when Haggard was nine, and by the age of fourteen he was on a freight train headed to nowhere—a place many of us can relate to! Not an ideal child by any means, he spent some time in reformatories and eventually three years in San Quentin. Paroled in 1960, he headed back to Bakersfield, California to work with his brother. Bored of digging ditches, Haggard started playing lead guitar in a local country band. He traveled to Las Vegas, backing singer Wynn Stewart, and by 1962 had decided he found a new career. He hooked up with Lewis Talley and Fuzzy Owen, the owners of Tally Records, a local independent label which showed interest in Haggard's work. From 1963 to 1965, Tally Records recorded Merle Haggard and by his second release, "Sing a Sad Song," which made it into the Top Twenty on the country charts, they were convinced they had found a talent. Not alone in their discovery, Capitol Records signed Haggard to a recording contract.

Okie from Muskogee (1969, Capital) marked his debut on a major record label and with it extensive touring began for Haggard and his newly-formed backing band. "The Fugitive" (#1 (C), 1966) became his first chart topper in 1966, and Haggard was named the Academy of Country Music's Top Male Vocalist of the Year. From 1966 to 1987 Merle Haggard has had at least one Top Five country hit each year, including "Mama Tried," "Hungry Eyes," "Everybody's Had the Blues," "It's All in the Movies," and "Big City." From popular country hallmarks like "Today I Started Loving You," to patriotic anthems like "The Fighting Side of Me," there are few topics and forms of music he hasn't touched.

Diverse, but yet loyal to his roots, Haggard has recorded tribute albums, gospel albums, and even Dixieland jazz albums. His musical prowess landed him at the White House, playing for President Carter in 1973, and even on tape aboard Apollo 16 on the way

to the moon. He has also appeared in other media, including television, on such shows as *The Waltons* and *Centennial*, and on film, in the movies *Killers Three* and *Bronco Billy*.

His career began to slow in the '80s when many new acts began edging him out of the charts he once dominated. His touring also slowed, because he preferred instead to enjoy his ranch near Lake Shasta. While he still kicks out an occasional album, others are now making tribute albums about him. I guess what goes around, really does come around!

AUTOGRAPHS
A CD, LP, magazine cover, ad, photo, or card signed by the artist: $15-$25

TOUR BOOKS/PROGRAMS/PASSES
Backstage Passes:
Cloth: $8-$10; Laminated: $10-$20

USED CLOTHING/EQUIPMENT
Guitar Picks: $10-$25

OFTEN OVERLOOKED MEMORABILIA
All items associated with Tally Records

Haircut 100

Formed 1980

Nick Heyward, Les Nemes, Graham Jones, Memphis Blair Cunningham, Phil Smith, and Mark Fox

When you mention Haircut 100 to most, images of the Bay City Rollers or the Monkees are often evoked. You know, pretty-faced English boys—clean-cut, dancing around someone's living room listening to the radio and drinking milk. All fun aside, the group did enjoy a level of short-lived success in the U.K. and even put a single in the U.S. Top Forty.

Nick Heyward penned the group's debut single, "Favourite Shirts (Boy Meets Girl)" (#4, U.K., 1981). It was contained on the debut album *Pelican West* (#2, 1982, U.K., Arista), which also spun off "Fantastic Day" (#2, U.K., 1982) and "Love Plus One" (#3, 1982). Albeit, some critics praised their mix of Latin rhythms infused with a touch of jazz and an occasional moment of funk, but most had trouble getting by the group's puppy dog purist image. Heyward never made it to the next album, choosing to bail out during high tide and opt for a solo career. He was replaced by his nemesis Mark Fox, who had previously left in a fallout with Heyward.

Haircut 100 then moved to Polydor Records while Arista retained Heyward who scored his first U.K. solo hit with "Whistle Down the Wind" (#13, U.K., 1983) off his *North of a Miracle* (#178, U.S., 1984) album. Meanwhile, *Paint on Paint*, the second Haircut 100 album, failed miserably, leading to the dissolution of the group. Most of the group members turned up in other bands over the years, leaving only Hey-

ward as a viable solo offering. He followed up his initial offering with *Postcards From Home*, *I Love You Avenue* (1989, Reprise), and *From Monday to Sunday* (1993, Epic), all while jumping around to various record companies.

AUTOGRAPHS
Group:
A CD, LP, magazine cover, ad, photo, or card signed by the band: $10-$20*
*Original lineup on first album.
Individual:
Nick Heyward: $10-$20

POSTERS/PRESS KITS
Promotional posters: $5-$10
Press Kits: $15-$20 (first album only!), $10 (Heyward solo)

USED CLOTHING/EQUIPMENT
Guitar Picks:
Nick Heyward: $10*
*Heyward seldom appears live

OFTEN OVERLOOKED MEMORABILIA
Movie memorabilia from *Nothing In Common* (featured a Heyward song); The Final Wham! concert at Wembley Stadium (U.K.)—supported by Heyward

Haley, Bill

Born: July 6, 1925, Died: February 9, 1981

Bill Haley, the rock pioneer and teen idol of the '50s who altered his country image in 1952 in favor of a "rockabilly rebel" as leader of Bill Haley and His Comets, is typically associated with the hits "Rock Around the Clock" (#1, 1955), "Shake, Rattle and Roll," "See You Later Alligator," Burn That Candle," "Dim, Dim the Lights," "Razzle-Dazzle," and "R-O-

Bill Haley and His Comets poster from a May 22, 1955, show in Womelsdorf, P.A. This 14" x 22" poster was printed by Posters, Inc. of Philadelphia. It is valued between $800 and $1,000. From the collection of Hank Thompson

C-K." Haley was so popular that within a twenty-four month time frame, he was averaging a new Top Forty record every two months! As his star faded in the U.S., it seemed to never dim in Europe where he was always treated as a star. Haley himself was overwhelmed by his greeting there in February 1957. At the time of his death his estimated record sales was 60 million.

Bill Haley was inducted into the Rock and Roll Hall of Fame in 1986.

AUTOGRAPHS

Group:

An LP, magazine cover, ad, photo, or card signed by the group: $300-$500

Individual:

Bill Haley: $200-$425

Autographed Bill Haley advertisement

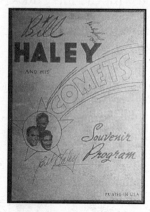

A scarce autographed Souvenir Program for Bill Haley and His Comets

OFTEN OVERLOOKED MEMORABILIA

Movie memorabilia from *Rock Around the Clock*, *Don't Knock the Rock*, and *Let the Good Times Roll*; memorabilia from the numerous nostalgia shows he played

REFERENCES/BOOKS

A few resources exist; begin with John Swenson's book *Bill Haley: The Daddy of Rock and Roll*. No dedicated collector books.

Hall, Aaron, Damion Hall: See Guy

Hall & Oates

Formed 1969

Daryl Hall, Born: October 11, 1949; John Oates, Born: April 7, 1949

Hall & Oates are the number one charting duo in rock & roll history. Both raised in the Philadelphia suburbs, Hall (the Temptones) meets Oates (the Masters) at a local battle of the bands. Oates, who earned a journalism degree at local Temple University, hooks up in Hall's band Gulliver, (Hall failed to complete his curriculum at the same university).

Gulliver recorded only one album on Elektra in 1969 before disbanding. Oates then heads to Europe while Hall becomes a studio musician, singing back-up for numerous acts including the Stylistics and the Delfonics. When Oates returns the two decide to pool their talents as Hall & Oates. Their live debut takes place at Hecate's Circle, a small Philadelphia club, on Saturday Night, December 5, 1970.

In November 1972, *Whole Oats* is released. Although it was produced by Arif Mardin, it gets little attention. The group begins the following year by relocating to Greenwich Village, NY, while *Abandoned Luncheonette*, their second album, also produced by Mardin, is released. The record yields one single, "She's Gone" (#60, 1974), later covered by Tavares who make it Number One on the U.S. R&B chart. In search of a change, the two choose Todd Rundgren to produce their third album, *War Babies* (#86, 1974). The album, more conceptual in nature, is an unexpected departure from their previous releases and results in Atlantic Records terminating their contract.

In 1975, *Daryl Hall and John Oates* (#17, 1976) is the duo's debut release on its new label, RCA. Spun off the album is the group's first big hit, "Sara Smile" (#4, 1976), prompting Atlantic to re-issue "She's Gone" (#7, 1976). *Bigger Than the Both of Us* (#13, 1976), the band's sophomore release for RCA, yielded "Rich Girl" (#1, 1977), which gives the band its first chart topper. Ironically, *Abandoned Luncheonette*, two years after release, reaches #33 on the album chart.

In 1977, Atlantic Records releases *No Goodbyes* (#92, 1977), still riding on the coat tails of the group's success on RCA, while the group begins work on *Beauty on a Back Street* (#30, 1977), which when released, stalls a bit and fails to yield a hit single. *Livetime* (#42, 1978), a collection of road activity, is released next and supported with extensive touring. *Along the Red Edge* (#27, 1978), produced by David Foster, spins off "It's a Laugh" (#20, 1978). The band follows up with another Foster production, *X-Static* (#33, 1979), with extracted "Wait for Me" (#18, 1980) selling well and reaching the Top Twenty. In a bold move, the band, disappointed it hasn't reached greater success, decides to produce the next album.

In September 1980, *Voices* (#17, 1980) peaks in sales, while spinning off four successful singles: "How Does It Feel to Be Back" (#30, 1980), "Kiss on My List" (#1, 1981), "You've Lost That Loving Feeling" (#12, 1980), and "You Make My Dreams" (#5, 1981). On a roll, with no rocks in the road, the band releases *Private Eyes* (#5, 1981), quickly recorded at Electric Lady Studios. The album, on the heels of its predecessor, is similarly successful with hits "Private Eyes" (#1,1981), "I Can't Go for That (No Can Do)" (#1, 1982), and "Did It in a Minute" (#9. 1982). H_2O (#3, 1982), the band's tenth album, spins off more hits including "Maneater" (#1, 1982), "Family Man" (#6, 1983), and "One on One" (#7, 1983).

In November 1983, RCA releases *Rock 'n' Soul (Part 1)*, a compilation of eleven Top 10 hits and two new songs, both of which break into the Top Ten: "Say It Isn't So" (#2, 1983) and "Adult Education" (#8, 1984). On April 7, 1984, the RIAA confirms the group as the most successful duo in U.S. recording history. Everything the two touch seems to turn to gold. Hall's written and produced "Swept Away," sung by Diana Ross, breaks into the Top Twenty (1984). At the same time *Big Bam Boom* (#5, 1984), the duo's first new album in two years is released and it also is crammed with hits, including "Out of Touch" (#1, 1984), "Method of Modern Love" (#5, 1985), "Some Things Are Left Better Unsaid" (#18, 1985), and "Possession Obsession" (#30, 1985).

The duo performs at the reopening of the legendary Apollo Theatre in Harlem in May 1985, and in July back Mick Jagger at the Live Aid concert in Philadelphia, Pennsylvania. The duo then opts for a sabbatical. Hall releases his sophomore solo effort *Three Hearts in the Happy Ending Machine* (#29, 1986) with extracted single "Dreamtime" (#5, 1986).

The band returns in 1988 with *Ooh Yeah!* (#24, 1988), followed by *Change of Season* (#61, 1990); each yields only one single hit. It is becoming increasingly clear that the 1990s may be best suited for each members' solo careers rather than the duo. With Hall & Oates' place in rock and roll history firmly secure, and for the most part unchallenged, there simply is nothing left to prove.

AUTOGRAPHS
Group:
A CD, LP, magazine cover, ad, photo, or card signed by the band: $40-$55*
*Reflects vintage or key memorabilia
Individual:
Daryl Hall: $30-$35
John Oates: $25-$30

TOUR BOOKS/PROGRAMS/PASSES
Tour Programs:
Big Bang Boom: $10-$12
Live Thru '85: $10-$12
Backstage Passes:
Cloth: $10-$12; Laminated: $15-$20

Two versions of Hall and Oates Big Bang Boom Live Thru '85 tour program (© 1984 Whole Oats Enterprises)

POSTERS/PRESS KITS
Promotional Posters: $10-$30*
Press Kits: $25-$40*
*Higher end of scale would be for #1 album memorabilia , a unique style, or Atlantic Records material

USED CLOTHING/EQUIPMENT
Guitar Picks:
Daryl Hall: $15-$25   John Oates: $15-$25

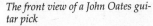

The front view of a John Oates guitar pick   *The back view of a John Oates guitar pick*

OFTEN OVERLOOKED MEMORABILIA
All early Atlantic Records promotional material; any news clippings regarding "Son of Sam" serial killer David Berkowitz's reference to the song "Rich Girl," which he said motivated his crimes; Care-Free chewing gum contest memorabilia (1978) for U.S. high schools who send the manufacturer the most wrappers, not rappers; *Outlaw Blues* movie memorabilia - soundtrack written by John Oates; Pontiac Fiero promotional materials in association with Big Bam Boom Tour Thru '85; posters - $5-$10; buttons - $3-$6; bandanna - $7-$10; video of the Temptones appearance on Jerry Blavat's afternoon television show on WCAV-TV - $25; a menu from the Rosedale Diner on Route 724 near Pottstown - $15; a Whole Oats handbill - $10-$20

REFERENCE BOOKS
Dangerous Dances, by Nick Tosches in cooperation with Daryl Hall and John Oates, 1984: $10-$15. Numerous other resources exist, but nothing that does justice to the band in my opinion. No dedicated collector books. The band's fan club is a must: The Daryl Hall - John Oates International Fan Club, P.O. Box 450, Mansfield, MA 02048 ($8 fee)

Hall, Tom T.

Born: May 25, 1936

This '70s country singer/songwriter, of which the latter he is known most for, was nicknamed "the Storyteller" for his detailed narratives best exemplified in his "Harper Valley P.T.A.," "I Washed My Face in the Morning Dew" (1967), "The Year That Clayton Delaney Died," "I Love" (#12, 1973), and "I Can't Dance," many of which have been covered by numerous artists.

AUTOGRAPHS
An LP, magazine cover, ad, photo, or card signed by the artist: $5-$10

USED CLOTHING/EQUIPMENT
Guitar Picks: $10

OFTEN OVERLOOKED MEMORABILIA
Artifacts relating to other artists' covers of his songs

REFERENCE BOOKS
The Laughing Man of Woodmont Cove by Tom T. Hall; *The Songwriter's Handbook* by Tom T. Hall

Hallyday, Johnny

(John Phillippe Smet)
Born: June 15, 1943

Mid-60s European rock star Johnny Hallyday is best known for his American covers such as "Viens Danser Ie Twist" (Let's Twist Again). He was formerly married to Sylvie Vartan, a popular singer who even opened concerts for the Beatles at Paris' Olympic Theatre in 1964.

AUTOGRAPHS
An LP, magazine cover, ad, photo, or card signed by the artist: $10-$20

Hamilton, Roy

Born: April 16, 1925, Died: July 20, 1969

Hamilton, the late-50s R&B singer with gospel roots, is best remembered for his songs "Don't Let Go" (#13, 1958), "Pledging My Love" (#45, 1958), "I Need Your Lovin'" (#62, 1959), and "You Can Have Her" (#12, 1961). Hamilton influenced many artists including Jerry Butler and the Righteous Brothers.

AUTOGRAPHS
An LP, magazine cover, ad, photo, or card signed by the artist: $20-$40

Hammer

(Stanley Kirk Burrell)
Born: March 30, 1963

Stanley Kirke Burrell, showman extraordinaire, dancer, rapper, and former batboy, proved that with a little luck and a lot of talent, you can become very successful in a relatively short period of time. Born out of a rough neighborhood in the suburbs in Oakland, Burrell developed two passions in life: entertainment and sports—particularly baseball. His second home soon became the Oakland Coliseum, where A's fans could catch the young man dancing in a parking lot and eventually shagging bats on the field as the team's bat boy. In fact, it was the Oakland A's baseball team that first began to call him "Little Hammer" because he resembled the baseball great "Hammerin' Hank" (Henry) Aaron.

After realizing that neither a career in baseball, nor in the United States Navy were going to emerge, "Hammer" chose the next logical alternative, entertainment. He formed a religious rap duo before he created his own record label (he asked two professional baseball players, Mike Davis and Dwayne Murphy, to invest in his career, which they did). He sold his debut single "Ring 'Em" from the trunk of his car while passing along ten percent of his earnings to the ballplayers.

While performing in the Oak Tree Cabaret club in Oakland (1988), he was spotted by Capitol Records executive Joy Bailey, who singed the musician to a recording contract that included a healthy advance. His debut release, *Let's Get It Started* (#30, 1989), was an updated version of his own label's *Feel My Power* plus four new songs. On April 8, 1989, the record topped the R&B charts and sold more than a million copies.

His second record, *Please Hammer Don't Hurt 'Em* (#1, 1990), included the hit "U Can't Touch This" (#8, 1989), his signature song patterned after Rick James' "Super Freak." It soon became a dance smash with M.C. Hammer's accompanying video, which was one of the hottest attractions on MTV. The record stayed at the top of the charts for a record twenty-one weeks, becoming the biggest-selling rap album ever.

Although his success was met with some criticism, his image was everywhere, even in his own kid's cartoon. Hammer also began diversifying his skills by delving into music management, horse racing, and even his own children foundation.

Now simply Hammer, *Too Legit to Quit* (#2, 1991) sold well, but his following seemed to be diminishing. His tour was marred by disappointments including an on-stage shooting (6/25/92). In 1994, as his stock faded, he returned to the moniker M.C. Hammer with *The Funky Headhunter* (#12, 1994)—now on Gi-

ant Records. The album included two extracted singles, "Pumps and a Bump"(#26, 1994) and "It's All Good" (#46, 1994). The latter was a far cry from the truth, because the musician filed for bankruptcy in an Oakland court on April 3, 1996.

Despite the adversity he has had to overcome at various times in his life, the musician is a fascinating subject to collect. His involvement in so many forms of entertainment and media give his followers numerous collecting paths. Those who have followed this talented man's career know that he will emerge once again—this is one Hammer that isn't through pounding!

M.C. HAMMER - SELECTED TELEVISION APPEARANCES

Date	Show
September 18, 1990	"All-Star Tribute to Oprah Winfrey" - ABC-TV
October 21, 1990	"News Special" - NBC-TV about Hammer
February 23, 1991	*Amen* - NBC-TV
May 1, 1991	*Wogan* - BBC1-TV
September 7, 1991	"Hammerman" - ABC-TV, premier of cartoon
October 6, 1991	"Ray Charles: 50 Years In Music" - FOX-TV, guests
November 17, 1991	*Saturday Night Live* - NBC-TV, musical guest
January 27, 1992	"19th Annual American Music Awards" - co-hosts
March 1, 1992	"Muhammad Ali's 50th Birthday" - ABC-TV, participates
March 30, 1992	"Hammer's MTV Birthday Bash" - MTV
April 3, 1992	"Hammer from the Heart" - CBS-TV special
October 31, 1992	*Out All Night* - NBC-TV, sings
June 9, 1993	*The Arsenio Hall Show*

AUTOGRAPHS

A CD, LP, magazine cover, ad, photo, or card signed by the artist: $10-$25

TOUR BOOKS/PROGRAMS/PASSES

Tour Book:
Too Legit to Quit, 1992: $10- $12
Backstage Passes:
Cloth: $8-$10; Laminated: $10-$20

POSTERS/PRESS KITS

Promotional Posters: $10-$20
Press Kits: $15-$25

OFTEN OVERLOOKED MEMORABILIA

Oakland A's memorabilia (team photos with him in the picture, yearbooks, etc.) from his years there as a bat boy; all British Knights athletic footwear and Pepsi-Cola promotional items featuring him; scorecard from October 8, 1990 - Oakland A's game - Hammer threw out first ball - $8; movie memorabilia from *Rocky V* and *The Addams Family*- includes a Hammer composition; race programs that include his horse Lite Light; Hammer memorabilia from MTV Rock 'n' Jock softball game (1/11/92); All

Bustin Productions memorabilia; backpack - $10-$20 (two styles); bubble gum - $5 (pack or tin); Mattel rap fashions - $5-$7; Mattel dolls - $25-$30 (two styles: cassette tape and boom box); fanny pack - $5; Milton Bradley jigsaw puzzles - $10 (500 pcs.), $5 (100 pcs.); lunch box w/thermos - $10 (thermos alone -$5); school notebooks - $5 (small), $8 (large, 8" x 10.5"); Simplicity sewing patterns - $8-$10; rap microphone (Impact) - $25; school folder - $3; school kit - $10; slap bracelet - $5; video game (Tiger Elec.) - $20; View-Master 3-D - $5; wallets - $10

REFERENCES/BOOKS

A few resources exist, but none do justice to the singer in my opinion.

Hammill, Peter: See Van Der Graaf Generator

Hammond, John

Born: November 13, 1943

Sixties blues singer John Hammond is perhaps best known as the artist who was backed by the Hawks (who later became the Band), before Bob Dylan lured them away. The Hawks were far from his only prestigious alumni—Jimi Hendrix also backed Hammond in the mid-60s. Hammond was a regular on the small concert venue circuit in the late '60s, while tackling other projects from soundtrack contributions to sessions. In 1973 he became part of the would-be and short-lived supergroup Triumvirate, which also included Dr. John and Mike Bloomfield, before continuing on with his contributions and releases.

AUTOGRAPHS

An LP, magazine cover, ad, photo, or card signed by the artist: $10-$25

OFTEN OVERLOOKED MEMORABILIA

Movie memorabilia from *Little Big Man* (1970); artifacts from his numerous contributions to other musicians recordings

Hancock, Herbie

Born: April 12, 1940

Herbie Hancock, the extraordinary keyboardist and creative composer, is often associated with The Miles Davis legendary mid-60s quintet, where, as a pianist, he helped shape postbop chamber jazz, which influenced him to later pursue a funk-fusion direction on his own. Hancock worked with Davis

from 1963 to 1968, before going solo, while also scoring motion picture soundtracks.

Headhunters was Hancock's breakthrough album and it spun off the extract "Chameleon" (#42, 1974). From this point onward, he released at least one album per year in his desired genre, occasionally accompanied by a soundtrack, until 1984. The years produced experimental and even one-off styled albums, such as "V.S.O.P." that played in the early Blue Note-Miles Davis style, most of which were consistent sellers and highly praised by critics.

Future Shock (1983) was an enormous success for Hancock, partially due to the extract "Rockit" (#71, 1983) and its creative promotional video that garnered good airplay on MTV. The single became a good example of just how in-line Hancock was to where music has been and where it may go, complete with funk rhythms and hip-hop "scratching." The '80s also saw the artist continue his work on soundtracks; he even earned an Oscar for *Round Midnight* in 1986. In 1994 he also won a Grammy for Best Jazz Instrumental Performance for his collaboration on *A Tribute to Miles*. As an artist and innovator he represents where his media has been, the challenges it has faced and overcome, and its future.

AUTOGRAPHS

An LP, magazine cover, ad, photo, or card signed by the artist: $10-$20

OFTEN OVERLOOKED MEMORABILIA

Movie memorabilia from *Blow-Up*, *A Soldier's Story* (1984), *Round Midnight* (1986), *Jo Jo Dancer Your Life Is Calling* (1986), and *Colors* (1987); memorabilia from the television show "Fat Albert Rotunda"; artifacts associated with his numerous contributions to other musicians' works

****

"On The Edge"

Hanson

Just as your subscription to *Teen Beat* expires, in the *"Middle of Nowhere"* (#2, 1997) arrives Hanson. Clark (Born: 11/17/80), Jordan (Born: 3/15/83), and Zachary (Born: 10/22/85) take their Tulsa harmonies from the dinner table, where they sang during supper, into the hearts of our nation's teenagers. From hip hop to "MMMBop" (#1, 1997), these three brothers prove that music evolves—or is it dissolves? "Where's the Love" you ask? Just consult my daughter Elizabeth, who demanded this entry.

POSTERS/PRESS KITS

Promotional Posters: $10-$30
Press Kits: $10-$20

****

Happy Mondays

Formed 1980

Bez (Mark Berry), Paul Davis, Mark Day, Paul Ryder, Shaun Ryder, and Gary Whelan

This late-80s British acid house rave scene group, which enjoyed success in the U.K. but had little impact here in America, is commonly associated with the songs "Tart Tart," "24 Hour Party People," "Cut 'Em Loose Bruce," and "Step On" (#57, 1991). The group split up in 1993.

AUTOGRAPHS

An LP, magazine cover, ad, photo, or card signed by the group: $8-$15

Hardin, Tim

Born: December 23, 1941, Died: December 29, 1980

This early-60s singer/songwriter, who became part of the folk-blues revival, attained little commercial success, but the songs he wrote did, including "If I Were a Carpenter," "Reason to Believe," and "Misty Roses." His only Top Fifty single was Bobby Darin's "Simple Song of Freedom," which he charted in 1969. His death came from a heroin overdose in 1980.

AUTOGRAPHS

An LP, magazine cover, ad, photo, or card signed by the artist: $20-$40

Harding, John Wesley

Born: October 22, 1965

Eighties British singer/songwriter John Wesley Harding was heavily influenced by post-punk and folk rock styles. He adopted his name from Bob Dylan's 1968 album. His work, on the Sire label, has received critical accolades but little commercial success.

AUTOGRAPHS

An LP, magazine cover, ad, photo, or card signed by the artist: $6-$12

Harper, Roy

Born: June 12, 1941

Roy Harper, the late-60s and early-70s eclectic British folksinger and songwriter, is best known in

the States as the subject of Led Zeppelin's "Hats Off to (Roy) Harper," from the group's third LP, and as the lead vocal in Pink Floyd's "Have a Cigar" from the 1975 *Wish You Were Here* LP.

AUTOGRAPHS

An LP, magazine cover, ad, photo, or card signed by the artist: $8-$15

OFTEN OVERLOOKED MEMORABILIA

Movie memorabilia from *Made*

Harper's Bizarre

Ted Templeman, Dick Scoppettone, Eddie James, Dick Yount, and John Peterson

This late-60s San Francisco pre-psychedelic five-part harmony pop-rock group is best known for its cover hit of Paul Simon's "The 59th Street Bridge Song (Feelin' Groovy)" (#13, 1967) and as the early home of lead singer Ted Templeman, who would go on to become one of Warner Brothers Records' most successful top in-house A&R men and producers.

AUTOGRAPHS

An LP, magazine cover, ad, photo, or card signed by the group: $10-$15

Harpo, Slim

(James Moore)
Born: January 11, 1924, Died: January 31, 1970

Bayou blues singer, songwriter, guitarist, and harp player Slim Harpo is best remembered for penning "I'm a King Bee," along with songs "Rainin' in My Heart" (#34, 1961) and "Baby, Scratch My Back" (#16, 1966). In the early '40s as Harmonica Slim, he played bars and clubs before meeting guitarist Lightnin' Slim, with whom he would tour and perform for the next two decades.

AUTOGRAPHS

An LP, magazine cover, ad, photo, or card signed by the artist: $20-$60

OFTEN OVERLOOKED MEMORABILIA

Artifacts associated with the numerous musicians who have covered his music

The Harptones

Best-known Lineup: William "Willie" Winfield, William "Bill" Dempsey, William "Dicey" Galloway, Bill Brown, Nicky Clark, and Raoul Cita

Fifties and early-60s New York jazz-tinged vocal group the Harptones are best remembered for the songs "My Memories of You," "Life Is But a Dream," and "What Will I Tell My Heart" (#96, 1961), before disbanding in 1964.

AUTOGRAPHS

An LP, magazine cover, ad, photo, or card signed by the group: $15-$35

Harris, Don "Sugarcane"/ Don and Dewey

(Don Harris)
Born: June 18, 1938

Talented instrumentalist, and veteran R&B performer as half of the duo Don and Dewey, Don Harris is commonly associated with the songs "Farmer John," "Big Boy Pete," and "I'm Leaving It All Up to You." As also a proficient blues-rock violinist he has also played with numerous others including Frank Zappa, Little Richard, and John Mayall.

AUTOGRAPHS

An LP, magazine cover, ad, photo, or card signed by the artist: $8-$15

OFTEN OVERLOOKED MEMORABILIA

Associated artifacts from his numerous contributions with other musicians

Harris, Emmylou

Born: April 2, 1947

This gifted country singer's beginnings can be traced back to early collaborations with Gram Parsons, who would have an enormous impact on the singer before his death in 1973. Emmylou Harris went on to form her own group—some members were even former Parsons sidemen—before signing on with Warner Brothers Records in 1975. She called her touring group the Hot Band, and indeed it was; it was made up of talented musicians such as Rodney Crowell, Emory Gordy, Jr., Hank deVito, Albert Lee, and Ricky Skaggs.

"If I Could Only Win Your Love" topped the country charts in 1975 and started her rolling on a series of hits including "Together Again" (#1, 1976), "One of These Days" (#3, 1976), "Sweet Dreams" (#1, 1976), and "To Daddy" (#3, 1977). During this period she also appeared in *The Last Waltz* and later teamed up with Roy Orbison on the song "That Lovin' You Feelin' Again" (#55, 1980).

"Beneath Still Waters" (#1, 1980), "If I Needed You" (#3, 1981), and "(Lost His Love) On Our Last Date" (#1, 1983) were just some of the numerous early-80s C&W hits for Harris, who also penned the somewhat biographical *The Ballad of Sally Rose*, a

country opera that was met with praise by critics. In 1987 the album *Trio* (#6) united three of the most gifted voices in music, Dolly Parton, Linda Ronstadt, and Emmylou Harris, and included the C&W hit extracts "To Know Him Is to Love Him" (#1, 1987), "Telling Me Lies" (#3, 1987), "Those Memories of You" (#5, 1987), and "Wildflowers" (#6, 1988). She had other hits by decade's end, most notable of which is "Happy Endings" (#1, C&W, 1988).

The '90s opened with Harris putting out a compilation of previously released pairings called *Duets* (#24, 1990), which had her alongside many of her favorites including Gram Parsons and George Jones. The Hot Band was replaced during the decade by the Nash Ramblers, an acoustic combination that she had felt more comfortable with at this time. Although the hits tailed off a bit there was still plenty of great material for fans to return to, which we did and even she did with *At the Ryman*, recorded live at the Grand Ole Opry (1992).

The signature of Emmylou Harris (obtained in-person)

AUTOGRAPHS

I caught her early in her career when she was flattered by autograph requests, but I have been told that in recent years she has been somewhat evasive.

An LP, magazine cover, ad, photo, or card signed by the artist: $15-$35

Harris, Wynonie

Born: August 24, 1915, Died: June 14, 1969

Powerful '40s vocalist and big-band blues shouter Wynonie Harris is best remembered for the songs "Good Morning Judge," "Lovin' Machine," "All She Wants to Do is Rock," and later for "Bloodshot Eyes."

AUTOGRAPHS

An LP, magazine cover, ad, photo, or card signed by the artist: $10-$30

Harrison, George

Born: February 25, 1943

Tinged in eastern-flavor, the soundtrack album *Wonderwall Music* (1968) began George Harrison's solo career. As the first LP released under the Apple umbrella, all related pieces of memorabilia are highly collectible. *Apple Gold* includes everything from stationery to matchbooks. *All Things Must Pass* (#1, 1970), a three-record set, was released in November 1970. The LP's success brought Harrison acclaim as the first ex-Beatle to top the album charts. The set spun off the extract, and quickly controversial, "My Sweet Lord" (#1, 1970). Also collectible are periodical clippings surrounding the plagiarism suit filed by the Chiffons—based on Ronnie Mack's song "He's So Fine."

Two releases, *The Concert for Bangla Desh* (#1, 1972) and *Living in the Material World* (#1, 1973), occupied the artist's time over the next couple years. Interrupted primarily by a February 28, 1972, automobile accident, Harrison also garnered numerous awards, tackled humanitarian issues, and complained about his taxes, before forming his own record label, Dark Horse. Little was made of his achievement of being the first artist in chart history to land two successive triple albums atop the LP chart.

Dark Horse (#4, 1974) and *Extra Texture (Read All About It)* (#8, 1975), the last on the Apple label, were Harrison's next two album releases. On December 18, 1976, *Thirty-Three and a Third* (#11, 1977) became the first LP released on his own Dark Horse label. *George Harrison* (#14, 1979) was his last LP release of the decade. In great contrast to his group days with the Beatles, Harrison had relatively little success on the singles chart.

Somewhere in England (#11, 1981), with the hit extract "All Those Years Ago" (#2, 1981), and *Cloud Nine* (#8, 1988), with its single "Got My Mind Set on You" (#1, 1988), thrust Harrison back into the spotlight. Nearly a quarter of the century since "I Want to Hold Your Hand" was a top the singles chart, the ex-Beatle executed one of the most significant comebacks in rock history. With his solo career in check, and the misery of the film *Shanghai Surprise* (1986) behind him, Harrison finished the decade as Nelson Wilbury of the Traveling Wilburys.

Tributes, contributions, and benefits were a mainstay of the humanitarian George Harrison in the '90s. While there was some time for projects, such as legal house cleaning, the Beatles Anthology series, and a one-off performance, the musician's public appearances seldom found him the focal point. Like so many successful musicians who have found themselves at a similar impasse, Harrison is content at

using his celebrity status to battle social issues or to benefit his fellow mankind.

A check signed by George Harrison

George Harrison's signature

AUTOGRAPHS

A CD, LP, magazine cover, ad, photo, or card signed by the artist: See the Beatles

TOUR BOOKS/PROGRAMS/ PASSES

Tour Books:
1974 Tour: $15

POSTERS/PRESS KITS

Promotional Posters:
$40-$85

George Harrison guitar picks can command $150

OFTEN OVERLOOKED MEMORABILIA

Movie memorabilia from *Wonderwall* (1968), *The Concert for Bangla Desh* (3/23/72) (Lobby Cards - $25, posters - $20-$125, pressbook - $25, stills - $5-$10), *The Life of Brian* (1979), *Water* (1985), *Porky's Revenge* (1985), *Shanghai Surprise* (1986), and *Lethal Weapon 2* (1989); videotapes from his numerous television appearances including *Rutland Weekend Television* (12/26/75), *Saturday Night Live* (11/20/76), *The Old Grey Whistle Test* (11/30/75), *This Is Your Life* (1/25/78), *Ringo* (4/26/78), *Aspel & Co.* (3/5/88), and *The Simpsons* (9/30/93); promotional items for the book *I Me Mine* (1979); a copy of the documentary *Life of George* (1989); items relating to the numerous social issues the artist has been involved with; artifacts from Friar Park; stationery from some of his numerous companies; The Traveling Wilburys guitar with case made by Gretsch (numerous variations)

REFERENCES/BOOKS

Numerous resources to choose from, but begin with Harrison's autobiography *I Me Mine;* no dedicated collector books

Harrison, Jerry: See Talking Heads

Harrison, Wilbert

Born: January 6, 1929, Died: October 26, 1994

This '50s jump-blues singer is best remembered for two hits, "Kansas City" (#1, 1959) and "Let's Work Together" (#32, 1969), although he also had a minor hit with "My Heart Is Yours" (#98, 1971).

AUTOGRAPHS

An LP, magazine cover, ad, photo, or card signed by the artist: $10-$40

Harry, Deborah: See Blondie

Hart, Grant: See Hüsker Dü

Hart, Mickey: See Grateful Dead

Hartford, John

Born: December 30, 1937

Late-60s singer, songwriter, and guitarsmith John Hartford is commonly associated with his penned "Gentle on My Mind," of which Glen Campbell garnered a Grammy, as well as other compositions including "California Earthquake" and "Natural to Be Gone." Hartford also became familiar as a television regular and later won a Grammy in the ethnic-traditional category for his 1976 *Mark Twang*.

AUTOGRAPHS

An LP, magazine cover, ad, photo, or card signed by the artist: $10-$20

OFTEN OVERLOOKED MEMORABILIA

Videotapes of his numerous television show appearances including *Smothers Brothers Comedy Hour*, *The Glen Campbell Goodtime Hour*, and *Something Else*—which Hartford hosted; associated artifacts from other musicians' covers of his material

Hartman, Dan

Born: 1951, Died: March 22, 1994

Talented mid-70s multi-instrumentalist, commonly associated with his bass playing for Edgar Winter and for penning "Free Ride," Hartman also scored hits with "Instant Replay" (#29, 1978) and "I Can Dream About You" (#6, 1984). Hartman was also a talented producer and owner of the Schoolhouse, a Westport, Connecticut, studio. During the '80s he also established himself as a gifted contributor to film, taking credits on many including *Bull Durham* and *Rocky IV*.

AUTOGRAPHS

An LP, magazine cover, ad, photo, or card signed by the artist: $10-$30

OFTEN OVERLOOKED MEMORABILIA

Movie memorabilia from *Fletch*, *Krush Groove*, *Bull Durham*, *Down and Out in Beverly Hills*, *Ruthless People*, and *Rocky IV*; artifacts associated with his production work; Schoolhouse artifacts

Harvey, PJ

Formed 1991

PJ (Polly Jean) Harvey, Rob Ellis, and Stephen Vaughan

This '90s English post-punk power trio, which bolted into the British spotlight by quickly landing two chart-topping singles with its raw rock sound, is led by the dynamic guitarist, singer, and songwriter Polly Jean Harvey, whose straight-forward approach to a variety of issues, including femininity, has drawn considerable attention. She later left the band in favor of a solo career.

AUTOGRAPHS

An LP, magazine cover, ad, photo, or card signed by the group: $10-$15

Hassell, Jon

Born: March 22, 1937

"Fourth World" composer and trumpeter, and technically driven musician, Jon Hassell—dedicated to primitive, yet futuristic sounds—has established himself in his own dimension of world music.

AUTOGRAPHS

An LP, magazine cover, ad, photo, or card signed by the artist: $8-$12

Hatfield, Juliana/Blake Babies

Formed 1986
Born: July 27, 1967

Juliana Hatfield, John Strohm, and Freda Boner

A college-radio star with the Blake Babies, Juliana Hatfield sought a harder sound upon her departure from the band in 1990. Noted for her tender voice, planted assertively against energetic guitar riffs, Hatfield has also garnered accolades for her introspective songwriting, specifically as it relates biographically. Adored by a fascinated media, she has also adorned numerous publication covers, giving collectors a wider range of memorabilia to choose from.

AUTOGRAPHS

An LP, magazine cover, ad, photo, or card signed by the artist: $6-$12

OFTEN OVERLOOKED MEMORABILIA

Copies of the numerous periodicals she has appeared in including *Sassy* and *Vogue*

Hathaway, Donny

Born: October 1, 1945, Died: January 13, 1979

This '70s talented singer, songwriter, and keyboardist is best remembered for his beautiful duets with Roberta Flack on songs such as "You've Got a Friend" (#29, 1971), "Where Is the Love" (#5, 1972), and "The Closer I Get to You" (#2, 1978). He died while working with the artist on the album *Roberta Flack Featuring Donny Hathaway* from an apparent fall.

AUTOGRAPHS

An LP, magazine cover, ad, photo, or card signed by the artist: $15-$50

OFTEN OVERLOOKED MEMORABILIA

All items relating to his work with Roberta Flack; movie memorabilia from *Come Back Charleston Blue*; a videotape from the television series *Maude*—Hathaway sang the theme song

Havens, Ritchie

Born: January 21, 1941

Late-60s folksinger and popular outdoor festival artist, whose aggressive guitar playing became his hallmark, Ritchie Havens is most identified with the song "Here Comes the Sun" (#16, 1971) and for his appearances at Woodstock (1969, 1994). Havens

would also later become associated with his successful commercial jingles.

AUTOGRAPHS

An LP, magazine cover, ad, photo, or card signed by the artist: $10-$15

OFTEN OVERLOOKED MEMORABILIA

Movie memorabilia from *Catch My Soul* (1974) and *Greased Lightning* (1977); theatrical memorabilia from the stage presentation of *Tommy*; videotapes of his numerous commercial jingles; major festival artifacts from the Newport Folk Festival (1966), the Monterey Jazz Festival (1967), the Isle of Wight Festival (1969), and Woodstock (1969, 1994)

Hawkins, Dale

Born: August 22, 1938

Late-50s rockabilly pioneer, singer, guitarist, and band leader Dale Hawkins is commonly linked with his hits "Suzie Q" (#27, 1957) and "Le Do-Dada" (#32, 1958), as well as the songs "My Babe" and "Liza Jane." He is also revered for the successful guitarists who played in his band including James Burton, Scotty Moore, and Roy Buchanan.

AUTOGRAPHS

An LP, magazine cover, ad, photo, or card signed by the artist: $8-$25

OFTEN OVERLOOKED MEMORABILIA

Associated artifacts from other musicians' covers of his work; artifacts from his production work

Hawkins, Eddie Singers

Formed 1967

This late-60s gospel group is best remembered for the legendary hit "Oh Happy Day" (#4, 1969), before fading into obscurity.

AUTOGRAPHS

An LP, magazine cover, ad, photo, or card signed by the group: $10-$25

Hawkins, Ronnie

Born: January 10, 1935

Seasoned veteran roadhouse rocker, who is best remembered as the man who assembled the Band, as well as for his hits "Mary Lou" (#26, 1959) and "Forty Days" (#45, 1959), Ronnie Hawkins has always been popular in Canada where his 1963 rendition of Bo Diddley's "Who Do You Love" is now

considered a classic. "Down in the Alley" (#75, 1970) was his last American chart single. Hawkins later hosted his own television series called *Honky Tonk*.

AUTOGRAPHS

An LP, magazine cover, ad, photo, or card signed by the artist: $10-$25

OFTEN OVERLOOKED MEMORABILIA

Movie memorabilia from *The Last Waltz*, *Heaven's Gate*, and *Renaldo and Clara*; videotapes of his television series *Honky Tonk*

Hawkins, Screamin' Jay

(Jalacy Hawkins)
Born: July 18, 1929

This late-50s unrestrained, rocking R&B showman is best remembered for his flamboyant and energetic performances and the songs "I Put a Spell on You" (1956), "Alligator Wine" (1958), and "Feast of the Mau Mau" (1967). Screamin' Jay Hawkins was a favorite on the Alan Freed package tours, because he was typically carried offstage in a flaming coffin.

AUTOGRAPHS

An LP, magazine cover, ad, photo, or card signed by the artist: $10-$30

OFTEN OVERLOOKED MEMORABILIA

Movie memorabilia from *Mister Rock and Roll* (1957), *American Hot Wax* (1978), and *Mystery Train* (1989); memorabilia from the Alan Freed package tours

Hawkwind/Hawklords

Formed 1969

Original members (Group X/Hawkwind Zoo): Terry Ollis, Nik Turner, Dave Brock, Dikmik, John Harrison, and Mick Slattery

Numerous personnel changes followed above line-up.

Hawkwind, the '70s English psychedelic rock band, has become known just as much for its longevity as for its musical contributions—especially the hits "Silver Machine" and "Urban Guerilla"—while building a substantial cult following. The group's prolific output has averaged about an album a year, despite numerous personnel changes. Many of the group's members have gone on to other successful ventures including Ian "Lemmy" Kilmister, who later formed heavy-metal giants Motorhead.

AUTOGRAPHS

An LP, magazine cover, ad, photo, or card signed by the group: $15-$30*

*Varies, lineup dependent

OFTEN OVERLOOKED MEMORABILIA

"Sonic Attack" UA promo, one-sided came with special cloth bag cover, 1972; "Hawfan," a special fan club issue with sticker, poster, and bag, limited to 600, 1986

REFERENCES/BOOKS

The Illustrated Collector's Guide to Hawkwind by Robert Goodwin is a must!

Hayes, Isaac

Born: August 6, 1938

Late-60s and early-70s songwriter, arranger, producer, pianist, and vocalist Issac Hayes can credit himself for laying the foundation for disco, while forming the roots of rap. Although "Hot Buttered Soul" (#8, 1969) brought him out of the background, "The Theme from Shaft" (#1, 1971) pushed him into the spotlight. He became the first African-American composer to win an Academy Award for his accomplishment. His flamboyant acceptance appearance at the ceremony is more memorable than the show itself, with the smoke, lights, and ladies. He would later land other songs on the R&B charts including "Never Can Say Goodbye" (#22, #5 R&B, 1971) and "Don't Let Go" (#21, 1979), while also cowriting Dionne Warwick's pop hit "Deja Vu" and beginning an acting career.

Isaac Hayes. Photo by Thierry Le Goues. Courtesy Pointblank.

AUTOGRAPHS

An LP, magazine cover, ad, photo, or card signed by the artist: $10-$15

OFTEN OVERLOOKED MEMORABILIA

Movie memorabilia from *Shaft* (1971), *Wattstax* (1973), *Truck Turner* (1974), *It Seemed Like a Good Idea at the Time* (1975), *Escape from New York* (1981), *I'm Gonna Get You Sucka* (1988), *Robin Hood: Men in Tights* (1993), *Posse* (1993), and *It Could Happen to You* (1994); television memorabilia from his numerous appearances including *The Rockford Files*, *Miami Vice*, and *The A-Team*

Haza, Ofra

Born: November 19, 1959

This late-80s international Israeli pop star, whose gifted voice has drawn numerous comparisons to the greats before her—even Barbra Streisand—had her first-major label release here in the U.S. with *Shaday* (#130, 1989), which spun off the minor U.S. dance hit single "Im Nin'alu."

AUTOGRAPHS

An LP, magazine cover, ad, photo, or card signed by the artist: $6-$10

Hazlewood, Lee

Born: July 9, 1929

Record producer, singer, and songwriter Lee Hazlewood is best remembered for his duets with Nancy Sinatra on "Jackson" (#14, 1967), "Summer Wine" (#49, 1967), "Lady Bird" (#20, 1967), and "Some Velvet Morning" (#26, 1968), while also producing her songs "These Boots Are Made for Walkin'" (#1, 1966) and "Sugar Town" (#5, 1966).

AUTOGRAPHS

An LP, magazine cover, ad, photo, or card signed by the artist: $5-$10

OFTEN OVERLOOKED MEMORABILIA

Artifacts from his label, Jamie Records, which he co-owned with Dick Clark; memorabilia associated with the numerous acts he produced including Duane Eddy

Head, Hands and Feet

Formed 1970

Albert Lee, Tony Colton, Ray Smith, Chas Hodges, Pete Gavin, and Mike O'Neil

This early-70s combination of British studio musicians—including guitarist Albert Lee, who would later embark on efforts with Emmylou Harris and Eric Clapton—released three albums. The last album peaked the most curiosity with the public, but

was not a commercial success. By this time the band had already begun focusing on other efforts.

AUTOGRAPHS
An LP, magazine cover, ad, photo, or card signed by the group: $10-$15

Healey, Jeff Band

Formed 1985

Jeff Healey (Norman Jeffrey Healey), Joe Rockman, and Tom Stephen

Late-80s blues-rock guitarist Jeff Healey, whose unique style of playing attracted the attention of Albert Collins and even Stevie Ray Vaughan, formed his own band to begin the long task of touring and generating label interest. The band finally landed with Arista and released *See the Light* (#22, 1988), which included the hit extract "Angel Eyes" (#5, 1989). The group later followed up with the album *Hell to Pay* (#27, 1990); it failed to yield a hit single. Interest seemed to be waning, and by *Feel This* (#174, 1992), the group's following was numb.

AUTOGRAPHS
An LP, magazine cover, ad, photo, or card signed by the group: $10-$15

OFTEN OVERLOOKED MEMORABILIA
Movie memorabilia from *Road House* (1988)

Heart

Formed 1970

Ann Wilson, Nancy Wilson, Roger Fisher, Howard Leese, Michael Derosier, and Steve Fossen*

*Mark Andes and Denny Carmassi replaced Derosier and Fossen in 1981, however, both left in 1993

Emerging from the Seattle suburbs, Ann (Ann Wilson & the Daybreaks, Bordersong) and Nancy Wilson merged talents with Steve and Roger Fossen, who along with Mike Fisher were in a band called Army, later changed to White Heart and finally Heart in 1974. Fisher moved into a position as the band's manager and sound engineer. In 1975, the band relocated to Vancouver, BC, Canada, added Michael Derosier, and upon establishing a strong live reputation, signed a record deal with the independent label Mushroom.

Dreamboat Annie (#7, 1976), which sold strong locally, was released in 1975. The album began to sell nationally due to improved distribution and an extracted single "Crazy on You" (#35, 1976), which began to get increased airplay, while moving into the Top Forty. When another single from the album, "Magic Man" (#9, 1976), began to climb up the charts,

larger record companies began to take notice. In December 1976, Heart moved back to Seattle and signed with CBS/Portrait Records. Legal battles ensued—Mushroom claimed a breach of contract and the group countersued to avoid the release of its second album, *Magazine*.

The debut Portrait album *Little Queen* (#9, 1977) yielded three singles: "Barracuda" (#11,1977), "Kick It Out" (#79, 1977), and the self-titled "Little Queen" (#62, 1977). In 1978, Mushroom reissued "Crazy on You" and won a court battle to release *Magazine* (#17,1978), which had already been heavily bootlegged. The album spun off "Heartless" (#24, 1978), while the band worked on its next release. *Dog and Butterfly* (#17, 1978) became the group's fourth million-seller and included the hit singles "Straight On" (#15, 1978) and the self-titled "Dog and Butterfly" (#34, 1979).

While completing its next album, the relationship between band members faltered, and Roger Fisher left. In March *Bebe Le' Strange* (#5, 1980, Epic) peaked high on the album charts while the group enjoyed a successful 77-date U.S. Tour. The band added Howard Leese and did its best to augment Fisher's departure. An extracted single from the album, "Even It Up" (#34, 1980), also climbed into the Top Forty.

The group's double album *Greatest Hits / Live* (#13, 1980) peaked in December and included a compilation of hits and six live tracks. The following year began well as "Tell It Like It Is" (#8, 1981) scored another hit single for the group. In May the group began an extensive six-month U.S. Tour. At tour's end, Steve Fossen departed from the band.

Private Audition (#25, 1982), the band's next album, included "This Man Is Mine" (#33, 1982) and marked the debut of the newly added Mark Andes (Spirit, Jo Jo Gunne, Firefall). The group also enjoyed a strong U.K. tour opening for Queen. *Passionworks* (#39, 1983) followed and yielded the single "How Can I Refuse" (#44, 1983). The group also had a new drummer, Denny Carmassi (Montrose), who replaced Michael Derosier.

In January 1985, the band, now signed with Capitol Records, began work on *Heart* (#1, 1985). The album included four Top Ten hits: "What About Love?" (#10, 1985), "Never" (#4, 1985), "These Dreams" (#1, 1986), and "Nothin' at All" (#10, 1986). *Bad Animals* (#2, 1987) also sold well and contained the singles "Alone" (#1, 1987), "Who Will You Run To" (#7, 1987), and "There's the Girl" (#12, 1987).

The next decade began with *Brigade* (#3, 1990), which yielded three hits: "All I Want to Do Is Make Love To You" (#2, 1990), "I Didn't Want to Need You" (#23, 1990), and "Stranded" (#13, 1990). On June 8, 1990, the group began the lengthy six-month North American "Brigade" Tour. *Rock the House Live!* (#107, 1991) was the band's next offering. The Lovemongers, an acoustic quartet and outlet for the Wil-

son sisters, played selected shows and released a four-song EP.

In 1993 the band emerged with *Desire Walks On* (#48, 1993), but was without Andes and Carmassi. They were later replaced by drummer Denny Fongheiser and bassist Fernando Saunders. This was also the year the band issued one of the first rock related CD-ROMs, *Twenty Years of Rock & Roll*—a multimedia biography. *The Road Home* (#87, 1995), produced by John Paul Jones (Led Zeppelin), was released. It was an acoustic reworking of familiar covers and Heart favorites.

The Seattle music scene has always benefited from the Wilson sisters charitable work and development of other local talent. Additionally, their Bad Animals studio has hosted some of the best names in the business including R.E.M., Soundgarden, and Pearl Jam.

AUTOGRAPHS

Group:
A CD, LP, magazine cover, ad, photo, or card signed by the band: $30-$45*
*Original lineup

Individual:

Ann Wilson: $15-$20	Nancy Wilson: $15
Roger Fisher: $5-$10	Howard Leese: $5-$10
Michael Derosier: $5-$10	Steve Fossen: $5-$10
Mark Andes: $5-$10	Denny Carmassi: $10

Ann Wilson's signature

Howard Leese's signature

Steve Fossen's signature

Bad Animals Tour program (1988) (© Heart Amalgomated, Inc.)

TOUR BOOKS/ PROGRAMS/PASSES

Tour Programs:
Bad Animals: $15
Brigade: $15
Passion Works: $25

Backstage Passes:
Cloth: $8-$15;
 Laminated: $15-$25*
*Tours before 1985

POSTERS/PRESS KITS
Promotional Posters:
$10-$45
Press Kits: $15-$40
Bad Animals: $20

USED CLOTHING/EQUIPMENT
Guitar Picks:

Ann Wilson: $15-$60	Nancy Wilson: $15-$60
Roger Fisher: $10-$25	Howard Leese: $10-$25
Steve Fossen: $15-$25	Mark Andes: $10-$20

Drum Sticks:

Michael Derosier $10-$15	Denny Carmassi $10-$15

Nancy Wilson guitar pick

A pair of guitar picks from Howard Leese

OFTEN OVERLOOKED MEMORABILIA
Brigade hanging mobile - $20; Brigade promotional cassette countertop dispenser - $17; Bebe Le' Strange songbook - $25-$30; Little Queen songbook - $30; Bad Animals, beret - $35; Dreamboat Annie songbook, 1978 - $40-$50; Dog and Butterfly (Portrait) promotional music box, 1978; Brigade (Capitol), Anne Klein promotional perfume, 1990

The Heartbreakers/Johnny Thunders

Formed 1975

Johnny Thunders (1952-1991), Walter Lure, Richard Hell, and Jerry Nolan (1946-1992)

Billy Rath replaced Hell in 1976, Ty Styz replaced Nolan in 1977

This late-70s pre-punk/punk band is best known for its inclusion of two former New York Dolls, drummer Jerry Nolan and guitarist Johnny Thunders, both of whom combined to continue the havoc they caused with their predecessor. The group built a

quick and large following, especially along the East Coast, before heading to the U.K. to join the landmark 1976 Anarchy Tour. When the group's debut album *L.A.M.F.* did little to excite even the band members, Nolan quit to form the Idols. Not long after, the band drifted apart. Thunders went on to pursue a solo career. The group later performed reunion/farewell gigs, the last of which was held in New York during 1990. A year later Thunders was dead of a lethal substance mixture, followed later by Nolan who was also suffering from drug-related health problems.

AUTOGRAPHS

An LP, magazine cover, ad, photo, or card signed by the group: $35-$75

Heaven 17

Formed 1979

Martyn Ware, Ian Craig Marsh, and Glenn Gregory

Eighties synth and techno-pop act Heaven 17, with two members from the Human League, is commonly associated with the song "(We Don't Need This) Fascist Groove Thing" (#45, U.K., 1981), its album *How Men Are's* (#12, U.K., 1984), and its extraordinary production talent in both Ware and Marsh.

AUTOGRAPHS

An LP, magazine cover, ad, photo, or card signed by the group: $10-$15

Heavy D. and the Boyz

Formed 1984

Heavy D. (Dwight Myers) , Eddie F. (Eddie Farrell), G-Whiz (Glen Parrish), and Trouble T-Roy (Troy Dixon)

This late-80s R&B, rap, and hip-hop group, which was originally thought of as more of a novelty act, surprised many critics with the success of the albums *Big Tyme* (#19, 1989) and *Peaceful Journey* (#21, 1991), aided by H. D.'s theme to *In Living Color*. Heavy D. and the Boyz are also known for the hit songs "We Got Our Own Thang" (#10, R&B, 1989), "Somebody for Me" (#8, R&B, 1989), "Now That We Found Love" (#11. 1991), "Is It Good to You" (#32, 1991), and "Got Me Waiting" (#20, 1994).

AUTOGRAPHS

An LP, magazine cover, ad, photo, or card signed by the group: $15-$25

POSTERS/PRESS KITS

Promotional Posters: $10-$25
Press Kits: $12

OFTEN OVERLOOKED MEMORABILIA

Videotapes of *In Living Color*

Hebb, Bobby

Born: July 26, 1941

Mid-60s singer/songwriter Bobby Hebb is best known for his hits "Sunny" (#2,1966), "A Satisfied Mind" (#39, 1966), and "Love Me" (#84, 1966). Hebb also toured the U.S. with the Beatles in 1966. His thousands of songs have been covered by numerous artists including Lou Rawl's 1971 Grammy winning "A Natural Man."

AUTOGRAPHS

An LP, magazine cover, ad, photo, or card signed by the artist: $8-$20

OFTEN OVERLOOKED MEMORABILIA

Associated artifacts from the numerous musicians who have covered his material

Hedges, Michael

Born: December 31, 1953

Sensational '80s Windham Hill recording artist Michael Hedges, a "New Age" acoustic guitarist, applies many of the principles pioneered by Eddie Van Halen, such as unusual tunings, two-handed fret board taping, and full-chord hammer-ons and pull-offs, to create a rich and full harmonic sound, more applicable to a full band than a solo artist. His *Aerial Boundaries* (1984) album was nominated for a Best Instrumental Grammy award.

AUTOGRAPHS

An LP, magazine cover, ad, photo, or card signed by the artist: $10-$15

POSTERS/PRESS KITS

Promotional Posters: $10
Press Kits: $10

USED CLOTHING/EQUIPMENT

Guitar Picks: $10-$20

OFTEN OVERLOOKED MEMORABILIA

His numerous contributions to other artists' albums

Hell, Richard and the Voidoids

Formed 1976

Richard Hell (Richard Myers), Marc Bell, Robert Quine, and Ivan Julian

These late-70s New York scene punk artifacts, who are best remembered as one of the CBGB regulars who didn't "make it," created a stir and a large tri-state cult following with anthems such as "Love

Comes in Spurts." While Hell had played with Johnny Thunders and the Neon Boys, who would later become Television, he sought the comfort of a haven to perform his own material, but by the mid-80s he dropped his pick in favor of a pen to give the literary world a little Hell.

AUTOGRAPHS

An LP, magazine cover, ad, photo, or card signed by the group: $10-$20

OFTEN OVERLOOKED MEMORABILIA

Movie memorabilia from the *Smithereens* (1982) and *What About Me?* (1993)

Helmet

Formed 1989

Page Hamilton, Peter Mengede, Henry Bogdan, and John Stanier

This '90s New York avant-garde heavy metal band's album *Meantime* (#68, 1992) was well-received by critics before personnel changes began to inflict the band. The group is led by the talented Page Hamilton, who has earned a master's degree in jazz from the Manhattan School of Music. It is still early in the game for these guys, despite their numerous contributions to film soundtracks, so put your Helmet on!

AUTOGRAPHS

An LP, magazine cover, ad, photo, or card signed by the artist: $15-$35

OFTEN OVERLOOKED MEMORABILIA

Movie memorabilia from *Judgment Day* (1993), *Johnny Mnemonic* (1995), and *The Jerky Boys*—the band makes a cameo with "The Wizard"

Hendrix, Jimi

Born: November 27, 1942, Died: September 18, 1970

Hendrix was born in Seattle, Washington, and was given the name Johnny Allen Hendrix by his mother Lucille. He was later renamed James Marshall Hendrix by his father Al on September 11, 1946. Hendrix obtained his first electric guitar in 1959—a Supro Ozark—from a music store in Seattle.

In 1961 Hendrix enlisted for a three-year stint with the army, but was discharged for medical reasons on July 2, 1962. Following his service duties he began working under the pseudonym Jimmy James. He recorded with Lonnie Youngblood in 1963 ("Go Go Shoes" - Fairmount Records) before moving to New York City in 1964. Having already played with legends such as Sam Cooke, B.B. King, Jackie Wilson, Wilson Pickett, and Ike and Tina Turner, he tackled

White-matte LP award for Jimi Hendrix's Axis—Bold as Love from 1968. It is valued at $5,000. From the Doug Leftwitch collection.

the New York club circuit with King Curtis, John Hammonds Jr., and Curtis Knight.

Jimmy James and the Blue Flames was formed in 1965 and entered the Greenwich Village coffeehouse circuit. On August 24, 1966, Chas Chandler of the Animals took him to London to arrange the foundation of the Jimi Hendrix Experience. Hendrix jammed at the Polytechnic of Central London with Cream on October 1st, just five days prior to the formation of the band. On October 12, 1966, the band debuted at the Olympia in Paris in support of Johnny Hallyday. Hendrix, who was now making a name for himself in Europe, played the Monterey Pop Festival (6/18/66) at the request of Beatle Paul McCartney.

The band briefly supported the Monkees in America during their summer tour in 1967 before headlining their first tour in the U.K. on November 14, 1967 (Royal Albert Hall, London). The band's final concert together was in Denver, Colorado, on June 29, 1969.

The Band of Gypsys (Hendrix, Cox, and Miles [Electric Flag]), debuted on New Year's Eve (1969) at New York's Fillmore East. The two-night gig provided important pieces for the Band of Gypsys' album. Drummer Mitch Mitchell rejoined Hendrix during the Cry of Love tour, which opened on April 25, 1970. Hendrix's last official concert was at the Love and Peace Festival (9/6/70) on the Isle of Fehmarn, Germany.

Photo taken of Hendrix at the Star Club in Hamburg (1967) (Hard Rock Café, Key West)

On September 18, 1970, Hendrix was pronounced dead on arrival at St. Mary Abbots Hospital in London (suffocation due to acute barbiturate intoxication). He was buried at Greenwood Memorial Park in Renton, Washington, on October 1. His grave still attracts about forty fans per day. Most leave behind artifacts of a generation still stunned by the early death of the guitar legend.

In the years since his death, the Hendrix legend has persisted, primarily fueled by more than a dozen books and nearly 100 albums. While these works have done much to comprehensively document the musician's life, they have also had the unfortunate circumstance of fueling litigation over the Hendrix estate. The posthumous works have also created some confusion among Hendrix collectors who often find themselves spending hours sorting out the details of each new artifact.

1966

France: 4 dates, 1 unconfirmed venue - 10/14, Support act with Johnny Hallyday
England: 9 dates, Includes a press concert (11/25) at the Bag O' Nails
Germany: 4 dates, All two shows at the Big Apple in München

Collectors Note:

Jimi Hendrix arrived in London (8/24/66) with sparse belongings and a Fender Stratocaster. The word "sparse" could also be applied to memorabilia from this period. A handful of photographs have survived, as well as some advertisements. "Hey Joe" b/w "Stone Free" was released on 12/16 accompanied by some associated direct marketing materials such as flyers and handouts.

Total 1966 Live Performances: 22 Shows, 17 Venues
Memorabilia from this period is scarce and highly prized by Hendrix ollectors

1967
January
24 Shows, 21 Venues
England: 21 dates; 5 shows at the 7-1/2 Club, Whitehorse Street, London
February
23 Shows, 22 Venues
England: 22 dates; 2/4 - played at two different venues
March
21 Shows, 17 Venues
England: 10 dates
France: 3 dates
Germany: 3 dates; 5 shows at Star Club in Hamburg
Belgium: 1 date

April*
48 Shows, 24 Venues
England: 22 dates
Scotland: 1 date
Wales: 1 date
*First major package tour with Walker Brothers, Cat Stevens, Engelbert Humperdinck, Californians, and Quotations. Entire month was two-show venues.

May
23 Shows, 17 Venues
England: 6 dates; 1 two-show venue
Germany: 4 dates; 3 two-show venues
Sweden: 5 dates; 2 two-show venues
Finland: 1 date
Denmark: 1 date
June
16 Shows, 9 Venues
England: 1 date
USA: 8 dates; 12 shows at the Fillmore West, San Francisco, California; 1 show at Monterey International Pop Festival (6/18) - USA debut; 1 free concert in the Golden Gate Park (6/25)

Collectors Note:

The Fillmore "Bill Graham Presents... (BGP)" poster is outstanding and relatively scarce. The poster, which is believed to have been printed only once, features a woman holding the main attractions in her hands: Jefferson Airplane, Garbor Szabo, Jimi Hendrix. In traditional Graham fashion, postcards bearing the identical design were also used to advertise the venue. Although BGP postcards typically outnumber the posters three to one, this design is not very easy to find. See Chapter 6 for pricing.

July*
19 Shows, 16 Venues
USA: 16 dates; 10 dates in New York City
*7/8 to 7/16: touring as the support act for the Monkees.
August
21 Shows, 15 Venues
USA: 13 dates; 10 shows in five days at the Ambassador Theatre in
Washington, DC; 2 shows at the Fifth Dimension Club in Ann Arbor, Michigan
England: 2 dates
September
17 Shows, 11 Venues
Sweden: 10 dates; 6 two-show venues
England: 1 date
October
8 Shows, 7 Venues
England: 6 dates
France: 1 date
November*
24 Shows, 14 Venues
England: 11 dates
Holland: 1 date
Wales: 1 date
N. Ireland: 1 date
*Ten two-show venues
December*
11 Shows, 6 Venues
*11/14 to 12/5: a package tour with The Move, Pink Floyd, Outer Limits, Amen Corner, Eire Apparent, and The Nice

Collectors Note:

If you're going to begin a Jimi Hendrix memorabilia collection, the year 1967 is a great starting point. Nearly half (48.4%) of the artist's career live performances occurred during these twelve months.

Total 1967 Live Performances: 254 Shows, 179 Venues

1968

January
9 Shows, 5 Venues
Sweden: 3 dates; 2 two-show venues
Denmark: 1 date; 2 shows at the Tivolis Koncertsal
France: 1 date; 2 shows in Paris at the Olympia

February
37 Shows, 25 Venues
USA: 24 dates
Canada: 1 date

Collectors Note:

The Fillmore/Winterland "Bill Graham Presents... (BGP)" poster is a classic. The poster, which has a complicated printing history, features a flying eyeball with tentacles. The poster reads (top to bottom): "BILL GRAHAM PRESENTS IN SAN FRANCISCO," "JIMI HENDRIX," "EXPERIENCE," JOHN MAYALL," "AND THE BLUESBREAKERS," design, "ALBERT KING," "4," "DAYS" (Underneath the "4")... The first and second printings of this poster vary primarily in the type of stock used and registration. This Rick Griffin design has been so popular that it has been reprinted several times and even pirated. In traditional Graham fashion, postcards bearing the identical design were also used to advertise the venue. The design was so popular that the postcard was also reprinted several times.
Posters for smaller venues, such as the February 8th Sacramento State College show, do occasionally surface in the marketplace. Much less information is often associated with these smaller shows, making authentication difficult for collectors.

March
23 Shows, 17 Venues
USA: 16 dates
Canada: 1 date

April
6 Shows, 5 Venues
USA: 4 dates
Canada: 1 date

May
13 Shows, 8 Venues
Italy: 4 dates; 4 shows at the Brancaccio Theatre.
USA: 2 dates; 5/10 - The Fillmore East, two shows (8:00 P.M. & 11:30 P.M.)
Switzerland: 2 dates

Collectors Note:

The Fillmore "BILL GRAHAM PRESENTS IN NEW YORK... (BGP)" poster is very popular with Hendrix collectors. The original artwork, done by David Byrd/ Fantasy Unlimited was sold in recent years. It is not unusual for original artwork such as this to command prices in the $2,750-$4,000 range. BGP posters for New York shows never commanded the intense collector interest exhibited by their West Coast counterparts, primarily due to the lack of an extensive numbered series. The graphic poster for this event reads as follows (top to bottom): "BILL GRAHAM PRESENTS IN NEW YORK," design - graphic head shots within a circle, "JIMI HENDRIX," "EXPERIENCE," "JOSHUA LIGHT SHOW," "BILL GRAHAM'S," "FILLMORE EAST," "SECOND AVENUE & SIXTH STREET," "ONE NIGHT ONLY," "FRIDAY MAY 10," "TWO SHOWS 8:00 P.M. & 11:30 P.M.," "FANTASY UNLIMITED 1968, BILL GRAHAM, N.Y. NO.7," "ALL SEATS RESERVED $3, $4, $5," "BOX OFFICE OPEN DAILY 12:00 NOON TO 10:00 P.M.," "INFORMATION: PHONE 777-5260"

July
5 Shows, 4 Venues
USA: 2 dates; 1 two-show venue in Baton Rouge, Louisiana
England: 1 date
Spain: 1 date

August
21 Shows, 16 Venues
USA: 16 dates; 5 two-show venues

September
11 Shows, 11 Venues
USA: 10 dates
Canada: 1 date

October
8 Shows, 5 Venues
USA: 5 dates; 6 shows at the Winterland in San Francisco, California

November
13 Shows, 12 Venues
USA: 12 dates; 1 two-show venue at Philharmonic Hall in New York City

December
1 Show, 1 Venue
USA: 1 date

Total 1968 Live Performances: 147 Shows, 109 Venues

1969

January
24 Shows, 14 Venues
Germany: 9 dates
Sweden: 2 dates
Denmark: 1 date
France: 1 date
Austria: 1 date

February
2 Shows, 2 Venues
England: 2 dates; both dates at the Royal Albert Hall (2/18 & 2/24)

Collectors Note:

A black & white "Souvenir Brochure" was sold during the two Royal Albert Hall performances for two shilling and six pence

April
8 Shows, 7 Venues
USA: 7 dates; 1 two-show venue in Memphis, Tennessee

Collectors Note:

Electric Church: A Visual Experience was a program ($125-$170) sold at a Hendrix concert during the spring. The unusual cover features a colorful graphic design in a tri-fold format that opens into the heart of the program.

May
15 Shows, 15 Venues
USA: 14 dates
Canada: 1 date; 1 show at the Maple Leaf Garden in Toronto

June
3 Shows, 3 Venues
USA: 3 dates; Included Newport 69 (6/10) and Denver Pop Festival (6/29)

Collectors Note:

Newport '69 poster ($75-$100) and flyer ($100-$150)

August
1 Show, 1 Venue
USA: 1 date; Woodstock Music and Art Fair in Bethel, New York

September
2 Shows, 2 Venues
USA: 2 dates

December
2 Shows, 1 Venue
USA: 1 date; Fillmore East (12/31) two shows
Total 1969 Live Performances: 57 Shows, 45 Venues

1970

January
3 Shows, 2 Venues
USA: 2 dates; Fillmore East (1/1) two shows; Winter Festival for Peace (1/28) at Madison Square Garden

April
2 Shows, 2 Venues
USA: 2 dates

May
11 Shows, 9 Venues
USA: 9 dates; 2 two-show venues—Norman, Oklahoma (5/8) and Berkeley, California (5/30); Holding Together benefit concert -
(5/4)

Collectors Note:

The Berkeley shows were captured on film as a way to pacify the public's demand for a live performance. The Jimi Plays Berkeley video was met with mixed reviews, but created a number of direct marketing pieces for Hendrix collectors. From cinema tickets to posters, Hendrix enthusiasts could enhance their collections with numerous paper-based collectibles.

June
12 Shows, 11 Venues
USA: 11 dates; 1 two-show venue at Albuquerque, New Mexico (6/19)

July
8 Shows, 6 Venues
USA: 6 dates; 2 two-show venues—Miami, Florida (7/5) and Haleakala Crater, Hawaii (7/30)

August
3 Shows, 3 Venues
USA: 1 date; Honolulu, Hawaii
England: 1 date; Isle of Wight
Sweden: 1 date; Stockholm

Collectors Note:

Although the Isle of Wight performance was heavily criticized, Polydor's official recording of the event created numerous collectible pieces including flyers, promotional posters, etc. Concert poster ($400) and promo flyer ($200)

September

5 Shows, 5 Venues
Germany: 2 dates; last live performance (9/6) at Love and Peace Festival in Isle of Fehmarn
Denmark: 2 dates
Sweden: 1 date
Total 1970 Live Performances: 44 Shows, 38 Venues
Career Live Performance Totals: 524 Shows, 388 Venues

HENDRIX AFFILIATIONS

Band/Group	Year	Comments
The Rocking Kings	1959	First formal band
King Casuals	1962	Bass player was Billy Cox
The Isley Brothers	1964	Hendrix joined the group in March
Little Richard's band	1965	Spent nearly six months with the band
Jimmy James and the Blue Flames	1966	Formed by Hendrix in the summer of 1966
Jimmy Hendrix Experience	1966	Formed the band on October 6 with bassist Noel Redding and drummer Mitch Mitchell
Gypsy Sun and Rainbows* (8/18)	1969	Hendrix played at the Woodstock Music and Art Fair
Band of Gypsys	1969	Billy Cox on bass and Buddy Miles on drums

*Also referred to as the Electric Sky Church

AUTOGRAPHS

Autographed pages from albums typically range in price from $800-$1,300 depending upon inscription, condition, etc. Jimi Hendrix typified "The '60s" with his common autographed inscriptions of "Stay Kool," "Be Sweet," "Be Groovy," and "Love Forever."

Autographed letters typically range in price from $1,750-$7,000, depending upon content and condition.

When authenticating the handwriting of Jimi Hendrix, I always look first at the formation of the lower case "a" -

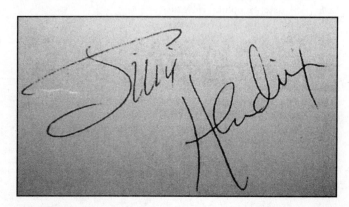

Jimi Hendrix's signature

unique with it's hooked beginning stroke, lower case "s" - often larger and unconnected to any other letters regardless of positioning. The hallmarks of his signature are the large two-stroke "J," the descending peaks of the lower case stroke of "imi," the large two or three stroke "H," and the large "e" in Hendrix.

While Jimi Hendrix was an excellent signer, collectors should still exercise caution when purchasing autographed material because numerous forgeries have been found in the market.

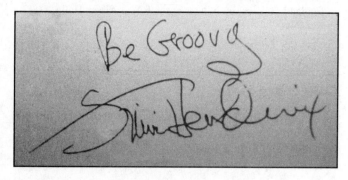

"Be Groovy" inscription from Jimi (and the Experience)

TICKETS

Full or unused tickets: $150-$250

The ticket from the Monterey Pop Festival (6/18/67) is perhaps the most sought after ticket by Hendrix collectors. This single-stubbed, non-illustrated ticket is horizontal in format with seating information on both portions. The "Orchestra" tickets that I have seen are printed on yellow stock and use red ink to designate Section number, Gate, and the text "ORCHESTRA," "$6.50 Tax Exempt," "No Refund." There has been speculation that some of the tickets were reprinted due to typographical errors.

TOUR BOOKS/PROGRAMS

Handbills can range in price from $275-$450 depending upon venue, design, and condition.

Concert programs can range in price from $150-$1,400 (condition dependent). Concert programs during this era were mainly published in conjunction with packaged tours. Popular with many Hendrix collectors is the program for the November/December 1967 package tour (Horizontal format, multicolor design) featuring JHE, The Move, Pink Floyd, The Amen Corner and The Nice, The Eire Apparant, and The Outer Limits. The illustration/design was created by A. Litri/Paul Martin & Associates.

POSTERS

Original concert posters can range in price from $750-$7,000 depending upon venue and condition. A rare concert poster (11" x 32") from his final concert can fetch top dollar ($7,000). Promotional posters, advertisements, and even sheet music should not be overlooked by collectors. Polydor produced some interesting early advertisements and promotional posters, while sheet music publishers (April Music Ltd.—"Hey Joe"—and A. Schroeder Music Publishing Ltd.—"The Wind Cries Mary," "Burning of the Midnight Lamp") issued some nice inexpensive (20p) collectible pieces.

PRESS KITS/PHOTOGRAPHS

Original Photographs (Unpublished): $250-$700

USED EQUIPMENT

Stage shirt: $2,000
Stage jacket: $5,000-$40,000
Stage hat: $10,000
Stage guitar strap: $7,500-$10,000

INSTRUMENTS

Guitars: $10,000-$80,000*

*Note: The Fender Stratocaster guitar (#13MAR68 C) used by Jimi Hendrix at the 1969 Woodstock festival sold in a 1990 auction for 198,000 pounds or about $300,000 (U.S.)

Portions of guitars (often smashed during performance): $10,000-$15,000

OFTEN OVERLOOKED MEMORABILIA

Italian trading card #207 (Cantanti); "The Jimi Hendrix Experience Official Fan Club of Great Britain" issued material including newsletter, stationery, and buttons; promotional material from the original *Electric Ladyland* double LP

REFERENCES/BOOKS

Jimi Hendrix, The Man, The Music, The Memorabilia by Caesar Glebbeek & Douglas J. Noble, 1996: $22; *Jimi Hendrix, The Complete Studio Recording Sessions, 1963-1970*, by John McDermott with Billy Cox and Eddie Kramer, 1995: $25. Both of these books are MUST purchases for Hendrix collectors! *Straight Ahead: The International Hendrix Fanzine* is also a must ($26 for six issues).

ASSORTED JIMI HENDRIX USED ELECTRIC GUITARS

Supro Ozark - first - (1959/1960)
Daneelctro (1961)
Fender Duosonic (1964/1965)
Fender Stratocaster (1966), white pickguard
Fender Stratocaster (Sweden, 1967) tortoiseshell pickguard
Hagstrom eight string bass guitar (No. 723006) (1967)
Gibson "Flying V" (1967) - primarily for blues songs
Les Paul, Fuzzface and Vox was-wah (1968)
Gibson SG (1968)
Dobro twelve-string electric steel guitar (1968/69)
Gibson "Flying V" (No. 932954) (1969)
Fender Stratocaster (#13MAR68 C) (1969)

Hendryx, Nona

Born: August 18, 1941

Versatile and talented performer, often associated with Patti LaBelle and the Bluebelles, and later La-Belle, Nona Hendryx is a singer, composer, and even a rocker. She is typically remembered for the songs "Keep It Confidential" (#22 R&B, 1983), the Grammy nominated "Rock This House," and "Why Should I Cry" (#5, R&B, 1987), as well as her numerous collaborations.

AUTOGRAPHS

An LP, magazine cover, ad, photo, or card signed by the artist: $10-$15

POSTERS/PRESS KITS

Promotional Posters: $10-$15
Press Kits: $12

OFTEN OVERLOOKED MEMORABILIA

Movie memorabilia from *Perfect* (1985) and *Coming to America* (1988)

Henley, Don: See the Eagles

Henry, Clarence "Frogman"

Born: March 19, 1937

This crafty New Orleans R&B singer and pianist is commonly associated with the songs "Ain't Got No Home" (1956), "But I Do" (a.k.a. "I Don't Know Why"), "You Always Hurt the One You Love," "Lonely Street," "On Bended Knee" (1961), and "A Little Too Much" (1962).

AUTOGRAPHS

An LP, magazine cover, ad, photo, or card signed by the artist: $10-$25

OFTEN OVERLOOKED MEMORABILIA

Memorabilia from his appearances at the New Orleans Jazz and Heritage Festival

---

Henry Cow/Fred Faith

Formed 1968

Original lineup: Fred Frith, Tim Hodgkinson, Chris Cutler, John Greaves, and Geoff Leigh

Seventies British eclectic band, whose small, very small, dedicated cult following contributed enormously to their longevity, Henry Cow opened for Captain Beefheart on a European tour in 1974—this piece of information alone should give you some sense of a band that had little before combining with Slapp Happy in 1975. The group's dedicated mission, whatever it happened to be at that time, carried it into the early '80s. To my knowledge, most of the members have survived into the '90s, struggling on various ancillary projects, most of which are hardly worthy of recognition.

AUTOGRAPHS

An LP, magazine cover, ad, photo, or card signed by the group. $10

The Heptones

Formed 1965

Barry Llewelyn, Earl Morgan, Leroy Sibbles

This '70s Jamaican trio's soul-style harmonies made them one of their homeland's most popular vocal acts of the period with songs such as "Baby (Be True)," "Why Must I," "Why Did You Leave," and "Cry Baby Cry," and later with songs such as "Young, Gifted and Black," "Hypocrites," "Freedom to the People," "I Miss You," "Book of Rules," and "Country Boy."

AUTOGRAPHS

An LP, magazine cover, ad, photo, or card signed by the group: $10-$20

OFTEN OVERLOOKED MEMORABILIA

Movie memorabilia from *Rockers* (1979)

Herman's Hermits

Formed 1963

Peter Noone, Karl Green, Keith Hopwood, Derek "Lek" Leckenby, and Barry Whitwam

Sixties British Invasion pop stars Herman's Hermits landed a dozen Top Ten hits between 1964 and 1967 including "I'm Into Something Good" (#13, 1964), "Mrs. Brown You've Got a Lovely Daughter" (#1, 1965), "I'm Henry the Eighth, I Am" (#1, 1965), "Can't You Hear My Heartbeat" (#2, 1965), "Wonderful World" (#4, 1965), "Silhouettes" (#5, 1965), "Just a Little Bit Better" (#7, 1965), "Listen People" (#3, 1966), "Dandy" (#5, 1966), "A Must to Avoid" (#8, 1966), "Leaning on the Lamp Post" (#9, 1966), and "There's a Kind of Hush" (#4, 1967) before disbanding in 1971.

Peter Noone returned to acting, which he had been successful with prior to the band's formation, and also worked on a few other recording projects, including two albums with the Tremblers and later even an album with Phil Ramone. His first British solo hit was "Oh You Pretty Thing" penned by David Bowie, who also sat in on the recording sessions. Noone also hosted the VH-1 program *My Generation*.

A signed contract from Herman's Hermits

AUTOGRAPHS

Group:

An LP, magazine cover, ad, photo, or card signed by the group: $25-$100

Individual:

Peter Noone: $20-$50

Hiatt, John

Born: 1952

Seventies singer and songwriter, the latter of which he is most noted for, Hiatt is also typically associated with his friend Ry Cooder, because they both often sang and toured together.

AUTOGRAPHS

An LP, magazine cover, ad, photo, or card signed by the artist: $5-$10

USED CLOTHING/EQUIPMENT

Guitar Picks: $10

Hicks, Dan and His Hot Licks

Formed 1968

Original lineup: Dan Hicks, David LaFlamme, Bill Douglas, Mitzy Douglas, and Patti Urban

This late-60s witty, pseudo-nostalgic saloon band is best remembered for the songs, "How Can I Miss You (When You Won't Go Away)," "Walkin' One and Only," and "I Scare Myself," before disbanding in the mid-70s.

AUTOGRAPHS

An LP, magazine cover, ad, photo, or card signed by the group: $10-$20

OFTEN OVERLOOKED MEMORABILIA

Associated artifacts from other musicians' covers of their material

Hill, Jesse

Born: December 9, 1932

Sixties Bourbon Street pianist Jesse Hill is best remembered for his song "Ooh Poo Pah Doo—Parts I & II" (#28, 1960), "Whip It on Me" (#91, 1960), "Sweet Jelly Roll," " I Got Mine," and "Can't Get Enough," many of which have been covered by other artists.

AUTOGRAPHS

An LP, magazine cover, ad, photo, or card signed by the artist: $10

OFTEN OVERLOOKED MEMORABILIA

Associated artifacts from other musicians' covers of his material

Hitchcock, Robyn/Soft Boys

Born: March 3, 1953

This '80s British eclectic cult band, with its folk-ballad style and bizarre bantering, has been cited as an influence to a few American bands who became far more successful than it did.

AUTOGRAPHS

An LP, magazine cover, ad, photo, or card signed by the group: $10

OFTEN OVERLOOKED MEMORABILIA

Associated artifacts from other musicians' covers of their material

Hole

Formed 1990

Courtney Love (Love Michelle Harrison), Born: July 9, 1965; Eric Erlandson; Jill Emery; and Caroline Rue*

*Patty Schemel and Kristen Pfaff replaced Rue and Emery in 1992. Melissa Auf Der Maur replaced Pfaff in 1994.

Love, who suffered a somewhat turbulent childhood, is the daughter of Grateful Dead associate Hank Harrison and therapist Linda Carroll. Her rebellious attitude, no doubt a result of her dysfunctional family, landed her in a number of reform schools. Inspired by the record *Never Mind The Bullocks* (Sex Pistols), she had the desire to start a band and moved into an apartment in Portland, Oregon. When her first attempt failed, she spent the first years of the 1980s traveling around the world, making pilgrimages to various historical music meccas like Liverpool, England. While there she tried to break into the local music scene, while making as many key contacts as possible. Soon after she returned to Portland, and after a brief stint with Faith No More, she formed Sugar Babylon with Jennifer Finch (L7), and Kat Bjelland (Babes in Toyland). When the combination failed, she opted for more traveling, often financed by her employment as a stripper. Her aspirations were to land a job in either music or acting, the latter of which she found first with a few bit parts in Alex Cox's films *Sid and Nancy* and *Straight to Hell*.

Love then returned to Los Angeles, California, in 1989 and ran an ad in the local *Recycler* newspaper in hopes of attracting the right combination for a band. Following auditions, Eric Erlandson, Caroline Rue, and Jill Emery successfully combined with Love to form Hole—a name actually taken from the play *Medea*. It was also during this period that Love married L.A. punk band Leaving Trains' lead singer James Morland; the relationship did not last.

The underground soon adopted the band—its live performances entranced the audience especially during set favorites "Dicknail" and "Retard Girl." In 1991, Caroline Records released the band's first album, *Pretty on the Inside* (#59, U.K., 1991), which firmly drove a stake in the hearts of the U.K. music media. Now the darlings of the rebellious music press, the group released the first single from the album, "Teenage Whore," much to the delight of its European fans.

The group soon took a backseat to Love's relationship with her new boyfriend, and eventual husband, Kurt Cobain (Nirvana). The two married in Hawaii on February 24, 1992, and Love gave birth to their daughter Frances Bean Cobain on August 19, 1992. An unfair press, which had been having a field day covering the king and queen of grunge, tossed allegations at the couple on a daily basis. Child custody battles ensued as allegations of drug use during pregnancy hovered over the couple, which finally won back Frances.

On February 28, 1992, following a gig in Los Angeles, Emery quit the band. It was just one of many personnel issues facing the band, which finally began recording *Live Through This* (#52, 1995, Geffen) with a new lineup: Love, Erlandson, Patty Schemel (Dumbhead), and Kristen Pfaff (replaces Leslie Hardy). One week prior to the release of the album, Cobain was found dead at the couple's Seattle home—a victim of suicide. As the album climbed the U.S. charts, tragedy struck again as Kristen Pfaff overdosed on heroin.

Amid tragedy, the band tried to re-group. Pfaff was replaced by bassist Melissa Auf Der Maur while the band prepared for an upcoming tour. Strong live performances, and opening up for acts such as the Lemonheads and Nine Inch Nails, secured the band's position amid end-of-year music poles. The album also spun off singles "Miss World" and "Doll Parts" (#65, 1994), which began to pick up better airplay.

The following year would prove to be a media fiasco for Hole: Love was first arrested for offensive behavior aboard an airplane, followed by a misdemeanor assault charge, then by a backstage brawl with Bikini Kill singer Kathleen Hanna. If all this weren't enough, her erratic behavior caused her to walk offstage twice (4/25/95, 7/31/95) and be carried off once following another incident with the audience (8/9/95).

She began 1996 by appearing in the film *Feeling Minnesota*, which opened in April and also starred Keanu Reeves. The year also found her trying to block the sale of some rock and roll memorabilia affiliated with her late husband including items such as prescription bottles and substance abuse rehabilitation papers. Just when you think the Hole can't get any deeper, it does. Perhaps it's time to cover it up and dig elsewhere.

AUTOGRAPHS

Group:
A CD, LP, magazine cover, ad, photo, or card signed by the band: $30-$85*
*Original lineup

A common counterfeit Hole backstage pass

Individual:
Courtney Love: $25-$35
Eric Erlandson: $10-$15
Jill Emery: $5-$10
Caroline Rue: $5-$10
Patty Schemel: $5-$10
Kristen Pfaff: $10-$25
Melissa Auf Der Maur: $5-$10

TOUR BOOKS/PROGRAMS/PASSES

Backstage Passes:
Cloth: $10-$12;
Laminated: $15-$20

POSTERS/PRESS KITS

Promotional Posters:
$10-$30
Press Kits: $15-$35

USED CLOTHING/EQUIPMENT

Guitar Picks: $10-$20
Drum Sticks: $15

OFTEN OVERLOOKED MEMORABILIA

All Sub-Pop and Caroline Records release associated items; Lollapalooza (1995) memorabilia; Courtney Love's cyberspace transcripts from America On-Line - $5-$10; movie memorabilia from *Feeling Minnesota* and *The People vs. Larry Flynt*

REFERENCE BOOKS

Look Through This, by Wilson - $20, *Hole* by Burrows - $10, *Kurt Cobain & Courtney Love, In Their Own Words* - $16; numerous other resources exist, but nothing that does justice to the band in my opinion; no dedicated collector books

Holiday, Billie

(Eleanora Fagan)
Born: April 7, 1915, Died: July 17, 1959

"Lady Day" and her golden voice broke every rule of jazz and then rewrote the book with newly improvised melodic lines that seemed so much more personal, refined, and purely delivered than those of any singer who went before her.

Holiday landed in New York during the Roaring '20s and hooked up later with talent scout John Hammond, who heard her in 1933 and arranged her first recording sessions. In 1935 she began working with Teddy Wilson (Benny Goodman pianist), and it was he who would handpick the best of the big band talent he was aware of to work with her, including Lester Young (Count Basie). It would be these sessions, which ran into the mid-40s, that would later become her hallmark with songs such as "Miss Brown to

You," "He's Funny That Way," "What a Little Moonlight Can Do," and "God Bless the Child."

She then landed in Count Basie's band for a year (1937), before moving on to work with Artie Shaw. But the country's segregation policies at the time quickly frustrated her enough to quit her stint with Shaw. She later chose to lead her own groups, culminating in an extended engagement at New York's Cafe Society in 1939. During the same year she also recorded her signature song "Strange Fruit" before she decided to leave Columbia for Decca Records.

Her personal life then crumbled, and her battles with heroin addiction only made matters worse. Imprisoned for a year, and later prohibited from working New York nightclubs, she was slowly loosing control, and by the late '50s, she seemed only a shadow of the talent she had been earlier. But even that too was better than most, as exemplified by the Verve recordings of that period. She died on July 17, 1959.

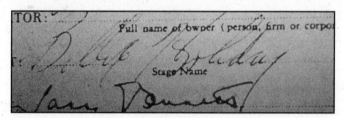

A contract signed by the legendary Billie Holiday

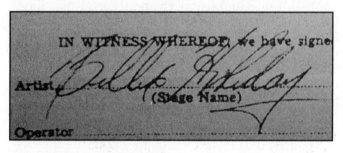

Another contract signed by Lady Day

AUTOGRAPHS

An LP, magazine cover, ad, photo, or card signed by the artist: $1,000-$2,000

OFTEN OVERLOOKED MEMORABILIA

Associated artifacts from her career are highly sought by collectors, few of which occasionally surface in the market

Holiday, Jennifer

Born: October 19, 1960

Thespian turned '80s R&B-based singer, Holiday is typically associated with the hits "And I Am Telling You I'm Not Going" (#22, 1982), both a Tony and Grammy winner, "I Am Love" (#2, R&B, 1983), and "Just Let Me Wait" (#24, R&B, 1983).

AUTOGRAPHS

An LP, magazine cover, ad, photo, or card signed by the artist: $10-$20

OFTEN OVERLOOKED MEMORABILIA

Associated artifacts from her theater work; videotapes of her television appearances including *The Love Boat* (1986); artifacts from her numerous contributions to other musicians' work

The Hollies

Formed 1962

Graham Nash, Allan Clarke, Anthony Hicks, Donald Rathbone, and Eric Haydock*

*Robert Elliott replaced Rathbone in 1963. Haydock was replaced by Bernard Calvert in 1966. Terry Sylvester replaced Nash in 1968. Clarke was replaced with Mikael Rikfors in 1971. Clarke was back in 1973 while Rikfors left again. Clarke left again in 1977, but returned the following year. In 1983 , Nash, Elliott, Hicks, and Clarke re-formed group.

Sixties British band whose consistency of hits falls short of few bands, the Hollies are best known for their successful series of songs including "Searchin," and "Stay" (both 1963), followed in 1964 by "Just One Look," "Here I Go Again," "We're Through," and "Yes I Will," "I'm Alive" (#1), and "Look Through Any Window" (1965).

"Bus Stop" (#5, 1966) then broke the band big in America; it was followed by "Stop Stop Stop" (#7, 1966), "Carrie-Anne" (#9, 1967), "On a Carousel" (#11, 1967), and "Pay You Back with Interest" (#28, 1967). But by the late '60s, "psychedelia" was in and the Hollies' "cutesy" manner was out, so the band shifted and with it came the departure of one of their main writers, Graham Nash.

Nash was replaced by Terry Sylvester, and the group bounced back with "He Ain't Heavy, He's My Brother" (#7, 1970) before Clarke left, leaving Hicks the last remaining member. Clarke returned in 1973 and with him the hits "Long Cool Woman (in a Black Dress)" (#2, 1972) and "The Air That I Breathe" (#6, 1974) before pulling another cycle of departure and return.

AUTOGRAPHS

An LP, magazine cover, ad, photo, or card signed by the group: $35-$110*

*Varies, lineup dependent

OFTEN OVERLOOKED MEMORABILIA

Associated artifacts from other musicians' covers of their material

Holly, Buddy and the Crickets

Band formed 1955

Buddy Holly (Charles Hardin Holley) Born: September 7, 1936, Died: February 3, 1959; Sonny Curtis; Don Guess; and Jerry Allison*

The Crickets also utilized the talents of Niki Sullivan, Larry Welborn, Joe B. Mauldin, Tommy Allsup, Glen D. Hardin, Jerry Naylor, and Waylon Jennings

With high school friends Bob Montgomery and Larry Welborn, Holley formed a country-oriented Western group with a touch of Bop. KDAV, a local radio station, gave them an opportunity to showcase their talents from late 1953 to 1955. During this period the group recorded various demo tapes and began to establish a reputation on the southwestern country circuit. The group's popularity led to a recording session in Nashville with Decca. Holly (having dropped the "e" from his last name), along with the lineup of Sonny Curtis and Don Guess, recorded "Blue Days, Black Nights"/"Love Me" (D 29854)* and "Modern Day Juan"/"You Are My One Desire" (D 30166)** by the end of 1956. Both singles went unnoticed, and Decca continued to refuse the release of "That'll Be the Day," which Holly had also recorded during the same period.

Buddy Holly's pair of black suede loafers. Photo courtesy Phillips Son & Neale.

The failed sessions with Decca did little to discourage Holly, who used the time to write prolifically. After returning home the duo of Holly and Allison (1956-57) shared numerous bills at the Lubbock Youth Center with many aspiring artists including Elvis Presley.

Everything soon changed for Holly. When he and the newly formed Crickets drove to Clovis, New Mexico, on February 25, 1957, to record a demo tape, Holly, along with Larry Welborn (bass), Jerry Allison (drums) and Niki Sullivan (rhythm guitar)*** recorded rock versions of "That'll Be the Day" and "I'm Looking for Someone to Love." "That'll Be the Day" attracted the attention of Coral/Brunswick records (New York City), which released it as a single (Br 5509). By September 1957 the record had reached the number one position on the New Musical Express's list of top thirty best-selling singles in Britain. The record's success promoted the group's first national tour in late 1957. Just prior to the tour, the Crickets played the Howard, Royal, and Apollo theaters, followed by Dick Clark's *American Bandstand*, Alan Freed's local New York City television show, along with the Brooklyn Paramount. The eight-day cross-country package tour, arranged by Irvin Feld-General Artists Corporation (GAC), was billed as "The Biggest Show of Stars for '57." Following the GAC tour, the Crickets returned to New York for an appearance on the *Ed Sullivan Show* (12/1/57).

By 1958, American rock 'n' roll was starting to capture the hearts of many worldwide. The success of "That'll Be the Day," "Peggy Sue," and "Oh Boy" promoted bookings in Australia and Great Britain. The Crickets, now Allison, Holly, and Mauldin, headed to Australia in late January 1958, stopping en route in Honolulu for a show. The five-day Australian Tour included shows in Melbourne, Sydney, and Brisbane. After leaving Australia, the band headed back to Lubbock. Following a brief stop in Florida, the band headed to Great Britain to begin a four-week tour at the end of February. The British tour included television stops on *Sunday Night at the London Palladium* and the BBC's *Off the Record*. The Crickets returned to the United States on March 25.

Buddy Holly married Maria Elena Santiago on August 15, 1958, and the two honeymooned in Acapulco. The Crickets appeared on the Alan Freed television show in October before setting out on a seventeen-day GAC package tour. Two television appearances followed the tour, both for Dick Clark - October 25 and 28. Following these shows Holly left his long-time producer Norman Petty and the Crickets.

Holly's interests at this time were shifting to other aspects of the music business. He decided to pursue the role of a producer and to work with young artists to develop their potentials. Waylon Jennings (9/58 - "Jole Blon"), the future country superstar, and Lou Giordano (12/58 - "Stay Close to Me") were Holly's initial efforts as a producer. He continued recording, mostly from his apartment in New York City, before legal and financial problems created by his departure from Petty forced him to join the Winter Dance Party Tour of the Midwest in early 1959.

A wintertime tour through the Midwest—Minnesota, Wisconsin, and Iowa—was by no means something any entertainer would look forward to, and such was the case with Holly. Sporting only five acts: Holly, Ritchie Valens, the Big Bopper, Dion and the Belmonts, and Frankie Sardo, the tour was far less impressive when compared with others he had been on. Holly formed a new band for the tour which included former Cricket Tommy Allsup, Waylon Jennings, and Charlie Bunch.

On Sunday, February 1, the tour played afternoon and evening shows in Appleton and Green Bay, Wisconsin, before setting out for Clear Lake, Iowa (350 miles away). Frustrated by the bus travel, Holly opted to charter a plane following their performance in Clear Lake. The Beechcraft Bonanza, piloted by Roger Peterson lifted off from the Mason City, Iowa, airport about 2:00 a.m.**** on February 3. Ritchie Valens, and J.P. (Big Bopper) Richardson were also on the plane. Six miles north of the airport the plane crashed in a cornfield, killing everyone aboard. Buddy Holly was buried in the Lubbock City Cemetery,

Lubbock, Texas, where some fifty people a month still visit his grave.

*Also featured Grady Martin and Faris Coursey
**Also featured Boots Randolph
***Also included Sullivan, June Clark, Gary and Romona Tollett, vocals
****Accounts vary on exact time

AUTOGRAPHS

Autographed pages from albums typically range in price from $750-$800. Unlike some other artists, Holly was not prone to inscriptions or personalizations. On album pages where the signatures of the entire band appear, his is usually the largest.

Autographed letters typically range in price from $2,000-$8,500 depending upon content and condition.

When authenticating the handwriting of Buddy Holly, compare the formation of the capitalized "T" which often resemble a tilted "2." Also worth note is that he almost always crosses over the ending stroke of his lower case "y"—the only exception being his signature. Hallmarks of his signature are consistent character slants, long ascenders in "dd" and "ll," and the lack of formation in the "y."

Band (Holly, Mauldin, Allison) autographed album page: $800-$875

Band (Holly, Mauldin, Allison) autographed Coral Records publicity card (1957): $1,000-$1,500

Band (Holly, Mauldin, Allison) autographed Coral Records promotional postcard (1958): $1,000-$1,250*

*"THE CRICKETS Exclusive Coral recording Artists" should appear underneath the photo as well as the word "COPYRIGHT" in the lower right hand corner beneath this text.

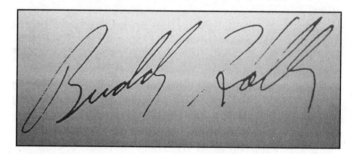

Buddy Holly's signature

Buddy Holly's signature

The signatures of Buddy Holly and the Crickets

TOUR BOOKS/PROGRAMS

Concert Programs:
"The Biggest Show of Stars for '57": $750-$1,000
Christmas Jubilee, 1957 (Alan Freed): $200
Concert Program (1958): $1,200-$1,500
Any advertisements, handbills/circulars, and programs from the major packaged tours are popular with Holly collectors. The two-colored (black and blue ink) 1958 Souvenir Programme is very popular with Holly collectors and has surfaced often in Great Britain auction houses.

Posters:
Original concert posters can range in price from $750-$2,000 depending upon venue and condition.

USED CLOTHING/EQUIPMENT

Prescription eyeglasses: $45,000-$55,000
Belt: $2,000-$2,300
Bow tie: $5,000-$6,000
Shoes: $750-$1,300
Guitar Strap: $7,500-$8,000
Microphone: $1,500-$2,500
Guitar: $200,000-$250,000

OFTEN OVERLOOKED MEMORABILIA

Business card (red, black, and white), 5.5" x 2" - $500-$550; autographed high school yearbook - $5,000-$6,000; Fan Club membership card - $200 - $275

REFERENCES/BOOKS

Numerous resources exist; no dedicated collector books; a must fanzine is *File,* Pastime Publications, 412 Main Road, Sheffield, S9 4QL England ($11 fee)

Holman, Eddie

Born: June 3, 1946

Late-60s R&B and soul vocalist Eddie Holman is best remembered for his songs "This Can't Be True" (#57, 1966), "Hey There Lonely Girl" (#2, 1970), and "Don't Stop Now" (#48, 1970), although he did have minor hits into the late '70s.

AUTOGRAPHS

An LP, magazine cover, ad, photo, or card signed by the artist: $10

The Holy Modal Rounders

Formed 1963

Peter Stampfel and Steve Weber

Late-60s tie-died folk and bluegrass enthusiasts, best known for their strange interpretations and associations within their music, exemplified in their trademark songs such as "If You Wanna Be a Bird," "Boobs a Lot," and "My Mind Capsized," The Holy Modal Rounders also became a home for many transient musicians, most of whom could handle the novelty of act for only a short period of time.

AUTOGRAPHS

An LP, magazine cover, ad, photo, or card signed by the group: $10-$15*
*Varies, lineup dependent

OFTEN OVERLOOKED MEMORABILIA

Movie memorabilia from *Easy Rider*

The Honeycombs

Formed 1963

Original lineup: Martin Murray, Alan Ward, Denis D'ell (Denis Dalziel), John Lantree, and Ann "Honey" Lantree

Sixties British band the Honeycombs is best remembered for the song "Have I the Right?" (#1, U.K., 1964) and for the fact it included a female drummer. The group disappeared nearly as fast as it arrived.

AUTOGRAPHS

An LP, magazine cover, ad, photo, or card signed by the group: $10-$15

The Honey Cone

Formed 1969

Carolyn Willis, Edna Wright, and Shellie Clark

This early-70s R&B vocal trio, made up of seasoned backup singers, is best remembered for the songs "Want Ads" (#1, 1971), "Stick-Up" (#11, 1971), and "One Monkey Don't Stop No Show, Part 1" (#15, 1971), as well as for a handful of minor hits before disbanding in 1973.

AUTOGRAPHS

An LP, magazine cover, ad, photo, or card signed by the group: $10-$20

The Hoodoo Gurus

Formed 1981

Original lineup: Dave Faulkner, Brad Shepard, Clyde Bramley, and James Baker*

*Mark Kingsmill replaced Baker in 1985 and Rick Grossman replaced Bramley in 1988

This '80s Australian pop band is best known for the college radio novelty songs "Television Addict," "Bittersweet," "Like Wow-Wipeout," "What's My Scene," "Come Anytime," "Another World," and "Baby Can Dance."

AUTOGRAPHS

An LP, magazine cover, ad, photo, or card signed by the group: $8-$15

Hooker, John Lee

Born: August 22, 1920

Pioneering blues musician, whose single-chord delta electric compositions helped bridged the gap to rock and roll, John Lee Hooker is typically associated with songs such as "Boogie Chillun," "I'm in the Mood," and "Boom Boom." He made his debut performance at the 1959 Newport Folk Festival, and his influence is indicative of the numerous rock acts that covered his music over the years including the Spencer Davis Group and George Thorogood.

He continued to tour throughout the '70s and '80s, opening many rock shows for acts like Foghat and Canned Heat, the latter of which he worked with on *Hooker 'n' Heat* (#73, 1970). "I'm in the Mood," a duet with Bonnie Raitt, extracted from his album *The Healer* (#62, 1989) earned him his first Grammy Award in 1989.

John Lee Hooker was inducted into the Rock and Roll Hall of Fame in 1991.

AUTOGRAPHS

An LP, magazine cover, ad, photo, or card signed by the artist $35-$100

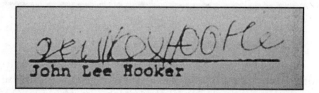

A rare signed contract from John Lee Hooker

OFTEN OVERLOOKED MEMORABILIA

Associated artifacts from other musicians' covers of his material; movie memorabilia from *The Blues Brothers* (1980); associated artifacts from the numerous festivals he attended

The Hooters

Formed 1978

Rob Hyman, Eric Bazilian, John Lilley, and David Uosikkinen*

*Fran Smith replaced Miller in 1987

Mid-80s pop rock band the Hooters is best known for its songs "And We Danced" (#21, 1985) and "Day by Day" (#18, 1986). The group's varied sound and multi-instrumentation has been better received in Europe than in its U.S. homeland. Both Hyman and Bazilian had been with the band Baby Grand, and following the group's dissolution, the two wrote and did session work together. One project they both participated in was Cyndi Lauper's 1983 breakthrough album *She's So Unusual*, which included the Hyman cowritten hit single "Time After Time."

The Hooters' first two albums for Columbia, *Nervous Nights* (#12, 1985) and *One Way Home* (#27, 1987), both sold gold, but follow-up U.S. efforts were less fruitful. The single "Satellite," extracted from the latter album, hit the Top Twenty-Five in the U.K. and also did well in Germany.

AUTOGRAPHS

An LP, magazine cover, ad, photo, or card signed by the group: $10-$25

TOUR BOOKS/PROGRAMS/PASSES

Backstage Passes: Cloth: $8 - $12, Laminated - $10 - $15

OFTEN OVERLOOKED MEMORABILIA

Associated artifacts from other musicians' covers of his material

Hootie & The Blowfish

Formed 1987

Darius Rucker, Mark Bryan, Dean Felber and Brantley Smith*

*Jimi "Soni" Sonefeld replaced Smith in 1989

Nineties rock/pop band, formed while the members were attending the University of South Carolina in Columbia, SC, Hootie & the Blowfish garnered a strong local following that quickly spread through the southeastern states before they signed with Atlantic Records on October 31,1993.

Following the release of their 11-track debut, *Cracked Rear View*, they were heard on New York radio station WNEW-FM by talk show host David Letterman, who booked them on his *Late Show*. Extensive television exposure helped guide the album extract "Hold My Hand" (#10, 1995) up the singles chart. Meanwhile the band's touring finally paid off—their debut album topped the charts on May 5, 1995.

"Let Her Cry" (#9, 1995), also from *Cracked Rear View*, preceded "Only Wanna Be With You" (#6, 1995) and "Time" (#14, 1996) as the group's next singles. Meanwhile, in January 1996, the band learned that their debut record was the third biggest-selling debut album of all-time.

Fairweather Johnson, the group's second album, was released on April 23, 1996. "Old Man & Me," a reworking of a song that appeared on the group's *Kootchpop* EP in July 1993, became the new album's first extract (Debuting at #28, 1996).

AUTOGRAPHS

A CD, LP, magazine cover, ad, photo or card signed by the group: $35-$110

TOUR BOOKS/PROGRAMS/PASSES

Backstage Passes: Cloth: $5-$10; Laminated: $10-$20

POSTERS/PRESS KITS

Promotional Posters: $10-$25
Press Kits: $15-$30

USED CLOTHING AND EQUIPMENT

Guitar Picks: $10-$20

OFTEN OVERLOOKED MEMORABILIA

Artifacts from the Wolf Brothers; University of South Carolina apparel; videotapes from the group's numerous television appearances including *Late Show With David Letterman* - CBS-TV (9/2/94, 5/5/95, 11/9/95, 4/23/96), *Tonight Show* (12/27/94), *New Year's Rockin' Eve '95* (12/31/94), *Live from the House of Blues* (1/27/95), and *Unplugged* - MTV - (4/22/96 - air date); Farm Aid VII artifacts; a copy of the band's first multi-media E-CD (Old Man & Me) - $4

Hopkin, Mary

Born: May 3, 1950

Late-60s teen pop star, whose good fortune—appearing on the BBC-TV variety show *Opportunity Knocks* and being seen by the model Twiggy, who told Paul McCartney about her—led to a recording contract with Apple Records, Mary Hopkin was in the right place at the right time. McCartney produced "Those Were the Days" (#2, 1968) and then wrote and produced "Goodbye" (#13, 1969) for Hopkin; both quickly pushed her into the spotlight.

Hopkin then went on to work with Mickie Most, after which she only scored minor hits before turning to acting. She married British record producer Tony Visconti at this time. The two concentrated on raising a family before eventually splitting up in 1981.

AUTOGRAPHS

An LP, magazine cover, ad, photo, or card signed by the artist: $5-$15

OFTEN OVERLOOKED MEMORABILIA

Associated artifacts from her work with Paul McCartney; memorabilia associated with her theatre work

Hopkins, Lightnin'

(Sam Hopkins)
Born: March 15, 1912, Died: January 30, 1982

Conventional blues pioneer Lightnin' Hopkins' career spanned more than three decades, yet recognition of his work and talent came later in life. He was well known locally for his hits "Short Haired Woman" and "Baby Please Don't Go" before songs such as "December 7, 1941," "Don't Embarrass Me, Baby," "Ball of Twine," "I'm Gonna Meet My Baby Somewhere" and "Little Antoinette" brought him wider exposure.

He worked during an era where cash in lieu of royalties was common, and as such he received little financial gain in comparison to his musical legacy. Having been an impoverished street singer, his return to the Downing Street area in Houston during tough times was not a difficult pill to swallow. When folks and blues were revived during the late '50s, he was rediscovered by Sam Charters, and a second career soon began.

Hopkins played the University of California Folk Festival in 1969, followed the next year by an appearance at Carnegie Hall with Joan Baez and Pete Seeger. Meanwhile he also became a regular at Houston nightspots the Sputnik Bar and Irene's. A 1969 documentary about the singer, *The Blues Accordin' to Lightnin' Hopkins*, brought greater attention to the artist and it won the Gold Hugo Award at the Chicago Film Festival.

He continued to perform sporadically into the late '60s and through the '70s, slowed only by an auto accident in 1970. In 1979 he capped his lengthy career with a performance at Carnegie Hall.

AUTOGRAPHS

An LP, magazine cover, ad, photo, or card signed by the artist: $40-$125

OFTEN OVERLOOKED MEMORABILIA

Associated artifacts from other musicians' covers of his material; movie memorabilia from *Sounder*; a videotape of the documentary *The Blues Accordin' to Lightnin' Hopkins* (1969)

Hopkins, Nicky

Born: February 24, 1944, Died: September 6, 1994

Noted studio session keyboardist and "sixth member" of the Rolling Stones, Hopkins had played with Lord Sutch's Savages (1960), followed by Cyril Davies R&B All-Stars until 1963, before an illness briefly sidelined him. He later returned and recorded with the Rolling Stones, the Beatles, the Who, the Small Faces, and the Kinks, before joining the Jeff Beck Group.

Hopkins then joined the Quicksilver Messenger Service in San Francisco and also recorded with Steve Miller and Jefferson Airplane, and he even performed with the latter at Woodstock. During the '70s he continued his efforts and collaborations with other noted musicians, including Jerry Garcia, but the majority of the time was taken by the Rolling Stones, which considered him an integral part, despite his non-member status.

AUTOGRAPHS

An LP, magazine cover, ad, photo, or card signed by the artist: $10-$25

OFTEN OVERLOOKED MEMORABILIA

Associated artifacts from other groups' works he contributed to, especially the Rolling Stones

Hornsby, Bruce and the Range

Formed 1984

Bruce Hornsby, David Mansfield, George Martinelli Jr., Joe Puerta, and John Molo*

*Peter Harris replaced Mansfield in 1988 and left in 1990

Bruce Hornsby studied music at the University of Miami (Coral Gables, Florida) and at the Berklee School of Music (Boston, Massachusetts), but he paid his dues playing the lounges and taverns below the Mason-Dixon line. In the process he spent years recording demonstration tapes and mailing them to every record company imaginable. But in 1980, at the invitation of Michael McDonald (Doobie Brothers), who was impressed when he heard him at a Steak & Ale bar, he headed to Los Angeles and began work at 20th Century Fox Publishing. In 1982 he befriended Huey Lewis, who asked the musician to add a composition to his new album *Sports*. Hornsby politely declined, as he was continually asked to join numerous other bands and projects.

Bruce Hornsby and the Range—David Mansfield, George Martinelli, Joe Puerta, and John Molo—got their big break and signed to RCA records in 1985. The group's debut album, *The Way It Is* (#3, 1987), was driven on the strength of intensive touring and the singles "Every Little Kiss" (#72, 1986), "Mandolin Rain" (#4, 1987), and the self-titled "The Way It Is" (#1, 1986). On February 24, 1987, the group won the award for Best New Artist at the 29th Annual Grammy Awards.

Scenes from the Southside (#5, 1988), the band's sophomore effort, included extracted singles "The Valley Road" (#5, 1988), "Look Out Any Window" (#35, 1988), and its own version of "Jacob's Ladder," which Huey Lewis had covered and topped the charts with in 1987. *A Night on the Town* (#20, 1990) soon followed and produced the single "Across the River" (#18, 1990). On August 16, 1990, RCA Records confirmed that Hornsby had agreed to help his longtime

friends the Grateful Dead get through a very tough time following the death of its keyboard player Brent Mydland. It was a bit ironic, because a as teenager Hornsby was a member of the Grateful Dead cover band Bobby Hightest & the Octave Kids.

BRUCE HORNSBY - CONTRIBUTIONS TO OTHER ARTISTS' ALBUMS
(Selected Entries)

Clannad (1987)	Tom Wopat (1987)
Patti Austin (1988)	Kim Carnes (1988)
Huey Lewis (1988)	Don Henley (1989)
Shawn Colvin (1989)	Nitty Gritty Dirt Band (1990)
Cowboy Junkies (1990)	The Peace Choir (1991)
Bonnie Raitt (1991)	Robbie Robertson (1991)
Bob Seger (1991)	Squeeze (1991)
Leon Russell (1992)	

Also Bob Dylan, Liquid Jesus, Willie Nelson, Phil Collins, Stevie Nicks, Crosby, Stills, Nash & Young, Chaka Kahn, and others

On May 1, 1993, Hornsby's fourth album, *Harbor Lights* (#46, 1993), peaked on the album chart; for the first time the Range was noticeably absent. His next offering was *Hot House* (#68, 1995) and it promoted his interest in jazz. It included numerous musicians, including Pat Metheny, Jerry Garcia, and Chaka Kahn, and was uniquely promoted by in-store performances at multi-media stores. During the summer of 1996 he partook in "Deadapalooza" with Los Lobos, Mickey Hart's new band Mystery Box, and Bob Weir's Ratdog.

AUTOGRAPHS

Bruce Hornsby has always greeted his fans warmly and doesn't hesitate to sign an autograph request in-person or via mail—outstanding!

A CD, LP, magazine cover, ad, photo, or card signed by the band: $25-$40

TOUR BOOKS/PROGRAMS/PASSES

Tour Programs:
Scenes From The Southside: $10

A Bruce Hornsby backstage pass (Printed by Perri Ent. Services Inc.)

Scenes from the Southside tour program (1988-89) (© 1988 Bruce Hornsby and The Range)

Backstage Passes:
Cloth: $8-$10;
Laminated: $15-$20

POSTERS/PRESS KITS

Promotional Posters: $10-$30

Scenes From The Southside, U.K. (40" x 60"): $30

Press Kits: $20-$30

Harbor Lights: $20

USED CLOTHING/EQUIPMENT

Guitar Picks: $10-$20 (The Range)
Drum Sticks: $15

OFTEN OVERLOOKED MEMORABILIA

His session work—if you're going to collect Hornsby you're going to have to try to keep up with his contributions to other work; free promotional compact disc that was part of Coca-Cola's Olympics advertising campaign and never commercially available

---

BRUCE HORNSBY ON TELEVISION - SELECTED ENTRIES

October, 1986	*Wogan*- BBC1-TV, opening for Huey Lewis and The News
January 31, 1987	*Saturday Night Live*- NBC-TV, musical guest
February 23, 1990	*Coast to Coast*- Showtime-TV, guest of Herbie Hancock
September 11, 1990	*Late Night With David Letterman*- NBC-TV
February 10, 1991	*NBA All-Star Game*- national anthem with Branford Marsalis
September 20, 1991	"A Comedy Salute to Michael Jordan"- NBC-TV
August 7, 1992	*1992 Olympic TV Coverage*- NBC-TV
May 3, 1993	*The Tonight Show*- NBC-TV
May 21, 1993	*Late Night With David Letterman* - NBC-TV
June 8, 1993	"Center Stage"- VH-1 TV
December 2, 1993	*Late Show With David Letterman*- CBS-TV
February 4, 1994	*The Tonight Show*- NBC-TV
April 1, 1995	Boston Celtics vs. Miami Heat- performs national anthem
June 7, 1995	Orlando Magic vs. Houston Rockets- performs national anthem
September 6, 1995	Cal Ripken Record Breaking Night at Camden Yards- performs national anthem
September 29, 1995	*The Tonight Show*- NBC-TV
December 3, 1995	"In the Spotlight"- PBS-TV, Bruce Hornsby and Friends
January 3, 1996	*Late Show With David Letterman*- CBS-TV

Horton, Johnny

Born: April 30, 1925, Died: November 5, 1960

Johnny Horton was one of country and western's first acts to make the successful transition to the pop charts with "The Battle of New Orleans" (#1, 1959). He was also associated with the songs "Johnny Reb" (#54, 1959), "Sink the Bismarck" (#3, 1960), and "North to Alaska" (#4, 1960).

In a bit of irony, Horton felt that his death was imminent, whether or not it had anything to do with his fascination with the occult or not is speculation, but he even went so far as to accelerate his schedule. While returning from a performance at the Skyline in Austin, Texas, he was involved in an automobile accident that took his life. The Skyline was also noted for being the place of Hank Williams' last performance; coincidental too is the fact that Horton's widow, Billy Jean, had also been married to Williams.

AUTOGRAPHS

An LP, magazine cover, ad, photo, or card signed by the artist: $20-$50

OFTEN OVERLOOKED MEMORABILIA

Associated artifacts from other musicians' covers of his material

Hot Chocolate

Formed 1970

Errol Brown, Patrick Olive, Larry Ferguson, Harvey Hinsley, Ian King, and Tony Wilson*

*Tony Connor replaced King in 1973. Tony Wilson departed in 1975

This '70s British soul band is best remembered for the hits "You Sexy Thing" (#3, 1976), "Brother Louie" (a hit for Stories), "Disco Queen" (#28, 1975), "Emma" (#8, 1975), and later for "Every 1's a Winner" (#6, 1979).

AUTOGRAPHS

An LP, magazine cover, ad, photo, or card signed by the group: $12-$25

OFTEN OVERLOOKED MEMORABILIA

Associated artifacts from other musicians' covers of their material

Hothouse Flowers

Formed 1986

Liam O'Maonlai, Fiachna O'Braonain, Peter O'Toole, Jerry Fehily, and Leo Barnes

This late-80s Irish band, which recorded its first single on U2's own label, garnered interest from fans and major record companies, including PolyGram's London label which signed the band. Although the group's debut album scored in Ireland, the group hasn't gained even minor cult status in America.

AUTOGRAPHS

A CD, LP, magazine cover, ad, photo, or card signed by the group: $10

Hot Tuna

Formed 1972- Officially left Jefferson Airplane

Jorma Kaukonen and Jack Casady

Additional personnel: Will Scarlet, Pap John Creach, Sammy Piazza, Bob Steeler, Nick Buck, and Michael Falzarano

Hot Tuna, a '70s branch of Jefferson Airplane, and pet project of both Jorma Kaukonen and Jack Casady, was an anomaly of sorts, which built a large cult following around its mediocre album releases and seemingly endless live and loud performances. The group disbanded in 1978, and Kaukonen resumed his solo career that he had begun in 1974 with the release of *Quah*.

Kaukonen and Casady temporarily reunited in 1983 for a series of club dates and later again in 1986; Michael Falzarano was added to a now firmer unit. As is typical with Airplane/Starship spinoffs, members were often interchanged within bands to form new offshoots or one-off projects.

The members of Hot Tuna

AUTOGRAPHS

An LP, magazine cover, ad, photo, or card signed by the group: $10-$30

OFTEN OVERLOOKED MEMORABILIA

Associated artifacts from members' numerous contributions to other musical efforts

House, Son

(Eddie House)
Born: March 21, 1902, Died: October 19, 1988

Pioneer Mississippi bluesman Son House was pivotal in laying the foundation for rock and roll prior to World War II. He was often referenced as an inspiration to the greats who followed including Muddy Waters, Robert Johnson, and Bob Dylan.

AUTOGRAPHS

An LP, magazine cover, ad, photo, or card signed by the artist: $25-$60

OFTEN OVERLOOKED MEMORABILIA

Associated artifacts from other musicians' covers of his material

The Housemartins/The Beautiful South/Beats International

The Housemartins- formed 1984
The Beautiful South- formed 1988
Beats International- formed 1989

Eighties British pop band the Housemartins were primarily associated with two songs, "Caravan of Love" (#1, U.K., 1986) and "Happy Hour" (#3, U.K., 1986), before dissolving in 1988.

Heaton and Hemingway went on to the Beautiful South, which landed on the U.K. charts with "Song for Whoever" (#2, 1989), "You Keep It All In" (#8, 1989), and "A Little Time" (#1, 1990).

Cook moved to the techno-dance outfit Beats International which put "Dub Be Good to Me" (#1, 1990) and "Won't Talk About It" (#9, 1990) on the U.K. charts

AUTOGRAPHS

An LP, magazine cover, ad, photo, or card signed by the group: $10-$20*
*Original lineup for The Housemartins

The House of Love

Formed 1986

Terry Bickers, Guy Chadwick, Pete Evans, Chris Groothuizen, and Andrea Heukamp*

*Heukamp left in 1987 and Simon Walker replaced Bickers in 1990. Simon Mawbey replaced Walker in 1991.

This late-80s British pop act has enjoyed some success in its homeland, but little more than a small cult following here in the U.S.

AUTOGRAPHS

An LP, magazine cover, ad, photo, or card signed by the group: $5-$10

House of Pain

Formed 1990

Everlast (Erik Schrody), Danny Boy (Daniel O'Connor), and Lethal (Leor DiMant)

Nineties Irish-American rap group House of Pain is commonly associated with the hit "Jump Around" (#3, 1992).

AUTOGRAPHS

An LP, magazine cover, ad, photo, or card signed by the group: $8-$15

POSTERS/PRESS KITS

Promotional Posters: $8
Press Kits: $8-$10

Houston, Cissy

Born: 1933

This gospel-soul singer is best known for her work as a member of the Sweet Inspirations, her solo hit "Be My Baby" (#92, 1971), her numerous contributions as a backup singer, and as the mother of Whitney Houston.

AUTOGRAPHS

An LP, magazine cover, ad, photo, or card signed by the artist: $5-$10

OFTEN OVERLOOKED MEMORABILIA

Artifacts from her numerous contributions to other musicians' work including, Chaka Kahn, Aretha Franklin, and Luther Vandross

Houston, Thelma

Seventies gospel-rooted disco diva Thelma Houston is best known for her smash disco hit "Don't Leave Me This Way" (#1, 1977). She also scored minor hits with "Saturday Night, Sunday Morning" (#34, 1979) and "You Used to Hold Me So Tight" (#13, R&B, 1984), and she has appeared in numerous films and on motion picture soundtracks.

AUTOGRAPHS

A CD, LP, magazine cover, ad, photo, or card signed by the artist: $10-$15

OFTEN OVERLOOKED MEMORABILIA

Movie memorabilia from *The Bingo Long Traveling All Stars & Motor Kings* (1976), *Norman...Is That You?*, *Death Scream*, and *The Seventh Dwarf*

Houston, Whitney

Born: August 9, 1963

Mid-80s and '90s premier R&B and pop diva Whitney Houston is best known for her chart topping hits "Saving All My Love for You" (#1, 1985), "How Will I Know" (#1, 1985), "Greatest Love of All" (#1, 1986), "I Wanna Dance with Somebody (Who Loves Me)" (#1, 1987), "Didn't We Almost Have It all" (#1, 1987), "So Emotional" (#1, 1987), "Where Do Broken Hearts Go" (#1, 1988), "I'm Your Baby Tonight" (#1, 1990), "All the Man That I Need" (#1, 1990), and "I Will Always Love You" (#1, 1992), along with numerous other Top Ten hits. She married singer Bobby Brown in 1992, the same year she made her acting debut in *The Bodyguard*.

AUTOGRAPHS

A CD, LP, magazine cover, ad, photo, or card signed by the artist: $35-$100

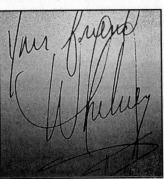

Whitney Houston's signature

TOUR BOOKS/PROGRAMS/PASSES

Programs:
1987 Tour: $10
Feels So Right (Japan) 1990: $40
One South Africa, 1994: $30
Live in Concert, 1994: $15
Backstage Passes:
Cloth: $10-$12; Laminated: $15-$20

POSTERS/PRESS KITS

Promotional Posters: $20-$40
1985 (40" x 60") $40;
Waiting to Exhale, U.K. (40" x 60"): $22
Press Kits: $15-$30

1987 Tour program (1987, Nippy Inc.)

OFTEN OVERLOOKED MEMORABILIA

Movie memorabilia from *The Bodyguard* and *Waiting to Exhale*; any and all artifacts from her modeling career which included shots for magazines such as *Glamour* and *Vogue*; any artifacts from her contributions backing Lou Rawls and Chaka Kahn; videotapes of her numerous television appearances

REFERENCES/BOOKS

Numerous resources exist, but nothing that does justice to the singer in my opinion; no dedicated collector books; serious fans should opt for her fan club: Whitney Houston Official Fan Club, Dept. Friend, P.O. Box 885288, San Francisco, CA 94188 ($18 fee)

Howlin' Wolf

(Chester A. Burnett)
Born: June 10, 1910, Died: January 10, 1976

A legendary Mississippi Delta bluesman, Wolf was monumental in the formation of electric Chicago blues. Upon his arrival there in 1952, following the recording of his first R&B hit "Moanin' at Midnight." His recordings with Chess Records—Willie Dixon penned many of the songs—during the '50s and '60s were among his best, including "Sitting on Top of the World," "Spoonful," "Smokestack Lightnin'," "Little Red Rooster," "Back Door Man," "Killing Floor," and "How Many More Years."

The late '60s and early '70s found Wolf appearing at rock and blues festivals where his music, which had been covered by numerous rock acts such as the Rolling Stones, the Doors, and Cream, was now appealing to an entirely new generation. He spent the final years of his life suffering from numerous ailments, including kidney disease, in his Chicago home on the crumbling South Side. One of his last shows was his appearance at the Chicago Amphitheater, with such luminaries as B.B. King, in November 1975, just months before he died at age 65.

Howlin' Wolf was posthumously inducted into the Rock and Roll Hall of Fame in 1991.

AUTOGRAPHS

An LP, magazine cover, ad, photo, or card signed by the artist: $275-$850*

*Items may fluctuate significantly depending upon the scarcity of the item

Humble Pie

Formed 1969

Steve Marriott (Born: January 30, 1947, Died: April 20, 1991) and Peter Frampton (Born: April 22, 1950),

Greg Ridley (Born: October 23, 1947) and Jerry Shirley (Born: February 4, 1952)*

*David "Clem" Clempson replaced Frampton in 1971. The group disbanded in 1975 and re-grouped in 1980 with: Marriott, Shirley, Bobby Tench, and Anthony Jones.

Steve Marriott left the Small Faces in 1968 and hooked up with Peter Frampton (Herd), Greg Ridley (Spooky Tooth), and Jerry Shirley to form Humble Pie. The band eventually formed a hard rock reputation augmented by Frampton's heavy guitar licks and Marriott's raspy vocals. It took a while, however, for the group to refine its sound and looks to get just the right mix to make it all work.

As Safe as Yesterday (1969, Immediate, U.K.) and Town and Country (1969, Immediate, U.K.) had little impact on the U.K. market and even less in America. In 1969, after finding its record company went under, the group found a new manager (Dee Anthony) and signed to a new label, A&M Records. When Humble Pie (1970, A&M) and Rock On (#118, 1971, A&M) failed to garner the attention the band felt it deserved, Anthony put a new loud and rougher edge on the band, and sent it out on tour. The result was Rockin' the Fillmore (#21, 1972), a powerful two album live set that really showcased the band's talent. Just when it appeared that everything was gelling, Peter Frampton left the band (before the album's release) for a solo career.

Smokin' (#6, 1972) featured new guitarist David "Clem" Clempson and became the band's most successful album, no doubt warmed up by the single "Hot 'n' Nasty" (#52, 1972). A&M Records saw the interest and reissued the first two albums as Lost and Found (#37, 1972). The group followed it up, in 1973, with the two album set Eat It (#13, 1973).

Following Thunderbox (#52, 1974) and Street Rats (#100, 1975) the band split up, and Shirley went to Natural Gas, while Clempson went to Greenslade and then to Strange Brew with Ridley. Marriott, meanwhile, started Steve Marriott's All-Stars and attended a Small Faces reunion in 1976, before reforming Humble Pie in 1980. The group disbanded permanently in 1981, after two poor selling albums, On to Victory and Go for the Throat.

On April 20, 1991, after reuniting with Peter Frampton and a brief mid-1980s jaunt with Packet of Three, Marriott died in a fire.

AUTOGRAPHS

Group:

A CD, LP, magazine cover, ad, photo, or card signed by the band: $150-$225*

*Original lineup on the Humble Pie (A&M) album

Individual:

Steve Marriott: $30-$50

Peter Frampton: $15-$45

Greg Ridley: $10

Jerry Shirley: $10

TOUR BOOKS/PROGRAMS/PASSES

Backstage Passes:

Cloth: $8-$20; Laminated: $15-$40

USED CLOTHING/EQUIPMENT

Drum Sticks: $15

Humperdinck, Engelbert

(Thomas Arnold George Dorsey)
Born: May 2, 1936

Late-60s crooner and geriatric sex symbol Engelbert Humperdinck is best remembered for his hits "Release Me (and Let Me Love Again)" (#4, 1967), "Am I That Easy to Forget" (#18, 1968), "A Man Without Love" (#19, 1968), "Winter World of Love" (#16, 1970), and "After the Lovin'" (#8, 1976). His longevity is no doubt attributable to one of the largest and most devoted followings of any one performer from his era.

AUTOGRAPHS

An LP, magazine cover, ad, photo, or card signed by the artist: $5-$15

TOUR BOOKS/ PROGRAMS/PASSES

Tour Books: $10 - $20

OFTEN OVERLOOKED MEMORABILIA

Videotapes of his numerous television appearances; a bottle of his Release Me fragrance for women.

An Engelbert Humperdinck tour program (Raydell Publishing, 1974)

Hunter, Alberta

Born: April 1, 1895, Died: October 17, 1984

This early American cabaret star is best known for her caustic charm, yet magical stage performance and songs such as "Down Hearted Blues," "A Good Man Is Hard to Find," My Castle's Rocking," and "You Can't Tell the Difference After Dark." She replaced Bessie Smith on Broadway in *How Come* in 1923, just one of many theatre productions she became involved in. By the '30s one could catch her at Harlem's Cotton Club or at Connie's Inn with Louis Armstrong.

Hunter recorded with many of the top orchestras of her era and spent most of World War II touring with the USO. She returned to club work in the '50s and picked up her recording career. Late in the decade, at the age of 82, she established a residency in New York's Greenwich Village, performing at the Cookery. In 1984 she died of natural causes in New York City.

AUTOGRAPHS

An LP, magazine cover, ad, photo, or card signed by the artist: $15-$40

OFTEN OVERLOOKED MEMORABILIA

Associated artifacts from her numerous theater productions including *How Come* (1923) and *Showboat* (1928); any and all Cotton Club and Connie's Inn memorabilia; a copy of the videotape *Jazz at the Smithsonian* (1985)

Hunter, Ian

Born: June 3, 1946

Ian Hunter is typically associated with his work as lead singer of Mott the Hoople, although he had enjoyed a modest solo career during the late '70s with songs such as "Once Bitten Twice Shy." Hunter also penned Barry Manilow's hit "Ships" before departing the scene.

AUTOGRAPHS

An LP, magazine cover, ad, photo, or card signed by the artist: $10-$25*
*High-end reflects a choice Mott the Hoople item

OFTEN OVERLOOKED MEMORABILIA

Memorabilia associated with other musicians' covers of his songs

Hunter, Ivory Joe

Born: October 10, 1914, Died: November 8, 1974

This '40s and '50s multi-talented pop-blues performer, whose creativity and musical prowess made him successful at translating country songs into an R&B flavored format, is typically associated with the recordings "Blues at Sunrise," "Landlord Blues," "I Almost Lost My Mind" (#1, R&B), "I Need You So" (#2, R&B, 1950), "Since I Met You Baby" (#12, 1956), "Empty Arms" (1957), "Yes I Want You" (1958), and "City Lights" (1959). His songs have been covered by everyone from Elvis Presley to Nat King Cole. He died in a Memphis hospital in 1974.

AUTOGRAPHS

An LP, magazine cover, ad, photo, or card signed by the artist: $25-$60

OFTEN OVERLOOKED MEMORABILIA

Memorabilia associated with other musicians' covers of his songs

Hurt, Mississippi John

Born: July 3, 1893, Died: November 2, 1966

Fingerpicking Mississippi blues singer John Mississippi Hurt, who is best remembered for the songs "Stack-O-Lee," "Candy Man Blues," "Coffee Blues," "Chicken," and "C.C. Rider," was rediscovered at the

age of 70, after having fallen into obscurity during the early-60s folk-blues revival.

AUTOGRAPHS
An LP, magazine cover, ad, photo, or card signed by the artist: $30-$125

OFTEN OVERLOOKED MEMORABILIA
Memorabilia associated with other musicians' covers of his songs; videotapes of his television appearance on the *Tonight Show* (1963); a copy of the Canadian documentary *This Hour Has Seven Days*; Newport Folk Festival memorabilia from 1963-1965

Hüsker Dü

Formed 1979

Bob Mould, Greg Norton, and Grant Hart

These '80s indie alt-rock pioneers from Minnesota provided five years worth of productive touring and releases that created some of the finest artifacts of the post-punk era. Many critics claim the group's pinnacle of creativity came with *Zen Arcade*, a double-disc punk concept album, which chronicled a youth's transformation to adulthood. On January 25, 1988,

Ian, Janis

(Janis Eddy Fink)
Born: May 7, 1951

Seventies pop singer and songwriter Janis Ian is best remembered first for her teen hit "Society's Child (Baby I've Been Thinking)" (#14, 1967) and later for "At Seventeen" (#3, 1975)—a Grammy award winner.

AUTOGRAPHS
A CD, LP, magazine cover, ad, photo, or card signed by the artist: $10-$20

Ian and Sylvia

Formed 1959

Ian Tyson, Born: September 25, 1933, and Sylvia Tyson (Fricker), Born: September 19, 1940

Canadian folksingers and songwriters, later turned country, Ian and Sylvia were active in the early '60s folk circuit and are typically identified with the songs "Four Strong Winds" and "You Were On My Mind." The married couple later divorced, and Ian went on to record cowboys songs.

Bob Mould quit the band to pursue a solo career before forming the band Sugar.

AUTOGRAPHS
A CD, LP, magazine cover, ad, photo, or card signed by the group: $10-$30

POSTERS/PRESS KITS
Promotional Posters: $10-$20
Press Kits: $13-$15

Hyland, Brian

Born: November 12, 1943

Early-60s pop novelty singer Hyland is best known for his first hit "Itsy Bitsy Teenie Weenie Yellow Polkadot Bikini" (#1, 1960) and later for "Let Me Belong to You" (#20, 1961), "Sealed with a Kiss" (#3, 1962), "Ginny Come Lately" (#21, 1962), "The Joker Went Wild" (#20, 1966), and "Gypsy Woman" (#3, 1970).

AUTOGRAPHS
An LP, magazine cover, ad, photo, or card signed by the artist: $10

AUTOGRAPHS
An LP, magazine cover, ad, photo, or card signed by the group: $6-$10

OFTEN OVERLOOKED MEMORABILIA
Memorabilia associated with other musicians' covers of Ian's songs

Ice Cube

(O'Shea Jackson)
Born: June 15, 1969*
*Unsure of exact year

When Ice left N.W.A., L.A.'s "bad boy" of rap, he knew that his reputation would precede him, but by 1990, he was significantly smarter to the scene. He took his group, Da Lench Mob, and joined hands with one of the best, the Bomb Squad production team. Just how good was the pairing? Just ten days after its release in the spring of 1990, *AmeriKKKa's Most Wanted* sold gold.

The album did its best to rip a hole a mile wide in just about every critical issue facing America's streets, from gang violence to a fantasy about an aborted pregnancy, nothing was sacred and nothing was solved, parents abhorred it, critics adored it, and the public bought it. Now considered a rap classic, it has been viewed in a different perspective.

Ice used the album to introduce his collaborator Yo Yo, who countered Cube's views from a female prospective, which landed her accolades and later a six-figure deal with Atlantic Records. Ice followed his debut with the *Kill at Will* EP, which included two of raps most controversial songs, "Black Korea" and "No Vaseline." Their inclusion, in retrospect, was not a particularly wise choice and led to the first public condemnation of an artist ever in the industry's premier periodical *Billboard*.

The Predator (#1, 1992), Cube's next album release, debuted at #1 on both the R&B and album charts, putting rap in the history books for reaching another major pinnacle.

AUTOGRAPHS

A CD, LP, magazine cover, ad, photo, , or card signed by the artist: $20-$40

OFTEN OVERLOOKED MEMORABILIA

Memorabilia associated with Cube's other projects including production work.

Ice-T

(Tracy Marrow)
Born: Late 1950s*
*Unsure of exact year

The "King of Controversy" first came under fire for "Cop Killer," a song by his thrash-metal side band (Body Count), in 1992. But the '80s rapper is also associated with songs such as "High Roller" (#76, R&B, 1989), "I'm Your Pusher" (#13, R&B, 1988), and the title song for the 1988 street film *Colors*. Ice has also appeared in numerous films, while working on his numerous ancillary projects.

AUTOGRAPHS

A CD, LP, magazine cover, ad, photo, or card signed by the artist: $15-$30

OFTEN OVERLOOKED MEMORABILIA

Movie memorabilia from *Colors* (1988), *New Jack City* (1991), *Ricochet* (1991), *Trespass* (1992), and *Surviving the Game* (1994); all artifacts associated with the controversy over "Cop Killers"

REFERENCES/BOOKS

The Ice Opinion, his autobiography (1994)

Icicle Works

Formed 1980

Robert Ian McNabb, Born: November 3, 1960, Chris Layne, and Chris Sharrock*

*Dave Green was added in 1985. Layne and Sharrock left in 1987, while Roy Corkhill and Zak Starkey were added. Both Green and Starkey left the following year and Dave

Baldwin, Paul Burgess, and Mark Revell were brought into the band.

This '80s British post-punk band is best remembered in the U.S. for the song "Whisper to a Scream (Birds Fly)" (#37, 1984) and for adding drummer Zak Starkey (Ringo Starr's son) to the lineup.

AUTOGRAPHS

A CD, LP, magazine cover, ad, photo, or card signed by the group: $6-$10

Ides of March

Formed 1964

James Peterik, Ray Herr, Larry Millas, Bob Bergland, John Larson, Chuck Somar, and Michael Borch

Ides of March, a '70s brass-pop band, is best remembered for the hit "Vehicle" (#2, 1970), which sounded extraordinarily close to the sound of Blood, Sweat and Tears, and minor hits "You Wouldn't Listen" and "Roller Coaster," before it faded from the music scene. Peterik, however, would surface later in Survivor, which scored a hit with "Eye of the Tiger" (#1, 1982).

AUTOGRAPHS

An LP, magazine cover, ad, photo, or card signed by the group: $8-$20

Idol, Billy/Generation X

(William Michael Albert Broad)
Born: November 30, 1955

Generation X formed in 1976. Members: Idol, Tony James, Bob Andrews, and John Towe

The '80s cyber-punk, sneering bad boy, and former frontman of Generation X ("Your Generation," "Ready Steady Go," "Wild Youth"), Billy Idol is typically associated with the songs "White Wedding" (#36, 1983), "Rebel Yell" (#46, 1984), "Eyes Without a Face" (#4, 1984), "To Be a Lover" (#6, 1986), "Mony Mony 'Live'" (#1, 1987), and "Cradle of Love" (#2, 1990).

Idol, who left Generation X—which was the first punk band to appear on the BBC's *Top of the Pops*, in 1981—maintained his rebellious image both on and off the stage; his tours were often filled with almost routine allegations. A serious motorcycle accident sidelined him in 1990, and even cost him a major role in Oliver Stone's movie *The Doors* (1991—he did manage a minor role), but thankfully he recovered. The latter half of the '80s found him fighting with his image, which was getting a bit worn.

In 1993 Idol regrouped and introduced *Cyberpunk* (#48, 1993). Whether he will remain on-line for the remainder of the decade will just have to be seen!

AUTOGRAPHS

An LP, magazine cover, ad, photo, or card signed by the artist: $10-$25

Tour program from Idol's Whiplash Smile Tour (© 1986 Whiplash Smile Prod. Group Ltd.)

Back of Billy Idol tour program 1990-91 (Awest/Lyn Bradley-Brass Ring Circus Gifford)

TOUR BOOKS/ PROGRAMS/PASSES

Programs:
Whiplash Smile Tour: $10-$15
The Tour 1991: $11
Backstage Passes:
Cloth: $8-$10;
Laminated: $12-$20

POSTERS/PRESS KITS

Promotional Posters: $10-$25
Press Kits: $10-$20

USED CLOTHING/ EQUIPMENT

Guitar Picks: $20-$25*
*Some of the "Cyber Corps" picks have been advertised at $75
Drum Sticks: $15

OFTEN OVERLOOKED MEMORABILIA

Memorabilia associated with Idol's performances of the Who's *Quadrophenia* (1996)

REFERENCES/BOOKS

Numerous resources exist, but nothing that does justice to the singer in my opinion; no dedicated collector books

Iglesias, Julio

(Julio Jose Iglesias de la Cueva)
Born: September 23, 1943

The Valentino of the '80s, whose suave crooning has made him an international star, is best known in America for his songs "Begin the Beguine," "To All The Girls I've Loved Before" (#5, 1984)—a duet with Willie Nelson—and "All of You" (#19, 1984)—a duet with Diana Ross. A perennial live attraction here in America, he can still sell out a venue in a heartbeat.

AUTOGRAPHS

An LP, magazine cover, ad, photo, or card signed by the artist: $15-$45

TOUR BOOKS/PROGRAMS/PASSES

Tour Books:
Starry Nights Tour, 1991: $17

OFTEN OVERLOOKED MEMORABILIA

Memorabilia associated with other musicians' covers of his songs

The Impressions

Formed 1957

Curtis Mayfield, Born: June 3, 1942; Jerry Butler, Born: December 8, 1939; Arthur Brooks; Richard Brooks; and Sam Gooden*

*Numerous personnel changes. Butler left in 1958-1959, both Brooks in 1961, and Mayfield in 1970.

This versatile, talented '60s soul and R&B vocal group, with big-band horn arrangements, is typically associated with the songs "For Your Precious Love" (#11, 1958), "Gypsy Woman" (1961), "Talking About My Baby" (#14, 1964), "I'm So Proud" (#14, 1964), "Keep On Pushin'" (#10, 1964), "People Get Ready" (#14, 1965), and "Amen" (#7, 1965). Although numerous other hits followed, including "Finally Got Myself Together" (#1, R&B, 1974), the band remained a far cry from its earlier days, despite having both Fred Cash and Sam Gooden.

AUTOGRAPHS

An LP, magazine cover, ad, photo, or card signed by the group: $30-$85

OFTEN OVERLOOKED MEMORABILIA

Memorabilia associated with other musicians' covers of their songs

The Incredible String Band

Formed 1965

Mike Heron, Robin Williamson, and Clive Palmer*

*Numerous personnel changes

The Incredible String Band, the diversely talented mid-60s Scottish folk group, drew inspiration from a variety of sources including traditional British and American ballads, and then blended it with an assortment of selected world sounds. The group's work has inspired many rock artists including Led Zeppelin, which cites the group as such in one of its tour programs, and the Rolling Stones, which even tried to sign the group to its Mother Earth label. The group's reputation was spread to America primarily through the efforts of Judy Collins and Tom Paxton, both of whom were impressed while performing with ISB at London's Royal Albert Hall in 1966. (Collins later even covered Williamson's "First Girl I Loved").

A cult audience then began to develop slowly for the band in the U.S., while in England ISB was con-

sidered a staple in the hippie movement of the late '60s. The group's last show together was in 1974, but by that time personnel changes and musical tastes had drastically altered the band's sound.

AUTOGRAPHS

An LP, magazine cover, ad, photo, or card signed by the group: $10-$25

OFTEN OVERLOOKED MEMORABILIA

Memorabilia associated with other musicians' covers of their songs

Indigo Girls

Formed 1980

Amy Ray, Born: April 12, 1964, and Emily Saliers, Born: July 22, 1963

This late-80s-early-90s female vocal pop rock duo, which draws on traditional folk roots while expressing contemporary feminine, social, or environmental issues, is typically associated with songs such as "Closer to Fine" and "Hammer and a Nail" and also for the albums *Rites of Passage* (#21, 1992)—which was nominated for a Grammy award, and *Swamp Ophelia* (1994). The Indigo Girls have enjoyed successful gold and platinum albums sales in America, which is a strong indicator of the loyal following they possess despite the lack of a successful smash hit single.

This group has not only an extremely strong cult following of fans, but also of collectors. Items offered for sale won't last long and you may be surprised at the prices they can command.

AUTOGRAPHS

A CD, LP, magazine cover, ad, photo, or card signed by the group: $10-$35

TOUR BOOKS/PROGRAMS/ PASSES

Programs:
Rites of Passion: $10
Backstage Passes:
Cloth: $10-$15; Laminated: $20-$25

POSTERS/PRESS KITS

Promotional Posters: $10-$20
Press Kits: $25

USED CLOTHING/EQUIPMENT

Guitar Picks: $20-$25

OFTEN OVERLOOKED MEMORABILIA

Memorabilia associated with other musicians' covers of the group's songs; Swamp Ophelia promo business card - $3; Swamp Ophelia counter display - $20; Sweet Relief II promo postcard - $2

Indigo Girls backstage pass (Printed by OTTO)

Indigo Girls guitar pick

Ingram, James

Born: February 17, 1952

James Ingram, the '80s and '90s pop singer and sex symbol, is so gifted that he won a 1981 Grammy without having released an album of his own—he won for "One Hundred Ways" (#14, 1981) from the Quincy Jones album *The Dude*. Ingram is best known for the songs "Just Once" (#17, 1981), "Yah Mo Be There"— a Grammy winning duet with Michael McDonald— "Somewhere Out There" (#2, 1986)—a duet with Linda Ronstadt—and "I Don't Have the Heart" (#1, 1990). The artist also has a flair for choosing the perfect duet partner for just the right songs and has established a strong reputation for himself for film contributions.

AUTOGRAPHS

A CD, LP, magazine cover, ad, photo, or card signed by the artist: $12-$25

POSTERS/PRESS KITS

Promotional Posters: $10-$30
(High end primarily movie related)
Press Kits: $15

OFTEN OVERLOOKED MEMORABILIA

Movie memorabilia from *The Color Purple*, *Best Friends*, *An American Tail*, *Beverly Hills Cop II*; videotapes of *General Hospital* that use the theme "Baby, Come to Me" (#1, 1982)—his collaboration with Patty Austin; associated artifacts from his numerous collaborations

The Ink Spots

Formed late 1920s

Prominent members have included: Jerry Daniels, Orville "Hoppy" Jones, Born: February 17, 1905, Died: October 18, 1944, Charles Fuqua, Ivory "Deek" Watson, and Bill Kenny (1915-1978)

Although the group's time came long before rock and roll, The Ink Spots were a precursor to doo-wop vocal groups of the '50s and are certainly worthy of mention in a book of this kind.

The Ink Spots are best remembered for the hits "If I Didn't Care," "My Prayer," "Maybe," "We Three," "Whispering Grass," "To Each His Own," "and "I Don't Set the World on Fire."

The original group was inducted into the Rock and Roll Hall of Fame in 1989.

AUTOGRAPHS

An LP, magazine cover, ad, photo, or card signed by the group: $275-$300

OFTEN OVERLOOKED MEMORABILIA

Memorabilia associated with other musicians' covers of their songs; a bottle of Chanel autographed by a former member or associate

Inspiral Carpets

Formed 1986

Stephen Holt, Graham Lambert, Clint Boon, David Swift, and Craig Gill

This late-80s British pre-rave psychedelic dance-rock scene group, that has built a slow but substantial cult following here in America through the early Mute label releases and later on Cow Records, is perhaps best known first for its albums such as *Life* (1990) and *The Beast Inside* (1991).

AUTOGRAPHS

An LP, magazine cover, ad, photo, or card signed by the group: $15-$25

POSTERS/PRESS KITS

Promotional Posters: $10-$20
Press Kits: $10-$15

OFTEN OVERLOOKED MEMORABILIA

She Comes In, 1990 Moo Cow! battery operated toy; Life promotional milk bottle, 1990; bumper sticker, "Cool as Fuck" - $5

The Intruders

Formed 1960

Phil Terry, Born: November 1, 1943, Robert "Big Sonny" Edwards, Born: February 22, 1942, Samuel "Little Sonny" Brown, and Eugene "Bird" Daughtry, Born: October 29,1939.

The Intruders, a talented '60s vocal act, are best known as the first group signed to Gamble Records and for numerous R&B and pop hits including "Cowboys to Girls," "Love is Like a Baseball Game," and "I'll Always Love My Mama" (#36, 1973).

AUTOGRAPHS

An LP, magazine cover, ad, photo, or card signed by the group: $15-$40

OFTEN OVERLOOKED MEMORABILIA

Memorabilia associated with other musicians' covers of their songs

INXS

Formed 1977

Garry Gary Beers, Born: June 22, 1957, Michael Hutchence, Born: January 22, 1960, Andrew Farriss, Born: March 27, 1959, Jon Farriss, Born: August 10, 1961, Tim Farriss, Born: August 16, 1957, and Kirk Pengilly, Born: July 4, 1958

This late-80s Aussie funk-rock pop band combined tasty guitar hooks with hip-hop beats to score a very commercially successful recipe exhibited best on hit songs such as "Original Sin," "What You Need," "Need You Tonight," "Devil Inside," "New Sensation," "Never Tear Us Apart," and "Suicide Blonde."

The band became so popular that in 1991 that it sold out Wembley Stadium in London. But rising so quickly to the top may have also hurt the group from a longevity standpoint. Some felt the group became far too commercial with all of its Top Ten hits and had just enough bubblegum taste to turn some people off. By the early '90s it was clear that INXS' appeal was weakening, especially because it couldn't place its tenth album in the Top Forty. Nonetheless, few groups ever have an album such as *Kick*, which contained four hit singles, including a Number One. Recently, the band has shown signs of awakening.

AUTOGRAPHS

A CD, LP, magazine cover, ad, photo, or card signed by the group: $30-$55

INXS 1987/88 World Tour "Kick" program (Nick Egan and Geoffrey Gifford design)

TOUR BOOKS/ PROGRAMS/PASSES

Programs:
Kick: $12- $15
The Dirt Honeymoon Tour: $10-$15
Multiplication Tour, 1989-90: $10

Backstage Passes:
Cloth: $10-$12;
Laminated: $15

POSTERS/PRESS KITS

Promotional Posters
$10-$40
Press Kits: $25-$40
Full Moon, Dirty Hearts: $25

USED CLOTHING/EQUIPMENT

Guitar Picks: $10-$15
Drum Sticks: $15

OFTEN OVERLOOKED MEMORABILIA

A copy of the videotape *Live Baby Live*; Need You Tonight, Mercury promotional PJs, 1988; Suicide Blonde promotional shampoo, 1990; *X Australia*, blue box set with cassette and 26 cards, tied with a blue ribbon, 1990 (100 sets only!)

REFERENCES/BOOKS

A few resources exist, but nothing that does justice to the band in my opinion; no dedicated collector books

Iron Butterfly

Formed 1966

Doug Ingle, Born: September 9, 1946, Ron Bushy, Born: September 23, 1945, Jerry Penrod, Darryl DeLoach, and Danny Weis.*

*Penrod, DeLoach, and Weis left in 1968, and Lee Dorman and Erik Braunn were added. Braunn left in 1969, while Mike Pinera and Larry "Rhino" Reinhardt joined the band. The group disbanded in 1971, but re-formed in 1974.

These late-60s hard-edged acid rockers got their first break as an opening act for both The Doors and Jefferson Airplane. The added exposure sustained the chart activity of the group's debut album *Heavy*, after which three of the original members departed. "In-A-Gada-Da-Vida," written by Doug Ingle who was the group leader and primary vocalist, was also the name of the group's second album. The song and album broke the band and catapulted it into stardom. The album alone stayed in the Top Ten for nearly two years!

While Iron Butterfly's next album effort, *Ball* (#3, 1969), sold gold, subsequent efforts failed and the band gave its farewell performance on May 23, 1971.

AUTOGRAPHS

An LP, magazine cover, ad, photo, or card signed by the group: $15-$50

TOUR BOOKS/PROGRAMS/PASSES

Tour Books:
Visual Thing, 1969: $60

OFTEN OVERLOOKED MEMORABILIA

Movie memorabilia from *Savage Seven* and *Easy Rider*

REFERENCES/BOOKS

Numerous resources exist, but nothing that does justice to the band in my opinion; no dedicated collector books; serious fans can communicate with the Iron Butterfly Information Network, Attention: Rick Gagnon, Biografix, 9745 Sierra Avenue, Fontana, CA 92335

Iron Maiden

Formed 1976

Paul Di'anno, Born: May 17, 1959, Steve Harris, Born: March 12, 1957, Dave Murray, Born: December 23, 1958, and Doug Sampson*

*Numerous personnel changes

Iron Maiden, the late-70s English metal merchants, were successful the old-fashioned way with piercing crisp guitar riffs with excessive volume, thundering bass chords under enormous volume, and ear drum crushing lyrics complimented by extreme volume. While other bands of the era were looking for their cosmetic cases, Maiden was looking for more voltage!

Killers (#12, 1981) was the first album to really introduce the band, although albeit it was going to take some time to warm up to these boys. With song titles reminiscent of Black Sabbath, Maiden fans delighted in tunes such as "Children of the Damned" and "The Number of the Beast,"—the band often drew inspiration from popular cult films.

The Number of the Beast, with new vocalist Bruce "Air Raid Siren" Dickinson, was the first in a series of seven albums that would "sell metal (gold or platinum)" in the U.S. despite virtually no radio airplay or MTV exposure. But by the late 80s, sales began to slip and although the band had suffered numerous personnel changes over the years, it had always managed to sustain itself. When Bruce Dickinson departed in 1993, though, everyone associated with the band became concerned. He was replaced by Blaze Bayley (Wolfsbane).

Iron Maiden has an enormous cult following and is heavily collected, so numerous unique items may command a significant price.

AUTOGRAPHS

An LP, magazine cover, ad, photo, or card signed by the group: $20-$60*
*Lineup dependent

TOUR BOOKS/PROGRAMS/PASSES

Programs:
1985 Japan Tour: $75
1992 Fear of the Dark (U.K.) $25
1990/91 No Prayer on the Road (U.K.): $25
1993 Real Live Tour: $20
Backstage Passes:
Cloth: $10; Laminated: $20

POSTERS/PRESS KITS

Promotional Posters: $10-$55
Press Kits: $20-$65
"Piece of Mind" - 1 photo, 9 pg. bio, scarce: $50

USED CLOTHING/EQUIPMENT

Guitar Picks: $10-$20
Drum Sticks: $15

OFTEN OVERLOOKED MEMORABILIA

Various necklaces - $15-$20, metal pins - $15-$25, buttons - $5; any and all artifacts surrounding the controversial and withdrawn Maragret Thatcher sleeve design for Women in Uniform/Invasion, 1980; Seventh Son, EMI promotional torch in a box, 1988; Somewhere in Time, Capitol promotional watch with Eddie on the face, 1986; The band's personal Christmas card with printed signatures - $20-$30

REFERENCES/BOOKS

Limited resources exist and nothing that does justice to the band in my opinion; no dedicated collector books

Isaak, Chris

Born: June 6, 1956

A mid-80s singer/songwriter typically associated with "Wicked Game" (#6, 1981), this retro-crooner and countrybilly enthusiast came to the light of many when *USA TODAY* included his self-titled debut among the Top Ten recommended albums of 1987. *Heart Shaped World* (#7, 1991) followed, due to strong sales resulting from the extract "Wicked Game," which was featured in the movie *Wild At Heart*. *San Francisco Days* (#35, 1993), his first album in more than three years, garnered some attention for its back-to-the-roots approach before the release of Isaak's next project, *Forever Blue* (#31, 1995). The extract "Somebody's Crying (#45, 1995) nearly sold into the Top Forty as the artist continued to maintain dual careers as an actor/musician.

Chris Isaak. Photo by Henry Diltz. Courtesy Reprise Records.

AUTOGRAPHS
An LP, magazine cover, ad, photo, or card signed by the artist: $20-$35

TOUR BOOKS/PROGRAMS/PASSES
Backstage Passes:
Cloth: $8; Laminated: $10-$12

POSTERS/PRESS KITS
Promotional Posters: $8-$20
Press Kits: $15

USED CLOTHING/EQUIPMENT
Guitar Picks: $10-$20

OFTEN OVERLOOKED MEMORABILIA
Wicked Game, Reprise promotional jigsaw puzzle 1990; Blues Hotel, Reprise promotional luggage tag 1991; movie memorabilia from *Let's Get Lost*, *Married to the Mob* (1988), *Blue Velvet*, *Wild At Heart*, *Silence Of The Lambs*, *Twin Peaks*, *Fire Walk With Me*, *Little Buddha*, and *Mr. Wrong*; videotapes from his numerous television appearances including *The Last Resort* (1987), *Days of Our Lives*, *The Preppie Murder*, *Private Eyes*, *The Tonight Show* (4/9/91, 5/18/93, 7/11/95), *Saturday Night Live* (5/11/91), "Coca-Cola Pop Music Backstage Pass to Summer" (6/16/91), *Late Show With David Letterman* (9/8/93, 5/25/94, 12/28/95), *Later With Jools Holland* (5/27/95), and *Friends* (1996); copies of his spreads in numerous fashion magazines including *Esquire*, *Elle*, and *People*.

The Isley Brothers

Formed Early 1950s

Rudolph Isley, Born: April 1, 1939, Ronald Isley, Born: March 21, 1941, O'Kelly Isley, Born: December 25, 1937, Died: March 31, 1986, and Vernon Isley, Died: 1955*

*Ernie and Marvin Isley were added in 1969 along with Chris Jasper and Everett Collins. Ernie and Marvin Isley, along with Chris Jasper, left in 1984. In 1990, Ronald, Rudolph, Ernie, and Marvin Isley reunited.

This enduring soul, R&B, and pop band's success has spanned generations not only to its audience, but also inside the band through its members. The Isley Brothers first came to light in the late '50s with the hit single "Shout," which was later followed by "Twist and Shout." It was during the early '60s that the band toured heavily, supported by a backup band which included Jimmy James (Hendrix). Hendrix spent most of 1964 with the band and made his first recordings with the group, much of which is contained on *In the Beginning...with Jimi Hendrix* (1971).

In 1965 the band moved to Motown and scored a hit with "This Old Heart of Mine" (#12, 1966) and after living in England for a few years, returned to release the songs "It's Your Thing" (#2, 1969)—also a Grammy winner—"I Turned You On" (#23, 1969), and "Pop That Thang" (#24, 1972).

During the next phase of the band, which included brothers Ernest and Marvin Isley, brother-in-law Chris Jasper, and drummer Everett Collins, the band moved first toward successful covers such as "Love the One You're With" (#18, 1971) and "Spill the Wine" (#49, 1971). The group later followed with the hits "The Lady (Part I)" (#6, 1973), "Fight the Power (Part I)" (#4, 1975), and Number One R&B hits "The Pride" (1977), "Take Me to the Next Phase (Part 1)" (1978), "I Wanna Be With You (Part 1)" (1979), and "Don't Say Goodnight" (1980).

Numerous other R&B hits followed into the '80s and '90s. Also during these decades, the group's members were involved in a variety of projects: Ronald remade "This Old Heart of Mine" (#10, 1990) with Rod Stewart; Earnest, Marvin, and Chris Jasper left for their own band that had a Number One R&B hit with "Caravan of Love" (1985). O'Kelly died of a heart attack in 1986, while Rudolph went on to join the ministry. The group reunited in 1990 and two years later was inducted into the Rock and Roll Hall of Fame.

AUTOGRAPHS

An LP, magazine cover, ad, photo, or card signed by the group: $30-$125*
*Lineup dependent - without Hendrix.

OFTEN OVERLOOKED MEMORABILIA

Memorabilia associated with other musicians' covers of their songs; an autographed copy of "Love Is a Wonderful Thing" by Michael Bolton

It's A Beautiful Day

Formed 1968

David LaFlamme, Linda LaFlamme, Val Fuentes, Patti Santos, Hal Wagenet, and Michael Holman*

*Numerous personnel changes

This late-60s pop vocal band is best remembered for the song "White Bird," penned by David LaFlamme, and for having two of the band's later members form Pablo Cruise in 1973 (Bud Cockrell and David Jenkins).

AUTOGRAPHS

An LP, magazine cover, ad, photo, or card signed by the group: $7-$10

Jackson, Alan

Born: October 17, 1958

Alan Jackson was born and raised in Newnan, Georgia. The youngest of five, he was the only boy. His father was a mechanic, so naturally the younger Jackson's first love was cars and by the age of ten he already had his first car—a toy '68 Mustang. His first real car was a white 1955 Thunderbird convertible; he got it about the same time his family purchased its first stereo. It was then that he slowly developed a greater interest in music. He graduated from Newnan High School in 1976 before a brief stint at West Georgia Community College.

While job hopping and dating his sweetheart Denise, Jackson joined his first band, Dixie Steel. At the time he was just singing and having fun, and had little interest in music as a career. Finally, when the urge was starting to take hold, he decided he had to head to Nashville. At a chance meeting in an airport, Denise cornered the Rhinestone Cowboy himself, Glen Campbell. He gave her some advice and a business card from Glen Campbell Music. Following an interview in Nashville, Alan was offered a job as a staff songwriter for the company.

His struggling artist phase came in 1985 and lasted until 1989. It was then that he found himself inspired by some of country music's heroes like Merle Haggard, Hank Williams, Jr., and George Jones. Fortunately for Jackson, during the '80s the world of country music was changing. The arrival of Randy Travis and George Strait found Nashville marketing artists' looks just as much as their music. "Country Hunks" were in, while "Opry Fossils" were out!

Strait was the first "hat act" (many others followed), and record companies jumped at a chance to sign fresh talent. While working at the music publishing firm was fun, it didn't pay the bills, so Jackson took a job as the mailboy at The Nashville Network. Jackson then went on to form a backup band, the Strayhorns, to play his compositions on the Nashville circuit.

In 1988, Arista Records decided to open a country division of its label while scouting for new talent in Nashville. The label's initial signings included Jackson, Pam Tillis, and Brooks and Dunn. *Here in the Real World* was originally released on February 27, 1989, and was far from an overnight success. "Blue Blooded Woman," the first extract, was released on September 29, but it wasn't until the title cut was released as a single that people really started to take notice. Now wearing a white Stetson, Jackson was also dubbed part of the "hat acts" movement, along with Garth Brooks and Clint Black. The end of 1990 saw Jackson firmly planted in the spotlight with a hit album and a popular video collection.

His sixteen Number One songs "Chattahoochee," "Gone Country," "She's Got The Rhythm (And I Got The Blues)," "Midnight In Montgomery," "Chasin' That Neon Rainbow," "Don't Rock The Jukebox," "Livin' On Love," "Summertime Blues," "Love's Got a Hold On You," "(Who Says) You Can't Have It All," "Home," "Wanted," "I Don't Even Know Your Name," "Dallas," "Here In The Real World," "Someday," "Mercury Blues," and "I'd Love You All Over Again" quickly established him as a force to be reckoned with in country music. So strong was Jackson's appeal that his *Alan Jackson: The Greatest Hits Collection* debuted at number one on the country charts and number five on the pop charts. "Everything I Love" (#12, 1997) was released in 1997, while *The Greatest Hits* still lingered on the Billboard 200.

AN ALAN JACKSON PILGRIMAGE TO NEWNAN, GEORGIA

Place	Comments
Elm Street School	Alan's mom worked there occasionally
The Newnan High School Auditorium	Where Alan got his first shot at show business
Dairy Queen	Where Alan met his high school sweetheart and future bride
Ford Dealership	Go in and grab a brochure at Alan's former employer

ALAN JACKSON COLLECTIBLE MAGAZINES
(Assorted and Selected Titles)

Magazine	Issue(s)
Country America	1/94, 11/95
Country Beat	Summer 1993, Winter 1993, 10/1/94
Country Confidential	1/1/93
Country Fever	3/93, 9 & 10/94, 7 & 8/95
Country Guitar	1994
Country Music	3 & 4/92, 1/93, 5/94, 11/95
Country Song Roundup	1/93, 5 & 6/95
Country Spirit	9/1/92
Country Weekly	4/5/94, 4/19/94, 9/20/94, 4/4/95, 10/31/95, 11/21/95, 11/21/95
Entertainment Weekly	3/20/92, 9/24/93, 11/6/93, 7/8/94
Headliner	Summer 1993
Modern Screen's Country Music	5/92, 5/1/92, 2/93, 6/21/92, 9/95, 12/95
Modern Screen's Country Music Special	6/92, 12/93
Music City News	8/90, 5/95
New Country	Holiday Special, 1994
New Country Music	3/94
People	Fall 1994, 9/2/91, 5/4/92
Rolling Stone	4/16/92
Starline's Garth Brooks & Country...	1/91
Tune-In	4/90, 1/91, 12/92, 8/94
Us	8/94

*Note: All range in price from $3-$7

AUTOGRAPHS
A CD, LP, magazine cover, ad, photo, or card signed by the artist: $25-$75

TOUR BOOKS/PROGRAMS
Tour Books: $10-$12
Backstage Passes:
Cloth: $8-$10; Laminated: $10-$15

POSTERS/PRESS KITS
Promotional Posters: $10-$25
Press Kits: $20 - $30

USED CLOTHING/EQUIPMENT
Guitar Picks: $10-$20

OFTEN OVERLOOKED MEMORABILIA
Videotapes of his television performances on: various award shows, *The Tonight Show* (11/7/95), *Home Improvement* (11/95); a box of Dixie Steel nails - $5; magazines (see below); all Fruit of the Loom associated items (1995); cookbook, *Who Says You Can't Cook It All?*; Alan Jackson Visa

Alan Jackson paper backstage pass

An Alan Jackson guitar pick

card (1-800-615-4101); videotapes *Alan Jackson: Livin', Lovin', and Rockin' That Jukebox* (1993)

REFERENCES/BOOKS
Country Hunks by Mark Bego, 1994: $20; *Alan Jackson: Gone Country* by Mark Bego, 1996: $20

The Jackson 5/The Jacksons/ The Jackson Family

Formed 1964

Jackie Jackson (Sigmund Esco), Born: May 4, 1951; Tito Jackson (Toriano Adaryll), Born: October 15, 1953; Marlon Jackson, Born: March 12, 1957; Jermaine Jackson, Born: December 11, 1954; and Michael Jackson, Born: August 29, 1958*

*Randy Jackson was added in 1975. The Jackson Family (mid-1970s), also included Maureen "Rebbie" Jackson, La Toya Jackson, and Janet Jackson.

Sixties Indiana family group, which rose to pop prominence with hit singles such as "I Want You Back" (#1, 1970), "ABC" (#1, 1970), "The Love You Save" (#1, 1970), "I'll Be There" (#1, 1970), "Mama's Pearl" (#2, 1971), "Never Can Say Goodbye" (#2, 1971), "Sugar Daddy" (#10, 1972), "Lookin' Through the Windows" (#16, 1972), and "Dancing Machine" (#2, 1974), the Jackson 5 set the precedence for the many similar acts that followed.

Although the brothers typically took the back seat to Michael, they too were a bundle of talent. Although Jackie's solo career wasn't much to write home about, Jermaine managed to put together a solid solo effort and found himself atop the R&B charts in 1980. Through the media, especially television, the Jacksons won over the hearts of American youth and adults. They slowly became role models for an entire new generation.

Eventually, like so many Motown artists, the label's heavy hand restricted the group's artistic control. After capturing thirteen Top Twenty hits for the record giant, the Jackson 5 departed for a lucrative deal with Epic Records. All Motown artifacts, most of which are scarce, are highly sought by Jackson collectors.

The group, now simply the Jacksons, moved over to Epic Records officially on March 10, 1976; their first single on the label was "Enjoy Yourself" (#6, 1977). "Shake Your Body (Down to the Ground)" (#7,

1979), and "Lovely One" (#12, 1980) landed on the charts just prior to the band taking some time off for a couple of years. "State of Shock" (#3, 1984), "Torture" (#17, 1984), and in particular the Victory Tour, brought the group back into the spotlight, but it was the beginning of the end for the band. The tour, produced by boxing legend Don King, was marred by so much controversy, that wasn't a surprise to learn that members went their separate ways following the event.

The Jackson dynasty began unraveling after the breakup, however, there were plenty of indications that it was inevitable. The next decade found the group members in the news more for controversy rather than for musical accomplishments. With the exception of Michael and Janet's careers, the family's halo became heavily tarnished. While the group's place in pop history is certainly secure, it's unfortunate that the circumstances couldn't have been better.

AUTOGRAPHS
A CD, LP, magazine cover, ad, photo, or card signed by the group: $275-$400

TOUR BOOKS/PROGRAMS
Backstage Passes:
Cloth: $12-$20; Laminated: $20-$40

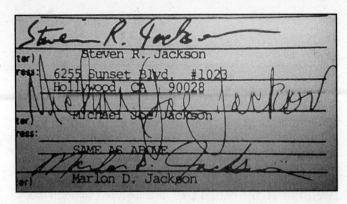

Signed contract from the Jackson 5

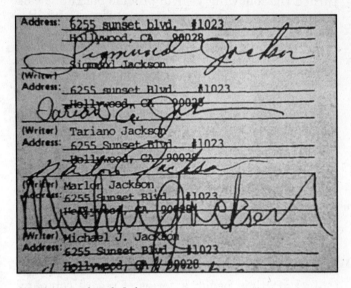

Signed contract from the Jacksons

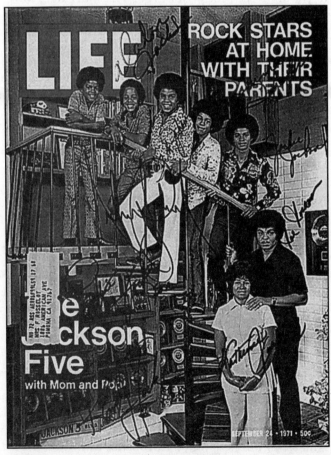

A Sept. 24, 1971 autographed copy of Life *magazine. (Includes signatures from the Jacksons' parents.) Photo courtesy Phillips Son & Neale.*

POSTERS/PRESS KITS
Promotional Posters: $15-$75
Press Kits: $20-$100

OFTEN OVERLOOKED MEMORABILIA
Artifacts from the numerous talent shows they participated in during the their early years; associated artifacts from Mr. Lucky's, the Gary, IN, nightclub where the group debuted; videotapes of the group's numerous television performances including *Hollywood Palace* (10/18/69) (national TV debut), *The Ed Sullivan Show* (12/14/69), *Diana!* (4/18/71), *Goin' Back to Indiana* (9/19/71), *Jackson 5* (animated cartoon series) (9/11/71-), *The Jacksons* (summer variety show) (June 1976-July 1976), *The Jacksons* (January 1977-March 1977), "25 Years of Motown" (5/16/83), "The Jacksons: An American Dream" (1992), and "The Jackson Family Honors" (1994); all artifacts from the group's first gig as a headliner at the Convention Center, Philadelphia, PA (5/2/70); a Jackson 5 Boulevard street sign; all Victory Tour memorabilia; "We Are the World" artifacts

REFERENCES/BOOKS
Numerous resources exist, but nothing that does justice to the band in my opinion; no dedicated collector books

Jackson, Freddie

Born: October 2, 1958

Like many of us, Jackson began singing in church, while growing up in Harlem. He left high school and began working in a bank as a computer operator, saving money where he could with dreams of pursuing his artistic career. He played the New York nightclub circuit in a band called LJE, but decided to head west in 1983 to join the R&B outfit Mystic Merlin. He returned the following year to provide backup vocals on numerous tours for artists including Harry Belafonte, Evelyn King, and Melba Moore. It was the latter who signed and inked him to a recording deal with Capitol Records.

Rock Me Tonight (#10, R&B, 1985), his debut release, included the hit extracts "Rock Me Tonight (For Old Times Sake)" (#18, 1985) and "You Are My Lady" (#12, 1985). The success of the album and supporting tour with Moore, catapulted Jackson into the spotlight. *Just Like the First Time* (#23, 1986), his sophomore release, picked up right where its predecessor left off—it went platinum, while the hits continued, including "Tasty Love" (#1, 1986), "A Little Bit More" (#1, 1986)—a duet with Melba Moore—"Do Me Again" (#1, 1991), and "Main Course"(#2, 1991). He was the only artist in the '80s to have six R&B chart-toppers.

Jackson then began a series of record company hopping, in hopes of furthering his chart success. *Here It Is* (#11, R&B, 1994) was his first release on the RCA label. He then moved on to the Scotti Bros. label for *Private Party* (#28, R&B, 1995), which barely made it into the Top Two Hundred album chart.

AUTOGRAPHS

A CD, LP, magazine cover, ad, photo, or card signed by the artist: $10-$20

TOUR BOOKS/PROGRAMS

Backstage Passes:

Cloth: $8; Laminated: $8-$12

POSTERS/PRESS KITS

Promotional Posters: $10-$15

Press Kits: $15

OFTEN OVERLOOKED MEMORABILIA

Videotapes of his television performances on *Melba and Friends* (1986), *Happy New Year America* (12/31/86), and *The Tonight Show* (5/7/91); memorabilia from his Up Close And Personal tour , which was part of the Budweiser Music Festival (1988); movie memorabilia from *Def By Temptation* (1989); memorabilia from his inclusion in the 1992 Benson & Hedges Blues concert series; items related to his Grand Marshall status at the Martin Luther King, Jr. National Parade of Celebration (1994)

Jackson, Janet

Born: May 16, 1966

No longer in the shadows of her brothers, Janet Jackson has emerged to forge her own brilliant career, untarnished, and shining brightly. The youngest of nine, she appeared in her brothers' stage show at the early age of seven. She made her television debut on *The Jacksons* (U.S., CBS-TV) summer variety show on June 16, 1976. The following year she would begin to appear on other shows and sitcoms including *Good Times*, *Different Strokes*, *Fame*, and *A New Kind of Family*.

Her debut album on A&M Records, *Janet Jackson* (#63, 1983), sold well and spun off her first two successful singles "Young Love"(#64, 1982) and "Come Give Your Love To Me" (#58, 1983). She was managed by her father Joseph—a legend in the entertainment business—who helped guide the early years of her career.

Dream Street (#147, 1984), her sophomore effort, like her first album, had moderate sales, but failed to generate the anticipated interest. The year was also marked by her first marriage, to James DeBarge of the musical group DeBarge. The marriage, however, was annulled seven months later.

The lack of interest in her first two albums had A&M executive and family friend John McClain suggesting a new production team made up of Jimmy Jam and Terry Lewis. In January 1986, *Control* (#1, 1986) was released and quickly raced to the top of the charts. The album contained numerous hits including "What Have You Done For Me Lately" (#4, 1986), "Nasty" (#3, 1986), "When I Think of You" (#1, 1986), "Control" (#5, 1987), "Let's Wait Awhile" (#2, 1987), and "The Pleasure Principle" (#14, 1987). Also driving the success of the album was her brilliantly choreographed videos, most of which were done by Paula Abdul.

In 1987, Janet dismissed her father from his responsibilities as manager before recording *Rhythm Nation 1814* (#1, 1989). Although following the success of *Control* seemed an impossible task, Jackson performed eloquently, while the album yielded the hit singles "Miss You Much" (#1. 1989), "Rhythm Nation" (#2, 1990), "Escapade" (#1, 1990), "Alright" (#4, 1990), "Come Back to Me" (#2, 1990), "Black Cat" (#1, 1990), and "Love Will Never Do (Without You)" (#1, 1990). The album marked the first time an artist achieved seven top five hits from the same album. To support the album, Jackson also embarked on her first major tour, The Rhythm Nation World Tour 1990. The tour included ninety-six sold-out North American dates, twenty European, and fifteen Far East.

On March 11, 1991, Jackson signed the most lucrative contract in recording history with Virgin

Two Janet Jackson autographed LPs. Estimated value for the two is between $300 and $500. © Butterfield & Butterfield, Auctioneers Corp., 1997.

Records. On June 5, 1993, *janet* (#1, 1993) exemplified the strength of her work and debuted at the top of the album charts. Extracted hit singles from the album included "That's the Way Love Goes" (#1, 1993), "If" (#4, 1993), and "Again" (#1, 1994). In contrast to her previous work, both her songs and stage presence took on a new sexual aura, which she managed to pull off successfully.

On June 17, 1995, "Scream," the Michael and Janet collaboration, became the highest debuting single in U.S. chart history, besting the Beatles' #6 "Let It Be." *Design of a Decade 1986/96* (#3, 1995) was released by A&M Records and included all of her hits and two new cuts. Extracted single "Runaway" (#3, 1995) quickly climbed up the singles chart.

As a subject, Janet Jackson, with her multiple talents, is fascinating to collect. As successful as her recording career has been, more can certainly be done on the marketing side. Collectors of her memorabilia are craving for more Janet! As the success of Terry Lewis, Jimmy Jam, and Janet Jackson continues to seem boundless, one wonders if there are any others challenges these three can not conquer!

Outstanding Janet tour program! (© 1993 Juggernaut Productions, Inc.)

AUTOGRAPHS

A CD, LP, magazine cover, ad, photo, or card signed by the artist: $25-$75

A few examples of Janet backstage passes (Printed by OTTO)

TOUR BOOKS/ PROGRAMS

Tour Books: Janet World Tour: $15 1990 Japan Tour: $35

Backstage Passes: Cloth: $8-$10; Laminated: $20

POSTERS/ PRESS KITS

Promotional Posters: $10-$30

Press Kits: $20-$45

OFTEN OVERLOOKED MEMORABILIA

Rhythm Nation set of four buttons - $6-$8; memorabilia from the movie *Mo' Money* (the soundtrack includes a Jackson song); memorabilia from movie *Poetic Justice*, Janet's movie debut; Rhythm Nation earrings - $10; set of five different Pro Stock rock cards - $2; Rhythm Nation hat - $25-$30; Design of the Decade giant cut-out (26" x 33") - $50; Rhythm Nation "flip" book - $10

REFERENCES/BOOKS

Numerous resources exist, but nothing that does justice to the singer in my opinion; no dedicated collector books; serious fans should opt for her fan club: Friends of Janet, P.O. Box 884988, San Francisco, CA 94188 ($19 fee)

Jackson, Joe

Born: August 11, 1954

Jackson began studying music at an early age, first the violin, then the piano. Although he later studied percussion instruments, he enjoyed the freedom he had in songwriting on the piano. He attended London's Royal Academy of Music on a scholarship from 1971 to 1974. After a short stint with a band called Arms and Legs, he became a featured performer and eventual music director at the local Playboy club in 1977.

In February 1978 he signed with A&M Records, having been overlooked by other record companies. *Look Sharp!* (#20, 1979) was his debut effort and included extracted singles "Is She Really Going Out With Him?" (#21, 1979), "Sunday Papers," and "One More Time." Released six months later, *I'm a Man* (#22, 1980) continued Jackson's momentum, but failed to include a U.S. hit single. Trying to avoid the incessant music labels being thrown at him, he released *Beat Crazy* (#41, 1980), a somewhat jazz, somewhat reggae, and somewhat confusing mix of music. Billed for the first time as The Joe Jackson Band, the new title and album did little commercially, and the band split in December.

Within months Jackson was back in the studio working on *Joe Jackson's Jumpin' Jive* (#42, 1981), a new album of swing tunes. Although Jackson toured the U.S. with a big band, no hit singles emerged from the work. In 1982, Jackson relocated to New York to record a more mainstream sound. *Night and Day* (#4, 1982) was the result and it catapulted the artist into the spotlight, supported by the hit singles "Steppin' Out" (#6, 1982) and "Breaking Us In Two" (#18, 1983). In a departure, Jackson tried his luck at a soundtrack, *Mike's Murder* (#64, 1983), which yielded one single, "Memphis" (#85, 1983).

Body and Soul (#20, 1984), his next studio offering, included two extracted U.S. singles, "Happy Ending" (#57, 1984) and "You Can't Get What You Want (Till You Know What You Want)" (#15, 1984). From this point his popularity began to diminish in the U.S. *Big World* (#34, 1986), was a strong live offering, but *Will Power* (#131, 1987), *Live 1980/86* (#91, 1988), *Blaze of Glory* (#61, 1989), and *Laughter and Lust* (#116, 1991, Virgin) all fell short of sales expectations.

Night Music (1994, Virgin) was his first album in three years. It had a classical twist including four instrumental nocturnes. Although not as commercially successful as past releases, his maturity and interest in a variety of music has enabled him to sustain a strong cult following in the U.S.

AUTOGRAPHS

A CD, LP, magazine cover, ad, photo, or card signed by the artist: $15-$35

TOUR BOOKS/PROGRAMS

Backstage Passes:

Cloth: $5-$7; Laminated: $10-$12

POSTERS/PRESS KITS

Promotional Posters: $10-$15

Press Kits: $10-$15

OFTEN OVERLOOKED MEMORABILIA

His soundtracks from films such as *Mike's Murder* (1983), *Tucker* (1988), *Queen's Logic* (1990), and *Three of Hearts* (1992); I'm the Man, A&M promotional watch, 1979; Look Sharp, A&M promotional comb, 1979

Jackson, Mahalia

Born: October 26, 1911, Died: January 27, 1972

Mahalia Jackson is regarded as one of, if not the, greatest gospel singer ever. Influenced by the likes of Ma Rainey and Bessie Smith, Jackson's dynamic vocal range warmed the hearts of everyone she came in contact with and became an inspiration for the many great singers who would follow.

She regularly attended New Orleans' Mount Moriah Baptist Church and had a stern upbringing. When she could, however, she would enjoy the richness of New Orleans' jazz and blues. She listened to the records of both Smith and Rainey when she could, picking up every inflection, while memorizing some of the arrangements. In 1927, she found herself heading to Chicago, spending her days as a domestic nurse, and singing where she could. Five years later some Decca Records scouts heard singing at a funeral and signed her to a recording contract. She later moved on to the Apollo label, where she recorded her hallmark "Move On Up." During this period she was accompanied by pianist Mildred Palls, who herself was nothing short of a legend, and often considered the greatest gospel accompanist that ever lived.

In 1954 Jackson hooked up with Mitch Miller at Columbia Records, who set out to back her with an extensive array of both strings and choirs. While the music brought greater commercial appeal, it was far from the foundation that Jackson had laid in her earlier years. Decades after her death, her appeal and music legacy continues to grow.

AUTOGRAPHS

A magazine cover, ad, photo, or card signed by the artist: $100-$200

Born: August 29, 1958

1971-1975: MICHAEL'S MOTOWN YEARS

In 1969, the Jackson 5 were signed to the legendary Motown label. The family then moved to Los Angeles, CA, where the label was headquartered, and the Jackson 5 began work on building a recording career. Two years later, the group now firmly established, Michael Jackson signed as a soloist to the Tamla-Motown label, where he made his debut hit "Got To Be There" (#4, 1971).

Got To Be There (#14, 1972), his debut album, with the eponymous hit extract, was a hit with his growing audience. "Rockin' Robin" (#2, 1972), "I Wanna Be Where You Are" (#16, 1972), and "Ain't No Sunshine" (#8, U.K., 1972) quickly followed, before his next album, *Ben* (#5, 1972), was released. The album's self-titled extract quickly topped the U.S. singles chart.

Music and Me (#92, 1973) and *Forever Michael* (#101, 1975) were his next and final studio albums for Motown. Disappointed by album sales and the lack of strength of the album extracts "With a Child's Heart" (#50, 1973) and "Were Almost There," Michael Jackson, signed to Epic Records in 1975.

1979-1992: OF EPIC PROPORTION

Off the Wall, his Epic Records debut, made him the first solo artist to release four Top Ten hits from a single album: "Don't Stop Till You Get Enough" (#1, 1979), "Rock With You" (#1, 1979), "Off the Wall" (#10, 1980), and "She's Out of My Life" (#10, 1980). The attention attracted by the record aided the Jacksons' album *Triumph* to sell more than a million copies, while the band also enjoyed a very successful tour. It was becoming increasingly clear, however, that Michael had become the focal point of the band.

In 1980, Jackson penned "Girlfriend" (#41, U.K., 1980) with Paul McCartney, and the duo later followed it up with "The Girl Is Mine" (#2, 1982) and "Say Say Say" (#2, U.K., 1983). Diana

Michael Jackson autographed Moonwalker poster. Estimated value for the poster is between $1,200 and $1,500. © Butterfield & Butterfield, Auctioneers Corp., 1997.

Ross took "Muscles" (#10, 1982), another Jackson song, up the singles chart, while Jackson waited for the release of his next album.

In 1983, Michael Jackson released *Thriller* (#1, 1982), a landmark album for both solo artists and the music industry. It spent a record thirty-seven weeks at the top of the U.S. album chart. From the album came a record seven Top Ten U.S. singles: "This Girl Is Mine" (#2, 1982), "Billie Jean" (#1, 1983), "Beat It" (#1, 1983), "P.Y.T. (Pretty Young Thing)" (#10, 1983), "Wanna Be Startin' Somethin'" (#5, 1983), "Human Nature" (#7, 1983),

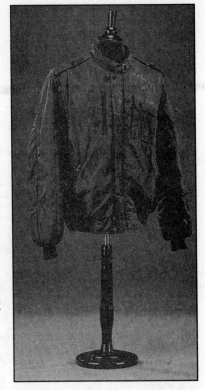

Michael's personal jacket from his Bad Tour. The jacket is signed on the upper left breast. Estimated value for the jacket is between $2,000 and $2,500. © Butterfield & Butterfield, Auctioneers Corp., 1997.

and "Thriller" (#4, 1983). The latter was the source for an elaborate fourteen-minute video, with state-of-the-art special effects, directed by John Landis. Jackson was later credited for breaking the de facto color line at MTV, where up to this point few black artists were receiving extensive play.

On January 27, 1984, Jackson was admitted at the Cedars-Sinai Medical Center with second-degree burns on his skull, following an accident on the set on the second day of filming a Pepsi commercial at the Shrine Auditorium. It was during this period that rumors abound regarding the artist's use of plastic surgery and other reconstructive work. These allegations, along with a constantly growing list of others, would continue to periodically haunt the artist.

Jackson then joined his brothers on a supporting tour for the Jacksons' *Victory*, while extracted single "State of Shock" (#3, 1984) featured a duet with Mick Jagger and was the first hit from the record. Although the Victory tour shows were nothing short of spectacular, the event itself was plagued by controversy. From financial to organizational issues, the tour, which was promoted by Hall of Fame Boxing promoter Don King, was a major source of dissatisfaction for the artist.

In 1985, a year that would see no new singles or album releases by the solo artist, Jackson cowrote "We Are the World" (#1, 1985) with Lionel Ritchie. He also starred in a fifteen-minute 3D sci-fi film,

Michael Jackson's stage-worn "Bad" outfit. Photo courtesy Phillips Son & Neale.

Captain Eo, which was featured in a special movie theatre at Disneyland and Disneyworld. Jackson finished the year by purchasing the ATV music publishing catalogue for $47.5 million. The prestigious catalog included more than 250 Lennon/McCartney songs.

Bad (#1, 1987) was Jackson's successful follow-up to *Thriller*. The record included five Number One hits: "I Just Can't Stop Loving You," "Bad," "The Way You Make Me Feel," "Man in the Mirror," and "Dirty Diana." The record was heavily promoted by a very expensive, yet successful tour. Large in comparison to similar tours, Jackson's entourage alone consisted of 250 people. By the end of the decade the artist had moved into his 2,700-acre "Neverland" California Ranch. The home, reportedly purchased for just under $30 million, includes a movie theater, amusement park rides, and an exotic menagerie, all under the watchful eye of a forty person security staff.

In 1991 Jackson signed a $65 million deal with the Sony Corporation. The contract promised him an extensive share of the profits from his next six albums, now on his own label. It also gave the artist a roll in developing software products, some movie options, and numerous other enticements. *Dangerous* (#1, 1991) included the hit extracts "Black and White" (#1, 1991), "Remember the Time" (#3, 1992), and "In the Closet" (#6, 1992). Jackson, determined to outsell his previous album, embarked on another extensive world tour. "Jam" (#26, 1992) also climbed the U.S. singles chart.

1993-PRESENT: MAKING HISTORY

On January 31, 1993, Michael Jackson performed during half-time of Super Bowl XXVII at the Rose Bowl in Pasadena, CA, in front of an estimated viewing audience of 133.4 million people. The year, however, will be remembered most for allegations made against the artist claiming the sexual abuse of a thirteen-year old boy. The incident would permanently haunt the enormously successful singer and humanitarian, and would take its toll on both Jackson and his devoted fans.

On January 25, 1994, a private settlement was announced between lawyers representing Jackson and the alleged victim. On May 26, 1994, Jackson and Lisa Marie Presley were married in La Vega, Dominican Republic, by civil judge Hugh Francisco Alvarez Perez. The event was denied during the numerous months that followed, and speculation regarding the sincerity of the event also surfaced in the media.

HIStory: Past, Present, and Future Book 1 (#1, 1995), featuring hit extracts "Scream" (#5, 1995) and

"You Are Not Alone" (#1, 1995), debuted at the top of the U.S. album chart. "You Are Not Alone" become the first ever single to debut at Number One in the U.S. On December 6, 1995, Jackson collapsed on stage while rehearsing for an upcoming HBO special. Once diagnosed he would remain in the hospital until December 12, 1995. On January 18, 1996, Lisa Marie filed for divorce from Michael Jackson in a Los Angeles Court claiming "irreconcilable differences." *Blood on the Dance Floor: History in the Mix* (#24, 1997) kept Jackson on the album charts as he sorted through his personal life.

Michael Jackson, simply defined, may be "The Greatest Living International Performer." He is a fascinating subject to collect, mysterious to a fault, yet successful beyond anyone's wildest imagination. His skills as a dancer, singer, and songwriter are un-paralleled in the field of entertainment. Entire books have been written about the performer; many could also address the numerous collectibles associated with his career.

Michael signed this black fedora—"All My Love 1998." Its estimated value is between $800 and $1,000. Courtesy Christie's Images.

An autographed album cover from Michael Jackson

AUTOGRAPHS

A CD, LP, magazine cover, ad, photo, or card signed by the artist: $200-$350
Drawing: $1,750-$3,000
Signed pillowcase:
$800-$900
Signed promotional poster:
$600-$700

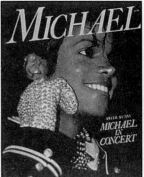

Outstanding Michael In Concert tour book (© 1984 Publications Int. Ltd.)

TOUR BOOKS/ PROGRAMS

Tour Books:
Michael In Concert:
$15-$20 (1984)
Japan Tour '87: $40
World Tour '88: $20
Backstage Passes:
Cloth: $12-$20;
Laminated: $20-$25
(1987-Present)

POSTERS/PRESS KITS

Promotional Posters:
$15-$25
1992 HBO Special promo poster
(27" x 40"): $20
Bad poster sold only on tour - stage shot
(23" x 35"): $10-$15
Press Kits: $40-$50
(Current Record)

USED CLOTHING/ EQUIPMENT

Backstage pass from the Dangerous World Tour (Printed by OTTO)

Clothing:
A rhinestone stage glove, white cotton, tagged:
$30,000-$35,000
"Bad" tour, personal jacket: $2,250-$2,500
Exotic stage jacket, worn in Pepsi commercial:
$12,750-$14,500
Leather jacket worn in Thriller video: $4,500-$5,000
Signed stage-worn fedora, 1989-90: $900-$1,200
Stage-worn shoes, signed: $7,000-$7,500

OFTEN OVERLOOKED MEMORABILIA

A videotapes from the following television appearances: *Diana* (1971), "25 Years of Motown," NBC-TV (5/16/83), "Michael Jackson - The Magic Returns" (1987), all his appearances at award ceremonies such as, *30th Annual Grammy Awards* (1988), *The Arsenio Hall Show* (11/16/89), *The Simpsons* (9/19/91), *MTV 10* - ABC-TV (11/27/91), "Entertainers '91" - ABC-TV (12/26/91), *Maury Povich Show* (9/2/92), "From Bucharest: The Dangerous Tour" (10/10/92), "An American Reunion: The 52nd Presidential Gala" (1/19/93) , *Oprah Winfrey* (2/10//93), "Michael Jackson Changes HIStory" - ABC-TV (7/28/1995); associated movie memorabilia from *Ben* (1972), *The Wiz* (1978), *Moonwalker* (1988), *Free Willy* (1993); any and all items associated with the storytelling record *ET* (1982) which was withdrawn due to a legal dispute, all items associated with his lucrative advertising deal with Pepsi Cola (1984, 1986); a copy of the Pepsi commercial that aired first on MTV (3/27/84); press clippings from his receipt of the Presidential Award from Ronald Reagan in June 1984; all items associated with his induction into *The Guinness Book of Records* at the American Museum of Natural History in New York; a jacket worn and autographed by elevator operator Hector Cormana; a rubbing from his Hollywood Star on the Walk of Fame, 6856, Hollywood, California; all *Captain Eo* artifacts; a copy of the September 21, 1986, *National Enquirer* - $10; all associated items from his brief relationship with L.A. Gear sportswear - included only one commercial; a copy of the Pepsi teaser commercial (2/24/87); all associated items surrounding his alleged interest in purchasing the remains of the Elephant Man (5/29/87); a copy of the Russian television commercial featuring Jackson (5/5/88); a copy of the California Raisins commercial featuring a "claymation" version of Jackson (9/18/89); all his commercially released videotapes including, *The Making of Michael Jackson's Thriller* and *The Legend Continues*; all copies of his promotional videos, especially those versions withdrawn such as the original "Black and White" (1991); newspaper accounts of his African Tour (1992); all items associated with MTV contest "My Dinner With Michael" (1992); *Ebony* magazine (5/30/92) issue - $7-$10; all items associated with Pepsi promotion "Someone Put Your Hand Out" single cassette offering; all associated items from his perfume line "Mystique de Michael Jackson" for women and "Legend de Michael Jackson" for men (1992); a videotape of Jackson's four-minute live satellite broadcast from Neverland Valley denying the charges made against him (12/22/93); the 1995 Michael Jackson calendar featuring the artist in a Boy Scouts of America scoutmaster's uniform - $10-$15; address book - $7; belts (LEE), 1984 - $20; binder - $10-$12; candy bar (1989) - $10; trading cards (Topps, Set of 33), 1984 - $20; Cassette and glove set (Motown, "16 Greatest Hits"), 1984 - $30; cereal box - (ET) - $50; cereal premium - $30-$45; COLORFORMS dress-up set - $20; comic book - $3; dolls (LJN) four varieties - $25-$50; doll cloths - $7-$17; folder - $5; glove (JC Penney) promotional 8" silver - $5; jigsaw puzzle (COLORFORMS), 500 pcs. - $10; key chains (various) - $7-$10; microphone (LJN) - $25; mug ("I (lips/love) Michael") - $15; notebook - $6; paper weight (Thriller) - $50; Michael's Pets (10 different) - $25-$32; Promotional Jacksons Pepsi cans - $5; radio (ERTL), 1984 - $30-$45; record player (1984), Vanity Fair - $125-$150; scarf (1983) - $5; stickers (various) - $1 each; View Master: GAF Talking, 1984 - $20-$30; GAF Thriller Gift Set - $20 $30; additional picture reels $5 each; wallet - $5; watch (LED) - $10; watch (Captain EO) - $20-$25; all items associated with Motown's release of Ben album with rat cover - withdrawn after one week; Magazines: *BAM* - $8, *Entertainment Weekly* - $6, *GQ* - $6-$8, *Musician* - $8, *NME* - $8-$15, *People* - $8-$10, *People Extra* - $15, *Record* - $8, *Rolling Stone* - $6-$12 (1983-Present), *Smash Hits* - $6, *Spin* - $8, *Spy* - $6, *Time* (3/19/84)- $20; Bad, Japan, 1987, Epic Records Box Set, includes CD, T-shirt, phone card, and tour book; Moonwalker promo hanging box display - $45

REFERENCES/BOOKS

Moonwalk, the artist's autobiography (1988); *Dancing the Dream*, also by Jackson (1992); *Michael Jackson, The Visual Documentary* by Adrian Grant: $20; *On the Road*

With Michael by Mark Bego: $10-$12; *The Michael Jackson Story*, Nelson George paperback, 1984: $10; *Live & Dangerous* by Grant: $10; *In His Own Words* by Dineen - $16; Tear Out Photo Book (U.K.): $15; *Complete Guide to the Music of Michael Jackson* by Brown: $8-$10; *The Michael Jackson Catalog* by Milt Machlin; *Sequins and Shades: The Michael Jackson Reference Guide* by Carol Terry. Serious fans should opt for his fan club: Michael Jackson Fan Club: The Legend Continues, P.O. Box 1160, 2301 Eb Leiden, Holland.

Jackson, Millie

Born: 1943

Jackson was born and raised in Georgia, where she lived with her grandfather who was a preacher. She ran away form home when she was fourteen and ended up in New York City, working as a model. Enticed by a bet, she began working as a singer, cut a single, and finally landed with Spring Records in 1971.

"A Child of God" (#22, R&B, 1972), "Ask Me What You Want"(#14, R&B, 1972), and "It Hurst So Good" (#3, R&B, 1973) were the first chart successes for this talented singer and songwriter. *Caught Up*, a concept live album that really showcased her abilities and brought her into the forefront in 1974. Extract "(If Loving You Is Wrong) I Don't Want To Be Right" (#42, 1974) nearly landed her in the Top Forty. The record also led to the successful sales of both *Feelin' Bitchy* and *Get It Out'cha System*. Unfortunately, Jackson's language often limited her airplay. "Royal Rappin's" (1979), a duet with Issac Hayes, was well received and picked up some ground for the performer.

In 1981 she headed to Nashville for *Just a Lil' Bit Country*, before she disappeared from the recording scene. She resurfaced on a duet with Elton John for his *To Be Continued* release and signed with Jive Records in 1985. *An Imitation of Love* (1986) managed a hit with "Hot! Wild! Unrestricted! Crazy! Love!" which climbed into the Top Ten R&B chart. She has not been able to regain the success that found her during the '70s.

AUTOGRAPHS

A magazine cover, ad, photo, or card signed by the artist: $10-$15

OFTEN OVERLOOKED MEMORABILIA

Movie memorabilia from *Cleopatra Jones* (1973)

Jackson, Wanda

Born: October 20, 1937

Wanda Jackson has had a diverse career. Often associated with her "Queen of Rockabilly" recordings of the late 50s, she has also worked as both a country and gospel singer. She was so gifted as a youth that by the age of fifteen she already had her own radio program on KLPR out of Oklahoma City. The following year she signed a record deal with Decca and eventually landed with Hank Thompson's swing band. She moved on to Capitol Records in 1956.

Although she had no Top Twenty hits, "Let's Have a Party (#37, 1960)—backed by Gene Vincent's Blue Caps—"Right or Wrong" (#29, 1961), and "In the Middle of a Heartache" (#27, 1961) all sold moderately well. She toured internationally and recorded in a variety of languages. During the '70s she became a born-again Christian and performed primarily religious based works at selected venues.

AUTOGRAPHS

A LP, CD or magazine cover, ad, photo, or card signed by the artist: $5-$10

Jagger, Mick: See the Rolling Stones

The Jaggerz/Donnie Iris

Formed 1965

Donald Iris, Ben Faiella, Thom Davies, James Ross, William Maybray, and James Pugliano*

*Iris departed in 1971

The Jaggerz are best remembered for the 1970 single and million seller "The Rapper" (#2, 1970). Led by frontman Donnie Iris, the group's debut single "Baby I Love You," with William Maybray on vocals, failed, as did the two follow-up singles to "The Rapper," "I Call My Baby Candy" and "What a Bummer." The departure of Iris in 1971 essentially ended the band's career.

Iris landed in Pittsburgh at a recording studio before joining Wild Cherry. "Play That Funky Music" gave Wild Cherry a platinum single, but Iris was still itching to get his solo career off the ground. His album Back on the Streets was eventually released by MCA, while his single "Ah! Leah" (#29, 1980) climbed into the Top Thirty. He followed the album up with King Cool, which yielded two Top Forty extracts: "Love Is Like a Rock" and "My Girl."

AUTOGRAPHS

A LP, CD, magazine cover, ad, photo, or card signed by the group: $20-$30*

*A single sleeve from "The Rapper"

The Jam/Paul Weller/Style Council

Formed 1973

Paul Weller, Born: May 25, 1958; Bruce Foxton, Born: September 1, 1955; and Rick Buckler, Born: December 6, 1955

Style Council formed in 1983

Paul Weller, Mick Talbot, and Dee Lee

Weller meets Buckler at a Sheerwater Secondary Modern school in 1975, where the two spend lunch hours jamming together, hence the name. They soon hook up with Foxton and Steve Brooks and begin performing at local social and mens' clubs. When Brooks leaves, Foxton moves to bass, while Weller establishes himself on guitar and lead vocal. They soon become a regular in London's top clubs, and even perform at the Marquee and 100 Club.

In 1977 they ink a deal with Polydor Records and release the debut single "In the City" (#40, U.K., 1977). The group resents the U.K. press which links it to the punk movement—the members instead fancy themselves more as members of a mod revival, wearing mohair suits and strumming Rickenbacher guitars. In the City (#20, U.K., 1977) is the band's debut album, and the band's exposure now extends to the BBC1-TV's Top of the Pops, where the band performs the single "All Around Town" (#13, U.K., 1977). "The Modern World" (#36, U.K., 1977) climbs into the U.K. Top Forty as the band embarks on a 16-date U.S. club tour that is far from impactful. This Is the Modern World (#22, U.K., 1977) is met with mild praise by critics, but still manages to aggressively climb the charts.

The band supports Blue Oyster Cult, in an odd pairing, on a U.S. tour during the spring of 1978. The band still has difficulty gaining any recognition in the U.S. despite high-volume U.K. singles production and Weller's unique guitar strokes. The band headlines the first day of the Reading Festival (8/25/78), prior to the release of singles "David Watts" (#25, U.K., 1978) and "Down in the Tube Station" (#15, U.K., 1978). The band finishes the year with the release of its next album All Mod Cons (#6, U.K., 1978). The band' string of U.K. hits continues in 1979 with "Strange Town" (#15, U.K., 1979), "When You're Young" (#17, U.K., 1979), and "The Eton Rifles" (#3, U.K., 1979).

The band starts out strong in the 1980s. Setting Sons (#137, 1980) becomes the group's first U.S. charting album and the U.K. single "Going Underground/The Dreams of Children" (#1, U.K., 1980) debuts at Number One. The band spends the summer attending numerous festivals, including the Pink Pop Festival. During the fall, "Start" (#1, U.K., 1980) tops the U.K. singles chart prior to the release of the next album, Sound Affects (#2, U.K., 1980).

"That's Entertainment" (#21, U.K., 1981) and "Funeral Pyre" (#4, U.K., 1981) highlight the band's single releases for 1981. The following year, while the band continues to slowly migrate up the U.S. charts, *The Gift* (#82, 1982) is released, which yields the Motownish single "Town Called Malice" (#1, U.K., 1982). On October 28, 1982, Weller announces that the band will split after the upcoming U.K. tour.

"Beat Surrender" (#1, U.K., 1982) sends the band off in style, but is ignored by U.S. radio. *Dig the New Breed* (#2, U.K., 1982), a 14-track live compilation, also takes little time to climb the U.K. charts. The band, now a rock legacy in the U.K., has left a definitive mark on music history, and it is certainly worth spending some time gathering artifacts, of which few surface in the U.S..

Weller then teams up with Mick Talbot in a duo they call Style Council. From 1983 to 1988, the band places seven hits in the U.K. Top Ten, while in similar contrast to Weller's former band, Style Council manages only one Top Thirty single stateside: "My Ever Changing Moods" (#29, 1984). The group eventually disbands in 1990, while Weller resurfaces in the Paul Weller Movement in 1991.

AUTOGRAPHS

Group:

A CD, LP, magazine cover, ad, photo, or card signed by the group: $35-$80

Individual:

Paul Weller: $20-$25

OFTEN OVERLOOKED MEMORABILIA

Videotapes from the group's television appearances on: BBC1-TV's *Top of the Pops* (8/20/77, 2/82), *Something Else* (August 1981), *The Tube* (11/5/82); copies of *Jamming* magazine (Est. 1981)

REFERENCES/BOOKS

Numerous resources exist, but nothing that does justice to the band in my opinion; no dedicated collector books

James, Elmore

(Elmore Brooks)
Born: January 27, 1918, Died: May 24, 1963

This slide guitarist and Chicago blues pioneer laid the foundation for his craft, most evident in songs such as "It Hurts Me Too," "Dust My Broom," "Shake Your Money Maker," and "The Sky Is Crying"—all now considered classics. His influence migrated into rock music, where Eric Clapton, John Mayall, and Duane Allman became his disciples.

AUTOGRAPHS

An LP, magazine cover, ad, photo, or card signed by the artist: $30-$100

James, Etta

(Jamesetta Hawkins)
Born: January 25, 1938

A dynamic soul singer whose work has spanned decades, Etta James is commonly associated with the songs "Roll With Me, Henry," "All I Could Do Was Cry," "My Dearest Darling," "If I Can't Have You," "At Last," and "Pushover," to name only a few. Through the mid-50s she was a mainstay with legendary R&B bandleader Johnny Otis, who also cowrote her first hit, "Roll With Me, Henry." She has played numerous festivals and even opened some dates for the Rolling Stones' 1978 U.S. Tour. In 1994 she picked up a Grammy for Best Jazz Vocal Performance for her album *Mystery Lady*.

In 1992 Etta James was inducted into the Rock and Roll Hall of Fame.

AUTOGRAPHS

A CD, LP, magazine cover, ad, photo, or card signed by the artist: $20-$40

OFTEN OVERLOOKED MEMORABILIA

Associated artifacts from other musicians covers of her work

James, Rick

(James Johnson)
Born: February 1, 1948

Late-70s punk funk showman, singer, songwriter, and performer Rick James is typically associated with his flamboyant stage image and the songs, "You and I" (#13, 1978), "Bustin' Out" (#6, 1979), "Give It to Me Baby" (#40, 1981), and "Super Freak (Part 1)" (#16, 1981). He had performed earlier in his career as Ricky Matthews, fronting the Canadian band the Mynah Birds, which also included Neil Young, Bruce Palmer, and Goldy McJohn—although they recorded, nothing was ever released.

James' pop career started sliding in the early '80s, and although he was often on the R&B chart, he also concentrated on other outside projects such as production. The '90s would be turbulent for the artist who would find himself doing jail time, although upon his release, he stated that the experience was significant in his drug rehabilitation.

AUTOGRAPHS

A CD, LP, magazine cover, ad, photo, or card signed by the artist: $10-$30

POSTERS/PRESS KITS

Promotional Posters: $8-$15
Press Kits: $10-$20

OFFEN OVERLOOKED MEMORABILIA

Associated artifacts from other musicians covers of his work; items relating to his legal battles with M.C. Hammer over sampling in "U Can't Touch This" (1990); periodical clipping relating to the legal problems that sent him to jail.

James, Tommy and the Shondells

Formed 1960

Tommy James (Thomas Jackson), Born: April 29, 1947; Ronald Rosman; Michael Vale; Vincent Pietropaoli; and George Magura*

*Pietropaoli and Magura left in 1965 and were replaced with Peter Lucia and Eddie Gray

This late-60s successful pop group, best remembered for the hits "Hanky Panky" (#1, 1966), "I Think Were Alone Now" (#3, 1967), "Mony Mony" (#3, 1968), "Crimson and Clover" (#1, 1969), and "Crystal Blue Persuasion" (#2, 1969), Tommy James and the Shondells disbanded after over a dozen Top Forty hits.

James later emerged as a solo act to score hits with "Draggin' the Line" (#4, 1971) and "Three Times in Love" (#19, 1980), while he watched numerous other musicians score hits with covers of his earlier material.

AUTOGRAPHS

A CD, LP, magazine cover, ad, photo, or card signed by the group: $15-$60

OFTEN OVERLOOKED MEMORABILIA

Associated artifacts from other musicians' covers of their work

The James Gang

Formed 1967

Jim Fox, Tom Kriss, and Glen Schwartz*

*Schwartz departed in 1969 and was replaced by Joe Walsh, Born: November 20, 1947. Kriss also departed and was replaced with Dale Peters. Walsh left in 1971 and was replaced by Dominic Troiano and Roy Kenner. Troiano left in 1973 and was replaced by Tommy Bolin, Born: 1951, Died: December 4, 1976. Group disbanded in 1974 then reformed in 1975 with Fox, Peters, Richard Shack, and Bubba Keith.

The James Gang, an early-70s Cleveland hardrock group, which built an enormous cult following that helped most of the group's releases sell gold and made them a popular live attraction, even opened for the Who in Europe in 1971. "Funk 49" and "Walk Away" were just a couple of the band's cult classics. The band's centerpiece was Guitarist Joe Walsh, who was integral to the group's success and when he departed in 1971, it was difficult for the band to sustain

itself despite the other strong members, many of whom would go on to other successful acts.

AUTOGRAPHS

A LP or magazine cover, ad, photo, or card signed by the group: $15-$35

Jan and Dean

Jan Berry, Born: April 3, 1941; and Dean Torrence, Born: March 10, 1941

Sixties surfing song duo Jan and Dean is best remembered for the songs "Baby Talk" (#10, 1959), "Surf City" (#1, 1963)—cowritten with Brian Wilson—"Honolulu Lulu " (#11, 1963), "Drag City" (#10, 1964), "Dead Man's Curve" (#8, 1964), "The Little Old Lady (from Pasadena)" (#3, 1964), and "Ride the Wild Surf" (#16, 1964). The duo charted more than a dozen Top Thirty singles.

The group's hit singles series came to an end when Berry, who handled the bulk of the duo's songwriting, crashed his Corvette into a parked truck at over 60 mph on Whittier Boulevard in Los Angeles, California on April 12, 1966. The three passengers with him were killed, and he sustained severe brain damage. It took years for Berry, who still suffers from partial paralyzation and speech difficulties, to recover. Torrence went on to design album covers, and even earned a Grammy for the feat, in his position as head of Kitty Hawk Graphics.

The group still performs, typically during summer oldies reunion tours. Surf's Up!

This 17" x 28" Jan and Dean poster for a June 15, 1963 show in Corte Madera, CA, was printed by Tilghman Press of Oakland, CA. Its estimated value is between $800 and $1,000. From the collection of Hank Thompson.

AUTOGRAPHS
A CD, LP, magazine cover, ad, photo, or card signed by the group: $20-$65*

*Vintage autographed on picture sleeve from "Ride The Wild Surf": $150-$200

OFTEN OVERLOOKED MEMORABILIA
Movie memorabilia from *Ride the Wild Surf* (1964) and *Back to the Beach*; videotapes of their numerous television appearances including *The T.A.M.I. Show*; a copy of the television movie *Dead Man's Curve* (1978); insert poster from "Jan and Dean," 1960 (Dore 101) scarce; all associated items from their Coca-Cola promo (1965); promotional items from "The Budweiser Fight Song (Be True to Your Bud)," (1984) Mike (Love) and Dean

---

Jane's Addiction/Porno for Pyros

Formed 1986

Perry Farrell (Bernstein), Born: March 29, 1959; Eric Avery, Born: April 25, 1965; David Navarro, Born: June 6, 1967; and Steve Perkins, Born: September 13, 1967

Porno for Pyros formed 1992

Farrell, Perkins, Peter DiStefano, and Martyn Le Noble

As a youth Perry Bernstein was no stranger to adversity. After his mother committed suicide, the family moved to Woodmere, Long Island, then onto Miami. He spent time working with his father who was jeweler in New York City's diamond district, before he decided to attend college. Following a nervous breakdown, he was forced to quit the college he was attending in Oceanside, California. He took the stage name Perry Farrell while working in a Newport Beach nightclub as an exotic dancer.

In 1981 he started Psi Com, which gained a strong local following. The group even released an indie-la-

bel EP before breaking up in 1985. Jane's Addiction was formed in Los Angeles, California, during the summer of 1986 after a mutual friend, who was also a prostitute, introduced Farrell to Eric Avery. The duo then added Stephen Perkins and Dave Navarro to complete the band. Fueled by the flamboyant and outrageous Ferrell, Jane's Addiction entered the L.A. arty rock scene, complimenting its Zeppelinesque sound with the lead singer's fetish for provocative undergarments.

Following the releases of *Jane's Addiction* (1987), a live set debut album on L.A.'s Triple X Records, the larger record companies began to take notice. Warner Brothers Records soon signed the band and it released *Nothing's Shocking* (#103, 1988). The band then supported the album by linking up with rock fossil Iggy Pop for a U.S. tour. The band's first extract, "Mountain Song," had its promotional video banned on MTV due to nudity.

"Been Caught Stealing" (#34, U.K., 1991), extracted from *Ritual de lo Habitual* (#19, 1990), raised some eyebrows, because the album featured Ferrell's nude sculptures. When some record chains refused to carry it, the band asked Warner Bros. to issue new cover art, simply a plain white wrapper with the First Amendment printed on it.

On July 18, 1991, the Ferrell-conceived Lollapalooza package tour opened in Phoenix, Arizona, while *Ritual de lo Habitual* became the group's first platinum certified album. Just over two months later, Ferrell decided to perform nude during the second half of what would turn out to be the band's final concert in Honolulu, Hawaii. The event preceded the lead singer's arrest and charge of being under the influence of a controlled substance on October 16, 1991.

In 1992, Ferrell decided to disband Jane's Addiction at the peak of its popularity, surprising both critics and fans. Ferrell and Perkins then went on to form Porno For Pyros, while Avery and Navarro formed the short-lived Deconstruction in 1993 (Navarro later joined the Red Hot Chili Peppers). *Porno for Pyros* (#3, 1993) debuted at its U.S. peak, in a strong initial sales performance.

AUTOGRAPHS
Group:
A CD, LP, magazine cover, ad, photo, or card signed by the group: $45-65
Individual:
Perry Ferrell: $15-$25

TOUR BOOKS/PROGRAMS
Backstage Passes:
Cloth: $8-$10; Laminated: $10-$15

POSTERS/PRESS KITS
Promotional Posters: $15-$25
Press Kits: $25

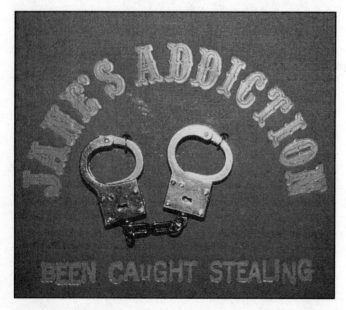

Been Caught Stealing handcuffs

The Ritual de lo Habitual Voodoo Doll in its original package

USED CLOTHING/EQUIPMENT

Guitar Picks:
Dave Navarro: $15-$25
Eric Avery: $5-$8

Drum Sticks:
Stephen Perkins: $15

OFTEN OVERLOOKED MEMORABILIA

A copy of the band's "Mountain Song" promotional video that was banned on MTV (1988); a copy of "Soul Kiss," a videomentary of the band (1989); all associated items surrounding the album release of *Ritual de lo Habitual* with original artwork; items associated with "Dedicated," a collection of Dead covers one of which is "Ripple" (#24, 1991) by Jane's Addiction; Ritual de lo Habitual Voodoo Doll - $35-$40; Been Caught Stealing handcuffs with key/CD single - $40-$45

Japan

Formed 1974

David Sylvian (Batt), Born: February 23, 1958; Steve Jansen (Batt), Born: December 1, 1959; Richard Barbieri; Mick Karn (Anthony Michaelides); and Rob Dean*

*Dean departed in 1981

Late-70s British forerunner to the New Romantic movement, Japan's synth-pop glam-rock is commonly associated with the songs "Quiet Life," "Ghosts," and "I Second That Emotion." The band had little impact in America, but sold well in the U.K. and Far East before it broke up in 1982.

AUTOGRAPHS

A CD, LP, magazine cover, ad, photo, or card signed by the group: $10-$25

****

"On The Edge"

Jars of Clay

Just when you thought you couldn't find an answer, behold it's right in front of you! Jars of Clay is proof that the simple path in life might just be the most rewarding. The music is fresh, simple, melodic, peaceful, and yet very inspirational. Dan Haseltine's lyrics compliment the group's pieces without trying to wrestle for dominance. If its silver lining doesn't tarnish with success, this group should shine for a long time. The group well worth watching, and it is perhaps even worthwhile to purchase a T-shirt, baseball cap, or poster. Contact: Jars of Clay Merchandise, c/o Zomba Merchandise Inc., P.O. Box 1771, New York, NY 10116-1771.

Jars of Clay. Photo by Norman Jean Roy. Courtesy Silvertone Records.

****

Jason and the Scorchers

Formed 1981

Jason Ringenberg, Warner Hodges, Jeff Johnson, and Perry Baggs*

*In 1986 Andy York and Ken Fox were added

Jason and the Scorchers, a mid-80s punk band, gained significant exposure while touring with R.E.M. in 1982. The band is typically associated with the songs "Absolutely Sweet Marie," "Lost Highway," and "19th Nervous Breakdown."

AUTOGRAPHS

A CD, LP, magazine cover, ad, photo, or card signed by the group: $5-$10

OFTEN OVERLOOKED MEMORABILIA

Memorabilia from the band's 1990 tour when it opened for Bob Dylan

Jay and the Americans

Formed 1961

John "Jay" Traynor, Kenny Vance (Rosenberg), Sandy Deane (Yagunda), and Howie Kane (Kirshenbaum)*

*In 1962 Marty Sanders and Jay Black were added, while Traynor departed.

Wholesome '60s vocal group, best remembered for the hits "She Cried" (#5, 1962), "Come a Little Bit Closer" (#3, 1964), "Cara Mia" (#4, 1965), and "This Magic Moment" (#6, 1969), Jay and the Americans stopped recording in 1970. Jay Black (David Blatt), who was actually the second Jay, later had a solo hit with "Love Is in the Air." The group also has the distinction of having both Donald Fagen and Walter Becker, the founders of Steely Dan, in its backup band in the early '70s.

AUTOGRAPHS

A CD, LP, magazine cover, ad, photo, or card signed by the group: $25-$65

OFTEN OVERLOOKED MEMORABILIA

Associated artifacts from other musicians' covers of their work

Jazzy Jeff and the Fresh Prince

Fresh Prince (Willard Smith), Born: September 25, 1969; and Jazzy Jeff (Jeff Townes), Born: January 22, 1965)

This late-80s "light rapping" duo, best known for the songs "Parents Just Don't Understand" (#12, 1988) and "Summertime" (#4, 1991), brought the multi-talented Will Smith into the spotlight. Smith landed a starring role in a television show *Fresh Prince*, which was followed shortly after by film roles in *Bad Boys* and later *Independence Day* and *Men in Black*, which have thrust him even further into the spotlight.

AUTOGRAPHS

A CD, LP, magazine cover, ad, photo, or card signed by the group: $15-$50

POSTERS/PRESS KITS

Promotional Posters: $10-$40
Press Kits: $15-$35

OFTEN OVERLOOKED MEMORABILIA

Movie memorabilia from *Six Degrees of Separation* (1993), *Bad Boys* (1995), *Independence Day* (1996), and *Men in Black* (1997)

Jefferson, Blind Lemon

Born: July, 1897, Died: December, 1930

Legendary pioneer bluesman of the '20s, arguably the most influential of all, Blind Lemon Jefferson influenced all of the greats who followed including Big Joe Williams, T-Bone Walker, and B.B. King. During the mid-20s he signed with Paramount Records where, thankfully, he laid down just some of his many great songs and even recorded religious songs under the moniker Deacon L.J. Bates. He is perhaps best known for songs such as "Black Snake Moan," "See That My Grave Is Kept Clean," "Long Lonesome Blues," and "Booger Rooger Blues."

AUTOGRAPHS

A related item from the period signed by the artist: $1,250-$2,500

OFTEN OVERLOOKED MEMORABILIA

Associated artifacts from other musicians' covers of his work

REFERENCES/BOOKS

Blind Lemon Jefferson by Bob Groom (1970)

Jefferson Airplane/Jefferson Starship/ Starship

Formed 1965

Original lineup: Marty Balin (Martyn Buchwald), Born: January 30, 1943; Paul Kantner, Born: March 12, 1941; Jorma Kaukonen, Born: December 23, 1940; Signe Anderson, Born: September 15, 1941; Skip Spence, Born: April 18, 1946; and Bob Harvey*

*Numerous personnel changes. See chart on page 396.

JEFFERSON AIRPLANE

Jefferson Airplane defined the psychedelic era of the '60s through its music. With a combination of folk, pop, jazz, and blues elements, the group established its sound with intricate vocal harmonies that migrated throughout its creative arrangements. Marty Balin (the Town Criers) formed the band in 1965 after meeting Paul Kantner at a local club, the Drinking Gourd. Kantner then recommended Kaukonen, whom he met at Santa Clara University. The group was then completed by the addition of vocalist Signe Anderson, Bob Harvey on bass, and Jer-

ry Peloquin on drums. The primary reason for the formation of the band was to play at a club (formerly the Honeybucket club) Balin had acquired at 3138 Fillmore St. in San Francisco.

The band made its live debut on August 13, 1965, at the opening of the Matrix club. A strong review of the performance in the newspaper resulted in the band receiving numerous record offers. A number of personnel changes occurred over the following months. Skip Spence replaced Peloquin, while Harvey was replaced by Jack Casady (the Triumphs). Meanwhile Kantner was impressed with Grace Slick, a singer from the band the Great Society, when he heard her sing at "A Tribute To Dr. Strange" dance on October 16, 1965.

On November 6, 1965, the band played at the first San Francisco Mime Troupe benefit, organized by Bill Graham, with whom the group developed a long and mutually respected relationship. On December 10, 1965, Jefferson Airplane, along with the Great Society, the John Handy Quintet, the Mystery Trend, and Sam Thomas & the Gentlemen's Band, played the inaugural concert held at Bill Graham's Fillmore Auditorium.

"It's No Secret," the band's debut single on RCA Records, was released on February 26, 1966, while the band quickly became one of the regular attractions at the Fillmore West. In May, Spence departed to head to Mexico, and was replaced by Spencer Dryden. Spence later returned to the Bay Area to form Moby Grape. In addition to showcasing its ability at the Fillmore during the year, the group also played at KFRC Presents The Beach Boys Summer Spectacular (6/24/66), the Berkeley Folk Festival (7/4/66) and the Monterey Jazz Festival—the first rock act to attend. Meanwhile, Anderson made her last appearances with the band during a fall stint at the Fillmore (10/15/66) and was replaced by Grace Slick, who made her debut with the band on October 16, 1966. Fortunately for the band, Slick brought with her two songs that she had been performing with the Great Society: "White Rabbit" and "Somebody To Love." *Jefferson Airplane Takes Off*, the group's debut album, was released in November of 1966.

In 1967, Bill Graham took over the management of Jefferson Airplane in what would prove to be a landmark year for the group. *Surrealistic Pillow* (#3, 1967), the first album featuring Slick, was released during the summer and featured the hits extracts "Somebody To Love" (#5, 1967) and "White Rabbit" (#8, 1967). *After Bathing at Baxter's* (#17, 1968) was a departure for the band and although it contained no hit singles, it did manage to break some new ground with "Spayre Change," a nine-minute psychedelic jam. It also marked the firing of Graham as manager and the group's first battle with RCA over obscene lyrics. On August 29, 1967, the band made its first European live performance at the Revolution club in London during a well-received overseas tour. *Crown of Creation* (#6, 1967), the band's next album, was an improvement over its predecessor with cuts like "Lather" and the David Crosby-penned "Triad." Personality clashes slowly developed at this point, with Slick garnering much of the attention. The end of the year found members Casady and Kaukonen forming the splinter band Hot Tuna.

Bless Its Pointed Little Head (#17, 1969), a live album, showcased the vocal battles between Balin and Slick and also became the group's first U.K. chart entry (#38, 1969). The band's extensive touring included stops at the Atlantic City Pop Festival (8/1/69), the Woodstock Music & Art Fair (8/17/69), and a concert with the Rolling Stones at Altamont Speedway, California (12/6/69). The year also found two band members, Jack Casady and Paul Kantner, facing drug possession charges. *Volunteers* (#13, 1969) was the band's most politically satired release.

The following year Dryden left and eventually formed the New Riders of the Purple Sage (1971). He was replaced by Hot Tuna drummer Joey Covington. By fall, Slick, who was pregnant by Kantner, was unable to make live gigs. The band then restructured itself and added violinist Papa John Creach. In November Kantner and Slick invited guests Jerry Garcia, David Crosby, and Graham Nash to contribute to their project *Blows Against the Empire* (#20, 1970), an album recorded as Paul Kantner & Jefferson Starship (the first use of the name).

The Worst of Jefferson Airplane (#12, 1971) and *Bark* (#11, 1971, Grunt) highlighted the year's recording releases for the band. Personnel issues still dogged the band, which now found Balin taking a year off, while Slick gave birth to daughter China, on January 25. Slick then crashed her Mercedes into a wall near the Golden Gate bridge on May 13—she required brief hospitalization. The band also launched its own label, Grunt Records, which was distributed by RCA.

Sunfighter (#89, 1972), a Kantner and Slick project, peaked in January, while *Burgers* (#68, 1972), a Hot Tuna release, peaked in May, during a year that found the band extremely fragmented. The band did manage to regroup for a recording session that resulted in *Long John Silver* (#20, 1972). On August 22, 1972, the final date of the band's U.S. Tour, the group performed at Winterland in what proved to be the band's last performance for seventeen years. Members of Hot Tuna also made their final break from the band, and went on to record six more albums before splitting up.

JEFFERSON STARSHIP

In February 1974, Slick and Kantner formed the Jefferson Starship with Freiberg (who had toured with Airplane), Creech, Barbeta, Peter Kaukonen (replaced in June by Pete Sears), and Craig Chaquico. *Dragon Fly* (#11, 1974), the new group's debut, was extremely well received and even included a guest appearance by Marty Balin (who tentatively rejoined in 1975).

Red Octopus (#11, 1975) became the group's big breakthrough, spurned by hit extract "Miracles" (#3,

1975). It was also the band members' first Number One album—the group seemed to be at the peak of its popularity. Friction between band members was still evident and by years end Slick and Kantner split up. Albums *Spitfire* (#3, 1976), which included the hit "With Your Love" (#12, 1976), *Flight Log (1966-1976)*, a compilation, and *Earth* (#5, 1978), with extract "Count On Me"(#8, 1978), followed, but by October 1978, only Kantner remained as an original member.

In 1979, Mickey Thomas, who was best known during the time for his lead vocals in Elvin Bishop's "Fooled Around And Fell In Love" took over the lead vocal duties, while Barbata was replaced by journeyman Aynsley Dunbar. The new lineup's *Freedom at Point Zero* (#10, 1979), with hit extract "Jane" (#14, 1980), was well received, but momentum was nearly halted when Kantner suffered a stroke in October, of which he fully recovered. *Modern Times* (#26, 1981), the group's next album, featured Slick, who rejoined the band in February, on one cut. The hits continued for the band which scored with "Find Your Way Back" (#29, 1981), "Be My Lady" (#28, 1982), "Winds of Change" (#38, 1983) and "No Way Out" (#23, 1984).

STARSHIP

In 1985, following an extensive legal battle, Kantner departed from the band with a lump sum of money and the provision that "Jefferson" be dropped from the group's name. Freiberg also departed, and the band released *Knee Deep in the Hoopla* (#7, 1985). "We Built This City" (#1, 1985), extracted from the new album, topped the U.S. singles chart, as did the band's next single, "Sara" (#1, 1986). "Tomorrow Doesn't Matter Tonight" (#26, 1986) was the last single from the Top Ten album.

No Protection (#12, 1987) included the group's third Number One single, "Nothing's Gonna Stop Us Now" (#1,1987), along with the hit "It's Not Over ('Til It's Over)" (#9, 1987). "It's Not Enough" (#12, 1989) was the last Top Forty single for the Starship lineup of Thomas, Chaquico, Baldwin, Brett Bloomfield, and Mark Morgan, before the band called it quits in 1990.

FLIGHT WRECKAGE

In 1989 Kantner, Slick, Balin, Casady, and Kaukonen pulled the old aircraft out of the hanger and released *Jefferson Airplane* (#85, 1989). Prior to this new flight plan, Kantner, Balin, and Casady had formed the KBC band and even released a self-titled album (#75, 1986). In 1991, Kantner reclaimed the moniker "Jefferson Starship" and put a new lineup together (Casady, Creach, Tim Gorman, Praire Prince, Slick Aguilar, Darby Gould, and later Balin). "Jefferson Starship-The Next Generation" was now ready to chart a new course.

JEFFERSON AIRPLANE ALUMNI/ALUMNAE 1965-1990

Date	Band Members
8/65-11/65	Balin, Kantner, Kaukonen, Anderson, Spence, Harvey
11/65-9/66	Balin, Kantner, Kaukonen, Anderson, Spence, Jack Casady
10/66-3/70	Balin, Kantner, Kaukonen, Casady, Grace Slick, Spencer Dryden
4/70-9/70	Balin, Kantner, Kaukonen, Casady, Slick, Joey Covington
10/70-4/71	Balin, Kantner, Kaukonen, Casady, Slick, Covington, Papa John Creach
5/71-4/72	Kantner, Kaukonen, Casady, Slick, Covington, Creach
5/72-8/72	Kantner, Kaukonen, Casady, Slick, Creach, John Barbata
8/72	Kantner, Kaukonen, Casady, Slick, Creach, Barbata, David Freiberg
8/72-2/74	Kantner, Slick, Creach, Barbata, Freiberg
2/74-5/74	Kantner, Slick, Creach, Barbata, Freiberg, Craig Chaquico, Peter Kaukonen
6/74-12/74	Kantner, Slick, Creach, Barbata, Freiberg, Chaquico, Pete Sears
1/75-8/75	Kantner, Slick, Creach, Barbata, Freiberg, Chaquico, Sears, Balin
9/75-6/78	Kantner, Slick, Barbata, Freiberg, Chaquico, Pete Sears, (Balin)*
6/78-10/78	Kantner, Barbata, Freiberg, Chaquico, Sears, (Balin)*
10/78-4/79	Kantner, Barbata, Freiberg, Chaquico, Sears
4/79-3/81	Kantner, Freiberg, Chaquico, Sears , Mickey Thomas, Aynsley Dunbar
3/81-10/82	Kantner, Freiberg, Chaquico, Sears , Thomas, Dunbar, Slick
10/82-3/85	Kantner, Freiberg, Chaquico, Sears , Thomas, Slick, Don Baldwin
3/85-8/89	Chaquico, Sears , Thomas, Baldwin
11/88-8/89	Slick, Kantner, Kaukonen and Cassady
8/89-11/89	Chaquico, Sears, Thomas, Baldwin, Brett Bloomfield, Mark Morgan
8/89-9/89	Slick, Kantner, Kaukonen, Cassady, Kenny Aronoff, Peter Kaukonen, Randy Jackson, Tim Gorman**
9/89-1990	Slick, Kantner, Kaukonen, Cassady, Aronoff
11/89-1990	Thomas, Baldwin, Chaquico, Morgan, Bloomfield

*Uncertainty regarding Balin's official position

**Uncertainty regarding status of Aronoff, P. Kaukonen, Jackson, and Gorman

Note: Various offshoots of the band perform and reunite during the following decade

AUTOGRAPHS

Group:

A CD, LP, magazine cover, ad, photo, or card signed by all members: $200-$250*

*Vintage autographed material

Individual:

Marty Balin: $20-$25	Paul Kantner: $20-$25
Jorma Kaukonen: $20	Signe Anderson: $5-$10
Skip Spence: $5-$10	Bob Harvey: $5-$10
Jack Casady: $20	Grace Slick: $20-$30
Spencer Dryden: $10	Joey Covington: $5-$8
Papa John Creach: $20-$35	Craig Chaquico: $10
Mickey Thomas: $10	Aynsley Dunbar: $10-$15
Others: $5-$7	

TOUR BOOKS/PROGRAMS

Backstage Passes:

Jefferson Airplane (1965-1972): $20-$30 (cloth/paper), $25-$50
(laminated) - scarce
Jefferson Starship (1974-1984): $12-$20 (cloth), $25-$30
(laminated)
Starship (1985-1990): $10-$12 (cloth), $20-$25
(laminated)

POSTERS/PRESS KITS

Promotional Posters:

Jefferson Airplane (1965-1972): scarce
Jefferson Starship (1974-1984): $15-$45
Starship (1985-1990): $15-$30

Press Kits:

Jefferson Airplane (1965-1972): scarce
Jefferson Starship (1974-1984): $25-$50
Starship (1985-1990): $15-$25

USED CLOTHING/EQUIPMENT

Guitar Picks:

Marty Balin: $20-$25	Paul Kantner: $20-$25
Jorma Kaukonen: $10-$30	Bob Harvey: $5-$10
Jack Casady: $8-$20	Craig Chaquico: $10-$20

Drum Sticks:

Skip Spence: $10-$15	Spencer Dryden: $10-$20
Joey Covington: $10-$15	Aynsley Dunbar: $10-$15

OFTEN OVERLOOKED MEMORABILIA

Associated memorabilia from the Honeybucket club, the Matrix club, the Carousel Ballroom (Fillmore West), and the Kaleidoscope club; a copy of the review of the band's first gig that appeared in the San Francisco Chronicle; videotapes from the group's television performances on *The Smothers Brothers Comedy Hour* - CBS-TV (5/7/67, 11/10/68); a copy of *Life* magazine (6/28/68) featuring the band on the cover; any associated items from the group's residence at 2400 Fulton, San Francisco, CA; a copy of the film *One P.M.*; memorabilia associated with Hugo Award nominated *Blows Against the Empire* (1970); items associated with Balin's rock opera *Rock Justice* (1980); copies of Major League Baseball's advertisements utilizing "It's Not Over ('Til It's Over)"; associated movie memorabilia from *Mannequin* (1987) and *Cocktail* (1989); "Count On Me," Grunt promotional Polish Calculator, 1977 (pencil, cord, and presentation box) - $25; Earth pop-up display, 1978 - $55

REFERENCES/BOOKS

Numerous resources exist, but nothing that does justice to the band in my opinion; no dedicated collector books

---

Jeffreys, Garland

Born mid-1940s

This '70s rock and roll vocalist is best known for his late-60s stint with Grinderswitch and FM staples "Wild in the Streets," "The Disco Kid," and "Matador." Jeffreys is a "poor man's Lou Reed,"—that is they are both former Orangeman and acquaintances, so I can get away with the comparison. Although he has a loyal and significant following in America, he has yet to garner commercial success here.

AUTOGRAPHS

A CD, LP, magazine cover, ad, photo, or card signed by the artist: $5-$10

OFTEN OVERLOOKED MEMORABILIA

Associated artifacts from other musicians' covers of his work

---

Jellybean

(John Benitez)
Born: November 7, 1957

Flamboyant club D.J. gone producer Jellybean is best known for his work at Studio 54, Xenon, and the Fun House and his innovative experiments in sound. Jellybean befriended Madonna, who later asked him to remix "Borderline," "The Gambler," and "Crazy for You," before they both went different routes in 1984.

AUTOGRAPHS

A CD, LP, magazine cover, ad, photo, or card signed by the artist: $5-$7

OFTEN OVERLOOKED MEMORABILIA

Movie memorabilia from *Spaceballs* (1987), *The Principal* (1987), *Carlito's Way* (1993), and *The Shadow* (1994)

Jennings, Waylon

Born: June 15, 1937

Waylon Jennings, pioneer, along with Willie Nelson, of the outlaw country movement, is commonly associated with the songs "MacArthur Park"—his first Grammy winner—"Luckenbach Texas," "Good Hearted Woman" and "Mamas Don't Let Your Babies Grow Up to Be Cowboys," (a Grammy winner) both with Willie Nelson, "Amanda," and "Will the Wolf Survive." He is also remembered for giving up his seat on the chartered plane that crashed, killing Buddy Holly, whom he backed as a member of the Crickets.

His 1976 album *Wanted: The Outlaws* featuring Waylon, Willie, Tompall Galser, and Jenning's wife Jessi Colter became the first certified platinum country album. He later paired with Willie Nelson again, along with Johnny Cash and Kris Kristofferson as the Highwaymen, who periodically release albums—when the dust settles. Jennings garnered attention in the '90s with the song "The Eagle" that became an anthem of sorts to Operation Desert Storm. By all accounts he is a living legend to his craft.

AUTOGRAPHS

A CD, LP, magazine cover, ad, photo, or card signed by the artist: $10-$25

TOUR BOOKS/PROGRAMS

Backstage Passes:
Cloth: $8-$10; Laminated:
$15-420 (1990-Present)

POSTERS/PRESS KITS

Promotional Posters:
$10-$20
Press Kits: $15-$55

USED CLOTHING/ EQUIPMENT

Guitar Picks: $20-$35

OFTEN OVERLOOKED MEMORABILIA

Memorabilia associated with his days with the Crickets

REFERENCES/BOOKS

A few resources exist. John L. Smith's book *The Waylon Jennings Discography* is a must!

Waylon Jennings guitar pick

TOUR BOOKS/PROGRAMS

Backstage Passes:
Cloth: $5-$10; Laminated: $10-$15

POSTERS/PRESS KITS

Promotional Posters: $8-$15
Press Kits: $15-$20

USED CLOTHING/EQUIPMENT

Guitar Picks: $10
Drum Sticks: $15

OFTEN OVERLOOKED MEMORABILIA

"Riot," Fierce (1984), includes drug paraphernalia, with a second issue containing a candy bar, badge, piece of cloth, and a postcard

Jesus Jones

Formed 1988

Mike Edwards, Jerry De Borg, Barry D. (Iain Baker), Al Jaworski, and Gen (Simon Matthews)

Nineties post-new-wave pop rock jocks Jesus Jones is best known for the songs "Info Freako" (#42, U.K., 1989), "Right Here, Right Now" (#2, 1991) and "Real, Real, Real" (#4, 1991).

AUTOGRAPHS

A CD, LP, magazine cover, ad, photo, or card signed by the group: $20-$35

POSTERS/PRESS KITS

Promotional Posters: $8-$10
Press Kits: $10

The Jesus and Mary Chain

Formed 1984

William Reid, Jim Reid, Douglas Hart, and Murray Dalglish*

*Dalglish departed in 1984 and Bobby Gillespie was added. Gillespie left in 1985 and drummer John Moore joined the band. Moore left in 1989 and Richard Thomas was added. Hart also left in 1989. Thomas left in 1994 and Ben Lurie and Steve Monti were added.

Mid-80s British press darlings and U.S. college-radio remnants, and another Velvet Underground progeny, The Jesus and Mary Chain, led by the Reid brothers (not as in Lou), is commonly associated with its thrashing but short live sets, and songs such as "Just Like Honey" and "Reverence." The band gained significant exposure in the U.S. during the second annual Lollapalooza Tour, and is slowly gaining ground commercially.

AUTOGRAPHS

A CD, LP, magazine cover, ad, photo, or card signed by the group: $25-$35

****

"On The Edge"

Jesus Lizard/Scratch Acid

Texas-laced jalapeño poppers and gonzo garage bands, these guys will make you happy you left your truck outside, so come on in and grab a lyric sheet to "Mary Had a Little Drug Problem," they're over there by the door. It's time for Scratch Acid karaoke. You can leave your woman and your Lone Star at your table, on second thought you better take the beer with you, and come on up on stage and sing with us. We'll start with an oldie but goodie first, you know that old Jesus Lizard tune, "Happy Bunny Goes Fluff-Fluff Along." What do you mean you don't want to? Then go back and sit down by your woman, if that's what you call it!

Start your collecting with Texas saloon posters if you can find them, and also local bar rags with adverts for the band!

****

Jethro Tull

Formed 1967

Ian Anderson, Born: August 10, 1947; Mick Abrahams; Glenn Cornick; and Clive Bunker*

*Numerous personnel changes. See chart below.

Ian Anderson forms the Blades with Michael Stephens (Atlantics), Jeffrey Hammond-Hammond, and John Evans, playing blues-rooted music in local clubs. The band later changes its name to the John Evan Band, then John Evan Smash, while heading to Luton to be closer to the London blues club. The band then falls apart leaving Cornick, who replaced Hammond-Hammond, and Anderson to pick up the pieces, while forming a new band which tries numerous names including Navy Blue and Bag of Blues before arriving at Jethro Tull (An 18th century agriculturist).

In February 1968 the band, which now also includes Mick Abrahams and Clive Bunker, releases "Sunshine Day" on the MGM label, with the now highly collectible first pressing crediting the band as "Jethro Toe." The group's fresh sound lands it a residency at London's Marquee club during the summer of 1968, which also finds the band stealing the show at the Sunbury Jazz & Blues Festival (8/11/68), garnering media accolades and even landing the group a recording contract on Island Records.

This Was (#10, U.K., 1968), the band's debut album, features extract "A Song For Jeffrey," which was dedicated to Hammond-Hammond. By now Anderson's extraordinary stage presence—dressed in long tattered overcoats, bearded, and often playing the flute while standing on one leg—is becoming the focal point of the band. Looking more like a Dicken's character than a rock musician, Anderson entices his audiences with his enthusiastic and choreographed performances. By the end of the year, Abrahams departs due to conflicts with Anderson, while the group is invited to perform in the Rolling Stones' Rock "n' Roll Circus.

Love Story (#29, U.K., 1969) is the band's sophomore effort and the last featuring Abrahams who is now replaced with Tony Iommi and then Davey O'List, before Martin Barre joins permanently. The group makes its U.S. debut on January 24, 1969, sharing the bill with Led Zeppelin, at the Fillmore East in New York, at the start of a two month tour. Meanwhile, Reprise issues *This Was* (#62, 1969) in the U.S. a month before the band's single "Living in the Past" (#3, U.K., 1969) is released. During the summer the band, like similar acts of the era, will play numerous festivals and prepare for the release of its next album, *Stand Up* (#20, 1969), released on the Chrysalis label.

"Sweet Dream" (#7, 1969), and "The Witch's Promise/Teacher" (#4, U.K., 1970) maintain the act's chart presence as Anderson marries Jennie Franks, a later contributor to *Aqualung*. The blues-flavored *Benefit*, the last release in this genre, features John Evan along with Anderson, Barre, Bunker, and Cornick. Personnel changes continue (see chart) as the band plays some prestigious gigs including the three-day Atlanta Pop Festival which also includes Jimi Hendrix.

Aqualung (#7, 1971) is the band's fourth album. It was penned by Anderson in a concept manner and the first clear rock release for the band. The album, the group's first Top Ten entry, receives heavy airplay on cuts such as "Hymn 43," the group's first chart single (#91), "Locomotive Breath," and "Cross-eyed Mary." The band's following is now growing at a significant rate, driven by its extensive touring and critical reviews.

Thick as a Brick (#1, 1972), the band's next album, is its first U.S. Number One and is quickly followed by *Living in the Past* (#3, 1972), a double compilation album consisting primarily of singles and a live side recorded at New York's Carnegie Hall.

"Living in the Past" (#11, 1973) is now released as a single in America as the band is preparing for its next album release, *Passion Play* (#1, 1973). The album, which is disliked by some critics who label it pretentious, nevertheless sells very well both in America and in the U.K. The title track, however, released as an edited single, fails to make it into the Top Forty. The band then claims it is retiring from live performances due to "critical abuse"—a surprising and eventually costly error.

War Child (#2, 1974), orchestral-based and supposedly developed in conjunction with a film that fails to surface, is released late in 1974. Album extract "Bungle in the Jungle" (#11, 1975) helps drive sales as the band follows with "Minstrel in the Gallery" (#7, 1975), which is recorded in the band's new mobile studio. The following year *M.U.—The Best of Jethro Tull Vol. 1* is released as singles "Rainbow Blues" (#13, 1976) and "Locomotive Breath" (#62, 1976) are released as singles.

Too Old to Rock 'n' Roll (#14, 1976) is the next album release by the band, which also release a seasonal EP, *Ring Out Solstice Bells* (#28, U.K., 1976). *Songs from the Wood* (#8, 1977), the heavily folk-oriented album, sells well as extract "The Whistler" (#59, 1977) struggles up the singles chart. The group then buys time with *The Best of Jethro Tull Vol.2* (#94, 1977) before releasing *Heavy Horses* (#19, 1978). The album is heavily supported and yields the group's next release *Live: Bursting Out* (#21, 1978).

Stormwatch (#22, 1979) is the group's next album, as the band endures tragedy with the death of John Glascock, who never played live with the band, while also facing other personnel changes. The album *A* (#30, 1980) follows, recorded as a solo project it will, however, be released as a group effort. *The Broadsword and the Beast* (#19, 1982) begins a period in which Anderson is writing with Peter-John Vettese,

who worked with him on his solo album *Walk into Light*. It is followed the next year by *Under Wraps* which continues the band's keyboard dominated sound and declining sales.

In 1984, Anderson's throat problems sideline him for three years, during a time in which salmon farming presided over songwriting. He returned in 1987 with *Crest of a Knave* (#32, 1987). The album garnered the band a gold record and even a Grammy award, while the group extensively toured in its support. Anderson, Barre, Pegg, and Martin Allcock embark on their next tour supporting *20 Years of Jethro Tull* (#97, 1988).

Rock Island (#56, 1989), *Catfish Rising* (#88, 1991) and *A Little Light Music* (#150, 1992) are the band's next albums, exhibiting a downward trend in the group's popularity, as its former audience is now concerning itself with adulthood and raising children rather than catfish. The band supports some compilation releases with an extensive silver-anniversary world tour which ends in mid-1994. Anderson releases a solo instrumental album in 1995, *Divinities: Twelve Dances With God*, while Tull releases *Roots to Branches* (#114, 1995).

With little left to prove, the group remains a rock legacy.

AUTOGRAPHS

Group:

A LP, CD or magazine cover, ad, photo, or card signed by the group: $40-$80

Individual:

Ian Anderson: $15-$30
Martin Barre: $10-$25

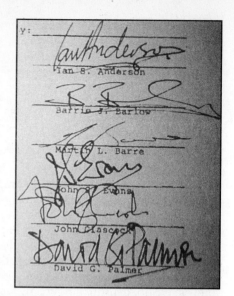

Contract signed by the members of Jethro Tull

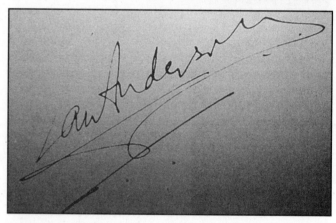

Ian Anderson's signature

JETHRO TULL ALUMNI - LIVING IN THE PAST

Date	Members
11/67-11/68	Ian Anderson, Clive Bunker, Glenn Cornick, Mick Abrahams
12/68-4/70	Cornick, Bunker, Anderson, Martin Barre
4/70-12/70	Cornick, Bunker, Anderson, Barre, John Evan
1/71-5/71	Bunker, Anderson, Barre, Evan, Jeffrey Hammond-Hammond
5/71-12/75	Anderson, Barre, Evan, Hammond-Hammond, Barriemore Barlow
12/75-10/76	Anderson, Barre, Evan, Barlow, John Glascock
10/76-8/79	Anderson, Barre, Evan, Barlow, Glascock***, David Palmer
8/79-6/80	Anderson, Barre, Barlow, Palmer, Evan, Dave Pegg
6/80-5/81	Anderson, Barre, Pegg, Eddie Jobson, Mark Craney
6/81-1984	Anderson, Barre, Pegg, Gerry Conway*, Peter-John Vettese
1984-6/88	Anderson, Barre, Pegg, Vettese, Doane Perry
6/88-1995	Anderson, Barre, Pegg**, Perry, Martin Allcock****
1995	Anderson, Barre, Perry, Andrew Giddings, Jonathan Noyce

*Paul Burgess added for Conway on U.S. Tour leg
**Matt Pegg fills in on occasion for his father
***Tony Williams filled in for Glascock in 1978 as his health deteriorated
****John Bundrick, Foss Peterson, and Dave Mattacks also enjoy stays with the band

TOUR BOOKS/PROGRAMS

Tour Books:

1973 A Passion Play, U.K.: $200, scarce

1974 Japan Tour, scarce: $200

1982 Tour: $10-$12

Rock Island (1989). $10-$15

Catfish Rising: $15

Backstage Passes:

Cloth: $10-$12; Laminated: $15-$20 (1984-Present)

Cloth: $15; Laminated: $15-30 (1978-1983)

Cloth/cardboard: $30-$50 (1968-1977) (scarce)

POSTERS/PRESS KITS

Promotional Posters:

1984-Present: $7-$10

1978-1983: $10-$20

1977-1968: $25-$100

Jethro Tull Rock Island tour book (©1989 Jethro Tull)

Press Kits:

1984-Present: $15

1978-1983: $15-$25

1977-1968: $30-$150, Example: A Passion Play: $125

USED CLOTHING/EQUIPMENT

Guitar Picks:

Martin Barre: $10-$20

OFTEN OVERLOOKED MEMORABILIA

The group's numerous television appearances on *Top of the Pops* (5/69, 12/76) and *The Tonight Show* (4/28/93); a copy of *The Scotsman* newspaper reporting that Anderson is buying Strathaird on the Isle of Skye, he will later turn the salmon processing plant into a real money maker, while expressing interest in numerous environmental issues; a videotape from the 31st annual Grammy Awards, where the band beats out Metallica and AC/DC for Best Hard Rock/Metal Performance; Heavy Horses, 1978 brass promotional horseshoe; Songs from the Wood, 1977, promotional wooden tree stumps; memorabilia from the 1991 National Association of Brick Distributors' second annual Brick Hall of Fame gala in New York - band inducted (10/10/91)

The Jets

Formed 1984

Leroy, Eddie, Eugene, Rudy, Haini, Kathi, Elizabeth, and Moana Wolfgramm

Eighties South Pacific-rooted family band, best known for the songs "Crush on You" (#3, 1986), "You Got It All" (#3, 1986), "Cross My Broken Heart" (#7, 1987), "Make It Real" (#4, 1988), and "Rocket 2 U" (#6, 1988), The Jets scored hits fast and furiously, before Eugene left the group to form the Boys Club—as Gene Hunt—and landing a single hit "I Remember Holding You" (#8, 1988). The Jets then began descending and by 1992 had crashed with a bankruptcy filing.

AUTOGRAPHS

A CD, LP, magazine cover, ad, photo, or card signed by the group: $10-$20

OFTEN OVERLOOKED MEMORABILIA

Movie memorabilia from *Beverly Hills Cop II*; 1987 World Series memorabilia (the group performed at the event)

Jett, Joan

Born: September 22, 1960

Joan Jett, the '80s solo glam rocker and former leader of the Runaways, is commonly associated with such songs as "I Love Rock 'n' Roll" (#1, 1982), "Crimson and Clover" (#7, 1982), "Do You Wanna Touch Me (Oh Yeah)" (#20, 1982), "I Hate Myself for Loving You" (#8, 1988), and "Little Liar" (#19, 1988). Although her popularity and hits have been sporadic, her longevity has been impressive and influential to many female performers who have followed. Jett still manages to surface occasionally with a hit or two and has even tried her luck at acting.

AUTOGRAPHS

A CD, LP, magazine cover, ad, photo, or card signed by the artist: $15-$35

TOUR BOOKS/PROGRAMS

Backstage Passes:

Cloth: $10; Laminated: $12-$15

Two Joan Jett backstage passes (Printed by OTTO)

POSTERS/PRESS KITS

Promotional Posters: $10-$25

Press Kits: $10-$30

USED CLOTHING/EQUIPMENT

Guitar Picks: $15-$20

Drum Sticks: $15

OFTEN OVERLOOKED MEMORABILIA

The Hit List counter display - $20; movie memorabilia from *Light of Day*; The Hit List promo lithograph, different colors - $40

REFERENCES/BOOKS

Limited resources exist; no dedicated collector books; serious fans should opt for her fan club: La Gajette International, 3104 Willow Knolls #203, Peoria, IL 61604 ($4 fee)

Jimmy Jam and Terry Lewis

Jimmy Jam (James Harris III) and Terry Lewis

One of the premier writing and production teams of the '80s and '90s, best known for their superstar packaging of Janet Jackson, for which they earned the1986 Grammy for Producer of the Year, Jimmy Jam and Terry Lewis were the nucleus of the band Flyte Time, which became Time when Prince came along. They later formed Flyte Tyme Productions primarily to write and produce other acts such as the S.O.S. Band, Gladys Knight, and Thelma Houston. In 1991 they even launched their own Perspective label through A&M Records and scored with their first release, *The Evolution of Gospel*, by the Minneapolis choir Sounds of Blackness, which won a 1992 Grammy. Although successful acts often change labels and producers, such hasn't been the case with this "dynamic duo."

AUTOGRAPHS

A CD, LP, magazine cover, ad, photo, or card signed by the artists: $25-$70*

*High-end for a key career piece

OFTEN OVERLOOKED MEMORABILIA

Associated artifacts from musicians they have produced, especially Janet Jackson

The Jive Five

Formed 1959

Original lineup: Eugene Pitt, Thurman "Billy" Prophet, Richard Harris, Norman Johnson, and Jerome Hanna*

*Harris departed in 1962. Group re-formed in 1971 and in 1979. Numerous personnel changes followed.

This early-60s New York doo-wop vocal group is best remembered for the songs "My True Story" (#3, 1961), "These Golden Rings," and "I'm a Happy Man," before fading from the music scene. The Jive Five later regrouped and remained active by touring in the '90s.

AUTOGRAPHS

A CD, LP, magazine cover, ad, photo, or card signed by the group: $10-$20

OFTEN OVERLOOKED MEMORABILIA

Associated artifacts from other musicians who have covered the artists' music

Jobriath

(Jobriath Boone)
Born: Late 1940s

One of the biggest hypes in rock history, Jobriath, a self-made glitter-rock god, inked a deal with Elektra Records for a figure reportedly near $500,000. The deal, mastered by his agent Jerry Brandt, included a Times Square billboard featuring the star's debut album cover (Jobriath, partially nude) and an expensive stage debut package. The show, which opened at the Paris Opera House, featured the singer doing mime to what turned out to be a 40-foot phallic symbol (the Empire State Building), with Jobriath playing the roll of King Kong. Needless to say the media had a field day with the event, enhanced by the performer's constant references to himself as a homosexual, and after a second album, which also bombed, he slipped away from the music scene much richer than when he arrived.

AUTOGRAPHS

A CD, LP, magazine cover, ad, photo, or card signed by the artist: $2-$10

OFTEN OVERLOOKED MEMORABILIA

Associated artifacts from his debut at the Paris Opera House

Jodeci

Formed 1988

K-Ci (Cedric Hailey), Jo-Jo (Joel Hailey), Devante Swing (Donald DeGrate), and Mr. Dalvin (Dalvin DeGrate)

Successful '90s romantic R&B vocal group, typically associated with the songs, "Forever My Lady" (#25, 1991), "Stay" (#41, 1991), "Lately" (#4, 1993), and "Cry for You" (#15, 1993), Jodeci was formed in Charlotte, North Carolina, when the Hailey and DeGrate brothers met while singing in different church choirs.

AUTOGRAPHS

A CD, LP, magazine cover, ad, photo, or card signed by the group: $15-$35

Joel, Billy

Born: May 9, 1949

William Martin Joel grew up in Hicksville, New York, and when he wasn't boxing or listening to a baseball game, you could find him playing piano. Inspired by the Beatles, he joined a series of bands including the Echoes/Emeralds and then the Lost Souls, before finally joining the Hassles in 1967. The Hassles signed to United Artists and released four singles and two albums (*The Hassles* and *Hour of the Wolf*) in the U.S., before disbanding.

Joel then joined drummer Jon Small to form the duo Attila, which released its self-titled debut on Epic Records in 1970. When the record failed, the two went their separate ways. *Cold Spring Harbor* (1971), released on Family Productions through Paramount, was Joel's debut album as a soloist. Joel assembled a band to support the release while he found out that the album was improperly pressed which resulted in a faster speed. Despite the flaw, the album was well received by critics. He then headed to Los Angeles, California, where he spent half of 1972 playing the piano bar at the Executive Room on Wilshire Boulevard—the inspiration for "Piano Man." In April, he had an opportunity to play the Mar Y Sol Festival in Puerto Rico, where he came to the attention of CBS Records executives. Columbia officer Clive Davis then went to see Joel play at the piano bar in Los Angeles, and signed him to a deal.

Piano Man (#27, 1974), with extracted title cut (#25, 1974), was Joel's debut album for Columbia. He supported the release through extensive touring with a strong stage band and found his first headlining home in Philadelphia. *Streetlife Serenade* (#35, 1975), his sophomore effort for CBS, included the hit single "The Entertainer" (#34, 1975). Joel then moved from Los Angeles back to New York, renewing his inspiration as a songwriter and producing such numbers as "New York State of Mind" in under a half hour.

Turnstiles (#1122, 1976), which included such songs as "Say Goodbye to Hollywood," was not as successful as its predecessor, but was extensively supported. Joel was becoming a regular favorite on the college and university circuit, especially in his home state of New York.

In September 1977 he appeared on NBC-TV's *Saturday Night Live* playing a new song, "Just The Way You Are" (#3, 1978). By November the song's parent album, *The Stranger* (#2, 1977), nearly topped the U.S. album chart. The record eventually became Columbia's second-biggest selling album of all time, behind only *Bridge Over Troubled Water* by Simon & Garfunkel.

In 1978 he enjoyed his U.K. debut performance at London's Theatre Royal in March, as "Movin' Out (Anthony's Song)" (#17, 1978), also from *The Stranger*, climbed the singles charts. It was followed by two other singles also from the same album: "Only the Good Die Young" (#24, 1978) and "She's Always a Woman" (#17, 1978).

52nd Street (#1, 1978), Joel's next album, included the hits "My Life" (#3, 1978), "Big Shot" (#14, 1979), and "Honesty" (#24, 1979). The Phil Ramone-produced *Glass Houses* (# 1, 1980) was his first album of the decade. It helped him continue his string of successful singles with "It's Still Rock and Roll To Me" (#1, 1980), "Don't Ask Me Why" (#19, 1980), "Sometimes a Fantasy" (#36, 1980) and "You May Be Right" (#7, 1980).

Joel's next album, *Nylon Curtain* (#7, 1982), had a much different flavor to it. Both politically and socially conscious, it included singles "Pressure" (#20, 1982), "Allentown" (#17, 1982) and "Goodnight Saigon" (#56, 1983). Joel, who was now divorced from his wife Elizabeth, met model Christie Brinkley during a Caribbean vacation. The two later wed on March 23, 1985.

An Innocent Man (#4, 1983) was his tribute album to the '60s stars of AM radio, which so influenced Joel, and included "Tell Her About It" (#1, 1983), "An Innocent Man" (#10, 1983), "The Longest Time" (#14, 1984), "Keeping the Faith" (#18, 1985), and "Uptown Girl" (#3, 1983). The promotional video for "Uptown Girl" featured Brinkley, Joel's then fiancée. *Greatest Hits Volumes 1 & 2* (#6, 1985) bought the artist some time to enjoy married life.

The Bridge (# 7, 1986) included an appearance with Ray Charles and contributions by Steve Winwood and Cyndi Lauper. The following year found Joel touring the Soviet Union and documenting the visit with the live album *Kohyept* (#38, 1987). *Stormfront* (#1, 1989) and its first single "We Didn't Start the Fire" (#1, 1989) both topped their respective U.S. charts simultaneously. The album was supported by an extensive world tour which more than 4 million people in sixteen countries viewed.

On June 22-23, 1990, he became the first rock act to perform at New York's Yankee Stadium and, in a fitting tribute, dedicated a song to the memory of #1 Yankee and namesake Billy Martin. *River of Dreams* (#1, 1993) was another departure for Joel, including a more philosophic outlook toward life.

During the summer of 1994 Joel toured the U.S. with Elton John, just prior to his divorce from Brinkley.

As an entertainer who is somewhat skeptical of the music business, following years of litigation surrounding his own career, he still manages to evolve and endure. He has been very fortunate to have always been labeled progressive, because his work seems to avoid the staleness so commonly associated with successful entertainers. His efforts in music education and his support of numerous charitable causes find him viewed now as both an educator and a humanitarian and maybe a "Big Shot" once in a while!

AUTOGRAPHS

A CD, LP, magazine cover, ad, photo, or card signed by the artist: $20-$70*

*Vintage items pre-1975

TOUR BOOKS/PROGRAMS

Tour Books:

Billy Joel, 1976 (black & white)*: $25-$35

Japan Tour, 1979: $50

Storm Front, 1989: $15

*Caricature of Joel with facsimile signature on cover

A Billy Joel tour book (© William Joel, 1989)

A few examples of Billy Joel backstage passes (Printed by OTTO (L), Perri (R), laminate is a common counterfeit.)

Backstage Passes:
Cloth: $10-$15; Laminated: $20-$30**
**Prices for 1977-present

POSTERS/PRESS KITS
Promotional Posters: $10-$50
Press Kits: $15-$75

USED CLOTHING/EQUIPMENT
Guitar Picks: $15-$40

OFTEN OVERLOOKED MEMORABILIA
Time Is the Time, Columbia promotional watch; We Didn't Start the Fire Columbia promotional cigarette lighter, 1989; We Didn't Start the Fire, Columbia promotional thermometer, 1989; *World News*, Columbia promotional newspaper, 1989 - used to market the "Storm Front" release; The Stranger Cbs, promotional T-shirt - $15; River of Dreams - counter standup - $10; an autographed bag of Bachman Pretzels signed by both Joel and Chubby Checker; a cocktail napkin from the Executive Room on Wilshire Blvd. in Los Angeles, CA - $5; copies of *Changes* magazine that include pieces from rock critic Billy Joel - $6-$10; videotapes of his television show appearances on: *Saturday Night Live* (9/77, 10/23/93), *The Old Grey Whistle Test* - BBC2-TV(3/78), *Moonlighting* (episode featuring "Big Man On Mulberry Street") (1986), and *Late Show With David Letterman* (8/30/93); newspaper clippings from Joel's visit to Leningrad (1987); a copy of *Playboy* featuring the Joel interview where he calls musician John Powers a jerk - $8-$10; movie memorabilia from *Oliver and Company* (1988), *Honeymoon in Vegas* (1992), and *A League of Their Own* (1992); memorabilia from Super Bowl XXIII (1/22/89) - Joel sang national anthem; all associated items with CBS Records release of "We Didn't Start the Fire" that include a ten minute talk by Joel with

Junior Scholastic and *Update* magazines (1990); a program from the ceremony where Billy Joel received an honorary doctorate of humane letters from Fairfield University - $10; a piece of sod from the Billy Joel Park in Huntington, Long Island - $1; memorabilia from his contributions to other projects such as "Simply Mad About The Mouse" (1991); all memorabilia associated with his music clinics; items associated with his being awarded his diploma at Hicksville High (6/24/92); a program from the ceremony where Billy Joel received an honorary degree at Berklee College of Music (5/8/93) - $10; a copy of the PBS documentary on the making of "The River of Dreams" (10/13/93); memorabilia from "An Evening of Questions and Answers and Perhaps a Few Songs" (10/3/94)

REFERENCES/BOOKS
Numerous resources exist, but nothing that does justice to the singer in my opinion; no dedicated collector books; serious fans should opt for his fan club: Streetlife Serenade, Wells Ink, P.O. Box 2075, Garden City, NY 11531 ($10 fee)

Johansen, David/Buster Poindexter

Born: January 9, 1950

If at first you can't succeed as yourself, or in a band, create a character. That is exactly what former New York Doll David Johansen did. His character's name is Buster Pointdexter, which sounds more like a shoe salesman than a rock star, but nonetheless Buster has been able to attract his fair share of attention. Prior to Buster, Johansen had really only scored one minor hit, with his Animals medley on his *Live It Up* (#148, 1982), although he did open at Shea Stadium for the Clash and the Who in '82.

Buster's eponymous debut album included an electrifying cover of "Hot Hot Hot" (#45, 1988) and was also responsible for him landing some acting roles and television spots. Thus far it's clear that Johansen has yet to filibuster his creativity!

AUTOGRAPHS
A CD, LP, magazine cover, ad, photo, or card signed by the artist: $10-$20*
*Item relating to the New York Dolls

POSTERS/PRESS KITS
Promotional Posters: $10
Press Kits: $10-$15

OFTEN OVERLOOKED MEMORABILIA
Movie memorabilia from *Married to the Mob* and *Scrooged*; videotapes of his numerous television appearances including *Saturday Night Live* and *The Tonight Show*, along with "Buster's Happy Hour" (VH-1).

John, Elton

(Reginald Dwight)
Born: March 25, 1947

Reginald Kenneth Dwight won a part-time scholarship to the Royal Academy of Music in 1958. He soon hooked up with local R&B act Bluesology, whose members included Stuart Brown, Rex Bishop, and Mike Inkpen. The band's first paying gig was at the Northwood Hills Hotel, which was a familiar venue for John who performed there regularly as a soloist. "Come Back Baby" (1965) was the band's first release on Fontana and was written by John. The band then turned professional in 1965 and found itself backing many R&B artists playing in U.K. clubs. By the end of 1966, Long John Baldry was now fronting the group, which expanded to nine members and was renamed the John Baldry Show.

The following year, a very bitter John, upset at the music the band was playing, auditioned for Liberty Records, which was seeking both artists and writers. Although he failed the audition, he did manage to get the name and some sample lyrics of Bernie Taupin. The duo then corresponded via mail, writing songs and finally meeting, before living together in John's parents' house. The duo first appeared together on the B-side of the John Baldry single "Lord You Made the Night Too Long."

In 1968 the duo then signed to Dick James Music Publishing (DJM) as staff writers. On March 1, 1968, "I've Been Loving You Too Long," John's first solo single, was released on Phillips. His second single on Phillips was "Lady Samantha," and while it did not chart, it did attract enough attention to have it covered by Three Dog Night in the U.S. It was during this period that John also unsuccessfully auditioned with Robert Fripp for his new band King Crimson.

"It's Me That You Need," John's next single on DJM Records, was released, as was his debut album on the same label, "Empty Sky." Extract "Border Song" did not chart despite strong airplay. During this period John also contributed session work for the Hollies and his song "From Denver to L.A." to a movie. On August 22, 1970, Elton John signed to MCA Records Uni subsidiary in the U.S.

Elton John, driven by the hit extract "Your Song" (#8, 1970) and his brilliant arrival in the United States, catapulted the artist into the public eye. Elton dropped four albums into the American Top Ten simultaneously, a feat not accomplished by any artist since the Beatles. "Rocket Man" (#6, 1972), "Crocodile Rock" (#1, 1973), "Daniel" (#2, 1973), "Goodbye Yellow Brick Road" (#2, 1973), "Bennie and the Jets" (#1, 1974), "Don't Let the Sun Go Down On Me" (#2, 1974), "The Bitch Is Back" (#4, 1974), "Lucy in the Sky with Diamonds" (#1, 1975), "Philadelphia Free-

dom" (#1, 1975), "Someone Saved My Life Tonight" (#4, 1975), and "Island Girl" (#1, 1975) sold Elton John into stardom. His extravagant shows and chart success sold out arenas and stadiums wherever he played. The hectic pace and business obligations—he now owned his own label—were taking a toll on the performer, and in November 1977, he announced his retirement from performing.

"A Single Man," now without lyricist Taupin, bombed in comparison to his previous albums. John then toured the Soviet Union before attempting a small hall comeback tour of the U.S. While "Mama Can't Buy You Love" (#9, 1979) landed him in the Top Ten, he couldn't sustain his presence. After his *Victim of Love* (#35, 1979) album peaked early, John landed with "Little Jeanie" (#3, 1980), his first Top Ten of the new decade, from the album *21 at 33* (#13, 1980). Unfortunately he failed to hit the Top Ten again in the U.S. until "Empty Garden (Hey Hey Johnny)" (#13, 1982). "Blue Eyes" (#12, 1982), "I'm Still Standing" (#12, 1983), "I Guess That's Why They Call It the Blues" (#4, 1984), "Sad Songs (Say So Much)" (#5, 1984), "That's What Friends Are For" (#1, 1986) with Gladys Knight, Dionne Warwick, and Stevie Wonder, "Nikita" (#7, 1986), "Candle in the Wind" (#6, 1988) (a live version), "I Don't Want to Go On With You Like That" (#2, 1988), and "Healing Hands" (#13, 1989) rounded out his bigger hits of the decade. Despite his early retirement from live performing, John toured heavily over the decade, attended many major charity events, received numerous awards, married, divorced, had throat surgery, and sold more than 2,000 items at a Sotheby's auction.

The Elton John AIDS Foundation was formed in 1992, during a decade that saw the performer turn heavily to humanitarian issues. *The One* (#8, 1992) became his highest charting album since *Blue Moves*, as the artist announced that he would donate all future royalties from sales of his U.S. singles to AIDS research. "Can You Feel the Love Tonight" (#4, 1994) earned the performer both a Grammy and an Oscar—the song was featured in the Disney film *The Lion King*. *Made in England* (#13, 1995) and *Love Songs* (#24, 1995) solidified his reputation mid-decade, prior to Billboard magazine honoring him in its October 4, 1997, issue. The periodical coincided with the 30th anniversary of his astonishing career. Arguably rock's premier performer, and no doubt its greatest humanitarian, the Elton John legacy continues—to that we are grateful.

AUTOGRAPHS

A CD, LP, magazine cover, ad, photo, or card signed by the artist: $75-$200*

*Vintage items pre-1975

Autographed letter signed (ALS): $500-$800

KEY DATES 1970-1979

August 25, 1970	U.S. debut at Doug Weston's Troubadour in Los Angeles, CA
October 31, 1970	First U.S. Tour date at the Boston Tea Party, Boston, MA
November 12-15, 1970	First date at the Fillmore West supporting the Kinks
November 20-21, 1970	First date at the Fillmore East supporting Leon Russell
November 28, 1974	John and Lennon sing "I Saw Her Standing There" at MSG in New York
October 26, 1975	John plays Dodger Stadium, Los Angeles, CA

ELTON JOHN - SELECTED TELEVISION APPEARANCES

Date	Show
3/11/71	*Andy Williams Show* - BBC-TV
4/3/71	"Aquarius" features a documentary about Elton John.
12/4/73	"Elton John And Bernie Taupin Say Goodbye Norma Jean and Other Things" - U.K. TV also on ABC-TV (1974)
2/16/75	*Cher* show
5/3/75	*Soul Train*
12/15/77	*Top of the Pops* - BBC1-TV
6/7/78	*Headliners with David Frost* - NBC
10/31/78	*The Old Grey Whistle Test* - BBC2-TV
10/9/86	*The Late Show Starring Joan Rivers* - FOX-TV
6/23/90	*Wogan* - BBC1-TV
11/22/91	*A Conversation with David Frost* - PBS-TV
11/24/91	Coca-Cola television advertising campaign begins for Diet Coke featuring Elton John.
12/31/92	"New Year's Eve Live" - FOX-TV
1/18/93	"Elton John Unplugged" - MTV
5/9/93	"Aretha Franklin: Duets"
9/4/93	"A Beacon in the War Against AIDS" - ABC-TV
9/20/93	*The Tonight Show* - NBC-TV
12/21/93	"X-mas in New York: Ru Paul's Christmas in New York" - C4-TV
2/25/95	*Live and Kicking* - BBC1-TV
3/27/95	"67th Annual Academy Awards"
5/15/95	*Late Show With David Letterman* - CBS-TV
11/15/95	*Late Show With David Letterman* - CBS-TV

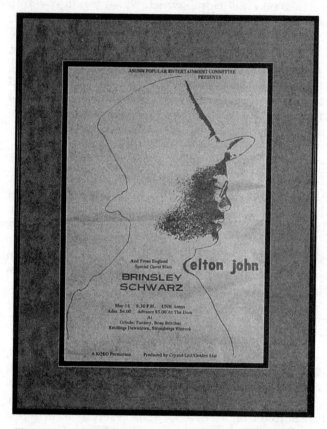

This very rare Elton John poster is from a 1971 concert at the University of New Mexico Arena. It is valued at $1,500. From the Doug Leftwitch collection.

Elton John's signature

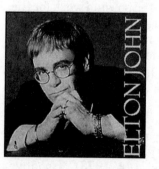

A classy Elton John tour program North America and Europe 1993.

An Elton John tour program (© 1974 Licensed Boutwell Ent. also includes "The Kiki Dee Band" insert.)

TOUR BOOKS/PROGRAMS

Tour Books:

World Tour, 1980: $35
Breaking Hearts, 1984: $15
1974 Tour: $25
1974 (Japan): $65
1988 Reg Strikes Back: $15
1989 Sleeping With The Past: $15
Rock of the Westies, 1975: $25
North America/ Europe, 1993: $15
1992-93 World Tour: $15 (Half Elton John, Half Eric Clapton)

Assorted of outstanding Elton John backstage passes (Otto)

Backstage Passes:

Cloth: $10-$15; Laminated: $20-$30*
*Prices for 1989-present

POSTERS/PRESS KITS

Promotional Posters: $10-$55
Press Kits: $15-$75

USED CLOTHING/EQUIPMENT

Stage-worn glasses: $2,500-$15,000
Stage-worn platform shoes: $150-$1,000*
Stage-worn hat: $600-$700
Stage-worn Bob Mackie outfit: $1,500-$12,250
Stage-worn Jean Paul Gaultier suit: $5,000-$7,000
Stage-used piano: $4,500-$25,000

*Most stage-worn platform shoes average $500, while unique pairs can fetch $7,000-$8,000

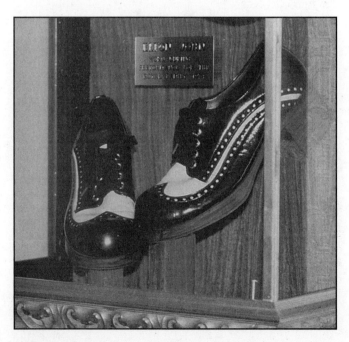

A classic pair of Elton's shoes (Hard Rock Care, Key West)

Note: Elton John was the most flamboyant entertainer to hit show business since Liberace. His extravagant costumes became his hallmark, thus many unique stage-worn items were designed specifically for particular tours and shows. Elton, who has always been philanthropic, often donates numerous items to charity auctions. On September 8, 1988, prestigious auction house Sotheby's sold 2,000 items of his personal memorabilia. The giant platform shoes worn by John in the movie *Tommy* fetched a respectable $11,000.

Guitar Picks:

Band member guitar picks: $20-$45
*Perhaps the most sought after pick is Davey Johnstone's "Sleeping with the Past" pink plectrum, with his signature on one side and a silhouette of Elton on the other.

OFTEN OVERLOOKED MEMORABILIA

Sad Songs promotional handkerchief, 1984; Madman Across the Water, 1971, promotional denim pillow; Honky Chateau, DJM promotional bottle of wine, 1972; Breaking Hearts, 1984, Rocket promo quartz watch; Duets, 1993, promotional backgammon game, complete; Captain Fantastic and the Brown Dirt Cowboy, promotional paperweight; Captain Fantastic and the Brown Dirt Cowboy, promotional pen holder; 21 At 33, MCA, 1980 promotional playing cards; *Rolling Stone* magazine (6/10/71); "Captain Fantastic" Bally professional pinball machine $1,000-$1,500; the advertisement in NME (6/67) that brings John in contact with Taupin; movie memorabilia from *The Game* (1969), *Friends* (1971), *Born to Boogie* (1972), and *Tommy* (1975); all Watford Football Club memorabilia; videotapes from television performances on: "Elton John and Bernie Taupin Say Goodbye Norma Jean and Other Things" (1973 U.K., 1974 U.S.), *Cher* (2/16/75), *Soul Train* (5/3/75),...(See chart); a rubbing from his star on Hollywood's Walk of Fame - $10; *Playboy* (1/78); *Captain Fantastic and the Brown Dirt Cowboy album,* MCA brown vinyl 2142, 1975, limited edition autographed (2,000); Promotional Ego watch; Louder Than a Concorde (1976) tie clip; Palm tree belt buckle (1974); Reg Strikes Back coffee mug; A Single Man diary book; a Blue Moves jacket patch; a Tommy bath towel; Sisco ceramic figurine (10", 1973); a commemorative mirror from the June 30, 1984, show at Wembley Stadium; Honky Chateau watch; Captain Fantastic jigsaw puzzle; limited edition Blue Moves print; sheet of Elton John stamps (Grenada, 1984); Reg Strikes Back baseball bat pen; Television Commercials: Sasson Jeans (1984), Cadbury Chocolates (1985-86), Diet Coke (two), VISA Gold (1995), and the state of Georgia (1995); copies of his numerous radio commercials; copies of his appearance in print advertisements including Roland Pianos, Pioneer, Ebony Menswear, and Chess King Men's Stores; movie memorabilia from *Alex: The Life of a Child, Alice's Restaurant, Aloha Bobby and Rose, And the Band Played On* (TV- HBO), *Candle in the Wind* (TV), *Days of Thunder, Dog Day Afternoon, Driving Me Crazy, Fandango, Ferngully, Four Weddings and a Funeral, Ghostbusters II, Goodbye Norma Jean, Ice Castles, Leap of Faith, Lethal Weapon 3, Love on the Orient Express, My Girl 2, My Own Private Idaho, Oh, Heavenly Dog, Rocky V, Slapshot, Smokey and the Bandit, Summer Lovers, The Cat's Eye, The Entity, The Lion King, The Lost Boys, The Ryan White Story* (TV), *To Die For, Welcome Home,* and *Young Guns II*

REFERENCES/BOOKS

Numerous resources exist; a must book is *The Complete Elton John Discography* by John DiStefano. Serious fans should opt for his fan club: East End Lights, Box 760, New Baltimore, MI 48047 ($20 fee)

John, Little Willie

(William J. Woods)
Born: November 15, 1937, Died: May 27, 1968

This late-50s, early-60s gospel-trained soul singer is best remembered for his songs "All Around the World," "Sleep" (#13, 1960), and "Fever" (he was the very first to record the classic), and numerous R&B hits along with his occasional appearances with the Duke Ellington and Count Basie orchestras. In 1966 he was convicted of manslaughter and sent to prison where he later died.

AUTOGRAPHS

A CD, LP, magazine cover, ad, photo, or card signed by the artist: $15-$35

Johnny and the Hurricanes

Formed 1950s

Johnny Paris, Paul Tesluk, David Yorko, Lionel "Butch" Mattice, and Don Staczek

The late-40s Ohio pop band Johnny and the Hurricanes is best remembered for the instrumental hits "Crossfire" (#23, 1959) and "Red River Rock" (#5, 1959), along with "Reveille Rock" (1959), "Beatnik Fly," "Rocking Goose," and "Down Yonder." The band is also associated with the "Fab Four" because the band traveled to Hamburg, Germany, in the early '60s and often appeared with the group.

AUTOGRAPHS

A CD, LP, magazine cover, ad, photo, or card signed by the group: $10-$45

OFTEN OVERLOOKED MEMORABILIA

Associated artifacts from the group's Hamburg days with the Beatles

Johnson, Robert

Born: May 8, 1911, Died: August 16, 1938

Delta bluesman Robert Johnson, whose life spanned only twenty-seven years, left a phenomenal legacy behind contained in a mere twenty-nine songs. These songs, which were recorded during three sessions in November 1936, include such classics as "Dust My Broom," "Sweet Home Chicago," "Ramblin' on My Mind," "Crossroads," "Love in Vain," "Stop Breaking Down," and "Terraplane Blues." During his lifetime he played with such greats as Robert Nighthawk, Elmore James, Howlin' Wolf, Memphis Slim, and Sonny Boy Williamson, the latter of which was with him during his final days.

He played his last show of his life in August 1938 and died three days later of strychnine poisoning and pneumonia.

AUTOGRAPHS

An ad, photo, or card signed by the artist: $1,500-$4,500* (scarce in all forms)

*High end for a key career piece

OFTEN OVERLOOKED MEMORABILIA

Associated artifacts from musicians who have covered his work

REFERENCES/BOOKS

Searching for Robert Johnson by Peter Guralnick (1988)

****

"On The Edge"

Daniel Johnston

Still amused by fundamental recording technology, this disjointed Texan developed a cult following in the early '80s by combining analog technology with "buy one, get one free" musical instruments. *Yip/Jump Music* (Homestead), recorded in 1983, but not released until 1988, is a good place for collectors to start their Johnston memorabilia hunt.

****

****

"On The Edge"

Freedy Johnston

Best described as "John Steinbeck trapped in a studio, tape running, with only one locked door—minus a door knob and three paper clips near a piece of aluminum foil." *Can You Fly* (Bar/None, 1992) is where Johnston uses the paper clips and aluminum foil to unlock the door. His belief in his music and ability are clear and respected, making the work a great place to begin a Johnston memorabilia collection. From here jump to *This Perfect World* (Elektra, 1994). While you may find more related memorabilia, you won't find a better way to fly!

****

Jo Jo Gunne

Formed 1971

Jay Ferguson, Born: May 10, 1947; Mark Andes, Born: February 19, 1948; Matt Andes; and Curley Smith*

*Mark Andes departed in 1972 and was replaced by Jimmy Randell. Matt Andes left in 1973 and Star Donaldson was briefly added on guitar in 1974 before John Staehely assumed responsibilities.

Jo Jo Gunne, the early-70s rockers led by Jay Ferguson and Mark Andes, both formerly with Spirit, (who had left in January 1971 to form a heavier ensemble), is best remembered for the song "Run Run Run" before Mark Andes departed. The group had little success beyond this first single and disbanded in 1974. The Andes brothers tried to restart Spirit in 1976, but without success, thus leaving each to different directions. Mark Andes would go on to score big with Firefall and later with Heart. Meanwhile, Ferguson's solo career picked up with his hit "Thunder Island" (#9, 1978).

AUTOGRAPHS

A LP, magazine cover, ad, photo, or card signed by the group: $10-$30

Jones, George

Born: September 12, 1931

One of the giants in country music, George Jones dominated the genre from the late '50s into the '80s with songs such as "Why Baby Why" (#4, 1955), "Just One More" (#3, 1956), "White Lightning"—his only pop hit—"Who Shot Sam" (#7, 1959), "The Window Up Above" (#2, 1960), "Tender Years" (#1, 1961), "She Thinks I Still Care" (#1, 1962), "Walk Through This World with Me" (#1, 1967), "A Good Year for the Roses" (#2, 1970), "He Stopped Loving Her Today" (#1, 1980), and "Yesterday's Wine" (#1, 1982) with Merle Haggard. These are just a few of the more than 150 chart entries the artist has placed.

Revered by all who have followed for his sincere, yet hauntingly honest approach, Jones ignored the fads that approached country music in favor of telling a story from his perspective, without all the fluff. Throughout his career he has had to battle substance abuse, and a highly publicized turbulent marriage and divorce from singer Tammy Wynette. In typical Jones fashion, he has taken the criticism like a man, admitted his faults, corrected them, and as a result of the entire experience, earned respect from both his peers and fans.

Although the four-year marriage with Wynette was rocky, it was also fruitful, producing hit songs such as "We're Gonna Hold On" (#1, 1973), "Golden

Ring" (#1, 1976), "Near You" (#1, 1976), and "Two Story House" (#2, 1980). He cleaned up his life in the '80s, re-examined his roots, and put a greater emphasis on achieving success in his fourth marriage. Jones underwent bypass surgery in 1994 and upon his recovery, returned to the studio to record *One*, an album of duets with Wynette. Both toured together for the first time in more than fifteen years.

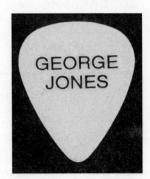

George Jones guitar pick

AUTOGRAPHS

A CD, LP, magazine cover, ad, photo, or card signed by the artist: $10-$25

USED CLOTHING/ EQUIPMENT

Guitar Picks: $8-$12

OFTEN OVERLOOKED MEMORABILIA

Associated artifacts from musicians who have covered his songs

Jones, Grace

Born: May 19, 1952

Eighties cult artist and erotic disco dance diva Grace Jones was the queen of the New York club scene with her stylish image, dipped just enough with S&M to taunt her salivating audiences. Of her songs, she is best known for "I Need a Man," "La Vie en Rose," and "Do or Die," as well as her more rock-oriented "Pull Up to the Bumper," "Nipple to the Bottle," "Slave to the Rhythm," and "I'm Not Perfect (But I'm Perfect for You)." Not surprisingly, her striking look landed her film opportunities and her acting talent has carried her farther than anyone had anticipated. She later returned to Island Records for her album *Sex Drive*; its extracted title cut topped the dance chart.

AUTOGRAPHS

A CD, LP, magazine cover, ad, photo, or card signed by the artist: $20-$40*
*Add 55 % on for a sexy pin-up style shot

OFTEN OVERLOOKED MEMORABILIA

Movie memorabilia from *Conan the Destroyer*, *A View to Kill*, and *Boomerang*; New York clubs rags (newspaper) with advertisements for their shows

Jones, Howard

(John Howard Jones)
Born: February 23, 1955

Mid-80s British synth-pop rock artist Howard Jones gave us habit forming melodies and hooks as

companied by passionate lyrics, best exhibited in songs such as "New Song" (#3, U.K., 1983), "What Is Love" (#2, U.K., 1983), "Things Can Only Get Better" (#5, 1985), and "No One to Blame" (#4, 1986). He is also remembered for his one-man shows, supplemented by a mime named Jed Hoile.

AUTOGRAPHS
A CD, LP, magazine cover, ad, photo, or card signed by the artist: $10-$25

Jones, Quincy

Born: March 14, 1933

Perhaps the most important figure in contemporary pop, Quincy Jones has carved out a legacy which few, if any, could follow. He has been a jazz musician and bandleader, as well as a composer, arranger, and producer, he has had a monumental impact on many of this generation's key performers from Frank Sinatra to Michael Jackson, from Jose Feliciano to B.B. King, and he has the instinctive capability of drawing out the best in an artist and bottling it before it is lost.

Jones himself is also a successful musician. His memorable bodies of work have included *Body Heat* (1974), *The Dude* (1981), *Back on the Block* (1989), and *Miles & Quincy Live at Montreaux (with Miles Davis)* (1993). Complimenting his solo work has been his numerous film scores including *In Cold Blood*, *Banning*, and *In the Heat of the Night*, an Academy Award winner. Jones also composed theme music for television shows, including *Ironside*, *The Bill Cosby Show*, and *Sanford and Son*.

He has been nominated for more Grammy Awards than any other artist—now approaching 100—and has won more than two dozen including a Legend award. His production work, of which he is perhaps most noted for, has included such memorable works as Michael Jackson's monster hit album *Thriller*, and singles "We Are the World," the anthem of USA for Africa, and "Fly Me to the Moon" from Frank Sinatra.

Jones also scored the 1978 film *The Wiz*, coproduced the film *The Color Purple*, and launched *Vibe* magazine. All this in just one lifetime!

AUTOGRAPHS
A CD, LP, magazine cover, ad, photo, or card signed by the artist: $15-$50

POSTERS/PRESS KITS
Promotional Posters: $10-$75
Press Kits: $25-$100

OFTEN OVERLOOKED MEMORABILIA
Jones is a fascinating subject to collect because of the diversity of his talents. You may want to specialize in a single body of his work, such as his solo career, film work, television work, or production work. I find his solo work, his early days with Ray Charles in the Seattle clubs, and his

membership in Lionel Hampton's big band intriguing. With such a body of work, space doesn't permit a comprehensive listing of all of his associated artifacts.

Jones, Rickie Lee

Born: November 8, 1954

Eclectic '80s pop artist Rickie Lee Jones is best remembered for her song "Chuck E's in Love" (#4, 1979). Jones has been both praised by critics who saw her as a visionary in the Joni Mitchell mold and scoffed as just another bohemian who fell out of a Laura Nyro album. The artist still manages to sustain a cult following in the '90s.

AUTOGRAPHS
A CD, LP, magazine cover, ad, photo, or card signed by the artist : $12-$25

TOUR BOOKS/PROGRAMS/PASSES
Backstage Passes:
Cloth: $5; Laminated: $8-$10

POSTERS/PRESS KITS
Promotional Posters: $8-$15
Press Kits: $15

Jones, Tom

(Thomas Woodward)
Born: June 7, 1940

The "Prince of Wales," the lean mean sexy soul machine of the '60s and '70s who created a new vision of men in tight pants, Tom Jones put the "y" in the male chromosome while landing such chart hits as "It's Not Unusual," "What's New Pussycat?," "Green, Green Grass of Home," "Delilah," "Love Me Tonight," "I'll Never Fall in Love Again," "Daughter of Darkness," "I (Who Have Nothing)," "Without Love (There is Nothing)," and "She's a Lady."

Not since Elvis have fathers wanted to lock both their daughters and wives in the house. Jones was a phenomenon, complemented by his hit television series *This is Tom Jones* which ran from February 7, 1969, to January 15, 1971. He had four albums sell gold in 1969 alone before he moved on to country and Las Vegas during the '70s, a quick comeback in the '80s led by two songs, "Kiss" and "Unbelievable," and a revival of his work in the '90s. To this I say, "Gwyn eich byd a dymunaf i chwi lawenydd bob amser," which in Welsh means "Can't these pants stretch any further?" - Just Kidding!

AUTOGRAPHS
A CD, LP, magazine cover, ad, photo, or card signed by the artist: $10-$25

TOUR BOOKS/PROGRAMS/PASSES

Tour Books: $20-$30
1973 Japan Tour: $40
1974 Japan Tour: $40
Backstage Passes:
Cloth: $8-$12; Laminated: $10-$20

POSTERS/PRESS KITS

Promotional Posters: $10-$30
Press Kits: $20-$45

OFTEN OVERLOOKED MEMORABILIA

Movie memorabilia from *What's Up Pussycat?*; videotapes of his hit variety show *This is Tom Jones*; tabloid clippings; videotapes of his "The Right Time" on VH-1; videotapes of his numerous television guest appearances including *The Simpsons*

REFERENCES/BOOKS

Limited resources exist, but nothing that does justice to the singer in my opinion; no dedicated collector books

Joplin, Janis

Born: January 19, 1943, Died: October 4, 1970

The early '60s find Janis Joplin actually earning a living by singing in both Austin and Houston, Texas area honky tonks. She becomes part of the Walter Creek Boys trio with R. Powell St. John and later a member of Mother Earth. When she finally accumulates enough money, she hitchhikes to San Francisco, California, where she sustains herself by singing in clubs with friends such as Roger Perkins and Jorma Kaukonen. Although she impresses many with her outstanding vocal range, she finds herself not progressing fast enough for her desires, and heads home to Texas. While at home she makes an attempt to modify her current hippie lifestyle in favor of school and the desire for marriage and a family.

During the summer of 1965, she abandons her plans and returns to San Francisco and accepts the job as lead singer of the blues/rock outfit Big Brother & the Holding Company. She performs for the first time with the band at the Avalon Ballroom on June 11, 1965, just months before the group signs a recording contract with Mainstream records. The following year the group will share the Avalon Ballroom stage with some of the top acts of the next few decades including Jefferson Airplane, Bo Diddley, and the Grass Roots.

In 1976 the band puts on an astounding performance at the Monterey International Pop Festival. Dylan manager Albert Grossman is so impressed that he signs the group. *Big Brother & The Holding Company* (#60, 1967), the group's debut album, is released in the fall. The band is now considered a major west coast draw, but has yet to leave an impact on the opposite side of the continent. In February the band heads to New York City to make its debut at the Anderson Theater. The following month the group plays at the opening of the Fillmore East (3/8/68) as CBS/Columbia Records buys up Big Brother's Mainstream contract and books studio time for the band.

Cheap Thrills (#1, 1968), originally titled *Dope, Sex and Cheap Thrills*, is a smash and driven up the charts by extracts "Down On Me" (#43, 1968) and "Piece of My Heart" (#12, 1968). Having announced that she is leaving the band at the end of the year, Joplin makes her last appearance with the band during the first week of December 1968 while in Hawaii.

Joplin plays four nights at New York's Fillmore East (2/11-14/69) with her new group, initially called Janis & the Joplinaires, which includes: Sam Andrews, Brad Campbell, Terry Clements, and Marcus Doubleday. During the year the band is renamed the Kozmic Blues Band, and the personnel changes. Prestigious gigs for the year include: the Fillmore West (3/20-23/69), London's Royal Albert Hall (4/21/69), the Newport '69 Pop Festival, the Texas International Festival, the Atlanta Pop Festival, and the New Orleans Pop Festival.

I Got Dem Ol' Kozmic Blues Again Mama! (#5, 1969), with extract "Kozmic Blues" (#41, 1969), climbs the chart, while the band struggles with live performances and finally splits before the end of the year. When Big Brother & the Holding Company reforms the following year, Joplin again appears with the band during performances at the Fillmore West and Avalon Ballroom. In May Joplin's new group, the Full-Tilt Boogie Band, debuts at a Hells Angels Benefit in San Rafael, California.

On August 6, 1970, Joplin participates in a 12-hour anti-war rock festival at Shea Stadium in New York. Two days later she buys a headstone for the grave of her idol, Bessie Smith, who is buried at the Mount Lawn cemetery in Philadelphia, Pennsylvania.

On October 4, 1970, Joplin is found dead at the Landmark Hotel, 7047 Franklin Ave., Hollywood, California. After partying the night before at Barney's Beanery (8447 Santa Monica Blvd.), she returned to her hotel where she died of an accidental heroin overdose. On February 27, 1971, *Pearl* (#1, 1971), compiled from her unfinished recording sessions, tops the album charts and is driven by sales of single extract "Me and Bobby McGee," penned by Kris Kristofferson.

Janis Joplin in Concert (#91, 1972), *Janis Joplin's Greatest Hits* (#37, 1973) and *Janis* (#54, 1975) are posthumous releases. The performer is inducted into the Rock and Roll Hall of Fame on January 12, 1995.

AUTOGRAPHS

An LP, magazine cover, ad, photo, or card signed by the artist: $600-$1,000

OFTEN OVERLOOKED MEMORABILIA

Movie memorabilia from *The Rose* (1979); a copy of the documentary *Janis* (1975); all associated items from the biographical play *Janis* (1991), which was forced to close due to a lawsuit

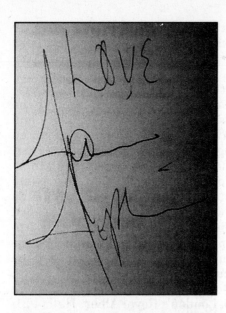

*A scarce signature
from "Pearl"*

REFERENCES/BOOKS

Numerous resources exist; *The Memorabilia Guide* is available through the address that follows. Serious collectors should opt for the fanzine *Pearl: The Janis Joplin Fanzine*, 178 Jarvis Street #506, Toronto, ON Canada

Jordan, Louis

Born: July 8, 1908, Died: February 4, 1975

Forties band leader Louis Jordan was the architect of the bridge between rhythm & blues and rock & roll. He is best remembered for his classics "Knock Me a Kiss," "I'm Gonna Move to the Outskirts of Town," "Five Guys Named Moe," "Caldonia," "Beware," "Choo Choo Cha Boogie," "Saturday Night Fish Fry," and "Let the Good Times Roll." His arrangements were inspired by swing and blues, then spiced by rock rhythms—all of his songs are indicative of the R&B "jump style." He later also landed the '50s hits "Ain't Nobody Here but Us Chickens," "Run Joe," Early in the Morning," and "School Days."

AUTOGRAPHS

A CD, LP, magazine cover, ad, photo, or card signed by the artist: $30-$75

OFTEN OVERLOOKED MEMORABILIA

Associated artifacts from others musicians' covers of his compositions

Journey

Formed 1973

Neal Schon, Born: February 27, 1954; Ross Valory; Gregg Rolie, Born: June 17, 1947; Prairie Prince, Born: May 7, 1950; and George Tickner*

*Prince departed in 1974 and Aynsley Dunbar was added. Tickner left in 1975, Robert Fleischman was briefly added in 1977, before Steve Perry, Born:1949 assumed responsibilities. Dunbar left in 1978 and Steve Smith joined the group. Rolie left in 1981 and Jonathan Cain took over on keyboards. Both Smith and Valory left in 1986. The band re-formed in 1996.

Former Santana road manager Walter Herbert brought former bandmates Neal Schon and Greg Rolie together again, while adding Ross Valory, George Tickner from Frumious Bandersnatch, to form Journey—a name picked from a radio contest on KSAN-FM. Tubes drummer Prairie Prince sat in on the group's first shows, before journeyman—no pun intended—Aynsley Dunbar was added. The band debuted at a 1974 New Year's Eve party held at San Francisco's Winterland and less than a year later found itself inked to a record deal with Columbia.

Following the completion of the group's first album, *Journey* (#138, 1975), Tickner left for medical school and was not replaced. *Look into the Future* (#100, 1975), the band's sophomore effort. The band continued its extensive touring schedule, and even supported Santana during a U.K. tour. *Next* (#85, 1977) followed, again with Rolie doing most of the singing from behind the keyboards. The lack of a dynamic frontman was a constant criticism, so a search was undertaken to find a lead singer. Robert Fleischmann was briefly recruited in June 1977 before the former lead singer of Alien Project, Steve Perry, was added.

Infinity (#21, 1978), the first album featuring Steve Perry, eventually charted for more than two years. Extract "Wheel in the Sky" (#57, 1978) became the band's first U.S. chart single. It was followed up by "Anytime" (#83, 1978), which featured Rolie on lead vocals, then "Lights" (#68, 1978). In October Dunbar departed and Steve Smith was added from the band Montrose.

Evolution (#20, 1979), the band's next album and second million seller, included singles "Just the Same Way" (#58, 1979) and "Lovin', Touchin', Squeezin'" (#16, 1979). *Departure* (#8, 1980) included the hit single "Any Way You Want It" (#23, 1980), while both "Walks Like a Lady" (#32, 1980) and "Good Morning Girl/Stay Awhile" (#55, 1980) also charted.

In 1981 the band decided to take advantage of its live appeal and released *Captured* (#9, 1981) with extract "The Party's Over (Hopelessly in Love)" (#34, 1981). Meanwhile, Rolie, tired of the band's extensive touring, decided to leave. He was replaced on keyboards by ex-Baby Jonathan Cain, who made his live debut on June 13, 1981, at the opening date of the "Escape" tour. *Escape* (#1, 1981) quickly topped the charts, driven by extracts "Who's Crying Now" (#4, 1981) and "Don't Stop Believin'" (#9, 1981), and a tour that saw the band supporting the Rolling Stones. "Open Arms" (#2, 1982), and "Still They Ride" (#19, 1982), also hit the singles chart, as did Perry's

duet with Kenny Loggins, "Don't Fight It" (#17, 1982).

Bolstered by music videos and a string of hit extracts, the Journey's post-1983 albums continued to sell at an outstanding pace. During this period the group's Top Twenty hits included: Separate Ways (Worlds Apart)" (#8, 1983), "Faithfully" (#12, 1983), "Only the Young" (#9, 1985), "Be Good to Yourself" (#9, 1986), "Suzanne" (#17, 1986), "Girl Can't Help It" (#17, 1986), and "I'll Be Alright Without You" (#14, 1987).

In 1984, Steve Perry released his first solo album, *Street Talk* (#12, 1984), which included the hit singles "Oh Sherrie" (#3, 1984), "She's Mine" (#21, 1984), "Strung Out" (#40, 1984), and "Foolish Heart" (#18, 1985). Meanwhile, havoc erupted within the band: Smith and Valory were fired, and recording sessions were disrupted due to the illness of Steve Perry's mother. Journey, now a trio, regrouped and recorded *Raised on Radio* (#4, 1986), which included the extracts "Be Good to Yourself" (#9, 1986), "Suzanne" (#17, 1986), "Girl Can't Help It" (#17, 1986), and "I'll Be Alright Without You" (#14, 1987).

In the spring of 1987, Journey members decided to go their separate ways. Not necessarily worlds apart, Schon and Cain headed to Bad English, and Smith fronted his own fusion band, Vital Information, before reuniting with Rolie and Valory in Storm. Perry released his second album, *For the Love of Strange Medicine* (#15, 1994).

In 1996, the band re-formed to record the album *Trial by Fire*. It was met with praise by critics and included cuts such as "Castles Burning," "Easy to Fall," and "It's Just the Rain."

AUTOGRAPHS

Group:

A CD, LP, magazine cover, ad, photo, or card signed by the group: $55-$160

Individual:

Neal Schon: $20-$30	Ross Valory: $10
Gregg Rolie: $15-$20	Prairie Prince: $5-$10
George Tinkner: $5	Aynsley Dunbar: 20-$25
Robert Fleischman: $5	Steve Perry: $30-$45
Steve Smith: $10	Jonathan Cain: $10

TOUR BOOKS/PROGRAMS/PASSES

Tour Books:

Evolution Tour (1979): $30-$35

1983 World Tour: $20-$25

Backstage Passes:

Cloth: $15-$20; Laminated: $20-$30 (1978-1984)

Cloth: $10-$12; Laminated: $15-$20 (1985-Present)

POSTERS/PRESS KITS

Promotional Posters:

1978-1984: $25-$60

1985-Present: $15-$25

Press Kits:

1978-1984: $35-$75

1985-Present: $20-$35

USED CLOTHING/EQUIPMENT

Guitar Picks:

Neal Schon: $25-$45

OFTEN OVERLOOKED MEMORABILIA

Associated memorabilia from the group's advertising deal with Budweiser beer (1979); movie memorabilia from *Vision Quest* (1985)

REFERENCES/BOOKS

Limited resources exist; no dedicated collector books

Joy Division/New Order

Formed 1976

Ian Curtis (1956-1980), Bernard Sumner (Albrecht), Peter Hook, and Stephen Morris

New Order formed 1980

Hook, Sumner, Morris, and Gillian Gilbert

This promising British '80s new-wave dance band is best remembered for the songs "She's Lost Control," "Transmission," and "Love Will Tear Us Apart," before the untimely suicide of Ian Curtis on May 18, 1980.

The remaining members regrouped as New Order and, in similar fashion, landed club hits such as "Everything's Gone Green" and "Temptation," before their breakthrough with "Blue Monday," which was an international hit and climbed to the Top Five on the Billboard dance chart.

The group followed with "Confusion," "True Faith" (#32, 1987), and the British World Cup Soccer theme "World in Motion..." (#1, U.K., 1990), before essentially parting company in lieu of solo projects. The group would later re-form in 1993 and tour the U.S.

AUTOGRAPHS

A CD, LP, magazine cover, ad, photo, or card signed by the group: $12-$35*

*New Order, original lineup. Double the price for Joy Division.

REFERENCES/BOOKS

A few resources exist; no dedicated collector books

Joy of Cooking

Formed 1967

Terry Garthwaite, Toni Brown, Ron Wilson, Fritz Kasten, and David Garthwaite*

*D. Garthwaite left in 1970 and Jeff Neighbore was added. Brown left in 1972.

This '70s folk-rock group, led by women, is best remembered for its one hit, "Brownsville."

AUTOGRAPHS

A CD, LP, magazine cover, ad, photo, or card signed by the group: $5

Judas Priest

Formed 1969

Kenneth "K.K." Downing, Born: October 27, 1951; and Ian Hill, Born: January 20, 1952*

*Rob Halford, Born: August 25, 1951, and John Hinch were added in 1971. Glenn Tipton was added in 1974, while Hinch departed. Alan Moore was also added in 1974. Moore left in 1977 and Simon Phillips was added. Phillips departed in 1978 and Les Binks was added. Binks left in 1979 and Dave Holland took over drumming responsibilities. Holland left in 1989 and Scott Travis was added. Both Halford and Travis left in 1992.

Late-70s British leather-metal band Judas Priest, known for its extravagant and outrageous live shows, is commonly associated with the songs "Living After Midnight," "Breaking the Law," and "You've Got Another Thing Comin'" (#67, 1982). The band's persistence proved worthwhile because by the mid-80s, it had successfully broken into the American market, although later in the decade it would lose ground to younger metal mavens.

In 1986, the wind was taken out of the band's "sales," by a lawsuit alleging that a song on the *Stained Glass* (1978) album contained subliminal messages that drove a Reno, Nevada, couple's sons to shoot themselves in 1985. Although the judge dismissed the charges in 1990, it took a considerable toll on the band.

Halford quit in 1992, and took Scott Travis with him, to form his own band, Flight. He would later reinvent himself as the leader of Gimp, an industrial-metal departure. Priest recruited Yank Tim "Ripper" Owens to fill Halford's slot.

AUTOGRAPHS
A CD, LP, magazine cover, ad, photo, or card signed by the group: $25-$55*
*Mid-80s lineup

TOUR BOOKS/PROGRAMS/PASSES
Tour Books:
World Tour 1984: $12
Mercenaries of Metal, 1988, U.K.: $15
The Painkiller Tour, 1990/91: $10
Backstage Passes:
Cloth: $10; Laminated: $12-$15

POSTERS/PRESS KITS
Promotional Posters: $8-$20
Press Kits: $10-$25

USED CLOTHING/EQUIPMENT
Guitar Picks: $20-$25
Drum Sticks: $15

OFTEN OVERLOOKED MEMORABILIA
Promotional pins - $5-$10; necklace - $12

REFERENCES/BOOKS
Limited resources exist; no dedicated collector books

The Judds/Wynonna

Formed 1983

Naomi (Dianna) Judd, Born: January 11, 1946; and Wynonna Judd (Christina Ciminella), Born: May 30, 1964

The Judds, the mid-80s mother and daughter act that hit like a tornado on an Oklahoma plain, exploded onto the country charts and into the hearts of many with their golden voices and "Dynasty" looks. As fate might have it, the group landed an RCA recording contract through a meeting with prominent Nashville producer Brent Maher when his daughter was injured in an auto accident. Naomi was compassionately nursing the child, and following her recovery, she gave a demo tape to Maher. The tape impressed him so much that he passed it to RCA executives, who signed the duo.

What followed was a C&W chart domination by the pair. Their Number One hits included "Mama He's Crazy" (1984), "Why Not Me" (1984), "Girls Night Out" (1985), "Love Is Alive" (1985), "Have Mercy" (1985), "Grandpa (Tell Me 'Bout the Good Old Days)" (1986), "Rockin' with the Rhythm of the Rain" (1986), "Cry Myself to Sleep" (1986), "I Know Where I'm Going" (1987), "Maybe Your Baby's Got the Blues" (1987), "Turn It Loose" (1988), and "Change of Heart" (1988). Numerous other hits also dominated the charts as the two made room on their mantles for their multiple Grammy Awards.

In 1991 Naomi announced her plans to retire as she faced chronic hepatitis. The result was a much publicized and emotional farewell tour. Wynonna then faced the task of tackling a solo career, which she did successfully with three Number One hits off her debut effort including "She Is His Only Need," "I Saw the Light," and "No One Else on Earth"—these were just the beginning to the success that followed. After taking some time off to have a baby, Wynonna returned to the road. Both Judds were reunited publicly during the half-time show of the 1994 Super Bowl. Naomi, whose illness was in remission, also published the book, *Love Can Build a Bridge*, which later became a highly-rated made-for-television movie in 1995.

AUTOGRAPHS
A CD, LP, magazine cover, ad, photo, or card signed by the group: $25-$45

TOUR BOOKS/PROGRAMS/PASSES
Backstage Passes:
Cloth: $10-$15; Laminated: $15-$25

POSTERS/PRESS KITS
Promotional Posters: $10-$35
Press Kits: $25-$75

USED CLOTHING/EQUIPMENT
Guitar Picks:: $15-$35

OFFTEN OVERLOOKED MEMORABILIA

OFTEN OVERLOOKED MEMORABILIA

Videotapes of their numerous television show appearances

REFERENCES/BOOKS

Love Can Build a Bridge, Naomi's memoir

The Jungle Brothers

Formed 1986

Mike G (Small); Afrika Baby Bambaataa (Nathaniel Hall), Born: June 22, 1970; and Sammy B (Burwell)*

*Torture (Colin Bobb) was added in 1993

K., Tonio

(Steve Krikorian)
Born: July 4, 1950

A member of a latter-day version of Buddy Holly's group the Crickets from (1972 to 1975), Krikorian turned to songwriting when the group disbanded. Hailed by Irving Azoff (the Eagles' manager), he signed to Full Moon, a subsidiary of Epic Records. *Life in the Foodchain* (1979), although enjoyed by critics, did little to bolster the claims of a new Bob Dylan. His follow-up albums *Amerika* (1980, Arista), *La Bomba* (1983, Capitol), *Romeo Unchained* (1986, A&M), and *Notes from the Lost Civilization* (1988, A&M) also did little to ignite greater sales, but again, most found a warm heart with a few critics. Meanwhile, Krikorian sustained his financial well-being by penning hits including "Love Is" (Vanessa Williams with Brian McKnight) and "You" (Bonnie Raitt).

AUTOGRAPHS

An LP, magazine cover, ad, photo, or card signed by the artist: $5-$10

Kaleidoscope

Formed 1966

Fenrus Epp (Max Buda), John Vidican, Solomon Feldthouse, David Lindley, and Chris Darrow*

*Numerous personnel changes

Known best as a springboard for David Lindley, who left the band to hook up with Jackson Browne, Kaleidoscope's eclectic albums were too much to recall, but not recalled enough—if you follow me. Basically the group was ignored and, despite an appearance at the 1968 Newport Folk Festival, it was still ignored, and although accompanied by a live act

This late-80s dance-rap act helped forge the '90s jazz-rap trend, while it ignited interest in the New York hip-hop underground with songs such as "Jim Browski" and "I'll House You." The Jungle Brothers efforts have garnered praise by critics, but as of yet the group has had little commercial success.

AUTOGRAPHS

A CD, LP, magazine cover, ad, photo, or card signed by the group: $10

OFTEN OVERLOOKED MEMORABILIA

Movie memorabilia from *Living Large*

that even included belly dancers—which weren't ignored—the albums still were.

Various line-ups continued the Kaleidoscope name throughout the years and even recorded into the late 1980s, with the same results. Whoever said "mediocrity doesn't breed mediocrity" never played in this band. As far as collecting, you may want to wait for *The Complete and Definitive Guide to Kaleidoscope Memorabilia,* coming to a bookstore near you, before starting!

AUTOGRAPHS

An LP, magazine cover, ad, photo, or card signed by the group: $5

Kansas

Formed 1970

Kerry Livgren, Born: September 18, 1949; Steve Walsh; Robby Steinhardt; Richard Williams; Phil Ehart; and Dave Hope*

*John Elefante replaced Walsh who left in 1981. The group disbanded in 1983 and then re-formed in 1986 as follows: Walsh, Ehart, Williams, Steve Morse, and Billy Greer.

Livgren, Hope, and Ehart, all buds from West Topeka High School in Topeka, Kansas, form the Gimlets with other local musicians. Inspired by Frank Zappa, the group plays the local dance circuit, although personnel changes plague the band—the only constant remains the trio. The following year they add classically-trained violinist Robby Steinhardt and relaunch themselves as White Clover. When Phil Ehart decides to visit the U.K. in 1972, the band splits, but re-forms when he returns a few months later.

In 1972 the re-formed White Clover adds Steve Walsh and Rich Williams to the last band configuration to now form Kansas. The group quickly begins to gel, and while refining their live skills and developing their own unique sound, they record a demo tape in 1974. The tape eventually lands in the hands

of a Kirshner Records executive who requests a live showcase, after which the band is signed to a recording contract.

Kansas (#174, 1974) (the group's debut album), *Songs for America* (#57, 1975), and *Masque* (#70, 1975) all sell well, which is attributable to extensive touring, but fail to garner that one big break that finally comes with the band's fourth effort. *Leftoverture* (#5, 1977) is driven up the album chart by extracted single "Carry On Wayward Son" (#11, 1977)—now a staple on FM classic radio.

Point of Know Return (#4, 1978) picks up right where *Leftoverture* left off and is driven up the charts by hit singles "Point of Know Return" (#28, 1978) and "Dust in the Wind" (#6, 1978), the group's only Top Ten single. *Two for the Show* (#32, 1979), a double-live album, follows as the band concentrates on its next self-produced effort *Monolith* (#10, 1979). Extracted single "People of the South Wind" (#23, 1979) helps sales, as does "Reason to Be" (#52, 1979).

Audio-Visions (#26, 1980) is the last album with Steve Walsh, who quits in January 1982. The band replaces him with John Elefante. *Vinyl Confessions* (#16, 1982) follows and is aided on the charts by the single "Play the Game Tonight" (#17, 1982). *Drastic Measures* (#41, 1983, CBS) doesn't sell as well as anticipated and is hurt by the falloff in concert attendance. A disappointed band comes off the road and decides to dissolve for awhile, while *The Best of Kansas* (#154, 1984) follows.

In the fall of 1986 Walsh, Ehart, and Williams resurrect Kansas and recruit Steve Morse (Dixie Dregs) and Billy Greer. The band signs to MCA Records and releases the comeback album *Power* (#35, 1987). The album also contains the hit single "All I Wanted" (#19, 1987). But follow-up *In the Spirit of Things* (#114, 1988) does little to excite a new legion of fans.

In 1992 *Live at the Whiskey* (Intersound) is released and appeals primarily to die-hard fans. It is followed by the now traditional summer tours. *Freaks of Nature* (Intersound, 1995) becomes the band's first studio offering in seven years, but does little to resurrect interest in the band, which now finally appears to be just "Dust in the Wind."

Contract signed by the members of Kansas

AUTOGRAPHS
Group:
A CD, LP, magazine cover, ad, photo, or card signed by the entire band: $50-$110*
*High end reflects vintage signed memorabilia

Individual:
Kerry Livgren: $20-$30 Steve Walsh: $15-$20
Robby Steinhardt: $15 Richard Williams: $10
Phil Ehart: $10-$15 Dave Hope: $10
John Elefante: $5

POSTERS/PRESS KITS
Promotional Posters: $15-$35
Press Kits: $10-$30

USED CLOTHING/EQUIPMENT
Guitar Picks:
Kerry Livgren: $10-$20
Richard Williams: $10-$15
Dave Hope: $10
Drum Sticks:
Phil Ehart: $10-$15

A couple of guitar picks from Kansas

OFTEN OVERLOOKED MEMORABILIA
Individual members' contributions to other albums (such as Walsh as guest vocalist on Steve Hackett's *Please Don't Touch*)

REFERENCES/BOOKS
Limited resources exist, but nothing that does justice to the band in my opinion; no dedicated collector books

Kantner, Paul : See Jefferson Airplane

Karn, Mike: See Japan

Kasenetz-Katz: See 1910 Fruitgum Company

Katrina and the Waves

Formed 1981
Katrina Leskanich, Kimberley Rew, Vince de la Cruz, and Alex Cooper

This band was seldom given credit for paying its dues, which it indeed did for years, before finally giv-

en its moment in the sun. Too clean cut for the British punk scene, the group honed its skills with a few indie label singles and two Canadian albums under the Attic Records label before it finally signed with Capitol Records.

Katrina and the Waves (#25, 1985) was driven up the charts by the extracted single "Walking on Sunshine" (#9, 1985), followed by "Do You Want Crying" (#37, 1985). Leskanich's powerful, clear vocals combined well with Rew's creative guitar work and gave the band a very likable sound, which matched its image. The problem was that by the time *Waves* (#49, 1986) hit in 1986, that wasn't what the public wanted anymore.

Dropped by Capitol, the band headed to England where *Break of Hearts* (#122, 1989, SBK), which landed a Top Twenty hit in "That's the Way" (#16, 1989), seemed more conducive for the band. As for collecting, memorabilia from early singles and the two Canadian albums is a good place to start, but a tough place to find relics. The Capitol material will be the easiest to run across in the form of press kits, promotional posters, etc.

AUTOGRAPHS
A CD, LP, magazine cover, ad, photo, or card signed by the group: $10-$15

POSTERS/PRESS KITS
Promotional Posters: $6-$10
Press Kits: $8-$12

USED CLOTHING/EQUIPMENT
Guitar Picks: $5

Kaz, Eric

Born 1946

Primarily known as a songwriter, Eric Kaz has been a member of numerous groups including the Blues Magoos and American Flyer. He was part of the Greenwich Village folk/rock scene in the mid-60s. Following the Blues Magoos, he tried his luck at soundtracks with *Greetings* (1968) and *Hi Mom* (1970) (both early efforts by Brian DePalma), before landing a contract with Atlantic in 1972.

Although his voice wasn't always memorable, his songs often were, and as such many were covered by other musicians—most is noteworthy "Love Has No Pride," popularized by Linda Ronstadt in 1973. In 1975 Kaz joined "to-be supergroup" American Flyer with Steve Katz (Blood, Sweat and Tears), Doug Yule (Velvet Underground), and Craig Fuller (Pure Prairie League) for two uneventful United Artists albums before disbanding.

"Hearts on Fire" (#19, 1981, co-written with Randy Meisner), "Heartbeat" (#5, 1986), "That's What Love Is All About" (#19, 1987), and "Cross My Heart" (#1 C&W, 1992) all have one thing in common—Eric Kaz

as author. His songwriting skills have continued to thrive, despite the hurdles he has faced in other bands. We will no doubt see many more hits from him before he retires his pen.

AUTOGRAPHS
All LP, magazine cover, ad, photo, or card signed by the artist: $10

KC and the Sunshine Band/KC

Formed 1973

Harry Wayne Casey, Born: January 31, 1951; Richard Finch; Jerome Smith; Robert Johnson; Fermin Coytisolo; Ronnie Smith; Denvil Liptrot; James Weaver; and Charles Williams

H.W. Casey, while working for Tone Distributors in 1973, met engineer and bassist Richard Finch, and the two formed a songwriting partnership as well as KC and the Sunshine Junkanoo Band. Junkanoo had a Caribbean-style, pop-oriented sound with heavy percussion that was popular. "Blow Your Whistle" (#27, R&B, 1973), the group's debut single, successfully entered the R&B chart and was followed by "Sound Your Funky Horn" (#17, U.K., 1974), this time recorded and released under the name KC and the Sunshine Band. Meanwhile, the duo of Finch and Casey, which penned George McCrae's "Rock Your Baby" (#1, 1974), watched the single top the U.S. chart. The band also made its U.K. chart debut with "Queen of Clubs" (#7, U.K., 1974).

"Get Down Tonight" (#1, 1974), the band's next single, became the group's breakthrough record, topping both the pop and R&B charts. Now an established band of nine members, the group spent the next three years delivering hit singles like "That's the Way (I Like It)" (#1, 1975) and "(Shake, Shake, Shake) Shake Your Booty" (#1, 1976). The band then became only the second group (the Jackson 5 is the other) to achieve four U.S. Number One singles in the '70s with the hit "I'm Your Boogie Man" (#1,1977). "Keep It Comin' Love" (#2, 1977), the band's next release, was nearly its fifth chart-topper.

Although it seemed like the band had run its course in 1978, it bounced back with the minor hits "Boogie Shoes" and "It's the Same Old Song." The following year the band delivered "Do You Wanna Go Party" (#8, R&B, 1979) and then struck with "Please Don't Go" (#1, 1980), followed by "Yes, I'm Ready" (#2, 1979) (featuring Teri De Sario).

In 1981, TK Records filed for bankruptcy and the group disbanded. Casey then signed to Epic Records and delivered *The Painter* under the group's name and *Space Cadet*, his solo debut. On January 15, 1982, Casey was seriously injured in a head-on collision near his home in Hialeah, Florida. Upon his full recovery he released *All in a Night's Work* with hit extract "Give It Up" (#1, U.K., 1983).

The duo of Finch and Casey also continued songwriting and production work and by the early '90s, they repackaged their act and took it on the road. *Oh Yeah!* and *Get Down Live!*, their next two albums, marked the band's return in 1995. The group now frequents disco revival shows, so break out your leisure suit and watch that polyester stretch!

AUTOGRAPHS

Group:
A CD, LP, magazine cover, ad, photo, or card signed by the entire band: $20-$40*
*High end reflects vintage signed memorabilia

Individual:
H.W. Casey and Richard Finch (duo): $20

TOUR BOOKS/PROGRAMS/PASSES

Backstage Passes:
Cloth: $5; Laminated: $7-$10 (1981-Present)
Cloth: $5-8; Laminated: $10-$15 (Prior to 1981)

POSTERS/PRESS KITS

Promotional Posters: $5-$7 (1981-Present), $10-$30 (1975-1980)
Press Kits: $10 (1981-Present), $15-$35 (1975-1980)

USED CLOTHING/EQUIPMENT

Guitar Picks:
Richard Finch: $10

OFTEN OVERLOOKED MEMORABILIA

Individual members' contributions to other albums; movie memorabilia form *Saturday Night Fever* (1978)

K-Doe, Ernie

(Ernest Kador, Jr.)
Born: February 22, 1936

Best known for chart-topper "Mother-in-Law," he was essential in bringing attention to the R&B New Orleans sound in the early '60s. He was raised in New Orleans and, like many others, he was heavily influenced by gospel music. Kador was a member of the Golden Chain Jubilee Singers and the Zion Travelers before he landed with the Moonglows and the Flamingos. By the time he joined with the Blue Diamonds, he changed his name to K-Doe.

While the Blue Diamonds became a popular attraction in New Orleans, K-Doe released solo efforts including the regional hit "Hello My Lover," followed by his Number One "Mother-in-Law" (#1, 1961). "Te-Ta-Te-Ta-Ta" (#21, R&B, 1961) and "I Cried My Last Tear" (#69, 1961) were his most successful follow-up singles on Minit. He bounced back in 1967 with "Later for Tomorrow" (#37, R&B, 1967) and remained active in the music scene into the '90s.

AUTOGRAPHS

An LP, magazine cover, ad, photo, or card signed by the artist: $10-$20*
*High end reflects vintage signed memorabilia

Keith

(James Barry Keefer)

"98.6" (#7, 1967) gave James Barry Keefer, who changed his name to Keith, his first and possibly last Top Ten single. His previous single, "Ain't Gonna Lie," didn't break into the Top Thirty. In 1969 the adventures of Keith included being picked up for draft evasion. He then spent a year stint in the army, before landing with Zappa's DiscReet Records—he even sang on tour with Frank. Once his temperature dropped, little more was seen of Keith.

AUTOGRAPHS

An LP, magazine cover, ad, photo, or card signed by the artist: $5-$10*
*High end reflects signed sleeve from "98.6"

Kelly, Paul

Born: January 13, 1955

Australian Paul Kelly, better known down under than here in the States, started out as a folk singer in the '70s. He established a reputation for himself while playing the local Melbourne music scene. He recorded two albums with the Dots before he finally ended up with the Coloured Girls/Paul Kelly and the Messengers (U.S.). While the critics typically praised his work, releases such as *Gossip* had low sales. When A&M dropped Kelly in 1989, he headed to the States, where he spent a decade looking for a recording deal. In 1994, he released *Wanted Man* on Vanguard—isn't that ironic!

AUTOGRAPHS

A CD, LP, magazine cover, ad, photo, or card signed by the artist: $5-$10

Kendricks, Eddie: See the Temptations

Kenner, Chris

Born: December 25, 1929, Died: January 25, 1976

Although he was a very talented vocalist—"I Like It Like That" (1961) can attest to such a claim—Kenner is best remembered for his songwriting. "Sick and Tired" (#22, 1958) was covered by Fats Domino, while "Land of 1000 Dances" (#6, 1966) landed Wilson Pickett in the Top Ten. He teamed up with Allen Toussaint at Minit Records for "I Like It Like That" (#2, 1961) in their very first collaboration. "Something

You Got" was a regional success in New Orleans where he had been active in the music scene since the '50s. He continued to record until 1969 and died seven years later.

AUTOGRAPHS

An LP, magazine cover, ad, photo, or card signed by the artist: $20-$30*

*High end reflects vintage signed memorabilia, hit related

Kentucky Colonels

Formed 1961

Clarence White, Born: June 7, 1944, Died: July 14, 1973; Billy Lathum; Roland White, Born: April 23, 1938; Roger Bush; LeRoty Mack; and Bobby Sloane

The Kentucky Colonels are best known for the brothers White, mandolinist Roland and guitarist Clarence (who found himself in the last edition of the Byrds). The brothers had been playing country music together since 1954 as the Country Boys, with brother Eric on bass. The Kentucky Colonels was formed when Eric left and was replaced by Roger Bush in 1961. The band then became a regular on the national folk circuit and familiar to many through the larger folk festivals. The band hit a pinnacle with the classic "Appalachian Swing!" (1964).

The following year Clarence left the band for session work in Los Angeles. He would then go on to the Byrds (1968) until their split in 1973. Meanwhile Roland made attempts to resurrect the band after his brother's departure. He even found himself working with Lester Flatt and Bill Monroe. The band regrouped with Clarence for occasional shows following the Byrds split. Tragically, Clarence was killed by a drunk driver while loading his equipment van in 1973. Various forms of the band continue to occasionally perform on the bluegrass and folk circuit.

AUTOGRAPHS

An LP, magazine cover, ad, photo, or card signed by the entire band: $15-$40*

*High end reflects vintage signed memorabilia, such as "Appalachian Swing!" related

OFTEN OVERLOOKED MEMORABILIA

Their television appearances on Andy Griffith's show (twice); Clarence White's work with the Byrds

The Kentucky Headhunters

Formed 1986

Greg Martin, Ricky Phelps, Doug Phelps, and Richard Young*

*Both Phelps departed in 1991 and were replaced with Anthony Kenny and Mark Orr

"Hillbilly Speed Metal" at its finest—the band crawled out of the Kentucky Hills as remnants of redneck bar band Itchy Brother, which had nearly landed a record deal with Zeppelin's Swan Song at one point. *Pickin' On Nashville*, the group's debut album, opened some eyes and crushed a few eardrums, as song such as Bill Monroe's "Walk Softly on This Heart of Mine" treaded a bit heavier than anticipated. The band's next single, "Dumas Walker" (#26, C&W), broke into the country Top Thirty, while its debut turned gold faster than any other country album. The result earned the Headhunters a Grammy for Best Country Performance by Duo or Group with Vocal.

Electric Barnyard (#29, 1991) went gold in one week, attributable to the group's growing popularity and extensive touring. Its release, however, marked the departure of the Phelps brothers. The Headhunters then recruited former Itchy Brothers Orr and Kennedy and released *Rave On!* before collaborating with the legendary Johnnie Johnson in 1994 on *That'll Work*.

AUTOGRAPHS

A CD, LP, magazine cover, ad, photo, or card signed by the entire band: $25-$40*

*High end includes Phelps brothers

POSTERS/PRESS KITS

Promotional Posters: $10

Press Kits: $10-$15

USED CLOTHING/EQUIPMENT

Guitar Picks: $6-$8

Kershaw, Doug

Born: January 24, 1936

Doug Kershaw, "The Premier Cajun Fiddler, " gleans his roots from the traditional swamp waters of the Louisiana bayous where he has lived since his migration from a tiny island in the Gulf of Mexico. He started practicing fiddle at an early age and has since taught himself more than twenty-five other instruments.

Kershaw, a graduate of McNeese State University with a degree in mathematics, formed the Continental Playboys with two of his siblings before he began recording as a duo with brother Rusty. By 1957, Rusty and Doug became regulars on the Grand Ole Opry. "Louisiana Man" climbed into the Country Top Ten and soon became his hallmark. The duo hit in 1961 with "Diggy Liggy Lo" before breaking up.

The Cajun Way (1969, Warner Brothers) brought him to the attention of a national audience, as did his numerous television appearances. He continues to tour and record during the '90s.

AUTOGRAPHS

An LP, magazine cover, ad, photo, or card signed by the artist: $8-$15

OFTEN OVERLOOKED MEMORABILIA

His numerous celluloid appearances: *Zachariah*, *Medicine Ball Caravan*, *We Have Come for Your Daughters*, and *Days of Heaven*; associated memorabilia from his Grand Ole Opry days

Khan, Chaka

(Yvette Marie Stevens)
Born: March 23, 1953

Khan was in her first band, the Crystalettes, by the age of 11. As a teenager she was member of the Afro-Arts Theater she even toured briefly with Mary Wells. She worked in bands Lyfe and the Babysitters before ending up in Rufus with Kevin Murphy (American Breed) and Andre Fisher in 1972.

Khan went solo in 1978, having already attained success with Rufus, and released *Chaka* (#12, 1978), with hit extract "I'm Every Woman" (#21, 1979), penned by Ashford and Simpson. Still under contract for two more albums with Rufus, she traded off between careers while also collaborating with numerous other musicians including Chick Corea, Freddie Hubbard, and Stanley Clarke.

I Feel for You (#14, 1984) yielded the hit single "I Feel for You" (#3, 1984), which was written by Prince. The album offered a diverse sound mix, with appearances by Melle Mel of Grandmaster Flash and the Furious Five, and Stevie Wonder, who played harmonica. While she garnered a Grammy for the track, her future efforts failed to meet expectations. Her album *Destiny* only reached #67 and *CK* didn't make the Top Hundred. She then moved to Europe, reappeared on Steve Winwood's "Higher Love," and began to resurrect her career. Eventually she picked up Grammys for her duet with Ray Charles ("I'll Be Good To You") and for "The Woman I Am" in the Best R&B Vocal Performance category. Her daughter is a member of the group Pretty in Pink.

Nothing short of a bundle of talent, she remains incredibly active in the music business and always seems to add her efforts to numerous humanitarian causes including AIDS research.

AUTOGRAPHS

An LP, magazine cover, ad, photo, or card signed by the artist: $10-$25

POSTERS/PRESS KITS

Promotional Posters: $10
Press Kits: $10-$12

OFTEN OVERLOOKED MEMORABILIA

Her numerous contributions to other musical efforts; associated movie memorabilia from: *Krush Groove* (1985), *Labyrinth* (1986), *Clockers* (1995), *To Wong Foo, Thanks for Everything, Julie Newmar* (1995), and *Waiting to*

Exhale (1996); related television appearances by her or her music on *Miami Vice* (1/25/86), "Celebrate the Soul of American Music" (6/29/91), *Summer Scene* (7/16/92) - BBC1-TV, *Tonight* (12/15/92), and numerous award show appearances

****

"On The Edge"

Nusrat Fateh Ali Khan

Khan, the eminent translator of qawwali, had been a fixture in music for more than a decade. Unfortunately, it had taken that long for him to gain any recognition here in the United States. Prodigious in physical stature and octave range, his concerts often seem hypnotic. He could both ignite and calm an audience with his arrangements. *Devotional and Love Songs* (Real World, 1989) is a good place to start your collecting. As his popularity has grown, more and more pieces of memorabilia have found their way into collectors' hands in the United States. Khan died in 1997.

****

Kid Creole and the Coconuts/ Dr. Buzzard's Original Savannah Band

Dr. Buzzard's Original Savannah Band Formed 1974

Kid Creole (August Darnell), Born: August 12, 1950; Andy Hernandez (Coati Mundi); Stony Browder Jr.; Cory Daye; and Mickey Sevilla

Kid Creole and the Coconuts Formed 1980

Darnell, Hernandez, Fonda Rae, Lourdes Cotto, Brooksie Wells, Franz Karuns, Andrew Lloyd, Winston Grennan, and Peter Schott

Kid Creole (a.k.a. August Darnell) formed the In-Laws and later Dr. Buzzard's Original Savannah Band, where he had some chart success with "Whispering/Cherchez la Femme/Se Si Bon" (#27, 1976). When future releases had limited success, the group disbanded. Originally conceived as a side project, Darnell and the Coconuts released *Off the Coast of Me*, its debut album. The group soon gained a reputation as an outstanding show band, sporting elaborate costumes while moving to a well-choreographed routine.

Fresh Fruit in Foreign Places (#180, 1981), the band's unique follow-up album, told a story of musical stops with accompanied rapping narratives. The material was presented at New York's Public Theater to solid reviews. *Wise Guy* (#145, 1982), the group's next album, included what was to be its only chart single, "I'm a Wonderful Thing, Baby" (#44, R&B, 1982). The album was originally conceived as

a Darnell solo album, although it retained the group's name. It was a good year for the band, especially in the U.K. where it scored three hits: "I'm a Wonderful Thing, Baby" (#4, 1982), "Stool Pigeon" (#7, 1982), and "Annie, I'm Not Your Daddy" (#2, 1982). Darnell currently remains active in the business.

AUTOGRAPHS

An LP, magazine cover, ad, photo, or card signed by the entire band: $10-$20

POSTERS/PRESS KITS

Promotional Posters: $5-$7
Press Kits: $10

OFTEN OVERLOOKED MEMORABILIA

Movie memorabilia from *Against All Odds* (1984) and *New York Stories* (1989)

Kid Frost

(Arturo Molina, Jr.)
Born: May 31, 1962

The multi-talented Kid Frost uses hip hop—he raps in both Spanish and English—to convey the issues facing urban life in East Los Angeles. He was raised on military bases and later moved to California. *Hispanic Causing Panic* (#67, 1990), his impressive album debut, included the powerful "La Raza" (#42, 1990). In 1989 he founded the Latin Alliance, a coalition of Hispanic rappers using their music for unification rather than violence.

East Side Story (#73, 1992), bit hard into urban issues and included a classic cover of Bill Withers "No Sunshine." Frost remains active in numerous social and political causes and like few others, practices what he preaches!

AUTOGRAPHS

An LP, magazine cover, ad, photo, or card signed by the artist: $10-$15

POSTERS/PRESS KITS

Promotional Posters: $8-$10
Press Kits: $10

OFTEN OVERLOOKED MEMORABILIA

Movie memorabilia from *American Me*

Kid 'n Play

Formed 1988

Kid (Christopher Reid) and Play (Christopher Martin)

In the early '90s Kid 'n Play made their mark with rap and dance performances in the *House Party* movies. In the mould of Jazzy Jeff and the Fresh Prince, they presented a more wholesome view of hip hop.

Hailing from the same neighborhood in Queens that spawned Eric B. (Eric B. and Rakim) and Hurby Azor (Producer), they landed solidly on the R&B charts with "Rollin' with Kid 'n Play" (#11, R&B, 1989), along with "2 Hype" (#46, R&B, 1989), "Fun House (The House We Dance In)" (#27, R&B, 1990), and "Ain't Gonna Hurt Nobody" (#51, 1991).

The group's debut album *2 Hype* was a finely mixed brew of go-go and house styles; it didn't take long for it to top the R&B album chart. When the two appeared in the movie *House Party*, they were accused of "going mainstream" by much of the adoring public, despite a strong performance.

AUTOGRAPHS

An LP, magazine cover, ad, photo, or card signed by the group: $15-$25

POSTERS/PRESS KITS

Promotional Posters: $10-$15
Press Kits: $10-$15

OFTEN OVERLOOKED MEMORABILIA

Movie memorabilia from *House Party* (1990), *House Party 2* (1991), *Class Act* (1992), and *House Party 3* (1994); videotape episodes of their Saturday morning cartoon *Kid 'n Play*

Johnny Kidd and the Pirates

Formed 1959

Prominent lineup: Johnny Kidd (Frederick Heath, 1939-1966), Mick Green, Johnny Spence, and Frank Farley

This late-50s British pop-rock singles band is best remembered for the classic hit "Shakin' All Over" (#1, U.K., 1960) and other minor hits including "You Got What It Takes," "Restless," "I'll Never Get Over You," and "Hungry for Love," before the Merseybeat sound came crashing down.

The band disbanded in April 1966, only to reunite weeks later, but in the fall Kidd was killed in an automobile accident. The group resurrected unsuccessfully years later.

AUTOGRAPHS

A CD, LP, magazine cover, ad, photo, or card signed by the group: $20-$55*
*Original lineup

Kihn, Greg/Greg Kihn Band

Formed 1975

Greg Kihn, Robbie Dunbar, Larry Lynch, and Steve Wright*

*Dave Carpender replaced Dunbar in 1976. Gary Phillips was added in 1980. Carpender left in 1982 and Greg Douglas was added.

One of the original acts on the Beserkley label of Berkeley, California, Kihn found his way to California from Baltimore in late 1974. The following year he contributed two songs to a record label anthology and also added his backup vocals on Jonathan Richman's "Roadrunner." For his debut album, he used labelmates Earth Quake as his support band—some members went on to join the artist fully as members of the Greg Kihn Band. The group's second album, *Greg Kihn Again* (1976), included a cover of Springsteen's "For You," which so impressed "The Boss," that he too adapted the arrangement.

The band's releases which followed sold moderately well, especially in the Bay Area, because the group had developed a cult following through its presence on the club circuit. The band's big break happened in 1981 as the album *Rockihnroll* (#32, 1981) was driven up the charts on the success of extract "The Breakup Song (They Don't Write 'Em)" (#15, 1981). "Jeopardy" (#2, 1983), from the album *Khinspiracy* (#15, 1983), was the band's next successful single. In 1985, Kihn landed his last Top Forty single with "Lucky" (#30, 1985), from the album *Citizen Kihn* (#51, 1985).

He released two original sets for Rhino, in between novel and screenplay projects. Praised by critics, *Mutiny* (1994) was an acoustic set that featured covers by a variety of artists.

AUTOGRAPHS
An LP, magazine cover, ad, photo, or card signed by the entire band: $10-$15

POSTERS/PRESS KITS
Promotional Posters: $7-$10
Press Kits: $10

USED CLOTHING/EQUIPMENT
Guitar Picks: $10

OFTEN OVERLOOKED MEMORABILIA
Copies of his fan newsletter *Rocklife*: $3-$5

Killing Joke

Formed 1978
Jaz Coleman, Geordie (K. Walker), Youth (Martin Glover), and Paul Ferguson*

*Geordie and Youth departed in 1982 and were replaced by Paul Raven. Ferguson left in 1988 and Geordie returned. Martin Atkins was added in 1988.

Eighties British punk-rock act with a disco beat, Killing Joke is perhaps best remembered for the showmanship of frontman Jaz Coleman, who was kind of like a cross between Adam Ant and the Village People—warpaint and all! The group's first single, "Wardance," garnered accolades from the legendary DJ John Peel, and it was followed by other songs such as "Psyche" and "Follow the Leader," the latter of which actually found itself on the disco chart. But by the third album, the group was unraveling: Coleman's occult interests and paranoia caused him to flee to Iceland before the Apocalypse, which I thought already happened during the '60s. Coleman, Geordie, and Youth eventually resurfaced as a three piece in 1994.

AUTOGRAPHS
A CD, LP, magazine cover, ad, photo, or card signed by the group: $6-$10

King, Albert

(Albert Nelson)
Born: April 25, 1923, Died: December 21, 1992

Sixties Blues legend Albert King is best remembered for songs like "Lonesome in My Bedroom," "Bad Luck Blues," "Don't Throw Your Love on Me Too Strong," and "Laundromat Blues," as well as for his extraordinary guitar craftsmanship. He had the unique distinction of playing both the first and last show at the Fillmore East (March 8, 1968 and June 27, 1971). He is so revered that his songs have been covered by numerous acts including Free, the Electric Flag, and John Mayall. He toured extensively through the '70s, '80s, and right up to his death in 1992 .

AUTOGRAPHS
A CD, LP, magazine cover, ad, photo, or card signed by the artist: $10-$40

OFTEN OVERLOOKED MEMORABILIA
Associated artifacts from the numerous other artists who covered his music

King, B.B.

(Riley B. King)
Born: September 16, 1925

B.B. King is the "King" of modern day blues. His trademark Gibson guitar "Lucille" passionately sings each note with such delicate perfection, that when combined his left-hand vibrato, you would swear the guitar was speaking directly to you completely unassisted. He has influenced, in one way or another, every major rock guitarist including legends such as Eric Clapton, David Gilmour, Mike Bloomfield, The Edge, and Buddy Guy.

King is the son of a sharecropper and was influenced in his youth by the early blues and jazz guitar pioneers. The self-taught guitarist found himself leading a trio in Memphis, Tennessee, where he had relocated (1946), to link up with Sonny Boy Williamson. After impressing a local radio station, he was given his own slot, *The Sepia Swing Show*, on WDIA. The radio station's publicity man dubbed King the

"Beale Street Blues Boy," which was later shortened to "B.B." Between the radio show and his live performances, trading licks with Johnny Ace and Bobby "Blue" Bland, King developed an impressive reputation.

In 1951, having already recorded some previous songs including "Miss Martha King," he released "Three O'Clock Blues" (#1, R&B, 1951), his eighth single and first chart topper. He followed it with "You Didn't Want Me" (#1, R&B, 1951), "Please Love Me" (#1, R&B, 1953), and "You Upset Me Baby"(#1, R&B, 1954). During this period he was catapulted into the spotlight and landed prestigious bookings. Part of his extensive touring schedule included Harlem's Apollo and Washington, D.C.'s Howard. He later stated that he played more than 300 one-nighters in 1956 alone.

In 1961 he took part in the Alan Freed Spectacular at the Hollywood Bowl, on the strength of single "Sweet Sixteen" (#2, R&B, 1961). The following year he moved from the Kent label to the larger ABC Record Company that was eventually absorbed by MCA in 1979. On November 12, 1964, he played a concert at the Regal Theater in Chicago, Illinois. The show was recorded and eventually released—it became regarded as one of the greatest classic blues records ever (*Live at the Regal*). Singles "Rock Me Baby" (#34, 1964), "Paying the Cost to Be the Boss" (#39, 1968), and "The Thrill Is Gone" (#15, 1969) showed the depth of his craftsmanship and his ability to transcend musical lines. By the end of the '60s he played nearly every festival and jammed with the greatest guitarists of the era including Jimi Hendrix.

By the '70s, all of King's albums were consistent sellers, and he even managed an occasional Top Forty single or two such as "Ask Me No Questions" (#40, 1971), "To Know You Is to Love You" (#38, 1973), and "I Like to Live the Love" (#28, 1973). On January 21, 1987, he was inducted into the Rock and Roll Hall of Fame and the following year he was presented with the Lifetime Achievement Award at the 30th Annual Grammy Awards. U2's "When Love Comes to Town" (#6, 1989) landed in the Top Ten on the U.S. singles chart and featured King as a prominent guest.

A vintage B.B. King poster from a July 29, 1955 concert at the Marine Room in Galveston, TX. It is valued at $6,000. From the collection of Dr. Dennis Hickey.

During his lifetime B.B. King has been honored with nearly every related music award, attended nearly every music festival, and jammed with the best there is in rock and roll music. If rock and roll had a Mt. Rushmore, B.B. King would be on it!

AUTOGRAPHS

A CD, LP, magazine cover, ad, photo, or card signed by the artist: $20-$100

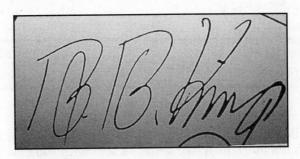

B.B. King's signature

TOUR BOOKS/PROGRAMS/PASSES

Tour Books:
Super Sessions '92 (European Tour): $10

POSTERS/PRESS KITS

Promotional Posters:
1990- Present: $20-$35

Press Kits:
1990-Present: $20-$30

USED CLOTHING/EQUIPMENT

Guitar Picks: $50-$75

A nice assortment of B.B. King guitar picks

OFTEN OVERLOOKED MEMORABILIA

An autographed bottle of Pepticon; movie memorabilia from *For the Love of Ivy* (1968), *Into the Night* (1985), and *Rattle and Hum* (1989) one sheets - $25; videotapes from his numerous television appearances including *Donahue Live* (1971), *Good Morning America* (1978) (includes lawyer F. Lee Bailey), *Late Night With David Letterman* (2/28/85, 8/1/89, 1/22/96), *Coast to Coast* (1990), *The Tonight Show* (12/31/90, 8/13/92), "Willie Nelson the Big Six-O" (5/22/93), "Apollo Theatre Hall of Fame" (8/4/93), *Austin City Limits* (5/11/95), "Blues Summit Concert" (9/28/95), "18th Annual Kennedy Center Honors" (12/3/95), and *Touched by an Angel* (2/3/96); memorabilia associated with *Happy Anniversary, Charlie Brown!* (1989) (includes the King song "Joe Cool") and *The Simpsons Sing the Blues* (1990); "Am I Cool, Or What?" (Garfield homage, 1991); memorabilia from the 1990 Rose Bowl Parade—King rides on a float; a rubbing from his star on the Hollywood Walk of Fame; all items associated with his relationship with

Gibson Guitars; all memorabilia from his restaurant and nightclub B.B. King's Memphis Blues Club, on Beale Street, Memphis; a sign from Interstate 55 through Jackson, MS—B.B. King Freeway; memorabilia from his many Hard Rock Cafe inaugurals; King's first CD-ROM (1996); a copy of his Wendy's television commercial (1996)

REFERENCES/BOOKS

A few resources exist, begin with Charles Sawyer's book, *B.B. King: The Authorized Biography;* no dedicated collector books

King, Ben E.

(Benjamin Nelson)
Born: September 23, 1938

Ben E. King, the former lead singer of the Drifters, left his mark as a solo artist as well with song such as "Spanish Harlem" (#10, 1961), "Stand By Me" (#4, 1961), "Don't Play That Song" (#11, 1962), and "I (Who Have Nothing)" (#29, 1963).

King emerged again in the '70s with Atlantic Records and scored with "Supernatural Thing, Part 1" (#5, 1975) and a handful of R&B hits including two with the Average White Band. His career was revived when "Stand By Me" was used in a film by Rob Reiner in 1986.

AUTOGRAPHS

A CD, LP, magazine cover, ad, photo, or card signed by the artist: $10-$25

OFTEN OVERLOOKED MEMORABILIA

Movie memorabilia from *Stand By Me* and *The Book of Love;* all Drifters artifacts; videotapes from his numerous television appearances including *Ready Steady Go!* (2/7/64, 10/15/65), "David Letterman's Sixth Anniversary Special" (1988), and the *Late Show With David Letterman* (3/2/94); memorabilia from the Genesis album The Lamb Lies Down On Broadway (King sang "On Broadway"); a copy of a Levi 501 jeans television commercial (1987)

King, Carole

(Carole Klein)
Born: February 9, 1940

Carole King is a gifted singer/songwriter whose career came in two phases—first as a prolific Brill Building songwriter and later as a successful solo artist. During her early years she worked with Gerry Goffin, who would later become her husband, writing songs together before both were hired to work with Neil Sedaka, Cynthia Weil, and Barry Mann at Don Kirshner and Al Nevin's Aldon Music in the Brill Building. They wrote more than one hundred songs, many of which were huge hits, such as "Will You Still Love Me Tomorrow?," "Chains," and "Don't Bring Me Down." In 1962 King-Goffin arranged, conducted, and produced "The Loco-Motion" for Little Eva, who

also just happened to be their baby-sitter. It was during this time that King began toying with the idea of a solo career.

King formed the City with Charles Larkey (her second husband) and Danny Kortchmar; they both played previously with the Fugs. The group released one unsuccessful album, but two songs from it would later yield hits for other artists: "Hi-De-Ho" (BS&T) and "You've Got a Friend" (James Taylor). James Taylor, who was also a part of the New York club circuit scene, encouraged King to write her own lyrics and not to give up on her solo career. Following her second album, *Writer* (1970), she entered the studio to produce *Tapestry* (#1, 1971), one of the most commercially successful and monumental albums in rock 'n' roll history. Not only did the album yield hits with "It's Too Late" (#1, 1971) and "So Far Away" (#14, 1971), but it set the tone for the music of the '70s.

Tapestry stayed on the album chart for nearly six years and it ignited interest in the artist's entire catalogue. "Jazzman" (#2, 1974) also proved a successful single for King, who was also writing songs for a children's program, *Really Rosie.* She later toured, which she had often been reluctant to do, with a band called Navarro. It was there that she collaborated with her next husband, Rick Evers, who later died of a heroin overdose in 1978.

In the years that followed, she worked on various projects, toured, and occasionally released an album, before even trying her luck on Broadway in 1994. She was inducted into the Rock and Roll Hall of Fame in 1990.

AUTOGRAPHS

A CD, LP, magazine cover, ad, photo, or card signed by the artist: $15-$25

OFTEN OVERLOOKED MEMORABILIA

Memorabilia from her Broadway acting debut in *Bloodbrothers;* Simple Things mobile: $50

REFERENCES/BOOKS

A few resources exist dating back to 1976, but none do justice to the singer in my opinion; no dedicated collector books

King Crimson

Formed 1969

Robert Fripp, Born: May 16, 1946; Greg Lake, Born: November 10, 1948; Ian McDonald, Born: June 25, 1946; Michael Giles; and Pete Sinfield*

*McDonald, Giles, and Lake departed in 1969. Gordon Haskell, Andrew McCulloch, and Mel Collins were added in 1970. Haskell and McCulloch left in 1971 and Boz Burrell and Ian Wallace joined the band. Sinfield also departed in 1971. Burrell, Wallace, and Collins left in 1972. Bill Bruford, Jamie Muir, John Wetton, David Cross, and Robert Palmer were recruited in 1972. Muir left in 1973, Cross in 1974, and then the group disbanded. The group reformed in 1981 as follows: Fripp, Bruford, Adrian Below,

and Tony Levin. The group disbanded in 1984. The group re-formed in 1994 as follows: Fripp, Bruford, Levin, Pat Mastelotto, and Trey Gunn.

King Crimson, the late-60s British progressive art-rock band, is best known for its only common denominator over the years—leader Robert Fripp. The band has been plagued by personnel changes since its inception. King Crimson's reputation seems to have manifested over time, no doubt attributable to Fripp's eccentric reputation, and a rediscovering of its older works, such as *In the Court of the Crimson King*, by a new generation.

The group's list of talented alumni reads like that of the New York Yankees, but like the legendary baseball team, notoriety and talent command a price and a significant share of the spotlight, neither of which was really available in the band. Fripp had numerous offers to leave the "big red dinosaur" to join bands such as Yes, but refused in favor of his project. With each new ensemble, fans hoped for a more stable environment, but such was never the case.

In 1974 Fripp officially declared King Crimson was dead! To that, fans responded if Fripp isn't dead, than neither is the band, and of course the buyer is always right. Frippertronics followed, as did session work for Fripp, with the usual "cranial committee" of Eno, David Bowie, Peter Gabriel, Talking Heads, and Blondie—don't ask me why on this! Fripp's next band of gypsies was the League of Gentleman, before King Crimson was again resuscitated, this time with Tony Levin, Adrian Below, and Bill Bruford. To this the fan response was simply awesome! The group lasted three albums before it disbanded.

Other flavors of the band continued in the years that followed, but by now most critics either worship Fripp as a creative genius, or dismiss him as a lunatic who is just plain difficult to deal with. As one critic put it, he's the Sugar Ray Leonard of music—how many comebacks can you make without a victory?

AUTOGRAPHS

A CD, LP, magazine cover, ad, photo, or card signed by the band - $50-$125*

*Lineup dependent

TOUR BOOKS/PROGRAMS/PASSES

Tour Book:
1995 European Tour: $20

REFERENCES/BOOKS

Limited resources exist, but nothing that does justice to the band in my opinion; no dedicated collector books; serious collectors should opt for fanzine: *Book of Saturday,* P.O. Box 221, Leeds, LS1 5LW, England

King Curtis

(Curtis Ousley)
Born: February 7, 1934, Died: August 13, 1971.

Definitive saxophonist and R&B session god, best known for his tooting on the Coasters 1957 hit "Yakety Yak," King Curtis went on to contribute his work to more than one hundred performers including Wilson Pickett, Eric Clapton, and the Allman Brothers. He was appointed musical director for Aretha Franklin just before his death in 1971. In addition to a moderately successful solo career, he was also a talented producer.

AUTOGRAPHS

A CD, LP, magazine cover, ad, photo, or card signed by the artist: $15-$45

OFTEN OVERLOOKED MEMORABILIA

Artifacts from the numerous sessions he contributed to

King, Earl

(Earl Silas Johnson)
Born: February 7, 1934

Earl King, one of New Orleans' major R&B singers, is best known for the songs "Those Lonely Lonely Nights," "Let's Make It a Better World" (later covered by Dr. John), "Don't Take It So Hard," "Everybody Has to Cry Sometime" (under the pseudonym Handsome Earl), "Come On" (later covered by Jimi Hendrix), and "Always First TiMaine" (later covered by Robert Palmer). All set the stage for future swamp rock.

King worked as a Motown session musician in the '60s and later returned to New Orleans where he played with Professor Longhair. He also became a staple at the New Orleans Jazz and Heritage Festival and was even nominated for a Grammy award in 1986 for his album *Glazed*.

AUTOGRAPHS

A CD, LP, magazine cover, ad, photo, or card signed by the artist: $8-$25

OFTEN OVERLOOKED MEMORABILIA

Artifacts associated with other musicians' covers of his work

King, Evelyn "Champagne"

Born: June 29, 1960

This late-70s pop soul singer is best remembered for her hits "Shame" (#9, 1978), "I Don't Know If It's Right" (#23, 1978), "I'm in Love" (#40, 1981), "Love Comes Down" (#17, 1981), and a handful of other R&B singles.

AUTOGRAPHS

A CD, LP, magazine cover, ad, photo, or card signed by the artist: $8-$15

King Floyd

Born: February 13, 1945

Seventies soul-funk singer King Floyd is best remembered for his hit "Groove Me" (#6,1971) and a couple of minor hits.

AUTOGRAPHS

An LP, magazine cover, ad, photo, or card signed by the artist: $5-$8

OFTEN OVERLOOKED MEMORABILIA

Artifacts from the numerous New Orleans sessions he has contributed to

King, Freddie

(Freddie Christian)
Born: September 3, 1934, Died: December 28, 1976.

Late-50s Texas pioneering blues guitarist, who later migrated to Chicago, Freddie King was a big influence on the British blues boom of the '60s with songs such as "Hideaway" and "Have You Ever Loved a Woman?," just a few of a stable of more than seventy-five songs he cut for the Federal label. Although he was without a recording contract by the mid-60s, interest in his work had been revived in Britain through numerous successful covers. King then traveled to the U.K. before landing a label contract with Cotillion, followed later by Leon Russell's Shelter Records. By the mid-70s he was on RSO and even worked with Eric Clapton on *Burglar* (1974) before passing away in 1976.

AUTOGRAPHS

A CD, LP, magazine cover, ad, photo, or card signed by the artist: $10-$30

OFTEN OVERLOOKED MEMORABILIA

Associated artifacts from the numerous artists who covered his work

This Freddie King poster is from the mid-1960s. From the collection of Dr. Dennis Hickey.

****

"On The Edge"

King Missile

Whether it is considered twisted brilliance, or simply another generation's reiterative spume of self professing rhetoric, King Missile with frontman John S. Hall can strike a nerve. Weaving spoken rock through overdrawn arrangements, King Missile forces us to draw deep within ourselves and imagine throwing darts at an Allen Ginsberg metaphor. A "word-slinger" at heart, Hall is living proof why we need to stop teaching Shakespeare in school systems and replace it with interpretations of Frank Zappa's record *Burnt Weeny Sandwich*. Put that in your Café Latte! Start your collection with Atlantic Record's *Happy Hour*, released in 1992.

****

The Kingsmen

Formed 1958

Lynn Easton, Jack Ely, Mike Mitchell, and Bob Nordby*

*Don Gallucci was added in 1962. Ely and Nordby departed in 1963 and were replaced by Norm Sundholm and Gary Abbott.

This early-60s Northwest pop rock group is best remembered for the classic hit "Louie Louie" (#2, 1963), penned by Richard Berry, along with "Money" (#16, 1964) and "The Jolly Green Giant" (#4, 1965). The Kingsmen retired in 1967, although Mitchell has managed to keep a version going in the '90s.

AUTOGRAPHS

An LP, magazine cover, ad, photo, or card signed by the group: $25-$75

Kingston Trio

Formed 1957

Bob Shane, Born: February 1, 1934; Nick Reynolds, Born: July 27, 1933; and Dave Guard (1934-1991)

These extremely popular late-50s preeminent folksingers are best known for their only Number One hit "Tom Dooley" and the success of their albums (five out of their first six reached the top of the album chart). John Stewart replaced Guard in 1961, and Guard later went on to form the Whiskeyhill Singers. When they began to slip on the charts, they altered their repertoire to include even contemporary protest songs such as "Where Have All the Flowers Gone" (#21, 1962). But their wholesome image made it a difficult pill for the public to swallow, and by 1967

both Reynolds and Stewart had left. Roger Gamble and George Grove then joined the new Kingston Trio, which was re-formed by Bob Shane.

AUTOGRAPHS

A CD, LP, magazine cover, ad, photo, or card signed by the group: $30-$100*

*Original lineup

OFTEN OVERLOOKED MEMORABILIA

A copy of the 1982 PBS TV special, bringing together all six members

King's X

Formed 1980

Jerry Gaskill, Doug Pinnick, and Ty Tabor

Late-80s Christian pop rockers King's X are commonly associated with their "metal and messages" approach to music and songs such as "It's Love" and "Junior's Gone Wild." The band's first two albums were a disappointment, but *Faith Hope Love by King's X* (#85, 1990) exhibited considerable promise. The group's Atlantic debut stalled and followed with *Dogman*, which showed even more promise. The band also played the Woodstock Festival the same year.

AUTOGRAPHS

A CD, LP, magazine cover, ad, photo, or card signed by the group: $10-$20

The Kinks

Formed 1963

Ray Davies, Born: June 21, 1944; Dave Davies, Born: February 3, 1947; Mick Avory, Born: February 15, 1944; and Pete Quaife, Born: December 27, 1943*

*Quaife departed in 1969 and was replaced by John Dalton. John Gosling was added on keyboards in 1971. Dalton left in 1976 and was replaced by Andy Pyle. Both Pyle and Gosling departed in 1978 and were replaced by Jim Rodford and Gordon Edwards. Edwards stayed only briefly before being replaced by Ian Gibbons in 1979. Avory left in 1984, and Bob Henrit joined the band. Gibbons left in 1988, and Mark Haley was added in 1989.

The Kinks were an integral part of the British Invasion of the 1960s. Like the Beatles and the Rolling Stones, their music paved the way for the numerous bands that would follow, particularly those of the hard rock genre. Ray Davies and younger brother Dave, while attending William Grimshaw Secondary School, joined classmate Pete Quaife and drummer John Start to form the Ray Davies Quartet. Ray Davies, while attending Hornsey Art College, met Alonio Korner, who helped him join the Hamilton King/Dave Hunt Band which was playing at the Piccadilly Club in January 1963.

Ray Davies, who continued to also play in the band with his brother, changed the Quartet's name to the Ravens, which was suggested by Dave, in early 1963. He soon became more assertive and essentially took over the band that he know called the Kinks. The brothers were joined by bassist Pete Quaife and drummer Mick Avory, and after a few unrecognized singles, the Kinks released "You Really Got Me" (#7, 1964). The record was a smash and quickly topped the U.K. charts. The band then followed with "All the Day and All of the Night" and "Tired of Waiting for You," which would begin the sequencing of their hard rock, followed by soft rock, singles releases. The group's successful formula led to other hits including "Who'll Be the Next in Line" and "Set Me Free," before the band moved to a somewhat whimsical mode with hits such as "A Well Respected Man," "Dedicated Follower of Fashion," "Til the End of the Day," and "Sunny Afternoon" (#14, 1966).

During the later portion of the decade, the band was prohibited from touring the U.S. as a result of a problem with the American Federation of Musicians that wasn't resolved until 1969. While the time away from America gave Ray Davies more time to write, which he did by moving more toward concept albums, it decreased the band's momentum. The first of Davies' concept albums to achieve a significant level of attention was *Lola Versus Powerman and the Moneygoround, Part One* (#35, 1970), which contained the hit extract "Lola" (#9, 1970).

With hit singles now more a novelty than a ritual, the band developed a more cult-oriented following, enhanced by its often saloon-spirited live performances. From 1971 to 1976, the band was floundering, albeit still composing its concept albums and supporting them with more theatrical shows. But the releases were left on the shelves, where in 1977, they left the recipe.

Misfits finally brought the band back on track and it even scored two hits with "A Rock 'n' Roll Fantasy" (#30, 1978) and "(Wish I Could Fly Like) Superman" (#41, 1979). The album sold gold, the group's first since the Reprise greatest-hits collection. Part of the success can also be attributed to the increased interest in the group's work as a result of successful covers by other bands, most notably Van Halen's "You Really Got Me."

The band then concentrated more on its live act and released *One for the Road* (#14, 1980), a double-live set that also included a video, followed by *Give the People What They Want* (#15, 1981). The next few years were filled with personal projects: for Ray it was production and scoring a film, and Dave released a solo album before it was back to the Kinks. *State of Confusion* (#12, 1983) spun off the group's first Top Ten hit since "Lola," the creative "Come Dancing" (#6, 1983), later followed by "Don't Forget to Dance."

By the mid-80s the band was running out of steam again, and despite poor albums sales, the band kept on touring. In 1990 the Kinks were inducted into the Rock and Roll Hall of Fame, and were once again in the spotlight. In 1993 the group undertook its first tour in three years in support of *Phobia*, its latest album.

AUTOGRAPHS

Group:

A CD, LP, magazine cover, ad, photo, or card signed by the entire band: $60-$150*

*High end reflects vintage signed memorabilia

The signature of Ray Davies

The signature of Dave Davies

Individual:

Ray Davies: $35-$50	Dave Davies: $25-$35
Mick Avory: $15-$20	Pete Quaife: $20-$25
John Dalton: $10-$15	John Gosling: $10
Andy Pyle: $10	Jim Rodford: $5-$10
Gordon Edwards: $5-$7	Ian Gibbons: $5-$8
Bob Henrit: $5	Mark Haley: $5

TOUR BOOKS/PROGRAMS/PASSES

Tour Books:

The Kinks on Tour, 1981: $15

Backstage Passes:

Cloth: $8-$10; Laminated: $10-$20 (1980-Present)
Cloth/paper: $10-$20; Laminated: $12-$30 (1970-1979)

POSTERS/PRESS KITS

Promotional Posters: $15-$25 (1978-Present)
Press Kits: $20-$30 (1978-Present)

USED CLOTHING/ EQUIPMENT

Guitar Picks:

Ray Davies: $25-$50
Dave Davies: $20-$30
Pete Quaife: $10-$15
John Dalton: $5
Andy Pyle: $5
Jim Rodford: $5

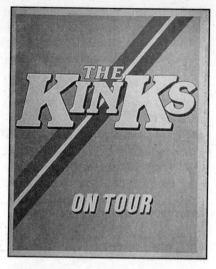

The Kinks On Tour program (© 1981 Kinks Productions, Inc.)

Drum Sticks:

Mick Avory: $15-$25
Bob Henrit: $10

A paper Kinks backstage pass common in form during the '70s.

OFTEN OVERLOOKED MEMORABILIA

Word of Mouth giant lips display - $35; Sleepwalker paperweight, 1977 - $35; Mirror of Love, RCA promotional heart-shaped mirror - $40-$45; Low Budget promotional ashtray, 1979 - $25; Give the People What They Want, Arista promotional yo-yo, 1981 - $20; Schoolboys in Disgrace, RCA promo notebook, stamps, photo, paper, and biography, 1975 - $40; Mirror of Love promo paperweight, 1974 - $35; associated artifacts from other musicians' covers of their compositions; God Save the Kinks, Reprise promotional box set, includes Arthur album and a piece of grass from Daviesland, a jigsaw puzzle, a sticker, six postcards, a consumers' guide, flag, biography, and a letter (two different versions), 1969

REFERENCES/BOOKS

Numerous resources exist, but begin with *X-Ray: The Unauthorized Autobiography* by Ray Davies (1994) and Doug Hinman and Jason Brabazon's *The Kinks Part One: You Really Got Me: An Illustrated World Discography of the Kinks, 1964-1993*. Serious collectors should opt for fan club: The Official Kinks Fan Club, P.O. Box 30, Atherstone, Warwickshire CV9 2ZX England.

Kiss

Formed 1972

Gene Simmons (Klein), Born: August 25, 1949; Paul Stanley (Stanley Eisen), Born: January 20, 1952; Peter Criss (Crisscoula), Born: December 20, 1947; and Ace (Paul) Frehley, Born: April 27, 1951*

*Criss left in 1980 and was replaced by Eric Carr (1950-1991). Frehley left in 1982 and was replaced by Vinnie Vincent. Vincent departed in 1984 and was replaced by Mark St. John. St. John left in 1985 and was replaced by Bruce Kulick. Eric Singer replaced Eric Carr, who died tragically from cancer at age 41. The Kiss lineup reunited on *MTV Unplugged* on August 9, 1995. Original line-up returned to its make-up and reunited in 1996.

PHASE I: STRAP ON YOUR FIRE EXTINGUISHER!

While in New York in 1972 teacher Gene Simmons and Paul Stanley formed the part-time rock outfit Wicked Lester. Criss was added when the duo responded to his ad of desperation in *Rolling Stone* magazine. Guitarist Frehley was added via a recruitment ad in the *Village Voice* to complete the line-up. (Both ads are highly sought by Kiss collectors). The band played its first gig as Kiss at the Popcorn Club in Queens, followed by a performance at Manhattan's Hotel Diplomat. The group's emphasis on theatrics proved to be a wise choice—the members were yet to hone in their musical skills.

On December 31, 1973, the band debuted at the Academy of Music in New York, along with Blue Oyster Cult, Iggy Pop, and Teenage Lust. The following year fledgling Casablanca Records signed the combustible band and released its debut *Kiss* (#87, 1974), while debut single "Kissin' Time" (#83, 1974) did little damage to the U.S. singles chart. The band's sophomore effort *Hotter Than Hell* (#100, 1974) was far from the conflagration needed to ignite the U.S. album chart. The band toured extensively and built up a strong cult following.

The members' unique leather costumes, creative countenances—used to disguise their identities and state-of-the-art pyrotechnics—quickly made them one of America's leading attractions, years before the opening of Universal Studios in Orlando. Each member's stage antics also highlighted a show that found bassist Gene Simmons vomiting blood and blowing fire, Ace Frehley playing his guitar until it "smoked," and Peter Criss consistently rising to the occasion.

Dressed to Kill (#32, 1975) was the band's breakthrough album and included the band's anthem and hallmark extract "Rock and Roll All Nite" (#68, 1975, studio version). *Alive!* (#9, 1975), the band's next album, included a live version of "Rock and Roll All Nite" (#12, 1976). Capitalizing on its enormous live appeal, the double disc package sold itself into the Top Ten! Meanwhile, on November 21, 1975, the Kiss Army fan club officially opened in Terry Haute, Indiana.

Kiss. Photo by Barry Levine. Courtesy Mercury Records.

Kiss members' footprints were placed in the pavement outside Grumman's Chinese Theater (a must plaster caster for Kiss Fans), while *Destroyer* (#11, 1976), which included singles "Shout It Out Loud" (#31, 1976) and the ballad "Beth" (#7, 1976). *The Originals* (#36, 1976), a repackaging of the first three discs with a comic-book history, bought the group time to concentrate on its next album, *Rock and Roll Over* (#11, 1976).

"Hard Luck Woman" (#15, 1977), "Calling Dr. Love" (#16, 1977), "Christeen Sixteen" (#25, 1977), and "Rocket Ride" (#39, 1978) were the band's next hit singles, while the four simultaneously released solo albums charted as follows: Gene (#22, 1978), Ace (#26), Paul (#40) and Peter (#43). Meanwhile, in ghoulish fashion, on October 30, 1978, *Kiss Meets the Phantom of the Park* aired on NBC-TV.

"I Was Made For Lovin' You" (#11, 1979) was the group's last Top Forty single before it began a new phase—without makeup—in 1983.

PHASE II: LOOK MOM, NO MORE FOUNDATION!

Lick It Up (#24, 1983) marked the beginning of the band's second wave of popularity and was followed by *Animalize* (#19, 1984) and *Asylum* (#20, 1985). Although album sales were consistently strong during this period, the band failed to land a single in the Top Forty and it also experienced personnel changes.

Albums *Crazy Nights* (#18, 1987), *Smashes, Thrashes, and Hits* (#21, 1988), and *Hot in the Shade* (#29, 1989) were all released before the ballad "Forever" (#8, 1990) became the group's first hit in fourteen years! *Revenge* (#6, 1992) was the band's next album. This period's greatest tragedy was the death of Eric Carr on November 24, 1991.

Alive III (#9, 1993) climbed the U.S. album charts, and the band went through a period of recognition by a number of artists who cited it as an influence. On July 13, 1994, the group appeared on *The Tonight Show* and performed "Hard Luck Woman" with Garth Brooks. The country star previously stated his admiration for the band and even included his version on the newly released *Kiss My Ass* tribute album. Less than two weeks later the group also appeared on the *Late Show With David Letterman* and performed with the Gin Blossoms.

On August 9, 1995, the group, with former members, reunited to tape *MTV Unplugged*. The album from the event charted at #15 the following year as the band began Phase III.

PHASE III: "DOES ANYBODY KNOW WHERE I LEFT MY EYELINER?"

The group, again consisting of all four original members, embarked on its historical 1996 U.S. summer tour. The band shattered nearly every attendance mark at the venues it played in what may prove to be one of the most successful live caravans of the decade!

AUTOGRAPHS
Group:
A CD, LP, magazine cover, ad, photo, or card signed by the entire band: $175-$275*

*High end reflects vintage signed memorabilia

Individual:
Gene Simmons: $30-$40
Peter Criss: $35-$45
Eric Carr: $40
Mark St. John: $10-$15
Eric Singer: $10-$15

Paul Stanley: $30-$40
Ace Frehley: $35-$45
Vinnie Vincent: $10-$15
Bruce Kulick: $10-$15

An autographed Kiss promotional handout

TOUR BOOKS/PROGRAMS/PASSES
Tour Programs:
Alive Tour, 1976: $45-$80
Destroyer/Rock and Roll Over Tour: $30-$45
(Two versions; Paul Stanley pictures vary)
Love Gun/ Alive II Tour: $25-$50
Dynasty Tour: $25-$38 (Three versions)
Creatures Tour: $65-$115
Lick It Up: $25-$40
Animalize Tour: $15-$30 (Two versions)
Asylum Tour: $15-$30
Crazy Nights Tour: $20-$30

A nice assortment of Kiss backstage passes (Cloth passes printed by OTTO; laminate is a common counterfeit)

Hot In The Shade: $10-$20
Revenge Tour: $10-$15
Alive/Worldwide, Europe, 1997: $45
Foreign Tour Books:
Rock and Roll Over Tour (Japan): $60-$110
Love Gun Tour (Japan): $60-$110
Unmasked Tour (Europe): $50-$90
Unmasked Tour (Australia): $50-$90
Lick It Up (Europe): $25-$40
Donington/Monsters of Rock Festival: $10-$25
Backstage Passes:
Cloth, Laminated
Alive Tour, 1976: $45-$50, $TBD
Destroyer/Rock and Roll over Tour: $30-$35, $35-$45
Love Gun/ Alive II Tour: $25-$30, $35
Dynasty Tour: $22-$25, $30-$33
Creatures Tour: $20-$23, $28-$34
Lick It Up: $17-$20, $27-$32
Animalize Tour: $15-$17, $25-$30
Asylum Tour: $12-$14, $20-$22
Crazy Nights Tour: $10-$12, $18-$20
Hot In The Shade: $8-$10
Revenge Tour: $8-$10

POSTERS/PRESS KITS
Promotional Posters: $10-$125
Honda Kissmobile
Motorcycle, 1980: $100-$125; Double Platinum: $55;
The Elder LP, U.S. (Clear plastic): $55
Press Kits: $45-$55 (makeup), $12-$20 (no makeup)

USED CLOTHING/EQUIPMENT
Guitar Picks:

Gene Simmons: $15-$60	Paul Stanley: $25-$50
Ace Frehley: $30-$40	Vinnie Vincent: $20-$30
Mark St. John: $20-$30	Bruce Kulick: $20-$35

Drum Sticks:
Peter Criss: $40-$50
Eric Carr: $40-$55
Eric Singer: $20-$25

Custom guitar picks used by Gene Simmons and Paul Stanley

Vinnie Vincent guitar pick

OFTEN OVERLOOKED MEMORABILIA
Kiss included a number of inserts in its recorded releases, and these should not to be confused with memorabilia unassociated with a specific title.
Postcards - $3-$5; scarves, headbands, etc.. $10 (Exceptions: 1984/Kiss World Tour/1985, knit - $38); jewelry $12-$15; belt buckles - $20; pins/buttons: small - $1, large - $3; stickers - $4-$10; patches - $5; Hotter Than Hell mobile - $110; Alive! mobile - $125; Love Gun standee of band - $125; Alive II mobile - $135; Double

Platinum arrow or cardboard logo - $30-$40; Solo Albums wall hanging (4') - $175 (scarce); Solo Albums wall hanging (2') or arrow - $30; Dynasty wall hanging (4') - $175; Dynasty cardboard w/logos (4') - $25; Unmasked cardboard cube - $75; Smashes, Thrashes, and Hits triangular standup - $25 (two sizes); Smashes, Thrashes, and Hits poster standup - $55; Hot in the Shade - cap - $27; Hot in the Shade "forever" sweatshirt - $80; Hot in the Shade sphinx - $25; Hot in the Shade pyramid paperweight - $125 (scarce); promotional jackets - $375-$450; Kiss comics (Marvel) - $32 (#1) (Published June 28, 1977), 25 (#2), Assorted comics - $3-$6; songbooks - $20 (Exception: The Originals - $45); sheet music - $12-$15; magazines - $8-$15 (Exceptions: Creem Special Edition, 1977 - $25/ Kiss Meets the Phantom, 1978 - $20); backpack - $75; towels - $50-$65; bedspread - $135; Chu-Bops (bubble gum) - $8; colorforms - $40; cups (Majik Market, set of 8) - $130; curtains - $155; dolls - $90-$100 each; On Tour game - $70; garbage can - $70; toy guitar - $125; Halloween costumes - $60; jackets - $75-$125; Dynasty key chain - $12; lunch box - $85; makeup kit - $60-$80; complete microphone kit - $125; mirrors - $20-$25; model van - $55; notebooks - $20; pencils (set of 4) - $15; pens - $15 each; Bally pinball machine - $1, 000-$1,250; poster art - $50; poster put-ons - $5-$10; Milton Bradley puzzles: individual - $15-$20 (4), Destroyer, or Love Gun - $30; radio - $50; record player - $225; remote control van - $80; rub & play set - $25; shoelaces - $15; sleeping bag - $165; Kiss Army sponge - $15-$20; View-Master - $40 and View-Master reels - $15-$20
*All above merchandise in mint condition with complete original packaging

REFERENCES/BOOKS
Kiss by Robert Duncan, (1978) - $15; Kiss, Headliner Series by John Swenson (1978) - $14-$18; *Rock Stars* by Scholastic Books (1979) - $5; *Rock's Biggest Ten* by Scholastic Books (1979) - $5; *Kiss: The Real Story* by Peggy Tomarkin (1979) - $35-$40; *Kiss, Shout It Out* by Nick Seymour (1985) - $25; *Kiss* by Paolo Piccini (1987) - $20; *Still on Fire* by Dave Thomas and Anders Holm (1988) - $25; *Kiss Collectibles* by Karen and John Lesniewski (1993) - $10—a must for all Kiss Collectors!

KISSTORY - UNIQUE ARTIFACTS
December 11, 1976: Ace Frehley's electric shock therapy during a gig in Lakeland, Florida (tickets, passes, etc. are all sought after)

Copies of *Playboy* magazine featuring Debra Svensk (Mrs. Peter Criss)

Newspaper clippings and propaganda material from the Free Fatherland Nationalist Commando movement exhibiting threats regarding a possible Kiss three-day tour of Argentina

A videotape of the September 18, 1983, MTV segment where Kiss finally reveals all—no makeup!

Gene Simmons movie memorabilia from *Runaway* (1984), *Never Too Young to Die*, *Trick or Treat*, and *Wanted Dead or Alive*

A videotape from the *Donahue* show airing February 5, 1991 - "The Criss Crisis"

A copy of *The Star* tabloid dated January 8, 1991 - "The Criss Crisis"

Klaatu

Formed 1973
John Woloschuk, Terry Draper, and Dee Long

Klaatu had a brief rise to stardom based on rumors—fueled by numerous sources—that they were in fact the Beatles. Recording on the Capitol label certainly didn't curtail any of the speculation or stop the company from fueling speculation itself. Capitol denied knowing the band members' true identities and also contrasting the band's styles to Magical Mystery Tour and other Beatles' classics.

The group splashed on the scene in 1976, but it wasn't until the following year that the hype began. The band's eponymous debut album sold into the Top Forty before researchers revealed that the band was a group of studio musicians from Toronto, Canada. Following four albums, the group disbanded in 1981. Rumors of an anthology series to be released on the twentieth anniversary of its demise remains to be seen; however, the group is proof enough of just how strong the "Fab Four's" reputation was years after its breakup.

AUTOGRAPHS

An LP, magazine cover, ad, photo, or card signed by the band: $5-$10

The KLF/The Orb

The KLF formed 1987
Bill Drummond (Butterworth) and Jimmy Cauty
The Orb formed 1990

This mischievous and controversial '90s British trance-dance duo, which has recorded under numerous monikers, is typically associated with songs such as "What Time Is Love" (#57, 1991), "3 A.M. Eternal" (#5, 1991), and "Justified and Ancient" (#11, 1992). The KLF broke up in 1992, but later continued as The K Foundation. The group was one of the early challengers of laws surrounding sampling and its legal use.

AUTOGRAPHS

A CD, LP, magazine cover, ad, photo, or card signed by the duo: $10-$20

OFTEN OVERLOOKED MEMORABILIA

Artifacts surrounding the releases that were pulled due to unauthorized sampling

The Knack

Formed 1978
Doug Fieger, Berton Averre, Bruce Gary, and Prescott Niles*

*Group disbanded in 1981 and re-formed in 1991

Double platinum in-house award for the Knack's Get the Knack, 1978, valued at $300. From the Doug Leftwitch collection.

Get the Knack, was in fact, a great debut attack, from an act, that got lots of flack, for its lack, of interviews. I know you're scolding me for my contrived approach, but it is certainly in line here, because this band was accused of being far too cynical to take seriously. "My Sharona" (#1, 1979) sold ten million copies before the "Knuke the Knack" movement, from the bowels of the L.A. club scene, crushed the group with eyeliner, stating that its lyrics were sexist.

Band members Doug Fieger and Berton Averre wrote together and similar to the other two members, Gary and Niles, had been successful session men before teaming up in 1978. The band established itself fairly quickly, playing the Southern California club circuit, and by year's end was being courted by numerous record companies. The Knack's debut, produced by Mike Chapman, was a huge success, driven obviously by a Number One extract. Unfortunately, the band was improperly packaged, and as such, couldn't shake the hype surrounding its image. Following a failed tour in 1981, the group disbanded.

Band members then went their separate ways. There were numerous failed attempts, in one form or another, to regain their initial success over the years. Gary had some success drumming for other musicians, Niles toured with Josie Cotton, and Fieger even ended up on the television show Roseanne. The band seems to attempt to resurrect itself every time "My Sharona" shows up somewhere in the media. I now find myself looking in a variety of directions before I play the song on the jukebox—just gotta have a little Sharona with my Corona! Alright, enough of this!

AUTOGRAPHS

A CD, LP, magazine cover, ad, photo, or card signed by the band: $8-$22

POSTERS/PRESS KITS

Promotional Posters: $8-$12
Press Kits: $10

USED CLOTHING/EQUIPMENT
Guitar Picks: $3-$5

The Knickerbockers

Formed 1964

Buddy Randell, Jimmy Walker, John Charles, and Beau Charles

Remember "Lies" (#20, 1966)? That was the Knickerbockers producing that Beatlesque beauty. The band formed initially as the Castle Kings in 1964 and included Buddy "Short Shorts" (#3, 1958) Randell. The group then changed its name, but following "Lies" with "One Track Mind" (#46) wasn't the solution, nor did the band have one, and thus it faded into obscurity. Walker then went on to the Righteous Brothers and replaced Bill Medley, which is about as fun and as logical as replacing Brian Wilson in the Beach Boys.

AUTOGRAPHS
A CD, LP, magazine cover, ad, photo, or card signed by the band: $5-$10

Knight, Gladys and the Pips

Formed 1952

Gladys Knight, Born: May 28, 1944; Merald "Bubba" Knight, Born: September 4, 1942; Brenda Knight; William Guest; and Elenor Guest*

*B. Knight and E. Guest departed in 1957 and Edward Patten and Langston George were added.

Seventies Atlanta-rooted pop-soul vocal group Glady Knight and the Pips was known in the earlier years for R&B songs such as "Every Beat of My Heart" and "Letter Full of Tears." The band faltered in the early '60s, but by mid-decade had gained wider appeal with hits such as "I Heard It Through the Grapevine" (#2, 1967), "The End of the Road," "Friendship Train," "If I Were Your Woman," and "Neither One of Us."

The band then moved from Motown to Buddah in 1973 where it released the smash hit album and multiple Grammy winner *Imagination*, which included three hit extracts: "Midnight Train to Georgia" (#1, 1973), "I've Got to Use My Imagination" (#4, 1974), and "Best Thing That Ever Happened to Me" (#3, 1974). The band was then thrust into the spotlight as its hits continued with "The Way We Were"/"Try to Remember" (#11, 1975) and "On and On" (#5, 1974). Gladys Knight then turned to acting in both film and television, while the latter '70s saw her prohibited from recording with the Pips due to an unsettled law suit.

During the '80s the band was reunited and delivered numerous hits including "Landlord" (#3, R&B, 1980), "Save the Overtime (for Me)" (#66, 1983), and "Love Overboard" (#13, 1987), which was a Grammy winner. By the '90s Gladys Knight had begun solo work—as the band had been suspended—and scored hits with "License to Kill" (#69, R&B, 1989), "Men" (#2, R&B, 1991), and "That's What Friends Are For," recorded with Dionne Warwick, Stevie Wonder and Elton John.

AUTOGRAPHS
A CD, LP, magazine cover, ad, photo, or card signed by the band: $25-$70

OFTEN OVERLOOKED MEMORABILIA
Movie memorabilia from *Pipe Dreams*; videotapes from group-related television appearances including *Charlie and Co.* (1977).

Knopfler, Mark: See Dire Straits

Kool and the Gang

Formed 1964

Robert "Kool" Bell, Born: October 8, 1950; Ronald Bell; Dennis "Dee Tee" Thomas; Claydes Smith; Robert "Spike" Mickens; Rickey Westfield; and George "Funky" Brown*

*Clifford Adams added in 1976. Westfield departed in 1977 and James "J.T." Taylor was added in 1979. Curtis Williams and Michael Ray were added in 1980. "J.T." Taylor departed in 1989 and Skip Martin, Odeon Mays, and Gary Brown were added.

This '70s and '80s funk-driven pop group scored a couple of early R&B hits before landing with its smash hit album *Wild and Peaceful*, which included three hit extracts: "Funky Stuff" (#29, 1973), "Jungle Boogie" (#4, 1974), and "Hollywood Swinging" (#6, 1974). Other hits followed including "Higher Plane" (#1, R&B, 1974), and "Open Sesame - Part 1" (#6, R&B, 1976), the latter of which was included on the soundtrack to *Saturday Night Fever*, before the disco sound slowly pushed the group out of the music picture.

By 1979 the band had chartered a new course, under new management and with a new lead singer, James "J.T." Taylor, before scoring hits with "Ladies Night" (#1, R&B, 1979), "Too Hot" (#5, 1980), "Celebration" (#1, 1980)—the perennial party and wedding reception classic—"Take My Heart (You Can Have It If You Want It)" (#17, 1981), "Get Down on It" (#10, 1982), "Big Fun" (#21, 1982), "Joanna" (#29, 1983), "Tonight" (#13, 1984), "Fresh" (#9, 1984), "Cherish" (#2, 1985), "Victory" (#10, 1986), "Stone Love" (#10, 1987), and "Holiday" (#9, 1987), before Taylor's departure in 1989.

During the '90s, the band, although still landing on the R&B charts, has yet to attain the success of the previous decade.

AUTOGRAPHS

A CD, LP, magazine cover, ad, photo, or card signed by the band: $25-$50*
*Lineup dependent

OFTEN OVERLOOKED MEMORABILIA

Movie memorabilia from *Saturday Night Fever* and *Pulp Fiction* (1994)

Kool Moe Dee

(Mohandas DeWese)

This New York rap artist is best known for his classic old school style debut album and the songs "Go See the Doctor" (#89, 1987) and "Wild, Wild West" (#4, R&B, 1988).

AUTOGRAPHS

A CD, LP, magazine cover, ad, photo, or card signed by the artist: $5-$12

POSTERS/PRESS KITS

Promotional Posters: $10-$15
Press Kits: $10-$15

Kooper, Al

Born: February 5, 1944

Kooper turns professional at the age of 15, proficient at both the guitar and keyboards, he joins the Royal Teens, best known for the single "Short Shorts" (#3, 1958). In the late '50s he leaves the band in favor of studio work and songwriting. Kooper co-pens "This Diamond Ring" (#1, 1965), which lands atop the singles chart for Gary Lewis and the Playboys, and adds keyboards on Bob Dylan's single "Like a Rolling Stone." Kooper also joins Dylan on projects such as *Highway 61 Revisited*, *Blonde on Blonde*, and *New Morning*.

The Blues Project is formed in 1965 (Kooper and Steve Katz) before the two move on to their next project in 1967—Blood, Sweat and Tears. Although Kooper is key in the foundation of B, S & T, he leaves before the band's commercial success. He then finds himself producing and collaborating on numerous projects during the years that follow, including *Super Session* (1968) with Mike Bloomfield and Stephen Stills, *Let It Bleed* with the Rolling Stones, and *Electric Ladyland* with Jimi Hendrix.

The decade that follows finds Kooper's role as a producer enhanced as he takes on three Lynyrd Skynyrd records, the Tube's debut, and Nils Lofgren's *Cry Tough*. He also cuts solo records in 1976,

1982, and in 1995, and appears at a variety of venues with numerous musicians.

AUTOGRAPHS

A CD, LP, magazine cover, ad, photo, or card signed by the artist: $10-$15

POSTERS/PRESS KITS

Promotional Posters: $10-$20
Press Kits: $10-$25

OFTEN OVERLOOKED MEMORABILIA

Associated artifacts from his numerous contributions to other musicians' works

REFERENCES/BOOKS

Backstage Passes, his autobiography (1974); limited other resources exist, but none do justice to the singer in my opinion; no dedicated collector books

Korner (Koerner), Alexis

Born: April 19, 1928, Died: January 1, 1984

Sixties British blues revival pioneer Alexis Korner is best remembered for his group Blues Incorporated, which is renowned for its prestigious musical alumni (who are typically associated for what they accomplished outside of the group). Korner was also successful in Europe with the band New Church and later with CCS (the Collective Consciousness Society). He also hosted his own popular radio show on BBC Radio 1.

AUTOGRAPHS

A CD, LP, magazine cover, ad, photo, or card signed by the artist: $15-$45

Kottke, Leo

Born: September 11, 1945

Leo Kottke can traverse a pair of guitar strings faster than anyone else you have ever seen. His proficient fingerpicking has earned him tremendous respect over the years and has established him a solid cult following. Having played guitar since he was 11, he entered St. Cloud State College in Minnesota following a stint in the navy. Three years later he dropped out and began hitchhiking across America, accompanied by his guitar.

Twelve String Blues (1969) was his first album, and while it earned him some respect, it was far from a huge commercial success. *Six and Twelve-String Guitar*, his only album on Tacoma, sold well, despite the lack of airplay or a hit single. Eventually the album sold close to a half a million copies.

He then signed with Capitol for six albums, followed by Chrysalis and Private Music. He continues

to tour as a soloist as new generations begin to recognize his profound ability.

AUTOGRAPHS
A CD, LP, magazine cover, ad, photo, or card signed by the artist: $8-$12

POSTERS/PRESS KITS
Promotional Posters: $10-$20
Press Kits: $10-$25

USED CLOTHING/EQUIPMENT
Guitar Picks: $15-$25

Kraftwerk

Formed 1970

Ralf Hutter, Florian Schneider, Klaus Dinger, and Thomas Homann*

*Dinger and Homann departed in 1971. Klaus Roeder and Wolfgang Flur were added in 1974. Roeder left in 1975 and Karl Bartos was added. Flur left in 1990 and Fritz Hijbert was added.

This mid-70s German synth-pop act is best remembered for the albums *Autobahn* (1974) and *Computer World* (1981), along with songs such as "Trans-Europe Express," "Showroom Dummies," and "Computer Love" (#1, U.K., 1981). During the group's musical career it has influenced many other artists including David Bowie and has sustained a large international cult following.

AUTOGRAPHS
A CD, LP, magazine cover, ad, photo, or card signed by the band: $25-$50

REFERENCES/BOOKS
Limited resources exist, but none do justice to the group in my opinion; no dedicated collector books

Kramer, Billy J. and the Dakotas

Formed 1963

Billy J. Kramer (William Ashton), Born: August 19, 1943; Tony Mansfield; Mike Maxfield; Robin Macdonald; and Raymond Jones

Early-60s British crooner Billy J. Kramer is best remembered for his association with the Beatles (they shared managers, producers, and songs) and also for the tunes "Do You Want to Know a Secret?," "Bad to Me," "Little Children" (#7, 1964), and "Trains and Boats and Planes" (#47, 1965).

AUTOGRAPHS
A CD, LP, magazine cover, ad, photo, or card signed by the group: $15-$60

OFTEN OVERLOOKED MEMORABILIA
Any and all items associated with the Beatles

Krauss, Alison

Born: July 23, 1971

Eighties bluegrass prodigy Alison Krauss is best known for her album *I've Got That Old Feeling* (1990), a Grammy winner for Best Bluegrass Album, and for her gifted production work on albums such as *I Know Who Holds Tomorrow* (with the Cox Family) (1994), which was also a Grammy winner. She also fronts the band Union Station. Collectors would be wise to start collecting her memorabilia now, because it looks like this gifted artist is here to stay!

AUTOGRAPHS
A CD, LP, magazine cover, ad, photo, or card signed by the artist: $5-$20

POSTERS/PRESS KITS
Promotional Posters: $10-$20
Press Kits: $10-$15

OFTEN OVERLOOKED MEMORABILIA
All items associated with her production work

Kravitz, Lenny

Born: May 26, 1964

Lenny Kravitz is commonly linked with actress Lisa Bonet—they were married from 1987 to 1991—and his mother actress Roxie Roker (*The Jeffersons*), but he has now forged a path of his own with his retro-rock, Elvis Costello-sounding music. He is commonly associated with his song "It Ain't Over Til It's Over" (#2, 1991).

AUTOGRAPHS
A CD, LP, magazine cover, ad, photo, or card signed by the artist: $5-$12

TOUR BOOKS/PROGRAMS/PASSES
Tour Books:
The Universal Love Tour: $15
Continental Tour: $15

USED CLOTHING/EQUIPMENT
Guitar Picks: $10

Lenny Kravitz guitar picks

Kris Kross

Formed 1991

Chris Kelly and Chris Smith

Early-90s Atlanta teenybopper hip-hop act Kris Kross is best remembered for wearing their clothes backwards and the songs "Jump" (#1, 1992) and "Warm It Up" (#13, 1993).

AUTOGRAPHS

A CD, LP, magazine cover, ad, photo, or card signed by the duo: $8-$12

POSTERS/PRESS KITS

Promotional Posters: $10
Press Kits: $10

Kristofferson, Kris

Born: June 22, 1937

Late-60s country-rock singer/songwriter, turned '70s film actor, turned '80s film and television actor, turned '90s aging country singer/desperado Kris Kristofferson is typically associated with the songs, "Me and Bobby McGee," "Sunday Morning," and "Help Me Make It Through the Night." When it was clear that his recording career had reached its peak with his fourth album, *The Silver-Tongued Devil and I* (1971), Kristofferson made his film debut in *Cisco Pike* (1972), followed by *Pat Garrett and Billy the Kid*, two years later.

He married Rita Coolidge, his second wife, in 1973—the marriage lasted until 1979. His film career seemed to peak during *A Star Is Born*, with Barbra Streisand in 1976, but following the disastrous *Heaven's Gate* (1980), Kristofferson seemed hard pressed to prove himself again. Numerous movies followed, as did a break with his record company Columbia. The late '80s and '90s found Kristofferson of-ten collaborating with his buddies, The Highwaymen, who have landed hits such as "Highwayman" (#1, C&W, 1985), "Desperados Waiting for a Train" (#15, C&W, 1985), and "Silver Stallion" (#25, C&W, 1990).

AUTOGRAPHS

A CD, LP, magazine cover, ad, photo, or card signed by the artist: $10-$35

OFTEN OVERLOOKED MEMORABILIA

Movie memorabilia from *Cisco Pike* (1972), *Pat Garrett and Billy the Kid* (1974), *Alice Doesn't Live Here Anymore* (1974), *The Sailor Who Fell From Grace with the Sea* (1976), *Semi-Tough* (1971), *Convoy* (1978), *A Star Is Born* (1976), *Heaven's Gate* (1980), *Rollover* (1981), *Trouble in Mind* (1985), *Song Writer* (1984), and *Lone Star* (1997)

REFERENCES/BOOKS

Few resources exist, but none do justice to the singer in my opinion; no dedicated collector books

KRS-One: See Boogie Down Productions

Jim Kweskin Jug Band

Formed 1963

Jim Kweskin, Born: July 18, 1940; Bill Keith; Mel Lyman; Fritz Richmond; Richard Greene; Geoff Muldaur; and Maria Muldaur, Born: September 12, 1943

This '60s "folk revival" cover band is best remembered for having Maria Muldaur as one of its numerous members.

AUTOGRAPHS

Group:
An LP, magazine cover, ad, photo, or card signed by the group: $5-$10

Labelle

Formed 1961

(Patti LaBelle and the Blue Belles)

Patti LaBelle; Nona Hendryx, Born: August 18, 1945; Sarah Dash, Born: May 24, 1942; Cindy Birdsong, Born: December 15, 1939

Traditional '60s all-female vocal group fashioned in the style of the Supremes, who evolved during the decade that followed into a spacy trio of funk divas, Patti LaBelle and the Blues Belles were associated first with songs such as "I Sold My Heart to the Junkman" (#15, 1962), "Danny Boy" (#76, 1964), and "You'll Never Walk Alone" (#4, 1964), before Florence Ballard left to join the Supremes. The band, although popular in familiar venues such as the Apollo Theatre, had little success beyond the soul circuit until Vicki Wickham repackaged the band and released them simply as Labelle. By 1975 they had toured the U.S. with the Who, debuted their glitter space suits, played New York's Metropolitan Opera House, and had a million-selling hit, "Lady Marmalade" (#1, 1975). The band broke up the following year to pursue their individual careers.

AUTOGRAPHS

A CD, LP, magazine cover, ad, photo, or card signed by the group: $25-$50

TOUR BOOKS/PROGRAMS/PASSES

Backstage Passes:
Cloth/paper: $10; Laminated: $15

POSTERS/PRESS KITS

Promotional Posters: $15-$30
Press Kits: $15-$35

LaBelle, Patti

(Patricia Louise Holt)
Born: October 4, 1944

When Labelle broke up in 1976, Patti LaBelle set her sights on a solo career. Although solo success eluded her for a time, she and her husband/manager Armstead Edwards persisted. Her confidence grew with each release and she also intertwined her music career with an attempt at acting. The Broadway revival of *Your Arm's Too Short to Box with God* aligned her with Al Green, and its success led to other opportunities, dismissing any concerns she may have had about her performing abilities. She played a blues singer in the movie *A Solider Story* and followed it with a strong performance as a star in the musical *House of Flowers*. She also appeared in numerous television shows during this period, including *A Different World* and *Out All Night*.

Ironically, after leaving a group for a solo career, duets with other performers were what solidified trust in her ability. From ex-Labelle member Nona Hendryx to Michael Bolton, she always seemed to bring a magical charm to the recording, as if she was fueled by the artist next to her. Although "New Attitude" (#15, 1985) from the *Beverly Hills Cop* soundtrack dropped her in the Top Twenty, "On My Own" (#1, 1986), her duet with ex-Doobie Brother Michael McDonald, put her right back where she belonged—on top of the charts.

Like so many successful performers, Patti LaBelle has also wanted to give something back. She has been the recipient of the Martin Luther King Lifetime Achievement Award, a spokeswoman for the National Cancer Institute, twice recipient of the NAACP Entertainer of the Year Award, chairwoman of the Black Health Research Foundation, and appeared at numerous charitable events including 1985 Live Aid.

Just when you think she can't get any more of our hearts, "My Love, Sweet Love" (#1, 1996) hits the chart. On March 29, 1996, she is honored with the Heritage Award for Outstanding Career Achievements and while at the Shrine Auditorium for the Tenth Annual Soul Train Music Awards, she sings "Over the Rainbow"—if this performance doesn't send a chill up your spine, nothing will!

AUTOGRAPHS

A CD, LP, magazine cover, ad, photo, or card signed by the artist: $15-$35

TOUR BOOKS/PROGRAMS/PASSES

Backstage Passes:
Cloth: $5-$0, Laminated: $10

POSTERS/PRESS KITS

Promotional Posters: $10-$25
Press Kits: $15-$30

OFTEN OVERLOOKED MEMORABILIA

Movie memorabilia from *Beverly Hills Cop* (1985); Broadway memorabilia from her revival of *Your Arm's Too Short to Box with God* (1982) as well as her other acting efforts

Ladysmith Black Mambazo

Formed 1964

Joseph, Hedaman, Jockey, and Ben Shabalala; also Albert and Abednego Mazibuko, Russel Mthembu, Inos Phungula, Jabulani Dubazana, and Geophrey Mdletshe

Best-selling South African Zulu mbube choir formed by Joseph Shabalala with his family, Ladysmith Black Mambazo (LBM) has released more than 25 albums in South Africa, and came to the attention of America when they sang on two tracks of Paul Simon's *Graceland* album, while also appearing with him on a Showtime TV special and *Saturday Night Live*. Their album *Shaka Zulu* (1987), produced by Simon, earned the group a Grammy award. The group has also been regular guests on *Sesame Street* and participated in award-winning commercials.

AUTOGRAPHS

A CD, LP, magazine cover, ad, photo, or card signed by the group: $20-$25

OFTEN OVERLOOKED MEMORABILIA

Movie memorabilia from *Coming to America* and *A Dry White Season*

Lake, Greg: See Emerson, Lake and Palmer

Lance, Major

Born: April 4, 1941, Died: September 3, 1994

Early-60s Chicago soul singer best remembered for his hits "The Monkey Time" (#8, 1963) and "Um, Um, Um, Um, Um, Um" (#5, 1964), as well as numerous R&B hits, Major Lance was the benefactor of a writer named Curtis Mayfield and a producer named Carl Davis.

Lanegan, Mark: See Screaming Trees

lang, k.d.

(Kathryn Dawn Lang)
Born: November 2, 1961

During her teens "k.d.," already insisting on the unique abbreviation of her name, becomes proficient at both the piano and guitar. It's not long before she sets her sights on career in country music, establishing a strong backing band and releasing her Canadian-only debut album *A Truly Western Experience*.

In 1987 she releases her second album, *Angel With A Lariat,* on Sire Records. While the traditional country market turns their back to the artist, many new country fans embrace the work. "Crying" (#42, U.S., Country), a popular duet with Roy Orbison included on the soundtrack to *Hiding Out,* begins to climb the charts and soon becomes a popular mainstay in her sets.

Shadowland (#73, 1988) is her next offering and her first album to enter the pop chart. The year 1988 also sees her perform at the closing ceremonies of the 1998 Winter Olympics and her first appearance on *Late Night With David Letterman* (NBC-TV). The following year she wins the Best Country Vocal Collaboration category at the 31st Annual Grammy Awards for the duet "Crying."

Absolute Torch And Twang (#69, 1990), credited to k.d. lang and the Reclines (her backing band named after Patsy Cline), is released in 1989 and allows her to collect the Best Country Vocal Performance at the 32nd Annual Grammy Awards. Lang also contributes "Damn Old Dog" to *Tame Yourself* (#165, 1991), a benefit album for People for the Ethical Treatment of Animals.

Ingenue (#44, 1992, #18, 1993), with its hit single "Constant Craving" (#38, 1992), is critically revered as Lang, who crosses into various types of music, fails to be labeled. On February 24, 1993, Lang collects the Best Pop Female Vocal trophy at the 35th Annual Grammy Awards—just one of many awards she receives during the year. She went on to contribute to worthy causes like the George Michael-organized "Concert Of Hope" benefit and to new initiatives such as the *Even Cowgirls Get The Blues* soundtrack.

In 1995 Lang releases the short but sweet *All You Can Eat* (#37, 1995) and on October 16th even caters to cyberfans with a chat on America OnLine. Her cross-genre albums and multifaceted talents make her a fascinating subject to collect. In 1997 her album *Drag* (#29) finds the entertainer far from one. Videotape collectors can have fun trying to track down all her guest appearances and award ceremony performances.

k.d. ON T.V. - SELECTED ENTRIES

2/28/88	Closing ceremonies of 1988 Winter Olympics, Calgary, Canada
7/7/88	*Late Night With David Letterman* - NBC-TV
11/23/90	*Late Night With David Letterman* - NBC-TV
7/14/91	*Town and Country* - C4-TV
4/3/92	*The Tonight Show* - NBC-TV
5/1/92	*Late Night With David Letterman* - NBC-TV
5/13/92	*Wogan* - BBC1-TV
8/10/92	*The Arsenio Hall Show* - syndicated
12/10/92	*The Tonight Show*-- NBC-TV
2/24/93	35th Annual Grammy Awards, performs
3/3/93	*Top Of The Pops* - BBC1-TV
6/21/93	*Bruce's Guest Night* - BBC1-TV
1/15/94	*Unplugged* - BBC2-TV
10/1/95	*South Bank* - ITV
12/3/95	Fashion and Music Awards - VH1-TV
3/7/96	*Late Show With David Letterman* - CBS-TV

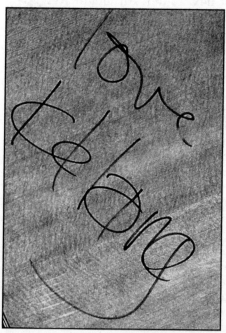

Guitar signed by k.d. lang

POSTERS/ PRESS KITS

Promotional Posters:
$12-$25
"Torch   Twag"
(23" x 35"): $15
"Angel With A Lariat"
(18" x 24"): $12
Press Kits:
$25-$35

USED CLOTHING/ EQUIPMENT

Guitar Picks:
$10-$15

k.d. lang backstage passes (Printed by OTTO)

OFTEN OVERLOOKED MEMORABILIA

Movie memorabilia from *Hiding Out, Dick Tracy, Coneheads, Even Cowgirls Get The Blues;* memorabilia from her movie acting debut in *Salmonberries;* 1988 Winter Olympic memorabilia, program, videotapes, etc. - she performed at the closing ceremony at McMahon Stadium in Calgary, Canada; *Entertainment Weekly* magazine, 2/18/90 (lang cover) - $5-$7; *Vanity Fair* (May, 1993) - lang and Cindy Crawford on controversial cover - $5-$10; *Friends - The Album* (1995) - lang contributes a song; "Touring Australia 1996" display, 17" x 24" - $50; All You Can Eat promo Chinese food container w/ patch - $25

REFERENCES/BOOKS

Illustrated Biography by David Bennahum: $12; a few other resources exist, but begin with Victoria Starr's *k.d.lang: All You Get Is Me;* no dedicated collector books

Lanois, Daniel

Born: September 19, 1951

One of the '80's pivotal producers, known for his subtleties and passion for spontaneous performances elicited by unique environmental surroundings, he is typically associated with his coproduction work with Eno on U2's *The Joshua Tree* and *The Unforgettable Fire,* and for shared production work on *So* and *Us* by Peter Gabriel. Lanois has had a few solo offerings, and although praised by critics, has found little commercial impact.

AUTOGRAPHS

A CD, LP, magazine cover, ad, photo, or card signed by the artist: $10-$15

OFTEN OVERLOOKED MEMORABILIA

Associated artifacts from his numerous productions

L.A. Reid and Babyface

Formed 1984

Antonio "L.A." Reid, Kenneth "Babyface" Edmonds

Late-80s Cincinnati duo and one of the most successful production and songwriting teams in R&B and pop history, L.A. and Babyface helped define New Jack Swing while working with acts such as TLC, Paula Abdul, the Jacksons, Bobby Brown, Boyz II Men, and Whitney Houston. In 1989 the pair moved to Hotlanta, Georgia, and formed a record company, releasing artists such as Damian Dame and TLC. Their work together and separately has earned them numerous Grammy awards for their associations with Boyz II Men, Whitney Houston, and Eric Clapton.

Babyface's solo career began in 1987 with the release of *Lovers,* followed by the smash *Tender Lover* (#14, 1989) that included the hit extracts "It's No Crime" (#7, 1989), "Tender Lover" (#14, 1989), "My Kinda Girl" (#30, 1990), and "Whip Appeal" (#6, 1990). *For the Cool in You* (#6, 1990) was his follow-up album and it contained the extracts "Never Keep Secrets" (#15, 1993) and "When Can I See You" (#4, 1994). "The Day" (#6, 1997) found daylight near the top of the chart for the artist.

Collectors would be wise to grab as many artifacts as possible from this duo, as there seems to be no end to their abilities. Does Babyface remind you of a young Quincy Jones?

AUTOGRAPHS

Group:
A CD, LP, magazine cover, ad, photo, or card signed by the duo: $20-$45
Individual:
Kenneth "Babyface" Edmonds: $15-$40

POSTERS/PRESS KITS

Promotional Posters: $15-$25
Press Kits: $25-$35

OFTEN OVERLOOKED MEMORABILIA

Movie memorabilia from *The Bodyguard;* all associated artifacts from their productions

Laswell, Bill/Material

Bill Laswell
Born: February 12, 1955

Material was formed in 1979. Original lineup: Laswell, Michael Beinhorn, and Fred Maher*

*Both Maher and Beinhorn eventually departed

This talented bassist and producer starts by throwing all of his musical elements into a music processor, sets it to "blend," then pours it over the rocks and right up to the rim before flavoring it with his current twist—Arabic, ambient, or whatever. Perhaps best known for cowriting and producing Herbie Hancock's hit "Rockit," he also won a Grammy for Hancock's following album, *Sound-System.* Laswell has played with numerous acts, including Brian Eno, David Byrne, and Peter Gabriel, while also produc-

ing for the Ramones, Mick Jagger, Motorhead, and Iggy Pop. He remains an eclectic producer of world music, experimental jazz, and numerous other forms. If music is ever produced on the planet Mars, look for his name in the credits.

AUTOGRAPHS

A CD, LP, magazine cover, ad, photo, or card signed by the artist: $10-$15

OFTEN OVERLOOKED MEMORABILIA

Assorted artifacts from his numerous productions and contributions

Lattisaw, Stacy

Born: November 25, 1966

Eighties teenage disco diva best known for hits "Dynamite" (#8, R&B, 1980), "Let Me Be Your Angel" (#21, 1980), "Love on a Two Way Street" (#26, 1981) and "Where Do We Go from Here" (#1, R&B, 1990), Stacy Lattisaw scored numerous other Top Twenty R&B hits before fading from the music scene.

AUTOGRAPHS

A CD, LP, magazine cover, ad, photo, or card signed by the artist: $10

Lauper, Cyndi

(Cynthia Anne Stephanie Lauper)

Born: June 22, 1953

Early-80s New York pop rocker, and the first woman to have four Top Five singles on a debut album, she is typically associated with her charm and "blue light special" wardrobe, as well as the songs, "Girls Just Want to Have Fun" (#2, 1983), "All Through the Night" (#5, 1984), "She Bop" (#3, 1984), "Time After Time" (#1, 1984), "True Colors" (#1, 1986), "Change of Heart" (#3, 1986) and "I Drove All Night" (#6, 1989).

She also later turned to acting, although it turned away. After being relatively quiet in the early '90s, she returned with releases in both 1993 and 1994, but thus far the CDs have only found a home in bargain bins.

AUTOGRAPHS

A CD, LP, magazine cover, ad, photo, or card signed by the artist: $20-$55

TOUR BOOKS/PROGRAMS/PASSES

Tour Books:

12 Deadly Cyns: $15

Backstage Passes:

Cloth: $5-$8; Laminated: $10

POSTERS/PRESS KITS

Promotional Posters: $8-$15
Press Kits: $15

OFTEN OVERLOOKED MEMORABILIA

Trading cards (set of 66, 1985) - $10; earrings, "Girls"/"Fun" - $15; movie memorabilia, not!

REFERENCES/BOOKS

Numerous resources exist, but none do justice to the singer in my opinion; no dedicated collector books

Leadbelly

(Huddie Ledbetter)

Born: 1885, Died: December 6, 1949

The "king of the 12-string guitar," Leadbelly was an inspiration for the blues and folk revivals of the '50s and '60s, while being a living artifact to the traditional blues of years past. He began playing with his mentor Blind Lemon Jefferson in Dallas at the turn of the century, before finding himself behind bars rather than playing in them. He spent part of three decades in prison on a variety of charges from assaulting a woman, to killing a man because of one—if that won't give you the blues, nothing will.

Leadbelly was finally released from jail in 1934, then brought by folklorists John and Alan Lomax to New York where he recorded his trademark songs, "The Rock Island Line," "The Midnight Special" and "Goodnight Irene." Whether or not they actually belonged to Leadbelly is anyone's guess, but he was the first to introduce them to the public. By 1939 he was back in the slammer on another assault charge, only adding to the lure surrounding the guitarist. He died of Lou Gehrig's disease in 1949.

AUTOGRAPHS

A photo or card signed by the artist: Unavailable

OFTEN OVERLOOKED MEMORABILIA

Associated artifacts from the numerous musicians who have covered his work

REFERENCES/BOOKS

Very limited resources exist; serious collectors should join the Lead Belly Society, P.O. Box 6679, Ithaca, NY 14851

Led Zeppelin

Formed 1968

Jimmy Page, Born: January 9, 1944; John Paul Jones (John Baldwin), Born: January 3, 1946; Robert Plant, Born: August 20, 1948; and John Bonham, Born: May 31, 1948, Died: September 25, 1980

Led Zeppelin is considered one of the most influential forces in the history of rock 'n' roll music. Although the flight of the dirigible lasted just a dozen years, the group remains as popular today as it was

during their touring days. Demand for their rarest recordings and obscure promotional items has increased with time, no doubt fueled by the band's now legendary status. The group definitely falls within the top ten in terms of number of collectors.

Numerous reference materials exist for both the Zeppelin fan and collector. From the excellent *Hammer of the Gods* by Stephen Davis, to the comprehensive *Led Zeppelin: A Celebration* by Dave Lewis, nearly every breath the band took has been documented or recorded. Numerous fanzines also still archive the band's reign as rock's premier band. Zeppelin collectors are urged to take full advantage of these publications.

That Jimmy Page and Robert Plant had always been avid record collectors was a bonus for Zeppelin fans, who could rely on each release to be collectible. Simplifying matters for collectors is a finite Zeppelin catalog that consists of only ten full-length albums, ten U.S. singles, and one boxed set.

The ten U.S. singles were distributed in most European markets, as well as Australia and Japan. Promotional materials associated with these issues are highly sought by collectors, as none of the band's 45s ever came with picture sleeves.

Notable Atlantic promotional pieces include the three inflatable blimps issued for the first three records. The Led Zeppelin I inflatable promo blimp alone can command $350. These items are now difficult to find, as is the inflatable blimp issued in Japan to promote *Physical Graffiti*.

It is an object (or should I say "The Object," used for promoting *Presence*) that attracts greater collector interest than the blimps. This small black ornament, featured on the album's cover, was produced as a promotional piece and limited to 1,000 pieces. Even "The Object" could not evade Zeppelin bootleggers, who produced counterfeit copies. Both pieces ironically are hard to find, with the latter distinguished only by a rougher finish.

Both promotional and concert posters are sought by Zeppelin collectors; both are heavily bootlegged. The two-color Atlantic Records poster (1969) is a favorite among promo collectors. This poster features the band in a classic promotional pose that produced the photograph that was included in the Led Zeppelin I Press Kit. The top of the poster reads, "NOW ON ATLANTIC/AMPEX STEREO TAPES 8-4 TRACK CARTRIDGE, & CASSETTE," "LED ZEPPELIN."

The famous Fillmore posters commissioned by promoter Bill Graham do appear regularly in the marketplace; however, these relics can carry hefty price tags. Of those concert posters produced by Graham, the September 2, 1970, show at the Oakland Coliseum remains the toughest to find. Concert posters are not only difficult to find, but also difficult to identify. Complicating the issue are counterfeits, limited-edition reproductions, and variations.

Other paper-based Zeppelin collectibles worth noting are magazines, newspapers, sheet music, and

White-matter RIAA gold award for Led Zeppelin's Led Zeppelin, 1969. This reverse-style matte award is valued at $3,000. From the Doug Leftwitch collection.

music books. Magazines such as *Cashbox* (9/15/79), *Modern Drummer* (7/84), *Music Life* - Japan (6/74), *Rock Steady* - Japan (9/78), and *Rockin' On* - Japan (3/78, 11/78, 11/79) have changed hands at over $100 each. A copy of *In Through the Out Door*, a color songbook, can even bring $60-$75.

THE LED ZEPPELIN ATLANTIC AND SWAN SONG CATALOG

Led Zeppelin. Atlantic Records. Recorded in October 1968, LP released in U.S. 1/12/69.

Led Zeppelin II. Atlantic Records. Recorded July-September 1969, LP released in U.S. 10/22/69.

Led Zeppelin III. Atlantic Records. Recorded May-August 1970, LP released in U.S. 10/5/70.

Four Symbols. Atlantic Records. Recorded December 1970-October 1971, LP released in U.S. 11/8/71.

House Of The Holy. Atlantic Records. Recorded April-May 1972, LP released in U.S. 3/28/73.

Physical Graffiti. Swan Song Records. Recorded November 1973-August 1974*, LP released in U.S. 2/24/75.

Presence. Swan Song Records. Recorded November 1975, LP released in U.S. 3/31/76.

The Song Remains The Same. Swan Song Records. Recorded July 27-29, 1973, N.Y.C., LP released in U.S. 10/22/76.

In Through The Out Door. Swan Song Records. Recorded November & December 1978, LP released in U.S. 8/15/79.**

Coda. Swan Song Records. Recorded June 1969-November 1978, LP released in U.S. 11/19/82.

*Some material dates back to 1971 & 1972
**Known by collectors for the six different LP covers

AUTOGRAPHS

At the height of its career, Led Zeppelin was elusive to autograph requests, making items signed by all four members particularly valuable. Solo careers by both Page and Plant have allowed collectors greater exposure to the artists through touring. Of the surviving original members, Jones is most elusive.

Group:
Entire band on single sheet: $1,000-$1,200
Page, Plant & Jones on single item: $450-$550

Individual:
Robert Plant: $45-$65
Jimmy Page: $45-$65
John Paul Jones: $55-$75

The signatures of Led Zeppelin

TOUR BOOKS/PROGRAMS/POSTERS/PASSES

1969:
Programs exist for the International Pop Festival 1969 (Texas), Bath Festival of Blues (U.K.) - 6/28, and Royal Albert Hall - 6/29 (Zeppelin headlining show). For the autumn tour a hardcover book was produced featuring Jimmy Page reaching out his hand. A reproduction of this 1969 tour program can be found in the market for about $20. It features a 12" x 12" softcover instead of the originally issued album-like hard cover. Original copies of this program are scarce and can command $150 each in excellent condition.

One the most sought after posters from this era is the original green color poster for the band's appearance at the Winterland Ballroom in San Francisco on April 25 & 26 and the Fillmore West on the 24th and 27th. It was designed by Tea Lautrec Litho in San Francisco. Another is the January Fillmore West poster that also included Taj Mahal and Country Joe and the Fish. This three-color design featured the front end of a car with the three bands listed in large text (curved) above it.

Atlantic records promotional posters from this era are also highly sought by collectors. Most are two-color and feature a publicity shot of the band.

1970:
A program was produced for the Bath Festival of Blues and Progressive Music on June 28, 1970. This program features a black & white cover illustration of a uniformed old-time band with super-imposed images. This scarce program, highly sought by collectors, is also difficult to find in excellent condition and can command $125-$165.

1971:
A program was issued for the Japan Tour, but plans for a program for the Wembley shows were abandoned in favor of a special poster. The 1971 program features the band dressed formally and standing in front of a "Zeppelin" backdrop. The text "LED ZEPPELIN" (red/white) in block 3-D letters appears above the band. This large (horizontally formatted/folded) program, produced by Koyodo Tokyo, is not particularly easy to find.

A popular poster from this era is the November 20, 1971, Wembley Empire Pool, "Electric Magic" show. This poster, which sold during the two-night stay for 30 pence, will cost a collector considerably more today.

1972:
Dedicated programs exist for both the Japan and Australian tours; however, the 1972/73 U.K. Tour had posters issued. Buyer beware! Bootleg programs have turned up on the market for the Alexandra Palace dates and the Knebworth shows.

The Japanese program features a high-contrast black & white photograph of Jimmy Page, with the text "LED ZEPPELIN" (white) appearing at the top right hand corner. A tough program to find in just about any condition.

The Australian Concert Tour (Feb '72) two-color (purple/black) program features the *Led Zeppelin I* cover. It's an outstanding program and also very difficult to find.

1975:
Both the U.S. Tour and Earl's Court had programs issued. An excellent reproduction of the 1975 Earl's Court concert has found its way into the market. Priced at about $15, this 14-page booklet with text and color photos is at least an alternative for program collectors who find the original very difficult to acquire. The 1975 U.S. Tour program has also been reproduced and can be picked up for about $15. It includes 38 color and black & white photographs along with a four-page biography on the band.

An Evening with Led Zeppelin counterfeit tour program

The 1975 "Physical Rocket" (steam train) posters sold at the Earl's Court shows are also highly sought by collectors. The poster features an illustration of an old steam train carrying four passengers. The top of the program reads as follows "MEL BUSH in association with PETER GRANT," "LED ZEPPELIN," "ZEPPELIN," "EXPRESS" (left), "EARL'S," "COURT" (right). Also sought by collectors is the "A Day On The Green" concert poster, August 23 and 24 at the Oakland Stadium. These shows were canceled due to Robert Plant's car crash.

1977:

A program was issued for the USA Tour. This twenty-page program has been frequently counterfeited. Reprints and counterfeits are often misregistered and include characteristic out-of-focus photographs.

1979:

The "OFFICIAL PROGRAMME" for Knebworth features a color picture of the band prominently on the black cover. The top of the program reads as follows, "FREDERICK BANNISTER IN ASSOCIATION WITH PETER GRANT" (yellow), "PRESENTS" (yellow), "LED * ZEPPELIN" (red/white), "AT" (yellow), "KNEBWORTH 1979" (yellow), photo, "OFFICIAL PROGRAMME 90p" (yellow).

1980:

Plans for a 1980 European Tour program were scrapped in favor of a couple tour posters. The most popular of the two posters is the horizontally formatted "LED ZEPPELIN," "Concert 80."

Collector's Note:

A package, *Led Zeppelin, Ten Years Gone,* came out of the U.S. and included all ten CDs in a cardboard box, a set of band photos (5), a poster of the *Chicago Tribune* advertisement, and a set of eight authentic concert tickets from the canceled 1980 Chicago concerts.

USED CLOTHING/EQUIPMENT
Guitar Picks:
Page: $35-$125 (Post-Zeppelin years)

OFTEN OVERLOOKED MEMORABILIA
Official press releases; marketing pieces such as the 3-D object issued (1000) to promote *Presence* ($500-$1,500) and its complimentary hanging mobile, or the Atlantic Records issued "Led Zeppelin II" inflatable airship (11/69); complete set of original Led Zeppelin *Tight but Loose* fan magazines (1-6); Knebworth button badges (1970); promo plastic carrier bag "Zeppelin at Knebworth" (1979);

newspaper ticket advertisements such as the one that appeared in the *Chicago Tribune* on Thursday, September 25—the day John Bonham died—or the full-page advertisement that appeared in *Melody Maker* (6/16/73) featuring the 56,800 people who attended their Tampa, Florida show; sheet music, especially the early years; postcards, trading cards, and even tour bags, such as the Swan Song official tour bag for "Led Zeppelin: The Eighties Part One"

Lee, Albert

Born: December 21, 1943

The dynamic British guitarist has played with some of the best in the business, from Eric Clapton to Emmylou Harris. His fascination for country music over blues separates him from some of his peers. He began by playing piano before switching to guitar in his teens. He hooked up with Chris Farlowe's back-up group, the Thunderbirds, in 1964. At that time, the popular R&B outfit also included Carl Palmer. When the band dissolved in 1968, he joined Country Fever, followed by Heads, Hands and Feet, then on to work with Jerry Lee Lewis, one of Lee's idols, on *The Session* album.

In the next decade he did session work and was found with Rick Grech and the Crickets, Don Everly, and Joe Cocker. Finally in 1975 A&M records offered him a solo contract, which he worked on while playing with Emmylou Harris' Hot Band. Before he could tour in support of the album, he was off on the road with Eric Clapton's band. His contributions with Clapton include *Just One Night* (1980), *Another Ticket* (1981), and *Money and Cigarettes* (1983). Lee managed to kick out three albums during the '80s, while touring with numerous other musicians.

AUTOGRAPHS
A CD, LP, magazine cover, ad, photo, or card signed by the entire band: $10-$15

POSTERS/PRESS KITS
Promotional Posters: $15
Press Kits: $10-$15

USED CLOTHING/EQUIPMENT
Guitar Picks: $25

OFTEN OVERLOOKED MEMORABILIA
His numerous contributions to other musicians work, most notably Eric Clapton.

Lee, Brenda

(Brenda Tarpley)
Born: December 11, 1944

Brenda Lee's career could fill this entire book, as she has attained decades of recording success and her

record sales are estimated at well over 100 million copies! Lee was singing before the age of ten, and by the age of 16 her single "Rockin Around the Christmas Tree" (#14, 1960) was an international hit, ultimately selling over five million copies.

During the '60s she scored numerous hit singles, including "Sweet Nothin's" (#4, 1960), "That's All You Gotta Do" (#6, 1960), "I Want to Be Wanted" (#1, 1960), "Emotions" (#7, 1961), "You Can Depend On Me" (#6, 1961), "Dum Dum" (#4, 1961), "Fool #1" (#3, 1961), "Break It to Me Gently" (#4, 1962), "Everybody Loves Me But You" (#6, 1962), "All Alone Am I" (#3, 1962), and "Losing You" (#6, 1963), before the British Invasion.

During the '70s she found comfort in country music and scored hits with "If This Is Our Last Time" (#30, C&W, 1971) and "Nobody Wins" (#3, C&W, 1973), among others. She also became a staple on television, tried her luck at acting—while continuing to record, and contributed to numerous other musicians' work.

"Little Miss Dynamite," who has played with everyone from Boots Randolph to Jimmy Page, has won numerous awards including the 1984 National Academy of Recording Arts and Sciences Governors Award, but most of all, has won over our hearts!

AUTOGRAPHS
A CD, LP, magazine cover, ad, photo, or card signed by the artist: $10-$30

POSTERS/PRESS KITS
Promotional Posters: $10-$12 (1980-Present)
Press Kits: $10-$15 (1980-Present)

OFTEN OVERLOOKED MEMORABILIA
Videotapes from her numerous television appearances on *Ozark Jubilee, The Perry Como Show,* and *The Ed Sullivan Show;* copies of her syndicated Nashville interview show; movie memorabilia from *Two Little Bears* (1962), *Smokey And The Bandit II* (1981), and *Dick Tracy* (1990); associated memorabilia from her appearance in the 1962 stage production of *Bye Bye Birdie;* a copy of Billboard's Brenda Lee special supplement

REFERENCES/BOOKS
The Brenda Lee International Fan Club, c/o Pat O'Leary, P.O. Box 2700, Murfreesboro, TN 37133 is a must for fans

Lee, Dickey

(Dick Lipscomb)
Born: September 21, 1941

Sixties country singer and songwriter typically associated with the songs "Patches" (#6, 1962), "I Saw Linda Yesterday" (#14, 1963) and "Laurie (Strange Things Happen)" (#14, 1965), Dickey Lee also penned the country hits, "9,999,999 Tears," "Angels, Roses and Rain," "Rocky," and "Never Ending Song of Love."

AUTOGRAPHS
A CD, LP, magazine cover, ad, photo, or card signed by the artist: $8-$15

OFTEN OVERLOOKED MEMORABILIA
Associated artifacts from other musicians' covers of his work, such as Elvis Presley ("She Thinks I Still Care")

Lee, Peggy

(Norma Egstrom)
Born: May 6, 1920

Late '40s and '50s versatile singing star who first gained notoriety for her work with the Benny Goodman Orchestra and her 1943 hit "Why Don't You Do Right?," Peggy Lee was also one of the first singers to write her own material—songs such as "I Don't Know Enough About You," "Mañana," and "It's A Good Day." She is perhaps best known for her songs "Fever" (#8, 1958) and "Is That All There Is?" (#11, 1969). Lee later turned her attention to film, both acting and contributing compositions, as well as her voice.

AUTOGRAPHS
A CD, LP, magazine cover, ad, photo, or card signed by the artist: $10-$30

OFTEN OVERLOOKED MEMORABILIA
Associated artifacts from other musicians' covers of her work; movie memorabilia from *Mr. Music* (1951), *The Jazz Singer* (1953) *Pete Kelly's Blues* (1955), *Johnny Guitar,* and *Lady and the Tramp* (1955) - she was the voice of Peg and also cowrote songs

REFERENCES/BOOKS
Miss Peggy Lee, her autobiography

The Left Banke

Formed 1965
Steve Martin, Tom Finn, Jeff Winfield, George Cameron, Michael Brown (Lookofsky), Born: April 25, 1949*

*Brown and Winfield depart in 1967 and Rick Brand is added

Keyboardist Michael Brown, who studied music at an early age, penned "Walk Away Renee" (#5, 1966) at age 16 and recorded it with The Left Banke two years later. The band's debut single was a smash and entered the Top Five on the U.S. singles chart. Follow-up single "Pretty Ballerina" (#15, 1967) was similar in its classically edged harmonious treatment, which was now being dubbed baroque rock. Following the first two albums, the bulk of which was written by Brown, he left the band. The Left Banke continued unsuccessfully and called it a career in 1969.

Brown would go to Montage, then Stories, before working as an A&R man for Mercury Records. He then formed the Beckies in 1976, before slipping out of sight. The band did try to reform without Brown in 1978, resulting in an incomplete recording session.

AUTOGRAPHS

A CD, LP, magazine cover, ad, photo, or card signed by the entire band: $15-$25*

*High end reflects original members on debut LP

OFTEN OVERLOOKED MEMORABILIA

A copy of *Left Banke, Too* autographed by backing vocalist Steven Tyler: $30

Lemonheads

Formed 1986

Evan Dando, Born: March 4, 1967; Ben Deily; and Jesse Peretz*

*Doug Trachten is added in 1986. Trachten departs in 1987 and John Strohm joins the band. Strohm leaves in 1989, as does Deily and Peretz. David Ryan is added in 1989. Juliana Hatfield is added on bass in 1991. Hatfield leaves in 1992 and is replaced by Nick Dalton.

A band whose line-up varied significantly over the first six years, finally centering around guitarist Evan Dando (formerly of the Whelps), who released the EP *Laughing All The Way to the Cleaners,* which landed them a record deal with indie label Taang! The band then proceeds to record three albums: *Hate Your Friends* (1987), *Creator,* featuring Charles Manson's "Home," and *Lick,* which includes the cover of Vega's "Luka." Personnel changes follow, as Dando signs the Lemonheads to Atlantic Records where they release *Lovey* (1990).

It's a Shame About Ray (#68, 1993), an instant college radio classic, is the band's second album on Atlantic, as the title track (#70, 1992) climbs the U.K. singles chart. Meanwhile, extract "Mrs. Robinson" becomes an MTV hit and also lands in the U.K. Top Twenty singles chart. *Come On Feel the Lemonheads* (#56, 1993), the band's next album release, includes numerous guests such as Juliana Hatfield, Belinda Carlisle, and Rick James.

The outspoken Dando, always a subject of media attention, continues his solo contributions to other artists' work and various compilations. Not surprisingly he has even pursued an acting career.

AUTOGRAPHS

Group:
A CD, LP, magazine cover, ad, photo, or card signed by the entire band: $25-$30

Individual:
Evan Dando: $10-$20

TOUR BOOKS/PROGRAMS/PASSES

Backstage Passes:
Cloth: $10-$20; Laminated: $20-$25

POSTERS/PRESS KITS

Promotional Posters: $7-$12
Press Kits: $10-$12

OFTEN OVERLOOKED MEMORABILIA

Videotape of television performances on *Top of the Pops* BBC1-TV (12/10/92), *The Big Breakfast* - C4-TV (5/6/94), and *Later With Jools Holland* - BBC2-TV (2/18/95); *Playboy* magazine (3/95)

REFERENCES/BOOKS

A few resources exist, but none do justice to the band in my opinion; no dedicated collector books

The Lemon Pipers

Formed mid-1960s

R.G. Nave, Ivan Browne, Bill Bartlett, Steve Walmsley, and Bill Albaugh

Late-60s pop group best remembered for their songs "Green Tambourine" (#1, 1968), "Rice Is Nice" (#46, 1968), and "Jelly Jungle (of Orange Marmalade)" (#51, 1968), before disbanding in 1968. In 1977 Bill Bartlett resurfaced with the band Ram Jam, which struck the Top Twenty with "Black Betty."

AUTOGRAPHS

A CD, LP, magazine cover, ad, photo, or card signed by the group: $15-$25

OFTEN OVERLOOKED MEMORABILIA

Associated artifacts from other musicians' covers of their work

Lennon, John and Yoko Ono

John Lennon, Born: October 9, 1940, Died: December 8, 1980
Yoko Ono, Born: February 18, 1933

Highly collected as a member of the Beatles, Lennon's solo career begins while he is still in the landmark group, when he issues *Unfinished Music No. 1: Two Virgins* (#124, 1969). The disjointed release is remembered most for its controversial packaging, featuring Lennon and companion Yoko Ono nude. The album, which is distributed by Track rather than EMI, is wrapped in a brown paper bag for retail sale. All items relating to the release become instant collectibles. Newspaper clippings from album seizures at various locations are also prized by collectors.

Following the duo's wedding and Lennon's subsequent name change, they release *Unfinished Music No. 2: Life With The Lions* (#174, 1969), a continuation of the first album, but on avant-garde imprint Zapple. During their Montreal "bed-in," "Give Peace A Chance" (#14, 1969) was recorded, and is now considered the definitive peace anthem. Publicity surrounding the "bed-ins" is also good material for collectors, from newspaper articles to magazine features.

In September 1969, Lennon, Ono, and the Plastic Ono Band (Eric Clapton, Alan White, and Klaus Voormann) played at the Rock 'n' Roll Revival show in Toronto, which was later released as *Live, Peace In Toronto, 1969*. The group also released "Cold Turkey" (#30, 1969), which the Beatles had declined to record. *The Wedding Album* (#178, 1969) was also released before the end of the year, as an extravagant gift to their fans. It included a press book, a replica of their marriage license, a photographic piece of wedding cake, and two discs, each with a blank B-side. As part of their continued peace campaign, they spoke to the press and even erected billboards on December 15, 1969 in twelve cities across the world stating "War Is Over! If You Want It"—now extremely sought after by collectors.

On January 17, 1970, an exhibition of Lennon lithographs being held in London is raided by police acting under the Obscene Publications Act. Nine days later, Lennon will write, record, and mix *Instant Karma* (#3, 1970) during a one-day session. Produced by Phil Spector, who at the time was still editing *Let It Be* for the Beatles, the record climbs up world singles charts. With the Beatles officially defunct by March, and Lennon's friendship with McCartney at odds, the Lennons begin a six-month course in primal scream therapy conducted by Dr. Arthur Janov. The period becomes a time for introspection for Lennon, who writes some of his most revealing songs, most of which, including the single "Mother" (#43, 1971), are found on his forthcoming album, *John Lennon and The Plastic Ono Band* (#6, 1971).

"Power to the People" (#11, 1971) is released in the spring, while in September his solo album *Imagine* (#1, 1971), commercially his most successful, is widely praised and extremely well received. *Some Time In New York City* (#11, U.K., 1972), his next album, features his new backing band, Elephant's Memory, as the Lennons continue to fight deportation by the U.S. Immigration and Naturalization Office in New York. The overtly political album included songs such as "Woman Is The Nigger Of The World" and "Sisters, O Sisters," and in such a format, sold poorly in comparison to his other works.

During the next two years he released *Mind Games* (#9, 1973) and *Walls and Bridges* (#1, 1974), the latter of which yields his only solo #1 hit, "Whatever Gets You Thru the Night" (#1, 1974). It also marks a dark period for the artist, who embarks on a haphazard lifestyle following a temporary split from Ono. On November 28, 1974, as a result of a bet he lost to Elton John (over the chartability of Lennon's latest single featuring John), Lennon makes his last public appearance, at John's Madison Square Garden concert. "Whatever Gets You Thru the Night," "I Saw Her Standing There" and "Lucy in the Sky with Diamonds" were later released as an EP (3/81).

Rock 'n' Roll (#6, 1975) was a controversial album due to litigation over its tapes, but is released during a year that will also find singles "#9 Dream" (#9,

1975) and "Stand By Me" (#20, 1975) continuing the artist's string of hits. He will also work with David Bowie on *Young Americans* while the new York Supreme Court votes to reverse his deportation order just days before the birth of his son Sean. For the next five years Lennon devotes his attention to his new son and his reconciled marriage, which survived despite the 18-month separation.

In August 1980, Lennon begins songwriting again and returns from a Bermuda vacation to begin recording at the Hit Factory in New York, for his forthcoming album *Double Fantasy* (#1, 1980), having now signed a contract with the newly formed Geffen Records. The album is released on November 29, 1980, to extremely positive reviews.

On December 8, 1980, the Lennons depart from the Record Plant studio at 10:30 p.m. for their home at New York's prestigious Dakota building and enter at the West 72nd Street entrance. Upon hearing the call "Mr. Lennon," he turns around and is shot four times by a 25-year-old, later identified as one Mark David Chapman. Struggling up six stairs to inside the building alcove, Lennon collapses at around 10:50 p.m. Upon answering the call of a shooting, police officer James Moran places Lennon in the back seat of his patrol car, and drives him fifteen blocks to the Roosevelt Hospital, where the musician is pronounced dead at 11:30 p.m.

It's peace that he sought, pieces of his soul which he gave, pieces of our heart which we lost, to the peace which he has now found.

AUTOGRAPHS

	Sig.	SP*	TLS**	ALS***
John Lennon	$700	$1,200	$2,500	$6,000
Yoko Ono	$40	$70	$85	$100

* = Signed photo
** = Typed letter signed
*** = Autographed (handwritten) letter signed

John Lennon signature with a classic caricature

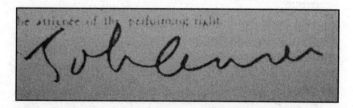

John Lennon signature on a legal contract

The signature of John Lennon

Specific items:

Handwritten and drawn note, includes self-portraits of John and Yoko: $15,000-$20,000

Same as above, self-portraits, only inscribed: $5,000

Same as above, self-portraits, minimal strokes (very quickly done): $1,000-$1,500

Self-portrait, John Lennon only, signed: $2,000

Autographed Christmas card: $800

Autographed "Two Virgins" photograph: $900-$1,200

Autographed handbill "WAR IS OVER!": $1,000

An unpublished lyric: $10,000-$15,000

Published lyrics: $20,000-$100,000

Autographed sheet music: $1,500-$1,750

Autographed "John & Yoko Calendar": $1,500-$1,750

Signed receipts: $1,400-$1,600

Signed publishing agreements: $1,500-$2,750

Pen and Ink drawings, nonformal (doodle) (8" x 10"): $600-$700 per figure

Pen and Ink drawing, formal with annotations: $4,000

Postcard with note, signed: $1,100-$1,900

Autographed single: $2,000-$4,000

Autographed album (solo years): $1,500-$1,800

"Bag One" series of lithographs (300): $14,000-$17,000

"Bag One" rug, 1988 (50): $900

Early (1960s) handwritten play list: $4,000

Autographed poster from *Imagine,* 1971: $2,000-$2,500

OFFEN OVERLOOKED MEMORABILIA

Movie memorabilia from *How I Won The War* (1967), *The Rolling Stones' Rock 'n' Roll Circus* (1968/1996), *Imagine* (1988 version); art exhibition memorabilia from Ono - catalogs, posters, etc., most notably her "Half Wind Show" at London's Lisson Gallery, which was sponsored by Lennon; all items associated with press conferences, such as John and Yoko conduct while sitting inside a white bag at London's Royal Albert Hall (12/18/68); copies of all legal documents surrounding the Lennon/Ono marriage on March 20, 1969 and Lennon's name change on April 22,

1969; stationary from the Hotel La Reine Elizabeth, Montreal, Canada (5, sheets, 5 envelopes) - $15; any associated items from room 1742 of the Hotel La Reine Elizabeth, Montreal, Canada - room key, etc.; *Oz* magazine associated items (1971); videotapes of his television appearances on *The Dick Cavett Show* (9/21/71), *The Mike Douglas Show* (2/15-18/72), *Monday Night Football* (12/9/74); a copy of the film *Imagine* (1972); clippings and accounts from the infamous Troubadour Club incident on March 12, 1974; a copy of his green card (no: A17-597-321) - $2; a copy of the full-page newspaper ad in May 1979 explaining his activities - $5; all associated items surrounding his assassination - newspaper and magazine accounts, etc.; a piece of sod from "Strawberry Fields - an area in Central Park - $1-$3; a rubbing from his star on Hollywood's Walk of Fame - $5-$10; memorabilia from Lennon's Restaurant in London - napkins, plates, menus, etc.; all associated posthumous memorabilia, much of which could fill a book of this size

REFERENCES/BOOKS

Come Together: John Lennon in His Time by Jon Wiener; a wealth of other resources exist, but none do justice to the singer in my opinion. Collectors may want to opt for John Robertson's book *The Art and Music of John Lennon.*

Lennon, Julian

(John Charles Julian Lennon)
Born: April 8, 1953

The son of John Lennon and his first wife Cynthia Twist, the subject of Paul McCartney's "Hey Jude," and a considerable talent in his own right, Julian is raised in a typically middle-class fashion, despite his father's wealth and fame. Blessed by heredity and ambition, he decides to capture some of his musical aspirations, following the tragic death of his father.

Valotte, his debut Atlantic offering, produced by veteran Phil Ramone, yields two hit extracts, the title

The signature of Julian Lennon, also a rock memorabilia collector

track (#9, 1984) and "Too Late For Goodbyes" (#5, 1984), and is an overwhelming success. Not surprisingly, his familiar looks and sound bear an uncanny resemblance to his father. His follow-up album, *The Secret Value of Daydreaming,* falls short of expectations, and his next two albums are virtually ignored.

A rock and roll memorabilia collector himself, he has found himself focusing on the many artifacts of his father that have turned up in prominent public auctions.

AUTOGRAPHS

A CD, LP, magazine cover, ad, photo, or card signed by the artist: $10-$20

TOUR BOOKS/PROGRAMS/PASSES

Backstage Passes:

Cloth: $5; Laminated: $7-$10

POSTERS/PRESS KITS

Promotional Posters: $7-$10

Press Kits: $10

REFERENCES/BOOKS

A few resources exist, but none do justice to the singer in my opinion; no dedicated collector books

Let's Active

Formed 1981

Mitch Easter, Faye Hunter, and Sara Romweber*

*Romweber departs in 1984 and is replaced with Eric Marshall, while Angie Carlson is also added. Hunter leaves in 1986 and John Heames is added on bass.

North Carolina bred Easter, who has always been influenced by the '60's British pop sound, finds himself playing in bands prior to opening a recording studio in his mom's garage during the late '70s. Mitch's Drive-In Studio includes customers such as the dB's, Pylon, and R.E.M., and while working with these acts he forms Let's Active with girlfriend Sara Romweber. While their music was met with mixed reviews—frankly too much it hard to swallow—Easter used the group as a vehicle for his studio creativity during the '80s, before touring with another outfit, Velvet Crush, in 1994.

AUTOGRAPHS

A CD, LP, magazine cover, ad, photo, or card signed by the band: $10-$12

POSTERS/PRESS KITS

Promotional Posters: $4-$6

Press Kits: $5

OFTEN OVERLOOKED MEMORABILIA

Mitch's Drive-In Studio memorabilia

The Lettermen

Formed 1958

Best known lineup: Tony Butala, Bob Engemann, and Jim Pike*

*Numerous personnel changes

The Letterman have captured the hearts of mature audiences for nearly four decades. Formed in 1960, its personnel has varied significantly over the years, but the lineup of Butala, Engemann, and Jim Pike seems to carry the distinction of being most remembered. Opening up for acts such as George Burns and Jack Benny, they slowly developed a solid foundation that has been built upon for decades. When they moved from Warner Brothers to Capitol in 1961, they put together a string of hits including "The Way You Look Tonight," "When I Fall In Love" and "Come Back Silly Girl." Their albums were consistent sellers for the label, as the group evolved with the music they presented.

When Engemann departed in 1968, he was replaced with Jim Pike's brother Gary, while the group's successful string of singles continued, most notably of which is the medley of "Goin' Out Of My Head/Can't Take My Eyes Off of You/Hurt So Bad" (#12, 1969). Although the group continued to record and perform, this single would be their last gold record. They also established themselves in the television commercial market, winning a Golden Globe Award for an airlines ad, while continuing their presence well into the '90s.

AUTOGRAPHS

A CD, LP, magazine cover, ad, photo, or card signed by the group: $15-$45*

*Original lineup

POSTERS/PRESS KITS

Press Kits: $10-$25

OFTEN OVERLOOKED MEMORABILIA

Their numerous television appearances including commercials, such as Pan Am Airlines*

Level 42

Mark King, Phil Gould, Boon Gould, and Mike Lindup*

*Phil and Boon Gould depart in 1987 and Alan Murphy and Gary Husband are added in 1988. Murphy dies in 1989, and Jakko Jakszyk joins in 1988.

Born out of the relationship of Mark King with the Gould Brothers (having migrated from the Isle of Wight to London), the band forms in 1980. Influenced by jazz-rock and adding a touch of fusion, their first albums were primarily instrumental, until finally commercial pressure led to King's vocalization. The

group's first international hit, the extract "Something About You" (#7, 1986), landed from *World Machine* (#18, 1986), which was followed up with the album *Running in the Family* (#23, 1987) and single "Lessons in Love" (#12, 1987). Their success led to a 1987 tour with Madonna, before going off and touring on their own.

King will go on to work with numerous other artists, including Midge Ure and Robert Palmer.

AUTOGRAPHS
A CD, LP, magazine cover, ad, photo, or card signed by the group: $20*
*Original lineup

TOUR BOOKS/PROGRAMS/PASSES
Backstage Passes:
Cloth: $5; Laminated: $10*
*Consult Madonna entry for their 1987 summer tour

POSTERS/PRESS KITS
Promotional Posters: $10
Press Kits: $10

Levert

Formed 1982
Gerald Levert, Sean Levert, and Marc Gordon

The singing Levert brothers, sons of O' Jays' Eddie Levert Sr., form a trio with keyboardist Marc Gordon, to carry the polished rich harmonies characteristic in the work of their father and other groups such as the Spinners. Adding a funkier, more progressive upbeat sound, the Leverts begin to tackle the Midwest club scene, as regional single "I'm Still" attracts the attention of Atlantic Records.

Their debut album *Bloodline* included the hit "(Pop, Pop, Pop, Pop) Goes My Mind" (#1, R&B, 1986). The band followed up with the album *The Big Throwdown* (#32, 1987), which contained three outstanding R&B singles: "Casanova" (#1, R&B, 1987),which also scored well on pop charts, "My Forever Lover" (#2, R&B, 1987), and "Sweet Sensation" (#4, R&B, 1988).

The band then topped the R&B charts the following year with "Addicted to You" from the film soundtrack to *Coming To America*. The same year Gerald Levert and Gordon formed Travel Productions, which produced and wrote for a variety of artists including Miki Howard, who scored with single "That's What Love Is" (#4, R&B, 1988). The Leverts released their album *Just Coolin'* in 1988, with the hit extract "Gotta Get the Money." The singles just kept on coming, including "Rope a Dope Style " (#7, R&B, 1990), "All Season" (#4, R&B, 1990), and the chart topper "Baby I'm Ready" (#1, R&B, 1991). Gerald's solo album, released in 1992, also landed three Top Ten R&B extracts: "School Me" (#3, R&B, 1992), "Can You Handle It" (#9, R&B, 1992) and "Baby Hold

On to Me" (#1, R&B, 1992), a duet with his father. The latter combination would also prove successful on the 1996 album *Father and Son*.

AUTOGRAPHS
Group:
A CD, LP, magazine cover, ad, photo, or card signed by the group: $20-$25
Individual:
Gerald Levert: $10-$15

POSTERS/PRESS KITS
Promotional Posters: $10
Press Kits: $10-$15

OFTEN OVERLOOKED MEMORABILIA
Movie memorabilia from *Coming to America* (1988)

Lewis, Bobby

Born: February 17, 1933

Midwest '60s pop star best remembered for his songs "Tossin' and Turnin'" (#1, 1961) and "One Track Mind" (#9, 1961), "I didn't sleep at all...

AUTOGRAPHS
A CD, LP, magazine cover, ad, photo, or card signed by the artist: $5-$20

OFTEN OVERLOOKED MEMORABILIA
All items associated with "Tossin' and Turnin'" (#1, 1961) and "One Track Mind" (#9, 1961)

Lewis, Furry

(Walter Lewis)
Born: March 6, 1893, Died: September 14, 1981

Memphis blues craftsman often cited as the first guitarist to play bottleneck, Walter "Furry" Lewis, born in Mississippi, but raised in Memphis, became a well-known local attraction. He toured the country in medicine shows, was playing Beale Street while still a teenager, and played the local saloons with Memphis Minnie and Blind Lemon Jefferson. He made his first recordings in the late '20s, but with the Depression came other forms of music, so Lewis looked to support himself with a regular job as a street cleaner.

As his earlier contributions became more acknowledged, he recorded with other labels, but never earned enough to quit his day job. The blues and folk festivals of the '60s and '70s were good for pocket money and he even landed on a Leon Russell television special. He was so influential later in his life that the Rolling Stones asked him to open their 1975 show in Memphis.

AUTOGRAPHS

An LP, magazine cover, ad, photo, or card signed by the artist: $20-$30

OFTEN OVERLOOKED MEMORABILIA

A videotape from his appearance on *The Tonight Show*; movie memorabilia from *W.W. and the Dixie Dance Kings*, and *This Is Elvis*

Lewis, Gary and the Playboys

Formed 1964

Best known lineup: Gary Lewis (Levitch), Born: July 31, 1945; Al Ramsey, Born: July 27, 1943; John R. West, Born: July 31, 1939; David Walkes, Born: May 12, 1943; and Dave Costell, Born: March 15, 1944*

*Numerous personnel changes

Gary Lewis, the eldest son of actor Jerry Lewis, decides to turn his attentions to rock 'n' roll as a teenager, while taking drum lessons from Buddy Rich. He forms the Playboys and the group plays a summer season at the Disneyland theme park, while also playing locally. In 1965, now signed to Liberty Records, they land a debut hit with "This Diamond Ring" (#1, 1965) and soon follow it with the Glen D. Hardin-penned "Count Me In" (#2, 1965).

Their debut album, *This Diamond Ring* (#26, 1965), surprises the chart watchers who are now used to having British artists dominate. "Save Your Heart For Me" (#2, 1965), "Everybody Loves A Clown" (#4, 1965), "She's Just My Style" (#3, 1966), "Sure Gonna Miss Her" (#9, 1966) and "Green Grass" (#8, 1966) follow as Lewis' series of seven consecutive U.S. Top Ten hits draws to a close. "My Heart's Symphony" (#13, 1966), "(You Don't Have To) Paint Me A Picture" (#15, 1966), and "The Words Come From" (#21, 1967) become his last hits before being drafted into the U.S. army, where he opts for a clerical job, rather than entertaining troops.

In the fall of 1968, just out of the service, he tries to revive the band. "Sealed With A Kiss" (#19, 1968) is successful on the singles chart, but the momentum is noticeably gone. He later opts for the oldies circuit during the '70s and '80s, while also running a music store and giving music lessons.

AUTOGRAPHS

A CD, LP, magazine cover, ad, photo, or card signed by the band: $15-$40

OFTEN OVERLOOKED MEMORABILIA

Associated movie memorabilia from *Rock-A-Bye-Baby* (1957), *A Swingin Summer, Out Of Sight* (1966), and *Way Way Out* (1966); videotapes from his television appearances on *The Ed Sullivan Show* (1965, 1967), *It's What's Happening Baby* (1965), *Ready Steady Go!* (1965), *Top of the Pops* (1965), and *Thank Your Lucky Stars* (1965); memorabilia from his lead role in *Bye Bye Birdie* musical in Kansas City, Missouri (1966); memorabilia from the "Why I Want To Give Gary Lewis His Last Kiss" national contest; cereal box record offer - $125

Lewis, Huey and the News

Formed 1979

Huey Lewis (Cregg III), Born: July 5, 1950; Chris Hayes; Mario Cipollina; Bill Gibson; Sean Hopper; and Johnny Colla

Mid-80s Bay Area funtime party band, Huey Lewis and the News sold well over ten million albums filled with predictable no-frills rock 'n' roll, and with it, became one of the most commercially successful acts of the decade. "Do You Believe In Love" (#7, 1982) and "Hope You Love Me Like You Say You Do" (#36, 1982) were extracted from the group's breakthrough second album, *Picture This* (313, 1982), and began a string of hits that would follow the group into the '90s.

Sports (#1, 1983), with five Top Twenty hits, included "Heart and Soul" (#8, 1983), "I Want A New Drug" (#6, 1984), "The Heart of Rock & Roll" (#6, 1984), and "If This Is It" (#6, 1984), and stayed on the chart for three years. The hits that followed included "The Power of Love" (#1, 1985) from the movie *Back to the Future,* "Stuck With You" (#1, 1986), "Hip to Be Square" (#3, 1986), "Jacob's Ladder" (#1, 1987)—penned by Bruce Hornsby, "I Know What I Like" (#9, 1987), "Doing It All for My Baby" (#6, 1987), "Perfect World" (#3, 1988), "Small World" (#25, 1988) and "Couple Days Off" (#11, 1991). By the '90s the band's momentum, despite the hits, had dissipated, best exemplified by the album *Four Chords and Several Years Ago,* which couldn't break into the Top Fifty.

Lewis, with his good looks and camera appeal, then turned to acting in the mid-90s.

AUTOGRAPHS

A CD, LP, magazine cover, ad, photo, or card signed by the group: $20-$45

TOUR BOOKS/ PROGRAMS/PASSES

Tour Books:
Small World Tour: $15

Backstage Passes:
Cloth: $10-$15;
Laminated: $15-$25

POSTERS/PRESS KITS

Promotional Posters: $10-$25

Press Kits: $20-$35

USED CLOTHING/ EQUIPMENT

Guitar Picks: $10-$20

Huey Lewis and the News World Tour program (© 1986 Hulex)

OFTEN OVERLOOKED MEMORABILIA

Movie memorabilia from *Short Cuts* (1994); "Small World" blow-up vinyl globe - $50; coffee mug (w/Melissa Etheridge) - $35

REFERENCES/BOOKS

A few resources exist, but none do justice to the band in my opinion; no dedicated collector books; serious collectors should opt for fan club: Newsline II, P.O. Box 99, Payson, UT 84651

Lewis, Jerry Lee

Born: September 29, 1935

"THE KILLER," cousin of both Mickey Gilley and Jimmy Swaggart, Jerry Lee Lewis, despite having only three Top Ten hits, helped redefine rock 'n' roll during his years on the legendary Sun Records label in the late '50s. His first single, "Crazy Arms," was a regional hit, but his follow-up cut "Whole Lotta Shakin' Going On" (#3, 1957), put him high on the chart and even landed him an appearance on the *Steve Allen Show*. "Great Balls of Fire" (#2, 1957) and "Breathless" (#7, 1958) continued his hit streak, before Lewis found himself in the movie *High School Confidential* (#21, 1958), where he also contributed the hit title track.

The strength of "Shakin'" and "Great Balls" landed him on three singles charts—pop, R&B and C&W—simultaneously. Unfortunately, his career nearly ground to a screeching halt when he married his thirteen-year-old third cousin, Myra Gale Brown, his third wife, in 1957. Now hounded by the press and condemned by the church, his career was in a tailspin. Through extensive touring, he tried to pick up his career, but instead picked up a bottle. He did land a modest hit in 1961 with "What'd I Say," but by the end of the decade he found himself abandoning rock in favor of country music.

His switch to country would prove very fruitful for Lewis, who scored hits with "Another Place, Another Time" and "What Made Milwaukee Famous (Made a Loser of Me)," followed by two and a half dozen country hits, such as "To Make Love Sweeter for You" (#1, C&W, 1968), "Would You Take Another Chance on Me" (#1, C&W, 1971) and "Chantilly Lace" (#1, C&W, 1972).

Periodic other releases also brought attention to him during the '70s, including the album *The Session,* which included a host of British stars such as Peter Frampton and Rory Gallagher, while even yielding the modest extract "Drinkin' Wine Spo Dee Odee."

On June 30, 1981, he was hospitalized in Memphis as a result of a hemorrhaging stomach ulcer. Given a 50/50 chance of survival, Lewis defied the odds. The decade would continue to be marred by tragedy: the drowning of his estranged fourth wife and the mysterious death of his fifth wife just over two months after their wedding. He would also become addicted to pain killers, eventually leading to a stint at the Betty Ford Clinic. By the end of the decade he would see attention in his career resurrected with the film *Great Balls of Fire* (1989) and his induction into the Rock and Roll Hall of Fame in 1986. During the Nineties Lewis has been evasive, pursuasive and occasionally pixilated.

AUTOGRAPHS

A CD, LP, magazine cover, ad, photo, or card signed by the artist: $35-$85

OFTEN OVERLOOKED MEMORABILIA

All items associated with the bizarre events that seem to follow the artist; movie memorabilia from *Great Balls of Fire* and *Dick Tracy* (1990); videotapes of his numerous television appearances; mail order goods available at 1-800-988-FIRE

REFERENCES/BOOKS

A few resources exist, but none do justice to the singer in my opinion; no dedicated collector books; serious collectors should opt for fan club: Jerry Lee Lewis International Fan Club, Wim de Boer, Jan Hendrikxstraat 22, NL-5684 XJ Best, Holland

Lewis, Linda

Seventies British singer/songwriter best remembered for "Rock-a-Doodle-Do" (#15, 1973), "It's In His Kiss (The Shoop Shoop Song)" (#6, U.K., 1975), and "Baby I'm Yours" (#33, U.K., 1976), Linda Lewis had little commercial success in America despite a bundle of talent.

AUTOGRAPHS

A LP, magazine cover, ad, photo, or card signed by the artist: $5-$10

OFTEN OVERLOOKED MEMORABILIA

All items associated with "Rock-a-Doodle-Do" (#15, 1973), "It's In His Kiss (The Shoop Shoop Song)" (#6, U.K., 1975), "Baby I'm Yours" (#33, U.K., 1976)

Lewis, Ramsey

Born: May 27, 1935

Lewis, formally trained on classical piano, found success in the mid-60s with pop-jazz rearrangements of numerous current hits. In 1965 the Ramsey Lewis Trio, formed in nearly a decade earlier, earns a Grammy award for "The In Crowd" (#5, 1965), and will earn another award nine years later for their cover of "Hang On Sloopy" (#11, 1965). The trio of Lewis, Eldee Young, and Issac Holt broke up in 1965. The following year Lewis forms another trio with Cleveland Eaton and Maurice White (Earth, Wind & Fire), who score a hit with "Wade in the Water" (#19, 1966), while Lewis earns another Grammy for "Hold it Right There."

His success continued into the '70s, where he landed "Sun Goddess" (#12, 1975), before exploring new

The signature of Ramsey Lewis

music during the '80s. By 1990 he was cohosting a jazz radio show in Chicago, while working with his son.

AUTOGRAPHS

A CD, LP, magazine cover, ad, photo, or card signed by the artist: $10-$20

OFTEN OVERLOOKED MEMORABILIA

All items associated with his Grammy-winning songs and his collaborations with other musicians

---

Lewis, Smiley

(Overton Lemons)
Born: July 5, 1920, Died: October 7, 1966

Well-known, talented, and deep rooted in the New Orleans R&B jazz scene, Lewis's work has been covered successfully for decades by everyone from Elvis Presley to Dave Edmunds. He began recording in New Orleans in 1947 for the Deluxe label under the name Smiling Lewis. Best remembered for songs such as "Shame Shame Shame," "The Bells Are Ringing," "I Hear You Knocking" and "One Night (of Sin)," the latter of which was cleaned up and recorded by Elvis Presley as "One Night (Of Love)." Lewis loved music and worked right up until his death in 1966.

AUTOGRAPHS

A LP, magazine cover, ad, photo, or card signed by the artist: $20-$45

OFTEN OVERLOOKED MEMORABILIA

All items associated with cover version of his songs

Lightfoot, Gordon

Born: November 17, 1938

Inspired by the folk movements of the early '60s, Lightfoot emigrated to Los Angeles in 1958 to attend college, before returning home to his native Canada and producing commercial jingles. Inspired to move from piano to guitar by the likes of such performers as Pete Seeger, Lightfoot now plays the local coffeehouse circuit.

His first Canadian hit "Remember Me" evoked his country influence and showcased his songwriting. Peter, Paul & Mary would later score with his song "For Lovin' Me" (#30, 1965), given to them by legendary manager Albert Grossman, who was also impressed with the talent he saw in Lightfoot so much so he signed on with Groscourt Productions in 1964. He began releasing albums in 1966, under the United Artists label, before moving on to Reprise in 1969, where the album *Sit Young Down Stranger* became his breakthrough. Aided by album extract "If You Could Read My Mind" (#5, 1971), album sales were brisk, and Lightfoot was now in the spotlight. His popularity peaked with the album *Sundown* (#1, 1974), which topped the U.S. chart, as did its title track. "Carefree Highway" (#10, 1974) and "Rainy Day People" (#26, 1975) continue the artist's series of hit singles. *Summertime Dream* (#12, 1976) also sold well and included the hit single "The Wreck of the Edmund Fitzgerald" (#2, 1976). From 1986 to 1993, Lightfoot didn't release an album, although his popularity, especially in Canada, seems to always have sustained itself. He toured the U.S. in 1995, while occasionally appearing at a variety of festivals.

AUTOGRAPHS

A CD, LP, magazine cover, ad, photo, or card signed by the artist: $12-$30

POSTERS/PRESS KITS

Promotional Posters: $10 (1993-Present)

USED CLOTHING/EQUIPMENT

Guitar Picks: $20-$25

OFTEN OVERLOOKED MEMORABILIA

All items associated with the wreck of the Edmund Fitzgerald (11/11/75); movie memorabilia from *Harry Tracy* (1982); videotapes of his variety show, which ran for eight weeks on BBC-TV (1963); a copy of *Let's Sing Out* (1963) on CTV; covers of his songs by other artists

REFERENCES/BOOKS

A few resources exist, but none do justice to the singer in my opinion; no dedicated collector books

---

****

"On The Edge"

Liliput/Kleenex

An adventurous Swiss foursome whose femininity was intertwined between pungent rhythmic riffs. Similar to their peers of the late '70s (Delta 5, the Raincoats, and

the Slits, all of which make an interesting study in human behavior), they were innovators of indie punk. As a movement, well worth some research, and the acquisition of any artifacts that you may be lucky enough to still find.

****

Lindisfarne

Formed 1969

Alan Hull, Born: February 20, 1945; Rod Clements; Ray Jackson; Simon Cowe; and Ray Laidlaw*

*Clements, Cowe, and Laidlaw leave in 1973 and are replaced with Kenny Craddock, Charlie Harcourt, and Paul Nichols. Group disbands in 1975. The original lineup reforms in 1978.

Seventies British pop folk-rock act best remembered for songs such as "Meet Me on the Corner" (#5, U.K., 1972), "Lady Eleanor" (#3, U.K., 1972) and "Run For Home" (#33, 1978), as well as for their album *Fog on the Tyne* (1971), Lindisfarne was popular in Britain, but never garnered much more than a cult following in America.

AUTOGRAPHS

An LP, magazine cover, ad, photo, or card signed by the group: $10-$30

Lindley, David: See Kaleidoscope

Lindsay, Arto: See DNA

Lipps, Inc.

Formed 1977

Steven Greenberg, Cynthia Johnson, David Rivkin, Tom Riopelle, Terry Grant, and Ivan Rafowitz

Eighties Twin Cities pop funk group best remembered for their hit "Funkytown" (#1, 1980), as well as for a handful of R&B minor hits, before disbanding.

AUTOGRAPHS

An LP, magazine cover, ad, photo, or card signed by the group: $10-$15

Lipscomb, Mance

Born: April 9, 1895, Died: January 30, 1976

Texas blues artist who wasn't discovered until 1960, Mance Lipscomb continued performing and recording until 1974, two years before his death. His body of work has been cited as an influence by many, including Bob Dylan and the Grateful Dead.

AUTOGRAPHS

An LP, magazine cover, ad, photo, or card signed by the artist: $20-$35

OFTEN OVERLOOKED MEMORABILIA

Copies of the documentaries he has appeared in: *The Blues* (1962), *The Blues Accordin' to Lightnin' Hopkins* (1969), *A Well Spent Life* (1971), *Blues Like Showers of Rain* (1970) and *Out of the Blacks into the Blues* (1972)

Lisa Lisa and the Cult Jam

Formed 1984

Latin-rooted, mid-80s New York dance-music scene act best remembered for their songs, "I Wonder If I Take You Home" (#34, 1985), "All Cried Out" (#8, 1986), "Head to Toe" (#1, 1987), "Lost in Emotion" (#1, 1987), "Someone to Love Me for Me" (#7, 1987), "Little Jackie Wants to Be a Star" (#29, 1989) and "Let the Beat Hit 'Em" (#37, 1991), before Lisa Velez departed for a solo career.

AUTOGRAPHS

A CD, LP, magazine cover, ad, photo, or card signed by the group: $10-$15

POSTERS/PRESS KITS

Promotional Posters: $8-$15
Press Kits: $10-$15

Little Anthony and the Imperials

Formed 1957

Anthony (Jerome Anthony) Gourdine, Born: January 8, 1940; Ernest Wright Jr.; Clarence Collins; Tracy Lord; and Glouster "Nate" Rogers*

*Lord and Rogers depart in 1961 and Sammy Strain is added. Gourdine also leaves in 1961 and is replaced by George Kerr. Group reunites in 1963. Additional changes follow.

Late-50s New York doo-wop group best remembered for their songs "Tears on My Pillow" (#4, 1958) and "Shimmy, Shimmy, Ko-ko Bop" (#24, 1960) before breaking up the first time, and "Goin' Out of My Head" (36, 1964), "Hurt So Bad" (#9, 1965) and "Take

Me Back" (#16, 1965), before slipping from the pop chart.

AUTOGRAPHS

An LP, magazine cover, ad, photo, or card signed by the group: $20-$40

Little Eva

(Eva Boyd)
Born: June 29, 1945

Early-60s pop baby-sitter best remembered for her debut smash "The Loco-Motion" (penned by King and Goffin), followed by "Keep Your Hands Off My Baby" (#12, 1962), "Let's Turkey Trot" (#20, 1963) and "Swingin' on a Star" (#38, 1963, a duet with Big Dee Irwin), before slipping away from both the music and babysitting scene.

AUTOGRAPHS

An LP, magazine cover, ad, photo, or card signed by the artist: $10-$20

Little Feat

Formed 1969

Lowell George (1945-1979); Billy Payne, Born: March 12, 1949; Richard Hayward; and Roy Estrada*

*Estrada departs in 1972 and Kenny Gradney along with Paul Barrere and Sam Clayton are added. Group disbands following the death of George. Group re-forms in 1988, adding Craig Fuller and Fred Tackett. Fuller leaves in 1994 and Shaun Murphy is added.

Lowell George and Roy Estrada, both former Mothers of Invention members, add Richie Hayward and Bill Payne to form Little Feat. George's rich blues sound, complemented by his playful approach to the band's sound—no doubt attributed to his former entourage—dominated the band. After signing with Warner Brothers, the band releases "Strawberry Flats/Hamburger Midnight" extracted from their debut album *Little Feat* (1971), which is hailed by critics. *Sailin Shoes* follows in 1972, after which Estrada leaves.

Dixie Chicken, the band's third album, features new personnel, who set out in support of the record, but soon find out that self-destructive behavior permeates, resulting in the band's break-up. Payne joins the Doobie Brothers briefly before going on to Bonnie Raitt's band. Most of the others go on to provide backing for singer Kathy Dalton, as rumors abound regarding the fate of the Feat. The following year the band regroups to produce the album *Feats Don't Fail Me Now* (#36, 1974), which quickly becomes the band's first charting record.

In 1975 the group hits the road as part of "The Warner Brothers Music Show" and manages to upstage many of the other acts. *The Last Record Album* (#36, 1975) is released in the fall of 1975 and is basically penned by both Payne and Barrere. The band plays the U.K. the following year, before *Time Loves A Hero* (#34, 1977), their next album, is released in 1977. *Waiting for Columbus* (#18, 1978), sells well despite the criticism of it; meanwhile George goes on to produce the Grateful Dead's *Shakedown Street* (#41, 1979).

In April, having completed the recording of their final album, Payne announces that Little Feat has disbanded. George then heads out on tour supporting his solo effort *Thanks, I'll Eat It Here* (#71, 1979). On June 29, 1979, two months after the band's breakup. George is found dead at the age of 34, from a heart attack influenced by drug abuse, in his Arlington, Virginia, hotel. The band then regrouped to perform a fundraiser for his widow, while also finishing *Down on the Farm* (#29, 1979), before disbanding again.

Following George's death, Hayward toured with both Joan Armatrading and Robert Plant. Payne returned to his solid studio work and very occasional tours. Barrere also went solo and toured with his own band. In 1988, Payne, Hayward, Barrere, Gradney, and Clayton re-formed Little Feat with the addition of Fred Tackett and Craig Fuller (Pure Prairie League), releasing *Let It Roll* (#6, 1988), *Representing the Mambo* (#45, 1990), and "Shake Me Up" (#126, 1991). Fuller then departs and Shaun Murphy is added, as the band, now signed to Zoo Records, releases their next album, *Ain't Had Enough Fun* (#154, 1995). While on tour to support the album, they will also be taping for a future live set, their first since 1978.

AUTOGRAPHS

Group:
A CD, LP, magazine cover, ad, photo, or card signed by the band: $60-$125*
*Original lineup

Individual:
Lowell George (1945-1979): $20-$40
Billy Payne: $15-$20
Richard Hayward: $10-$15
Roy Estrada: $5-$10
Kenny Gradney: $5-$7
Paul Barrere: $5-$10
Sam Clayton: $5
Craig Fuller: $7-$12
Fred Tackett: $5
Shaun Murphy: $5-$7

A Little Feat backstage pass (Printed by OTTO)

TOUR BOOKS/PROGRAMS/PASSES

Tour Book:
1978 Concert Tour - $100

OFTEN OVERLOOKED MEMORABILIA

Videotapes from television appearances on *Ted Mack's Amateur Hour* (George), *Austin City Limits* (3/30/91) and *The Tonight Show* (9/13/95); covers of the band's songs, especially "Willin'"

Little Milton

(Milton Campbell)
Born: September 7, 1934

Sixties blues artist commonly associated with the songs "So Mean to Me" (#14, R&B, 1962), "We're Gonna Make It" (#25, 1965), "Who's Cheating Who" (#43, 1965), "Feel So Bad" (#7, R&B, 1967) and "Walkin' the Back Streets and Cryin'," Little Milton also had some of his Checker hits arranged by Donny Hathaway.

AUTOGRAPHS

A CD, LP, magazine cover, ad, photo, or card signed by the artist: $5-$10

OFTEN OVERLOOKED MEMORABILIA

Movie memorabilia from *Wattstax* (1973)

Little Richard

(Richard Penniman)
Born: December 5, 1932

This 1956 poster for Little Richard is the earliest known to exist —and it is in mint condition. It's estimated value is $4,000. From the collection of Dr. Dennis Hickey.

This Little Richard poster is one of only two known. Majestic Press of Hollywood printed this 14" x 22" poster for a July 24, 1957, poster. From the collection of Hank Thompson.

One of rock 'n' roll's apostles, this exotic late-50s performer seemed to harbor his rebelliousness before releasing it during one of his legendary energetic stage shows. Little Richard is best remembered for his hits "Tutti Frutti" (#17, 1956), "Long Tall Sally" (#6, 1956), "Rip It Up" (#17, 1956), "Lucille" (#21, 1957), "Jenny, Jenny" (#10, 1957), "Keep a Knockin'" (#8, 1957) and "Good Golly, Miss Molly" (#10, 1958), before quitting at the height of his popularity to become an ordained minister.

He returned to the music business with gospel recordings in 1964, but when they failed to capture the public interest he was looking for, he attempted a resurrection of his rock career. Despite his continued recording and extensive touring, he was unable to match his previous success.

A tough to obtain autographed photo of Little Richard

Little Richard tried his hands at acting in both film and television, while exerting his charm doing commercials and later even worked on children's recordings. He was inducted into the Rock and Roll Hall of Fame in 1986, and is the recipient of numerous awards.

AUTOGRAPHS

A CD, LP, magazine cover, ad, photo, or card signed by the artist: $25-$75

OFTEN OVERLOOKED MEMORABILIA

Movie memorabilia from *Down and Out in Beverly Hills* (1985); videotapes of his numerous television appearances including *Miami Vice, Martin,* and *Full House;* copies of his marketing efforts, such as television commercials and print ads; associated artifacts from his work in the ministry

REFERENCES/BOOKS

The Life and Times of Little Richard, his autobiography (1984); a few other resources exist, but none do justice to the singer in my opinion; no dedicated collector books

Little River Band

Formed 1975

Beeb Britles, Graham Goble, Glenn Shorrock, Roger McLachlan, Derek Pellicci and Rick Formosa*

*Numerous personnel changes.

Late-70s Australian pop vocal act, the Little River Band broke in the States after signing with Capitol in 1976. They are best known for their hits "It's a Long Way There" (#28, 1976), "Help Is On Its Way" (#14, 1977), "Reminiscing" (#3, 1978), "Lady" (#10, 1979), "Lonesome Loser" (#6, 1979), "Cool Change" (#10, 1979), "Take It Easy on Me," "Night Owls" and "Man On Your Mind" (the last three all from 1981), before falling prey to personnel changes.

AUTOGRAPHS

An LP, magazine cover, ad, photo, or card signed by the group: $20-$45

OFTEN OVERLOOKED MEMORABILIA

"Time Exposure" triangular mobile - $50; videotapes from their numerous television appearances; artifacts from band members' earlier days, such as Shorrock's work with the Twilights

Little Walter

Marion Walter Jacobs (1930-1968)

Legendary '50s Delta-Chicago bluesman and harmonica player best known for his classic hits "Juke," "Sad Hours," "Blues with a Feeling," "Mean Old World," "You Better Watch Yourself," "You're So Fine," "Key to the Highway," and "My Babe," Little Walter often recorded and toured with Muddy Wa-

ters. He was one of the first harmonica players, if not the very first, to "plug-in" (play under amplification). His influence was widespread, as he set the precedence for all who would follow. He died from head injuries suffered in a street fight in 1968.

AUTOGRAPHS

An LP, magazine cover, ad, photo, or card signed by the artist: $20-$50

OFTEN OVERLOOKED MEMORABILIA

All associated artifacts from his days with Muddy Waters and from other musicians' covers of his compositions

Live

Formed circa 1990

Chad Taylor, Born: November 24, 1970; Edward Kowalczyk, Born: July 17, 1971; Patrick Dahlheimer, Born: May 30, 1971; and Chad Gracey, Born: July 23, 1971

One of the '90's premier rock bands, Live, who started by playing in a high school band called Public Affection before changing the group's name following their graduation, began via the bar circuit before finding a residency at Lancaster, Pennsylvania's popular night spot the Chameleon Club. The band members, three whom of hail from York, Pennsylvania, and Kowalczyk from Lancaster, began spreading their wings and it wasn't long after performing at the famed CBGB club in New York that they were signed to Radioactive Records.

In January 1992, the band's four-track EP *Four Songs* is released, and eventually hits #9 on the U.S. Modern Rock chart. It is quickly followed by the band's debut album *Mental Jewelry* (#73, 1992), produced by ex-Talking Head keyboardist Jerry Harrison. The album gets a warm reception on college airways, as the band tours extensively in its support. The group's exposure is increased by a slot on MTV's "120 Minutes" U.S. caravan, before returning to the studio to begin work on their sophomore effort.

Throwing Copper (#1, 1995), also produced by Harrison and fueled by extracts "Selling the Drama" (#43, 1994), "I Alone" (#48, 1995) and "Lightning Crashes" (#1, U.S. Modern Rock chart), takes fifty-two weeks to reach the top of the chart. The group, which has had heavy MTV rotation, performs on the channel's popular *Unplugged* series, taped at the Brooklyn Academy of Music on April 19, 1995.

The group's first U.S. tour ends on May 13, 1995, which is followed by U.K. dates and even an appearance at the "Glastonbury Festival." Upon their return the group begins a 33-date, 32-city tour on July 21, 1995, at Hershey Park Stadium, Hershey, Pennsylvania, with the tour set to end on September 20, 1995. For collectors the most sought after ticket for this event becomes a warm-up gig at the Chameleon Club ($10 admission). In December 1995, Billboard

names Live the Top Rock Artist during a live award show broadcast on Fox-TV.

The band begins 1997 by purchasing their own building adjacent to the Lancaster Market, just blocks from their former residency at the Chameleon Club. They also prepare for the release of their new album by making their second appearance on *Saturday Night Live,* performing "Lakini's Juice" from their new album *Secret Samadh* (#1, 1997), produced by Jay Healy and Live. On April 2, 1997, the band begins their European Tour, which runs until April 18, followed by festival dates and two more tour legs.

Live and Let Live!

AUTOGRAPHS

A CD, LP, magazine cover, ad, photo, or card signed by the group: $25-$45

TOUR BOOKS/ PROGRAMS/ PASSES

Backstage Passes:
Cloth: $8-$10;
Laminated: $15

POSTERS/ PRESS KITS

Promotional Posters: $8-$12
"Throwing Copper" album cover art, 26" x 28": $10
Press Kits: $15-$25

USED CLOTHING/EQUIPMENT

Guitar Picks:
Edward Kowalczyk: $10-$25
Patrick Dahlheimer: $15-$20
Drum Sticks:
Chad Gracey: $15

OFTEN OVERLOOKED MEMORABILIA

Videotapes from their numerous television appearances including *Saturday Night Live* (1/21/95, 2/97), *MTV Unplugged* (4/19/95), the *Late Show with David Letterman* (7/18/97), and *Woodstock '94* (8/14/94); all associated items from their appearance on the MTV "120 Minutes" U.S. Caravan; early handbills/club calendar from the Chameleon Club - $5; promotional pin - $5; Secret Samadhi tour poster - $5

A couple of examples of Live backstage passes (Left: printed by OTTO)

Living Colour

Formed 1983

William Calhoun, Corey Glover, Vernon Reid, and Muzz Skillings*

*Skillings departs in 1992 and is replaced by Doug Wimbish

Late-80s Brooklyn rock act best remembered for their hits "Cult of Personality" (#13, 1989) and "Glamour Boys" (#31, 1989), Living Colour's break came when Mick Jagger heard them play at CBGB in 1987 and financed a demo tape that led to their signing on Epic Records. Their exposure was dramatically increased when they opened for the Stones on their 1989 Steel Wheels Tour, as well as their creative promotional videos. The band broke up in 1995.

AUTOGRAPHS

A CD, LP, magazine cover, ad, photo, or card signed by the group: $15-$25

POSTERS/PRESS KITS

Promotional Posters: $10-$20
Press Kits: $15-$25

USED CLOTHING/EQUIPMENT

Guitar Picks: $20-$35

OFTEN OVERLOOKED MEMORABILIA

Movie memorabilia from *Platoon* - Corey Glover has a part in the film; any artifacts from their CBGB days

---

L.L. Cool J

(James Todd Smith)
Born: August 16, 1968

Mid-80s New York rapper and heartthrob who smashed the charts with his groundbreaking debut Def Jam album *Radio* (#6, R&B, 1985), which included the street anthem "I Can't Live Without My Radio" (#15, R&B, 1985). L.L. Cool J is also associated with his hits "I Need Love" (#14, 1987), "Going Back to Cali" (#31, 1988), "I'm That Type of Guy" (#15, 1989), "Around the Way Girl" (#9, 1990) and "Mama Said Knock You Out" (#17, 1991).

Considered a pioneer of his craft, he also became the first rap artist to perform on MTV's *Unplugged*. From his Grammy-winning album *Mama Said Knock You Out* (#16, 1990) to *14 Shots to the Dome* (#5, 1993), which yielded no Top Twenty singles, he seemed to have floundered a bit with direction, but as talented as he is, the album still was a commercial success.

AUTOGRAPHS

A CD, LP, magazine cover, ad, photo, or card signed by the artist: $20-$40

POSTERS/PRESS KITS

Promotional Posters: $10-$20
Press Kits: $15-$20

OFTEN OVERLOOKED MEMORABILIA

Movie memorabilia from *The Hard Way* (1991) and *Toys* (1992); artifacts from the artist's numerous children's welfare programs

Lofgren, Nils

Born: June 21, 1952

Nils Lofgren, a student of classical music at an early age, releases two singles with Paul Dowell & the Dolphin before forming Grin with Bob Berberich and Bob Gordon in 1969. In February 1970, after being seen by Neil Young, Lofgren is invited to play on his *After The Goldrush* album. Lofgren doesn't join Young permanently, opting instead to stay with Grin.

In August 1971 the group's debut, *Grin* (#192, 1971), is released and supported by a tour with Edgar Winter. It is followed by *1+1* (#180, 1972), which includes the single "White Lies" (#75, 1972). The following year Lofgren's younger brother Tom is added to the band as second guitarist and appears on the group's third album *All Out* (#186, 1973). The album is followed by *Gone Crazy,* the group's first effort for A&M Records. The album's commercial failure leads to the destruction of the band that same year, with Lofgren eventually joining Crazy Horse for Young's "Tonight's The Night" tour.

Public speculation has Lofgren joining the Rolling Stones when Mick Taylor departs, but the rumors silence when Ron Wood fills the bill. Lofgren goes solo and releases *Nils Lofgren* (#141, 1975), a good first effort that is supported with extensive touring. *Cry Tough* (#32, 1976), unsupported by a hit single, sells well, as Lofgren's reputation and following continue to grow. *I Came To Dance* (#36, 1977), *Night After Night* (#44, 1977), and *Nils* (#54, 1979) are all consistent sellers, while Lofgren finishes his obligation to A&M Records.

In the fall of 1981 Lofgren signs with the Backstreet label and releases *Night Fade Away* (#99, 1981), which is followed by the poorly selling *Wonderland* (1983), which essentially ends his relationship with the record company. In a turn of events, Nils Lofgren joins Bruce Springsteen's E Street Band, replacing Steve Van Zandt, and rejuvenating his career. He signs to indie label Towerbell and releases *Flip* with extracted single "Secrets in the Street" (#53, U.K.). It's followed by *Code Of The Road,* which stalls because his record company folds. Lofgren then goes back on the road with Springsteen until 1991.

In 1991 Lofgren releases *Silver Lining* (#153, 1991), his first album in half a decade, with Bruce Springsteen gracing the vocals on "Valentine." He will then move to his own Essential label for his next offering, *Crooked Line* (1992), but fails to hit a chord. Numerous other non-related projects also fail to come to fruition, and Lofgren doesn't release another album until 1994 *(Every Breath).*

AUTOGRAPHS
A CD, LP, magazine cover, ad, photo, or card signed by the artist: $10-$25

TOUR BOOKS/PROGRAMS/PASSES
Backstage Passes:
Cloth: $5-$8; Laminated: $10-$15

POSTERS/PRESS KITS
Promotional Posters: $10
Press Kits: $10-$12

USED CLOTHING/EQUIPMENT
Guitar Picks: $10-$15

OFTEN OVERLOOKED MEMORABILIA
Early Grin work

Loggins, Kenny

Born: January 7, 1948

Loggins majors in music at Pasadena City College in Pasadena, California, where he also played in folk groups, before landing in Gator Creek, Second Helping, and the Electric Prunes (which he joins in a 1969 one-off tour). He then moves on to songwriting at Wingate Music, a division of ABC Records, where he scores his first compositional success "House On Pooh Corner," covered by the Nitty Gritty Dirt Band. Subsequently signed to CBS/Columbia Records as a solo performer, he meets producer Jim Messina, setting the stage for a long and very successful collaboration (see Loggins and Messina).

In 1976 Loggins and Messina split, but remain signed as solo acts to CBS/Columbia Records. In July 1977, *Celebrate Me Home* (#27, 1977), Loggins's first solo effort, sells very well and lands him into the Top Thirty on the album charts. Extracted single "I Believe In Love" (#66, 1977) helps drive album sales as Loggins tours in support of the album.

In the fall of 1978 *Nightwatch* (#7, 1876) climbs into the Top Ten on the album charts, as Loggins solidifies his reputation as a solo act. The album also includes "What A Fool Believes" (#1, 1979), written by Loggins and Doobie Brother Michael McDonald. Loggins drives album sales with the extracted single "Whenever I Call You Friend" (#5, 1979), cowritten with Melissa Manchester, but sung with Stevie Nicks.

Keep the Fire (#16, 1980), driven by the single "This Is It" (#11, 1979), does just as its title states and continues Loggins's presence on all sales charts. The year also finds Loggins's side projects equally successful as "I'm Alright" (#7, 1980), the theme from the movie *Caddyshack,* climbs into the Top Ten. Loggins finishes the year with the release of a double-live album, *Kenny Loggins: Alive* (#11, 1980), which is confirmed platinum just days before Christmas.

High Adventure (#13, 1982), with the extracted single "Don't Fight It" (#13, 1982) is Loggins's only

major studio effort of the year. The album's success is followed by the theme song to the movie *Footloose* (#1, 1984), penned by Loggins and Dean Pitchford, which tops the chart for three consecutive weeks. Success at the movies continues for Loggins with "I'M Free (Heaven Help the Man)" (#22, 1984) also from *Footloose*, "Danger Zone" (#2, 1986) from *Top Gun*, "Meet Me Halfway" (#11, 1987) from *Over the Top*, and "Nobody's Fool" (#8, 1988) from *Caddyshack 2*.

Loggins's studio albums—*Vox Humana* (#41, 1985), *Back To Avalon* (#69, 1988), *Leap Of Faith* (#71, 1991), *Outside: From The Redwoods* (#60, 1993) and *Return To Pooh Corner* (#65, 1994)—are less successful than his movie work, although many include extracted cinema singles to help drive sales. *Yesterday, Today, Tomorrow: The Greatest Hits of Kenny Loggins* (#39, 1997) and *The Unimaginable Lite* find the artist back on the album charts in 1997.

AUTOGRAPHS

A CD, LP, magazine cover, ad, photo, or card signed by the artist: $10-$25

TOUR BOOKS/PROGRAMS/PASSES

Tour Books:
Vox Humana, 1985: $20
Backstage Passes:
Cloth: $5-$8; Laminated: $10-$15

POSTERS/PRESS KITS

Promotional Posters: $10-$20
Press Kits: $10-$20

USED CLOTHING/EQUIPMENT

Guitar Picks: $10-$15

OFTEN OVERLOOKED MEMORABILIA

Movie memorabilia from *Caddyshack, Footloose, Top Gun, Over The Top, Caddyshack 2;* "Celebrate Me Home" mobile - $50

Loggins and Messina

Kenny Loggins, Born: January 7, 1948; Jim Messina, Born: December 5, 1947

Highly successful '80s country-pop power duo best remembered for their songs "Danny's Song," "Vahevala," "Your Mama Don't Dance" (#4, 1972) and "Thinking of You" (#18, 1973), the two met when Jim Messina (Poco) agreed to produce Kenny Loggins's solo debut. Loggins would go on to a successful solo career after the duo, while Messina's efforts would garner less accolades before he rejoined Poco in 1989 for their acclaimed reunion album *Legacy*.

AUTOGRAPHS

A CD, LP, magazine cover, ad, photo, or card signed by the artist: $25-$50

TOUR BOOKS/PROGRAMS/PASSES

Tour Books: In Concert, Fall 1975 - $45

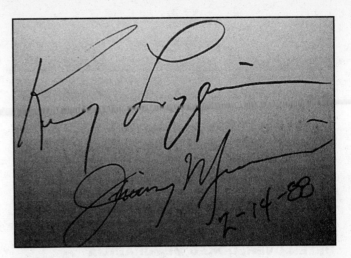

The signatures of Kenny Loggins and Jimmy Messina

OFTEN OVERLOOKED MEMORABILIA

Any associated artifacts from their live debut at L.A.'s famed Troubador; "Mother Lode" or "Native Sons" mobiles - $45; "Native Sons" bin divider - $30; playing cards (white on blue, 54 cards) - $40

Lomax, Jackie

Born: May 10, 1944

Late-60s British blues-rooted rock singer best remembered for his association with the Beatles: same manager, Brian Epstein, first to sign with the Beatles Apple Records; and his single "Sour Milk Sea," written by George Harrison.

AUTOGRAPHS

A CD, LP, magazine cover, ad, photo, or card signed by the artist: $5-$10

OFTEN OVERLOOKED MEMORABILIA

All artifacts associated with the Beatles

Lone Justice

Formed 1983

Maria McGee, Ryan Hedgecock, Marvin Etzioni, and Don Heffington*

*Numerous personnel shifts in 1986 find Etzioni, Heffington, and Hedgecock departing and the addition of Shayne Fontayne, Gregg Sutton, Rudy Richman, and Bruce Brody.

Early-80s club scene rockers best remembered for Maria McKee's powerful and impressive soprano and as the opening act for U2's 1985 tour. Fontayne later joined Bruce Springsteen's band (1982).

AUTOGRAPHS

A CD, LP, magazine cover, ad, photo, or card signed by the group: $5-$10

Long Ryders

Formed 1982

Sid Griffin, Stephen McCarthy, Greg Sowders, and Tom Stevens

Mid-80s L.A. underground cowpunk act, best known for not garnering the attention Island Records was hoping for!

AUTOGRAPHS

A CD, LP, magazine cover, ad, photo, or card signed by the group: $5

OFTEN OVERLOOKED MEMORABILIA

There is none.

REFERENCES/BOOKS

Gram Parsons: A Musical Biography by Sid Griffin (1985)

Loose Ends

Formed early 1980s

Original lineup: Carl McIntosh, Jane Eugene, and Steve Nichol*

*Only McIntosh remained in 1990

Eighties British pop-funk outfit best remembered for their songs "Hanging on a String (Contemplating)," "Slow Down" (#1, R&B, 1986), "Watching You" (#2, 1988), "Don't Be a Fool" (#10, R&B, 1990) and "Cheap Talk" (#28,1991). Loose Ends' members also wrote and produced material for other pop artists before a new configuration of the group emerged to challenge the '90s—good luck!

AUTOGRAPHS

A CD, LP, magazine cover, ad, photo, or card signed by the group: $15

OFTEN OVERLOOKED MEMORABILIA

Associated artifacts from members' production work for artists such as Juliet Roberts, Five Star, and Cheryl Lynn

Los Bravos

Formed 1965

Michael Kogel, Manuel Fernandez, Miguel Danus, Pablo Sanllehi (Gomez), and Antonio Martinez

Sixties Spanish rock band best remembered for their international hit "Black is Black" (#4, 1966) and a handful of minor hits including "I Don't Care" (#16, 1966)—do you?

AUTOGRAPHS

A CD, LP, magazine cover, ad, photo, or card signed by the group: $10-$15

Los Lobos

Formed 1973

Cesar Rosas, David Hidalgo, Luis Perez, and Conrad Lozano*

*Steve Berlin is added in 1984

Late '70s and '80s Chicano-rooted L.A. club band turned retro rockers, Los Lobos is typically associated with the songs "Anselma" (a Grammy winner), "Will the Wolf Survive?" (a hit for Waylon Jennings), "La Bamba" (#1, 1987), and "Come On, Let's Go" (#21, 1987). The band's compositions can also be found on numerous film soundtracks.

AUTOGRAPHS

A CD, LP, magazine cover, ad, photo, or card signed by the group: $20-$35

POSTERS/PRESS KITS

Promotional Posters: $10-$15
Press Kits: $15-$20

USED CLOTHING/EQUIPMENT

Guitar Picks: $10

OFTEN OVERLOOKED MEMORABILIA

Movie memorabilia from *La Bamba, Eating Raoul, The Mambo Kings, Alamo Bay,* and *Chan Is Missing;* associated artifacts from other musicians' covers of their work

Loudermilk, John D.

Born: March 31, 1934

Late-60s singer/songwriter best known for his songs "Tobacco Road," "A Rose and a Baby Ruth," "Abilene," "Sittin' in the Balcony," "Waterloo," "Indian Reservation," "Ebony Eyes," "Break My Mind" and "Bad News." Loudermilk has had his songs covered by the Everly Brothers, Eddie Cochran, and Paul Revere and the Raiders.

AUTOGRAPHS

A CD, LP, magazine cover, ad, photo, or card signed by the artist: $10-$15

OFTEN OVERLOOKED MEMORABILIA

Associated artifacts from the numerous musicians who have covered his work

Lounge Lizards

Formed 1979

John and Evan Lurie, Arto Lindsay, Anton Fier, and Steve Piccolo*

*Numerous personnel changes

Eighties downtown New York "fake jazz" (feel over structure) group who were popular in New York and Europe, where they sustained a large cult following. They are probably best remembered for their longevity, personnel changes, and John Lurie, who scored films, acted, and fished with unique guests. Pass me the bait!

AUTOGRAPHS

A CD, LP, magazine cover, ad, photo, or card signed by the group: $10*

*Add $5 for Lurie's signature

OFTEN OVERLOOKED MEMORABILIA

Lurie's film work and later television work

Love and Rockets: See Bauhaus

Love/Arthur Lee

Formed 1965

Arthur Lee, Bryan MacLean, John Echols, Ken Forssi, and Don Conka*

*Numerous personnel changes

Late-60s, British-influenced Sunset Strip act led by guitarist Arthur Lee and best known for their songs "My Little Red Book," the twenty-minute-long "Revelation," "7 and 7 Is," and their album *Forever Changes*. The band was plagued by personnel problems right from the start, with Lee the common link. At one point Lee recorded a full album with Jimi Hendrix but, plagued by legal issues, it has never been released in its original form.

AUTOGRAPHS

A CD, LP, magazine cover, ad, photo, or card signed by the group: $10-$15

OFTEN OVERLOOKED MEMORABILIA

Any associated items surrounding Lee's work with Jimi Hendrix

Love, Darlene

(Darlene Wright)
Born: July 26, 1938

Sixties singer best remembered for singing some lead vocals with the Crystals, Bob B. Soxx, the Blue Jeans, and the Blossoms, Darlene Love is commonly associated with the songs "He's a Rebel" (#1, 1962), "He's Sure the Boy I Love" (#11, 1963), "Zip-A-Dee Doo-Dah" (#8, 1963), "Wait till My Bobby Gets Home" (#26, 1963), "(Today I Met) The Boy I'm Gonna Marry" (#39, 1963) and "A Fine Fine Boy" (#53, 1963). She

worked in Phil Spector's stable and appears on his classic Christmas album. With the Blossoms she appeared regularly on "Shindig" and even toured with Elvis Presley. Love later turned to acting in both film and on the stage.

AUTOGRAPHS

A CD, LP, magazine cover, ad, photo, or card signed by the artist: $5-$15

OFTEN OVERLOOKED MEMORABILIA

Movie memorabilia from *Song of the South* and the *Lethal Weapon* films; artifacts from Love's appearance in Broadway's *Leader of the Pack;* any and all artifacts associated with her work with Phil Spector

Love, Monie

(Simone Johnson)
Born: July 2, 1970

Nineties British transplanted, Brooklyn rapper, Monie Love is perhaps best known for her hit "It's a Shame (My Sister)" (#26, 1991) and for her contributions to numerous artists, including the Jungle Brothers and Queen Latifah.

AUTOGRAPHS

A CD, LP, magazine cover, ad, photo, or card signed by the artist: $10

OFTEN OVERLOOKED MEMORABILIA

Associated artifacts from her numerous contributions to other artists' work

Loverboy

Formed 1979

Paul Dean, Mike Reno, Doug Johnson, Matt Frenette, and Scott Smith

Successful '80s Canadian hard pop group best remembered for their songs "Turn Me Loose" (#35, 1981), "Working for the Weekend" (#29, 1981) and "When It's Over" (#26, 1982), and their Top Ten hits "Lovin' Every Minute of It," "This Could Be the Night" and Reno's duet with Ann Wilson on "Almost Paradise." Loverboy disbanded first in 1988.

AUTOGRAPHS

A CD, LP, magazine cover, ad, photo, or card signed by the group: $15-$30

TOUR BOOKS/PROGRAMS/PASSES

Backstage Passes:
Cloth: $10-$12; Laminated: $15

POSTERS/PRESS KITS

Promotional Posters: $10-$20
Press Kits: $10-$20

USED CLOTHING/EQUIPMENT

Guitar Picks: $10-$20

OFTEN OVERLOOKED MEMORABILIA

Movie memorabilia from *Footloose* (1984); "Keep It Up" school book cover - $7

Lovett, Lyle

Born: November 1, 1957

Late-80s Texas eclectic country singer/songwriter commonly associated with the C&W hits "Farther Down the Line" (#21, C&W, 1986), "Cowboy Man" (#10, C&W, 1986), "God Will" (#18, C&W, 1987), "Why I Don't Know" (#15, C&W, 1987), "Give Back My Heart" (#13, C&W, 1987), "She's No Lady" (#17, C&W, 1988) and "I Loved You Yesterday" (#24, C&W, 1988), Lyle Lovett is gradually gaining more interest in his work from a wider audience, as evidenced by albums such as *Lyle Lovett and his Large Band* (#62, 1989) and *Joshua Judges Ruth* (#57, 1992). His increased exposure during the '90s through features on VH-1, film roles, and even his marriage/divorce with Julia Roberts, has boosted his popularity.

AUTOGRAPHS

A CD, LP, magazine cover, ad, photo, or card signed by the artist: $25-$70

OFTEN OVERLOOKED MEMORABILIA

Movie memorabilia from *Bill: On His Own, The Player, Leap Of Faith, The Crying Game, Short Cuts, Dead Man Walking*; copies of the numerous tabloids who exploited his marriage to actress Julia Roberts; videotapes from his numerous television appearances including *Late Night With David Letterman* (2/2/92, 6/16/93), *The Tonight Show* (5/12/92, 7/25/92, 2/17/93, 12/7/95), "Tom Jones: The Right Time" (6/27/92), Whoopi Goldberg show (2/2/92), "Willie Nelson The Big Six-O" (5/22/93), *Late Show With David Letterman* (4/19/94, 3/7/96), *Mad About You* (2/2/95), 1992 World Series memorabilia - Lovett sings the "Star Spangled Banner" (10/22/92); a copy of the documentary "A Day In the Life of Country Music", videotapes of his appearances on ESPN's *Motor World*

Lovich, Lene

(Lili Premilovich)
Born: March 30, 1949

Late-70s Stiff label singles artist commonly associated with the songs "Lucky Number," "Say When," "Bird Song," and "New Toy," Lene Lovich has found far greater success in the U.K. than in America. She has tried her luck acting, in both film and on stage, while also writing a novel.

AUTOGRAPHS

A CD, LP, magazine cover, ad, photo, or card signed by the artist: $10

OFTEN OVERLOOKED MEMORABILIA

Movie memorabilia from *Cha-Cha* (1979); television memorabilia from the film *Rock;* stage artifacts from the London play *Mata Hari* (1983); associated material from her work of behalf of the People for the Ethical Treatment of Animals (PETA)

The Lovin' Spoonful

Formed 1965

John Sebastian, Born: March 17, 1944; Steve Boone; Zal Yanovsky; and Joe Butler*

*Yanovsky departs in 1967 and is replaced by Jerry Yester

Late-60s New York folk rockers and "everything's fine" practitioners, The Lovin' Spoonful is best remembered for their songs "Do You Believe in Magic" and "You Didn't Have to Be So Nice," "Daydream," "Did You Ever Have to Make Up Your Mind?," "Summer in the City" (the group's only #1), "Rain on the Roof," "Darling Be Home Soon" (#15), "Nashville Cats" and "Six O'Clock" (#18). The success of the band virtually stopped in 1967 after the adverse publicity surrounding the arrest of Steve Boone and Zal Yanovsky for drugs. The band rebounded with one minor hit, "She Is Still a Mystery" (#27, 1967), before Sebastion departed for a solo career in 1968 and the group disbanded. The band reunited for an apperaance in the movie *One Trick Pony* (1980).

AUTOGRAPHS

A CD, LP, magazine cover, ad, photo, or card signed by the group: $15-$50*
*Original lineup

TOUR BOOKS/PROGRAMS/PASSES

Tour Books: $80-$100

OFTEN OVERLOOKED MEMORABILIA

Movie memorabilia from *You're a Big Boy Now, What's Up, Tiger Lily?* and *One Trick Pony;* periodical clippings regarding the arrest of Boone and Yanovsky and the boycott of their records; items relating to Butler's acting career

---

Lowe, Nick

Born: March 25, 1949

Late-70s British pop rocker best known for his association with Brinsley Schwarz, Rockpile, and his launching of Stiff Records, as well as his productions work, Nick Lowe is remembered for his songs "Cruel to Be Kind" (#12, 1979), "(I Love the Sound of) Breaking Glass," and " I Knew the Bride (When She Used to Rock and Roll)" (#77, 1985). The '90s find him in

demand for his production skills, while still touring in various configurations.

AUTOGRAPHS
A CD, LP, magazine cover, ad, photo, or card signed by the artist: $10

POSTERS/PRESS KITS
Promotional Posters: $8-$12
Press Kits: $12-$15

USED CLOTHING/EQUIPMENT
Guitar Picks: $10-$20

OFTEN OVERLOOKED MEMORABILIA
All his associated artifacts from Stiff Records and his work for other artists

L7

Formed 1985

Suzi Gardner, Jennifer Finch, Donita Sparks, and Roy Koutsky*

*Koutsky departs in 1990 and is replaced by Demetra Plakas

Late-80s and early-90s all female L.A. grunge act and part of the decade's fascination for women rockers, L7 has built a substantial cult following both in the U.S. and Europe through extensive touring, indie releases, and flagrancy. The band is typically associated with the songs "Pretend We're Dead" and "Shove," as well as their often controversial live shows. In 1994 they also gained recognition via Lollapalooza appearances, while supporting their album *Hungry for Stink*.

AUTOGRAPHS
A CD, LP, magazine cover, ad, photo, or card signed by the group: $10-$30

POSTERS/PRESS KITS
Promotional Posters: $10-$15
Press Kits: $15-$20

USED CLOTHING/EQUIPMENT
Guitar Picks: $10

OFTEN OVERLOOKED MEMORABILIA
Movie memorabilia from *Serial Mom* (1994); Lollapalooza memorabilia; Camel Lips artifacts

Lulu

(Marie McDonald McLaughlin Lawrie)
Born: November 3, 1948.

Late-60s teen pop star, Lulu is commonly associated with her hit songs "To Sir with Love" (she also costarred in the film), "On Me, Oh My, I'm a Fool for You, Baby," "The Man Who Sold the World," "I Could Never Miss You (More than I Do)" (#18, 1981), "If I Were You" and numerous other minor hits.

She was married to Bee Gee Maurice Gibb from 1969 to 1973, during a time when she had established herself in television. She continued touring in the early '70s and even hosted her own prime-time BBC-TV weekly music series. The '90s find her still charting singles in the U.K.

AUTOGRAPHS
A CD, LP, magazine cover, ad, photo, or card signed by the artist: $10-$25*
*Vintage photograph

OFTEN OVERLOOKED MEMORABILIA
Movie memorabilia from *To Sir With Love;* videotapes of her weekly television series

Lunch, Lydia

Born: June 2, 1959

Eighties New York "no wave" prodigy and underground apostle, commonly associated with the bands Teenage Jesus and the Jerks, 8 Eyed Spy, Devil Dogs, 13.13., and her appearances in Vivienne Dick super-8mm movies, Lunch then moved to poetry and spoken-word performances. Still drowning in limbo, the '90s find Lunch packing pixels over proverbs.

AUTOGRAPHS
A CD, LP, magazine cover, ad, photo or card signed by the artist: $10

OFTEN OVERLOOKED MEMORABILIA
Movie memorabilia from her numerous films including *The Right Side of My Brain* and *Fingered*

REFERENCES/BOOKS
Adulterers Anonymous by Lunch and Cervenka

Lurie, John: See Lounge Lizards

Lush

Formed 1988

Miki Berenyi, Meriel Barham, Emma Anderson, Christopher Acland, and Steve Rippon*

*Barham leaves in 1989 and Rippon follows in 1990. Phil King is added on bass in 1990.

Late-80s London "shoegazing" band who developed a strong cult following in the city's club scene, Lush is commonly associated with their appearance at the 1992 Lollapalooza Tour, as they have yet to have a substantial impact in the U.S.

AUTOGRAPHS

A CD, LP, magazine cover, ad, photo or card signed by the group: $10

OFTEN OVERLOOKED MEMORABILIA

Memorabilia from Lollapalooza '92

Lymon, Frankie and the Teenagers

Formed 1955

Frankie Lymon (1942-1968), Sherman Garnes (1940-1978), Joe Negroni (1940-1977), Herman Santiago, and Jimmy Merchant

Mid-50s talented R&B pop vocal act best remembered for their hits "Why Do Fools Fall In Love?" (#6, 1956), "I Promise to Remember" (#10, 1956), "I Want You to Be My Girl" (#13, 1956), "The ABC's of Love" (#14, 1956) and "I'm Not a Juvenile Delinquent." The group found success when Lymon was only thirteen years old, but their popularity slipped fast and by the age of eighteen Lymon was looking for a new career. After a minor hit with "Goody Goody" (#20, 1957), follow-up flops, a stint in the army, and a marriage, he was found dead of a heroin overdose while on a lounge circuit attempt at resurrecting his career. In 1993 the group was inducted into the Rock and Roll Hall of Fame.

AUTOGRAPHS

A CD, LP, magazine cover, ad, photo or card signed by the group: $35-$75

Lynn, Barbara

(Barbara Lynn Ozen)
Born: January 16, 1942

Early-60s East Texas R&B singer, commonly associated with the songs, "You'll Loose a Good Thing" (#8, 1962), "You're Gonna Need Me" (#13, R&B, 1963), "It's Better to Have It" (#26, R&B, 1965), "(Until Then) I'll Suffer" (#31, R&B, 1971) and "Oh! Baby (We Got a Good Thing Goin')"—covered by the Rolling Stones. Barbara Lynn has sporadically surfaced during the '80s and '90s.

AUTOGRAPHS

A CD, LP, magazine cover, ad, photo or card signed by the artist: $5-$10

OFTEN OVERLOOKED MEMORABILIA

Associated artifacts from other artists' covers of her work

Lynn, Loretta

(Loretta Webb)
Born: April 14, 1935

Talented mid-60s singer and songwriter Loretta Lynn is one of country music's living legends. Born out of the hills in Butcher Hollow, Kentucky, and raised on a shoestring, she was married by thirteen, a mother at fourteen, and a grandmother eighteen years later. Her break came from a self-promoted single, "Honky Tonk Girl," and an appearance on the Grand Ole Opry in October of 1960. She then signed to Decca Records (now MCA) where she released thirteen records over two decades, including sixteen #1 C&W hits. Her classics include "Don't Come Home a Drinkin' (With Lovin' on Your Mind)" (1966), "Fist City" (1968), "Woman of the World (Leave My World Alone)" (1969) and "Coal Miner's Daughter" (1970).

The '70s found her touring with Conway Twitty, as both dueted on numerous smash C&W hits, such as "After the Fire Is Gone," "Lead Me On," "Louisiana Woman, Mississippi Man" (1973) and "Feelins'" (1975), while she also maintained her own string of chart-toppers that lasted into the '80s.

In 1980 her life was put to film in the successful *Coal Miner's Daughter,* for which actress Sissy Spacek won the Best Actress Oscar. Lynn herself also made a few television appearances, while sustaining herself as one of country music's most loved and cherished artists.

AUTOGRAPHS

A CD, LP, magazine cover, ad, photo or card signed by the artist: $5-$15

OFTEN OVERLOOKED MEMORABILIA

Movie memorabilia from *Coal Miner's Daughter* (1980); Grand Ole Opry memorabilia from her numerous appearances there; videotapes of her appearances on television, including *Fantasy Island, The Dukes of Hazzard,* and even *The Muppet Show*

REFERENCES/BOOKS

Coal Miner's Daughter, her autobiography with George Vecsey; no dedicated collector books; serious collectors should opt for fan club: The Loretta Lynn Swap Shop, c/o Lenny Mattison/Andy Comer, 87 Hong Kong Road, Parish, NY 13131

Lynyrd Skynyrd

Formed 1966

Ronnie Van Zant (1949-1977), Gary Rossington, Allen Collins (1952-1990), Billy Powell, Leon Wilkeson (replaced Larry Jungstrom [.38 Special]), and Bob Burns*

*Ed King (Strawberry Alarm Clock) joins the band on guitar in 1972. Burns leaves in 1974 and Artimus Pyle is

added. King leaves in 1975. In 1976 Steve Gaines (deceased, 1977) joins the band. The group disbands in 1977 following the tragic crash of their aircraft. In 1991 the group re-forms: Rossington, Pyle, Wilkeson, King, Powell, Johnnie Van Zant, Dale Krantz-Rossington, Randall Hall, and Custer

Lynyrd Skynyrd was the first major success to follow the Allman Brothers into the newly created Southern rock market. Unlike the Allman Brothers, however, who enjoyed roots deep in the blues, "Skynyrd" chose to rough up the edge of their sound with heavy guitar riffs. The group was founded in Jacksonville, Florida, by classmates Van Zant, Collins, and Rossington, who were playing in a band called My Backyard (1965) before merging with Wilkeson and Powell. The group immortalized their old school gym teacher, Leonard Skinner, by choosing the alternative spelling.

Al Kooper (Blood Sweat & Tears) was looking for discoverable talent for his new Sounds of the South label (MCA) in 1972, when as fate would have it, he would find the band playing at Funocchio's bar in Atlanta. MCA launched the band in 1973 and put them on the Who undercard during their "Quadrophenia" supporting tour. Later that fall, the group's debut album *Pronounced Leh-Nerd Skin-Nerd* (#27) aggressively charts and produces the band's first gold disc. The album's hallmark is the lengthy tribute to the late Duane Allman, now a considered a rock classic: "Free Bird."

The band's first chart placement was "Sweet Home Alabama" (#8, 1974), a creative southern-style answer to Neil Young's redneck, down-home, river banked, Crimson tide slander of a song called "Southern Man" (1971). The creative single was spun off the band's second disc *Second Helping* (#12, 1974), another Kooper-produced album that mined more gold for the band and even managed to produce a run on replacement volume stereo dials ("Turn It UP"!).

"Free Bird" by now had become the band's anthem, and was issued as a belated single in 1975. *Nuthin' Fancy* (#9, 1975) becomes the band's next gold album. The group makes their U.K. debut in 1975 supporting the Dutch "Radar Love" crooners Golden Earring. While the "Torture Tour" seems like a bad recipe, King falls prey to drug and alcohol problems part way through the stint. The band returns home for a record-breaking non-stop U.S. tour that continues to bolster their image while driving "Saturday Night Special" (#27, 1975) up the singles chart.

In 1976 the band, now managed by Peter Rudge (the Who), begins a short tour of the U.K. in February. *Gimmie Back My Bullets* (#20, 1976), produced by Tom Dowd, keeps the band on track with their fourth gold disc. The band's often liquor-enhanced barroom reputation is by now preceding itself, as Van Zant becomes notorious for his saloon brawling. The group's double live set, *One More For The Road* (#9, 1976), recorded the following year during a three-night stay at Atlanta's Fox Theatre, soon becomes the group's biggest seller. The disc spotlights the group's new third guitarist Steve Gaines, introduces fans to an added all female back-up vocal trio, and spins off a live version of "Free Bird" (#38, 1976).

Early 1977, the beginning of a long U.K. visit is marred by scuffle between guests and the band. Both Rossington and Pyle are knocked unconscious during the melee that included the Metropolitan Police Boxing Team, who were attending a dinner at the Royal Lancaster Hotel in London. The band redeems itself in the public's eye when it returns to Atlanta, Georgia, on April 15, 1977, to present the mayor Maynard Jackson and the Fox Theatre with gold discs earned from *One More for the Road*.

While en route from Greenville, South Carolina, to Baton Rouge, Louisiana, on October 20, 1977, the group's rented twin-engined propeller-driven Convair 240 plane crashes into a swamp in Gillsburg, Mississippi. Van Zant, Steve Gaines, his sister Cassie Gaines (one of the three back-up singers) and manager Dean Kilpatrick are among six passengers killed. Rossington, Collins, Powell, and Wilkeson are all seriously injured and eventually recover. The event has ominous undertones, as just three days prior MCA released *Street Survivors* (#5, 1977), the band's next album, featuring the group standing amid flames. The event sparks the withdraw of the sleeve, creating an instant collectible.

The album spins off the hit single "What's Your Name" (#13, 1978); however, the incident changes the course of the band forever. Posthumous releases of older material follow, positioning the band in rock history, while giving surviving members an opportunity to heal. The Rossington-Collins Band emerges from the ashes in 1979 and features four of the surviving members. The band's debut *Anytime, Anyplace, Anywhere* (#13, 1980) spins off the single "Don't Misunderstand Me" (#55, 1980), while the band closes its live act with an instrumental version of "Free Bird."

Tragedy continues to haunt the band as Collins's wife Katy dies in 1980, and Collins himself is paralyzed from the waist down in a car accident that also claims the life of his girlfriend in 1986. Collins dies on January 23, 1990, at Jacksonville's Memorial Medical Center of respiratory failure due to pneumonia.

To mark the ten year anniversary (1987), the band re-forms and plays a thirty-two-date reunion tour. The success tour unites older fans with newer followers and hails the new line-up's double live album *Southern By the Grace of God / Lynyrd Skynyrd Tribute Tour* (#68, 1988). The band undertook a variety of projects during the 1990s, most of which centered around maintaining Lynyrd Skynyrd's legacy in rock history.

Pre-accident memorabilia is highly sought by Skynyrd fans, most of which centers around the *Street Survivors* release. The original flames cover (MCA-3029) was withdrawn after the fatal crash, thus any related items would be highly collectible (the cover was reinstated by DCC Compact Classics in 1994). The band's rise to prominence, cultivated through many bizarre events, and unfortunate trail of hard luck create an unusual sense of intrigue about the group. From Ronnie Van Zant's 300-pound stolen headstone taken from his grave (2/82) and later retrieved from a nearly dried-up riverbed, to the now classic tales of barroom brawls, the legend of Lynyrd Skynyrd forever endures. "You Got That Right!"

A handful of Gary Rossington's picks— play it pretty for Atlanta!

AUTOGRAPHS

Group:
A CD, LP, magazine cover, ad, photo or card signed by the entire band: $225-$275*

*High end reflects vintage signed memorabilia

Post-Accident Lineup:
A CD, LP, magazine cover, ad, photo or card signed by the entire band: $45-$55

Individual:
Ronnie Van Zant: $150-$200
Gary Rossington: $25-$30
Leon Wilkeson: $20
Allen Collins: $20-$30
Artimus Pyle: $10-$15
Steve Gaines: $45-$60
Billy Powell: $20
Bob Burns: $10
Ed King: $10-$15

TOUR BOOKS/ PROGRAMS/PASSES

Tour Books:
1976 "Give Me Back My Bullets," U.K.: $25
1977 Tour: $12-$18

Backstage Passes:
Cloth: $8-$15; Laminated: $15-$25 (Post-accident)

POSTERS/PRESS KITS:

Promotional Posters:
Street Survivors (40" x 40"): $200-$300

A Lynyrd Skynyrd tour program (Designed by Kosh © 1977)

USED CLOTHING/EQUIPMENT

Guitar Picks:
Generic band pick, post-accident: $15-$20
Gary Rossington: $20-$25
Allen Collins: $25-$40
Leon Wilkeson: $15-$20
Steve Gaines: $100-$125*

*Scarce and difficult to authenticate

OFTEN OVERLOOKED MEMORABILIA

One More from the Road MCA promotional mug, globe paperweight and map, 1976; Ten from the Swamp Atlantic promotional rubber snake, 1991; Pendant with chain, 1977 - sold at shows; 24-page, four-color and black and white photos, souvenir booklet, 1977; a promotional rabbit's foot keychain (recalled, didn't work)

REFERENCES/BOOKS

Very few resources exist; no dedicated collector books; serious collectors should opt for fan club: Lynyrd Skynyrd Fan Club, P.O. Box 120855, Nashville, TN 37212

MacColl, Kristy

Born: October 10, 1959

This crafty '80s British vocalist/songwriter, who has sung with the Rolling Stones, Talking Heads, and Van Morrison, is commonly associated with the songs "Fairytale of New York" (#2, U.K., 1987)—a duet with Shane McGowan—"They Don't Know," which was a hit for Tracey Ullman, and "A New England" (#7, U.K., 1985).

She married noted producer Steve Lillywhite in 1984, but they eventually split.

AUTOGRAPHS

A CD, LP, magazine cover, ad, photo, or card signed by the artist: $5-$10

OFTEN OVERLOOKED MEMORABILIA

Associated artifacts from the musicians who have covered he work; memorabilia associated with her numerous contributions to other artists' work.

Mack, Lonnie

(Lonnie McIntosh)
Born: July 18, 1941

Sixties rockabilly guitarist and cult legend Lonnie Mack is commonly associated with songs "Memphis" and "Wham!." He has also contributed to session for James Brown, Freddie King, and the Doors. His hallmark sound, ignited by the use of his whammy bar on his Gibson Flying V, was an inspiration to Stevie Ray Vaughan and many guitarists over the past few decades.

AUTOGRAPHS

A CD, LP, magazine cover, ad, photo, or card signed by the artist: $8-$15

OFTEN OVERLOOKED MEMORABILIA

All associated artifacts from his numerous musical contributions

---

Madness

Formed 1978

Lee Thompson, Chris Foreman, Mike Barson, Dan Woodgate, Mark Bedford, Graham "Suggs" McPherson, and Chas Smash (Cathal Smythe)*

*Barson left in 1983. Group disbanded in 1986, then re-formed in 1988.

Late-70s British ska and vaudevillian pop cult act, best known in the States for songs such as "One Step Beyond," "Our House" (#7, 1983), and "It Must Be Love" (#33, 1983), Madness had placed numerous hit singles on the U.K. charts, but had relatively minimal impact in America.

AUTOGRAPHS

A CD, LP, magazine cover, ad, photo, or card signed by the group: $8-$15

TOUR BOOKS/PROGRAMS/PASSES

Tour Books:
1983 U.K. tour: $25

Madonna

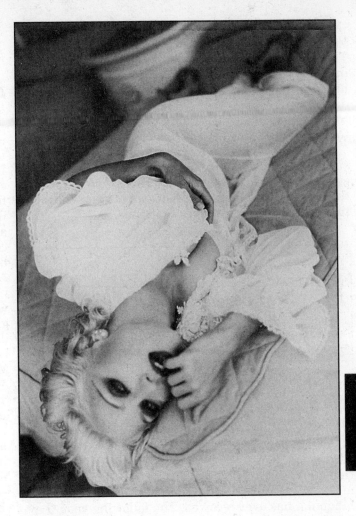

Madonna. Photo by Patrick DeMarchellier. Courtesy Maverick Recording Company.

(Madonna Louise Veronica Ciccone)
Born: August 16, 1958

A creative force who has successfully managed to combine all the key elements of the arts into one compact package—this is how I define Madonna. Simply a "marketing genius," perhaps, her innate ability to smash all boundaries, be it sexual or social, does defy one's imagination.

One of six children, at age six she faced was the death of her mother. She began studying dance at fourteen, and following her high school graduation (1976), she pursued the performing arts at the University of Michigan. In 1978 she headed to New York City where she studied briefly with the Alvin Ailey dance troupe.

In 1979 she landed a job as a backup singer and dancer briefly in the "Patrick (Born to be Alive) Hernandez Revue." Her first-ever band, The Breakfast Club, was born during this time. The band consisted of Dan and Ed Gilroy, Madonna, and Angie Smit. She left the band and Dan Gilroy—whom she had been involved with—in 1980. She started her own band under the name The Millionaires/Emmenon/Emanon, later shortened to Emmy, and began to focus on songwriting. During this time she hooked up with a former boyfriend from Detroit (Steve Bray) and began work on a demo tape.

A break came when Mark Kamins, a DJ/Producer at a club called Danceteria, introduced her to Sire Records, which signed Madonna. The very first Madonna song ever commercially available was "Everybody" (intended to be "Ain't No Big Deal"). It was released as a 12-inch dance single in 1982 and reached Number Three on the dance charts. Her follow-up release, "Burning Up/Physical Attraction," was also a club hit. Her self-titled debut album, produced by John "Jellybean" Benitez, peaked at Number Eight. "Holiday" was released in June 1983 and became Madonna's first Top Twenty hit.

Madonna recruited famed manager Freddie DeMann, typically associated with Michael Jackson, to director her career. Sensual and controversial videos soon followed with "Borderline" (#10) and "Lucky Star" (#4). Both propelled Madonna into the entertainment spotlight. At this time she also began work on her first major film role in Susan Seidelman's *Desperately Seeking Susan*. In late 1984, "Like a Virgin" (#1, 2/85 - U.S.) was released and immediately charted high and spun off the title song to Number One.

"Material Girl" was the second smash from *Like a Virgin*. In April 1985 Madonna began her first tour, The Virgin Tour. It reached more than 350,000 fans in twenty-seven cities. Originally slated for smaller halls, the bookings had to bump up to larger facilities due to the overwhelming ticket demand. The hits continued in 1985 with "Angel," "Crazy for You," "Into the Groove," and "Dress You Up."

Madonna married actor Sean Penn on her twenty-sixth birthday. The unlikely pairing became an instant tabloid target, as the paparazzi waged war on the couple. More than one photographer was the victim of one of Penn's temper tantrums.

A contract signed as "Madonna Penn"

In 1986, "Live to Tell" (#1), "Papa Don't Preach" (#1), "True Blue" (#3), and "Open Your Heart" (#1) all struck pay dirt. Other projects included George Harrison's disastrous *Shanghai Surprise*, a movie that starred both Madonna and Sean Penn. The movie was a flop and garnered some of the worst reviews Madonna has ever received. The following year "La Isla Bonita" (#4), "Who's That Girl" (#1), and "Causing a Commotion" (#2) were released. "Who's That Girl" was linked to an album of the same name, which was a soundtrack for her third major movie. The movie was badly received in America, but did recoup some losses overseas.

Madonna filed divorce papers against Sean Penn the first time on December 4, 1987, which were withdrawn on the 16th, and filed them again on January 25, 1989. The divorce was finalized on September 14, 1989. The time between legal filings was filled with projects. Madonna opened on Broadway on March 29, 1988 in *Speed the Plow*. The Royale Theatre playbill of the show is now a collectors item. The show ran until September and was considered a phenomenal success.

On March 2, 1989, the entertainer began her $5 million sponsorship deal with Pepsi-Cola and "Like a Prayer" aired prior to its release during *The Cosby Show*. The two-minute commercial aired only twice before Pepsi canned the deal, creating a real videotape collectible. The first of three commercials proposed in the deal became the last; however, the company did air the commercial in Canada throughout the Summer. The associated promotional video caused a religious controversy worldwide—it was eventually even banned by the Vatican. As a result of the conflict, her proposed 1989 tour was canceled.

The parent album *Like a Prayer* spun off four other Top 20 Hits: "Express Yourself" (#2), "Cherish" (#2), "Oh Father" (#20), and "Keep It Together" (#8).

Madonna's 54-date worldwide Blond Ambition tour opened in Tokyo, Japan, on April 13, 1990, with the U.S. leg slated for the first week in May. Meanwhile "Vogue," from the forthcoming *I'm Breathless* album, climbed nearly every chart imaginable and finally reached Number One on the big board (5/12, U.S.). In addition to her extensive tour, she wrote the soundtrack for and appeared in *Dick Tracy*, the 1990 film based upon the Chester Gould comic strip. The film extracted single "Hanky Panky" (#10) did well, as did the movie. The multi-media blitz did much to enhance her megastar status and silenced many of her critics. On August 5, the Madonna—Live! Blond Ambition World Tour '90 concert aired on HBO and instantly became the most watched show in the network's history. *The Immaculate Collection*, her greatest hits, was released concurrently with a similar video package on November 2. The newly released "Justify My Love" (#1) video was banned on MTV and created an uproar over scenes it depicted. As if the controversy wasn't enough, the star oversaw the production of a film documenting her world tour, later released as *Truth or Dare* (1991).

In 1992 Madonna signed a multimillion-dollar deal with Time Warner, an insurance policy of sorts for the release of all albums, films, and books under her Maverick Production Company. The first project was a controversial book, *Sex*, which featured the unclad star. The book was released virtually simultaneously with *Erotica*, her sixth full-length studio album. *Erotica* launched four singles: the title track (#2), "Deeper and Deeper" (#6), "Bad Girl" (#35), and "Rain" (#14).

Late 1993 found the artist launching a 19-city world tour—The Girlie Show Tour. The elaborate tour sold out every venue, required 1,500 costumes and a 24-hour stage set-up time. The following year found Madonna creating a stir on *The Late Night Show With David Letterman*, the release of "I'll Remember" (#2) from the 1994 film *With Honors*, and another album, *Bedtime Stories* (#3). The album spun off singles "Secret" (#4, 1994) and "Take a Bow" (#1, 1995).

In 1996 she accepted the role of Eva Peron in the movie adaptation of *Evita*, opposite Antonio Banderas. Despite an outstanding performance in the lengthy film, she was shunned during the year's Oscar nominations. Now a mother of a baby girl born to her and personal trainer Carlos Leon, she has turned her interests toward family matters.

Despite any controversy, any barrier she might cross, or any truth she may uncover, Madonna remains one of the most creative sources of the last two decades. Her dedication to many humanitarian efforts, especially AIDS research, transcends any critical assault. Madonna is nothing short of a fascinating memorabilia subject. Her participation

in various forms of media creates thousands of collectibles world-wide. From picture discs, perfumes, and programs, to passes, photographs, and periodicals, nearly everything imaginable has had an association with the star.

AUTOGRAPHS

Madonna has never been thrilled with signing autographs, and when confronted with the task, takes little interest. She's an impossible acquisition by mail, so in-person seems like the only acquisition mode feasible, if of course you can get by her bodyguards (Often GSS Security Services, Inc.).
Signature (index card, paper): $150-$200
Photograph, CD, album, magazine cover, etc.: $225-$300
Calendar—large item: $350-$450

The signature of Madonna—good luck authenticating this one!

TOUR BOOKS/PROGRAMS/PASSES

Tour Books:
Who's That Girl (1987): $20
Blond Ambition World Tour (1990): $20-$22
The Girlie Show Tour (1993): $25

The gorgeous 1987 tour program is nothing short of fantastic and one of rock's finest (1987 Music Tours Inc.; designed by John Coulter Design, Inc.)

When it comes to programs this diva is first class. Her 1990 tour book is one the best ever—a must for every collector. (1990 Boy Toy/ Music Tour Inc.; designed by John Coulter Design, Inc.)

1987 Who's That Girl backstage passes (Printed by OTTO)

Backstage pass for the Girlie Show tour (Printed by OTTO)

Backstage Passes:
Backstage passes vary in price based on venue, significance, and access. Pass availability depends upon the performer, management, site, and crew—remember , the Blonde Ambition Tour carried more than one hundred crew members.
$8-$12 (Cloth), $20-$25 (Laminated), Example: Bedtime Stories - VIP - $20 (laminated)

POSTERS/PRESS KITS
Promotional Posters: $10-$25 (Post 1985)
Handbills range $10-$25. Example: In Bed With - Laminated 2-sided Japanese handbill - $25

Press Kits:
Madonna (Sire), 1981: $100*
Like a Virgin, 1984: $60-$75
True Blue,1986: $50
Who's That Girl, 1987: $45
You Can Dance, 1987: $45
Like a Prayer, 1989: $40
I'm Breathless, 1990: $35
The Immaculate Collection, 1990: $40-$50
Erotica (1992): $30
Bedtime Stories, 1994: $27
Truth or Dare, scarce w/ 6 color slides: $100
*Has shown significant
 price variation
EVITA press book,
32 pages $65

USED CLOTHING/ EQUIPMENT
Undergarments:
Stage brassiere: $1,000-$12,000*
Stage bustier: $4,000-$15,000
Brief one-piece (leather): $5,000-$7,000
Negligee: $15,000-$17,000
*High-end: Jean Paul Gaultier custom made
Outfits:
$3,000 - $20,000*

Madonna blouse from the Blonde Ambition tour. © Butterfield & Butterfield, Auctioneers Corp., 1997.

Blond Ambition World Tour (1990)
Blouse: $3,500-$4,500
Video worn dresses: $4,500-$6,500
The Girlie Show Tour (1993)
Two-piece (blouse, shorts): $7,500-$9,000
*High-end: Jean Paul Gaultier custom outfits, etc.

Shoes:
Dolce & Gabbana: $3,500-$6,000
Stage worn shoes: $2,000

Jewelry:
Crucifix pendant: $7,500-$9,000
Hats/Caps/Berets: $2,750-$4,000
Wigs: $1,000-$1,500
Note: Madonna often donates personal objects to charity auctions. Rumor has it that she spends over $200,000 a year on clothes and nearly $50,000 annually on shoes - Go Girl!

OFTEN OVERLOOKED MEMORABILIA

Lock of Madonna's hair - $50-$75; Breathless earrings - $10; Like a Prayer - Japanese only promo shirt - $40-$50; Like a Virgin promo jacket - $200; Like a Prayer promo jacket - $450; Truth or Dare promo 6' banner - $200; *League of Their Own* promo 10' banner - $200; In Bed With Madonna - Japanese counter display - $40; *League of Their Own* - baseball bat pen - $3; buttons - $1-$4; 1957 Thunderbird given to Madonna from Sean Penn - $60,000; Madonna Quartz Watch - $40; Vogue 250-piece jigsaw puzzle - $8-$10; reproduction Boy Toy belts; Madonna: Sex Goddess comic book from Friendly Comics, Inc.; Crazy for You - Madonna's first ever picture disc; Madonna trading cards; Madonna money used during Virgin Tour; Mitsubishi memorabilia (1986/87) includes: print ads, oversized poster book, and silk banners; "ITALIANS DO IT BETTER" T-shirts - $15; Passion Pack from *Body of Evidence* - a hard to find memorabilia piece; Erotica U.K. picture disc - a very tough find as an estimated 40 exist;

Speed the Plow Playbill - $10; postage stamps - Granada, St. Vincent, and even Gambia have honored her; Madonna magazine covers: *Harper's Bazaar*, *Island* (her first and toughest cover!), *Rolling Stone*, etc.; Breathless Mahoney puzzle - $20; beach towels - $30; button pack (2", set of 6) - $10; calendars - $10; canteen (Breathless) - $12; club card (Breathless) - $5; comics (Revolutionary) - $5; dolls: (Playmates, 1990) - $30, (Applause, three sizes, Breathless) 14" - $25, 9" - $15, 3.5" - $5; earrings, (Play it by ear) - $8; emblem - $5; fan club kit - $25 (Includes: two 8x10s, card, newsletter, product catalog, folder); fanny pack (Breathless) - $15; Flippy Flyer (Breathless) - $10; Superstars puzzle, 500 pcs. - $10; key chains, various - $3-$8; lighter - $10; magazines: *Penthouse* (9/85) - $15, *Playboy* (9/85) - $20; Like a Virgin mirror- $5; mugs, various (plastic) - $5; necklaces - $ varies; patches - $5; pillows: Breathless - $20, Vogue - $35; plaques, various - $ varies; poster books - $15; postcards, various - $5-$10; sports bottle - $5; stickers, various - $3; tote (bag), two sizes, Breathless - $5 (sm.) - $8 (lg.); trash can "Truth or Dare" - $20; tumblers, various - $7; wallets, various $10; wall hangings: Desperately Seeking Susan - $20, Vogue - $15; watches: (Nelsonic)- $15, (Timex) Breathless - $75, (quartz - plastic) - $30, (quartz - metal) - $40; "Sex" party invitation - $100, *Evita* large cloth store display banner $65 - $100, Like A Prayer promotional candle $100, *Dick Tracy* promo hat $75,

REFERENCES/BOOKS

Sex (Warner Brothers) in mylar cover - $55; Numerous resources exist, but none do justice to the singer in my opinion. There are no dedicated collector books. Serious collectors should opt for the wealth of Fan Clubs: Madonna Mania, Attention: Gavin Coe, 3 Beaumont Vale, Haverhill, Suffolk CB9 8QG, England; also the fanzine Everybody: A pro-Fan Madonna Zine, 3100 S. 208th St. #A-304, Seattle, WA 98198

A VIRGIN TOUR OF NEW YORK

Selected Memorabilia Sites:

*Madonna's Apartment - 1 West 64th St., home to many stars

*Her first apartment - 232 E. 4th St.

*Cafe Tobac - East Village, 232 E. 9th St. - trendy star-heavy cafe, numerous Madonna sightings

*Lucky Strike - 9th and Third Ave. - Madonna very briefly tended bar here

*Barney's - 106 Seventh Ave., upscale department store, a Madonna sighting

*Melting Pot - 29 E. 29th St. - formerly Danceteria, a Madonna early-80s club favorite

*Empire Diner - 10th Ave. and 22nd St., where part of "Bad Girl" video was shot

*Inglis, Ledbetter & Gower - 611 W. 6th St., represented Madonna in her divorce from Sean

*Laura Belle - 120 W. 43rd St. at Sixth Ave., one of her favorite restaurants

*Private Eyes - once situated at 12 W. 21st St., video club and site of first date with Sean

*The Shelter - 157 Hudson St., *Truth or Dare* post-premiere party site

*Royale Theatre - 224 W. 45th St., site of her Broadway debut in *Speed the Plow*

*The Ziegfeld - 141 W. 54th St., legendary movie theatre, a Madonna premier site

... not intended to be comprehensive, but just a starting point for trophy hunting.

Memorabilia Spotlight

Tour Program

Who's That Girl - World Tour 1987
Size: Height: 14", Width: 11", 32 Pages
An excellent 1980s program, well laid out with photography by some of the best in the business. This full-color program includes both movie and video stills along with well-groomed text. It does what many program fall short of doing: successfully flattering and selling the subject. The tour book was designed by John Coulter, John Coulter Design, Inc.
A program of average production, based on the tour, and a must for both fans and collectors!
Value: $20

Tour Program

Blond Ambition World Tour 1990
Size: Height: 15-1/2", Width: 12", 54 Pages
Larger than the program above, this may be one of the decade's finest programs! First-class in every way—photography, layout, design, paper stock, etc. Excellent touches include varied paper stock (translucent opening page), full-page color imagery, two-page (center)color spread poster, movie stills (Dick Tracy), and beautiful designed images of her supporting cast of dancers and singers. The tour book was designed by John Coulter, John Coulter Design, Inc.
A program of average production, based on the tour, and a must for both fans and collectors! A real collectors item and an industry hallmark for excellence!
Value: $20-$22

Magazine

Formed 1977

Howard Devoto, John McGeoch, Dave Formula, Barry Adamson, and Martin Jackson

This late-70s British punk band, formed by former Buzzcocks Howard Devoto, is typically associated with the song "Shot by Both Sides," before band members went their separate ways. Formula, McGeoch, and Adamson went on to some success with Visage before separating again.

AUTOGRAPHS

A CD, LP, magazine cover, ad, photo, or card signed by the group: $10-$15

****

"On The Edge"

Magnetic Fields

Travel with the Magnetic Field, first on *The Charm of the Highway Strip* (Merg, 1994), but pay attention to mile markers, as Stephin Merritt takes you on your synth journey, which is somewhat more intriguing than making animals from your truck-stop-vending-machine-purchased cheese puffs. So what if you don't eat junk food, grab yourself a state-shaped keychain and get on the damn bus, we're goin' on *Holiday* (Feel Good All Over, 1994), first to Las Vegas to contemplate casino electric bills with Merritt, then it's up to you find another ride.

****

Mahal, Taj

(Henry Fredericks)
Born: May 17, 1942

Late-60s multi-talented instrumentalist, deeply moved by Black American and Caribbean music, Taj Mahal has pushed and pulled his music between genres for more than three decades. His creativity and experimentation have contributed significantly to his longevity, as has his international appeal.

AUTOGRAPHS

A CD, LP, magazine cover, ad, photo, or card signed by the artist: $10-$15

OFTEN OVERLOOKED MEMORABILIA

Artifacts associated with his contributions to other musicians' works

Mahavishnu Orchestra/ John McLaughlin

Formed 1971

Original lineup: John McLaughlin, Born: January 4, 1942, Rick Laird, Jerry Goodman, Billy Cobham, Born: May 16, 1944, and Jan Hammer, Born: April 17, 1948

This innovative '70s jazz-rock fusion band formed by John McLaughlin is perhaps best known for the outstanding musicianship of its jazz-oriented players and its founder's creative lyricism. The group's second album, *Birds of Fire* (#14, 1973), sold extremely well and landed in the Top Twenty, but success was fleeting as band members split up following

the third album, allegedly due to conflicts over composer credits.

McLaughlin went on to form other flavors of the band, however, none could reach the critical acclaim and sales of the original lineup. Of all who left the original lineup, Cobham and Hammer remained most active in the music scene, with the former going on to sessions, new bands, and touring with the Grateful Dead, and the latter probably best known for his scoring of the television theme to *Miami Vice* (#1, 1985).

AUTOGRAPHS

A CD, LP, magazine cover, ad, photo, or card signed by the group: $35-$100*

*Original lineup

OFTEN OVERLOOKED MEMORABILIA

Associated artifacts from works by the bands' original members, such as Hammer's work on *Miami Vice*

Mahogany Rush

Formed 1971

Frank Marino, Born: August 22, 1954, Paul Harwood, and Jimmy Ayoub

These '70s Canadian rockers, revered for guitar god and Hendrix-styled apostle Frank Marino, have endured by the strength of a strong cult following while producing moderate record sales.

AUTOGRAPHS

A CD, LP, magazine cover, ad, photo, or card signed by the group: $15-$20*

*Original lineup

USED CLOTHING/EQUIPMENT

Guitar Picks:

Frank Marino: $20-$35

The Main Ingredient/The Poets

Formed early 1960s (the Poets)

Enrique Antonio "Tony" Silvester, Luther Simmons, Don McPherson (1941-1971), and Cuba Gooding*

*Additional personnel included Carl Tompkins and Jerome Jackson

This '70s R&B vocal act is best remembered early in its career for the songs "You've Been My Inspiration" (#25, 1970), "I'm So Proud" (#13, 1970), and "Spinning Around" (#7, 1971) before the death of lead singer Don McPherson, and later for the pop hits "Everybody Plays the Fool" (#3, 1972), "Just Don't Want to Be Lonely" (#10, 1974), and "Happiness Is Just Around the Bend" (#35, 1974) with lead singer Cuba Gooding. The band scored a handful of other R&B hits before splitting in 1976.

AUTOGRAPHS

A CD, LP, magazine cover, ad, photo, or card signed by the group: $ 15-$45*

*Original lineup

Malmsteen, Yngwie

Born: June 30, 1963

Mid-80s Swedish guitar hero Yngwie Malmsteen, who is often compared to Ritchie Blackmore, is perhaps most associated with the album *Odyssey* (#40, 1988).

AUTOGRAPHS

A CD, LP, magazine cover, ad, photo, or card signed by the artist: $15

USED CLOTHING/EQUIPMENT

Guitar Picks: $15-$20

Malo

Formed 1971

Original Lineup: Jorge Santana, Arcelio Garcia, Abel Zarate, Roy Murray, Pablo Tellez, Rich Spremich, Richard Kermode, and Luis Gasca*

*Numerous personnel changes

Early-70s Latin-rock band Malo is best remembered for being formed by Carlos Santana's brother Jorge and for the song "Suavecito" (#18, 1972). The band was no longer by mid-decade.

AUTOGRAPHS

A CD, LP, magazine cover, ad, photo, or card signed by the group: $ 10-$15*

*Original lineup

The Mamas and the Papas

Formed 1965

John Phillips, Born: August 30, 1935, Dennis Doherty, Born: November 29, 1941, Michelle Phillips (Holly Gilliam), Born: April 6, 1944, and Cass Elliot, Born: September 19, 1943, Died: July 29, 1974*

*Group disbands in 1968. Group reforms in 1971 only to disband again the same year. In 1981 the group reformed: J. Phillips, Doherty, Mackenzie Phillips and Elaine "Spanky" McFarlane.

This late-60s Greenwich Village folk pop act is best remembered for two years worth (1966/67) of classic hits such as "California Dreamin'" (#4), "Monday, Monday" (#1), "I Saw Her Again" (#5), "Words of Love" (#5), and "Dedicated to the One I Love" (#2) (all in 1966) and "Creeque Alley " (#5, 1967). The Mamas

A great presentation piece of a Mamas and Papas signed agreement (Hard Rock Café, Key West)

and the Papas also made a memorable closing act appearance at the 1967 Monterey Pop Festival. John Phillips is also associated with the decade's anthemic "San Francisco (Be Sure to Wear Flowers in Your Hair)" (#4, 1967), which he wrote. The band disintegrated in 1968, because John Phillips went on to film production. John's former wife Michelle also went on to acting and even latter married Dennis Hopper for eight days, although she is best known for her TV role on *Knots Landing*. Mama Cass continued her solo career, but choked to death in 1974.

John Phillips also garnered significant publicity over his substance abuse problems through the years. Following his recovery, he lectured about his life with his daughter, actress Mackenzie Phillips. John also cowrote the Beach Boys' hit "Kokomo" in 1988. John and Michelle Phillips are parents to

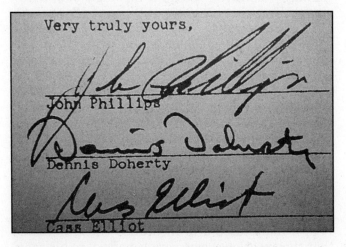

A close-up of the signatures of John Phillips, Dennis Doherty, and Cass Elliot

Chynna Phillips, who formed the vocal group Wilson Phillips.

AUTOGRAPHS

Group
A CD, LP, magazine cover, ad, photo, or card signed by the group: $350-$500*
*Original lineup

Individual
Cass Elliott: $150

OFTEN OVERLOOKED MEMORABILIA

Associated artifacts from members' numerous side ventures following the group's split; movie memorabilia from *Brewster McCloud*, *The Last Movie*, *Dillinger*, *Brewster McCloud*, *Pufnstuf*, *The Man Who Fell to Earth*, *Bloodline*, *The Man with Bogart's Face*, *Savage Harvest*, *American Anthem*, *Let It Ride*, and *For the Love of Ivy*; videotapes of *Knots Landing*; memorabilia from the 1967 Monterey Pop Festival; videotapes of the group's numerous television show appearances; periodical clippings regarding members' numerous legal problems (*Post* (3/67) - $10); dolls (Hasbro) - $100 (Show Biz Babies)

REFERENCES/BOOKS

A few resources exist; choose either of the Phillips autobiographies

Manchester, Melissa

Born: February 15, 1951

This mid-70s pop singer/songwriter and former backup singer for Bette Midler is typically associated with the songs "Midnight Blue" (#6, 1975), "Don't Cry Out Loud' (#10, 1979), and "You Should Here How She Talks About You" (#5, 1982). Melissa Manchester also cowrote "Whenever I Call You Friend" with Stevie Nicks and became the first performer to have recorded two of the movie themes nominated for an Academy Award for *Ice Castles* and *The Promise*.

AUTOGRAPHS

A CD, LP, magazine cover, ad, photo, or card signed by the group: $ 10-$25

TOUR BOOKS/PROGRAMS/PASSES

Tour Books:
'81 Tour: $20

OFTEN OVERLOOKED MEMORABILIA

Movie memorabilia from *Ice Castles*, *The Promise*, and *For the Boys*; videotapes of her appearances in the television series *Blossom*.

Mandrill

Formed 1968

Original Lineup: Lou Wilson, Ric Wilson, Carlos Wilson, Omar Mesa, Bundie Cenac, Claude Cave, and Charlie Padro*

*Numerous personnel changes

This '70s Brooklyn R&B band, formed by the talented Wilson Brothers, is typically associated with the R&B songs "Fencewalk" (#19, R&B, 1973) and "Too Late" (#37, R&B, 1978). Mandrill also played with Duke Ellington at the 1973 Newport Jazz Festival.

AUTOGRAPHS

A CD, LP, magazine cover, ad, photo, or card signed by the group: $10

OFTEN OVERLOOKED MEMORABILIA

Movie memorabilia from *The Greatest*

Mangione, Chuck

Born: November 29, 1940

Seventies pop-jazz star Chuck Mangione is best remembered for his Grammy-winning instrumental *Feels So Good* (1978). His smooth, clean brass sound and loyal following have allowed him to maintain fairly consistent sales. He garnered an Emmy in 1976 for his background music to the 1976 Olympic television coverage on ABC-TV and two years later won a Grammy for Best Pop Instrumental Performance for his album *Children of Sanchez*.

AUTOGRAPHS

A CD, LP, magazine cover, ad, photo, or card signed by the artist: $5-$15

OFTEN OVERLOOKED MEMORABILIA

Evening of Magic mobile: $30

The Manhattans

Formed 1961

George "Smitty" Smith, Winfred "Blue" Lovett, Edward "Sonny" Bivens, Kenneth Kelley, and Richard Taylor*

*Gerald Alston was added in 1970, while Smith left the following year. Taylor left in 1977. Alston left in 1988 and Roger Harris was added. Group re-formed in 1993: Alston, Harris, and various other personnel.

Late-60s and '70s vocal group, commonly associated with the R&B hits "I Wanna Be (Your Everything)," "Searchin' for My Baby," "Follow Your Heart," "Can I," "Kiss and Say Goodbye," and "Shining Star" (#5 pop, 1980), The Manhattans, despite consistent and numerous hits, have never enjoyed the popularity you would think a group this well accomplished deserves.

AUTOGRAPHS

A CD, LP, magazine cover, ad, photo, or card signed by the group: $ 15-$35*

*Hit associated item, with Smith

The Manhattan Transfer

Formed 1969

Tim Hauser, Pat Rosalia, Erin Dickens, Gene Pistilli and Marty Nelson*

*Additional personnel included Alan Paul, Janis Siegel, Laurel Masse, and Cheryl Bentyne.

Originally conceived as a nostalgia group in 1969, it broke up before anything significant transpired, leading Hauser to form a new Manhattan Transfer in 1972. The group quickly became a favorite on the New York cabaret scene and was enormously successful, especially among easy-listening and jazz radio- formatted radio stations. The multiple Grammy Award winners are typically associated with songs such as "Operator," "Chanson d'Amour," "Twilight Zone/Twilight Tone," "Birdland," "Boy from New York City," "Until I Met You (Corner Pocket)," "Route 66," "Why Not!," and "Spice of Life." The group's pinnacle may have been the album *Vocalese*, which garnered twelve Grammy nominations and won two. Whatever successes that may lie ahead for the group are of little concern to a combination that has already left a significant mark in music history.

AUTOGRAPHS

A CD, LP, magazine cover, ad, photo, or card signed by the group: $ 30-$85*

*Original 1972 lineup

Manilow, Barry

(Barry Pinkus), Born: June 17, 1946

Highly successful '70s pop singer and songwriter Barry Manilow is typically associated with the songs "Mandy" (#1, 1975), "Could It Be Magic" (#6, 1975), "It's a Miracle" (#12, 1975), "I Write the Songs" (#1, 1976), which was penned by Bruce Johnston, and "Tryin' to Get the Feeling Again" (#10, 1976). Manilow also had later hits including "The Old Songs" and "Let's Hold On."

Manilow's career began after he left the Julliard School: he wrote an Off-Broadway musical adaptation of *The Drunkard* before taking the job as musical director of the television series *Callback*. After meeting Bette Midler, he became her musical director, arranger, and pianist, and played a pivotal role in her 1972 Grammy-winning debut album. Manilow also picked up some extra cash from writing many well-known commercial jingles, including those for Dr. Pepper and State Farm Insurance—he later stated that the experience was very beneficial to his songwriting.

Endlessly talented, and recipient of an Emmy, a Tony, and a Grammy, this multifaceted performer continues to set new standards for his craft.

AUTOGRAPHS

A CD, LP, magazine cover, ad, photo, or card signed by the artist: $20-$75

TOUR BOOKS/PROGRAMS/PASSES

Tour Books:
'89 On Broadway: $15
Big Fun: $10
1995 Tour: $10
World Tour (1996): $12
Backstage Passes: $10 (cloth/paper), $15-$20 (laminated)

POSTERS/PRESS KITS

Promotional Posters: $10-$40
Press Kits: $12-$50

OFTEN OVERLOOKED MEMORABILIA

Movie memorabilia from *Thumbelina*; artifacts from his numerous stage productions including *The Drunkard* and *Barry Manilow's Copacabana—The Musical*; videotapes of commercials utilizing his jingles; any and all artifacts from his days with Bette Midler; videotapes of his numerous television appearances and specials; copies of his commercially available videotapes; promotional pins - $10; ad-pad inc. 4 LPs - pad of paper - $40.

REFERENCES/BOOKS

Sweet Life: Adventures on the Way to Paradise - his autobiography (1987)

Manfred Mann

Formed 1964

Manfred Mann (Michael Lubowitz), Born: October 21, 1940, Paul Jones (Paul Pond), Mike Hugg, Born: August 11, 1942, Michael Vickers, and Tom McGuinness*

*Additional personnel included: Jack Bruce, Born: May 14, 1943, Klaus Voormann, Born: April 29, 1942, Michael D'Abo, Mick Rogers, Colin Pattenden, Chris Slade, Chris Thompson, Dave Flett, Pat King, Steve Waller, and John Lingwood

This mid-60s British rock act is best remembered for the songs "5-4-3-2-1" (#5, U.K., 1964)—the theme song to *Ready Steady Go*—"Do Wah Diddy Diddy" (#1, 1964), "Come Tomorrow" (#50, 1965), "Pretty Flamingo" (#29, 1966), and "The Mighty Quinn" (#10, 1968), before splitting into other entities including Manfred Mann's Earth Band, which scored hits with "Blinded by the Light" and "Joybringer." The band is also commonly associated with the numerous musicians who played with the group, some of which went on to score success in other areas, such as Jack Bruce who departed to form Cream.

AUTOGRAPHS

A CD, LP, magazine cover, ad, photo, or card signed by the group: $85-$165*
*Lineup dependent

OFTEN OVERLOOKED MEMORABILIA

Copies of videotapes of *Ready Steady Go!* using the group's theme songs; movie memorabilia from *Privilege* and *Up the Junction*; associated memorabilia from Michael D'Abo's covered compositions including "Build Me Up Buttercup" and "Handbags and Gladrags"

REFERENCES/BOOKS

A few resources exist. Start with Greg Russo's book *Mannerisms: The Five Phases of Manfred Mann*

****

"On The Edge"

Barbara Manning

Start with *Lately I Keep Scissors* (Heyday, 1989)—Manning will lead you through snippets of intricately woven fibers, before pulling out the shears and cutting through the tapestry with her plain-spoken, yet crisp verses. Like an artful paper doll surgeon, she's creative, yet precise, smooth, but non-committal. Manning then moved on to the San Francisco Seals, dropping her cutlery for a slab of ash, where she recorded the *Baseball Trilogy* EP, which is a must for all followers of the national pastime, that is more reminiscent of a "fielder's choice" than a "hit." Like the most famous Seal of all, without the hits you may be destined to sell coffee makers!

****

Manson, Marilyn

Marilyn Manson, Daisy Berkowitz, Madonna Wayne Gacy, and Gidget Gein. Sara Lee Lucas was added on drums. Twiggy Ramirez replaced Gidget Gein. Ginger Fish replaced a pissed off Lucas.

One of the '90s premier shock rock acts, Marilyn Manson members are self-defined "freak supremacists." Picking up the pieces, although decades later, where Ozzy Osbourne and Jim Morrison left off, their stage antic of self-mutilation and indecent exposure lacks the creativity of their predecessors, but nonetheless garners a few local headlines. Working first as the foursome Marilyn Manson and the Spooky Kids in 1990, band members took their first names from famous females, and last from serial killers— Marilyn Manson, Daisy Berkowitz, Madonna Wayne Gacy, and Gidget Gein.

The band gained a strong cult following in Florida—not so much for its music as for its unpredictable stage antics. From peanut butter and jelly sandwiches tossed into the audience to skinned goat heads, the band's culinary delights often found their way onto audiences' plates. When a drum machine just wasn't cutting it, probably due to the minimal trajectory of its food tosses, it was replaced with drummer Sara Lee Lucas. The band then trimmed its name to just Marilyn Manson.

In May 1993, the band was signed to Trent Reznor's—the band's guardian angel—new label Nothing (Interscope). Reznor also added the band to the opening slot for the Nine Inch Nails 1994 Self-Destruct tour. Reznor, who actually owns the home where the original Manson family murdered actress Sharon Tate in 1969, claims the parallelisms between himself and the band are purely circumcisional.

Portrait of an American Family was released in July 1994. The thirteen tracks on the album, which Reznor executive produced, included such classics as "Cake and Sodomy," "Get Your Gunn," and "My Monkey." The album also showcased Twiggy Ramirez (a.k.a. Jeordie White, Amboog-A-Lard), who replaced Gidget Gein.

The band's inclusion on the Nine Inch Nails tour included the daily fill of contumely and numerous controversial incidents from tearing up the Mormon Bible to the now Morrison classic "Violation of the Adult Entertainment Code." Needless to say it sparked quite an interest in the band, which followed the stint with NIN with its own controversial tour. On January 13, 1994, it was reported that a live chicken had been thrown into the crowd of frenzied moshers who dismembered it. Although reports of the incident varied, one mosher overheard a security guard asking a colleague how he liked his wings, "mild, medium, or hot?"

The next to last gig of the tour also found pyromaniac Manson setting fire to Sara Lee Lucas's drum kit. Lee, who values his life, was not heard from again, and was later replaced by Ginger Fish. The band then headed out on tour from March through May 1995, supporting Danzig.

Smells Like Children, with extract Eurythmics cover "Sweet Dreams (Are Made of This)" landed the band more airplay on both MTV and radio, while the band also supported the effort in the fall by extensive touring. *Antichrist Superstar* was released on October 8, 1996, and debuted at Number Three on the charts. Divided into three cycles, Manson classics include "The Beautiful People," "Wormboy," and "Scabbed Wings." Whether the band's macabre brand of decadence will endure or not remains to be seen. Thankfully, most of us have endured Alice Cooper, lived through a real Manson ("Charles"), and seen more tragedy unfold live on CNN than this group could ever manage to muster.

The band is definitely worth collecting now, and if and when they hit a crescendo, or each other, it would be worth selling your collection to the first sap you can find! The band is possibly the Kiss of the 1990s, but not until they appear on an authentic METAL lunchbox!

AUTOGRAPHS
Group
A CD, LP, magazine cover, ad, photo, or card signed by the entire band: $20-$35
Individual
Marilyn Manson: $10-$15

TOUR BOOKS/PROGRAMS/PASSES
Backstage Passes: $5-$10 (cloth), $10-$12 (laminated)

POSTERS/PRESS KITS
Promotional Posters: $10-$15
Press Kits: $20-$30

USED CLOTHING/EQUIPMENT
Guitar Picks: $10

OFTEN OVERLOOKED MEMORABILIA
A Lite-Brite toy spelling out "Kill God" - $15; all items associated with their self-produced promotional cassettes (scarce); soundtrack to the film *S.F.W.*; a copy of *The Devil's Notebook* by Dr. Anton LaVey; a copy of *SPIN* America On-Line transcript for November 2, 1995; newspaper clippings from October 18, 1994, Manson Bible tearing incident; copies of the Marilyn Manson newsletter (began fall 1994); all items associated with the June 22, 1995, fire setting incident on the *Jon Stewart Show*.

****

"On The Edge"

Thomas Mapfumo

"The Doctor of Chimurenga Music" and Zimbabwe musical rebel, he is certainly worthy of mention for releases such as *The Chimurenga Singles, 1976-1980* (Shanachie, 1983) and *Corruption* (Mango, 1989).

****

Marie, Teena

(Mary Brockert)
Born: March 5, 1956

Teena Marie, the '70s and '80s Motown/Epic vocalist, is commonly associated with her songs "Lovergirl" (#4, 1985) and "Ooo La La La" (#1, 1988).

AUTOGRAPHS
A CD, LP, magazine cover, ad, photo, or card signed by the artist: $10

POSTERS/PRESS KITS
Promotional Posters: $10
Press Kits: $12

OFTEN OVERLOOKED MEMORABILIA
Videotapes of her appearances on television commercials early in her career

Mark-Almond Band

Formed 1970

Jon Mark, Johnny Almond, Rodger Sutton, and Tommy Eyre*

*Additional personnel included: Dannie Richmond, Ken Craddock, Colin Gibson, Geoff Condon, Alun Davies, Wolfgang Melz, and Bobby Torres

This '70s British blues-rooted jazz-folk group is typically associated with the FM hit "The City." Mark-Almond developed a cult following here in the States, but was unable to find a major audience.

AUTOGRAPHS
A CD, LP, magazine cover, ad, photo, or card signed by the group: $ 10-$15*
*Original lineup

OFTEN OVERLOOKED MEMORABILIA
Artifacts from both Jon Mark and Johnny Almond's work with John Mayall's Bluesbreakers and from Mark's early work with Marianne Faithfull and Sweet Thursday

The Mar-Keys

Formed 1957

Original Lineup: Terry Johnson, Steve Cropper, Born: October 21, 1941, Donald Dunn, Born: November 24, 1941, Jerry Lee Smith, Charles Axton, Don Nix, Wayne Jackson, and Charlie Freeman

The Mar-Keys, the late-50s and early-60s pre-Memphis sound act, are best remembered for the Top Ten hit single "Last Night" and for being formed by a young Steve Cropper.

AUTOGRAPHS
A CD, LP, magazine cover, ad, photo, or card signed by the group: $10-$35*
*Original lineup

Marky Mark and the Funky Bunch

Formed 1991

Marky Mark (Mark Wahlberg), Born: June 5, 1971, Scott Ross, Hector Barrons, and Terry Yancy

Nineties Boston rapper and younger brother of New Kid on the Block Donnie Wahlberg, Marky Mark is typically associated with the songs "Good Vibrations" (#1, 1991) and "Wildside" (#10, 1991)—before negative publicity and a lack of hits pushed him from the spotlight. He later turned to acting and as a model he has even appeared in Calvin Klein ads.

AUTOGRAPHS
A CD, LP, magazine cover, ad, photo, or card signed by the artist: $10-$25

OFTEN OVERLOOKED MEMORABILIA
All items associated with the artists work for Calvin Klein; movie memorabilla from *The Basketball Diaries*; a copy of his workout tape; periodical clippings of his public tirades

REFERENCES/BOOKS
A few resources exist, but none do justice to the group in my opinion.

Marley, Bob and the Wailers

Formed 1963

Robert Marley, Born: April 6, 1945, Died: May 11, 1981, Peter Tosh, Born: October 9, 1944, Died: September 11, 1987, Bunny (Neville) Livingstone, Junior Braithwaite, and Beverly Kelso*

*Numerous personnel changes

An icon in the world of reggae music, Bob Marley was an international star and a homeland hero. His songs embodied the spirit of the streets and the determination among individuals to succeed. Bob Marley and the Wailers are best remembered for the songs "No Woman No Cry"(1975), "Exodus" (1977), "Jamming" (1977), "Is This Love" (1978), "Roots, Rock, Reggae" (#51, 1976), and "Could You Be Loved" (#56, R&B, 1980). Performers such as Eric Clapton introduce the band to their own audiences through songs like "I Shot the Sheriff."

Marley, who fended off a murder attempt in 1976, collapsed while jogging. He then discovered he had cancer, which killed him eight months later. Both Peter Tosh and Carlton Barrett were murdered in separate incidents (1987).

AUTOGRAPHS
Group
A CD, LP, magazine cover, ad, photo, or card signed by the group: $1,250-$3,000*
*Original lineup
Individual
Bob Marley: $1,000

A scarce signature—Bob Marley

TOUR BOOKS/PROGRAMS/PASSES

Tour Books:
Kaya '78: $22

POSTERS/PRESS KITS

Promotional Posters: $15-$20 (Posthumous)
Press Kits: $15-$25 (Posthumous)

OFTEN OVERLOOKED MEMORABILIA

Exercise caution because many unlicensed products and counterfeit items exist. Rastaman Vibration, Island promo box set which includes: album, scrapbook, and press kit, with textured cover, 1976

REFERENCES/BOOKS

Numerous resources exist. Timothy White's book *Catch a Fire: The Life of Bob Marley* is a must read.

Marley, Ziggy and the Melody Makers

Formed 1979

David "Ziggy" Marley, Born: October 7, 1968, Stephen Marley, Cedella Marley, and Sharon Marley

Bob and Rita Marley's eldest son and multiple Grammy winner is perhaps best identified with the song "Tomorrow People" (#39, 1988) and the albums *Conscious Party* (#42, 1988) and *One Bright Day* (#18, 1989).

AUTOGRAPHS

A CD, LP, magazine cover, ad, photo, or card signed by the group: $ 10-$15

POSTERS/PRESS KITS

Promotional Posters: $10
Press Kits: $15-$35, Example: One Bright Day (1989) - $30

OFTEN OVERLOOKED MEMORABILIA

"Jah Mak Ya" (green/yellow/red) flag - $25

Marsalis, Branford

Born: August 26, 1960

Late-80s saxophonist, and older brother of Wynton, Branford appeared on his brother's first five recordings before leaving and touring with Sting. With Sting he contributed to the albums *The Dream of the Blue Turtles* (1985) and *Nothing Like the Sun* (1987) and he also appeared in his rockumentary *Bring On the Night*. He started his own quartet in 1986, while he continued his contributions to other musicians' work. In 1992 he became the musical director for *The Tonight Show*. He left briefly in 1995, but returned.

AUTOGRAPHS

A CD, LP, magazine cover, ad, photo, or card signed by the artist: $ 10-$20

POSTERS/PRESS KITS

Promotional Posters: $10-$15
Press Kits: $12-$15

OFTEN OVERLOOKED MEMORABILIA

Assorted artifacts from his numerous contributions to other musicians' works; videotapes of his appearances on *The Tonight Show*.

Marsalis, Wynton

Born: October 18, 1961

One of the pivotal performers in modern day jazz, Wynton Marsalis attended New York's Julliard School of Music and by the early '80s he was spending time with Art Balkey's Jazz Messengers and Herbie Hancock's V.S.O.P. quartet.

Columbia Records quickly inked him to a deal, and his self-titled debut was released in 1982. The following year he began winning his string of Grammy Awards, which now number in double figures, while attracting some of the largest jazz crowds seen in years to his live shows. When his brother Branford departed the group in 1985, he pushed himself more toward traditional jazz roots, echoing many greats who have gone before him from Ellington to Coltrane.

He was appointed the artistic director at the Lincoln Center in 1988, for a program he has helped develop, and by the early '90s he found himself interested in scoring for dance.

AUTOGRAPHS

A CD, LP, magazine cover, ad, photo, or card signed by the group: $ 15-$25

POSTERS/PRESS KITS

Promotional Posters: $10-$15
Press Kits: $20

OFTEN OVERLOOKED MEMORABILIA

Assorted artifacts from his numerous contributions to other musicians' works; videotapes of his television performances.

Marshall Tucker Band

Formed 1971

Toy Caldwell (1948 - 1994), George McCorkle, Doug Gray, Paul Riddle, Jerry Eubanks, and Tommy Caldwell (1950-1980)*

*Frank Wilkie was added on bass following the death of Tommy Caldwell. Numerous changes follow 1982.

This successful '70s Spartanburg, South Carolina, classic southern rock band was built from two outfits, the Rants and the New Generation, with the nucleus of the band being the Caldwell brothers. The Marshall Tucker Band is best remembered for such clas-

sics as "Can't You See," "Take the Highway," "24 Hours at a Time," "Long Hard Ride," "Fire on the Mountain" and "Heard It in a Love Song' (#14, 1977). Following its 1973 tour (opening for the Allman Brothers), the band gained enormous exposure and headlined the following year. The band was the most popular college and university act during the late '70s and in 1979 after years with Capricorn, it signed to Warner Brothers Records.

At the peak of the band's popularity, tragedy struck with the death of Tommy Caldwell on April 28, 1980, from injuries suffered during an automobile accident days earlier. Ironically, and just weeks prior, another Caldwell brother, Tim, had perished in an automobile accident. Franklin Wilkie, who had also played with the Rants, replaced Tommy on bass. The band's next album, *Dedicated*, was in remembrance of Tommy Caldwell.

In 1983, Toy Caldwell, George McCorkle, and Paul Riddle sold their interest in the band, which for all intents and purposes, had gone the distance.

AUTOGRAPHS

A CD, LP, magazine cover, ad, photo, or card signed by the group: $30-$85*

*Original band

TOUR BOOKS/PROGRAMS/PASSES

Backstage Passes: $10-$15 (cloth/paper), $15-$20 (laminated)

POSTERS/PRESS KITS

Promotional Posters:

(1973-1980): $35-$50

Press Kits:

(1973-1980): $40-$60

OFTEN OVERLOOKED MEMORABILIA

All of the band's early artifacts during its Spartanburg club circuit days; beer mug - $20.

Martha and the Vandellas/ Martha Reeves

Formed 1962

Martha Reeves, Born: July 18, 1941, Annette Beard, and Rosalind Ashford*

*Beard departed in 1963 and Betty Kelly was added. Kelly left in 1967 and Lois Reeves was added. Ashford left in 1969 and Sandra Tilley joined the group. Tilley died during surgery for a brain tumor in 1981.

One of Motown's principal "girl groups," and perhaps its most soulful, Martha and the Vandellas is best remembered for the hits "Come and Get These Memories" (#29, 1963), "Heat Wave" (#4, 1963), "Quicksand" (#8, 1963), "Dancing in the Street" (#2, 1964), "Nowhere to Run" (#8, 1965), "I'm Ready for Love" (#9, 1966), "Jimmy Mack" (#10, 1967), and "Honey Chile" (#11, 1967).

A farewell performance on December 21, 1972, at Detroit's Cobo Hall would mark the end of the group. The group had benefited tremendously, like others at Motown, from Holland-Dozier-Holland compositions. Reeves went on to solo work in 1974, and although her work was praised by critics, she never regained the success she had with The Vandellas.

AUTOGRAPHS

A CD, LP, magazine cover, ad, photo, or card signed by the group: $25-$75

REFERENCES/BOOKS

Limited resources exist, but none do justice to the singer in my opinion.

Martyn, John

Born: 1948

This '70s deviated Scottish folk-rocker is known for his ability to sustain a modest cult following throughout his career, his consistent praise from critics, and his inability to capture commercial success.

AUTOGRAPHS

A CD, LP, magazine cover, ad, photo, or card signed by the artist: $5-$10

The Marvelettes

Formed 1960

Gladys Horton, Katherine Anderson, Georgia Dobbins, Juanita Cowart, and Wanda Young*

*Dobbins and Cowart left in 1963, Horton left around 1969, and Anne Bogan was brought into the group. Dobbins died on January 6, 1980.

One of Motown's '60s "girl groups," the Marvelettes are best remembered for the hits "Please Mr. Postman" (#1), "Playboy" (#7), "Beechwood 4-5789" (#17), "Someday, Someway" (#9, R&B), "Too Many Fish in the Sea" (#25), "Danger Heartbreak Dead Ahead" (#11, R&B), during the first part of the decade, followed by "Don't Mess with Bill" (#7), "The Hunter Gets Captured by the Game" (#13), "My Baby Must Be a Magician" (#17), and "Her I Am Baby" (#14, R&B, 1968) during the latter half.

AUTOGRAPHS

A CD, LP, magazine cover, ad, photo, or card signed by the artist: $20-$70*

*Original lineup

Marx, Richard

Born: September 16, 1963

Eighties pop-rock vocalist, who is somewhat commercially cliché, but extremely successful, Richard Marx is typically associated with the hit songs "Don't Mean Nothing" (#3, 1987), "Should've Known Better" (#3, 1987), "Endless Summer Nights" (#2, 1968), and "Hold On to the Nights" (#1, 1988), which were all from his self-titled debut album (#8,1987), "Satisfied" (#1, 1989), "Right Here Waiting" (#1, 1989), "Angelia" (#4, 1989), "Too Late to Say Goodbye" (#12, 1990), and "Children of the Night" (#13, 1990), from his second album, *Repeat Offender*, and "Keep Coming Back" (#12, 1991), "Hazard" (#9, 1992), and "Take This Heart" (#20, 1992) from his third album, *Rush Street* (#35, 1991).

"Now and Forever" (#7, 1994), featured in the movie *The Getaway*, continued his chart activity as he released his fourth album, *Paid Vacation* (#37, 1994). "The Way She Loves Me" (#20, 1994) was his final release of 1994. In 1996 he released *Flesh and Bone*.

AUTOGRAPHS

A CD, LP, magazine cover, ad, photo, or card signed by the artist: $15-$40

An over produced 1994-95 Paid Vacation World Tour program (Designed by Larry Vigon and Brian Jackson)

TOUR BOOKS/ PROGRAMS/PASSES

Tour Books:
Paid Vacation: $10
Backstage Passes:
$8-$10 (cloth),
$12 (laminated)

POSTERS/PRESS KITS

Promotional Posters:
$8-$15
Press Kits: $15-$30

USED CLOTHING/ EQUIPMENT

Guitar Picks: $15

OFTEN OVERLOOKED MEMORABILIA

Repeat Offender standee - $60; movie memorabilia from *Staying Alive*

A Richard Marx guitar pick

REFERENCES/BOOKS

Limited resources exist, but none do justice to the singer in my opinion.

Mason, Dave

Born: May 10, 1946

This well-traveled British singer/songwriter and guitarist, who was a member of Traffic in the mid-60s where he penned "Hole in My Shoe," "You Can All Join In," and "Feelin' Alright," finished the decade as part of Delaney and Bonnie Bramlett and their Friends tour (1969). Mason opened the '70s with his hit "Only You Know and I Know" (#42, 1970), tackled numerous other projects such as playing with Derek and the Dominos, George Harrison, and again with Traffic, while sporadically maintaining a solo career, which began to take shape mid-decade with the release of his albums *Dave Mason* (#25, 1974), *Split Coconut* (#27, 1975), and *Let It Flow* (#37, 1977), the latter of which included the hit extract "We Just Disagree" (#12, 1977). The '80s saw his career slip considerably—he even resorted to singing radio commercials for Miller Beer—but by the '90s he was right back in the swing of things as a member of Fleetwood Mac.

AUTOGRAPHS

A CD, LP, magazine cover, ad, photo, or card signed by the artist: $12-$35

TOUR BOOKS/PROGRAMS/PASSES

Tour Books:
1975-76 Split Coconut Tour - $45
Backstage Passes: $8-$10 (cloth), $10-$12 (laminated)

POSTERS/PRESS KITS

Promotional Posters: $8-$25
Press Kits: $15-$30

USED CLOTHING/EQUIPMENT

Guitar Picks: $20

OFTEN OVERLOOKED MEMORABILIA

Associated artifacts from his numerous contributions to other artists' work; tour jacket - $75; Split Coconut mobile - $35.

Mason, Nick: See Pink Floyd

Material : See Bill Laswell

Material Issue

Formed 1986

Jim Ellison, Ted Ansani, and Mike Zelenko

This late-80s Chicago power pop-rock trio is typically associated with songs like "Valeries Loves Me,"

"Diane," and "What Girls Want." Material Issue has built a strong cult following in the Midwest through extensive touring and energetic shows.

AUTOGRAPHS

A CD, LP, magazine cover, ad, photo, or card signed by the group: $5-$10

Mathis, Johnny

Born: September 30, 1935

This late-50s ballad crooner, who is known for his career longevity and songs such as "Wonderful Wonderful" (#14, 1957), "It's Not for Me to Say" (#5, 1957), "Chances Are" (#1, 1957), "The Twelfth of Never" (#9, 1957), "Misty" (#12, 1959), and "What Will Mary Say" (#9, 1963), continues his recipe of covering popular MOR songs right into the '90s. Later in his career he found success again dueting with Deniece Williams on songs such as "Too Much, Too Little, Too Late" (#1, 1978) and "Without Us," used as the theme to the popular television show *Family Ties*.

The '90s find Mathis headlining casino shows on the circuit, mixed with occasional tours and selected one-off performances. Over the years he has sustained such a large following that it still can be tough getting tickets for some of his choice venues.

AUTOGRAPHS

A CD, LP, magazine cover, ad, photo, or card signed by the artist: $10-$35*

*Add $10 for key related album

TOUR BOOKS/PROGRAMS/PASSES

Tour Books:

1961 Tour: $42

1962 Tour: $40

1963 Tour: $38

1964 Tour: $40

OFTEN OVERLOOKED MEMORABILIA

Videotapes of his numerous television appearances

Mattea, Kathy

Born: June 21, 1959

Late '80s and '90s versatile country singer Kathy Mattea is typically associated with the songs "Love at the Five and Dime" (#3, C&W, 1986), "Goin' Gone" (#1, C&W, 1987), "Eighteen Wheels and a Dozen Roses" (#1, C&W,1988), "Untold Stories" (#4, C&W, 1988), and "Where've You Been" (#10, C&W, 1989), which was a Grammy-winner. The singer has ventured into other genres of country music during the '90s and successfully returned to the mainstream.

AUTOGRAPHS

A CD, LP, magazine cover, ad, photo, or card signed by the artist: $10-$20

POSTERS/PRESS KITS

Promotional Posters: $8-$12

Press Kits. $12

****

"On The Edge"

Dave Matthews Band

Starting small, sinking clothespins, loose sheets, framed pottery, soup can eyes, Richmond now, Richmond then, dental floss, floating saucers with plastic bath towels! The Dave Matthews Band is Carter Beauford, Stefan Lessard, David Matthews, Leroi Moore, and Boyd Tinsley. Originating from the heart of the confederacy, the band hit pay dirt with *Under the Table And Dreaming* and didn't forget the recipe once it got there. It is one of the few bands smart enough to include a merchandise flyer inside its releases. A Dave Matthews collector should start first by dialing (804) 971-4829 and asking for what type of merchandise is currently available. From 2-Tone Brushed Twill Hats ($18.00) to a Mouse Pad ($15.00), your "DMB" collection is just a phone call away, or write Bama Rags Records, Inc., P.O. Box 1911, Charlottesville, VA 22903. Always remember a "Typical Situation" is to "Pay For What You Get"!

Promotional Posters: $10

Press Kits: $14

****

Matthews, Iain

(Ian MacDonald), Born: June 16, 1946

Founding member of British folk-rock band Fairport Connection, Matthews left following the group's second LP and formed Matthews Southern Comfort, which had a hit with "Woodstock" (#23, 1971).

He found himself involved in numerous projects during the '70s: he had his solo career, he worked with various bands, and he even landed the hit "Shake It" (#13, 1979). The '80s found him active in the music business, but primarily as a talent scout. He returned to a heavier recording schedule throughout the early '90s.

AUTOGRAPHS

A CD, LP, magazine cover, ad, photo, or card signed by the artist: $5-$10

May, Brian: See Queen

Mayall, John/John Mayall's Bluesbreakers

Born: November 29, 1933

The Bluesbreakers formed 1963

John Mayall, Davy Graham, John McVie, Born: November 26, 1945, and Peter Ward*

*Graham stayed a very short time and was replaced by Bernie Watson

Additional personnel included: Hughie Flint, Roger Dean, Eric Clapton, Born: March 30, 1945, Peter Green (Greenbaum), Born: May 14, 1943, Aynsley Dunbar, Born: January 10, 1946, Mick Fleetwood, Born: June 24, 1947, Mick Taylor, Born: January 17, 1948, Keff Hartley, Chris Mercer, Rip Kant, Henry Lowther, Dick-Heckstall-Smith, Paul Williams, Keith Tillman, Andy Fraser, Tony Reeves, Jon Hiseman, Colin Allen, Steve Thompson, Jon Mark, Johnny Almond, Harvey Mandel, Alex Dmochowski, Larry Taylor, Don Harris, Jimmy McCulloch, Freddie Robinson, Blue Mitchell, Ron Selico, Clifford Solomon, Victor Gaskin, Fred Jackson, Charles Owens, Ernie Watts, Red Holloway, Hightide Harris, Randy Resnick, Soko Richardson, Dee McKinnie, Rick Vito, Jay Spell, Gary Rowles, Frank Wilson, Warren Bryant, Pepper Watkins, Patty Smith, James Q. Smith, Steve Thompson, Chris Cameron, Christian Mostert, Angus Thomas, Ruben Alvarez, and Maggie Parker. Numerous personnel changes after 1980

John Mayall is the ambassador of the British blues movement. His career has spanned more than three decades, during which time he has built the foundation for numerous pivotal acts that would follow and their members. Musicians such as Eric Clapton, Mick Taylor, Jack Bruce, Aynsley Dunbar, Peter Green, Mick Fleetwood, and John McVie have all paid homage to Mayall as members of his band. Now with more than forty albums to his credit, he has surpassed the output of most of his peers. His longevity—he formed his first band at the age of thirty—can be attributed to his steadfast convictions to his roots. His inspiration, however, is provided by the youth to which he still influences and the gratification provided by his disciples.

His career landmark may have been *The Turning Point* (#32, 1969), which included the song "Room to Move." During the years numerous reunions of various lineups have taken place, but perhaps the most noteworthy was the 1982 Mayall, McVie, and Taylor Bluesbreakers short series of dates in both America and Australia. This event was finally commemorated with the release of the album *The 1982 Reunion Concert*.

He has continued to tour and record into the '90s, while his albums, such as *Wake Up Call* (1993), still can manage to garner significant attention and even Grammy nominations. By all accounts Mayall remains one of rock's living legends.

AUTOGRAPHS

A CD, LP, magazine cover, ad, photo, or card signed by the artist: $20-$45

POSTERS/PRESS KITS

Press Kits: Varies, Example: A Sense of Place - $20

REFERENCES/BOOKS

Limited resources exist, but none do justice to the singer in my opinion.

Mayfield, Curtis

Born: June 3, 1942

Gifted singer, songwriter, producer, and label owner Curtis Mayfield has helped define generations of music, from his early days with the Impressions, to his later years as a solo artist in the '90s, with albums such as *new world order* (1997). During the early and mid-60s, his prolific output built the foundation for the Chicago sound with songs such as "It's All Right" (#4, 1963), "Amen" (#7, 1964), "People Get Ready" (#14, 1965), and "We're a Winner" (#14, 1968). He also wrote hits for Major Lance, Gene Chandler, and the Fascinations.

Mayfield covered the '70s as a solo act. He released three albums before his landmark soundtrack to *Superfly* (#1, 1972), which included the hits extracts "Freddie's Dead" (#4, 1972) and the title cut, "Superfly" (#8, 1972). The album marked Mayfield's interest in scoring films, which he continued throughout the remainder of the decade. He also landed numerous hits on the R&B chart such as "Kung Fu" (#3, R&B, 1974) and "Only You Babe" (#8, R&B, 1976).

He moved from Chicago to Atlanta in 1980 and signed with Boardwalk Records. Mayfield landed a few more R&B hits before joining the Impressions for a 1983 reunion tour. His career slowed during the later part of the decade, starting with the bankruptcy of Boardwalk. Attempts to start his own label, and even resurrecting others, went unnoticed.

The '90s began in turbulent fashion for Mayfield: first he scored the failed movie *Return of Superfly*, then he suffered a horrible accident on August 14, 1990, when a lighting rig fell from above him while he was performing at an outdoor concert. The accident left him permanently paralyzed from the neck down and sidelined him for years. The decade has had its high moments, though. The Impressions were inducted into the Rock and Roll Hall of Fame, and Mayfield was given a lavish tribute at the 1994 Grammy Awards. But that wasn't all. Shanachie Records released an all-star tribute album to the artist in 1994, *People Get Ready*, and his work saw a resurgence of interest. From hit covers to video documentaries, a Mayfield mania movement was underway; it was topped off by the artist himself who reentered the studio and released *new world order* (1997), featuring guest vocalists Aretha Franklin, Mavis Staples, and Sandra St. Victor. Mayfield was back in a triumphant return to form!

AUTOGRAPHS

A CD, LP, magazine cover, ad, photo, or card signed by the artist: $20-$45

POSTERS/PRESS KITS

Press Kits.

Varies, Examples: Artists Honor a Legend - $20, People Get Ready - $20

OFTEN OVERLOOKED MEMORABILIA

Movie memorabilia from *Superfly* (1972), *Claudine* (1974), *Let's Do It Again* (1975), *Sparkle* (1976), *Short Eyes* (1977), *Almighty Fire* (1978), and *Return of Superfly* (1990); associated artifacts from his numerous productions or covers of his material; all of his earlier work, particularly with the Impressions.

McCartney, Paul

Born: June 18, 1942

Wings formed in 1971
Paul and Linda McCartney (Linda L. Eastman), Born: September 24, 1942, Denny Laine (Brian Hines), Born: October 29, 1944, and Denny Seiwell*
*Henry McCullough was added in 1972. McCullough and Seiwell left in 1973 and Jimmy McCulloch and Geoff Britton were added in 1974. Britton left the same year and Joe English was added on drums. McCulloch and English departed in 1976. Steve Holly and Laurence Juber joined the band in 1978.

Rock 'n' Roll's premier composer!

PAUL McCARTNEY KEY COLLECTOR DATES

1971	8/3: Announced the formation of Wings 11/8: *Wings Wildlife* album launched
1972	2/9: Embarked on 11-date U.K. tour to end on 2/23 7/9: Began 25-date European and Scandinavian tour to end 8/24
1973	3/8: *James Paul McCartney* filmed for airing on ITV on 5/10 5/11: Band embarked on 15-date U.K. tour 8/9: McCullough and Seiwell left Wings
1974	5/74: Wings added Jimmy McCulloch and Geoff Britton
1975	2/75: Joe English added on Drums replacing Britton 9/9: Wings began 13 month, 10 country Tour to end on 10/21/76
1976	5/3: Wings Over America arrived in the U.S.
1977	9/8: McCulloch quit Wings 12/17: David Ackroyd purchased one millionth copy of "Mull of Kintyre" and became first record buyer to receive gold disc.
1979	3/16: *Wings Over the World* aired on U.S. television 11/24: Wings began 18-date U.K. tour ending 12/17/79
1980	1/16: McCartney jailed in Tokyo for marijuana possession 11/26: *Rockshow* premier
1984	1/16: The McCartneys arrested for drug possession in Barbados 11/16: McCartney hosted NBC-TV's "Friday Night Videos" with Julian Lennon
1989	9/28: Began world tour ending in Chicago on 7/29/90
1990	1/25: Appeared on *48 Hours* (CBS-TV) 4/21: Played before largest paying audience in rock history (184,000) in Rio de Janeiro, Brazil 11/18: McCartney's birth certificate sold for $18,000 in Houston, TX
1991	1/25: Recorded acoustic set for MTV *Unplugged* in London 5/10: Played smallest concert hall since the Cavern at London's Mean Fiddler. All items from this gig are highly sought by collectors. 6/27: *Liverpool Oratorio* performed in Liverpool cathedral 9/18: *Get Back* world premier in Hamburg, Germany
1992	12/10: Announced first tour of Australia since 1975 and gave first hints of Anthology project!
1993	2/13: McCartney on Saturday Night Live (NBC-TV) 3/5: Australian tour began 4/14: U.S. tour leg began in Las Vegas, NV, ending on 6/4 6/15: *Paul McCartney Live in the New World*; first live televised concert broadcast on FOX-TV
1994	1/19: McCartney inducted John Lennon into the Rock and Roll Hall of Fame in New York
1995	9/14: Hand-written lyrics to "Getting Better" sold for $249, 200 at Sotheby's in London
	11/19: First portion of Anthology aired on ABC-TV

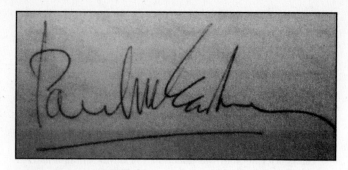

Paul McCartney's autograph

AUTOGRAPHS

A CD, LP, magazine cover, ad, photo, or card signed by the artist: $200

This Paul McCartney backstage pass is a common counterfeit!

TOUR BOOKS/ PROGRAMS/PASSES

Tour Books:

Over Europe '72, U.K.: $50
Over the World Tour '79: $20
World Tour '89 (Magazine format): $25-$30
Flowers in the Dirt 1989 Japan: $25
World Tour '89-90 (die cut cover): $12

POSTERS/PRESS KITS

Promotional Posters:

1970-1971: $Unavailable
1980-1984: $20-$45
1986-1991: $15-$40
1991-Present: $10-$35

Press Kits:

1970-1971: $Unavailable
1986-1991: $30-$45
1980-1984: $35-$55
1991-Present: $25-$30

REFERENCES/BOOKS

Numerous resources exist. Edward Gross's book *Paul McCartney: 20 Years on His Own* may prove useful. Serious fans should opt for this Fan Club: Club Sandwich, P.O. Box 110, Westcliff, Essex SSO 8NW England

McClinton, Delbert

Born: November 4, 1940

Texas saloon singer whose career has spanned nearly four decades, McClinton has backed up such greats as Howlin' Wolf, Lightnin' Hopkins, and Big Joe Turner on guitar before moving to harmonica in the early '60s. He worked with Bruce Channel in the early '60s, then the Ron Dels and Delbert and Glen, and finally he worked solo. McClinton is typically associated with the songs "Two More Bottles of Wine," "B Movie Boxcar Blues," "Giving It Up for Your Love" (#8, 1980), and later for his duets "Good Man, Good Woman" with Bonnie Raitt, which won a Grammy, and "Tell Me About It" with Tanya Tucker.

AUTOGRAPHS

A CD, LP, magazine cover, ad, photo, or card signed by the artist: $10-$20

McCoo, Marilyn and Billy Davis Jr.: See the Fifth Dimension

McCoy, Van

Born: January 6, 1944, Died: July 6, 1979

This '60s and '70s songwriter, producer, and disco don is best known for his hits "The Hustle" (#1, 1975), "Change with the Times' (#46, 1975), and "Party" (#69, 1976). Van McCoy had worked with Aretha Franklin, Gladys Knight and the Pips, and Melba Moore before he died in 1979.

AUTOGRAPHS

A CD, LP, magazine cover, ad, photo, or card signed by the artist: $10-$25

OFTEN OVERLOOKED MEMORABILIA

Associated artifacts from his numerous productions

McDonald, Michael

Born: February 12, 1952

Talented singer, songwriter, and keyboardist Michael McDonald is typically associated with the Doobie Brothers, although he is also recognized for his work with Steely Dan. He is best known for songs such as "I Keep Forgettin' (Every Time You're Near)" (#4, 1982), "Yah Mo B There" (#19, 1984) with James Ingram, "Sweet Freedom" (#7, 1986), and also for his duet "On My Own" (#1, 1986) with Patti LaBelle. His career slid when he failed to follow-up his *No Lookin' Back* (#45, 1985) until 1990 when he released *Take It to Heart* (#110, 1990). Following his *Blink of an Eye*, which was nothing short of a disaster, he turned back to the Doobie Brothers, who are trying to turn back the clocks.

AUTOGRAPHS

A CD, LP, magazine cover, ad, photo, or card signed by the artist: $15-$25

POSTERS/PRESS KITS

Promotional Posters: $8-$12
Press Kits: $12

OFTEN OVERLOOKED MEMORABILIA

His numerous contributions to other artists' recordings; movie memorabilia from *Running Scared*.

McDowell, Mississippi Fred

Born: January 12, 1904, Died: July 3, 1972

Blues singer/guitarist who didn't record until the age of fifty-five, Mississippi Fred McDowell is typically associated with his song "You Got to Move," which was covered by the Rolling Stones. He was a particular favorite of Bonnie Raitt, who toured with him and covered many of his songs. McDowell also attended many folk and blues festivals in the '60s.

AUTOGRAPHS

A CD, LP, magazine cover, ad, photo, or card signed by the artist: $15-$60

OFTEN OVERLOOKED MEMORABILIA

Copies of the numerous films he has appeared in including *The Blues Maker* (1968) and *Fred McDowell* (1969)

McEntire, Reba

Born: March 28, 1955

Eighties country music sweetheart and lovable redhead Reba was best known in the early part of the decade for her C&W hits "Can't Even Get the Blues" (#1, 1982) and "You're the First Time I've Thought About Leaving" (#1, 1983) before landing hits such as "How Blue" (#1, 1984), "Somebody Should Leave" (#1, 1985), "Whoever's in New England" (#1, 1986), "Little Rock" (#1, 1986), "What Am I Gonna Do About You" (#1, 1986), "One Promise Too Late" (#1, 1987), "The Last One to Know" (#1, 1987), "Love Will Find Its Way to You" (#1, 1988), "I Know How He Feels" (#1, 1988), "New Fool at an Old Game" (#1, 1988), "Cathy's Clown" (#1, 1989), "You Lie" (#1, 1990), "For My Broken Heart" (#1, 1991), and "Is There Life Out There" (#1, 1992).

She has persevered through numerous obstacles in her career including the 1991 death of eight members of her band when a twin-engine jet they were flying in crashed into a mountain side.

AUTOGRAPHS

A CD, LP, magazine cover, ad, photo, or card signed by the artist: $15-$30

TOUR BOOKS/PROGRAMS/PASSES

Tour Books:
1993-94 tour book: $10

POSTERS/PRESS KITS

Promotional Posters: $8-$25
Press Kits: $15-$32

USED CLOTHING/EQUIPMENT

Guitar Picks: $10-$15

REFERENCES/BOOKS

Reba: My Story (written with Tom Carter) - her autobiography

OFTEN OVERLOOKED MEMORABILIA

Artifacts from the 1974 National Rodeo finals held in Oklahoma City, OK - where she sings the national anthem, movie memorabilia from *Tremors*, *North*, *The Little Rascals*, videotapes of her numerous television appearances including on *Luck Of The Draw*, *The Gambler Returns* (1990), *The Tonight Show* (11/1/94, 12/4/95), *Reba* (11/25/94), *Buffalo Girls* (1995), *Reba: Starting Over* (1995), a pack of Fritos which features the artist on the front.

McFadden and Whitehead

Gene McFadden, Born: 1948 and John Whitehead, Born: 1948

This prolific songwriting team is commonly associated with its work with Gamble and Huff's Philadelphia International Records (PIR) which included "Bad Luck," "Where Are All My Friends," "Wake Up Everybody," "Back Stabbers," and "I'll Always Love My Mama." The two also later wrote "Ain't No Stoppin' Us Now" (#13, 1979).

AUTOGRAPHS

A CD, LP, magazine cover, ad, photo, or card signed by the duo: $20-$45

OFTEN OVERLOOKED MEMORABILIA

Associated artifacts from their numerous collaborations and productions

McFerrin, Bobby

Born: March 11, 1950

Late-80s jazz singer and one-man band Bobby McFerrin is best known for his novelty hit "Don't Worry Be Happy" (#1, 1988). He is also familiar to many through singing *The Cosby Show* theme and numerous television commercials.

AUTOGRAPHS

A CD, LP, magazine cover, ad, photo, or card signed by the artist: $5-$10

POSTERS/PRESS KITS

Promotional Posters: $8-$12
Press Kits: $10

OFTEN OVERLOOKED MEMORABILIA

Videotapes featuring his television work

MC5

Formed 1965

Rob Tyner (Rob Derminer), Born: December 12, 1944, Died: September 17, 1991, Wayne Kramer, Born: April 30, 1948, Fred "Sonic" Smith, (Died November 5, 1994) Michael Davis, and Dennis Thompson

One of rock's most influential bands, which only missed its mark by a decade, these late-60s hard rockers were precursors to punk. Known for its political fashion, revolutionary slogans, and as the house band for John Sinclair's radical White Panther Party, the "Motor City Five" scored with the debut album *Kick Out the Jams* (#30, 1969). The record created great controversy over the title tune's noticeable scream of "Kickout the Jams, motherfuckers!," which resulted in many stores refusing to stock the album, and eventually, the band's departure from Elektra.

The band then moved to Atlantic and released *Back in the USA*, which is considered by many as the very best hard-rock album ever, although it sold poorly. When Atlantic also dropped the band, it went to England and fell apart. Band members then went in separate directions, many to projects involving music, but most with minimal success. Tyner died of a heart attack in 1991, Davis went to another obscure band, Thompson had a short-lived solo career, Smith married rocker Patti Smith and died in 1994, and Kramer spent two years in jail and later hooked up with Johnny Thunders.

MC5 will always be remembered as the super-group that wasn't, because music already had Grand Funk Railroad.

AUTOGRAPHS

A CD, LP, magazine cover, ad, photo, or card signed by the group: $100-$250

McGarrigle, Kate and Anna

Kate, Born: 1946 and Anna, Born: 1944

These late-70s Canadian folk-pop sisters are best known for penning "Heart Like a Wheel," "Mendocino," "You Tell Me That I'm Falling Down," "The Work Song," and "Cool River." The two had little luck cracking the U.S. market, despite having both Linda Ronstadt and Maria Muldaur cover their work.

AUTOGRAPHS

A CD, LP, magazine cover, ad, photo, or card signed by the duo: $8-$15

OFTEN OVERLOOKED MEMORABILIA

Associated artifacts from other artists' covers of their compositions; film artifacts from *Helicopter Canada*.

McGuinn, Roger: See The Byrds

McGuire, Barry

Born: October 15, 1935

Sixties protest singer and '80s Christian crooner McGuire is best known for one song, "Eve of Destruction" (#1, 1965), although he was also instrumental in aiding the Mamas and the Papas and was a former member of the New Christy Minstrels.

AUTOGRAPHS

A CD, LP, magazine cover, ad, photo, or card signed by the artist: $5-$10

McKee, Maria: See Lone Justice

****

"On The Edge"

Sarah McLachlan

Celtic influenced, she jumps "Into The Fire", dribbling or is it *Fumbling Towards Ecstasy*, she's "Good Enough" to find her way onto *Letterman* (3/24/92) and into celluloid with her ballad "I Will Remember You". McLachlan, in 1997, finds her "Building A Mystery" and a substantial following in the process. Buy now, especially promotional posters, press kits, etc... I see a trip to Canada in your future!

****

McLaren, Malcolm

Born: January 22, 1946

The "Brian Epstein of the '70s," and one of post-punk's true legendary figures, McLaren began managing the New York Dolls in late 1974. Shortly thereafter he relocated to New York from London, although he returned to London when things weren't working out. He had previously operated a clothing store in the early '70s called Let It Rock; he then opened another called Sex, while setting about to form his next venture, the Sex Pistols.

A brilliant marketer, his handling of the British press may have been the best since Brian Epstein with the Beatles. When the Pistols split after their horrendous 1987 U.S. Tour, McLaren concocted Bow Wow Wow, built around the nucleus of Annabella, but that too was short-lived. He also was involved in the early stages of both Adam Ant and Culture Club, but was now more apprehensive about getting totally enveloped with a group.

He then toyed with numerous forms of music, releasing songs such as "Buffalo Girls" (#9, U.K., 1982), "Double Dutch" (#3, U.K., 1983), and "Madame Butterfly" (#13, U.K., 1984) before deciding to try his

luck in Hollywood. When his film bubble burst in the States, it was back to music with the release of *Paris* (1995).

AUTOGRAPHS

A CD, LP, magazine cover, ad, photo, or card signed by the artist: $10 $40*
*Item relating to the Sex Pistols

OFTEN OVERLOOKED MEMORABILIA

Periodical clippings from his numerous appearances in U.K. tabloids

McLaughlin, John: See Mahavishnu Orchestra

McLean, Don

Born: October 2, 1945

This '70s singer/songwriter is forever linked with "American Pie" (#1, 1972). He also penned "And I Love You So," which Perry Como made into an international hit, and he found success with songs such as "Vincent," a cover of Roy Orbison's "Crying" (#5), "Castles in the Air," and "Since I Don't Have You." In 1997, McLean makes a surprise appearance at Garth Brooks heralded Central Park free concert, along with others including Billy Joel.

AUTOGRAPHS

A CD, LP, magazine cover, ad, photo, or card signed by the artist: $10

OFTEN OVERLOOKED MEMORABILIA

His work with Pete Seeger boating along the Hudson River on ecology campaigns

The signature of Don McLean

McLenna, Grant: See the Go-Betweens

MC Lyte

(Lana Moorer), Born: October 11, 1971

This late-80s Brooklyn female rap star is best known for her songs "When in Love" (#14, R&B, 1991), "Poor Georgie" (#83, 1992), "Eyes Are the Soul" (#84, R&B, 1992), and "Ruffneck" (#35, 1993). MC Lyte began her own management company in the early '90s.

AUTOGRAPHS

A CD, LP, magazine cover, ad, photo, or card signed by the artist: $5-$10

POSTERS/PRESS KITS

Promotional Posters: $10
Press Kits: $10

McNabb, Ian : See Icicle Works

McNeely, Big Jay

(Cecil McNeely), Born: April 29, 1927

The "King of the Honkers," the late '40s and '50s saxophonist, is best remembered for his wild style of playing and his songs "Deacon's Hop" (#1, R&B, 1949), "Wild Wig" (#12, R&B, 1949), as well as the two part "There Is Something on Your Mind" (#44, 1959) and "There's Something on Your Mind, Part 2" (#31, 1960). After a retirement from music for two decades he returned to performing of enthusiastic crowds in 1983.

AUTOGRAPHS

A CD, LP, magazine cover, ad, photo, or card signed by the artist: $10-$15

OFTEN OVERLOOKED MEMORABILIA

Any and all artifacts from his early days

REFERENCES/BOOKS

Nervous Man Nervous: Big Jay McNeely and the Rise of the Honking Sax by Jim Dawson

McPhatter, Clyde: See the Drifters

McTell, Ralph

Born: December 3, 1944

Seventies British folk artist McTell is best remembered for the song "Streets of London" (#1, U.K., 1975) and later for his work on children's television. He had little to no impact in the States.

AUTOGRAPHS
A CD, LP, magazine cover, ad, photo, or card signed by the artist: $5-$10

Meat Loaf

(Marvin Aday), Born: September 27, 1947

Meat Loaf, the '70s and '90s sporadic hell raiser, is best remembered for his albums *Bat Out of Hell* (1977) and *Bat Out of Hell II: Back into Hell* (1993) and the songs "Paradise by the Dashboard Light" (#39, 1977), "Two Out of Three Ain't Bad" (#11, 1977), "You Took the Words Right Out of My Mouth" (#39, 1977), and "I'd Do Anything for Love (But I Won't Do That)" (1993), which was a Grammy winner. He is also known for his extremely energetic stage shows, which often end with the performer passing out from exhaustion. Meat Loaf has had two musical careers thus far, primarily due to his business relationship with songwriter Jim Steinman.

Between both *Bat* releases, Meat Loaf virtually disappeared from sight, declared bankruptcy, and underwent physical and psychological therapy to regain his voice, all while releasing sporadic mediocre albums that contained no Steinman material. Ironically, the comeback album sold faster than the original—ten million copies in the first three months! On the current schedule, the duo's next release is anticipated in the year 2009 and is allegedly titled *Get the Hell Out of Here With That Bat*.

AUTOGRAPHS
A CD, LP, magazine cover, ad, photo, or card signed by the artist: $15-$35

TOUR BOOKS/PROGRAMS/PASSES
Tour Books:
Born to Rock the World Tour: $15

POSTERS/PRESS KITS
Promotional Posters: $8-$30
Press Kits: $15-$40

USED CLOTHING/EQUIPMENT
Guitar Picks: $12-$15

OFTEN OVERLOOKED MEMORABILIA
The singer's early work in bands Meat Loaf Soul and Popcorn Blizzard; artifacts from his early stage productions in *Hair* (West Coast) and Off-Broadway appearance in *Rainbow in New York* (1973) and *More Than You Deserve* (written by Steinman); movie memorabilia from *The Rocky Horror Picture Show*, *Americathon* (1979), and *Roadie* (1980); artifacts from Ted Nugent's album *Free for All* - Meatloaf sang lead vocals on one side; artifacts from the touring National Lampoon Road Show; memorabilia from

the Kennedy Center's performance of *Never Land* (1977) (written by Steinman)

Meat Puppets

Formed 1980
Curt Kirkwood, Born: January 10, 1959, Cris Kirkwood, Born: October 22, 1960, and Derrick Bostrom, Born: June 23, 1960

Eighties Phoenix trash triumvirate, with a hint of country, the Meat Puppets garnered significant exposure while guesting on Nirvana's December 1993 *Unplugged* performance and later had three songs on the resulting CD. Following the *Monsters* release in 1989, the group was signed to London Records.

AUTOGRAPHS
A CD, LP, magazine cover, ad, photo, or card signed by the group: $10-$25

TOUR BOOKS/PROGRAMS/PASSES
Backstage Passes: $5 (cloth), $8 (laminated)

POSTERS/PRESS KITS
Promotional Posters: $8-$12
Press Kits: $15-$20

USED CLOTHING/EQUIPMENT
Guitar Picks: $8

Megadeth

Formed 1983
Dave Mustaine, Born: September 13, 1961, David Ellefson, Born: November 12, 1964, Chris Polland, and Gars Samuelson*

*Poland and Samuelson left in 1986 and Jeff Young and Chuck Behler were added. Both Behler and Young left in 1988 and Marty Friedman and Nick Menza joined the band.

Late-80s thrash metal band, formed by former Metallica member Dave Mustaine, Megadeth developed a growing following right from start and by its third album, *So Far, So Good...So What?* (#28, 1988), had an album in the Top Thirty. By this point Mustaine had a substance abuse problem, and while correcting it, the band released *Rust in Peace* (#23, 1990). The band then erupted with *Countdown to Extinction* (#2, 1992), with Mustaine and the band sounding better than ever, perhaps attributable to a more stable lineup. *Youthanasia*, which debuted at Number Four, followed in 1994. Collectors went nuts when they found out that the album's press release was penned by novelist Dean Koontz—*Real Prose or Just Cryptic Writings* (#10, 1997).

AUTOGRAPHS
A CD, LP, magazine cover, ad, photo, or card signed by the artist: $30-$50

TOUR BOOKS/PROGRAMS/PASSES
Backstage Passes: $10 (cloth), $15-$20 (laminated)

POSTERS/PRESS KITS
Promotional Posters: $10-$25
Press Kits: $15-$30, Example: Youthanasia - $15

USED CLOTHING/EQUIPMENT
Guitar Picks:
Dave Mustaine: $10-$30
Dave Ellefson: $10-$20
Marty Friedman: $10-$20

OFTEN OVERLOOKED MEMORABILIA
Rust in Peace counter display and static window sticker - $20; Rust in Peace CD in coffin box - $75; giant metal die cut bottle opener, 1990 - $60

REFERENCES/BOOKS
Limited resources exist, and there are no dedicated collector books. Serious fans should opt for a Fan Club: Megadeath CyberArmy, P.O. Box 883488, San Francisco, CA 94188

The Mekons

Formed 1977

Jon Langford, Born: October 11, 1957, and Tom Greenhalgh*

Sally Timms and Susie Honeyman were added in 1985

Perpetual British indie punk band, adored by the press and best known for its longevity, has never stepped beyond cult status. Both Greenhalgh and Langford have been the band's only constants during their first two decades.

AUTOGRAPHS
A CD, LP, magazine cover, ad, photo, or card signed by the group: $10-$15

Mel and Tim

Formed Mid 1960s

Mel Harden and Tim McPherson

Two cousins from St. Louis best remembered for three songs: "Backfield in Motion" (#10, 1969), "Good Guys Only Win in the Movies" (#17, R&B, 1970), and "Starting All Over Again" (#4, R&B, 1972).

AUTOGRAPHS
A CD, LP, magazine cover, ad, photo, or card signed by the duo: $6-$10

Melanie

(Melanie Safka), Born: February 3, 1947

Late-60s singer/songwriter Melanie is best remembered for her songs "Lay Down (Candles in the Rain)" (#6, 1970), "Peace Will Come (According to the Plan)" (#32, 1970), "Brand New Key" (#1, 1971), "Ring the Living Bell" and for penning "What Have They Done to My Song, Ma."

AUTOGRAPHS
A CD, LP, magazine cover, ad, photo, or card signed by the artist: $10-$20

Mellencamp, John

Born: October 7, 1951

This Midwest successful singer/songwriter, whose hometown all-American image and pure rock attitude has served him well over the years, is typically associated with the songs "I Need a Lover" (#28, 1979), "This Time" (#27, 1980), "Ain't Even Done With the Night" (#17, 1981), "Hurts So Good" (#2, 1982), "Jack and Diane" (#1, 1982), "Hand to Hold On To" (#19, 1982), "Crumblin' Down" (#9, 1983), "Pink Houses" (#8, 1983), "Authority Song" (#15, 1984), "Lonely Ol' Night" (#6, 1985), "Small Town" (#6, 1985), "R.O.C.K. in the U.S.A." (#2, 1986), "Rain on the Scarecrow" (#21, 1986), "Rumbleseat" (#28, 1986), "Paper in Fire" (#9, 1987), "Cherry Bomb" (#8, 1987), "Check It Out" (#14, 1988), "Pop Singer" (#15, 1989), "Get a Leg Up" (#14, 1991), "Again Tonight" (#36, 1992), and "Wild Nights" (#3, 1994).

During his career he has been a co-organizer for Farm Aid, testified on behalf of the farmer's plight before a congressional subcommittee, an outspoken critic of beer and cigarette concert sponsorship, and nearly never turned his back on a humanitarian cause. In 1994 he canceled plans for a large North American tour after he suffered a heart attack. Oddly, little has slowed him down and despite his already impressive career, he still continues to show signs of even greater talent.

AUTOGRAPHS
A CD, LP, magazine cover, ad, photo, or card signed by the artist: $20-$55

TOUR BOOKS/PROGRAMS/PASSES
Tour Books:
Whenever We Wanted: $10
Backstage Passes:
$10 (cloth), $15 (laminated)

POSTERS/PRESS KITS
Promotional Posters:
$8-$20
Press Kits: $15-$25

The Whenever We Wanted tour book (© Mellencamp Merchandising Corp. 1992.)

A 1995 Farm Aid program (Design by Reiner Design Consultants Inc.)

USED CLOTHING/ EQUIPMENT

Guitar Picks: $15-$25

OFTEN OVERLOOKED MEMORABILIA

Lonesome Jubilee promotional divider display - $15; Mr. Happy Go Lucky promo display pack, includes: poster, mobile, cloth banner, and 7 flats - $35; Dance Naked promo postcard - $3; movie memorabilia from *Falling from Grace* (1992), his directorial debut; programs from the numerous art exhibits where his paintings have been exhibited; a copy of the book *Musicians as Artists*; Farm Aid memorabilia; any items relating to his congressional appearance; videotapes of his numerous television appearances

REFERENCES/BOOKS

Limited resources exist, but none do justice to the singer in my opinion, and there are no dedicated collector books. Serious fans should opt for a Fan Club: The John Mellencamp Official International Fan Club, P.O. Box 679, Branford, CT 06405

Melvin, Harold and the Blue Notes

Formed 1955

Harold Melvin, Born: June 25, 1939, Bernard Wilson, Jesse Gills Jr., Franklin Peaker, and Roosevelt Brodie*

*Numerous personnel changes. Additional musicians included: John Atkins, Lawrence Brown, Teddy Pendergrass, Born: March 26, 1950, Lloyd Parks, Jerry Cummings, David Ebo, Dwight Johnson, Bill Spratley, Rufus Thorne, and Anthony Quarterman

Founded as a doo-wop group in the mid-50s, the group didn't attain widespread popularity until the mid-70s with the addition of lead singer Teddy Pendergrass. In 1971 the group signed with Kenny Gamble and Leon Huff's Philadelphia International Records and began to form the roots of the Philadelphia sound. From 1972 to Pendergrass' departure in 1976, the group enjoyed success with hits such as "If You Don't Know Me by Now" (#3, 1972), "The Love I Lost" (#7, 1973), "Wake Up Everybody" (#12, 1976), and "Bad Luck" (#15, 1975).

David Ebo replaced Pendergrass, but his shoes were far from easy to fill, and the group slowly faded from the R&B charts, yet it remained touring.

AUTOGRAPHS

An LP, magazine cover, ad, photo, or card signed by the group: $30-$65

OFTEN OVERLOOKED MEMORABILIA

All items associated with Pendergrass' stint with the band

Memphis Slim

(Peter Chatman), Born: September 3, 1915, Died: February 24, 1988

One of the first American bluesman to leave home and build a significant European following, this singer and pianist is perhaps best remembered for the songs "Every Day (I Have the Blues)" and "Beer Drinkin' Woman." Willie Dixon had a stint in Slim's band during the late '50s and early '60s, at a time that saw Slim garner a standing ovation at the 1959 Newport Folk Festival. Slim also spent some time with Pete Seeger at New York's Village Gate and first toured Europe in 1960. He died in 1988 of kidney failure.

AUTOGRAPHS

An LP, magazine cover, ad, photo, or card signed by the artist: $20-$45

OFTEN OVERLOOKED MEMORABILIA

Memorabilia from the 1959 Newport Folk Festival

Men at Work

Formed 1979

Colin Hay, Born: June 29, 1953, Ron Strykert, Jerry Speiser, Greg Ham, and John Rees*

*Speiser and Rees departed in 1984

This early-80s Australian pop band is best remembered for the songs "Who Can It Be Now?" (#1, 1982), "Down Under" (#1, 1982), "Overkill" (#3, 1983), "It's a Mistake" (#6, 1983), and "Dr. Heckyll and Mr. Jive" (#28, 1983) and also for picking up the 1982 Grammy for Best New Artist. Men at Work also are known for breaking the Monkees' 1966 record for longest run at Number One for a debut album.

The group, suffering from numerous personnel conflicts, disintegrated by the mid '80s.

AUTOGRAPHS

An LP, magazine cover, ad, photo, or card signed by the group: $15-$30

TOUR BOOKS/PROGRAMS/PASSES

Tour Books:
World Tour 1983: $20

POSTERS/PRESS KITS

Promotional Posters: $10-$15
Press Kits: $15

USED CLOTHING/EQUIPMENT

Guitar Picks: $10

OFTEN OVERLOOKED MEMORABILIA

Business as Usual do not disturb doorhanger - $20; Business as Usual book cover - $10.

Merchant, Natalie: See 10,000 Maniacs

The Merseybeats

Formed 1963

Tony Crane, Aaron Williams, Bill Kinsley, and John Banks*

*Kinsley departed in 1964 and Gustafson was added

Early-60s Liverpool pop act, best remembered for the U.K. songs "It's Love That Really Counts" (#24, 1963), "Wishin' and Hopin'" (#13, 1964), "I Think of You" (#5, 1964), "Don't Turn Around" (#13, 1964), "Last Night" (#40, 1964), and later (as the Merseys) with "Sorrow" (#4, U.K., 1966), The Merseybeats broke up in 1966. Only Crane and Kinsley continued as the Merseys.

AUTOGRAPHS

An LP, magazine cover, ad, photo, or card signed by the group: $10-$30

Metallica

Formed 1981

James Hetfield, Born: August 3, 1963, Ron McGovney, Dave Mustaine, Born: September 13, 1961, and Lars Ulrich, Born: December 16, 1963*

*Mustaine and McGovney departed in 1983 and Kirk Hammett, Born: November 18, 1962, and Clifford Burton, Born: February 10, 1962, Died: September 27, 1986 were added. Following Burton's death Jason Newsted, Born: March 4, 1963 was added on bass.

The Lords of Metal came out of the suburbs of Los Angeles in 1982 to introduce the city to a new form of subversive music. Heavy on aggression and light on style, they attacked their instruments with such vehemence that were initially known for their attitude, rather than for their music. James Hetfield (Obsession and Leather Charm)and Lars Ulrich, both from varied backgrounds, formed a relationship built around their interest in the heavy rock sound— Motörhead, Diamond Head, etc. originating out of the U.K. Ulrich recruited Hetfield from an ad placed in a Los Angeles magazine. Both recorded "Hit the Lights," first with guitarist Lloyd Grant. They later added guitarist Dave Mustaine and bassist Ron McGovney and began writing songs for a demo tape. Their first recorded effort came from indie label Metal Blade Records which included them on a compilation of L.A. metal bands called *Metal Massacre* (6/14/82).

Their first performance was at Radio City in Anaheim, California, on March 14, 1982, followed by two shows opening up for Saxon on March 28 at the Whis-key-A-Go-Go. During their fourth show, at The Factory in Costa Mesa (4/23), they were joined on stage by guitarist Brad Parker in his only appearance with the band.

No Life Till Leather, a seven-track demo, was the band's next recording effort. McGovney quit soon after and was replaced four months later by Cliff Burton (Trauma). Burton asked the band to relocate to San Francisco, which it did. The band's following grew quickly and soon Metallica headlined three shows (11/25-27) in Palo Alto, Berkeley, and San Francisco. In pursuit of a record deal the band was convinced to relocate on the east coast. The band headed across the country on April 1, 1983. Sensing the band's recipe just wasn't right, Dave Mustaine left the band and was replaced by Kirk Hammett (Exodus). Mustaine later successfully resurfaced with Megadeth.

In May 1983 the band began recording its debut album, *Kill 'em All* (Megaforce U.S./Music For Nations U.K.). The recording was met with great interest in the U.K. and soon the band departed for a short European tour in support of the effort. The band began immediate work on the follow-up album *Ride the Lightning*, which was first released on Megaforce in the U.S., followed by Elektra three months later.

The album (#100 U.S., #87 U.K.) solidified the band's reputation as a pioneering force in the "thrash/speed" metal movement. The band's 1984 European tour in support of the new release made twenty-four stops before the final show at the London Lyceum on December 20.

The advent of the new year summoned the group back on the road for an early tour, followed by a series of summer festival appearances. The first summer gig was the prestigious Castle Donington Monsters of Rock festival in the U.K. on August 17. The band was fourth on a bill that included ZZ Top, Bon Jovi, Ratt, Magnum, and Marillion.

Master of Puppets, Metallica's third album, was released on February 21, 1986, and hit Billboard's Top Thirty chart. The band combined the successful charting of the new album with an opening slot for Ozzy Osbourne to bring greater arena exposure. Later that year, during a European tour, James Hetfield was sidelined by a skateboarding injury and the band's guitar tech John Marshall filled in during twelve shows. On September 27, 1986, the band's tour bus skidded off an icy road in Sweden, killing bassist John Burton.

In November 1986, Metallica toured Japan and the U.S. with newly added Jason Newsted (Flotsam and Jetsam) on bass. January of the following year found them completing the postponed (due to Burton's death) tour in Europe and heading back to California in March. As fate might have it, Hetfield broke his arm again skateboarding in an empty pool, while the band tackled the problem of where to record its next product. *The $5.98 EP Garage Days Revisited* was recorded in Ulrich's garage and consisted of cov er material from the group's favorite bands. Newsted's playing brought a tighter and thicker sound to the band that would contribute nicely to the group's success during the years that followed.

... And Justice for All became the group's first Top Ten album and yielded a successful single, "One." Following a three-year hiatus, the band returned with *Metallica*, which entered the chart at Number One. The album delivered three singles including "Enter Sandman," which reached Number Sixteen. *Live Shit* (#26, 1993), recorded during three shows in Mexico City, was the band's first live album, although it, like so many other successful bands, had been bootlegged to death over the years. *Load*, the band's next major effort, also quickly topped the album charts.

Metallica collectors have seen Brian Schroeder's (Pushead) work follow in the path of creative gods Rick Griffin, Stanley Mouse, and Derek Riggs. Skeletal imagery has become a staple in metal merchandising, especially with T-shirts. The toughest Metallica T-shirts may be the ones adorned with the logo and the phrase "The Young Metal Attack." Classic offerings include the "Metal Up Your Ass" slogan shirts and the official "Kill 'em all for One" (1983) shirt. Mark DeVito's "Cap'ns of Krunch" and "Trails We Crept" merchandise are also musts for all Metallica collectors.

AUTOGRAPHS

Metallica has always been fairly accessible to fans. I have seen some earlier Megaforce Records promotional photographs autographed by Hammett, Burton, Ulrich, and Hetfield. Authentic examples can land in the $250-$300 range. Hetfield typically signs very large, followed by Ulrich. Authentic Burton signatures are usually condensed and the smallest to appear on a group photograph.

Group

A CD, LP, magazine cover, ad, photo, or card signed by the entire band $70-$200*

*Current line-up

Individual

James Hetfield: $30-$35	Ron McGovney: $10-$15
Dave Mustaine: $30	Kirk Hammett: $25-$30
Clifford Burton: $40*	Jason Newsted: $25
Lars Ulrich: $30	

*Difficult to acquire

TOUR BOOKS/PROGRAMS/PASSES

Tour Books:

Damaged Justice 1988/89: $12-$15

"Masters of Rock" 1991: $15-$18

Backstage Passes*:

*Metallica backstage passes are fairly easy to acquire in the market. One of my favorites is the "CAP'NS OF KRUNCH WORLD TOUR - LASER FOIL, which can be had for $25.

$10 (Cloth), $20-$25(Laminated), Example: Wherever I May Roam - Europe - Laser Foil: $25

POSTERS/PRESS KITS

Promotional Posters: $10-$35

Press Kits: $20-$60

Metallica cloth backstage passes printed by OTTO

USED CLOTHING/EQUIPMENT

Guitar Picks:

James Hetfield: $20-$40	Ron McGovney: $10
Dave Mustaine: $10-$15	Kirk Hammett: $20-$40
Clifford Burton: $100-$150	Jason Newsted: $15-$20
John Marshall: $50-$75	

Drum Stick:

Lars Ulrich: $50-$65

OFTEN OVERLOOKED MEMORABILIA

Embroidered crew shirt - $125; copies of *Metal Mania* fanzine; *Aaardschok* and *Whiplash* fanzines; painter's can, patches, badges, marble paperweight, plastic dagger, a snake-in-a-bag promotional souvenir and concert flyers; *...And Justice For All*, Japan, Mercury CD, includes T-shirt in tin "Metallicab," 1988.

REFERENCES/BOOKS

Metallica by Jon Hotten - $9; *Metallica, In Their Own Words* by Mark Putterford - $16; *Complete Guide to the Music of Metallica* by Wall & Dome - $8; Chris Crocker's book *Metallica: The Frayed Ends of Metal* is a MUST!

The Meters

Formed 1967

Original lineup: Art Neville, Leo Nocentelli, Joseph Modeliste and George Porter, Jr.

Prominent late-60s New Orleans R&B backup band gone feature act, formed by Art Neville, the quartet is best remembered for songs such as "Sophisticated Cissy" (#34, 1969), "Cissy Strut" (#23, 1969), "Look-Ka Py Py" (#11, R&B, 1969), and "Chicken Strut" (#11, R&B, 1970). The group backed numerous artists including Dr. John, Robert Palmer, Labelle, and Paul McCartney and Wings. The Meters also opened shows for the Rolling Stones on their 1975 American and 1976 European tours before breaking up in 1977.

AUTOGRAPHS

An LP, magazine cover, ad, photo, or card signed by the group: $20-$35

OFTEN OVERLOOKED MEMORABILIA

Associated items from the numerous contributions the group has made to other artists' works

Metheny, Pat

Born: August 12, 1955

Late 70s contemporary jazz guitarist Pat Metheny built a solid and increasingly respectable following on his way to becoming one of the most influential artists in his genre. His early days were spent playing twelve-string guitar in vibist Gary Burton's band before he set out to form a band of his own. Metheny hooked up with keyboardist Lyle Mays, who became a staple in the group, and other bandmates following the release of his first two albums, on which drummer Bob Moses and bassist Jaco Pastorius accompanied him.

Metheny clearly established himself by the turn of the decade with albums such as *New Chautauqua* (#44, 1979), *American Garage* (#53, 1979), and *As Falls Wichita, So Falls Wichita Falls* (#50, 1981). His broad based appeal due to his occasional rock riffs also found him tackling the pop market with each new release, without forsaking his jazz roots. During the '80s he turned to world music and even scored the film *The Falcon and the Snowman* (1985). Through it all he has sustained his outstanding reputation.

AUTOGRAPHS
A CD, LP, magazine cover, ad, photo, or card signed by the artist: $15-$40

POSTERS/PRESS KITS
Promotional Posters: $8-$20
Press Kits: $12-$30

USED CLOTHING/EQUIPMENT
Guitar Picks: $20-$30

OFTEN OVERLOOKED MEMORABILIA
Movie memorabilia from *The Falcon and the Snowman* (1985); associated artifacts from his numerous contributions to other artists work.

MFSB

Formed Early 1970s

This early-70s band of Philadelphia sound musicians, MFSB is best known for the song "TSOP" (#1, 1974)—"The Sound of Philadelphia"—a Gamble-Huff composition that was the theme to *Soul Train*, and for backing of numerous artists responsible for the genre.

AUTOGRAPHS
A CD, LP, magazine cover, ad, photo, or card signed by the group: $10-$20

OFTEN OVERLOOKED MEMORABILIA
Associated artifacts from the numerous musicians the backup group has supported

Miami Sound Machine: See Gloria Estefan

Michael, George

(George Panayiotou)
Born: June 25, 1963

Eighties British sex symbol and solo artist, formerly half of the pop duo Wham!, Michael made a successful migration from teen heartthrob to mature singer/songwriter. He is best known for his hits, "I Knew You Were Waiting (For Me)" (#1, 1987), a Grammy winning duet with Aretha Franklin, "I Want Your Sex" (#2, 1987), "Faith" (#1, 1987), "Father Figure" (#1, 1988), "One More Try" (#1, 1988), "Monkey' (#1, 1988), "Kissing a Fool" (#5, 1988), "Heaven Help Me" (#5, 1989), "Praying for Time" (#1, 1990), "Freedom" (#8, 1990), and his duet with Elton John on "Don't Let the Sun Go Down on Me" (#1, 1991).

Faith, his first solo album, was 1988's best-selling release and also a Grammy winner for Album of the Year. He followed it with *Listen Without Prejudice Vol.1* (#2, 1990) and essentially turned his back to the media. He has spent most of the '90s battling with Sony to terminate his record contract. Michael's appearance at the Freddie Mercury tribute concert in 1992, where he played with the surviving members of the band Queen, was nothing short of spectacular. The event resulted in a *Five Live* EP released by Hollywood Records, with Sony's permission, in 1993.

Michael's legal battles with Sony have been tragic, not just for the parties involved, but also for music fans in general. Despite the lack of releases, George Michael remains one of the most outstanding voices in rock and roll history!

AUTOGRAPHS
A CD, LP, magazine cover, ad, photo, or card signed by the artist: $25-$85

TOUR BOOKS/PROGRAMS/PASSES
Tour Books:
The Faith Tour, 1988 (Japan) - $45
Cover to Cover, 1991 - $15
Backstage Passes:
$8-$12 (cloth), $15-$20 (laminated)

POSTERS/PRESS KITS
Promotional Posters: $9-$25
Press Kits: $25-$40

OFTEN OVERLOOKED MEMORABILIA
Five Live promo box with CD & video press kit - $30; Older two-sided window display - $15; 1988 promo counter display - $15; puzzle (Milton Bradley) - $5; notebook - $5; folder - $3; periodical clippings associated with his Sony contract conflict.

Michaels, Lee

Born: November 24, 1945

Late-60s hard rockin' organist Lee Michaels is best remembered for the songs "Do You Know What I Mean?" (#6, 1971), "Can I Get a Witness" (#39, 1971), "Heighty Hi," and "Stormy Monday."

AUTOGRAPHS

A CD, LP, magazine cover, ad, photo, or card signed by the artist: $8-$12

OFTEN OVERLOOKED MEMORABILIA

Stand-up display (A&M) Records: $45

Mickey and Sylvia

Mickey (McHouston) Baker and Sylvia Robinson (Vanderpool)

This late-50s R&B duo is typically associated with the songs "Love Is Strange" (#11, 1956), "There Oughta Be a Law" (#46, 1957), and "Baby You're So Fine" (352, 1961). After the break-up Mickey went on to write several guitar instruction books, while Sylvia married Joe Robinson, founded All Platinum Records and Studios, become a successful producer, and even landed on the charts again as a solo artist with "Pillow Talk" (#3, 1973), "Sweet Stuff" (#16, R&B, 1974), and "Automatic Lover" (#43, R&B, 1978).

When All Platinum Records began to flounder, Sylvia renamed the label Sugarhill and formed the Sugar Hill Gang, which landed on the charts with "Rapper's Delight" (#26, 1979). She later also signed and produced other top rap acts, including Grandmaster Flash and the Furious Five.

AUTOGRAPHS

A CD, LP, magazine cover, ad, photo, or card signed by the duo: $10-$15

OFTEN OVERLOOKED MEMORABILIA

Associated artifacts from All Platinum/Sugarhill Records; copies of Mickey Baker's instruction books.

Midler, Bette

Born: December 1, 1945

Seventies pop singer and sexy retro-diva turned 80s film star, the multi-talented "Divine Miss M" is typically associated with the songs "Boogie Woogie Bugle Boy" (#8, 1973), "The Rose," "Wind Beneath My Wings" (#1, 1989), which was a Grammy winner, and "From a Distance" (#2, 1991). She began her ca-

Two Bette Midler outfits from the movie For the Boys. The dress at left has an estimated value between $600 and $800 while the outfit at right has an estimated value between $700 and $900. © Butterfield & Butterfield, Auctioneers Corp., 1997.

reer early, even appearing in a bit part in the movie *Hawaii*, before moving on to the stage in Off-Broadway and Broadway roles. She developed a strong cult following in New York City, while polishing her act. Her debut album, *The Divine Miss M* (1972), sold gold and earned her a Grammy for Best New Artist.

When her record sales began to tail off, she turned to acting and her appearance in *The Rose* (1979) earned her an Oscar nomination. A concert film and even a best-selling book followed before her career dipped in the early '80s. Midler rebounded quickly with a series of comedies for the Walt Disney Studio-Touchstone Pictures followed by the drama *Beaches*.

By the '90s she had established a trend of appearing in strong film productions, accompanied by a related hit song, which typically also garnered both Oscar and Grammy nominations. In 1992 she earned a well-deserved Emmy for her appearance on one of the final *Tonight Show* broadcasts with Johnny Carson. The event will go down in history as one of television's truly magical moments. Midler continues to impress new legions of fans who still can't get over the depth of her talent.

AUTOGRAPHS

A CD, LP, magazine cover, ad, photo, or card signed by the artist: $15-$45

POSTERS/PRESS KITS
Promotional Posters: $10-$50
Press Kits: $15-$60, Example: Bette of Roses - $15

OFTEN OVERLOOKED MEMORABILIA
Movie memorabilia from *Hawaii*, *The Rose*, *Divine Madness*, *Down and Out in Beverly Hills* (1986), *Ruthless People* (1986), *Outrageous Fortune* (1987), *Big Business* (1988), *Beaches*, *Scenes from a Mall* (1991), *Stella* (1991), and *For the Boys* (1991); theater memorabilia from *Tommy* and *Fiddler on the Roof*; a copy of *Newsweek* magazine (1973) with Bette on the cover; videotapes of her numerous television appearances including *The Tonight Show* (1992).

REFERENCES/BOOKS
A View from a Broad - her memoirs; *The Saga of Baby Divine* - a children's book (1983); Limited resources exist, but none do justice to the singer in my opinion.

Midnight Oil

Formed 1976

Peter Garrett, Rob Hirst, Jim Moginie, Martin Rotsey, and Andrew James*

*James left in 1980 and Peter Gifford was added. Gifford left in 1990 and Dwayne Hillman was added.

Late-80s Australian rock band Midnight Oil is best remembered for the songs "Beds Are Burning" (#17, 1987) and "Blue Sky Mine" (#47, 1990) and the albums *Diesel and Dust* (#21, 1987) and *Blue Sky Mining* (#20, 1990), before fading from the music scene.

AUTOGRAPHS
A CD, LP, magazine cover, ad, photo, or card signed by the group: $15-$45

POSTERS/PRESS KITS
Promotional Posters: $10
Press Kits: $10

Mighty Clouds of Joy

Formed late 1950s

Joe Ligon, Johnny Martin, Elmo Franklin, Ermant Franklin, Richard Wallace, Leon Polk, and Jimmy Jones

*Paul Beasly was added in the early 1980s and leaves in 1987. Others are added to the group including Wilbert Williams. Martin died in 1987.

Multiple Grammy award winning Gospel vocal unit, which has backed numerous top pop artists including Marvin Gaye, Aretha Franklin, and the Rolling Stones, the Mighty Clouds of Joy have spent decades touring extensively and recording.

AUTOGRAPHS
A CD, LP, magazine cover, ad, photo, or card signed by the group: $15-$45*
*Original lineup

OFTEN OVERLOOKED MEMORABILIA
Associated artifacts from their numerous contributions to other artists' work

The Mighty Diamonds

Formed 1973

Donald "Tabby" Shaw, Lloyd "Judge" Ferguson, and Fitzroy "Bunny" Simpson

This late-70s "second wave" Jamaican reggae vocal threesome typically associated with its homeland hits "Jah Jah Bless the Dreadlocks," "Let's Pull It All Together," "Right Time," "Have Mercy," " I Need a Roof," "Wise Son" (#1, 1980), and "Pass the Kouchie/ Knowledge" (#1, 1981).

AUTOGRAPHS
A CD, LP, magazine cover, ad, photo, or card signed by the group: $15

Mike and the Mechanics: See Genesis

Milburn, Amos

Born: April 1, 1927, Died: January 3, 1980

Mid-40s and '50s R&B vocalist Amos Milburn is best remembered for his song "Chicken Shack Boogie," as well as his numerous tavern related tunes including "Bad Bad Whiskey" (#1, R&B, 1950), "One Scotch, One Bourbon, One Beer" (32 R&B, 1953), "Thinking and Drinking" (#8, 1952), and "Let Me Go Home Whiskey" (#3, 1953).

AUTOGRAPHS
An LP, magazine cover, ad, photo, or card signed by the artist: $15-$35

Miles, Buddy

Born: September 5, 1946

Multi-talented singer/drummer, whose resume included stints with Wilson Pickett's backup band, the Electric Flag, the Buddy Miles Express, Hendrix's Band of Gypsys, Hardware, and even the California Raisins, Buddy Miles is typically remembered for his work with Carlos Santana, the album *Band of Gypsys*, and the songs "Them Changes" and "I Heard It Through the Grapevine."

AUTOGRAPHS
A CD, LP, magazine cover, ad, photo, or card signed by the artist: $25-$60

OFTEN OVERLOOKED MEMORABILIA
The numerous pieces of memorabilia associated with The California Raisins

Miller, Steve Band

Formed 1966

Steve Miller, Born: October 5, 1943, James "Curly" Cooke, Lonnie Turner, Born: February 24, 1947, and Tim Davis*

*In 1967 Boz Scaggs, Born: June 8, 1944 and Jim Peterman were added, and Cooke left. Both Scaggs and Peterman left in 1968 and Ben Sidran was added. Numerous changes follow.

Late-60s blues rocker, best remembered for the songs "Brave New World," "Space Cowboy," and "My Dark Hour," turned late-70s/early-80s successful pop rock artist, Steve Miller is typically associated with the songs "The Joker" (#1, 1973), "Fly Like an Eagle" (#2, 1976), "Rock 'n Me" (#1, 1976), "Take the Money and Run" (#11, 1976), "Jet Airliner" (#8, 1977), "Swingtown" (#17, 1977), "Jungle Love" (#23,1977), "Heart Like a Wheel" (#24, 1981), and "Abrcadabra" (#1, 1982). The transition in his career came during a convalescence following a serious automobile accident, in which he broke his neck. Although his hits stopped by the mid-80s, his music has remained a staple on classic-rock radio and a must-cover for an entirely new music generation.

AUTOGRAPHS
A CD, LP, magazine cover, ad, photo, or card signed by the artist: $15-$40

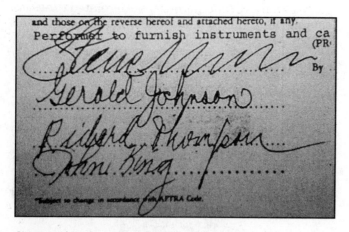

Signatures from the members of the Steve Miller Band

TOUR BOOKS/PROGRAMS/PASSES
Tour Books:
Tour '77: $20
Backstage Passes:
$10-$15 (cloth/paper), $22 (laminated)

POSTERS/PRESS KITS
Promotional Posters:
1967-1972: $20-$30
1973-Present: $10-$30

Press Kits:
1967-1972: $20-$30
1973-Present: $15-$40

USED CLOTHING/EQUIPMENT
Guitar Picks: $20

OFTEN OVERLOOKED MEMORABILIA
Styrofoam display (Miller's head w/name): $50

Milli Vanilli

Formed 1988

Fabrice Morvan and Rob Pilatus

Late-80s lip synch hoax Milli Vanilli is typically associated with the songs "Girl You Know It's True" (#2, 1989), "Baby Don't Forget My Number" (#1, 1989), "Blame It on the Rain" (#1, 1989), and "Girl I'm Gonna Miss You" (#1, 1989). The two will forever be remembered for hits they didn't sing.

AUTOGRAPHS
A CD, LP, magazine cover, ad, photo, or card signed by the group: $10

OFTEN OVERLOOKED MEMORABILIA
Periodical clippings associated with the hoax

Mills, Stephanie

Born: March 22, 1957

Late-70s R&B vocalist, commonly associated with the songs "I'll Never Knew Love Like This Before" (#6, 1980), "Sweet Sensation" (#3, R&B, 1980), "Two Hearts" (#3, R&B, 1981), which was a duet with Teddy Pendergrass, "The Medicine Song," and numerous other R&B hits, Stephanie Mills has also been linked to the Broadway production of *The Wiz*, which was responsible for bringing her into the spotlight.

AUTOGRAPHS
A CD, LP, magazine cover, ad, photo, or card signed by the artist: $10-$20

POSTERS/PRESS KITS
Promotional Posters: $8-$12
Press Kits: $10-$12

OFTEN OVERLOOKED MEMORABILIA
All associated artifacts from her appearances in *The Wiz*

Mimms, Garnet and the Enchanters

Formed 1963

Garnet (Garrett) Mimms, Sam Bell, Charles Boyer, and Zola Pearnell

This early-60s Philadelphia R&B group is best remembered for the songs "Cry Baby" (#4, 1963), "For Your Precious Love" (#26, 1963), "Baby Don't You Weep" (#30, 1963), and "A Quiet Place" (#78, 1964) before Mimms split from the group to score hits with "Tell Me Baby" (#69, 1964), "One Girl" (#67, 1964), "Look Away" (#73, 1964), and "I'll Take Good Care of You" (#30, 1966). One of the group's biggest fans was Janis Joplin, who scored with numerous songs it recorded including "Try (Just a Little Bit Harder)" and "Piece of My Heart." The group had also been backed by numerous female singers including Dionne Warwick and Cissy Houston.

AUTOGRAPHS

A CD, LP, magazine cover, ad, photo, or card signed by the artist (Mimms): $15-$40

OFTEN OVERLOOKED MEMORABILIA

All items relating to the group's unique affiliation with fan Janis Joplin

The Mindbenders: See Wayne Fontana and the Mindbenders

Ministry

Formed 1981

Al Jourgensen, Lamont Welton, and Stevo*

*Numerous personnel changes. Additional musicians included: Stephen George, Paul Barker William Rieflin, Roland Barker, and Mike Scaccia.

Early-80s British synth industrial group, best known for their album *Psalm 69: The Way to Succeed and the Way to Suck Eggs*, which entered the chart in the Top Thirty and its extract "Jesus Built My Hotrod," Ministry gained significant exposure when it appeared on the 1992 Lollapalooza Tour. The band is also notorious for its offshoot projects such as 1,000 Homo DJs, Acid Horse, and Pailhead.

AUTOGRAPHS

A CD, LP, magazine cover, ad, photo, or card signed by the group: $25-$40

POSTERS/PRESS KITS

Promotional Posters: $8-$12
Press Kits: $15

USED CLOTHING/EQUIPMENT

Guitar Picks: $15-$20

Mink DeVille/Willy DeVille

Formed 1974

Willy DeVille (William Boray), Louis X. Erlanger, Bobby Leonards, Ruben Siguenza, and T.R. "Manfred" Allen*

*Numerous personnel changes. In 1978 only DeVille and Erlanger remained of above lineup. Erlanger left in 1980, while Rick Borgia, Kenny Margolis, Joey Vasta, Thommy Price, and Louis Cortelezzi joined the group.

Late-70s New York punk rockers—albeit a bit softer—are best remembered for their appearance on the 1976 *Live from CBGB* compilation and the song "Spanish Stroll." Willy DeVille later went solo and was often been identified with the song "Storybook Love."

AUTOGRAPHS

A CD, LP, magazine cover, ad, photo, or card signed by the group: $10-$15

OFTEN OVERLOOKED MEMORABILIA

Movie memorabilia from *The Princess Bride*

Minutemen/Firehose

Minutemen formed 1979

D. Boon (Dennes Boon, (1958-1985)), Mike Watt, and George Hurley

fIREHOSE

formed 1986

Watt, Hurley, and Ed Crawford

This '80s San Pedro free-form hard-core punk trinity, the second band to release from the indie label SST, is perhaps best remembered for the 45-song and American punk classic album *Double Nickels on the Dime* (1984) and for being at a career pinnacle when Boon was tragically killed in a van accident. The surviving members, reluctant at first to continue, decide to go on as fIREHOUSE before disbanding in 1994.

AUTOGRAPHS

A CD, LP, magazine cover, ad, photo, or card signed by the group: $30-$60*
*Original lineup on *Double Nickels* related piece

Missing Persons

Formed 1980

Dale Bozzio (Consalvi), Warren Cuccurullo, Chuck Wild, Patrick O'Hearn, and Terry Bozzio

Early-80s synth pop show band—with a heavy MTV rotation—Missing Persons was led by former Playboy Bunny Terry Bozzio, who gave a new meaning to plexi-glass bowl bras, hot-pink hair, and seemingly endless legs. In addition to Terry Bozzio, the band included three former Zappa alumni, including Terry's husband Dale. The band is best remembered for two songs, "Words" and "Destination Unknown," before it broke up. Many of the band's members found success with other projects.

AUTOGRAPHS

A CD, LP, magazine cover, ad, photo, or card signed by the group: $15-$25

POSTERS/PRESS KITS

Promotional Posters: $10
Press Kits: $15

Mission of Burma

Formed 1979

Clint Conley, Roger Miller, Martin Swope, and Pete Prescott

This '80s North-east indie post-punk act is best remembered for the classic songs "Academy Fight Song" and "That's When I Reach for My Revolver." Mission of Burma split-up in 1983.

AUTOGRAPHS

A CD, LP, magazine cover, ad, photo, or card signed by the group: $10-$25

Mr. Big

Formed 1988

Eric Martin, Paul Gilbert, Billy Sheehan, and Pat Torpey

Late-80s L.A. hard-rockers Mr. Big are best remembered for their 1991 Number One hit "To Be With You," as well as their unusual antics of playing their instruments with power equipment fitted with picks. Mr. Big has since done little.

AUTOGRAPHS

A CD, LP, magazine cover, ad, photo, or card signed by the group: $10

Mitchell, Joni

(Roberta Anderson)
Born: November 7, 1943

Late-60s/Early-70s Canadian folk-pop disciple Joni Mitchell is best remembered for such classics as "Both Sides Now," "Michael from Mountains," "Woodstock," "Eastern Rain," "The Circle Game," "Big Yellow Taxi," "You Turn Me On (I'm a Radio)," and "Help Me" (#7, 1974)—just to name a few. Mitchell has been cited by numerous artists as an influence and her decades of creativity have set new standards for her genre.

Mitchell has always appealed to both her fans and critics for her ability to migrate to other forms of music with little regard to the ventures' commercial success. Her conviction in attacking an issue, altering her song structures, or even embracing an extremely

Joni Mitchell. Photo by Gregory Heisler. Courtesy Reprise Records.

difficult task has always garnered respect. To think that the same artist who released the album *Court and Spark* (#2, 1974) would even attempt a project as diverse and challenging as *Mingus* (#17, 1979) is beyond the comprehension of many, and the abilities of most.

It is my guess that her career will be analyzed, re-analyzed, and dissected for many years following its completion—an outstanding subject for a Master's thesis.

AUTOGRAPHS

A CD, LP, magazine cover, ad, photo, or card signed by the artist: $10-$30

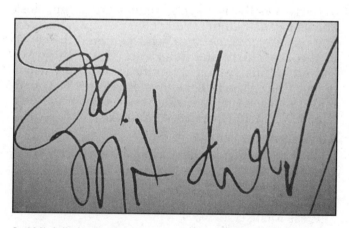

Joni Mitchell's signature

OFTEN OVERLOOKED MEMORABILIA

Night Ride Home Geffen promo CD in special packaging that includes title sheet, lyrics, and 4 self-portrait prints, 1991; *Inside Information* Geffen promo box set contains, cassette, photo, and biography, 1988

REFERENCES/BOOKS

Limited resources exist, but none do justice to the singer in my opinion.

Mitchell, Willie

Born: January 3, 1928

Willie Mitchell, the '60s Memphis soul and R&B bandleader, is best remembered for the R&B hits "Buster Browne" (#29, 1965), "Bad Eye" (#23, 1966), "Soul Serenade" (#10, 1968), and "Prayer Meetin'" (#23, 1968) and also for his trumpet solo on B.J. Thomas's hit "Raindrops Keep Falling on My Head." He went on to become vice president of Hi Records. Mitchell also discovered and produced the talented Al Green.

AUTOGRAPHS
A CD, LP, magazine cover, ad, photo, or card signed by the artist: $15

OFTEN OVERLOOKED MEMORABILIA
Artifacts and souvenirs from Willie Mitchell's Rhythm & Blues Club on Beale Street in Memphis

Moby

(Richard Hall)
Born: September 11, 1965

Nineties DJ gone king of techno, Moby is best known for his song "Go" (#10, U.K., 1991) and for his album *Everything Is Wrong* (1995).

AUTOGRAPHS
A CD, LP, magazine cover, ad, photo, or card signed by the artist: $5-$10

Moby Grape

Formed 1966

Skip Spence, Born: April 18, 1946, Peter Lewis, Born: July 14, 1945, Jerry Miller, Born: July 10, 1943, Bob Mosley, Born: December 4, 1942, and Don Stevenson, Born: October 15, 1942*

*Spence departed in 1968. Group later transformed into the Melvilles, followed by the Legendary Grape.

This late-60s Bay Area psychedelic folk-rock act is perhaps best remembered as one of the few local acts with a major record deal not to make it. The haphazard launch of its debut record, which included eight simultaneously released singles and a poster of Stevenson with his middle finger pointing upward, did much to convince many to simply ignore the band, which they did.

The group's second album, *Wow*, picked up where the first left off, including gimmicks such as a cut that had to be played at 78 rpm and a bonus LP, *Grape Jam*—most were confused of its significance. Moby Grape then went through a series of breakups and reunions, all with little significance. Spence, who had also played with Jefferson Airplane, was later committed to New York City's Bellevue Hospital for schizophrenia and later released to a residential-care home.

AUTOGRAPHS
A CD, LP, magazine cover, ad, photo, or card signed by the group: $15-$40

Modern English

Formed 1979

Robbie Grey, Gary McDowell, Stephen Walker, Mick Conroy, and Richard Brown*

*Walker and Brown left in 1984 and Aaron Davidson was added

Eighties British post-punk band Modern English is best remembered for two minor hits, "I Melt With You" (#78, 1983) and "Hands Across the Sea" (#91, 1984), before splitting up after the 1990 album *Pillow Lips*.

AUTOGRAPHS
A CD, LP, magazine cover, ad, photo, or card signed by the group: $10-$15

Molly Hatchet

Formed 1975

Dave Hlubek, Duane Roland, Steve Holland, Danny Joe Brown, Banner Thomas, and Bruce Cramp*

*Brown left in 1980 and Jimmy Farrar was added only to have the situation reverse itself in 1981. In 1982 both Thomas and Crump left, while Barry Borden and Riff West were added.

Late-70s Sunshine State rock band Molly Hatchet is best remembered for its extensive touring and beer drinkin' attitudes. These Southern rockers built a strong cult following that helped sell its debut album platinum and the follow-up double platinum. The group also garnered significant FM airplay and was a popular act on the college circuit for many years.

AUTOGRAPHS
A CD, LP, magazine cover, ad, photo, or card signed by the group: $15-$35

POSTERS/PRESS KITS
Promotional Posters: $7-$10
Press Kits: $10

USED CLOTHING/EQUIPMENT
Guitar Picks: $5

The Moments/Ray, Goodman and Brown

Formed mid-1960s

Best known lineup: Billy Brown, Al Goodman, and Johnny Morgan

Late-60s Garden State R&B vocal act, best remembered for songs such as "Not on the Outside" (#57, 1968), "Love on a Two-way Street" (#3, 1970), "Sexy Mama" (#17, 1974), and later as Ray, Goodman and Brown, for "Special Lady" (#5, 1980), The Moments were plagued by personnel changes and litigation, both of which contributed significantly to their inability to sustain momentum. Ray died of a stroke in 1992.

AUTOGRAPHS

A CD, LP, magazine cover, ad, photo, or card signed by the group: $12-$40*

*Lineup dependent

Money, Eddie

(Edward Mahoney)
Born: March 21, 1949

Former New York Police Academy student turned rocker, Eddie Money gave up his dream to be a cop in favor of a musical career. He then moved to Berkely and became a regular on the Bay Area circuit before he was signed by the legendary promoter Bill Graham.

Money is typically associated with the songs "Baby, Hold On" (#11, 1978), "Two Tickets to Paradise" (#22, 1978), "Take Me Home Tonight" (#4, 1986), which was a duet with Ronnie Spector, "Think I'm in Love" (#16, 1982), "I Wanna Go Back" (#14, 1987), "Walk On Water" (#9, 1988), and "Peace in Our Time" (#11, 1990)

AUTOGRAPHS

A CD, LP, magazine cover, ad, photo, or card signed by the artist: $15-$30

TOUR BOOKS/PROGRAMS/PASSES

Backstage Passes:
$8-$12 (cloth/paper), $15-$20 (laminated)

POSTERS/PRESS KITS

Promotional Posters: $9-$22
Press Kits: $15-$30

The Monkees

Formed 1965

David Jones, Born: December 30, 1945, Michael Nesmith, Born: December 30, 1942, Peter Tork, Born: February 13, 1944, and Mickey Dolenz, Born: March 8, 1945*

*Tork left in 1969 and the group disbanded. Group reformed in 1986 with Jones, Dolenz, and Tork.

The premier "Pre-fab(ricated) Four" pop group of the '60s and '70s, manufactured by television executives to combat the "British Invasion," wasn't taken seriously as either a music group, or a remedy for the Beatles, until some very talented songwriters were able to come to their recording assistance. Enter Neil Diamond, Tommy Boyce, Bobby Hart, and even their own Michael Nesmith, who all contributed some of the finest pop songs of the era including "I'm a Believer," "(I'm Not Your) Steppin' Stone," and "Pleasant Valley Sunday."

Jones, Nesmith, Dolenz, and Tork were signed in October 1965 after successfully auditioning for sessions advertised in industry trade publications. The goal was to build a show based around a Beatles-type group, using the film *A Hard Day's Night* as the key example. On January 17, 1966, NBC-TV bought *The Monkees* television series.

The television show began filming over the summer, while Don Kirshner took over the series and appointed Bobby Hart and Tommy Boyce as producers. Kirshner brought with him his staff of music writers which included Carole King, Gerry Goffin, Neil Diamond, Neil Sedeka, and many others. On September 1, 1966, the group began a ten-day promotional tour to launch the show, which premiered September 12, 1966, on NBC-TV.

The Monkees (#1, 1966) topped the U.S. LP chart for the first of thirteen weeks on November 12, 1966, while "Last Train to Clarksville" reached the pinnacle of the singles chart one week ahead of the album. "I'm a Believer" (#1, 1966) quickly followed, and the group began to make live performances. Its first was on December 3, 1966, to a sellout crowd (8,364) at the International Center Arena, Honolulu, Hawaii.

More of the Monkees (#1, 1967), with advance orders of 1.5 million, dislodged *The Monkees* at the top of the U.S. album chart. The group, with an all-star support cast, gained confidence in its musical ability and began to insist that it should be allowed to play on its own records. *Headquarters* (#1, 1967) was released in May and quickly became the band's third consecutive million seller. The group played on the album with a limited support crew—the members hoped for the time when they would need none. On July 8, 1967, the Monkees began a 29-date U.S. Tour, supported by (but only briefly) the Jimi Hendrix Experience. The second season of the Monkees began on September 11, 1967, while the band prepared to release *Pisces, Aquarius, Capricorn & Jones Ltd*. On March 25, 1968, the 58th, and final, episode of the television series was broadcast, while the band enjoyed watching its single "Valerie" (#3, 1968) become its sixth million seller.

An in-house Gold 45 Disc Award Ltd. Award for the Monkees' "Last Train to Clarksville," 1966. It is valued at $1,000. From the Doug Leftwitch collection.

The Birds, the Bees and the Monkees (#3, 1968) quickly followed the release of the fourth album, while the band revived the Coasters' "D.W. Washburn" (#19, 1968) and released it as a single. The group played its last performance as a quartet on October 8, 1968, in Japan at Festival Hall, Osaka. The movie *Head* premiered in New York on November 6, 1968. Expected to be a standard teen flick starring the Monkees, it instead revealed a bizarre fragmented film documenting the group's deception. Columbia Pictures was furious as critics attacked from all sides. Meanwhile, the movie flopped at the box office. The soundtrack album did manage to make it into the Top Fifty, recouping some loses, while collectors grabbed as much memorabilia from the film as they could get their hands on.

On December 30, 1968, Peter Tork quit the group by buying out his contract. The maneuver essentially wiped out Tork, whose conspicuous lifestyle had always come under fire. He went on to start the new group Release. The Monkees, now a trio, released *Instant Replay* (#32, 1969), however, it was becoming increasingly clear that the band was faltering. Amidst concerts being canceled due to poor ticket sales, *The Monkees Greatest Hits* (#89, 1969) was released.

On November 30, 1969, the group made its last live appearance for fifteen years, at the Oakland-Alameda County Coliseum, Oakland, California. The sparse crowd of 2,000 listened as the band members announced their new plans: Nesmith was going to a new band, while the other two opted to continue the Monkees. Nesmith moved on to a fairly successful solo career, while Jones and Dolenz appeared sporadically at festivals and events. In 1986 and 1987 the band enjoyed a revival of sorts, because its catalog was reissued on CD, MTV broadcasted the original television show episodes, and a new anthology was released (*That Was Then, This Is Now*), which contained three new songs, one of which charted to Number Twenty.

The Monkees compiled eleven Top Forty hits, sold millions of albums, had a hit television show, and delighted millions of fans world-wide. The group's memorabilia also sold well and was aggressively marketed—standing next to only the Beatles and

Kiss in popularity. The fact that many of the members are still active in music only draws greater attention to the group's older artifacts. To little surprise, and even lesser anticipation, all four members reunited in the middle of the 1990s.

AUTOGRAPHS

Group
A CD, LP, magazine cover, ad, photo, or card signed by the entire band: $150-$225*
*High-end reflects vintage signed memorabilia

Individual
David Jones: $25-$35
Michael Nesmith: $35-$55
Peter Tork: $20-$30
Mickey Dolenz: $25-$35

TOUR BOOKS/ PROGRAMS/PASSES

Tour Books:
1966: $45-$55
1967: $45-$55
Backstage Passes:
$8-$10 (cloth),
$10-$12 (laminated)*
*Post 1969

POSTERS/PRESS KITS
Promotional
Posters: $12-$30
(Post 1969)
Press Kits: $12-$15
(Post 1969)

USED CLOTHING/ EQUIPMENT
Guitar Picks:
Mike Nesmith: $10-$25

A scarce Monkees tour program (1966). (1966 Raypert Prods. Inc., trademark Screen Gems, Inc.)

OFTEN OVERLOOKED MEMORABILIA
September 9, 1965 issue of *Hollywood Reporter* - $10; September 10, 1965 issue of *Daily Variety* - $10; Early Davy Jones BBC television work, stage work, and U.S. television work; Nesmith material associated with singles released as Michael Blessing; Mickey Dolenz television work under the name Mickey Braddock; Peter Tork's work with Richie Furay in the Au GoGo Singers; copies of the U.K. fanzine *Monkees Monthly*; assorted paperback books - $5-$10; badges (Donruss, set of 44) - $200-$275; buttons - $5-$10; clothes tag - $30; coins (cereal premium, set of 12) - $100-$125; comics - $10 (Exception Dell #1 - $37); dolls (Hasbro), set of 4 - $125 (packaged); fan club kit (intact) - $175; finger puppets (set of 3 - no Peter) - $90; glasses - $45; game (Transogram) - $100; flip books (Topps, set of 16) - $140; guitars (Mattel): $150 (14"), $200 (20"); trading cards (Donruss, set): $75 (Set A), $100 (Set

"I'm a Monkees Fan" button

B), $70 (Set C); Halloween costumes (Bland Charnas Inc.) - $150-$175; hanger (cardboard) - $50; lunch box - $180, thermos (metal) - $50, thermos - $250; Monkeemobiles: $350-$450 (APC), $225 (Corgi, 6"), $100 (Corgi), $100 (Remco), $100 (Husky); model kit - $250; mug - $60; necklace (Raybert) - $45; oil paint set - $150; pajamas - $140; pen - $7; pencil - $5; pencil by number - $165; pencil sharpener - $7; playing cards - $60; punchout book - $100; jigsaw puzzle (Fairchild) - $35; record cut-outs (Post) - $2-$5; record carrying case - $100; plastic ring - $10; metal ring - $40; shirt - $150; sweater - $175; talking hand puppet - $150 (includes box); tambourine (Raybert) - $150; Three-ring binder - $100; View-Master 3-D - $50; stickers - $3-$5; Monkee related commercials Kodak (1980), Pizza Hut (1995) etc.; (That Was) Then... And Now, Arista promo pack, 1986, includes: shoulder bag, wool scarf, monkey mask, blow-up banana, rubber monkey head, a rosette, and a fact sheet

REFERENCES/BOOKS

Numerous resources exist. *The Monkees - A Manufactured Image: The Ultimate Guide to Monkee Memories and Memorabilia* by Edward Reilly, Maggie McManus, and William Chadwick is a MUST! Serious collectors will also want subscribe to Monkee Business Fanzine, Attention: Maggie McManus, 2770 S. Broad St., Trenton, NJ 08160, and join the Head of the Monkees Fan Club c/o Teresa Jones, 262 Baltimore Ave., Baltimore, MD 21222

Monro Threat: See Fugazi

Monroe, Bill

Born: September 13, 1911, Died: September 9, 1996

"The Father of Bluegrass," Bill Monroe is best remembered for such American classics as "Kentucky Waltz" (#3, C&W, 1946), "Footprints in the Snow" (#5, C&W, 1946), "Blue Moon of Kentucky" (1947), which Elvis Presley covered, and "Wicked Path of Sin" (#13, C&W, 1948). He formed the Kentuckians, and later the Blue Grass Boys in 1938, and joined the Grand Ole Opry in 1939, while also touring in the road show. His landmark group quickly became the launching pad for other legends such as Lester Flatt and Earl Scruggs—more than one hundred musicians claim time with Monroe. He was elected to the Country Music Hall of Fame in 1970 and has garnered numerous honors and awards since.

AUTOGRAPHS

A CD, LP, magazine cover, ad, photo, or card signed by the artist: $35-$100

Montrose

Formed 1974

Ronnie Montrose, Sammy Hagar, Born: October 13, 1947, Bill Church, and Denny Carmassi*

*Church left in 1974 and was replaced by Alan Fitzgerald. Hagar departed in 1975 and both Jim Alcivar and Bob James were added. Randy Jo Hobbs was added on bass in 1976. Group re-formed in 1987: Montrose, Johnny Edwards, James Kottack, and Glen Letsch.

Ronnie Montrose, who had contributed his guitar prowess to efforts by Van Morrison, Gary Wright, Dan Hartman, and Boz Scaggs, landed himself a job with the Edgar Winter Group in 1972. The following year, after turning down an offer as lead guitarist with Mott the Hoople, he decided to form his own band.

If ever there was a guitarist ahead of his time, it was Ronnie Montrose. His debut album *Montrose*, and although it yielded no singles, it went platinum at a time when such a feat was unheard of. Ironically, if the album had been put out five years later, it probably would have received a greater welcome and Montrose praised in the same breath as Eddie Van Halen and maybe even Jimmy Page. Despite the lack of greater accolades, Montrose persisted with a band that contained Denny Carmassi on drums, Bill Church on bass, and Sammy Hagar on vocals. Many people had actually been caught off guard by the band's initial release, because Montrose's blazing lead guitar work was in stark contrast to the work he had done in earlier sessions with various musicians.

Paper Money followed in 1974 with the only change in personnel being Alan Fitzgerald, who replaced Church on bass. Montrose's writing remained solid with "I Got the Fire," in which complimented by Hagar's vocals, was cutting edge at the time and provided listeners with great interplay between both rising talents. The thriving Bay Area scene in San Francisco had manicured Montrose well and the strong production provided by Ted Templeman was a bonus.

The magic dissipated quickly when Hagar (later with Van Halen) departed to pursue a solo career following *Paper Money*. Church, Fitzgerald, and Carmassi (Heart, Coverdale/Page, Ted Nugent) eventually landed with Hagar (1978), while Montrose was caught trying to pick up the pieces. Montrose answered with a new band, Gamma, which released three albums worth of an identity crisis, before finally breaking up. Gamma, however, was the first sign that Montrose was going to try to branch the boundaries of both jazz and rock—a task that he would never successfully accomplish.

In 1987 he failed at an attempt to resurrect Montrose (with himself as the only original member). He later reverted to solo work, releasing little known ef-

forts that took him into the next decade. Whether anything else ever comes of Montrose or not, one thing is certain, for two albums this band had a magic that transcended anything else of its time, while spotlighting some extraordinary musical talent.

AUTOGRAPHS

Group
A CD, LP, magazine cover, ad, photo, or card signed by the entire band: $60-$75*

*High-end reflects vintage signed memorabilia, first album signed by all four original members

Individual
Ronnie Montrose: $30

The signature of Ronnie Montrose

TOUR BOOKS/PROGRAMS/PASSES

Backstage Passes:
$10 (cloth), $15 (laminated) - if you can find any!

USED CLOTHING/EQUIPMENT

Guitar Picks: $15-$25

OFTEN OVERLOOKED MEMORABILIA

Ronnie Montrose's earlier work with Van Morrison, Beaver and Krause, the Beau Brummels, Gary Wright, Dan Hartman, and Kathi McDonald; Paper Money money clip- $35.

The Moody Blues

Formed 1964

Denny Laine, (Brian Hines) Born: October 29, 1944, Mike Pinder, Born: December 27, 1941, Ray Thomas, Born: December 29, 1941, Clint Warwick(Eccles), Born: June 25, 1939, and Graeme Edge, Born: March 30, 1941*

*Laine and Warwick left and were replaced by Justin (David) Hayward, Born: October 14, 1946 and John Lodge, Born: July 20, 1945. Pinder left in 1978 and was replaced by Patrick Moraz, Born: June 24, 1948. Moraz left in 1992.

Initially formed as blues band in the early '60s, at a time when both Denny Laine and Mike Pinder were writing a majority of the group's work, the band backed many American blues musicians during their U.K. tours. Although the group finally scored a hit with "Go Now" (#10, 1965), subsequent releases were less successful, and both Laine and Warwick departed. Both Hayward and Lodge were then recruited and, following the purchase of a Mellotron, the group entered the studio. Instead of recording a rock adaptation of Dvorak's Symphony No. 9, it emerged with the album *Days of Future Passed*, which included the extracted hit single "Tuesday Afternoon" (#24, 1968).

From this point onward the band scored hits with "Nights in White Satin" (#2, 1972), "Question" (#21, 1970), "The Story in Your Eyes" (#23, 1971), "Isn't Life Strange?" (#29, 1972), "I'm Just a Singer (In a Rock and Roll Band)" (#12, 1973), while numerous other compositions became FM staples, including "Ride My See Saw." Following *Seventh Sojourn* the band took some time off to pursue individual and collaborative projects.

Mike Pinder departed following the release of the album *Octave* (1978) and Patrick Moraz was added. The group then continued with its series of hits which included "Gemini Dream," "The Voice," and "Sitting at the Wheel," and later with "Your Wildest Dreams" (#9, 1986) and "I Know You're Out There Somewhere" (#30, 1988). Moraz then departed in 1992, the year the band celebrated the silver anniversary of *Days of Future Passed* with a tour featuring a full orchestra.

AUTOGRAPHS

Group
A CD, LP, magazine cover, ad, photo, or card signed by the entire band:
$40-$125*

*High-end reflects vintage signed memorabilia, original lineup

An autographed photo of the Moody Blues

Individual

Denny Laine: $20-$30
Mike Pinder: $10-$20
Ray Thomas: $10
Clint Warwick: $5-$10
Graeme Edge: $15-$20
Justin Hayward: $15-$25
John Lodge: $15-$25
Patrick Moraz: $10-$15

TOUR BOOKS/ PROGRAMS/ PASSES

Tour Books:

Murray the K's Christmas Show, 1965: $150-$200
MCMXC Tour: $10
Days of Future Past: $10-$12
Sur La Mer: $10

John Lodge's autograph (obtained in-person). Courtesy Patsy Morrison.

A Night at Red Rocks Tour: $20-$22
Time Traveler: $15-$17
U.K. tour March 1997: $20
U.S. tour 1997: $15

Backstage Passes:

$8-$12 (cloth),
$12-$20 (laminated)*
*1980-1970 add $5-$10
Before 1970 (scarce) add an additional $10, plus above

POSTERS/PRESS KITS

Promotional Posters:

1972-Present: $12-$50

Press Kits:

1972-Present: $25-$60,
Example: Night at Red Rocks (w/deluxe bio folder) - $25

Cloth 1987 Moody Blues pass (Printed by OTTO)

Days of Future Passed tour book. Photo courtesy Patsy Morrison. (Designed by Sunset Graphics/Richard Nelson)

Sur La Mer tour book. Photo courtesy Patsy Morrison. (Produced by CMC, cover painting © Adagp, Paris/Dacs, London)

Poster for a free Moody Blues concert in Austin, TX, 1988. Photo courtesy Patsy Morrison.

Red Rocks tour book. Photo courtesy Patsy Morrison. (Printed by Hill Shorter Ltd.)

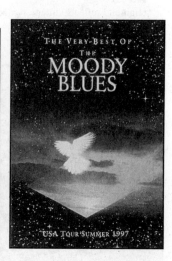

1997 USA Summer tour book. Photo courtesy Patsy Morrison. (Designed by Connexion. Printed by Hill Shorter Ltd.)

USED CLOTHING/EQUIPMENT

Guitar Picks:

Denny Laine: $25-$40   Clint Warwick: $20
Justin Hayward: $25-$35   John Lodge: $20-$30

Drum Sticks:

Graeme Edge: $25-$30

*Guitar picks from
John Lodge and
Justin Hayward*

OFTEN OVERLOOKED MEMORABILIA
Blue World/Going Nowhere, 1983, promotional T-shirt

REFERENCES/BOOKS
Limited resources exist. Serious collectors should opt for
the fanzine *Higher & Higher: The Moody Blues Magazine*,
P.O. Box 829, Geneva, FL 32732, or join The Moody Blues
Fan Club, 53055 High Street, Cobham Surrey KT11 3DP
England

Morissette, Alanis

Born: June 1, 1974

Morissette, an agitated feminist with an attitude,
used her voice and disconcerting lyrics to rip another
orifice in an industry where such vacuums have become commonplace. Hats off to Maverick Records,
whose CEO happens to be Madonna, for having the
guts to ingest a *Jagged Little Pill* (#1, 1996) and spit
out six 1995 Grammy nominations and four awards.

*Alanis Morissette. Photo by Michelle Lavrita. Courtesy Maverick Re-
cording Company*

Morissette, born in Canada, spent much of her early childhood in West Germany before returning home
at the age of six. She was just ten years old she landed
a starring role on the Nickelodeon cable TV show *You
Can't Do That on Television*. She used her finances
to eventually fund a recording. Under the name of
Lamor Records, her own label, she pressed copies
(2,000) of a song called "Fate Stay With Me." During
this period of time she also had the good fortune of
hooking up with producer Stephan Klovan who was
working out of Ottawa. It was Klovan who used his
marketing savvy to increase the artist's exposure
whenever and wherever possible.

Klovan underwrote the cost of a videotape for
Morissette's song "Walk Away" that helped ice a
record deal with MCA. At that time Alanis had been
singing with a cover band named the New York Fries.
Alanis (MCAAD - 10253, 10 songs), the self-titled debut of the fourteen year old, was released in April
1991 and went double platinum. It featured her first
single, appropriately named, "Too Hot," a step forward for the performer who landed a Juno Award for
"Most Promising Female Vocalist."

Now Is the Time (MCAD-10731, 10 songs) followed
with far less success and spun the artist into a state
of confusion. An unsuccessful attempt was made during this period to launch both of Morissette's album
in the U.S. (1993). Time passed quickly as the artist
moved first to Toronto, then on to Los Angeles where
she finally hooked up with Glen Ballard in February
1994. MCA helped arrange the now legendary encounter. Ballard, who has worked with some of the
industry's finest, is perhaps best known as the cow-
riter of Michael Jackson's "Man in the Mirror."

Jagged Little Pill (Maverick Records 9 45901-2)
was the result, a product of both Ballard and Morissette. Her band, formerly Mother Tongue, consisted
of Jesse Tobias, Nick Lashley, Chris Chaney, and
Taylor Hawkins, none of whom played on the studio
album. Intensive touring and good media exposure
helped place the release at Number One, a position
it even reverted to following the 1995 Grammy
Awards show.

With success comes detractors—it seems like it's
part of the recipe—and with Alanis they have even
established an Internet address for those people
against her music. Alanis Morissette collectors
would like to politely suggest the following return net
address at www. shoveit.com—this girl is here to
stay! Collect Now!

You can't collect Alanis artifacts without making
a pilgrimage to Canada to buy her first two releases
and all their associated relics.

AUTOGRAPHS
It has taken very little time for her to establish an elusive
attitude toward autograph requests. Considered now to be a
tough signature.
A CD, LP, magazine cover, ad, photo, or card signed by the
artist: $50-$100

TOUR BOOKS/PROGRAMS/PASSES

Backstage Passes:
$4-$8 (cloth), $8-$12 (laminated) - not a lot around yet!

POSTERS/PRESS KITS

Promotional Posters: $10-$20
Press Kits: $25

OFTEN OVERLOOKED MEMORABILIA

Videotapes of her singing the Canadian National Anthem at major sporting events, such as the opening ceremonies of the 1988 World Figure Skating Championships, also of her appearance on *Star Search* singing "One Bad Apple"; magazines, such as *Grammy Magazine* (Spring 1996), *Rolling Stone* (November 2, 1995), *Details* (October 1995), and *Swing* (May 1996) can still be had for just a few bucks; 3-D counter display of Alanis with her hand to her chin, wearing those great vinyl pants, 16' high - $25; Jagged Little Pill counter display - $25; Jagged Little Pill promo counter display - $15

REFERENCES/BOOKS

The Story of Alanis Morissette, by Kalen Rogers (Omnibus Press, 1996) $12

Morrison, Van

Born: August 31, 1945

This early-60s temperamental Irish pop icon, who depending upon which critic you talk to, or how you interpret his work, is either a moody, aloof, introverted '60s fossil with no stage presence living off old royalty checks, or the greatest living artist next to Bob Dylan. My guess is that a majority would choose the latter.

Morrison is commonly associated with the songs "Gloria," "Mystic Eyes," "Brown Eyed Girl," "Moondance," "Come Running," "Domino," "Blue Monday," "Wild Night," "Jackie Wilson Said," "Listen to the Lion," and "Whenever God Shines His Light on Me," a duet with Cliff Richard, and also with the classic albums *Astral Weeks* and *Moondance*—frankly he has produced so many strong releases during his career, though, that it is often difficult to choose and somewhat dependent upon your mood.

As his career has been dissected in virtually every manner conceivable, by thousands of critics using the same old garbage clichés and comparisons, I'll spare you from my rhetoric.

AUTOGRAPHS

A CD, LP, magazine cover, ad, photo, or card signed by the artist: $25-$50

OFTEN OVERLOOKED MEMORABILIA

Movie memorabilia from *The Last Waltz* and *Avalon Sunset*; Polydor promo box set that includes: CD, cassette, biography, photo, two slides, and a pen, 1989; "The Healing Game" plastic bottle with vitamin C tablets - $15

REFERENCES/BOOKS

Limited resources exist, but none do justice to the singer in my opinion, and there are no dedicated collector books. Wavelength: The Van Morrison Newsletter, P.O. Box 80, Winsford Cheshire CW7 4ES England, is a MUST for serious collectors ($32 fee)!

Morrissey: See The Smiths

The Motels

Formed 1972

Original lineup: Martha Davis, Dean Chamberlain, and Richard D'Andrea*

*Numerous personnel changes

Late-70s L.A. first generation punk band The Motels is best known for its longevity, numerous personnel changes, and for not landing a hit single until a decade after its formation. The band is associated with the songs "Only the Lonely" (#9,1982), "Suddenly Last Summer" (#9, 1983), and "Shame" (#21, 1985). The group later disbanded following the announcement that Davis was suffering from cancer.

AUTOGRAPHS

A CD, LP, magazine cover, ad, photo, or card signed by the group: $15-$25*
*Lineup dependent

Mother Love Bone: See Pearl Jam

Mothers of Invention: See Frank Zappa

Mötley Crüe

Formed 1981

Tommy Lee (Bass), Born: October 3, 1962, Mick Mars (Bob Deal), Born: April 3, 1956, Vince Neil (Wharton), Born: 1961, and Nikki Sixx (Frank Ferranno), Born: December 11, 1958*

*Neil departed in 1992 and was replaced by John Corabi, Born: April 26, 1959. Neil returned in 1997 and Corabi was out!

This early-80s L.A. hedonistic saloon, or is it salon, band, is best known for the albums *Dr. Feelgood* (#1, 1989), *Girls, Girls, Girls* (#2, 1987), and *Decade of Decadence—'81-'91*. Mötley Crüe scored first on the singles chart with an updated version of Brownsville Station's "Smokin' in the Boys Room" (#16,1985), followed by the power ballad "Home Sweet Home" (#89,

1985). It was clear, however, that the Crüe was an album band, leveraged by extensive touring, energetic live shows, and popular promotional videos.

Despite their "hair act" look, they were "bad boys" through and through, living the rock and roll lifestyle of sex, drugs, and music to the max. From celebrity marriages, to substance abuse problems and even wrongful termination lawsuits, the Crüe pushed life to the edge, and sometimes even fell over!

AUTOGRAPHS
A CD, LP, magazine cover, ad, photo, or card signed by the group: $45-$100*
*Lineup dependent

TOUR BOOKS/PROGRAMS/PASSES
Tour Books:
Shout 1984 World Tour: $25
Japan tour, 1984: $30
Japan tour, 1986: $35
Dr. Feelgood World Tour: $12
Backstage Passes: $8-$10 (cloth), $10-$15 (laminated)

POSTERS/PRESS KITS
Promotional Posters: $10-$25
Press Kits: $15-$30

USED CLOTHING/EQUIPMENT
Guitar Picks:
Mick Mars: $20-$25
Vince Neil: $30-$35
Nikki Sixx: $20-$35
Drum Sticks:
Tommy Lee: $15-$20

OFTEN OVERLOOKED MEMORABILIA
Girls, Girls, Girls cardboard banner - $35; promotional pin (guitar w/logo) - $8; lapel pin - $10; necklace - $12

REFERENCES/BOOKS
Limited resources exist, but none do justice to the band in my opinion.

Motörhead

Formed 1975
Lemmy (Ian) Kilmister, Born: December 24, 1945, Eddie Clark, and Phil "Philthy Animal" Taylor, Born: September 21, 1954*

*Numerous personnel changes. Additional members have included: Brian Robertson, Phil Campbell, "Wurzel," Pete Gill, and Mikkey Dee

Late-70s British ear crushing precursors to the thrash and speed-metal genres, formed by bassist and vocalist Lemmy Kilmister (formerly of Hawkwind), Motörhead has developed a strong U.S. cult following despite its inability to make a dent on the charts.

AUTOGRAPHS
A CD, LP, magazine cover, ad, photo, or card signed by the group: $25-$65

TOUR BOOKS/PROGRAMS/PASSES
Tour Books:
1982 Japan Tour: $35
Backstage Passes:
$8-$10 (cloth/paper), $12 (laminated)

POSTERS/PRESS KITS
Promotional Posters: $10
Press Kits: $10-$20

USED CLOTHING/EQUIPMENT
Guitar Picks: $20-$25

OFTEN OVERLOOKED MEMORABILIA
Orgasmatron, 1986, vinyl box set that includes a T-shirt and other inserts; The Complete Motörhead Kit, Canada, 1982, vinyl with book, poster, and patch

REFERENCES/BOOKS
A few resources exist, but *The Illustrated Collector's Guide to Motorhead* by Alan Burridge and Mick Stevenson is a starting point!

The Motors

Formed 1977
Nick Garvey, Andy McMasters, Bram Tchaikovsky (Peter Bramall), and Ricky Slaughter

Late-70s British pub rockers the Motors are typically associated with the songs "Dancing the Night Away," "Airport," and "Love and Loneliness." The group had little impact in the States.

AUTOGRAPHS
A CD, LP, magazine cover, ad, photo, or card signed by the group: $15

Mott the Hoople

Formed 1968
Stan Tippens, Mick Ralphs, Born: May 31, 1944, Overend Pete Watts, Dale Griffin, and Verden Allen*

*Tippens left in 1969 and was replaced by Ian Hunter, Born: June 3, 1946. Allen and Ralphs left in 1973 and were replaced by Morgan Fischer and Ariel Bender. Bender left in 1974 and was replaced by Mick Ronson (1946-1993). Both Hunter and Ronson left in 1974. The name of the band was changed to Mott and included Ray Major and Nigel Benjamin.

This late-60s British glam-rock act, best remembered for the songs "All the Young Dudes," "Honaloochie Boogie," and "All the Way from Memphis," nearly split up after a few poorly received albums when David Bowie stepped in and helped package the group—he even offered it what would be its breakthrough single, "All the Young Dudes."

The group's next album, *Mott*, was its finest and is considered by some as a key release for the era. But

despite the album's success, the band began to fall apart: first Allen left, followed by Ralphs, who was upset over Allen's departure, and both upset over the group's lack of interest in their songs or capability to record them. Ralphs went on to join Bad Company, while the band filled the gap with Ariel Bender (Luther Grosvenor), who stayed only briefly (he was replaced by Mick Ronson in 1974). The band later fell apart, as both Hunter and Ronson split together.

AUTOGRAPHS
A CD, LP, magazine cover, ad, photo, or card signed by the group: $15-$40*
*Lineup dependent

TOUR BOOKS/PROGRAMS/PASSES
Tour Book:
Mott Tour, 1974: $50-$65

OFTEN OVERLOOKED MEMORABILIA
Pair of dice - $30; associated artifacts from other musicians' covers of the group's work.

Mould, Bob: See Hüsker Dü

Mountain

Formed 1969

Felix Pappalardi (1939-1983), Lesile West (Weinstein), Born: October 22, 1945, and N.D. Smart*

*Smart left in 1970 and Corky Laing and Steve Knight were added. Group disbanded in 1972, then re-formed in 1974, only to disband again. The band re-formed in 1985.

Authoritative New York power-triumvirate Mountain is best remembered for the song "Mississippi Queen" (#17, 1970) and its fourth live performance—Woodstock.

A guitar pick from Mountain's Leslie West valued at $15

AUTOGRAPHS
A CD, LP, magazine cover, ad, photo, or card signed by the group: $25-$50*
*Original lineup

TOUR BOOKS/ PROGRAMS/PASSES
Tour Book:
1973 Japan tour, scarce: $100

OFTEN OVERLOOKED MEMORABILIA
Woodstock memorabilia, tickets, posters, etc.

The Move/Roy Wood

Formed 1966

Roy (Ulysses) Wood, Born: November 8, 1946, Bev Bevan, Born: November 25, 1944, Carl Wayne, Born: August 18, 1944, Trevor Burton, Born: March 9, 1944, and Chris Kefford, Born: December 10, 1946*

*Kefford left in 1968. Burton left in 1969 and Rick Price was added. Wayne left in 1970 and Jeff Lynne, Born: December 30, 1947, was added. Price left in 1971. The group disbanded in 1972 and became the Electric Light Orchestra (ELO).

Late-60s versatile British pop act the Move is best remembered for the songs "Night of Fear," "Flowers in the Rain," "Blackberry Way," "Hello Susie" (later recorded by Amen Corner), and "Brontosaurus." The group later transformed into the Electric Light Orchestra. While the band scored just over a handful of U.K. hits, it was hardly noticed in the U.S. until ELO broke through. During the band's early years, Wood was the primary focus and principle songwriter. He combined numerous psychedelic elements with classical music to produce his compositions, many of which were in stark contrast to the group's zany stage act.

Wood later became the first fallout member of ELO; he preferred instead to move on to a more nostalgic '50s sound.

AUTOGRAPHS
Group
A CD, LP, magazine cover, ad, photo, or card signed by the group: $25-$45*
*Lineup dependent

Mudhoney

Formed 1988

Mark Arm, Born: February 21, 1962, Dan Peters, Born: August 18, 1967, Steve Turner, Born: March 28, 1965, and Matt Lukin, Born: August 16, 1964

Mudhoney is yet another relic from the early-90s Seattle "grunge" scene. Arm and Turner left Green River, a key band of the era that also spawned Mother Love Bone and Pearl Jam, to join forces with leftovers Matt Lukin and Dan Peters. Band nepotism was prevalent during this era, as any formula was better than nothing at all, sometimes.

Heavy distorted guitars and anti-everything attitudes were characteristic of the "grunge sound" which was fueled by remnants of dysfunctional single-parent households, who were simply pissed at what life had dealt them. Until Nirvana came along, Mudhoney moved more vinyl for underworld indie gods Sub Pop than any other group. The group was extremely popular in England, where Mudhoney toured with Sonic Youth in 1989. Following its debut

EP *Superfuzz Bugmuff*, the band went on to release *Mudhoney* (1989), *Boiled Beef & Rotting Teeth* (1990), and *Every Good Boy Deserves Fudge* (1991). Financial problems at Sub Pop drove Mudhoney to a major label, which to its members was about as entertaining as having your nose hairs removed with a claw hammer.

Piece of Cake, the group's debut on Reprise, was like listening to a hung-over subcontractor removing your dishwasher before he's had his first Bloody Mary.

AUTOGRAPHS

A CD, LP, magazine cover, ad, photo, or card signed by the band: $35-$55

POSTERS/PRESS KITS

Promotional Posters: $15-$30
Press Kits: $20

USED CLOTHING/EQUIPMENT

Guitar Picks:
Mark Arm: $10-$20
Steve Turner: $10-$15
Matt Lukin: $15
Drum Sticks:
Dan Peters: $10-$15

OFTEN OVERLOOKED MEMORABILIA

A videotape of the Russ Meyer film the band took its name from - $40; authentic handbills - $10.

Murphy, Michael Martin

Born: March 14, 1945

Murphy is a cosmic country pioneer and survivor of the '70s. A native Texan, he was raised on a staple diet of Hank Williams, Bob Willis, and Woody Guthrie. He played pop while studying writing at UCLA in an outfit called the Lewis and Clarke Expedition. He was also a staff screenwriter at Screen Gems, where he penned "What Am I Doing Hangin' Round" for the Monkees. A champion of Indians' rights, he penned the now classic protest song "Geronimo's Cadillac," which was also the name of his debut record on A&M.

"Wildfire" (#3, 1975), "Carolina in the Pines" (#21, 1975), and "Renegade" (#39, 1976) found him refining his sound, which became more distinctive and showcased his songwriting ability. The next decade saw Murphy establish himself as a country and western superstar, blasting out hits such as "What's Forever For?" (#1, 1982), "Still Taking Chances," (#3, 1982), "Love Affairs" (#11, 1983), "Don't Count the Rainy Days" (#9, 1983), "Will It Be Love by Morning" (#7, 1984), "What She Wants" (#8, 1984), "A Face in the Crowd" (#4, 1987) (a duet with Holly Dunn), "A Long Line of Love" (#1, 1987), "I'm Gonna Miss You Girl" (#3, 1987), "Talkin to the Wrong Man" (#4, 1988) (a duet with his son), and "From the Word Go" (#3, 1988)—just to name a few!

AUTOGRAPHS

A CD, LP, magazine cover, ad, photo, or card signed by the artist: $10-$30

POSTERS/PRESS KITS

Promotional Posters: $10-$25
Press Kits: $15

USED CLOTHING/EQUIPMENT

Guitar Picks: $20-$30

OFTEN OVERLOOKED MEMORABILIA

Movie memorabilia from *Urban Cowboy* (1980), *Take This Job and Shove It*, *Hard Country*, and *Pink Cadillac*; videotapes of his numerous television appearances.

Murray, Anne

(Morna Anne Murray)
Born: June 20, 1945

Murray was the first Canadian vocalist to earn a gold record in the United States. Murray, who taught physical education on Prince Edward Island, also sang in small clubs, where she honed her skills. She debuted in America, following a deal with Canadian label Arc, with the album *Snowbird* and single (#8). The record pushed her into the spotlight and she soon found herself appearing regularly on the Glen Campbell variety television show, which also led to a joint recorded and tour project with the Rhinestone Cowboy in 1971.

"Danny's Song," a cover of the Loggin's classic, brought her back into the Top Ten in the spring of 1973. "You Won't See Me" (#8, 1974), "Love Song" (#12, 1975), and "I Just Fall in Love Again" (#12, 1979) soon followed. She then took some time off to raise her family, before bouncing back with *Let's Keep It That Way*, which included the hit extracts "You Needed Me" (#1, 1978) and "Walk Right Back," a Top Five country hit. Her next albums also went platinum, but her streak of U.S. hit pop singles ended. She then turned her full attention to country music with songs like "A Little Good News" (#1, C&W, 1983), which garnered many awards including a Grammy.

"Nobody Loves Me Like You Do" (#1, C&W, 1985), a duet with Dave Loggins, also was a chart topper and winner of numerous awards. Success in her newly found field continued as she blasted off a series of C&W hits including "Just Another Woman in Love" (#1, 1984), Time Don't Run Out On Me" (#2, 1985), "I Don't Think I'm Ready for You" (#7, 1985), "Now and Forever (You and Me)" (31, 1986), "Feed This Fire" (#5, 1990), a duet with Kenny Rogers, and "If I Ever Fall in Love Again" (#28, 1989). She was named Country Female Vocalist of the year from 1979 to 1986 in Canada and continues to enjoy an extremely successful career.

AUTOGRAPHS

Anne Murray has always been obliging to autograph requests in-person or through the mail!
A CD, LP, magazine cover, ad, photo, or card signed by the artist: $7-$18

TOUR BOOKS/PROGRAMS/PASSES

Backstage Passes:
$5-$7 (cloth), $7-$12 (laminated)

POSTERS/PRESS KITS

Promotional Posters: $10-$20
Press Kits: $15-$20

OFTEN OVERLOOKED MEMORABILIA

Videotapes of her numerous television appearances, especially on Glen Campbell's show

---

Nash, Graham: See Crosby, Stills, Nash and Young

Nash, Johnny

Born: August 19, 1940

Recording since 1957, Texan Johnny Nash was pivotal in spicing up American pop music with a little Jamaican hot sauce through reggae-flavored songs such as "I Can See Clearly Now" (#1, 1972) and "Stir It Up" (#12, 1973).

AUTOGRAPHS

A CD, LP, magazine cover, ad, photo, or card signed by the artist: $8-$12

POSTERS/PRESS KITS

Promotional Posters: $6-$10
Press Kits: $8

OFTEN OVERLOOKED MEMORABILIA

Videotapes from his appearances on television's *Arthur Godfrey Show* (1956-1963); associated memorabilia from his earlier hits such as "A Very Special Love" (#23, 1958) and covers of his songs performed by other artist including Joey Dee's 1962 hit with "What Kind of Love Is This"; movie memorabilia from *Take a Giant Step*, *Love Is Not a Game*, and *Key Witness*.

Naughty by Nature

Formed 1986

Treach (Anthony Criss), Vinnie (Vincent Brown), and Kay Gee (Kier Gist)

Garden State rap triad which hit the charts with one of the most popular cheating anthems of the '90s in "O.P.P.," which was a mix of urban rap laid down atop of samplings from the Jackson 5's "ABC." The group's debut *Naughty by Nature* (#16, 1991) also included extract "Ghetto Bastard," later filtered on the FM waves as "Everything's Gonna Be Alright." The band followed up with *19NaughtyIII* (#3, 1993), with hit extract "Hip Hop Hooray" (#8, 1993), and then *Poverty's Paradise* (#3, 1995).

AUTOGRAPHS

A CD, LP, magazine cover, ad, photo, or card signed by the group: $15-$20

TOUR BOOKS/PROGRAMS/PASSES

Backstage Passes: $5-$7 (cloth), $7-$10 (laminated)

POSTERS/PRESS KITS

Promotional Posters: $10-$12
Press Kits: $15

OFTEN OVERLOOKED MEMORABILIA

Movie memorabilia from *Juice* and *Who's the Man?*

Nazareth

Formed 1968

Dan McCafferty, Manny Charlton, Darrel Sweet, and Pete Agnew*

*Zal Cleminson was added in 1978, and departed in 1980. Billy Rankin and John Locke were added in 1981. Locke left in 1982. Rankin left in 1983 but returned in 1990 when Charlton departed.

These Scottish rockers managed to combine the distinguished vocal style of McCafferty with a heavy guitar sound to successfully cover a diverse range of music and score some U.K. singles and one successful U.S. hit, "Love Hurts" (#8, 1976). Despite personnel changes, the group's sound remained relatively full and its following fairly consistent for decades.

AUTOGRAPHS

A CD, LP, magazine cover, ad, photo, or card signed by the group: $20-$35

TOUR BOOKS/PROGRAMS/PASSES

Tour Books:
No Mean City poster/program: $30
Backstage Passes: $5-$7 (cloth), $7-$10 (laminated)

POSTERS/PRESS KITS

Promotional Posters: $10-$15
Press Kits: $10

USED CLOTHING/EQUIPMENT

Guitar Picks: $10

OFTEN OVERLOOKED MEMORABILIA

Play the Game display mobile - $50; No Mean Entry fold-up poster - $20.

The Naz

Formed 1967

Todd Rundgren, Born: June 22, 1948, Stewkey (Robert Antoni), Thom Mooney, and Carson Van Osten

Best known as Todd Rundgren's first recording group, The Naz produced three albums worth of material, which was heavily influenced by the Beatles and early Who, which garnered good press and even appearances in teen magazines, but no hit singles. Conflicts, mainly between Rungren and Mooney, essentially put an end to the band, although versions lasted into the mid-70s. Mooney later played with other bands including Paris with Bob Welch, while Van Osten became an animator, and Stewkey went on to bands that would later be acknowledged as early branches of Cheap Trick. As for Rundgren, see his entry.

AUTOGRAPHS

A CD, LP, magazine cover, ad, photo, or card signed by the group: $20-$30

Neil, Vince: See Mötley Crüe

Nektar

Formed 1968

Derek Moore, Roy Albrighton, Alan Freeman, Ron Howden, and Mick Brockett

These British musicians migrated to Germany to form the band Nektar, in the melodic art rock vein. The band's U.S. releases came during the mid-70s, a period that found a cult interest in this style of band in America. Both *Remember the Future* (1974) and *Down to Earth* (1975) sold into the Top Forty, however, steady sales decline eventually led to the group's break up.

AUTOGRAPHS

An LP, magazine cover, ad, photo, or card signed by the band: $15-$20

OFTEN OVERLOOKED MEMORABILIA

Bin Divider: $25

Nelson

Formed 1988

Matthew Nelson and Gunnar Nelson, both Born: September 20, 1967, Brett Garsed, Joey Cathcart, Paul Mirkovich, and Bobby Rock

Matthew and Gunnar Nelson, leaders of the band Nelson, are identical twin sons of the late rock star Rick Nelson in a family that spans four generations of entertainment success. In 1988 the group landed a record deal with DGC and released *After the Rain* (#17, 1988), a successful debut that was driven by hit extracts "(Can't Live Without Your) Love and Affection" (#1, 1990), "After the Rain" (#6, 1990), "More Than Ever" (#14, 1991), and "Only Time Will Tell" (#28, 1991).

AUTOGRAPHS

A CD, LP, magazine cover, ad, photo, or card signed by the group: $10-$15

TOUR BOOKS/ PROGRAMS/PASSES
Backstage Passes: $5 (cloth), $7 (laminated)

POSTERS/PRESS KITS
Promotional Posters: $10
Press Kits: $15

USED CLOTHING/ EQUIPMENT
Guitar Picks: $5

OFTEN OVERLOOKED MEMORABILIA

A Nelson guitar pick

Videotapes from the television appearances, especially *Saturday Night Live* (1986); school folder - $3; jigsaw puzzle, Milton Bradley (100 piece) - $5; bubble gum related (pack, tin box, etc.) - $5.

Nelson, Rick

(Eric Nelson)
Born: May 8, 1940, Died: December 31, 1985

Rick Nelson was an American teen idol long before his first album—he appeared in the popular television show *The Adventures of Ozzie and Harriet*. He was the son of a famous band leader, and he and his older brother David began playing themselves on their parents popular radio comedy series before it went to television. Ricky quickly became the program's most popular character and even gave birth to the popular fad phrase "I don't mess around boy." He began singing on the show in 1957, to a growing audience which quickly accepted the singer into their hearts.

"I'm Walkin'" (#4) with its hit flipside "A Teenager's Romance" (#2) was his debut record. Aided by a television performance of the song it quickly sold a million copies. This was the first in a series of numerous hits, many double-sided, for the artist including "Be-Bop Baby" (#3, 1957), "Stood Up" (#2, 1958)/ "Waitin' in School" (#18, 1958), "Believe What You Say" (#4, 1958) "My Bucket's Got a Whole in It" (#12,

1958), "Lonesome Town" (#7, 1958)/"I Got a Feeling" (#10, 1958), "It's Late" (#9, 1959)/"Never Be Anyone Else But You" (#6, 1959), "Just a Little Too Much" (#9, 1959), "Poor Little Fool" (#1, 1958), "Sweeter Than You" (#9, 1959), and "Travelin' Man" (#1, 1961)/ "Hello Mary Lou" (#9, 1961).

"Young World" (1962), "Teenage Idol" (1962), "It's Up to You" (1962), and "For You" (1964) became his last Top Ten hits for a while, as he then concentrated on his marriage and raising a family. His twin sons Matthew and Gunnar later found a home in the rock world. Ricky continued his acting, appearing in some films, and recording. Hanging out at L.A.'s Troubadour, he soon hooked on to what would later be known as country rock and formed the Stone Canyon Band, which would land the hit "She Belongs to Me" (#33, 1969). He earned critical acclaim for his double live album *Rick Nelson in Concert* (1970), which finally laid to rest that he was more than a packaged teen dream.

"Garden Party" (#6, 1972), his first hit in over a decade, also became a hallmark for the artist. When his follow-up albums failed to have any significant impact, he lost his contract with MCA. He then toured extensively during the late '70s and early '80s and even landed on the *Interviews from "The Class of '55" Recording Session*, which won a Grammy in 1986 for Best Spoken Word or Nonmusical Recording—ironically his only one!

In 1985 he formed a new band and seemed revitalized, recording *Memphis Sessions* (released posthumously). En route to a New Year's Eve show in Dallas, Texas, on December 31, 1985, his DC-3 crashed in a field near DeKalb, Texas. The NTSB determined that the crash was a result of a malfunctioning gas heater. Nelson was buried in Los Angeles' Forrest Lawn Cemetery.

As a teen idol, he was always a subject of numerous collections. He has been cited by many musicians as a large influence on their work. On January 21, 1987, Rick Nelson was inducted into the Rock and Roll Hall of Fame.

The now scarce signature of Rick Nelson

AUTOGRAPHS

An LP, magazine cover, ad, photo, or card signed by the artist: $100-$300

OFTEN OVERLOOKED MEMORABILIA

Movie memorabilia associated with *The Story of Three Loves, Here Come the Nelsons, Rio Braco* (1959), *The Wackiest Ship in the Army* (1960), *Love and Kisses* (1964), and *Pulp Fiction* (1994); copies of the television series *The Adventures of Ozzie and Harriet* and his appearances in other television shows including *McCloud, Petrocelli,* and the NBC-TV movie *High School USA* (1983); a copy of *LIFE* magazine with him on the cover - $10; paper dolls, Whitman, 1957 - $60; iron-on patch - $50; souvenir book, 1959 - $60 (tour program)

REFERENCES/BOOKS

A few resources exist. Begin first with *Ricky Nelson: Idol for a Generation*. There are no dedicated collector books.

Nelson, Sandy

Born: December 1, 1938

This West coast rocking guitarist's drum-fused instrumentals landed him hits with "Teen Beat" (#4, 1959), "Let There Be Drums" (#7, 1961), "Drums Are My Beat" (#29, 1962), and "Teen Beat '65" (#44, 1964).

AUTOGRAPHS

An LP, magazine cover, ad, photo, or card signed by the artist: $10-$12

OFTEN OVERLOOKED MEMORABILIA

Memorabilia associated with his work on other musicians' albums such as Gene Vincent's *Wild Cat* and the Hollywood Argyles' *Alley-Oop*

Nelson, Tracy

Born: December 27, 1944

Tracy Nelson is a powerful female singer who garnered a good reputation with bands such as Mother Earth in the late '60s. Her song "Down So Low" has been covered by numerous artists including Linda Ronstadt. From her 1974 Atlantic Records debut she scored a Grammy nomination for her duet with Willie Nelson on "After the Fire Is Gone." She reemerged in 1993 with the acclaimed *In the Here and Now* and in 1995 with *I Feel So Good*.

AUTOGRAPHS

A CD, LP, magazine cover, ad, photo, or card signed by the artist: $10

OFTEN OVERLOOKED MEMORABILIA

Memorabilia associated with her work with other artists

Nelson, Willie

Born: April 30, 1933

Willie Nelson is a country and western living legend whose rusted desert voice and generic delivery helped him transcend musical barriers to become extremely popular and prolific both as a songwriter and a performer. He began writing songs at the age of seven and by age ten joined Johnny Paycheck's Bohemian Polka Band on a part-time basis. He joined the air force in 1952, serving briefly in Korea, before attending Baylor University in Waco, Texas, where he studied agriculture and business. In 1955, Nelson began broadcasting a radio show in Washington state while financing his own recording of "No Place for Me," which he plugged consistently on the radio.

In 1958, Nelson went to Houston, where he worked as a DJ and performed at the Esquire nightclub. His songwriting became prolific, but his poor financial condition required him to sell some of his songs including "Family Bible" ($50) and "Night Life" ($150). In 1960 Nelson headed to Nashville where he met other struggling musicians including Mel Tillis and Kris Kristofferson, while playing in Tootsie's Orchid Lounge. Late in 1961 he signed a publishing contract with Pamper Music, having watched his "Hello Walls" (#2, 1961) and "Crazy" (#2, 1961) jump into the Top Ten for Faron Young and Patsy Cline respectively. Nelson did manage to land a recording contract, but his tattered tenor voice and fascination with simplicity often yielded far less than commercial success.

With stardom still eluding him, Nelson inaugurated his annual Fourth of July Picnic, which was held every year until 1980 in different Texas locations, and it even eventually found itself in Syracuse, New York, in 1983. *Red Headed Stranger* (#28, 1975), his debut record for CBS/Columbia Records, quickly topped the country charts driven by extract "Blue Eyes Crying in the Rain" (#21, pop, #1, C&W, 1975). Nelson then shifted to the ground-breaking record *Wanted: The Outlaws* with Waylon Jennings, Tompall Glaser, and Jessi Colter—the first country album to sell one million copies!

"Good Hearted Woman" (#25, 1976), "Mama Don't Let Your Babies Grow Up to Be Cowboys" (#42, 1978), and "Georgia on My Mind" (#84, 1978) catapulted the artist into the mainstream, reinforced by his appearances in a variety of movies, particularly *Electric Horseman* (1980). The movie also yielded the creative single "My Heroes Have Always Been Cowboys" (#44, 1980).

"On the Road Again" (#20, 1980), "Angels Flying Too Close to the Ground" (his tenth C&W #1), "Always on My Mind" (#5, 1982), "Let It Be Me" (#40, 1982), "To All the Girls I've Loved Before" (#5, 1984), and "Nothing I Can Do About It Now" (#1, C&W, 1989) rounded out some of his '80s hit singles.

In 1990, Nelson went back out on the road to support *Highwayman 2*, the sequel to the successful *Highwayman*, he did with his old pals Waylon Jennings, Johnny Cash, and Kris Kristofferson. By the end of the year the IRS has seized his bank accounts and real estate holdings to satisfy a $16.7 million tax debt. The following year he wed for the fourth time and pulled out all the stops to raise money for his tax bill.

Throughout the decades he has maintained his cowboy attire and love for the road—many believe after all of his financial woes, it is probably all he has left.

Nelson has made numerous contributions to duets and fund raisers in the '90s. In 1996 he became the first country artist to sign with Island Records. Despite all of his own financial problems, Nelson is forever an advocate for both the farmer and the downtrodden and is never afraid to lend a helping hand. His "outlaw" image is often overshadowed by his big heart. He is a fascinating individual to collect and a living legend in every sense of the words!

AUTOGRAPHS

A CD, LP, magazine cover, ad, photo, or card signed by the artist: $15-$45

A signed photograph from the Highwaymen

TOUR BOOKS/ PROGRAMS/PASSES

Tour Books:
Farm Aid 1985: $10
Backstage Passes:
$10-$15 (cloth),
$15-$25 (laminated)

POSTERS/PRESS KITS

Promotional Posters:
$15-$30
Press Kits: $20-$35

USED CLOTHING/ EQUIPMENT

Guitar Picks: $10-$25

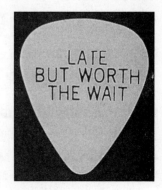

A Willie Nelson guitar pick

OFTEN OVERLOOKED MEMORABILIA

Memorabilia associated with his movie appearances in *Electric Horseman* (1980), *Honeysuckle Rose* (1980), *Barbarosa* (1982), *Songwriter* (1984), *Red Headed Stranger* (1987), and *Honeymoon in Vegas* (1992); his numerous television appearances including "In the Jailhouse Now" (1982), *Miami Vice* (11/7/86), "Another Pair of Aces: Three of a Kind" (1991), "Ray Charles: 50 Years in Music" (1991), *Delta* (1992), "A Country Celebration" (1993), "Academy of Country Music's Hits" (1993), *Saturday Night Live* (5/15/93), "Willie Nelson the Big Six-O" (1993), *The Tonight Show* (6/25/93, 3/23/94, 2/20/96), "A Day in the Life of Country Music" (10/1/93), and the *Late Show With David Letterman* (1/23/94, 8/15/95); a copy of the BBC-TV's *Edge of Darkness* featuring "Time of the Preacher"; his advertisements on radio and television for Taco Bell

REFERENCES/BOOKS

Numerous resources exist. Begin first with Nelson's autobiography. There are no dedicated collector books.

The Nerves: See The Beat

Nesmith, Michael

Born: December 30, 1942

Songwriter, video guru, and producer Michael Nesmith is best remembered as part of the Monkees. Linda Ronstadt scored her first big hit with the Nesmith penned "Different Drum" in 1968. When the Monkees split, Nesmith formed the First National Band, which released *Magnetic South* with hit extract "Joanne" (#21, 1970), followed by the Second National Band. The Pacific Arts Corporation was his next project, which released the concept album *The Prison*. *Elephant Parts* (1980), a unique combination of music, conceptual rock, and dance, met with critical acclaim and also won a 1981 Grammy award—the first ever for a video.

AUTOGRAPHS

A CD, LP, magazine cover, ad, photo, or card signed by the artist: $25-$50

POSTERS/PRESS KITS

Promotional Posters: $15-$20
Press Kits: $10-$15

USED CLOTHING/EQUIPMENT

Guitar Picks: (see the Monkees)

OFTEN OVERLOOKED MEMORABILIA

Memorabilia associated with his days in the Monkees; copies of all of his associated videos; movie memorabilia from *Repo Man* and *Tapeheads*; a bottle of Liquid Paper.

Nevil, Robbie

Born: October 2, 1960

The multi-talented Robbie Nevil landed briefly on the charts with his self-titled debut album (#37, 1986) with smash hit extract "C'est la Vie" (#2, 1986), followed by "Dominoes" (#14, 1986) and "Wot's It to Ya" (#10, 1987). His follow-up was *A Place Like This* (#118, 1988) which yielded "Back on Holiday" (#34, 1988) and "Somebody Like You" (#63, 1989). His third album failed to chart despite extracts "Just Like You" (#25, 1991) and "For Your Mind" (#86, 1991).

AUTOGRAPHS

A CD, LP, magazine cover, ad, photo, or card signed by the artist: $10-$15

POSTERS/PRESS KITS

Promotional Posters: $5
Press Kits: $10

USED CLOTHING/EQUIPMENT

Guitar Picks: $5

The Neville Brothers/Aaron Neville

Formed 1977

Arthur Neville, Born: December 17, 1937, Charles Neville, Aaron Neville, Born: January 24, 1941, and Cyril Neville

Well known for years on the Bourbon St. R&B scene first as the Hawketts and later as the Neville Sounds, the Neville Brothers, led by Aaron, released their debut record on Capitol. Marketed with a disco flavor, when the record didn't meet expectations, the group was dropped from the label's roster. Aaron Neville, a successful solo artist, who had scored in 1960 with "Over You" (#21, R&B, 1960) and six years later with "Tell It Like It Is" (#2, 1966), emerged at the forefront of the band. He attracted fans who still marveled at his tender voice emerging from his imposing muscular physique.

After opening some dates for the Rolling Stones in 1982, the band's reputation began to spread, although only "Yellow Moon" (#66, 1989) and "Brother's Keeper" (#60, 1990) managed to make it in the Top One Hundred. "Don't Know Much" (#2, 1989) resurrected Aaron's solo career when the duet with Linda Ronstadt found a home in the Top Five on the U.S. singles chart. He also enjoyed chart success with singles "Everybody Plays the Fool" (#8, 1991) and "Don't Take Away My Heaven." In 1991 Aaron took home a Grammy for his work with Trisha Yearwood on "I Fall to Pieces."

AUTOGRAPHS

Group
A CD, LP, magazine cover, ad, photo, or card signed by the group: $25-$35

Individuals
Aaron Neville: $10-$15

TOUR BOOKS/PROGRAMS/PASSES
Backstage Passes: $6 (cloth), $8-$12 (laminated)*

*See also Rolling Stones passes

POSTERS/PRESS KITS
Promotional Posters: $10-$15
Press Kits: $12

OFTEN OVERLOOKED MEMORABILIA
Movie memorabilia from *Bird on the Wire* (1990); videotapes of their television commercials; associated memorabilia from the numerous festivals they have performed at including Woodstock II and Farm Aid VII; videotapes of their numerous television appearances including *Saturday Night Live* (12/15/90), *Late Night With David Letterman* (9/1/92), *48 Hours* (3/10/93), "Apollo Theatre Hall of Fame" (9/6/94), *The Tonight Show* (7/7/94); Mardi Gras to the World scarf - $20.

The New Christy Minstrels

Formed 1961

This group is perhaps best known as a development band, because many former members, such as Kenny Rogers, John Denver, Gene Clark, Kim Carnes, and even actress Karen Black, went on to their own successful careers. As a very commercial folk-based group, it was formed by Randy Sparks in 1961, and hit the charts in 1963 with "Green Green" (#14, 1961), "Saturday Night" (#29, 1963), and "Today" (#17, 1964).

AUTOGRAPHS
A CD, LP, magazine cover, ad, photo, or card signed by the artist: $35-$50*

*Varies depending on which lineup.

OFTEN OVERLOOKED MEMORABILIA
Videotapes from their own summer television show (1964); associated members other works.

New Edition

Formed 1981

Bobby Brown, Born: February 7, 1966, Michael Bivens, Ricky Bell, Ronnie DeVoe, and Ralph Tresvant*

*Brown left in 1988 and Johnny Gill was added

The group's five original members met while attending junior high school in Boston. While performing at a talent show, they were spotted by the promoter Maurice Starr, who landed them a deal with hip-hop label Streetwise. The group's debut album *Candy Girl* (1983) scored two Top Ten R&B hits in "Candy Girl" (#1, 1983) and "Is This the End" (#8, 1983). But by the end of the year, the group broke

ties with Starr and moved on to a deal with MCA Records. Starr went on to form the New Kids on the Block.

In 1984, New Edition's eponymous MCA debut went to #6 and yielded hits "Cool It Now" (#4, 1985), "Mr. Telephone Man" (#12, 1985), and "Lost in Love" (#6, R&B, 1985). Other hits followed including "Count Me Out" (#2, 1985), "A Little Bit of Love (Is All It Takes)" (#3, 1986), "With You All the Way" (#7, 1986), "Earth Angel" (#3, 1986), and "Once in a Lifetime Groove" (#10, 1986).

By 1986, however, tensions were developing in the band, leading to Brown's departure to a successful solo career. His replacement, Johnny Gill, was also very talented and landed the group in the Top Ten with "If It Isn't Love" (#7, 1988) before he eventually went solo. Tresvant was also working on solo projects and hit the charts with "Sensitivity" (#4, 1990), "Stone Cold Gentleman" (#3, 1991), and "Do What I Gotta Do" (#2, 1991). In 1988 the remaining members of New Edition went on to from Bell Biv DeVoe.

Collecting the history of this group and all of its members should prove fascinating and fruitful. Be sure to watch for one-off reunions of the original members. Also, grab what you can now of items relating to the group's early releases.

AUTOGRAPHS
A CD, LP, magazine cover, ad, photo, or card signed by the group: $50-$100*

*Original members

TOUR BOOKS/PROGRAMS/PASSES
Backstage Passes: $8-$10 (cloth), $10-$15 (laminated)

POSTERS/PRESS KITS
Promotional Posters: $10-$30
Press Kits: $15-$30

OFTEN OVERLOOKED MEMORABILIA
Associated movie memorabilia from *Karate Kid II* (1986), *Dragnet* (1987), and *Boomerang* (1992); videotapes of their numerous appearances on televised music award shows, especially the "MTV Awards" (1990) and the "18th Annual American Music Awards" (1991), and additional television appearances on *The Tonight Show* (4/16/91) (Gill) and *The Arsenio Hall Show* (1993); all items associated with the Budweiser Superfest (1991) (Bell Biv DeVoe)

REFERENCES/BOOKS
Limited resources exist, but none do justice to the band in my opinion.

New Kids on the Block

Formed 1985

Donnie Wahlberg, Jonathan Knight, Jordan Knight, Danny Wood, and Joe McIntyre

Determined to find a replacement for his loss of New Edition, pop guru Maurice Starr gathered New Kids on the Block, who released their 1986 epony-

mously titled album (which didn't sell well). The group followed up with *Hangin' Tough* (#1, 1988) written, arranged, and produced by Starr, and included the hit extracts "Please Don't Go Girl" (#10, 1988) and "You Got It (The Right Stuff)" (#3, 1989).

"I'll Be Loving You (Forever)" (#1, 1989), "Hangin' Tough" (#1, 1989), "Didn't I Blow Your Mind" (#8, 1989), "Cover Girl" (#2, 1989), and "This One's for the Children" (#7, 1990) soon followed as the band began a "can't miss" period. *Step by Step* (#1, 1990) also shot up the charts and landed the hits "Tonight" (#7, 1990) and "Step by Step" (#1, 1990). During this period, however, numerous problems surfaced from personality conflicts between members, to even charges of hotel room arson against Wahlberg. Once the problems were swept under the carpet, a repackaged group emerged, "NKOTB," and struck first with single "If You Go Away" (#16, 1992). *Face the Music* (#37, 1994) was released under better album reviews, but less sales, as the group slowly faded out of the picture.

This band was heavily merchandised and makes a fascinating subject to collect because of the diverse range of products you may encounter. Like similar packaged bands of this nature, over time they may prove a worthy investment.

AUTOGRAPHS
A CD, LP, magazine cover, ad, photo, or card signed by the group: $15-$50

TOUR BOOKS/PROGRAMS/PASSES
Tour Books:
Hangin' Tough Tour: $15
Magic Summer Tour, 1990: $12
Backstage Passes:
$6-$8 (cloth), $10 (laminated)

POSTERS/PRESS KITS
Promotional Posters: $15-$25
Press Kits: $20-$25

OFTEN OVERLOOKED MEMORABILIA
Movie memorabilia from *Free Willy* (1993) and *The Fantasticks* (McIntyre); videotapes from their appearances at numerous award shows; all associated magazines, newspaper, and magazine articles featuring the band; copies of their numerous court documents - those in public record; all of the band's related work for Coca-Cola; a copy of *Forbes* magazine (9/91, 10/90) - $8; Super Bowl XXV memorabilia - the band provided half-time entertainment; copies of their publicly released videotapes *Hangin' Tough*, *Step by Step*, and *Hangin' Tough Live*; copies of their pay-for-view concerts; advertisements relating to their "900" telephone calling line; videotapes of their television appearances including *Unsolved Mysteries* (11/7/90); videotapes of the New Kids cartoon series; copies of the 1990 Harvard Crimson - $3; a copy of the WRBQ playlist from March, 1988 autographed by Randy Kabrich - the program director who "got the ball started, so to speak" - $4; back pack - $10; balloons - $3; binder - $5; blanket - $15; book covers (8) - $8; bubble gum cassettes - $14 (full box); button pack (6) - $5; card game - $5; cassette player - $25; coloring book - $5; colorforms - $15; comics $2 (each); dolls: Hasbro (5") - $10 (each), Hasbro (12") - Hangin' Loose - $17 (each), Hasbro (12") - In Concert - $22 (each),

Hasbro (18")- $25 (each); fanny pack - $10; fashion plates - $12; game (Milton Bradley) - $10; gift wrap set - $10; hat - $3; jigsaw puzzles: (100 pcs.) - $5, (500 pcs.) - $10; keychain - $8; keychain viewer - $15; lapel pins - $4; locker mirror - $4; lunch boxes - $10; microphone - $22; mugs - $4; mylar balloons - $4; notebook - $4; party pac - $12; pillow - $7; poster book - $4; radio - $25; rad "marbles" rollers - $4; school kit - $10; shoelaces - $7; sleeping bag - $25; slippers - $15; socks - $6; sports bottle - $3; stage set - $20; stickers -$1 (each); Thank-You notes (8) - $5; trading cards - $.10 (each); telephone - $20; thermos (plastic) - $3; watches - $15; yo-yo - $10

REFERENCES/BOOKS
Limited resources exist, but none do justice to the band in my opinion.

Newman, Randy

Born: November 28, 1944

Talented, and often satirical, songwriter and composer Randy Newman is perhaps best known for his novelty single "Short People" (#2, 1978), as well as "The Blues" (#54, 1983), "I Love L.A.," and "It's Money That Matters" (#60, 1988). People took note of the artist first as a songwriter when he penned the hits "I Think It's Going to Rain Today," covered by Judy Collins, "Love Story," covered by Peggy Lee, and "Mama Told Me (Not to Come)" (#1), covered by Three Dog Night. His infamous tour with friend Harry Nilsson also brought him recognition as a popular campus attraction.

Coming from a musical family—his uncles scored numerous films—it was no surprise when Newman turned to the cinema. I do think, however, it shocked many when they heard just how incredibly talented he was at scoring films. His efforts have garnered a number of Grammy Award nominations and his work has included such films as *Ragtime* and *The Natural*.

AUTOGRAPHS
A CD, LP, magazine cover, ad, photo, or card signed by the artist: $10-$25*
*A significant item autographed, such as one of his Grammy nominated soundtracks

POSTERS/PRESS KITS
Promotional Posters: $10-$15
Press Kits: $15

OFTEN OVERLOOKED MEMORABILIA
Memorabilia associated with the numerous films he has scored such as *Ragtime* (1982), *The Natural* (1984), *The Three Amigos* (1986), *Her Alibi* (1990), *Major League* (1990), *Awakenings* (1990), *The Paper* (1995), *Toy Story* (1996), and *James and the Giant Peach* (1996); videotapes of his numerous television appearances on *Late Night With David Letterman* (11/12/92), the *Late Show With David Letterman* (1994), and *Later With Jools Holland* (11/11/95); videotapes of commercials using his song "I Love L.A." (used for the Los Angeles 1984 Olympics); videotapes of ABC-TV's *Cop Rock* series

New Order: See Joy Division

New Riders of the Purple Sage

Formed 1969

John "Marmaduke" Dawson, David Nelson, Jerry Garcia, Mickey Hart, and Phil Lesh (Phil Chapman)*

*Numerous personnel changes; members have included: Spencer Dryden, Dave Torbert, Buddy Cage, Skip Battin, Stephen Love, Allen Kemp, Rusty Gauthier, Gary Vogensen, and Evan Morgan

The New Riders of the Purple Sage had an offbeat origin. The group was formed as an offshoot of the Grateful Dead in the spring of 1969 when Jerry Garcia, who had acquired a pedal steel guitar, quickly learned that if he didn't have a country band to play it in, he had just wasted his money. Garcia recruited David Nelson, songwriter John Dawson, plus Dead members Mickey Hart and Phil Lesh. Both Nelson and Dawson had roots with the Dead dating back to 1962, so their inclusion was no surprise, nor was it to find the Riders touring with the Dead. By the time the band landed a recording contract, Spencer Dryden had replaced Hart and Dave Torbert had taken over for Lesh, while Garcia bowed out after the band's debut.

Anthemic tunes such as "Panama Red" and the band's affiliation with the Grateful Dead captured the hearts of deadheads who now had another band to follow across the country. *The Adventure of Panama Red* was the group's only album to sell gold—the band was more of a live attraction than a singles pusher. The band's lineup remained fairly consistent until 1974 when numerous personnel changes took place. Dawson, Nelson, and Cage reunited in 1994 for the first time in more than a decade.

AUTOGRAPHS
A CD, LP, magazine cover, ad, photo, or card signed by the group: $200-$300*
*Original lineup with Garcia, Lesh, and Hart

OFTEN OVERLOOKED MEMORABILIA
Memorabilia associated with the Grateful Dead

Newton, Juice

(Judy Newton)
Born: February 18, 1952

Self-taught on acoustic guitar while a teenager, Newton moved from Virginia to California during the late '60s and formed the band Dixie Peach, followed by Silver Spur. The latter found the band releasing its debut on RCA as *Juice Newton and Silver Spur* (1975), followed by *After the Dust Settles* (1976), both of which received little attention. The group then moved to Capitol Records and, following an initial effort, disbanded, leaving Newton as a solo act. She then released *Well Kept Secret* (1978) and *Take Heart* (1979), which yielded her first country hit, "Sunshine."

Her breakthrough album came in 1979 with *Juice*, which included the hit extract "Angel of the Morning" (#4, 1981) and the rockabilly flavored "Queen of Hearts" (#2, 1981). From this point on she delivered C&W hits faster than cold beers during Friday night happy hour, including "The Sweetest Thing" (#7, 1981), "Love's Been a Bit Hard on Me" (#7, 1982), "Break It to Me Gently" (#11, 1982), "A Little Love" (#44, 1984), followed by four country and western Number Ones "You Want Me to Want to Make You Mine," "I'm So Hurt," "Old Flame," and "Both to Each Other (Friends and Lovers)." She also had hits with "Cheap Love" (#9, C&W, 1986), "What Can I Do With My Heart" (#9, C&W, 1986), and "Tell Me True" (#8, C&W, 1987).

AUTOGRAPHS
A CD, LP, magazine cover, ad, photo, or card signed by the artist: $20-$30

OFTEN OVERLOOKED MEMORABILIA
The Sweetest Thing candy bar w/photo on wrapper: $35

Newton-John, Olivia

Born: September 26, 1948

Born of a prestigious blood line which includes her grandfather Max Born the Noble Prize winning physicist and her father who is headmaster of Ormond College in Melbourne, Australia, Newton-John, who grew up in Melbourne, formed her first band with three other girls, the Sol Four, before quitting school and winning a talent contest which sent her to London. There she hooked up with Don Kirshner who at the time was trying to piece together Toomorrow—a British Monkees—which she joined briefly.

She then spent some time touring with Cliff Richard and appearing regularly on his series *It's Cliff Richard*. The appearances bode well for her as she tried to boost sales of her single "If Not for You" (1971), a Dylan cover. She also scored with covers of George Harrison's "What Is Life" and John Denver's "Take Me Home Country Roads."

Let Me Be There (1973), her first American LP, was her breakthrough album and included the title track hit (#6, 1973) which also won her a Grammy. She followed with the album *If You Love Me, Let Me Know*, with its hit title track (#5, 1974) and the tender "I Honestly Love You" (#1, 1974). She then moved to the U.S. and took up residency in Malibu, California.

"Have You Ever Been Mellow" (#1, 1975) and "Please Mr. Please" (#3, 1975)— her fifth million-selling single in a row! continued her string of hits

both on the pop and country and western charts. She then turned her interest to film and starred in *Grease*, which became the most profitable movie musical ever made and yielded Newton-John three hit singles: "You're The One That I Want" (#1,1978), sung with John Travolta, "Summer Nights" (#5, 1978), also with Travolta, and "Hopelessly Devoted to You" (#3, 1978).

"Suddenly" (#20, 1981), a duet with Cliff Richard, was extracted from the *Xanadu* hit soundtrack, although the film was a catastrophe. Newton-John then released the sexier *Totally Hot* and *Physical*, the latter of which included the Number One title single and two other hits. She then reunited with Travolta in the film *Two of a Kind*, which failed miserably, but the soundtrack delivered the two charting singles "Twist of Fate" (#5, 1983) and "Livin' in Desperate Times" (#31, 1984).

Her personal life then took center stage—she married actor Matt Lattanzi in 1984 and gave birth to a daughter in 1986. She also opened a chain of clothing stores, Koala Blue. Her last album of the '80s was *The Rumour* (#67, 1988), followed by her first release on Geffen Records, *Warm and Tender* (#124, 1990), a collection of nursery rhymes and lullabies. She confirmed in1992 that she was suffering from breast cancer and in 1995 she released her first studio set in five years, *Gaia (One Woman's Journey)*.

AUTOGRAPHS

A CD, LP, magazine cover, ad, photo, or card signed by the artist: $15-$50*

TOUR BOOKS/PROGRAMS/PASSES

Tour Books*:
1975 Tour: $35-$40
Physical: $40
Backstage Passes:
$12-$20 (cloth), $20-$40 (laminated)*
*Note: She rarely tours

POSTERS/PRESS KITS

Promotional Posters: $15-$35
Press Kits: $20-$45

OFTEN OVERLOOKED MEMORABILIA

Memorabilia associated with her movie appearances including *Tomorrow* (1970), *Grease* (1978), *Xanadu* (1980), and *Two of a Kind* (1984); videotapes of her numerous television appearances including *It's Cliff Richard* (1972), her television "Specials" (11/17/76, 5/78, 12/81) "A Gift of Song - The Music for UNICEF Concert" (1/79), *Saturday Night Live* (5/22/82), "A Mom for Christmas " (12/90), "A Call to Action in the War Against AIDS" special (7/4/92), and "A Christmas Romance" (12/18/94); a rubbing from her star on the Hollywood Walk of Fame; mobiles (assorted) - $50-$65; foam stickers, promo heart-shaped - $20

REFERENCES/BOOKS

Numerous resources exist. *Olivia: More Than Physical: A Collector's Guide* by Gregory Branson-Trent is a MUST for collectors! Serious collectors should also opt for one of her Fan Clubs: Belgian Olivia Newton-John Fan Club,

Attention: Kristin va de Wijer, Zonneboslaan 82, 1950 Kraainem, Belgium, or Olivia: Dutch Olivia Newton-John Fan Club, Karekiethof 20, 6005 JM Weert England.

The New York Dolls

Formed 1971

Johnny Thunders (John Genzale), Born: July 15, 1952, Died: April 23, 1991, Arthur Kane, Billy Murcia (1951-1972), Rick Rivets, and David Johansen, Born: January 9, 1950*

*Sylvain Sylvain (Syl Mizrahi) and Jerry Nolan were added in 1972, when Rivets and Murcia departed.

What do you get when you cross Ru Paul with Gary Glitter? The answer is the New York Dolls, well, sort of. "The Dolls" helped form the early glitter era and the foundation of punk, while suffering from an identity crisis in New York City. Well, if you're from The Big Apple, you say, "So what else is new?" But the music scene, a bit confused at the time, wasn't really sure what was happening.

The band developed a strong cult following in a city where outlandish clothing and men wearing women's makeup was simply no big deal. The band's music was very catchy, and critics often tried to describe it as Iggy Pop mixed with the Rolling Stones, mixed with, well, you get the picture. They really didn't know what the recipe was, but one thing was for sure: something was going on here, "Something musta be happening over Manhattan."

While playing its first tour of the U.K., Murcia died of suffocation (actually a deadly combination of pills and alcohol) and the band replaced him with Jerry Nolan. The albums *New York Dolls* (Mercury, 1973) and *Too Much Too Soon* (Mercury, 1974) were both well received in the media, but commercial bombs that sent Mercury Records packing. The first effort was well produced by Todd Rungren, and the latter by girlie group famed Shadow Morton. Sparkling moments in the first effort included "Trash" and "Personality Crisis," and before your make-up could run, "Too Much Too Soon" yielded "Chatterbox." Now considered cult classics, any artifacts relating to these releases are highly sought after, not only by Dolls collectors, but also by the many fans of this early New York-based punk movement.

Before you could say, control-top pantyhose, poof (or is it puff?), the band's magic seemed to have disappeared. *Lipstick Killers* (ROIR cassette, 1981) was more like lipstick smears and *Red Patent Leather* (Fan Club, 1984) sounded like it was recorded in a bathroom stall in Coney Island. Not even the famed Malcolm McLaren, who managed the group for awhile, could make-over the band.

Thunders and Nolan soon left to form the Heartbreakers before turning to other projects. Thunders died of a drug overdose in 1991. Nolan, who played at a memorial concert for Thunders, died shortly

thereafter of a stroke. Johansen, still suffering from an identity crisis, retired his platform shoes for penny loafers and returned as Buster Poindexter. For no apparent reason, Johansen, who clearly has enormous talent including acting ability, opted for the lounge lizard Poindexter, as if he were possessed by Mel Torme.

While there have been bits of solo excellence by nearly every member, the first two Dolls albums seem to wrap around you like a sari in a wind storm. Like the Ramones, no one can take away the "foundation" and influence the New York Dolls had on so many other musicians. Like so many defunct acts, some posthumous material surfaced like a "magical moon" in a bowl of Lucky Charms—by the time it gets to the top it's just too mushy to take seriously.

For Doll collectors, all artifacts are tough to come by.

AUTOGRAPHS

An LP, magazine cover, ad, photo, or card signed by the group: $250-$400

REFERENCES/BOOKS

Limited resources exist, and there are no dedicated collector books.

The Nice

Formed 1967

Keith Emerson, Born: November 1, 1944, Lee Jackson, , Brian "Blinky" Davison, and David O'List

The Nice is remembered for the foundation it laid for Keith Emerson and for joining the psychedelic sounds of the '60s with classical-infused art rock. For much of the band's existence it was a three-piece power trio, with Emerson as the focal point. The group gained a respectable level of popularity in Europe but failed to do much in the U.S. Emerson soon grew frustrated with carrying the weight of an unsuccessful band and upon meeting Greg Lake, he set a course for ELP.

AUTOGRAPHS

A CD, LP, magazine cover, ad, photo, or card signed by the group: $30-$45

OFTEN OVERLOOKED MEMORABILIA

Concert reviews that often referred to the group's outlandish stage antics, most of which was attributed to Emerson.

Nicks, Stevie: See Fleetwood Mac

Nico

(Christa Paffgen)
Born: October 16, 1938, Died: July 18, 1988

Over time she has taken on cult status among followers and historians. Forever linked with the Factory, Andy Warhol, and the Velvet Underground, she had somewhat of a vagabond life. She began modeling in Paris and landed in the music scene when she became a friend of Rolling Stone Brian Jones and group manager Andrew Loog Oldham. She cut the single "The Last Mile" (1965) for Oldham. Pop artist Andy Warhol became enthralled with Nico, perhaps entranced by her dry but mesmorizing voice, and led her to Lou Reed and John Cale. She stayed with the Velvet Underground for only one album before going solo, but she remained close to the band.

Like her work, she surfaced sporadically and garnered little attention, yet some respect. During the late '70s and early '80s, she played the club circuit before releasing her first album in seven years, *Drama of Exile* (1981), which included an interesting mix of music from Velvet cuts to Bowie's "Heroes." She spent the last year of her life in Manchester, England, where rumors abounded regarding her substance addiction. While on holiday in Ibza, a Spanish island, she had a bicycle accident and was later found by a cab driver. A misdiagnosis led to her death on July 18, 1988, of cerebral hemorrhage. Her cremated ashes were buried in her mother's Berlin grave.

AUTOGRAPHS

A CD, LP, magazine cover, ad, photo, or card signed by the artist: $30-$75

OFTEN OVERLOOKED MEMORABILIA

Movie memorabilia from *The Chelsea Girls* and *La Dolce Vita*

Night Ranger: See Damn Yankees

Nile, Willie

(Robert Noonan)
Born: June 7, 1948

Poet, singer, and songwriter Willie Nile, another Dylan disciple, spent seven years on the Greenwich Village folk scene before a 1978 *New York Times* review was strong enough to land him a contract with Arista records. His self-titled debut (1980) release was praised by critics, as was his sophomore *Golden Down* (1981). His debut was so strong that an impressed Pete Townshend asked him to do a few stadium openers for the Who. A decade between his

second and third albums was enough time to diminish any momentum he might have stirred up!

AUTOGRAPHS

A CD, LP, magazine cover, ad, photo, or card signed by the artist: $10-$15

USED CLOTHING/EQUIPMENT

Guitar Picks: $2-$5

OFTEN OVERLOOKED MEMORABILIA

Memorabilia associated with his numerous live appearances

Nilsson, Harry

(Harry Nelson)
Born: June 15, 1941, Died: January 15, 1994

An extremely successful singer and songwriter, Harry Nilsson learned to play the guitar while working at a bank. Using the name Nilsson, he was successful enough to sell Phil Spector three songs and earned extra money singing on demos and commercials. While working on his debut album for RCA, the Monkees covered his "Cuddly Toy," and his "One" scored well for Three Dog Night. While his debut received rave reviews and even caught the attention of John Lennon, it sold poorly. Nilsson answered with his follow-up *Aerial Ballet*, which included the smash hit "Everybody's Talkin'," which also appeared as the theme to the film *Midnight Cowboy*.

From this point onward numerous hits followed for Nilsson including "Me and My Arrow" (#34, 1971), "Coconut" (#8, 1972), "Jump into the Fire" (##27, 1972), and "Space Man" (#23, 1972). He faded from the recording scene during the '80s to concentrate on his family of seven children and emerged following Lennon's death to lobby for gun control. He recorded an album in 1988, his only release of the decade. In 1993, after suffering a heart attack, he became extremely committed to his songwriting and recording and even contributed to *The Fisher King* soundtrack. His death in 1994 was followed by a tribute album and the respect for his work consistently grows with each passing year!

AUTOGRAPHS

A CD, LP, magazine cover, ad, photo, or card signed by the artist: $30-$100

POSTERS/PRESS KITS

Promotional Posters: $20-$45
Press Kits: $20-$30

USED CLOTHING/EQUIPMENT

Guitar Picks: $70-$100
*Note: He never performed a public concert and rarely made television appearances!

OFTEN OVERLOOKED MEMORABILIA

Memorabilia associated with covers of his songs by other musicians; movie memorabilia from *Midnight Cowboy*, which earned him a Grammy, *Skidoo* (1968), *Son of*

Dracula (1974), *In God We Trust* (1976), and *The Fisher King* (1992); associated memorabilia from his television work including "The Courtship of Eddie's Father" (1969) and "The Point"; his work on behalf of the Coalition to Stop Handgun Violence; a brochure from the Security First National Bank in Van Nuys, CA - $.25; a handbill from "The Point."

Nine Inch Nails

Formed 1987
Trent Reznor, Born: May 17, 1965

The multifaceted and talented Trent Reznor began playing the piano at the age of five and slowly added more instruments to his resume. During high school he was in the band Option 30. He graduated from local Allegheny College in computer engineering before moving to Cleveland, Ohio, where he worked at a local musical instrument store, Pi Corporation, while he played keyboards in the band Innocent. He played on the group's album *Livin' on the Streets* before the band split. Then he hooked up with Urge before landing with the Exotic Birds, which released the EP *L'Oiseau* on the Pleasureland label.

Thereafter, he was a member of the Problems, Slam Bam Boo, and Lucky Pierre for a short stint. He mixed his bands with his work at Right Track Studio in Cleveland. Working at the studio enabled him to put together a three-song demo tape during the summer of 1988 as Nine Inch Nails, which was then signed to a recording deal with TVT Records. *Industrial Nation*, Reznor's debut effort was a declaration to industrial rock which solidified the foundation for his future work. Mixing anguish, remorse, and deep seeded anger, he delivered visions of catastrophic mental suffering and despair faster than Goebels could deliver Nazi rallies.

Nine Inch Nails (NIN), whose line-up was in a constant state of flux, had only Reznor as the common denominator. In 1989 the group began a seemingly endless trek of touring which ended some three years later. The band succeeded in garnering some adventurous college airplay with "Down In It," and found itself entering the U.S. Modern Rock survey.

Pretty Hate Machine (#75, 1991) slowly climbed the U.S. album charts driven by touring and extracts, including "Head Like a Hole" (#45, U.K., 1991). The band's stint with Guns n' Roses during its 1991 European tour provided enormous exposure for the band as did its controversial "Sin" video clip.

Following legal disputes over recording rights, EP *Broken* (1992), which included singles "Happiness in Slavery" and "Wish," debuted at U.S. Number Seven. "Wish" picked up a Grammy the following year for Best Metal Performance. Meanwhile Reznor was concentrating on songwriting for the next NIN release. The first extract from the forthcoming album was "March of the Pigs" (#59, 1994). It successfully

set the stage for the bleak release *The Downward Spiral* (#2, 1994).

The band embarked on a six-date U.K. tour as the soundtrack for the movie *The Crow* (#1, 1994) climbed up the U.S. album chart and included a NIN cover of "Dead Souls." The band then headed out on its Self Destruct Tour, which also included a stop at Woodstock II (8/13/94). Reznor also produced the soundtrack to the controversial thriller *Natural Born Killers* (#19, 1994), which included the NIN cuts "Something I Can Never Have" and "Burn."

In the fall of 1995, NIN joined David Bowie on The Outside Tour during its six-week U.S. trek. The band picked up its second Grammy award the following year, again in the category of Best Metal Performance—this time for "Happiness in Slavery." In 1997 Reznor contributed "The Perfect Drug" to the soundtrack *Lost Highway* as NIN.

Collect and collect now, as NIN relics ain't gonna get any easier to find!

AUTOGRAPHS

A CD, LP, magazine cover, ad, photo, or card signed by the artist: $35-$65

TOUR BOOKS/PROGRAMS/PASSES

Backstage Passes:
$10-$12 (cloth), $12-$25 (laminated)

POSTERS/PRESS KITS

Promotional Posters:
$15-$35, Example: U.K., Trent on Stage, (40" x 60") - $30
Press Kits: $20-$25

USED CLOTHING/EQUIPMENT

Guitar Picks: $15-$25

OFTEN OVERLOOKED MEMORABILIA

Movie memorabilia from *Light of Day* (1987), *The Crow* (1994), *Natural Born Killers* (1994), and *Lost Highway* (1997) ; copies of rejected MTV videotapes; an unpublished photo of Reznor's dog Maide - $5; Broken promo postcard - $5; "The Perfect Drug" promo prescription bottle - $20

REFERENCES/BOOKS

A couple resources exist, but none do justice to the artist in my opinion. There are no dedicated collector books.

1910 Fruitgum Company

Formed 1968

Joey Levine, Bruce Shay, Frank Jeckell, Mark Gutkowski, Larry Ripley, Rusty Oppenheimer, Pat Karwan, Floyd Marcus, and Chuck Travis

This discreet novelty act, formed by pop gurus Jerry Kasenetz-Jeff Katz, score hits with "Simon Says" (#4, 1968), "1,2,3 Red Light" (#5, 1968), "Goody, Goody, Gumdrops" (#37, 1968), "Indian Giver" (#5, 1969), and "Special Delivery" (#38, 1969)

AUTOGRAPHS

A CD, LP, magazine cover, ad, photo, or card signed by the producers: $10-$35*
*Kasenetz and Katz only on a hit single sleeve

OFTEN OVERLOOKED MEMORABILIA

Covers of the band's material

Nirvana

Formed 1987

Kurt Cobain (a.k.a. Kurdt Kobain), Born: February 20, 1967, Died: April 5, 1994, Krist Anthony Novoselic (a.k.a. Chris Novoselic), Born: May 10, 1965, Jason Everman, and Chad Channing*

*Everman departed in 1989. David Grohl replaced Channing in 1990. Other drummers were also used: Aaron Burckhard (1988), Dale Crover (1988, 1990), Dave Foster (1988), and Dan Peters (1990)

Nirvana picked up where R.E.M. and Jane's Addiction left off, fueling a generation that was sick of having condescending corporate rock shoved down its throat. During the late '80s, indie labels caught on like flip-top beer cans. At one point there were more record executives in Seattle than in both New York and Los Angeles. With Nirvana, twentysomethings finally had something to listen to that seemed to echo their feelings of hopelessness.

Cobain and Novoselic were raised in Aberdeen, Washington, about an hour and a half outside of Seattle. Both were products of broken families and they bonded together and formed Nirvana. Cobain had formed earlier bands such as Fecal Matters, Skid Row, and Brown Towel (Brown Cow, as it was misspelled one time) as local outlets for his creativity and played with these bands in nearby Olympia. While Cobain and Novoselic gelled well together, drummers became a commodity. The first drummer to stay awhile was Chad Channing.

Seattle's independent label Sub Pop finally signed the band and released its first single, "Love Buzz/Big Cheese," in November 1988. The single was a limited edition of 1,000 hand-numbered copies and sold out quickly, making it an instant collector's item. "Spank Thru," the band's next release, was included on *Sub Pop 200*, a compilation album the following month. Nirvana's first album, *Bleach*, was released in June 1989 and was praised by the underground rock community. Selling 35,000 copies initially, it was considered a success by indie-label standards. The first 1,000 copies were pressed on white vinyl, while the next 2,000 included a limited edition poster. The poster featured various images of the band and had "NIRVANA" in one corner (bottom - depending upon how you look at it) and the "S>U>B>, P<O<P" logo in the opposite corner. The "NIRVANA" logo first appeared in Bodoni Extra Bold Condensed Type on *Bleach*.

Following the release of *Bleach*, the band went on its first U.S. Tour (1989) of 26 dates beginning June 22 in San Francisco, California. A European tour with TAD began on October 20, 1989, in Newcastle, England. Weak distribution and limited marketing skills were common on indie labels, and Sub Pop was no exception. As such the group's records were hard to find.

Nirvana recorded a tape in early April 1990, supposedly its second Sub Pop album. Later it was known as "the demo tape" that the band shopped around to major record labels. Although the band was opposed to major labels, it was the only way it felt it could get its message across to larger audiences. A major-label bidding war soon ensued and Geffen/DGC was finally chosen.

The "Smells Like Teen Spirit/Even in His Youth/Aneurysm" single was released on September 10, 1991, just prior to the album *Nevermind* (September 24, 1991). An initial shipment of 50,000 copies was soon eclipsed and the album eventually sold ten million copies worldwide. Relics from the September 13, 1991, infamous *Nevermind* release party at the Re-bar club in Seattle are collector's items, especially the "smiley face" invitations.

The band set off for a European Tour on November 2, the same day *Nevermind* leaped into the Top Forty. At this time DGC was doing an excellent job of stepping up distribution of promotional items such as posters and mobiles, now all of which are collector's items. During the week of January 11, 1992, *Nevermind* hit Number One on the Billboard album chart.

"Smells Like Teen Spirit" soon became an anthem for a new generation, now clad with flannels shirts and torn jeans. Moshing, tattoos, and anarchy were "in," and everything else was "out." Soon band members, especially Cobain, became concerned that the band's antiestablishment messages were not being heard. Unfortunately, while the commercial success of *Nevermind* did much to deliver the band's message, it also did much to contradict it.

Cobain married Courtney Love, singer for the underground band Hole, on February 24, 1992. From the beginning of their relationship, the couple was deluged with media which quickly made them the "John and Yoko" of the '90s. Rumors persisted that both were "slam-dancing with Mr. Brownstone"—Guns n' Roses slang for doing heroin. Collectors can have a field day with all of the publications that plastered the couple's photos on their covers.

Amidst the chaos surrounding the birth of the couple's daughter on August 18, 1992, the band released *Incesticide* (December 15) . This was a collection of early singles and outtakes, issued primarily to "beat the bootleggers."

Chronic stomach problems, depression, and bouts with drug addiction were getting the best of Cobain. On September 14, 1993, *In Utero* was released as Nirvana's follow-up to its legacy *Nevermind*. It debuted at Number One and included hits like "Heart-Shaped Box" and "All Apologies." The band's last American concert was on January 8, 1994, at the Seattle Center Arena. Naturally, all items associated with the event are highly sought by collectors.

On April 8, 1994, Cobain was found dead in a room above his and Love's garage in Seattle. His death was due to a self-inflicted gun shot wound to the head. The event was marked by weeks of media coverage and worldwide tributes. In November 1994, *MTV Unplugged in New York* (#1, 1994), the acoustic show Nirvana had taped in 1993, was released.

*AUTOGRAPHS

Group
A CD, LP, magazine cover, ad, photo, or card signed by the group: $400-$600

Individual
Kurt Cobain: $350-$400
Krist Novoselic: $30-$35
Dave Grohl: $25-$30

An autographed photo from Nirvana's Kurt Cobain, who typically singed "Kurdt" or "Kurt"

TOUR BOOKS/PROGRAMS/PASSES
Backstage Passes:
$15-$20 (cloth), $20-$50 (laminated)

POSTERS/PRESS KITS
Promotional Posters: $25-$75
Press Kits: $35-$75

USED CLOTHING/ EQUIPMENT

Guitar Picks:
Cobain: $100-$150
Novoselic: $50-$100

Drumsticks:
Grohl: $35*-$75
*From Foo Fighters

A common Nirvana counterfeit backstage pass

OFTEN OVERLOOKED MEMORABILIA

Nevermind DGC promotional jar with floating doll and dollar bill, 1991; Bleach 1991 Australian release of 500 copies in a cloth bag; Kurt Cobain junk mail - $50-$500 (varies); Kurt Cobain prescription bottle - $750-$1,200; videotapes of the band's television appearances including *Rapido* (12/18/91) - BBC2-TV, *Saturday Night Live* (1/11/ 92, 9/25/93), and the "MTV Video Music Awards" (9/9/ 92); an autographed copy of Nevermind signed by Spencer Elden - $25; a copy of the Date House Bill 2554 signed by Washington Governor Booth Gardener - $20-$25; memorabilia from *The Beavis and Butt-Head Experience* - Nirvana contributes "I Hate Myself and Want to Die"; associated items from Suite 541 at the Excelsior Hotel in Rome, Italy (suicide attempt); an autographed burglar alarm by Gary Smith - the electrician who found Cobain's body - $5.

REFERENCES/BOOKS

Come As You Are by Michael Azerrad - $17 (A must for any Nirvana fan!); *Nirvana, Nevermind* by Susan Wilson - $20; *Nirvana, The Legacy* by Mick Wall and Malcolm Dome - $15; *Nirvana & The Sound of Seattle* by Brad Morrell - $20; *Nirvana* by Paul Haus - $10; Ltd. Ed. CD Sized book & Interview CD - $18; *Tribute to Nirvana* by Suzi Black - $12; *The Story of Nirvana* by Black - $12.

A Kurt Cobain Drug Prescription Bottle for Ampicillan—do collectors have to draw the line between what is tasteful and what is not? An item like this is very difficult to authenticate. Photo courtesy Executive Collectibles Gallery, Inc.

Formed 1966

Jeff Hanna, Born: July 11, 1947, Jimmie Fadden, Born: march 9, 1948, Jackson Browne, Born: October 9, 1948, Ralph Barr, Les Thompson, and Bruce Kunkel*

*Browne was only in the band briefly before being replaced by John McEuen. Numerous other personnel changes. Musicians included: Chris Darrow, Jimmy Ibbotson, , John Cable, Jackie Clark, Bob Carpenter, Al Garth, Richard Hathaway, Merle Brigante, Rick Schlosser, Vic Mastriani, Michael Gardner, and Bernie Leadon.

Surviving transitions in both music and members, "The Dirt Band" was most stable during the '70s when Hanna, Fadden, and McEuen laid a foundation for the group. The Dirt Band's debut LP scored a modest hit with "Buy for Me the Rain" (#45, 1967) and was released after Jackson Browne's short stint with the band. *Uncle Charlie and His Dog Teddy* was the band's breakthrough album and included the hit Walker cover "Mr. Bojangles," which landed in the Top Ten.

Will the Circle Be Unbroken (1972), a three record set with country legends, went gold and to this day is considered a monumental release. It was followed up more than sixteen years later with *Will the Circle Be Unbroken, Vol.2* (#95, 1989), which was in a similar format with updated country legends. Always a popular live band, the Dirt Band became the first rock group to tour the Soviet Union in 1977. The following year it helped Steve Martin bring to life his version of "King Tut." "An American Dream" (#13, 1980), a duet with Linda Ronstadt, was a success for the band just months before it landed again with "Make a Little Magic."

In 1983 the band focused more on the country and western charts and yielded a series of hits including the chart toppers "Long Hard Road (Tha Sharecropper's Dream)" (1984), "Modern Day Romance" (1985), and "Fishin' in the Dark" (1987).

AUTOGRAPHS

A CD, LP, magazine cover, ad, photo, or card signed by the group: $12-$40*
*Hadden, Fadden, and McEuen

TOUR BOOKS/PROGRAMS/PASSES

Backstage Passes: $5-$7 (cloth), $7-$10 (laminated)

POSTERS/PRESS KITS

Promotional Posters: $8-$20
Press Kits: $10-$15

OFTEN OVERLOOKED MEMORABILIA

Movie memorabilia from *Paint Your Wagon* (1968); associated memorabilia from all of the band's alumni.

Nixon, Mojo

(Neill McMillan, Jr.)
Born: August 2, 1957

A former bike racing champion, Nixon is content only when fueling a fire, rather than putting one out. Mojo settled in San Diego and formed a duo with Skid Roper. The two released their first self-titled effort and, although the release contained the legendary cut "Jesus at McDonald's," the album failed to reach Number One. (I wonder who picked up the check.)

Frenzy (1986, Restless), their sophomore effort, featured the MTV classic "Stuffin' Martha's Muffin," an ode to VJ Martha Quinn. (She should have sued their asses for this!) *Bo-Day-Shus!!!* (1987) followed and included an assault on "The King" with the cut "Elvis Is Everywhere."

Root Hog or Die (1989) actually landed the band MTV airplay with the cut "Debbie Gibson Is Pregnant with My Two-Headed Love Child," no doubt attributable to the ingestion habits Nixon became infamous for. The video featured actress Winona Ryder as Debbie Gibson—how's that for casting?

Nixon split with Roper and went solo in 1990 with *Otis*, which included the controversial cut that nearly got the musician shot ("Don Henley Must Die"), although the two are now friends—supposedly. Nixon then formed the Toad Liquors before moving on to a project with Jello Biafra.

AUTOGRAPHS

A CD, LP, magazine cover, ad, photo, or card signed by the artist: $10-$20

OFTEN OVERLOOKED MEMORABILIA

Memorabilia associated with any controversy surrounding his hits; copies of his MTV promotional spots; a couple bottles of "that green stuff."

Nova Mob: See Hüsker Dü

NRBQ

(New Rhythm and Blues Quintet) Formed 1967

Terry Adams, Joey Spampinato, Steve Ferguson, Tom Staley, and Frank Gadler*

*Numerous personnel changes

More than twenty-five years without commercial success has not diminished NRBQ's spirit. Since the late '60s the band has played its outlandish from of music, a blend the band dubbed "omnipop." "Get the Gasoline Blues" (#70, 1974) has been its only charting single.

AUTOGRAPHS

A CD, LP, magazine cover, ad, photo, or card signed by the band: $10-$15

OFTEN OVERLOOKED MEMORABILIA

Memorabilia associated with the Grateful Dead

Nugent, Ted/Amboy Dukes

Born: December 13, 1948

The original Amboy Dukes: Nugent, Greg Arama, Steve Farmer, Dave Palmer, and Andy Soloman

What do you get when you cross Daniel Boone with a Gibson Byrdland guitar and spice it up with a little "Wango Tango" sauce? The Motor City Madman himself, Ted Nugent. Some say he was born with a guitar in one hand and a Bowie knife in the other. Whatever the case, by the age of nine he was rockin' out in his Detroit garage. He started first with the Royal High Boys (1960-61), followed by the Lourdes (1962-64). At age fourteen he had already played Cobo Hall, opening for the Supremes and the Beau Brummels. Nugent's family moved to Chicago in 1965 where he formed the Amboy Dukes.

The Amboy Dukes gained regional attention with "Baby Please Don't Go" (Them) in 1967. The release *Journey to the Center of the Mind* (#74, 1968) spun off the same titled single that reached Number Sixteeen in the U.S. The band's extensive touring, primarily in the Northeast and South, enhanced Nugent's reputation as an outstanding guitarist—a reputation he tried to bolster with his live stage "guitar battles" (1973) against metal merchants Mike Pinera (Iron Butterfly), Wayne Kramer (MC5), and Frank Marino (Mahogany Rush).

In 1974, Ted Nugent's Amboy Dukes switched to Frank Zappa's DiscReet label to release *Call of the Wild* and *Tooth, Fang, and Claw*. Both titles played off of Nugent's highly-publicized image as an outdoorsman. As adept with bow and arrow as he was on his Gibson Howard Roberts Fusion ax, he wielded a notorious passion for blood-sports. Nugent is an active supporter of the NRA—any associated memorabilia, such as advertisements, are worthy of Nugent collections. Publicity for his archery prowess was enhanced in 1974 when he won the U.S. National Squirrel-Shooting Contest by downing a critter at 150 yards.

The Dukes split in 1975, and Ready Teddy was signed to a solo deal with Epic Records. Add to this his switch to Aerosmith's Leiber-Krebs management and you had a recipe better than venison soup on a cold winter's day. Now heavily supported both on and off the stage, Nugent attacked the public through Blitzkrieg touring. Most wanted to see him in person just to see if he was for real. Hit singles "Free For All," "Dog Eat Dog," and "Cat Scratch Fever" put him into the Top Forty and he ground his way into the hearts of an increased audience now craving for more Gonzo!

Double Live Gonzo! (#13, U.S.), *Weekend Warriors* (#24, U.S.), and *State of Shock* (#18, U.S.) found him well-established going into the next decade. *Scream Dream* reached Number Thirteen in the United States in 1980 with the single "Wango Tango," which

made it into the Top One Hundred. But Gonzomania was cooling, so he signed a new record deal and revamped his band in hopes of creating greater interest. Between 1980 and 1984 he became a Michigan County Deputy Sheriff, a noted public speaker, and an advocate of having the right to bear arms. The end of the decade found Nugent exploring other media. He appeared on an episode of *Miami Vice* in January 1984, sex therapist Dr. Ruth Westheimer's television show (5/13/86), and on *Late Night With David Letterman* (12/25/87). The decade ended with the rocker forming a new band called Damn Yankees with Tommy Shaw (Styx), Jack Blades (Night Ranger), and drummer Michael Cartellone.

The '90s found Nugent again successful, this time with Damn Yankees. "High Enough," from the self-titled debut album, hit in the U.S. at Number Three in 1991. The band's follow-up album *Don't Tread* spun off "Where You Goin' Now" (#20, 1992). On December 31, 1995, Nugent celebrated the tenth anniversary of the Whiplash Bash at the Cobo Arena in Detroit, Michigan.

The forever flamboyant Detroit carnivore is certainly a fascinating topic for collecting, whether it's a piece of venison he donated to a Salvation Army soup kitchen (12/31/91) or part of one of the flaming arrows he shot off during a show in Cincinnati (1/11/93). Collecting memorabilia from the Motor City Madman is certainly not dull. My sentimental favorite has always been a copy of the horror movie *State Park* where Nugent sings the tender ballad "Love Is Like a Chain Saw." Gonzomaniacs will also want to pick up a Ted Nugent pinball machine introduced by Stern Electronics, the book *Blood Trails: The Truth About Bowhunting* (authored by Nugent), a subscription to *Ted Nugent World Bowhunters Magazine*, and a copy of "Fred Bear—American Hunter's Theme Song" (through his mail-order business). Another must for Nugent collectors is the four part "Spirit of the Wild" television special aired by Midwestern Public Broadcasting in 1994. Nugent hosted the series and continued his role as an outdoors advocate. The guitarist was also active in several anti-drug programs including D.A.R.E. (Drug Abuse Resistance Education).

A nice variety of Ted Nugent guitar picks including one from his days with Damn Yankees

AUTOGRAPHS

Ted Nugent has always been obliging to autograph requests. He typically signs his name very large, with flamboyant strokes.

A CD, LP, magazine cover, ad, photo, or card signed by the artist: $20-$30

TOUR BOOKS/PROGRAMS/PASSES

Tour Books:
TNT - Ted Nugent Tour: $20
Backstage Passes:
$5-$10 (cloth), $8-$15 (laminated)

POSTERS/PRESS KITS

PromotionalPosters: $10-$30
Press Kits:
$15-$35

USED CLOTHING/ EQUIPMENT

Guitar Pick:
$10-$20
*His zebra skin guitar picks are musts for all Nugent collectors

"Personality in Picks"—a typical Nugent trademark

OFTEN OVERLOOKED MEMORABILIA

Used Nugent weaponry, bows, arrows, etc. (prices vary); display box mobile (Up to Double Live) - $40

REFERENCES/BOOKS

Limited resources exist, and there are no dedicated collector books.

Numan, Gary

(Gary Webb)
Born March 1958

Synth guru Numan, departed early from his guitar infused sound and into the world of synthesizers. His band Tubeway Army scored with its second album, *Replicas* (1979), which yielded the British Number One extract "Are 'Friends' Electric?" and was the prelude to the electropop trend of the early '80s.

The Pleasure Principle (1979) found Numan going solo and it entered the U.K. charts at Number One, driven by the single "Cars" (#9, 1979). His 1980 follow-up *Telekon* (#64, 1980) was indicative of America's lack of appreciation for his craftsmanship. He announced his retirement from performing in 1980, but continued his recording, before becoming a professional pilot.

AUTOGRAPHS

A CD, LP, magazine cover, ad, photo, or card signed by the artist: $15-$35

TOUR BOOKS/PROGRAMS/PASSES

Tour Books:
Teletour '80: $40
Warriors (1983): $40

POSTERS/PRESS KITS

Promotional Posters: $15-$25
Press Kits: $20-$30

OFTEN OVERLOOKED MEMORABILIA

Promotional pins: $2

REFERENCES/BOOKS

A couple resources exist, but none do justice to the artist in my opinion. There are no dedicated collector books.

NWA

Formed 1986

Ice Cube (O'Shea Jackson), M.C. Ren (Lorenzo Patterson), Eazy-E (Eric Wright), Dr. Dre (Andre Young), and D.J. Yella (Antoine Carraby)*

*Ice Cube departed in 1990

Straight Outta Compton threw gangsta rap right smack on main street and offered a first hand perspective on the gang-infested streets of South Central Los Angeles. Songs like "Fuck tha Police" and "Gangsta Gangsta" shoved the first amendment down the throats of the establishment and even foreshadowed the 1992 L.A. riots.

Ice Cube met Dr. Dre., who was in-line with his perspective and shared the same direction for their music, before hooking up with Eazy-E. *Straight Outta Compton* sold nearly a million copies before the band embarked upon a tour. N.W.A. (Niggaz With Attitude) was quickly thrown into controversy over their controversial subject matter and lyrics to the extent that the FBI became involved.

Never a group to avoid controversy, the group's 1991 album *Efil4zaggin* (Niggaz 4 Life backward) shot to the top of the charts two weeks after its release. During this period group members also began to experience their own share of misfortune. Dr. Dre was charged with attacking a television rap-show host, while Eazy-E drifted off and died of complications due to AIDS in 1995.

Dr. Dre went solo with *The Chronic* (#3, 1993), which included hits "Nuthin' but a G'Thang" (#2, 1993) and "Dre Day" (#8, 1993), which introduced the rapper Snoop Doggy Dog.

AUTOGRAPHS

A CD, LP, magazine cover, ad, photo, or card signed by the group: $35-$55*

*Original members

OFTEN OVERLOOKED MEMORABILIA

Memorabilia associated with each members' solo careers

Nyro, Laura

(Laura Nigro)
Born: October 18, 1947, Died: April 8, 1997

Talented singer and songwriter Laura Nyro was one of the most important women in rock music. Her music included shades of gospel, jazz, and a very occasional hint of folk, mixed with early rock undertones. At the young age of nineteen she recorded her first album, *More Than a New Discovery*, and although it eluded commercial success, it included some classic songs that were cover hits by other artists such as "Wedding Bell Blues" and "Blowin' Away" (both by the Fifth Dimension), "Stoney End" (Barbara Streisand), and "When I Die" (Blood, Sweat and Tears).

Eli and the Thirteenth Confession (1968) followed the same road as her first release and included "Sweet Blindness" and "Stoned Soul Picnic" (both hits for the Fifth Dimension) and "Eli's Comin" (a hit for Three Dog Night). By now Nyro's reputation of rapid rhythm changes and complex lyrics preceded her. *New York Tendaberry* (1969), her third album, included the classics "Time and Love" and "Save the Country." Her lyrics now winning considerable respect for their depth and expression and, in retrospect, were far ahead of their time.

Christmas and the Beads of Sweat (1970) brought her in contact with the Muscle Shoals musicians and yes, that's Duane Allman's distinctive guitar on "Beads of Sweat." *Smile* (1975), *Seasons of Lights* (1977), and *Nested* (1978), like all of her previous albums, won the hearts of critics, but failed to achieve expected commercial sales. She then slipped away and concentrated on her private life and reemerged for *Mother's Spiritual* (1984), *Live at the Bottom Line* (1989), and *Walk the Dog and Light the Light* (1993). Nyro died in 1997.

AUTOGRAPHS

A CD, LP, magazine cover, ad, photo, or card signed by the artist: $20-$40

OFTEN OVERLOOKED MEMORABILIA

Memorabilia associated with covers of her music; memorabilia from the 1967 Monterey Pop Festival

Oasis

Formed 1991

Liam Gallagher, Born: September 21, 1972, Noel Gallagher, Born: May 29, 1967, Paul "Bonehead" Arthurs, Born: June 23, 1965, Paul "Guigs" McGuigan, Born: May 9, 1971, and Tony McCarroll

Liam Gallagher joins forces with Arthurs, McGuigan, and McCarroll first as the band Rain, then eventually as Oasis. Noel, after presenting his terms to the band and it agrees, joins Oasis. On October 19, 1991, the quintet plays its first gig at Manchester's Boardwalk club where the band, minus Noel, had played for the first time as Oasis.

On October 22, 1993, Creation Records finally signs Oasis after seeing the band play at the King Tut's Wah Wah Club in Glasgow, Scotland, on May 31. Early on, sibling rivalry among the Gallaghers and group infighting rumors emerge about the band. Whether the allegations are true is a matter of speculation, but it is known for certain the increased media exposure is helpful to the band. On May 23, 1994, a U.K. tour, co-headlining with Whiteout, begins in Bedford and runs until April 13. This is followed on April 29 and June 1 with two additional U.K. tours.

In April 1994, the group's first single, "Supersonic" peaks at Number Thirty-One on the U.K. charts. It is followed by "Shakermaker" (#11, 1994, U.K.) and "Live Forever" (#10, 1994, U.K.), while the band performs its debut U.S. gig on July 21, 1994, at the New Music Seminar held at the Wetlands club in New York City. Already selling-out dates in the U.K., the group releases its debut album *Definitely Maybe* (#1, 1994, U.K.) on August 30, 1994.

Now labeled BritPop pioneers, the band releases the single "Cigarettes and Alcohol" (#7, 1994, U.K.) backed by Beatles cover "I Am the Walrus," while finishing a five-week U.S. Tour. The single is followed by "Whatever" (#3, 1994, U.K.), and the group's U.S. exposure pushes *Definitely Maybe* (#58, 1994) into the Top Sixty on the album chart.

The Gallaghers, now known as the "Bruise Brothers," have it out with McCarroll in the spring of 1995, which leads to his firing from the band. New drummer Alan White (5/23/95 debut) joins the band in May, the same month that finds single "Some Might Say" (#1, U.K., 1995) topping the British singles chart. Internal band affairs are soon replaced with an ongoing media feud between Blur and Oasis, both of which occupy the top two slots on the singles chart the final week of August 1995.

On October 1, 1995, the band (minus a sick McGuigan) performs acoustically at London's Virgin Megastore to promote its new album *(What's The Story) Morning Glory* (#1, 1995, U.K.). Extracted single "Wonderwall" (#2, 1995, U.K.) climbs the charts. The band also finds success in Australian sales.

On February 24, 1996, *(What's The Story) Morning Glory?* (#4, U.S., 1996) lands high on the U.S. album charts driven by single "Wonderwall" (#8, 1996). In 1997, *Be Here Now* draws significant attention as its extract "D'You Know What I Mean" climbs the charts. While the band is selling better in the United States, it still remains relatively unknown in many areas. While somewhat reminiscent of the Who in the earlier years, Oasis will need to cross some critical junctures in the years to come to insure sustained success. The group's success so far should not be ignored by U.S. collectors, because Oasis memorabilia is still both attainable and affordable.

OASIS ON TELEVISION

Selected Dates

*December 10, 1994	*Later With Jools Holland* - BBC2-TV
*May 9, 1995	*Late Show With David Letterman* - CBS-TV (U.S. Debut)
*April 17, 1995	*The White Room* - C4-TV
*October 9, 1995	*Late Show With David Letterman* - CBS-TV
*December 2, 1995	*Later With Jools Holland* - BBC2-TV, taped
*December 31, 1995	"The White Room New Year Special" - C4-TV

The band also appeared on C4-TV's *The Word* in Spring 1994 and BBC-TV's *Top of the Pops* in the spring of 1995.

AUTOGRAPHS
Group
A CD, LP, magazine cover, ad, photo, or card signed by the entire band: $50-$90

Individual
Liam Gallagher: $15-$25	Noel Gallagher: $20-$35
Paul Arthurs: $10-$20	Paul McGuigan: $10-$20
Tony McCarroll: $10	Alan White: $10

TOUR BOOKS/PROGRAMS/PASSES
Tour Programs:
Knebworth & Loch (U.K.): $20-$25
Maine Road, April 1996 (U.K.): $18
Backstage Passes: $8-$10

POSTERS/PRESS KITS
Promotional Posters: $10-$25
Press Kits: $10-$30

USED CLOTHING/EQUIPMENT
Guitar Picks:
Noel Gallagher: $15-$25
Paul Arthurs: $10
Paul McGuigan: $10
Drum Sticks:
Tony McCarroll: $10-$15
Alan White: $15

OFTEN OVERLOOKED MEMORABILIA
New Musical Express and *Melody Maker* issues (April 1994) choosing "Supersonic" as single of the week - $5-$10; the issue of *The Observer* (October 1995) with Noel's alleged death quotes about Blur. $5-$10.

REFERENCES/BOOKS

Lost Paradise by Paul Moody, 1996: $10-$20

Ocasek, Ric: See the Cars

Ocean, Billy

(Lesile Charles)
Born: January 21, 1950

In 1976 Billy Ocean's "Love Really Hurts" (#22, 1976) landed high in the charts, but he couldn't sustain himself there until 1984 when he began to land singles into the Top Ten. He had a total of seven in the Top Ten: "Caribbean Queen" (#1,1984), "Loverboy" (#2, 1984), "Suddenly" (#4, 1984), "When the Going Gets Tough, the Tough Get Going" (#2, 1986), "There'll Be Sad Songs (to Make You Cry)" (#1, 1986), "Love Zone" (#10, 1986), and "Get Outta My Dreams, Get Into My Car" (#1, 1988). On June 13, 1993, *Time to Move On*, his first album in four years, was released but it failed to vault him back into the limelight.

AUTOGRAPHS

A CD, LP, magazine cover, ad, photo, or card signed by the artist: $10

TOUR BOOKS/PROGRAMS/PASSES

Backstage Passes: $5 (cloth), $5-$8 (laminated)

POSTERS/PRESS KITS

Promotional Posters: $5-$8
Press Kits: $10

OFTEN OVERLOOKED MEMORABILIA

Movie memorabilia from *The Jewel of the Nile* (1986)

Ochs, Phil

Born: December 19, 1940, Died: April 9, 1976

When the folk-protest movement was in full bloom during the '60s, so was Phil Ochs. A vehement critic of "the establishment," he criticized, publicized, and romanticized, all without compromise. Like his Greenwich Village peers, he knew when to "tune out," "tune in," and even "plug-in," as if it were instinctive.

Ochs studied journalism at Ohio State University, wrote songs, and accompanied a few folk groups, including the Swinging Socialists/Sundowners, all before moving to New York City in 1961. He became part of the elite folk circle at the time—its most noteworthy participant was, of course, Bob Dylan. His journalistic nature contrasted well with his songwriting, and the voice he chose to speak with became his music. His antiwar anthems included "I Ain't a'Marchin'" and "Draft Dodger Rag."

Joan Baez covered Ochs' "There but for the Fortune" which landed in the Top Fifty. His *Pleasures of the Harbor* (A&M, 1967) album included two of his more popular tunes: "Outside of a Small Circle of Friends" and "The Party." Following its release, Ochs headed west to L.A. where he teamed up with producer Van Dyke Parks for *Tape from California*. This album was followed by *Rehearsals for Retirement* (1969), *Greatest Hits* (1970), and *Gunfight at Carnegie Hall* (1971).

During the early '70s, Ochs lived outside of the U.S., worked on his writing, and occasionally performed. He reunited with Dylan in 1974 at a show protesting against the military junta in Chile. It ironically came just after what was to be his last release during his lifetime: "Here's to the State of Richard Nixon." Suffering from severe depression, Ochs hung himself at his sister's home on April 9, 1976.

While Ochs makes a fascinating subject to study and collect, there is little memorabilia to reflect his brilliant career.

AUTOGRAPHS

A single, LP, magazine cover, ad, photo, or card signed by the artist: $50-$100

OFTEN OVERLOOKED MEMORABILIA

The articles he wrote for *Time Out* (London); any items relating to his mysterious assault while traveling in Africa in 1973; any items from his last public appearance at New York's Folk City on October 23, 1975

REFERENCES/BOOKS

Limited resources exist. *Death of a Rebel: Phil Ochs and a Small Circle of Friends* by Marc Eliot is a good place to begin! There are no dedicated collector books.

O'Connor, Sinéad

Born: December 12, 1966

A tough childhood finds O'Connor facing a myriad of problems at young age before she runs away to Dublin to attend the Dublin College of Music. She begins to perform on her own in 1985, often in Dublin pubs, before joining local band Ton Ton Macoute. It is there that she is spotted by Ensign Records executives who persuade her to travel alone to London to work at the label's office before beginning her recording career.

Virgin Records releases the movie soundtrack to *Captive*, which features lyrics by O'Connor, in September 1986. She begins work on her debut record the following year, while parenting a son and being featured on World Party's debut album *Private Revolution*. In January 1988 *The Lion and the Cobra* (#36, 1988) is released and includes breakthrough single "Mandinka" (#17, 1988, U.K.). Media attention persists around her, prompted by her short haircut, formless clothing, and vehement opinions.

In January 1990, O'Connor releases "Nothing Compares 2 U" (#1, 1990), a Prince cover, from her sec-

ond album, *I Do Not Want What I Haven't Got* (#1, 1990). The album is an enormous world-wide success. She tours extensively in support of it and participates at various events including the Glastonbury Festival and Roger Water's performance of *The Wall*.

On August 24, 1990, O'Connor, as a protest, refuses to perform at a show in Holmdel, New Jersey, if the American national anthem is played. The incident evokes international headlines, while radio stations across the United States refuse to play her records. She continues the media frenzy by casting allegations that Prince physically threatened her during a visit.

Am I Not Your Girl? (#27, 1992) is released in 1992, but is overshadowed when O'Connor tears up a picture of the Pope at the end of a song while performing on the NBC-TV show *Saturday Night Live*. The act creates an uproar in the catholic community and results in her being banned from the show for life. She is now booed virtually everywhere she travels in the U.S. but refuses to apologize for the event.

Universal Mother (#36, 1994) is a twist for the performer who now combines political prophecy amongst her compositions. She continues to be plagued by vicious rumors from suicide attempts to abortions by a seemingly endless stream of media. The good she does do, which is often considerable, from giving away homes to benefit performances, is often overlooked because of her misguided provocative statements and foolish actions.

AUTOGRAPHS

A CD, LP, magazine cover, ad, photo, or card signed by the artist: $30-$35

TOUR BOOKS/PROGRAMS/PASSES

Backstage Passes: $5-$8 (cloth), $8-$12 (laminated)

POSTERS/PRESS KITS

Promotional Posters: $8-$15
Press Kits: $10-$15

OFTEN OVERLOOKED MEMORABILIA

Movie memorabilia from *Captive*, *Married to the Mob*, and *In the Name of the Father*; her June 3, 1988, concert videotape *The Value of Ignorance*; a videotape from her acting debut in C4-TV film *Hush-A-Bye-Baby* (1990); all memorabilia from Roger Water's July 21, 1990, performance of *The Wall*; press clippings from her "I tore up the Pope" incident; her numerous contributions, video messages, and advertisements on behalf of AIDS research and education; *Q* magazine December 1990 issue - $5-$10; a videotape from her performance in *The Ghost of Oxford Street* C4-TV aired December 25, 1991; memorabilia from her contributions to other artists' albums such as *Two Rooms—Celebrating the Songs of Elton John & Bernie Taupin*; a copy of "Sinéad O'Connor—Coffee and Cigarettes" program on the making of her 1992 album; a copy of her written statement following the *Saturday Night Live* performance - $5; *Time* magazine (December 9, 1992) includes interview - $5; *Irish Times*, June 10, 1993, issue that includes her full-page ad - $5; Lollapalooza '95 memorabilia - she was part of eight dates

REFERENCES/BOOKS

Limited resources exist, but none do justice to the singer in my opinion. There are no dedicated collector books.

Ohio Express

Formed 1968

Joey Levine, Dale Powers, Doug Grassel, Jim Pfayler, Dean Kastran, and Tim Corwin

The Ohio Express shared producers with the 1910 Fruitgum Company (Kasenetz-Katz) along with vocalist Joey Levine in the era of bubblegum-based pop. While "Yummy, Yummy, Yummy" (#4, 1968) and "Chewy Chewy" (#15, 1968) were devoured by the public, many of the group's other singles were not equally consumed, including "Beg Borrow and Steal" (#29, 1967), "Try It" (#83, 1967), "Down at Lulu's" (#33, 1968), "Mercy" (#30, 1969), and a few others.

AUTOGRAPHS

A single, LP, magazine cover, ad, photo, or card signed by the group: $10-$15

POSTERS/PRESS KITS

Promotional Posters: $10

The Ohio Players

Formed 1959

Best-known lineup: Billy Beck, Clarence Satchell, Jimmy "Diamond" Williams, Leroy "Sugar" Bonner, Marvin Pierce, Marshall Jones, and Ralph "Pee Wee" Middlebrooks*

*Numerous personnel changes

Formed as Greg Webster and the Untouchables, the group spent a time as the backing band for the Falcons (Wilson Pickett), and following the addition of some personnel, the band became The Ohio Players. Working as a studio band for Compass Records in 1967, it worked diligently on a demo tape with hopes of landing a major recording contract of its own, which it did with Capital Records.

It wasn't until the group landed with Westbound Records of Detroit in the early '70s that things really started to happen. When the group hit the top of the R&B charts with "Funky Worm," which also made it to Number Fifteen on the pop charts, Mercury Records took notice and signed the act in 1974.

For three years, from 1974 to 1976, the band produced a consecutive run of hits including "Skin Tight" (#13, 1974), "Fire" (#1, 1974), "Love Rollercoaster" (#1, 1975), "Fopp" (#9, 1976), and "Who'd She Coo" (#18, 1976). "O-H-I-O" (#45, 1977) was the group's last big hit with Mercury Records before it moved to Arista. Although "Let's Play (From Now On)" (#33, 1988) did manage to make the Top Forty, it was clear that by this time the band had run its course.

While the group will be forever remembered for its hits, it also made an impression with the public

through its provocative album covers. Often, scantly glad women suggestively tangled with the elements, many of which were album subjects, including both fire and honey. More than one critic at the time suggested that at least a few albums were sold on the merits of the cover design alone—a point this author certainly can not dispute.

AUTOGRAPHS

A single, LP, magazine cover, ad, photo, or card signed by the group: $20-$45*

* High-end prices for "fire" or "honey" album covers

TOUR BOOKS/PROGRAMS/PASSES

Backstage Passes:
$5 (cloth), $5-$8 (laminated)

POSTERS/PRESS KITS

Promotional Posters: $10-$25
Press Kits: $10-$25

Oingo Boingo/Danny Elfman

Formed 1979

Danny Elfman, Born: May 19, 1953, Steve Bartek, Kerry Katch, Rich Gibbs, Johnny "Vatos" Hernandez, Sam Phipps, Leon Schneiderman, and Dale Turner*

*Gibbs and Katch left in 1983 and John Avila joined the band

Formerly a unique theatre group made up of a comedy troupe called the Mystic Knights of Oingo Boingo, the group joined the new-wave movement of the late '70s by adding a horn section and cross-pollinating its music with diverse influences while addressing strange topics. Often compared to Frank Zappa—for lack of a better choice—the band accomplished relatively little.

"Weird Science" (#45, 1985) became its highest charting single and the popularity of the song landed it on numerous soundtracks. Perhaps it was a portent of things to come, but Elfman did concentrate on his composition for both television and film. His credentials now include *Batman*, *The Nightmare Before Christmas*, and *James and the Giant Peach*. He is now considered one of Hollywood's most successful composers, and rightfully so because his music has been extremely popular, especially with children.

Oingo Boingo, now just Boingo, continues to produce records, but as of yet its greatest legacy will remain Danny Elfman, and everything considered, that in itself is pretty damn impressive!

AUTOGRAPHS

Group

A CD, LP, magazine cover, ad, photo, or card signed by the artist: $25-$35

Individual

Danny Elfman: $20-$35*

*High-end reflects key movie items

TOUR BOOKS/PROGRAMS/PASSES

Backstage Passes:
$5-$8 (cloth), $8-$15 (laminated)

POSTERS/PRESS KITS

Promotional Posters: $10-$15
Press Kits: $10

OFTEN OVERLOOKED MEMORABILIA

Movie memorabilia from all films Elfman has been involved with. This will not be cheap because the popularity of his films has drawn significant attention to his work and its relics.

The O'Jays

Formed 1958

Bobby Massey, Walter Williams, Eddie Levert, Bill Isles, and William Powell*

*Massey departed in 1972. Powell left in 1976 and Sammy Strain was added. Strain left in 1991 and Nathaniel Best joined the band.

The O'Jays helped forge the sound of the '70s as one of America's most popular vocal groups—it reflected the talent of not only the group's members but also of masterminds Gamble and Huff. Eddie Levert and Walter Williams, who were previously members of a gospel group, formed the Mascots, a doo-wop group, in 1958 with William Powell, Bobby Massey, and Bill Isles. The group eventually assumed its name in appreciation of fan and Cleveland DJ Eddie O'Jay. The O'Jays recorded with Imperial from 1963 to 1967, and scored its biggest hit with "Stand in for Love" (#12, R&B, 1966).

In 1965 the group became a quartet when Isles left, and the remaining members signed on with Bell, but following only one R&B hit, they were growing increasingly discouraged. That's when Kenny Gamble and Leon Huff stepped in and signed them to their Neptune label where the group landed four hits including "One Night Affair" (#15, R&B, 1969) and "Looky Looky (Look at Me Girl)" (#17, R&B, 1970). They then moved on to Gamble and Huff's new Philadelphia International label where they scored eight Number One R&B hits from 1972 to 1978 including "Back Stabbers" (#3, 1972), "Love Train" (#1, 1973), "For the Love of Money" (#9, 1974). "I Love Music (Part 1)" (#5, 1975), and "Use ta Be My Girl" (#4, 1978). The precious metal was rolling in faster than the O'Jays could find walls to hang all of their awards on.

Tragedy struck in 1975 when William Powell was diagnosed with cancer and died two years later. His replacement was Sammy Strain from Little Anthony and the Imperials. Levert and Williams were now assuming more responsibility within the band although they continued working with Gamble and Huff up until "Love Fever" (1975). After some time off the pop chart, they struck hard at the R&B list at the end of the decade with "Lovin' You" (#1, R&B, 1987), "Let Me

Touch You" (#5, R&B, 1987), "Have You Had Your Love Today" (#1, R&B, 1989), "Out of My Mind" (#11, R&B, 1989), and "Serious Hold on Me" (#9, R&B, 1989). They still seem to manage to reach deep inside their songbooks to land a top R&B tune almost on demand! In 1997, "What's Stopping You" finds its way to the singles chart, as a second generation is introduced to the band.

AUTOGRAPHS

A CD, LP, magazine cover, ad, photo, or card signed by the group: $35-$80*
*Original members

TOUR BOOKS/PROGRAMS/PASSES

Tour Programs:
In Concert (1976): $25

Oldfield, Mike

Born: May 15, 1953

Late-60s British composer Mike Oldfield is commonly associated with the album *Tubular Bells*, of which an edited version was released as a single (#7, 1974) and also used as the theme to the hit movie *The Exorcist*. He has also been successful at placing numerous singles on the U.K. chart including "In Dulce Jubilo" b/w " On Horseback" (#4, 1975)

AUTOGRAPHS

A CD, LP, magazine cover, ad, photo, or card signed by the artist: $10-$25

OFTEN OVERLOOKED MEMORABILIA

Movie memorabilia from *The Exorcist*

O'Neal, Alexander

Born: November 15, 1953

Emersed in his R&B roots, O'Neal originated out of Minneapolis with Flyte Time (Time) before landing solo with the R&B hit "Saturday Love" (1986), a Top Five duet with Cherrelle. "Never Knew Love Like This" (#28, 1988) and "Fake" (#25, 1987), off *Hearsay* (1987), also in collaboration with Cherrelle, landed successfully on the charts before the artist slipped outta sight.

AUTOGRAPHS

A CD, LP, magazine cover, ad, photo, or card signed by the artist: $10-$12

TOUR BOOKS/PROGRAMS/PASSES

Tour Book:
All True Man World Tour, 1991: $10

POSTERS/PRESS KITS

Promotional Posters: $7
Press Kits: $10

The Only Ones

Formed 1976

Peter Perrett, John Perry, Alan Mair, and Mike Kellie

Originating out of the British punk-rock movement, the band with a veteran rhythm section released two albums—*The Only Ones* (1978) and *Even Serpents Shine* (1979)—and became somewhat recognized for the single "Another Girl, Another Planet" (#57, 1992) before slipping into obscurity.

AUTOGRAPHS

A CD, LP, magazine cover, ad, photo, or card signed by the band: $10-$20

POSTERS/PRESS KITS

Promotional Posters: $7
Press Kits: $10

Ono, Yoko: See John Lennon

Orbison, Roy

Born: April 23, 1936, Died: December 6, 1988.

With his thick, dark sunglasses and smooth black pompadour, Roy Orbison charmed his way into our hearts with his crescendoing falsetto which ran smoothly across his often tender ballads. Although he often vacillated between blues-rooted rock and just pure rockabilly, his quavering tenor was the hallmark of many of his hits and immediately identifiable.

Although he scored numerous hits, Orbison is typically associated with the songs "Only the Lonely" (#2, 1960), "Running Scared" (#1, 1961), "Crying" (#2, 1961), "Dream Baby" (#4, 1962), and "Oh, Pretty Woman" (#1, 1964). His career slipped during the latter part of the '60s, and he suffered numerous personal tragedies, such as the loss of his wife and the death of two children, but Orbison somehow found the inner strength to continue. He toured Britain with the Beatles in 1963 and developed an extremely strong following which never seemed to dissipate over his entire career.

In 1980 he opened for the Eagles and landed a hit dueting with Emmylou Harris on "That Lovin' You Feelin' Again," extracted from the soundtrack to *Roadie*. His comeback show in New York the following year was an enormous success and it seemed as if the old wheels were turning again. Other artists were returning to his catalog, and even newer acts such as Van Halen were successfully covering songs such as "Oh, Pretty Woman." Many of his compositions even found their ways to movie soundtracks.

The '80s were good for Orbison: he was inducted into the Rock and Roll Hall of Fame, became a member of the Traveling Wilburys, taped an all-star tribute show, and had his first Top Twenty hit in twenty-five years with "You Got It" (#9, 1989), which was included on his solo album *Mystery Girl* (#5, 1989). The album was tragically released posthumously—the singer died of a sudden heart attack in 1988.

AUTOGRAPHS
A CD, LP, magazine cover, ad, photo, or card signed by the artist: $125-$225

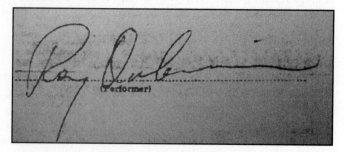

The signature of the legendary Roy Orbison

TOUR BOOKS/PROGRAMS/PASSES
Tour Programs:
Arthur Howe Presents, 1965: $55
Also see the Beatles

POSTERS/PRESS KITS
Promotional Posters:
(1980-1988) $10-$20, Example: Mystery Girl - $12
Press Kits: (1980-1988) $12-$25

OFTEN OVERLOOKED MEMORABILIA
Laminar Flow, Asylum promo sunglasses with "Orbison" on one side - $40; Mystery Girl, Australia, Virgin (1989) CD came with printed ribbon and card for Mother's day

REFERENCES/BOOKS
Limited resources exist, but none do justice to the artist in my opinion, and there are no dedicated collector books. Serious collectors should subscribe to: In Dreams: Roy Orbison Magazine, Attention: Burt Kaufman, 484 Lake Park #80, Oakland, CA 94610

Orchestral Manoeuvres in the Dark (OMD)

Formed 1978
Andy McCluskey, Paul Humphreys, David Hughes, and Malcolm Holmes*

*Numerous personnel changes

This perpetual post-punk synth party was formed by Paul Humphreys and Andy McCluskey, two Kraftwork junkies who first landed with VCL XI in 1976, followed by Hitler's Underpantz and the Id. In 1978 they adopted the name Orchestral Manoeuvres in the Dark (OMD). The group's debut single "Electricity" was a Top Forty British hit and was heavily played in American new-wave clubs. It set the groundwork for the second *Album Architecture and Morality* (#144, 1982). Praised by critics and a growing cult following, it wasn't until the album *Crush* (#38, 1985) hit, with extracts "So In Love" (#26, 1985) and "Secret" (#63, 1985), that anyone really took notice. The following year the group scored its biggest hit with "If You Leave" (#4, 1986), which was followed by two other singles, "(Forever) Live and Die" (#19, 1986) and "Dreaming" (#16, 1988), before the band split up.

AUTOGRAPHS
A CD, LP, magazine cover, ad, photo, or card signed by the group: $15-$25

POSTERS/PRESS KITS
Promotional Posters: $7-$15
Press Kits: $10-$15

OFTEN OVERLOOKED MEMORABILIA
Movie memorabilia from *Pretty in Pink* (1986)

Oregon

Formed 1970
Ralph Towner, Paul McCandless, Glenn Moore, and Colin Walcott*

This instrumental limb of the Paul Winter Consort managed some commercial success with its lightly jazz-infused arrangements before going splitting up.

AUTOGRAPHS
A CD, LP, magazine cover, ad, photo, or card signed by the group: $10

The Orioles

Formed 1946
Sonny Til, (1925-1981), George Nelson, Alexander Sharp, Johnny Reed, and Tommy Gaither*

*Gaither died in 1950 and Ralph Williams was added. Nelson left in 1953 and Gregory Carol joined the band along with Charlie Hayes.

Often cited as a frontrunner to the doo-wop sound of the '50s, this R&B vocal group was extraordinarily talented. In 1948 it signed with Natural Records and changed its name from the Vibranaires to the Orioles. Several singles quickly scored for the group including "It's Too Soon to Know" (#13, 1948), which was a landmark for black acts at this time, "Lonely Christmas" (#8, R&B, 1949), the classic "Tell Me So" (#1, R&B, 1949), the first use of a wordless falsetto technique indicative of doo-wop, "A Kiss and a Rose" (#12, R&B, 1949), "Forgive and Forget" (#5 R&B, 1949), and "What Are You Doing New Year's Eve" (#9, R&B, 1949). Tragedy struck the following year when Gaither was killed in an automobile accident that also injured Nelson and Reed.

Nelson then quit, and the group added two other members before recording "Crying in the Chapel" (#11, 1953), one of the first successful cross-over records in rock music. It was followed by "In the Mission of St. Augustine," the group's final hit before the original group disbanded. The group was inducted into the Rock and Roll Hall of Fame in 1995.

AUTOGRAPHS

A CD, LP, magazine cover, ad, photo, or card signed by the group: $100-$250

OFTEN OVERLOOKED MEMORABILIA

Videotapes of their appearances on *Arthur Godfrey's Talent Scouts* television program

Orlando, Tony and Dawn

Formed 1970

Tony Orlando (Michael Cassavitis), Born: April 3, 1944, Telma Hopkins, and Joyce Vincent-Wilson

Orlando, who had charted in the '60s with the songs "Halfway to Paradise" and "Bless You", was asked to record the lead vocal to the song "Candida" (#3, 1970), which had been recorded by the unknown group Dawn in 1970. "Knock Three Times" (#1, 1971) by Dawn was the trios next smash hit, although it was released prior to all three members even having met in-person. On Orlando's insistence, the three united for live performances. Numerous singles follow including "I Play and Sing" (#25, 1971), "Summer Sand," and "What Are You Doing Sunday" before "Tie a Yellow Ribbon Round the Old Oak Tree" (#1, 1973) catapulted the group into superstardom.

"Say, Has Anybody Seen My Sweet Gypsy Rose" (#3, 1973) and "Steppin' Out" (Gonna Boogie Tonight) (#7, 1974), along with a four-week variety show pilot on CBS-TV, kept the group in the public's eye. "Look in My Eyes Pretty Woman" (#11, 1975), "He Don't Love You (Like I Love You)" (#1, 1975), "Mornin' Beautiful" (#14, 1975), and "Cupid" (#22, 1976) sustained the band just prior to Orlando's surprise announcement in 1977 that he would no longer perform. Having suffered the loss of his sister and the suicide of his good friend Freddie Prinze, Orlando was extremely depressed. Although the artist returned to live performing and even reunited with Dawn in 1988, the group never again regained its previous success. Hopkins then embarked on what would be a very successful television acting career, while Orlando also occassionally tested the waters.

AUTOGRAPHS

A CD, LP, magazine cover, ad, photo or card signed by the group: $40-$100

OFTEN OVERLOOKED MEMORABILIA

Videotapes from the group's numerous television appearances including their own series, July 3, 1974- December 28, 1976

Orleans

Formed 1972

Lance Hoppen, Wells Kelly , Larry Hoppen, Jerry Marotta, and John Hall, Born: October 25, 1947*

*Hall and Marotta left in 1977. Bob Leinbach and R.A. Martin were added. Wells died in 1984.

Orleans was founded by Larry Hopen, Wells Kelly, and John Hall, who along with his wife Johanna, wrote some of the group's finest music and even songs for other musicians including Janis Joplin's "Half Moon."

Larry's brother Lance joined later, and the band quickly developed a large cult following, especially in the East. The group's second album, *Let There Be Music*, scored its first hit single with "Dance With Me" (#6, 1975), while follow-up album *Walking and Dreaming* struck pay dirt with extract "Still the One" (#5, 1976). Hall then left the band to pursue a solo career, signed to Elektra Records, and turned his focus to MUSE (Musicians United for Safe Energy).

"Love Takes Time" (#11, 1979), extracted from *Forever*, was the band's last hit single, but it continued to tour and sustain a fairly large following. The group endured some personnel changes and the tragic death of Wells Kelly in 1984. Hall returned to perform with Orleans during the summer of 1995.

AUTOGRAPHS

A CD, LP, magazine cover, ad, photo, or card signed by the group: $25-$40*
*Original members

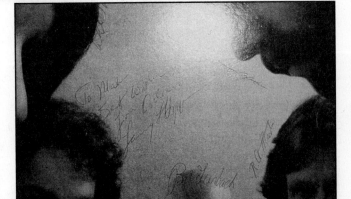

An autographed album from the band Orleans

TOUR BOOKS/PROGRAMS/PASSES
Backstage Passes:
$6-$8 (cloth), $8-$10 (laminated)

POSTERS/PRESS KITS
Promotional Posters: $15-$25
Press Kits: $10-$20

USED CLOTHING/EQUIPMENT
Guitar Picks
John Hall: $10

Videotapes of the ABC television commercials using "Still the One"; assorted MUSE memorabilia.

Orr, Ben: See The Cars

****

"On The Edge"

Osborne, Joan

After paying her dues in Manhattan clubs, she recorded on her own Womanly Hips label in 1992, before moving over to Gorilla to release *Relish* (#9, 1996). She toured with Rusted Root (1995) and key television appearances such as *Saturday Night Live* (1/13/96) helped sell extract "One of Us" (#4, 1996) up the charts, while even pushing Osborne on to the cover of *Rolling Stone* magazine. Already established in numerous humanitarian efforts, Joan Osborne has charmed her way into our hearts. Whether it's her sexual spunk, or just that cute nose piercing, you can't afford to ignore her. By now, you should know better. Autograph: $20-$50

Joan Osborne. Photo by Frank Ockenfels 3. Courtesy Mercury Records.

****

Osborne, Jeffrey

Born: March 9, 1948

This soulful baritone captured hearts through his tender ballads such as "On the Wings of Love" (#29, 1982), "You Should Be Mine (The Woo Woo Song)" (#13, 1986), and "Love Power"(#12, 1987), a duet with Dionne Warwick. Osborne had previously spent a decade with L.T.D. (Love, Togeth-erness, Devotion). L.T.D. scored hits with "Love Ballad" (320, 1976) and "(Every Time I Turn Around) Back in Love Again" (#4, 1977) over the course of six albums—all displayed Osborne's heavy Motown influences.

AUTOGRAPHS
A CD, LP, magazine cover, ad, photo, or card signed by the artist: $15-$20

OFTEN OVERLOOKED MEMORABILIA
All of his work with L.T.D.

Osbourne, Ozzy

(John Osbourne)
Born: December 3, 1948

The "Wizard of Oz" left Black Sabbath after seven albums and enormous success, but oscillated and returned briefly later after plans to form his own band fell apart. In 1980, after a permanent split from Black Sabbath, Osbourne formed the Blizzard of Ozz and embarked on a U.K. mini-tour supporting the group's self-titled debut (#21, 1981), which was driven up the charts by the singles "Crazy Train" (#49, U.K., 1980) and "Mr. Crowley" (#46, U.K., 1980).

Diary of a Madman (#16, 1981) fared well the album charts as the band continued to be plagued by personnel changes and problems. *Mr. Crowley* (#120, 1982), a picture disc live EP, climbed the U.S. charts while Osbourne recorded and released *Talk of the Devil* (#14, 1983), a compilation of old Sabbath tunes.

Bark at the Moon (#19, 1983) was his next album. Again, personnel changes persisted. On July 13, 1985, Osbourne reunited with Tony Iommi, Geezer Butler, and Bill Ward for a day as Black Sabbath at Live Aid. His next album was *The Ultimate Sin* (#6, 1986)—the Oz master drove sales through his extensive touring. *Tribute* (#6, 1987), the group's next double disc, was dedicated to guitarist Randy Rhoads who was killed in a 1982 tour plane crash. *No Rest for the Wicked* (#13, 1988), his last album of the decade, followed.

Just Say Ozzy (#58, 1990), *No More Tears* (#7, 1991), *Live and Loud* (#22, 1993), and *Ozzmosis* (#4, 1995) rounded out his album offerings during the '90s.

AUTOGRAPHS
A CD, LP, magazine cover, ad, photo, or card signed by the artist: $20-$40

OZZY OSTENTATION - Notable Events (Un)Worthy of Generating Ozzy Artifacts

*1981	Not an Osprey, but a bat is beheaded before CBS/Columbia executives at a meeting in L.A. While osmosis is not a concern, portions of the bat seem to ossify during this ostensible act which prompts the band members to carefully examine the chicken wings in the dressing room.
*1982	While traveling near Orlando, Florida, the party's tour plane begins buzzing its tour bus, like the Luftwaffe over London, however, during the last pass the wing clips the bus, throwing the plane out of control, and killing three occupants.
*1984	Osbourne accidentally swallows glass during the filming of the video for the single "So Tired" (#20, U.K., 1984). While there appears to be no permanent ill effects, the singer is allegedly seen drinking Windex during a routine sound check.
*1986	A lawsuit against Osbourne and CBS Inc., seeking to implicate Osbourne in the suicide of a California teenager on the basis that he was influenced by the singer's song "Suicide Solution," is refused reinstatement.
*1987	The Wizard is mugged in New York's Time Square by an assailant who thrusts a knife through an open window of the taxi cab he is riding in. The cab driver, who allegedly has just moved to this country and can speak little English, jumps out of the car screaming "War Pigs."
*1988	Ozzy announces his intent to tour the world's insane asylums. While nothing amounts to the tour, his next tour opens in Omaha, Nebraska, creating speculation as to the intent of the opening date.
*1989	On September 2, 1989, Ozzy is charged with threatening to kill his wife, but is later released under the condition that he enter a detox center and avoid contact with her. The case is later dropped when the two reconcile. Allegations that Ozzy was going to do it in the library, with a candlestick, are later denied!
*1991	Ozzy breaks his foot onstage during a show, forcing him to cancel the remaining dates of the Theater of Madness tour. The musician later claims it happened as a result of his song "Suicide Solution" and decides to sue himself!
*1992	Oz invites the first two rows of his audience to join him on stage, while the maestro crawls off stage, the mob racks up $100,000 worth of damage. Osbourne later claims he was trying to break the record for a table dance! What the hell was this guy thinking anyway? Osbourne, in a landmark decision, is allowed to perform in San Antonio, Texas, his first concert in more than a decade, after he was ostracized for urinating on a wall at the Alamo. Allegations that he was told it was the car rental place, and not the historical landmark, are later disproven.
*1996	Osbourne receives whiplash and is knocked unconscious when his car is rear-ended after a show at The Summit in Houston on January 7

TOUR BOOKS/PROGRAMS/PASSES

Tour Programs:
Bark at the Moon Tour '84: $35
Ultimate Sin World Tour '86: $25
1989 Japan Tour: $50

Backstage Passes:
$10-$12(cloth), $15-$25 (laminated)

POSTERS/PRESS KITS
Promotional Posters: $15-$25
Press Kits: $15-$20

USED CLOTHING/EQUIPMENT
Guitar Picks: $10-$40*
*Geezer Butler primarily!

OFTEN OVERLOOKED MEMORABILIA
A personal copy of *Diary of a Madman* by occultist Aleister Crowley, along with Ozzy's autobiography of the same name; copies of Ozzy issued videotapes *The Ultimate Ozzy* (1987); a copy of Sam Kinison's video "Under My Thumb" featuring "The Oz" (1990); videotapes from ITV's cartoon series *The Dreamstone* featuring "The Urpney Song"; videotapes from his numerous television appearances including *Parker Lewis Can't Lose* (1990), "Halloween Jam at Universal Studios" (10/31/92), "Halloween Jam II" (10/23/93), and "Faith & Music" (5/16/93); memorabilia associated with "Kermit Unplugged" (1994); No Rest for the Wicked counter display - $12, Diary of a Madman Epic, 1989 promo diary; Bible of Ozz, Japan, Epic promo box includes CD, belt buckle, patch, and diary, 1988; Bark at the Moon set of 5 promo postcards - $15

REFERENCES/BOOKS

Limited resources exist, but none do justice to the singer in my opinion. There are no dedicated collector books.

Osibisa

Formed 1969

Teddy Osei, Sol Amarfio, Mac Tontoh, Robert Bailey, Wendell Richardson, Spartacus R., and Loughty Amao*

*Numerous personnel changes

Osibisa gained some recognition for crossing pop and with traditionally-rooted African music. Teddy Osei formed the band, and it signed to Decca Records in 1970. The band developed a cult following based on its live act and numerous television appearances which were often enhanced by members' ornate costuming. Its biggest hit was "Sunshine Day."

AUTOGRAPHS

A CD, LP, magazine cover, ad, photo, or card signed by the group: $15-$20

OFTEN OVERLOOKED MEMORABILIA

Movie memorabilia from *Superfly TNT*; associated artifacts from musicians who have covered their songs; videotapes of their numerous television appearances especially in the U.K.

The Osmonds/Donny Osmond/ Marie Osmond

Formed 1957

Alan Osmond, Wayne Osmond, Merrill Osmond, Jay Osmond, Donny Osmond, Born: December 9, 1957, Marie Osmond, Born: October 13, 1959, and Jimmy Osmond

Like the Jacksons, the Osmonds contributed significantly to rock and roll music, leaving behind a legacy and family dynasty. During the '70s, the family scored more than twenty gold records (in numerous combinations), positioning the family securely in the entertainment business. Now well into their fourth decade, the Osmonds' members have gone on to solo careers and on to the Osmond Boys and the Osmonds Second Generation.

The family carries on the rich tradition of the parents, George and Olive, who always felt music education was an important part of a child's development. Raised in a strict Morman environment, the family began singing religious and barbershop-quartet songs. As fate would have it, it landed a spot on "Disneyland After Dark," a segment of *Walt Disney's Wonderful World of Color*—it was the family's television debut. The group then auditioned with Andy Williams for his popular television variety show, and once invited, made numerous appearances from 1962 to 1971.

During the '60s, now with Donny, the group made other television appearances (*The Jerry Lewis Show* 1967 to 1969) and even toured with celebrities including Pat Boone. By the time the band was ready to record, it had developed a respectable level of musical prowess. The group's self-titled debut quickly sold gold, as did Donny's single "Sweet and Innocent" (#7, 1971). The group also took musical rivals the Jacksons' song "One Bad Apple" (#1, 1971) to the top of the singles chart, while working in conjunction with Donny's solo career. Other hits followed including "Double Lovin'"(#14, 1971), "Yo-Yo" (#3, 1971), and Donny's "Go Away Little Girl" (#1, 1971).

During the following years, Donny struck pay dirt with "Hey Girl/I Knew You When" (#9, 1972), "Puppy Love" (#3, 1972), "Why" (#13, 1973), "Too Young" (#13, 1972), "The Twelfth of Never" (#8, 1973), and "A Million to One/Young Love" (#23, 1971), while the group released the hits "Down by the Lazy River" (#4, 1972), "Hold Her Tight" (#14, 1972), and "Goin' Home" (#36, 1973). During this period Marie also made her recording debut, which included "Paper Roses" (#5, 1973), although her focus was more toward country and western. Little Jimmie also had a hit with "Long Haired Lover from Liverpool" (#38, 1972).

The family's success led to jealous assaults which claimed the Osmonds' clean-cut family image was just a bubble gum fad, but many were proven wrong during the next decade. Marie updated her image and teamed with Donny on television work and in the film *Goin' Coconuts* (1978). She also scored some country hits including "Meet Me in Montana" (#1, 1985), a duet with Dan Seals, "There's No Stopping Your Heart" (1985), and "You're Still New to Me," a duet with Paul Davis. Donny also appeared on Broadway and maintained his recording career with hit singles "Soldier of Love" (#2, 1989) and "My Love Is a Fire" (#21, 1990). Meanwhile, The Osmond Brothers (without Donny and Jimmy), focused on country music, where Billboard's top new singles group award was handed them in 1992. Working out of Branson, Missouri, they own, operate, and perform at the Osmond Family Theater. Rumored in 1997: Donnie and Marie are returning to television!

AUTOGRAPHS

Group
A CD, LP, magazine cover, ad, photo, or card signed by the group: $25-$55
Individual
Marie Osmond: $10-$25
Donny Osmond: $10-$20

TOUR BOOKS/PROGRAMS/PASSES

Tour Books:
1982 Tour: $10-$12
Backstage Passes:
$5-$8 (cloth/paper), $10-$20 (laminated)

POSTERS/PRESS KITS

Promotional Posters: $7; $10-$20 (1971-1973)
Press Kits: $10; $10-$25 (1971-1973)

OFTEN OVERLOOKED MEMORABILIA

A videotape of the Osmonds in their television debut on "Disneyland After Dark"; copies of their appearances on *The Andy Williams Show* from 1962 to 1971; videotapes and memorabilia from *The Osmonds* cartoon series on ITV (1972-1974) and from their six live BBC-TV shows (1974); videotapes of the *Donny and Marie* show (1976) - ABC-TV and the *Marie* show (1980); movie memorabilia from *Goin' Coconuts* (1978); videotapes from additional television appearances including 48 Hours (3/13/91) (Marie), "Bob Hope's Yellow Ribbon Party" (4/6/91) (Marie), and *Parker Lewis Can't Lose* (4/28/91) (Donny); a playbill from *Joseph and the Amazing Technicolor Dreamcoat*; a program from

the boxing match of the decade "Osmond vs. Bonaduce" (1/17/94); **Osmond Artifacts:** Jimmy doll - $80; coloring book - $25; trading cards (Donruss) - $60 (set); Jimmy Halloween Costume - $25; lunch box (Aladdin) - $100; photo activity albums - $17; stationary - $50; thermos - $20-$30 (2 styles); wall decoration (Rocky Mt. Rainbow Corp.) - $60; **Donny and Marie Artifacts:** books (Golden Press) $7, (Whitman) - $10; lunch bag - $100; buttons (Osbro) - $10; color book (Whitman) - $12; colorforms (dress-up set) -$40; Country & Rock Rhythm Set (tambourine and microphone, Gordy) - $20; doll carry case (vinyl) - $55; doll clothes (Mattel 10" x 13") boxed - $15; dolls (all Mattel) 12" Donny - $25, 12" Marie - $25, Boxed together $80, 30" Marie modeling doll - $80; dress patterns (Butterick) - $8; fan club kit (1976) - $50; game (Mattel TV show) - $25; guitar (1977) - $90; Halloween costume - $30; key chains - $5; lunch boxes - $100; makeup set (Marie) - (Mattel) - $25; notebook (Westab) loose-leaf - $25; paper dolls - Marie - $35, Donny & Marie (Whitman) - $25; puzzle (Whitman) - $12; radio (LJN AM) portable - $70; record cases (Perrless, two sizes) large- $45, small - $25; record player (1977) - $40; string puppets (Madison Ltd., 1978) - Donny - $55, Marie - $45, set w/both - $110; thermoses (two versions, long & short hair) each - $20; tooth brush (battery operated) - $75; television show play set (Mattel) - $75; vanity set - Marie - $50; assorted magazines featuring the two entertainers

TOUR BOOKS/PROGRAMS/PASSES

Tour Books:
1982 Tour $10 -$12

REFERENCES/BOOKS

Numerous resources exist, but there are no dedicated collector books.

O'Sullivan, Gilbert

(Raymond O'Sullivan)
Born: December 1, 1946

Pop singer and songwriter, formerly with Rick's Blues, scored his first solo hit in Britain with "Nothing Rhymed" (#8, 1970), followed by his breakthrough U.S. hits "Alone Again (Naturally)" (#1, 1972) and "Clair" (#2, 1972). "Out of the Question" (#17, 1973), "Get Down" (#7, 1973), and "Ooh Baby" (#25, 1973) followed before he slipped into obscurity. He briefly re-emerged with "I Don't Love You, But I Think I Like You" and "What's in a Kiss?" in 1980. O'Sullivan was one of the first artists to challenge the sampling of recorded music in 1991.

AUTOGRAPHS

A CD, LP, magazine cover, ad, photo, or card signed by the artist: $20-$35

The Other Two: See Joy Division

Otis, Johnny

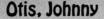

(John Veliotes)
Born: December 8, 1921

An integral figure in rhythm and blues, rock and roll pioneer Johnny Otis has been a successful songwriter, producer, performer, bandleader, and even a talent scout! "Harlem Nocturne" was his first regional hit in 1945, well before his hits "Double Crossing Blues" (#1, R&B, 1950), "Mistrustin' Blues" (#1, R&B, 1950), "Deceivin' Blues" (#4, R&B, 1950), "Dreamin' Blues" (#8, R&B, 1950), and "Wedding Boogie" (#6, R&B, 1950)—many more followed.

Johnny Otis Rhythm and Blues Caravan toured America from 1950 to 1954, with many then unknown performers including Hank Ballard and Jackie Wilson. Otis produced Big Mama Thornton's version of "Hound Dog" and watched his penned "Every Beat of My Heart" become Gladys Knight and the Pips' first hit in 1961.

He quit the road in 1954 and took a job as a DJ before landing his own television show. It was during this period that he had his biggest hit, "Willie and the Hand Jive" (#9, 1958). He then became active in the civil rights movement of the '60s and began to work with his guitarist son Johnny Otis, Jr. In 1978 he became an ordained minister and also progressed as both a painter and sculptor. A mutli-faceted individual, possessing incredible creativity, he found his proper home when he was inducted into the Rock and Roll Hall of Fame in 1994.

AUTOGRAPHS

A CD, LP, magazine cover, ad, photo, or card signed by the artist: $20-$45

OFTEN OVERLOOKED MEMORABILIA

Any artifacts from his popular Watts nightclub, The Barrelhouse Club; all memorabilia, posters, etc. from the Johnny Otis Rhythm and Blues Caravan (1950-1954); videotapes of his television shows; memorabilia from artists who have covered his material; one of his original paintings or sculptures.

REFERENCES/BOOKS

Listen to the Lambs, his autobiography

Otis, Shuggie

(Johnny Otis, Jr.)
Born: November 30, 1953

Shuggie Otis, the son of Johnny Otis, was a child prodigy who has contributed to numerous sessions with other musicians including Frank Zappa, while recording a few albums of his own. He watched the Brothers Johnson take his penned "Strawberry Letter 23" to a Top Five hit in 1977, although by this time he had turned his attention elsewhere.

AUTOGRAPHS

A CD, LP, magazine cover, ad, photo, or card signed by the artist: $10-$12

USED CLOTHING/EQUIPMENT

Guitar Pick: $10

OFTEN OVERLOOKED MEMORABILIA

Items relating to his work with his father and the numerous sessions he has appeared on including Frank Zappa's *Hot Rats*.

Otway, John

Born: October 2, 1952

"(Cor Baby, That's) Really Free" (#27, U.K., 1977), John Otway's only hit, classifies the musician as an "OHW," a one hit wonder, which has so annoyed him that he has spent his entire career trying to score another.

AUTOGRAPHS

A CD, LP, magazine cover, ad, photo, or card signed by the artist: $5

REFERENCES/BOOKS

Cor Baby, It's Really Me by John Otway (1990)

Hughie Thomasson from the Outlaws

The Outlaws

Formed 1974

Hughie Thomasson, Billy Jones, Henry Paul, Frank O'Keefe, and Monte Yoho*

*O'Keefe and Paul departed in 1977 and Harvey Dalton Arnold and David Dix joined the band. Freddie Salem was added in 1978, then left in 1979. Arnold left in 1979 and Rick Cua was added. Yoho departed in 1980, and Jones in 1981. Group re-formed in 1983: Paul, Thomasson, Chris Hicks, Barry Borden, and Jeff Howell. Paul left again in 1986. O'Keefe and Jones both died in February 1995.

Clive Davis' first Arista Records signing, this Tampa-based band, structured in a traditional (Allman Brothers style) country rock format with two twin engine driving guitars, could soothe you with a soft country ballad, or "brand your behind" with the riveting opening chords of "Green Grass and High Tides," a country rock classic. Enormously talented, the band was "all go" and "no show," letting the music speak for itself.

Popular on the college and university circuit, The Outlaws landed some chart success with "There Goes Another Love Song" (#34, 1975) and "(Ghost) Riders in the Sky" (#31, 1980), but their FM audience really

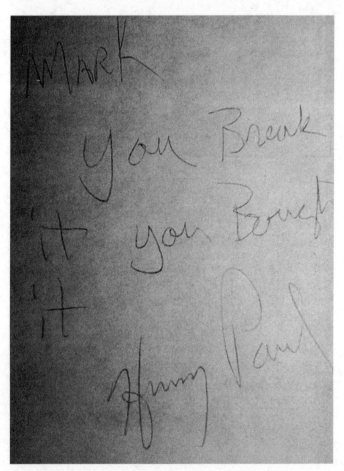

An autograph from Outlaw Henry Paul

drove the sales of their albums. Henry Paul left in 1977, but often joined the band on tour. Tragically the band lost two founding members in February 1995.

AUTOGRAPHS

A CD, LP, magazine cover, ad, photo, or card signed by the group: $20-$45*

*Original Members, scarce because O'Keefe left in 1977

Owens, Buck

(Alvis Edgar Owens, Jr.)
Born: August 12, 1929

One of the founding fathers of the "Bakersfield Sound," the other of course being Merle Haggard, he is a country music living legend, who ironically is probably best remembered as the cohost of the popular television show *Hee Haw* (1969-1986).

Buck, a name he took from his favorite mule, migrated to Bakersfield from Arizona when he was twenty-one. There he played sessions with musicians such as Gene Vincent and Sonny James, and even recorded a little rockabilly on his own under the name Corky Jones.

"Under Your Spell Again" (#4, 1959) started things off for Owen, now recording under his own name, and was the first of an amazing seventy-five charting country singles that continued into the '80s. Backed by the Buckaroos, he scored twenty Number One hits including "Act Naturally," "I've Got a Tiger by the Tail" (1965), and "Open Your Heart" (1966). His commitment to his traditional approach of drums, pedal steel, two guitars, and an occasional fiddle, combined with his tenor voice, was his magic recipe.

Pablo Cruise

Formed 1973
Dave Jenkins, Cory Lerios, Bud Cockrell, and Steve Price*
*Cockrell leaves in 1977 and Bruce Day is added. Day departs in 1980 and is replaced with Angelo Rossi and John Pierce

This is a band rich in the laid back, "soak up the sun" California sound, which enjoyed quick notoriety and solid radio airplay with hits such as "Watcha Gonna Do?" (#6, 1977), "Love Will Find a Way" (#6, 1978), "Don't Want to Live Without It" (#21, 1978), "I Go to Rio" (#46, 1979), and "Cool Love."

AUTOGRAPHS

A CD, LP, magazine cover, ad, photo, or card signed by the group: $20-$32

Owens spent most of the late '70s in semi-retirement, but was lured out in 1987 by "hat act" Dwight Yoakam to duet on the hit "The Streets of Bakersfield." The non-Nashville performers took the song into the Top Ten and even provided old Buck the enticement of picking up the old guitar one more time. "Ladies and Gentleman, Alvis is back in the building!"

AUTOGRAPHS

A CD, LP, magazine cover, ad, photo, or card signed by the artist: $10-$25

USED CLOTHING/EQUIPMENT
Guitar Pick: $20-$40

OFTEN OVERLOOKED MEMORABILIA

Videotapes of old *Hee Haw* episodes; memorabilia associated with covers of his songs.

Ozark Mountain Daredevils

Formed 1971
John Dillon, Steve Cash, Randle Chowning, Michael Granda, Buddy Bryfield, and Larry Lee

Whatya get when you mix a little Missouri moonshine with hillbilly picking and a pinch of snuff? Try the Cosmic Corncob and His Amazing Mountain Daredevils, later known as the Ozark Mountain Daredevils. They first came down from the hills with the single "If You Wanna Get to Heaven" (#25, 1974) before landing with their biggest hit "Jackie Blue" (#3, 1975). They then slipped away again—probably went huntin'!

AUTOGRAPHS

A CD, LP, magazine cover, ad, photo, or card signed by the group: $10-$20

POSTERS/PRESS KITS
Promotional Posters: $15-$20
Press Kits: $20-$30

OFTEN OVERLOOKED MEMORABILIA

Videotapes of television specials using their music as a soundtrack; a copy of the surfing documentary *Free Ride*; movie memorabilia from *An Unmarried Woman* and *Dreamer*.

Page, Jimmy

Born: January 9, 1944

Since the demise of Led Zeppelin, Jimmy Page, considered one of rock's finest guitar players, writers, and producers, has been involved in numerous collaborations intermixed with solo outings. In 1982 he scored with the primarily instrumental *Death Wish II*. The following year he joined the 1983-84 ARMS (Action and Research in Multiple Sclerosis) tour to benefit ex-Faces bassist Ronnie Lane—it was the first time he had been on a concert stage since 1980.

Page then contributed to Robert Plant's first solo album, *Pictures at 11*, in 1982, followed two years later by his founding of the Firm with Paul Rodgers. The group released two albums and did one tour, both with little impact. Page then picked up another cocaine possession arrest, his second, in 1984.

The latter half of the decade found Page releasing *Outrider* (#26, 1988), his first real solo album, which garnered a Grammy nomination and even prompted a tour. During the '90s he released an album with David Coverdale (Whitesnake) (#5, 1993) and reunited with Robert Plant for the album *No Quarter* and on the *MTV Unplugged* special "Unledded."

AUTOGRAPHS

A CD, LP, magazine cover, ad, photo, or card signed by the artist: $35-$155

A Page/Plant backstage pass (Printed by OTTO)

TOUR BOOKS/ PROGRAMS/ PASSES

Tour Programs:
Page & Plant World Tour 1995: $15

Backstage Passes:
Outrider: $9 (cloth); The Firm (1985, rectangular, red, green, blue): $4-$5 (cloth)

POSTERS/PRESS KITS

Promotional Posters:
No Quarter cover - $5, No Quarter personality posters - $6, No Quarter tour poster (Miller Genuine Draft) - $5, MTV Unplugged poster -$15 (sm.), $20 (lg.), Coverdale/ Page - $3-$6, Outrider - $4-$12, ARMS Concert - $5, Firm - $6
Press Kits: $25-$50, Example: "Unledded" - $25

A Coverdale/Page guitar pick

OFTEN OVERLOOKED MEMORABILIA

Outrider promotional print of the album cover, autographed (Limited to 300) - $500, unsigned - $20; Outrider, Geffen promo lunch pail (black w/JP logo) with CD, cassette, and video, 1988; Coverdale/Page road sign - $30 (40" square); Coverdale/Page display - $25; Ourider regional display - $12; **Page & Plant Artifacts:** No Quarter tour cup (plastic) - $5; concert flyer - $5; No Quarter keychain - $2; No Quarter banner - $4; No Quarter table tent - $3; No Quarter tour pennants - $20; No Quarter Tour mobile with blimp - $30; No Quarter counter display - $20; No Quarter tour banner - $35; No Quarter tour banner "day of show" - $75; No Quarter cardboard display, U.K. - $150.

Palmer, Robert

(Alan Palmer)

Born: January 19, 1949

Forever eclectic, Palmer has sustained and enriched his career through a series of transformations, contributions, collaborations, dissertations, luck, and fine tailored suits. He went professional in 1968 with the Alan Bown set before joining Dada, which released three albums before splitting up. Palmer then went solo with *Sneakin' Sally Through the Alley* (1974), *Pressure Drop* (1975), *Some People Can Do What They Like* (1976), and *Double Fun* (1978), the latter of which yielded "Every Kinda People" (#16, 1978). "Bad Case of Loving You (Doctor, Doctor)" (#14,1979) was extracted from *Secrets*, his first self-produced work.

His next phase came when he joined Power Station, where he rocked on tunes "Get It On" and "Some Like It Hot" (#2, 1986) before he departed due to his reluctance to tour. Palmer then transformed himself into a sex symbol of sorts with *Riptide*, which yielded hit extracts "Addicted to Love" (#1, 1986) and "I Didn't Mean to Turn You On" (#2, 1986). His MTV promotional videos, featuring sensuous deadpan female models in short skin tight skirts, backing up the sharp-dressed singer, were instant hits. *Heavy Nova*, his next album, picked up where its predecessor left off, scoring hits with "Simply Irresistible" (#2, 1988) and "Early in the Morning" (#19, 1988). He continued to evolve over the years that followed, exploring diversions into Tin Pan Alley and other forms of music.

AUTOGRAPHS

A CD, LP, magazine cover, ad, photo, or card signed by the artist: $20-$40

OFTEN OVERLOOKED MEMORABILIA

Movie memorabilia from *Sweet Lies*

Paris

(Oscar Jackson)

Born: October 29, 1967

This controversial Bay Area rapper gained notoriety when his second album for Warner Brothers Records was rejected due to the controversial subject matter with the songs "Coffee, Donuts & Death" (a cop killing fantasy) and "Bush Killa" (about an assassination on then President Bush). The "Black Panther of Rap" and founder of the Scarface label, Paris has been heavily influenced by the ideology of the '60s Black Panther Party.

AUTOGRAPHS

A CD, LP, magazine cover, ad, photo, or card signed by the artist: $10-$15

OFTEN OVERLOOKED MEMORABILIA

All items associated with his rejected effort *Sleeping with the Enemy* (1992, Scarface)

Paris, Mica

(Michelle Wallen)
Born: April 27, 1969

A British pop singer with roots in soul, Paris swaggered on to the music scene in the '80s with her extract "My One Temptation" from her *So Good* (1988) debut. She has had numerous other hits, but remains far more successful in Britain.

AUTOGRAPHS

A CD, LP, magazine cover, ad, photo, or card signed by the artist: $10-$15

Parker, Charlie

Born: August 29, 1920, Died: March 12, 1955

The "bird," or "Yardbird," was not only the most adored musician of his time, but an important figure in be-bop, and perhaps the finest alto saxophonist ever. His innovations in jazz harmony and rhythm were integral to music's development during the era.

Parker began playing at the age of eleven. Heavily influenced by Count Basie's saxophonist Lestor Young, he quickly developed and refined his skills. By his late teens found himself working with the Kansas City band of Buster Smith. He spent time in New York during the late '30s, picking up pointers from Art Tatum, before returning to Kansas City and joining Jay McShann's big band.

The lure of the big city and the New York music scene soon overcame Parker, who returned and then called it home. In 1943 he played in bands led by Earl Hines and an offshoot band led by Hines' singer Billy Eckstine. During this period he was also sewing the seeds of bop with pianist Thelonious Monk and drummer Kenny Clarke at the Harlem Jazz sessions.

Parker then found himself alongside probably one of the few who could a hold a candle to him, Dizzy Gillespie. The two made a series of recordings in 1945 that lay the foundation for the transformation of dance-driven jazz to be-bop with songs such as "Shaw 'Nuff," "Sale Peanuts," and "Hot House." "Now's the Time," "Billie's Bounce," and "Koko" soon took New York by a storm, but when the duo took their show on the road, they were met with mixed emotions, which eventually led to quarreling between Parker and Gillespie. Parker then slid into a dark shadow of his past—drug addiction. The problem eventually led to a mental breakdown in 1946 and hospitalization in California.

When he was released, he produced "A Night in Tunisia," "Relaxing at Camarillo," "Orinthology," and the superb "Yardbird Suite" before heading back to New York. Back in the Big Apple he formed a band with drummer Max Roach and trumpeter Miles Davis and delivered some of his finest recordings for Dial. Hailed now as one of the greatest musicians alive, the critical acclaim, however, was in great contrast to his personal life. Although the great music continued, so did his appetite for the "fast lane"—drugs and alcohol. He made legendary tours and one-off reunions with Gillespie, who himself had reached stardom, before bottoming out. When his daughter Chan died in 1954, the first nail in his coffin was in place. His erratic behavior even got him tossed from the club that was named after him, Birdland. He died of a hemorrhage related to pneumonia while watching television in 1955.

AUTOGRAPHS

A CD, LP, magazine cover, ad, photo, or card signed by the artist: $375-$3,250

The scarce signature of Charlie Parker on a publicity photo

Parker, Graham

Born: November 18, 1950

This singer/songwriter born from the British pub-rock scene in the mid-70s and garnered critical praise, but little commercial success. His early years with Mercury Records (1976-1978) were filled with confrontation between himself and management, primarily centering around the promotion and distribution of his work. *Squeezing Out Sparks* (#40, 1979), his Arista debut, was his commercial and artistic pinnacle and included such Parker classics as "Local Girls" and "Passion Is No Ordinary Word." Parker did manage a minor hit with "Wake Up (Next to You)" (#39, 1985) and has released respected and heralded albums well into the '90s.

AUTOGRAPHS

A CD, LP, magazine cover, ad, photo, or card signed by the artist: $10-$25

Parker, Junior

(Herman Parker)

Born: March 3, 1927, Died: November 18, 1971

Extremely talented and admired blues vocalist and harmonica player Junior Parker played with the Sonny Boy Williamson show, Howlin' Wolf (he led the band which included Ike Turner and M.T. Murphy), the Beale Streeters with B.B. King, Johnny Ace, and Roscoe Gordon, and his own band in 1952, the Blue Flames. He scored in 1953 with "Feelin' Good," followed by "Mystery Train," which Elvis drove up the charts in 1955. He joined the Johnny Ace Revue in 1953; it included Big Mama Thornton. He took over the following the accidental death of Ace and changed the name to Blues Consolidated. His R&B hits included "Next Time You See Me" (#7, 1957), "Driving Wheel" (#5, 1961), "In the Dark" (#7, 1961), and "Annie Get Your Yo-Yo" (#6, 1962).

AUTOGRAPHS

A CD, LP, magazine cover, ad, photo, or card signed by the artist: $35-$115

OFTEN OVERLOOKED MEMORABILIA

Memorabilia associated with covers of his songs by other musicians

Parker, Maceo

Born: February 14, 1943

"Maceo, blow your horn!" This noted saxophonist built a legacy around his work with James Brown. When Brown was imprisoned in 1993, Parker released two extraordinary solo releases that quickly shot to Number One on the jazz chart.

AUTOGRAPHS

A CD, LP, magazine cover, ad, photo, or card signed by the artist: $10-$20

POSTERS/PRESS KITS

Promotional Posters: $10-$15
Press Kits: $10-$15

OFTEN OVERLOOKED MEMORABILIA

All items associated with his involvement with James Brown

Parker Jr., Ray

Born: May 1, 1954

Another multi-faceted talent to emerge from the L.A. pop music scene, Parker is noted as an excellent session guitarist/writer and as a talented producer. By his teenage years he was already sitting in on a few Motown sessions before he hooked up with Holland-Dozier-Holland. He appeared on Stevie Wonder's *Talking Book* and also joined him on tour with the Rolling Stones. Having successfully written for a number of artists, he formed Raydio in the late '70s and landed a hit, "Jack and Jill" (#8, 1978), off its self-titled album. Other hits soon followed including "You Can't Change That" (#9, 1979), "Two Places at the Same Time" (#30, 1980), and the instrumental "For Those Who Like to Groove" (#14, R&B).

"Ghostbusters" (#1, 1984) has been his biggest chart success to date—it landed him on top of the U.S. singles chart. "Jamie" (#14, 1984), "Girls Are More Fun" (#34, 1985), and "I Don't Think That Man Should Sleep Alone" (#5, R&B, 1987) were other chart successes during the decade. His production work also increased and he did work for Diana Ross and Randy Hall.

AUTOGRAPHS

A CD, LP, magazine cover, ad, photo, or card signed by the artist: $10-$25

OFTEN OVERLOOKED MEMORABILIA

Movie memorabilia from *Uptown Saturday Night* (1974), *Ghostbusters* (1984), and *Quicksilver* (1986); items associated with his production work and contributions for other artists; videotapes of his television appearances on *Berrenger's*, NBC-TV (1985); sheet music for "I Want a New Drug" - $6.

Parks, Van Dyke

Born: January 3, 1943

An eclectic personality with more than three decades in the music business, Parks' talents extends from songwriting and arranging to producing. Having been closely associated with the Beach Boys, his verbal collages are perhaps best exemplified on "He-

roes and Villains" and "Surf's Up." A meticulous producer, he has worked with Judy Collins, Randy Newman, and many others, establishing himself as a local legend of sorts in L.A. His solo work on Warner Brothers, while often praised by critics and colleagues, has ignited little interest commercially.

AUTOGRAPHS

A CD, LP, magazine cover, ad, photo, or card signed by the artist: $6-$15

OFTEN OVERLOOKED MEMORABILIA

Movie memorabilia from *Popeye*, *Goin' South*, and *The Two Jakes*; associated memorabilia from his numerous contributions to other musicians' work; all items associated with his work with the Beach Boys.

Parsons, Alan

Born: 1949

Alan Parsons Project formed 1975

Parsons, a talented producer and engineer is renowned for his work on the Beatles' *Abbey Road* and later for Paul McCartney's *Wildlife* and *Red Rose Speedway*. He formed a creative outlet for his keyboards and occasional vocals with various session players in 1975 called the Alan Parson Project.

I Robot, *Card*, and *Eye* were all successful selling albums and yielded a variety of hits including "Games People Play" (#16, 1980), "Time" (#15, 1981), "Eye in the Sky" (#3, 1982), and "Don't Answer Me" (#15, 1984).

AUTOGRAPHS

A CD, LP, magazine cover, ad, photo, or card signed by the artist: $15-$30

TOUR BOOKS/PROGRAMS/PASSES

*He rarely performs live, but in recent years did some European and U.S. dates.

POSTERS/PRESS KITS

Promotional Posters: $10-$15
Press Kits: $10-$15

OFTEN OVERLOOKED MEMORABILIA

Memorabilia associated with other projects he has been involved with; artifacts from sources he has based his work on, for example a paperback book of Assimov's *I, Robot*.

REFERENCES/BOOKS

Difficult to find information; serious collectors should opt for the fan club: The Avenue, 65 Front Street, Suite 0116, Box 201, Toronto, Ontario M5J 1E6, Canada ($3.50 per issue)

Parsons, Gram

(Ingram Connor III)
Born: November 5, 1946, Died: September 19, 1973

This creative and insightful singer/songwriter brought traditional country music to the attention of rock's mainstream and pioneered the genre "country rock" in groups such as the International Submarine Band, the Flying Burrito Brothers, the Byrds (in a brief stint), and through his solo work. Although not commercially successful, his music and image have lived through the music of Emmylou Harris, Bernie Leadon, Elvis Costello, and numerous others, creating a cult figure of Parsons who died in 1973 at the young age of twenty-six.

AUTOGRAPHS

A CD, LP, magazine cover, ad, photo, or card signed by the artist: $50-$225

OFTEN OVERLOOKED MEMORABILIA

Associated memorabilia from other musicians' covers of his work; news clippings relating to the theft and burning of his coffin by his friend and road manager Phil Kaufman

REFERENCES/BOOKS

Limited resources exist. *Hickory Wind: The Life and Times of Gram Parsons* by Ben Fong-Torres is a suggested read. There are no dedicated collector books.

****

"On The Edge"

Arvo Part

Part is a reclusive minimalist who spins mystic chords like a pile of duck feathers falling from a six story building. Progressive jazz producer Manfred Eicher has released numerous Part efforts on his ECM label—the most impressive are *Tabula Rasa* and *Passio*. *Passio* is an interpretation of the New Testament with an epiphany which tops off the piece like a three-part swirl of whip cream on a double chocolate fudge brownie. The popularity of mystic minimalists has often been a bit trendy, but Part seems to successfully pull it off with out selling out his traditional roots. Undoubtedly, the best Part of any memorabilia collection!

****

Parton, Dolly

Born: January 19, 1946

Seventies major country and western star, turned '80s pop star and actress, Dolly Parton has established herself soundly in both music and film. As a country artist, she has landed more than twenty C&W Number One hits including "Joshua" (#1, 1970), "I Will Always Love You" (#1, 1974), while also teaming up with Porter Wagoner on hits such as "Just Someone I Used to Know" (1969) and "Daddy

Was an Old Time Preacher Man" (1970). "Miss Dolly" joined Wagoner's syndicated country-music show and became extremely popular with viewers.

Parton left Wagoner in 1974 and took the single "Jolene" to the top of the C&W chart. As she saw more and more pop artists cover her songs, she began toying with the idea to cross over, which she did with the single "Here You Come Again" (#3, 1978). She landed other pop singles, without ignoring C&W releases, and found herself playing Las Vegas by the turn of the decade.

During the '80s she intertwined record releases with acting jobs and landed roles in such films as *9 to 5* (she earned an Oscar nomination), *Rhinestone*, and *Steel Magnolias*. Parton also did some made-for-television movies and even her own prime-time variety shows. Some of her more memorable '80s hits include "But You Know I Love You" (1981), "Islands in the Stream" (#1, 1983) and "Real Love" (1985), both duets with Kenny Rogers, and "Yellow Roses" (1989).

During the '90s she recorded her most successful album, *Trio*, with Emmylou Harris and Linda Ronstadt, which earned her a Grammy. She also collaborated with Loretta Lynn and Tammy Wynette on *Honky Tonk Angels* (1993). She opened up a theme park called Dollywood, established a foundation, and released her autobiography.

AUTOGRAPHS

A CD, LP, paper, photo, or card signed by the artist: $10-$25

OFTEN OVERLOOKED MEMORABILIA

Movie memorabilia from *9 to 5* (1980), *The Best Little Whorehouse in Texas* (1982), *Rhinestone* (1984), *Steel Magnolias* (1989), and *Straight Talk* (1992); videotapes of her numerous television show appearances, particularly on Porter Wagoner's syndicated show; Dollywood souvenirs.

REFERENCES/BOOKS

Dolly: My Life and Unfinished Business - her autobiography (1994); Numerous resources exist. There are no dedicated collector books. Serious collectors should opt for her Fan Club: The Dollywood Ambassadors, The Dollywood Foundation, 1020 Dollywood Lane, Pigeon Forge, TN 37863 ($20 fee)

The Partridge Family

Formed 1970

David Cassidy, Born: April 12, 1950; and Shirley Jones, Born: March 31, 1934

More of a marketing concept than an actual band, The Partridge Family, consisting of only two entertainers with musical ability (David Cassidy and his stepmother Shirley Jones), gained notoriety through its ABC network television show that premiered on September 25, 1970 and ran until September 7, 1974 (96 shows).

While the rest of the family/band consisted of Danny Bonaduce, Brain Foster, Suzanne Crogh, and ex-model Susan Dey, it was Cassidy, with his teen idol image, who was featured singing the group's releases on the television shows. "I Think I Love You" (1970) was the first indication of the success that was to follow—it quickly rose up the singles chart to Number One. The group's self-titled debut album went gold, the first of an eventual five, while the singles kept coming: "Doesn't Somebody Want to Be Wanted" (#6, 1971), "I'll Meet You Half Way" (#9, 1971), "I Woke Up in Love This Morning" (#13, 1971), and "Looking Through the Eyes of Love" (#39, 1973).

When the show ended in 1974, Cassidy continued with his solo career that he had begun while appearing in the show, Susan Dey made film appearances before landing on the television series *L.A. Law*, and the others occasionally resurface in projects.

AUTOGRAPHS

Group:

A CD, LP, magazine cover, ad, photo, or card signed by the group: $50-$100

Individuals:

David Cassidy: $7-$18

Shirley Jones: $10-$30

USED CLOTHING/EQUIPMENT

Guitar Pick:

David Cassidy: $10-$25

OFTEN OVERLOOKED MEMORABILIA

Movie memorabilia from *Carousel*, *Oklahoma*, and *Elmer Gantry*; videotapes of their 96 shows; videotapes of their numerous other television appearances, such as *Mayberry R.F.D.*, *Bewitched*, etc.; copies of the commercials they have appeared in, particularly Jones and Dey; beach towel (Cassidy) - $45; bus (Remco), plastic - $175; book cover (album insert) - $12; books; (Curtis) (#1-16) - $8, (#17) - $20; *Young Mr. Cassidy* - $18; bracelet (charm style) - $70; bulletin board - $40; button set ("Family Tree" each $18) - $55; clock (Cassidy) - $100; colorforms (Cassidy) - $40; coloring book - $20; comic books; (#1) - $20, others - $7, David Cassidy - $7; dolls (Laurie) - $125 (Patty) - $170; fan club kit - $75; game (Milton Bradley) - $20; guitar (Cassidy) - $80; *LIFE* magazine (Cassidy cover, 10/71) - $15; lunch box (Thermos), steel - $75; luv beads - (1971, mail-in offer) - $60; paper dolls (Saalfield) - $45 (Artcraft) "Laurie" - $35, Cassidy "paint & color" - $30, "activity album" - $30, "The Partridge family" - $40; posters (Topps) - (Set of 24) - $195; puzzle (APC) (Cassidy) - $40; record cabinet (American Toy) - $250; shopping bag (album insert) - $7; stickers (Mail-in offer) (Cassidy)- $40; thermos; (steel) - $30, (plastic) - $20; *TV Guides* - $15 (Add $5, 1970); View-Master -$20-$30 (all styles)

REFERENCES/BOOKS

Numerous resources exist, but there are no dedicated collector books. Serious collectors should opt for one of the numerous Fan Clubs: Friends of the Cassidys, c/o Cheryl Corwin, 2601 E. Ocean Blvd., #404, Long Beach, CA 90803, or The Shirley Jones Fan Club, Martina Schade - President, 2295 Maple Rd., York, PA 17404

Patton, Charley

Born: April 1891, Died: April 28, 1934

Patton was an early Delta blues singer, whose mastery of the bottleneck slide playing and songs such as "Pony Blues," "Tom Rushen Blues," and "Moon Going Down" influenced many including Howlin' Wolf. He has now reached near legendary status for his poetic portrayal of southern rural living that so embodied his rich blues.

AUTOGRAPHS

A paper, photo, or card signed by the artist: Unavailable.

Paul, Billy

(Paul Williams)

Born: December 1, 1934

Paul is best known for his smash hit "Me and Mrs. Jones" (#1, 1972), which was critical in establishing Kenny Gamble and Leon Huff's Philadelphia International label. His later releases included "Thanks for Saving My Life" (#9, R&B, 1974) and "Let's Make a Baby" (#18, R&B, 1976).

AUTOGRAPHS

A CD, LP, magazine cover, ad, photo, or card signed by the artist: $10-$15

OFTEN OVERLOOKED MEMORABILIA

His work with the Flamingos and the Blue Notes

Paul and Paula

(Ray Hildebrand) Paul and Paula (Jill Jackson)

Paul and Paula are best known for their smash "Hey Paula" (#1, 1963) before slowly slip into obscurity, despite the release of a handful of other singles.

AUTOGRAPHS

A magazine cover, ad, photo, or card signed by the artists: $10-$15

Pavement

Formed 1989

Stephen Malkmus, Scott Kannberg, and Gary Young*

*Mark Ibold and Bob Nastanovich were added in 1991. Young left in 1993 and Stephen West replaced him on drums.

Pavement is one of the late-80s "come as you are" bands which combined distorted and diverse sounds with typical pop hooks. It gained some attention with the album *Slanted and Enchanted* (1992); it became a favorite with many critics. "Cut Your Hair," extracted off of *Crooked Rain, Crooked Rain* (#121, 1994), was also successful in picking up some decent airplay, while also catching the attention of Warner Bros. Records, which signed the band. The group's label debut *WOWEE ZOWEE* charted briefly before the band embarked on the Lollapalooza '95 tour.

AUTOGRAPHS

A CD, LP, magazine cover, ad, photo, or card signed by the group: $10-$20

Paxton, Tom

Born: October 31, 1937

Tom Paxton is another singer who emerged out of the early-60s Greenwich Village folk revival. A talented singer and songwriter, his topical songs, such as "Going to the Zoo," have been covered by a range of performers from Peter, Paul & Mary to Judy Collins. Paxton's prolific writing, now surpassing its third decade, finds the artist recording and writing music and books for children. He has served as the honorary chairman of the board for the World Folk Music Association and has even hosted his own BBC radio series.

AUTOGRAPHS

A CD, LP, magazine cover, ad, photo, or card signed by the artist: $10-$15

OFTEN OVERLOOKED MEMORABILIA

Associated memorabilia from other artists' covers of his music; copies of his numerous children's books.

Payne, Freda

Born: September 19, 1945

Freda Payne is best known for her early-70s soul hits with the Holland-Dozier-Holland production team, including "Band of Gold" (33, 1970) and "Bring the Boys Home" (#12, 1971). She is also known for "Deeper and Deeper" (#24, 1970), "Cherish What Is Dear to You (While It's Near to You)" (#99, 1971), and "You Brought the Joy" (#52, 1971).

AUTOGRAPHS

A CD, LP, magazine cover, ad, photo, or card signed by the artist: $10-$20

OFTEN OVERLOOKED MEMORABILIA

Videotapes of her syndicated television talk show *For You Black Woman*

Peaches and Herb

Formed 1965

Herb Fame (Herb Feemster), Peaches (Francine Barker), Marlene Mack, and Linda Green

Peaches and Herb Phase I (1967-1969)

Francine Barker (the Sweet Thing) and Herb Fame formed Peaches and Herb at the insistence of producer Van McCoy. Together they landed a series of hit singles beginning in 1967 including "Let's Fall in Love" (#21, 1967), "Close Your Eyes" (#8, 1967), "For Your Love" (#20, 1967), "Love Is Strange" (#13, 1967), "United" (#46, 1968), and "When He Touches Me" (#49, 1969).

Peaches and Herb Phase II

Marlene Mack filled in for Barker, but by this time, the group's appeal is dissipating and the group splits up.

Peaches and Herb Phase III

Fame, who took a job as a D.C. police officer, later found a new Peaches, Linda Green, and returned to music full time. The duo then signed on with Polydor Records and released *2 Hot!* (#2, 1978) with hit extracts "Shake Your Groove Thing" (#5, 1978) and "Reunited" (#1, 1979). Other singles followed through the early '80s including "I Pledge My Love" (#19, 1979) and "Remember" (#35, 1983).

AUTOGRAPHS

A CD, LP, magazine cover, ad, photo, or card signed by the duo: $12-$40*

*phase I or III

Pearl Jam

Formed 1990

Jeff Ament, Born: March 10, 1963; Stone Gossard, Born: July 20, 1965; Dave Krusen; Mike McCready; and Eddie Vedder (Edward Louis Severson Junior), Born: December 23, 1966*

*Krusen left in 1991 and was replaced on drums briefly by Matt Chamberlain before Dave Abbruzzese was added. Abbruzzese left in 1994 and Jack Irons was added.

Mother Love Bone: Ament, Gossard, Bruce Fairweather, Andrew Wood, Born: January 8, 1966, Died: March 19, 1990, and Greg Gilmore

Temple of the Dog: Ament, Gossard, McCready, Matt Cameron, and Chris Cornell

Combine Seattle punk with generic Northwest metal and then stir it up with Kiss and you have the sound that would be exemplary of the grunge era. The first band from Seattle to usher in this era was the Melvins. It influenced many including a young Aberdonian named Kurt Cobain. It was Cobain who delivered Nirvana and Andrew Wood who gave life to Mother Love Bone—a Pearl Jam predecessor. Seattle's roots run deep and to appreciate the sum of the whole, you must understand its parts.

In 1985, Jeff Ament (formerly with Deranged Diction) and Stone Gossard (formerly with the Ducky Boys) were members of Green River, one of the seeds of the early Seattle sound. The group split up in 1987 and Ament and Gossard joined forces with singer Andrew Wood to first form the Lords of the Wasteland (1987) and then Mother Love Bone (1987-1990). Mother Love Bone was one of the earliest Seattle bands to sign with a major label (Polydor). Two weeks prior to the release of the band's only album, *Apple*, Wood died of a heroin overdose. Without Wood the band refused to continue and Mother Love Bone was extinguished.

Ament, Gossard, and Seattle veteran Mike McCready began work on a demo tape in late 1990. Through a friend (Jack Irons), Eddie Vedder (Surf and Destroy/the Butts/Bad Radio) received the tape and added his own lyrics to it before he mailed it back to Seattle. Ament, Gossard, and McCready liked what they heard and invited Vedder and drummer Dave Krusen to join their band—first Mookie Blaylock (named for after the New Jersey Nets basketball player), then Pearl Jam.

The band's (Mookie Blaylock) first gig came on December 22, 1990, opening for Alice in Chains at the Moore Theater in Seattle. The band played about fifteen shows before the Blaylock moniker was retired in favor of Pearl Jam. Growing interest in the Seattle scene, combined with the reputation of both Ament and Gossard, led Epic Records to signing the band in 1991. Krusen departed following the recording sessions for the band's debut album *Ten* (Blaylock's uniform number) and returned to his previous band, Son of Man, and Matt Chamberlain filled on drums during the tour that followed the record's release. Drummer Dave Abbruzzese was later added to the band.

The band toured extensively and following opening gigs for the Red Hot Chili Peppers, Neil Young, and U2, it later headlined the 1992 Lollapalooza Tour. Vedder, Gossard, and Ament even found themselves backing actor Matt Dillon in the 1992 Seattle-based movie *Singles*.

The band followed up its successful debut album *Ten* with *Vs.* (1993), which sold more than a million copies during the first two weeks of release. Last minute title changes actually led to some initial quantities of the album arriving in stores with no title on the sleeve at all. *Vs.* also became what I refer to as a "mission" album. The band wanted to protest the state of the U.K. singles chart by releasing "Go" as its first single and having Epic take various steps to ensure that it was ineligible for charting. All items surrounding this incident are certainly collectible,

for example: stickers reading "NOT ELIGIBLE FOR THE CHART THAT COUNTS" which were put on "Go," advertising pieces that carry the single's chart bar code, and even T-shirts. The band did choose to ignore any major promotion for *Vs.* (issuing no videos, etc.) in favor of returning to the studio to begin work on the next album.

The demands of stardom were starting to become evident in members of Pearl Jam during 1993. Noticeably uncommunicative, the band shunned interviews and even began distributing contracts to be signed by both journalists and photographers. Vedder was also arrested in New Orleans for public drunkenness and disturbing the peace after a barroom brawl.

The band's 1994 summer tour was shelved when a public dispute erupted over service charges initiated by Ticketmaster. The band even testified against the company before Congress. *Vitalogy*, the next Pearl Jam album, was released on Halloween in 1994. All formats of the 14-track release included a booklet that contained advertising reproductions from a book of the same title published in the 1890s—a must acquisition for all Pearl Jam collectors.

In 1995, Gossard announced his own record label, Loosegroove, designed to offer acts maximum creative control. Mike McCready also teamed up with Layne Staley (Alice in Chains) to form Mad Season. Both efforts were not considered conflicts of interest and Pearl Jam set out on its next tour. Plagued with problems, the tour included bad rumors, poor weather, and even Vedder walking off stage at the San Diego Sports Arena after only five songs. The only positive event of the summer was the release of Neil Young's *Mirrorball*; it included various members of Pearl Jam backing him.

The album *No Code* was Number Fifty-seven on the Billboard Top 200 albums of 1996 chart.

AUTOGRAPHS
Group:
A CD, LP, magazine cover, ad, photo, or card signed by the entire band $150-$400*
*High end reflects vintage signed memorabilia
Individual:
Jeff Ament: $30-$35
Stone Gossard: $30-$35
Mike McCready: $20-$25
Eddie Vedder: $40-$55*
Dave Abbruzzese: $20-$25
*Before being deluged, Vedder replied to fans' "problem" letters personally

TOUR BOOKS/PROGRAMS/PASSES
Backstage Passes:
Cloth: $8-$15;
Laminated: $15-$30

POSTERS/PRESS KITS
Promotional Posters:
$12 (stock) to $30
(U.K. promo for "Dissident")
Press Kit: $25

A Pearl Jam backstage pass

USED CLOTHING/EQUIPMENT
Guitar Picks:
Jeff Ament: $20-$25
Stone Gossard: $30-$35
Mike McCready: $20-$25
Eddie Vedder: $30
Drum Stick:
Dave Abbruzzese: $20-$25

OFTEN OVERLOOKED MEMORABILIA
Vitalogy 6-piece hanging mobile - $30; Promo mini-basketball for Ten - $95; Promo mini-basketball and hoop for Ten - $195; photographer's agreement - $5-$10; No Code stamp and stamp pad - $40; Ten, Epic, 1992 promotional door mat - $150; movie memorabilia from *Dead Man Walking* (1996) and *Singles* (1992); all articles relating to the "Pearl Jam vs. Ticketmaster" riff; videotapes of the group's numerous television appearances including *Saturday Night Live* (4/11/92, 4/16/94) and the tenth annual *MTV Video Music Awards* show (9/2/93, 9/9/92); a complete run of Mookie Blaylock basketball cards; 1992 Lollapalooza artifacts; Japanese promo booklet for *No Code* - $25

Eddie Vedder guitar pick

No Code stamp and stamp pad

REFERENCES/BOOKS
Pearl Jam by Mick Wall - $18; *The Story of Pearl Jam* by Morrell - $12; *Pearl Jam Live* by Lorenzo - $10; *Pearl Jam* by Mark Blake - $10; *Pearl Jam Illustrated Biography* by Brad Morrell - $10; Release: An International Fanzine for Pearl Jam Fans, 410 A Gilbert St., Bryan, TX 77801 is a MUST! ($24 fee)

Peebles, Ann

Born: April 27, 1947

A soul singer with deep gospel roots, Ann Peebles is best known for her 1973 hit "I Can't Stand the Rain" (#38), although she also had rhythm and blues hits with "Walk Away," "Part Time Love," "I Pity the Fool," and "Breaking Up Somebody's Home." Peebles recorded through the late '70s before she turned her attention to family life. She and her husband still remain active in the Memphis gospel scene.

AUTOGRAPHS

A CD, LP, magazine cover, ad, photo, or card signed by the artist: $10-$15

OFTEN OVERLOOKED MEMORABILIA

Movie memorabilia from *The Commitments* (1991)

Pendergrass, Teddy

Born: March 26, 1950

"Teddy Bear" not only became a major star following his departure from Harold Melvin and the Blue Notes, but he was also a late '70s sex symbol. A gifted singer and instrumentalist, he became the Blue Notes' frontman in 1970 and helped take many classic Gamble and Huff productions up the charts. He quit the band in 1976 and produced a string of alluring and mesmerizing singles including "I Don't Love You Anymore" (#41, 1977), "Close the Door" (#25, 1978), and "Turn Off the Lights" (#48, 1979). He had more lipstick in his audiences than most department store cosmetic counters!

The hits continued with "Love TKO" (#44, 1980), "Two Hearts" (#40, 1980), and "Your My Latest, My Greatest Inspiration" (#4, R&B, 1982). His fans were given white chocolate teddy bear lollipops—how's that for a collectible!

On March 18, 1982, he suffered a serious car accident that left him paralyzed from the waist down, and only limited use of his arms. After a courageous and successful therapy, he returned with his album *Love Language* in 1984. The album continued right where he left off. Pendergrass delivered a string of beautiful R&B singles of which "Joy" (#1) and " Hold Me" (#4), a duet with Whitney Houston, melt your heart faster than a stick of butter!

AUTOGRAPHS

A CD, LP, magazine cover, ad, photo, or card signed by the artist: $15-$25

POSTERS/PRESS KITS

Promotional Posters: $10-$15
Press Kits: $15

OFTEN OVERLOOKED MEMORABILIA

Movie memorabilia from *Soup for One* (1982) and *The Adventures of Ford Fairlane* (1990); associated

memorabilia from his return to performing following the accident at Live Aid (7/13/85); videotapes of his numerous television show appearances including *The Arsenio Hall Show* (3/13/91), *Apollo Theatre Hall of Fame* concert (6/1/593), and *The Tonight Show* (11/2/93).

Pentangle/Bert Jansch/John Renbourn

Formed 1967

Bert Jansch, Born: November 3, 1943; John Renbourn, Born: August 8, 1944; Jacqui McShee; Danny Thompson; and Terry Cox*

*Numerous personnel changes

Pentagle achieved cult status with its extraordinary repertoire of music, from traditional folk to jazz and blues, led by talented acoustic guitarists Bert Jansch and John Renbourn.

AUTOGRAPHS

A CD, LP, magazine cover, ad, photo, or card signed by the group: $10-$20

Pere Ubu

Formed 1975

David Thomas (a.k.a. Crocus Behemoth), Tom Herman, Peter Laughner, Tim Wright, Allen Ravenstine, and Scott Krauss*

*Numerous personnel changes. Laughner died in 1977.

Late-70s Midwest synth-rock group, founded by two music journalists (Thomas and Laughner), the group is best remembered for the album *The Modern Dance* (1978), which has been cited as an influence to bands like R.E.M. and the Pixies. Pere Ubu maintained a strong cult following, particularly in England, but was continually plagued by personnel problems. Many of the band members went on to greater success with other acts.

AUTOGRAPHS

A CD, LP, magazine cover, ad, photo, or card signed by the group: $10-$25*
*Original Group

Perkins, Carl

Born: April 9, 1932

One of Sam Phillips' first artists on his Sun label, Perkins is typically associated with his monster hit "Blue Suede Shoes" (#2, 1956), although he has penned numerous other rock classics such as "Matchbox," "Honey Don't', "Your True Love," and "Everybody's Trying to Be My Baby," all of which were covered by Perkins' good friends the Beatles. When his rockabilly style fell out of fashion, he opted like

many for country music. He worked extensively with Johnny Cash in the late '60s, did some sessions with Paul McCartney in 1981, and even cowrote the Judds' 1989 hit "Let Me Tell You About Love." Perkins overcame a bout with throat cancer in 1992 and went on to continue his writing and recording. Memorabilia buffs will want to stop by the Suede restaurant in Jackson, Tennessee, which is filled with the singer's relics. In 1987, Carl Perkins was inducted into the Rock and Roll Hall of Fame.

AUTOGRAPHS
A CD, LP, magazine cover, ad, photo, or card signed by the artist: $10-$30

Carl Perkin's signature

USED CLOTHING/ EQUIPMENT
Guitar Picks: $30

OFTEN OVERLOOKED MEMORABILIA
Periodical clippings surrounding his near fatal automobile accident in the late '50s; associated artifacts from the numerous musicians who have covered his work, especially Elvis Presley and the Beatles

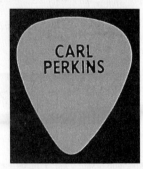

Carl Perkins guitar picks are valued at around $30

REFERENCES/BOOKS
Limited resources exist. The singer's autobiography is good place to begin your study. There are no dedicated collector books.

Perry, Joe Project: See Aerosmith

Perry, Lee "Scratch"

(Rainford Perry)
Born: 1940

A multi-talented force in modern reggae music, Lee Perry has had numerous Jamaican hits including "People Funny Boy," "Live Injection," and "Return of Django" (#5, U.K., 1969). During the late '60s he began working with Bob Marley and the Wailers and penned songs such as "Duppy Conquer," "Small Axe," "Kaya," and "Sun is Shining." He was a pioneer in Jamaican dubbing and is also known for his '70s songs "Station Underground News" and "Roast Fish and Corn Bread."

AUTOGRAPHS
A CD, LP, magazine cover, ad, photo, or card signed by the artist: $10-$30*

*Vintage item relating to his work with the Wailers

The Persuasions

Formed 1962
Jerry Lawson, Jayotis Washington, Joseph "Jesse" Russell, Herbert "Tubo" Rhoad, and Jimmy "Bro" Hayes*

*Washington left in 1974 and Willie Daniels was added, only to be reversed in 1977. Rhoad died in 1988.

Late-60s a cappella vocal act and popular backup singers the Persuasions are perhaps best remembered for their album *Chirpin'* (1977), the songs "I Really Got It Bad for You" (1974) and "One Thing on My Mind" (1975), and for backing successful artists like Stevie Wonder.

AUTOGRAPHS
A CD, LP, magazine cover, ad, photo, or card signed by the group: $10-$25

OFTEN OVERLOOKED MEMORABILIA
A videotape of Spike Lee's documentary *Do It A Capella* (1990); associated artifacts from the numerous projects the group has worked on with other artists.

Pet Shop Boys

Formed 1981
Neil Tennant, Born: July 10, 1954; and Chris Lowe, Born: October 4, 1959

Late-80s British synth-pop act the Pet Shop Boys are commonly associated with the songs "West End Girls" (#1, 1985), "Opportunities (Let's Make Lots of Money)" (#10, 1986), "It's a Sin" (#9, 1987), "What Have I Done to Deserve This" (#2, 1987), and "Always on My Mind" (#4, 1987). *Behavior*, *Discography* (1991), *Very* (1993), and *Bilingual* (1996) have been the band's album legacy thus far during the decade.

AUTOGRAPHS
Group:
A CD, LP, magazine cover, ad, photo, or card signed by the group: $10-$25
The Pet Shop Boys Compiled five track compilation given away through the radio (25 autographed copies, scarce)

TOUR BOOKS/PROGRAMS/PASSES

Tour Programs:
1989 Tour: $10
MCMLXXXIX Tour: $15

Backstage Passes:
Cloth: $8-$10; Laminated: $12

POSTERS/PRESS KITS

Promotional Posters: $10-$20
Press Kits: $10-$35, Examples: Disco $2-$16

OFTEN OVERLOOKED MEMORABILIA

Vinyl Beach Bag, inflatable - $35; Disco, Parlophone Christmas pack with socks, candy, and gift tag, 1987; Very, Parlophone promotional yellow golfing umbrella, 1993; It's a Sin, West Germany, EMI box set with mini-scarf, 1987; In Depth, Japan, EMI, 6 track promo copy with a Pet Shop Boys phone card

REFERENCES/BOOKS

Limited resources exist, but none do justice to the band in my opinion. There are no dedicated collector books. Serious collectors should opt for a Fan Club: Pet Shop Boys Club, P.O. Box 102, Stanmore, Middlesex HA7 2PY England

Pete Rock and C.L. Smooth

Formed 1984

Pete Rock (Phillips), Born: June 21, 1970; and C.L. Smooth (Corey Penn), Born: October 8, 1968

Nineties rappers and producers Pete Rock and C.L. Smooth are typically associated with the song "They Reminisce Over You (T.R.O.Y.)" (#10, R&B, 1992). The two are building a strong reputation for their production work, which has included Kid 'n Play, Shabba Ranks, and Heavy D.

AUTOGRAPHS

A CD, LP, magazine cover, ad, photo, or card signed by the group: $10-$25

Peter and Gordon

Formed 1963

Peter Asher, Born: June 22, 1944; and Gordon Waller, Born: June 4, 1945

Mid-60s British act Peter and Gordon is best remembered for the songs "A World Without Love" (#1, 1964) (penned by Paul McCartney), "Nobody I Know" (#12, 1964), "I Don't Want to See You Again" (#16, 1964), "I Go to Pieces" (#9, 1965) (penned by Del Shannon), "True Love Ways" (#14, 1965) (penned by Buddy Holly), "Woman" (#14, 1966), "Lady Godiva" (#6, 1966), and "Knights in Rusty Armour" (#15, 1967). The group broke up in 1968. Asher went on to be a successful manager and Grammy winning producer of artists such as Linda Ronstadt and James Taylor, while Gordon slipped away from the music scene.

AUTOGRAPHS

A CD, LP, magazine cover, ad, photo, or card signed by the group: $15-$40

OFTEN OVERLOOKED MEMORABILIA

Associated artifacts from Asher's numerous productions

Peter, Paul and Mary

Formed 1961

Peter, Paul and Mary. Courtesy Warner Bros. Records Inc.

Peter Yarrow, Born: May 31, 1938; Noel Paul Stokey, Born: November 30, 1937; and Mary Travers, Born: November 7, 1937

Hailing from the Greenwich Village music scene, Peter, Paul and Mary quickly found their way into the hearts of a new generation. The trio landed classic hits such as "Lemon Tree" (#35, 1962), "If I Had a Hammer" (#10, 1962), "Blowin' in the Wind" (#2, 1963) (penned by Bob Dylan), "Don't Think Twice It's Alright" (#9, 1963), "Puff the Magic Dragon" (#2, 1963), "Leaving on a Jet Plane" (#1, 1969) (penned by John Denver), "I Dig Rock and Roll Music" (#9, 1967), and "Day Is Done" (#21, 1969) before breaking up in 1970.

The group's members went on to numerous other projects. Stokey landed the hit "Wedding Song (There Is Love)" (#24, 1971), Yarrow coproduced and wrote Mary MacGregor's hit "Torn Between Two Lovers" (#1, 1977), and Travers turned to television work. The group has had numerous one-off reunions and has starred in three PBS specials.

AUTOGRAPHS

A CD, LP, magazine cover, ad, photo, or card signed by the group: $10-$45

OFTEN OVERLOOKED MEMORABILIA

Videotapes of their PBS Specials; press clipping from their activist activities such as the March on Washington with Dr. Martin Luther King, Jr.

Peterson, Ray

Born: April 23, 1939

This late-50s singer with a dynamic vocal range is best remembered for the songs "The Wonder of You" (#25, 1959) (written by Baker Knight), "Tell Laura I Love Her" (#7, 1960), "Corinna, Corinna" (#9, 1961), "Missing You" (#29, 1961), and "I Could Have Loved You So Well" (#57, 1962). Peterson looked toward country when his pop hits stopped, but it looked the other way.

AUTOGRAPHS

A CD, LP, magazine cover, ad, photo, or card signed by the artist: $10-$30

Petty, Tom and The Heartbreakers

Formed 1975

Tom Petty, Born: October 20, 1952; Mike Campbell, Born: February 1, 1954; Benmont Tench, Born: September 7, 1954,; Ron Blair, Born: September 16, 1952; and Stan Lynch, Born: May 21, 1955*

*Blair left in 1982 and Howie Epstein was added. Lynch left in 1994 and Steve Ferrone joined the band.

Tom Petty and the Heartbreakers are best known for their hits "Breakdown," "American Girl," "Don't Do Me Like That" (#10, 1979), "Refugee" (#15, 1980), "Stop Draggin' My Heart Around" (#3, 1981) (duet with Stevie Nicks), and "Don't Come Around Here No More" (#13, 1985). The group has landed numerous singles on the charts and has faced seemingly endless legal battles with record companies.

The group garnered significant attention in the late '70s, through extensive touring, which included a noteworthy tour with Nils Lofgren—it was fruitful in breaking the band and its California Byrds-like sounding singles. With momentum really picking up for the band, Petty waged a legal battle with MCA, trying to renegotiate his contract. The company had bought ABC Records, and by mid-1979, he was filing for bankruptcy.

Fortunately, he returned strong with *Damn the Torpedoes* (#2, 1979) before beginning another battle with MCA over the company's intent to raise the list price of his record, which he later won. During the years, Petty has been steadfast on his convictions and never afraid to prove a point.

During the '80s Tom Petty and the Heartbreakers guested on Stevie Nicks' album *Bella Donna*, underwent a personnel change, and embarked on a 1986 world tour with Bob Dylan. Petty also joined the Traveling Wilburys, released a solo album, *Full Moon Fever* (1989), and tragically lost many of his belongings in a house fire—thankfully his wife and two children escaped.

The group opened the '90s with *Into the Great Wide Open* (1991), and while Petty released a second Wilbury's album, the group members ventured into other creative and successful projects, from production to songwriting. Petty also incurred more legal woes from more record company battles to allegations of copyright infringement (later upheld in Petty's favor). In 1993 the group released a greatest hits package before Steve Ferrone replaced Stan Lynch on drums. Meanwhile, Petty kicked out another solo album, although like always, the Heartbreakers contributed to the record.

Tom Petty signed acoustic guitar

AUTOGRAPHS
Group:
A CD, LP, magazine cover, ad, photo, or card signed by the group: $40-$110
Individual:
Tom Petty: $30-$80

Tour program from the Southern Accents tour (Design by Steele Works)

TOUR BOOKS/ PROGRAMS/PASSES
Tour Programs:
Hard Promises, 198: $15-$20
Southern Accents, 1985: $15
Dogs with Wings, 1995: $12
Backstage Passes:
Cloth/paper: $10-$12;
Laminated: $15-$20

POSTERS/PRESS KITS
Promotional Posters:
(1976-1982): $15-$40
(1985-Present): $10-$20

Press Kits:
(1976-1982): $25-$50
(1985-Present): $18-$30

USED CLOTHING/EQUIPMENT
Guitar Picks:
Tom Petty: $20-$35
Mike Campbell: $20
Howie Epstein: $25
Drum Stick:
Stan Lynch: $10-$15

OFTEN OVERLOOKED MEMORABILIA
Learning to Fly MCA promotional Frisbee, 1991; Into the Great Wide Open MCA promo box set, includes CD, bio, photo copy of album cover, tie, bird-shaped knife, and "Gone Gator" sampler, 1991; Damn the Torpedoes promo button - $3; periodical clippings regarding Petty's legal battles with record companies

REFERENCES/BOOKS
Limited resources exist; there are no dedicated collector books. Serious collectors should opt for a Fan Club: Makin' Some Noise, c/o Amanda Saladine, 69 Crofthill Rd., Slough, SL2 1HG, England

Phair, Liz

Born: April 17, 1967

Nineties New York indie savvy female cult rocker, whose bite can be just as bad as her bark, Phair tackles the male-dominated rock scene with her typical aggressive attitude. Her first two albums, *Exile in Guyville* and *Whip-Smart* (#27, 1994), have been praised by the music press and have been significant in building her strong cult following.

AUTOGRAPHS
A CD, LP, magazine cover, ad, photo, or card signed by the artist: $10-$25

POSTERS/PRESS KITS
Promotional Posters: $10
Press Kits: $15

Phillips, Little Esther

(Esther Jones)
Born: December 23, 1935, Died: August 7, 1984.

Impressive Texas R&B singer Little Esther Phillips scored first in the '50s with songs like "Double Crossing Blues" (#1, R&B, 1950) and "Cupid's Boogie" (#2, R&B, 1950) (a duet with Mel Walker), in the '60s with tunes like "Release Me" (#8, 1962) and "You Never Miss Your Water (Until Your Well Runs Dry)" (a duet with Big Al Downing), and again in the '70s with "Home Is Where the Hatred Is" and "What a Difference a Day Makes" (#20, 1975).

AUTOGRAPHS
A CD, LP, magazine cover, ad, photo, or card signed by the artist: $15-$35

****

"On The Edge"

Phish

Pass out, pass on, go fish! Can you pass the acid test? What relics we seek may be in a new ocean. Phish, not fish, just Phish, smells like dead fish, dead what? What Dead? Who's dead? Jerry's dead, is he? He who? Billy. Billy Breathes, he does! How? Through his gills of course, like all Phish.

A couple of Phish backstage passes that typically run about $10 each (Printed by OTTO)

Putting everything aside this is one Phish which is getting bigger and better with time! Start collecting now—don't wait! Remember how long we waited before starting our Family Dog collection? Now look what those posters are going for!

****

Pickett, Bobby "Boris"

Born: February 11, 1938

Early-60s novelty singer, best remembered for the song "Monster Mash" (#1, 1962), Pickett also penned "Monster's Holiday" (#30, 1962) and "Graduation Day" (#88, 1963).

AUTOGRAPHS

A CD, LP, magazine cover, ad, photo, or card signed by the artist: $10-$30

OFTEN OVERLOOKED MEMORABILIA

Movie memorabilia from *It's a Bikini World* (1967); videotapes of his numerous television appearances in *Bonanza*, *The Beverly Hillbillies*, and *Petticoat Junction*; perhaps the most sought of Pickett's items are relics from his very last performance of "Monster Mash" at a Sunset Strip club, backed by Van Halen!

Pickett, Wilson

Born: March 18, 1941

Late-60s soul singer Wilson Pickett is typically associated with the vocal group the Falcons ("I Found a Love") and later for the songs he scored with during his solo career like "In the Midnight Hour" (#21, 1965), "634-5789" (#13, 1966), "Land of 1,000 Dances" (#6, 1966), and "Funky Broadway" (#8, 1967) and with Gamble and Huff for "Engine Number 9" (#14, 1970), "Don't Let the Green Grass Fool You" (#17, 1971), "Don't Knock My Love" (#13, 1971) and "Fire and Water" (#24, 1972). In 1991 Wilson Pickett was inducted into the Rock and Roll Hall of Fame.

AUTOGRAPHS

A CD, LP, magazine cover, ad, photo, or card signed by the artist: $15-$50

OFTEN OVERLOOKED MEMORABILIA

All artifacts from "The Wicked Pickett" participation in the package show "Music In The 5th Dimension" (Murray The K, 1967), movie memorabilia from "Soul To Soul" (1971), videotapes of his television appearances including "Late Night With David Letterman" (1/15/86), newspaper clippings surrounding his legal battles.

Pink Floyd

Formed 1965

Syd (Roger) Barrett, Born: January 6, 1946; Richard Wright, Born: July 28, 1945; Roger Waters, Born: September 9, 1944; and Nick Mason, Born: January 27, 1945*

*David Gilmour was added in 1968, Born: March 6, 1944. Barrett left in 1969. Wright departed in 1982, but returned in 1987. Waters departed in 1984.

The group, minus Barrett, first managed to link up while attending Regent Street Polytechnic in London. With architecture as a common denominator, the group began as Sigma 6, then T-Set, the Meggadeaths, Adabs, Architectural Abdabs, and even the Screaming Abdabs. It was as the Architectural Abdabs, now with Syd Barrett, that collectors can begin a Floyd collection with a copy of the band's first interview which appeared in the *Regent Street Poly Magazine* (c. 1965).

By combining the names of two bluesman, Pink Anderson and Floyd Council, whom Barrett owned records of, the band's new name "Pink Floyd" was coined by "El Syd." Under the new moniker the band played its first gig at the Countdown Club, Palace Gate, London. It was the Spontaneous Underground, a psychedelic Sunday afternoon groove fest held at the Marquee Club on Wardour Street, Soho, where the band ultimately distinguished itself from it's peers with a highly experimental sound and innovative look.

The group's first appearance at a large venue was at the Royal Albert Hall in London on December 12, 1966. For collectors, this highly sought ticket, which rarely appears in the market, was three-stubbed and reads as follows, "YOU'RE JOKING?," "A Show for Oxfam," "Monday, 12th December, 1966," "At 7:30 P.M., Doors open at 7." Having seen very few, expect to pay $300 plus for an unused example. Following the gig the band made its debut at the UFO club, kinda the British Fillmore if you will. Here the band was advertised with psychedelic rainbow day-glow posters—now highly sought by collectors—indicative of the transition the band was undergoing.

For collectors 1967 has some choice pieces, first all items surrounding the release of the band's debut album *The Piper At the Gates of Dawn* (8/67), singles artifacts from "Arnold Layne" (3/11/67), "See Emily Play" (6/16/67), and "Apples and Oranges" (11/18/67), videotapes of the band's television appearances on *The Rave* (3/6/67), *Top of the Pops* (4/6/67), *American Bandstand*, and *The Pat Boone Show*, a copy of the promotional film shot for *Arnold Layne*, and all items associated with its first U.S. dates (the band arrived on October 1, 1967). Obviously, all items associated with the Fillmore West (10/26-28/67), Fillmore Auditorium (11/2/67), and Winterland (11/3-4/67) are highly sought and often costly. The band returned home and did a package tour with the Jimi Hendrix Experience as headliners, from 11/14-12/5/67, although scarce and highly sought, many items from this tour have turned up in auctions over the years.

In 1968 David Gilmour (Ramblers, Jokers Wild) joined Pink Floyd, primarily due to the unmanageable and unpredictable Syd Barrett who was finally

asked to leave in April—although it remained a mystery as to the extent of his departure. The year was marked by the release of *A Saucerful of Secrets* (6/29/68), a transitional album for the group. Depending on which source you believe, Barrett appeared on one, two, or three tracks of the seven-track release. The cinema, always an interesting medium to band members, became an additional creative outlet as they worked on the soundtracks to *The Committee* and *Tonight Let's Make Love in London*. The band also played the first free concert ever by a rock group held in Hyde Park on June 29, 1968.

Pink Floyd contributed to several soundtracks over the next few years including *More* (1969), *Zabriskie Point* (1970), and *The Valley* (1972), while starring in its own *Pink Floyd Live At Pompeii* (1972). Albums during this period include *Ummagumma* (10/25/69), *Atomic Heart Mother* (10/10/70), *Relics* (5/71), *Meddle* (11/71), and *Obscured by Clouds* (6/72)—the soundtrack to *The Valley*.

In March 1973, the entire face of rock music was transformed with the release of *The Dark Side of the Moon*, which remained on the album charts for 741 weeks. The group toured extensively in support of the work, and performed the album in its entirety with an elaborate stage production. Naturally, all items associated with this monumental release are highly sought by collectors. To celebrate the 20th Anniversary of the release, a limited edition box set was created and marketed. It contained a new booklet (also released with the *Shine On* box) and five art-cards. The album still evokes intrigue, and in recent years has even drawn parallels to the movie *The Wizard of Oz*—I guess we're not in Kansas anymore, Toto!

Wish You Were Here (9/15/75), the alternative to a scrapped *Household Objects* project, explored much of the same ground as its predecessor, and also included a tribute to Syd Barrett, "Shine On You Crazy Diamond," sung by Roy Harper. The year's live highlight, by most accounts, was the Knebworth Festival, where the band, in its first U.K. performance of the year, delighted fans with a spectacular show, including a Spitfire aircraft put to quadrophonic sound.

The most sought after Pink Floyd collectible of 1976 was a forty foot pig that broke loose from its mooring above the Battersea Power Station during a sleeve film shoot and was last seen over Chatham, Kent, headed toward Germany at a cruising altitude of 18,000 feet. Please fasten your seat belts and return your tray tables to the upright and locked position, or was it the stewardess, I can never remember. The band's Animals tour opened in West Germany on January 23, 1977, during a time period that found its members somewhat distracted by outside projects, including production work and solo efforts.

Pink Floyd, following the collapse of an investment company, Norton Warburg, found itself in dire straits financially, and turned to Roger Waters, who composed the only thing that could hold him back, *The Wall* (11/30/79). The successful and immense project, which even included a film adaptation featuring designs by Gerald Scarfe, became an enormous undertaking. Cost prohibitive, *The Wall* was performed only twenty-nine times in three different cities: New York, Los Angeles, and London. Tour artifacts became instant collectibles as fans scrambled primarily for tickets. Increasingly clear that tension had developed within the group, Wright departed over conflicts with Waters. The movie adaptation of the work premiered in London on July 14, 1982.

The Final Cut (3/21/83), penned by Waters, marked his bitter, although believed acrimonious, departure from the band. With little water under the dam, litigation was filed to dissolve the group's partnership, and prohibit Mason and Gilmour from using the name Pink Floyd. Waters lost his suit, while the others, including Wright, joined forces and released *A Momentary Lapse of Reason* (9/7/87). *Delicate Sounds of Thunder* (11/21/88), a live offering, even found its way aboard the MIR space station, prior to Christie's Rock & Roll Memorabilia auction that found one of the band's inflatable pigs, which together with an Animals tour jacket, garnered about $1,500 (4/27/89).

Meanwhile Waters assembled an all-star cast to perform *The Wall* in Berlin at the site of the newly fallen relic in 1990. Following the performance, Christie's Auction House in London (9/21/90) offered nearly 300 lots worth of foundation material, on behalf of Waters and Scarfe, who raised more than 100,000 pounds—currency that is!

In 1994, Pink Floyd took to the road with a crew of two hundred in sixteen trailers worth of equipment and eleven trucks filled with staging, in support of *The Division Bell* (3/29/94). The record, which debuted atop the album chart in the U.S., was supported by a North American tour that entertained more than three million people, while selling out all but seven of the groups 59 shows. In May 1994, *Record Collector* magazine offered Syd Barrett's very first guitar (1963 Harmony Sovereign acoustic) for sale at a mere $7,500—the diamond still shines! On November 1, 1994, the band played *The Dark Side of the Moon* at Earls Court for a large pay-per-view audience.

In 1995 *Pulse* (#1, 1995) became the first release ever to be packaged with a flashing light bulb incorporated into the packaging. Enjoying the novelty, the band watched as the Smashing Pumpkin's Billy Corgan inducted it into the Rock and Roll Hall of Fame during its annual January ceremony (1996). With nearly ever breath of each member documented by some Floyd enthusiast, collectors will find numerous resources available to assist their craving for collectibles, so "Shine On"!

AUTOGRAPHS

For Pink Floyd, Syd Barrett has become a cult figure, similar to what Brian Wilson is considered to the Beach Boys. Sightings of the original "Crazy Diamond" have been

rare—if of course you recognize him—so needless to say, autographs are less than plentiful.

Group:

A CD, LP, magazine cover, ad, photo, or card signed by the entire band: $600-$700*

*High end reflects vintage signed memorabilia by Wright, Waters, Mason, and Gilmour

Individual:

Syd (Roger) Barrett: $150-$300*
Richard Wright: $50-$65
Roger Waters: $80-$100
Nick Mason: $50-$65
David Gilmour: $100

*Extremely difficult to acquire and authenticate

TOUR BOOKS/PROGRAMS/PASSES

Tour Books/Programs:

On Stage/Hollywood Bowl, 9/22/72: $45-$65
1972 Japanese Tour Program: $250-$300
Knebworth 1975: $250-$300
The Wall '80/'81 (London version-blue cover): $22-$25
Momentary Lapse of Reason (1987/88 World Tour): $15-$17
The Division Bell/European Tour 1994: $20

1990s Backstage Passes:

Cloth: $15-$35; Laminated: $20-$45
World Tour 1994, VIP, laser foil: $20-$35

POSTERS/PRESS KITS

The early "UFO" concert posters are in great demand and can command a price range of $400-$500 depending significance, supply, and design.

Promotional posters, post-1990, are relatively easy to find in the $10-$35 range.

Complete promo merchandising kits (displays, posters, etc.) are highly sought by collectors and can command significant prices (Example: Animals - $250-$325)

USED CLOTHING/EQUIPMENT

Guitar Picks:

Roger Waters: $100-$125
David Gilmour: $150

Drum Stick:

Nick Mason: $50-$65

OFTEN OVERLOOKED MEMORABILIA

Sigma 6 business cards; early newspaper interviews and articles; copies of the *International Times*; animation cels from The Wall - $1,500-$10, 000 - depending on size, background vs. overlays, etc.; Momentary Lapse of Reason promo white coffee mug - $65; Momentary Lapse of Reason promo pig shaped cushion - $50-$65; Discover What's Beyond the Dark Side of the Moon mobile- 16" tall - $20-$25; The Division Bell cast-iron metal faces (limited to 2,000) with CD - $99; The Wall limited edition lithographs (3,800) plate signed by Waters and Scarfe - $40-$50; songbooks - $15-$30; comic books - $3-$4; calendars - $6-$8; postcards - $1-$3, however, The Wall movie set postcards (4) - 1982 - $7-$10; stamp sheet , 25 stamps - $4-$5; Christmas tree ornaments - $10; The Division Bell promotional shirt (PINK FLOYD WILL COMMUNICATE COMMUNICATION BEGINS APRIL 5, 1994) - $25; Pink Floyd backpack - $25; Fillmore poster art necktie - $30, bandanna - $7-$10, and metal jewelry - $10; Animals pig mobile - $100-$125; Dark Side of the Moon EMI promotional Swatch, 1993 (limited to 100); Dark Side of the Moon Frisbee, pyramid design; Delicate Sound promo

counter display - $15; Pulse promo double-sided banner - $10.

Pitney, Gene

Born: February 17, 1941

Talented early-60s singer and songwriter Gene Pitney landed more than twenty charting singles and penned numerous other hits for some of the era's biggest stars. Pitney is best remembered for the songs "Town Without Pity" (#13, 1962), "(The Man Who Shot) Liberty Valance" (#4, 1962), "Only Love Can Break a Heart" (#2, 1962), "Half Heaven—Half Heartache" (#12, 1963), "Mecca" (#12, 1963), "It Hurts to Be in Love" (#7, 1964), and "I'm Gonna Be Strong' (#9, 1964) and for writing "Hello Mary Lou" for Rick Nelson and "He's a Rebel" for the Crystals. He befriended many pivotal people in the music business early in his life, such as Phil Spector, Roy Orbison, and the Rolling Stones, and achieved far greater success in England and Italy than in the U.S. He continued to tour throughout the years, as his hits subsided, while he tended to his rather large portfolio of businesses.

AUTOGRAPHS

A CD, LP, magazine cover, ad, photo, or card signed by the artist: $10-$30

OFTEN OVERLOOKED MEMORABILIA

Associated artifacts from the numerous musicians who have covered his work

Pixies/The Breeders/Frank Black

Formed 1986

Black Francis, a.k.a. Frank Black (Charles Thompson IV), Joey Santiago, Kim Deal, and David Lovering.

The Breeders formed in 1990

These "bean town" college cult rockers are best remembered for their album *Doolittle* (1989) and songs like "Monkey Gone to Heaven" and "Velouria." The group became far more popular in England than in the U.S. and even landed minor hits there. The group split up in 1992, but remained an influence for the numerous bands that followed including Nirvana.

Thompson, under the moniker Frank Black, suffering from a Brian Wilson "Pet Sounds" stage, attempted to mark through his eponymous debut (1993). Meanwhile the Breeders struck pay dirt on their second full-length release, *Last Splash* (#33, 1994), which included the extract "Cannonball" (#44, 1994).

AUTOGRAPHS

A CD, LP, magazine cover, ad, photo, or card signed by the group: $20-$40*

*Original lineup on significant piece

TOUR BOOKS/PROGRAMS/PASSES

Tour Book:
1991 Tour: $10

OFTEN OVERLOOKED MEMORABILIA
Doolittle nine postcard set, 1989

Plant, Robert

Born: August 20, 1948

Since the fall of Led Zeppelin, Robert Plant has been the most active former-member on the music scene. He has released a progression of innovative and current works, starting first with a group of local R&B musicians called the Honeydrippers. Plant released *Pictures at 11* (#5, 1982) followed by *The Principle of Moments* (#8, 1983), which included the hit extracts "Big Log" (#20, 1983) and the classic "In the Mood" (#39, 1983) before he embarked on his debut solo tour.

The following year was filled with numerous projects including a contribution to the *Porky's Revenge* soundtrack and a Honeydrippers EP, which enjoyed donations from Jimmy Page, Jeff Beck, and Nile Rodgers, as well as two hit extracts, "Sea of Love" (#3, 1984) and "Rockin' at Midnight" (#25,1985). In 1995, the surviving members of Led Zeppelin played a one-off stint at Live Aid, while Plant also released *Shaken 'n' Stirred* (#20, 1985).

Plant then restructured his band and worked closely with Phil Johnstone on *Now and Zen* (#6, 1988), which yielded the nostalgic hit "Tall Cool One" (#25, 1988), praised for its sampling of old Zeppelin tunes, it was later even used in a Coca-Cola commercial. Plant also later contributed a song to Page's *Outrider* album. Following a one-off all-star band release of "Smoke on the Water," Plant re-entered the studio to record *Manic Nirvana* (#13, 1990), which sold gold, and was followed by *Fate of Nations* (1993).

Plant then joined forces again with Jimmy Page in 1994. The duo released the album *No Quarter*, which was complimented by an appearance on MTV *Unplugged* and a heavily promoted tour. Needless to say the collaboration met with a warm response from Zeppelin fans and collectors, who now had a whole new wave of music and memorabilia to add to their collections.

AUTOGRAPHS
A CD, LP, magazine cover, ad, photo, or card signed by the artist: $35-$70

TOUR BOOKS/PROGRAMS/PASSES

Tour Programs:
Manic Nirvana: $8-$10
Non-Stop Go Tour, 1988: $10-$12 (blue cover)*
Non-Stop Go Tour, 1988: $8-$10 (later cover)
Principle of Moments, 1983: $7-$12 (U.S. and Canada)
Shaken 'n' Stirred: $10-$15

A Robert Plant tour program. (Icon, London, Reiner Design, N.Y., Controlled Media Co.)

Fate of Nations: $12-$15
Page and Plant World Tour: $15
*Two cover styles exist: original blue cover sold on British tour leg and some American gigs before it was changed.

Backstage Passes:
Manic Nirvana: $5-$7 (cloth) (VIP passes are high end); $20 (laminated) - VIP clip-on
Non-Stop Go Tour: $6-$8 [cloth, All Purpose (green, orange), After Show (orange, pink, yellow), Working Personnel (orange, green, yellow)]; $13-$15 (laminated, 2 var.: blue, black)
Shaken 'n' Stirred: $4-$5 (cloth), $15 (laminated)
Principle of Moments: $6 (cloth, North American); $10 (cloth, other countries); $15 (laminated, 3 different)

POSTERS/PRESS KITS

Promotional Posters:
Washburn Guitar poster: $7
Fate of Nations, Atlantic promo: $6
Manic Nirvana, various: $4-$13 (Except Canadian Molson, neon poster - $20)
Now and Zen:, various: $3-$15 (High end for large U.K. posters)
Shaken 'n' Stirred: $5-$8 (Only a few styles)
Honeydrippers: $3-$5
Principle of Moments: $6-$15
Pictures at Eleven: $8-$10

OFTEN OVERLOOKED MEMORABILIA
Now and Zen Atlantic promotional pennant - $10; Now and Zen red banner - $5; wall tapestries - $10-$15; Manic Nirvana mobile - $15; Now and Zen CD display - $2

Page & Plant Artifacts
No Quarter tour cup (plastic) - $5; concert flyer - $5; No Quarter keychain - $2; No Quarter banner - $4; No Quarter table tent - $3; No Quarter tour pennants - $20; No Quarter Tour mobile with blimp - $30; No Quarter counter display - $20; No Quarter tour banner - $35; No Quarter tour banner "day of show" - $75; No Quarter cardboard display, U.K. - $150.

The Plasmatics

Formed 1978

Wendy Orleans Williams, Richard Stotts, Chosei Funahara, Wes Beech, and Stu Deutsch*

*Funahara left in 1980 and was replaced by Jean Beauvoir. Beauvoir and Deutsch both left in 1981.

Late-70s New York heavy metal band, best remembered for its erotic and typically minimally clad lead singer Wendy O. Williams (W.O.W.) and outrageous stage show, the Plasmatics debuted at CBGB

on July 26, 1978. From cutting guitars in half with chain saws, to driving automobiles in the Hudson River, the band was long on media marketing, but short on hits. The band endured into the late '80s on the strength of a large cult following, some of which monitored Williams' acting career in films such as *Reform School Girls* (1986).

AUTOGRAPHS

A CD, LP, magazine cover, ad, photo, or card signed by the group: $10-$30*

*Original lineup on significant piece

****

"On The Edge"

Plastic People of the Universe (PPOTU)

This the legendary Czech group, the Ann Frank of Bozi Mlyn, if you will. My favorite of course is Egon Bondy's Happy Hearts Club Banned (Bozi Mlyn, 1977). More allegorical than political, yet hauntingly totalitarian, this band did have an influence on its society.

Just picture Frank Zappa hosting ESPN's *Sportscenter*, with the theme show music now "Phill Esposito" by PPOTU. "It's time for our Did You Know segment, hosted of course by Captain Beefheart," says Zappa, "take it Beef." "Thanks Frank, Did you know Vaclav Havel actually flosses his teeth while listening to Bez Onhu Je Underground!" It is not an easy band to collect, due to accessibility of material, but it is worth a mention!

****

The Platters

Formed 1953

Tony Williams, Born: April 15, 1928, Died: August 14, 1992; David Lynch (1929-1981); Herbert Reed; and Alex Hodge*

*Zola Taylor was added in 1954. Hodge left in 1955 and was replaced by Paul Robi. Williams departed in 1960 and Sonny Turner was added. Both Robi and Taylor left in 1962 and Nate Nelson and Sandra Dawn joined the group.

Outstanding late-50s vocal group, led then by Tony Williams, The Platters set the standard by which all other acts of the era were measured. The group scored hits such as "Only You," "The Great Pretender" (#1, 1956), "The Magic Touch" (#4, 1956), "My Prayer" (#1, 1956), "You'll Never Know" (#11, 1956), "I'm Sorry" (#23, 1957), "Twilight Time" (#1, 1958), "Smoke Gets in Your Eyes" (#1, 1958), and "Enchanted" (#12, 1959).

The group's hits stalled when allegations of sexual misconduct found four members arrested in Cincin-

nati. Although they were later acquitted, the charges diminished the group's image with the public. Later hits followed, such as "Harbor Lights" and "With This Ring," but the group was never able to regain its earlier momentum.

The Platters were inducted into the Rock and Roll Hall of Fame in 1990.

AUTOGRAPHS

A CD, LP, magazine cover, ad, photo, or card signed by the group: $100-$275*

*Original lineup

Plimsouls: See Peter Case

PMD: See EPMD

PM Dawn

Formed 1989

Prince Be, a.k.a. "the Nocturnal" (Attrell Cordes) and DJ Minutemix, a.k.a. "J.C. the Eternal" (Jarrett Cordes).

This early-90s "alternative rap" group is commonly associated with the songs "Set Adrift on Memory Bliss" (#1, 1991), "Paper Doll" (#28, 1992), "I'd Die Without You" (#3, 1992), and "Looking Through Patient Eyes" (#6, 1993). PM Dawn was perhaps the most pop-flavored act of its genre, and also altruistic, as they seldom turned their back to a good cause. "Jesus Wept" (#119, 1995) fell short of sales expectations before the band added a cut to "Songs In The Key Of X" - inspired by the smash FOX-TV show "The X-Files."

AUTOGRAPHS

A CD, LP, magazine cover, ad, photo, or card signed by the group: $12-$20

Poco

Formed 1968

Richie Furay, Born: May 9, 1944; Jim Messina, Born: December 5, 1947; Rusty Young, Born: February 23, 1946; George Grantham, Born: November 20, 1947; Randy Meisner, Born: March 8, 1946*

*Meisner left in 1969. Timothy B. Schmit, Born: October 30, 1947, added in 1970. Messina left in 1970 and Paul Cotton was added. Furay left in 1973. Both Schmit and Grantham left in 1977 and Steve Chapman, Charlie Harrison, and Kim Bullard joined the band. Original quintet re-formed in 1989

This promising late-60s L.A. country-rock act was probably best known during its first decade of existence for its rotating personnel. Poco finally broke through on its fourteenth album. Only one original member played on it—Rusty Young. The album spun off the hit singles "Crazy Love" and "Heart of the Night," but its success was only brief, as subsequent albums reverted to old sales levels.

In 1989, the original members of the band united, all except George Grantham, to release *Legacy*, which yielded two hit singles, "Call It Love" (#18, 1989) and the Richard Marx penned "Nothin' to Hide" (#39, 1989). The group then set out on tour in 1990, but tensions with Furay resulted in his departure. The band now only has Young as its original member.

AUTOGRAPHS

A CD, LP, magazine cover, ad, photo, or card signed by the group: $25-$60*

*Original lineup on significant piece

OFTEN OVERLOOKED MEMORABILIA

Associated memorabilia from other musicians' covers of their compositions

The Pogues

Formed 1982

James Fearnley, Jeremy "Jem" Max Finer, Shane MacGowan, Andrew Ranken, Cait O'Riordan, and Peter "Spider" Stacy*

*Philip Chevron was added in 1985. O'Riordan left in 1986 and Darryl Hunt, along with Terry Woods, joined the group. MacGowan departed in 1991 and Joe Strummer (John Mellor) briefly joined the band.

An '80s British punk band with traditional Irish roots, the Pogues garnered significant attention when they opened for the Clash's 1984 tour. The band is perhaps best identified with the *Rum Sodomy & the Lash* (1985) and *If I Should Fall from Grace with God* (#88, 1988) albums and the song "Fairytale of New York." Former Clash singer Joe Strummer had a brief stint with the band.

AUTOGRAPHS

A CD, LP, magazine cover, ad, photo, or card signed by the group: $15-$20*

*Original lineup

REFERENCES/BOOKS

Limited resources exist; there are no dedicated collector books.

Poindexter, Buster: See David Johansen

The Pointer Sisters

Formed 1971

Ruth, Anita, Bonnie, and June Pointer*

*Bonnie left the group in 1978

Dynamic Bay Area '70s vocal group, best known for the hits "Fairytale" (#13, 1974) (Grammy award for Best Country Single) and "How Long (Betcha' Got a Chick on the Side)" (#20, 1974), before Bonnie Pointer went solo, and "Fire" (#2, 1979), "Happiness" (#30, 1979), "He's So Shy" (#3, 1980), "Slow Hand" (#2, 1981), "Should I Do It" (#13, 1982), "Automatic" (#5, 1984), "Jump (for My Love)" (#3, 1984), "I'm So Excited" (#9, 1984), and "Neutron Dance" (#6, 1984), the Pointer Sisters were discovered by Jerry Wexler when they were backing Elvin Bishop at Los Angeles' Whiskey-a-Go-Go. They garnered significant attention with their self-titled debut record, which included extracts "Yes We Can Can" (#11, 1973) and "Wang Dang Doodle" (#61, 1973), as well as for their stage show that had a flair for nostalgic costuming. When the hits finally subsided, the group took some time off before returning with *Only Sisters Can Do That* (1993) and going back on the road.

AUTOGRAPHS

A CD, LP, magazine cover, ad, photo, or card signed by the group: $25-$50

TOUR BOOKS/PROGRAMS/PASSES

Tour Programs:
Contact '85 Tour: $20
The Pointer Sisters, 1987: $18

POSTERS/PRESS KITS

Promotional Posters: $10-$25
Press Kits: $15-$30

OFTEN OVERLOOKED MEMORABILIA

Videotapes of their 1974 PBS documentary; all associated items from their performance at the Grand Ole Opry; all memorabilia associated with their days singing backup to the likes of Dave Mason, Boz Scaggs, and Tower of Power.

Poison

Formed 1983

Bret Michaels (Bret Sychak), Matt Smith, Bobby Dall (Kendall), and Rikki Rockett (Richard Ream)*

*Smith departed in 1985 and C.C. DeVille (Bruce Johannesson) was added. DeVille left in 1991 and Richie Kotzen joined the band. Kotzen left in 1993 and Blues Saraceno was added.

Late-80s Pennsylvania pop-metal group and precursor to the '80s glam-rock bands, Poison is typically associated with the songs "Talk Dirty to Me" (#9, 1987), "I Won't Forget You" (#13, 1987), "Nothin' But

a Good Time" (#6, 1988), "Fallen Angel" (#12, 1988), "Every Rose Has Its Thorn" (#1, 1988), "Your Mama Don't Dance" (#10, 1989), "Unskinny Bop" (#3, 1990), and "Something to Believe In" (#4, 1990). The band's popularity on the L.A. metal-club circuit was key in landing its record deal. With the '90s came drastically reduced record sales, the band has since struggled to sustain consistency in both chart placement and personnel. A dark cloud also seemed to hang over Bret Michaels, who introduced his Ferrari to a telephone poll on May 24, 1994, prior to beginning litigations against Capitol Records.

AUTOGRAPHS

A CD, LP, magazine cover, ad, photo, or card signed by the group: $25-$40*
*Original lineup

TOUR BOOKS/PROGRAMS/PASSES

Backstage Passes: $10 (cloth)

Two Poison backstage passes (Printed by T-Bird Entertainment Printing)

POSTERS/PRESS KITS

Promotional Posters: $10-$20
Press Kits: $15-$25

USED CLOTHING/EQUIPMENT

Guitar Picks: $10-$20

OFTEN OVERLOOKED MEMORABILIA

Flesh and Blood promo counter display cube - $10; necklace w/logo - $10; I Won't Forget You notepad, Capitol promo, 1987 - $25; Open Up and Say Ahhh!, tongue depressor - $15.

The Police

Formed 1977

Stewart Copeland, Born: July 16, 1952; Sting (Gordon Sumner), Born: October 2, 1951; and Andy Summers (Somers), Born: December 31, 1942

This '80s rock-reggae pop act is best remembered for the songs "Roxanne" (#32, 1979), "Message in a Bottle," "Walking on the Moon," "De Do Do Do, De Da Da Da" (#10, 1980), "Don't Stand So Close to Me" (#10, 1981), "Every Breathe You Take" (#1, 1983), "Synchronicity II" (#16, 1983), "King of Pain" (#3, 1983), and "Wrapped Around Your Finger" (#8, 1984). The Police managed to blend cultivating hooks and with British good looks to create their own style of music. Sting's thundering bass lines interwoven through Summer's mystic Rastafarian chords and Copeland's intricate drumming gave their music an international and fresh feel that became extremely popular with listeners.

The band, as an entity, has been idle since the end of their triumphant Synchronicity world tour, with each member pursuing their own individual efforts. Sting has had an impressive solo career, Copeland has scored both film and television, and Summers has explored new directions in rock-fusion. The development each member has undergone, while maybe not yet conducive to another group structure, certainly would add intrigue to a Police reunion.

AUTOGRAPHS

A CD, LP, magazine cover, ad, photo, or card signed by the group: $50-$115

TOUR BOOKS/PROGRAMS/PASSES

Tour Programs:
Ghost in the Machine : $15
Synchronicity Tour (U.S.): $10
Synchronicity Tour (U.K.): $20
Japan Tour (1980): $50

POSTERS/PRESS KITS

Promotional Posters: $15-$50
Press Kits: $25-$60

Ghost in the Machine tour program (© The Police)

USED CLOTHING/EQUIPMENT

Guitar Picks:
Sting: $20-$30
Andy Summers: $15-$30
Drum Stick:
Stewart Copeland: $20-$30

OFTEN OVERLOOKED MEMORABILIA

Promotional whistle (A&M) - $35 (at least two variations); videotapes of their numerous television performances; a copy of their infamous chewing gum commercial; Ghost in the Machine tour mood necklace - $10

REFERENCES/BOOKS

Numerous resources exist, but none do justice to the band in my opinion. There are no dedicated collector books.

Ponty, Jean-Luc

Born: September 29, 1942

Noted French space-age-fusion violinist and composer Jean-Luc Ponty has worked with numerous artists including Elton John, Frank Zappa, and the Mahavishnu Orchestra during a career that has spanned three decades. During the last few years he has been more intrigued with synthesizers, while interacting with computers to create conceptual world music than playing the violin.

AUTOGRAPHS

A CD, LP, magazine cover, ad, photo, or card signed by the artist: $10-$20

Formed 1967

Iggy Pop (James Osterberg), Born: April 21, 1947; Ron Asheton; Dave Alexander (1947-1975); and Scott Asheton*

*Alexander left in 1970 and James Williamson was added. Group disbanded in 1970, then re-formed in 1972. Scott Thurston was added in 1973. Group disbanded again in 1974.

The godfather of punk, Iggy Pop (and the Stooges), has endured decades without falling into commercialism, while sustaining a large cult following and becoming a living rock icon. Whether respected as a precursor of '70s punk and '90s grunge, or just for his ability to survive, Pop has managed to portray the role of rock misfit, as if Charles Dickens himself had created him. Iggy Pop and the Stooges debuted on Halloween in Ann Arbor, Michigan, in 1967. Iggy's stage antics were nothing short of lunacy—from spreading peanut butter all over his body to belting out primal screams that could wake the dead—one thing was certain, though, if you had been to a Stooges show, you would have remembered it.

He is perhaps best remembered for the albums *Raw Power* (1973), *The Idiot* (#72, 1977), and *Blah Blah Blah* (#75, 1986) and maybe even for some of his movie roles, such as his character in *Sid and Nancy*.

Iggy, at 50, is still Iggy, but he is showing signs of looking for his successor, which most bet will be Henry Rollins, although they maybe tough shoes to fill, but Pop seldom wore shoes anyway, or anything for that matter.

AUTOGRAPHS

A CD, LP, magazine cover, ad, photo, or card signed by the artist: $15-$40

POSTERS/PRESS KITS

Promotional Posters: $8-$30
Press Kits: $15-$40

OFTEN OVERLOOKED MEMORABILIA

Instinct, West Germany, promotional Coca-Cola can, 1988, scarce; All artifacts associated with Iggy and the Stooges live debut in Ann Arbor, MI (10/31/67); videotapes of his numerous television appearances including *The Dinah Shore Show* (4/5/77), *Late Night With David Letterman* (7/21/88, 5/26/93) also *Shannon's Deal*, *Tales From The Crypt*, *Miami Vice*, "Elvis Aaron Presley: The Tribute" (10/8/94), movie memorabilia from *Rock 'n' Rule*, *Repo Man*, *Sid and Nancy*, *The Color Of Money*, *Dogs In Space*, *Cry Baby*, *American Dreamer*, *Coffee And Cigarettes*, *Dead Man*, *City Of Angels*, *The Brave* ; a copy of the book *I Need More* penned with Anne Wehrer; memorabilia from his appearance in John Moran's opera *The Manson Family* (1991); Iggy Halloween mask (1986) — part of promotional package for *Blah Blah Blah*.

REFERENCES/BOOKS

Limited resources exist. *The Wild One: The True Story of Iggy Pop* by Per Nilsen and Dorthy Sherman is a MUST read! There are no dedicated collector books.

Pop Will Eat Itself

Formed 1986

Graham Crabb, Clinton Mansell, Richard March, and Adam Mole*

*Fuzz (John) Townshend was added in 1992

Late-80s English indie-rock band that evolved significantly over the years, Pop Will Eat Itself is best known for the U.K. hits "Dance of the Mad" (#32, 1990), "X Y and Zee" (#15, 1991), "Karmadrome" (#17, 1992), and "Get the Girl! Kill the Baddies!" (#9, 1993).

AUTOGRAPHS

A CD, LP, magazine cover, ad, photo, or card signed by the group: $12-$15

****

"On The Edge"

Pooh Sticks

Out of Swansea, Wales, emerges Pooh Sticks, an indie band headed by Hue and his collaborator Steve Gregory, with a sound similar to "Weird Al" Yankovic singing with a mouth full of jawbreakers. Lets face it, any group that has the nerve to name its debut effort *Multiple Orgasm* can't possibly live up to its expectations. *Million Seller* (Zoo, 1993), which also fell short of its title, is at least worth a listen. With each release an almost self-serving satire of itself, expect titles such as "Number One With a Bullet," "The Greatest Album of All-Time," and the soundtrack to "The Last Supper."

The scary thing is the Pooh Sticks are actually getting better with age. Buy low and sell high!

****

Porno for Pyros: See Jane's Addiction

Power Station: See Duran Duran; Robert Palmer

Praxis: see Bill Laswell

Prefab Sprout

Formed 1982

Paddy McAloon, Martin McAloon, Wendy Smith, and Neil Conti

This late-80s British post modern pop band, fronted by the talented voice of Paddy McAloon, is com-

monly associated with the albums *Swoon* and *Two Wheels Good* (*Steve McQueen* - outside U.S.), both of which have had significant media play, but little sales in the U.S.

AUTOGRAPHS

A CD, LP, magazine cover, ad, photo, or card signed by the group: $10

POSTERS/PRESS KITS

Promotional Posters: $10
Press Kits: $10

OFTEN OVERLOOKED MEMORABILIA

Hey Manhattan! promo snow-shaker, 1988; Looking for Atlantis promo snorkel, 1990; We Let the Stars Go promo sparklers, 1990; Carnival 2000 promo tub with silly string, party poppers, balloons, etc., 1990.

Presley, Elvis

Born: January 8, 1935, Died: August 16, 1977

Elvis on Film

A fascinating area of Elvis collectibles is that relics from his movie career. He appeared in thirty-three films, and collectibles range from one sheet (27" x 41") movie posters and lobby cards, to press books and invitations. All items associated with these film releases are highly sought by both movie buffs and Elvis collectors. Among the most popular forms of movie memorabilia are the standard movie posters commonly referred to as "one-sheets." One-sheets were produced for all thirty-three of Elvis Presly's films. It is worth noting that more than one style of one-sheet may exist for a film—for example, *Viva Las Vegas* and *Elvis on Tour*—and when a film is re-released a reissue poster, which can vary substantially from the original, is often made available to cinemas.

One-sheets are not to be confused with other forms of posters, such as a three-sheet (41" x 81"), six-sheet (81" x 81"), or 24-sheet (9' x 13-1/2'), which may have been issued for Presley films. These other forms of advertising can vary significantly in value from one sheets, depending upon scarcity, quality, and condition. Billboard size advertising—24-sheet posters—are extremely scarce because many were destroyed via the creation process.

Window cards (14" x 22"- heavy paper), lobby cards (11" x 14"), insert posters/cards (14" x 36"), and half-sheets (22" x 28") and posters (40" x 60") are other forms of movie memorabilia. Unlike one sheets, not all of these forms may be used in the promotion of a film. Window cards are attractive to collectors because of their size and heavier paper stock. Occasionally window cards will use different illustrations from those used on a related one sheet, such is the case with both *Loving You* and *Frankie and Johnny*.

Lobby cards or scene cards, which are made of cardboard, were released in sets of eight. Most sought among lobby cards are key movie scenes or outstanding shots of Elvis. If a lobby card depicts a poor scene or fails to depict Presley as the key image, it may be referred to as a "dead" card and is of little interest to the collector.

Insert posters are also popular with collectors because of their vertical format and heavier paper stock. Most insert posters were folded, thus creating unwanted creases with possible paper cracking. Occasionally insert posters were rolled, thus solving the crease issue. A rolled poster does command greater value than a folded variation.

Lobby photo cards, or display posters, are often referred to as half-sheet posters. This style of poster may also vary in design, and such was the case with *Jailhouse Rock*, *King Creole*, and *Loving You*.

One of the most popular forms of posters comes in a large (40" x 60") format and was produced on heavy cardboard stock. Styles do vary in this form—for example the poster for *Blue Hawaii* has a different color scheme than those produced in other forms. While durability is an advantage in this form, the posters larger size can be cumbersome to collectors.

Other forms of movie memorabilia include panels (201" x 60"), stand-ups, still photos, press books, handbills, flyers, banners, hats, and even Hawaiian leis—guess which film this is for!

AUTOGRAPHS

Elvis Presley, as popular as he was, was as accommodating as possible to autograph requests. His signature varied greatly during his lifetime, primarily in capitalization, character formation, and flamboyance. Most notable is the lack of flamboyance when signing legal documents, as compared to simple in-person autograph requests. Presley commonly inscribed photos to the recipient, and although many examples of "Best Wishes, Elvis Presley" or "Sincerely, Elvis Presley" have been found in the market, most have been proven to have been facsimiles or forgeries. Additionally worth noting is that Presley associates sometimes signed for him. These, however, are easier to identify as forgeries than many well-executed printed facsimiles. By the late '70s his handwriting had shown considerable degradation, with much of the flamboyance missing. Examples from this period can be very difficult to authenticate.

Autographed piece of paper: $450-$550

Autographed photograph: $500-$800

Autographed Tour Program: $500-$600

Autographed picture sleeve: $700-$1,200

Autographed hound dog: $750-$1,250

Autographed Las Vegas menu: $500-$1,500

Autographed fan magazine: $500-$1,650

Autographed associated postcard: $2,000

Autographed publicity photos: $600-$3,50
(depends on scarcity of photo)

Movies

Blue Hawaii (1961)
Insert Card: $35-$45
Lobby Card: $40-$55
Lobby Photo: $30-$50
One-Sheet: $75-$115
Still: $10-$20
Window Card: $125-$200

Change of Habit (1969)
Insert Card: $15-$25
Lobby Card: $10-$20
Lobby Photo: $15-$30
One-Sheet: $50-$80
Still: $5-$10
Window Card: $40-$50

Charro (1969)
Insert Card: $15-$25
Lobby Card: $10-$20
Lobby Photo: $15-$30
One-Sheet: $50-$80
Still: $5-$10
Window Card: $50-$100

Clambake: (1967)
Insert Card: $20-$30
Lobby Card: $10-$20
Lobby Photo: $15-$30
One-Sheet: $60-$90
Still: $5-$10
Window Card: $40-$80

Double Trouble (1967)
Insert Card: $20-$30
Lobby Card: $10-$20
Lobby Photo: $15-$30
One-Sheet: $60-$90
Still: $5-$10
Window Card: $40-$80

Easy Come, Easy Go (1967)
Insert Card: $20-$30
Lobby Card: $10-$20
Lobby Photo: $15-$30
One-Sheet: $60-$90
Still: $5-$10
Window Card: $50-$80

Elvis on Tour (1972)
Insert Card: $20-$30
Lobby Card: $15-$30
Lobby Photo: $30-$70
One-Sheet: $65-$120
Still: $5-$10
Window Card: $55-$90

Follow That Dream (1962)
Insert Card: $30-$70
Lobby Card: $20-$30
Lobby Photo: $30-$50
One-Sheet: $75-$125
Still: $10-$15
Window Card: $125-$200

Flaming Star (1960)
Insert Card: $30-$60
Lobby Card: $40-$60
Lobby Photo: $30-$75
One-Sheet: $75-$125
Still: $10-$15
Window Card: $100-$175

Frankie and Johnny (1966)
Insert Card: $15-$28
Lobby Card: $10-$20
Lobby Photo: $15-$30
One-Sheet: $50-$80
Still: $10-$15
Window Card: $60-$100

Fun in Acapulco (1963)
Insert Card: $25-$60
Lobby Card: $15-$25
Lobby Photo: $25-$35
One-Sheet: $50-$85
Still: $10-$15
Window Card: $50-$125

Fun in Acapulco/Girls! Girls! Girls! (1966)
Insert Card: $15-$25
Lobby Card: $10-$20
Lobby Photo: $15-$30
One-Sheet: $50-$70
Still: $10-$15
Window Card: $60-$100

G.I. Blues (1960)
Insert Card: $35-$60
Lobby Card: $40-$55
Lobby Photo: $30-$70
One-Sheet: $75-$130
Still: $10-$20
Window Card: $150-$225

Girls! Girls! Girls! (1962)
Insert Card: $30-$70
Lobby Card: $20-$30
Lobby Photo: $30-$50
One-Sheet: $70-$110
Still: $10-$15
Window Card: $115-$200

Girl Happy (1965)
Insert Card: $20-$30
Lobby Card: $10-$25
Lobby Photo: $15-$35
One-Sheet: $50-$85
Still: $10-$15
Window Card: $60-$110

Harum Scarum (1965)
Insert Card: $20-$30
Lobby Card: $10-$25
Lobby Photo: $15-$35
One-Sheet: $50-$90
Still: $10-$15
Window Card: $60-$115

It Happened at the World's Fair (1963)
Insert Card: $25-$50
Lobby Card: $15-$22
Lobby Photo: $25-$35
One-Sheet: $100-$165
Still: $10-$15
Window Card: $50-$125

Jailhouse Rock (1957)
Insert Card: $100-$125
Lobby Card: $60-$75
Lobby Photo: $50-$125
One-Sheet: $175-$425
Still: $10-$20
Window Card: $200-$375

Kid Galahad (1962)
Insert Card: $30-$70
Lobby Card: $20-$30
Lobby Photo: $30-$50
One-Sheet: $70-$110
Still: $10-$15
Window Card: $120-$225

King Creole (1958)
Insert Card: $120-$220
Lobby Card: $50-$70
Lobby Photo: $120-$200
One-Sheet: $200-$450
Still: $10-$20
Window Card: $120-$250

Kid Creole (second run) (1959)
Insert Card: $80-$140
Lobby Card: $30-$45
Lobby Photo: $80-$150
One-Sheet: $100-$225
Still: $10-$20
Window Card: $200-$275

Kissin' Cousins (1964)
Button: $45-$60
Insert Card: $25-$35
Lobby Card: $10-$25
Lobby Photo: $15-$35
One-Sheet: $50-$90
Still: $10-$15
Window Card: $70-$140

Live a Little, Love a Little (1968)
Insert Card: $15-$25
Lobby Card: $10-$20
Lobby Photo: $15-$30
One-Sheet: $50-$75
Still: $10-$15
Window Card: $45-$65

Love Me Tender (1956)
Insert Card: $100-$170
Lobby Card: $75-$110
Lobby Photo: $100-$175
One-Sheet: $300-$650
Still: $15-$30
Window Card: $150-$300

Loving You (1957)
Insert Card: $75-$125
Lobby Card: $70-$90
Lobby Photo: $70-$100
One-Sheet: $200-$500
Still: $10-$25
Window Card: $100-$250

Paradise Hawaiian Style (1966)
Insert Card: $15-$25
Lobby Card: $10-$20
Lobby Photo: $15-$30
One-Sheet: $50-$85
Still: $10 -$15
Window Card: $65-$120

Roustabout (1964)
Insert Card: $30-$50
Lobby Card: $15-$22
Lobby Photo: $20-$30
One-Sheet: $100-$165
Still: $10-$15
Window Card: $70-$140

Speedway (1968)
Insert Card: $15-$25
Lobby Card: $10-$20
Lobby Photo: $15-$30
One-Sheet: $50-$75
Still: $10-$12
Window Card: $35-$60

Spinout (1966)
Insert Card: $15-$25
Lobby Card: $10-$18
Lobby Photo: $15-$30
One-Sheet: $50-$70
Still: $8-$12
Window Card: $40-$75

Stay Away Joe (1968)
Insert Card: $15-$25
Lobby Card: $10-$20
Lobby Photo: $15-$30
One-Sheet: $50-$75
Still: $10-$15
Window Card: $40-$60

That's the Way It Is (1970)
Insert Card: $45-$60
Lobby Card: $30-$45
Lobby Photo: $30-$45
One-Sheet: $75-$110
Still: $5-$10
Window Card: $30-$45

Tickle Me (1965)
Insert Card: $20-$30
Lobby Card: $10-$20
Lobby Photo: $15-$35
One-Sheet: $50-$80
Still: $10-$15
Window Card: $60-$100

Trouble with Girls (1969)
Insert Card: $15-$20
Lobby Card: $10-$20
Lobby Photo: $15-$30
One-Sheet: $40-$75
Still: $5-$10
Window Card: $40-$80

Viva Las Vegas (1964)
Insert Card: $45-$60
Lobby Card: $25-$35
Lobby Photo: $45-$65
One-Sheet: $100-$150
Still: $10-$20
Window Card: $50-$80

Wild in the Country (1961)
Insert Card: $35-$45
Lobby Card: $40-$55
Lobby Photo: $35-$45
One-Sheet: $125-$200
Still: $10-$20
Window Card: $125-$200

Presley, Elvis

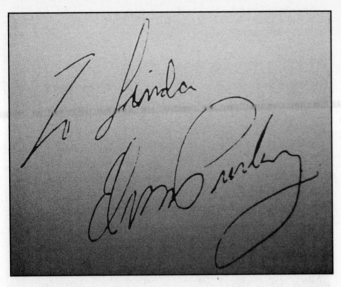

A personalized Elvis autograph

An extremely rare Elvis concert poster from Madison Square Garden, 1972. This poster is possibly a one-of-a-kind. Its estimated value is $4,000. From the Doug Leftwitch collection.

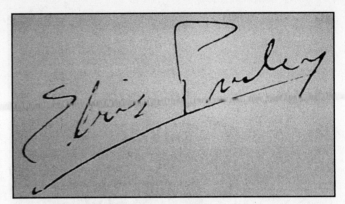

Elvis Presley autographed piece of paper

TOUR BOOKS/PROGRAMS/PASSES

Las Vegas Menus:

1969

$400-$550: Opening engagement at International Hotel in Las Vegas, vertical format
$1,000-$1,350: International Hotel gift box set with contents, invited guests only (7/31 & 8/1)**

1970

$150-$200: Black and white cover.

1971

$100-$125: Black and white cover, International Hotel
$100-$125: "ELVIS" colored dots in background, 1/26 - 2/23
$100-$125: Sahara Tahoe, no photo on cover, text only, 7/20 - 8/2
$60-$80: International Hotel, 8/9-9/6

1972

$70-$100: Las Vegas Hilton, 1/26-2/23, round, red background.
$65-$70: Las Vegas Hilton, Red, White and Blue, Summer Festival Menu

1973

$40-$50: Las Vegas Hilton - "Now Elvis" (7" x14") - 1/26-2/23
$45-$55: Las Vegas Hilton - "Now Elvis" (4 " x 7 1/2") - 1/26-2/23, same design as above
$95-$110: Sahara Tahoe, 5/4-5/20, round (91/2"), album format
$100-$115: Sahara Tahoe, 5/4-5/20, round (8"),same design as above
$40-$50: Las Vegas Hilton, 8/6-9/3, Summer Festival, round

1974

$45-$65: Las Vegas Hilton, 1/26-2/9, color picture cove.
$45-$65: Sahara Tahoe, 5/16-26, same cover as above with text changes
$40-$50: Las Vegas Hilton, 8/19-9/2, Summer Festival

1975

$55-$70: Las Vegas Hilton, fold-open color cover of Elvis with facsimile signature
$150-$175: Las Vegas Hilton, 8/18- Labor Day, with insert, album format
$135-$170: Hilton Showroom, 12/2-15, horizontal format
$60-$75: International Hotel, color cover of Elvis in chair*
*This cover is identical to Photo Album and RCA Records Photo Album, only text varies
**This scarce collectible was given to invited guests only on the first two opening nights. It included:

The King's leather jacket worn on "ELVIS" (NBC) on 12/3/68. (Hard Rock Café, Key West)

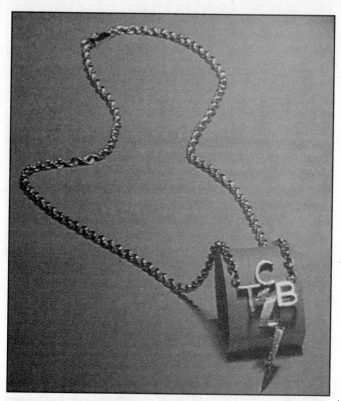

Elvis' "T.C.B." (Taking Care of Business) Lightning Bolt Gold Pendant. Its estimated value is between $8,000 and $10,000. © Butterfield & Butterfield, Auctioneers Corp., 1997.

Elvis (NBC-TV) and *Elvis in Memphis* albums, a nine-page letter from Elvis and Colonel Parker, 1969 discography with tapes, two black and white photos (8"x10"), a 1969 pocket calendar, and a color handout/photo. A similar box was also handed out the following year, however, it had different contents.

Elvis used this guitar on tour in 1976 and 1977. It has an estimated value between $50,000 and $70,000. © Butterfield & Butterfield, Auctioneers Corp., 1997.

POSTERS/PRESS KITS

See chart below

USED CLOTHING/EQUIPMENT

Cufflinks - $2,000; watch - $2,500-$4,000; bracelet - $3,000-$3,250; Graceland ashtray - $2,500; personalized sunglasses $14,000-$27,500; unpersonalized sunglasses $1,500-$1,700; suit jacket - limited use - $1,500-$2,000; karate outfit - used $17,500-$20,000; used acoustic guitar - $40,000-125,000-$165,000 (depends on model and significance); belt - $5,000-$11,000; hat - $5,000 (price varies due to material and craftsmanship); leather coat - $20,000-$25,000 (full-length); leather coat - $2,000-$2,750 (blazer); shirt - $1,500-$2,000; ring - $4,000-$10,000; smoking jacket - $5,000; money clip - $10,000; custom one-piece stage suit - worn - $45,000-$120,000; suit - $4,000-$10,000

OFTEN OVERLOOKED MEMORABILIA

1953 Humes High School autographed yearbook - $4,000-$4, 250; unpublished photographs - $400-$1,000 (high end assumes negative and copyright); Graceland television - $800-$1,000; Graceland lamp - $1,000-$1,5000; guitar pin - $500-$650; karate certificates - $850-$1,500; souvenir pillow - $500; personally owned vehicle - $100,000; badges (special deputy) - $2,000-$12,000; Elvis in concert, red winter tour jacket - $5,000; Elvis Alive pinball machine $2,500-$3,000

REFERENCES/BOOKS

Numerous resources exist, including many dedicated to collectibles. Serious King fans can take their pick from the many Elvis Fan Clubs.

L to R: Elvis Presley karate Gi (estimated value between $10,000 and $15,000), an Elvis stage shirt (estimated value between $1,200 and $1,500), and Elvis' Kenpo Karate jacket (estimated value between $20,000 and $30,000). © Butterfield & Butterfield, Auctioneers Corp., 1997.

ELVIS PRESLEY SELECTED ASSORTED MEMORABILIA

*Consult a more specific source
EPE = Elvis Presley Enterprises

Anklets (EPE 1956), two pairs attached to card: 850-$1,250

Anklets (EPE 1956), card/package by itself: $225-$375

Ashtray (EPE 1956), autographed photo in glass: $400

Balloon CA. TOYTIME 1962, 1963, Various: $*

Belt (EPE 1956), leather: $625-$750

Belt (EPE 1956), plastic: $600-$650

Belt Buckle (EPE 1956) $200-$275

Billfold (EPE 1956) $450-$525

Binder (EPE 1956), zipper model "Love Me Tender": $900-$1,250*

Bolo Tie (EPE 1956) $175-$225

Book (EPE 1956),autograph: $600-$650

Bookends (EPE 1956), both: $550-$675

Bookends (EPE 1956), single: $275-$350

Books, with dust cover: $15-$55*

Books, without dust cover: $10-$30*

Bracelet (EPE 1962) various styles: $30-$65*

Browser Box, RCA VICTOR 1956, "Now...Everything Elvis Presley Has Recorded...Available Here On RCA Victor Single Recordings": $200-$400

Bubble Gum Card (TOPPS 1957) "Hit Stars" Card - Individual: $30-$40

Bubble Gum Card Counter Display (EPE 1956) display Box with 24 packs of gum/cards: $800-$1,300

Bubble Gum Card Counter Display (EPE 1956) box alone: $300-$600

Bubble Gum Wrapper (EPE 1956) 5 cent: $50-$75

Bubble Gum Wrapper (EPE 1956) 1 cent: $25-$50

Bubble Gum Cards (EPE 1956) full color - unopened 1 cent: $50

Bubble Gum Cards (EPE 1956) full color - unopened 5 cent: $125

Bubble Gum Cards (EPE 1956) full color - any card: $8-$15

Bubble Gum Wrapper (TOPPS 1957) "Hit Stars" card: $20-$30

Buttons, various sizes, styles, colors, etc.: $*

Carrying Case (EPE 1956) includes insert: $600-$700

Ceramic Tile (EPE 1956) "Best Wishes, Elvis Presley" - 6" square: $850-$900

Charm Bracelet (EPE 1956) bracelet with card: $100-$200

Charm Bracelet (EPE 1956) bracelet alone: $75-$110

Numerous Christmas items exist, consult a more specific resource

Numerous charms exist, consult a more specific resource

Coaster (EPE 1956) autographed photo in the glass: $100-$200

Coin Purse/Keychain, Elvis pictured in striped shirt: $100-$200

Coloring contest (Girls! Girls! Girls!), watch for counterfeits!

Consult a more specific source for details, sizes, etc., watch for counterfeits!

Concert Placards 1954-56 Elvis not listed as headliner: $*

Concert Placards 1956-58 The Elvis Presley Show: $*

Concert Placards 1960-61 The Elvis Presley Show: $*

Concert Placards 1969-77 Elvis in Concert: $*

Concert Placards "Elvis—Extra special show by popular demand. Sunday morning, Sept. 2nd at 3:00 AM—Make Your Reservations Now. Las Vegas Hilton": $*

Cuff Links (EPE 1958) cuff links in original box: $275-$425

Cuff Links (EPE 1958) without box: $200-$250

Diary (EPE 1956) one year: $425-$550

Dog Tag (EPE 1962) "I'm An Elvis Fan": $30- $45

Dog Tag (EPE 1962) "Presley, Elvis - 53310761": $30-$50

Dog Tag Anklet (EPE 1958) anklet attached to card: $45- $50

Dog Tag Anklet (EPE 1958) anklet alone: $15-30

Dog Tag Bracelet (Boy's) (EPE 1958) bracelet attached to card: $25-$40

Dog Tag Bracelet (Boy's) (EPE 1958) bracelet alone: $20-$25

Dog Tag Bracelet (Girl's) (EPE 1958) bracelet attached to card: $20-$30

Dog Tag Bracelet (Girl's) (EPE 1958) bracelet alone: $15-$20

Dog Tag Keychain (EPE 1958) keychain attached to card: $75-$100

Dog Tag Keychain (EPE 1958) key chain alone: $20-40

Dog Tag Necklace (EPE 1958) necklace attached to card ("Authentic" - $1 price): $75-$100

Dog Tag Necklace (EPE 1958) necklace attached to card (no "Authentic" or $1 price): $25-$50

Dog Tag Necklace (EPE 1958) necklace alone: $15-$35

Dog Tag Sweater Holder (EPE 1958) sweater holder attached to card: $150-$250

Dog Tag Sweater Holder (EPE 1958) sweater holder alone: $100-$150

Doll (EPE 1957) with all clothing, original box: $1500-$2,000

Doll (EPE 1957) with all clothing, no box: $,1000-$1,500

Earrings (EPE 1956) picture of Elvis, attached to card: $200-$300

Earrings (EPE 1956) picture of Elvis, earrings alone: $100-200

Easter related item, see more specific source

Elvis Special Electric Display (NBC-TV 1968) promotional store display: $100-$300

Fan Club Membership Package (1956) one personal note to you from EP with "Elvis Presley, National Headquarters, Madison, Tenn" on bottom: $100-$150

One Elvis Presley Complimentary Fan Club Membership Card: $40-$50

One Elvis Presley National Fan Club - I Like Elvis And His RCA Records pin-on button: $75-$100

Complete Package: $275-$600

Framed Portrait (EPE 1956) "Love Me Tender, Sincerely Elvis Presley": $400-$575

GI Blues LP Special Electric Display, promotional Store Display: $200-$375

Board Game (EPE 1956) "The Elvis Presley Game—A Party Game for the Young at Heart": $750-$1,250

Drinking Glass (EPE 1956): $150-$225

Guitar (EPE-EMENEE 1956-57) with carrying case: $1,200-$2,000

Guitar alone: $750-$1,200

Song book "For EMENEE Guitar Including Elvis Presley Song Hits": $35-$50

Handbag (EPE 1956) clutch style: $375-$700

Handkerchief (EPE 1956) $250-$400

Hats (EPE-MAGNET 1956) with mfg. tag: $100-$125

Hats, without tag: $50-$125

Hats, tag alone: $20-$25

Hat, Paper Army/GI Blues Theater Ticket (1960) promoted GI Blues film and soundtrack

Hat with box office stub: $45-$80

Hat without box office stub: $25-$50

Hat, styrofoam straw, with "Elvis Summer Festival" Band: $15-$20

Hound Dog (EPE 1956) "10" dog with "Hound Dog" hat: $200-$300

Hound Dog (1972) small "Elvis Summer Festival" dog with ribbon: $35-$45

Hound Dog (1972) "12-15" "Elvis Summer Festival" dog with ribbon: $175-$350

Jar, AML, 112060, "Love Me Tender": $50-$75

Jeans (EPE-BLUE RIDGE 1956) with "Elvis Presley Jeans" tag: $100-$175

Jeans, without tag: $75-$125

Jeans, Tag alone: $15-$30

Keychain (EPE-PICTORIAL PRODUCTS 1956) flasher: $15-$25

Lei, Elvis pictured on one side, Blue Hawaii LP promoted on the other: $100-$125

Lipstick (EPE-TEEN-AGER LIPSTICK CORP. 1956) tube attached to card: $800-$1,000

Lipstick, tube alone: $250-$300

Locket (EPE 1957) heart-shaped Elvis Presley: $25-$50

Magazines, numerous exist, consult more specific resource

Selected Key Magazines

1956	Amazing Elvis Presley: $50-$75
June 56	Best Songs: $25-$65
1957	Cool: Special Issue on Elvis Presley: $40-$65
July 55	Country Song Roundup: $40-$70
1956-58	Dig (covers): $40-$65
1956	Elvis and Jimmy (Dean): $75 $150
1956	Elvis Answers Back - with cardboard 78 RPM attached: $300-$325
1956	Elvis Answers Back - with record removed: $150-$250
1957	Elvis: His Loves & Marriage: $50-$80
1959	Elvis in the Army: $50-$85
1956	Elvis Photo Album 125 Photos Never Before Published: $50-$75
1956	Elvis Presley More Than 100 Pictures, Etc.: $50-$75
1956	Elvis Presley: Hero or Heel: $150-$175
1956	Elvis Presley in Hollywood: $50-$80
1956	Elvis Presley Speaks!: $50-$80
1957	Elvis: The Intimate Story: $50-$100
1960	Elvis: The King Returns: $25-$55
1965	Elvis vs The Beatles: $75-$150
1960	Elvis Yearbook: $25-$50
1956-58	Hep Cats (covers) $65-$100
1966	I Love You #60: Here Comes Elvis: $40-$75
1956	Lowdown: $25-$45
1961	Movie Teen: Special Elvis Issue: $20-$50
1956	Official Elvis Presley Album: $60-$100
1957	Personalities: $45-$70
1956	Record Whirl $25-$50
1957	Rock and Roll Roundup: $40-$65
1956	Rock & Roll Stars #1—The Real Elvis Presley Story: $40-$60
1957	Rock & Roll Stars #2—Elvis Answers...Teenage Questions: $25-$50
1958	Rock & Roll Stars #3—Elvis in the Army?: $25-$50
1956	Rock 'n' Roll Battlers: $40-$75
1956	Rock 'n' Roll Jamboree: $40-$70
1957	Rock 'n' Roll Rivals: $40-$70
	Sixteen (covers): $20-$50
1956	Souvenir Photo Album "Elvis Presley 'Mr. Dynamite' Nation's Only Atomic Powered Singer": $75-$120
1956	Suppressed Annual: $25-$50
1956	TV Guide (various): $125-$200
1960	TV Guide (various): $50-$85
1957	Teen Life: $50-$75
Oct. 56	Teenage Rock and Roll Review: $40-$75
Dec. 56	Teenage Rock and Roll Review: $40-$75
1957	Tommy Sands vs. Belafonte and Elvis: $50-$75
1957	Young Lovers #18: The Real Elvis Presley Complete Life Story: $150-$200

Medallion (EPE-1956) "I Want You, I Need You, I Love You - Don't Be Cruel - Hound Dog - Heartbreak Hotel": $100-$200

Menus: See chart above

Mittens (EPE-Nolan 1956) pair: $325-$400

Mittens (EPE-Nolan 1957) single: $50-$125

Necklace (EPE 1956) heart-shaped, engraving of Elvis - attached to card: $150-$275

Necklace alone: $125-$175

Necklace (EPE 1962) "Follow That Dream": $30-$50

Opening night invitations, Las Vegas and Lake Tahoe - printed paper: $10-$15

Felt 3 foot banner invitation (1/26/72): $65-$100

Paint Set (EPE 1956) prenumbered, oil colors: $500-$600

Pajamas (EPE) singing Elvis pictured, lists "Heartbreak Hotel," "Don't be Cruel," "Hound Dog," "I Want You, I Need You": $275-$550

Paperweights, 'Sincerely Yours, Elvis': $12

Patches (EPE 1956) heart-shaped, "My Heart Belongs to Elvis Presley," "I Love Elvis Presley," or "Elvis Presley is a Doll" Display card with patches attached: $50-$125

Single patch: $20-$30

Tour patches/ribbons (EPE 1970-77) $20-$30

Pens, various, see more specific resource

Pencil (EPE-Union Pencil Co. 1956) complete box, one dozen packs of Elvis Presley Pencils: $1,500-$2,500

Pencil box alone: $75-$125

Wrapped 12 pack of pencils: $200-$350

Single pencil: $10-$15

Pencil Sharpener (EPE 1956): $100-$150

Pennants, various, see more specific resource

Perfume (EPE 1957) Elvis Presley's Teddy Bear Eau de Parfum 1957 picture of Elvis on label: $200-$325

Perfume (EPE 1965) Elvis Presley's Teddy Bear Eau de Parfum 1965 picture of Elvis on label: $30-$50

Phonograph (EPE 1956) portable, autograph model Manual record change player: $750-$950

Automatic record change player: $800-$1,100

Printed instructions: "How to Use and Enjoy Your RCA Victor Portable Phonograph": $50-$100

Photo Album (EPE 1956) $300-$400

Photo Albums (souvenir tour & concert) (1956) "In Person - Elvis Presley, Country Music's Mr. Rhythm": $275-$450

Photo Albums (1956) "Elvis Presley—Mr. Dynamite": $250-$400

Photo Albums (1956) "Souvenir Photo Album - Elvis Presley": $250-$350

Photo Albums (1957) "Elvis Presley Photo Folio": $125-$250

Photo albums (1970-77): $20-$45

Photos, various, see more specific resource

Pillow (EPE 1956) $450-$650

Pin (EPE 1956) framed picture of Elvis attached to a guitar with card: $265-$400

Pin alone: $175-$250

Pin (EPE-Vari-Vue 1956) flasher: $20-$40

Pin (EPE-Pictorial Productions 1956) flasher: $20-$40

Pinball Machine, see more specific resource

Plastic Bags (1970-72) Nevada hotels, complimentary, LP-sized bags: $15-$20

Plate, various, see more specific resource

Pocket Calendars, see more specific resource

Pocket Watch (1964) picture of Elvis wearing a jacket & playing guitar-polished finish: $125-$225

Picture of Elvis (1964) wearing a jacket & playing guitar-knurled finish: $25-$35

Picture of Elvis singing (EPE 1956) Lists: "Heartbreak Hotel," "Don't Be Cruel," "Hound Dog," "I Want You, I Need You": $150-$250

Purse (EPE 1956) clutch style, 3 pictures of Elvis, lists "Hound Dog," "Heartbreak Hotel," "I Want You, I Need You": $300-$400

Record Case (EPE 1956) $350-$450

Ring (adjustable) (EPE 1956) 12 rings in counter display: $2,000

Single ring: $75-$125

Display card without rings : $300-$450

Ring (1957) flasher: $50-$75

Scarves (EPE 1956) 3 drawings of Elvis, lists "I Want You, I Need You," "Love Me Tender," "Don't Be Cruel," "You're Nothing But a Hound Dog," reads: "Best Wishes, Elvis Presley": $175

Concert souvenir autographed, with/without Hilton logo: $20-$30

Scrap Book (EPE 1956): $250-$350

Sheet Music (Elvis) (1956-59): $25-$50

1960-77 with Elvis picture: $15-$30

1960-77 without Elvis picture: $8-$12

Sheet Music (other) "Elvis Presley For President," Lou Monte: $50-$75

Shirt (EPE-Blue Ridge 1956) green and white striped: $100-$125

RCA Records (1976) "For the Heart/Elvis": $20-$40

Shoes (EPE-Faith Shoe Co. 1956) pumps, pair with box: $400-$500

Single pump: $100-$125

Pair without box: $300-$425

Box alone: $100-$150

Shoes (EPE 1956) sneakers, pair with box: $400-$600

Single sneaker: $100-$130

Pair without box: $300-$450

Box alone: $100-$150

Side Burns Machine Label, see more specific resource

Skirt (EPE-Little Jeans Togs 1956) $500-$750

Song Folios, magazines, similar items, see more specific resource

Socks, bobby (EPE 1956) 2 pair attached to card: $150-$250

Card/package alone: $25-$50

Statuette (EPE1956) bronze, 8 inch: $500-$600

Tag (EPE 1956) used for shirt and jeans, pictures Elvis w/guitar: $30-$35

Teddy Bears (EPE 1957) 24 inch with "Elvis Presley" and "Teddy Bear" ribbons: $225-$300

1971 International Hotel bear, pink/white with pin on badge: $35-$50

Tickets, see more specific resource, this is a book by itself!

Title "Juke Strips" Sheets of 10 strips, front/back side of single printed on each strip

Releases from 1955-59: $20-$30

Releases from 1960-69: $15-$25

Releases from 1970-79: $5-$10

Releases from 1980-current: $5

Tour Patches, etc., see more specific resource

Wallet, coin purse, and keychain (EPE 1956) Elvis Presley - Rock 'n' Roll, 2 drawings/1 photo of Elvis: $350-$425

Wallet (EPE 1956) clutch, folding with 2 coin compartments: $250-$300

Wallet (EPE 1956) cash: $250-$350

Wallet (EPE 1956) photos: $250-$350

Preston, Billy

Born: September 9, 1946

Rock music's premier session guest and talented singer/songwriter Billy Preston is probably first remembered for his contributions to other key musicians efforts (Ray Charles, the Beatles, and the Rolling Stones), however, it won't take you long to also associate him with hits like "Outaspace" (#2,

1972) (a Grammy winner), "Will It Go Round in Circles" (#1, 1973), "Space Race" (#4, 1973), "Nothing from Nothing" (#1, 1974), and for his duet with Syretta Wright on "With You I'm Born Again." It was also Preston who penned Joe Cocker's biggest solo hit "You Are So Beautiful."

AUTOGRAPHS

A CD, LP, magazine cover, ad, photo, or card signed by the artist: $10-$20

OFTEN OVERLOOKED MEMORABILIA

Artifacts associated with the numerous contributions Preston has made to other performers' works; all items associated with his work for the Beatles.

Preston, Johnny

(John Courville)

Born: August 18, 1930

This Texas pop star is typically associated with the novelty hit "Running Bear" (#1, 1960), which came complete with "oom-pah-pah" vocals by the "Big Bopper" (J.P. Richardson). Preston also had a handful of other hits including "Cradle of Love" (#7, 1960) and "Feel So Fine" (#14, 1960).

AUTOGRAPHS

A CD, LP, magazine cover, ad, photo, or card signed by the artist: $10-$25

The Pretenders

Formed 1978

Chrissie Hynde, Born: September 7, 1951; Pete Farndon (1953-1983); James Honeyman-Scott (1957-1982); and Martin Chambers*

*Numerous personnel changes after 1982

A successful late-70s British new wave act, The Pretenders are commonly associated with the songs "Brass in Pocket," "Talk of the Town," "Back in the Chain Gang" (#5, 1983), "Middle of the Road" (#19, 1984), "Don't Get Me Wrong" (#10, 1986), and "I'll Stand by You" (#16, 1994). The group's rise to stardom was far from smooth, as delayed follow-up records, controversy regarding Hynde's relationship with Ray Davies, a postponed tour when Martin Chambers badly injured his hand, and the drug overdose death of James Honeyman-Scott, followed by the death of former member Pete Farndon, also due to a drug overdose, took a toll on the group.

Despite adversity, both Hynde and Chambers persevered—they looked forward, rather than back. Just when many had written the band off, the group released *Last of the Independents* (1994), its first album in four years, which was praised by critics, sold gold, and yielded two singles. *The Isle of View* (#100,

1995), an acoustic album, followed as Hynde even found herself guest starring on the NBC sitcom *Friends* (11/2/95).

AUTOGRAPHS

A CD, LP, magazine cover, ad, photo, or card signed by the group: $50-$200*

*Original lineup on significant piece

TOUR BOOKS/ PROGRAMS/PASSES

Tour Programs:
1987 Tour: $20-$22
On Tour (1981): $14-$18

POSTERS/PRESS KITS

Promotional Posters: $10-$25
Press Kits: $15-$30

USED CLOTHING/ EQUIPMENT

Guitar Picks: $15

OFTEN OVERLOOKED MEMORABILIA

Pretenders 1987 Tour program (© 1986 The Pretenders)

Scarf, includes facsimile signatures: $20; Copies of Hynde's written work that appeared in the New Musical Express, artifacts from Hynde's earlier bands the Frenchies, Jack Rabbit and Berk Brothers, all tabloid articles referencing Hynde's on-again-off-again relationship with Kinks frontman Ray Davies, newspaper clippings documenting Hynde's fight with a Memphis bouncer (5/80), movie memorabilia from King Of Comedy, and Indecent Proposal, a videotape of the press conference held on June 8, 1989 where vegetarian Hynde states she once firebombed McDonalds, copies of media coverage surrounding the firebombed McDonalds in Milton Keynes on June 9, 1989, videotapes of the group's appearances on television including *Saturday Night Live* (5/7/94), *The Danny Baker Show* (10/8/94), *The Tonight Show* (10/14/94), *Friends* (11/2/95) and *Late Show With David Letterman* (11/3/95), a copy of the 1995 C4-TV documentary *The Pretenders: No Turn Left Unstoned* and artifacts from the third game of the 1995 World Series - Hynde sings the national anthem.

REFERENCES/BOOKS

Numerous resources exist, but none do justice to the band in my opinion. There are no dedicated collector books.

The Pretty Things

Formed 1963

Phil May, Dick Taylor, Brain Pendleton, John Stax, Peter Kitley (replaced by Vic Andrews, who was then replaced by Vic Prince)*

*Numerous personnel changes

This late-60s British pop-rock band is commonly associated with the songs "Rosalyn" (banned in U.S.), "Don't Bring Me Down," and "Honey I Need You" (#13, 1965). The Pretty Things had little impact in the States and weren't really noticed until the album *S.F. Sorrow* (1969).

AUTOGRAPHS

A CD, LP, magazine cover, ad, photo, or card signed by the group: $10-$25

Price, Alan

Born: April 19, 1942

Typically identified as the keyboardist with the Animals, Price score a few U.K. hits with his own band such as "Jarrow Song" (#6, 1974) before he went on to score films and established himself as an actor.

AUTOGRAPHS

A CD, LP, magazine cover, ad, photo, or card signed by the artist: $10-$15

OFTEN OVERLOOKED MEMORABILIA

Movie memorabilia from *O Lucky Man!* and *Alfie Darling*; theater memorabilia from *Home*.

Price, Lloyd

Born: March 9, 1934

A pivotal figure during the early years of the New Orleans rock scene, Price is best remembered for his songs "Lawdy Miss Clawdy" (1952), "Stagger Lee" (#1, 1959), "Personality," "I'm Gonna Get Married," "Lady Luck," and "Question" before he turned his interest to his business affairs during the '60s.

AUTOGRAPHS

A CD, LP, magazine cover, ad, photo, or card signed by the artist: $10-$45*

*On a significant piece pertaining to "Lawdy Miss Clawdy" or "Stagger Lee"

OFTEN OVERLOOKED MEMORABILIA

Souvenirs from his New York nightclub called the Turntable

Priest, Maxi

(Max Elliott)
Born: June 10, 1960

Late-80s British reggae singer Maxi Priest is typically associated with the songs "Hey Little Girl," "Wild World" (#25, 1988), a Cat Stevens cover, and "Close to You" (#1, 1990).

AUTOGRAPHS

A CD, LP, magazine cover, ad, photo, or card signed by the artist: $5-$10

Primus

Formed 1984

Tim "Herb" Alexander, Les Claypool, and Todd Huth*

*Huth departed in 1989 and was replaced by Larry LaLonde

These Bay Area '90s alt-rockers garnered significant attention by headlining the 1993 Lollapalooza tour. Primus is typically associated with the album *Pork Soda* (#7, 1993), which helped push it to the forefront of its music genre. In 1997, Primus struck pay dirt with *Brown Album*, which nearly missed debuting in the Top Twenty album chart.

AUTOGRAPHS

A CD, LP, magazine cover, ad, photo, or card signed by the group: $20-$40*

*Original lineup on significant piece

POSTERS/PRESS KITS

Promotional Posters: $10-$15
Press Kits: $15-$20

Prince

(Prince Rogers Nelson)
Born: June 7, 1958

One of rock and roll's key movers during the last two decades, his work is closely monitored, analyzed, and reanalyzed always in reverence, even if its not always acclaimed. Sexy, mysterious, controversial, cutting-edge—the adjectives seem endless when describing this performer. This Midwest singer/songwriter's first bands were Grand Central and Champagne. He moved on to a solo career on the Warner Brothers label and landed the early hits "I Wanna Be Your Lover," "Why You Wanna Treat Me So Bad?," and "Let's Work."

The album *1999* (#9, 1982) catapulted the artist into the spotlight and yielded the hit extracts "Little Red Corvette" (#6, 1983), "Delirious" (#8, 1983), and "1999" (#12, 1983). His pursuit of superstardom seemed fulfilled by his follow-up album and soundtrack *Purple Rain* (a Grammy winner), of which the artist starred in the film of the same title. The album, which spent nearly a half of a year atop the chart, spun off the hits extracts "When Doves Cry" (#1, 1984), "Let's Go Crazy" (#1, 1984), "Purple Rain" (#2, 1984), "I Would Die 4 U" (#8, 1984), and "Take Me With U" (#25, 1985). The album also marked the first time Prince had involved a backing band with a release, a group he named the Revolution.

Around the World in a Day (#1, 1985), his follow-up to the enormously successful *Purple Rain*, spun off two singles, "Raspberry Beret" (#2, 1985) and "Pop Life" (#7, 1985). Although the record topped the al-

bum chart, it yielded far less accolades than its predecessor. Following an announcement that he was quitting live performances, which lasted only two years, he opened his own studio and record label, both called Paisley Park.

"Kiss" (#1, 1986), extracted from his next film *Under the Cherry Moon*, landed him back atop the singles chart, while the soundtrack to the movie *Parade* (#3, 1986) landed only two minor hits, no doubt attributable to the film's lack of success. In 1987 Prince fired the Revolution, with the exception of Matt Fink, and hired all new musicians for *Sign 'O' the Times* (#6, 1987), which proved to be a critical factor in the success of the album, which both critics and fans adored, while driven in sales by the three hit extracts, "Sign 'O' the Times" (#3, 1987), "U Got the Look" (#2, 1987), a duet with Sheena Easton, and "I Could Never Take the Place of Your Man" (#10, 1987).

Prince's next project *The Black Album* (1987), wasn't officially released until 1994, but became one of the best selling bootleg albums of all-time—the tapes were stolen from Warner Brother's German pressing plant! Consult your *Hot Wacks* guides for further details! *Lovesexy* (#11, 1988), his next album, fell short of expectations and yielded only one hit, "Alphabet Street" (#8, 1988). Wisely, as is typically the case with Prince, when he saw his momentum slip, he decided to go back out on the road.

In 1989, the King, I mean Prince, was back on top with *Batman*, which included the hit "Batdance" (#1, 1989). Unfortunately the momentum he had built with the release was quickly flattened by both the

Prince. Photo by Jeff Katz. Courtesy Warner Bros. Records Inc.

film and soundtrack (#6, 1990) to *Graffiti Bridge*, Prince's next offering. Although the soundtrack yielded two hit singles, the film was a disaster, leaving many critics scratching their heads and asking "Why?"

Prince began the next decade by opening the Grand Slam nightclub in Minneapolis, unveiling his new band (the New Power Generation), filing a lawsuit against his former managers, and releasing the album *Diamonds and Pearls* (#3, 1991), which spun off the hit extracts "Get Off" (#21, 1991), "Cream" (#1, 1991), and "Diamonds and Pearls" (#3, 1992). More of his personal eccentricities surfaced when he named his next album with a symbol (#5, 1992), which yielded the hits "7" (#8, 1992), "My Name is Prince" (#36, 1992), and "Sexy M.F." (#66, 1992), and was a prelude to his name change.

Warner Brothers dropped the distribution of his records in February 1994 and Paisley Park went into a tailspin, but the label later released *Come*, a compilation album, and the now infamous *The Black Album*. The artist's next major release was *emancipation*, which included his single "The Holy River." The year 1997 finds the artist cyber-marketing his recordings.

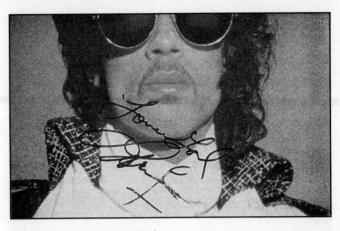

A scarce Prince autograph

AUTOGRAPHS

A CD, LP, magazine cover, ad, photo, or card signed by the artist: $100-$225

TOUR BOOKS/PROGRAMS/PASSES

Tour Programs:
Purple Rain '84-'85: $45
Lovesexy: $15
New Power Generation: $20

Backstage Passes:
Cloth: $8-$17; Laminated: $15-$35

POSTERS/PRESS KITS

Promotional Posters: $10-$60
Press Kits: $25-$75

USED CLOTHING/EQUIPMENT

Guitar Picks: $35-$75

Two examples of Prince backstage passes (Printed by OTTO)

VERY OFTEN OVERLOOKED PRINCE PARAPHERNALIA

12/10/82:	Items associated with Prince-sponsored $50 a head benefit to Marva Collins, Chicago, IL
8/3/83:	Items associated with Benefit concert for Minnesota Dance Theatre (MDT)
6/7/84:	Prince's birthday party celebration at a sculptor's studio in Minneapolis, MN—any purple napkins left?
7/26/84:	Premiere memorabilia from *Purple Rain* at Graumann's Chinese Theatre, Hollywood, CA
3/30/85:	Concert transmitted live to several European countries from Syracuse, NY
4/2/85:	Press Release stated that Prince would quit live performing following his 4/7/85 gig
4/22/85:	*Around the World in a Day* became the first album on Prince's Paisley Park label
3/6/86:	An unexpected Prince appearance at a Sheila E. show, Universal Amphitheater, Los Angeles, CA (one-off concert appearance memorabilia is often scarce)
7/1/86:	Premiere memorabilia from *Under the Cherry Moon*, held in Sheridan, Wyoming, and all MTV and Warner Bros. contest sponsored items (10,000th caller won event!)
9/11/87:	Memorabilia surrounding the opening of the Paisley Park studios, designed by Boto Design of California
10/29/87:	Premiere memorabilia from *Sign 'O' the Times*, Detroit, MI
9/24/88:	Church people hand out programs condemning the artists' lyrics—they're now collectibles!
6/19/89:	Opening night of *Batman* movie in Los Angeles, attended by Prince
11/1/90:	Premier of *Graffiti Bridge* at the Ziegfeld Theater in New York
6/94:	Comptons New Media launched the artist's first interactive CD
2/14/96:	Married his fiancée, dancer Mayte Garcia in Minneapolis, MN—reception memorabilia?
1997:	Cyber printing from the artist's web site

PRINCE IN PRINT

Assorted and Selected Appearances

4/30/78: *Minneapolis Tribune* published its first interview with Prince since he signed with Warner Brothers

2/19/81: *Rolling Stone* published first article on Prince

6/6/81: Three major U.K. papers, *NME* (*New Musical Express*), *MM* (*Melody Maker*), and *Sounds*

12/21/81: *Newsweek*, first article on Prince

4/28/83: Prince and Vanity appear on cover of *Rolling Stone*

10/84: *Musician* and *Rolling Stone* (#429), Prince on cover

11/84: *Rock & Soul*, *Ebony*, and *People*, Prince on cover

1/85: *Black Beat*

2/4/85: *Jet*

5/7/85: *The National Enquirer*

9/12/85: *Rolling Stone* (first interview since 1982)

10/18/90: *Rolling Stone* (First interview since 1985)

*The artist has appeared in thousands of related periodicals

OFTEN OVERLOOKED MEMORABILIA

Work by his protégés the Time, Sheila E. and Carmen Electra; 1985 Grammy Awards promo pack with B&W photo, press sheet, and color photo; Batdance, Warner Bros. (WB), 1989 promo picture CD in tin with ten page booklet; Purple Rain, WB, promo purple and white umbrella; Batman WB promo pack with CD, cassette, badge, and T-shirt, 1989; Diamonds and Pearls Paisley Park (PP) promo pair of cuff-links, 1991; Lovesexy, WB promo album with black knickers with emblems, 1988 - limited to 100 pairs; Graffiti Bridge, PP promo, Australia, double-album with embroidered jacket, 1990.

PRINCE ON THE TUBE

Assorted Selected Appearances

1/26/80: *American Bandstand*

12/11/80: *The Midnight Special*

2/21/81: *Saturday Night Live*

1/29/83: *Solid Gold*

5/13/83: *Solid Gold*

11/15/85: *MTV Presents Prince*

7/1/86: MTV Post-movie screening party broadcast live

9/11/87: *MTV Music Video Awards* - performed a ten minute set

9/24/89: *Saturday Night Live* Fifteenth Year Anniversary, broadcast live

9/27/89: U.K. Broadcast of nine-minute documentary preview for *Prince: Musical Portrait*

9/5/91: *MTV Video Music Awards*

9/9/91: *The Arsenio Hall Show*

12/13/91: Prince Rogers Nelson, a documentary in BBC TV's *Omnibus* series.

1/26/92: Super Bowl Today, pre-game show included "Willing and Able" video

2/25/93: *The Arsenio Hall Show*, taped

7/12/94: *The Tonight Show*, duets with Nona Gaye on "Love Sign"

12/24/94: *MTV European Music Awards*

12/13/94: *Late Show With David Letterman*

REFERENCES/BOOKS

Prince: A Documentary by Per Nilsen (1993) - $20 (Awesome!); Numerous resources exist. Uptown: The Magazine for Prince Fans and Collectors, P.O. Box 43, Cuyahoga Falls, OH 44222 is a MUST subscription!

PRINCE - ON TOUR

Selected Key Dates

*6/78: Promotional tour of the U.S., interviewed with media, signed autographs at public appearances

*11/28/79: Roxy Theater, Los Angeles, CA

*2/9/80: Orpheum Theater, Minneapolis, MN

*2/15-16/80: Bottom Line, New York

*Winter/ Spring 1980: Supported Rick James' Battle of Funk

*12/4/80: First headlining tour opened in Buffalo at Shea's (clubs, small theaters)

*5/29/81: First concert in Europe, Paradiso club in Amsterdam

*10/5/81: Sam's Minneapolis, MN, under name "Controversy," Stones warm-up gig

*10/9/81: Opens for Rolling Stones at Los Angeles Memorial Coliseum

*10/11/81: Opens for Rolling Stones' second show at Los Angeles Memorial Coliseum

*11/20/81: Controversy tour began at Pittsburgh's Stanley Theatre

*11/11/82: 1999 tour began at the Memorial Auditorium in Chattanooga, TN

*11/4/84: Purple Rain tour began with seven sold-out shows in Detroit, MI

*4/7/85: Final show of Purple Rain tour, Orange Bowl, Miami, FL

*5/86: Hit & Run tour series of surprise shows (announced day of show) began

*8/12/86: Parade European tour began in London

*9/9/86: Last ever performance with the Revolution

*5/8/87: Sign 'O' Times tour opened in Stockholm

*7/8/88: Lovesexy tour opened at the Paris Palais Omnisport

*7/25/88: Prince played the first of seven appearances at London's Wembley Arena

*9/9/88: European leg of Lovesexy tour ended—the show was filmed and broadcast live!

*9/14/88: The American leg of tour began in Minneapolis, MN

*11/29/88: The American Lovesexy tour concluded in Dallas' Reunion Arena

*2/1/89: The Japanese leg of "Lovesexy" tour begins at Sendai Stadium

*2/13/89: The last date of the "Lovesexy" tour

*6/2/90: The Nude tour opened at Rotterdam's Stadion Feijenoord

*6/19/90: Prince began record-breaking sixteen-night engagement at London's Wembley Arena

*7/7/90: Prince's first ever concert in Ireland at Cork's Pairc U Chaoimh

*9/10/90: The Nude tour closed at Yokohama Stadium, Japan

*4/3/92: Diamonds and Pearls world tour opened in Tokyo, Japan

*7/12/92: Diamonds and Pearls world tour concluded in Paris, France

*3/8/93: Opened North American tour in Sunrise, FL—a ten-city trek

*3/27/93: Played for the very first time at the Apollo Theatre in Harlem, NY

*3/3/95: Embarked on an eleven-date U.K. and Irish tour set to end 3/30/95

*Does not include the artist's numerous one-off appearances, surprise appearances, post gig bashes, fund raisers, etc.

Prine, John

Born: October 10, 1946

Dynamic Midwest singer/songwriter John Prine recorded his self-titled debut album in 1971, but it wasn't until other artists began recording his work that people really took notice. The Everly Brothers covered "Paradise," while both Bette Midler and Joan Baez recorded "Hello in There." Typically pegged as a folk artist, he caught many off guard when he moved toward hard rock or diversified into other genres. His 1983 album *German Afternoons* earned him a Grammy nomination for Best Contemporary Folk Recording, an award he finally won with his *The Missing Years* album in 1991. During a career that has spanned two and half decades, Prine has managed to sustain a considerable cult following.

AUTOGRAPHS

A CD, LP, magazine cover, ad, photo, or card signed by the artist: $10-$15

OFTEN OVERLOOKED MEMORABILIA

Movie memorabilia from *Falling from Grace* (1992)

Proby, P.J.

(James Marcus Smith)

Born: November 6, 1938

Early-60s singer, better known in Britain than the U.S., P.J. Proby is best remembered for his songs "Hold Me" (#3, U.K, 1964) and "Niki Hoeky" (#23, 1967).

AUTOGRAPHS

A CD, LP, magazine cover, ad, photo, or card signed by the artist: $5-$10

OFTEN OVERLOOKED MEMORABILIA

Associated stage memorabilia from a production he may have appeared in, or revival show souvenirs

The Proclaimers

Formed 1983

Craig Reid and Charlie Reid, both Born: March 5, 1962

These twin brothers finally broke in America with their hit "I'm Gonna Be (500 Miles)" (#3, 1993). It was released in 1988, didn't hit until it was included in the film soundtrack to *Benny and Joon*. The Proclaimers have scored a few other U.K. hits and have looked for a repeat performance on the U.S. singles chart.

AUTOGRAPHS

A CD, LP, magazine cover, ad, photo, or card signed by the duo: $10-$20

POSTERS/PRESS KITS

Promotional Posters: $8-$10
Press Kits: $10

OFTEN OVERLOOKED MEMORABILIA

Movie memorabilia from *Benny and Joon* (1993)

Procol Harum

Formed 1966

Gary Brooker, Keith Reid, Matthew Fisher, Ray Royer, Dave Knights, and Bobby Harrison*

*Numerous personnel changes

This late-60s classic-rock band, best remembered for the hits "A Whiter Shade of Pale" (1967) and "Conquistador" (1972), was consistently plagued by personnel problems. Of all of its previous alumni, the most notable was perhaps Robin Trower, who stayed with the group from 1967 to July 1971, and is still performing in 1997. Occasional offshoots of the band periodically join together to both record and perform.

AUTOGRAPHS

A CD, LP, magazine cover, ad, photo, or card signed by the group: $40-$75*
*Original lineup

****

"On The Edge "

Prodigy

Bringing new meaning to the phrase "having a bad hair day," Keith Flint makes Cyndi Lauper look like the girl next door. The punkin' instigator Flint, teams with Liam Howlett, Leeroy Thornhill and Maxim (Keith "Keeti" Palmer) to form the rock-techno band Prodigy. Now living off *The Fat of the Land*, Prodigy has watched "Firestarter" and "Breathe" crown them the disciples of dance-punk. With the band also feeding off criticism and condemnation, songs such as "Smack My Bitch Up" and "Funky Shit," mixed with liner note quotes from Nazi Herman Goering, find listeners putting down the gun and slowly backing away, rather than catering to their appetite. Whether or not the band will ever be more than a portentous event, remains to be seen. Anyway picking up a few copies of the August 21, 1997 issue of *Rolling Stone*, featuring Keith Flint - stone, may be worth the bucks.

****

Professor Longhair

(Henry Roeland Byrd) (1918-1980)

While his left hand did boogie-woogie bass lines, his right hand plays rolling arpeggios—Professor Longhair pioneered one of the classic styles of rock and roll piano playing, influencing disciples such as Fats Domino, Huey "Piano" Smith, and Allen Toussaint. In 1950 Longhair signed to Mercury and released "Baldhead," which rose to Number Five on the R&B chart. He is noted for other songs including "Mardi Gras in New Orleans" and "Big Chief." He left the music business in the mid-60s and didn't return until 1971, when he was rediscovered by some festival talent scouts. Thereafter he appeared regularly at the New Orleans Festival and numerous other similar events including the Newport Folk Festival in 1973. Prior to his death he was actually making plans to tour with the Clash. He was inducted into the Rock and Roll Hall of Fame in 1991.

AUTOGRAPHS

A CD, LP, magazine cover, ad, photo, or card signed by the artist: $75-$200

OFTEN OVERLOOKED MEMORABILIA

Associated festival memorabilia

Psychedelic Furs

Formed 1978

Richard Butler, Tim Butler, Duncan Kilburn, and Roger Morris

This late-70s British punk band is typically associated with the songs "Pretty in Pink," "Love My Way," and "Heartbreak Beat" and for the albums *Forever Now* (#61, 1982) and *Midnight to Midnight* (#29, 1987), before it broke up in 1991. The group was plagued by personnel changes, and although it received significant MTV rotation and college-radio airplay, it wasn't translating into sufficient enough sales to sustain the band.

AUTOGRAPHS

A CD, LP, magazine cover, ad, photo, or card signed by the group: $15-$35

Public Enemy

Formed 1982

Chuck D (Carlton Ridenhour), Flavor Flav (William Drayton), Terminator X (Norman Rogers), and Professor Griff (Richard Griffin)

Eighties rap innovators, who put the "i" in hip-hop (for "intensity"), Public Enemy is best known for its songs "Bring the Noise," "Don't Believe the Hype" (#18 R&B, 1988), "Fight the Power" (#20 R&B, 1989), "Welcome to the Terrordome" (#15 R&B, 1990), "911 Is a Joke" (#15 R&B, 1990), "Brothers Gonna Work It Out" (#20 R&B, 1990), "Can't Truss It" (#50, 1991), and "Shut Em down" (#26 R&B, 1992).

The group garnered significant positive attention in the pop community when it opened for U2's Zoo TV Tour, but was often plagued by controversy over racial epithets. By the mid-90s the group's chart staying power was diminishing, and member Flavor Flav was convicted of an assault charge, followed by another charge of attempted murder during a domestic squabble. While charges from the latter incident were later dropped, bad luck seems to follow Flav.

AUTOGRAPHS

A CD, LP, magazine cover, ad, photo, or card signed by the group: $35-$50

OFTEN OVERLOOKED MEMORABILIA

Periodical clipping surrounding the controversies the group has faced over the years; black cap with silver logo - $20.

Public Image Ltd. (PiL)

Formed 1978

John Lyndon (Johnny Rotten), Keith Levene, Jah Wobble (John Wordle), Jim Walker, Jeanette Lee, and Dave Crowe*

*Numerous personnel changes

Late-70s "anti-rock" group, led by former Sex Pistol frontman Johnny Lyndon, PiL made its live debut in London on Christmas Day in 1978, but couldn't ignite interest in America until the release of *Second Edition* (#171, 1980). The album was praised by critics, and the band toured the U.S. in the spring of the same year. Personnel conflicts began to arise during the early '80s, and by 1983, of the original lineup, only Lyndon remained. The band did land one club hit, "This Is Not a Love Song," but by the '90s PiL's charter seemed clouded, as did Lyndon.

AUTOGRAPHS

A CD, LP, magazine cover, ad, photo, or card signed by the group - $40-$65

TOUR BOOKS/PROGRAMS/PASSES

Tour Programs:

Europe '83: $25

OFTEN OVERLOOKED MEMORABILIA

Happy?, Virgin promo tin can, includes mug, pen, can opener, and keychain, 1987; 9, Virgin promo jigsaw puzzle, 1989.

Puckett, Gary and the Union Gap

Formed 1967

Gary Puckett, Born: October 17, 1942; Dwight Bement; Kerry Chatter; Gary Withem; and Paul Wheatbread

Garbed in civil war uniforms, this late-60s Southern California pop act is best known for the hits "Woman, Woman" (#4, 1967), "Young Girl" (#2, 1968), "Lady Willpower" (#2, 1968), "Over You" (#7, 1968), "Don't Give Into Him" (#15, 1969), and "This Girl Is a Woman Now' (#8, 1969) before disbanding in 1971.

AUTOGRAPHS

A CD, LP, magazine cover, ad, photo, or card signed by the group: $35-$60

Purify, James and Bobby

James Purify and Bobby Purify (Robert Lee Dickey)

This mid-60s Florida duo, also cousins, is best remembered for the hits "I'm Your Puppet" (#6, 1966), "Shake a Tail Feather" (#25, 1967), "I Take What I Want" (#41, 1967), and "Let Love Come Between Us" (#23, 1967).

AUTOGRAPHS

A CD, LP, magazine cover, ad, photo, or card signed by the duo: $10-$15

Quarterflash

Formed 1980

Rindy Ross, Marv Ross, Jack Charles, Rick DiGiallonardo, Brian David Willis, and Rick Gooch

Made up of two popular Portland bands, Seafood Mama and Pilot, Quarterflash debuted aggressively with a Top Ten platinum album which included two smash extracts, "Harden My Heart (#3, 1981) and "Find Another Fool" (#16, 1981). While its sophomore effort was less successful, it did yield a Top Twenty hit with "Take Me to Heart" (1983).

AUTOGRAPHS

A CD, LP, magazine cover, ad, photo, or card signed by the group: $10-$20

Purim, Flora

Born: March 6, 1942

Dynamic '70s Brazilian jazz singer, with an incredible vocal range, Purim has worked with Stan Getz, Chick Corea, and Santana, while gaining exposure in the U.S. An eighteen month prison sentence for cocaine possession slowed her career during the '70s, but during the following decade she spent time working with David Sanborn, Airto Moreira (her husband), and Mickey Hart.

AUTOGRAPHS

A CD, LP, magazine cover, ad, photo, or card signed by the artist: $10-$15

Pylon

Formed 1979

Vanessa Briscoe Hay, Vanessa Ellison, Randy Bewley, Michael Lachowski, and Curtis Crowe

This late-70s Athens, Georgia, funk-rock act is best remembered for the songs "Cool," "Dub," "Crazy" (later covered by R.E.M.), "Beep," and "Yo-Yo." Pylon disbanded in 1984, but reunited in 1988.

AUTOGRAPHS

A CD, LP, magazine cover, ad, photo, or card signed by the group: $15-$20

OFTEN OVERLOOKED MEMORABILIA

A copy of the 1987 film *Athens, Georgia: Inside/Out*

Quatro, Suzi

(Suzi Quatrocchio)
Born: June 3, 1950

Suzi Quatro was an icon to the glitter (bubble gum) pop sound of the early '70s. Born into a musical family, she quit high school and formed her first band with her sisters, an all-girl unit called Suzi Soul (Quatro) and the Pleasure Seekers—they later changed the name to Cradle. When the cradle couldn't get rocked enough, the band split, leaving Suzi to head to England and start a solo career.

She scored in Britain with singles "Can the Can" (#1, U.K., 1973), "Daytona Demon" (#14, U.K., 1973), "48 Crash" (#3, U.K., 1973), "Devil's Gate Drive" (#1, 1974), and "The Wild One" (#7, U.K., 1974), but Americans were less impressed with her tough '50s attire. Determined to break through in the U.S., Suzi toured with Alice Cooper in 1974 and 1975, but failed to light a fire under her audience. Meanwhile, her British audience was also slipping.

In 1977 she turned her attention to another media, television. She became a semi-regular on the hit series *Happy Days* as character Leather Tuscadero. She also managed to pick up another record deal, this time with RSO and released *If You Knew Suzi*, which managed a hit with "Stumblin' In" (#4, 1979), a duet with Chris Norman. She also had a minor hit with "Lipstick" (#51, 1981, Dreamland), before giving up touring in favor of having a family. Quatro later extended her horizons to theatre.

AUTOGRAPHS

A CD, LP, magazine cover, ad, photo, or card signed by the artist: $10-$25

OFTEN OVERLOOKED MEMORABILIA

Videotapes of her performances on the television series *Happy Days*; copies of her 1983 British television show *Gas*; programs from her theatre appearances including *Annie Get Your Gun* and *Tallulah Who?*

Queen

Formed 1971

Freddie Mercury (Frederick Bulsara), Born: September 5, 1946, Died: November 24, 1991; Brian May, Born: July 19, 1947; John Deacon, Born: August 19, 1951; Roger Meddows-Taylor, Born: July 26, 1949

This glam rock band combined a custom hard rock edge with intricate vocal harmonies to produce some of rock 'n' rolls classic songs. The band united two members of the band Smile, Roger Taylor and Brian May, with John Deacon and singer Freddie Mercury of Wreckage. All four Queen members were college graduates, who originally preferred to attend classes over playing the local club circuit. In June 1971 they played as the band Queen for the first time at the College of Estate Management in the U.K.

In 1973 the band recorded its debut *Queen* (#41, U.S.), which was released on July 13. The band's first single "Keep Yourself Alive/Son and Daughter" received virtually no airplay—any related items are extremely collectable. The group entered the studio during the summer to record its second album, *Queen II*, and then embarked on its first U.K. tour as a support act for Mott the Hoople. Its following manifested, but the press didn't take the band seriously until "Seven Seas of Rhye," which was included on the first album, then re-recorded and released as a single. On April 12, 1974, the group began a second tour with Mott the Hoople, however, it was cut short when guitarist Brian May collapsed with hepatitis in New York.

Sheer Heart Attack (11/1/74), Queen's third album, hit pay dirt and spun off the single "Killer Queen" (#12, U.S.). On February 5, 1975, the band opened up its first headlining U.S. Tour in Columbus, Ohio,

Queen. Photo by Douglas Puddifoot. Courtesy Hollywood Records.

and closed in Portland, Oregon, on April 7. This was followed by a Japanese tour (4/19-5/1) before the group headed into the studios for the recording of its fourth album, *A Night at the Opera* (12/3/75). This breakthrough album yielded the hit six-minute single "Bohemian Rhapsody" (#9, U.S.), and with it, the birth of the video era. The band produced what is now regarded as the first-ever pop promo video made by any performer or group.

A U.K. tour preceded the album's release. Queen's next extensive U.S. tour began on January 27, 1976. A Japanese tour followed (3/22- 4/4), and then an Australian tour (4/11-4/22). Another single was released ("You're My Best Friend," #16, U.S.), before the band entered the studio again to begin work on its next album. A few concerts preceded the release of *A Day at the Races* (10/10/76), and then the group went on to America on January 13, 1977.

The band's chart success continued with the hits "Somebody to Love" (#13, 1976), "We Are the Champions"/"We Will Rock You" (#4, 1977), "Fat Bottomed Girls"/"Bicycle Race" (#24, 1978), "Crazy Little Thing Called Love" (#1, 1979), "Another One Bites the Dust" (#1, 1980), "Under Pressure" with David Bowie (#29, 1981), "Body Language" (#11, 1982), and "Radio Ga-Ga" (#16, 1984).

Queen memorabilia collectors had a field day with the release of *Jazz* on November 11, 1978. The album included the single "Fat Bottomed Girls"/"Bicycle Race," which has many controversial pieces of memorabilia including a banned album insert, a promotional film of nude girls racing bicycles at Wimbledon Stadium, an innocuous rear view photo of a girl that is used as the single sleeve, an advertising poster, and even on stage passes associated with it.

The band accepted the soundtrack duties for the film *Flash Gordon* (#23), which was released on December 8, 1980. Neither the film, nor the soundtrack, were overly successful, but did provide collectors with another form of media.

During the '80s Queen released the albums *Greatest Hits* (10/26/81), *Hot Space* (5/23/82), *The Works* (2/27/84), *The Complete Works* (12/85), *A Kind of Magic* (5/86), *Live Magic* (12/86), *The Miracle* (5/89), and *Queen at the Beeb* (12/89). Of all of the decade's releases, *Hot Space* fell short of expectations both by fan accounts and members of the band.

In early 1991 *Innuendo* shot to number one in Britain, but was far less successful in America. Rumors were also circulating that Mercury was gravely ill. Unfortunately the news was confirmed from Mercury himself just two days prior to his death—he tested HIV positive. At the young age of 45, Freddie Mercury died of bronchial pneumonia, which had crippled his immune system, at his London home.

The Freddie Mercury Tribute Concert, A Concert for Life, was held at Wembley Stadium on April 20, 1992. The concert was attended by nearly every friend of the band and some of the greatest names in the music world. A crowd of 70,000 watched it live while the concert was beamed via satellite to 70 countries worldwide. Brian May closed the emotional show with only the guitar part to "God Save the Queen"—vocals were supplied by the audience and tears were provided by everyone who was watching.

In 1995 the band assembled and revised tracks that were recorded prior to Mercury's death. The result was *Made in Heaven* (#58, U.S.).

AUTOGRAPHS

Queen was elusive, but obliging to autograph requests
A CD, LP, poster, or photograph signed by the entire band: $400-$700

Freddie Mercury: $225-$650	Brain May: $40-$50
John Deacon: $35	Roger Taylor: $30-$40

A Paiste Power crash 19" cymbal signed by all members: $800

A stage-used Roger Taylor snare drum signed by entire band: $1,200

A nice sampling of Queen backstage passes

TOUR BOOKS/PROGRAMS/BACKSTAGE PASSES

Tour Programs: $30-$70
1977 U.S. tour program: $75-$100
1978 Jazz U.S. Tour: $35-$45
1979 Japan Tour: $90
1980 U.S. Tour: $25
1981 Japan Tour: $85
Backstage Passes:
Cloth: $10-$25; Laminated: $15-$35

POSTERS/PRESS KITS

Promotional Posters: $15-$70
Press Kits: $20-$80

USED CLOTHING/EQUIPMENT

Guitar Picks:
Brian May: $125-$200
John Deacon: $100-$125
Drum Stick:
Roger Taylor: $30-$45
A Freddie Mercury two-piece stage-worn suit: $5,000-$6,500

OFTEN OVERLOOKED MEMORABILIA

News of the World promotional clock - $300-$350; News of the World giant deluxe press kit - $75; Jazz LP poster insert - $10; Made in Heaven U.K. promotional lyric book - $10; Queen II, Celebrating 20 years, U.K. promotional style book - $65; movie memorabilia from *Flash Gordon* (1980), *Metropolis* (1986), *Teachers* (1985), *Iron Eagle* (1985), *The Highlander* (1986), and *Biggles* (1986); videotapes of their numerous television appearances including *Top of the Pops* BBC1-TV (4/13/74), *Hammersmith Odeon* BBC-TV (12/2/475), *Milton Keynes Bowl* (5/82), and "Ibiza '92" (1992); a copy of the film *Queen at the Rainbow* (4/76); a copy of the promotional video *Fat Bottomed Girls* and all associated items; a copy of the 1980 *The Guinness Book of Records*; copies of Shell television commercials using "I Want to Break Free"; copies of the numerous international fanzines; Bohemian Rhapsody, 1978, Queen's award cover, special scarf and goblets (scarce); Innuendo promotional calendar, 1991; Greatest Hits, Volume Two promotional double set with wallet containing six photos; Capitol Welcomes Queen, Capitol promo quill pen, 1983; Queen Mania, West Germany, EMI Sixteen CD set in metal flight case, includes T-shirt and badge, 1990 (limited to 1,500).

REFERENCES/BOOKS

Queen, The New Visual Documentary by Ken Dean - $20; *Complete Guide to the Music of Queen* by Peter Hogan - $8; *Queen, In Their Own Words* by Mick St. Michael - $16; A Tear Out Photo Book - $15; *Queen, The Early Years*, by Hodkinson - $23. Numerous additional resources exist. *Queen: These Are the Best Days of Our Lives* by Stephen Rider and *Queen Live: A Concert Documentary* ($20) are MUST purchases for Queen fans.

QUEEN EIGHTIES VIDEOGRAPHY

Queen's Greatest Flix (October 1981)
We Will Rock You (September 1984)
The Works EP (November 1984)
Live in Rio (May 1985)
A Kind of Magic (October 1986)
Live in Budapest (February 1987)
Bohemian Rhapsody (May 1987)
The Magic Years - Volume 1 (November 1987)
The Magic Years - Volume 2 (November 1987)
The Magic Years - Volume 3 (November 1987)
The Magic Years - Vols. 1-3 boxed(December 1987)
Rare Live Video (August 1989)
We Will Rock You reissue (September 1989)
The Miracle Video EP (December 1989)
Freddie Mercury Video EP (July 1986)
The Great Pretender (March 1987) (with Montserrat Caballe)
Barcelona (February 1989)
The Golden Boy (1989)

Queen Latifah

(Dana Owens)
Born: March 18, 1970

"Delicate and sensitive" Queen Latifah, former star of her high school basketball team, began her early hip-hop days while in a group called Ladies Fresh. She was fortunate enough to have some tracks she recorded end up at Tommy Boy Records, which then released her debut record *All Hail the Queen* (1989). The album included the Queen classic "Ladies First." Her flamboyance quickly led to her "princess to the press" appeal, and she became an ad hoc spokeswoman for youth cultures and her art of hip-hop.

The Queen was coronated when she rapped with David Bowie on a remake of "Fame" and scored with a cover of the O'Jays' "For the Love of Money" (#12, R&B, 1992), from the *New Jack City* soundtrack. *Nature of a Sista* was her somewhat softer sophomore offering and included extracts "Latifah's Had It Up 2 Here" (#13, R&B, 1992) and "Fly Girl" (#16, 1992).

Her third album, *Black Reign* (#15, R&B, 1994), found her at Motown. The album landed her two hit singles with "Just Another Day" (#37, R&B, 1994) and "U.N.I.T.Y." (#23, 1994), the latter of which won her a 1994 Grammy for Best Solo Rap Performance. From there she turned her sights to acting in both television and film.

AUTOGRAPHS

A CD, LP, magazine cover, ad, photo, or card signed by the artist: $10-$20

POSTERS/PRESS KITS

Promotional Posters: $10
Press Kits: $12-$15

OFTEN OVERLOOKED MEMORABILIA

Movie memorabilia from *New Jack City*, *Jungle Fever*, *Juice*, and *House Party 2*; videotapes of her television sitcom *Living Single*.

Queensrÿche

Formed 1981
Chris DeGarmo, Eddie Jackson, Scott Rockenfield, Geoff Tate, and Michael Wilton

Formed in 1981, this art-metal band with a sound that is hauntingly reminiscent of Pink Floyd, shunned the local club scene in favor of crafting its sound through extensive rehearsing. *Queen of the Reich*, the group's self-financed EP, was a success and led to the band inking a deal with EMI and releasing *Queensrÿche* (#81, 1983), followed by *The Warning* (#61, 1984), *Rage for Order* (#47, 1986) and *Operation: Mindcrime* (#50, 1988). By now its extensive touring, which included stints with acts such as Kiss and Metallica, catapulted sales.

Empire (#7, 1990) became the group's breakthrough album, and extract "Silent Lucidity" was seen on MTV more often than Kurt Loder. It became one of the most popular rock songs of 1991. The band's extensive tour support of the album also included the Monsters of Rock Tour (1991). The next album, *Operation: Livecrime* (#38,1991)*, captured the group's now blossoming live act and was followed by the Number Three debut release *Promised Land* (#3, 1994), with its multimedia version two disc CD-Rom version during the summer of 1995.

*Included album, 44 page booklet, and one hour video.

AUTOGRAPHS

A CD, LP, magazine cover, ad, photo, or card signed by the artist: $25-$85

TOUR BOOKS/PROGRAMS/PASSES

Tour Programs:
The Warning Tour: $15
Monsters of Rock, 1991: $15

Backstage Passes:
Cloth: $8-$10;
Laminated: $10-$15

POSTERS/PRESS KITS

PromotionalPosters:
$12-$17
Press Kits:
$15-$25

USED CLOTHING/EQUIPMENT

Guitar Picks:
Chris DeGarmo: $15-$25
Eddie Jackson: $15-$25
Michael Wilton: $15-$25
Drum Sticks:
Scott Rockenfield: $15-$25

Queensrÿche guitar picks

OFTEN OVERLOOKED MEMORABILIA

Movie memorabilia from *The Last Action Hero* (1993); videotapes of their television appearances including the Eighth Annual *MTV Video Music Awards* (9/5/91); Promised Land static window sticker - $10.

? (Question Mark) and the Mysterians

Formed 1962

? (Question Mark), Robert Martinez, Larry Borjas, also Robert Balderrama, Frankie Rodriguez Jr., Frank Lugo, and Edward Serrato

The band best identified with a distinctive Vox Continental organ line hook that took "96 Tears" (#1) to the top of the charts in 1966. The band has forever been shrouded in mystery, due to its unidentified lead singer who legally changed his name to "?." Most of the band members migrated from Mexico to Detroit where they became local favorites and eventually landed a national vinyl deal with Cameo Records.

Later in 1966, they also had a minor hit with "I Need Somebody" (#22). While the group was slipping out of the limelight, a young bassist named Mel Schacher (Grand Funk Railroad) became a member.

RIAA Gold 45 white-matte award for ? and the Mysterians' "96 Tears," 1966. It is valued at $4,000. From the Doug Leftwitch collection.

AUTOGRAPHS

A CD, LP, magazine cover, ad, photo, or card signed by the group: $20-$35*
*Original band on an item related to "96 Tears"

OFTEN OVERLOOKED MEMORABILIA

Memorabilia associated with those numerous bands which covered "96 Tears"

Quicksilver Messenger Service

Formed 1965

Original lineup: Gary Duncan, Jartohn Cipollina (1943-1989), David Freiberg, Greg Elmore, and Jim Murray*
*Numerous personnel changes

This is one of the few San Francisco psychedelic spin bands of the late '60s that failed to achieve the national recognition of its contemporaries such as the Grateful Dead and the Jefferson Airplane, although Freiberg did fly with the latter for a period

of time. The group received critical acclaim in the Bay Area, primarily due to its long instrumental jams, particularly evident on songs such as "The Fool" (1968). *Just for Love* (#27, 1970), with cut "Fresh Air," slowly became one of the group's best selling albums. The group, constantly plagued by personnel changes, disbanded after *Solid Silver* (1975), although there have been unsuccessful attempts to resurrect QMS.

QMS was a Bill Graham favorite, so collectors should plan on dishing out some serious cash for vintage QMS posters, postcards, and handbills.

AUTOGRAPHS

A CD, LP, magazine cover, ad, photo, or card signed by the group: $30-$60*
*Original members

Signatures from the members of the Quicksilver Messenger Service

OFTEN OVERLOOKED MEMORABILIA

Movie memorabilia from *Revolution* (1968)

Quiet Riot

Formed 1975

Original lineup: Kevin DuBrow, Randy Rhoads, Kelly Garni, Drew Forsyth*

*Numerous personnel changes

One of the mid-70s premier Hollywood screaming saloon bands, Quiet Riot rivaled peers Van Halen and the Knack, but failed to land record deals any faster. Collectors should try to grab any artifacts surrounding the bands two out-of-print early albums issued only in Japan. The original band suffered when Rhoads departed to join Ozzy Osbourne. He later died in a bizarre Florida plane incident in 1982, one week before he was going to rejoin the band in the studio.

The new QR's first release was *Metal Health* (#1, 1983), which smashed the U.S. charts, primarily driven by Slade remake extract "Cum on Feel the Noize" (#5, 1983). The single seemed to appear more often on MTV than its claymation promo segments. The album's second extract was "Bang Your Head (Metal Health)" (#31, 1983) *Condition Critical* (#15,

1984), the group's next album, included another Slade extract, "Mama Weer All Crazee Now" (#51, 1984). The band then experienced numerous personnel issues, and sales began to slip. When *QR III* (#31, 1986) failed to land a hit single, the riot was quiet.

AUTOGRAPHS

A CD, LP, magazine cover, ad, photo, or card signed by the group: $25-$35

REFERENCES/BOOKS

Limited resources exist, but none do justice to the band in my opinion. There are no dedicated collector books.

Rabbitt, Eddie

(Edward Thomas)
Born: November 27, 1944

Edward Thomas migrated to Nashville in 1968 and landed a job writing at music publisher Hill and Range. One of his dreams came true in 1970 when Elvis Presley recorded his "Kentucky Rain." His songwriting continued, and when Ronnie Milsap took Rabbitt's penned "Pure Love" to the top of the C&W charts, he knew it was time to establish himself as a performer.

His self-titled debut album on Elektra hit in 1975, and from that point on, he just cranked out the hits including "Forgive and Forget," "Drinkin' My Baby (Off My Mind)," "Rocky Mountain Music," and "Two Dollars in the Jukebox." He crossed over to the pop audience in 1979 with the theme to Clint Eastwood's *Every Which Way but Loose.*

"Suspicious" (#13, 1979), "Drivin' My Life Away" (#5, 1980), "I Love a Rainy Night" (#1, 1980), "Step by Step" (#5, 1981), and "Someone Could Lose a Heart Tonight" (#15, 1981) continued his success on the singles chart. Rabbitt then charted with two duets, the first with Crystal Gayle on "You and I" (#1, C&W, 1982), followed by "Both to Each Other (Friends and Lovers)" (#1, C&W, 1986), which was the theme to the daytime soap *Days of Our Lives.*

Tragedy struck in 1985 when his son, who was born two years earlier, died from a rare liver disease. It put the entertainer's career on hold, but also gave him the inspiration to share his crisis with others—he became a spokesman for many children's causes.

Rabbitt returned to the C&W charts in 1988 with his remake of "The Wanderer" (#1), "We Must Be Doin' Somethin' Right" (#7), "On Second Thought" (#1, 1989), and "Runnin' with the Wind" (#8, 1990).

AUTOGRAPHS

A CD, LP, magazine cover, ad, photo, or card signed by the artist: $10-$25

TOUR BOOKS/PROGRAMS/PASSES

Backstage Passes:
Cloth: $5-$7; Laminated: $8-$10

POSTERS/PRESS KITS

Promotional Posters: $10-$15
Press Kits: $15

USED CLOTHING/EQUIPMENT

Guitar Picks: $10-$20

OFTEN OVERLOOKED MEMORABILIA

Movie memorabilia from *Every Which Way but Loose* (1979)

****

"On The Edge"

Radiohead

Radiohead is proof "Anyone Can Play Guitar"! Taking their name from a Talking Heads album, Thom E. Yorke, Ed O'Brien, Johnny Greenwood, and Phil Selway formed the band in 1991 and released their debut EP on Parlophone, *Drill.* Heavy rotation on MTV sent *Pablo Honey* up the album charts, although the group's follow-up *The Bends* fell short of expectations. Heavy exposure through both the media and touring ignited interest in the band, as *OK Computer* (#21, 1997) brought the band back on-line!

****

Rafferty, Gerry

Born: April 16, 1947

Rafferty had the hit "Stuck in the Middle with You" while playing with Stealers Wheel. But when his solo album *City to City* (#1, 1978) hit, Rafferty was thrust in the spotlight with hits extracts "Baker Street" (#2, 1978) and "Right Down the Line" (#12, 1978). Few realized that he had recorded his debut solo effort back in 1971. Although he has yet to match the album's success, he has managed a couple of hit singles: "Days Gone Down (Still Got the Light in Your Eyes)" (#17, 1979) and "Get It Right Next Time" (#21, 1979).

AUTOGRAPHS

A CD, LP, magazine cover, ad, photo, or card signed by the artist: $15-$25

TOUR BOOKS/PROGRAMS/PASSES*

*Rarely tours or performs live

POSTERS/PRESS KITS
Promotional Posters: $10-$15
Press Kits: $10-$15

****

"On The Edge"

Rage Against the Machine

This Southern California band, with members of impressive pedigree, turned heads at Lollapalooza II, and not just because they were on the second stage. A controversial cover to their impressive self-titled debut album, which brought kudos from the alt music media, showed that the rage was simply uncompromising. In 1993 the band took a *Bullet in the Head* as far as it could, while bringing a new meaning to the phrase "just duct tape" during a Philadelphia Lollapalooza gig. Three years later, the machine's *Evil Empire* debuted atop the album chart, sold there through an extensive cult following that is only too happy to silence the critics! Still considered spare parts, all artifacts from the band's debut are a must.

****

Rainbow: See Ritchie Blackmore

The Raincoats

Formed 1977
Original Lineup: Gina Birch, Ana Da Silva, Ross Crichton, and Nick Turner*
*Numerous personnel changes. Became all-female band in 1979

This all-female British punk group's crude music spawned a cult following and even inspired Nirvana's Kurt Cobain, who would later encouraged the band's label to reissue all three of its albums. Two members of the group also managed to re-form for an East Coast tour of the U.S. in 1994.

AUTOGRAPHS
A CD, LP, magazine cover, ad, photo, or card signed by the group: $20-$30

Raitt, Bonnie

Born: November 8, 1949

A multitalented musician and composer, Bonnie Raitt, daughter of Broadway singer John Raitt, es-

tablished a strong reputation for herself in the northeast, which lead to a recording agreement with Warner Brothers Records and her acclaimed self-titled debut album in 1971. One of the few women who plays bottleneck, her choice of music has always impressed both fans and critics alike.

Sweet Forgiveness (1977), her sixth album, yielded a single with cover "Runaway," but her subsequent work didn't give her the push she needed to step up to the next level. Ironically, it wasn't until she lost her agreement with Warner Brothers and moved on to Capitol that she had her breakthrough album *Nick of Time*. Her Capitol debut was so impressive that she won a Grammy for Album of the Year. This then set the stage for her next album, *Luck of the Draw* (#2, 1991), with hit extracts "Something to Talk About" (#5, 1991) and "I Can't Make You Love Me" (#18, 1991).

"Longing in Their Hearts" (#1, 1994) continued her string of hit albums and contained the single "Love Sneakin' Up On You" (#19, 1994). *Road Tested* (#44, 1995), a live set, fared less well, but she followed it up strongly with her first multimedia work *Burning Down the House* (E-CD) in 1996.

She is a gifted performer, who has finally reached the level of recognition she deserves. It is well worth the effort of sticking a few top Raitt artifacts into a time capsule!

A Bonnie Raitt backstage pass (Printed by Perri Entertainment Services Inc.)

AUTOGRAPHS
A CD, LP, magazine cover, ad, photo, or card signed by the artist: $5-$30

TOUR BOOKS/ PROGRAMS/ PASSES
Backstage Passes:
Cloth: $8-$10;
Laminated: $10-$15

POSTERS/PRESS KITS
Promotional Posters: $10-$20
Press Kits: $15

USED CLOTHING/EQUIPMENT
Guitar Picks: $15-$20

OFTEN OVERLOOKED MEMORABILIA
Movie memorabilia from *Urban Cowboy* (1980), *Heart Condition* (1990), and *Boys on the Side* (1995); videotapes of her numerous television appearances including *The Tonight Show* (9/17/91, 12/11/92, 1/23/96), *Saturday Night Live* (10/26/91, 10/1/94), *Wogan* (11/25/91), *Late Night With David Letterman* (8/20/92), "The Winans Real Meaning of Christmas" (12/7/92), "Aretha Franklin: Duets" (4/27/93), "Willie Nelson the Big Six-O" (5/22/93), *Late Show With David Letterman* (3/2/94, 10/24/95), and *Austin City Limits* (5/11/95)

REFERENCES/BOOKS
Limited resources exist, but none do justice to the singer in my opinion. There are no dedicated collector books.

The Ramones

Formed 1974

Joey Ramone (Jeffrey Hyman) Born: May 19, 1951; Johnny Ramone (John Cummings) Born: October 8, 1951; Dee Dee Ramone (Douglas Colvin) Born: September 18, 1952; and Tommy Ramone (Tom Erdelyi) Born: January 29, 1952*

*Marky Ramone replaced Tommy Ramone in 1977, then Richie Ramone replaced Marky in 1983. Marky returned in 1987 and replaced Richie. C.J. Ramone replaced Dee Dee Ramone in 1989.

Best stated, "The Ramones are the Grateful Dead of Punk!." They were instrumental in forming the punk rock scene in New York at clubs such as Mother's, Kenny's Castaways, Max's Kansas City, and CBGB ("Country, Bluegrass and Blues"), "the mecca" for underground bands during the mid-70s. The group was another link in the chain, that is if you allow me to use such a banal analogy, between the '60s rock scene and the "new wave" movement. Fast music, basic chords, and mundane lyrics have always been the core of the Ramones. Choosing never to leave the neighborhood, they have watched as their peers opt for new forms of music or simply retire.

The band's first album *Ramones* (1976, Sire) is now considered a classic. The release contained fourteen tracks including "Beat on the Brat," "Blitzkrieg Bop," and "Now I Wanna Sniff Some Glue," at a combined length of twenty-eight minutes and fifty-two seconds. Such was "the minimalist style" that they not only invented, but perfected!

The band's first gig was at the Performance Studio on March 30, 1974. The band sent out its own flyers, now collectors items, that stated the admission was two dollars. The band chose the name Ramones, because Paul McCartney called himself Paul "Ramone" when he was with the Silver Beetles (the Beatles). Since the band members figured that no one would remember, or even care about their last names, they simply used the logical surname.

The band essentially picked up where the New York Dolls left off, seizing the moment with its brief, but loud, repertoire. In fact the band didn't even have a song over three minutes until the fourth album. It seemed like the main purpose of doing a song was to get it over with as fast as possible.

Although not easy to authenticate, the Ramones "handmade handbills," which the band posted up around CBGBs and other clubs, are real collectors items. Additionally, collectors may want to pick up copies of periodicals that advertised the band. C.B.G.B. advertisements often listed about a weeks worth of bands and included names like Blondie, Talking Heads, and Television. CBGBs was to the '70s what the Fillmore East was to the '60s.

Artist Arturo Vega was the creative source behind early Ramones memorabilia. He created the band's logo and many of the T-shirt designs ("Hey, ho! Let's go!"). The earlier T-shirts are a must purchase for all Ramones collectors, if of course you can find them.

On July 4, 1976, the Ramones played their first gig in England, at the Roundhouse in London. The U.K. gigs were attended by virtually every musician who shaped the years to come, from members of the Sex Pistols and the Clash to those of the Pretenders and Generation X. All items associated with this tour are also worth collecting. Before the year ended, *Ramones Leave Home* hit the shelf. Early pressings, now extremely collectible, included "Carbona Not Glue," later replaced by "Babysitter" (U.K.) and "Sheena Is a Punk Rocker" (U.S.), due to possible trademark infringement. Following the band's third album, *Rocket to Russia*, Tommy Ramone left and was replaced by Marky Ramone (Bell). *Road to Ruin* followed in 1978, and although it featured improved production, it did little to attract a greater audience. The band's torrid touring pace continued as the band played more than 150 dates in 1978. The band also starred in Roger Corman's *Rock 'n' Roll High School* the following year, but failed to garner a single Academy Award or nomination. Memorabilia from the movie included notebooks ($20) and hall passes ($5-$10) and are not particularly easy to find.

While the Ramones waited for commercial success, the '70s came and went. Now faced with a new decade, the band tried working with noted producers Phil Spector for *End of the Century* (1980) and Graham Gouldman for *Pleasant Dreams* (1981). Neither met with commercial success, nor did *Subterranean Jungle* (1983), after which Marky Ramone left the band. *Too Tough to Die* (1984) produced an energetic single "Howling at the Moon," and *Animal Boy* (1986) cut deep into political satire with "Bonzo Goes to Bitburg," but both brought little bounty by the decade's conclusion.

Best-selling author Stephen King brought the band the title track to the movie adaptation of *Pet Sematary* in 1989. The exposure helped considerably, but soon the departure of Dee Dee Ramone seemed to curtail any advances it had made. C.J. Ramone, fourteen years younger than Johnny and Joey, replaced Dee Dee, as the band looked to the '90s.

While watching bands it had influenced during the earlier years slowly pass by commercially, the Ramones meander through the '90s. "Gabba Gabba Hey"!

AUTOGRAPHS

Group:

A CD, LP, magazine cover, ad, photo, or card signed by the entire band: $70-$85

Individual:

Joey Ramone: $20-$25	Johnny Ramone: $20
Dee Dee Ramone: $20	C.J. Ramone: $10-$15
Tommy Ramone: $15-$20	Marky Ramone: $15
Richie Ramone: $10	

TOUR BOOKS/PROGRAMS/PASSES

Backstage Passes:

Cloth/paper: $8-$15; Laminated: $10-$30

POSTERS/PRESS KITS

Promotional posters: $0-$30

The first promotional posters are tough to find; one even came from a full-page *Village Voice* ad that included sixty-two choice quotes. Promotional posters produced in the '90s range in price from $8 to $10.

Tour posters from the '80s usually bring $25-$40.

Press Kits:

$15-$40

USED CLOTHING/ EQUIPMENT

Guitar Picks:

Johnny Ramone: $10

Dee Dee Ramone: $10

C.J. Ramone: $8

Drum Sticks:

Tommy Ramone: $20

Marky Ramone: $15

Richie Ramone: $10-$15

A Johnny Ramone guitar pick

OFTEN OVERLOOKED MEMORABILIA

Copies of *Punk* magazine; homemade handbills, advertisements (such as the full-page Billboard ad for Blitzkrieg Bop); Beat on the Brat miniature Louisville Sluggers, later changed to Blitzkrieg Bop (U.S.) - $30-$40; old issues of the *Sniffin Glue* fanzine; Rocket to Russia full-size album cover stand-up display for record stores - $30-$40; Road to Ruin promotional push-pin box - $20-$30; Ramones Leave Home pen/knife letter opener - $20-$35; Blitzkrieg Bop Bud Light promo items, button - $3, bumper sticker - $5, and Ramones baseball hat - $15-$20; movie memorabilia from *Blank Generation* (1976) and *Rock 'n' Roll High School* (1979) (including the Sire promotional note pad - $15-$20), and *Roadkill* (1989); videotapes of the band's television appearances on *The Simpsons* (10/21/93) and the *Late Show With David Letterman* (2/9/96).

REFERENCES/BOOKS

Limited resources exist. *Ramones: An American Band* ($15) by Jim Bessman is a MUST read for Ramones fans. There are no dedicated collector books.

Rank and File

Formed 1981

Chip Kinman, Tony Kinman, Alejandro Escovedo, and Slim Evans

Rank and File, consisting of members of the Dils ("I Hate the Rich" and "Class War") and the Nuns, was formed in 1981 as a pulsating pop act, with just enough country edge to get labeled a "cowpunk" band. *Sundown*, the band's debut album on Slash records, received good reviews but fell short of sales expectations. The band then split up. The Kinmans relocated in Los Angeles and eventually recorded un-

der the name Blackbird. Meanwhile, Alejandro Escovedo, from the famous Escovedo extended family, pursued a solo career with Austin label Watermelon.

AUTOGRAPHS

A CD, LP, magazine cover, ad, photo, or card signed by the group: $10

Ranking Roger: See English Beat

Ranks, Shabba

(Rexton Ralston Fernando Gordon)
Born: January 17, 1966

Shabba Ranks was born from Saint Ann's Parish and the Trenchtown ghetto that yielded Bob Marley and was influenced by reggae rappers Josey Wales and Yellowman before he began performing in Kingston in 1980. *As Raw as Ever* (#89, 1991) included hit extracts "Housecall (Your Body Can't Lie to Me)" (#37, 1991) and "The Jam" (#52, 1992). It won 1991's Best Reggae Grammy, making Ranks the first dancehall artist to accomplish such a task.

Rough and Ready, Volume I (#78, 1992), his sophomore Epic album, spun off the hit "Mr. Loverman" (#40, 1992), while follow-up *X-tra Naked* (#64, 1992) scored a hit with "Slow and Sexy" (#33, 1992). Ranks took some hits in 1993 for his alleged gay-bashing comments. Despite the indicent, his album *A Mi Shabba* (1995) was very well received.

AUTOGRAPHS

A CD, LP, magazine cover, ad, photo, or card signed by the artist: $10-$15

POSTERS/PRESS KITS

Promotional Posters: $8-$10

Press Kits: $10-$15

Rare Earth

Formed 1969

Original Lineup: Gil Bridges, Pete Rivera, John Persh, Rob Richards, and Kenny James*

*Numerous personnel changes

Rare Earth, which hails from Detroit and was even signed to a Motown subsidiary, released *Get Ready* (#12, 1969), its well-received debut effort in 1969. The album's title cut (#4) was extracted and landed in the Top Ten. Albums *Ecology* and *One World*, released the following year, scored hits with "(I Know) I'm Losing You" (#7, 1970), "Born to Wander" (#17, 1970), "I Just Want to Celebrate" (#7,1970), and "Hey, Big Brother" (#19, 1970). The band was ham-

pered during its development by numerous personnel changes. The band is still active today, but Gil Bridges it the last original member still remaining.

AUTOGRAPHS

A CD, LP, magazine cover, ad, photo, or card signed by the group: $25-$60

The Rascals/The Young Rascals

Formed 1965

Original Lineup: Felix Cavaliere, Born: November 29, 1944; Eddie Brigati, Born: October 22, 1946; Gene Cornish, Born: May 14, 1945; and Dino Danelli, Born: July 23, 1945*

*Brigati and Cornish left in 1971 and were replaced by Buzzy Feiten, Robert Popwell, and Ann Sutton

Cavaliere met Danelli, who as a teenage drummer played with Lionel Hampton, in New York before the two migrated to Las Vegas in search of work with a casino band. When they returned to New York, Cavaliere joined Joey Dee and the Starlighters, which included Eddie Brigati and Gene Cornish. The three Starlighters then left the band in 1964 to form the Rascals with Danelli.

The band quickly became popular playing the tri-state circuit, and by the end of 1965, it was known as the Young Rascals. "I Ain't Gonna Eat Out My Heart Anymore" (#52, 1965), the debut single, was followed by "Good Lovin'" (#1, 1966), one of the year's biggest hits. The Young Rascals then put nine more Top Twenty hits on the charts including "You Better Run" (#20, 1966), "(I've Been) Lonely Too Long" (#16, 1967), "Groovin'"(#1, 1967), and "A Girl Like You" (#10, 1967).

In 1967 the band tried altering its image by dropping the word "Young" from its name, while polishing up its sound with the release of *Freedom Suite*. The result was three more Top Five hits, "How Can I Be Sure" (#4, 1967), "A Beautiful Morning" (#3, 1968), and "People Got to Be Free" (#1, 1968), which was the group's last Top Twenty hit.

When record sales and concert attendance plummeted, Cornish and Brigati left the band. Although the group continued, success eluded it and by the early '70s, the band diminished.

AUTOGRAPHS

A CD, LP, magazine cover, ad, photo, or card signed by the group: $45-$125

OFTEN OVERLOOKED MEMORABILIA

Videotapes of the group's numerous television appearances including *The Ed Sullivan Show* (4 times), *Hullabaloo* (4/14/66), *Ready Steady Go!* (1966), and the *Saturday Club* (1966); memorabilia from the well-attended Shea Stadium show (8/15/65) (the Beatles also performed); memorabilia from the Newport '69 Rock Festival (6/20/69) (Jimi Hendrix also performed).

The Raspberries/Eric Carmen

Formed 1970

Original Lineup: Eric Carmen, Born August 11, 1949; Wally Bryson, Born: July 18, 1949; Jim Bonfanti, Born: December 17, 1948; and Dave Smalley, Born: July 10, 1949*

*Michael McBride and Scott Carl replaced Bonfanti and Smalley in 1973

In 1970, Carmen, Bryson (the Mods), Bonfanti (the Outsiders, the Mods), and Smalley (the Mods), all familiar with each other as part of the Cleveland music scene, formed the Raspberries. The group's debut album was a hit, driven by its Beatlesque sound and extracted single "Go All the Way" (#5, 1972). Fresh, its sophomore effort, spun off two singles, "I Wanna Be with You" (#16, 1972) and "Let's Pretend" (#35, 1973).

By *Side 3* (1973) internal conflicts, revolving around the band's very commercial image, began to cause friction. The result was the departure of both Bonfanti and Smiley. The two were replaced and by *Starting Over*, it seemed like everything was back on track. The album, despite yielding the single "Overnight Sensation (Hit Record)" (#18, 1974), fell short of expectations and the band ceased.

Eric Carmen (1975, Arista) was the singer's first solo effort and resulted in three hit singles, "Sunrise" (#34, 1976), "Never Gonna Fall in Love Again" (#11, 1976), and "All By Myself" (#2, 1976). *Change of Heart* (#19, 1978) followed, but by now the momentum had slid away. Carmen did manage to pen "That's Rock 'n' Roll" and "Hey Deanie" (#7, 1977) for Shaun Cassidy, along with "Almost Paradise," the love theme from *Footloose*. "Hungry Eyes" (#4, 1987), from the movie *Dirty Dancing*, landed Carmen back in the Top Five on the singles chart. Follow-up "Make Me Loose Control" (#3, 1988) also faired well for the singer/songwriter.

AUTOGRAPHS

Group:
A CD, LP, magazine cover, ad, photo, or card signed by the group: $15-$40
Individual:
Eric Carmen: $10-$30

OFTEN OVERLOOKED MEMORABILIA

Movie memorabilia from *Footloose* (1984) and *Dirty Dancing* (1987); memorabilia from other artists who have covered Carmen's songs

REFERENCES/BOOKS

Limited resources exist, but none do justice to the band in my opinion. There are no dedicated collector books.

Ratt

Formed 1981

Bobby Blotzer, Robbin Crosby, Juan Croucier, Warren De Martini, and Stephen Pearcy

This L.A. metal band scored big with the albums *Out of the Cellar* (#7, 1984), which included extract "Round and Round" (#12, 1984) and *Invasion of Your Privacy* (#7, 1985). The band was successful until Stephen Pearcy left in 1992.

AUTOGRAPHS

A CD, LP, magazine cover, ad, photo, or card signed by the group: $10-$15

TOUR BOOKS/PROGRAMS/PASSES

Backstage Passes:
Cloth: $6-$8; Laminated: $10

POSTERS/PRESS KITS

Promotional Posters: $10
Press Kits: $10-$15*
*For Top Ten album

USED CLOTHING/EQUIPMENT

Guitar Picks: $6-$10

REFERENCES/BOOKS

Limited resources exist, but none do justice to the band in my opinion. There are no dedicated collector books.

Ravan, Genya

(Goldie Zelkowitz)

A person of diverse talents, Ravan formed Goldie and the Gingerbreads (an all-female rock band), sang hits for the band Ten Wheel Drive ("Morning Much Batter" (#74, 1970)), and became a major female record producer.

AUTOGRAPHS

A CD, LP, magazine cover, ad, photo, or card signed by the artist: $10

OFTEN OVERLOOKED MEMORABILIA

Movie memorabilia from *The Warriors*

The Ravens

Formed 1945

Original Lineup: Warren Suttles, Jimmy Ricks, Leonard Puzey, and Ollie Jones

Forties R&B vocal group the Ravens sang a unique variety of material, featuring two vocal leads, and was the first group to add choreographed moves to its act. Its slick harmonies were characteristic of their peers the Mills Brothers. "Write Me a Letter" (#24, 1947) and "Old Man River" (#10, R&B, 1947), two of the group's first big hits, are now considered classics. "I Don't Have to Ride No More" (#9, R&B, 1950) and "Rock Me All Night Long" (#4, R&B, 1952) finished its chart success before Ricks sold the Ravens name, which allowed countless groups to perform under the heading in the years that followed.

AUTOGRAPHS

A CD, LP, magazine cover, ad, photo, or card signed by the group : $60-$150*
*Original line-up

Rawls, Lou

Born: December 1, 1935

Ageless multiple Grammy-winning singer, whose work has spanned over three decades, Lou Rawls began his career in the mid-50s with the L.A. based Pilgrim Travelers gospel group. Following a stint in the army, he toured with Sam Cooke and was in the car with the singer in an automobile crash that nearly claimed both of their lives in 1958.

He signed a solo contract with Capitol in 1962 and scored with "Love Is a Hurtin' Thing" (#13, 1966) and "Dead End Street" (#29, 1967), a Grammy winner. The smooth perfected tenor then moved on to MGM and picked up another Grammy for "A Natural Man" (#17, 1971).

He found himself with Kenny Gamble and Leon Huff on their Philadelphia International label in 1976 where he hit pay dirt with "You'll Never Find Another Love Like Mine" (#2, 1976), "Groovy People" (#19, R&B, 1976), "See You When You Get There" (#8, R&B, 1976), "Lady Love" (#24, 1977), and "Let Me Be Good to You" (#11, R&B, 1979).

The following years found him doing voice overs for television and radio commercials, sponsoring his annual *Lou Rawls' Parade of Stars* telethon, and raising money for the United Negro College Fund. His last charting record was "I Wish You Belonged to Me" (#28, R&B,1987).

AUTOGRAPHS

A CD, LP, magazine cover, ad, photo, or card signed by the artist: $15-$35

OFTEN OVERLOOKED MEMORABILIA

Movie memorabilia from *Believe in Me* (1971); videotapes of his numerous television appearances including *77 Sunset Strip*; associated Garfield the Cat soundtrack albums and specials.

Ray, Johnny

Born: January 10, 1927, Died: February 24, 1990

Johnny Ray was a popular vocalist and teen idol in the early and mid-50s who scored hits with "Cry" (#1, 1952), "Please Mr. Sun," "Such a Night," "Just Walking in the Rain," "Yes, Tonight, Josephine," and "You Don't Owe Me a Thing." He became far more popular in Britain than in the U.S.—he landed twenty-nine chart appearances in the Top Forty in the U.K.

AUTOGRAPHS

A CD, LP, magazine cover, ad, photo, or card signed by the artist: $20-$45

Raydio: See Ray Parker Jr.

Rebennack, Mac: See Dr. John

Redbone

Formed 1968

Original Lineup: Lolly Vegas, Pat Vegas, Anthony Bellamy, and Peter DePoe*

*DePoe was replaced by Butch Rillera in 1974

A band made up of Native Americans, Redbone scored hits with "Maggie" (#45, 1971), "Witch Queen of New Orleans," and "Come and Get Your Love" (#5, 1974), but its albums never sold up to expectation despite the success of its singles. The group later focused more on its roots and its sound became more of a traditional Indian sound.

AUTOGRAPHS

A CD, LP, magazine cover, ad, photo, or card signed by the group: $10-$25

OFTEN OVERLOOKED MEMORABILIA

Videotapes from television appearances on *Shindig*

****

"On The Edge"

Red Crayola/Krayola

Formed in late 1966, this band consisted of Mayo Thompson, Frederick Barthelme, and Steve Cunningham. The Houston trio churned out *The Parable of Arable Land* (International Artists) in 1967, a now classic Texas relic, not at the Alamo level, but certainly a must for all rental car companies. The group was occasionally joined by a counter throat culture dubbed "the Family Ugly," which felt compelled to join the band on stage, often during the last song, and performed a strange ritualistic armadillo road kill dance. Mayo, like the clinic, resurfaces occasionally in attempt to recapture that old Crayola spirit, but similar to an old crayon, he is often found dull, broken, and funny smelling.

****

Redding, Otis

Born: September 9, 1941, Died: December 10, 1967

One of the few outstanding male soul singers of the '60s, and perhaps the greatest of all-time, Otis Redding was influenced by Sam Cooke and Little Richard (Redding was a member of his former backing band the Upsetters). He moved to L.A. in 1960 and recorded and took odd jobs until he landed with his first big record "These Arms of Mine" (#20, R&B, 1963). He quickly became one of the favorite black entertainers of the mid-60s and scored numerous hits such as "Fa-Fa-Fa-Fa-Fa-(Sad Song)" (#29, 1966) and "(Sittin' on) The Dock of the Bay" (#1, 1968).

He was a staple on the R&B charts from 1965 to 1967. His single "I've Been Loving You Too Long" (#2, R&B, 1965) placed the highest during this period. Of all of his albums during this time, *Dictionary of Soul* (1966) is often referred to as a landmark album for Memphis soul. His appearance at the Monterey Pop Festival in 1967 brought him before a whole new audience, which couldn't help but to fall in love with the entertainer. On December 6, 1967, he recorded "(Sittin' on) The Dock of the Bay" with his old buddy session guitarist Steve Cropper, who was nice enough to fill in some classic whistling during the fadeout of the song. Redding and four members from his backup band, the Bar-Kays, died four days later when his chartered plane crashed into the frigid waters of Lake Monona, WI.

Otis Redding was inducted into the Rock and Roll Hall of Fame in 1989 by Little Richard.

A rare autographed Otis Redding souvenir program

AUTOGRAPHS

A CD, LP, magazine cover, ad, photo, or card signed by the artist: $200-$500

OFTEN OVERLOOKED MEMORABILIA

Memorabilia from the Monterey Pop Festival (1967)

REFERENCES/BOOKS

Limited resources exist. *The Otis Redding Story* by Jane Schiesel is a MUST for fans. There are no dedicated collector books.

Redd Kross

Formed 1978

Original Lineup: Greg Hetson, Jeff McDonald, Steve McDonald, and Ron Reyes*

*Hetson and Reyes left in 1982. Gere Fennelly, Eddie Kurdziel, and Brain Reitzell joined in 1993.

Redd Kross, formerly Red Cross, are thrash bashers led by the McDonald brothers, whose first recording came in 1980 with their self-titled EP on Posh Boy. At that time the group also included Greg Hetson and Ron Reyes, who departed for the Circle Jerks and Black Flag, respectively. The McDonalds continued their work by utilizing various musicians from the L.A. music scene. Following *Born Innocent* (1982), *Teen Babes from Monsanto* (1984), and *Neurotica* (1987), their label Big Time folded, which slowed some considerable momentum the band had built. *Third Eye* (1990) found them on Atlantic Records. The group then returned to an indie label for *Phaseshifter* (1993).

AUTOGRAPHS

A CD, LP, magazine cover, ad, photo, or card signed by the group: $10-$15

OFTEN OVERLOOKED MEMORABILIA

Redd Kross promotional sticker: $3

Reddy, Helen

Born: October 25, 1941

Helen Reddy will forever be linked with her feminist anthem "I Am Woman" (#1, 1972), but it only represents a small part of this complete performer. She migrated from Australia in the late '60s, already a star in her native country where she had even hosted her own television show. Following an impressive performance on *The Tonight Show* in 1970, it took less than twelve months to land her first hit in America, a cover of "I Don't Know How to Love Him" (#13, 1971) from the rock opera *Jesus Christ Superstar*.

She then put together a series of hits including "Peaceful," (#12, 1973), "Delta Dawn" (#1, 1973), "Leave Me Alone" (#3, 1973), "Keep on Singing" (#15, 1974), "You and Me Against the World" (#9, 1974), "Angie Baby" (#1, 1974), "Emotion," (#22, 1975), "Bluebird" (#35, 1975, "Ain't Now Way to Treat a Lady" (#8, 1975), "I Can't Hear You No More" (#29, 1976), and "You're My World" (#18, 1977). By the end of the decade she was spending more time honing her acting skills than releasing music.

AUTOGRAPHS

A CD, LP, magazine cover, ad, photo, or card signed by the artist: $10-$20

OFTEN OVERLOOKED MEMORABILIA

Videotapes of her Australian series *Helen Reddy Sings*, from her 1973 variety show series on NBC-TV, and her work on *The Midnight Special*; movie memorabilia from *Airport 1975* (1974), *Pete's Dragon* (1977), and *Sgt. Pepper's Lonely Hearts Club Band* (1978).

The Red Hot Chili Peppers

Formed 1983

Original Lineup: Flea (Michael Balzary) Born: October 16, 1962; Jack Irons, Born: July 18, 1962; Anthony Kiedis, Born: November 1, 1962; and Hillel Slovak, Born: April 13, 1962, Died: June 25, 1988*

Slovak and Irons were replaced by Jack Sherman and Cliff Martinez in 1983, but returned to reverse the sequence of changes in 1985 before both left again in 1988. Blackbyrd McKnight and D.H. Peligro were added in 1988, but left the following year. John Frusciante and Chad Smith were added in 1989. Frusciante left in 1992 and Arik Marshall was added. He left the following year. Jesse Tobias joined in 1993 and departed the same year. Dave Navarro replaced Tobias.

The Red Hot Chili Peppers (RHCP) are a combustible mix of highly toxic puissance packaged as if they fell out of a television commercial for ESPN's *Extreme Games* rather than a rock band. After a shaky start, the band finally emerged from its bastion personal and personnel problems to become on of the '90's premier acts. Cultivated at L.A.'s Fairfax High, Flea, Slovak, Irons, and Kiedis played their first show, which was an impromptu single song jam at an L.A. club in 1983.

The Uplift Mofo Party Plan (#148, 1987), the group's second album, was its first chart entry and included the popular anthem "Party on Your Pussy." The following year EMI released *The Abbey Road* EP, which mimicked the fab four's original sleeve, featured the Chili Peppers appearing only wearing strategically placed socks. While the sleeve became an instant collector's item, nobody remembers the record.

Tragedy struck on June 25, 1988, when Hillel Slovak died of a heroin overdose. Irons was so upset that he quit the band. He later emerged with Eleven and Pearl Jam. The band then stumbled through more personnel changes before *Mother's Milk* (#52, 1989) was released. The band consisted then of Flea, Anthony Kiedis, drummer Chad Smith, and guitarist John Frusciante. The album extracts "Knock Me Down" (#6, 1989) and "Higher Ground" (#4, 1989) from the album climbed the singles charts. The following year was marred by another unfortunate in-

The Red Hot Chili Peppers. Photo by Marina Chavez. Courtesy Warner Bros. Records Inc.

cident—while the band was filming "MTV's Spring Break," the members were arrested and charged with battery for sexually harassing a woman.

BloodSugarSexMagik (#3, 1992), the band's next album, yielded the extracts "Give It Away" (#76, 1992) and "Under the Bridge" (#2, 1992), which drove record sales. The album was also helped by the group's extensive touring and numerous television show appearances. In May 1992, Frusciante announced he was leaving and was temporarily replaced by Zander Schloss for the band's forthcoming Lollapalooza II summer tour before Arik Marshall joined permanently in July.

What Hits!? (#22, 1992), an EMI-issued retrospective, was the band's next release. Marshall quit and was replaced briefly by Jesse Tobias, who then quit by mutual decision and was finally replaced by Dave Navarro, formerly of Jane's Addiction. "Soul to Squeeze" (#22, 1993), from *The Coneheads* soundtrack, climbed while the band and its members worked on numerous other projects. The band performed at Woodstock '94 on August 14, 1994, before releasing *Out in L.A.* (#82, 1994) (out-takes, remixes, etc.), in the fall.

One Hot Minute (#4, 1995) entered the album charts at its peak, just months before the band postponed its forthcoming tour because Smith broke his wrist. The band began its postponed tour on February 6, 1996, in Philadelphia, Pennsylvania, and ended it on April 16 in San Diego.

AUTOGRAPHS
A CD, LP, magazine cover, ad, photo, or card signed by the band: $45-$110

TOUR BOOKS/PROGRAMS/PASSES
Backstage Passes:
Cloth: $10; Laminated: $15-$20

POSTERS/PRESS KITS
Promotional Posters: $12-$30
Press Kits: $15-$25

USED CLOTHING/EQUIPMENT
Guitar Picks: $15-$25

OFTEN OVERLOOKED MEMORABILIA

Mother's Milk notepad in the shape of a milk carton

All newspaper and periodical articles surrounding the band, its personnel changes, and problems; videotapes of the band's numerous television appearances including *Late Night With David Letterman* (10/11/91, 2/13/96), *Rapido* - BBC2-TV (11/20/91), *Saturday Night Live* (2/22/92), *The Word* (3/6/92) - ITV, "Rock the Vote" (8/23/92), *The Ben Stiller Show* (12/13/92), and *The Arsenio Hall Show* (5/14/93); movie memorabilia from *F.I.S.T.* (1976), *Point Blank, Thrashin', Tough Guys, The Decline of Western Civilization, Suburbia, Wayne's World,* and *The Coneheads*; "a copy of the band's recruiting advertisement placed in the *Los Angeles Weekly* (8/93); associated artifacts from *The Beavis And Butt-Head Experience* (1993); a copy of Smith's chatter on America On-Line (12/12/95); Mother's Milk notepad in shape of milk carton - $12; BloodSugarSexMagik promotional tattoo - $3; BloodSugarSexMagik promotional hanging mobile - $17; Uplift Mojo Party Plan, nudie pen w/ nudie card - $20

REFERENCES/BOOKS
A few resources exist, but none do justice to the band in my opinion. There are no dedicated collector books.

Reed, Jerry

(Jerry Hubbard)
Born: March 20, 1937

The guitarist is a fast-pickin', quick-witted, good natured, down-home country boy who has made a mark for himself as a creative songwriter and talented actor. At the age of eighteen he was handed a recording contract with Capitol Records and gained his first real attention with "Crazy Legs," which Gene Vincent recorded in 1956. He moved to Nashville in the early '60s landed two minor hits with "Hully Gully Guitars" and "Goodnight Irene." He signed to RCA while he worked as session guitarist in 1965. From here he was lucky enough to have Elvis Presley cover his "Guitar Man" and later "U.S. Male."

"Amos Moses" (#8, 1970) quickly became Reed's first gold single. His exposure was noticeably increased through his appearances on *Glen Campbell's Goodtime Hour* (1970-1972). "When Your Hot, You're Hot" was a novelty release that topped the country charts in 1971 and won the artist a Grammy. The following year he scored another Number One C&W with "Lord, Mr. Ford" and received accolades for his Grammy winning duet album with Chet Atkins, *Me and Jerry*. By this time he focused more attention on his acting, but later scored a Number One C&W hit with "She Got the Goldmine (I Got the Shaft)" (#1, C&W, 1982).

AUTOGRAPHS
A CD, LP, magazine cover, ad, photo, or card signed by the artist: $5-$15

USED CLOTHING/EQUIPMENT
Guitar Picks: $10-$15

Jerry Reed's signature

OFTEN OVERLOOKED MEMORABILIA
Videotapes of his numerous television performances including *Glen Campbell's Goodtime Hour* (1970-1972), *The Jerry Reed When Your Hot You're Hot Hour* (1972), *Dean Martin Presents Music Country* (1973), *Nashville 99* (1977), and *Concrete Cowboys* (1981); movie memorabilia from *WW and the Dixie Dance Kings* (1975), *Gator* (1976), and *The Smokey and the Bandit* Series (1977-1983).

Reed, Jimmy

Born: September 6, 1925, Died: August 29, 1976

Legendary blues harpist and composer Jimmy Reed is best remembered for his classic R&B hits "Big Boss Man," "Honest I Do" (#10, 1957), "Bright Lights, Big City," and "Baby, What You Want Me to Do" (#10, 1960). He began performing in the Chicago area in the late '40s and early '50s before he signed to Vee Jay Records in 1953 and released his first big hit "You Don't Have to Go" (#9, R&B, 1955). His work has been covered by many major artists including Elvis Presley and the Rolling Stones.

AUTOGRAPHS
A CD, LP, magazine cover, ad, photo, or card signed by the artist: $35-$100

OFTEN OVERLOOKED MEMORABILIA
Memorabilia associated with other artists' covers of his songs

Reed, Lou

(Louis Firbank)
Born: March 2, 1942

Another Godfather of punk, Reed is best known as the lead singer and songwriter of the '60s group Velvet Underground. He began his solo career in 1970 after leaving the Velvets. Since then he has released a wide variety of product—some acclaimed as "genius," others scorned as "junk." Through it all, though, he has always been viewed as "cutting edge" and revered as a rock icon, rather than a fossil. *Transformer* (#29, 1972) was his breakthrough record and yielded his only Top Twenty hit, "Walk on the Wild Side," an ode to his ole' soup can buddy Andy Warhol. With Bowie manning the knobs on the record, Reed successfully made the transition to glitter rock, no doubt aided by his bleach-blond hair and black nail polish.

Reed's work is like a box of chocolates, unpredictable but still sweet—even when you don't particularly care for it. *Rock 'n' Roll Animal* (#45, 1974) metal plated some Velvet classics, and Reed's rebellious attitude began to take on a greater presence on the stage—he even pretended to shoot up while performing his cult classic "Heroin." Following a few uneventful releases, he moved to Arista in 1976 and a few years later released *Street Hassle* (#89, 1978), which picked some modest airplay.

Reed went through his mid-life crisis during the '80s while he watched a new breed of musicians, such as R.E.M. and U2, praise "The Godfather" for his instrumental role in music and his inspiration. It seemed to breathe new life into Reed, who released *New Sensations* (#56,1984) and *Mistrial* (#47,1986). Both albums garnered acclaim and fairly good sales. Reed then moved to Sire and released *New York, Songs for Drella*, a creative pinnacle perhaps, and a tribute to his friend Andy Warhol.

The first half of the '90s found Reed more somber, political, and refined until his Warner Bros. debut Christian-bashing release *Set the Twilight Reeling* (#110, 1996) with extract "Sex with Your Parents (Motherfucker)" (#26, U.K., 1996).

AUTOGRAPHS

A CD, LP, magazine cover, ad, photo, or card signed by the artist: $25-$55

TOUR BOOKS/PROGRAMS/PASSES

Tour Books:
New York: $10

Backstage Passes:
Cloth: $10-$20; Laminated: $12-$30

POSTERS/PRESS KITS

Promotional Posters: $10-$35
Press Kits: $15-$30

USED CLOTHING/EQUIPMENT

Guitar Picks: $15-$25

OFTEN OVERLOOKED MEMORABILIA

Movie memorabilia from *One Trick Pony* (1981), *Damned in the USA* (1992), and *Blues in the Face* (1995); associated memorabilia from the "butt biting incident" at a concert in Buffalo, NY (3/24/73); videotapes of his television appearances including *Saturday Night Live* (11/15/86), *Late Night With David Letterman* (5/4/89, 1/14/92), *Late Show With David Letterman* (2/21/94, 2/2//96), *Tales of Rock 'n' Roll* (5/1/93) - BBC2-TV, and *The Tonight Show* (3/19/96); a copy of his lecture given at the New York School of Research (2/12/91).

REFERENCES/BOOKS

Between Thought and Expression by Lou Reed; *Transformer: The Lou Reed Story* by Victor Bockris; Numerous other resources exist. There are no dedicated collector books.

Reeves, Martha: See Martha and the Vandellas

R.E.M.

Formed 1980

Michael Stipe (John Michael Stipe), Born: January 4, 1960; Peter Buck, Born: December 6, 1956; Mike Mills, Born: December 17, 1958; and Bill Berry, Born: July 31, 1958

Athens, Georgia, is a college town that gave rise to a rock and roll renaissance during the late '70s. Bands such as the B52's, Pylon, and the Side Effects brought a fresh sound for a new decade—so did R.E.M. The band is also a product of the town, yet not one member of the band was born in or raised in the Southern portion of the U.S. On the site at 394 Oconee St., now marked only by a lone steeple, a converted Episcopal church gave birth to a new congregation. As fate would have it, and with a bit of irony, the four musicians met and joined together in March of 1980. A mutual friend (Kathleen O'Brien who lived at the converted church with Peter Buck and Michael Stipe) provided the introductions, then coaxed the newly formed band into playing its first gig at her birthday party on April 5, 1980. After agreeing to comply with her request, the band managed to compose some fundamental songs and combine them with some popular cover versions to form the set for the debut. This performance led to a booking at a local club called Tyrone's on May 5, 1980.

Now the band needed a name. The group chose R.E.M. Although it is an acronym for "Rapid Eye Movement," the band later claimed that its choice was based only on simplicity and lack of typecasting. Contradicting this claim, however, was the band's early advertising that often used eyes as the main motif.

The earliest known recording of a live R.E.M. show was made on October 4, 1980, at Tyrone's. Although recordings (bootlegs) exist from this era, little memorabilia has survived. Handbills, advertisements, and posters from this era are highly sought by collectors. Beginning in late 1980, R.E.M. played at Tyrone's at 110 Foundry St. nearly every weekend.

R.E.M. Photo by Chris Bilheimer. Courtesy Warner Bros. Records Inc.

Unfortunately the club caught fire and burned down in January 1982.

Ignoring the premier markets for success in the music business, R.E.M.'s unorthodox approach of touring focused on many Southern dive bars and off-beat venues. Despite the success of other Athens bands (the B52's and Pylon who used a different marketing method), the R.E.M. missionary approach brought its music straight to America's heartland rather than to New York or Los Angeles. Whereas this approach may have slowed the band's rise to national prominence, it no doubt has contributed to the longevity of its success.

The group began touring during the latter part of 1981. In July, "Radio Free Europe" was released on Hib-Tone (HT-0001). Far from a hit, the record ($2.25 purchase price), with sales of about 7,000, became a cornerstone for the group's recording catalog. A decade after its release, copies of the record were changing hands at $125 to $150. Advertisements and flyers for the single are highly sought by collectors. Most feature a photograph of the band used on the back sleeve of the single.

The band signed with the IRS label in New York on May 31, 1982. It then chose tracks for a mini-album (EP), *Chronic Town*, which was released on August 24, 1982. The EP met with critical praise, and R.E.M. continued its non-stop touring. The band had most of December and the first two months of 1983 off from the road to prepare for its first album *Murmur*.

From the start, the marketing of the band was a paramount concern for members of R.E.M., and in particular Michael Stipe. Stipe, who came from an artistic background, not only generated much of the artwork used as part of the bands releases, but also directed operations toward the final product. As such, the packaging of the band's products also added to the R.E.M. intrigue. From visual jokes to hidden images, the band never fails to add a bit of personality to each release. For example, the 1986 Pageantry tour program has a sketch of a turtle reproduced conventionally on the inside front cover and again without notice on the second to last page.

The band's first ever tour program, "R.E.M. Ponders Perpetual Motion," was published in 1985 and is a real collector's item, as are tickets form the "1985 Preconstruction Tour"

"Stand" compass

An Automatic for the People coaster and various buttons

and previous tours. Because non-stop touring characterized the band's first five years of existence, collectors can expect to encounter a wide array of tickets, flyers, and promotional materials from this period.

In addition to programs, tickets, passes, videotapes, flyers, posters, and unique promo items, R.E.M. memorabilia collectors often add artifacts to their collection from Athens, Georgia. (See chart)

Following the release of *Green* (1988), it took the band three years to return with *Out of Time* (1991). This album was then followed by *Automatic for the People* in 1992. In 1994 R.E.M. returned to the limelight with *Monster* and commenced its first world tour in five years. The tour, however, was interrupted briefly when Berry was stricken with a brain aneurysm.

Scarce U.K. record release invitation with ticket and Monster pin

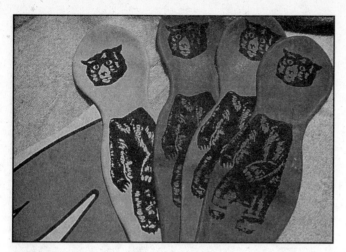

"Monster" balloons

New Adventures in Hi-Fi was an outstanding release for memorabilia buffs who could stare into their "Sterophonic on Film" (View-Master, #946320-1), write notes on their official note pads, send out New Adventures in Hi-Fi postcards (set of 6), place their coffee on New Adventures in Hi-Fi coasters, or hang wall banners in their family rooms. With rock 'n' roll memorabilia more popular than ever, more limited edition packages are finding their ways into the marketplace, containing both a CD and non-recorded novelties. For example, the limited edition New Adventures in Hi-Fi (#2-463210) package contained a hard cover 64-page color book of artwork, exclusive band photographs, and a CD. Originally this package hit the market at $30 to $35, but stories of damaged production and a far more limited distribution than anticipated have driven up into the $80 to $90 range.

With product and tour frequency diminishing, collectors may want to begin by acquiring older material (Pre-1989). Contrary to what many believe, memorabilia from the band is not as readily available as one might expect. The acquisition of these items will require some time, research, and dedicated finance.

Front of the "To make a Monster" dehydrated T-shirt promo item

AUTOGRAPHS

The key to getting signatures from all members of the band on any item begins with Michael Stipe. Unlike the other members of R.E.M., Stipe is an evasive and reluctant signer.

Group:

A CD, LP, magazine cover, ad, photo, or card signed by the entire band: $75-$100

Individual:

Michael Stipe: $45-$55
Peter Buck: $20-$25
Mike Mills: $20-$25
Bill Berry: $20-$25

*Green World Tour program
(© 1989 R.E.M.)*

TOUR BOOKS/ PROGRAMS/PASSES

Programs:

Reconstruction Tour: $25
Work Tour, 1987: $25
Green World Tour 1989: $13-$15
Monster Tour, U.K., 1995: $18-$20
(Hologram 3-D cover)

Backstage Passes:

Cloth: $10-$20;
Laminated: $15-$35

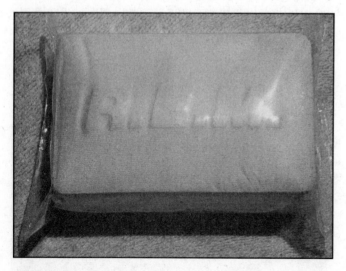

Back side of the "To make a Monster…" promo item that was shaped to resemble a bar of soap

*Monster Tour program
(© 1995 R.E.M.)*

A great selection of R.E.M. backstage passes

POSTERS/PRESS KITS

Promotional Posters:
$10-$30, Examples:
Dead Letter Office: $15-$18
Out of Time: $10-$12
Monster: $10
Press Kits: $25-$50

USED CLOTHING/EQUIPMENT

Guitar Pick:
Mills: $15-$25

OFTEN OVERLOOKED MEMORABILIA

Videotape of *Out of Time*; Promo only boxed pillow case $40-$50; Out of Time promotional coffee mug, Warner Bros., $15-$18; Monster promotional coasters, 1994 - $3; New Adventures in Hi-Fi View-Master - $35-$50 (many of the boxes were damaged); New Adventures in Hi-Fi coasters - $3; New Adventures in Hi-Fi, 1996, promotional notepad - $8-$10; New Adventures in Hi-Fi postcard set (6 photographs) - $10-$12; New Adventures in Hi-Fi hanging banner - $35-$40; New Adventures in Hi-Fi large window sticker - $25-$30; Stand, Warner Bros. promotional compass, 1989 - $15; Losing My Religion, Warner Bros. promotional prayer book (black/gold), with notepad inside - $25-$32; Green, Warner Bros. promotional tin of seeds -

The New Adventures in Hi-Fi View-Master

$20-$25; Automatic for the People, Warner Bros. promotional bag of peanuts, 1992; Murmur, IRS promotional stethoscope; videotapes of their numerous television appearances including *The Tube* (11/18/83), MTV *Unplugged* (4/10/91), *Saturday Night Live* (4/13/91, 11/12/94), *The Adventures of Pete and Pete* (9/8/91), and *MTV 10* (11/27/91); a lock of hair from a Distipel; movie memorabilia from *Get a Life* (1989), *Until the End of the World* (1992), *Desperation Angels* (1992), *The Coneheads* (1993), and *Backbeat* (1993); television segments utilizing the band's "Stand" as the theme; an authentic "Delicious Fine Foods - Automatic for the People" sign from Weaver D's; all associated items from the Hershey Foods corp. promotion "Kit Kat/R.E.M. Concert" marketing campaign; artifacts from the release *Songs in the Key of X* (1996); a copy of *Monster* signed by William Tager - infamous as the "What's the frequency, Kenneth?" Dan Rather stalker;

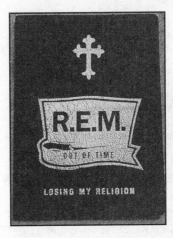

The Losing My Religion prayer book

Monster and New Adventures in Hi-Fi coasters

Green promotional tin of seeds

Promotional "Out of Time" coffee mug

New Adventures in Hi-Fi promotional items (note pad, postcards, coaster)

ehydrated "Monster" T-shirt (in the shape of a bar of soap) - $25, "?" Issues 1995 book - $5, "Monster" interactive disk (MAC/IBM) - $40, "Monster" balloons with feet (4 colors) - $30 - $40 (set), "Monster" inflatable orange punching bag - $85 - $100, "Monster" WEA Records custom invitation with round pin, 1995 - $85; see text above for additional items.

REFERENCES/BOOKS

An R.E.M. Companion, It Crawled from the South by Marcus Gray, 1992 - $17; *Talk About the Passion, R.E.M. an Oral History* by Denise Sullivan, 1994 - $13; *Remarks - The Story of R.E.M.* by Tony Fletcher, 1989, 1993 - $18; *R.E.M. Documental* by Dave Bowler & Bryan Dray, 1995 - $20; *R.E.M. Behind the Mask* by Jim Greer; there are no dedicated collector books.

THE OFFICIAL R.E.M. ATHENS, GEORGIA, PILGRIMAGE TOUR CHECKLIST
Memorabilia for the Masses

❑ The Church, 394 Oconee Street (only the steeple remains)

❑ The University Art Department, Jackson St.: Stipe attended from 1/79 to 3/82; the band played one of its early shows here

❑ Wuxtry Records, 197 E. Clayton St. and 510 Baxter St.: where Peter met Michael; often a meeting place for the band

❑ Reed Dormitory, Reed St.: the co-ed dormitory where Bill lived when he moved to Athens to attend the university in January 1979; also home to many future R.E.M. employees

❑ Tyrone's (O.C.—Old Chameleon club), 110 Foundry St.: site of R.E.M.'s third ever performance (now a parking lot)

❑ The Memorial Hall, UGA Campus: the band's fifth gig on May 15, 1980

❑ The 40 Watt Club, 171 College Ave. (1978)

❑ The 40 Watt East, 100 College Ave. (1980): with only a capacity of 75, it became a locally recognized live venue; R.E.M. played here on numerous occasions

❑ The 11.11 Koffee Klub/The 40 Watt Club, 256 W. Clayton St.: R.E.M.'s second ever concert was here on April 18, 1980. The site became the 40 Watt Club in 1981, vacated two years later, then back in 1987 under different management (Jared Bailey and Barrie Greene (Mrs. Peter Buck)). The band played here many times, and as it grew in popularity, appeared only during a surprise or unadvertised show. The club moved again in 1991.

❑ The 40 Watt Uptown, 382 E. Broad St.: the club's home from 1983-1987; eventually converted into University office space

❑ The 40 Watt Club, 285 Washington St.: an ex-furniture store bought by Peter Buck and opened in

❑ April 1991. The largest of the 40 Watt Clubs has also played host to the band under the pseudonym William.

❑ Walter's Bar-B-Q, 1660 W. Broad St.: a Peter Buck favorite; this eatery was featured in "Walter's Theme," a song which appeared on the band's *Dead Letter Office* LP. Also used as a photographic backdrop for the band.

❑ The Railway Trestle Bridge: situated on the eastern end of town, this bridge is an Athens landmark. It appeared on the back cover of the bands debut LP *Murmur*.

❑ The Madhatter, 450 E. Hancock Ave.: with a capacity of 1,200, it was considered a premier Athens club in the early '80s. R.E.M. played here once it outgrew the smaller clubs in town. It closed in 1986.

❑ John Keane Studios, 165 Hillcrest Ave.: a regular demo site since the mid-80s. The band recorded part of *Out of Time* here.

❑ R.E.M./Athens Ltd., 250-252 W. Clayton: Mecca for R.E.M. fans and purchased by the band in 1986. It houses management and fan club offices, conference, storage, and rehearsal rooms. When in Athens, the band often rehearses here.

❑ The Uptown Lounge, 140 E. Washington St.: a live music venue where the band had occasionally turned up unadvertised. It closed in 1990.

❑ The Lucy Cobb Chapel, Milledge Ave.: where R.E.M. performed in the documentary film, *Athens, GA*, Inside-Out.

❑ The G.A. Bar, 159 W. Clayton: an accessible and frequented bar for the band's three musicians

❑ Prince Avenue Baptists Church, 595 Prince Ave.: a political adversary

❑ The Grit, 113 Hoyt St.: a restaurant frequented by Michael and featured in the video "The One I Love" in July 1987. In 1990 the restaurant moved to Prince Ave.

❑ The Night Gallery Coffee Club/The Grit, 199 Prince Ave.: The Night Gallery had been frequented by Stipe, who eventually bought the building in 1990.

❑ Allen's Hamburgers, 1294 Prince Ave.: a favorite hangout of Peter Buck.

The Remains

Formed 1965

Darry Tashian, Dill Briggs, Vern Miller, and N.D. Smart

This Boston cult band scored with local classic single "Don't Look Back" and even opened concerts for the Rolling Stones (1965) and the Beatles (1966). The group broke up in 1967.

AUTOGRAPHS

A CD, LP, magazine cover, ad, photo, or card signed by the group: $5-$20

Renaissance

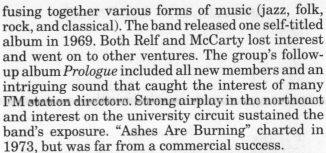

Formed 1969

Original lineup: Keith Relf, Born: March 22, 1943, Died: May 14, 1976; Jim McCarty; Jane Relf; John Hawken; and Louis Cennamo

Next lineup (1972): Rob Hendry, Jon Camp, John Tout, Terry Sullivan, and Annie Haslam*

*Hendry left in 1972 and Michael Dunford was added. Both Sullivan and Tout left in 1979, and Peter Gosling and Peter Barron joined the band.

Former Yardbirds members Keith Relf and Jim McCarty formed Renaissance as a creative outlet for fusing together various forms of music (jazz, folk, rock, and classical). The band released one self-titled album in 1969. Both Relf and McCarty lost interest and went on to other ventures. The group's follow-up album *Prologue* included all new members and an intriguing sound that caught the interest of many FM station directors. Strong airplay in the northeast and interest on the university circuit sustained the band's exposure. "Ashes Are Burning" charted in 1973, but was far from a commercial success.

The band then switched to the Sire label and delivered *Turn of the Cards* (#94, 1974) and *Scheherazade* (#48, 1975). By this point Hendry left and songwriter/guitarist Michael Dunford was just coming into his own. Dunford's unique approach to songwriting found him penning the music and then sending the sheets to British poet Betty Thatcher, who wrote the lyrics. The collaboration was genuinely unique and produced some beautiful pieces.

Much emphasis was placed on the band's next offering, *Live at Carnegie Hall*, which sold well, but failed to really draw the attention both the band and its label were hoping for. The group continued to tour during the late '70s on the college and university circuit where it typically found a warm reception.

AUTOGRAPHS

A CD, LP, magazine cover, ad, photo, or card signed by the group: $15-$30

TOUR BOOKS/PROGRAMS/PASSES

Backstage Passes:
Cloth/paper: $5-$8; Laminated: $10-$15

POSTERS/PRESS KITS

Promotional Posters: $10-$20
Press Kits: $10

OFTEN OVERLOOKED MEMORABILIA

Memorabilia from Annie Haslam's solo work

Annie Halsam of Renaissance

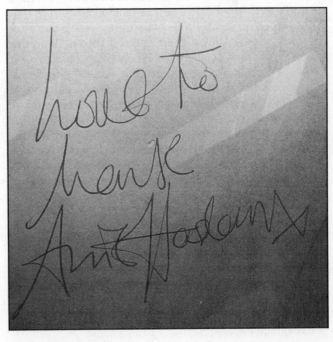

Annie Halsam's signature

REO Speedwagon

Formed 1968

Terry Luttrell; Greg Philbin; Gary Richrath, Born: October 18, 1949; Neal Doughty; and Alan Gratzer, Born: November 9, 1948*

*Luttrell departed in 1971 and Kevin Cronin, Born: October 6, 1951 was added. Cronin left the following year and was replaced by Michael Murphy. Cronin returned in 1975 and Murphy left. Philbin left in 1976 and Bruce Hall was added. Gratzer left in 1988 and Graham Lear was added on drums. Richrath and Lear left in 1990 and were replaced by Bryan Hitt, Dave Amato, and Jesse Harms. Harms departed in 1991.

Neal Doughty and Alan Gratzer formed the band, named after a high-speed fire engine, while they were students at the University of Illinois in 1968. The band quickly became a popular local attraction before it inked a deal with Epic in 1971. The band then toured extensively for years, while producing seven mediocre selling albums. *You Can Tune a Piano, but You Can't Tuna Fish* was a breakthrough record for the band and contained the hit extract "Roll with the Changes" (#58, 1978). It was followed by *Nine Lives* (1979) and the highly successful *High Infidelity* (#1, 1980), which yielded four hit extracts, "Keep on Lovin' You" (#1, 1980), "Take It on the Run" (#5, 1981), "Don't Let Him Go" (#24, 1981), and "In Your Letter" (#20, 1981).

The group's heavy ballading, attributable primarily to Cronin who seemed refreshed following his brief stint away from the band (1972-1975), became a staple with the band's releases. *Good Trouble* (#7, 1982), mustered only one hit single, "Keep the Fire Burnin'," as the band then headed into a two year sabbatical. It returned with *Wheels Are Turnin'* (#7, 1984), which included the group's second chart topper, "Can't Fight This Feelin'" (#1, 1984). A handful of Top Twenty singles followed through 1988, but the group's record sales slowly diminished. Both Gratzer and Richrath departed, leaving the band's future uncertain. Although each was replaced, success was fleeting. The band, however, does remain a solid draw, particularly in the Midwest and in '80s package tours.

AUTOGRAPHS

A CD, LP, magazine cover, ad, photo, or card signed by the group: $20-$45

TOUR BOOKS/PROGRAMS/PASSES

Tour Books:

Good Trouble: $20
Nine Lives Tour, 1979: $15

Backstage Passes:

Cloth: $6-$8; Laminated: $10-$12

Signatures from the members of REO Speedwagon

POSTERS/PRESS KITS

Promotional Posters: $10-$20
Press Kits: $10-$20

USED CLOTHING/EQUIPMENT

Guitar Picks: $10-$15*
*Richrath only

OFTEN OVERLOOKED MEMORABILIA

Movie memorabilia from *FM* (1978)

The Replacements

Formed 1980

Paul Westerberg, Bob Stinson (1959-1995), Tommy Stinson, and Chris Mars*

*B. Stinson left in 1987 and Slim Dunlap was added. Mars left in 1990 and Steve Foley joined the group.

Minneapolis mayhem at its best—the Replacements, led by Paul Westerberg, terrorized local clubs, where its rowdy behavior often preceded its musical integrity. The group played everything from Cher to Kiss and landed an indie record deal with Twin/Tone Records in 1981. It released its album debut *Sorry Ma, Forgot to Take Out the Trash* (which kinda' summed up the release). The group's self-destructive attitude, often alcohol infused, delighted an audience that wasn't sure if it was going to make it through the concert alive. A major label signing with Sire in 1985 still couldn't catapult the group into the mainstream, however, it was becoming obvious that Westerberg was refining his musicianship.

In 1987 Stinson was replaced for his excessive use of alcohol; Slim Dunlap replaced him. Stinson was found dead in 1995 in his apartment from a drug overdose. The band's breakthrough came with *Don't Tell a Soul* (1989) and its extract "I'll Be You" (#51,

1989). By now tension was developing in the band, which was now more of a Westerberg support group, and Mars departed. Westerberg released his solo debut in 1993 with *14 Songs* (#44, 1993)—the Replacements had essentially been replaced.

AUTOGRAPHS

Group:

A CD, LP, magazine cover, ad, photo, or card signed by the group: $10-$25*

*Original members

OFTEN OVERLOOKED MEMORABILIA

Movie memorabilia from *Singles* (1992); associated memorabilia from the *Friends* soundtrack (1995).

The Residents

Formed 1970

The Residents are four unidentified musicians who broke out of the San Francisco music scene in 1970 to record and release albums only available through the mail-order Ralph label. Shrouded by mystery, their self-intriguing releases were as if they fell out of a Diana Arbus photography book, topical yet fragmented. The group's infatuation with moles came in 1981, nearly a decade after Michael Jackson found Ben and decades after Walt Disney found Mickey. "Mark the Mole," possibly in reference to a group member, became a storyline integrated into a Mole Trilogy. The band endures and even released an interactive CD-ROM in 1994.

AUTOGRAPHS

A CD, LP, magazine cover, ad, photo, or card signed by the group: $4-$10

Revenge: See Joy Division

Paul Revere and the Raiders

Formed 1960

Paul Revere, Born: January 7, 1938; Mark Lindsay, Born: March 9, 1942; Phil Volk, Michael Smith; and Drake Levin*

*Levin left in 1966 and Jim Valley was added. Big changes in 1967: Volk, Smith, and Valley left. Joe Correro Jr., Charlie Coe, and Freddy Weller joined the band. Coe left in 1968 and Keith Allison was added. Correro left in 1971 and Omar Martinez and Robert Woolley were added. Smith also rejoined the band. Weller left in 1973 and Lindsay left in 1976.

Paul Revere and the Raiders emerged from the Northwest, where they were well-known for songs such as "Like, Long Hair" (1961), and moved to Cal-

ifornia in early 1965 and released their first hit single "Steppin' Out" (#46, 1965). The band garnered attention through Mark Lindsay's sex appeal and its appearances on Dick Clark's *Where the Action Is*. The hits just kept on coming: "Just Like Me" (#11, 1965), "Kicks" (#4, 1966), "Hungry" (#6, 1966), "The Great Airplane Strike" (#20, 1966), "Good Thing" (#4, 1966), "Ups and Downs" (#22, 1967), and "Him or Me - What's It Gonna Be?"(#5, 1967).

By 1967 the group was billed as Paul Revere and the Raiders featuring Mark Lindsay, who by 1969 had undertaken a solo career in conjunction with the band. Lindsay scored with "Arizona" (#10, 1970), while the Raiders struck again with "Indian Reservation" (#1, 1971). The lead singer finally quit the band in 1975, though he returned on occasion.

AUTOGRAPHS

Group:

A CD, LP, magazine cover, ad, photo, or card signed by the group: $25-$80*

*Original members

OFTEN OVERLOOKED MEMORABILIA

Videotapes form the groups numerous television appearances including *Where the Action Is* - ABC-TV (1965), *Hullabaloo* -NBC-TV (7/25/66), *Batman* - ABC-TV (11/2/66), *Coliseum with Woody Allen* - CBS-TV (2/16/67), *The Smothers Brothers Comedy Hour* - CBS-TV (3/5/67), *The Ed Sullivan Show* - CBS-TV (4/30/67), *Happening '68* - the group's series (1/68 - 9/69), and *Make Your Own Kind of Music* (7/20/71).

Revolting Cocks: see Ministry

Rhinoceros

Formed 1968

John Finley, Michael Fonfara, Danny Weis, Alan Gerber, Doug Hastings, Jerry Penrod, and Billy Mundi

This Elektra Records manufactured "supergroup" consisting of John Finley, Michael Fonfara (the Electric Flag), Danny Weis (Iron Butterfly), Alan Gerber, Doug Hastings (Buffalo Springfield), Jerry Penrod (Iron Butterfly), and Billy Mundi (Frank Zappa's Mothers of Invention) proved that money is not the key factor for success in the music business. When the group's self-titled debut could barely scrap a minor instrumental hit, personnel changes began and eventually led to the band's demise.

AUTOGRAPHS

An LP, magazine cover, ad, photo, or card signed by the group: $15*

*Original members

Rich, Charlie

Born: December 14, 1932, Died: July 25, 1995

Like many, Rich's musical education and development came as a youth while attending church. He formed his own pop band, the Velvetones, while in the air force and eventually the band even earned its own television show. Rich, through his wife's encouragement, eventually signed to Sun Records. There he played with legends such as Johnny Cash and Roy Orbison and eventually even landed a hit of his own, "Lonely Weekends" (#22, 1960).

"Mohair Sam" and "Big Boss Man" were his next successful singles. He then label hopped a bit before finally landing at Epic. There he struck pay dirt with "Behind Closed Doors" (#15, 1973), "The Most Beautiful Girl" (#1, 1973), and later with "There Won't Be Anymore" (#18, 1974), "A Very Special Love Song" (#11, 1974), "I Love My Friend" (#24, 1974), and "Every Time You Touch Me (I Get High)" (#19, 1975).

AUTOGRAPHS

A CD, LP, magazine cover, ad, photo, or card signed by the artist: $15-$30
*Original members

OFTEN OVERLOOKED MEMORABILIA

Movie memorabilia from *Every Which Way But Loose* (1978)

Richard, Cliff

(Harry Webb)
Born: October 14, 1940

Often referred to as Britain's Elvis Presley, Cliff Richard has placed more than one hundred hit singles in the U.K. Top Forty, a majority of which were Top Ten hits, and enjoyed more than a dozen chart toppers. It all started in 1958 when Richard put together a back-up group, first called the Drifters and later the Shadows, to record a demo and release his first record, "Move It" (#2, U.K., 1958). Following a television appearance and a tour, Richard was embraced by teens as a rock idol, which was only solidified by two follow-up Number One records in 1959, "Living Doll" and "Travelin' Light." During this period he also turned to film and made two movies during the same year (1959).

His near-constant presence on the singles chart and exposure on television and motion pictures pushed his popularity all across Europe. Ironically, only two of his dozens of hits made it into the U.S. Top Forty, "Living Doll" (#30, 1959) and "It's All in the Game" (#25, 1964). Despite his rockabilly image, he managed to survive through the '60s while most American '50s rock icons fell prey to the British In-

vasion. By the mid-60s Richard had embraced Christianity, cleaned up his image, and began to intertwine his rock releases with gospel recordings. In 1968 he parted company with the Shadows, although they reunited during several one-off occasions. The latter half of the decade continued to see Richard land more than his fair share of hit singles in Britain including "In the Country," "Its All Over," "The Day I Met Marie," "All My Love," and "Congratulations"(#1), which became an international hit everywhere except in the U.S.

During the '70s and '80s Richard made greater progress in the States with songs such as "Devil Woman," "We Don't Talk Anymore," "Dreaming," "Daddy's Home," and "Suddenly," a duet with Olivia Newton-John. He also sustained his popularity in Britain with numerous charting singles, an appearance in the Dave Clark musical *Time*, and numerous outstanding album releases including *Always Guaranteed* and *Stronger*.

During the '90s we saw the performer celebrate his 50th birthday, receive his knighthood, and even perform a song at Wimbledon (1996). In 1993 *The Album* (#1 U.K.) quickly rose to the top of the album chart. Richard seems impervious to failure and is truly a living rock and roll legend.

AUTOGRAPHS

A CD, LP, magazine cover, ad, photo, or card signed by the artist: $20-$70

TOUR BOOKS/PROGRAMS/PASSES

Tour Book:
Wired for Sound Tour, 1981: $30

OFTEN OVERLOOKED MEMORABILIA

Movie memorabilia from *A Serious Charge, A Touch of Hell, Expresso Bongo, The Young Ones, Summer Holiday, Wonderful Life,* and *Xanadu*; theatre memorabilia from *Time*; videotapes of his numerous television appearances; Always Guaranteed EMI box set includes: album, singles, poster, print, and postcards, 1987 - $40.

REFERENCES/BOOKS

Which One's Cliff? - his autobiography (1981); Numerous resources exist. *Cliff* by Patrick Doncaster and Tony Jasper is an excellent place to start any research. There are about a dozen European fan clubs to choose from, take your pick! There are no dedicated collector books.

Richards, Keith: See the Rolling Stones

Richman, Jonathan/Modern Lovers

Jonathan Richman, Born: 1951

Late-70s Boston singer, songwriter, and guitarist Jonathan Richman is typically associated with the

band Modern Lovers, which made a marginal impact before first disbanding in 1972, and again in 1978. Richman then moved on to quieter music, such as the instrumental hit "Egyptian Reggae," made with the acoustic version of Modern Lovers, before he began a solo career. While he has developed a cult following in the States, he has yet to achieve mass acceptance.

AUTOGRAPHS

A CD, LP, magazine cover, ad, photo, or card signed by the artist: $5-$10

Ridgeley, Andrew: See Wham!

Righteous Brothers

Formed 1962

Bill Medley, Born: September 19, 1940; and Bobby Hatfield, Born: August 10, 1940

Late-60s masters of blue-eyed soul, both performers broke away from the group the Paramours to form the now legendary duo in 1962. They called themselves the Righteous Brothers, and following the release of their first single, "Little Latin Lupe Lu" (#49, 1963), they signed with Phil Spector to his Phillies Records, where they cut "You Lost That Lovin Feelin'" which quickly topped the singles chart. From this point onward the hits just kept coming, including "Unchained Melody" (#4, 1965), "Ebb Tide" (#5, 1965), "Just Once in My Life" (#9, 1965), followed by the Verve Records hit, "(You're My) Soul and Inspiration" (#1, 1966) before the duo split apart in 1968. While Hatfield kept the name, Medley kept up the hits, although only minor ones. The duo then reunited for a record in 1974, *Give it to the People*, which spun off the title track (#20), "Dream On" (#32), and "Rock and Roll Heaven" (#3).

In-house Gold 45 Disc Award Ltd. award for "You've Lost that Lovin' Feeling," 1964. It is valued at $1,500. From the Doug Leftwitch collection.

Following the 1976 murder of his wife, Medley retired from the business for five years. The duo did make an appearance on the *American Bandstand* anniversary television special in 1981 and set out on tour two years later. Two films then reignited interest in the duo. *Dirty Dancing* (1987) had Medley singing with Jenni-

In-house Gold LP Disc Award Ltd. award for the Righteous Brothers' You've Lost that Lovin' Feeling, 1964. It is valued at $2,000. From the Doug Leftwitch collection.

fer Warnes on the Grammy winning "(I've Had) The Time of My Life" (#1, 1987), and *Ghost* (1990) put "Unchained Melody" back on the charts.

AUTOGRAPHS

A CD, LP, magazine cover, ad, photo, or card signed by the duo: $45-$125

OFTEN OVERLOOKED MEMORABILIA

Movie memorabilia from *Dirty Dancing* (1987) and *Ghost* (1990); videotapes of their numerous television appearances including *Shindig*.

Riley, Billy Lee

Born: October 5, 1933

This pioneer Sun Records session player and artist found himself backing his labelmates such as Jerry Lee Lewis, Johnny Cash, and Roy Orbison. Billy Lee Riley is typically associated with the songs "Red Hot" and "Flying Saucer Rock 'n' Roll." Both tunes were revived by Robert Gordon and Link Wray in 1978. Riley later moved to L.A. where he contributed to session by Herb Alpert, the Beach Boys, Rick Nelson, and numerous others. Although he released several albums in Europe, no new material surfaced here until his 1994 *Blue Collar Blues*.

AUTOGRAPHS

A CD, LP, magazine cover, ad, photo, or card signed by the artist: $10-$35

OFTEN OVERLOOKED MEMORABILIA

Associated artifacts from the numerous sessions he has contributed to for other artists

Riley, Jeannie C.

(Jeanne Stephenson)
Born: October 19, 1945

This late-60s singer's big break came when she recorded Tom T. Hall's "Harper Valley PTA" (#1, 1968), which won her a Grammy for Best Female Country Vocal Performance. Jeannie Riley also had a few lesser hits including "The Girl Most Likely," "There Never Was a Time," and "Good Enough to Be Your Wife."

AUTOGRAPHS

A CD, LP, magazine cover, ad, photo, or card signed by the artist: $5-$20

OFTEN OVERLOOKED MEMORABILIA

A videotape of the short-lived *Harper Valley* television series, as well as movie memorabilia from a related film.

Riley, Terry: See Guy

Riley, Teddy

Born: June 24, 1935

Late-60s Bay Area exotic minimalist of modern classical music Riley, along with Steve Reich and Phillip Glass, had a profound impact on much of the New Age genre. He is typically associated with his works *In C*, *A Rainbow in Curved Air*, and *Church of Anthrax*, as well as his all-night concerts.

AUTOGRAPHS

A CD, LP, magazine cover, ad, photo, or card signed by the artist: $15-$35

Riperton, Minnie

Born: November 8, 1947, Died: July 12, 1979

This '70s singer, with her noteworthy vocal range, is best remembered for the song "Lovin' You" (#1, 1975). Minnie Riperton, who was diagnosed with breast cancer in 1976, eventually succumbed to the disease in 1979.

AUTOGRAPHS

A CD, LP, magazine cover, ad, photo, or card signed by the artist: $20

Ritchie, Lionel: See the Commodores

Rivers, Johnny

(John Ramistella)
Born: November 7, 1942

Sixties singer and songwriter Johnny Rivers is best remembered for the songs "Memphis" (#2, 1964), "Seventh Son," "Poor Side of Town"(#1, 1966), "Secret Agent Man," "Baby I Need Your Lovin'," "The Tracks of My Tears," and later for "Rockin' Pneumonia and the Boogie Woogie Flu" and "Swayin' to the Music (Slow Dancin')." He is also an astute businessman and owner of a song publishing and record company. His talent discoveries include the Fifth Dimension and Jimmy Webb.

AUTOGRAPHS

A CD, LP, magazine cover, ad, photo, or card signed by the artist: $5-$25

The Rivingtons

Formed 1953

Carl White (1932-1980), John "Sonny" Harris, Al Frazier, and Turner Wilson

Early-60s Southern California vocal group The Rivingtons are best known for two novelty songs, "Papa-Oom-Mow-Mow" and "The Bird's the Word."

AUTOGRAPHS

An LP, magazine cover, ad, photo, or card signed by the group: $10-$15

Rob Base & D.J. E-Z Rock

Formed 1982

Rob Base (Ginyard) and D.J. E-Z Rock (Rodney Bryce)

These late-80s New York rappers are best known for their songs "It Takes Two" (#36, 1988), "Get on the Dance Floor," and "Joy and Pain." Base went solo and sold *The Incredible Base* (#50, 1989) gold before he reunited with E-Z Rock in 1994.

AUTOGRAPHS

A CD, LP, magazine cover, ad, photo, or card signed by the duo: $10-$15

The Robins: See the Coasters

Smokey Robinson and the Miracles/ The Miracles

Formed 1957

William "Smokey" Robinson, Born: February 19, 1940; Ronnie White, Born: April 5, 1939; Bobby Rogers, Born: February 19, 1940; Warren "Pete" Moore, Born: November 19, 1939; and Claudette Rogers Robinson*

*Claudette Robinson left in 1964. Robinson left in 1972 and William Griffin was added.

One of music's most gifted singers, songwriters, and producers, Smokey Robinson was instrumental in the success of Motown Records. He not only placed more than two dozen Top Forty hits with the Miracles, but also lent his music and business skills to the label. Robinson's relationship with Barry Gordy, Jr. really began with the release of "Shop Around" (#2, 1960), and although they had met earlier, it marked their first real project together. Robinson went on to write and produce many of the company's acts including Marvin Gaye, Mary Wells, and the Temptations, while the Miracles scored with a variety of singles including "Mickey's Monkey" (#8, 1963), "Going to a Go-Go" (#11, 1966), "You've Really Got a Hold on Me" (#8, 1963), "The Tracks of My Tears" (#16, 1965), "I Second That Emotion" (#4, 1967), "Baby, Baby Don't Cry" (#8, 1969), and "The Tears of a Clown" (#1, 1970) before Robinson decided to leave the group and record on his own.

For most of the '70s he handled his responsibilities as a Motown vice president. Later in the decade, he returned to his own music career with "Cruisin'" (#4, 1979), "Being With You" (#2, 1981), "Just to See Her," and "One Heartbeat." He resigned as Motown V.P. in 1988 and left the label in 1990. Nearly every major group or artist that appeared during Robinson's music career covered one of his songs, and the list of his achievements alone could fill this book, but it is safe to say he is probably most proud of being awarded the Grammy's Living Legend Award and for being inducted into the Rock and Roll Hall of Fame with the Miracles in 1987.

AUTOGRAPHS

A CD, LP, magazine cover, ad, photo, or card signed by the artist: $25-$50

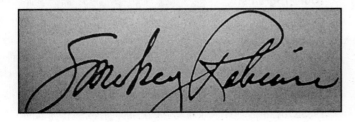

Smokey Robinson's signature

OFTEN OVERLOOKED MEMORABILIA

Associated artifacts from Robinson's numerous contributions to other artists, as well as from those artists who covered the The Miracle's compositions.

REFERENCES/BOOKS

Smokey: Inside My Life - his autobiography (1989); A few other resources exist. There are no dedicated collector books. Serious collectors should opt for a Fan Club: The Smokey Robinson and the Miracles Fan Club and Newsletter, 8 Hillside Rd., Narragansett, RI 02882

The Tom Robinson Band/Sector 27

Formed 1977

Tom Robinson, Danny Kustow, Mark Ambler, and Brian Taylor*

*Taylor and Ambler left in 1978 and Nick Plytas joined briefly before being replaced by Ian Parker. Preston Heyman was added on drums in 1978. Group disbanded in 1979 and Robinson formed Sector 27, which last for about a year.

This late-70s British punk act is best known for the songs "Glad to Be Gay" and "2-4-6-8 Motorway" before it split up in July 1979. After the failed group Sector 27, Robinson turned to a solo career that included the U.K. hit "War Baby," and he also hosted his own BBC Radio program.

AUTOGRAPHS

A CD, LP, magazine cover, ad, photo, or card signed by the artist: $10

The Roches

Formed late-1960s

Maggie Roche, Born: October 26, 1951; and Terre Roche, Born: April 10, 1953*

*Suzzy Roche was added in 1976

This late-70s folk trio, best remembered for its 1979 Warner Brothers debut LP *The Roches*, which contained the song "The Married Men" and was met with rave reviews (but yielded no hit single), managed to build a strong underground cult following, that judging by album sales, probably spent most of its funds attending the group's concerts. The Roches later went on to record music for theatre, television, and film.

AUTOGRAPHS

A CD, LP, magazine cover, ad, photo, or card signed by the group: $12-$25

OFTEN OVERLOOKED MEMORABILIA

Movie memorabilia from *Crossing Delancy* and *The Land Before Time*; videotapes from their voice overs on the '90s cartoon television series *Tiny Toons*; associated artifacts from their work on other artists' albums including Paul Simon.

Rockpile

Formed 1976

Dave Edmunds, Born: April 15, 1944; Nick Lowe, Born: March 25, 1949; Terry Williams; and Billy Bremner

Late-70s British rock band Rockpile's extensive touring built it a strong cult following in the U.S. The group recorded only one album, but was instrumental in generating interest in England's pub rock movement. The band split in 1981, and Lowe and Edmunds resumed their solo careers, Williams joined Dire Straits, and Bremner filled in a temporary gap with the Pretenders.

AUTOGRAPHS

A CD, LP, magazine cover, ad, photo, or card signed by the group: $15-$45

Rodgers, Jimmie

Born: September 8, 1897, Died: May 26, 1933

Jimmie Rodgers, the late-20s pivotal pioneer of country music, is typically associated with the songs "The Soldier's Sweetheart," "Sleep Baby Sleep," "Blue Yodel," and "Brakesman's Blues." He was one of the few musicians successful at mixing country, folk, and traditional blues. Rodgers suffered from deteriorating health, but managed to work right up until his death in 1933. He became one of the first inductees to the Country Music Hall of Fame.

AUTOGRAPHS

An ad, photo, or card signed by the artist: $425-$900

REFERENCES/BOOKS

Numerous resources exist. *Jimmie the Kid: The Life of Jimmie Rodgers* by Mike Paris and Chris Cober is a MUST! There are no dedicated collector books.

Roe, Tommy

Born: May 9, 1942

This '60s singer and songwriter is best remembered for his songs "Sheila" (#1, 1969), "Dizzy" (#1, 1969), "Sweet Pea" (#8, 1966), "Hooray for Hazel" (#6, 1966), and "Jam Up and Jelly Tight" (#8, 1969). Tommy Roe relocated to England when his hits stopped in the U.S.

AUTOGRAPHS

An LP, magazine cover, ad, photo, or card signed by the artist: $10-$30

REFERENCES/BOOKS

Limited resources exist. There are no dedicated collector books. Serious collectors should opt for a Fan Club: Tommy Roe International Fan Club, P.O. Box 813, Owatonna, MN 55060

Rogers, Kenny

Born: August 21, 1938

Multitalented late-60s pop act (New Christy Minstrels), turned country rock (First Edition), turned country solo act, and successful actor, Kenny Rogers has had a phenomenal career that has spanned over three decades. Rogers really broke first with the First Edition, which landed hits such as "Just Dropped in (to See What Condition My Condition Was In)" (#5), "Ruby Don't Take Your Love to Town," "Reuben James" (#26, 1969), "Something's Burning" (#11), and "Tell It All Brother" (#17, 1970). The group picked up its own Canadian produced syndicated television show *Rollin' on the River* (1971-1973, 52 episodes)

When the First Edition split up, Rogers pursued a country career and landed numerous hits including "Lucille" (#5, 1977), "Don't Fall in Love With a Dreamer" (#4, 1980) (a duet with Kim Carnes), "Lady" (#1) (penned by Lionel Ritchie), "I Don't Need You" (#3), and "Islands in the Stream" (#1, 1983) (with Dolly Parton). He raked up sales of more than $100 million during the latter part of the '70s alone.

By the mid-80s, Rogers' record sales had slowed, so he then concentrated on just the C&W chart where he scored more than his fair share of top records. The decade also saw the artist delve into acting, both in television and film, and appear in more than a dozen television specials. Other projects have included his rotisserie-chicken fast-food franchise, and hosting an Arts & Entertainment Network series on the Old West, and even working with the QVC shopping channel.

AUTOGRAPHS

A CD, LP, magazine cover, ad, photo, or card signed by the artist: $10-$30

TOUR BOOKS/ PROGRAMS/ PASSES

Tour Programs:
Monumental Tour (w/ First Edition): $25
Transition Tour (w/ First Edition): $35
1982 Tour: $10
1983 "Jovan Present...": $10

Kenny Rogers tour program (© Kenny Rogers)

Backstage Passes:
Cloth: $8-$10;
Laminated:
$10-$12

POSTERS/ PRESS KITS

Promotional
Posters: $10-$30
Press Kits:
$20-$40

OFTEN OVERLOOKED MEMORABILIA

Videotapes of his numerous television show appearances including *American Bandstand, The Smothers Brothers Comedy Hour* (11/5/67), *Rollin' On the River*, 1971-1973 (52 episodes), *The Gambler* (1980), *Coward of the County* (1981), his "1983 Kenny Rogers HBO Special," *The Gambler II* (1983), "A Christmas to Remember" with Dolly Parton (12/2/84), *Late Night With David Letterman* (11/26/85), "Welcome Home America" (4/14/91), *The Gambler Returns: The Luck of the Draw* (113-4/91), *Hot Country Nights* (11/24/91), "Christmas in the Ozarks" (12/18/92), "A Country Music Celebration' (1/13/93), *Rio Diablo* (2/28/93), *Dr. Quinn Medicine Woman* (5/22/93), "A Day in the Life of Country Music" (10/1/93), *The Tonight Show* (2/7/94), and *MacShayne: Winner Take All* (2/11/94); artifacts from his days in the New Christy Minstrels; movie memorabilia from *Fools*, and *Six Pack* (1982); a copy of his book with Len Epand, *Making It With Music*; a rubbing from his star on the Hollywood Walk of Fame; a casting from his footprints at the Country Place in Toledo, Ohio; copies of the documentary *Kenny Rogers and the American Cowboy* (1979) and the 13-part series *The Real West* (1992); a videotape from *A Current Affair* (2/11/93) and the assorted tabloids covering his 1993 divorce; all of his associated items with the QVC shopping channel.

REFERENCES/BOOKS

Your Friends and Mine - by Kenny Rogers (1987); *Kenny Rogers' America* - by Kenny Rogers (1986); Numerous other resources exist, but none do justice to the singer in my opinion. There are no dedicated collector books. Serious collectors should opt for a Fan Club: Kenny Rodgers International Fan Club, P.O. Box 24240, Nashville, TN 37202

Kenny Rogers tour program (© Kenny Rogers)

The Rolling Stones

Formed 1962

Mick Jagger, Born: July 26, 1943; Keith Richards, Born: December 18, 1943; Brian Jones (Lewis Hopkins-Jones), Born: February 28, 1942, Died: July 3, 1969; Bill Wyman,

Born: October 24, 1936; and Charlie Watts, Born: June 2, 1941*

*Mick Taylor, Born: January 17, 1948, was added following the death of Brian Jones. Jones was buried in the Priory Road Cemetery. Taylor left in 1975 and was replaced by Ron Wood, Born: June 1, 1947. Wyman left in 1992 and was replaced by Darryl Jones.

The Rolling Stones are considered the "World's Greatest Rock & Roll Band"!

The Rolling Stones. Photo by Anton Corbijn. Courtesy Virgin Records.

TOUR SPECIFICS AND PROGRAMS

1963

10/29-11/3: Begin first British Tour - 32 dates supporting the Everly Brothers and Bo Diddley. Little Richard also made an appearance. Last gig at Hammersmith Odeon, London 11/3. All memorabilia from this tour is very scarce and highly sought by Stones collectors. The Tour Programme cover features black and white photographs of the Everly Brothers (top), Bo Diddley (bottom left), and Little Richard (bottom right). The Rolling Stones are not mentioned on the cover. Another variation of the program exists without Little Richard. The group did play extensive club dates throughout the entire year.

Programs:
*U.K. (10.5" x 8"), two cover variations: $250-$350
*U.K. (7.5' x 10"), 4 Cities Show-City Hall, Nov.13th '63: $275-$325

1964

1/6-1/27: The Rolling Stones begin their second U.K. tour called Group Scene 1964. The 14-date tour has them

A Rolling Stones poster from the first year the group toured the U.S. (1964). Murray Poster Printing Co. of New York City printed this poster for a show in Dayton, Ohio. It is valued between $2,000 and $2,500. From the collection of Hank Thompson.

headlining and supported by numerous groups including the Ronettes. The official souvenir program (yellow/blue) from this tour featured a duotone picture of the band dressed in shirts and ties on the front cover.

2/8-3/7: The Roiling Stones begin their second U.K. tour of the year scheduled for 28 dates. All Stars '64 (U.K.)

3/15-5/31: A series of short U.K. Tours and selected dates

6/1-6/20: The band's first North American tour begins as it lands in New York's Kennedy airport

7/11-8/30: A series of selected U.K. dates

9/5-9/11: The group begins a 31-date, twice-nightly, U.K. Tour, The Rolling Stones Show

10/9/64: The band cancels its South African Tour

10/16-10/20: Selected European dates, West German, Belgium and France

10/23-11/15: The Rolling Stones begin their Second North American Tour

Programs:
*June '64 (10" x 13"), USA: $200-$300
*U.K. Group Scene (9.25" x 7"), Ronettes and Stones: $200-$300
*October/November, USA (10" x 13"): $200-$300
*U.K. All-Stars '64 (8.5" x 11"): $250-$300

1965
1/21-2/17: The group arrives in Sydney, New South Wales, Australia, to begin a 16-date tour of Australia, New Zealand, and the Far East

3/5-18: The Rolling Stones begin a 14-date, twice-nightly U.K. tour. The Hollies are one of the supporting acts.

3/26-4/18: Scandinavian tour and France

4/23-5/29: The group begins its third North America tour, 21-dates

6/15-29: The band embarks on a short Scottish and 4-date Scandinavian Tour

8/1/65: The group's London Palladium debut. It plays two shows supported by acts such as the Moody Blues and the Walker Brothers.

9/3-17: Ireland, West Germany, and Austrian tour

9/24-10/17: The Rolling Stones begin their sixth U.K. Tour, 24-date, twice-nightly

10/29-12/5: The band begins a 37-date Rolling Stones '65, its fourth North American tour

White-matte award for the Rolling Stones' Out of Our Heads, 1965. It is valued at $7,500. From the Doug Leftwitch collection.

Programs:
*USA (11" x 11.5"), USA: $125-$150
*Australian (8" x 10.5"): $250-$350
*Europe (8" x 10.25"): $200-$225
*New Zealand, "Big Beat 65": $250-$300

1966
2/18-3/2: The band begins an 11-date tour of Australia and New Zealand

3/26-4/5: The Stones start a 7-date, 11-show European tour

6/24-7/28: The Stones return to North America (fifth tour) for a 31-date tour, ending in Hawaii

9/23-10/9: The group returns home for Rolling Stones '66, a 12-date, twice-nightly U.K. tour that is heavily supported with Ike and Tina Turner, the Yardbirds, and others

Programs:
*USA (10.5" x 11.5"): $125-$150
*Belgium, Brussels - Da Lais Des Sports (8.25" x 11.5"): $115-$125
*U.K. Tour (8" x 10.5"): $175-$200

1967
3/25-4/17: The band begins a 16-date European tour. It also includes the band's first gig behind the Iron Curtain in Poland.

In-house Gold award for the Rolling Stones' "Jumping Jack Flash," 1968. It is valued at $1,000. From the Doug Leftwitch collection.

1969

11/7-12/6: The Rolling Stones begin their sixth U.S. tour, a 17-date journey. The colorful program from this tour is highly sought by collectors because the design is so indicative of the times. The close of their U.S. tour is a free concert at the Altamont Speedway Track in Livermore, CA. The concert is marred by violence and a stabbing death.

Programs:
*USA (12" x 12"): $35

1970

8/31-10/11: European Tour 1970

1971

3/4-3/14: The group begins British Tour, 11-date, (6) twice-nightly

1972

6/3 - 7/26: The Rolling Stones begin the North American Tour 1972, 38-date, (3) twice-nightly. The tour includes a stop in Montreal, which is marred by an explosion under the group's equipment van. The show also produces thousands of fake tickets and many unhappy would-be concert goers. The poster from this tour was mass produced across America and sold in just about every college and university bookstore.

Programs:
*USA, (9" x 12"): $45

1973

1/18-2/27: The Rolling Stones 1973 Winter tour begins at the Inglewood Forum. It includes 1 continental U.S. date, 2 Hawaii dates, then an 11-date Far East leg.
9/1-10/19: The Rolling Stones 29-date 1973 European tour opens in Vienna, Austria

Programs:
*USA (12" x 12"), Hawaii: $30-$35

1975

6/1 - 9/8 "1975 Tour of the Americas" begins in Louisiana. The 45-date tour includes major stops in New York and Los Angeles. The band announces the tour in New York City on May 31 during a press conference which includes the band playing live on a flat-bed truck in the street.

Programs:
*USA (9' x 14"): $25-$35

1976

"Rolling Stones Tour of Europe '76" opens in Frankfurt, West Germany. The 40-date sweep includes major stops in London and Paris, along with the Open Air Festival at Knebworth on August 21.

Programs:
*Europe (9" x 13"): $50-$60
*Knebworth Fair (8.5" x 11.5"): $150-$200

1978

6/10-7/26: The band begins a 26-date tour of the U.S. in Lakeland, Florida

Programs:
*USA (11.75" x 11.75"): $25

1981

9/25-12/19: The band starts an extensive 51-date tour across America. The tour has numerous multiple date gigs, creating less havoc for the band.

Programs:
*USA (12" x 12"): $20

Tour program from the 1981 American Tour (© 1981 Raindrop Products, Inc.)

1982

5/26-7/25: "The Rolling Stones, Europe '82," a 36-date continental slide begins in Aberdeen, U.K.

Programs:
*Europe (12" x 12"): $40-$50

1986

2/23/86: "Tribute for Ian Stewart," 250 invited guests, 100 Club, London, U.K.

1989

8/31-12/20: "1989 Steel Wheels U.S. Tour" begins in New Haven, CT, an extensive 59-date tour that includes numerous multiple date stops.

Programs:
*USA - Steel Wheels (12" x 16") - $15 - $20

1990

2/14-2/27: "Steel Wheels Japan Tour 1990"
5/18-8/26: "1990 Urban Jungle Tour" starts in Rotterdam, Netherlands. The 45-date tour through Europe ends in London on August 25.

Programs:
*Hungarian, Urban Jungle (8.5" x 11.75"): $25-$30
*Tokyo (11" x 14"): $75-$100
*European (11" x 14"): $15-$25

1994

8/1-12/18: "Voodoo Lounge" North American tour opens in Washington, DC

Programs:
*USA - Voodoo Lounge (9.5" x 12"): $15-$20
*Japan - Voodoo Lounge (9.5 " x 12"): $25-$35

World Tour program from the Voodoo Lounge Tour (1994/95) (© RZO Prods. Inc.)

1995

1/14-4/17: "Voodoo Lounge World Tour" (continued)
5/26-8/30: "Voodoo Lounge European Tour '95"

A rare signed program from the Stones' 1965 U.K. tour. Courtesy Phillips Son & Neale.

AUTOGRAPHS

The band has always been elusive and reluctantly obliging to autograph requests.

Group:

A CD, LP, magazine cover, ad, photo, or card signed by the entire band: $500-$1,500*

*Original lineup on a vintage item such as a poster

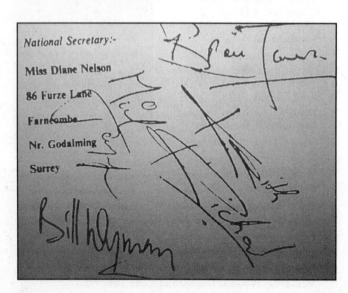

Signatures of the members of the Rolling Stones

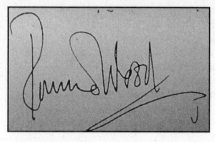

Ron Wood's signature

Individual:

Mick Jagger: $65-$100	Brian Jones: $150-$400
Keith Richards: $50-$75	Bill Wyman: $30-$45
Charlie Watts: $30-$45	Mick Taylor: $15-$25
Ron Wood: $20-$30	Ian Stewart: $20-$30
Darryl Jones: $12-$20	

TOUR BOOKS/PROGRAMS/PASSES

Programs: See chart
1990s Backstage Passes:
1990's Backstage Passes:
Steel Wheels, cloth: $15-$20, laminates: $35-$40
Urban Jungle, cloth: $15-$17, laminates: $25-$35
Voodoo Lounge, cloth: $12, laminates: $25-$30

POSTERS/PRESS KITS

See chart

USED CLOTHING/EQUIPMENT

Clothes:
Keith Richards hat: $900-$1,750
Keith Richards belt: $500-$1,000
Keith Richards blazer: $4,000-$5,000
Keith Richards suit: $1,500-$2,500
Mick Jagger jacket: $4,500-$6,500
Mick Jagger suit: $1,300-$3,000

Guitar Picks:

Keith Richards: $50-$75	Ron Wood: $50-$60
Bill Wyman: $50-$65	Brain Jones: $350-$550
Mick Taylor: $30-$40	Mick Jagger: $50-$65
Darryl Jones: $25-$30	

*The Rolling Stones are notorious for creative guitar pick quotes. Here's a sample: "Billy Wymold/The Roly Stokers," "Woody's Pecker/Enorum," "Zip Mouth Jagger/At The Vodoo Lounge," "The Biff Hitler Trio/(blank)," "Lord Richards/Thru and Thru," "Not Bill Wyman/Munch" and "Talk is Cheap/Touring Ain't."

Drum Stick:
Charlie Watts: $45-$60
Original bass drumskin, 1960s with group's name hand-painted: $10,000

OFTEN OVERLOOKED MEMORABILIA

Voodoo Lounge Flight Jacket - $100; Slide on Live (R. Wood) Zippo Lighter - $50; The Rolling Stones Fan Club Pack (reprint) - $15-$20; 1960s felt pennant - $75-$120; Hooded promo poncho - $12; Stripped promo postcard - $7; Urban Jungle European postcard - $7; Voodoo Lounge promo button - $5-$7; Voodoo Lounge promo matches - $10-$12; Voodoo Lounge lightbox promo piece - $230-$250; Voodoo Lounge European foldout - $15; Bill Wyman Monkey Grip display box - $100-$125; movie poster - T.A.M.I. - $200-$250; High Tides and Green Grass - alternate cover, rare (script title and artist) - $4,000-$6,000; Satanic Majesties, 3-D promo flasher (14.25" x 14.25") - $750-$1,000; Let It Bleed in-store promo stand-up - $200-$250; tongue stick pin (circa '72) - $25-$35; tongue key

Trinkets from the World's Greatest Rock Band including buttons, match books, 3-D glasses, and an air freshener

cardboard stand-up - $55-$75; Free Jack watch - $75-$100; Free Jack promo poster - $25-$35; postcard At the IMAX - $10-$15; metal lapel pin skull (Richard) - $20-$25; She's the Boss promo alarm clock, 1985; Primitive Cool Columbia promo magic mug (changes color), 1987 - $55.

REFERENCES/BOOKS

Hundreds of reference books exist about the band; Numerous resources exist, but every Rolling Stone collector has two must purchases: *Heart of Stone: The Definitive Rolling Stones Discography* by Felix Aeppli and *The Rolling Stones Album: 30 Years of Music and Memorabilia*. Beggar's Banquet, P.O. Box 6152, New York, NY 10128 is also a MUST publication! Also, *Keith Richards: The Biography* by Victor Bockris is a good place to begin research.

ASSORTED AND SELECTED MEMORABILIA
Period I: 1963-1970 "The Decca Records Years"

Advertisements: Newspaper and Periodical; Fan Club official membership card, lapel pin button, and photograph; Christmas cards; Unofficial Postage Stamps
Displays: Decca, concertina-style shop-counter display, promotes (5) singles
Magazines: *The Rolling Stones Book* (30) issues to a complete set, (6/64-11/66)
Mobile: hanging, U.K., featuring 12 albums, 5 individual hanging photos
Music Books: Photoramas/Foldbook, super glossy pictures
Press Kits: Gimme Shelter (two color, orange/black), 20th Century-Fox: $100-$125
Puzzle: jigsaw Puzzle, 350 pieces, approximate size: 17" x 11"
Trading cards: $500-$600
Songsheets: issued 1963-1969, Mirage Music Ltd.

Phase II: 1971-1985 "Sucking in the Seventies"
Recording Specific

Sticky Fingers (April 1971)
Promotional Posters: U.K. $500-$600

Exile on Main Street (May 1972)
Promotional Posters: $200-$250
Press Kit: $100
Other Items: Set of (12) postcards, undetached, album insert

Goat's Head Soup (August 1973)
Promotional Posters: $175-$200
Press Kit: $70-$75
Other Items: Goat's Head, flat insert: $10-$15

It's Only Rock 'n' Roll (October 1974)
Promotional Posters: $150-$175
Press Kit: $50-$65

Made in the Shade (June 1975)
Promotional Posters: $125-$150
Press Kit: $40-$55
Counter Display: w/ Foil Flat Poster, 21" x 22": $95-$125

chain (circa '72) - $20-$25; movie poster, Ladies & Gentlemen - $125-$150; Let's Spend the Night Together press kit - $50-$75; '81 U.S. tour posters - $10-$25; Let's Spend the Night Together poster $65-$85; Let's Spend the Night Together movie program - $30-$35; photo stickers (Musidor) - $8-$10; rub off transfers (27) tongues - $8-$10; butane lighter (Feudor) - $15-$20; napkin pack w/logo - $15; Chew-Bops mini LP covers (gum) - $5; Just Another Night (Jagger) clock - $75-$100; Willie/Poor Boys motorized counter display - $125-$150; acrylic display Harlem Shuffle (8" x 8") - $50-$75; trophy Ruthless People (7" - The Big Screw) - $85-$115; poster (ABKO) Stones CDs - $35-$45; poster, Hail! (Richards) - $25-$35; Urban Jungle

A package of 27 rub-off tongues

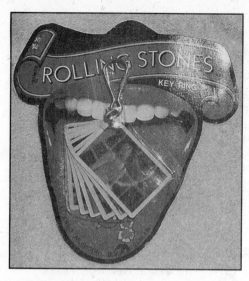

*A Rolling
Stones key ring
(© 1983)*

Tattoo You (October 1981)
Promotional Posters: $30-$40
Press Kit: $25-$45
Other Items: key ring - $15-$20; metal pin - $15-$20

Undercover (November 1983)
Promotional Posters: $45-$50

Non-Recording Specific: Car Deodorant, logo - $10-$12; Fan Club (1983) complete membership kit, card, postcards and 7" record - $45-$55; jigsaw puzzle, "The Shmuzzle Puzzle," 168 pieces - $20-$50; key ring - (Still being sold) - $10-$12; pinball machine, Bally, circa 1982 - $5,000-$6,000; telephone, Tristar, #1040, tongue shaped telephone - $150-$175; watch, Quartz Precision, Tristar, #6002, "Time is on my side" - $65-$85

Black and Blue (April 1976)
Promotional Posters (Controversial): $100 -$125
Press Kit: $40-$60

Love You Live (September 1977)
Promotional Posters: $125-$150
Press Kit: $35-$55
Other Items: promotional "Chattering Teeth" - $75-$100; promotional stickers, handed out at launch party

Some Girls (June 1978)
Promotional Posters: $65-$85 (sm.), $95-$115 (lg.)
Press Kit: $30-$50
Other Items: Buttons (2) - $12-$15

Emotional Rescue (June 1980)
Promotional Posters: (Three styles)
Press Kit: $25-$45
Other Items: poster, insert; metal buttons - $5-$7; plastic buttons - $10-$15

*Various pieces of Rolling
Stones memorabilia
including the Voodoo
Lounge CD ROM*

*More items from the Stones
including the tongue-shaped
telephone*

Phase III: 1986-1992 "Mixed Emotions"
Recording Specific

Steel Wheels (August 1989)
Other Items: Tongue CD counter display: $8-$10; floor display: $75-$100

Flashpoint (April 1991)
Other Items: matches - $12-$15; sparklers - $25-$35; Zippo lighter - $75-$100; metal badge - $65-$110

Non-recording Specific
At the Max, press kit, includes badge, clothing, etc. $30-$50; Rolling Stone 3-D glasses - $6-$10; Rolling Stones popcorn (7- Eleven, Fox) - $15-$20

Voodoo Lounge Miscellaneous Items: promotional postcard - $8-$10; keychain viewers (5) - $35 (set); postcard CD-ROM promo - $8-$10; match box (Brazil) - $35-$50; matches - $10-$12; keychain "spiky tongue" - $15; pins/pendant, various - $15; button (metal) - $6; window decal - $10-$15; counter display - $35-$55; cardboard stage display w/bulb - $200-$250; die-cut metal sign (Budweiser) (30" x 19") - $125-$150; neon sign - $275-$350

Rock and Roll Circus Items (Dec. 11, 1968): plastic popcorn tub - $30; plastic cup - $15-$25; movie ticket (special screening) - $20-$25; promo stand-up (3' x 4') - $45-$55

SELECTED TELEVISION AND FILM APPEARANCES

Television

7/7/63:	*Thank Your Lucky Stars* - TV debut on ITV, perform "Come On"
8/28/63:	*Ready Steady, Go!*
1/2/64:	*Top of the Pops* - BBC-TV, first edition of program, perform "I Wanna Be Your Man"
6/13/64:	*The Hollywood Palace* - ABC-TV, perform "I Just Wanna Make Love to You"
7/4/64:	*Juke Box Jury* - BBC-TV, five panelists
10/25/64:	*The Ed Sullivan Show* - CBS-TV
10/28-29/64:	*TAMI Show*
1/20/65:	*Shindig* - ABC-TV
4/9/65:	*Ready Steady Goes Live!* - ITV
5/2/65:	*The Ed Sullivan Show* - CBS-TV, The band performs while in the midst of their North American Tour. They also appear on "Hollywood A Go-Go" and "Shindig."
9/10/65:	*Ready Steady, Go!* - ITV, entire show devoted to the band
11/15/65:	*Hullabaloo* - NBC-TV
10/7/66:	*Ready Steady, Go!* - ITV, the band's final appearance. Jagger appears on 12/23 show.
1/15/67:	*The Ed Sullivan Show* - CBS-TV, the now legendary "Let's Spend Some Time Together" appearance.
1/22/67:	*Sunday Night at the London Palladium* - ITV, only appearance ever
6/25/67:	*All You Need Is Love* - The Beatles, Jagger, and Richard appear
12/11-12/68:	*Rock and Roll Circus*, television show never transmitted. All-star lineup!
9/20/77:	*The Old Grey Whistle Test* - BBC2-TV airs 1976 Paris concert
10/7/78:	*Saturday Night Live* - NBC-TV
1/14/83:	*Faerie Tale Theatre* series - Showtime TV, Jagger appears in "The Nightingale"
10/28/83:	*The Tube* - C4-TV, Jagger appears as guest
10/8/88:	*Saturday Night Live* -NBC-TV, Richards makes appearance
6/2/89:	*Wogan* - BBC1-TV - Bill Wyman and new bride appear on chat show
9/6/89:	*MTV Music Awards*, Stones appear live via satellite from Pittsburgh, PA
2/6/93:	*Saturday Night Live* -NBC-TV, Jagger makes guest appearance
2/6/93:	*In Concert* -ABC-TV, Jagger showcases in tapped appearance
9/8/94:	*MTV Music Awards* - MTV, band performs live at New York's Radio City Music Hall
11/13/94:	*60 Minutes*, the band is interviewed by Ed Bradley
12/7/94:	*Billboard Music Awards*, band plays via satellite from Montreal

Film

9/9/67:	*We Love You* promotional film, banned by the BBC
7/5/69:	*The Stones in the Park*, Mick Taylor debut at free concert in Hyde Park, London
9/69:	*Sympathy for the Devil* - Jean-Luc Goddard's impressionistic film
3/11/70:	*One Plus One* - band documentary opens in U.S.
7/28/70:	*Ned Kelly* premieres in Australia. Cast includes Mick Jagger.
8/1/70:	*Performance* premieres after two years of delays. Cast includes Mick Jagger.
12/6/70:	*Gimme Shelter* concert film opens in New York and documents the 1969 tour
4/6/76:	*Ladies and Gentleman: The Rolling Stones* opens in New York
3/24/83:	*Let's Spend the Night Together* premieres in New York
10/16/86:	*Hail! Hail! Rock 'n' Roll*, Richards makes appearance
4/20/91:	*Free Jack* begins filming in Atlanta and includes Mick Jagger
10/25/91:	*At the Max* film documentary from the last world tour opens at selected North American theaters

****
"On The Edge"

Henry Rollins

The former Black Flag singer screams like a fifth grade gym teacher suffering from mad cow disease. The Marky Mark of the testosterone-infested low self-esteemed burger flipping generation has taken his sweet, or should I say sweat, time getting to a point where he can finally carry his *Weight* (Imago, 1994). The Rollins Band now spews venomous chords over Hank's self-injected croons like Tabasco sauce over a hot tamale. While pre-1990 Rollins relics may not be worthy of unearthing, the Rollins band is at least worth some excavation. Bring a shovel!

REFERENCES/BOOKS

Get in the Van: On the Road with Black Flag by Henry Rollins is a MUST purchase!

****

The Romantics

Formed 1977

Wally Palmar, Mike Skill, Richard Cole, and Jimmy Marinos*

*Skill departed in 1981 and was replaced by Cos Canter. Marinos left in 1983 and David Patratos was added. Skill returned in 1985. Patratos left in 1989 and Clem Burke joined the band.

Eighties Midwest puffy hair power-pop band the Romantics was rooted in an English sound, although they were from Detroit. The group is typically identified with the songs "Talking in Your Sleep" (#3, 1983) and "What I Like About You" (#49, 1980), which has endured through numerous advertising campaigns. The band hit its commercial peak with the album *In Heat* (#14, 1983), which had a more pop flair than previous releases. During the same year Marinos, who sang lead on "What I Like About You," departed.

AUTOGRAPHS

A CD, LP, magazine cover, ad, photo, or card signed by the group: $15-$30

OFTEN OVERLOOKED MEMORABILIA

Videotapes of commercials using the band's compositions

Romeo Void

Formed 1979

Debora Iyall, Frank Zincavage, Peter Woods, Jay Derrah, and Ben Bossi*

*Derrah left in 1980 and John Stench was added on drums. Stench left the following year and Larry Carter was added.

This '80s Bay Area ecclectic post-punk dance act is commonly associated with the songs "Never Say Never" and "A Girl in Trouble (Is a Temporary Thing)" (#5, 1984). Romeo Void became null and void in 1985, and Debora Iyall went on to release a solo album. The band re-formed in 1993.

AUTOGRAPHS

A CD, LP, magazine cover, ad, photo, or card signed by the group: $10

OFTEN OVERLOOKED MEMORABILIA

Iyall's published literary work, poems, short stories, etc.

The Ronettes/Ronnie Spector

Formed 1959

Veronica Bennett (Ronnie Spector), Born: August 10, 1943; Estelle Bennett, Born: July 22, 1944; and Nedra Talley, Born: January 27, 1946

Traditional mid-60s girl group and Phil Spector's most accomplished act, the Ronettes consisted of the two Bennett sisters and their cousin Talley, who sang first together as the Darling Sisters, followed by Ronnie and the Relatives, and then the Ronnettes. Spector signed the group to his Phillies label in 1963 where the group performed background vocals before releasing hits such as "Be My Baby" (#2, 1963), "Baby I Love You" (#24, 1963), "Walking in the Rain" (#23, 1964), and "Do I Love You." Spector married Ronnie Bennett in 1966 when the group was near breaking up. The couple divorced in 1974, and Ronnie Spector pursued a solo career during the '70s. Spector was pushed back into the spotlight in 1986 when her duet with rocker Eddie Money, "Take Me Home Tonight" (#4, 1986), became a big hit, accompanied by its heavily played promotional video. During the '80s she also performed in the "legendary ladies of rock" with Martha Reeves, Lesley Gore, Mary Wilson, and others.

AUTOGRAPHS

A CD, LP, magazine cover, ad, photo, or card signed by the group: $25-$50

OFTEN OVERLOOKED MEMORABILIA

Associated memorabilia from other artists' covers of their material; a copy of Ronnie Spector's autobiography *Be My Baby*

REFERENCES/BOOKS

Limited resources exist, but none do justice to the group in my opinion. There are no dedicated collector books.

Ronson, Mick

(1946-1993)

Early-70s power guitarist Mick Ronson was in Bowie's Spiders from Mars, before launching an unsuccessful solo career and joining one of the later Mott the Hoople lineups. Mick Ronson also played in the Hunter-Ronson Band, Bob Dylan's Rolling Thunder Revue, and produced numerous records. He was told he had liver cancer in 1991 and died in 1993.

AUTOGRAPHS

A CD, LP, magazine cover, ad, photo, or card signed by the artist: $10-$25

OFTEN OVERLOOKED MEMORABILIA

Associated memorabilia from his numerous contributions to other artists' works

Ronstadt, Linda

Born: July 15, 1946

The Stone Poneys, consisting of Linda Ronstadt (Three Ronstadts, the New Union Ramblers, Kimmel Brothers), Bob Kimmel (Kimmel Brothers), and Kenny Edwards (Kimmel Brothers), performed regularly in 1965 at the Troubadour Club in L.A. They were spotted by Promoter Herb Cohen, who soon managed the act. In 1966 Cohen managed to bring them to the attention of Capitol Records, which signed the act to a recording contract.

The Stone Poneys was released in 1964, but failed to garner anticipated attention. It was not until *Evergreen, Volume 2* (#100, 1968), with extracted single "Different Drum" (#13, 1968) penned by Monkee Mike Nesmith, that the group gained any momentum. It supported the album by touring with the Doors assisted by session musicians (Edwards had departed from the band). "Up to My Neck in High Muddy Water" (#93, 1968) was the next single taken from the album and Ronstadt soon found herself as a solo artist.

Hand Sown, Home Grown, her debut solo album, was followed by *Silk Purse* (#103, 1970), which included hit "Long Long Time" (#25, 1970). In April 1971 she recruited Bernie Leadon, Glenn Frey, Randy Meisner, and Don Henley, who eventually become the Eagles, as her tour band. In March 1972 *Linda Ronstadt* (#163, 1972) was released and included single "Rock Me on the Water" (#85, 1972). She also spent time contributing vocals to Neil Young's *Harvest* album. Heavily in debt, her next project *Don't*

Cry Now (#45, 1973) floundered until Peter Asher (Peter & Gordon) took over the management reins and delivered the final product. Extracted Eric Katz penned "Love Has No Pride" (#51, 1974) helped drive album sales. Meanwhile Capitol spun out the Stone Poney/Ronstadt compilation *Different Drum* (#92, 1974).

The Asher/Ronstadt combination, with a song recipe that included new material mixed with covers of older hits accompanied by a superb recording ethic, turned out *Heart Like a Wheel* (#1, 1975). The album included hits "You're No Good" (#1, 1975), "When Will I Be Loved" (#2, 1975), "I Can't Help It If I'm Still in Love With You" (#2, Country, 1975), and "It Doesn't Matter Anymore" (#47, 1975). Her refined recording was accompanied by an upgraded personal image, which created a greater stage presence and a bit more sex appeal with her new fans. She certainly turned a few heads when she wore a cub scout outfit on September 20, 1977, at the Universal Amphitheater in California.

Prisoner in Disguise (#4, 1975) followed and featured a strong studio lineup including Andrew Gold, Kenny Edwards, and Russ Kunkel and the extracted singles "Heat Wave/Love Is a Rose" (#5, 1975) and "The Tracks of My Tears" (#25, 1976). The singles were brilliantly marketed and positioned Ronstadt well for future releases. *Hasten Down the Wind* (#3, 1976) showcased the songwriting of Karla Bonoff on three tracks including "Someone to Lay Down Beside Me" (#42, 1977). Ronstadt's Buddy Holly cover of "That'll Be the Day" (#11, 1976) continued her string of cover hits.

Enjoying worldwide success, *Greatest Hits* (#6, 1977) (an Asylum/Capitol compilation), bought some time for her to work on other projects including albums by Andrew Gold and Karla Bonoff. *Simple Dreams* (#1, 1977), with hits "Blue Bayou" (#3, 1977) and "Poor, Poor Pitiful Me" (#31, 1978), now found the artist at the height of her career, and *Living in the U.S.A.* (#1, 1978) solidified her position there. She became increasingly visible as a star and even shared the cover of *Time* magazine with California governor Jerry Brown, whom she was romantically linked to.

When the music scene around her began to change, Ronstadt released the harder-edged *Mad Love* (#3, 1980), backed by the Cretones. Extracted single "How Do I Make You" (#3, 1980) climbed into the Top Five, while critics were mixed in their opinions regarding her derivation in styles. Ronstadt also made her acting debut as Mabel in the New York Shakespeare Festival's production of *The Pirates of Penzance*. She followed the play into film production, and even tried a bit of opera in *La Boheme*.

Get Closer (#31, 1982), her least successful release of new material in a decade, included numerous guest vocalists, but often appeared fragmented. Ronstadt, whether coerced, disappointed by the criticism, or simply bored, decided to plunge into the "adult contemporary" market. Lavishly orchestrated

releases followed: *What's New* (#3, 1983), *Lush Life* (#13, 1984), and *Sentimental Reasons* (#46, 1986) arranged by veteran Nelson Riddle. Each sold less than their predecessors.

"Somewhere Out There" (#2, 1987), a ballad duet with James Ingram from the film *An American Tail*, rebounded her into the Top Ten U.S. singles. Ronstadt, the daughter of Mexican/German parents, then reached back to her roots and released Canciones De Mi Padre (#42, 1988), made up of thirteen traditional Mexican songs sung in Spanish in tribute to her father.

Trio (#6, 1988), a Ronstadt, Emmylou Harris, Dolly Parton collaboration, landed her another Grammy Award. She began work on *Cry Like a Rainstorm, Howl Like the Wind* (#7, 1989). The album contained hits "I Don't Know Much" (#2, 1989), a duet with Aaron Neville, and "All My Life" (#11, 1990). Ronstadt, then reverted back for two more Spanish-language albums, *Mas Canciones* (#88, 1992) and *Frensi* (#193, 1992). The mediocre sales of these albums contributed significantly to both her fall in popularity and her dissipating sales momentum.

Winter Light (#92, 1993) was a return to English, but a disappointment commercially. *Feels Like Home* (#75, 1995) was a bit better, but didn't have the strength to catapult her into the top chart ranks. In 1996 Ronstadt released *Dedicated to the One I Love* (#78, 1996), another indication of her struggling career and lack of direction. Whether she can get her ship back on course remains to be seen. If she doesn't, it certainly has nothing to do with lack of talent!

As a collecting subject, her diverse range of abilities and musical mix make her interesting to collect. She has had an enormous impact during her four decade career on furthering many musicians' careers and has also returned interest to the nostalgic songs of the past.

AUTOGRAPHS

Linda Ronstadt is somewhat apprehensive when people approach her for autographs. Once she realizes your autograph request is sincere, she typically obliges.

A CD, LP, magazine cover, ad, photo, or card signed by the artist: $30-$45

TOUR BOOKS/PROGRAMS/PASSES

Programs:
Summer Tour, 1977: $40
1988 Tour: $15-$17
Cry Like a Rainstorm Tour: $15
Mad Love Tour, 1980: $25

Backstage Passes:
Cloth: $8-$10; Laminated: $12-$15 (1990 to present)
Cloth: $10-$12; Laminated: $15-$20 (1982-1990)
Cloth/paper: $12-$15; Laminated: $20-$30 (1981-1969)

POSTERS/PRESS KITS

Promotional Posters:
$10 (1990 to present)
$10-$12 (1982-1990)
$15-$35 (1981-1969)

Press Kits:
$10 (1990 to present)
$10-$15 (1982-1990)
$15-$50 (1981-1969)

OFTEN OVERLOOKED MEMORABILIA

Memorabilia from Game 1 of the 1977 World Series between the Los Angeles Dodgers and the New York Yankees (Ronstadt sang "The Star Spangled Banner"); a copy of Mr. Blackwell's list of "Worst Dressed Women of 1978" (one of the few charts she didn't top that year) $5; movie memorabilia from *FM* (Ronstadt contributes "Tumbling Dice" and "Love Me Tender"—all Ronstadt collectors must have the DJ-spliced version with Elvis also), *The Pirates of Penzance* (1983), *Hail! Hail! Rock 'n' Roll* (1986), *An American Tail*, and *The Mambo Kings* (1992); a copy of *Rolling Stone* magazine (12/2/76); all memorabilia associated with her numerous contributions to albums by Neil Young, Karla Bonoff, Nicolette Larson, Andrew Gold, Emmylou Harris, Warren Zevon, Phillip Glass, Paul Simon, Frank Sinatra, and many others; newspaper clippings and tabloid accounts of romping with California Governor Jerry Brown; all politically-related fund raising memorabilia; a playbill and soundtrack (1981) from *The Pirates of Penzance* (1980/1981); memorabilia from her operatic debut in *La Boheme* (1984); memorabilia associated with *Kermit Unplugged* (1994) (Ronstadt dueted with the popular green amphibian); movie memorabilia associated with Disney's newly-released *Cinderella* (1995) (Ronstadt contributed); items associated with "The NAPA Presents a Concert Behind Prison Walls" (1978), posters, displays, etc.; *Don't Know Much* Elektra promotional dictionary, 1989, both U.S. and U.K. versions; bookcover - $6

REFERENCES/BOOKS

Limited resources exist, but none do justice to the singer in my opinion. There are no dedicated collector books.

Ross, Diana

Born: March 26, 1944

Former lead vocalist of the Supremes, one of the most successful trios in music history, Diana Ross made her solo stage debut on March 8, 1970, in Framingham, Massachusetts. Her departure from the trio was carefully calculated and crafted, often attributed to Motown president Berry Gordy, Jr. Her initial solo efforts were produced by the talented Nick Ashford and Valerie Simpson.

"Reach Out and Touch (Somebody's Hand)" (#20, 1970) was her first solo single, followed by "Ain't No Mountain High Enough" (#1, 1970). Both were extracted from her solo album *Diana Ross* (#19, 1970). It was followed by *Everything Is Everything* (#42, 1971) with single "Remember Me" (#16, 1971). *Diana* (#46, 1971), a television soundtrack from her special, allowed her enough time to concentrate on preparations for her role of Billie Holiday in *Lady Sings the Blues* (Motown Films, 1972).

Surrender (#56, 1971), was followed by the soundtrack to *Lady Sings the Blues* (#1, 1973) with single "Good Morning Heartache" (#34, 1973). Her next two solo* albums both included Top Twenty title songs "Touch Me in the Morning" (#5, 1973) and "Last Time I Saw Him" (#52, 1974). The soundtrack album for her movie *Mahogany* (#19, 1975) included the hit "Do You Know Where You're Going To" (#1, 1976), which in retrospect was actually the best component of the effort—the movie fell short of expectations.

Diana Ross (#5, 1976) was highlighted by the inclusion of smash hit "Love Hangover" (#1, 1976). It preceded *An Evening with Diana Ross* (#29, 1977), also a television special, and gave Ross time to star as Dorothy in *The Wiz*. Unfortunately for the star, who was criticized for her age, the movie was a critical and commercial failure.

Baby, It's Me (#18, 1977) and *The Boss* (#14, 1979) slowly built back her momentum, and when *Diana* (#2, 1980) hits she was back on top. The album included "Upside Down" (#1, 1980) and "I'm Coming Out" (#5, 1980). The following year she recorded "Endless Love" (#1, 1981), a duet with Lionel Ritchie, her last Motown hit.

Why Do Fools Fall in Love (#15, 1981), her debut RCA offering, yielded the self-titled cover hit (#7,1981) and "Mirror, Mirror" (#8, 1982). *Silk Electric* (#27, 1982) came next and included the Michael Jackson-penned single "Muscles" (#10, 1982). *Ross* (#32, 1983), *Swept Away* (#26, 1984), *Eaten Alive* (#45, 1985), and *Red Hot Rhythm and Blues* (#73, 1987) were successful in producing some hits, but didn't meet the expectations of everyone involved.

In 1989 she left RCA and returned to Motown and released *Workin' Overtime* (#116, 1989) on her newly-formed Ross Records. Although her concerts were well attended and the publicity surrounding her return was brisk, the album failed to chart on the Top One Hundred. *The Force Behind the Power* (#102, 1991) and *Take Me Higher* (#114, 1995) also failed to live up to expectations and fueled new rumors and ignited old ones regarding Ross's ability to handle her own career.

If she has indeed run her course, so be it, but her stature among her fans remains undiminished. As one of the top entertainers of all-time, she has nothing left to prove anyway! As a collecting subject, she is a must, especially her early Motown years.

*She recorded an album of duets with Marvin Gaye in 1973.

AUTOGRAPHS

A CD, LP, magazine cover, ad, photo, or card signed by the artist: $50-$60

TOUR BOOKS/PROGRAMS/PASSES

Programs:

Always Is Forever (U.K.): $20
Timepiece Tour: $25
1985 Volume Two Tour: $25
The Force Behind the Power, 1991. $20

Backstage Passes:

Cloth: $8-$10; Laminated: $10-$15 (1989-Present)

POSTERS/PRESS KITS

Promotional posters: $10-$25, Examples: Take Me Higher (16" x 24") - $10; Ultimate Collection (20" x 30") - $18

Press Kits: $15-$20 (1989-Present)

OFTEN OVERLOOKED MEMORABILIA

Movie memorabilia from *Lady Sings the Blues* (1972), *Mahogany* (1975), *The Wiz* (1977), *Endless Love* (1981), and *The Land Before Time* (1988); television videotapes from her various performances; memorabilia from the 1982 Superbowl in Pontiac, Michigan (Ross sang the National Anthem); a videotape of the "Motown 25" - NBC-TV special (516/83) (the Supremes reunited); memorabilia, posters, newspaper articles surrounding her controversial free concert in New York's Central Park (7/22/83); copies of her television GAP commercials produced by Herb Ritts (1991); a copy of her statement to the House Select Committee on Children, Youth & Families on September 30, 1991; items associated with her opening of the annual Harrods' January sale in London (1992); a rubbing from her star on the Sidewalk of the Stars outside Radio City Music Hall - $5-$10; a copy of her performance on *Out of Darkness* - ABC-TV (1/16/94); memorabilia from the 1994 World Cup Match at Chicago's Soldier Field (Ross headlined pre-game festivities); items from her performance on December 10, 1994, to conclude an Amway convention at the Tokyo Dome, Japan; a videotape from Superbowl XXX (1/28/96) (Ross was the half-time entertainment); Workin' Overtime Motown promotional lunch box that included cassette, CD, video, and biography, 1989 - $55; Take Me Higher giant 3D display (42 " x 40") - $100; Take Me Higher promo postcards - $3-$5; dolls: (Ideal), 1969, 18" - $275-$300, (Mego), 1977, 12-3/4" - $100; For One & For All opera glasses - $25

REFERENCES/BOOKS

Numerous resources exist, but none do justice to the singer in my opinion. There are no dedicated collector books. Serious collectors should opt for a Fan Club: Reach Out International: Celebrating the Music That Is Diana Ross, Subscription Department, P.O. Box 4562, Portland, OR 97208 ($23 fee)

The Rossington-Collins Band

Formed 1979

Gary Rossington, Allen Collins, (1952-1990), Billy Powell, Leon Wilkeson, Barry Harwood, Derek Hess, and Dale Krantz

This '80s Jacksonville country-rock group, formed from four of the five surviving members of the Lynyrd Skynrd band, had its debut album sell gold, but following the second record, The Rossington-Collins band folded.

AUTOGRAPHS

A CD, LP, magazine cover, ad, photo, or card signed by the group: (See Lynyrd Skynrd)

TOUR BOOKS/PROGRAMS/PASSES

Backstage Passes:
Cloth: $10-$12; Laminated: $15

POSTERS/PRESS KITS

Promotional Posters: $12-$25

Roth, David Lee: See Van Halen

Roxette

Formed 1986

Marie Frederiksson, Born: May 30, 1958; and Per Gessle, Born: January12, 1959

Late-80s Swedish rock duo Roxette is typically associated with the songs "The Look" (#1), "Listen to Your Heart" (#1), "Dangerous" (#2), "It Must Have Been Love" (#1, 1990), "Joyride" (#1), and "Fading Like a Flower (Every Time You Leave)" (#2). The group took America by a storm in 1989 with an impress series of successful hits, but by its fourth album *Tourism* (#117, 1992), it failed to spin off a single and was rapidly fading from view in the U.S.

AUTOGRAPHS

A CD, LP, magazine cover, ad, photo, or card signed by the group: $10-$30

TOUR BOOKS/PROGRAMS/PASSES

Tour Books:
Join the Joyride, 1991: $20

POSTERS/PRESS KITS

Promotional Posters: $10-$15
Press Kits: $15-$25

Roxy Music

Formed 1971

Original lineup: Bryan Ferry, Born: September 26, 1945; Graham Simpson; Brain Eno, Born: May 15, 1948; Andy Mackay, Born: July 23, 1946; Dexter Lloyd; and Roger Bunn*

*Numerous personnel changes. Additional musicians have included: Paul Thompson, David O'List, Phil Manzanera, Rik Kenton, John Porter, Sal Maida, Eddie Jobson, John Gustafson, John Wetton, Rick Wills, Gary Tibbs, David Skinner, Paul Carrack, Alan Spenner, and Andy Newmark.

This '70s British creative synth group, whose crafted look and sound never really caught on in America, is typically associated with the songs "Virginia Plain," "Love Is the Drug" (#30, 1976), "Dance Away," "Angel Eyes," "More Than This," and "Jealous Guy." The band was extremely successful in England and was often cited as an influence to many acts who followed. Despite an enormous cult following, Roxy Music never found the worldwide commercial success it so richly deserved.

A scarce Roxy Music backstage pass

AUTOGRAPHS

A CD, LP, magazine cover, ad, photo, or card signed by the group: $35-$125*
*Original members

TOUR BOOKS/ PROGRAMS/ PASSES

Tour Programs:
Autumn '74 Tour, U.K.: $75

Backstage Passes:
Cloth/paper: $15-$20

REFERENCES/BOOKS

Limited resources exist. There are no dedicated collector books.

Royal Guardsmen

Formed mid-1960s

Billy Taylor, Barry Winslow, Chris Nunley, Tom Richards, Bill Balogh, and John Burdette

Late-60s novelty act, best remembered for the novelty hits "Snoopy vs. the Red Baron" (#2, 1966) and "The Return of the Red Baron" (#15, 1967), the Royal Guardsmen's subsequent dog-related tunes were shot down, ending the battle and their career.

AUTOGRAPHS

A CD, LP, magazine cover, ad, photo, or card signed by the group: $10-$20

OFTEN OVERLOOKED MEMORABILIA

Associated *Peanuts* memorabilia

Royal Teens

Formed 1956

Bob Gaudio, Joe Villa, Tom Austin, Bill Crandall and Bill Dalton. Additional musicians included Larry Qualaino, and Al Kooper

Late-50s New Jersey group the Royal Teens are best remembered for the innovative hit "Short Shorts" (#3, 1958). The group tried for a couple years to repeat its success but could not. Gaudio departed

for an enormously successful career with the Four Seasons, while Kooper found a home with the Blues Project and Blood, Sweat and Tears.

AUTOGRAPHS

A CD, LP, magazine cover, ad, photo, or card signed by the group: $25-$40

****

"On The Edge"

Royal Trux

Neil Hagerty (Pusy Galore) and Jennifer Herrema formed Royal Trux as a creative outlet, or should I say alternative rather than a permanent fixture—kinda like building a carport instead of a garage. *Twin Infinitives* (Drag City, 1990) and *Cats and Dogs* (Drag City, 1993) proved that even if you drive a BMW under a carport it can still look pretty damn good. Trux's major label debut was *Thank You* (Virgin, 1995), an impressive mix of Hagerty's riffs and Herrema's snips, it is an excellent place to begin your collecting. If this band continues to park impressive automobiles under the carport, it's going to be time to build a garage.

****

Ruffin, David: See the Temptations

Rufus: See Chaka Khan

The Rumour

Formed 1975

Rob Andrews, Stephen Goulding, Andrew Bodnar, Brinsley Schwarz, and Martin Belmont.

Late-70s English pub rockers the Rumour, best remembered as Graham Parker's backup band, have backed numerous musicians including Garland Jeffreys.

AUTOGRAPHS

A CD, LP, magazine cover, ad, photo, or card signed by the group: $10-$20

OFTEN OVERLOOKED MEMORABILIA

Associated memorabilia from their numerous contributions to other artists' works

The Runaways

Formed 1975

Joan Jett, Born: September 22, 1960; Sandy West; and Micki Steele*

*Steele departed in 1975 and Cherie Currie was added, along with Lita Ford and Jackie Fox. Fox and Currie left in 1977 and Vicki Blue joined the group.

Late-70s L.A. all-girl teen rockers, whose tough girl charm and blatantly sexual presentation garnered them an enormous cult following, the Runaways found their best audience in Japan. While the group gained its greatest exposure by opening for the Ramones in 1978, by New Year's Eve the same year, the group had played its last show.

Currie went on to a basically straight-to-video film career, while both Ford and Jett landed solid solo efforts. Steele later joined the Bangles.

AUTOGRAPHS

A CD, LP, magazine cover, ad, photo, or card signed by the group: $25-$50

Rundgren, Todd/Utopia

Born: June 22, 1948

Todd Rundgren, a proficient guitar player in high school, joined Woody's Truck Stop bandmate Carson Van Osten, Robert Stewkey Antoni, and Thom Mooney to form the Nazz, which made its live debut supporting the Doors in 1967. *Nazz* (#118, 1968) was the group's debut product on Screen Gems/Columbia subsidiary label SGC.

"Hello It's Me" (#71, 1969/#66, 1970, #5, 1973), the B-side of its first single "Open My Eyes," was released in March 1969, preceding the next album *Nazz Nazz* (#80, 1969). Following disagreements with Mooney, Rundgren left before the release of the album, but returned briefly for a promotional tour before finally being replaced by future Cheap Trick member Rick Nielsen.

Rundgren then moved on to become in-house producer at Albert Grossman's Bearsville Studios. He traded studio time in lieu of his production skills and cut *Runt* (#185, 1971), which included extracted hit single "We Gotta Get You a Woman" (#20, 1970). *The Ballad of Todd Rundgren*, his second solo effort, followed before Rundgren headed to the U.K. to finish production of Badfinger's *Straight Up*.

Something/Anything (#29, 1972) sold well and included single "I Saw the Light" (#16, 1972). *A Wizard, A True Star* (#86, 1973) was recorded at his own Secret Sounds Studio in New York and included twenty-six songs joined together in *Abbey Road* fashion. Rundgren then produced Grand Funk's million dollar

We're an American Band and watched single "Hello It's Me" chart for the third time.

His next effort, *Todd* (#54, 1974), a double album, was recorded half solo, half with a group. The album included popular ballad "A Dream Goes on Forever" (#69, 1974). Rundgren then reverted back to a group structure and formed Utopia. The debut album *Todd Rundgren's Utopia* (#34, 1974) showcased a new art-rock sound more conducive to the artist's creativity.

Initiation (1975), a new solo offering, preceded Utopia's live second album *Another Live* (#66, 1975), which included a variety of material including the Move's "Do Ya" and even a song from *West Side Story*. *Faithful* (#34, 1976) was Rundgren's next solo album. It included a side dedicated to '60s classics, of which a cover of the Beach Boys' "Good Vibrations"(#34, 1976) became his next hit single.

In 1977, Utopia's *Ra* (#79, 1977), an Egyptian-inspired release, featured a new line-up: Rundgren, Kasim Sultan, Roger Powell, and John Wilcox. *Oops! Wrong Planet* (#73, 1977) followed; it was shorter in its song format and was considered more "radio friendly." Included on the record was "Love Is The Answer," which later was a hit for England Dan and John Ford Coley. While the album moved on the chart, Rundgren entered the studio to produce Meat Loaf's *Bat Out of Hell*.

Hermit of Mink Hollow, a solo album effort featuring Rundgren playing all instruments, contained the hit single "Can We Still Be Friends"(#29, 1978). He quickly followed with *Back to the Bars* (#75, 1979), a live double-album that featured a variety of musicians including Hall & Oates, Stevie Nicks, and Spencer Davis. *Adventures in Utopia* (#32, 1980), conceived as a soundtrack, included extracted single "Set Me Free" (#27, 1980). The single "The Very Last Time" (#76, 1980) followed.

Deface the Music (#65, 1980) lived up to its title—it featured Beatlesque snippets written, recorded, and forgotten hastily. Rundgren's next solo offering, *Healing* (#48, 1981), was filled with religious undertones and a Rundgren classic "Time Heals." *Swing to the Right* (#102, 1982) and *Utopia* (#84, 1982, U.S. Network), which included Utopia's final single "Feet Don't Fail Me Now" (#82, 1983), ended an era for the artist.

The Ever Popular Tortured Artist Effect (#66, 1983), with extracted single "Bang the Drum All Day" (#63, 1983) was his last Bearsville offering and last solo hit single. After releasing *Utopia Oblivion* (#74, 1985), *P.O.V.*, and *Trivia*, the group disbanded. Rundgren, who released *A Cappella* (1985), a vocal-based album, *Nearly Human* (#102, 1989), and *2nd Wind* (#118, 1991), released the world's first conventional music CD, with interactive CD companion *No World Order* on Rhino's Forward label and Phillips' CD-1 system. The release was the first to signal the artist's next creative direction.

The Individualist, a multi-media CD, was released in September 1995. He supported the release with his own one-man show accompanying his Apple Mac.

AUTOGRAPHS

Todd Rundgren frequents numerous computer shows and can often be spotted walking the floors looking for his next new source of inspiration.
A CD, LP, magazine cover, ad, photo, or card signed by the artist: $20-$30

TOUR BOOKS/PROGRAMS/PASSES

1990s Backstage Passes:
Cloth: $5-$8; Laminated: $8-$10

POSTERS/PRESS KITS
Promotional posters: $10-$25

USED CLOTHING/EQUIPMENT
Guitar Picks: $10-$25

OFTEN OVERLOOKED MEMORABILIA

Flowflazer Mac software package invented by Rundgren (1990); videotapes from appearances on *Late Night With David Letterman* (7/17/86, 4/26/91); memorabilia from the musical *Up Against It*; Video Toaster multi-media studio - $4,000 (original price); a copy of his keynote address given at the 13th Annual Billboard Music Video Conference (11/6/91); any assorted CompuServe online chats with Rundgren.

Run-D.M.C.

Formed 1981

Run (Joseph Simmons), D.M.C. (Darryl McDaniels), and Jam Master Jay (Jason Mizell)

Native New Yorkers Simmons, McDaniels, and Mizell, formed the rap trio Run D.M.C. following their graduation from St. Pascal's Catholic School. Rejected by many labels, "It's Like That/Sucker M.C.'s" was released on Profile Records in the spring of 1983, and *Run D.M.C.* (#53, 1983), the group's debut album, was released in June. The group supported the record by touring in a package with L.L. Cool J. (7/83).

On December 17, 1984, *Run D.M.C.* became the first rap album to reach RIAA gold certification. The group's follow-up album *King of Rock* (#52, 1985), however, failed to extract a crossover hit. Also that year the group contributed to "Sun City" (#28, 1985) for the Artists Against Apartheid effort.

Raising Hell (#3, 1986) did exactly what it stated—it topped the U.S. R&B chart and became the first rap album to make the Top Ten in the U.S. Meanwhile the group enjoyed an enormous media presence appearing on *Saturday Night Live* and even co-rapped with the hostess on *The Late Show Starring Joan Rivers*. The band's update of Aerosmith's "Walk This Way" (#4, 1986) saturated MTV and even resurrected the career of the "Bad Boys from Boston."

"You Be Illin'" (#29, 1986) and "It's Tricky" (#57, 1987) solidified the group on the singles chart while

it prepared for its next major release *Tougher Than Leather* (#9, 1988). While the album reached the Top Ten, it failed to live up to expectations, and the film by the same name was a bomb. It was the group's first step toward decline, which also saw some band members treated for substance abuse. Personal problems, some of which were just too public, took a toll on the group's popularity. When a band this talented released a *Greatest Hits 1983-1991* package that failed to get beyond #199 on the album chart, it was very clear that something had gone terribly wrong.

In 1993 the group made a return with its Christian-themed seventh album *Down with the King* (#7, 1993). Additionally, Simmons, an ordained minister, released the first album on his new gospel label REV RUN, titled *REV RUN Presents*. With the group now back on track, we can certainly expect much more from rap's pivotal first major act.

If you are a music historian, collecting memorabilia from this group is a must. Despite the troubles the members have faced, they were instrumental in the development of rap as an accepted musical form. Should rap continue in its popularity, artifacts from its early years will become scarcer with each passing year. Simply put, "they're not going to get any cheaper than they are now."

AUTOGRAPHS

The group has come to the aid of many causes and has always tried to be accessible to its fans.

Group:
A CD, LP, magazine cover, ad, photo, or card signed by the entire band: $30-$50

Individual:
Jason Mizell: $10-$20
Joseph Simmons: $10-$20
Darryl McDaniels: $10-$20

TOUR BOOKS/PROGRAMS/PASSES

Backstage Passes:
Cloth: $8-$10; Laminated: $12-$15

POSTERS/PRESS KITS

Promotional Posters: $15-$25
Press Kits: $20-$30 (Pre-1988), $10-$15 (1988-Present)

OFTEN OVERLOOKED MEMORABILIA

Memorabilia from the first rap movie *Krush Groove*, and movie memorabilia from *Ghostbusters II* and *Tougher Than Leather*, and promotional items from *The Beavis and Butt-Head Experience* (1993) (the group contributed "Bounce"); all items associated with the group's Adidas promotions.

RuPaul

(RuPaul Andre Charles)
Born: November 17, 1960

In the age of Dennis Rodman, "hair cams," Elvis sightings, control top pantyhose, and cyber sex, why not RuPaul? The tall, shapely, neo-disco, new age drag queen has shown all of us that with a lot of talent, and of course a pair of heels, you can have it all.

Familiar to everyone in Atlanta's night life in the early '80s, RuPaul was performing in various cabarets as a comedy act and with a rock group (RuPaul and the U-Hauls). He crossed the Mason-Dixon line on the way to New York in the latter half of the decade. It was the glitter of the Big Apple, with its fashion conscience and no-holds-barred night life, that really brought out her personality—I bet you thought I was going to say out of the closet—to the public's attention. RuPaul signed with Tommy Boy and released *Supermodel of the World*, with extracted hit single "Supermodel (You Better Work)" (#45, 1993). The song became a staple on video channels and in dance clubs.

Soon a regular on the talk-show circuit, RuPaul became a media favorite and popular with the public. In 1993 the singer recorded a duet with Elton John for his *Duets* album and contributed to numerous projects including the cable television special "RuPaul's Christmas Ball."

In 1995 the artist became the first cross-dresser to land a promotional contract with a major cosmetics company. With popularity soaring, VH-1 offered RuPaul his very own show, which was graciously accepted. Just when you think RuPaul can't get any better, he does. Grab all the memorabilia you can find now, because it looks like this artist is on a roll. You just go girl!

AUTOGRAPHS

A CD, LP, magazine cover, ad, photo, or card signed by the artist: $15-$25

TOUR BOOKS/PROGRAMS/PASSES

Backstage Passes:
Cloth: $8-$10; Laminated: $12-$15

POSTERS/PRESS KITS

Promotional Posters: $10-$25
Press Kits: $10-$15

OFTEN OVERLOOKED MEMORABILIA

Videotapes from all RuPaul's VH-1 shows; movie memorabilia from *The Addams Family Values* and *Crooklyn*; all associated cosmetics marketing items, posters, displays, etc.

REFERENCES/BOOKS

Lettin It All Hang Out by RuPaul (1995, Hyperion)

Rush

Formed 1969

Alex Lifeson (Alex Zivojinovich), Born: August 27, 1953; Geddy Lee (Gary Lee Weinrib), Born: July 23, 1953; and John Rutsey*

*Rutsey left in 1974 and was replaced by Neil Peart, Born: September 12, 1952

Various configurations of the band took place prior to 1971 when the band became regulars at the Abbey Road Pub in downtown Toronto, Canada. Lee (Rush, Ogilvie, Judd) had even been kicked out of the band at one point (1969). The group's first professional recording was done at Eastern Sound Studios in Toronto in 1973, which led to a single (Moon Records) and eventually an album in January 1974 (*Rush*). The strength of its Canadian album sales and slow but consistent growth in America, eventually led to a contract with Mercury Records.

The band had initially been scoffed at due to Lee's high-pitched vocals and the band's complex and lengthy song arrangements, which were often epic in comparison to what most successful acts were offering. Never an airplay favorite, Rush's early live performances, diligent touring, and commitment to its music gradually enabled the band to build a strong foundation first with Canadian listeners. The current lineup was formed on July 29, 1974, when Peart was added. *Fly By Night* was released in early 1975, and by this point, the band had gained considerable attention from opening for acts such as Kiss and Aerosmith. *Caress of Steel* followed but was met with a lukewarm response.

The band managed to turn things around with its fourth album *2112* (#61, 1976) and *All the World's a Stage*. By the release of *Permanent Waves* (#4, 1980), the trio's popularity had skyrocketed and the recipe was just right. Rush has always impressed its critics by forging in different directions musically without harming its musical foundation. *Signals* (#10, 1982) did much to refine the group's sound and provided a crisper, less strained, vocal line. It even spun off the single "New World Man" (#21, 1982). The end of the decade found the group, which was notorious for heavy touring, finally scaling back a bit. The group's next five albums were all successful and reached gold or platinum status. *Counterparts* (#2, 1993) was a fresh breath for the band and a return to an earlier sound. Once again Rush took a right turn when it had to!

Rush has never been overly marketed to its fans, and as such, it chose to skip the "ashtray and keychain" approach and concentrate on the music. Early tickets, handbills, and programs, especially during the "opening act era" for Kiss and Aerosmith, are often overlooked by Rush fans. Unfortunately, while playing on the same bill with these metal giants probably increased the likelihood that these items survived, it won't do anything to reduce the price.

AUTOGRAPHS

The band has always been responsive, and when possible, accessible to its fans.

Geddy Lee is also an avid sporting fan. Time permitting, he can be found at baseball spring training in Florida, or even at an NHL game.

Neil Peart has been active in his craft, working with *Modern Drummer* magazine, or putting on a clinic.

Alex Lifeson is a pilot, so you may just catch him sometime at his home airfield.

Group:
A CD, LP, magazine cover, ad, photo, or card signed by the entire band: $175-$250
Individual:
Alex Lifeson: $50-$65
Geddy Lee: $50-$65
Neil Peart: $50-$65

1991-1992 tour program (© 1991 Anthem Enterprises)

A few Rush backstage passes (Printed by OTTO)

TOUR BOOKS/ PROGRAMS/PASSES
Programs:
Roll the Bones: $15
Backstage Passes:
Cloth: $8-$15;
Laminated: $12-$25

POSTERS/PRESS KITS
Promotional Posters:
$10-$30, the high-end being primarily Canadian. For Example: Moving Pictures Canadian promo poster (24" x 38") - $30
Press Kits: $18-$40

USED CLOTHING/ EQUIPMENT
Guitar Picks:
Alex Lifeson: $20-$50
Geddy Lee: $20-$50
Drum Stick:
Neil Peart: $30*
*Stick collectors take note Peart has often played with the butt end of his sticks.

A Rush guitar pick

OFTEN OVERLOOKED MEMORABILIA
The Defenders by Marvel Comics, (Vol. 1, No. 45) dedicated to Rush and based on the lyrics to 2112; bumper stickers - $3; Roll the Bones crew flight bag - $300; Roll the Bones pinwheel promo calendar - $20; Crew Members jacket (1981) - $200; handbills; YYZ baggage claim check; an autographed band portrait from Yousuf Karsh (See "Grace Under Pressure"); Presto Atlantic promo pencil, 1991; Power Windows autographed promo lithograph - $500

REFERENCES/BOOKS
Limited resources exist. There are no dedicated collector books. A Show of Fans: A Rush Fanzine for and by Rush Fans, 5411 E. State St., Suite #309, Rockford, IL 61108 is a MUST publication! ($15 fee)

Rush, Tom

Born: February 8, 1941

Tom Rush, a graduate of Harvard, began working the Cambridge coffee house circuit in the early '60s. As an innovator and contributor to the folk-rock movement which spawned Bob Dylan, Joan Baez, and Joni Mitchell, he was one of the first artists to produce a concept album, *The Circle Game* (1968). The album yielded two songs which will always be identified with the artist: "No Regrets" and "The Circle Game" (written by Joni Mitchell).

He is now looked upon as a creative force for many successful acts including James Taylor, Joni Mitchell, and Jackson Browne. In 1980 he formed Maple Hill Productions, primarily to promote a concert series and later Night Light Recordings, his own mail-order record label. He tours and records regularly and is involved in many humanitarian causes.

AUTOGRAPHS

A CD, LP, magazine cover, ad, photo, or card signed by the artist: $10-$15

Rushing, Jimmy

Born: August 26, 1903, Died: June 8, 1972

Swing era blues-based vocalist, best remembered for his days with the Count Basie Orchestra (1935-1950), Rushing also sang with Jelly Roll Morton, Walter Page's Blue Devils, and Bennie Moten's Kansas City Orchestra (1929-1935). He recorded with Johnny Otis in 1946 and by the early '50s had his own showcase at New York's Savoy Ballroom. His tours also included stints with Eddie Condon's All Stars and Benny Goodman's orchestra.

AUTOGRAPHS

A CD, LP, magazine cover, ad, photo, or card signed by the artist: $40-$60

OFTEN OVERLOOKED MEMORABILIA

Videotapes of his numerous television appearances; movie memorabilia from *The Learning Tree* (1969).

Russell, Leon

(Hank Wilson)
Born: April 2, 1941

This late-60s Tulsa key tickler and frequent super sessionman has worked with just about everyone in the business, at least it seems that way. Leon Russell is typically associated with two songs, "Tight Rope" and "This Masquerade," later a Grammy winner for George Benson.

AUTOGRAPHS

A CD, LP, magazine cover, ad, photo, or card signed by the artist: $10-$25

OFTEN OVERLOOKED MEMORABILIA

Associated memorabilia from his numerous contributions to other artists' works; Concert for Bangla Desh memorabilia (1971); items associated with his touring with the Rolling Stones in 1971.

Rydell, Bobby

(Robert Ridarelli)
Born: April 26, 1942

A late-50s key figure in the Philadelphia sound, teen idol Bobby Rydell is best remembered for his hits "Kissin' Time," "Volare," "Sway," "Swingin' School," "Wild One," and "Forget Him." His music career, similar to that of Frankie Avalon and Fabian, was put to bed by the British Invasion of the '60s.

AUTOGRAPHS

A CD, LP, magazine cover, ad, photo, or card signed by the artist: $10-$15

OFTEN OVERLOOKED MEMORABILIA

Movie memorabilia from *Bye Bye Birdie*; videotapes from Paul Whitman's local *Teen Club*.

Ryder, Mitch and the Detroit Wheels

Formed 1965

Mitch Ryder (William Levise, Jr.), Born: February 26, 1945; James McCarty; Joseph Cubert (1947-1991); Earl Elliot; and Johnny "Bee" Badanjek

Late-60s Detroit brash soul crooner Mitch Ryder is best remembered for songs like "Jenny Takes a Ride," "Devil with a Blue Dress On," "Good Golly Miss Molly" (#4, 1966), "Too Many Fish in the Sea," "Three Little Fishes," and "Sock It to Me Baby" (#6, 1967). He split up his band at what appeared to be the peak of his success. His efforts at a solo career went relatively unnoticed.

AUTOGRAPHS

A CD, LP, magazine cover, ad, photo, or card signed by the group: $10-$40

OFTEN OVERLOOKED MEMORABILIA

Associated memorabilia from the numerous artists' who have covered their work

Sade

(Helen Folasade Adu)
Born: January 16, 1959

Sade Adu joins her first band, Arriva, while attending St. Martin's School of Art in the U.K. Having written songs for years, Adu and guitarist Ray St. John notice that their song "Smooth Operator" continues to be a set favorite. After quitting Arriva to briefly join the band Pride, Adu decides in 1983 to form her own band, but she signs to CBS/Epic Records as a solo artist in January 1984.

Singles "Your Love Is King" (#6, 1984, U.K.) and "When Am I Going to Make a Living" (#36, 1984, U.K.), accompanied by some strong media exposure, ignite interest in her debut album *Diamond Life* (#2, 1984, U.K.), making it one of the most successful female artist first efforts of all time. In February 1985, *Diamond Life* (#5, 1985) enters the U.S. album charts and is driven into the Top Five by the success of extracted single "Smooth Operator" (#5, 1985).

Promise (#1, 1986), with extracted hit singles "The Sweetest Taboo" (#5, 1986) and "Never As Good As the First Time" (#20, 1986), climbs to the top of the charts amid extensive touring in its support. The following year Adu appears in the cult film *Absolute Beginners* and also contributes "Killer Blows" to the soundtrack. Following the effort she relocates to Spain to begin work with the band on her third album.

Stronger Than Pride (#7, 1988), with extracted single "Paradise" (#16, 1988), is supported in the U.S. by a 40-date Summer Tour. Unfortunately, much momentum is lost and the band doesn't surface with another product until four years later. *Love Deluxe* (#3, 1992) proves the band hasn't lost as much appeal as anticipated. "No Ordinary Love" (#28, 1993) climbs the singles chart aided by its inclusion on the soundtrack of *Indecent Proposal*.

The Best of Sade (#9, 1994) buys some time for the band as former drummer Paul Cook issues legal proceedings during the summer of 1995, seeking a share of lost royalties.

AUTOGRAPHS

A CD, LP, magazine cover, ad, photo, or card signed by the artist (Sade Adu): $15-$20

OFTEN OVERLOOKED MEMORABILIA

Movie memorabilia from *Absolute Beginners* (1987) and *Indecent Proposal* (1993); cover of Time (April 1986) that has Sade Adu pictured with other artists - $5

REFERENCES/BOOKS

Limited resources exist, but none do justice to the singer in my opinion. There are no dedicated collector books.

Sadler, Barry Staff Sergeant

(1940-1989)

Sadler is best known, at least in the music world, as author of the patriotic novelty single "The Ballad of the Green Berets" (#1, 1966) (album of the same name also topped the charts). Sadler wrote the song with the help of writer Robin Moore (lyrics) while he recovered from a leg wound suffered in Vietnam. Moore went on to author a best-selling book by the same name.

Sadler then disappeared as fast as he arrived and didn't surface again until 1978 when he was involved in a shooting incident that left songwriter Lee Bellamy dead. No charges were filed against Sadler, who disappeared again until he was involved in another shooting incident in 1981, involving an ex-business partner. He himself was shot in 1988 during a robbery attempt in Guatemala. Suffering from brain damage and paralysis due to the shooting, he died the following year of heart failure. Considerable mystery still surrounds the final decade of his life.

AUTOGRAPHS

An LP, magazine cover, ad, photo, or card signed by the artist: $10-$35

OFTEN OVERLOOKED MEMORABILIA

Newspaper clipping regarding the shootings he was involved in

REFERENCES/BOOKS

The Green Berets by Robin Moore

Sainte-Marie, Buffy

Born: February 20, 1941

(See Biographical Information Below)

AUTOGRAPHS

A CD, LP, magazine cover, ad, photo, or card signed by the artist: $8-$20*

*"The Universal Soldier" and "Up Where We Belong" related material

Individual Items

OFTEN OVERLOOKED MEMORABILIA

Any items associated with her work on behalf of Native Americans; any material associated with covers of her songs such as "Until It's Time for You to Go," "The Universal Soldier," "Cod'ine," and "Up Where We Belong" (#1, 1982 by Joe Cocker and Jennifer Warnes); episodes of *Sesame Street* that she appeared on (1976-1981); movie memorabilia from *The Broken Circle* (1994); box of 10 greeting cards - $40

The Saints

Formed 1975

Chris Bailey, Ed Kuepper, Kym Bradshaw, and Ivor Hay*

*Bradshaw left in 1977 and Alisdair Ward was added. Kuepper left in 1978. Ward and Hay left in 1987, while Archie Larizza, Baz Francis, Iain Shedden, and Joe Chiofalo joined the band.

Late-70s Australian punk band The Saints are best remembered for their debut single "(I'm) Stranded."

AUTOGRAPHS

A CD, LP, magazine cover, ad, photo, or card signed by the group: $10-$12

POSTERS/PRESS KITS

Promotional Posters: $10-$12
Press Kits: $10-$12

USED CLOTHING/EQUIPMENT

Guitar Pick: $5-$7

OFTEN OVERLOOKED MEMORABILIA

Any artifacts from their "I'm Stranded" release; a copy of *Sounds* magazine that got them signed to EMI - $6

Sakamoto, Ryuichi

Born: January 17, 1952

An outstanding composer, producer, and actor, Sakamoto is proficient in a variety of music genres including pop and movie soundtracks.

AUTOGRAPHS

A CD, LP, magazine cover, ad, photo, or card signed by the artist: $10-$25

OFTEN OVERLOOKED MEMORABILIA

Items associated with the Yellow Magic Orchestra and the single "Computer Game (Theme from The Invaders)"; memorabilia from *Merry Christmas Mr. Lawrence*, *The Last Emperor*, and *High Heels*

Salt-n-Pepa

Formed 1985

Cheryl "Salt" James and Sandy "Pepa" Denton, and Pamela Greene*

*Greene left in 1988 and Deidre "Dee Dee" Roper was added.

This late-80s and '90s New York City female rap/pop group broke with its third album *Black's Magic* (#38, 1990), which included the hits extracts "Expression" (#26, 1990) and "Let's Talk About Sex" (#13, 1991). Salt-n-Pepa took their own career reigns on *Very Necessary* (#4, 1993); the rap divas landed with hits "Shoop" (#4, 1993) and "Whatta Man" (#3, 1994). The group also performed at Woodstock II on August 13, 1994, just prior to taking home three awards at the 11th Annual MTV Video Music Awards. The following year the group performed "Whatta Man" at Frank Sinatra's 80th birthday celebration at the Shrine Auditorium.

AUTOGRAPHS

A CD, LP, magazine cover, ad, photo, or card signed by the group: $25-$50

POSTERS/PRESS KITS

Promotional Posters: $10-$20
Press Kits: $15-$25

OFTEN OVERLOOKED MEMORABILIA

Videotapes of the group's numerous television appearances including *The Arsenio Hall Show* (10/19/93), *Saturday Night Live* (2/5/94), and *The Late Show With David Letterman* (10/25/95); movie memorabilia from *Colors* and *Stay Tuned*

Sam and Dave

Samuel Moore, Born: October 12, 1935; and David Prater, Born: May 9, 1937, Died: April 9, 1988

Late-60s vocal act, best remembered for the hits "Hold On! I'm Comin'" (#1, R&B, 1966), "Said I Wasn't Gonna Tell Nobody" (#8, R&B, 1966), "You Got Me Hummin'" (#7, R&B, 1966), "When Something Is Wrong with My Baby" (#2, R&B, 1967), "Soul Man" (#2, 1967), and "I Thank You" (#9, 1968), Sam and Dave broke up in 1970, but reunited for select one-off events. The Blues Brothers ignited interest in their career during the early '80s, which the group tried to take advantage of until its final split in 1981. Prater later died in an automobile accident. The group was inducted into the Rock and Roll Hall of Fame in 1992.

AUTOGRAPHS

An LP, magazine cover, ad, photo, or card signed by the group: $35-$85

OFTEN OVERLOOKED MEMORABILIA

Blues Brothers memorabilia; all items relating to their final show on New Year's Eve 1981, at San Francisco's Old Waldorf

Sambora, Richie: See Bon Jovi

Sample, Joe: See the Crusaders

Sam the Sham and the Pharaohs

Formed Early 1960s.

Sam the Sham (Domingo Samudio), David Martin, Ray Stinnet, Jerry Patterson, and Butch Gibson

Tex-mex rockers of the mid-60s who achieved brief and rapid success primarily with "Wooly Bully" and "Li'l Red Riding Hood," led by main pharaoh Domingo Samudio.

AUTOGRAPHS

A CD, LP, magazine cover, ad, photo, or card signed by the group: $10-$40*

*Vintage material

OFTEN OVERLOOKED MEMORABILIA

All memorabilia associated with the hits "Wooly Bully" (#2, 1965), "Juju Hand" (#22, 1965), "Ring Gang Doo" (#33, 1965), "Li'l Red Riding Hood" (#2, 1966), and "The Hair on My Chinny Chin-Chin" (#22, 1966); movie memorabilia from *The Border*; items associated with other artists covering their songs

Sanborn, David

Born: July 30, 1945

Proficient alto saxophonist Sanborn's sound is one of pop music's most recognizable. He is a brilliant composer, session contributor, and multiple Grammy award winner.

AUTOGRAPHS

A CD, LP, magazine cover, ad, photo, or card signed by the artist: $10-$25*

*Grammy related material

POSTERS/PRESS KITS

Promotional Posters: $10-$15
Press Kits: $10-$15

OFTEN OVERLOOKED MEMORABILIA

Woodstock memorabilia; items associated with his work with the Paul Butterfield Blues Band and his session work with Stevie Wonder, James Taylor, and David Bowie; television episodes of *Night Magic* and his appearances on *The Late Show With David Letterman*

Santana/Carlos Santana

Formed 1967

Carlos Santana, Born: July 20, 1947; Gregg Rolie; David Brown; Michael Shrieve; Mike Carbello; and Jose Chepito Areas*

*Neal Schon, Born: February 27, 1954 and Coke (Tommy) Escovedo (1941-1985) were added in 1971. Brown left in 1971 and Tom Rutley was added.

Carlos Santana grew up in Tijuana, Mexico, and San Francisco, California, where he discovered his true love for music. Upon leaving his high school band, he formed the Santana Blues Band in 1966, playing extensively around San Francisco's club circuit and eventually at the famed Avalon Ballroom. He soon shortened the band's name to Santana and shifted personnel until satisfied that his Latin rock sound, which was heavily blues based, was the recipe he was looking for.

Having established itself in the San Francisco music scene by regularly playing at the Fillmore West and a few festivals, the band signed to CBS/Columbia Records and appeared at the Woodstock Music & Art Fair in Bethel, New York on August 15, 1969. Boosted by this performance, *Santana* (#4, 1969) was released in the fall. Extracted singles "Jingo" (#56) and "Evil Ways" (#9, 1970) aided sales.

Abraxas (#1, 1970) quickly became a smash sophomore follow-up with extracted hits singles "Black Magic Women" (#4, 1971) (a Fleetwood Mac cover) and "Oye Como Va" (#13, 1971). The group's sound was now richer, as guitarist Neal Schon (a future member of Journey) joined the band. While other personnel changes took place, Carlos Santana produced the group's third offering *Santana III* (#1, 1971), with hit single "Everybody's Everything" (#12, 1971) and "No One to Depend On" (#36, 1972). By the end of the year, the group broke up as live unit, but re-grouped for recording.

Carlos Santana and Buddy Miles (#8, 1972), *Caravanserai* (#8, 1972), *Love Devotion Surrender* (#14, 1973) (a fusion super session with John McLaughlin and others), and *Welcome* (#25, 1973) exhibited the artist's transformation into jazzier directions. *Santana's Greatest Hits* (#17, 1974), *Illuminations* (#40, U.K.), and *Borboletta* (#20, 1974) became the artist's offering for 1974, with only *Illuminations* disappointing some critics.

In 1975 the legendary Bill Graham became Santana's manager, in a year that included the artist's monumental triple-live album release *Lotus* (1975), released only during the year in Japan. *Amigos* (#10, 1976), *Festival* (#27, 1977), and *Moonflower* (#10, 1977) followed, and the group enjoyed the U.K. and U.S. success of single "She's Not There" (#27, 1977). The decade finished for the band/artist with albums *Inner Secrets* (#27, 1978), *Oneness / Silver Dreams - Golden Reality* (#55, U.K., 1979), and *Marathon* (#25, 1979). All exhibited some forms of success. Meanwhile, Carlos Santana pondered his direction for the '80s.

The Swing of Delight (#74, 1980) was followed by the well-received *Zebop!* (#9, 1981), which included extracted singles "Winning" (#17, 1981) and "The Sensitive Kind" (#56, 1981). *Shango* (#22, 1982) came next and included hit single "Hold On" (#15, 1982). Carlos Santana then followed it with solo offering *Havana Moon* (#84, 1983) with guests including Willie Nelson, Booker T. Jones, and the Fabulous Thunderbirds.

Beyond Appearances (#50, 1985), with extracted single "Say It Again" (#46, 1985), indicated that the artist's popularity was slipping. *Freedom* (#95, 1987), extensively supported, still couldn't muster any chart strength. Both *Blues for Salvador* (#195, 1987), an instrumental solo offering, and *Viva Santana* (#142, 1988), an anthology, failed to live up to expected sales, although the former earned him a Grammy in 1989.

Spirits Dancing in the Flesh (#85, 1990) was the group's first offering for the decade and gained some momentum for the artist. Unfortunately the band lost the services of Bill Graham who died in 1991. The artist then moved to Polygram and appeared first on Polydor then Island in January 1992. *Millagro* (#102, 1992) was followed by *Sacred Fire—Live in South America* (#181, 1993), which exhibited the band's enormous popularity and loyal Latin American following.

On August 14, 1994, 25 years after appearing at the original event, Santana performed at Woodstock II in Saugerties, New York. *Santana Brothers* (#191, 1994) charted only briefly and was followed by a 34-track, three-CD boxed retrospective called *Dance of the Rainbow Serpent* (1995), which also included a 64-page booklet. Santana became only the fifth recipient of the coveted Century Award for Lifetime achievement at the Fifth Annual Billboard Music Awards in 1996.

The artist, as a subject of collecting, is not only intriguing, but a very historical element in the course of rock 'n' roll history. The band's affiliation to the San Francisco area, and the entire scene that was developing there during the late '60s and early '70s, makes associated memorabilia highly sought after. Of particular interest to collectors are "Bill Graham presents" and "Family Dog" memorabilia (posters, tickets, handbills, etc.), most of which can command significant prices.

Festival memorabilia and associated items, particularly from the Woodstock Music & Art Fair (8/69), can also command high prices and are often difficult to find in better grades. Additionally, since many items associated with this group can be expensive, the collector can expect to encounter counterfeits, reproductions, and forgeries. All collectors are advised to educate themselves thoroughly on associated memorabilia to avoid the unfortunate circumstance of purchasing a reproduction or counterfeit.

AUTOGRAPHS

A CD, LP, magazine cover, ad, photo, or card signed by the artist: $35-$50

TOUR BOOKS/PROGRAMS/PASSES

Tour Books:

The Freedom Concert 1987: $20

Backstage Passes:

Cloth: $8-$10; Laminated: $10-$15 (1990-Present)
Cloth: $8-$12; Laminated: $12-$20 (1983-1989)
Cloth/Paper: $10-$15; Laminated: $15-$30 (1975-1982)

POSTERS/PRESS KITS

Promotional Posters: $10-$15 (1990-Present)

Press Kits:

(1969-1974) $35-$65   (1975-1982) $25-$35
(1983-1989) $20-$30   (1990-Present) $20-$25

USED CLOTHING/EQUIPMENT

Guitar Pick: $35-$55

OFTEN OVERLOOKED MEMORABILIA

All Lotus promotional Japanese materials; Shango, Columbia promotional sliding puzzle, 1982; movie memorabilia from *La Bamba* (music produced by Carlos Santana); a copy of *Carlos Santana: Influences*, a three-part video documentary hosted by Carlos; Zebop! die-cut Santana logo (2') - $15; any Altamont related items (12/6/69) (Santana was on the bill); The Sensitive Kind bottle of massage oil - $35

REFERENCES/BOOKS

Limited resources exist, but none do justice to the Santana in my opinion. There are no dedicated collector books. Serious collectors should opt for a Fan Club: Santana International Fan Club, P.O. Box 88163, San Francisco, CA 94188

Satriani, Joe

Born: July 15, 1957

Satriani made his recording debut in 1984 with a self-titled EP, before a brief time with pop band the Squares. He followed the effort with a couple of instrumental albums that went relatively unnoticed before he landed a job with Mick Jagger. The increased exposure helped push the sales of his next album *Surfing with the Alien* (#29, 1987), which ended up being the first instrumental album to enter the Top Forty in seven years. Both *Flying in a Blue Dream* (#23, 1989) and *The Extremist* (#22, 1992) also sold well, as the guitarist's fan base and respect continued to grow.

Satriani's guitar prowess now precedes him, often attributable to a former students of his such as Steve Vai. Inspired by Jimi Hendrix, Satriani, who is proficient on a number of instruments, continues to carve out his musical legacy.

AUTOGRAPHS

A CD, LP, magazine cover, ad, photo, or card signed by the artist: $30-$40

TOUR BOOKS/PROGRAMS/PASSES

Tour Books:

Flying In A Dream (Japan): $25

Backstage Passes:

Cloth: $8-$10; Laminated: $10-$15

POSTERS/PRESS KITS

Promotional Posters: $10-$25

Press Kits: $15-$25

USED CLOTHING/EQUIPMENT
Guitar Picks: $30-$60

OFTEN OVERLOOKED MEMORABILIA
Session work and contributions of his music students; Surfing with the Alien items: bumper sticker - $5, banner (12" x 24") - $20, and promo T-shirt - $15; Time Machine promo postcard - $5

Savoy Brown

Formed 1966

Original lineup: Kim Simmonds, Bruce Portius, Martin Stone, Ray Chappell, Leo Mannings, and Bob Hall*

*Numerous personnel changes

Additional members include: "Lonesome" Dave Peverett, Chris Youlden, Rivers Jobe, Roger Earl, Tony Stevens, Paul Raymond, Dave Walker, Dave Bidwell, Andy Pyle, Andy Silvester, Jackie Lynton, Ron Berg, Eric Dillon, Stan Webb, Miller Anderson, Jimmy Leverton, and others.

Exhaustive touring was responsible for what little commercial success this blues-rock band had. The band did far better in the U.S. than in its U.K. home. The only steadfast member of the band has been guitarist Kim Simmonds, whose longevity is certainly noteworthy. Formed originally as the Savoy Brown Blues Band, it evolved from pre-1970s blues into post-1970s boogie-rock. The band soon earned the reputation as a breeding ground for future artists, because some of its members left to form the successful band Foghat in 1971.

Savoy Brown has since fallen into that John Mayall and the Bluesbreakers mold, recruiting talent when necessary from other prominent British blues bands. As Simmonds goes, Savoy Brown follows!

AUTOGRAPHS
A CD, LP, magazine cover, ad, photo, or card signed by the entire band: $30-$40*
*High-end reflects vintage signed memorabilia (pre-1970s)
Individual:
Kim Simmonds: $8-$10

USED CLOTHING/EQUIPMENT
Guitar Picks:
Kim Simmonds: $3-$5

OFTEN OVERLOOKED MEMORABILIA
Pre-1970s tickets, posters, handbills, etc.

Sayer, Leo

(Gerard Sayer)
Born: May 21, 1948

Roger Daltry's self-titled debut album was written almost entirely by Leo Sayer (lyrics) and David Courtney (music). In August 1973, the now Chrysalis Records signed Sayer and released his debut single

"Why Is Everybody Going Home." It was followed by "The Show Must Go On," which Three Dog Night later took up the chart. His debut album *Silver Bird* (#2, U.K., 1974) sold well in the U.K., but when he tried to promote the album in the U.S. wearing a clown costume, it bombed.

Just a Boy (#16, 1975), with extracted hit single "Long Tall Glass (I Can Dance)" (#9, 1975) became Sayer's U.S. chart debut. It was followed by *Another Year* (#125, 1975), which sold poorly primarily because Sayer couldn't support it with a tour—he was hospitalized for a wisdom tooth operation. *Endless Flight* (#10, 1977), his breakthrough album, yielded three smash hit singles: "You Make Me Feel Like Dancing" (#1, 1977), "When I Need You" (#1, 1977), and "How Much Love" (#17, 1977).

Sayer followed it with *Thunder in My Heart* (#37, 1977). It sold gold in the U.K., but failed to reach the Top Thirty in the U.S. As his audience began to dwindle, *Leo Sayer* (#101, 1978) sold poorly despite heavy media exposure by Sayer. *The Very Best of Leo Sayer* (#1, 1979, U.K.) bought him some time to work on his next album *Here* (#44, U.K.), but that too was a disappointment.

Sayer finally returned to the U.S. chart in 1980 with a cover of the Bobby Vee tune "More Than I Can Say" (#2, 1980). But by the end of the decade he was without a recording contract. He returned with his first album in seven years, in 1993, with *Cool Touch*. As if a predestined title, the album did little to restore his career.

AUTOGRAPHS
A CD, LP, magazine cover, ad, photo, or card signed by the artist: $6-$15

TOUR BOOKS/PROGRAMS/PASSES
Backstage Passes:
Cloth: $2-$5; Laminated: $5-7

POSTERS/PRESS KITS
Promotional Posters: $2-$15
Press Kits: $5-$20

OFTEN OVERLOOKED MEMORABILIA
Movie memorabilia from *Car Trouble* (1984) (Sayer contributed a cover of "Unchained Melody"); episodes of BBC-TV series *Leo Sayer* and BBC1-TV's *Leo*; Silverbird Leo mask with string - $10

Scaggs, Boz

(William Scaggs)
Born: June 8, 1944

While growing up in Texas, Boz Scaggs meets Steve Miller at a school in Dallas and joins his band, the Marksmen. Both musicians attend the University of Wisconsin in 1961 and play in R&B cover group the Ardells, which eventually becomes the Fabulous Night Train. Scaggs then returns to Texas

to form his own band, which then travels to Britain with hopes of striking it rich, but when hopes fade, the band splits, and Scaggs relocates in Europe.

In 1965 Scaggs records his debut album *Boz* for Polydor, which releases it only in Europe. When little is made of the release he eventually goes to San Francisco, California, where he rejoins the Steve Miller Band. In 1968 Scaggs contributes to two of the band's chart albums, *Children of the Future* (#134, 1968) and *Sailor* (#24, 1968), before leaving the band due to musical differences with Miller.

In 1969, encouraged and aided by Rolling Stone guru Jann Wenner, Scaggs secures a solo record deal with Atlantic Records. In August 1969, *Boz Scaggs*, featuring top session players including Duane Allman, is released to critic acclaim but lackluster sales, causing the label to drop him.

Scaggs, who travels extensively, eventually lands back on the West Coast and forms the Boz Scaggs Band. Signed to CBS/Columbia, the band releases *Moments* (#124, 1971), which includes the singles "We Are Always Sweethearts" (#61, 1971) and "Near You" (#96, 1971). *Boz Scaggs and Band* (#198, 1971) follows with mediocre album sales before *My Time* (#138, 1972) with single "Dinah Flo" (#86, 1972) is released. This album is supported by extensive touring that also occasionally includes Steve Miller. Searching for the answer as to why he hasn't had greater success, Scaggs forms a new band with Les Dudek, Jimmy Young, Tom Rutley, Rick Schlosser, and Jack Schroer.

Slow Dancer (#81, 1974) becomes his first album to chart in the Top One Hundred and signals that the foundation for his sound has finally been laid. "It's Over" (#38), from his forthcoming album, charts successfully into the Top Forty and sets the stage for what is to follow. *Silk Degrees* (#2, 1976) also spins off "Lowdown" (#3, 1976), "What Can I Do'" (#42, 1976), and "Lido Shuffle" (#11, 1977) and charts for a 115-week run.

Down Two Then Left (#11, 1978) sells relatively well but fails to yield a Top Forty single. *Middle Man* (#8, 1980) follows and brings Scaggs right back on track. It includes the hit singles "Breakdown Dead Ahead" (#15, 1980) and "Jo Jo" (#17, 1980). The compilation album *Hits* (#24, 1981) comes next. Scaggs' last single for seven years, "Miss Sun" (#14, 1981), features a duet with Lisa Del Bello.

In 1983 Scaggs retires from the music business and opens his own Southern-style down home restaurant in San Francisco. Persuaded to return to music, *Other Roads* (#47, 1988), including the single "Heart of Mine" (#35, 1988), is his comeback effort. Although he makes a rare television appearance on *Late Night With David Letterman* (11/23/88), he essentially slips out of sight once again.

He emerges once again in 1994, this time with his Virgin records debut *Some Change* (#91, 1994), his second album in fourteen years. He supports the album with a tour and numerous television appearances, but fails to drive the album into the Top Forty.

He performs a brief West Coast tour in 1996, but then slips quietly away once again.

AUTOGRAPHS

A CD, LP, magazine cover, ad, photo, or card signed by the artist: $30-$40

TOUR BOOKS/PROGRAMS/PASSES

Backstage Passes:

Cloth: $10; Laminated: $10-$25

POSTERS/PRESS KITS

Promotional Posters:

$15-$20 (1988-present)

$20-$45 (pre-1988)

Press Kits:

$20-$30 (1988-present)

$30-$60 (pre-1988)

OFTEN OVERLOOKED MEMORABILIA

Movie memorabilia from *Urban Cowboy* (1980); memorabilia from Slim's (Scaggs' San Francisco nightclub); copies of any of his television appearances which were scarce until 1994; all of his work with Steve Miller; store sign for Down 2 Then Left - $35

Scandal: See Patty Smyth

Scarface: See the Geto Boys

Schenker, Michael: See Scorpions; UFO

Schoolly D

(Jesse Weaver)
Born: June 22, 1966

Schoolly D pioneered gangsta rap while "throwin ya inta da streets, ta fen fa ya seff, genst violence." His eponymously titled debut included the gangsta staples "PSK - What Does It Mean?" and "I Don't Like Rock 'n' Roll." Weaver released the first two albums on his own before signing with Jive and kicking out the compilation album *The Adventures of Schoolly D* and *Saturday Night*.

Critics praised his straight-to-the-heart approach when addressing sex and violence. Never afraid to duck an issue, Schoolly D hit home on *Am I Black Enough for You?* (1989). In 1994 he released *Welcome to America*, backed by a talented band including Mike Tyler and Chuck Treece (Urge Overkill). The record also featured rapper Cheese. If you want to smoke some kill, Schoolly D is your man!

AUTOGRAPHS

A CD, LP, magazine cover, ad, photo, or card signed by the artist: $10-$20

Schulze, Klaus: See Tangerine Dream

Scorpions

Formed 1971

Original lineup: Lothar Heimberg, Klaus Meine, Jurgen Rosenthal, Michel Schenker, and Rudolf Schenker*

*Numerous personnel changes

The Scorpions release their debut album *Lonesome Crow* (1972) on the German Metronome label. Follow-up *Fly to the Rainbow* finds them with RCA Records, and despite some personnel changes, the band remains a fairly solid five piece powerhouse. The group ventures out of Germany for the first time to promote its third album *In Trance*. The extensive touring philosophy, typically more than one hundred gigs per year, begins to pay off—the group enjoys a strong following in both Europe and Japan.

Virgin Killer, the group's fourth album, strikes gold in Japan the very first week of its release. *Taken By Force* follows as drummer Rudy Lenners quits and is replaced by Herman Rarebell in 1977. A five-day tour of Japan, where the band is red hot, sells out. The band records two gigs at Sun Plaze, which are released as *The Tokyo Tapes*. Uli Roth, who replaced Michael Schenker who joined UFO, quits by year's end to form Electric Sun.

Lowdrive (#69, U.K., 1979), featuring new member Mathias Jabs and a briefly returning Michael Schenker, is a strong offering and the first album to really bring the band into the world-wide spotlight. The band supports the album in the U.S. at its live debut in Cleveland, Ohio, at the World Series of Rock festival, followed by a tour supporting Ted Nugent. If you collect in the U.S., this is a good place to begin your collecting.

Animal Magnetism (#52, 1980) and *Best of Scorpions* (#180, 1980) follow, but when *Blackout* (#10, 1982) is released and supported by a lengthy seven-month world tour, the poisonous sting of this arachnid is felt world-wide. With *Blackout* certified platinum in 1984, *Love at First Sting* (#6, 1984) is released, powered by the single "Rock You Like a Hurricane" (#25, 1984). It is followed by the double-live set *World Wide Live* (#14, 1985) which gives the band some time to prepare for the next album.

Savage Amusement (#5, 1988), a swan song production work by cohort Dieter Dierks, is released in 1988 and supported first by the Monsters of Rock package, followed by 50 headlining dates. The year ends with the band being invited to perform ten concerts in Leningrad, USSR. The experience so moves vocalist Klaus Meine that he pens his first composition for the group, "Wind of Change."

Mercury Records compilation *Best of Rockers 'N' Ballads* (#43, 1990) is released in 1990 as the band participates in Roger Waters *The Wall* spectacular at the site of the Berlin Wall on July 21, 1990. The ballad "Wind of Change" (#4, 1991), extracted from *Crazy World* (#21, 1990), becomes a world-wide hit and when then-Soviet premier Mikhail Gorbachev hears the group's Russian version, he invites the band for a personal visit.

Face the Heat (#24, 1993), the highly-charged album revolving around the problems facing German reunification, includes the popular "Alien Nation" (#51, U.K., 1993). In 1996 the band releases *Pure Instinct* as the group ponders its direction as it approaches the end of the decade.

The Scorpions is the most popular band to ever come out of Germany. If you're collecting Scorpions memorabilia you may want to grab a pen pal from Germany to aid in your search for earlier artifacts. All items associated with the band, especially any pieces of memorabilia issued before its days with RCA (1974), are highly sought after and very difficult to find.

AUTOGRAPHS

Group:

A CD, LP, magazine cover, ad, photo, or card signed by the group: $100-$150*

Original lineup: Lothar Heimberg, Klaus Meine, Jurgen Rosenthal, Michel Schenker, and Rudolf Schenker*

Individual:

Rudolf Schenker: $30-$45

TOUR BOOKS/PROGRAMS/PASSES

Tour Books:

Blackout Tour '82: $25
Blackout Tour '82 (U.K.): $30
1982 Japan: $30
1985 Japan: $30
Crazy World Tour '90-91: $12

Backstage Passes:

(1990 to present)
Cloth: $8-$12; Laminated: $12-$20

POSTERS/PRESS KITS

Promotional Posters: $10-$25*
*Japanese promotional posters are highly sought by collectors
Press Kits: $20-$35, Example: Face The Heat: $20

USED CLOTHING/EQUIPMENT

Guitar Picks: $15-$30

OFTEN OVERLOOKED MEMORABILIA

Any scarce Billingsgate label (Lonesome Crow, 1972) promotional pieces; *World Wide Live* tape display - two parts - $40; magazines - $8-$10; any German fanzines - $15-$20; stickers - $5-$10; promotional pins - $5-$10 (various); Savage Amusement, pair of promo banners - $12 and whip - $40

REFERENCES/BOOKS

Metal Mania, U.K. - $20

Scott-Heron, Gil

Born: April 1, 1949

This politically conscious, funk-jazz based writer-singer has been cited as an influence for the spoken word artists of the 90s.

AUTOGRAPHS

A CD, LP, magazine cover, ad, photo, or card signed by the artist: $10-$20

POSTERS/PRESS KITS

Promotional Posters: $10-$15
Press Kits: $10

OFTEN OVERLOOKED MEMORABILIA

Associated items from his R&B hits "Johannesburg" (#29, 1975), "Angel Dust" (#15, 1978), and "Shut' Um Down" (#68, 1980); items associated with *Sun City* and the 1979 MUSE Benefit

REFERENCES/BOOKS

Items associated with written work, novels *The Vulture* and *The Nigger Factory* and his book of rap verse *Small Talk at 125th and Lenox*

Screaming Trees

Formed 1984

Mark Lanegan, Van Conner, Gary Lee Conner, and Mark Pickerel*

*Pickerel left in 1991 and was replaced by Barrett Martin

Northwest indie rockers Screaming Trees paired the buffet-binging Conner brothers with singer Mark Lanegan and drummer Mark Pickerel. Before "grunge" landed in Seattle, there was "gruel" in Ellensburg, whose origins could be traced to the Screaming Trees. The bands first release in 1985 was the cassette-only *Other Words* on SST, which failed to chart in spite of Lanegan's Jim Morrison infected vocals.

A hard-drinking volatile band, that broke up and regrouped almost routinely, the Screaming Trees fought their way to a good reputation, while often fighting each other along the way. By the 1988 SST *Invisible Lantern* release they had climbed the indie-rock heap and were waiting for the big deal. It happened in 1990 when the band was signed to Epic and released the debut *Something About Today* (EP).

Uncle Anesthesia, produced by Terry Date (Metal Church) and Chris Cornell (Soundgarden), moved the band into a better hard rock groove and produced some excellent cuts. While Nirvana and Pearl Jam were breaking, the Trees awaited their turn. *Sweet Oblivion*, released at the height of "Seattlemania" was the group's breakthrough album. Produced by Don Fleming (Teenage Fanclub) and mixed by Andy Wallace (*Nevermind*) the album was crammed with catchy songs such as "Nearly Lost You." Unfortu-

nately for the Screaming Trees, the album never hit, although it did garner a fair amount of new followers and exposure on MTV's "grungemania." It's now considered a must for every grunge created time-capsule. If you're going to collect "leaves from the trees," *Sweet Oblivion* is a great place to start.

Also worth keeping an eye on is Mark Lanegan's solo career, both *The Winding Sheet* and Whiskey for the Holy Ghost were strong first offerings on Sub Pop.

AUTOGRAPHS

A CD, LP, magazine cover, ad, photo, or card signed by the group: $10-$20

OFTEN OVERLOOKED MEMORABILIA

Movie memorabilia from *Singles* (1992)

Seal

(Sealhenry Samuel)
Born: February 19, 1963

Seal. Photo by David Sandison. Courtesy Warner Bros. Records Inc.

Seal was initially a member of England's house-music scene, where he first scored big with "Killer" (#1, U.K., 1990). He had previously worked with funk band Push and a blues band in Thailand. He signed to Sire and he released his debut *Seal* (#24, 1991), which included Top Ten hit "Crazy" (#7, 1991).

His sophomore effort, again self-titled, produced by Trevor Horn, peaked at Number Twenty and yielded hit extract "Prayer for the Dying" (#21, 1994). "Kiss From A Rose" (#1, 1995), featured in the movie *Batman Forever* was reissued and soon topped the U.S. singles chart. Seal's follow-up "Don't Cry" (#33, 1996) climbed into the Top Forty as he continued to collect numerous Grammy Awards.

AUTOGRAPHS

A CD, LP, magazine cover, ad, photo, or card signed by the artist: $20-$35

TOUR BOOKS/ PROGRAMS/PASSES

Backstage Passes:
Cloth: $5-$8;
Laminated: $8-$12

POSTERS/PRESS KITS

Promotional Posters:
$10-$25
(*Batman Forever* related)
Press Kits: $15-$18

Backstage pass from Seal's Holding the Sun Tour '94-'95 (Printed by OTTO)

OFTEN OVERLOOKED MEMORABILIA

Associated items from his time with Push; movie memorabilia from *Toys* (1991) and *Batman Forever* (1995); videotapes of his television appearances on *Wogan* (1991), *Big 30* - ITV (1991), and *The Late Show With David Letterman* (6/8/95); copies of ATP tennis Tour events featuring Seal's "Bring It On"; videotape of his 1992 environmental-awareness public service spot for MTV with Madonna

Sea Level: See the Allman Brothers Band

Seals and Crofts

Formed 1969

Jim Seals, Born: October 17, 1941; and Dash (Darrell) Crofts, Born: August 14, 1940

This '70s pop duo went on to become one of the decade's most successful acts after playing in numerous groups including the Champs ("Tequila") in 1958. The duo gained its success with hits like "Summer Breeze" (#6, 1972), "Hummingbird" (#20, 1972), "Diamond Girl" (#6, 1973), "We May Never Pass This Way (Again)" (#21, 1973), "I'll Play for You" (#18, 1975), "Get Closer" (#6, 1976), "My Fair Share" (#28, 1977), and "You're the Love" (#18, 1978). Following the release of *The Longest Road* (1980), an album

that failed to chart, Warner Brothers dropped them from the company's roster.

With the exception of a short 1991-92 reunion tour, and an occasional one-off gig, the two have not played together. Crofts has lived all over the world, while Seals has spent the years on his coffee farm in Costa Rica.

AUTOGRAPHS

A CD, LP, magazine cover, ad, photo, or card signed by the duo: $40-$75

OFTEN OVERLOOKED MEMORABILIA

White plastic Frisbee w/picture, Warner Brothers promo item - $35; movie memorabilia from *One on One*; promotional mobiles - $35-$45

The Searchers

Formed 1961

John McNally, Mike Pender (Pendergast), Tony Jackson, and Chris Curtis*

*Jackson left the band in 1964 and Frank Allen was added. Curtis left in 1966 and John Blunt joined the group briefly before being replaced by Billy Adamson. Pender left in 1985 and Spencer James was added.

Late-60s British pop act, best remembered in the U.S. for the hits "Needles and Pins" (#13, 1964), "Don't Throw Your Love Away" (#16, 1964), and "Love Potion Number 9" (#3, 1965), The Searchers scored numerous other U.K. hits before resigning to the club and cabaret circuit

AUTOGRAPHS

An LP, magazine cover, ad, photo, or card signed by the group: $20-$50

REFERENCES/BOOKS

Limited resources exist, but none do justice to the group in my opinion. There are no dedicated collector books. Serious collectors should opt for a Fan Club: Mike Pender's Searchers Fan Club, 14 Goldfields Close, Greetland, Halifax, West York's England HX4 8LD

Sebastian, John

Born: March 17, 1944

Late-60s pop vocalist and former member of the Lovin' Spoonful John Sebastian garnered attention from both his solo debut album and his unscheduled appearance at Woodstock, but from that point onward he went virtually unnoticed until his first hit single in close to a decade, "Welcome Back" (#1, 1976) (used as the television theme to *Welcome Back, Kotter*).

He then went on to tour, opening for numerous acts, and worked on many diverse projects, from writing a children's book to scoring television shows.

AUTOGRAPHS

An LP, magazine cover, ad, photo, or card signed by the artist: $10-$25

OFTEN OVERLOOKED MEMORABILIA

Videotapes from *Welcome Back, Kotter*, as well as from his numerous television appearances

Secada, Jon

(Juan Secada)
Born: October 4, 1963

'90s Miami singing sensation, who got his big break by cowriting six songs on Gloria Estefan's *Into the Light* album including two chart-toppers, "Coming Out of the Dark" and "Can't Forget You," Jon Secada is typically associated with the songs "Just Another Day," "Do You Believe in Us," "Angel," and "I'm Free," all Top Forty singles. Secada also landed a Grammy for Best Latin Pop Album in 1992, for his debut Spanish album *Otro Dia Mas Sin Verte* (he recorded two versions of his successful debut—one in English and one in Spanish).

AUTOGRAPHS

A CD, LP, magazine cover, ad, photo, or card signed by the group: $10-$25*

*Secada is extremely responsive to both in-person and mail autograph requests

POSTERS/PRESS KITS

Promotional Posters: $10-$15
Press Kits: $14-$20

Sedaka, Neil

Born: March 13, 1939

One of music's most prolific songwriters, who has often found himself often caught between penning or performing, both of which he has been successful at during his long career, Neil Sedaka is typically associated early in his career with the songs "Stupid Cupid," "Where the Boys Are" (both hits for Connie Francis), "The Diary" (#14, 1959), "Oh! Carol" (#9, 1959), "Stairway to Heaven" (#9, 1960), "Calendar Girl" (#4, 1961), "Little Devil" (#11, 1961), "Happy Birthday Sweet Sixteen" (#6, 1961), "Breaking Up Is Hard to Do" (#1, 1962), and "Next Door to an Angel" (#5, 1962).

When his hits dissipated as a performer, he returned to writing songs for others, including "Puppet Man" for Tom Jones, "Workin' on a Groovy Thing" for the Fifth Dimension, and he even collaborated with his good friend Carole King on "Crying in the Rain" for the Everly Brothers. Encouraged by Elton John not to abandon his performing, *Sedaka's Back* (#23, 1974) and *The Hungry Years* (#16, 1975) became his

triumphant return, and yielded a Number One hit with "Laughter in the Rain." During the same period Captain and Tennille won a Grammy for Record of the Year with Sedaka's "Love Will Keep Us Together" (#31, 1975).

Sedaka's later singles included "Bad Blood" (#1, 1975), "Love in the Shadows" (#16, 1976), and a hit with his daughter, "Should've Never Let You Go."

AUTOGRAPHS

An LP, magazine cover, ad, photo, or card signed by the artist: $10-$25

OFTEN OVERLOOKED MEMORABILIA

Associated artifacts from the numerous songs he has had covered over his long career; videotapes of his numerous television show appearances; Greatest Hits mobile - $45; Rocket Records store late '60s display w/Cliff Richard and others - $50

The Seeds

Founded 1965

Sky Saxon (Richard Marsh), Jan Savage, Daryl Hooper, and Rick Andridge

Late-60s L.A. rock act, best remembered for the songs "Pushin' Too Hard," "Mr. Farmer," "Can't Seem to Make You Mine," and "Thousand Shadows," The Seeds disbanded before bearing fruit.

AUTOGRAPHS

An LP, magazine cover, ad, photo, or card signed by the group: $10

Seeger, Pete

Born: May 3, 1919

A living legend and pivitol in American folk music, Pete Seeger is a singer, songwriter, performer, stringsmith, archivist, ecologist, and humanitarian. His work with the Weavers alone made him a cultural hero—his anti-war attitudes and commitment to civil rights have always run deep. Most impressive to me has been his appreciation for history and his passion for never loosing sight of the mission, no matter what it may be.

Seeger is typically identified with the songs "If I Had a Hammer," "Where Have All the Flowers Gone?," "On Top of Old Smokey," "Goodnight Irene," and "Turn! Turn! Turn!" He is one of the few who has worked with both Woody Guthrie and his son Arlo. Arlo and Seeger are known for their infamous cruises along the Hudson River on the schooner Clearwater.

For what this wonderful man has given us, there simply aren't enough Thank Yous!

AUTOGRAPHS

An LP, magazine cover, ad, photo, or card signed by the artist: $20-$45

OFTEN OVERLOOKED MEMORABILIA

Read the book below, then begin an exploration into the numerous causes he has defended and their associated artifacts.

REFERENCES/BOOKS

Where Have all the Flowers Gone - his autobiography (1993); Numerous resources exist. Start first with *How Can I Keep Singing* by David Dunaway. There are no dedicated collector books.

Seger, Bob

Born: May 6, 1945

A working man's rocker from Michigan, Bob Seger was a local hero during the early '70s, but his return to Capitol record in 1975 for *Beautiful Loser* changed all of that. Backed by the talented Silver Bullet Band, he decided to see if he could capture some of the excitement he was famous for during his live shows, thus 1976's *Live Bullet*. Recorded in Detroit, this double-album set stayed on the charts for more than three years. Next to *Frampton Comes Alive*, this was one of the most popular live efforts of the era.

Success for Seger came quickly after the live album, sparked by its follow-up *Night Moves*, which catapulted the artist into national prominence, aided by the singles "Night Moves" (#8, 1977) and "Mainstreet" (#24, 1977). "Still the Same" (#4, 1978), "Hollywood Nights" (#12, 1978), "We've Got Tonite" (#13, 1978), and "Old Time Rock and Roll" (#28, 1979), all extract from his album *Stranger in Town*, continued the momentum, as did *Against the Wind* (#1, 1980) with its rich ballads "Fire Lake" (#6), "Against the Wind" (#5), and "You'll Accomp'ny Me" (#14). *Nine Tonight*, Seger's second live LP, was also his fifth consecutive multi-platinum release. After its release came the first signs that his sales were tapering off. It also marked the end of the original Silver Bullet Band and the beginning of a vast rotation of members, including two former members of Grand Funk Railroad, Craig Frost and Don Brewer.

Seger's later hits include "Even Now," "Roll Me Away," "Understanding," "Like a Rock," "The Little Drummer Boy," and "The Real Love."

AUTOGRAPHS

A CD, LP, magazine cover, ad, photo, or card signed by the group: $30-$60*
*High end reflects original Silver Bullet Band item

TOUR BOOKS/PROGRAMS/PASSES

Backstage Passes:
Cloth/paper: $10-$15; Laminated: $20-$35

POSTERS/PRESS KITS

Promotional Posters: $10-$40
Press Kits: $15-$50

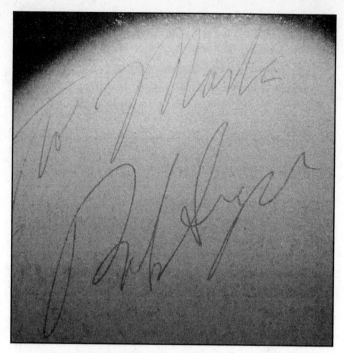

The autograph of Bob Seger

OFTEN OVERLOOKED MEMORABILIA

Night Moves flight jacket - $150; Like a Rock, Capitol promo pet rock, 1986 - $30; movie memorabilia from *Beverly Hills Cop II*; videotapes of television commercials utilizing his songs; promotional beach towel - $75; Live Seger triangular mobile - $45

The Seldom Scene

Formed 1971

John Duffy, Mike Auldridge, Ben Eldridge, John Starling, and Tom Gray*

*Starling departed in 1977 and Phil Rosenthal was added. Rosenthal and Gray left in 1986 and Lou Reid and T. Michael Coleman were added. Numerous changes followed.

Seventies progressive "new grass" group, founded by folk disciple John Duffy, the Seldom Scene is perhaps best remembered for its longevity and consistent releases. The group has recorded with such guests as Linda Ronstadt, Ricky Skaggs, and Emmylou Harris. As for the seldom seen hits, the group has been content with its mission throughout the years.

AUTOGRAPHS

A CD, LP, magazine cover, ad, photo, or card signed by the group: $10-$15*
*Lineup dependent

The Selecter

Formed 1979

Noel Davies, Charley Anderson, Pauline Black, Charley "H" Bembridge, Compton Amanor, Arthur "Gaps" Hendrickson, and Desmond Brown*

*Group disbanded in 1981, then re-formed in 1992

Late-70s British ska-influenced indie act the Selector is probably best remembered for the U.K. hit "Three Minute Hero" and members Pauline Black, who later turned to acting, and Noel Davies, who founded and nurtured the 2-Tone label into one of England's most successful independent record companies.

AUTOGRAPHS

A CD, LP, magazine cover, ad, photo, or card signed by the group: $15-25

The Sex Pistols

Formed 1975

Johnny Rotten (Lyndon), Born: January 31, 1956; Steve Jones, Born: September 3, 1955; Glen Matlock; and Paul Cook, Born: July 20, 1956*

*Matlock departed in 1977 and Sid Vicious (John Simon Ritchie), Born: May 10, 1957, Died: February 2, 1979, joined. Matlock returned in 1996.

The Sex Pistols, like so many other bands that have changed the course of rock and roll, were unique, controversial, expressive, revolting, turbulent, crude, and yet, oddly appealing. As Britain's youth faced monumental economic and social adversities, the Sex Pistols became an outlet for their expression. The brainchild of entrepreneur Malcolm McLaren, it was through his guidance that the group was marketed and packaged properly—to cater to the youth by rebelling against traditional norms. McLaren, owner of a popular London clothes boutique known as Sex (formerly Let It Rock and Too Fast To Live, Too Young To Die) was familiar with the task at hand, having managed the New York Dolls.

Cook, Jones, and Matlock, along with two others, formed the Swankers in 1973. The group's brief existence drew McLaren to the band, who suggested some key personnel changes. The Sex Pistols played their first gig at St. Martin's School of Art in London on November 6, 1975. The band's newly formed lineup included Cook, Jones, Rotten, and Matlock. The following summer the band built on their cult following, while packaging themselves in anti-fashion garb such as torn clothes, safety-pins through pierced orifices, and bondage paraphernalia. With the seeds of punk now sewn, it was time to cultivate the crop.

The Sex Pistols made their first U.K. television appearance on So It Goes (1976). The increased exposure included Johnny Rotten gracing the cover of New Musical Express (NME) (now considered a collector's item). The added attention also flagged EMI Records, which signed the band in October. Additional television exposure included Nationwide (BBC1-TV), London Weekend Show (ITV), and Today (ITV). The appearance on Today drew newspaper headlines throughout the country, because the band's verbal assault on interviewer Bill Grundy was laced with profanities. This event happened within a week of the band beginning the Anarchy in the U.K. Tour. Of the nineteen scheduled shows, which also featured the Clash, the Damned, and the Heartbreakers, only three actually took place. Posters for this tour are tough to find and highly sought by Sex Pistol collectors. No doubt the shortened tour and controversy surrounding the band contributed greatly to the scarcity of associated relics.

In 1977 EMI no longer felt it could market the band properly, or continue to handle the controversy surrounding them. Although their single "Anarchy In The UK" has sold over 50,000 copies, the company withdrew it. Sid Vicious joined the band in March 1977, and bass player Matlock was dismissed. The band then hopped to A&M Records, which pressed 25,000 copies of "God Save the Queen" before firing the band. This single, of which a hundred are allegedly surviving, can now command big money ($1,500). The next stop was Virgin Records which managed to sell 30,000 copies per day of the single in its first five days of release. The record company also hired a boat for a June 15 party along the Thames river. The Sex Pistols performed "Anarchy in the U.K." while floating outside the Houses of Parliament. The publicity stunt, and party, came to end as the boat docked and members of the party were arrested. Unfortunately, this event was only a prelude to a series of misfortunes that followed. Members of the band were attacked during the weeks that follow, and although all survived, some like Paul Cook did so with stitches and bruises.

On July 21, 1977, the band made its debut on Top of the Pops singing "Pretty Vacant." They also undertook a U.K. tour the following month under the names the Spots, Tax Exiles, Special Guest, Acne Rabble, and even the Hampsters. In October "Holidays in the Sun" reached Number Eight in the U.K., but copyright problems with the record's sleeve forced it to be withdrawn—another collector's item! On November 12, 1977, the band's first and only original album Never Mind the Bollocks Here's the Sex Pistols entered the U.K. chart at the top. The following month they planned to head to America, but were denied entry two days before a scheduled Saturday Night Live appearance. On Christmas Day the band played their last ever U.K. gig at a charity event held at Ivanhoe's in Huddersfield, York.

The Sex Pistols began a U.S. Tour in Atlanta, Georgia, at the Southeast Music Hall on January 5, 1978. More of a curiosity item than rock idols, they were met in America with little anticipation and even less adulation. After a handful of dates a dissatisfied Johnny Rotten announced the breakup of the band following a gig at the Winterland Ballroom in San

Francisco (1/14). Rotten headed to New York, while Cook and Jones headed to South America. Both Jones and Cook remained active in the punk movement, but with far less commercial success. Rotten, using his real name (John Lyndon), formed Public Image Ltd. Vicious, who was fighting substance abuse, moved to New York. On October 12, he called police from his room (100) at the Chelsea Hotel to inform them that someone had stabbed his girlfriend. Vicious was then arrested and charged with murdering Nancy Spungen. After a few days in jail, where he tried to commit suicide twice, he was finally bailed out by McLaren. On February 2, 1979, while out on bail, Vicious died of a heroin overdose, never seeing a trial.

The Great Rock 'n' Roll Swindle, a film documenting the band's rise to fame, premiered in October 1979. McLaren appeared in the film, claiming the entire phenomenon was nothing more than his creative hype. The film also included some animation portraying the band as pirates. Fortunately for collectors some of these cels have found their way into the market. Both film and promotional cels (often indicated as such with stickers on the reverse) can command $1,000 to $1,500.

Former band members and Vicious's mother sued McLaren and won royalties. The bio-film *Sid and Nancy* premiered in London on July 20, 1986. In addition to this film, a video documentary of the group was packaged as *Buried Alive* and released in 1988.

On March 18, 1996, a press conference was called to announce the Sex Pistol's forthcoming comeback tour. With their role as punk radicals played out fully, and their images already etched upon the rock 'n' roll slate, one wonders if there is really "Something Else," or is this comeback just a "Silly Thing."

AUTOGRAPHS
Group:

An LP, magazine cover, ad, photo, or card signed by the entire band: $800-$900*

*High-end reflects vintage signed memorabilia - *Never Mind the Bullocks...*

An autographed promotional poster for *Never Mind the Bullocks*: $1,800-$2,000

Individual:

Johnny Rotten: $50-$75 Sid Vicious: $400-$650
Paul Cook: $30-$40   Steve Jones: $35-$45
Glen Matlock: $20-$25

POSTERS/PRESS KITS

Early promotional handbill, two-color (Rotten, Jones, and Matlock): $700-$800

Early concert (single date) posters are scarce and can command $500-$1,000

Tour posters, such as Anarchy in the U.K. Tour (1976): $400-$500

Press Kits:

Deluxe 1978 Press Kit: $75-$100

USED CLOTHING/EQUIPMENT

Stage worn shirt (Jones): $800-$925
Stage worn shirt (Rotten) $850-$950

Guitar Picks:

Steve Jones: $30-$50
Glen Matlock: $20-$35
Sid Vicious: $350-$450

Drum Stick:

Paul Cook: $30-$65

OFTEN OVERLOOKED MEMORABILIA

M. Moorcock Rock and Roll Swindle newspaper - $20; an original artist's proof (Jamie Reid) for *Never Mind the Bullocks Here's the Sex Pistols* - $550-$600, original promo handbills average about $100 each; pair of *Sid &Nancy* used handcuffs- $630; promo paper Union Jack flags for "God Save The Queen"-$0-50; & cel from *The Great Rock'n Roll Swindle*- $1,000.

REFERENCES/BOOKS

Numerous resources exist. *England's Dreaming: Anarchy, Sex Pistols, Punk Rock and Beyond* by Jon Savage is a MUST read. There are no dedicated collector books.

Sexton, Charlie/Arc Angels

Born: August 11, 1968

Eighties teen idol and guitar prodigy Charlie Sexton is typically associated with his hit "Beat's So Lonely" (#17, 1985) from the debut album *Pictures for Pleasures* (#15, 1985). He faded from the music scene following the disappointing sales of his sophomore self-titled release. He briefly resurfaced later with the Arc Angels, which disbanded in 1994, and later with the Charlie Sexton Sextet.

AUTOGRAPHS

A CD, LP, magazine cover, ad, photo, or card signed by the artist: $10-$15

POSTERS/PRESS KITS

Promotional Posters: $8-$12
Press Kits: $10-$15

USED CLOTHING/EQUIPMENT

Guitar Picks: $8

The Shadows

Formed 1958 (the Drifters)

Hank B. Marvin, Born: October 28, 1941; Bruce Welch; Ian Samwell; Terry Smart; and Ken Payne*

*Numerous personnel changes

This late-50s British act, Cliff Richard's back-up band, is best remembered for the instrumental U.K. hits and songs "Apache," "F.B.I.," "KonTiki," "Atlantis," and "Frightened City," all in 1961, followed by "Shindig" (1963) and "Don't Make My Baby Blue" (1965). The Shadows, with their now trademarked guitar riffs of Hank B. Marvin, influenced numerous acts that would follow. The band was consistently

plagued by personnel changes—many members went out on their own individual successes. Periodic resurrections of the band have been frequent over the decades following the initial breakup.

AUTOGRAPHS
An LP, magazine cover, ad, photo, or card signed by the group: $15-$50

The Shaggs

Formed late-1960s

Betty, Dorothy, and Helen Wiggin

Bizarre late-60s New England act, consisting of the sisters Wiggin, whose over-exerted zeal for recording over shadowed the end result, the Shaggs have a minor, but loyal, cult following.

AUTOGRAPHS
A CD, LP, magazine cover, ad, photo, or card signed by the group: $12-$15

Shai

Formed 1990

Garfield Bright, Marc Gay, Carl Martin, and Darnell Van Rensalier

Nineties D.C. vocal group, whose gifted four-part harmonies have scored hits such as "If I Ever Fall in Love" (#2, 1992), "Comforter" (#10, 1993), and "Baby I'm Yours" (#10, 1993), Shai's overnight success has found it often compared to Jodeci and Boyz II Men, and justifiably so because this talented quartet has a very promising future.

AUTOGRAPHS
A CD,LP, magazine cover, ad, photo, or card signed by the group: $20-$35

POSTERS/PRESS KITS
Promotional Posters: $10-$15
Press Kits: $10-$15

Shalamar

Formed 1977

Jeffrey Daniels, Born: August 24, 1957; Jody Watley, Born: January 30, 1959; and Howard Hewett*

*Daniels and Watley departed in 1984 and Delisa Davis and Micki Free joined the group. Hewett left in 1985 and Sidney Justin was added.

Late-70s and '80s L.A. vocal trio and teen idols Daniels, Watley, and Hewett made Shalamar a household name (on its second try) with hits like "The Second Time Around" (#8, 1979), "Make That Move"

(#6 R&B, 1979), "Dead Giveaway" (#22, 1983), and "Dancing in the Sheets" (#17, 1984). Teen magazines drooled over the real-life love triangle between Watley, Daniels, and singer Stephanie Mills, who finally married, albeit briefly, before a divorce. Hewett, the last remaining original member, left in 1985 to pursue solo ambitions similar to his predecessors. His later hits included "I'm Not for Real," "Stay," and "Show Me" during a period that found him marrying actress Nia Peeples. Watley built a solid solo career (see entry), while Daniels turned his attentions to television and the stage.

AUTOGRAPHS
A CD, LP, magazine cover, ad, photo, or card signed by the group: $25-$50*
*Second lineup

POSTERS/PRESS KITS
Promotional Posters: $15-$25
Press Kits: $15-$30

OFTEN OVERLOOKED MEMORABILIA
Movie memorabilia from *Footloose*

Sha Na Na

Formed 1968

Original lineup: Johnny Contardo, Scott Powell, Frederick Dennis "Denny" Greene, Don York, Bruce Clarke, John "Jocko" Marcellino, Ritchie Joffe, Elliot Cahn, Henry Gross, Chris Donald, Screamin' Scott Simon, John "Bowser" Baumann, and Lennie Baker*

*Numerous personnel changes

Late-60s 1950s revival act Sha Na Na is best remembered for its live shows, one of which included Woodstock (1969), and for its successful syndicated television show that ran from 1977 to 1981 (97 episodes). The group has also seen alumni garner significant attention in other areas, such as Baumann in television, Simon cowriting "Sandy" for the movie *Grease*, and Henry Gross landing his 1976 hit single "Shannon" and numerous others. The group remains a staple on the oldies circuit.

AUTOGRAPHS
A CD, LP, magazine cover, ad, photo, or card signed by the group: $20-$35

OFTEN OVERLOOKED MEMORABILIA
Videotapes of episodes from the group's successful syndicated television show (1977-1981)

The Shangri-Las

Formed 1964

Mary Ann Ganser, Marge Ganser, Liz "Betty" Weiss, and Mary Weiss

This early-60s female vocal group, which scored numerous hits, is typically identified with the songs "Remember (Walkin' in the Sand)" (#5, 1964), "Leader of the Pack" (#1, 1964), "Give Him a Great Big Kiss" (#18, 1964), and "I Can Never Go Home Anymore" (#6, 1965). The Shangri-Las faded from the music scene by the late '60s.

AUTOGRAPHS

An LP, magazine cover, ad, photo, or card signed by the group: $25-$75*

*Original lineup

Shannon, Del

(Charles Westover)
Born: December 30, 1939, Died: February 8, 1990

Early-60s talented singer and songwriter, typically identified with his hits "Runaway" (#1, 1961), "Hats Off to Larry" (#5, 1961), and "Little Town Flirt" (#12, 1962), Del Shannon scored numerous other hits throughout a career that even found him on the chart in 1982 with "Sea of Love." When he wasn't touring or charting, he was often handling production work or arranging for other acts. The artist's cover of "From Me to You" made him the first American to cover a Beatles song. Shannon was reportedly suffering from severe depression when he took his own life in 1990.

AUTOGRAPHS

A CD, LP, magazine cover, ad, photo, or card signed by the artist: $40-$85

Shante, Roxanne

(Lolita Shante Gooden)
Born: March 8, 1970

Late-80s New York "bad girl" and teen rapper Shante is typically identified with the songs "Roxanne's Revenge" (#22, R&B, 1985) and "Loosey's Rap" (#1, R&B, 1988). She has gained moderate success with her first two albums.

AUTOGRAPHS

A CD, LP, magazine cover, ad, photo, or card signed by the artist: $10-$15

Sharkey, Feargal: See the Undertones

Shear, Jules

Born: March 7, 1952

Eighties singer and songwriter, formerly of the Funky Kings, Jules and the Polar Bears, and Reckless Sleepers, Shear is typically identified with the songs he has authored such as "All Through the Night" (#5, 1984) (covered by Cyndi Lauper) and "If She Knew What She Wants" (#29, 1986) (covered by the Bangles).

Shear was also instrumental in the birth of MTV's *Unplugged* series, which he found himself hosting from 1989 to 1991.

AUTOGRAPHS

A CD, LP, magazine cover, ad, photo, or card signed by the artist: $7-$12

OFTEN OVERLOOKED MEMORABILIA

Associated artifacts from other artists' covers of his compositions; videotapes of his hosting MTV's *Unplugged* series

Shelley, Pete: See the Buzzcocks

Shep and the Limelites

Formed 1961
James "Shep" Sheppard (1936-1970), Clarence Bassettand, and Charles Baskerville

Sixties New York vocal trio, fronted by the talented James Sheppard (formerly of the Heartbeats), Shep and the Limelites are best remembered for the hit "Daddy's Home" (#2, 1961), although they also charted with a handful of minor hits before breaking up in 1967. The Sheppard penned classic "A Thousand Miles Away" surfaces periodically and was featured on the soundtrack of *Diner*. The talented singer and songwriter was later found dead in 1970, a victim of an apparent robbery.

AUTOGRAPHS

An LP, magazine cover, ad, photo, or card signed by the group: $25-$75

OFTEN OVERLOOKED MEMORABILIA

Movie memorabilia from *Diner*

Sherman, Bobby

Born: July 18, 1943

Multi-talented teen heartthrob, typically identified with his television appearances in *Shindig!* (1964-1966) and *Here Come the Brides* (Jeremy Bolt), Sherman also recorded in the late '60s and landed numerous hits including "Little Woman" (#3, 1969), "La La La (If I Had You)" (#9, 1969), "Easy Come, Easy Go" (#9, 1970), "Julie, Do You Love Me" (#5, 1970), and "Cried Like a Baby" (#16, 1971). When the hits dissipated and some of his associated television series failed (*Getting Together*), he resigned himself to the typical guest appearance rolls on television shows such as *Love Boat*, *Fantasy Island*, *Lobo*, and even *Emergency*, which proved ironic, because he is now an emergency training officer for the Los Angeles Police Department.

AUTOGRAPHS

An LP, magazine cover, ad, photo, or card signed by the artist: $5-$15

OFTEN OVERLOOKED MEMORABILIA

Movie memorabilia from *Get Crazy* (1983); fan club kit includes: record, membership card, mini-poster, portraits, booklet, secret decoder, and stickers - $80; love beads - $40; ad for love beads - $5; lunch box w/steel Thermos - $100; necklaces (various) - $45; paint and color album (Artcraft) - $35; private photo album - $45; ad for private photo album - $5; records, "cut-outs" from Kellogg's Rice Krispies - $15 each; ring, premium send-away - $40; *Secret of Bobby Sherman* book - $20; stickers (hearts and flowers) - $20; Topps trading cards (both sets test marketed and scarce) gum cards - $950 (set of 55), plak cards - $750 (set of 35); numerous magazines featured his likeness, most ranging in price from $10-$20; videotapes of *Here Come the Brides* (9/25/68-9/18/70) and *Getting Together* (9/18/71-1/8/72), where Bobby played Bobby Conway

Shinehead

(Edmund Carl Aiken)
Born: April 10, 1962

Late-80s Jamaican reggae-rap artist Shinehead is typically associated with his Rastafarian-styled version of Michael Jackson's "Billie Jean" (1984), "Who the Cap Fits," and "Try My Love." He headlined the summer of 1993's Reggae Sunsplash Tour.

AUTOGRAPHS

A CD, LP, magazine cover, ad, photo, or card signed by the artist: $10

The Shirelles

Formed 1958

Shirley Alston, Born: June 10, 1941; Addie "Micki" Harris, Born: January 22, 1940, Died: June 10, 1982; Doris Kenner, Born: August 2, 1941; and Beverly Lee, Born: August 3, 1941

This late-50s and '60s all-female vocal group scored numerous hits, but is perhaps best known for the songs "Tonight's the Night" (#39, 1960), "Will You Love Me Tomorrow" (#1, 1961), "Dedicated to the One I Love," "Mama Said" (#4, 1961), "Soldier Boy" (#1, 1962), and "Foolish Little Girl" (#4, 1963). The Shirelles broke up in the late '60s. In 1994 the three living members sang together at a Rhythm and Blues Foundation awards ceremony for the first time in nineteen years

AUTOGRAPHS

An LP, magazine cover, ad, photo, or card signed by the group: $35-$110

Shirley and Lee/Shirley and Company

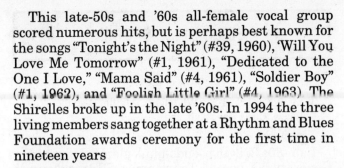

Shirley Goodman (Pixley), Born: June 19, 1936; and Leonard Lee (1935-1976)

Late-50s New Orleans R&B duo, best remembered for the songs "Let the Good Times Roll" (#20, 1956), "I'm Gone" (#2, R&B, 1952), and "I Feel Good" (#38, 1956), Shirley and Lee also scored a few other minor hits before splitting up in 1963. Shirley later resurfaced in the mid-70s with the disco dance hit "Shame, Shame, Shame" (#12, 1975).

AUTOGRAPHS

An LP, magazine cover, ad, photo, or card signed by the duo:- $25-$40

Shocked, Michelle

(Michelle Johnston)
Born: February 24, 1962

Late-80s vagabond rocker, typically associated with "The Texas Campfire Tapes," which ran to the top of the U.K. indie chart, Shocked has had greater exposure in the States with her album *Short Sharp Shocked*. The album was applauded by critics and received some airplay with the tunes "When I Grow Up" and "Anchorage." Her later efforts moved in a variety of directions, but were less well-received. Shocked by her lack of creativity in her work, she shocked her record company by suing it, and also her manager, whom she fired. Future Shocked fans were shocked when her self-released album *Kind-Hearted Woman* was only offered for sale at her performances.

AUTOGRAPHS

A CD, LP, magazine cover, ad, photo, or card signed by the artist: $12

POSTERS/PRESS KITS

Promotional Posters: $10-$12
Press Kits: $12

Sigue Sigue Sputnik

Formed 1982

Tony James, Neal X (Whitmore), Martin Degville, Ray Mayhew, Chris Kavanagh, and

Yana Ya Ya

Late-80s British pseudo-punk glam act, formed by Generation X bassist Tony James, SSS was long on look, flamboyance, and marketing, but short on talent. The hype reached such proportion that EMI reportedly signed the act for $6 million. The group's first album *Flaunt It*, quickly topped the U.K. chart, but it wasn't long before the backlash caught up to the band—some members were still learning how to play instruments. By the time its sophomore effort rolled out, the band was nearly rolled over.

AUTOGRAPHS

A CD, LP, magazine cover, ad, photo, or card signed by the group: $5

OFTEN OVERLOOKED MEMORABILIA

Clippings from industry-related periodicals hyping the band

The Silos

Formed 1985

Bob Rupe, Walter Sala-Humara, and Mary Rowell*

*Rowell departed in 1990. Rupe departed in 1991 and Rowell returned.

Mid-80s New York folk-rock band, which received accolades for its indie mentality, the Silos entrepreneur skills were key in handling its self-financed debut record. Positive reviews of the release helped get the group signed with RCA in1989, but when its major label debut stalled, the group was eventually dropped, and band members departed.

AUTOGRAPHS

A CD, LP, magazine cover, ad, photo, or card signed by the group: $10

Simon, Carly

Born: June 25, 1945

Carly Simon, a '70s and '80s prolific and successful composer, singer, and songwriter, is typically associated with the hits "That's the Way I've Always Heard It Should Be" (#10, 1971), "You're So Vain" (#1, 1972), "Nobody Does It Better" (#2, 1977), and "You Belong to Me" (#6, 1978). She has landed numerous hits on the charts over the past decades and has established herself in other media including film and children's literature. On November 3, 1972, she married singer James Taylor. Although their vows lasted just over a decade, the relationship was fruitful musically, as exhibited on duets such as "Mockingbird."

Simon's battles with stage fright often reached epic proportion, causing shows to be cancelled and, in some cases, even tours. She eventually overcame this, to the delight of her fans who seldom had the chance to attend her limited live performances. "Let the River Run" garnered Simon an Oscar for Best Original Song, giving her another creative outlet for her work. As the daughter of the cofounder of Simon & Schuster publishers, it was no surprise to see the artist look toward printed media, and as a mother it was only natural that she chose to write children's books. Now having successfully published many books, she has also found herself exploring opera for young people. Her *Romulus Hunt* debuted at the Metropolitan Opera and the Kennedy Center for the Performing Arts in 1993. As to her next venture, her fans and collectors wait in anticipation.

AUTOGRAPHS

ACD, LP, magazine cover, ad, photo, or card signed by the artist: $20-$55

TOUR BOOKS/PROGRAMS/PASSES

Simon stated in 1995 that she had given only sixty concerts in her entire career, making most live artifacts scarce.

POSTERS/PRESS KITS

Promotional Posters: $10-$40
Press Kits: $15-$50

TYPICALLY OVERLOOKED CARLY SIMON ARTIFACTS

Movie memorabilia from her cameo roll in Taking Off (1972), *The Spy Who Loved Me* (1977) (she provided the theme), *Perfect* (1985) (she poured water on John Travolta), *Heartburn* (she provided the song, "Coming Around Again"), *Working Girl* (1989) (Simon contributed the theme), *This Is My Life* (1992) (Simon composed and recorded the soundtrack); memorabilia from the MUSE concerts held at Madison Square Garden beginning on (9/19/79); auction artifacts from the 1988 annual Martha's Vineyard Celebrity Auction (Simon contributed lot that included a private performance of a song in the home of the winning bidder); an autographed copy of her children's book, *Amy and the Dancing Bear* (Simon does selected book signings); an autographed copy of her second children's book, *The Boy of the Bells* (1990); an autographed copy of her next children's book *The Fisherman's Song* (1992); videotape of U.K. Dunlop Tires commercial, includes "You're So Vain" (1991); associated items from the opera *Romulus Hunt* (1993); associated items from the American Repertory Theatre's production of *Cakewalk* in Cambridge, MA (Simon contributed music) (1993); videotape of *Phenom* (Simon contributed theme) ABC-TV (1993); associated artifacts from Simon's induction into the Songwriters Hall of Fame, New York (6/1/94); any and all artifacts from her five-month 1976 stay at 360 Rockingham Ave, Brentwood, CA; any and all associated items from her performance at New York's Grand Central Station for a cable special on Lifetime; any items related to Livestock '95, a benefit concert that reunited Simon and Taylor on stage

REFERENCES/BOOKS

Limited resources exist. There are no dedicated collector books. Serious collectors should opt for a Fan Club: The Official Carly Simon International Fan Club, P.O. Box 679, Branford, CT 06405 ($22 fee)

SOME RARE CARLY SIMON TELEVISION APPEARANCES

"Carly in Concert—My Romance" HBO-TV Special (4/15/90)
Late Night With David Letterman (1/31/90)
The Late Show With David Letterman (11/14/94)
"Christmas at Home With the Stars" ABC-TV (12/17/94)
The Tonight Show (3/2/95)
The Late Show With David Letterman (5/4/95)

Simon, Paul

Born: October 13, 1941

Having already recorded a solo album between the first two Simon and Garfunkel albums, Paul Simon only reaffirmed his status as a premier songwriter and performer during his solo years. "Mother and Child Reunion" (#4, 1972), "Loves Me Like a Rock" (#2, 1973), "Kodachrome" (#2, 1973), and "Slip Slidin' Away" (#5, 1977) have been among the numerous hits the artist has been identified with during the last two and a half decades. As for his album production, the one that sticks out in most everyone's mind is *Graceland* (#3, 1987), winner of the 1986 Grammy for Album of the Year, a reflection of South African dance music.

Throughout his solo career Simon has been creative, controversial, altruistic, introspective, and progressive. Although he is commonly linked with Garfunkel, his solo career has now eclipsed the duo's

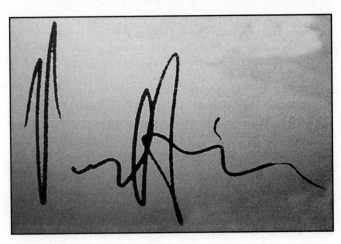

A very quick Paul Simon signature

work in many areas. As an artist and a humanitarian, his work will be studied for many years to come.

AUTOGRAPHS

A CD, LP, magazine cover, ad, photo, or card signed by the artist: $25-$75

TOUR BOOKS/PROGRAMS/PASSES

Tour Books:
Born at the Right Time: $10

SIMPLE SIMON SOLO ITEMS

Selected Forgotten Artifacts from Paul Simon's Solo Years

All items associated with his class on songwriting and recording given at New York University for one semester in 1970 including course catalogs, flyers, etc.; Concert for Peace related items (8/6/70); a menu from the 456 restaurant in Chinatown, New York—Simon says, "answer to inspiration for 'Mother and Child Reunion' is an egg and chicken dish"; first solo date since break with Garfunkel, Boston, MA (5/6/73); a press release from the BBC stating the reasons why it will not air "Kodachrome"; BBC-TV Special (1976) related items; artifacts from the Inaugural Eve Gala Performance for President Carter (1/19/77); all items associated with Simon's acting debut as Tony Lacey in Woody Allen's movie *Annie Hall* (1978); movie memorabilia from *All You Need Is Cash* (1978) (Simon made cameo appearance) and *One Trick Pony* (1980); videotapes of his 1978 appearances on *Saturday Night Live* also on 9/10/86, the 15th Anniversary special (9/24/89), and 5/15/93; souvenirs from the Philadelphia Furies soccer team (Simon is part owner); a plastic drink cup from his appearance at London's Hammersmith Odeon (11/6/80) (Simon bought the entire audience drinks); memorabilia from his induction into the Songwriters Hall of Fame (3/15/82); a copy of the press release given at his press conference on January 30, 1987, regarding his black listing for recording in South Africa; copies of both the film and home video *The Graceland Concert* (1987); videotape of NBC-TV's "Coca Cola Presents Live: The Hard Rock" (9/13/88); videotape of his appearance on *Late Night With David Letterman* (11/24/88); videotape of Shelly Duvall's "Mother Goose Rock 'n' Rhyme" (1989); Montauk Point Lighthouse preservation find items (Simon performed at benefit); Evian Music Festival items, programs, handouts, etc. (Simon previews his new album) (9/90); an autographed Senator Bill Bradley bumper sticker (Simon has been active in his campaign) (1990); all items associated with his Central Park Concert on August 15, 1991; a copy of his speech given at the Country Music Hall of Fame (1991) or related items; all items relating to his industrious international (27 country) tour, Born at the Right Time; all artifacts, program, tickets, etc. from Farm Aid V; videotape from his appearance on MTV *Unplugged* (6/3/92); a ticket to the Tennessee Inaugural Ball in Washington, D.C. (1/20/93); a ticket from the Tibet House Benefit Concert (2/10/94); all items relating to his annual Back to the Ranch benefits held in Montauk Point; contest info from his a cappella group search held (5/31/95); videotape of the *Oprah Winfrey* syndicated TV show featuring the Simon-penned theme

REFERENCES/BOOKS

A few resources exist, but none do justice to the singer in my opinion. There are no dedicated collector books.

Simon and Garfunkel

Formed 1962

Paul Simon and Art Garfunkel

Sixties New York vocal duo, whose poetic songs and pristine harmonies not only defined their era, but transcended generations with their appeal, Simon and Garfunkel are typically associated with their hits "Sounds of Silence," "Homeward Bound," "I Am a Rock," "The Boxer," "Cecilia," and the monumental "Bridge over Troubled Water" (#1, 1970).

The 1970 album *Bridge over Troubled Water* yielded four hit singles and was honored with the prestigious British Britannia Award as Best International Pop Album of the past 25 years. Most consider the title track to be one of the most memorable songs of the century. The duo was inducted into the Rock and Roll Hall of Fame in 1990 and has performed sporadically since the initial 1970 breakup.

AUTOGRAPHS

A CD, LP, magazine cover, ad, photo, or card signed by the duo: $55-$125

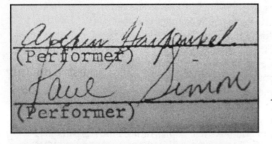

Signatures from the duo Simon and Garfunkel

TOUR BOOKS/PROGRAMS/PASSES

Tour Books:
An Evening With... (Japan, 1993): $25

SELECTED AND OFTEN OVERLOOKED COLLECTIBLES

All items associated with their attendance at Forest Hills High School in New York, especially a handbill from the performance of *Alice in Wonderland* in which both performed; videotape of their performance as "Tom and Jerry" on Dick Clark's *American Bandstand*; videotape from their appearance on *The Smothers Brothers Comedy Hour* (5/14/67 and 10/15/67); memorabilia from the Monterey International Pop Festival (6/16/67); all items relating to the song "You Don't Know Where Your Interest Lies" (B-side to "Fakin It"); movie memorabilia from *The Graduate* (1968); videotape from their first television special (11/30/69); Simon and Garfunkel reunite at a political fund raiser for Senator George McGovern (4/72); videotape from their appearance on *Saturday Night Live* (10/19/75); all items from their concert in New York's Central Park (9/19/81); all items from their 9-date European Tour (6/8-6/19/82); all items from their 1983 U.S. reunion tour; all items relating to the duo's induction into the Rock and Roll Hall of Fame (1/17/90); memorabilia from their benefit performances (5/4/92 and 3/1/93); videotape of television commercial advertising The Complete Collection, 1974; a copy of the Sears catalog

that included their special *Simon and Garfunkel* (SP-435); Fry's chocolate premium advertising for "Sounds of Silence" single, 1968; Pepsi advertising offering "The 59th Street Bridge Song" as a premium offer, 1968

REFERENCES/BOOKS

Numerous resources exist. Start first with *Simon and Garfunkel* by Joseph Morella and Patricia Barey. There are no dedicated collector books.

Simone, Nina

(Eunice Waymon)
Born: February 21, 1933

The late-50s "High Priestess of Soul" is typically identified with the songs "I Love You, Porgy," "Ain't Got No—I Got Life," and "My Baby Just Cares for Me," which was used for a Chanel No.5 television commercial. Nina Simone has enjoyed a long and productive career, with greater attention paid to her work in recent years.

AUTOGRAPHS

A CD, LP, magazine cover, ad, photo, or card signed by the artist: $10-$15

OFTEN OVERLOOKED MEMORABILIA

Movie memorabilia from *Point of No Return* (1993); videotape of the Chanel No. 5 commercial featuring her song "My Baby Just Cares for Me."

REFERENCES/BOOKS

I Put a Spell on You - her autobiography (1991)

Simple Minds

Formed 1978

Jim Kerr, Born: July 9, 1959; Charlie Burchill, Born: November 27, 1959; Duncan Barnwell; Mick McNeil, Born: July 20, 1958; Tony Donald; and Brian McGee*

*Barnwell and Donald departed in 1978 and Derek Forbes was added. McGee left in 1980 and Kenny Hyslop was briefly added before Mike Ogletree took over on drums. Ogletree left in 1982 and Mel Gaynor was added. Forbes left in 1984 and John Giblin, Robin Clark, and Sue Hadjopoulos were added. Clark, Hadjopoulos, and McNeil left in 1989 and Peter Vitesse was added. Vitesse departed in 1993.

Late-70s and '80s Scottish synth-based pop group, best remembered for the songs "Promised You a Miracle," "Don't You (Forget About Me)" (#1, 1985), "Alive & Kicking" (#3, 1985), and "Sanctify Yourself" (#14, 1986), Simple Minds has faced numerous personnel changes over the years, working both to its advantage and disadvantage. Interest in the group's work has dissipated in the '90s.

Simple Minds. Photo by Bob Sebree. Courtesy Virgin Records.

AUTOGRAPHS

A CD, LP, magazine cover, ad, photo, or card signed by the group: $25-$35*

*Lineup dependent

TOUR BOOKS/PROGRAMS/PASSES

Tour Books:
Sparkle in the Rain: $20
Street Fighting Years, Europe: $15
Good News From The Next World: $15

Backstage Passes:
Cloth/paper: $10-$15; Laminated: $15-$20

POSTERS/PRESS KITS

Promotional Posters: $6-$20
Press Kits: $12-$25

OFTEN OVERLOOKED MEMORABILIA

Once Upon a Time, Virgin promo magnetic jigsaw, 1985; movie memorabilia from *The Breakfast Club*

REFERENCES/BOOKS

A few resources exist, but none do justice to the singer in my opinion. There are no dedicated collector books.

Simply Red

Formed 1982
Mick Hucknall, Born: June 8, 1960

Late-80s British soul act, best remembered for the songs "Holding Back the Years" (#1, 1986), "The Right Thing," "Ev'ry Time We Say Goodbye," and "If You Don't Know Me by Now" (#1, 1989), Simply Red has been far more successful in the U.K., but well-respected for its ability in the States.

AUTOGRAPHS

A CD, LP, magazine cover, ad, photo, or card signed by the group: $20-$35

TOUR BOOKS/PROGRAMS/PASSES

Tour Books:
U.K Tour, 1992. $15

Backstage Passes:
Cloth: $8-$10; Laminated: $12-$15

POSTERS/PRESS KITS

Promotional Posters: $7-$15
Press Kits: $14-$18

OFTEN OVERLOOKED MEMORABILIA

Men and Women, Elektra promo bath robe

Sinatra, Frank

Born: December 12, 1915

"Ol' Blue Eyes" is perhaps the greatest singer of the Twentieth Century, and although he denounced rock music in the late '50s, he later embraced it by recording songs from Stevie Wonder, Billy Joel, and George Harrison. Suave and sophisticated, cool and romantic, Sinatra was an interpreter and the first bona-fide pop idol.

The Early Years: Chart Breakers and Broken Hearts

Sinatra joined the Harry James orchestra on July 13, 1939, and scored hits with "From the Bottom of My Heart" and "All or Nothing at All" (#2, 1943) before he joined Tommy Dorsey for two years. During this period the band placed fifteen songs in the Top Ten, including "I'll Never Smile Again" (#1). The performer's radio work catapulted his career, while he melted more than his fair share of hearts on Lucky Strike's *Hit Parade*. Over a three year period (1943-1946), "The Sultan of Swoon" dropped seventeen Top Ten singles onto the chart before he faded from the scene at the end of World War II. Devastated when Columbia Records dropped his contract in the early '50s, he turned to Hollywood, which finally took him seriously after his roll in *From Here to Eternity* garnered him a 1953 Oscar.

The Capitol Years

Capitol Records signed Sinatra in 1953 and teamed him with Nelson Riddle, and although the strategy was to focus on album production, the hit singles just kept coming, including, "Young at Heart" (#2, 1954), "Learnin' the Blues" (#1, 1955), "Hey! Jealous Lover" (#3, 1956), "All the Way" (#2, 1957), and "Witchcraft" (#6, 1958). Still a movie star, he won critical acclaim for his role in *The Man with the Golden Arm* (1958), but by the late '50s the singles failed and so did his second marriage to Ava Gardner. He left Capitol with plenty of capital and established his own company, Reprise, in 1961.

Rat Pack and Reprise

The '60s found Sinatra gaining some momentum on the charts, headlining the 1965 Newport Jazz Festival, and landing a series of successful television specials, including the Emmy winning "Frank Sinatra: A Man and His Music." "Strangers in the Night" (#1, 1966), "That's Life" (#4, 1966), and "Somethin' Stupid" (#1, 1967), a duet with his daughter Nancy, allowed him to hold is own against the British Invasion.

Gold Disc Award Ltd. award for Nancy and Frank Sinatra's "Somethin' Stupid," 1966. It is valued at $750. From the Doug Leftwitch collection.

During the '60s he also made his Las Vegas debut at the Sands, followed by Caesar's Palace, and led the notorious "Rat Pack" (Sinatra, Sammy Davis Jr., Dean Martin, Peter Lawford, and Joey Bishop). "My Way" (#27, 1968) became his hallmark song of the decade and evidence of his willingness to record younger material. Sinatra also married actress Mia Farrow in 1966, although it lasted for only two years.

Come Back

His gala farewell came on June 13, 1971, following his retirement announcement, but the decision was quickly overturned in 1973 with the release of *Ol' Blue Eyes Is Back*. The following year he mounted an eight-city, 13-date sold-out U.S. tour and even performed in Japan and Australia. In 1976 he married Zeppo Marx's widow Barbara. His career slowed down the end of the decade.

Following a five year hiatus from recording, he released *Trilogy: Past, Present, Future*, which included his next hallmark song, "New York, New York" (#32, 1980). *She Shot Me Down* (1981) and *L.A. Is My Lady* (1984) were his successful follow-ups, and many critics pondered just how much longer he would continue recording.

Frank Sinatra Duets (1993) and *Duets II* (1994), were his legacy in the '90s. Still touring, now in his late seventies, Sinatra was noticeably hampered, but persevered to the delight of his fans. By the middle of the decade, following hospitalization, it was clear that his career was drawing to a close. Having been awarded every conceivable award, there was simply nothing left to prove. The Trilogy was complete!

AUTOGRAPHS

A CD, LP, magazine cover, ad, photo, or card signed by the artist: $200-$375

POSTERS/PRESS KITS

Sinatra 80th, Italian: $25

Frank Sinatra's signature

OFTEN OVERLOOKED MEMORABILIA

Memorabilia from Sinatra's career can, and has, filled books. Most collectors, myself included, believe one of the most treasured items is *A Man and His Music*, Reprise promotional copy, double album box set, FS-1016, 1965. Limited to only 500, this item includes a 30-page book, autographed and numbered; *Duets* promo baseball cap-$25; *Duets* I & II center display- $20

REFERENCES/BOOKS

(Visit your local library)

Sinatra, Nancy

Born: June 8, 1940

Late-60s singer, and daughter of legendary crooner Frank Sinatra, Nancy Sinatra first came to the attention of the music scene with "These Boots Are Made for Walkin'" (#1, 1966), followed by "Sugar Town"/ "Summer Wine" (#5), "You Only Live Twice" (the theme to a James Bond movie), "Jackson" (#14, 1967), a duet with Lee Hazelwood, and a duet with father, "Somethin' Stupid" (#1, 1967). Sinatra later appeared in both television and film, before essentially retiring from show business by the end of the '60s.

AUTOGRAPHS

A CD, LP, magazine cover, ad, photo, or card signed by the artist: $5-$25

OFTEN OVERLOOKED MEMORABILIA

Movie memorabilia from *For Those Who Think Young*, *Get Yourself a College Girl*, *Bikini Party in a Haunted House*, *Last of the Secret Agents*, *The Oscar*, and *Speedway* (w/ Elvis Presley); videotapes of her numerous television show appearances such as *Hullabaloo* and *American Bandstand*; a copy of her appearance in *Playboy* magazine; a copy of *Sinatra, My Father*, which she authored

Siouxsie and the Banshees

Formed 1976

Siouxsie Sioux (Susan Dallion), Born: May 27, 1958; Sid Vicious (John Simon Ritchie), Born: May 10, 1957, Died: February 2, 1979; Steve Severin, Born: September 25, 1959; and Marco Pirroni, Born: April 27, 1959*

*Numerous personnel changes

Late-70s British rock group, typically associated with the songs "Kiss Them for Me" (#23, 1991), "Dear Prudence" (#3, U.K., 1983), and "Peek-a-Boo" (#53, 1988), the band has gone through numerous person-

nel changes. By the mid-70s it only included Siouxsie and Steve Severin from the original lineup. The group's music has gone from an art-punk sound to techno dance, which is perhaps a blessing considering the band's longevity.

AUTOGRAPHS
A CD, LP, magazine cover, ad, photo, or card signed by the group: $15-$35*
*Lineup dependent

POSTERS/PRESS KITS
Promotional Posters: $10-$25
Press Kits: $14 -$30

Sir Douglas Quintet/Doug Sahm

Formed 1964

Original lineup: Doug Sahm, Born: November 6, 1941; Augie Meyers, Born: May 31, 1941; Francisco Moran, Born: August 13, 1946; and Harvey Kagan and Johnny Perez*

*Group re-formed in 1994

Late-60s Tex-mex crooners, best remembered for the songs "Mendocino" (#27, 1969), "The Rains Came" (1966), and "She's About a Mover," was/is led by "cosmic cowboy" Doug Sham.

AUTOGRAPHS
An LP, magazine cover, ad, photo, or card signed by the group: $10-$15

Sir Mix-a-Lot

(Anthony Ray)
Born: August 12, 1963

Sir Mix-a-Lot Courtesy American Records

Late-80s Seattle rapper, typically associated with the songs "Square Dance Rap" (#82, 1988), "Posse on Broadway" (#70, 1988), and "Baby Got Back" (#1, 1992), Sir Mix-a-Lot also teamed up with Mudhoney on "Freak Mama" for the soundtrack of *Judgment Night*

AUTOGRAPHS
A CD, LP, magazine cover, ad, photo, or card signed by the artist: $5-$20

Sister Sledge

Formed late 1950s

Joni, Kathie, Kim, and Debra Sledge

Late-70s Philadelphia sister act, best remembered for the songs "He's the Greatest Dancer" (#9, 1979), "My Guy," "Frankie"(#1, U.K., 1985), and the anthem "We Are Family" (#2, 1979), Sister Sledge first started singing together in the late '50s while attending church.

AUTOGRAPHS
A CD, LP, magazine cover, ad, photo, or card signed by the group: $15-$35*
*Item relating to "We Are Family"

OFTEN OVERLOOKED MEMORABILIA
All related Pittsburgh Pirates memorabilia from 1979 (the team used the group's hit "We Are Family" as its anthem)

Sisters of Mercy

Formed 1980

Andrew Eldritch (Taylor), Ben Gunn (Matthews), Craig Adams, and Gary Marx (Mark Pearman)*

*Gunn left in 1984 and Wayne Hussey (Jerry Lovelock) was added. Hussey, Adams, and Marx left in 1987 and Patricia Morrison was added. Morrison departed in 1990 and Tony James, Andreas Bruhn, and Tim Bricheno joined the band. Numerous changes followed.

The '80s British goth morbid metal act, typically associated with the macabre classics "Vision Thing" and "More," Sisters of Mercy has undergone numerous personnel changes.

AUTOGRAPHS
A CD, LP, magazine cover, ad, photo, or card signed by the group: $10-$20*
*Lineup dependent

POSTERS/PRESS KITS
Promotional Posters: $8-$20
Press Kits: $12-$25

OFTEN OVERLOOKED MEMORABILIA
Floodland, Merciful promo bag set (1987) includes: CD, video, and T-shirt

Skaggs, Ricky

Born: July 18, 1954

This late-70s and '80s bluegrass player, who as a solo artist has landed more than a dozen C&W Top Ten hits, is typically associated with "Uncle Pen" (#1, 1984), the first bluegrass recording to top the country charts since 1963. Skaggs is also known for the popular Number One C&W albums *Highways & Heartaches*, *Don't Cheat in Our Hometown*, and *Country Boy* and for being an alumnus of the Hot Band, which backed Emmylou Harris. He later married performer Sharon White, and both duetted on "Love Can't Ever Get Any Better Than This" (#10, 1987). By the mid-90s his career was pushed into the background by Nashville's "hats acts."

AUTOGRAPHS
A CD, LP, magazine cover, ad, photo, or card signed by the artist: $10-$20

POSTERS/PRESS KITS
Promotional Posters: $8-$15
Press Kits: $14-$20

USED CLOTHING/EQUIPMENT
Guitar Pick: $10

The Skatalites

Formed 1963

Don Drummond, Rico Rodriguez, Baba Brooks, Johnny "Dizzy" Moore, Raymond Harper, Bobby Ellis, Lester Sterling, Karl Bryan, Roland Alphonso, Tommy McCook, Ernest Ranglin, Jah Jerry (Jerome Hines), Lloyd Brevette, Jackie Mittoo, Theophilus Beckford, Gladstone Anderson, Lloyd Nibbs, and Hugh Malcolm

Late-60s ska pioneers and inspiration for the British two-tone movement, the Skatalites were one of the first Jamaican acts signed to Island Records. The group is typically associated with the song "Guns of Navarone" (1967).

AUTOGRAPHS
A CD, LP, magazine cover, ad, photo, or card signed by the group: $15-$35

Skid Row

Formed 1986

Matt Fallon, Dave "Snake" Sabo, Scotti Hill, Rachel Bolan, and Rob Affuso*

*Fallon departed in 1987 and Sebastion Bach (Bierk), Born: April 3, 1968, was added

These late-80s New Jersey rancid rockers are typically associated with Bon Jovi, because the band includes the its former guitarist Dave Sabo, and with the controversy that typically looms around frontman Sebastion Bach. The group is best remembered for the songs "Youth Gone Wild," "18 and Life" (#4, 1989), and "I Remember You" (#6, 1989).

AUTOGRAPHS
A CD, LP, magazine cover, ad, photo, or card signed by the group: $25-$40

POSTERS/PRESS KITS
Promotional Posters: $8-$15
Press Kits: $15-$25

USED CLOTHING/EQUIPMENT
Guitar Pick: $10-$25

OFTEN OVERLOOKED MEMORABILIA
Newspaper and periodical clippings surrounding Bach's controversies

REFERENCES/BOOKS
Limited resources exist. There are no dedicated collector books. Serious collectors should opt for a Fan Club: Skid Row: Chain Gang, P.O. Box 884464, San Francisco, CA 94188 ($19 fee)

The Skids: See Big Country

Slade

Formed 1968

Noddy (Neville) Holder, Born: June 15, 1950; Dave Hill, Born: April 4, 1952; Jimmy Lea, Born: June 14, 1952; and Don Powell, Born: September 10, 1950

Early-70s British hard rock, glam and glitter band Slade is commonly associated with hits "Gudbuy T'Jane" (#2, U.K., 1972), "Cum On Feel the Noize" (#1, U.K., 1973), "Skweeze Me Pleeze Me," "Take Me Bak 'Ome" (#1, U.K., 1972), and "Mama Weer All Crazee Now" (#1, U.K., 1972), all with the band's hallmark misspellings. While "Slademania" pounded Britain, the group had relatively little impact in the States, although some of us were known to paint letters on our fists and fingers, and even alter our wardrobe.

A Slade tour program (The Concert Pub. Co.)

Undaunted by waning sales numbers, the band endured and even starred in the film *Flame* (1974). The group's later hits included "Lock Up Your Daughters," "My Oh My," and "Run Runaway," before it split up.

AUTOGRAPHS

A CD, LP, magazine cover, ad, photo, or card signed by the group: $35-$60

OFTEN OVERLOOKED MEMORABILIA

Movie memorabilia from the straight to video classic *Flame*; associated artifacts from other groups' covers of their compositions

---

Slayer

Formed 1982

Tom Araya, Born: June 6, 1961; Jeff Hanneman, Born: January 31, 1964; Kerry King, Born: June 3, 1964; and Dave Lombardo, Born: February 16, 1965*

*Lombardo departed in 1992 and Paul Bostaph was added on drums

Eighties L.A. head-bangers and Def Jam recording stars, typically associated with their macabre song subjects and aggressive albums such as *South of Heaven* (#57, 1988), *Seasons in the Abyss* (#40, 1990), and *Decade of Aggression* (#55, 1991), Slayer has garnered a significant cult following, some

Slayer. Courtesy American Recordings.

through negative references to the band that only seem to feed teenage obsession with the group. The band's album *Divine Intervention* (#8, 1994) was its first to sell into the Top Ten.

AUTOGRAPHS

A CD, LP, magazine cover, ad, photo, or card signed by the group: $25-$50

TOUR BOOKS/PROGRAMS/PASSES

Tour Books:
World Sacrifice Tour (Europe): $20

POSTERS/PRESS KITS

Promotional Posters: $8-$20
Press Kits: $20-$30

USED CLOTHING/EQUIPMENT

Guitar Pick: $8-$10

Sledge, Percy

Born: November 25, 1940

Mid-60s Alabama R&B/pop vocalist, typically associated with the hits "When a Man Loves a Woman" (#1, 1966), "Warm and Tender Love" (#17, 1966), "It Tears Me Up" (#20, 1966), and "Take Time to Know Her" (#11, 1968), Percy Sledge's career took off following his departure from the Esquires. During the '70s his hits dissipated, although a couple found their way to the R&B chart. Renewed interest in his career took place following the 1987 film *Platoon*, which included "When a Man Loves a Woman."

AUTOGRAPHS

A CD, LP, magazine cover, ad, photo, or card signed by the artist: $10-$30

OFTEN OVERLOOKED MEMORABILIA

Movie memorabilia from *Platoon* (1986); momentos from his days with the Esquires combo

---

Slick, Grace: see the Jefferson Airplane

Slick Rick

(Rickey Walters)
Born: January 14, 1965

Late-80s Def Jam rapper, typically associated with his smash album *The Great Adventure of Slick Rick* (#31, 1989) which featured the songs "Teenage Love" (#16, R&B, 1988), "Children's Story" (#5, R&B, 1989), and "Treat Her Like a Prostitute," Slick Rick's career was somewhat hampered by a sentence for attempted murder in 1991. Despite the circumstance he still managed to record prior to sentencing and during a work-release program.

AUTOGRAPHS

A CD, LP, magazine cover, ad, photo, or card signed by the artist: $10

The Slits

Formed 1976

Ari Up, Kate Korus, Palmolive, and Suzi Gutsy

Korus and Gutsy departed in 1977 and Tessa Pollit and Viv Albertine were added. Palmolive left in 1978 and Budgie was added on drums.

Late-70s British punk-rock all-female band, which made its stage debut by opening for the Clash (1977), the Slits are best remembered for the album *Cut*, its only major label release, which featured the band in just thongs and mud on the cover—an instant collectible! The Slits split in 1981.

AUTOGRAPHS

An LP, magazine cover, ad, photo, or card signed by the group: $20-$45*

Cut related item and lineup!

Sloan, Phillip (P.F.)

Born 1946

Late-60s singer/songwriter Sloan has written extensively for the Grass Roots, given the Turtles "You Baby," and provided songs to the Searchers and Herman's Hermits.

AUTOGRAPHS

An LP, magazine cover, ad, photo, or card signed by the artist: $10

OFTEN OVERLOOKED MEMORABILIA

Associated memorabilia from the numerous groups that have recorded his songs

Sly and the Family Stone

Formed 1967

Original lineup: Sly Stone (Sylvester Stewart), Born: March 15, 1944; Freddie Stone (Stewart); Larry Graham Jr.; Cynthia Robinson; Greg Errico; Rosie Stone; and Jerry Martini

Late-60s Bay Area act which invented '70s funk with its racial, overtly sexual, and ornate compositions and arrangements, Sly and the Family Stone are best remembered for hits such as "Dance to the Music" (#8, 1968), "Everyday People" b/w "Sing a Simple Song" (#1, 1968), "I Want to Take You Higher" (#38, 1969), "Hot Fun in the Summertime" (#2, 1969), "Thank You Falettinme Be Mice Elf Agin" b/w "Ev-

erybody Is a Star" (#1, 1970), "Family Affair" (#1, 1971), and "If You Want Me to Stay" (#12, 1973).

The band's appearance at Woodstock (1969), captured on the soundtrack, was one of the most invigorating performances of the event and an excellent example of the group's live power. During the late '60s the band had a phenomenal impact not only on music, but also on the culture of the era. But by the early '70s, Sly garnered a reputation for not always being timely or even in attendance at key events, such as concerts, resulting in band dissatisfaction and the departure of Graham and Errico. By the middle of the decade Sly's reputation was tarnished significantly by drug arrests, and his career significantly derailed in 1987 with a jail sentence. The group was inducted into the Rock and Roll Hall of Fame in 1993.

AUTOGRAPHS

A CD, LP, magazine cover, ad, photo, or card signed by the group: $15-$40

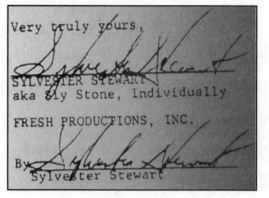

Sylvester Stewart's signature

OFTEN OVERLOOKED MEMORABILIA

All Woodstock related items; promo mobiles (1970s) - $40-$50; book cover Stand - $30

Small Faces/Faces

Formed 1965

Steve Marriott, Born: January 30, 1947, Died: April 20, 1991; Jimmy Winston (Langwith); Ronnie Lane, Born: April 1, 1946; and Kenney Jones, Born: September 16, 1948*

*Winston departed in 1965 and Ian McLagan, Born: May 12, 1945, was added. Marriott left in 1968. In 1968 the name was changed to Faces. In 1976 Small Faces re-formed: Marriott, Jones, McLagan, Rick Wills, and Joe Brown. Brown departed in 1978 and Jimmy McCulloch (1953-1979) was added. Group disbanded.

Faces formed 1969

Lane; McLagan; Jones; Rod Stewart, Born: January 10, 1945; and Ron Wood, Born: June 1, 1947*

Lane departed in 1973 and Tetsu Yamauchi was added. Stewart left in 1975 and Wood followed him a year later. The group disbanded in 1976.

Mid-60s British pop act, formed by Steve Marriott and Ronnie Lane, the Small Faces are best remembered for the U.K. hits "Sha La La La Lee," "Hey Girl," "All or Nothing," "My Mind's Eye," and "Itchycoo Park" (#16, 1967), which was the only hit that garnered any attention in America. The Small Faces quickly got tired of their image as a singles band and moved toward producing a conceptual album in 1968 with *Ogden's Nut Gone Flake*, but tensions inside the group led to Steve Marriott's departure in 1969. While Marriott was forming Humble Pie, the Small Faces became simply the Faces with the addition of two new members, Rod Stewart and Ron Wood, both of whom had played in the Jeff Beck Group.

With Stewart, who himself was coming of age as a performer, the Faces earned a solid reputation, albeit it a little on the rowdy side, from 1969 to 1975. Although band members later claimed they were overshadowed by Stewart's incredible success, the fact of the matter was that the band's exposure grew exponentially with the addition of the new members, especially in America. The Faces landed hits such as "Stay with Me" (#17, 1971) and "Cindy Incidentally" (#48, 1973), and the group's extensive touring in America with Stewart, in fact, broke the band.

In 1973 Lane decided to leave and was replaced by ex-Free bassist Tetsu Yamauchi. Lane later recorded a handful of albums before being diagnosed with debilitating multiple sclerosis. The Faces endured more changes, however, when Ron Wood, who had played with the Rolling Stones on their 1975 tour, accepted an invitation to join the world's greatest rock and roll band as a full member the following year. The loss of Wood was inevitable for the band, who had seen his soul-mate Stewart leave the year before. McLagen, who had also worked with the Rolling Stones and their various offshoots, went on to solo and session work before becoming a component in the Austin, Texas, music scene. Jones later found himself drumming with the Who following the death of Keith Moon. Marriott later died in a fire in his home. At the time he was pondering a reunion of Humble Pie.

AUTOGRAPHS

A CD, LP, magazine cover, ad, photo, or card signed by the group: $100-$225

*While I have seen items priced much higher, this seems more realistic

REFERENCES/BOOKS

Limited resources exist. *Small faces: The Young Mods' Forgotten Story* by Paolo Hewitt is a MUST for fans! There are no dedicated collector books.

Smashing Pumpkins

Formed 1989

Billy Corgan, Born: March 17, 1967; James Iha, Born: March 26, 1968; D'arcy Wretzky, Born: May 1, 1968; and Jimmy Chamberlain, Born: June 10, 1964

Smashing Pumpkins. Photo by Yelena Yumchuk. Courtesy Virgin Records.

The Smashing Pumpkins, the '90s Midwest "sophisticated grunge" act, catapulted into the limelight with the release of their major label debut *Siamese Dream* (#10, 1993). The Smashing Pumpkins were a household word by 1996, following the release of the album *Mellon Collie and the Infinite Sadness*. The band's greater interest in complex arrangements and melodies, laced with streamlined production, has separated it from its peers. Always evolutionary the band lost much of its indie edge in favor of a more progressive sound. They are now considered one of the major movers in rock music, with each of their releases thoroughly dissected, and often imitated. In 1997 the band even accepted some opening dates on the Rolling Stones *Bridges to Babylon Tour*.

AUTOGRAPHS

A CD, LP, magazine cover, ad, photo, or card signed by the group: $25-$80

TOUR BOOKS/ PROGRAMS/PASSES

Backstage Passes:
Cloth: $10; Laminated: $15

POSTERS/PRESS KITS

Promotional Posters:
$10-$25
Press Kits: $20-$35

USED CLOTHING/ EQUIPMENT

Guitar Pick: $15-$20

A Smashing Pumpkins guitar pick

REFERENCES/BOOKS

A few resources exist, but none do justice to the group in my opinion. There are no dedicated collector books,

Smith, Bessie

Born: April 15, 1894, Died: September 26, 1937

Bessie Smith was arguably the greatest and most influential of all blues singers. She was also a talented dancer and performer, but when she sang the blues, none could match her. She met her mentor, Gertrude "Ma" Rainey, while working on a vaudeville-type show, and although stories abound of their rivalry, they were friends. While parts of her life are sketchy, we know she moved to Philadelphia in the early '20s, about the same time as the release of "Gulf Coast Blues" b/w "Down Hearted Blues," her most successful record. The release not only was responsible for catapulting her career, but also lined the pockets of Columbia Records and compelled it to develop more talent in its "race" records division. Smith alone put 160 songs in the Columbia archives while working with such greats as Louie Armstrong and Fletcher Henderson.

Smith traveled the country in her custom-designed rail car, broadening her already large following. But when the stock market crashed, so did the salaries of many of the performers. By 1931 she had no recording contract, but by the mid-30s interest in her career resumed until a devastating automobile accident claimed both her dreams and life. Her funeral attracted thousands, yet her grave went unmarked for years until Janis Joplin and a woman who worked for the singer named Junita Green, paid for a headstone. On it reads, "The Greatest Blues Singer in the World Will Never Stop Singing."

Her life is nothing short of absolutely fascinating. Edward Albee even wrote a play about the performer, "The Death of Bessie Smith." Although relics from her career are scarce, they certainly won't get easier to find, so if you're going to collect, start now.

AUTOGRAPHS

A CD, LP, magazine cover, ad, photo, or card signed by the artist - values are undetermined

Smith, Curt: see Tears for Fears

Smith, Huey "Piano"

Born: January 26, 1934

Fifties New Orleans R&B pianist Huey "Piano" Smith, along with his vocal group the Clowns, laid down some of the finest R&B tunes of all-time including "Rockin' Pneumonia and the Boogie Woogie Flu" (#52, 1957), "Don't You Just Know It" (#9, 1958), and a record not credited to the group, Frankie Ford's "Sea Cruise." Other hits, like "Don't You Know Yock-omo" (#56, 1959), followed before he faded from the national music scene.

AUTOGRAPHS

A CD, LP, magazine cover, ad, photo, or card signed by the artist: $20-$65

Smith, Kendra: See the Dream Syndicate

Smith, Patti

Born: December 31, 1946

Eccentric '70s cult rocker and poet Patti Smith was an integral element of the burgeoning CBGB punk-rock movement. Her 1974 indie single "Hey Joe" b/w "Piss Factory" is considered by many historians to be THE first punk-rock record. The single, and her migration toward rock and roll, led to her debut release *Horses* (#47, 1975) on Arista. It is now considered one of the finest alternative records of all-time. Her mission was to take the spoken voice above and beyond where Jim Morrison left it, and with songs such as "Gloria" and "Land of 1000 Dances," she succeeded. The album was produced by John Cale, and his magic was left all over the album. While other artists have tried to respond to the work, all have failed, including subsequent Smith releases.

Radio Ethiopia (#122, 1976), her follow-up album, fell rungs short of her debut. In 1977 Smith fell twelve feet off a Florida stage and required hospitalization and three months in a neck brace, which impeded her ability to tour. During this period she wrote her fourth book of poetry and prepared for her next release *Easter* (#20, 1978). While the album sold well and spun off the Springsteen cover "Because the Night" (#13, 1978), it failed to meet many fans expectations who were hungry for more *Horses*. *Wave* (#18, 1979) was nothing more than a ripple and was a prelude to her departure from the music scene.

She returned to music in 1988, after she gave it up for domestic life with her husband Fred "Sonic" Smith, formerly of the MC5, with *Dream of Life* (#65, 1988), a trite expression that even included lullabies to her children. If Smith fans wanted this, they could've just turned on *Sesame Street*. They wanted the stuffed sole and all they got was a bowl of seafood gumbo. Smith turned up in 1993 reading poetry at Central Park's Summerstage on July 8, 1993, and dedicated the performance to two of her deceased friends, Robert Mapplethorpe and Richard Sohl. Tragically, Smith's younger brother and her husband died the following year.

Instead of retreating from music following the tragedies, she used it as a vehicle for her mourning, similar to how she has handled her prose. She made numerous appearances including an unannounced Lollapalooza gig in New York (7/28/95). New compositions from the artist have found there way to numerous projects, including the film soundtrack to *Dead Man Walking* (1996). A new Patti Smith was emerging, stronger, deeper, and more introspective—"I can here the sound of Horses in the distance."

AUTOGRAPHS
A CD, LP, magazine cover, ad, photo, or card signed by the artist: $35-$110

REFERENCES/BOOKS
A few resources exist, but none do justice to the singer in my opinion. There are no dedicated collector books.

The Smithereens

Formed 1980

Jim Babjak, Dennis Diken, Pat DiNizio, and Mike Mesaros

This '80s pop group is typically identified with the album *11* (#41, 1989) and the hit extract "A Girl Like You" (#38, 1989).

Guitar picks from the Smithereens

AUTOGRAPHS
A CD, LP, magazine cover, ad, photo, or card signed by the group: $15-$25

POSTERS/PRESS KITS
Promotional Posters: $10-$15
Press Kits: $12

USED CLOTHING/ EQUIPMENT
Guitar Pick: $5

REFERENCES/BOOKS
Limited resources exist, but none do justice to the group in my opinion. There are no dedicated collector books. Serious collectors should opt for a Fan Club: The Smithereens Fan Club, P.O. Box 35226, Richmond, VA 23235

A Mike Mesaros guitar pick

The Smiths/Morrissey

Formed 1982

Morrissey (Stephen Morrissey), Born: May 22, 1959; Johnny Marr (Maher), Born: October 31, 1963; Mike Joyce; and Andy Rourke*

*Craig Gannon was added in 1985, but left in 1987

Late-80s British trashy guitar band, fronted by the alluring and charismatic Morrissey, the Smiths became a pivotal band on the U.K. rock scene and known for songs such as "Hand in Glove" and "Heaven Knows I'm Miserable Now" (#10, U.K., 1984). The band's overwhelming acceptance was no better exemplified than with the album *Meat Is Murder*, which debuted at Number One on the British charts. "Sheila Take a Bow" was a Top Ten U.K. hit just prior to the band splitting in 1987. Morrissey went on to solo work which has yet to reach critical expectations.

AUTOGRAPHS
A CD, LP, magazine cover, ad, photo, or card signed by the group: $25-$65

TOUR BOOKS/PROGRAMS/PASSES
Tour Books:
U.K. Meat Is Murder Tour: $25
Meat is Murder (1985): $20
Kill Uncle: $20

POSTERS/PRESS KITS
Promotional Posters: $10-$40
Press Kits: $20-$45

REFERENCES/BOOKS
Numerous resources exist. *Morrissey & Marr: The Severed Alliance* by Johnny Rogan is a MUST read! There are no dedicated collector books.

Smyth, Patty/Scandal

Born: June 26, 1957
Scandal formed 1982

Smyth, Zack Smith, Ivan Elias, Benji King, and Frankie LaRocka

Eighties New York pop band Scandal is best remembered for the songs "Goodbye to You" (#65, 1982), "Love's Got a Line on You" (#59, 1983), and "The Warrior" (#7, 1984). The band split up after its first album when its initial release was the best selling EP in Columbia Records history. Smyth later turned up on "Sometimes Love Just Ain't Enough" (#2, 1992), a duet with Don Henley. She is married to punk legend Richard Hell.

AUTOGRAPHS
Group: A CD, LP, magazine cover, ad, photo, or card signed by the group $15-$30
Individuals: Patty Smyth $5-$15

Snap

Formed 1989

Turbo B. (Durron Butler), Penny Ford, Jackie Harris, and Arlissa Harris

Ford left in 1992 and was replaced by Thea Austin

This '90s techno-fabrication of two German producers is typically associated with the hits "The Pow-

er" (#2, 1990), "Rhythm Is a Dancer" (#5, 1992), and "Exterminate." The group, although affected by personnel changes, has still been able to land hits atop the charts.

AUTOGRAPHS

A CD, LP, magazine cover, ad, photo, or card signed by the group: $15-$25*

*Lineup dependent

Snoop Doggy Dogg

(Calvin Broadus)
Born: October 20, 1972

Nineties controversial, yet highly-successful rapper who landed the smash rap album *Doggystyle* (#1, 1993), which broke all previous sales records for a rap album, Snoop Doggy Dog debuted in 1992 as a collaborator on Dr. Dre's *The Chronic*. Never far from controversy, Snoop was arrested in connection with a 1993 murder while out on a million dollars bail. He continued his work which included contributions to the film soundtrack of *Murder Was the Case* (#1, 1994). Prior to his acquittal on the murder case, he was charged with drug possession, as the

AUTOGRAPHS

A CD, LP, magazine cover, ad, photo, or card signed by the artist: $20-$40

Snow, Phoebe

(Phoebe Laub)
Born: July 17, 1952

This late-70s vocalist is typically associated with her hit single "Poetry Man." Her career was curtailed by the responsibilities of being a single parent. She later surfaced on the vocal tracks of radio and television commercials and appeared in the early '90s with Donald Fagen's Rock and Soul Revue.

AUTOGRAPHS

A CD, LP, magazine cover, ad, photo, or card signed by the artist: $5-$15

OFTEN OVERLOOKED MEMORABILIA

Videotapes of the numerous commercials she has been heard on

Social Distortion

Formed 1979

Mike Ness, Dennis Danell, Brent Liles, and Derrick O'Brien.

Liles and O'Brien left in 1988, and Chris Reece and John Maurer were added.

Late-80s California punk rockers, best known for their alternative hit "Bad Luck" and their better-late-than-never attitude, Social Distortion endured for years before finally landing a major label debut in 1990.

AUTOGRAPHS

A CD, LP, magazine cover, ad, photo, or card signed by the group: $10

Soft Cell/Marc Almond

Formed 1980

Marc Almond (Peter Marc Almond), Born: July 9, 1959; and David Ball, Born: May 3, 1959

Eighties techno-pop duo Soft Cell is commonly associated with the song "Tainted Love" (#8, 1982). The duo scored numerous Top Ten singles in England before splitting up.

AUTOGRAPHS

A CD, LP, magazine cover, ad, photo, or card signed by the group: $10-$20

REFERENCES/BOOKS

Limited resources exist. There are no dedicated collector books. Serious collectors should opt for a Fan Club: Vaudeville & Burlesque: The Official Marc Almond Fan Club, P.O. Box 4RX, London W1A 4RX, England

Soft Machine/Robert Wyatt

Formed 1966

Original Lineup: Mike Ratledge, Robert Wyatt (Ellidge), Kevin Ayers, and Daevid Allen

Numerous personnel changes

Late-60s British progressive-fusion unit, perhaps known best for its longevity despite numerous personnel changes, Soft Machine garnered significant attention opening for Jimi Hendrix's 1968 tour. Wyatt left after recording *Fourth* (1971) to pursue a solo career. Although hampered by a near fatal fall, Wyatt went on to be an established cult hero and is typically identified with the songs "I'm a Believer" (#29, U.K., 1974) and "Shipbuilding" (#35, U.K., 1983).

AUTOGRAPHS

A CD, LP, magazine cover, ad, photo, or card signed by the group: $10-$25

Sonic Youth

Formed 1981

Kim Gordon, Lee Ranaldo, Thurston Moore, and Richard Edson

Edson departed in 1982 and Bob Bert was added. Bert left in 1985 and was replaced by Steve Shelley.

Eighties New York indie guitar group Sonic Youth is commonly associated with the albums *Dirty* (#83, 1992) and *Experimental Jet Set, Trash and No Star* (#34, 1994)

AUTOGRAPHS

A CD, LP, magazine cover, ad, photo, or card signed by the group: $15-$35

POSTERS/PRESS KITS

Promotional Posters: $8-$15
Press Kits: $15

USED CLOTHING/EQUIPMENT

Guitar Pick: $10

OFTEN OVERLOOKED MEMORABILIA

Experimental Jet Set...: promo cloth briefcase - $15, promo T-shirt - $15; No Star promo button -$3; Washing Machine promo sticker and clothes pin - $10; Daydream Nation, Blast First promo box set, 1988, includes numerous goodies, as well as a T-shirt and tour poster

REFERENCES/BOOKS

Limited resources exist. *Confusion is Next: The Sonic Youth Story* by Alec Foege is a MUST read! There are no dedicated collector books.

Sonny and Cher

Salvatore Bono, Born: February 16, 1935; and Cherilyn Sarkasian, Born: May 20, 1946

This late '60s husband and wife duo is often remembered for their wild wardrobe and cabaret-style singing and standup comedy, as well as for the songs "I Got You Babe" (#1, 1965), "Baby Don't Go" (#8,

Sonny and Cher dolls in the original boxes. Courtesy Phillips Son & Neale.

An autograph from Sonny and Cher

1965), and "The Beat Goes On" (#6, 1967). Sonny and Cher garnered tremendous attention through their successful television variety series *The Sonny and Cher Comedy Hour* (1971-1974). The duo performed their last show at the Houston Astrodome in 1974 before they divorced the following year. Sonny went on to an acting career, various entrepreneur ventures, and a successful political career, while Cher went on to create a legacy in both music and film.

AUTOGRAPHS

A CD, LP, magazine cover, ad, photo, or card signed by the group: $35-$100

OFTEN OVERLOOKED MEMORABILIA

Dolls: Cher, (Mego, 1976) 12," style #1 in (6" x 17" box) - $50, style #2 in (4" x 13" box) - $35, growing hair variety - $125, Sonny (Mego, 1976) 12" - $60, Cher (O.K. Toys, 12") - $15; dressing room (Mego) playset - $60; make-up center - $80; doll outfits - $15 each, numerous styles; theater in the round, Cher - $85; numerous magazines; a menu from Aldo's Coffee Shop, where the two met; any items relating to Caesar & Cleo, the duo's first moniker; an advertisement for their gig opening for Ike & Tina Turner at L.A.'s Purple Onion; any item from their only public U.K. appearance at the 100 Club in London (8/5/65) during first promotional visit; videotape of their appearance on *Ready, Steady, Go!* (8/6/65); all items from the Sonny & Cher clothing line become available at your local department store (2/66); newspaper clippings regarding their private audience with Pope Paul VI (9/14/66); 1967 Rose Bowl Parade memorabilia—they become first pop duo to ride on a float!; movie memorabilia from *Good Times* (1967); videotape of their appearance on *The Smothers Brothers Comedy Hour* (5/21/67); videotape of their appearance on *The Man From U.N.C.L.E.* (10/67); artifacts from their cabaret show at the Eden Roc Hotel in Miami Beach, FL (12/67); memorabilia from the 1968 Newport Pop Festival—they appeared on bill; videotape of their appearance on *This Is Tom Jones* (5/4/69); videotapes of their series *The Sonny and Cher Comedy Hour* - CBS-TV (8/1/71-8/29/77); videotape of *The Sonny Comedy Revue* (9/22/74-12/29/74); videotapes of *The Sonny and Cher Show* (2/76-8/77); videotape of their appearance on *Late Night With David Letterman* (11/14/87)—the duo sang "I Got You Babe" for the first time in a decade

REFERENCES/BOOKS

Numerous resources exist, but none do justice to the group in my opinion. There are no dedicated collector books.

S.O.S. Band

Formed 1977

Mary Davis, Jason "TC" Bryant, Bruno Speight, Billy Ellis, Willie "Sonny" Killebrew, John Simpson, and James Earl Jones III*

Abdul Raoof was added in 1980, and Jones departed in 1981. Jerome "JT" Thomas was added in 1981. Davis left in 1986 and Penny Ford joined the band.

Eighties Atlanta funk disco act the S.O.S. Band is best remembered for the songs "Take Your Time (Do It Right) Part 1" (#3, 1980), "S.O.S." (#20, R&B, 1980), "Just Be Good to Me" (#55, 1983), "Tell Me If You Still Care" (#65, 1983), and "The Finest" (#44, 1986). The group is also commonly referenced for being the band produced by Jimmy Jam and Terry Lewis, who while working on tracks for the act, missed a plane (due to bad weather) resulting in their employer, Prince, firing the duo.

Jam and Lewis later moved on to other lucrative ventures in 1986, while the S.O.S. band, without Mary Davis, continued to place songs on the R&B singles chart.

AUTOGRAPHS

A CD, LP, magazine cover, ad, photo, or card signed by the group: $10-$15

Soul Asylum

Formed 1981

Dave Pirner, Dan Murphy, Karl Mueller, and Grant Young

Young departed in 1994 and Sterling Campbell was added in 1995

This Minneapolis thrash band, which after some near fatal years with A&M Records, finally landed with the Columbia album *Grave Dancers Union* (#11, 1993), which included the hit extract "Runaway Train" (#5, 1993). Soul Asylum scored again in 1995 with the album *Let Your Dim Light Shine* (#6, 1995) with its hit extract "Misery" (#20, 1995).

AUTOGRAPHS

A CD, LP, magazine cover, ad, photo, or card signed by the group: $25-$35

POSTERS/PRESS KITS

Promotional Posters: $10-$15
Press Kits: $15

USED CLOTHING/EQUIPMENT

Guitar Pick: $20-$30

OFTEN OVERLOOKED MEMORABILIA

Movie memorabilia from *Reality Bites*; copies of various tabloids covering the Dave Pirner/Winona Ryder relationship

Soul II Soul

Formed 1982

Original lineup: Jazzie B (Beresford Romeo), Daddae (Phillip Harvey), Nellee Hooper, Caron Wheeler, and Simon Law*

*Numerous personnel changes

Late-80s British club music pioneer Soul II Soul is typically identified with the songs "Keep On Movin'" (#11, 1989) and "Back to Life (However Do You Want Me)" (#4, 1989) and the album *Keep On Movin'* (#14, 1989), a multiple Grammy winner. The group has also grown into a commercial enterprise including a studio, shop, and even fashion lines. The group's leader Jazzie B views its identity more as a concept than an act, no doubt attributable to the numerous personnel changes.

AUTOGRAPHS

A CD, LP, magazine cover, ad, photo, or card signed by the group: $10-$25
Lineup dependent

OFTEN OVERLOOKED MEMORABILIA

Artifacts from their numerous enterprises

Soundgarden

Formed 1984

Matt Cameron, Born: November 28, 1962; Chris Cornell, Born: July 20, 1964; Kim Thayil, Born: September 4, 1960; and Hiro Yamamoto*

*Yamamoto departed in 1989 and Jason Everman was added. Everman left in 1990 and Ben (Hunter) Shepard was added.

One of the earliest seeds of the late '80s Seattle grunge scene, Soundgarden had platinum success with *Badmotorfinger* (#39, 1991). The group was also one of the first to sign with the now legendary Sub Pop indie label, which released its two EPs, *Screaming Life* (1987) and *Fopp* (1988). Finding it hard to stick with its indie roots, the group went to SST for its debut album *Ultarmega OK* before finally signing on with A&M for *Louder Than Love* (#108, 1990). The increased exposure allowed the group to pick up a Grammy nomination.

In 1989 Yamamoto left the band and was replaced by Nirvana alumnus Jason Everman, followed by Ben Shepard. Three key elements then ignited interest in the band: the release of *Badmotorfinger*, the extract "Outshined" being chosen as an MTV "Buzz Clip," and an opening stint on the Guns 'n' Roses Lose Your Illusion Tour. Now catapulted to stardom, Soundgarden's next album release, *Superunknown*, debuted at Number One and earned the group two Grammies.

Just prior to the band's participation in the 1996 Lollapalooza tour, it released the self-produced *Down on the Upside*.

AUTOGRAPHS

A CD, LP, magazine cover, ad, photo, or card signed by the group: $35-$80

POSTERS/PRESS KITS

Promotional Posters: $10-$35
Press Kits: $15-$40

USED CLOTHING/EQUIPMENT

Guitar Pick: $30-$40

OFTEN OVERLOOKED MEMORABILIA

All associated Lollapalooza memorabilia; Alive in the Superunknown multi-media enhanced CD; Temple of the Dog artifacts; all Sub Pop related items; Superunknown bumper sticker - $3

REFERENCES/BOOKS

A few resources exist. *Soundgarden: New Metal Crown* by Chris Nickson is a MUST read! There are no dedicated collector books. Serious collectors should opt for a Fan Club: Soundgarden Fan Club, P.O. Box 61275, Seattle, WA 98121

The Soup Dragons

Formed 1985

Sean Dickson, Jim McCulloch, Sushil Dade, and Paul Quinn

All departed with the exception of Dickson in 1994

Mid-80s Scottish punk band the Soup Dragons are typically associated with the hits "I'm Free," "Divine Thing" (#35, 1992), and "Pleasure" (#69, 1992).

AUTOGRAPHS

A CD, LP, magazine cover, ad, photo, or card signed by the group: $10-15

POSTERS/PRESS KITS

Promotional Posters: $8-$10
Press Kits: $12

South, Joe

(Joe Souther)
Born: February 28, 1940

Late-60s songwriter, performer, and gifted sessionman Joe South is typically associated with his songs "Untie Me," "Down in the Boondocks," "Hush," "Games People Play," "Walk a Mile in My Shoes," and "Rose Garden," most of which were big hits for other artists including Billy Joe Royal, Deep Purple, and Lynn Anderson.

AUTOGRAPHS

A CD, LP, magazine cover, ad, photo, or card signed by the artist: $10-$30

Southside Johnny and the Asbury Jukes

Formed 1974

Southside Johnny (Johnny Lyon), Born: December 4, 1948; Billy Rush; Kevin Kavanaugh; Al Berger; Kenny Pentifallo; Carlo Novi; Eddie Manion; Tony Palligrosi; Ricky Gazda; and Richie "La Bamba" Rosenberg*

*Both Pentifallo and Novi left in 1977, and Steve Becker and Joe Gramalin were added. Berger departed in 1980 and Gene Bacia joined the band.

Late-70s Asbury Park bar and party band, typically associated with Bruce Springsteen—as Lyon and "Boss" guitarist Miami Steve Van Zandt played together in bands during the late '60s—the Jukes have released numerous albums over the years and toured, while still nurturing their large cult following and enhancing their reputation as an outstanding live show group.

AUTOGRAPHS

A CD, LP, magazine cover, ad, photo, or card signed by the group: $15-$30

OFTEN OVERLOOKED MEMORABILIA

Any and all Springsteen related items, Stone Pony relics, etc.

Soxx, Bob B. and the Blue Jeans

Formed 1963

Bob B. Soxx (Robert Sheen), Darlene Love (Wright), and Fanita James

Early-60s Wall of Sound vocal group, best remembered for its swinging version of the song "Zip-A-Dee Doo-Dah" (#8, 1963), Bob B. Soxx and the Blue Jeans was made up of talented members with strong provenance—all part of the Blossoms' heritage.

AUTOGRAPHS

A CD, LP, magazine cover, ad, photo, or card signed by the group: $10-$25

OFTEN OVERLOOKED MEMORABILIA

Movie memorabilia from the Disney classic *Song of the South*; Blossoms related items

Spandau Ballet

Formed 1979

Tony Hadley, Gary Kemp, Martin Kemp, Steve Norman, and John Keeble

Late-70s British dance-pop band and member of the New Romantic scene, Spandau Ballet scored numerous U.K. hits, but is typically identified in the

U.S. with the songs "True" (#4, 1983), "Gold" (#29, 1983), and "Only When You Leave" (#34, 1984). The band essentially feel apart in 1990 when the talented Kemp brothers opted instead for acting careers.

AUTOGRAPHS

A CD, LP, magazine cover, ad, photo, or card signed by the group: $10-$35

OFTEN OVERLOOKED MEMORABILIA

Movie memorabilia from *The Krays* and *The Bodyguard*; videotapes of *The Larry Sanders Show*

REFERENCES/BOOKS

Numerous resources exist, but none do justice to the group in my opinion. There are no dedicated collector books.

The Spaniels

Formed 1952

James "Pookie" Hudson, Gerald Gregory, Opal Courtney Jr., Ernest Warren, Willis C. Jackson*

*Numerous personnel changes

Mid-50s Hoosier doo-wop R&B vocal group the Spaniels are best remembered for the songs "Baby, It's You" and "Goodnite Sweetheart, Goodnite," which was popularized at the closing of the film *American Graffiti* (1973). During the late '50s the group was a mainstay on the R&B charts and popular for years later on the oldies circuit.

AUTOGRAPHS

A CD, LP, magazine cover, ad, photo, or card signed by the group: $10-$40

OFTEN OVERLOOKED MEMORABILIA

Movie memorabilia from *American Graffiti* (1973)

REFERENCES/BOOKS

Numerous resources exist, but none do justice to the group in my opinion. There are no dedicated collector books.

Spanky and Our Gang

Formed 1966

Elaine "Spanky" McFarlane, Born: June 19, 1942; Malcolm Hale; Kenny Hodges; Nigel Pickering; Lefty Baker; and John Seiter*

*Hale died from cirrhosis in 1968

Late-60s folk-rock vocal group, best remembered for the hits "Sunday Will Never Be the Same" (1967), "Making Every Minute Count" (1967), "Lazy Day" (1967), "Like to Get to Know You" (1968), and "Sunday Mornin'"(#30, 1968), Spanky and Our Gang performed until the hits stopped in 1970. McFarlane later took part in a reunion of the Mamas and the Papas, filling in for her friend Cass Elliot.

AUTOGRAPHS

A CD, LP, magazine cover, ad, photo, or card signed by the group: $35-$60

Sparks

Formed 1971

Ron Mael, Russell Mael, Earle Mankey, Jim Mankey, and Harley Feinstein*

*Numerous personnel changes

Early-70s L.A. art-pop rockers and creative outlet for the Mael brothers, Sparks was extremely successful in England with the songs "This Town Ain't Big Enough for Both of Us" (#2, 1974), "Amateur Hour" (#7, 1974), "Never Turn Your Back on Mother Earth" (#13, 1974), and numerous others.

"Cool Places" (#49, 1983) was the group's most successful American hit—the band failed to ignite commercial success here.

AUTOGRAPHS

A CD, LP, magazine cover, ad, photo, or card signed by the group: $10-$25

OFTEN OVERLOOKED MEMORABILIA

Movie memorabilia from *Rollercoaster*; Russell Mael fake mustache (Japan) - $15; promotional mirrored pins - $15; Big Beat promotional "sparking" toy, 1976

The Specials

Formed 1977

Jerry Dammers (Gerald Dankin), Sir Horace Gentleman (Horace Panter), Lynval Golding, Roddy Radiation (Byers), Terry Hall, Neville Staples, and John Bradbury*

*Group disbanded in 1981, only to later re-form as the Special AKA.

Late-70s pivotal players in the British two-tone movement (1979-1981), the Specials are remembered for the songs "Too Much Too Young," "Rat Race," "Stereotype," and "Do Nothing," all of which were U.K. hits. The band had little impact in America.

AUTOGRAPHS

A CD, LP, magazine cover, ad, photo, or card signed by the group: $10-$20

Spector, Phil/The Teddy Bears

Born: December 25, 1940

The Teddy Bears formed 1958

Spector, Marshall Lieb, Annette Kleinbard, and Harvey Goldstein*

*Goldstein stayed only briefly

By overdubbing scores of musicians, Phil Spector created his Wall of Sound and changed the course of pop-record production. Spector, who was part of a late-50s trio known as the Teddy Bears, had a Top Ten hit with his first production "To Know Him Is to Love Him." But when the group's next singles flopped, he turned to production at the young age of eighteen. Under the watchful eyes of Lester Sill and Lee Hazlewood, Spector was sent to New York, where he worked with the hit making team of Jerry Leiber and Mike Stoller.

The experience in New York proved invaluable to Spector, who cowrote "Spanish Harlem" with Leiber and even played the guitar on the Drifters recording of "On Broadway." During this period he became staff producer for Dunes Records, followed by his frequent roll as a freelance producer, and later filled an A&R position at Atlantic Records. His hit production work continued with artists such as Gene Pitney, Curtis Lee, and the Ducanes, quickly establishing the youth as a hit maker.

With Les Still, Spector then formed Philles Records (combining both of their first names), and set their sights first on recording a female vocal group called the Crystals. "There's No Other (Like My Baby)," "Uptown," "He Hit Me (and I Felt Like a Kiss)," and "He's a Rebel" were bug hits for the Crystals and helped make Spector a millionaire.

Spector then bought out Sill's part of Philles and headed to the West Coast to work his magic. While there he fine-tuned his Wall of Sound, while posting twenty straight hits in less than forty months. From "Be My Baby" and "Da Doo Ron Ron," to "You've Lost That Lovin' Feelin'," all had Spector's magic touch. In 1966, after working on what he considered his finest work, Ike and Tina Turner's "River Deep - Mountain High," Spector, furious that the record wasn't a hit in the U.S., entered a period of seclusion. With the exception of working for one group and a cameo appearance in the film *Easy Rider*, he was quiet for most of the remainder of the decade. The Beatles managed to lure him out to remix "Let It Be," and he also worked on individual members' projects into the early '70s.

During the years that followed he worked with other artists, survived two near-fatal automobile accidents, and ventured into a variety of business ventures. Phil Spector was inducted into the Rock and Roll Hall of Fame in 1989.

AUTOGRAPHS

A CD, LP, magazine cover, ad, photo, or card signed by the artist: $65-$80

OFTEN OVERLOOKED MEMORABILIA

Associated memorabilia from his numerous productions

REFERENCES/BOOKS

Numerous resources exist, but none do justice to the singer in my opinion. *Collecting Phil Spector: The Man, the Legend, and the Music* by John Fitzpatrick and James Fogerty is the first place to begin research.

Spector, Ronnie: See the Ronettes

Spedding, Chris

Born: June 17, 1944

Highly-praised three decade British guitarist for hire Chris Spedding has built a legacy around session work. A member of numerous bands during his career, with many notable musicians, none have proved to have any staying power. Spedding has also worked as a producer, journalist, actor, and composer, while trying to occasionally contribute to his solo career.

AUTOGRAPHS

A CD, LP, magazine cover, ad, photo, or card signed by the artist: $10-$15

USED CLOTHING/EQUIPMENT

Guitar Pick: $10-$20

OFTEN OVERLOOKED MEMORABILIA

Artifacts from his session work.

Spinal Tap

Formed 1967

David St. Hubbins (Michael McKean), Nigel Tufnel (Christopher Guest), and Derek Smalls (Harry Shearer) Various drummers were added to lineup

One of rock and roll's most successful parodies, conducted by some highly talented actors, Spinal Tap developed a large cult following and evolved into a successful parody of itself.

AUTOGRAPHS

A CD, LP, magazine cover, ad, photo, or card signed by the group: $10-$30

REFERENCES/BOOKS

Numerous resources exist, but none do justice to the group in my opinion. There are no dedicated collector books. Serious collectors should opt for a publication: This is the Spinal Tap Zine, Attention: Chip Rowe, P.O. Box 11967, Chicago, IL 60611

Spin Doctors

Formed 1988

Aaron Comess, Chris Barron (Gross), Mark White, and Eric Schenkman

Schenkman departed in 1994 and Anthony Krizan was added.

Early-90s New York pop and "Dead Clone Act" (DCA), typically associated with the hit "Little Miss Can't Be Wrong," the Spin Doctors are notorious for their energetic and seemingly endless shows. Simi-

lar to the Grateful Dead, the band doesn't discourage the taping of their shows, so warm up your recorder!

AUTOGRAPHS
A CD, LP, magazine cover, ad, photo, or card signed by the group: $15-$30

TOUR BOOKS/PROGRAMS/PASSES
Backstage Passes:
Cloth: $8-$10; Laminated: $12

POSTERS/PRESS KITS
Promotional Posters: $10
Press Kits: $15-$20

USED CLOTHING/EQUIPMENT
Guitar Pick: $10

The Spinners

Formed 1957

Bobbie Smith, Pervis Jackson, Henry Fambrough, Billy Henderson, and George W. Dixon

Dixon departed in 1962 and Edgar "Chico" Edwards was added. He left the following year and G.C. Cameron was added. Cameron left in 1972 and Phillipe Wynne (1941-1984) joined the band. Wynne left in 1977 and John Edwards was added.

Legendary Detroit vocal act, which prior to its move to Atlantic Records during the '70s was primarily known for two songs, "That's What Girls Are Made For" (#27,1961) and "It's a Shame" (#14, 1970), the Spinners were overlooked at Motown, despite its hits. In 1972 the group moved to Atlantic Records and dominated the both the pop and R&B charts until 1979 with numerous hits, including "I'll Be Around" (#3, 1972), "Could It Be I'm Falling in Love" (#4, 1972), "One of a Kind (Love Affair)" (#11, 1973), "Then Came You" (#1, 1974), "They Just Can't Stop It (the Games People Play)" (#5, 1975), "Rubberband Man" (#2, 1976), and "I'm Working My Way Back to You" (#2, 1979)—to name only a few!

By 1980 the pop hits began tailing off, so the group focused on the R&B chart until the mid-80s. Into the '90s the group was still touring and recording with the same lineup since the late '70s. Next stop Cleveland!

AUTOGRAPHS
A CD, LP, magazine cover, ad, photo, or card signed by the group: $40-$80

Spirit

Formed 1967

Randy California (Wolfe), Born: February 20, 1951; Jay (John) Ferguson, Born: May 10, 1947; John Locke, Born: September 25, 1943; Mark Andes, Born: February 19, 1948; and Ed Cassidy, Born: May 4, 1924*

Numerous personnel changes

Late-60s eclectic rock act Spirit was known primarily for its album *The Twelve Dreams of Dr. Sardonicus* and its one hit "I Got a Line on You" before the original lineup split during the early '70s.

AUTOGRAPHS
A CD, LP, magazine cover, ad, photo, or card signed by the group: $20-$35

Jay Ferguson's signature

OFTEN OVERLOOKED MEMORABILIA
A copy of Ed Cassidy's *Musicians' Survival/Resource* manual!

Split Enz/Tim Finn

Formed 1972

Tim Finn, Born: June 25, 1952; Phil Judd; Eddie Raynor; Wally Wilkinson; Jonathan Chunn; Emlyn Crowther; and Noel Crombie*

*Numerous personnel changes

Mid-70s New Zealand eclectic art-pop act, best remembered for the songs "I Got You" and "History Never Repeats," the group disbanded in 1985. Tim Finn later hooked up with Crowded House after a brief and lackluster solo stint.

AUTOGRAPHS
A CD, LP, magazine cover, ad, photo, or card signed by the group: $10-$20

POSTERS/PRESS KITS
Promotional Posters: $10-$15
Press Kits: $14

Spooky Tooth

Formed 1967

Mike Harrison, Born: September 3, 1945; Gary Wright, Born: April 26, 1943; Luther Grosvenor (a.k.a. Ariel Bender); Greg Ridley, Born: October 23, 1947; and Mike Kellie*

*Ridley departed in 1969 and Andy Leigh was added. Wright left in 1970 and Henry McCullough joined the band. Chris Stainton and Alan Spenner were also added the same year. Numerous changes followed.

Late-60s British hard-rock band, best remembered for its talented alumni including Mick Jones (Foreigner), Luther Grosvenor (Mott the Hoople), Greg Ridley (Humble Pie), and Gary Wright, Spooky Tooth never had a hit single or album.

AUTOGRAPHS

A CD, LP, magazine cover, ad, photo, or card signed by the group: $10-$40

Springfield, Dusty

(Mary O'Brien)
Born: April 16, 1939

Early-60s British pop singer Dusty Springfield is best remembered for "I Only Want to Be with You" (#12, 1963), "I Just Don't Know What to Do with Myself," "Wishin' and Hopin'," "Some of Your Lovin'," "Goin Back," "You Don't Have to Say You Love Me" (#4, 1966), and "Son of a Preacher Man." She compiled more than two dozen U.S. and U.K. hits before she slipped from the music scene in the early '70s. She surfaced on a variety of projects since, most notably dueting with Pet Shop Boy Neil Tennant on "What Have I Done to Deserve This?" (#2, 1987), and teaming with B.J. Thomas on "As Long As We Got Each Other"—the theme to the television series "Growing Pains." The nineties find her recovering from cancer and even releasing *A Very Fine Love* (1995), her first album in five years.

AUTOGRAPHS

A CD, LP, magazine cover, ad, photo, or card signed by the artist: $15-$25

OFTEN OVERLOOKED MEMORABILIA

Movie memorabilia from *Scandal*; videotapes of her numerous television appearances including *The Ed Sullivan Show*

Springfield, Rick

Born: August 23, 1949

Early-80s solo artist and soap opera star Rick Springfield is typically associated with the songs "Jessie's Girl" (#1, 1981), "I've Done Everything for You" (#8, 1981), "Don't Talk to Strangers" (#2,1982), "Affair of the Heart," "Human Touch," and "Love Somebody." The regular on *General Hospital* found his popularity slipping by the mid-80s and has been relatively quiet thus far in the '90s.

AUTOGRAPHS

A CD, LP, magazine cover, ad, photo, or card signed by the artist: $5-$15

REFERENCES/BOOKS

Limited resources exist, but none do justice to the singer in my opinion. There are no dedicated collector books. Serious collectors should opt for Fan Club - Rick's Loyal Supporters, c/o Vivian Acinelli, 4530 E. Four Ridge Rd., Imperial, MO 63052 ($15 fee)

Springsteen, Bruce

Born: September 23, 1949

Bruce Springsteen is rock and roll's John Steinbeck, forever empathizing with the working-class hero while never overlooking his trials and tribulations. His sincerity and emotion earned him the reverence of entire generations who found it easy to relate to his small-town philosophy. Amazingly, whenever he has found himself wondering away from home, he has never gotten lost, and has returned refreshed, wiser, and even more determined to convey his message.

Bruce Frederick Springsteen was born in Freehold, New Jersey, on September 23, 1949. The eldest of three children, he was affected by a very influential era in American music and auditioned and joined his first band, The Castiles, in 1965. He graduated from Freehold Regional High School in 1967 and formed a new band, first called Earth and later Steel Mill. In the summer of 1969, Steel Mill, which included bassist Steve Van Zandt and Danny Federici, traveled to California and played gigs at the Fillmore West and Esalen. In early 1971 Steel Mill broke up, but by that summer the Bruce Springsteen Band took shape.

In January 1972 Springsteen met New York City writer/producers Mike Appel and Jim Cretecos. Four months later Springsteen auditioned for famed CBS Records talent scout John Hammond and found himself inking a ten-album contract with Columbia Records on June 9, 1972.

A BRUCE SPRINGSTEEN CHRONOLOGY

Selected Significant Events 1973-1985

1973

Greetings From Asbury Park (LP) was released on January 5
"Blinded By The Light"/"The Angel" (45) was released on February 23
"Spirit In The Night"/"For You" (45) was released on May 11
May 30-June 15, 1973: Springsteen on tour with Chicago as the opening act
June 15: First appearance at Madison Square Garden
The Wild, The Innocent and The E Street Shuffle (LP) was released on September 11

Collectors Note:

During the first half of the year Springsteen appeared at numerous small venues including: The Main Point, Paul's Mall, The Quiet Knight, Max's Kansas City (1/31-2/4) with Bob Marley and the Wailers), Olivers, Shaboo, Childe Harold, and Ahmanson Theatre. The college circuit included: Villanova, Seton Hall, and Monmouth. Springsteen toured extensively the second half of the year with larger venues added. Key dates included: Madison Square Garden (6/14, 6/15), Max's Kansas City (7/18-7/23), and My Father's Place (7/31). Numerous small clubs and universities filled in the dates between large venues. On February 14 in Richmond, VA, Bruce and his band back Chuck Berry. It's event such as this that many "Boss Collectors" want to center their interests around. Additionally, collecting posters and tickets from venues where certain songs were first played "live" is also an alternative. For example: The first known versions of "The E Street Shuffle" were played during a stint (10/29-10/31) at The Main Point in Bryn Mawr, PA. Springsteen, who's every appearance is thoroughly documented or recorded, is an easy artist to collect in this manner.

1974

April 9-11: The band played a benefit at Charley's Place at Harvard Square in Boston, MA. On the evening of the tenth Springsteen was introduced to rock critic Jon Landau.

May 9: After witnessing Springsteen play some new songs live, Landau wrote a column claiming Springsteen was the future of rock and roll. Columbia Records jumped on the claim for its marketing campaign.

July: David Sancious and Ernest Carter left Springsteen's band. "Mighty" Max Weinberg and Roy Bittan were added on August 23, 1974, and the band was billed as Bruce Springsteen and the E Street Band.

Collectors Note:

Small colleges and venues remained the norm for 1974, although the group did play the Schaefer Music Festival in Central Park (8/3). Some posters, handbills, and tickets have survived, but the lack of accurate print run information and familiarity with design make many collectors apprehensive—as well it should. Using the venue as a reference point can be useful, and it is usually easy to speculate at the availability of tickets (if tickets were used). The lack of a consistent manufacturer and style of the ticket make them very easy to counterfeit.

1975

Born to Run (LP) was released on August 25
"Born To Run"/"Meeting Across The River" (45) was released on August 29
"Tenth Avenue Freeze-Out"/"She's the One" (45) was released on December 12

Collectors Note:

A pivotal year for the artist—larger and key venues became common on tour. Key dates included his five night run at New York's Bottom Line (8/13-17) (tons of publicity and a gig that helped break the artist), along with his four night residence at the Roxy in Los Angeles, CA (10/16-19), and the second Hammersmith Odeon gig in London, England (11/24). On October 27, 1975, both *Time* and *Newsweek* featured Bruce on the cover—a real collectors' item! All items associated with the smaller venues, many of which were booked months in advance, are difficult to both find and authenticate. Difficult items to find include Born to Run promo tennis-shoe key chains and tour jackets. Both items are heavily counterfeited.

1976

Collectors Note:

Larger venues and one-off performances made up a less hectic year on tour. Key dates included the Ellis Auditorium in Memphis, TN (4/29), where Bruce garnered press after the show by trying to thwart the security at Graceland, and New York's Palladium (11/2-4), where on the third night Bruce was joined on stage by Ronnie Spector. Off stage, the year was best remembered for its legal proceedings—Springsteen vs. Appel.

1977

Collectors Note:

Lesser gigs, mid-size halls, with the key dates being the four sensational sets delivered on March 22-25 at the Music Hall in Boston, MA. Plagued by legal issues, which ended on May 28, the band toured until April, after which Springsteen appeared only at impromptu one-off events. In November, recording sessions

for what will be Darkness On the Edge of Town began.

1978

Darkness on the Edge of Town (LP) was released on June 2
"Prove It All Night"/"Factory" (45) was released on June 9
"Badlands"/"Streets of Fire" (45) was released on August 14

Collectors Note:

Springsteen began his next trek on May 23 at Shea's Theatre in Buffalo, NY, during a year that was tour extensive. Although numerous gigs stand out (the Palladium, the Capitol Thaetre, etc.), the three-night stand at Madison Square Garden (8/21-23), where the artist had played in 1973 in support of Chicago, really set the media on fire. By then Springsteen's image adorned numerous covers from *Crawdaddy* (10/78) to *Creem* (10/78). As live broadcasts became common during 1978, associated items, such as radio generated PR pieces, all are highly sought by collectors. Watch out for reproductions!

1979

Collectors Note:

The band completed The Darkness Tour in Cleveland, OH, after completing 109 shows in 86 cities—all soldout! The year was marred with the unfortunate, from a freak motorcycle accident forcing the Boss to take some time off, to bootlegger battles. The artist celebrated his 30th birthday performing at the MUSE concert held in Madison Square Garden on September 23. A *No Nukes* triple album set and film commemorated the event. He entered the studio in the fall to begin work on his next release.

1980

The River (LP) was released on October 10
"Hungry Heart"/"Held Up Without a Gun" (45) was released on October 20

Collectors Note:

The River tour began on October 3 in Ann Arbor, Michigan. The tour was commemorated by a tour book, his first

official, although programs do exist for individual shows he has participated in over the years. CBS Records also issued a couple tour jackets and a cardboard die-cut of Springsteen's name. The year also was marked by a collector item, as Dave March's biography of the artist became the first rock 'n' roll book to enter the *New York Times* bestseller list. A variety of very attractive and collectible Otto-produced passes were used during the year. Beware of counterfeit radio station promotional passes, for example: WPLJ and concert passes, especially in geometric shapes. Die cut variations, such as "the pumpkin" versions used for the Halloween gig in Los Angeles are easier to authenticate.

1981

"Fade Away"/"Be True" (45) was released on February 3

Collectors Note:

Springsteen headed back to Britain in March for the first time since 1975, generating considerable excitement and numerous paper-based collectibles in the form of newspapers and magazines. When Springsteen fell ill, the tour was postponed with many March dates moving to May. The artist completed his 32-date European tour in Paris, France, on May 11, 1981. Worth noting is that many of European tickets are very easy to counterfeit, so watch your step! My favorite gigs remain the opening of Big Man's West in Red Bank, NJ—Clarence Clemons' new nightclub—where Bruce took the stage for six songs, and his heartfelt performance at a six-night benefit show for the Vietnam Veterans in Los Angeles, CA (8/20, 21, 23, 24, 27, 28).

1982

Nebraska (LP) was released on September 20

Collectors Note:

Nebraska, a set of solo acoustic compositions, a second Springsteen produced Gary U.S. Bonds album and one-off performances highlighted the year for the performer. Key performances included Springsteen's participation in the Rally for Disarmament held in Central Park, New York on June 12.

1984

"Dancing in the Dark"/"Pink Cadillac" (45) was released on May 11

Born in the U.S.A. (LP) was released on June 4*

*Marketing campaign materials for this release are highly sought by collectors. "Born in the U.S.A. 6/84" T-shirts were sent out during the month of May. Baseball caps, posters, badges, and a "Cover Me" (5' x 3') blanket were distributed.

"Cover Me"/"Jersey Girl" was released on July 31

"Born in the U.S.A. "/"Shut Out the Light" (45) was released on November 4

Collectors Note:

Born in the USA, his first new material in two years, catapulted the artist back into the spotlight after essentially publicly taking the previous year off. Promotional goodies included a T-shirt, cap, and even a blanket issued for "Cover Me." Worth noting to collectors is prior to this release he had only licensed ONE commercial poster. Unfortunately, many of the artist's earlier promotional posters by this time had also been reproduced. Bring a magnifying glass with you when you purchase any paper based collectible! The Born in the USA tour began on June 29 at the Civic Centre in St. Paul, Minnesota, as Patti Scialfa (his first female backing singer) also debuted.

1985

"I'm On Fire"/"Johnny Bye Bye" (45) was released on February 4

"Glory Days"/"Stand On It" (45) was released on May 22

Collectors Note:

The Born in the USA tour ended on October 2, 1985, at the Memorial Coliseum, Los Angeles, CA. Springsteen spent most of the year in the press—tabloids had a field day speculating about his romance with actress and model Julianne Phillips, whom he wed on May 13. In addition to collecting wedding gifts, he also managed to win nearly every award conceivable during the year.

AUTOGRAPHS

As one might expect, Bruce Springsteen is very obliging to in-person signature requests.

Bruce Springsteen's autograph

A CD, LP, magazine cover, ad, photo, or card signed by the artist: $65-$225

Springsteen has always had a very fragmented signature. In the early '70s, many examples of his signature have nearly every letter in his name as a separate stroke. The large "B" in Bruce resembles the "r" in its formation. The "S" in Springsteen often resembles a "J" and the flamboyant "t" is similar in formation to the letter "v." By the mid-70s his signature had gotten larger and much more flamboyant, although it still remained fragmented.

Born in the USA tour book (© 1984 T-shirt Merchandise Inc.)

TOUR BOOKS/ PROGRAMS

Tour Books

River (sold on the 1980-81 tour): $20
Born in the USA (sold on first leg of tour): $15
World Tour 1984-85 (sold at '85 U.S. stadium tour): $15
1992-93 World Tour: $15
Tunnel of Love Tour: $15
World Acoustic Tour, '95-'96: $20

Backstage Passes

River: $25-$50
Born in the USA: $10-$12
Born In The USA, '84-85 World Tour: $25

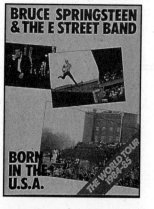

World Tour '84-'85 tour book (© 1985 T-shirt Merchandise Inc.)

Tunnel of Love tour book (© 1988 T-shirt Company)

World Tour 1984-85: $10
Tunnel of Love: $10-$15
High-end for key dates only, also some gold foil stamp passes
Note: Springsteen is believed to be the first artist to use four-color (full-color) passes and the first to have foil stamped passes. Jack Otto and Sons (c. 1980) has designed many award winning passes for Springsteen and his work is highly sought by collectors. Pre-1980 passes are rare, because many were never even used. If found they are usually local promoter passes or CBS issued. For the Darkness tour, the folks at CBS created several (about four) generic designs in different colors. The River tour broke new ground with backstage passes, because daily foil stamping, advanced die cutting, and unique inks did much to curtail counterfeit attempts. European tour passes of this era are scarce and employ individual designs for each major gig.

POSTERS/PRESS KITS

Concert Posters:

Early concert posters are scarce, however, a few legitimate examples do occasionally surface. When Springsteen played the State University of New York at Oswego on December 16, 1975, I was a member of the University concert board. We had ordered a few hundred posters in advance of the show, but as soon as the first few were put up, they soon disappeared. This led to us tearing the posters into numerous pieces before stapling them up around campus. It's my guess that fewer than twenty-five of these posters exist in one piece. I'm sure other universities which booked Springsteen during this period can relate to the story.

Promotional posters:

(1980-Present): $10-$40
Examples: The River album cover (37 x 47) - $40, Human Touch album cover (24 x 24) - $10

Press Kits:

(1980-Present): $25-$50, Examples: The River - $50

OFTEN OVERLOOKED MEMORABILIA

Greetings from Asbury Park, N.J. postcards; E Street, Kingsley, and Ocean Avenue Street signs; a tape recording of you having your fortune read by Madam Marie; all Stone Poney artifacts; copies of the fanzines *Point Blank*, *Candy's Room*, *Thunder Road*, and of course *Backstreets* (one of, if not THE premier fanzine—simply fantastic!); the Darkness four-by-four giant promotional square; 1976 *Playboy* promotional poster - $100-$200; "Live" denim jacket, coffee mug, and laminated listening pass; Tunnel of Love two promo jackets, promo bolo tie, and even a Swiss Army Knife, also Tunnel of Love U.K. Tour 1988 promotional life-size die-cut - $175; Born in the USA/Glory Days promo baseball shirt - $100-$125; Greatest Hits lighter - $80, key chain - $40 and pen - $50; "Born to Collect!"

REFERENCES/BOOKS

Numerous resources exist, take your pick. Backstreets, P.O. Box 51225, Seattle, WA 98115 is a MUST publication for Boss fans! ($18 fee)

Squeeze

Formed 1974

Chris Difford, Born: April 11, 1954; Glenn Tilbrook, Born: August 31, 1957; Julian "Jools" Holland; Harry Kakoulli; and Gilson Lavis, Born: June 27, 1951*

*Kakoulli departed in 1979 and John Bentley was added. Holland left in 1981 and Paul Carrack joined the band. He left the following year and Don Snow joined the band. Group re-formed in 1985: Difford, Holland, Lavis, and Keith Wilkinson. Andy Metcalfe was also added. Holland left in 1990 and Matt Irving was added briefly before leaving along with Metcalfe. Lavis left in 1993 and Carrack returned with Pete Thomas.

Late-70s and '80s British pop group and FM staple, typically associated with the songs "Tempted," "Hourglass," "Pulling Mussels (from a Shell)," "Another Nail in My Heart," "If I Didn't Love You," "Black Coffee in Bed," "I Can't Hold On," and "853-5937," Squeeze never gained the broad-based commercial success in America that many critics predicted. Holland went on to a successful television career, while Carrack pursued a solo career and found a home with Mike + the Mechanics before returning to the band.

AUTOGRAPHS

A CD, LP, magazine cover, ad, photo, or card signed by the artist: $25-$55

TOUR BOOKS/PROGRAMS/PASSES

Tour Books:
Babylon and On Tour: $20

OFTEN OVERLOOKED MEMORABILIA

Play Reprise promo picture CD w/clay pot and seeds; videotapes of Jools Holland's numerous television appearances

Squier, Billy

Born: May 12, 1950

Eighties New England rocker Billy Squier is best remembered for the songs "The Stroke," "My Kinds Lover," "In the Dark," "Everybody Wants You," and "Rock Me Tonite" (#15, 1984). He continues to record and tour into the late '90s. While catering to a large cult following, he remains identified with the eighties.

AUTOGRAPHS

A CD, LP, magazine cover, ad, photo, or card signed by the artist: $10-$35

TOUR BOOKS/PROGRAMS/PASSES

Tour Books:
Signs of Life Tour: $10-$15

POSTERS/PRESS KITS
Promotional Posters: $9-$20
Press Kits: $14-$30

USED CLOTHING/EQUIPMENT
Guitar Pick: $10-$15

OFTEN OVERLOOKED MEMORABILIA
Don't Say No book cover - $8

Stansfield, Lisa

Born: April 11, 1966

Early-90s British pop and R&B vocalist Stansfield is typically associated with the songs "This Is the Right Time" (#21, 1990), "All Around the World" (#3, 1990), "You Can't Deny It" (#14, 1990), "Change" (#27, 1991), "All Woman" (#1, R&B, 1992), and "A Little More Love" . "Someday (I'm Coming Back)" was featured in the movie *The Bodyguard*, as album releases such as *So Natural* (1993) and *Lisa Stansfield* (1997), along with numerous contributions to tribute releases, helped keep the entertainer in the forefront.

AUTOGRAPHS
A CD, LP, magazine cover, ad, photo, or card signed by the artist: $10-$15

TOUR BOOKS/ PROGRAMS/PASSES
Tour Books:
1990 Tour: $10

POSTERS/PRESS KITS
Promotional Posters: $7-$10
Press Kits: $13

OFTEN OVERLOOKED MEMORABILIA
Videotapes of her numerous television appearances including *Late Night With David Letterman* (2/19/91), *The Tonight Show* (11/21/91), "Amnesty International's Big 30 Concert" (12/28/91), *Des O'Connor Tonight* (12/30/91), "Dance Energy Christmas House Party" (12/21/92), "Total Relief: A Night of Comic Relief" (3/12/93), and *Top of the Pops* (6/10/93); movie memorabilia from *The Bodyguard* and *The Pagemaster*

"Around the World - 1990" tour book (© Lisa Stansfield)

The Staples

Formed 1953

Roebuck "Pop," Mavis, Cleo, and Pervis Staples

Yvonne Staples was later added, and "Pops" left in 1971

Late-50s gospel group turned '70s soul-pop act, the Staples are typically associated with the songs "Re-spect Yourself" (#12, 1971), "I'll Take You There" (#1, 1972), "If You're Ready (Come Go with Me)" (#1, R&B, 1973), and "Let's Do It Again" (#1, 1974).

AUTOGRAPHS
A CD, LP, magazine cover, ad, photo, or card signed by the group: $15-$40

OFTEN OVERLOOKED MEMORABILIA
A copy of the 1971 documentary *Soul to Soul*; movie memorabilia from *Wattstax* (1973), *The Last Waltz* (1978), and *Let's Do It Again*

Starr, Edwin

(Charles Hatcher)
Born: January 21, 1942

This late-60s pop/R&B singer and songwriter is commonly associated with the songs "Agent Double-O-Soul" (#21, 1965), "Twenty-five Miles" (#6, 1969), "War" (#1, 1970), "Stop the War Now' (#26, 1970), "H.A.P.P.Y. Radio" (#79, 1979), and "Contact" (#65, 1979).

AUTOGRAPHS
A CD, LP, magazine cover, ad, photo, or card signed by the artist: $10-$15

Starr, Ringo

(Richard Starkey)
Born: July 7, 1940

The "backbeat" of the "Fab Four," the post-Beatle Ringo Starr is typically associated with the songs "It Don't Come Easy" (#4, 1971), "Back Off Boogaloo" (#9, 1971), "Photograph" (#1, 1973), "You're Sixteen" (#1, 1973), "Oh My My" (#5, 1973), "No No Song" (#3, 1974), and "Only You" (#6, 1974). After appearing in three films with the Beatles, it was only logical for him to pursue a complimentary acting career, which he did during the '70s in films such as *The Magic Christian, Stardust*, and *Caveman*. Starr had little success as a recording artist during the '80s and '90s, but has never been out of the public eye. From appearing in Paul McCartney's *Give My Regards to Broad Street* (1984) to even playing himself on the television series *The Simpsons* (1990), this is one Starr that still shines.

AUTOGRAPHS
A CD, LP, magazine cover, ad, photo, or card signed by the artist: $100-$200

TOUR BOOKS/ PROGRAMS/PASSES
Tour Books:
Ringo Starr & His Allstarr Band Tour: $15
Ringo Starr & His Allstarr Band Tour, 1992: $15

The autograph of Ringo Starr

OFTEN OVERLOOKED MEMORABILIA

Ringo's Rotogravure, Polydor promo magnifying glass; Ringo Starr & His Allstarr Band Big League trading cards; Scouse the Mouse coloring page; Movie memorabilia from *Candy, The Magic Christian, Blindman, Concert for Bangla Desh, 200 Motels,*

Ringo Starr trading cards set

Born to Boogie, Listztomania, The Last Waltz, Sexette, Caveman, Give My Regards to Broad Street, and *Curly Sue*; videotapes from his numerous television appearances including *Rowan & Martin's Laugh-In* (1/27/70), *Cilla* (4/25/71), *The Smothers Brothers Comedy Hour* (4/28/75), *Ringo* (4/26/78), *Midnight Special* (6/8/79), *Parkinson* (12/12/82), *Princess Daisy* (11/6-7/83), *Thomas the Tank Engine and Friends* (1984, 1986), *Shining Time Station* (1989), *Saturday Night Live* (12/8/84), *Blue Suede Shoes* (10/21/85), *Alice in Wonderland* (12/9/85), *Aspel & Co.* (3/3/88), *Late Night With David Letterman* (6/20/89, 4/3/92, 5/25/95), and *The Simpsons* (4/12/90); artifacts from the Brasserie restaurant in Atlanta, GA; copies of his appearances in commercials including Pizza Hut

REFERENCES/BOOKS

Numerous resources exist, but none do justice to the singer in my opinion. There are no dedicated collector books, but numerous Beatle books cover his solo career.

Status Quo

Formed 1962

Francis Rossi, Richard Parfitt (Harrison), Alan Lancaster, John Coghlan, and Roy Lynes

Lynes departed in 1970. Coghlan left in 1981 and was replaced by Pete Kircher. Lancaster left in 1983. The group then re-formed.

Sixties British rock fossils Status Quo is typically associated with its longevity, its more than three dozen U.K. charting singles, and its only U.S. hit "Pictures of Matchstick Men" (#12, 1968). From high-harmony hooks to heavy-metal riffs, the band has altered its sound in order to appeal to its next generation of fans, but never so radically as to offend. While personnel changes can be expected over a thirty-five year time span, the band has somehow managed to maintain a moderate sales level.

AUTOGRAPHS

A CD, LP, magazine cover, ad, photo, or card signed by the group: $30-$65

OFTEN OVERLOOKED MEMORABILIA

Ain't Complaining, Vertigo promo box set, includes sampler, cassette, video, photo, and press sheet, 1988; Anniversary Party Pack, Vertigo promo carrier bag, includes cap, streamers, and numerous other party supplies, 1990

Stealers Wheel

Formed 1972

Gerry Rafferty, Born: April 16, 1947; Joe Egan; Rab Noakes; Ian Campbell; and Roger Brown*

*Numerous personnel changes

Mid-70s British pop group, best remembered for the song "Stuck in the Middle with You" (#2, 1973), Stealers Wheel basically crumbled with the departure of both Rafferty and Egan.

AUTOGRAPHS

A CD, LP, magazine cover, ad, photo, or card signed by the group: $12-$25

OFTEN OVERLOOKED MEMORABILIA

Movie memorabilia from *Reservoir Dogs*

Steele, Tommy

(Thomas Hicks)
Born: December 17, 1936

Premier late-50s teen idol and Britain's first rock and roll star Tommy Steele is typically associated with the songs "Rock with the Caveman" (1956), "Singing the Blues" (1957), "Nairobi" (1958), "Come On Let's Go" (1958), "Little White Bull" (1959), and "What a Mouth" (1960). When he quickly became upset with the direction of his life, he moved on to studying dance and acting. He later became a staple in British musicals.

AUTOGRAPHS

A CD, LP, magazine cover, ad, photo, or card signed by the artist: $15-$35

OFTEN OVERLOOKED MEMORABILIA

Memorabilia from his numerous theatrical roles.

Steel Pulse

Formed 1975

Selwyn "Bumbo" Brown, David Hinds, and Stephen "Grizzly" Nisbett

Late-70s British rock-reggae punk band Steel Pulse is typically associated with the album *Babylon the Bandit* which won the 1986 Grammy for Best Reggae Album.

AUTOGRAPHS

A CD, LP, magazine cover, ad, photo, or card signed by the group: $10-$20

Steely Dan

Formed 1972

Walter Becker, Born: February 20, 1950; Donald Fagen, Born: January 10, 1948; Denny Dias; and Jim Hodder*

*David Palmer and Jeffrey "Skunk" Baxter, Born: December 13, 1948, were added in 1972. Palmer departed in 1973, and Hodder left the following year. Michael McDonald, Born: February 12, 1952, was added in 1974. Jeff Porcaro (1954-1992) was also added. Baxter left in 1975, and the band resorted to sessionmen only to fulfill recording duties.

Seventies concept pop group, with jazz undercurrents, Steely Dan was essentially Walter Becker, Donald Fagen, and producer Gary Katz. Becker and Fagen began touring and composing together in the early '70s, while backing Jay and the Americans under the monikers Tristan Fabriani (Fagen) and Gustav Mahler (Becker). The duo then met indie producer Katz who recruited them as staff songwriters at ABC/Dunhill Records.

Steely Dan. Photo by Matthew Rolston. Courtesy Giant Records.

Can't Buy a Thrill (#17, 1972), the group's debut record, spun off two hit singles, "Do It Again" (#6, 1972) and "Reeling in the Years" (#11, 1973). The group's first tour in support of the release so frustrated the band that it was reluctant to repeat the process following its next album *Countdown to Ecstasy* (#35, 1973). *Pretzel Logic* (#8, 1974) then followed and contained the single "Rikki Don't Lose That Number" (#4, 1974), a hit the group is often associated with. In 1974 Steely Dan embarked on what was thought to be its last tour. It ended on July 4, and the group retired from live work for the next few years. Anticipating that their services would be of minimal use, both Baxter and Hodder departed.

Katy Lied (#13, 1975), with the hit extract "Black Friday" (#37, 1975), was Becker and Fagen's first Steely Dan release using session musicians. It was during this session that the group's expectations of recording perfection surface, indicated primarily by the enormous recording costs. *The Royal Scam* (#15, 1976) followed and yielded the U.K. only extract "Haitian Divorce" (#17, U.K., 1977), the group's best selling U.K. single.

Upset over the group's perfectionist attitudes, ABC sets the delivery date for the next album. Although the band missed the date, *Aja* (#3, 1977), a seven-song only LP, was the duo's first official album release as such. The entire album became an FM staple, while the hit extracts "Peg" (#11, 1977), "Josie" (#26, 1978), and "Deacon Blues" (#19, 1978) helped sell it platinum. The same year saw the band contribute the song "FM (No Static at All)" (#22) to a the movie *FM. Gaucho* (#9, 1980) followed and spun off the hit extract "Hey Nineteen" (#10, 1980). "Time Out of Mind" (#22, 1981), ectracted from Gaucho, became the duo's final U.S. charting single—both announced on June 21, 1981, the decision to split apart.

Becker will go on to production , while Fagen begins work on his first solo release "The Nightfly" (#11, 1982), which is followed by "Kamakiriad" (#10, 1993). On August 13, 1993, following a 15-year layoff, Steely Dan reforms and begins a U.S. Tour. The group will tour again in 1994 (18-dates) and in 1996.

AUTOGRAPHS

A CD, LP, magazine cover, ad, photo, or card signed by the duo: $75-$150

TOUR BOOKS/PROGRAMS/PASSES

Tour Books:
1994 Japanese Tour: $20
Art Crimes '96: $16

POSTERS/PRESS KITS

Promotional Posters: $10-$45,
Example: "Alive in America" - $10
Press Kits: $25-$60

OFTEN OVERLOOKED MEMORABILIA

Movie memorabilia from *FM, Bright Lights Big City, The King of Comedy,* and *Arthur 2: On the Rocks*; a copy of the William Burrough's novel *The Naked Lunch,* where the bands name originates from; the license plate of the car that hit Becker outside his Manhattan apartment in 1980; a copy of the press release of the group's split (6/21/81); videotapes

of commercial hawking band compilations; copies of *Premiere* with Fagen articles as music editor; artifacts from the annual New York Rock & Soul Revue (1990-Present); a videotape of Steely Dan's appearance on *The Late Show With David Letterman* (10/20/95); Rikki Don't Lose That Number, ABC promo garter belt, 1978

REFERENCES/BOOKS

Limited resources exist, but none do justice to the group in my opinion.

Steppenwolf

Formed 1967

John Kay (Joachim Krauledat), Born: April 12, 1944; Micahel Monarch, Born: July 5, 1950; Goldy McJohn (John Goadsby); Rushton Moreve (1948-1981); and Jerry Edmonton (McCrohan) (1946-1993)*

*Moreve departed in 1968 and John Russell Morgan was added. Monarch and Morgan left in 1969 and Larry Byrom and Nick St. Nicholas (Klaus Karl Kassbaum) were briefly added before George Biondi took over on bass. Byrom left in 1971 and Kent Henry was added. Group re-formed in 1974. Numerous personnel changes followed.

Late-60s L.A. hard rock band, forever linked with such classics as "Born to be Wild" (#2, 1968), "Magic Carpet Ride" (#3, 1968), "The Pusher," "Rock Me" (#10, 1969), "Move Over" (#31, 1969), and "Hey Lawdy Mama" (#35, 1970), Steppenwolf continued as a popular live draw after the big hits diminished in 1970. The group disbanded first in early 1972, but re-formed after unsuccessful solo ventures in 1974. That year the group had its last Top Forty single with "Straight Shootin' Woman" (#29, 1974).

AUTOGRAPHS

A CD, LP, magazine cover, ad, photo, or card signed by the group: $35-$75*
*Original lineup

TOUR BOOKS/PROGRAMS/PASSES

Tour Books:
'69 The Visual Thing (hardcover, 12 x 12"): $55
'69 The Visual Thing (softcover, foldout): $50

REFERENCES/BOOKS

A few resources exist. *Magic Carpet Ride: The Autobiography of John Kay and Steppenwolf* by John Kay and John Einarson is a MUST read! There are no dedicated collector books. Serious collectors should opt for a Fan Club: The Wolfpack: Official Fan Club of John Kay and Steppenwolf, P.O. Box 271496, Nashville, TN, 37227 ($10 fee)

Stetsasonic

Formed 1981

Daddy-O (Glenn Bolton), Delite (Martin Wright), Fruitkwan (Bobby Simmons), Wise (Leonard Roman), Prince Paul (Paul Houston), and DBC (Marvin Nemley)

Eighties New York hip-hop act Stetsasonic is typically associated with the album *Blood, Sweat & No Tears* and the single "Sally" (#25 R&B, 1988). Stetsasonic broke up in 1991.

AUTOGRAPHS

A CD, LP, magazine cover, ad, photo, or card signed by the group: $10-$15

Stevens, Cat

(Steven Demetri Georgiou)
Born: July 21, 1947

Seventies singer/songwriter Cat Stevens is typically associated with the songs "I Love My Dog," "Matthew and Son," "The First Cut is the Deepest," "Here Comes My Baby," and "I'm Gonna Get My Gun" (#6, U.K., 1968) from early in his career. Following a near-fatal case of tuberculosis in late 1968, he unveiled a wealth of new materials leading to the songs he is most remembered for: "Lady D'Arbanville" (#8, U.K., 1970), "Wild World," "Morning Has Broken" (#6), "Peace Train," "Moon Shadow," and "Oh Very Young."

During the mid-70s he was led, and then converted, to the Moslem religion and changed his name to Yusef Islam. By the end of the early '80s, he has withdrawn from music completely and sold all his material possessions. By the end of the decade he was silenced from most American radio stations in a boycott of his material over his comments regarding author Salman Rushdie. In 1995 Yusef signed copies of his new album *The Life of the Last Prophet*, a primarily spoken word release, in a London suburb. Rumors that he anticipates a return to his music have circulated since the mid-90s.

AUTOGRAPHS

A CD, LP, magazine cover, ad, photo, or card signed by the artist : $25-$75*
*Extremely scarce in any form, although this appears that it may be changing

OFTEN OVERLOOKED MEMORABILIA

Promo yo-yo - $30; *Teaser and the Firecat*, Scholastic softcover, scarce- $100

Stewart, Al

Born: September 5, 1945

Late-60s and '70s British folk-rocker, commonly associated with his American breakthrough album *The Year of the Cat* (1976) and the songs "The Year of the Cat," "Time Passages," "Song on the Radio," and "Midnight Rocks," Al Stewart saw his album sales dissipate during the '80s. Although he toured intermittently, he gradually turned away from the business to concentrate on his love for collecting wine.

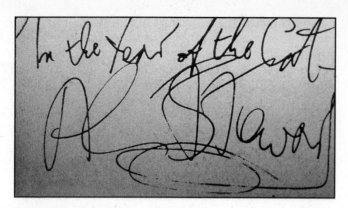
Al Stewart's autograph

AUTOGRAPHS

A CD, LP, magazine cover, ad, photo, or card signed by the artist: $10-$30

OFTEN OVERLOOKED MEMORABILIA

The Year of the Cat standup - $75

REFERENCES/BOOKS

Limited resources exist. There are no dedicated collector books. Serious collectors should opt for the publication *Al Stewart Chronicles*, Attention: Kim Dyer, 4656 Wilcox Road, Holt, MI 48842

Stewart, Billy

Born: March 24, 1937, Died: January 17, 1970

Late-50s and '60s rock scat man "Motormouth" is typically associated with his songs "Summertime"(#10, 1966), "Secret Love" (#29, 1966), and "Everyday I Have the Blues." Stewart also played with Bo Diddley for a couple of years and sang in the with the Rainbows before activating his solo career. He, along with two other band members, were tragically killed when the car they were traveling in plunged into a river.

AUTOGRAPHS

An LP, magazine cover, ad, photo, or card signed by the artist: $15-$40

Stewart, John

Born: September 5, 1939

Late-60s singer and songwriter, who is perhaps best remembered as a member of the Kingston Trio and composer of the Monkees' hit "Daydream Believer," John Stewart also landed a few solo hits including "Gold" (#5, 1979), "Midnight Wind' (#28, 1979), and "Lost Her in the Sun" (#34, 1980). Stewart replaced Dave Guard in the Kingston Trio in July 1961 and stayed until 1967. Still active in the business, he now records under his own Homecoming label.

AUTOGRAPHS

A CD, LP, magazine cover, ad, photo, or card signed by the artist: $10-$25

OFTEN OVERLOOKED MEMORABILIA

Memorabilia associated with his Kingston Trio days; "Daydream Believer" artifacts

Stewart, Rod

Born: January 10, 1945

Rod "The Mod" Stewart, a true megastar in every sense of the word, he may be rock 'n' roll's greatest interpretive singer, and if not, he certainly ranks among the finest. His ability to transcend generations by moving from one musical style to the next, by intricately intertwining his roots to sustain his music foundation, is a phenomena.

Before the age of twenty, Rod joined the Birmingham-based band the Dimensions as a backing vocalist and harmonica player in the fall of 1963. During this period he worked for his brother Bob as a picture framer during the day. He played less than fifty gigs billed as Jimmy Powell and the Fifth Dimensions in numerous prestigious London clubs, including The Marquee. He then hooked up with Long John Baldry and the Hoochie Coochie Men (with Rod "The Mod" Stewart), at the beginning of 1964 following the

Rod Stewart. Photo by Guzman. Courtesy Warner Bros. Records Inc.

death of the band's harmonica player and R&B pioneer Cyril Davies. This was Stewart's first full-time job, necessitating his departure from his brother's shop.

On June 19, 1964, he made his unaccredited recording debut on Long John Baldry's United Artists single (UP-1056) singing on Sister Rosetta Thorpe's "Up Above My Head I Hear Music in the Air/You'll Be Mine." Stewart's debut recording for Decca Records was "Good Morning Little Schoolgirl/I'm Gonna Move to the Outskirts of Town" (F 11996, 1964). He was now billed in a number of fashions including "An Evening With the Blues," "Rod Stewart and the Ad Lib," and "Rod Stewart with the Soul Agents." If you're looking for related material during this period it can be a bit confusing, especially old advertisements.

On July 16, 1965, the Steam Packet, consisting of Rod, Julie Driscoll, Brian Auger, Rick Brown, Mickey Waller, Long John Baldry, and Vic Briggs, made its debut in support of the Rolling Stones in Exeter. As reports hit the media of Rod's departure from Steam Packet, "The Mod" played a one-off gig billed as "The Peter B's with guest Rod Stewart" (3/17/66). In May 1966 Rod joined the Shotgun Express, consisting of Bertyl Marsden, Dave Ambrose, Peter Green, Mick Fleetwood, and Peter Bardens. Personnel changes were a constant battle, resulting in a loss of momentum. The group's debut on Columbia was the single "I Could Feel the Whole World Turn Underneath Me/Curtains" (DB 8025, 1966).

In February 1967 "The Mod" joined the Jeff Beck Group, which consisted of Beck, Ron Wood, and Roger Cook. Throughout the two and half years of life, the band went through six drummers. The group toured extensively and built a strong base of fans both in Europe and America. During the summer of 1968 the band was even joined on stage numerous times by Jimmy Page, who went on to form Led Zeppelin. Stewart became disillusioned when Beck fired Ron Wood and Micky Waller in 1969 during the recording of Beck Ola.

In June 1969 Rod made his first appearance with the Faces, billed as Quiet Melon, led by Ron Wood's brother Art. During this period Rod also signed a solo deal with Mercury Records, while claiming he was still a part of the Jeff Beck Group. Stewart left Beck's band the following month, and October 18, 1969 was announced as the Small Faces' new singer. The group consisted of Rod, Ron "Woody" Wood, Ronnie Lane, Ian McLagan, and Kenny Jones.

The group released its debut single "Flying/Three Button Hand Me Down" (WB 8005, 1970), and on February 13, 1970, Stewart's first solo album An Old Raincoat Won't Ever Let You Down (#139, 1970) was released. Stewart followed later with Every Picture Tells a Story (#1, 1971), as "Reason to Believe/Maggie May" (#1, 1971) was released as his new single. During the fall of 1971, Stewart-mania began as the rocker was constantly seen in the tabloids! The Faces

released the breakthrough album A Nod Is as Good as a Wink to a Blind Horse, which included a later withdrawn poster—a must for collectors—and extract "Stay With Me."

A collection of Rod Stewart concert tickets valued at $5-$7 each

Never a Dull Moment (#2, 1972) with hit extract "You Wear It Well" (#13, 1972) was also extremely well-received as Stewart's role with the Faces slowly became strained. His albums were consistently outselling the group's, which slowly became better known for its on-stage drinking antics and shoddy playing than its music. The beginning of the end started with Lane's departure in 1973, who was replaced by Tetsu Yamauchi, an incident that results in labor strains, and legal battles between Mercury and Warner over Stewart's work. Late in 1974 Mercury released Smiler (#13, 1974), his last album for the company.

On April 15, 1975, Ron Wood announced he was joining the Rolling Stones on a temporary basis, replacing Mick Taylor, on the Stones' forthcoming American tour. The situation caused friction with Stewart who felt the situation was not conducive to the Faces.

On November 21, 1975, Rod Stewart signed perhaps the most monumental record agreement of his career that started with Warner Brothers' release of Atlantic Crossing (#9, 1975) (released prior to referenced contract), and he moved to Los Angeles to escape British income taxes. This period also began the "Blondes Have More Fun" phase of Stewart's career, also referred to as "Does anyone know a good attorney?" phase—he was linked with Swedish starlet Britt Ekland (Mrs. Peter Sellers), Alana Hamilton (Mrs. George Hamilton), Kelly Emberg, and Rachel Hunter.

A Night on the Town (#2, 1976) with Number One extract "Tonight's the Night (Gonna Be Alright)" (#1, 1976) was the artist's next album release, and the situation with the Faces was very unclear. "The First Cut Is the Deepest" (#21, 1977) and "The Killing of Georgie (Part I & II)" (#30, 1977) were his next single releases. The Faces now history, Stewart released the risque "Hot Legs" (#28, 1978), ballad "You're in My Heart (The Final Acclaim)" (#4, 1977), and disco dance "Da Ya Think I'm Sexy" (#1, 1979) to finish out the decade.

The next decade's notable album releases include Foolish Behaviour (#12, 1980), Tonight I'm Yours (#11, 1982), and Out of Order (#20, 1988), along with singles "Passion" (#5, 1980), "Baby Jane" (#14, 1983), "Infatuation" (#6, 1984), "My Heart Can't Tell You

No" (#4, 1989), "Forever Young " (#12, 1988), and "Crazy About Her" (#11, 1989).

The '90s found Stewart releasing the following albums *Storyteller/The Complete Anthology: 1964-1990* (#54, 1990), *Vagabond Heart* (#10, 1991), *Unplugged ... And Seated* (#2, 1993), *A Spanner in the Works* (#35, 1995) and hit singles "Downtown Train" (#3, 1990), "This Old Heart of Mine" (#10, 1990), "Rhythm of My Heart" (#5, 1991), "The Motown Song" (#10, 1991), "Broken Arrow" (#20, 1992), "Have I Told You Lately That I Love You" (#5, 1993), "Reason to Believe" (#19, 1993), "All for Love" (#1, 1994) with Sting and Bryan Adams, and "Having a Party" (#36, 1994).

AUTOGRAPHS

Rod Stewart has varied in his attitude toward autograph requests over the years. He has been very obliging to autograph requests both in-person and through the mail in recent years.

An autographed LP, CD, poster, photograph, or tour book: $35-$75

TOUR BOOKS/ PROGRAMS/ BACKSTAGE PASSES

1978/79 Tour - a great tour book!: $10-$15
(U.S. version)
1984 U.S. Tour: $10-$12
1991 Vagabond Tour: $15-$17
Blondes Have More Fun, 1978-79: $25
(a great tour book!)
Foolish Behavior, 1980-81 World Tour: $20 - $25
Le Grande Tour of America & Canada, 1981-82: $25
Levi's Cords Present Labour Day Live'84: $15
Camouflage, 1984: $20
Every Beat of My Heart, 1986 Europe: $25
Lost in America, 1989: $15
Out of Order, 1988: $15
1995 A Spanner in the Works: $15-$17
Four versions of this program exist (U.K., Australia, Japan, and the U.S.)

Backstage Passes:

Cloth: $8-$11; Laminated: $11-$20 (Post-1990)
Pre-1990 assorted passes:
Fall Tour 1973: $18-$22 (cloth)
Australian Tour 1974: $18-$22 (cloth)
Faces Christmas Tour, '74: $13-$17 (stickers)
The Concert, 1977: $15-$20 (cloth, laminated crew pass add $5-$10)

The Blondes Have More Fun '78-'79 tour book (Winterland/Top-Billing Pubs. Ltd.)

Tour book from the Vagabond Tour (Rod Stewart, 1991)

POSTERS/PRESS KITS

Promotional Posters: $10 - $30 range. Example: "Vagabond Heart" (23" x 35") - $10

Press Kits:

(1990-Present): $15-$20
(1980-1989): $20-$25
(1969-1979): $25-$65

USED CLOTHING/EQUIPMENT

Guitar Picks:

Rod Stewart Group: $5

Drum Sticks:

Carmine Appice: $20

A used leopard skin suit, early '70s, pants and jacket: $5,000-$6,000

OFTEN OVERLOOKED MEMORABILIA

Out of Order embroidered jacket - $350; copies of *Melody Maker* (1963 onward), *Record Mirror* and *New Music Express*; artifacts from his U.S. visit during "Rod Stewart Visits His Friends" (1970); his numerous television appearances including *London Rock* (1970) and *German WDR-TV* (12/7/70) (also see below); artifacts from Stewart's appearance at *Tommy*, Rainbow Theatre (12/9/72); associated items from launch party for Ooh La La (4/73); a film of Ronnie lane's last performance (6/473); a copy of BBC2 documentary in its Lively Arts series "Rod The Mod Has Come of Age—A Profile of Rod Stewart" (9/1976); movie memorabilia from *All This & World War II* (1976), *Nightshift* (1982), *Innerspace* (1987), and *The Three Musketeers* (1994); newspaper and periodical clippings from Stewart's "DC-10 Pig Pen" incident; copies of his home video titles: *Live at the Los Angeles Forum* (1981), *Tonight He's Yours* (1982), *The Rod Stewart Concert Video* (1986), *Rod Stewart & The Faces Video Biography 1969-1974* (1988), and *Rod Stewart Videos 1984-1991* (1991); all items associated with his performance on 7/5/86 for the Faces reunion; copies of "*The Sun*" cartoon *Striker* that included "The Mod"; all items associated with appearance at Wembley Stadium charity soccer match (5/21/88); all Pepsi advertising featuring Rod used only in South America (2/89), also Pepsi It Takes Two duet with Tina Turner commercial spots (1990); a copy of the documentary *The Story of Rod Stewart* (4/4/89); copies of *News of the World* featuring the Stewart's sunbathing in his back garden; copies of fanzines *Foolish Behaviour* (Note: These were photocopied making originals difficult to determine) and *Smiler*—awesome!—a must for every collector; his contribution to other artists' work; jigsaw puzzle - $35; copies of the numerous lawsuits he has been involved in—fascinating as a collection on its own!; ceramic mug; Every Picture Tells a Story, 1971, $125; A Nod's as Good as a Wink pillow and sewing kit, 1972 - $75; lighter, 1975 - $25; photo mirror, 1975 - $60; Blondes Have More Fun wallet - $25; Tonight I'm Yours black jacket - $425, scarf (plaid, 5') - $45, scarf (nylon, 21") - $30, suspenders - $25, backpack - $35, frisbee - $25; Camouflage R-O-D promo letters - $40; 1986 European Tour: scarf - $40; headband - $25; 1986 World Tour scarf - $50; stand-up displays: Atlantic Crossing - $85, Blondes Have More Fun - $125, Body Wishes - $25, Downtown Train/Storyteller - $50, Tonight I'm Yours - $30

REFERENCES/BOOKS

The Rod Stewart Story by George Tremlett (1976); *Rod Stewart & The Changing Faces* by John Pidgeon (1976); *Rod Stewart* by Richard Cromelin (1976); *A Life on the Town* by Peter Burton (1977); *Rod Stewart* by Tony Jasper (1977); *Rod Stewart* by Paul Nelson & Lester Bangs (1982); *Rod Stewart* by Jurgen Selbold (1991), *Rod Stewart—A Biography* by Tim Ewbank & Stafford Hildred (1991); *Rod Stewart—The Visual Documentary* by John Gray (1992); There are no dedicated collector books.

ROD STEWART: SELECTED TELEVISION APPEARANCES

The Beat Room: U.K. TV debut with the Hoochie Coochie Men (8/6/64)

Ready, Steady Go!: promoting his first single and meeting Ron Wood for the first time (10/64) and with the Steam Packet (8/6/65)

An Easter With Rod: 30 minute portrait (11/2/65)

Steam Packet Show (11/15/65)

Top of the Pops: with the Faces (2/70, 11/70, 1/13/72, 2/8/73, 12/20/73), five consecutive appearances, backed by the Faces (10/71), Stewart and John backing Long John Baldry (2/72), backed by the Faces (8/10/72 , 11/16/72— minus Lane (cardboard cut-out used)— and 12/25/72), solo (6/24/93)

Russell Harty Show - ITV: (9/18/73, 9/18/74)

Old Grey Whistle Test - BBC2: (12/24/74, 12/76)

Supersonic: (3/1/75)

"Rod Stewart and The Faces" (12/28/75), live concert filmed (12/23/74)

Sounds of Scotland - BBC1: (8/7/76)

"A Night on the Town": (10/76) television special

The Kenny Everett Show: (1/79)

Russell Harty Show - BBC2: (11/20/80)

Saturday Night Live: 10/81

Late Late Breakfast Show - BBC1: (12/83)

Spitting Image: (2/9/86) in puppet form only!

Wogan - BBC1-TV: (5/86)

Terry Wogan Show: (6/23/86, 5/20/88)

Michael Aspel Show: (1/27/90, 3/9/91)

"Valentine Vagabond: Rod Stewart Live on Valentine's Day": (2/14/92) pay-for-view

Unplugged - MTV: (2/5/93, broadcast 5/5/93)

"Aretha Franklin: Duets" - Fox-TV: (4/27/93)

The Tonight Show - NBC-TV: (7/16/93, 5/13/95)

The Late Show With David Letterman - CBS-TV: (9/16/93)

"A Free New Year's Eve Show" - Brazilian TV: 12/31/94

*Not intended to be comprehensive

A ROD STEWART FAMILY PORTRAIT

Jimmy Powell's Five Dimensions: Stewart, Barry Wilson, Louis Cennamo, Martin Shaw, Jimmy Powell (1963)

Long John Baldry's Hoochie Coochie Men: Stewart, John Baldry, Ernie O'Malley, Johnnie Parker, Jeff Bradford, Cliff Barton (1964)

Steampacket: Stewart, John Baldry, Vic Briggs, Mickey Waller, Rick Brown, Brian Auger, Julie Driscoll (1965)

Shotgun Express: Stewart, Beryl Marsden, Dave Ambrose, Peter Green, Mick Fleetwood, Peter Bardens (1966)

Jeff Beck Group I: Stewart, Jeff Beck, Ron Wood, Mickey Waller (1967)

Jeff Beck Group II: Stewart, Jeff Beck, Ron Wood, Tony Newman, Nicky Hopkins (2/69-7/69)

Faces I: Stewart, Ron Wood, Ian McLagan, Kenny Jones, Ronnie Lane (6/69-5/73)

Faces II: Stewart, Ron Wood, Ian McLagan, Kenny Jones, Tetsu Yamauchi (5/73-12/75)

Rod Stewart Group: Stewart, Gary Grainger, Billy Peek, Jim Cregan, Carmine Appice, Phil Chen, Kevin Savinger (1977-79)*

*Other personnel involved

Sting

(Gordon Sumner)
Born: October 2, 1951

Late-80s and '90s singer, songwriter, and performer, who dissolved the Police at the height of its popularity, Sting's desire to explore and experiment with other forms of music overcame his willingness to continue on as principal songwriter for the group. *The Dream of the Blue Turtles* (#2, 1985), with its jazz and funk undercurrents, was his debut solo album and exhibited a pretentious side to his work, complimented by more complex arrangements. The two hit extracts from the record were "If You Love Somebody Set Them Free" (#3, 1985) and "Fortress Around Your Heart" (#8, 1985).

"We'll Be Together" (#7, 1987), "All This Time" (#5, 1991), "If I Ever Lose My Faith in You" (#17, 1993) (a Grammy winner), "Fields of Gold" (#23, 1993), and "All for Love" (#1, 1993) with Rod Stewart and Bryan Adams, were the hits that followed the artist into the mid-90s. During this period Sting suffered the loss of both of his parents, and his work reflected his mourning with religious imagery, haunting ballads, and an introspective return to tradition English folk roots.

Parallel to his music career, he remained active as an actor in both film and theater, and most importantly as a humanitarian. From environmental issues to his devotion for human rights, "The Best of Sting" is more likely to be found within efforts such as the Rainforest Foundation, rather than in any record store.

AUTOGRAPHS

A CD, LP, magazine cover, ad, photo, or card signed by the artist: $25-$75

TOUR BOOKS/PROGRAMS/ PASSES

Tour Books:
Three Penny Opera, 1989: $10
World Tour 1985: $10

Backstage Passes:
Cloth: $8-$10;
Laminated: $12-$15

POSTERS/PRESS KITS

Promotional Posters:
$10-$25
Press Kits: $15-$30

USED CLOTHING/ EQUIPMENT

Guitar Pick: $35-$75

OFTEN OVERLOOKED MEMORABILIA

Movie memorabilia from *Dune* (1984), *Stormy Monday* (1988), *Plenty* (1985), *The Three Musketeers* (1994), *Quadrophenia, Radio On, Artemis '81, The Secret Policeman's Other Ball, Bring on the Night* (1985), *Stars and Bars* (1988), *Julia Julia* (1988), *Lethal Weapon 3* (1992), *Demolition Man* (1993), *Ace Ventura: When Nature Calls* (1995), and *Leaving Las Vegas* (1995); videotapes of television projects including "Brimstone and Treacle"; videotapes of his numerous television appearances including *Late Night With David Letterman* (11/10/82, 9/4/91), *The Late Show With David Letterman* (2/28/94, 11/9/94, 4/10/96), *Saturday Night Live* (1/19/91, 2/20/93, 2/24/96), MTV *Unplugged* (4/10/91), *Rock Steady* (6/1/91), *The Simpsons* (1/9/92), *The Tonight Show* (5/13/93), and *Top of the Pops* (6/17/93); memorabilia from Live Aid; Police reunion memorabilia (6/1/86) and (8/22/92) at Sting's wedding; a copy of the CD-ROM "All This Time"; guitar pick earrings - $12; The Dream of the Blue Turtles bin display - $25

REFERENCES/BOOKS

A few resources exist, but none do justice to the singer in my opinion. There are no dedicated collector books.

Sting backstage pass common in couterfeit form

The Stone Roses

Formed 1985

Ian Brown, John Squire, Andy Couzens, Pete Garner, and Reni (Alan Wren)*

*Couzens and Garner departed in 1987, and Mani was added. Reni departed in 1995.

Late '70s product of the British psychedelic rave scene, the Stone Roses became overnight sensations in England while America slept. The group is typically associated with the songs "Elephant Stone," "What the World Is Waiting For/Fool's Gold" (#8, U.K., 1989), and "One Love" (#4, U.K., 1990).

AUTOGRAPHS

A CD, LP, magazine cover, ad, photo, or card signed by the group: $15-$30

Stone Temple Pilots

Formed 1987

Scott Weiland, Born: October 27, 1967; Dean Deleo; Robert DeLeo; and Eric Kretz

Early-90s Seattle hard-rock act, with an enormous cult following, the Stone Temple Pilots are typically associated with the albums *Core* (#3, 1993) and *Purple* (#1, 1994) and the songs "Sex Type Thing" and "Plush." *Tiny Music: Songs from the Vatican Gift Shop* (#4, 1996) was well-received, although the band failed to support the release due to Weiland's drug dependency. Temple-arily grounded, the band waited for clearance on Weiland before its next major departure.

AUTOGRAPHS

A CD, LP, magazine cover, ad, photo, or card signed by the group: $25-$50

POSTERS/PRESS KITS

Promotional Posters: $8-$12
Press Kits: $15

REFERENCES/BOOKS

A few resources exist, but none do justice to the group in my opinion. There are no dedicated collector books

---

Stone the Crows

Formed 1969

Maggie Bell, Les Harvey, Jon McGinnis, Jim Dewar, and Collin Allen*

*Numerous personnel changes

Late-60s and early-70s English soul band Stone the Crows is best remembered for members Maggie Bell and later Jimmy McCulloch.

AUTOGRAPHS

A CD, LP, magazine cover, ad, photo, or card signed by the group: $25*
*Original lineup

Stories

Formed 1972

Michael Brown (Lookofsky), Steve Love, Ian Lloyd (Buoncocglio), and Bryan Madey*

*Numerous personnel changes

Early-70s New York pop group the Stories are typically associated with one song, "Brother Louie" (#1, 1973), and occasionally for their talented alumni.

AUTOGRAPHS

A CD, LP, magazine cover, ad, photo, or card signed by the group: $10-$15

The Strangeloves

Formed 1965

Richard Gottehrer, Robert Feldman, and Jerry Goldstein

Mid-60s Brooklyn pop act, best remembered for one song, "I Want Candy" (#11, 1965), the Strangeloves also had a couple of follow-up minor hits before splitting up. All three band members went on to successful careers in various facets of the music business.

AUTOGRAPHS

A CD, LP, magazine cover, ad, photo, or card signed by the group: $10-$20

The Stranglers

Formed 1974

Jet Black (Brain Duffy), Jean-Jacques Burnel, Hugh Cornwell, and Dave Greenfield*

*Numerous changes in 1990 and after

Late-70s British keyboard infested punk act, better known in the U.K. where it has impressively compiled more than a dozen Top Forty hits including "Peaches" b/w "Go Buddy Go" and "Golden Brown," the Stranglers left the first mark in the U.S. with "Dreamtime" (#172, 1987)—better late than never!

AUTOGRAPHS

A CD, LP, magazine cover, ad, photo, or card signed by the group: $20-$30

OFTEN OVERLOOKED MEMORABILIA

96 Tears, Epic promo paint tray, 1990; Aural Sculpture, Epic cassette, includes computer game at the end of the tape; promotional pins - $15-$20

The Strawberry Alarm Clock

Formed 1967

Ed King, Lee Freeman, Mark Weitz, Gary Lovetro, George Bunnel, and Randy Seol*

*Numerous personnel changes

Late-60s California psychedelic rock act the Strawberry Alarm Clock is best remembered for the songs "Incense and Peppermints" (#1, 1967) and "Tomorrow" (#23, 1968), Randy Seol's outrageous stage antic of playing the bongos with his hands lit on fire,

and as the former home to Lynyrd Skynyrd's guitarist Ed King.

AUTOGRAPHS

A CD, LP, magazine cover, ad, photo, or card signed by the group: $15-$15

OFTEN OVERLOOKED MEMORABILIA

Movie memorabilia from *Beyond the Valley of the Dolls* (1970)

The Strawbs

Formed 1967

Dave Cousins, Born: January 7, 1945; Tony Hooper; and Arthur Phillips*

*Numerous personnel changes

Late-60s British progressive-rockers the Strawbs are typically associated with the songs "Lay Down" (1972) and "Part of the Union" (1973). Plagued by personnel changes, one of which was Rick Wakeman, the band somehow managed to endure into the late '70s before splitting up.

AUTOGRAPHS

A CD, LP, magazine cover, ad, photo, or card signed by the group: $10-$30*
*Lineup dependent

The Stray Cats

Formed 1979

Brian Setzer, Slim Jim Phantom (McDonnell), and Lee Rocker (Drucker)

Eighties Long Island rock-retro act, best remembered for the songs "Runaway Boys," "Stray Cat Strut," "Rock This Town," "Sexy + 17" (#5, 1983), and "I Won't Stand in Your Way," the Stray Cats garnered significant attention while opening the 1981 North American tour for the Rolling Stones. By the mid-80s the band had broken up, only to re-form in 1986 for two casually received albums.

AUTOGRAPHS

A CD, LP, magazine cover, ad, photo, or card signed by the group: $40-$75

USED CLOTHING/ EQUIPMENT

Guitar Pick: $15-$20

A Brian Setzer guitar pick

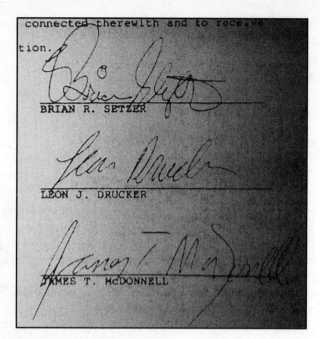

Contract signed by the Stray Cats

OFTEN OVERLOOKED MEMORABILIA

Gonna Ball, Arista promo hubcap, 1981; movie memorabilia from *La Bamba* (1987); Brian Setzer USA EMI, promo suntan lotion, 1988; Rant & Rave promo pin - $15

Streisand, Barbra

Born: April 24, 1942

Having sold more than 50 million albums in the U.S. alone, it's not hard to believe why Barbra Streisand is the top-selling female artist in history. Her multi-faceted career has now spanned over three decades, from the Broadway stage, to appearing in well over a dozen films. A consummate entertainer of now legendary status, her extraordinary degree of sophistication and professionalism have yet to be matched, and may never be.

When you think of her contribution to rock and roll, you typically turn toward songs such as "You Don't Bring Me Flowers" (#1, 1978) (a duet with Neil Diamond) and "No More Tears (Enough is Enough)" (#1, 1979) with Donna Summer, or albums such as *Stoney End* and *Streisand Superman*, or even movies like *A Star is Born* or *The Way We Were*, but with such an enormous and significant body of work to choose from, it certainly can vary.

Streisand is Simply Streisand!

AUTOGRAPHS

A CD, LP, magazine cover, ad, photo, or card signed by the artist: $150-$250

TOUR BOOKS/PROGRAMS/PASSES

Tour Books:
The Concert 93/94: $40
Landover, MD '94 Tour: $40

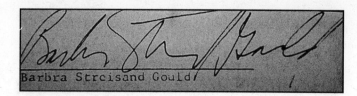

The autograph of Barbra Streisand Gould

Another Barbra signature

Movie Souvenir Books:
For Pete's Sake (Japan) $100
Funny Lady: $50
Hello Dolly: $50

Backstage Passes:
Varies significantly, because her appearances are rare with extensive security, Examples; MGM Grand 93/94 Guest and VIP laminates: $20-$50

POSTERS/PRESS KITS

Promotional Posters:
(1985-Present): $10-$15
(1974-1984): $20-$40

Press Kits:
(1985-Present): $20-$50, Example: The Concert w/deluxe Folder: $50, The Concert-$50, The Broadway Album-$20, Back to Broadway-$15
(1974 - 1984): $30-$70, Example: *Prince of Tides*

OFTEN OVERLOOKED MEMORABILIA

As an entire book could be written here, I will only touch on a handful of items before suggesting that you move to another source. *Hello Dolly*, complete set of stills from the movie - $125; *For Pete's Sake* lobby card sets $40-$60; *The Main Event* movie lithograph - $50; *The Broadway Album* songbook - $20; personality posters $15-$40; The Concert MGM Grand promotional postcards- $25

Strong, Barrett

Born: February 5, 1941

Talented '60s and '70s singer/songwriter, typically associated with his songs "Money," "I Wish It Would Rain," "Papa Was a Rolling Stone," "Just My Imagination (Running Away with Me)," "War," and "I Heard It Through the Grapevine" (many of which were collaborations with Norman Whitfield), Barrett Strong was one of the most significant song writers of his era.

AUTOGRAPHS

A CD, LP, magazine cover, ad, photo, or card signed by the artist: $15-$50

OFTEN OVERLOOKED MEMORABILIA

All items associated with his numerous compositions, particularly his Motown work

Stryper

Formed 1983

Oz Fox (Richard Martinez), Tim Gaines (Hagelganz), Micahel Sweet, and Robert Sweet

Eighties Orange County Christian rockers, typically identified with the album *To Hell with the Devil* (#32, 1986) and the song "Honesty" (#23, 1987), Stryper faded from the music scene by the '90s.

AUTOGRAPHS

A CD, LP, magazine cover, ad, photo, or card signed by the artist: $15-$30

POSTERS/PRESS KITS

Promotional Posters: $8-$10
Press Kits: $12

USED CLOTHING/EQUIPMENT

Guitar Pick: $12-$20

OFTEN OVERLOOKED MEMORABILIA

In God We Trust, promotional poster & banner - $15

The Stylistics

Formed 1968

Russell Thompkins Jr., Airrion Love, James Smith, Herbie Murrell, and James Dunn*

*Dunn departed in 1978

Late-60s and '70s "Philadelphia sound" vocal act, best remembered for the hits "You Are Everything" (#9, 1971), "Betctha By Golly Wow" (#3, 1972), "I'm Stone in Love with You" (#10, 1972), "Break Up to Make Up" (#5, 1973), and "You Make Me Feel Brand New" (#2, 1974), the Stylistics turned to Europe where they remained popular throughout the decade when domestic sales dissipated by the mid-70s. The group remained active as a trio in the '80s.

AUTOGRAPHS

A CD, LP, magazine cover, ad, photo, or card signed by the group: $25-$50

Styx

Formed 1963

James Young, John Curulewski, Dennis DeYoung, Chuck Panozzo, and John Panozzo (d. 1996)*

*Curulewski departed in 1975 and was replaced by Tommy Shaw. Group disbanded in 1984.

Late-70s Midwestern rock act, best remembered for the hits "Lady" (#6, 1975), "Come Sail Away" (#8, 1977), "Babe" (#1, 1979), "The Best of Times" (#3, 1981), and "Too Much Time on My Hands" (#9, 1981), Styx had enormous commercial success with its album sales—5 consecutive platinum releases. Following *Kilroy Was Here* (#3, 1983), the band essentially split up after loosing valuable momentum. Later reunions, although moderately successful, couldn't hold a candle to the group's previous success.

AUTOGRAPHS

A CD, LP, magazine cover, ad, photo, or card signed by the group: $30-$75

TOUR BOOKS/PROGRAMS/PASSES

Tour Books:
Kilroy Was Here Tour '83: $20
Paradise Theater (Japan): $45

Backstage Passes:
Cloth/paper: $8-$12;
Laminated: $12-$25

Platinum award for Cornerstone by Styx. The award from 1979 was made by DeJay Products. It is valued at $150. From the Doug Leftwitch collection.

POSTERS/PRESS KITS

Promotional Posters: $10-$35
Press Kits: $25-$45, Example: Styx Greatest Hits: $25, Greatest Hits 2: $10

USED CLOTHING/EQUIPMENT

Guitar Pick: $15-$30

OFTEN OVERLOOKED MEMORABILIA

Mirror - $10

Sugar: See Hüsker Dü

****

"On The Edge"

The Sugarcubes/Björk

An Icelandic additive, the Sugarcubes proved that *Life's Too Good* (#54, 1988), especially when it's your "Birthday." While *Here Today, Tomorrow, Next Week!* (#70, 1989) proved that even talented people who live in cold climates can be wrong, Björk Gudmundsdottir took exception. The entranced singer's first solo effort *Debut* (#61, 1993) spun off the single "Human Behavior," which was embraced by the modern-rock charts. Collectors who refuse to acknowledge Björk, will have to pay the prices later! The Icewoman has cometh! Press Kits: $10-$20, Promotional Posters: $15-$25

****

The Sugar Hill Gang

Formed 1977

Master Gee (Guy O'Brien), Wonder Mike (Michael Wright), and Big Bank Hank (Henry Jackson)

Late-70s New York selected rappers, best remembered for the hit "Rapper's Delight" (#4, R&B, 1979), a pivotal release in rap history because it really brought the genre into musicology, the Sugar Hill Gang had only two other minor hits, "8th Wonder" (#15, R&B, 1981) and "Lover in You."

AUTOGRAPHS

A CD, LP, magazine cover, ad, photo, or card signed by the group: $10-$15*

*A "Rapper's Delight" related item

Suicide

Formed 1972

Alan Vega and Martin Rev

Late '70s enigma, best remembered for being pelted with garbage while opening up British tour in 1978 for the Clash and Elvis Costello, Suicide's biggest, o.k., most noteworthy fan was Ric Ocasek, who even convinced the duo to open the Cars' 1980 U.S. tour. The band practically caused riots everywhere it played. By inciting conflict and humiliating its audience, nearly every concert promoter in the country tried to have it removed from the bill. The duo broke up in the early '80s, but got back together at the end of the decade.

AUTOGRAPHS

A CD, LP, magazine cover, ad, photo, or card signed by the group: $15-$25

OFTEN OVERLOOKED MEMORABILIA

"stage wingage," official stage struck relics dislodged by irate fans

Summers, Donna

(Donna Gaines)
Born: December 31, 1948

Mid-70s Boston dance diva, typically associated with the songs "Love to Love You Baby" (#2, 1975), "I Feel Love" (#6, 1977), "MacArthur Park" (#1, 1978), "Last Dance" (a Grammy winner), "Bad Girls" (#1, 1979), "Hot Stuff" (#1, 1979), "No More Tears (Enough Is Enough)" (a duet with Barbra Streisand), "Heaven Knows" (#4, 1979), "Dim All the Lights" (#2, 1979), "The Wanderer" (#3, 1980), "She Works Hard for the Money" (#3, 1983), and "Forgive Me" (a Gram-

my winner), Donna Summer was one of disco's few stars to cross successfully into pop genre and sustain herself over a long period of time—over two decades! She ended the '80s by placing "This Time I Know It's for Real" (#7,1989) into the Top Ten and certainly wouldn't bet against her repeating the feat by the end of the '90s. Afterall, "Melody Of Love (Wanna Be Loved) topped the dance charts in 1995.

AUTOGRAPHS

A CD, LP, magazine cover, ad, photo, or card signed by the artist: $15-$25

TOUR BOOKS/PROGRAMS/PASSES

Tour Books:
Bad Girls Tour '77: $40

POSTERS/PRESS KITS

Promotional Posters: $10-$35
Press Kits: $15-$45, Example: Another Place: $25

OFTEN OVERLOOKED MEMORABILIA

Movie memorabilia from *Thank God It's Friday* and *Fast Times at Ridgemont High*; all memorabilia from her Casablanca days (1975/77-1979/80)

REFERENCES/BOOKS

A few resources exist. *Donna Summer: An Unauthorized Biography* by Jim Haskins and J.M. Stifle is a MUST read! There are no dedicated collector books. Serious collectors should opt for a Fan Club: The Donna Summer Fan Club, P.O. Box 40965, Redford, MI 48240

Summers, Andy: See the Police

Supertramp

Formed 1969

Original Lineup: Roger Hodgson, Born: March 21, 1950; Richard Davies; Richard Palmer; and Bob Miller*

*Band restructured in 1974

Late-70s British pop act, bankrolled by Dutch millionaire Stanley August and formed by Rick Davies, Supertramp endured through a very unsuccessful beginning to become one of the early '80s most accomplished acts. Typically identified with songs such as "Dreamer," "Bloody Well Right," "Give a Little Bit" (#15, 1977), "The Logical Song" (#6, 1979), "Goodbye Stranger," "Take the Long Way Home" (#10, 1979), and "Cannonball," Supertramp was consistent in its chart presence until the departure of singer/songwriter Rodger Hodgson for a solo career in 1983. When Hodgson fared with less success than anticipated, he returned briefly to help promote the group's compilation *The Autobiography of Supertramp*. The group's later efforts have failed to chart with any substantive promise.

AUTOGRAPHS

A CD, LP, magazine cover, ad, photo, or card signed by the group: $40-$85*

*1979 lineup: Davies, Hodgson, Helliwell, Thomson, and Siebenberg

TOUR BOOKS/ PROGRAMS/ PASSES

Tour Books:
Supertramp in America, 1979: $10-$15
World Tour, 1983: $10

OFTEN OVERLOOKED MEMORABILIA

Breakfast in America matchbook - $20 and menu - $20; Crime of the Century, acetate for lightbox - $15; Umbrella Club member kit: patch, card, photo, breakdown sheet, (4) newsletters - $15 (1979)

REFERENCES/BOOKS

A few resources exist, but none do justice to the group in my opinion. There are no dedicated collector books

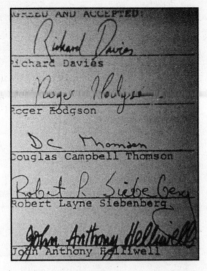

A contract signed by the members of Supertramp

The Supertramp in America tour book (Supertramp; designed by Sue Davies)

Supremes/Diana Ross and the Supremes

Formed 1959

As the Primettes: Diana Ross, Born: March 26, 1944; Florence Ballard (1943-1976); Mary Wilson, Born: March 6, 1944; and Betty McGlown*

*McGlown departed in 1960, and was replaced by Barbara Martin. Without Martin in 1963 as the Supremes. Ballard left in 1967 and Cindy Birdsong was added. Ross left in 1969 and Jean Terrell was added. Other changes followed.

Sixties Motown female vocal group, which went on to become one of the most successful acts of the decade and one of rock 'n' roll's all time premier groups, the Supremes had a dozen Number One hits including "Where Did Our Love Go" (1964), "Stop! In the Name of Love" (1965), "Back in My Arms Again" (1965), "I Hear a Symphony" (1965), "You Can't Hurry Love" (1966), "You Keep Me Hangin' On" (1966), "Love Is Here and Now You're Gone," and "The Happening" (1967). They were prolific performers and were often featured weekly on either a stage or in front of a television camera on virtually every major show of the era.

With Ross viewed in the public's eye as the star, despite members' claims that they were equals, by 1967 the group was billed as Diana Ross and the Supremes. Tensions ran high internally and in 1967 the group found itself without Ballard. She was replaced by Cindy Birdsong (Patti LaBelle and the Blue Belles) during a period that also saw the departure of the legendary Holland-Dozier-Holland team from Motown. The group's next Number One was "Love Child," as speculation of Ross' departure was finally confirmed in early 1969. "Someday We'll Be Together" became the Supremes' final chart topper before Ross departed. On January 14, 1970, at Las Vegas' Frontier Hotel, the group made its final appearance with Ross.

Ross was replaced by Jean Terrell, but the Supremes, for all intents and purposes, was nearing the end of the road. Although the group scored more hits, none topped the singles chart and by 1983 only Wilson remained as the final link to the legendary group. In 1976, the Greene-Wilson-Payne lineup released the final Top Forty single for the Supremes, "I'm Gonna Let My Heart Do the Walking." On February 21, 1976, Ballard died of cardiac arrest at the age of 32. The Wilson-Ross-Birdsong combination reunited for the taping of "Motown 25" in 1983. In 1988 the Supremes were inducted into the Rock and Roll Hall of Fame, but Ross chose not to attend.

BPI Platinum award for Diana Ross & the Supremes 20 Golden Greats, 1977. This award was presented to Cindy Birdsong. It is valued at $1,000. From the Doug Leftwitch collection.

AUTOGRAPHS

A CD, LP, magazine cover, ad, photo, or card signed by the group - $100-$275

OFTEN OVERLOOKED MEMORABILIA

Naturally there could be a book about the artifacts associated with a group as talented as the Supremes, but I will only touch on a few items. All artifacts from the group's inclusion in early package tours are highly sought by collectors, especially 1962 U.S. Motown Records Tour, 1964 Dick Clark's Calvalcade of Stars, Murray the K's 1964 ten-day Rock 'n' Roll Spectacular, and the 1965 UK 24-day Motown Package Tour; videotapes from the group's numerous television appearances including *Ready Steady Go!* (10/9/64, 4/65,), *T.A.M.I. Show* (1964), *The Ed Sullivan Show* (12/27/64, 10/10/65, 1968, 12/21/69), *It's What's Happening Baby* (6/28/65), *Tarzan* (1968), *Sunday Night at the London Palladium* (1/28/68), and "The Supremes Live at the Talk of the Town" (2/3/68); all artifacts with from their controversial performance at the "Royal Variety

Performance" (11/19/68); all artifacts from significant live performances including a member's first or final. As an early Motown act, and highly successful one at that, little or no promotional items exist from the group's pinnacle of popularity—a characteristic of the label.

REFERENCES/BOOKS

Numerous resources exist, but begin with Mary Wilson's autobiographies. There are no dedicated collector books.

Surface

Formed 1983

David Townsend, David Conley, and Karen Copeland*

*Copeland departed in 1988 and was replaced by Bernard Jackson

Late-80s New Jersey R&B soul group, formed by Dave Townsend and Dave Conley (both also talented producers), Surface is typically associated with the songs "Happy" (#20, 1987), "Shower Me with Your Love" (#5, 1989), and "Never Gonna Let You Down" (#17, 1991).

AUTOGRAPHS

A CD, LP, magazine cover, ad, photo, or card signed by the group: $12-$15

The Surfaris

Formed 1962

Original lineup: Pat Connolly, Jim Fuller, Bob Beryhill, Ron Wilson (1945-1989), and Jim Pash

Early-60s California surf act, typically remembered for only one hit—"Wipe Out" (#2, 1963)—the Surfaris also had a minor hit with "Point Panic" (#49, 1963) before disbanding in the mid-60s. "Wipe Out" has become a summertime classic, covered countless times, and used in numerous advertisements.

AUTOGRAPHS

A CD, LP, magazine cover, ad, photo, or card signed by the group: $25-$50

OFTEN OVERLOOKED MEMORABILIA

All items associated with the numerous covers of "Wipe Out," as well as copies of related items using the song

Sutherland Brothers and Quiver

Formed 1973

Iain Sutherland, Gavin Sutherland, Peter Wood, Tim Renwick, Willie Wilson, and Bruce Thomas*

*Numerous personnel changes

This early-70s British pop group, formed from two bands—Sutherland Brothers and Quiver—is best re-membered for the songs "(I Don't Want to Love You But) You Got Me Anyway" (#48, 1973), "Sailing" (covered by Rod Stewart), and "Arms of Mary." The band did gain considerable exposure by opening for Elton John's 1973 U.S. Tour, but never had enough to achieve an acceptable level of commercial success. Most group members found far greater satisfaction following the band's split.

AUTOGRAPHS

LP, magazine cover, ad, photo, or card signed by the group: $10-$15

Swan, Billy

Born: May 12, 1944

Swan, a '60s and '70s Nashville journeyman, wrote his first hit, "Lover Please" (covered by Clyde McPhatter in 1962), at the age of 16. He later traveled to Nashville and produced Tony Joe White's first three records. In 1970 he was in Kris Kristofferson's band at the Isle of Wight Festival, before he landed with Kinky Friedman in 1973. The following year he had a smash hit with "I Can Help" (#1, 1974), and after two follow-up minor hits and some successful tours, slipped from the music scene. He surfaced nearly a decade later in the supergoup Black Tie with Randy Meisner (Eagles) and James Griffin (Bread), but like many such configurations, nothing really amounted from it.

AUTOGRAPHS

A CD, LP, magazine cover, ad, photo, or card signed by the artist: $10

OFTEN OVERLOOKED MEMORABILIA

Associated artifacts from other artists' covers of his compositions

Sweat, Keith

Born: July 22, 1961

New York R&B singer Sweat is typically associated with his early R&B hits "I Want Her" (#1, R&B, 1987), "Something Just Ain't Right" (#3, R&B, 1988), and "Make It last Forever" (#2, R&B, 1988), before he crossed into pop with song such as "Make You Sweat" (#14, 1990), "I'll Give All My Love to You" (#7, 1990), and "Keep It Comin'" (#17, 1991).

Sweat then formed Keia Records in 1992, based in New York and Atlanta and distributed by Elektra. His goal was to record new R&B and rap acts. His 1994 album *Get Up on It* (#8, 1994) became his second album to sell into the Top Ten , driven by the hit extract "How Do You Like It?" (#48, 1994). It was followed by his smash self-titled hit album in 1996, which included the extracts "Twisted," and "Nobody."

AUTOGRAPHS

A CD, LP, magazine cover, ad, photo, or card signed by the artist: $20-$40

POSTERS/PRESS KITS

Promotional Posters: $10-$20
Press Kits: $15-$25

****

"On The Edge"

Sweet, Matthew

Another University of Georgia alumnus, who following a stint in Lynda Stipe's band Oh-OK, landed a solo recording deal. Sweet's early efforts were sugar-coated to critics, but sour in sales. Not until the album *Girlfriend* (#100, 1992) did anyone take notice. Since this time the artist has slowly climbed his way up the album charts with each subsequent effort. Sweet is worth watching and always *100% Fun.* Press Kits: $15, Promotional Posters: $10 - $15

****

Sweet

Formed 1968

Brian Connolly, Mick Tucker, Andy Scott, and Steve Priest*

*Connolly departed in 1978, and Gary Moberley was added

Seventies British bubblegum hard-rockers, best remembered in the States for "Little Willy," "Fox on the Run," "Love is Like Oxygen," "Blockbuster" and "Ballroom Blitz," this Nicky Chin and Mike Chapman group scored numerous hits in the U.K., but soon had difficulty shedding its novelty rock image and disbanded.

AUTOGRAPHS

A CD, LP, magazine cover, ad, photo, or card signed by the group: $15-$30

The Sweet Inspirations

Formed during the '50s as the Drinkard Sisters

Emily "Cissy" Houston, Sylvia Shemwell, Judy Clay, Dede Warwick, and Dionne Warwick*

*Numerous personnel changes

Late-60s R&B-rooted pop group and notable back-up vocalists, the Sweet Inspirations are best remembered for their hit "Sweet Inspiration" (#18, 1968) and their numerous and notable back-up appearances such as on Elvis Presley's "Suspicious Minds."

AUTOGRAPHS

A CD, LP, magazine cover, ad, photo, or card signed by the group: $20-$60

OFTEN OVERLOOKED MEMORABILIA

Associated artifacts from their numerous contributions to other artists' records

The Swingin' Blue Jeans

Formed 1958

Original lineup: Ray Ennis, Ray Ellis, Les Braid, Norman Kuhlke, and Paul Moss*

*Numerous personnel changes

Early-60s British pop act, best remembered for the hits "Hippy Hippy Shake" (#2, U.K., 1963), "Good Golly Miss Molly" (#11, 1964), and "You're No Good" (#3, 1964), the Swingin' Blue Jeans faded as fast as a fresh pair of Levi's hit with a quart of bleach. Terry Sylvester, who had joined the band in 1964, later replaced Graham Nash in the Hollies.

AUTOGRAPHS

A CD, LP, magazine cover, ad, photo, or card signed by the group: $15-$25

Swing Out Sister

Formed 1986

Corinne Drewey, Andy Connell, and Martin Jackson

Late-80s British dance-pop act Swing Out Sister is typically associated with the hits "Breakout" (#6, 1987), "Twilight World" (#31, 1987), "Waiting Game" (#86, 1989) and "Am I the Same Girl" (#45, 1992).

AUTOGRAPHS

A CD, LP, magazine cover, ad, photo, or card signed by the group: $15-$25

Tackhead

Formed 1987

Keith LeBlanc, Doug Wimbish, Skip McDonald, Bernard Fowler, Gary Clail, and Adrian Sherwood

A menagerie of sounds put on a techno-dance and hip-hop foundation, Tackhead was put together in the mid-80s. The group consisted primarily of members of the Sugarhill house band and dub producer Adrian Sherwood, while other vocalists were added later. "The Game" was the group's breakthrough in 1987. Worth noting is that the group's debut album was released under Keith LeBlanc's name, because its moniker wasn't used until 1987.

AUTOGRAPHS

A CD, LP, magazine cover, ad, photo, or card signed by the group: $5-$15

Take 6

Formed 1987

Alvin Chea, Born: November 2, 1967; Mervyn Warren; David Thomas; Cedric Dent; Claude McKnight; and Mark Kibble*

*Warren left in 1991 and Joel Kibble was added.

Take 6 is an a cappella gospel act which achieved extraordinary success with the debut album *Take 6*, featuring "Spread Love," a multiple Grammy Award winner. Take 6 also landed a Grammy for its sophomore effort *So Much 2 Say* (#72, 1990), before Mervyn Warren departed in 1991. The group's *He Is Christmas* album also picked up another Grammy, while the 1994 record *Join the Band* (#86) sold well and featured numerous guests including Ray Charles and Stevie Wonder.

AUTOGRAPHS

A CD, LP, magazine cover, ad, photo, or card signed by the group: $15-$30

Talking Heads

Formed 1975

David Byrne, Born: May 14, 1952; Tina Weymouth; Chris Frantz; and Jerry Harrison

One of the most highly creative and eccentric bands to emerge from the new wave movement, the Talking Heads drew from a variety of inspirations and sounds. Their debut album featured the hit extract "Psycho Killer" which helped sell the album into the Top 100, while every release that followed had little trouble making it to the Top Forty.

Their sophomore album *More Songs* contained the hit extract "Take Me to the River" (#26,1978), but is most noteworthy as their first effort for new producer Brian Eno. *Fear of Music* (#21, 1979) and *Remain in Light* (#19, 1980) were creative departures for the band during a period that saw band members also pursuing solo efforts. For example, both Frantz and Weymouth recorded under the moniker Tom Tom Club and landed a disco hit with "Genius of Love."

The band then ended the relationship with Brain Eno and entered the studio to produce *Speaking in Tongues* (#15, 1983), the first album of new material in three years. It was the group's highest charting effort and included the hit extract "Burning Down the House" (#9, 1983). The group toured in support of the album and put their efforts on film with *Stop Making Sense*—the soundtrack sold very well (#41, 1984). Having extended the band numerous times to accommodate their sound,the band returned to basics on , *Little Creatures* (#20, 1985), which sold platinum.

The band's next effort was *True Stories*, a film directed by David Byrne. The soundtrack landed the hit single "Wild Wild Life" (#25, 1986). *Naked* (#19, 1988) was produced by Steve Lillywhite and included heavy African and Caribbean influences, while the band's final tracks were released as part of the *Popular Favorites* box-set retrospect.

AUTOGRAPHS

A CD, LP, magazine cover, ad, photo, or card signed by the group: $30-$90

TOUR BOOKS/PROGRAMS/PASSES

Tour Books:

Are You There, 1980 (Europe, Australia, Japan): $50

POSTERS/PRESS KITS

Promotional Posters: $10-$25
Press Kits: $15-$30

OFTEN OVERLOOKED MEMORABILIA

Fear of Music hospital bracelet - $10; More Songs jigsaw puzzle - $25; More Songs pocket protector - $25; More Songs 1978 tour matches - $20; Speaking in Tongues, set of 6 buttons - $20; *Stop Making Sense* film strips - $10; No Talk Just Head promo pack, (3 posters & 5 flats)-$25, Little Crewtures (Set of 7 buttons with card)-$20; Rhode Island School of Design and Harvard artifacts; a copy of the *TV Guide* the band took its name from; artifacts from CBGBs; videotapes of the group's numerous television appearances including *Rock from CBGBs* (1975), *Old Grey Whistle Test* (1/31/78), *South Bank* (12/23/79), *Ile' Aiye* (The House of Life), *Late Night With David Letterman* (8/14/92) (Tom Tom Club), and *The Tonight Show* (9/15/92) (Byrne); all festival artifacts including the 1979 Dr. Pepper Festival in Central Park; artifacts from Twyla Tharp's ballet *The Catherine Wheel* (1981); movie memorabilia from *Stop Making Sense* (1983), *Down and Out in Beverly Hills* (1986), *True Stories* (1986), *The Last Emperor*, *Until the End of the World* (1991), and *Blue in The Face*; copies of Byrne's lecture "Speaking of Music & Other Things" (1990) and his photography book *Strange Ritual* (1995); No Talk Just Head promo pack (3 posters 7 5 flats) - $25;

REFERENCES/BOOKS

Numerous resources exist, but none do justice to the group in my opinion. There are no dedicated collector books.

Tangerine Dream

Formed 1967

Edgar Frose, Klaus Schulze, and Konrad Schnitzler*

*Schulze and Schnitzler left in 1971and Christopher Franke and Steve Shroyder were added. Peter Baumann was added in 1972 and Shroyder departed. Baumann left in 1978 and Steve Jollife and Klaus Kreiger joined the band. Johannes Schmoelling was added in 1979 then left in 1985. Paul Haslinger joined in 1985 on keyboards. Franke left in 1988 and was replaced with Ralf Wadephal.

A German ensemble notorious for its experimentation with synthesizer music and forerunners of both New Age and techno music, Tangerine Dream built up a considerable cult following, especially in Europe where its cathedral tours were typically sold out well in advance. During the group's evolution it has experienced numerous personnel changes.

AUTOGRAPHS

A CD, LP, magazine cover, ad, photo, or card signed by the group: $15-$45

OFTEN OVERLOOKED MEMORABILIA

Movie memorabilia from *Sorcerer* (1977) and *Thief* (1981)

Tavares

Formed 1959

Ralph Tavares, Born: December 10, 1948; Arthur "Pooch" Tavares, Born: May 18, 1953; Perry Lee Tavares, Born: October 24, 1954; and Antone "Chubby" Tavares, Born: June 2, 1947

Tavares is best known for its string of R&B and disco hits during the '70s including "Check It Out" (#35, 1973), "She's Gone" (#50, 1974), "It Only Takes a Minute" (#10, 1975), "Heaven Must Be Missing an Angel" (#15, 1976), "Whodunit" (#22, 1977), and "More Than a Woman" (#32) (from the successful *Saturday Night Fever* soundtrack album).

The harmonizing Tavares brothers also later scored with the following R&B hits: "Bad Times" (#10, 1979), "A Penny for Your Thoughts" (#16, 1982), "Deeper in Love" (#10, 1983), and "Words and Music" (#29, 1983).

AUTOGRAPHS

A CD, LP, magazine cover, ad, photo, or card signed by the group: $15-$40

Taylor, James

Born: March 12, 1948

James Taylor was one of the '70s most successful singer/songwriters. His sensitive tenor voice combined delicately with his intricate acoustic guitar accompaniments produced numerous hits including "Fire and Rain" (#3, 1970), "Carolina in my Mind" (#), "You've Got a Friend" (#1, 1971), "How Sweet It Is" (#5, 1975), "Mockingbird" (#4, 1973) with wife Carly Simon, "Don't Let Me Be lonely Tonight" (#14, 1973), and "Handy Man." He also scored hits with "Wonderful World" with Paul Simon and Art Garfunkel, "Up on the Roof," "Her Town Too" (#11, 1981) with J.D. Souther, and "Everyday" (#61, 1985).

Success did not come easy for Taylor, who battled heroin addiction, visits to mental institutions, and a divorce with his former wife Carly Simon. He persevered despite the odds which were often not in his favor. He lost a contract with Apple Records early in his career and under the guidance of Peter Asher was able to sign on to Warner Brothers Records. Never one for the spotlight, Taylor's periodic retreats from stardom have included little live tour exposure and often one-off appearances for charity or political causes. "Hourglass" (#9,1997) brought him back to the spotlight in 1997, during a year that would find the artist on nearly every conceivable television variety show.

AUTOGRAPHS

Very accommodating to autograph requests in-person and extremely pleasant to deal with!

A CD, LP, magazine cover, ad, photo, or card signed by the artist: $30-$75

TOUR BOOKS/PROGRAMS/PASSES
Tour Books:
JT (1977): $27-$35

POSTERS/PRESS KITS
Promotional Posters: $9-$30
Press Kits: $15-$50

OFTEN OVERLOOKED MEMORABILIA

Movie memorabilia from *Two-Lane Blacktop* (1971) and *No Nukes*; all of his associated promotional items with Apple Records

Taylor, Johnnie

Born: May 5, 1938

Soul singer whose unique vocal style made him a consistent entity on the R&B charts beginning in the mid-60s and a "disco daddy" by the mid-70s, Johnnie Taylor scored with numerous diverse hits including

"Who's Making Love" (#5, 1968), "Take Care of Your Homework" (#20, 1969), "Jody's Got Your Girl and Gone" (#1, R&B, 1971), "Somebody's Gettin' It" (#33, 1976), and "Disco Lady" (#1, 1976).

AUTOGRAPHS

A CD, LP, magazine cover, ad, photo, or card signed by the artist: $5-$15

Taylor, Koko

(Cora Walton)
Born: September 28, 1935

Taylor, the "Queen of the Blues," was working with Buddy Guy and Junior Wells while still a teenager in Chicago. Discovered by Willie Dixon, who produced her classic and million-selling hit "Wang Dang Doodle" (1965), Taylor has been nominated for numerous Grammy Awards and won for Best Traditional Blues Recording in 1984. As a female blues artist, she has won the most W.C. Handy Awards.

AUTOGRAPHS

A CD, LP, magazine cover, ad, photo, or card signed by the artist: $10-$40

OFTEN OVERLOOKED MEMORABILIA

Movie memorabilia from *The Blues Is Alive and Well in Chicago* (1970) and *Wild at Heart* (1990); associated memorabilia from the numerous festivals she has performed at

Tchaikovsky, Bram: See the Motors

Teardrop Explodes: See Julian Cope

Tears for Fears

Formed 1982

Roland Orzabal, Born: August 22, 1961; and Curt Smith, Born: June 24, 1961

Melodic British techno-pop duo whose breakthrough came with their second album, *Songs from the Big Chair*, which landed the two Number One hits "Everybody Wants to Rule the World" and "Shout" and also "Head Over Heals" (#3, 1985). Four years then passed, and Smith left before *Elemental* (#45, 1993) was released. It yielded hit extract "Break It Down Again" (#25, 1993).

AUTOGRAPHS

A CD, LP, magazine cover, ad, photo, or card signed by the group: $10-$30

TOUR BOOKS/PROGRAMS/PASSES

Tour Books:
The Seeds of Love Tour: $15

Technotronic

Formed 1989

Ya Kid K (Manuela B. Kamosi), Jo Bogaert (Thomas de Quincy), and MC Eric

Of bizarre and somewhat confusing origins, Technotronic is best known for dance-to-pop crossover hit "Get Up! (Before the Night is Over)" (#7, 1990), featuring Ya Kid K of "Pump Up the Jam" fame.

AUTOGRAPHS

A CD, LP, magazine cover, ad, photo, or card signed by the group: $5-$15

OFTEN OVERLOOKED MEMORABILIA

Movie memorabilia from *Teenage Mutant Ninja Turtles*; a videotape of their song "Move This" being featured in Cindy Crawford's Revlon commercial

Teenage Fanclub

Formed 1989

Norman Blake, Gerard Love, Francis MacDonald, and Raymond McGinley*

*Additional personnel include Brendan O'Hare and Paul Quinn

Hairdressers gone grunge, Teenage Fanclub is best known for the album *Bandwagonesque* (#22, U.K., 1991) and for opening Nirvana's 1992 tour. The band's albums *Thirteen* and *Grand Prix* also have sold well in the U.K. where it is far more popular than in the U.S.

AUTOGRAPHS

A CD, LP, magazine cover, ad, photo, or card signed by the group: $5-$15

Television

Formed 1973

Tom Verlaine (Thomas Miller), Richard Lloyd, Richard Hell (Richard Myers), and Billy Ficca

Another mid-70s CBGB seed that had an effect on British postpunk rock, Television's accomplished guitar work, imaginative songwriting, and clever lyrics have been cited by many bands as an early influ-

ence. However, Television couldn't tune the reception in enough to establish any commercial success and broke up in 1978 after three albums.

AUTOGRAPHS

An LP, magazine cover, ad, photo, or card signed by the group: $10-$40

The Temptations/David Ruffin/ Eddie Kendricks

Formed 1961

Otis Williams (Otis Miles), Born: October 30, 1949; Eddie Kendrick(s), Born: December 17, 1939, Died: October 5, 1992; Paul Williams, Born: July 2, 1939, Died: August 17, 1973; Melvin Franklin (David English), Born: October 12, 1942, Died: February 23, 1995; and Elbridge Bryant*

*Additional personnel included: David Ruffin (Davis Ruffin), Born: January 18, 1941, Died: June 1, 1991; Dennis Edwards, Born: February 3, 1943; Ricky Owens; Damon Harris; Richard Street; Glenn Leonard; Louis Price; Ron Tyson; Ali Woodson; Theo Peoples; and Ray Davis

The Motown Model

The dominating male vocal group of the '60s and early '70s, and without question one of the greatest rock and roll acts of all-time, the Temptations was formed in 1961, (the group was first called the Elgins). The group had a rocky start out of the gates, which included numerous flops and even the departure of Bryant. The Temptations, now with David Ruffin and working with writer/producer Smokey Robinson, scored a hit with "The Way You Do the Things You Do" (#11), only the first of many that would follow. "My Girl" (#1, 1965), "Since I Lost My Baby" (#17, 1965), "Get Ready" (#29, 1966), "Ain't Too Proud to Beg" (#13, 1966), "Beauty's Only Skin Deep" (#3, 1966), "(I Know) I'm Losing You" (#8, 1966), "All I Need" (#8, 1967), "You're My Everything" (#6, 1967), "I Wish It Would Rain" (#4, 1968), and "I Could Never Love Another (After Loving You)" (#13, 1968) were only a few of the hits during this early period. Following the taping of the memorable Supremes-Tempts TV special, one of television's finest moments, Ruffin found himself no longer a part of the Temptations.

A Rough Departure: 1968-1971

Dennis Edwards then took over for Ruffin, and although many critics were writing the band's epitaph, the addition of Edwards wound up working in the band's favor. His more aggressive than smooth approach lent itself well to the atmosphere of the late '60s. "Cloud Nine," "Run Away Child, Running Wild" (#6, 1969), "Psychedelic Shack" (#7, 1970), and "Ball of Confusion (That's What the World is Today)" (#3, 1970) were harder-edged songs for the Tempts, who also intertwined their new sound with other less ag-

gressive hits such as "I'm Gonna Make You Love Me" (#2, 1968)—a duet with the Supremes recorded before Ruffin's departure—"I Can't Get Next to You" (#1, 1969), and "Jusy My Imagination (Running Away with Me)" (#1, 1971). This marked the end of another period for the band, which watched Kendricks depart for a solo career and Williams leave due to his health and some personal problems.

The Move From Motown: 1971-present

Damon Harris was then added briefly, but departed before ever recording with the band, and was followed by Richard Street. The band's next wave of singles included "Papa Was a Rollin' Stone" (#1, 1972), "Masterpiece" (#7, 1973), "Let Your Hair Down" (#27, 1973), and "Shakey Ground" (#32, 1975) during a period that found them more often atop the R&B listing than pop chart. *The Temptations Do the Temptations*, was the group's last release under their original Motown contract, because the group was becoming more disillusioned with the label.

Dennis Edwards, who left and returned often, did so for the first time just before the group signed with Atlantic. Louis Price was added as the band the tried to latch on to the disco sound with the albums *Bare Black* and *Hear to Tempt You*. When the group's efforts failed, Edwards returned, and the band returned to Motown and released the first hit single in seven years, "Power" (#43, 1980). When the subsequent album failed to meet expectations, projects were shelved in anticipation of a Reunion Tour. With Kendricks and Ruffin back, the now seven man outfit recorded *Reunion* (#37, 1982), under the watchful eye of Rick James.

Glory was fleeting, however, because both Kendricks and Ruffin returned to their solo careers. Both had already had already seen the bulk of their solo success, though: Ruffin had "Walk Away from Love" (#9, 1969), and Kendricks had "Keep on Trukin' (Part 1)" (#1, 1973) and "Boogie-Down" (#2, 1974). Both had to be satisfied with the R&B chart until Hall and Oates invited them for a Temptations medley recorded live at the Apollo Theatre. Ruffin, Kendricks, and Edwards later scored with their successful Temptations package tour during the '80s. On June 1, 1991, Ruffin, who had been battling a drug problem, overdosed, lapsed into a coma, and died at the age of 50. Kendrick died the following year from lung cancer at the age of 52.

The Temptations later joined the Four Tops in a battle of the bands format known as the T'n'T Tour. The three year stint, which began in 1983, included sold-out shows on Broadway. Of their latter hits, "Treat Her Like a Lady" (#48, 1984) and "Sail Away" (#54, 1984) stand out amongst numerous chart entries. The Temptations were inducted into the Rock and Roll Hall of Fame in 1989. Franklin died in 1995 following a rash of health problems. Williams carries the Temptations eternal light into the '00s.

AUTOGRAPHS

A CD, LP, magazine cover, ad, photo, or card signed by the group: $50-$125*

*A recent lineup, as an original lineup would command a far greater price

REFERENCES/BOOKS

Numerous resources exist. *Temptations* by Otis Williams and Patricia Romanowski is a MUST read. There are no dedicated collector books.

10cc

Formed 1972

Eric Stewart, Born: January 20, 1945; Lol Creme (Lawrence Creme); Graham Gouldman; and Kevin Godley*

*Godley and Creme left in 1976 and Paul Burgess was added. Burgess left in 1977 and Rick Fenn, Tony O'Malley, and Stuart Tosh joined the band. Group re-formed in 1991.

A very talented group of musicians that included Graham Gouldman, best known for his songwriting on classics such as "For Your Love," "Heart Full of Soul," "Evil Hearted You," "Look Through Any Window," "Bus Stop," and "No Milk Today," 10cc evolved from a group called Hotlegs that had a 1970 U.K. hit with "Neanderthal Man." The band scored early hits with "Donna" (#2, U.K., 1972), "Rubber Bullets" (#1, U.K., 1973), "Dean and I" (#10, U.K., 1973), "Wall Street Shuffle" (#10, U.K., 1974), "I'm Not In Love" (#1, U.K., 1975), and "Art for Art's Sake" (#5, U.K., 1975). It took time for the band to break in America, but it finally did with "I'm Not in Love" (#2, 1975) and later with "The Things We Do for Love" (#5, 1977) and "Dreadlock Holiday" (#44, 1978). The group disbanded in the early '80s, and Gouldman joined Andrew Gold in the duo Wax before turning to his outstanding video work.

AUTOGRAPHS

Group:

A CD, LP, magazine cover, ad, photo, or card signed by the artist: $15-$45*

*Original band members

Individual:

Graham Gouldman: $5-$15

10,000 Maniacs

Formed 1981

Natalie Merchant, Born: October 26, 1963; Robert Buck; Dennis Drew; Steven Gustafson; and Jerome Augustyniak; and John Lombardo*

*Lombardo, who left the band in 1985, and Mary Ramsey also appeared on *MTV Unplugged* (1994) release.

A talented alt band which created a strong cult following through extensive tour exposure and college airplay, 10,000 Maniacs is best known for songs such as "Like the Weather" (#68, 1988), "What's the Matter Here" (#80, 1988), "Trouble Me" (#44, 1989), and "These Are Days" (#66, 1992). Although it has never landed a Top Ten hit, its album sales strength was strong as was there live appeal. Natalie Merchant later decided to go solo and released *Tigerlily* (#13, 1995). The group returned in 1997 with *Love Among the Ruins*, which debuted on the charts beneath the Top 100 albums.

AUTOGRAPHS

Group:

A CD, LP, magazine cover, ad, photo, or card signed by the band: $15-$60*

*Original band

Individual:

Natalie Merchant: $15-$40

OFTEN OVERLOOKED MEMORABILIA

State University of New York at Fredonia artifacts; memorabilia from the group's 1987 tour with R.E.M.; Cambridge Folk Festival tickets, posters, etc.; artifacts from the group's numerous ecological concerns; videotapes of the group's numerous television appearances including *Saturday Night Live* (10/31/92), *The Tonight Show* (11/5/92), *Late Night With David Letterman* (11/19/92, 6/23/93), *Regis & Kathie Lee* (12/15/92), "MTV Drops The Ball '93" (12/31/92), and MTV *Unplugged* (6/1/93)

REFERENCES/BOOKS

Numerous resources exist, but none do justice to the group in my opinion. There are no dedicated collector books.

Ten Years After/Alvin Lee

Formed 1967

Alvin Lee, Born: December 19, 1944; Chick Churchill; Leo Lyons; and Rick Lee

A staple among the many hard working and hard rocking blues bands of the late '60s, the group is most remembered for Alvin Lee's lightening guitar speed, the "I'm Going Home" performance at the 1969 Woodstock Festival, and the hit song "I'd Love to Change the World" (1971).

AUTOGRAPHS

A CD, LP, magazine cover, ad, photo, or card signed by the group: $20-$50*

*Original band members

Individuals:

Alvin Lee: $10-$30

Terrell, Tammi

(Thomasina Montgomery)
Born: January 24, 1946, Died: March 16, 1970

Terrell is best known as Marvin Gaye's singing partner on Ashford and Simpson duets such as "Ain't No Mountain High Enough" (#19, 1967), "Your Precious Love" (#5, 1967), "Ain't Nothing Like the Real Thing" (#8, 1968), "You're All I Need to Get By" (#7, 1968), "Keep On Lovin' Me Honey" (#24, 1968), "Good Lovin Ain't Easy to Come By" (#30, 1969), and "What You Gave Me" (#6, 1969). Her somewhat tumultuous personal life that included failed marriages to other well-known musicians left her scarred. She was later diagnosed with a brain tumor that required multiple operations and extensive rehabilitation. Following her death on March 16, 1970, it was revealed by Gaye that Valerie Simpson had actually stepped in for the artist on occasional recording sessions.

AUTOGRAPHS

An LP, magazine cover, ad, photo, or card signed by the artist: $15-$40

Terry, Sonny and Brownie McGhee

Teddell Saunders "Sonny" Terry (1911-1986), and Walter Brown "Brownie" McGhee, Born: November 30, 1915

Early-40s influential folk-blues duo, which worked under a variety of pseudonyms before being discovered during the '50s folk revival movement, both performers went on to tour extensively including appearances at numerous colleges, clubs, and festivals, while also making dozens of records.

AUTOGRAPHS

A CD, LP, magazine cover, ad, photo, or card signed by the duo: $10-$30

OFTEN OVERLOOKED MEMORABILIA

Festival memorabilia

Tesla

Formed 1984

Jeff Keith, Tommy Skeoch, Frank Hannon, Brian Wheat, and Troy Luccketta

Late-80s California hard rock band, typically associated with the songs "Love Song" (#10, 1989), "Little Suzie" (#91, 1987), and "Signs" (#8, 1991), Tesla has enjoyed enormous exposure through many key tours and heavy MTV rotation. The group's strong following has translated to very successful album sales, exhibited best with *Five Man Acoustical Jam* (#12, 1991) and *Psychotic Supper* (#13, 1991).

AUTOGRAPHS

A CD, LP, magazine cover, ad, photo, or card signed by the group: $15-$35

TOUR BOOKS/PROGRAMS/PASSES

Tour Books:
In Japan: $15

BACKSTAGE PASSES:

Cloth: $8; Laminated: $10-$15

POSTERS/PRESS KITS

Promotional Posters: $8-$15
Press Kits: $12-$20

USED CLOTHING/EQUIPMENT

Guitar Pick: $5-$10

Tex, Joe

(Joseph Arrington [Hazziez], Jr.)
Born: August 8, 1933, Died: August 12, 1982

Texas soul singer, typically associated with his latter career dance hits, Joe Tex is popular for songs such as "Hold What You've Got" (#5, 1965), "I Want to (Do Everything for You)" (#1, R&B, 1965), "The Love You Save" (#10, 1965), "I Gottcha" (#2, 1972), and "Ain't Gonna Bump No More (with No Big Fat Woman)" (#12, 1977), although he scored numerous other R&B hits.

AUTOGRAPHS

An LP, magazine cover, ad, photo, or card signed by the artist: $15-$30

Texas Tornados

Formed 1989

Freddy Fender (Baldemar Huerta), Born: June 4, 1937; Augie Meyers, Born: May 31, 1940; Doug Sahm, Born: November 6, 1941; and Flaco Jimenez, Born: March 11, 1939

Early-90s Tex-Mex combination, made up of notable members, the Texas Tornados released a handful of albums, of which the first self-titled release garnered a Grammy. It was anticipated from the start that the venture may ignite interest in each member's solo career, and to an extent it did work, but never fulfilled expectations.

AUTOGRAPHS

A CD, LP, magazine cover, ad, photo, or card signed by the group: $20-$35

POSTERS/PRESS KITS

Promotional Posters: $8-$10
Press Kits: $12

That Petrol Emotion: See the Undertones

Them

Formed 1963

Billy Harrison, Alan Henderson, Ronnie Millings, Eric Wrixen, and Van Morrison, Born: August 21, 1945*

*Additional personnel also included Jackie and Patrick McAuley

This early-60s Irish pop act is best remembered for having included Van Morrison in the original lineup and the songs "Baby Please Don't Go" (#10, U.K., 1965), "Here Comes the Night" (#24, 1965), "Mystic Eyes" (#3, 1965), and "Gloria" (#71, 1966). Plagued by personnel changes, which at one point included Jimmy Page, the group eventually disbanded.

AUTOGRAPHS

An LP, magazine cover, ad, photo, or card signed by the group: $35-$100*

*Original lineup

The The

Formed 1979

Matt Johnson, Born: August 15, 1961

Eighties musical configuration that has included hundreds of members, the The's common link has been singer/songwriter Matt Johnson. Following the release of *Mind Bomb* (#138, 1989), Johnson put the band on the road for the first time, reaching a broader audience, while cultivating his cult following.

AUTOGRAPHS

A CD, LP, magazine cover, ad, photo, or card signed by the artist: $10-$15

TOUR BOOKS/PROGRAMS/PASSES

Tour Books:
Mind Bomb: $20

POSTERS/PRESS KITS

Promotional Posters: $10-$20
Press Kits: $15-$30

OFTEN OVERLOOKED MEMORABILIA

Infected, Epic promo first aid kit, 1987

They Might Be Giants

Formed 1984

John Flansburgh and John Linnell*

*Tony Maimone was added in 1993

New York novelty act and gimmick gurus, typically identified with "Don't Let's Start," "Ana Ng," "Istanbul (not Constantinople)," and "Snail Shell," the band has developed a large cult following thanks to media advocates and MTV.

AUTOGRAPHS

A CD, LP, magazine cover, ad, photo, or card signed by the group: $10-$15

POSTERS/PRESS KITS

Promotional Posters: $10
Press Kits: $15-$20

Thin Lizzy

Formed 1970

Phillip Lynott (1951- 1986), Brian Downey, and Eric Bell*

*Numerous personnel changes; former members have included Snowy White and Gary Moore.

Seventies Irish hard-rock group, fronted by Phil Lynott and best known for its breakthrough 1976 album *Jailbreak* and songs such as "The Boys Are Back in Town" (#12, 1976), "Whiskey in a Jar" (#6, U.K., 1973), "Waiting for an Alibi" (#9, U.K., 1979), and "Killer in the Loose" (#10, U.K., 1980), Thin Lizzy scored numerous U.K. hits before disbanding in 1983.

Lynott went on to a solo career and recorded with a new group called Grand Slam ("Out in the Field" (#5, U.K., 1985)). He died of heart failure in early 1986 following a drug overdose. Moore has gone on to record with many bands, while forging an outstanding reputation for himself as a blues artist. He is perhaps best known for the song "Still Got the Blues."

AUTOGRAPHS

A CD, LP, magazine cover, ad, photo, or card signed by the group: $100*

*Lineup dependent

TOUR BOOKS/PROGRAMS/PASSES

Tour Books:
Renegade Tour, 1981: $40

USED CLOTHING/EQUIPMENT

Guitar Pick:
Gary Moore: $25-$40

A Thin Lizzy guitar pick

REFERENCES/BOOKS

Songs for While I'm Away by Phil Lynott; *Philip* by Phil Lynott (Both are poetry books); there are no dedicated collectors books.

3rd Base

Formed 1988

M.C. Search (Michael Berrin), Prime Minister Pete Nice (Peter Nash), and Daddy Rich (Richard Lawson)

This late-80s racially mixed rap trio is best remembered for the song "Pop Goes the Weasel" (#29, 1991), its third and final album before disbanding,

Derelicts of Dialect (#19, 1991), and for being the first rap group to release a remix album, *The Cactus Revisited*.

AUTOGRAPHS
A CD, LP, magazine cover, ad, photo, or card signed by the group: $12-$20

13th Floor Elevators: See Roky Erickson

.38 Special

Formed 1975

Original lineup: Donnie Van Zant, Don Barnes, Jeff Carlisi, Ken Lyons, Jack Grondin, and Steve Brookins*

*Numerous personnel changes

Late-70s blues-rooted Southern-rock band, best remembered for the songs "Hold On Loosely" (#27, 1981), "Caught Up in You" (the group's first Top Ten single), "Like No Other Night" (#14, 1986), and "Second Chance" (#6, 1989), .38 Special featured lead vocalist Donnie Van Zant (brother of Ronnie), along with twin lead guitarists and two drummers.

AUTOGRAPHS
A CD, LP, magazine cover, ad, photo, or card signed by the group: $20-$35

TOUR BOOKS/PROGRAMS/PASSES
Backstage Passes:
Cloth: $10; Laminated: $12

POSTERS/PRESS KITS
Promotional Posters: $10-$20
Press Kits: $12-$25

USED CLOTHING/EQUIPMENT
Guitar Pick: $10-$15

Thomas, B.J.

Born: August 7, 1942

Late-60s vocalist and multiple Grammy Award winner B.J. Thomas is typically associated with the songs "Raindrops Keep Fallin' on My Head" (#1, 1970), "Hooked on a Feeling" (#5, 1968), "I'm So Lonesome, I Could Cry" (#8, 1966), "I Just Can't Help Believing" (#9, 1970), and "Rock and Roll Lullaby" (#15, 1972), although he has charted with numerous others. During the '70s he successfully moved toward gospel and earned two Dove Awards, while a decade later he also found himself on the country charts with songs such as "What Ever Happened to Old Fashioned Love" (#1, C&W, 1983) and "New Looks from an Old Lover" (#1, C&W, 1983).

AUTOGRAPHS
A CD, LP, magazine cover, ad, photo, or card signed by the artist: $5-$10

USED CLOTHING/EQUIPMENT
Guitar Pick: $10

OFTEN OVERLOOKED MEMORABILIA
Movie memorabilia from *Butch Cassidy and the Sundance Kid*

Thomas, Carla

Born: 1942

Early '60s queen of soul and daughter of musician Rufus Thomas, Carla Thomas is typically associated with the songs "Gee Whiz (Look at His Eyes)" (#10, 1961), "I'll Bring It Home to You" (#41, 1962), "B-A-B-Y" (#14, 1966), "Tramp" (#26, 1967), and "Knock on Wood" (#30, 1967). A star member on the Stax Record roster, she stopped recording in the '70s.

AUTOGRAPHS
A CD, LP, magazine cover, ad, photo, or card signed by the artist: $10-$25

Thomas, David: See Pere Ubu

Thomas, Mickey: See Jefferson Airplane

Thomas, Rufus

Born: March 26, 1917

Memphis music scene veteran who landed his first R&B hit in 1953 with "Bear Cat" (Sun Records), Rufus Thomas and his daughter Carla helped establish Stax Records. He is perhaps best associated with the songs "Walking the Dog," "Do the Funky Chicken," "(Do the) Push and Pull," and "The Breakdown."

AUTOGRAPHS
A CD, LP, magazine cover, ad, photo, or card signed by the artist: $15-$25

Thompson, Richard

Born: April 3, 1949

Founding member of the British folk-rock group Fairport Convention, Richard Thompson is best known for his eccentric releases that linked Celtic folk music to rock. Along with Linda Peters (his former wife) the two collaborated on numerous projects that often included contributions by ex-Fairport members. His experimentation has been lauded by many music critics and peers, but has never resulted in commercial success.

AUTOGRAPHS

A CD, LP, magazine cover, ad, photo, or card signed by the artist: $10-$30

POSTERS/PRESS KITS

Promotional Posters: $10-$20
Press Kits: $15-$30

USED CLOTHING/EQUIPMENT

Guitar Pick: $10-$20

The Thompson Twins

Formed 1977

Tom Bailey, John Roog, Pete Dodd, and Chris Bell*

*The band was restructured in 1982 when everyone departed but Bailey, while Alannah Currie and Joe Leeway were added. Leeway departed in 1986. Matthew Seligman played only briefly in 1982.

Eighties technopop group the Thompson Twins has had numerous incarnations, but the greatest success came as a trio with songs such as "Love on Your Side" (#45, 1983), "Hold Me Now" (#3, 1984), "Doctor Doctor" (#11, 1984), "Lay Your Hands on Me" (#6, 1985), and "King for a Day" (#8, 1986). Leeway departed in 1986, leaving Bailey and Currie, who were also a couple with a child. The duo later turned up in a band called Babble.

AUTOGRAPHS

A CD, LP, magazine cover, ad, photo, or card signed by the group: $20-$50

TOUR BOOKS/PROGRAMS/PASSES

Tour Books:
Tour 1984: $22
The Tour of Future Days: $20
Backstage Passes:
Cloth: $10; Laminated: $15

POSTERS/PRESS KITS

Promotional Posters: $10-$15
Press Kits: $15-$20

OFTEN OVERLOOKED MEMORABILIA

Here's to Future Days handkerchief - $20; Get That Love counter display - $30

REFERENCES/BOOKS

Numerous resources exist, but none do justice to the group in my opinion. There are no dedicated collector books.

Thornton, Big Mama

(Willie Mae Thornton)
Born: December 11, 1926, Died: July 25, 1984

Singer/songwriter and blueswoman Big Mama Thornton is best remembered for two songs, "Hound Dog," written by Lieber and Stoller and made famous by Elvis Presley, and her own "Ball and Chain," a hit for Janis Joplin. She toured with Sammy Greene's Hot Harlem Revue (1941-1948), and worked numerous package tours during the '50s including a stint with the Johnny Otis band. During the '60s she played numerous festivals including the Monterey Jazz Festival and the Newport Folk Festival. The following decade found her adding television to her repertoire including appearances on the Dick Cavett talk show and even the *Midnight Special*.

Her albums *Chicago Blues* (1967) and *Jail* (1975) are considered among her finest, the latter of which includes the classics "Ball and Chain," "Little Red Rooster," and "Hound Dog." She died of a heart attack in 1984.

Poster for a May 10, 1953, performance by Johnny Ace and "Big Mama" Thornton in L.A. Elvis recorded, and had a huge hit with, her song "Hound Dog" in 1956. Printed by J. Warner of New York, NY, this poster is valued at $1,500. From the collection of Hank Thompson.

AUTOGRAPHS

A CD, LP, magazine cover, ad, photo, or card signed by the artist: $20-$50

OFTEN OVERLOOKED MEMORABILIA

Videotapes of her numerous television appearances, most in the '70s; a copy of the PBS documentary *Black White and Blue*; assorted festival artifacts from her appearances, programs, tickets, etc.

Thorogood, George and the Destroyers

Formed 1973

Original lineup: George Thorogood, Born: December 31, 1952, Ron Smith, Billy Blough, and Jeff Simon.*

*Smith departed in 1980 and Hank Carter was added. Steve Chrismar was added in 1985.

Late-70s energetic retro rock group, led by slide-guitarist George Thorogood, the group gained national exposure when it opened several dates on the 1981 Rolling Stones tour. Typically associated with the raucous saloon slamin' songs such as "Bad to the Bone," "I Drink Alone," "Move It On Over," and "Willie and the Hand Jive" (#63, 1985), George Thorogood and the Destroyers have built a large cult following across the country that they continue to sustain through extensive touring. The group is known more for its live performances than for its records.

AUTOGRAPHS

A CD, LP, magazine cover, ad, photo, or card signed by the group: $15-$30

POSTERS/PRESS KITS

Promotional Posters: $8-$15
Press Kits: $12 -$20

USED CLOTHING/EQUIPMENT

Guitar Pick: $20

OFTEN OVERLOOKED MEMORABILIA

The Maverick (black on white) Frisbee - $35

Three Dog Night

Formed 1967

Danny Hutton, Born: September 10, 1942; Chuck Negron, Born: June 8, 1942; Cory Wells, Born: February 5, 1942; Mike Allsup, Born: March 8, 1947; Jimmy Greenspoon, Born: February 7, 1948; Joe Schermie; and Floyd Sneed*

*Schermie departed in 1973 while Jack Ryland and Skip Konte were added. Numerous changes in 1976.

Singles-oriented late-60s to early-70s dominant soul-influenced pop rockers Three Dog Night ran a streak of eighteen consecutive Top Twenty hits, which included three chart toppers, songs such as "One" (#5, 1969), "Easy to Be Hard" (#4, 1969), "Eli's Coming" (#10, 1969), "Mama Told Me (Not to Come)" (#1, 1970), "Joy to the World" (#1, 1971), "The Show Must Go On" (#14, 1974), "Liar" (#7, 1971), "An Old Fashioned Love Song" (#4, 1971), "Never Been to Spain" (#5, 1972), "Black and White" (#1, 1972), and "Shambala" (#3, 1973), to just name a few. Some critics shunned them due to their over commercialism and hits that almost always consisted of covers, but their exposure brought light to numerous songwriters including Randy Newman, Hoyt Axton, Laura Nyro, Leo Sayer, and Elton John and Bernie Taupin.

By the mid-70s the band was slipping and friction between the three lead singers was reaching a breaking point which finally climaxed with Hutton's departure and three new band members, before the group disbanded in 1977. In June 1981 the three original vocalists reunited for an EP entitled *It's a Jungle*. Band members then pursued individual projects, with Negron hitting such hard times that he was even sleeping on the streets for a portion of his life. A victim of substance abuse problems, he has since miraculously turned himself around and become quite an inspiration to others in need.

AUTOGRAPHS

A CD, LP, magazine cover, ad, photo, or card signed by the group: $45-$125

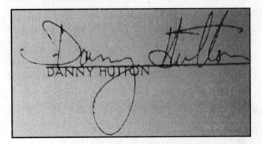

Danny Hutton's signature

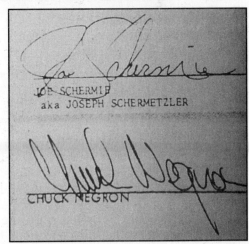

The signatures of Joe Schermie and Chuck Negron

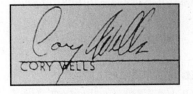

Cory Wells' signature

TOUR BOOKS/PROGRAMS/PASSES

Tour Book: 1972 Japan Tour-$50

OFTEN OVERLOOKED MEMORABILIA

American Pastime display - $40; movie memorabilia from *The Big Chill*; Super Bowl XXV memorabilia; videotapes of their numerous television appearances including "American Bandstand's 20th Anniversary" (1973)

REFERENCES/BOOKS

Numerous resources exist, but none do justice to the group in my opinion. There are no dedicated collector books.

Throwing Muses/Belly

Formed 1980

Kristin Hersh, Tanya Donelly, David Narcizo, and Elaine Adamedes*

*Adamedes departed in 1986 and Leslie Langston was added. Langston departed in 1991 and Fred Abong was added. Numerous changes followed. Belly was formed in 1991.

Mid-80s pseudo-dreamy group Throwing Muses is best remembered for their alternative radio classic "Counting Backwards." Throwing Muses' member Tanya Donelly later left the band to form Belly with brothers Tom and Chris Gorman, and scored with the MTV hit "Feed the Tree," while even being nominated for a Grammy for Best New Act of 1993. Hersh went on to produce an acclaimed solo effort *Hips and Makers*, that even included a visit from Michael Stipe of R.E.M.

AUTOGRAPHS
A CD, LP, magazine cover, ad, photo, or card signed by the group: $10-$15 (Throwing Muses), $15-$30 (Belly)

USED CLOTHING/EQUIPMENT
Guitar Pick: $10

Thunderclap Newman

Formed 1969

Andy Newman, Jimmy McCulloch (1953-1979), John Keen, and Jim Avery

Late-60s one album and one tour band, assembled by Pete Townshend, had one hit, "Something in the Air" (#37, 1970), before breaking up one time. Of all the band members, McCulloch went on to the greatest musical success with Paul McCartney's Wings (1975-1978), before passing away the following year.

AUTOGRAPHS
A CD, LP, magazine cover, ad, photo, or card signed by the group: $30-$45

OFTEN OVERLOOKED MEMORABILIA
Movie memorabilia from *The Magic Christian* and *The Strawberry Statement*

Tiffany

(Tiffany Renee Darwish)
Born: October 2, 1971

Late-80s bubble-gum teen queen, best remembered for her hits "Could've Been" (#1), "I Think We're Alone Now" (#1), and "All This Time" (#6,

1988). Tiffany was the creative element of George Tobin's brilliant marketing. When her third album flopped in 1990, she faded from the music scene.

AUTOGRAPHS
A CD, LP, magazine cover, ad, photo, or card signed by the artist: $5-$10

OFTEN OVERLOOKED MEMORABILIA
Movie memorabilia from *The Jetsons: The Movie* (Tiffany is the voice of Judy Jetson)

'Til Tuesday/Aimee Mann

Formed 1983

Aimee Mann, Robert Holmes, Joey Pesce, and Michael Hausman*

*Pesce departed in 1986, while Clayton Scobel, Jon Brion, and Michael Montes were added.

These late-80s Boston pop-rockers are best remembered for the hits "Voices Carry" (#8, 1985), "What About Love" (#49, 1986), and "Coming Up Close" (#59, 1987), before breaking up after their third album.

AUTOGRAPHS
A CD, LP, magazine cover, ad, photo, or card signed by the group: $10-$20

Timbuk 3

Formed 1984

Pat MacDonald and Barbara MacDonald*

*Wally Ingram was added in 1991

Timbuk 3, the late-80s Midwest novelty act, is best remembered for the hit "The Future's So Bright I Gotta Wear Shades" (#19, 1986).

AUTOGRAPHS
A CD, LP, magazine cover, ad, photo, or card signed by the group: $10-$15

The Time

Formed 1981

Morris Day, Jesse Johnson, Jimmy Jam, Monte Moir, Terry Lewis, and Jellybean Johnson*

*Numerous personnel changes

Eighties amusing, yet fashionable group of Prince protégés, The Time, also became ambassadors of the "Minneapolis Sound," scoring hits such as "Get It Up" (#6, R&B, 1981), "Cool" (#90, 1982), and "777-9311" (#88, 1982), while gaining tremendous exposure

opening the 1999 Tour (Prince). In March 1983, the duo of Jam and Lewis was fired when they missed a tour date while moonlighting as free-lance producers. They went on to be one of the most successful production teams ever, so in hindsight, missing a plane once in awhile ain't all bad. Moir also departed during the same period.

The band was the restructured and featured in Prince's film *Purple Rain*, which yielded the group two hits, "Jungle Love" (#20, 1984) and "The Bird" (#36, 1985), and were included on the album *Ice Cream Castle* (#24, 1984). When Morris Day then decided to leave the band, followed by Jesse Johnson, there was just no time left.

Day had some solo success with hits such as "Fishnet" (#23, 1988), and he also tried his luck at acting. The Time did briefly reunite for an appearance in the movie *Graffiti Bridge* and to record *Pandemonium* (#18, 1990), which included the hit extract "Jerk Out" (#9, 1990).

AUTOGRAPHS

A CD, LP, magazine cover, ad, photo, or card signed by the group: $40-$65

POSTERS/PRESS KITS

Promotional Posters: $10-$20
Press Kits: $15-$25

OFTEN OVERLOOKED MEMORABILIA

Movie memorabilia from *Purple Rain* and *Graffiti Bridge*

Tiny Tim

(1930-1996)

Late-60s ukulele player, singer, and television guest, best remembered for his hit "Tip-Toe thru' the Tulips with Me" (#17, 1968) and for his marriage to Miss Vicky (Victoria May Budinger) on the December 17, 1969 *Tonight* show, Tiny Tim tipped his last toe in 1996.

AUTOGRAPHS

A CD, LP, magazine cover, ad, photo, or card signed by the artist: $25-$45

OFTEN OVERLOOKED MEMORABILIA

Videotapes of his numerous television appearances including *The Tonight Show*, *Laugh-In*, and *Lip Service* (MTV)

Toad the Wet Sprocket

Formed 1988

Glen Phillips, Todd Nichols, Dead Dinning, and Randy Guss

This late-80s and '90s Southern California rock group broke through with its third album *Fear* (#49, 1991), which included the hit extracts "All I Want" (#15, 1991) and "Walk on the Ocean" (#18, 1991). Through extensive touring, the band was slowly gaining the recognition they deserved. Toad the Wet Sprocket also succeeded with the follow-up release *Dulcinea* (#34, 1994), which included the hit "Fall Down" (#33, 1994). In 1997, *Coil* (#8, 1997) debuted high on the album charts, but sank faster then expected.

AUTOGRAPHS

A CD, LP, magazine cover, ad, photo, or card signed by the artist: $15-$35

TOUR BOOKS/PROGRAMS/PASSES

Backstage Passes:
Cloth: $8-$10; Laminated: $12

POSTERS/PRESS KITS

Promotional Posters: $10-$20
Press Kits: $15-$25

OFTEN OVERLOOKED MEMORABILIA

Movie memorabilia from *So I Married an Axe Murderer* (1993); videotapes of the group's television numerous appearances including the *Late Show With David Letterman* (12/1/94, 1/5/96)

The Tokens

Formed 1958

Phil Margo, Hank Medress, Jay Siegel, Joseph Venneri, and Mitchell Margo

Late-50s vocal group, best remembered for the songs "The Lion Sleeps Tonight" (#1, 1961) and "Tonight I Fell in Love," the Tokens also backed numerous musicians including Connie Francis and Bob Dylan. The group also produced works for the Chifons and recorded many memorable jingles.

AUTOGRAPHS

A CD, LP, magazine cover, ad, photo, or card signed by the group: $25-$50

OFTEN OVERLOOKED MEMORABILIA

Movie memorabilia from *The Lion King*

Tom Tom Club: See Talking Heads

Tone-Loc

(Anthony Smith)
Born: March 3, 1966

Late-80s sandpaper-voiced rapper Tone-Loc is typically associated with the songs "Wild Thing" (#2, 1989) and "Funky Cold Medina" (#3, 1989), both ex-

tracted from his debut album *Loc-ed After Dark* which became the first album by a black rap artist to hit Number One on the pop chart. Following the disappointing sales of his second album *Cool Hand Loc* (#46 R&B, 1991) he pursued an acting career in both television and film.

AUTOGRAPHS

A CD, LP, magazine cover, ad, photo, or card signed by the artist: $15-$35

OFTEN OVERLOOKED MEMORABILIA

Movie memorabilia from *Posse*, *Poetic Justice*, and *Bebe's Kids*; videotapes of his numerous television appearances including *Roc*

Tones on Tail: See Bauhaus

Too Short

(Toss Anthony Shaw)
Born: April 28, 1966

Late-80s successful hip-hop act, typically associated with the songs "The Ghetto" and "Ain't Nothin' But a Word to Me," along with the albums *Shorty the Pimp* (#6, 1992), *Get It Where You Fit In* (#1, R&B, 1993), and *Cocktails* (#6, 1995), Too Short's pimp image and violent raps have pushed him further and further into gangsta rap.

AUTOGRAPHS

A CD, LP, magazine cover, ad, photo, or card signed by the artist: $10-$20

Toots and the Maytals

Formed 1962

Frederick Toots Hibbert, Nathaniel Matthias, and Ralphus Gordon*

*Matthias and Gordon left in 1981

Sixties Jamaican vocal trio, best known for the songs "Do the Reggay," "Monkey Man," "Sweet and Dandy," and "Pressure Drop," Toots and the Maytals gained significant exposure opening shows for the Who during their 1975 U.S. tour, despite being booed off many a stage during the trek.

AUTOGRAPHS

A CD, LP, magazine cover, ad, photo, or card signed by the group: $15-$20

OFTEN OVERLOOKED MEMORABILIA

Movie memorabilia from *The Harder They Come* (1972)

The Tornadoes

Formed 1962

George Bellamy, Heinz Burt, Alan Caddy, Clem Cattini, and Roger Lavern

Early-60s backup band, which is best remembered for the instrumental hit "Telstar" (#1), the Tornadoes also had a minor hit with "Ride the Wind" (1963) before breaking up. "Bustin Surfboards" found its way to the soundtrack of *Pulp Fiction* in 1994.

AUTOGRAPHS

An LP, magazine cover, ad, photo, or card signed by the group: $10-$25

Tosh, Peter

(Winston MacIntosh) (1944-1987)

Former Wailer Peter Tosh, who had maintained a solo career in Jamaica for years during the '60s, didn't garner significant attention in America until the late '70s when Mick Jagger and Keith Richards signed him to Rolling Stones Records where he released *Bush Doctor* (1978). The album included the popular extract and Temptations' cover "(You Got to Walk and) Don't Look Back," a duet by Tosh and Jagger. They sang the song together on *Saturday Night Live*. Tosh also toured America with the Stones the same year.

Outspoken and aggressive, Tosh had his fair share of confrontations with the law, typically relating to his advocacy for the legalization of "ganja." On September 11, 1987, three men entered his Jamaican home and murdered him, along with two guests, and injured four others.

AUTOGRAPHS

An LP, magazine cover, ad, photo, or card signed by the artist: $45-$110

OFTEN OVERLOOKED MEMORABILIA

All Rolling Stones Records related items; obviously his Wailer related items command premium price; videotapes of his television appearances including *Saturday Night Live*; periodical clippings regarding his murder and accusations that he was executed continually surface

Toto

Formed 1978

David Paich, Steve Lukather, Bobby Kimball (Toteaux), Steve Porcaro, David Hungate, and Jeff Porcaro (1954 - 1992)*

*Numerous personnel changes

Late-70s power-pop group, built around highly-respected and experienced sessionmen, Toto broke onto the music scene in full force, quickly racking up sales of more than two million copies of its self-titled debut. The group is typically associated with the hits "Hold the Line" (#5, 1979), "Rosanna" (#2, 1982), "Africa" (#1, 1982), and "I Won't Hold You Back" (#10, 1983). Throughout the years as a group, members continued their outside work of contributing to other artists' work, for example, Steve Porcaro penned "Human Nature" with Michael Jackson.

AUTOGRAPHS

A CD, LP, magazine cover, ad, photo, or card signed by the group: $30-$160

TOUR BOOKS/PROGRAMS/PASSES

Tour Book: 1986 Japan Tour-$30

Backstage Passes:

Cloth/paper: $10-$20; Laminated: $15-$25

POSTERS/PRESS KITS

Promotional Posters: $10-$40

Press Kits: $15-$50, Example: Tambu - $15

OFTEN OVERLOOKED MEMORABILIA

Movie memorabilia from *Dune*; logo button - $4

Tourists: See Eurythmics

Toussaint, Allen

Born: January 14, 1938

The multi-talented Allen Toussaint was a pivotal icon in the music of New Orleans during the '60s as house songwriter, arranger, and producer for Minit Records. He later opened Sea-Saint Studios in 1972, where Paul Simon, Paul McCartney and Wings, and others recorded. He produced '70s sessions for Dr. John, Labelle, Joe Cocker, and John Mayall. As a songwriter he is typically associated with the songs "Java," "Whipped Cream," "Fortune Teller," "A Certain Girl," "Southern Nights," and "High Life."

AUTOGRAPHS

A CD, LP, magazine cover, ad, photo, or card signed by the artist: $15-$30*

*Toussaint seldom appears live

OFTEN OVERLOOKED MEMORABILIA

Artifacts from the mid-80s musical *Stagger Lee*; movie memorabilia from *Pretty Baby* (1978)

Tower of Power

Formed 1968

Popular lineup: (1993) Emilio Castillo, Steve Kupka, Francis "Rocco" Prestia, Greg Adams, Lee Thornberg, Nick Milo, Russ McKinnon, Carmen Grillo, Tom Bowes, and David Mann*

*Numerous personnel changes

Late-70s Bay Area R&B band, prominently known for its talented and well-crafted horn section and hits such as "You're Still a Young Man" (#29, 1974), "So Very Hard to Go" (#17, 1973), and "Don't Change Horses (In the Middle of a Stream)" (#26, 1974), Tower of Power's core membership has remained relatively intact and includes Emilio Castillo, Steve Kupa, and Rocco Prestia. Although the hits have subsided, the band remains an extremely popular live draw and prolific in its musical contributions.

AUTOGRAPHS

A CD, LP, magazine cover, ad, photo, or card signed by the group: $25-$45

OFTEN OVERLOOKED MEMORABILIA

Associated artifacts from their numerous contributions to other artists work; videotapes of their numerous television performances

Townshend, Pete: See the Who

The Toys

Formed Early '60s

June Montiero, Barbara Harris, and Barbara Parritt

This late-60s all-female R&B group is commonly associated with the hits "A Lover's Concerto" (#2, 1965) and "Attack" (#18, 1966), before fading from the music scene.

AUTOGRAPHS

An LP, magazine cover, ad, photo, or card signed by the group: $10

OFTEN OVERLOOKED MEMORABILIA

Movie memorabilia from *The Girl in Daddy's Bikini*; videotapes of their television show appearances like *Shindig!*

Traffic

Formed 1967

Steve Winwood, Born: May 12, 1948; Chris Wood (1944 - 1983); Dave Mason, Born: May 10, 1946; and Jim Capaldi, Born: August 24, 1944*

*Mason departed then returned in 1967, but left again in 1968. Rick Grech (1946-1990) was added in 1970. Numerous changes then ensued.

Traffic. Photo by Anton Corbijn. Courtesy Virgin Records.

Late-60s British pop band, fronted by Dave Mason and Steve Winwood, and typically associated first with early hits such as "Paper Sun" (#5, U.K., 1967), "Hole in My Shoe" (#2, U.K., 1967), and "Feelin' Alright," and later (without Mason) for "Glad," "Freedom Rider," "Empty Pages," and "Rock & Roll Stew," Traffic's album work on *John Barleycorn Must Die* (#5, 1970), *The Low Spark of High-Heeled Boy* (#7, 1971), and *Shoot Out at the Fantasy* (#6,1973), became a staple of "progressive" FM radio. Following *When the Eagles Flies* (#9, 1974), both Winwood and Capaldi began solo careers. Of Traffic alumni, both Winwood and Mason have enjoyed the greatest solo success.

A Traffic backstage pass (Printed by OTTO)

AUTOGRAPHS

An LP, magazine cover, ad, photo, or card signed by the group: $75-$225*
*Original lineup

OFTEN OVERLOOKED MEMORABILIA

Movie memorabilia from *Here We Go Round the Mulberry Bush* (1968)

The Trammps

Formed Mid-60s

Popular lineup: Earl Young, Jimmy Ellis, Robert Upchurch, and Stanley Wade

Late-70s R&B group, best remembered for the hits "Hold Back the Night" (#35, 1975), "That's Where the Happy People Go" (#27, 1976), and "Disco Inferno" (#11, 1977), the Trammps had scored a hit earlier in their career with "Storm Warning" under the name the Volcanoes, but had far greater success during the late '70s disco explosion. When disco faded, so did the Trammps.

AUTOGRAPHS

A CD, LP, magazine cover, ad, photo, or card signed by the group: $20-$40*
*On a copy of "Saturday Night Fever."

OFTEN OVERLOOKED MEMORABILIA

Movie memorabilia from *Saturday Night Fever* (1977)

The Traveling Wilburys

Formed 1988

Nelson/Spike Wilbury: George Harrison; Lucky/Boo Wilbury: Bob Dylan; Otis/Clayton Wilbury: Jeff Lynne; Charlie T./Muddy Wilbury Jr.: Tom Petty; and Lefty Wilbury: Roy Orbison; also Jim Keltner

Late-80s supergroup, consisting of three established legends and two key contributors, the Traveling Wilburys were a casual off shoot of each musicians existing career. The group's debut album was an instant hit (#3, 1988), with sales somewhat aided by the extract "Handle with Care" (#45, 1988). The sophomore effort, *Vol.3* (#11,1990), with its clever title, was released without Roy Orbison, who had suffered a fatal heart attack just one month following the release of the group's debut album. Orbison was never replaced in the band, whose future remains a mystery.

AUTOGRAPHS

A CD, LP, magazine cover, ad, photo, or card signed by the group: $500-$1,750*
*Original lineup

POSTERS/PRESS KITS

Promotional Posters: $10-$20
Press Kits: $30-$45

OFTEN OVERLOOKED MEMORABILIA

Volume One, Wilbury Record Co. promo travel bag, 1988; Wilbury Twist promotional licorice, 1990; Volume One jar of jam, 1988; car window sign "Traveling Wilbury on Board" - $20; Gretsch-TW 300 sticker autographed guitar in original box - $500

Travis, Randy

(Randy Bruce)
Born: May 4, 1959

Randy Travis. Photo by Firooz Zahedi. Courtesy Warner Bros. Records.

Late-80s country music artist, typically associated with the Number One C&W hits "Forever and Ever, Amen," "I Won't Need You Anymore (Always and Forever)," "Too Gone Too Long," "I Told You So," "Honky Tonk Moon," " Deeper Than the Holler," "Is It Still Over?," and "It's Just a Matter of Time," Randy Travis became the first (C&W) performer to sell a million copies of his major-label debut. His nearly immediate superstar status garnered him numerous awards in 1988, while his sales slipped during the '90s primarily due to the popularity of "hat acts."

AUTOGRAPHS
A CD, LP, magazine cover, ad, photo, or card signed by the artist: $10-$30

TOUR BOOKS/PROGRAMS/PASSES
Backstage Passes:
Cloth: $8-$10; Laminated: $12

POSTERS/PRESS KITS
Promotional Posters: $10-$20
Press Kits: $15-$25

USED CLOTHING/EQUIPMENT
Guitar Pick: $10

The Tremeloes

Formed 1959

Brain Poole, Alan Blakely, Alan Howard, Dave Munden, and Rick Westwood*

*Poole and Howard left in 1966 and Len Hawkes was added.

Late-60s British trio, formerly the backup band for Brian Poole ("Do You Love Me"), the Tremeloes are best remembered for the 1967 hits "Silence Is Golden," "Even the Bad Times Are Good," and "Here Comes My Baby." When the hits faded, the Tremeloes turned to playing nightclubs and the nostalgia circuit.

AUTOGRAPHS
A CD, LP, magazine cover, ad, photo, or card signed by the group: $20-$35

T. Rex/Tyrannosaurus Rex/Marc Bolan

Formed 1967

Marc Bolan (Mark Feld), (1948-1977) and Steve Peregrine Took (1949-1980)*

*Took departed in 1969 and Mickey Finn was added.

Late-60s British glam-rockers, fronted by the charismatic Marc Bolan, T.Rex placed eleven U.K. Top Ten hits from 1970 to 1974, including "Bang a Gong (Get It On)" (#1), "Jeepster" (#2), and "Telegram Sam" (#1), while creating teen hysteria not seen since Beatlemania. Although the group had a sizable cult following in the U.S., as exhibited by the sales for *The Slider* (#17, 1992), the band could not duplicate its British success in America. By the mid-70s the group's star was fading. Bolan then broke the band up in 1975, followed by a reformed T. Rex (1977) and a solo career, both of which stalled. On September 16, 1977, Bolan was killed in an automobile accident.

AUTOGRAPHS
A CD, LP, magazine cover, ad, photo, or card signed by the group: $150-$450*
*Original lineup

OFTEN OVERLOOKED MEMORABILIA
Movie memorabilia from *Born to Boogie* and *Crimson Moon*; mail-order poster, 1978; Crimson Moon picture bag (used in redemption for poster), 1978; Christmas Bop, Japan, CD release with T-shirt and Christmas card, 1989; Christmas Box 1990, Japan, Warner Brothers, CD and digital watch; numerous other trinkets, most of which were released in the U.K., also exist

REFERENCES/BOOKS
Twentieth Century Boy by Mark Paytress—a must! Numerous other resources exist dating back to 1969 with Bolan's *The Warlock of Love*. No dedicated collector books.

A Tribe Called Quest

Formed 1988

Ali (Ali Shaheed Muhammad), Phife (Malik Taylor), Q-Tip (Jonathan Davis), and Jarobi*

*Jarobi departed in 1990.

A Tribe Called Quest. Photo by Christian Lantry. Courtesy Jive Records.

Nineties "jazz rap" pioneers, who successfully combined jazz samples with hip-hop, A Tribe Called Quest is typically associated with the songs "Scenario" and "Award Tour," the album *Midnight Marauders* (#8, 1993), and an appearance on MTV's *Unplugged.*

AUTOGRAPHS

A CD, LP, magazine cover, ad, photo, or card signed by the group: $15-$25

Trinity: See Brian Auger

Tritt, Travis

(James Travis Tritt)
Born: February 9, 1963

Nineties country artist, typically associated with the songs "Help Me Hold On" (#1, 1990), "I'm Gonna Be Somebody" (#2, 1990), "Drift Off to Dream" (#3, 1991), "Here's a Quarter (Call Someone Who Cares)" (#2, C&W, 1992), "On T-r-o-u-b-l-e" (#27, 1992), and "Foolish Pride" (#1, 1994), Travis Tritt shunned the "hat acts" in favor of an outlaw sound that often carried him on to the pop charts.

AUTOGRAPHS

A CD, LP, magazine cover, ad, photo, or card signed by the artist: $15-$40

TOUR BOOKS/PROGRAMS/PASSES

Tour Books:
Tritt/Yearwood, 1993: $12
Ten Feet Tall Tour, 1994- $10

POSTERS/PRESS KITS
Promotional Posters:
$10-$20
Press Kits: $15-$30

USED CLOTHING/ EQUIPMENT
Guitar Pick: $5-$10

A Travis Tritt guitar pick

The Troggs

Formed 1965

Original lineup: Reg Presley (Ball), Chris Britton, Peter Staples, and Ronnie Bond (Bullis)*

*Numerous personnel changes

Mid-60s British Invasion group, best remembered for the songs "Wild Thing" (#1, 1966), "With a Girl Like You" (#29, 1966), "I Can't Control Myself" (#43, 1966), "Love Is All Around" (#7, 1968), and "Summertime," the Troggs never quit playing and since have been involved with numerous projects from television commercial work to collaborating with members of R.E.M. on *Athens Andover.*

The Troggs in Bonn, Germany, 1995. Photo by Amy Tincher-Durik.

AUTOGRAPHS

A CD, LP, magazine cover, ad, photo, or card signed by the group: $25-$50

REFERENCES/BOOKS

Limited resources exist. There are no dedicated collector books. Serious collectors should opt for a Fan Club: Trogg Times, c/o Jacqueline Ryan, 56 Waite Davies Rd., Lee, London SE12 OND England

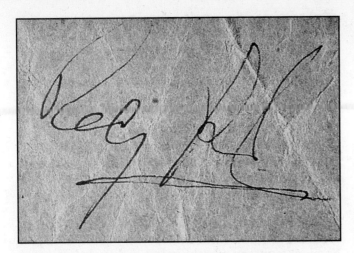

Reg Presley's autograph (obtained in-person). Courtesy Amy Tincher-Durik.

Trower, Robin

Born: March 9, 1945

Guitar hero and Hendrix disciple, who forged his identity with Procal Harum before forming his power trios of the early '70s, Trower is typically associated with his commercially successful albums *Bridge of Sighs* (#7, 1974), *For Earth Below* (#5, 1975), and *Live!* (#10, 1976). Trower also briefly collaborated with ex-Cream bassist Jack Bruce and drummer Bill Lordan in B.L.T. during the early '80s. The nineties find the guitar god still touring!

AUTOGRAPHS
A CD, LP, magazine cover, ad, photo, or card signed by the artist: $15-$30

The Tubes

Formed Late 60s

Fee Waybill (John Waldo), Bill Spooner, Roger Steen, Vince Welnick, Michael Cotton, Prairie Prince, Rick Anderson, and Re Styles*

*Numerous personnel changes in re-formed band 1993

Late-70s novelty act, best remembered for outrageous stage shows and songs such as "White Punks on Dope," "Don't Touch Me There," "Don't Want to Wait Anymore," "Talk to You Later," and "She's a Beauty," the Tubes had trouble sustaining themselves by the mid-80s. Vince Welnick later joined the Grateful Dead, replacing Brent Myland.

AUTOGRAPHS
A CD, LP, magazine cover, ad, photo, or card signed by the group: $20-$50

Tucker, Tanya

Born: October 10, 1958

Early-70s teenage country-pop star, whose early hits included "Delta Dawn," "What's Your Mama's Name," "Blood Red and Goin' Down," and "Would You Lay with Me (in a Field of Stone)," Tucker then tried to make it as a rock singer in the late '70s and early '80s. When the effort failed she turned once again to country music and scored C&W hits like "Just Another Love" (#1, 1986), "I Won't Take Less Than Your Love" (#1, 1987), "Highway Robbery" (#2, 1988), "What Do I Do with Me" (#2, 1991), "Some Kind of Trouble" (#3, 1992), "It's a Little Too Late" (#2, 1993), and "Soon" (#2, 1993). Having weathered a storm of problems, from tabloid exploitation to treatment at the Betty Ford Center in 1989, Tanya Tucker has emerged a mature, impressive, and extremely popular country star.

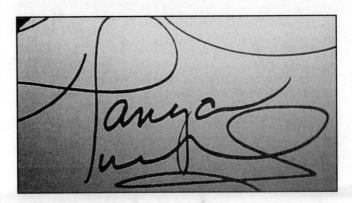

Tanya Tucker's signature

AUTOGRAPHS
A CD, LP, magazine cover, ad, photo, or card signed by the artist: $7-$20

OFTEN OVERLOOKED MEMORABILIA
Movie memorabilia from *Jeremiah Johnson*

Turner, Ike and Tina/Tina Turner

Ike Turner (Izear Luster Turner), Born: November 5, 1931; Tina Turner (Annie Mae Bullock), Born: November 26, 1939

Late-60s and early-70s soul revue, formed by talented session guitarist and producer Ike Turner—formerly of Kings of Rhythm—the group first recorded together in 1960, and landed hits such as "A Fool in Love" (#27, 1960), "It's Gonna Work Out Fine" (#14, 1961), "I Idolize You" (#5, R&B, 1961), "Poor Fool" (#38, 1962), "Tra La La La La" (#9, R&B, 1962), and followed later by "I Want To Take You Higher," "Proud Mary," "Come Together," and "Nutbush City

Poster for an Ike and Tina Turner Revue show on July 3, 1969 in L.A. This 19" x 23" poster was printed by Colby Poster Printing Co. of Los Angeles and is valued between $1,500 and $,2000. From the collection of Hank Thompson.

Limits." The group opened for the Rolling Stones on their 1969 tour, which garnered tremendous exposure for the act, but the couple's rocky marriage put an end to the group by the late '70s.

Following an initial struggle, a few opening dates for both Rod Stewart and the Rolling Stones helped Tina Turner get back on her feet. In 1984 she catapulted into the spotlight with her Capitol Records debut *Private Dancer* (#3, 1984)—Grammy winner for Record of the Year—which included the hit extracts "Let's Stay Together" (#26, 1984), "What's Love Got to Do with It" (#1, 1984)—Grammy winner for Song of the Year—"Better Be Good to Me" (#5, 1984), "Private

Dancer" (#7, 1985), and "Show Some Respect" (#37, 1985). Her follow-up singles "We Don't Need Another Hero (Thunderdome)" (#2, 1985) and "One of the Living" (#15, 1985) came from the movie *Mad Max Beyond Thunderdome*, in which Tina costarred.

Tina finished out the decade with numerous hits including "Typical Male" (#2,1986), "What You Get Is What You See" (#13, 1987), "It's Only Love," a duet with Bryan Adams, and "The Best" (#15, 1989). In 1992 Tina signed with Virgin Records and released her first hit for the label, "I Don't Wanna Fight" (#9, 1993).

Unfortunately, Ike Turner's road has been much rockier—his studio was destroyed by fire in 1982 and he spent eighteen months in jail on drug-related convictions. He was in prison in 1991 when he and Tina were inducted into the Rock and Roll Hall of Fame.

AUTOGRAPHS

Group:
A CD, LP, magazine cover, ad, photo, or card signed by the group: $50-$175

Individual:
Tina Turner: $20-$45

TOUR BOOKS/PROGRAMS/PASSES

Tour Books:
1984 World Tour: $45
Wildest Dreams Tour, 1996: $15

Backstage Passes:
Tina: Cloth: $10-$12; Laminated: $15-$20

POSTERS/PRESS KITS

Promotional Posters: Tina: $10 - $20
Press Kits: Tina: $15 - $35

OFTEN OVERLOOKED MEMORABILIA

Movie memorabilia from *What's Love Got To Do with It* and *Mad Max Beyond Thunderdome*; videotapes of their numerous television show appearances; Grow Your Own Nutbush, UA promo peanut growing kit with instructions

REFERENCES/BOOKS

Numerous resources exist, but start with her autobiography *I, Tina: My Life Story*, cowritten with Kurt Loder (1986). There are no dedicated collector books. Serious collectors should opt for a Fan Club: Simply the Best: Tina Turner Fan Club, Attention: Mark Lairmore, 4566 S. Park Ave., Springfield, MO 65810 ($8 fee)

Tina Turner. Photo by Peter Lindbergh. Courtesy Virgin Records.

Turner, Big Joe

(1911-1985)

One of rock and roll's pivotal pioneers and bluesman, Turner's jump-blues and crafty delivery helped him score numerous R&B hits—now considered classics—such as "Sweet Sixteen," "Honey Hush," "T.V. Mama," "Shake, Rattle and Roll," "Flip, Flop, Fly," "The Chicken and the Hawk," "Corina, Corina," and

"Rock a While." Having sung for two decades, before recording for Atlantic Records during the early '50s, Turner had crafted his art and successfully linked blues with rock and roll.

AUTOGRAPHS

An LP, magazine cover, ad, photo, or card signed by the artist: $50-$125

OFTEN OVERLOOKED MEMORABILIA

Movie memorabilia from *The Last of the Blue Devils*

The Turtles/Flo and Eddie

Formed 1963

Original lineup: Howard Kaylan, Mark Volman, Al Nichol, Chuck Portz, and Donald Murray

Early-60s California pop act, which transformed from a surf group to folk-rock, the Turtles are best remembered for the hits "Happy Together" (#1, 1967), "She'd Rather Be with Me" (#3, 1967), "You Know What I Mean" (#12, 1967), "She's My Girl" (#14, 1967), "Elenore" (#6,1968), and "You Showed Me" (#6, 1969). The band broke up for good during the mid-70s. Volman and Kaylan joined Frank Zappa and satisfied their alter egos as Flo and Eddie.

After leaving Zappa in 1972, the pair became more of a parody and novelty act, although occasional background vocals—probably done to pay the bills—exhibited both members' genuine talent. The two also had their hands in numerous projects from syndicated radio shows to children's records.

AUTOGRAPHS

A CD, LP, magazine cover, ad, photo, or card signed by the group: $40-$75

OFTEN OVERLOOKED MEMORABILIA

Movie memorabilia from *Get Crazy* and *Cheap*; associated artifacts from their numerous contributions, primarily on background vocals, to the works of other artists; copies of their music columns that have appeared in numerous periodicals; artifacts from their children's records; memorabilia from their annual New Year's Eve shows at New York City's Bottom Line, etc.

Twilley, Dwight

Born: June 6, 1952

Mid-70s Tulsa rockabilly-pop artist, best remembered for his songs "I'm On Fire" (1975), "Girls" (#16, 1984), and "Why Do You Wanna Break My Heart," Dwight Twilly has been plagued by record company problems during his career. He and partner Phil Seymour had developed an outstanding reputation with the release of "I'm On Fire," but a faltering Shelter Records wasn't in a position to capitalize on the duo's

momentum. Seymour did have a solo hit in 1981 with "Precious to Me," before his death in 1993 at the young age of 41. Twilly has gone on to work on children's books and is also a gifted artist who has had many of his works exhibited.

AUTOGRAPHS

A CD, LP, magazine cover, ad, photo, or card signed by theartist: $10-$20

OFTEN OVERLOOKED MEMORABILIA

Movie memorabilia from *Wayne's World*; a copy of Twilley's *Questions from Dad: A Really Cool Way to Communicate with Kids*; art exhibition catalogs associated with Twilley's works

Twisted Sister

Formed 1973

Jay Jay French (John Segall), Mark Mendoza, Eddie Ojeda, Tony Petri, and Dee Snider*

*Petri departed in 1982 and A. J. Pero was added. Pero later left and was replaced by Joe Franco in 1987.

Late-70s glitter-rock and saloon band, best remembered for the song "We're Not Gonna Take It" (#21, 1984), Twisted Sister had developed an avid cult following in the Tri-State/New York City area before landing a major record deal with Atlantic in 1983. Fronted by the not so user friendly Dee Snider, whose antiestablishment rhetoric led many parents to install dead-bolt locks on their homes, Twisted Sister took full advantage of the media to drive the *Stay Hungry* album into the Top Twenty. When the group's subsequent albums garnered little interest, the band broke up (1987).

AUTOGRAPHS

A CD, LP, magazine cover, ad, photo, or card signed by the group: $15-$25

OFTEN OVERLOOKED MEMORABILIA

A videotape of Snider's appearance at the Senate subcommittee on communications hearings; a copy of Snider's and Phillip Bashe's book *Dee Snider's Teenage Survival Guide: How to Be a Legend in Your Own Lunchtime*

Twitty, Conway

(Harold Lloyd Jenkins)
Born: September 1, 1933, Died: June 5, 1993

Twitty was initially a rockabilly and pop singer, who scored hits with "It's Only Make Believe" (#1, 1957) and "Lonely Blue Boy" (#6, 1960), and when the hits slowed, he formed a country band (1964). Through extensive touring, and an incredible amount of talent, the band built an enormous follow-

ing in the South and Southwest. Beginning in 1968, he began a series of country hits, including "Next in Line," "I Love You More Today," "To See My Angel Cry," "That's When She Started to Stop Loving Me," and "Hello Darlin'."

During the '70s he also scored with the duet "After the Fire is Gone," which was just one of many he sang with Loretta Lynn, followed by other hits including "She Needs Someone to Hold Her," "I Can't Stop Loving You," and "(Lost Her Love) On Our Last Date." Twitty inevitably became country's all-time greatest seller of records, with a dozen Number Ones during the '80s alone, including "Tight Fittin' Jeans" (1981), "The Clown" (1982), and "Somebody's Needin' Somebody" (1984).

The artist opened a nine-acre theme park outside Nashville, the popular Twitty City, in 1982. While U.S. presidents build libraries, country acts typically opt for cotton candy and roller coasters. Twitty died on June 5, 1993, following a performance in Branson, Missouri.

AUTOGRAPHS

A CD, LP, magazine cover, ad, photo, or card signed by the artist: $40-$75

OFTEN OVERLOOKED MEMORABILIA

Twitty City souvenirs; videotapes of the artist's numerous television show appearances

2 Live Crew

Formed 1985

Luke Skywalker (Luther Campbell), Fresh Kid Ice (Christopher Wong-Won), Brother Marquis (Mark Ross), and Mr. Mixx (David Hobbs)*

*Numerous personnel changes

Controversial late-80s pioneers of the bass-heavy Miami rap sound, "The Crew" is typically remembered for the albums *As Nasty As They Wanna Be* (#29, 1989) and *Sports Weekend* (#22, 1991), the single "Me So Horny" (#26, 1989), and its constant and often highly-visible legal battles. The original 2 Live Crew disbanded in 1991, while Campbell continued his solo career and even announced a new 2 Live Crew, before filing for bankruptcy.

AUTOGRAPHS

A CD, LP, magazine cover, ad, photo, or card signed by the group: $25-$50

OFTEN OVERLOOKED MEMORABILIA

Press clippings and legal documents from their numerous court battles

2 Pac

(Tupac Amaru Shakur) (1971-1996)

Nineties New York City gangsta rapper, who both lived hard and died hard, Tupac was a victim of a random drive-by shooting that killed him in 1996. He is perhaps best remembered for his 1985 chart-topping album *Me Against the World*, as well as for *All Eyez On Me* (1996), his hits such as "I Get Around" (#11, 1993), "Keep Ya Head Up" (#12, 1993), and "How Do You Want It/California Love" (#1, 1996), and finally for being the victim of a tragic and senseless crime.

Tupac was no stranger to controversy or violence, having been arrested numerous times on charges ranging from the shooting of two off-duty police officers in Atlanta, to sexual assault. He became the first artist to reach Number One on the Billboard charts while serving out a prison sentence.

AUTOGRAPHS

A CD, LP, magazine cover, ad, photo, or card signed by the artist: $50-$100

POSTERS/PRESS KITS

Promotional Posters: $10-$25
Press Kits: $20-$35

OFTEN OVERLOOKED MEMORABILIA

Movie memorabilia from *Juice* (1992) and *Poetic Justice* (1993)

Two Tons of Fun: See Weather Girls

The Tymes

Formed 1959

Original lineup: George Hilliard, Donald Banks, George Williams, Albert Berry, and Norman Burnett

Late-50s and '60s R&B/pop vocal group, best remembered for the songs "So Much In Love" (#1), "Wonderful! Wonderful!" (#7, 1963), "Somewhere" (#19, 1963), "People" (#39, 1968), and "You Little Trustmaker" (#12, 1974), the Tymes have endured generations, although they have seen numerous personnel changes.

AUTOGRAPHS

An LP, magazine cover, ad, photo, or card signed by the group: $10-$15

UB40

Formed 1978

Astro (Terrence Wilson), James Brown, Ali Campbell, Robin Campbell, Earl Falconer, Norman Hassan, Brian Travers, and Mickey Virtue

This successful British band best known for its reggae flavored covers such as "Red Red Wine" (#1, 1988), "Can't Help Falling in Love" (#1, 1993), "The Way You Do The Things You Do" (#6, 1990), and "Higher Ground" (#45, 1993).

AUTOGRAPHS

A CD, LP, magazine cover, ad, photo, or card signed by the group: $10-$20

TOUR BOOKS/PROGRAMS/PASSES

Tour Books: 1988/89 World Tour: $10

UFO

Formed 1969

Phil Mogg, Mick Bolton, Peter Way, and Andy Parker*

*Numerous personnel changes. Musicians have included: Michael Schenker, Danny Peyronel, Paul Raymond, Paul Chapman, Neil Carter, Paul Gray, Jim Simpson, Atomic Tommy M, Lawrence Archer, and Clive Edwards

This British heavy metal band scored a Japanese hit single with "C'mon Everybody" (1972) and a minor hit with "Back into My Life" (1982), before breaking up in 1983, disappointed with its marginal success.

AUTOGRAPHS

A CD, LP, magazine cover, ad, photo, or card signed by the group: $20-$30

Ugly Kid Joe

Formed 1990

Whitfield Crane, Klaus Eichstadt, Roger Lahr, and Mark Davis*

*Cordell Crockett was added in 1991. Lahr departed the same year and was replaced by Dave Fortman.

More of a novelty act than a bonafide act, Ugly Kid Joe is best known for its anti-love anthem "Everything About You" (#9, 1992), which turned up on the *Wayne's World* soundtrack.

AUTOGRAPHS

A CD, LP, magazine cover, ad, photo, or card signed by the group: $5-$10

OFTEN OVERLOOKED MEMORABILIA

Movie memorabilia from *Wayne's World*

U.K.

Formed 1977

Eddie Jobson, Born: April 28, 1955; John Wetton, Born: July 12, 1949; Alan Holdsworth; and Bill Bruford, Born: May 17, 1949*

*Holdsworth and Bruford departed in 1979 and Terry Bozzio was added.

This classic "sweventies"—second-wave '70s—band, made up of well-known recycled remnants, became an immediate hit with progressive rock fans with its impressive and commercially successful self-titled debut album. U.K. lasted only for a brief period of time. As is typically the case with bands such as this, when other more promising opportunities arose, members departed. Jobson (Roxy Music) went on to tour with Jethro Tull, Wetton (King Crimson, Roxy Music, Uriah Heep) went on to form the "sw80s" act Asia, while Bruford (Yes, King Crimson) and Holdsworth (Gong, Soft Machine) worked together briefly.

AUTOGRAPHS

A CD, LP, magazine cover, ad, photo, or card signed by the group: $25-$50*

*Original members

Ulmer, James Blood

Born: February 2, 1942

Innovative and talented guitarist of the early '80s, who combined Hendrix-like style vocals with his roots in "harmolodic" theory, James Blood Ulmer had played in Art Blakey's Jazz Messengers and recorded with other gifted jazz musicians, while maintaining a cult following made up of primarily jazz enthusiasts.

AUTOGRAPHS

A CD, LP, magazine cover, ad, photo, or card signed by the artist: $5-$10

****

"On The Edge"

Ultramagnetic MCs

This futuristic funk group combines off-beat rhyme flows with rap and then adds some down home Bronx flavor to deliver its message. Collectors should begin at *Critical Beatdown* (Next Plateau, 1988), the band's debut release, and pick up associated items from singles "Space Groove" and "Something Else."

****

Ultravox

Formed 1973

John Foxx (Dennis Chorley), Steve Shears, Billy Currie, Chris Cross (Christopher Allen), and Warren Cann*

*Shears left in 1978 and Robin Simon joined the band. In 1980 Foxx and Simon left and Midge (James) Ure was added. Cann departed in 1986 and Mark Brzezicki was added on drums.

A foundation for the "electropop" sound of the early '80s, Ultravox was founded by synthesizer influenced John Foxx who helped shape the band's sound on U.K. hits "All Stood Still" (1981), "Reap the Wild Wind" (1982), "Hymn" (1982), "Visions in Blue" (1983), "Lament" (1984), and "Love's Great Adventure" (1984). Of these, only "Reap the Wild Wind" (#71, 1983) managed to attract any U.S. interest, and was extracted from the group's highest charting U.S. album *Quartet* (#61, 1983), which was produced by George Martin. The band split up in 1987, with only Midge Ure managing to capture any solo success thus far.

AUTOGRAPHS

A CD, LP, magazine cover, ad, photo, or card signed by the group: $12-$25

Uncle Tuepelo

Formed 1987

Jeff Tweedy, Jay Farrar, and Michael Heidorn*

*Heidorn departed in 1993 and Ken Coomer, John Stirratt, and Max Johnson joined the band. Wilco was formed in 1994: Tweedy, Coomer, Stirratt, and Johnson. Son Volt formed in 1994: Farrar, Heidorn, Dave Boquist, and Jim Boquist.

This Midwestern alt rock band had just enough twang to attract R.E.M. guitarist Peter Buck to produce its *March 16-20, 1992* album release. The in-

terplay between Tweedy and Farrar's harmonies was intriguing until tensions between the two led to Farrar's departure in June 1994. Tweedy then transformed the band into Wilco, while Farrar formed Sun Volt.

AUTOGRAPHS

A CD, LP, magazine cover, ad, photo, or card signed by the group: $5-$10

The Undertones/Feargal Sharkey/ The Petrol Emotion

Formed 1975

Feargal Sharkey, John O' Neill, Damian O' Neill, Michael Bradley, and Billy Doherty. The Petrol Emotion was formed in 1986: John and Damian O' Neill, Reamann O'Gormain, Ciaran McLaughlin, and Steve Mack

An Irish group of sorts, whose buzzsaw guitars could rip a chord faster than Paul Bunyan on amphetamines, the Undertones' message was delivered by Sharkey's high-pitched vocals most notably on "Teenage Kicks" (#31, U.K., 1978). Still failing to kick in commercially, the band broke up after its fourth album, *The Sin of Pride* (#43, U.K. , 1983). Sharkey went on to the Assembly, which landed with "Never Never" (#4, U.K., 1983), before heading solo and landing with the single "Listen to Your Father (#23, U.K., 1984) and "A Good Heart" (#74, 1986). John and Damain went on to the Petrol Emotion.

AUTOGRAPHS

A CD, LP, magazine cover, ad, photo, or card signed by the group: $10-$22

****

"On The Edge"

Unrest

An indie-punk band searching for a good mouthwash, is my *SPIN* on Unrest. The group's debut *Tink of S.E.* (Teen Beat, 1987) is a tough find, as are associated items. *Malcolm X Park* (Caroline, 1988) is a logical next step for collectors. *Perfect Teeth* (Teen Beat/4AD, 1993) was the band's last effort before breaking up. Any project by Mark Robinson (guitar, vocals) is probably worth the unrest it might cause you.

****

Uriah Heep

Formed 1970

David Bryon, (1947-1985); Mick Box, Born: June 8, 1947; Ken Hensley, Born: August 24, 1945; Paul Newton; and Alex Napier*

*Numerous personnel changes. Members have included: Keith Baker, Lee Kerslake, Mark Clarke, Gary Thain, John Wetton, John Lawton, Trevor Bolder, John Sloman, Chris Slade, Greg Dechert, Bob Daisley, Pete Goalby, John Sinclair, Bernie Shaw, and Phil Lanzon

If Spinal Tap weren't Spinal Tap, it would be Uriah Heep, one of rock music's premier opening acts which has survived decades and numerous personnel changes, while selling consistently during the '70s and even scoring decade compilation favorites such as "Easy Livin'" (#39, 1972), "Sweet Lorraine" (#91, 1973), "Blind Eye" (#97, 1973), and "Stealin'" (#91, 1973).

AUTOGRAPHS

A CD, LP, magazine cover, ad, photo, or card signed by the group: $15-$50*

*High-end for 1972 - 1974 lineup

Contract signed by Uriah Heep

****

"On The Edge"

Urge Overkill

National Kato (Nathan Katruud) and King Roeser (Eddie Roeser) are the band's principals. Kato, not Kaelin, formerly roomed with Steve Albini whose *Strange, I...* (Ruthless, 1986) was somewhat reflective of the sounds of the Chicago rock underground during the 1980s. Collectors should start with *Supersonic Storybook* (Touch and Go, 1991)—actually anything prior to the band's

move to Geffen Records in 1993 is probably worth putting away. They drew considerable attention popping up on the soundtrack to *Pulp Fiction,* covering " Girl, You'll Be A Woman Soon." Exit the Dragon (collage of band shots, 12" x 22") and Saturation (group shot, yellow background, 24" x 26") promotional posters can be picked up for just under ten bucks. Concert posters run about $12-$15. Example: Urge Overkill/Veruca Salt - May 21 at Univ. of Chicago, flying saucer, 22" x 17" - $15.

****

U.T.F.O.

Formed 1982

Kangol (Shawn Fequiere), Dr. Ice (Fred Reeves), Educated Rapper (Jeffrey Campbell), and Mix-master Ice (Maurice Bailey)

"Roxanne, Roxanne" (#10, R&B, 1985), Untouchable Force Organization's second single, catapulted the group into the rap spotlight. The group followed with "The Real Roxanne," "Leader of the Pack," and "Fairytale Lover," all extracted from its debut album. Although its music evolved over the next few albums, even touching gangsta rap, the failure of *Bag It and Bone It* in 1990 led to the collapse of the group.

AUTOGRAPHS

A CD, LP, magazine cover, ad, photo, or card signed by the group: $5-$10

U2

Formed 1978

Bono Vox (Paul Hewson), Born: May 10, 1960; The Edge (David Evans); Adam Clayton, Born: March 13, 1960; and Larry Mullen, Born: October 31, 1961

The 1980s spawned many a successful band, but perhaps none has gained as much widespread acceptance as U2. They have bridged the gap between the late 1970s punk/postpunk era and the 1980s MTV generation, without selling out their principles or their music. Something very few bands can claim with any sense of integrity.

Their music adolescence was marked by the now traditional rebellious stage—*Boy*, *October*, and *War*—but as they matured both musically and personally, they were able to become more introspective. Already politically conscious by the time *The Unforgettable Fire* hit, the band transcended generations with songs such as "(Pride) In the Name of Love" (#33, 1984), which was a salute to 1960s slain civil rights leader Martin Luther King Jr., a cause which U2 was eager to pursue.

The label "super group" become synonymous with the band following the release of the critically acclaimed and commercially successful *The Joshua Tree*. The album spun off three hit singles: "With or Without You" (#1, 1987), "I Still Haven't Found What I'm Looking For" (#1, 1987), and "Where the Streets Have No Name" (#13, 1987). The album, like its predecessor, was produced by Brian Eno and Daniel Lanois, and garnered many Grammy Awards including Album of the Year (1988).

Rattle and Hum followed next and was a project that seemed to humble the band a bit. Tracing traditional American blues and rockabilliy roots, it brought with it everything from recording sessions in Sun Studios to duets with B.B. King. The LP, with its many complimentary media projects, shot to Number One and spun off a hit single "Desire" (#3, 1988).

Acthung Baby was an opportunity for the band to take a few chances without feeling guilty. It was also successful, with hits such as "Mysterious Ways" (#9, 1992), "One" (#10, 1992), "Even Better Than the Real Thing" (#32, 1992), and "Who's Gonna Ride Your Wild Horses" (#35, 1992).

By 1992 Bono's alter ego, MacPhisto (a stage character he had created), had attacked him full-time and Zoo TV was born—with or without our permission. By all accounts the event was a success with its elaborate staging (a jungle of TV monitors). While the tour was winding down the band came up with the idea of slipping into the studio to make an EP. *Zooropa*, an album that should have been an EP, was the result. Although it reached Number One, it was described best as "MacPhisto with an intestinal blockage." The album spun off the memorable "Stay (Faraway, So Close)" (#61, 1993).

In 1995 the band contributed "Hold Me, Thrill Me, Kiss Me, Kill Me" (#16, 1995) to the *Batman Forever* soundtrack. It was a nice return for the band which was exploring numerous avenues both individually and collectively, from duets with Luciano Pavarotti on *Original Soundtracks 1* (1995), to an updated theme of *Mission: Impossible* (1996).

In 1997, the band gave us *POP* (#1, 1997), and while we were looking for our disco outfits, "Staring at the Sun" (#26, 1997) as if it were the "Last Night on Earth" (#57, 1997), we attempted to understand this migration from "New Zooland."

The band's work with many world-wide organizations, including Greenpeace, AIDS research, and Amnesty International, is to be commended with utmost appreciation. They remain one of the few bands which can be acknowledged equally as both musicians and humanitarians. There is no better compliment!

U2 - A TOUR OVERVIEW

Date/Tour

1976-79: Ireland, The Early Years and the Clubs

Memorabilia from this era is scarce even if you live in Ireland. Any items pertaining to the band's first record, a three-song EP (U2-3) released only in Ireland, are highly sought after. The band's television debut took place on October 5, 1979, at the Cork Opera House. A copy of this event is a must for collectors. U2 also received their first cover story outside Ireland in the popular U.K. music paper *Record Mirror* (November 1979)—another must for any U2 collection. Advertisements from the group's London Club Tour, 1979, still can be found in various music periodicals from this time. An additional must for videotape collectors is the band's appearance on the *Late Late Show*, January 15, 1980 (RTE Studios, Dublin).

1980: 11 O'clock Tick Tock Tour

On May 23, 1980, the band's debut single on Island Records, "11 O'clock Tick Tock"/"Touch," was released. In support of the record they toured the U.K. Promotional items for the tour included some nice posters produced by Island Records. One vertically formatted poster includes their May and June tour dates and advertises the single. Another one I have seen is horizontally formatted and includes a picture of the band accompanied by tour dates. The band's first date at an open-air festival took place on July 27, 1980, in Dublin, Leixlip Castle.

1980-81: Boy Tour

Having just completed work on their debut album *Boy*, the band set out on a lengthy U.K. tour to preview the music and visit places they had never played at before. Gigs in Holland and Belgium were also added. The tour featured the band's first use of a backdrop which was a copy of the *Boy* sleeve. On September 8, 1980, the band played the first of four Monday evening shows at the Marquee in London. Their debut album was released on October 20, 1980, in the U.K. and Ireland. On November 21, 1980, the group played their first gig in Scotland at the Edinburgh Nite Club. The band's first performance in France was in Paris on December 3, 1980, at the Baltard Pavilion. The group's American debut was on December 6, 1980, at the Ritz in New York. Television performances during this era included *Magdagsborsen* (Swedish TV), *Rock Follies* (2/10/81), *Old Grey Whistle Stop* (U.K.-TV, 2/28/81), and *The Tomorrow Show* (5/30/81).

1981-82: October Tour

The band's October Tour had three legs: U.K. and Europe (Fall 1981), America (Fall 1981), and America (Winter/Spring 1982). The tour was to promote the band's new album which was released on October 12, 1981. Most of the dates on the first leg were in smaller clubs or at university halls. Television appear-

ances included *Generation 80* - RTBF - Belgian/ French station (10/25/81) and *Rockblast* - German TV (11/4/81). During this period the band was starting to outgrow clubs and moved to theatres in some cities to meet fan demand. During the third leg of their tour U2 supported the J. Geils Band at fourteen shows. The increased exposure helped push album sales and impressed a new legion of fans. It also marked the first time the band played an arena. Television performances included *Countdown in Concert* - Dutch TV (5/14/82), *Something Else* and *Get Set for Summer* both U.K.-TV (May, 1982), *The Tube* (7/31/82), and Dutch TV recorded performances on July 2, 1982, and July 4, 1982.

This tour was a good starting point for U2 ticket collectors, because of the size of the venues — bigger arenas equal more tickets. During this period Island Records released a live version of "I Will Follow" in an attractive picture sleeve that quickly became both a hit and a collector's item (only released in Holland). All memorabilia associated with this item is a must for collectors.

The band began a four-week, 20-date stint as a warm-up for the larger planned tour on December 1, 1982. It gave the band a chance to polish key songs from their new album. While in Sweden they shot a video clip for "New Year's Day," their first single off the *War* album. They appeared in January 1983 on the *Top of the Pops* (U.K.).

1983: War Tour

The first leg of the War Tour saw nineteen shows, all sold out, across the U.K. The photo from the *War* record sleeve was used as a stage backdrop for the band. On March 16, 1983, the band entered the Tyne Tees TV Studios in Newcastle for a live session for *The Tube*. On March 31, 1983, the group appeared on *Top of the Pops* U.K.-TV.

The second leg was in North America during the Spring. Advertisements, now highly collected stated "U2 DECLARE WAR." The ten-week tour saw the band moving into larger theatres and even performing in open-air festivals. When they began the tour in Hartford, CT, on April 23, 1983, U2 was in support of Todd Rundgren — their name didn't even appear on the ticket. Posters and backstage passes were also inconsistent in design. On May 21, 1983, while in Chicago, IL, the band visited the Chicago Peace Museum, which was exhibiting "The Unforgettable Fire." The exhibition was a collection of artwork made by the survivors of the Hiroshima and Nagasaki nuclear bombings of August 1945. The exhibition, along with the museum's representation of Dr. Martin Luther King, had a lasting impact on the band. On May 30, 1983, the band played in front of 125,000 people at the U.S. Festival in Devore, CA — the largest crowd the band has ever played for. The concert was aired on radio, with some songs also broadcast on television. On June 5, at the Red Rocks Amphitheatre in Denver, CO, the show was videotaped for the British TV rock program *The Tube*. The show also became a Showtime broadcast, a promotional video, a mini-live album, and *U2 Live At Red Rocks: Under A Blood Red Sky,* a videotape release (11/83). The band's first headlining show at a sports arena was on June 17 in Los Angeles, CA. The finale for this leg occurred in New York at Pier 84. The Show was promoted by Ron Delsner along with the sponsorship of Miller Beer.

The band then returned to Europe for the tour's final leg. The show on August 20, 1983, in Germany was aired live on WDR-TV and also on the radio *Rockpalast* concert series. It was the first time such an event had taken place for the band. Five songs from the event found their way to inclusion on the mini-live album *Under a Blood Red Sky*. While in Osaka, Japan, the band was interviewed on a TV show, after which they begin a chaotic version of New Year's Day complete with a broken guitar — a must for videotape collectors. The work for the band's next album was completed on August 5, 1984. During this period a 45-minute documentary videotape, *The Unforgettable Fire Collection* (1985), captured the events for posterity.

1984: Under Australian Skies Tour

Following the final mixing for their fourth album, *The Unforgettable Fire* (10/1/84), the band hastily prepared for an Australian Tour which began on August 19, 1984. The band was thrust immediately into sports arenas because of the pent-up demand for their live performances. During this tour they gradually introduced newer material into the previous *War* set.

1984-85: The Unforgettable Fire Tour

The tour that put the band on the map began on October 18, 1984*. The visual nature of the show attempted, and succeeded, to bring the album's message to the audience. It was a transformation for the band and a critical step in their career. Because of this, any and all items associated with the tour are prized collectibles. Numerous shows on the first leg were recorded for the mini-album *Wide Awake in America* (5/85). The show on November 21, 1984, in Germany was recorded for German TV. The second leg was North America, which began on December 1, 1984, at the Tower The-

ater in Philadelphia, PA. The following night's show in Worcester, MA, became a part of U2 history—it was the band's first completely sold out arena in America. The short American leg ended at Long Beach, California on December 16, 1984. It was back to Europe in the winter for the third leg of the tour. Issue #443 of *Rolling Stone* magazine featured U2, "Our Choice Band of the 80's," on the cover ($5-7). The fourth leg—America, Winter/Spring 1985—an all-arena tour, began on February 25 in Dallas, TX. The band's overwhelming success became apparent as fans flocked anywhere, at anytime, just for a glimpse of their new idols. The final leg, a Spring/Summer swing through Europe, was filled with various festivals. The band also managed to underwrite the cost of bringing "The Unforgettable Fire" art exhibition to Europe. The show ran from June 29 to July 5 at the Grapevine Arts Centere in Dublin, Ireland. Naturally, the association with the band makes artifacts from the exhibit also of interest to U2 collectors. The last official performance of "The Unforgettable Fire" tour came on July 7, 1985, in Belgium. The band gave a brief performance on Irish-TV's *TV Gaga* on January 30, 1986. Not a part of the tour, U2 attended and played at Live Aid on July 13 (1985) at Wembley Stadium, at the Lark by the Lee festival on August 25, and the Self Aid festival in Dublin, Ireland, in May.

*Some dates early in the tour were postponed to give the band more time to rehearse the new material (October 1, 4, 5, 6, 8, 10, 11, 12, 14, 15, 17, 18, 19, 21, 22, 24, and 25).

1986: A Conspiracy of Hope Tour

The band joined A Conspiracy of Hope, concerts for Amnesty International during the Summer of 1986. The shows began in San Francisco, CA, on June 4. The June 15 show held at Giant's Stadium in East Rutherford, NJ, was simulcast on MTV America, and broadcast on the Westwood One Radio Network. It became a 12-hour media presentation creating enormous interest in the cause. It was also the final event of the six-show tour. On March 8, 1987, the band performed live for the *Old Grey Whistle Test* television program and previewed a few songs from the next album, *The Joshua Tree* (3/9/87). Following the event, the band appeared at the Bellfast branch of Tower Records to meet with fans and autograph the first copies of *The Joshua Tree*. On March 16 the band performed on *The Late Late Show* (Irish -TV).

1987: The Joshua Tree Tour

On March 27, 1987, U2 appeared on the rooftop of a liquor store at 7th Avenue and Main St. in Los Angeles, CA, to film a video for "Where the Streets Have No Name." In Beatlesque fashion, the event attracted tremendous interest in the upcoming tour and drew attention to the new album. The first leg of The Joshua Tree Tour opened in Tempe, AZ, at the State University Activity Center. During this period the band was interviewed and photographed for an upcoming cover story in *Time* magazine (4/27/87), the fifth rock act ever to make the prestigious cover of the publication ($5-$7). On April 12, while performing in Las Vegas, NV, the band shot the promotional clip for "I Still Haven't Found What I'm Looking For" while they walked down the casino-laden streets. Following their April 14 show in San Diego, CA, the band recorded their final installment on *The Tube* rock program. The band's show at the Michigan Silverdome on April 30 became U2's first headlining stadium show in America. The second leg of the tour began on May 27 in Rome, Italy*. Despite their numerous scheduled stadium appearances, demand for the band exceeded expectations. Songs from the band's stop in Paris, France (7/4/87) at the Hippodrome de Vincennes, were fed via satellite to British TV for the Island Records 25th birthday celebration. During this leg of the tour the band played their first gig in Spain (7/15/87). The third leg of the tour was an extensive run through America in the fall.** On November 1, 1987, in Indianapolis, IN, the band pulled off a prank they had been planning for a time. They appear in disguises as "The Dalton Brothers"—their own support band. Although the crowd later realized and acknowledged the stunt, the band repeated the ploy. Another worthy incident was when the band decided to play a free show at the Justin Herman Plaza in the heart of San Francisco's financial district (11/11/87). Although the crowd, estimated at over 20,000 people, enjoyed the show, local officials were less amused when during "Pride" Bono decided to spray paint a statue. He was later charged for malicious mischief, a misdemeanor. Following an apology, and a sponsored cleanup of his expression, Bono's charges were dropped. The group's appearance at the Memorial Coliseum in L.A. was also noteworthy because the Olympic Flame was lit in the band's honor—a ceremony also attributed to a papal visit. While visiting Austin, TX (11/22/87) the band headed to Antone's, a prominent blues club, and ended up jamming with Stevie Ray Vaughan, Dr. John, and T-Bone Burnett. The band also visited Elvis Presley's Graceland estate, for some filming for *Rattle and Hum*. During the visit the band also stepped into the legendary Sun (Records) Studios to record a few new tracks.

The shows at Sun Devil Stadium in Tempe, AZ, on December 19 and 20 were filmed for the color portion of their videotape *Rattle and Hum*. To ensure that both shows sold out the band reduced tickets to $5. These shows concluded this leg of the tour, with only three out of fifty shows failing to sell out.

"The Official Book of the U2 Movie" (© 1988 Not Us Limited)

The extensive touring prompted the band to cancel an Australian leg of the journey in early 1988. The band's only official concert in 1988 was at the Smile Jamaica benefit on October 16. The world premiere of *Rattle and Hum* (film/video) took place in Dublin on October 27, 1988. The band appeared for the event outside and performed an impromptu show prior to and after the premiere. The band also appeared on the *Late Late Show* during a live broadcast on December 16, 1988.

*Official tour T-shirts included a 6/18/87 show that did not take place.
**Official tour program included a second show on 9/25/87 that did not take place.

1989-90: Lovetown Tour

The first leg of the Lovetown Tour was in Australia, followed by New Zealand and Japan. Chilean mural artist Rene Castro was hired to design and produce the band's stage backdrops. Blues legend B.B. King was invited to join the band for support during the tour. The tour began in Perth on September 21, with the band's multiple show format giving numerous fans an opportunity to see the group. The second night's show was hampered by a bomb threat. Four cities in Europe were chosen for the second leg of the tour: Paris, Amsterdam, Dublin, and Dortmund. The New Year's Eve Dublin show was aired live on the radio. The band encouraged listeners to tape the show and even took out advertising space in various publications to print a cut-and-fold cassette sleeve designed specifically to house the tape ($5-$8). U2's seventh album, *Achtung Baby*, was released on November 18, 1991.

*The shows held in Sydney on November 17, 18, and 19 are particularly noteworthy because they were filmed for a tour documentary that aired in Australia and Europe the following year.
**The October 17, 1989, show printed in the tour book did not take place. Shows scheduled for October 22, 24, and 25 in Sydney were also postponed.

1992: Zoo-TV Tour

The highly anticipated tour was announced in early 1992—the group did not perform publicly in 1991. The Zoo TV Tour began in Florida and included 32 arena dates. Tour merchandise included "Achtung Baby" condoms. While they generated controversy, they also generated cash—all revenues from sales were donated to AIDS research. On March 27, 1992, Bono spotted a pizza advertisement crossing the band's elaborate video screens and ordered 10,000 pizzas from his cell phone during "Even Better Than the Real Thing." During the encore the pizzas were delivered and flung into the crowd. The incident was commemorated on a now very collectable U2 T-shirt. During the tour the band recorded a segment for *Top of the Pops* (2/27/92) and for the "Live for Life" Freddie Mercury Tribute (4/18/92). The second leg of the tour touched down in Europe during the Spring of 1992. This primarily indoor tour served as a teaser for the outdoor Summer leg. Probably the most collectible item from this leg was the advertisement that appeared in *Select* magazine saying tickets for a June 20 show were going on sale May 9 ($10). The event was going to be a large open-air festival at Manchester's Heaton Park, but was eventually re-scheduled for the indoor G-Max Centre on June 19.

Zoo TV: Outdoor Leg

The outdoor leg headed back to America in August. The band rehearsed in Hershey, PA, and following a few days of hard work, tickets went on sale for an Outdoor Rehearsal to be held on August 7. The tickets, now sought by collectors ($5-$10), were priced at $15 with all proceeds going to local charities. A satellite link to L.A. was set up for the band's September 9 show at the Silverdome in Pontiac, MI. Zoo TV was beamed to L.A. for the MTV Awards show. A unique collectible from this leg is *The El Paso Times* concert survival guide ($5).

1993: Zooropa Tour

This tour was U2's first full stadium tour of Europe and included more than forty shows. The shows held in Dublin on August 27 and 28 were noteworthy first because the Department of Health stated that it was taking legal action against the band for their promotional posters that included Bono smoking a cigar, and second, the show on the 28 was transmitted live on radio in America and most of Europe. A specially designed cassette cover was printed in *Hot Press* magazine to encourage the taping of the event ($3-5). Also any collectible associated with Foster's lager for these shows is now collectible, because when the band found out about the collaboration, they were furious and

promptly chose another spirit—the band typically refuses to link themselves with such products.

"Zoomerang"/"New Zooland"

The final leg of the tour hit Australia, followed by New Zealand and Japan. The shows held on November 26 and 27 in Sydney are worthy of note. The first shows mark the first time the band had ever performed without one of its members. Adam fell prey to an illness and bass tech Stuart Morgan stood in for him. The following night included a live broadcast to America on a Thanksgiving pay-for-view special; it was also broadcast to nearly fifty countries in the following weeks. Eventually *Zoo TV Live Ärom Sydney* was released into the home video market.

> *The biggest zoo on the Zooropa Tour ended up being the July 6th date in Rome, Italy.
> **A Budapest show held on July 23, 1993, was not included on tour T-shirts or programs.

1997: POP Tour

With many major acts not even attempting a large venue tour due to poor ticket sales, U2 put POP on the road. The tour, which garnered rave reviews, failed to sellout.

AUTOGRAPHS

U2 has always been obliging to autograph requests. It's not unusual for Bono to show up somewhere, such as outside a hall exit, to sign a few autographs.

Group:

A CD, LP, magazine cover, ad, photo, or card signed by the entire band: $150-$250*

*High-end reflects vintage signed memorabilia

Individual:

Bono Vox (Paul Hewson): $45-$60
The Edge (David Evans): $40-$55
Adam Clayton: $30-$40
Larry Mullen: $30-$40
Autographed letter handwritten signature- Bono: $350-$500
Watercolor painting - Bono: $1,250-$2,500

TOUR BOOKS/PROGRAMS/PASSES

Tour Books:

1983 Japan: $75
ZOO TV (Japan), 1993:$35
ZOO TV (North America), 1992:$15
ZOO TV, 1993 (New Zooland, Japan, Zoomerang): $18
ZOO TV, U.S., Outside Broadcast, 1992: $16

Programs:

The Unforgettable Fire - U.S. Tour, 1986: $25-$30
The Joshua Tree - Spring Tour: $20

Backstage Passes:

The Joshua Tree: Cloth $15-$18, Laminated $35-$40
Lovetown Tour: Cloth $12-$15, Laminated $30-$35
ZOO Tours: Cloth $10-$12, Laminated $25-$30
POP Tour: Cloth $8-$10, Laminated $20-$25

The Joshua Tree tour program (© U2)

An often counterfeited U2 Zoo-TV pass

POSTERS/PRESS KITS

Posters:

Numerous promotional posters have been issued for both recordings and tours. Most range in price from $12 (stock posters) to $50 (tough to find tour posters). For example: Achtung Baby - European stock poster (24" x 34") - $12; Achtung Baby- European promotional poster for video (23" x 33") - $25; Zooropa - Rare Withdrawn tour poster, has group photo and includes all tour dates, (40" x 60"), only 400 assumed made - $50; *Rattle & Hum* - Movie one-sheet (22" x 34") - $25-$30

Press Kits:

Rattle and Hum, 1988: $30-$35
Achtung Baby, 1991: $25-$30
Zooropa, 1993: $15-$20
POP, 1997: $20

USED CLOTHING/EQUIPMENT

Guitar Picks:

Bono Vox: $150-$200
The Edge: $150
Adam Clayton: $100-$125

Drum Stick:

Larry Mullen Jr.: $30-$45
A complete set of stage equipment used by U2 in the recording studio (circa *Rattle and Hum*) sold in 1989 for more than $15,000, and is now estimated at $23,000-$25,000.

OFTEN OVERLOOKED MEMORABILIA

Set of five buttons sold on Unforgettable Fire Tour - $10; Unforgettable Fire enamel pin - $3; Rock 'n' Roll Comics Pt. 1 - $3; Promoter issued Joshua Tree embroidered hooded top - $100-$150; The Joshua Tree numbered limited edition (9,800) art print - $100-$125; War promo button-down long sleeve shirt - $90-$100; War white and red promo flag - $20; Achtung Baby condoms $3-$6; Achtung Baby funny money dollar bills - $3-$5; "I'D LIKE TO PURCHASE 10,000 PIZZAS" ("ACHTUNG BABY TOUR") T-shirts - $15-$20; Zoo Ecu funny money bill - $3; U2 Pop set of promo items: (balloon, pens, sticker, flyer, counter display & cube- $35; *Joshua Tree* envelope - $25; *War* promo baseball cap- $25; U2 Pop Special, double CD Rom includes video clips, photography & program info plus CD Rom for Stephen King's *Shining* - $200;

POP set of promotional items (balloons, pins, sticker, flyers, counter display, and cube) - $35; ZOO TV inflatable car - $150; Staring at the Sky promo kaleidoscope in box (U.K. only) - $80; The Joshua Tree Island promo sports bag, 1987, includes The Talkie cassette, sampler cassette, and a program; Rattle and Hum Island promo briefcase, 1988, includes album, cassette, and CD (only 250 made); The Fly, Island promotional fly swatter, 1991; Mysterious Ways, Island (French), promo single, picture CD with jigsaw puzzle, 1994; Rattle and Hum, Island (Spain), promotional pack that includes poster, biography, sticker, etc., 1988

REFERENCES/BOOKS

Numerous resources exist, but none do justice to the group in my opinion. There are no dedicated collector books

---

Vai, Steve

Born: June 6, 1960

With a well established image as a "guitarist for hire," Vai has worked with Frank Zappa, David Lee Roth, and Whitesnake. He was fortunate as a youth to have Joe Satriani as both a neighbor and guitar teacher. The lessons obviously worked, because by the age of 18 Vai was playing riffs in Zappa's band. Vai collectors will want to pick up anything associated with his debut album *Flex-Able* (Akashic, 1984).

His appearance with Alcatrazz was brief in 1985. He soon moved on to David Lee Roth's band in 1986 where he spent a comfortable three years. Vai also was a member of Whitesnake long enough to put out *Slip of the Tongue* (1989). Solo releases followed with *Passion and Warfare* (#18, 1990) and *Sex & Religion* (#48, 1993).

AUTOGRAPHS

A CD, LP, magazine cover, ad, photo, or card signed: $10-$20

TOUR BOOKS/PROGRAMS/PASSES

Programs:
Japanese Tour 1994: $25
Backstage Passes:
Cloth: $8-$15; Laminated: $15-$20

POSTERS/PRESS KITS

Numerous promotional posters have been issued for both recordings and tours. Most range in price from $5 (stick poster) to $10 (concert poster)
Press Kits: $10

USED CLOTHING/ EQUIPMENT

Guitar Picks: $10-$20*
*I have seen earlier picks go for as high as $75 (from the early Zappa days)

OFTEN OVERLOOKED MEMORABILIA

Associated memorabilia from his Zappa days, "Passion & Warfare" giant life-size display (autographed) $75

A Steve Vai guitar pick

Valens, Ritchie

(Richard Valenzuela)
Born: May 13, 1941, Died: February 3, 1959

Valens was one of the first successful Latin rockers to appear on the scene in the late '50s. His first band was the Silhouettes, a Mexican band that played around the San Fernando Valley area of California. In May 1958 he stepped into Gold Star Studios to record "Come On, Let's Go" for the Hollywood, CA-based Del-Fi label. In August he asked to appear on Dick Clark's *American Bandstand* to sing the song which entered the Top Fifty. During the same month he began his first U.S. tour. Following the tour he returned to California to record "Donna/La Bamba" (#2/#22, 1959). In December 1958 he was recorded during a concert he gave at his old school and even appeared briefly in Alan Freed's movie *Go, Johnny, Go*. Following his second appearance on *American Bandstand*, he began a ten-day run at New York's Lowe's State Theater with his friend Eddie Cochran, Bo Diddley, and the Everly Brothers.

In January 1959 he recorded a few tracks for an album before joining a package tour called The Winter Dance Party. On February 3, 1959, following a show in Clear Lake, IA, he boarded a plane chartered by Buddy Holly. On the

Concert poster for a show featuring, among others, Ritchie Valens. This 14" x 22" poster is valued at $2,000. From the collection of Hank Thompson.

way to the next stop on the tour—Moorhead, MN—the plane crashed, killing all aboard. He is buried in San Fernando Mission Cemetery.

A resurgence in Valens' work was sparked by the 1987 Taylor Hackford motion picture *La Bamba*. In the picture actor Lou Diamond Phillips portrayed Valens, while Chicano rockers Los Lobos made a cameo appearance singing an updated version of the title.

AUTOGRAPHS

An LP, magazine cover, ad, photo, or card signed: $450-$750*

*The low-end range would be simply a signed piece of paper

An autographed high school yearbook: $2,500-$3,000

USED CLOTHING/EQUIPMENT

Valens built his own solid-body guitar, which he used before he could finally afford a Fender Stratocaster.

OFTEN OVERLOOKED MEMORABILIA

Any Pacoima Junior High School memorabilia; *La Bamba* movie memorabilia; a one-sheet - $3-$6; autographs of Donna Ludwig ("Donna" subject) and Bob Keane (producer), 1960 high school yearbook- $500

Van der Graaf Generator/Peter Hammill

Formed 1967

Peter Hammill, Born: November 5, 1948; Hugh Banton; Chris Smith; Keith Ellis; and Guy Evans*

*Smith left in 1968. Ellis departed in 1969 and Nic Potter and David Jackson joined the band. Potter left in 1971 but returned in 1978. Graham Smith was also added in 1978.

Van der Graaf Generator split and reconciled more times than Liz Taylor and Richard Burton, and typically with the same personnel. Forever distinguished as one of the few art rock groups not to make it, it did manage to create a cult following in America, despite only playing one U.S. concert.

The group came together while at Manchester University in 1967. Founded by Chris Judge, the group's name came from a device that actually created electricity. Judge left the band before it could create any of its own, though. Hammill and other members came together once again to release the debut album *The Aerosol Grey Machine*, followed by personnel shifts, then *The Least We Can Do Is Wave* (1969).

H to He Who Am the Only One (1970) saw Robert Fripp sit in, and it was followed by *Pawn Hearts* (1971) before the band once again split. Hammill then aggressively pursued his solo career, however, it too was met with little response. The band reformed in 1975 for *Godbluff, Still Life, World Record* (1976), *The Quiet Zone* (1977), and *Vital/Live* (1978) before dissolving once again.

Hammill continued to record but is viewed as more of a cult phenomenon than anything else.

AUTOGRAPHS

Group:

A CD, LP, magazine cover, ad, photo, or card signed by the artist: $15-$25

Individual:

Pete Hammill: $10-$15

Vandross, Luther

Born: April 20, 1951

Luther Vandross, born into an extremely talented family of musicians, was quickly inspired at an early age to pursue a career in music. While still attending William Howard Taft High School in the Bronx, he assembled a group with his friends which became Listen My Brother, a musical theatre workshop at the Apollo Theatre. The group broke up in the early '70s, and the members went their separate ways.

In 1974, former bandmate Carlos Alomar, now working with David Bowie, invited both Vandross and Robin Clark to Philadelphia for the recording of "Young Americans." Impressed with the two, Bowie invited Vandross to provide a greater contribution including backing vocals and arranging. Vandross would also join the established Bowie on tour as the opening act. Through Bowie, Vandross then contributed vocals to Bette Midler's *Songs for the New Depression* (1975), and through producer Arif Mardin, he was added to numerous recording sessions.

Cotillion records then signed Vandross in 1976. As the leader of the group Luther, Vandross released *Luther*, which included singles "It's Good for the Soul" (#28, R&B, 1976) and "Funky Music (It's a Part of Me)" (#34, R&B, 1976), followed by the second album, *This Close to You*. When the latter failed to generate any interest, the group was dropped from the label. Without a recording contract he worked on jingles and contributed to a number of key projects before the end of the decade.

In 1980, Vandross emerged as the lead singer of Change, which released *The Glow of Love* (1980), containing the two hits "Searchin'" and "The Glow of Love," before he decided to embark on a solo career. In 1981, now under the Epic label, he released *Never Too Much* (#19, 1981) with the self-titles cut reaching into the Top Forty. *Forever, for Always, for Love* (#20, 1982) was his successful second album; it eventually sold platinum. He then followed with albums *Busy Body* (#32, 1983) and *The Night I Fell in Love* (#19, 1985), which contained the hit "'Til My Baby Comes Home" (#29, 1985).

As single "Stop to Love" (#15, 1987) peaked, Vandross was nominated, but failed to win a Grammy Award. His next album release was *Any Love* (#9, 1988). The title track fell just short of the Top Forty.

"She Won't Talk to Me" (#30, 1989) climbed the chart and was his last Top Forty hit of the decade.

The artist began the new decade with *The Best of Luther Vandross, The Best of Love* (#26, 1990), his first album chart entry, while single "Here and Now" (#6, 1990) became his first Top Ten U.S. hit. The following year he released *Power of Love* (#7, 1991), and its title cut landed in the Top Five on the singles chart, followed by "Don't Want to Be a Fool" (#9, 1991).

Never Let Me Go (#6, 1993) was followed by *Songs* (#5, 1994), which contained the hit single "Endless Love" (#2, 1994). The following year started with "Always and Forever" (#18, 1995) climbing the singles chart on both sides of the ocean, and ended with *This Is Christmas* (#28, 1995), a seasonal collection that included seven original compositions.

Vandross has received numerous awards during his career—far too many to list here. He is an outstanding talent to collect because of his diversity. There is little doubt that his contributions to music will continue, as will his extraordinary commitment to numerous humanitarian efforts.

AUTOGRAPHS

A CD, LP, magazine cover, ad, photo, or card signed by the artist: $15-$30

TOUR BOOKS/PROGRAMS/PASSES

Tour Books: Never Let Me Go Tour, 1993-1994: $10

POSTERS/PRESS KITS

Promotional Posters: $10-$25

Press Kits: $15-$20

OFTEN OVERLOOKED MEMORABILIA

The very first episode of *Sesame Street* included Vandross; movie memorabilia from *The Wiz* (1975) (Vandross contributed "Everybody Rejoice (A Brand New Day)"), *Bustin' Loose* (1981) (Vandross penned "You Stopped Lovin' Me"), *Ruthless People* (1986) (included "Give Me the Reason" (#57, 1986)), and *Mo' Money* (#10, 1992) (duetted with Janet Jackson); a copy of the Kodak promotional campaign using the Vandross' song "Everybody Rejoice (A Brand New Day)"; copies of jingles he participates in including those for AT&T, Burger King, Kentucky Fried Chicken, Pepsi-Cola, Seven-UP, the US Army, and Miller Beer (c.1977); a videotape of his performances on *Saturday Night Live* - NBC-TV (2/20/82), the very first *The Arsenio Hall Show* (1/3/89) (Vandross sang) and the 7/30/91episode devoted to Patti La Belle, *Out All Night* (9/26/92), "Gala for the President" (10/30/94) (actual date; Vandross took part), *Late Night With David Letterman* (11/28/94), and *The Tonight Show* (12/14/95); Power of Love cap - $20

REFERENCES/BOOKS

Limited resources exist. There are no dedicated collector books. Serious collectors should opt for a Fan Club: The Luther Vandross Official International Fan Club, P.O. Box 679, Branford, CT 06405 ($22 fee)

Vangelis

(Evangalos Papathanassiou)
Born: March 29, 1943

Evangalos Papathanassiou was a music prodigy as a youth. He attended the Academy of Fine Arts in Athens, Greece, before joining the group Formynx in the early '60s. He then teamed up with Demis Roussos and Lucas Sideras as Aphrodite's Child, before he moved to France. There the band signed a recording contract and scored a few European hits before splitting in 1972.

Vangelis, having released both *The Dragon* and *Hypothesis* in 1971, released *L'Apocalypse Des Animaux* in 1972, before he signed with Vertigo Records and moved to Britain in 1974. There he released *Earth* before signing on with RCA Records the following year. Vangelis' *Heaven and Hell* (#31, U.K., 1976) would be his first successful solo UK charting effort. *Albedo 0.39* (#18, U.K., 1976) was followed by *Spiral* (1977) and *Beauborg* (1978), before he released *China*, on Polydor Records (1979). In 1980 he teamed up with Yes-vocalist Jon Anderson to record *Short Stories* (#125, 1980), and later that year he released the solo album *See You Later*.

His breakthrough year was 1981 when Vangelis composed the soundtrack album *Chariots of Fire* (#1, 1982). The extracted title theme became his first hit single (#12, U.K., 1981). The following month his music from *Heaven and Hell* and *Third Movement* were used in Carl Sagan's BBC1-TV series Cosmos; the series' soundtrack climbed the charts (#48, U.K., 1981). Additionally, Vangelis and Anderson's follow-up album *The Friends of Mr. Cairo* (#64, 1981) made an impressive showing. Extract "I'll Find My Way Back Home" (#51, 1982) landed on the singles chart. The duo then released *Private Collection* (#148, 1983) before the compilation *The Best of Jon and Vangelis* (#42, U.K., 1984) hit the charts.

Soil Activities (#55, U.K., 1984), *Mask* (#69, 1985), and *Rhapsodies* (1985) soon followed. *Opera Sauvage* (#19, 1987), recorded nearly a decade before, charted in the U.S., primarily driven by the use of two songs in beer commercials. *Direct*, his first offering on Arista, was released in 1988 and was followed by the Polydor soundtrack compilation *Themes* (#11, U.K., 1989).

Vangelis then reunited with Anderson for *Page of Life* (1991), followed by the charity album *Polar Shift: A Benefit for Antarctica* (1991) and *Voices* (#58, U.K., 1996). *Portrait (So Long Ago, So Clear)* (#14, U.K., 1996) was released during the third week of April 1996.

AUTOGRAPHS

A CD, LP, magazine cover, ad, photo, or card signed by the artist: $30-$50

POSTERS/PRESS KITS
Promotional Posters: $10-$35
Press Kits:$10-$40
*High-end here for Chariots of Fire memorabilia.

OFTEN OVERLOOKED MEMORABILIA
Movie memorabilia from *Chariots of Fire* (1981), *Mask* (1985), *Blade Runner* (1982), *Missing* (1982), *The Bounty* (1984), *City* (1989), *1492—Conquest of Paradise* (#33, U.K., 1992), *Bitter Moon* (1994); associated items from the television series *Cosmos*; copies of the three (believed to be) Jacques Cousteau documentaries that included his music; memorabilia from his Royal Albert Hall appearance in March 1976 (he seldom is seen in public)

Van Halen/David Lee Roth

Formed 1974

David Lee Roth, Born: October 10, 1955; Edward Van Halen, Born: January 26, 1955; Alex Van Halen, Born: May 8, 1953; and Michael Anthony, Born: June 20, 1955*

*Roth departed in 1985 and was replaced by Sammy Hagar. Hagar left in 1996 and Roth returns very briefly before moving on.

By 1975 Van Halen was known as one of the loudest hard rock bands in L.A. The Van Halen brothers had recruited vocalist David Lee Roth for their band Mammoth in 1974, and played together for awhile before adding Snake bassist Michael Anthony to the band. The group's live reputation, made up primarily of heavy rock covers, landed the group numerous op-

Van Halen. Photo by F. Scott Schafer. Courtesy Warner Bros. Records Inc.

portunities to open for well-established acts. In 1976 Kiss bassist Gene Simmons, who was overwhelmed after seeing Van Halen, agreed to produce a demo tape for the band. Although the tape was rejected by every major label, the group's songwriting continued, as did the live performances. In 1977, while playing at the Starwood Club, Eddie Van Halen's guitar prowess and Roth's flamboyance attracted Warner Brothers Records' producer Ted Templeman. It was Templeman who saw to it that the band was signed to a record contract and produced the band's debut work.

The band's debut *Van Halen* (#19, 1978), which sold two million copies during the year, was the group's lowest charting album of its career to date. The first album spun off two singles, "Runnin' With The Devil" (#84) and a cover of the Kinks smash "You Really Got Me" (#36), which was eventually used by Nissan in a popular 1996 car commercial. Fans who could look beyond Roth's swashbuckling stage antics were soon impressed with Eddie Van Halen's mastery of the guitar. His hand-built guitars, with their custom-finished bodies, soon became one of his hallmarks. His thundering riffs and tapping harmonics were idolized and mimicked by virtually every would-be rocker.

The group embarked on its first U.S. tour on March 3, 1978, followed by a U.K. tour in support of Black Sabbath. The group entered the studio in the Spring of 1979 and finished recording its next album, *Van Halen II* (#6), in less than one week. On April 8, 1979, Van Halen, in support of the new album, pack up more than 20 tons of equipment for a ten-month world tour. Two singles were taken off *Van Halen II*: "Dance the Night Away" (#15, 1979) and "Beautiful Girls" (#84). *Women and Children First* (#6), released in 1980, was once again supported by an extensive tour. During an Italian TV special in June, Roth's versatility found him breaking his nose when he was introduced to some low hanging stage lights while lunging into one of his now infamous flying squirrel leaps.

Fair Warning was released in Spring 1981, following Eddie Van Halen's marriage to actress Valerie Bertinelli. A cover of Roy Orbison's "(Oh) Pretty Woman" topped the U.K. charts and almost climbed into the Top Ten in America. *Diver Down* (#3, 1982) was released the following year and was supported by the Hide Your Sheep tour that began at the U.S. Festival on September 3 although few farmers were comfortable, some did attend. In 1983 the band toured South America and was paid $1 million to perform once at the second U.S. Festival. As a favor to Michael Jackson, Eddie contributed a solo during "Beat It" (#1). The year ended with a bang as Van Halen released *1984* (#2, 1984) on New Year's Eve.

Memorabilia buffs will want to grab anything associated with the album's promotion in the U.K.—the album and its related items were banned in many

outlets due to the baby-smoking cover shot. The album spun off a Number One single with "Jump," while "Panama" (#13) and "I'll Wait" (#13) also dove into the Top Twenty. Van Halen collectors will want to pick up memorabilia associated with the group's U.K. release of "All I Need Is Everything" (the B-side includes a version of "Jump" by Aztec Camera). Also worth exploring are items related to Roth's presidency in the Jungle Studs club.

Overwhelmed by the interest in his babe-busting "California Girls" (#3, 1985) video—at least that's what some think—Roth officially departed from the band on April Fools Day in 1985. The following year the band recruited red rocker Sammy Hagar, formerly with Montrose and now a successful solo act, to take Roth's place. Hagar's presence added a new dimension to the band, because he also played guitar. *5150* —an NYPD term for the criminally insane— was released in 1986 and topped the charts. It yielded the singles "Why Can't This Be Love" (#3), "Dreams" (#22), and "Love Walks In" (#22). Hagar made his live debut with the band on the Third Annual MTV Music Awards, but his tour debut didn't come until March 27, 1987, in Shreveport, LA.

Meanwhile, Roth hit the Top Twenty with his Jolson medley of "Just a Gigolo/"I Ain't Got Nobody." He also covered Sinatra's "That's Life" from his mini-album *Eat 'Em and Smile*. Roth also took his solo act on the road with a talented backing band that included Steve Vai, Billy Sheehan, and Gregg Bissonette. Roth's "Yankee Rose" (#16) hit the Top Twenty. *Skyscrapper* (#6), Roth's third solo effort, was released in 1988.

Hagar, while a member of Van Halen, never abandoned his solo career. His "Winner Takes All" (#54) from Sylvester Stallone's movie *Over the Top* was well received. His "Give to Live" (#23) came from his self-titled solo album, while his work in Van Halen continued to draw more attention to his earlier projects.

OU812 (#1, 1988) included the hit singles "Black and Blue"(#34), "When It's Love" (#5), "Finish What You Started (#13), and "Fells So Good" (#35). The band began an aggressive album support tour in the Fall of 1988 that includes some 45-dates. Van Halen collectors will also want items the first World Music Invitational Pro/Am celebrity golf tournament at Stonebridge Ranch in Dallas, TX, because both Eddie and Michael participated. Can you say Van Halen "round-used golf tees, balls, and ball markers?" Why Not?

Speaking of unique Van Halen collectibles, how about a cocktail napkin from the Cabo Wabo Cantina restaurant and bar in Cabo San Lucas, Mexico. The group purchased the business and even played opening night there on April 21, 1990.

With *For Unlawful Carnal Knowledge* (#1, 1991), Van Halen became the first act to hit Number One with three consecutive studio albums since Madon-

na. The record included "Top of the World" (#27, 1991) and "Right Now" (#55, 1992), which was eventually used in a Pepsi television commercial. *Right Here, Right Now* (#5), a double-live release, hit stores during the Spring of 1993. The first leg of the group's support tour opened on March 30, 1993, in Munich, Germany, followed by its first U.K. tour in almost ten years.

Balance (#1) was released in the Spring of 1995, and was followed by a major U.S. tour beginning in Pensacola, FL, on March 11. The album included the singles "Can't Stop Lovin' You" (#30) and "Not Enough" (#97). In May 1996 the band contributed "Humans Being" to the soundtrack of the movie *Twister*. Another typhoon struck in June of 1996, as the band announced the departure of Sammy Hagar and a subsequent search for a new lead singer began. Speculation erupted when Roth was invited to work with the band on two contributions, "Can't Get This Stuff No More" and "Me Wise Magic," for the *Van Halen Best of Volume I* released in October. Publicly the feud continued because both Van Halen brothers assaulted Hagar for his work ethic and Roth for making fun of Eddie Van Halen's hip. Word is that Gary Cherone of Extreme will be the band's third lead singer, but even he knows that there are *III Sides To Every Story*. As for Roth, when "A Little Ain't Enough," lived up to its name, he fired his band and headed to New York, where he ponders his destiny.

AUTOGRAPHS

Van Halen is one of the few groups you still might be able to get an autographed photograph from a mail request. The group is elusive, yet compliant with in-person autograph requests. Individually, Sammy Hagar has been the most compliant to autograph requests.

Group:
A CD, LP, magazine cover, ad, photo, or card signed by the entire band: $150-$200*
* High-end reflects vintage signed memorabilia

Individual:
David Lee Roth: $30-$40
Edward Van Halen: $30-$45
Alex Van Halen: $25-$30
Michael Anthony: $20-$30
Sammy Hagar: $30-$40
Gary Cherone: $10-$20
Autographed Kramer electric guitar, not concert-used: $1,500-$2,000

Eddie Van Halen's signature.

TOUR BOOKS/ PROGRAMS/PASSES

Programs:
5150 Tour, 1986: $18-$20
OU812 Tour: $18-$20
David Lee Roth programs: $15-$20

Backstage Passes:
Cloth: $8-$15;
Laminated: $15-$20
1979 World Tour - Access All Areas (cloth): $15;
1982-1983 Tour - Backstage (cloth): $10

OU812 tour program (© Van Halen)

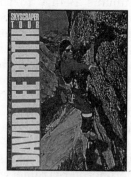

A David Lee Roth tour program (Diamond Dave Merchandising)

A common Van Halen backstage pass from 1981

A later backstage pass example that is often counterfeited

POSTERS/PRESS KITS

Numerous promotional posters have been issued for both recordings and tours. Most range in price from $10- $40
Examples: Balance (20" x 30") - $10; German Concert Poster - Hamburg, 1993 (23" x 33") - $20
Press Kits: $15-$40
Example: Right Here, Right Now - $25, Van Halen I, 1978 - $40

USED CLOTHING/EQUIPMENT

Guitar Picks*:
Edward Van Halen: $35-$200
Michael Anthony: $15-$40
Sammy Hagar: $25-$35
*Van Halen is another band notorious for its pick variation and unique quotations. Most of its picks utilize the "VH Logo" and tour name. Take your pick from a few of these examples: Eddie -

"Logo w/ring, Have A Nice Day/ Signature, See Ya Next Time," "Peavey, EVH Wolfgang/I Saw IT!"; Michael - "Mad Anthony's Cafe/ Kevin Expresso Dugan," "F***'n Mosh '93/ F***'n Mosh, Signature '93," "Face****'n Down In Cabo/Signature, Logo"; Sammy - "VH logo, Signature/ Gettin Off In Your Eye Live."
Drum Stick:
Alex Van Halen: $30-$45

Eddie Van Halen's hand-built Kramer Guitar, 1986, custom-finished body, Floyd Rose bridge with tremolo - $18,000-$20,000.

OFTEN OVERLOOKED MEMORABILIA

VH Logo - 3" promotional button for first album - $6-$8; Van Halen Comic Book - June 1990 - $3; Balance Tour Bomber Style Jacket - embroidered - $400; Van Halen stickers - $5; Black plastic 3x binoculars w /VH logo - $6-$7; 1979 Color Christmas Card - $20; OU812 Darwin's Age Ape + skull statue (price varies) - $150-$275; 1984 World Tour Promotional ring - $400; bag of M&M candies minus the brown ones - $3; a copy of the litigation papers filed by Linda Duke claiming "acoustic trauma" suffered during a Roth concert - $4; a menu from Cab Wabo Cantina restaurant and bar - $5-$10; copies of the legal papers filed by Van Halen against 2 Live Crew for the alleged use of a guitar riff - $10; David Lee Roth Eat' Em And Smile promotional clear glass plate, 1986; OU812 die-cut numbers - $18; OU812 keychain - $10; glowing ring on black handkerchief - $10 Warner Brothers 1984 promotional jacket - $195; life size "Eddie" (66") stand-up; Peavey promotional display, 1991 - $150; promotional postcards: 1978 - $5, 1979 - $.50 each; "Drink Milk" ad; set of 4 fan club photos - $15

REFERENCES/BOOKS

Numerous resources exist, but none do justice to the group in my opinion. There are no dedicated collector books. Serious collectors should opt for the publication *The Inside: The International Van Halen Magazine*, 784 N. 114 St., Suite 200, Omaha, Nebraska 68154

Vanilla Fudge

Formed 1966

Vince Martell, Born: November 11, 1945; Mark Stein; Tim Bogert; and Carmine Appice, Born: December 15, 1946

Bogert and Stein formed a group, the Pigeons, and Martell joined as guitarist and Appice replaced the original drummer. The group signed to Atlantic Records which renamed the band Vanilla Fudge. It became one of the first East Coast bands to join the growing California psychedelic rock movement.

On July 22, 1967, Vanilla Fudge made its New York debut at the Village Theater (Fillmore East) with the Byrds and the Seeds, while the group's debut single, the Supremes' cover "You Keep Me Hangin' On" (#67, 1967, #6, 1968), moved up the charts. In the fall the group released its debut album *Vanilla Fudge* (#6, 1967), and like many albums of this genre, it included long, drawn-out cover versions of well-known songs.

The Beat Goes On (#17, 1968), a concept record, tried to compress a quarter century of music into twelve minutes of playing time— a bit ambitious for a sophomore effort. It was followed by *Renaissance* (#20, 1968), with extracts "Take for a Little While" (#38, 1968) and "Season of the Witch" (#65, 1968).

The following year the group released *Near the Beginning* (#16, 1969), a half studio, half live album, that included the single "Shotgun" (#68, 1969). *Rock and Roll* (#34, 1969) followed, and soon internal problems caused the band to split up. Bogert and Appice move on to Cactus before both hooked up with Jeff Beck. Stein formed his own band before working with Alice Cooper and Tommy Bolin, while Martell slowly drifted out of the business. The band did eventually re-form and even recorded another album, *Mystery*, in 1984.

AUTOGRAPHS

A CD, LP, magazine cover, ad, photo, or card signed by the group: $50-$75

USED CLOTHING/EQUIPMENT

Guitar Pick:
Vince Martell: $10-$20
Tim Bogert: $10-$20
Drum Stick:
Carmen Appice: $15-$20

Van Ronk, David

Born: June 30, 1936

Van Ronk is acknowledged as a key conributor to the New York early '60s folk-rock boom, although his deep blues and jazz roots never bore the anticipated fruits. Though commercial success avoided him, he was a recognized performer, teacher, and scholar.

He grew up in a musical family and, while attending high school in Brooklyn, found it hard to avoid his growing interest in traditional jazz. He performed in jazz groups, took a stint in the merchant marines, but landed back in the city during the mid-50s. He began performing on the folk circuit, playing at festivals, and collaborating on a recording or two. He even performed at the 1964 Newport Folk Festival, and later formed the Ragtime Jug Stompers.

During this time he was a close friend of Bob Dylan and even occasionally appeared with him. He even turned down an opportunity to join the band that later became Peter, Paul and Mary. He tried acting, before returning to the comfort of touring. A gifted song interpreter, he has performed around the world and taught guitar.

AUTOGRAPHS

A CD, LP, magazine cover, ad, photo, or card signed by the artist: $10-$20

OFTEN OVERLOOKED MEMORABILIA

A copy of the set *Fingerpicking Folk, Blues, and Ragtime Guitar* (6 tapes)

Van Zandt, Little Steven

Born: November 22, 1950

The garden state guitarist Van Zandt was raised in Middletown, New Jersey. The Source was his first band in 1966, before moving on to Steel Mill and Southside Johnny's Asbury Jukes, followed then by Bruce Springsteen's E Street Band. Often linked with Springsteen as his powerful guitarist during the height of Brucemania, he also is a good songwriter and an excellent producer, the latter of which he executed for the first three Jukes albums.

He formed Little Steven and the Disciples of Soul, a 12-piece band, in 1982. They released *Men Without Women*, which was warmly received and followed it with the politically tainted *Voice of America* (1984). The same year he made two visits to South Africa that so deeply moved him that he gathered fifty performers to form Artists Against Apartheid. The group recorded Van Zandt's "Sun City," which eventually grew into an album.

His protest albums continued (*Freedom—No Compromise* (1987) and *Revolution* (1989)) and although the message was sincere and succinct, sales were not. He since has slipped back to the producer role, which he has been very comfortable and fruitful with.

AUTOGRAPHS

A CD, LP, magazine cover, ad, photo, or card signed by the artist: $15-$20

POSTERS/PRESS KITS

Promotional Posters: $10
Press Kits: $10

USED CLOTHING/EQUIPMENT

Guitar Pick: $15-$25

Van Zandt, Townes

(John Townes Van Zandt)
Born: March 7, 1944

Van Zandt, the J.D. Salinger of the folk world, began playing guitar at the early age of 15, influenced like so many other youths by the swivel-hipped Elvis Presley. He soon began playing Texas saloons, and quickly earned a reputation for being sharp witted, a bit crazy, and a keeper of the almighty drink songbook. He developed a cult following that was introspective in nature, likening him more as a Leonard Cohen than a Bill Monroe.

In 1967 he headed to Nashville and released an album a year until 1974 for the small and poorly distributed Poppy/Tomato label. He then moved on to Austin, Texas, where artists who were covering his songs were beginning to gain him some exposure. His penned "Poncho and Lefty" was covered by Emmylou Harris (1977) and turned into a major country hit in the early 1980s by Merle Haggard and Willie Nelson. Others soon followed as Van Zandt covers became as common as armadillos in Texas.

In 1986 he returned to Nashville to record *At My Window*, his first album of new material in eight years. He hooked up with Canada's Cowboy Junkies and toured with them in 1990 and even contributed a few songs to their *Black Eyed Man* (1992) release.

AUTOGRAPHS

A CD, LP, magazine cover, ad, photo, or card signed by the artist: $20-$60

USED CLOTHING/EQUIPMENT

Guitar Pick: $45-$75

Vaughan, Stevie Ray

Born: October 3, 1954, Died: August 27, 1990

At the age of 14, Stevie Ray was already playing local blues clubs in Dallas in bands such as Blackbird, the Shantones, and the Epileptic Marshmallow. Both he and his older brother Jimmie, who later helped form the Fabulous Thunderbirds, were heavily influenced by the work of such blues greats as B.B., Freddie, and Albert King, along with Lonnie Mack (Vaughan later produced his comeback album *Strike Like Lightning* in 1985). After dropping out of high school in 1972, Vaughan decided to relocate to Austin where his brother was living. The Austin "blues scene" was happening at that time and everyone including the Vaughans knew it was the place to be.

Vaughan first formed the Nightcrawlers, followed by the Cobras, then Triple Threat, which lasted for three years, until he and vocalist Lou Ann Barton formed Double Trouble. Barton, who had solo ambitions, left Double Trouble and Vaughan restructured the group. Double Trouble was then a powerful trio that included Vaughan, Chris Layton on drums, and bassist Tommy Shannon (formerly with Johnny Winter).

The three toured extensively around the Texas club circuit, where they developed a strong following based upon their sheer energy level and the blues guitar prowess of Vaughan. While they played at the Montreux Jazz Festival in Montreux, Switzerland— the first time an unsigned and unrecorded did so— they caught the eye of Epic Records talent scout John Hammond. Hammond took care of the circumstance and signed the band, which released the debut album *Texas Flood* (#38) in July of 1983.

The band's non-stop touring helped promote the successful sales of the first album (ultimately reaching 1,000,000 copies). The year 1984 saw a couple of unsuccessful Grammy Award nominations and the release of the album *Couldn't Stand the Weather* (#31). The album included a now classic cover version of the Hendrix classic "Voodoo Chile (Slight Return)." In 1985 the band added keyboardist Reese Wynans to augment its style a bit. Also that year Vaughan become the first white performer to win the prestigious W.C. Handy Blues Foundation's Blues Entertainer of the Year and he shared a Grammy Award for Best Traditional Blues Recording for his contribution of "Flood Down in Texas" on Atlantic Records' *Blues Explosion*.

On February 15, 1986, Double Trouble even performed on *Saturday Night Live* (NBC-TV). During the year, the group toured extensively, which took a toll on Vaughan and enhanced his ongoing drug and alcohol problem. A series of incidents found him entering a treatment center in Atlanta in September 1986—an event later commemorated in his song "Wall of Denial" (1989).

The group's double-live release *Live Alive* (#52) hit stores early in 1987 and included the Grammy nominated track "Say What." During the year Vaughan made a rare film appearance in *Back to the Beach*, trading guitar licks with fame surf-guitar jockey Dick Dale. In 1989 Vaughan stepped into the studio for the first time in four years to record *In Step* (#33). On October 25 the band went on tour in support of the album with Jeff Beck. On February 21, 1990, *In Step* won a Grammy for Best Contemporary Blues Recording. The band began its Power and the Passion Tour on June 8 with Joe Cocker in Mountain View, CA. The group also attended and played at the Benson & Hedges Blues '90 Festival in Dallas on June 18.

In July 1990, Vaughan completed his forthcoming album *Family Style* (#7, 1990). On it, he played with his brother Jimmie and even allowed him to contribute a rare vocal track. The album later earned the two numerous awards including a pair of Grammys.

Following a concert at the Alpine Valley Music Theatre in East Troy, WI, on August 27, 1990, Stevie Ray Vaughan was killed when the Bell 206 helicopter in which he was traveling crashed. Also killed were three members of Eric Clapton's entourage, along with the pilot. His memorial service was held on August 31, 1990, at the Laurel Land Memorial Park in Oak Cliff, Dallas, Texas.

AUTOGRAPHS

Stevie Ray Vaughan was very obliging to autograph requests and very fond of his fans. He typically inscribed "Soul to Soul" above his extremely flamboyant signature. Characteristic of an authentic signature is large capitalization—the "S" in Stevie was typically the largest letter in his name—a single-stroke unique formation to the "t" in Stevie, and very rounded flamboyant strokes.

His hotel pseudonyms were: Mr. Tone, Lee Melone, I.B. Clean, and Iza Newman

A CD, LP, magazine cover, ad, photo, or card signed $450-$550*
* High-end reflects vintage signed memorabilia

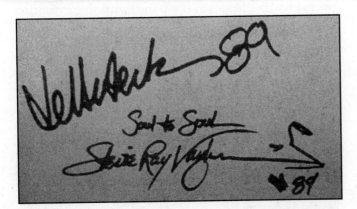

Paper signed by Stevie Ray Vaughan and Jeff Beck (Beck's autograph is valued at $25 to $60) in 1989.

TOUR BOOKS/PROGRAMS/PASSES

Programs:
First Tour of Australia (1984): $20-$35

Backstage Passes:
Cloth: $12-$15;
Laminated: $15-$25
*Popular with pass collectors is the "Stevie Ray Vaughan and Double Trouble" pass followed by "Jeff Beck with Terry Bozzio and Tony Hymas" pass—when you flip them over, the order is reversed ($20). The "Live Alive Tour" and "Soul-To-Soul" tour passes are nicely designed, and also very popular ($25).

Counterfeit backstage pass from Vaughan's Japan Tour '85

POSTERS/PRESS KITS

Early promotional posters from clubs like Antones, although getting increasingly difficult to find, are popular with Vaughan collectors. Expect to pay from $75-$200 for a club poster, depending upon the style, condition, and significance of the gig. Perhaps the most popular is the rare commemorative poster for his October Birthday celebration at Antones.
The Soap Creek Saloon was one of Vaughan's favorite gigs and its monthly calendars that include "Stevie Vaughn—Triple Threat Revue (also spelled Review) are collector's items, despite their obvious misspellings. ($25-$50)
Press Kits: $15-$50

USED CLOTHING/EQUIPMENT

Guitar Picks: $300-$375
Guitars used by Stevie Ray Vaughan include: 1959 Stratocaster ("Number One"), hollow yellow 1964 Stratocaster ("Lenny"), 1958 dot-neck 335 Gibson, and a National Duolian Stell-body acoustic. He also owned a '48 Airline, 1960 orange Strat, a 1957 Strat, a rare prototype Rickenbacker, a Cherryburst Hamilton Lurktame, and a Kay Barney Kessel model guitar.*

*Because he used large strings, his guitars were modified with bass frets to reduce wear.
In February 1992, Fender Musical Instruments introduced the Stevie Ray Vaughan Signature Series Stratocaster with a suggested retail price of $1,299.99.

OFTEN OVERLOOKED MEMORABILIA
The Austin Chronicle, June 1983 (Stevie on cover) - $5-$10; *Guitar Player* magazine, October 1984 (SRV's first cover) - $2-$5; his "Don't Mess With Texas" television public service announcements, "The Sky Is Crying"- promotional 2' guitar mobile- $20

REFERENCES/BOOKS
Numerous resources exist. *Stevie Ray, Soul to Soul* by Keri Leigh is a MUST for fans! There are no dedicated collector books. Serious collectors should opt for a Fan Club: Stevie Ray Vaughan Fan Club, Attention: Lee Hopkins, P.O. Box 800353, Dallas, TX 75380 ($8 fee)

Vee, Bobby

(Robert Velline)
Born: April 30, 1943

Early-60s teen idol, whose band the Shadows filled in for Buddy Holly following the singer's tragic death—which led to its first successful single "Suzie Baby" (#77, 1959)—Vee was groomed for solo stardom and achieved it with his hits "Take Good Care of My Baby" (#1, 1961), "Run to Him" (#2, 1961), "Punish Her" (#20, 1962), "The Night Has a Thousand Eyes" (#8, 1963), "Charms" (#13, 1963), and "Come Back When You Grow Up"(#3, 1972).

AUTOGRAPHS
A CD, LP, magazine cover, ad, photo, or card signed by the artist: $5-$20

OFTEN OVERLOOKED MEMORABILIA
Videotapes of his numerous television appearances

Vega, Suzanne

Born: July 11, 1959

As a young child growing up in Spanish Harlem, Vega fell in love with both music and dance. She studied at the High School of Performing Arts, and by age 16, she was playing the Greenwich Village scene. She went on to attend Barnard College where she studied literature. In 1983, while working as a temporary receptionist, she met Ron Fierstein and Steve Addabbo, who were starting their own music promotion company. The trio decided to pool their efforts and work together, which resulted in an A&M Records contract.

In 1985, the critically praised *Suzanne Vega* (#11, U.K., 1985) established her as a cult favorite. *Soli-*

tude Standing (#11, 1987), her breakthrough album, contained the extracted hit single "Luka" (#3, 1987). She was quickly hailed as a member of the new female folk movement that was taking place.

Days of Open Hand (#50, 1990) was not as well received and contained no hit singles. When funk rhythm track "Tom's Diner," a song from Solitude, found its way into the market via bootleg, A&M and Vega capitalized on its success and rode it up the charts. No doubt influenced by the new dance craze, Vega released 99.9F. (#86, 1992), a different and unexpected twist for the artist, which was welcomed with only a warm reception. Having contributed to numerous projects during the nineties, she adds songs to the soundtracks Dead Man Walking and The Truth About Cats and Dogs, before the release of her album Nine Objects Of Desire.

AUTOGRAPHS
A CD, LP, magazine cover, ad, photo, or card signed by the artist: $10-$15

POSTERS/PRESS KITS
Promotional Posters: $5-$10
Press Kits: $7-$10

USED CLOTHING/EQUIPMENT
Guitar Pick: $10-$20

OFTEN OVERLOOKED MEMORABILIA
Movie memorabilia from Pretty in Pink (1986); memorabilia surrounding her contributions to other musicians' albums

Velvet Underground

Formed 1965
Lou Reed (Louis Firbank), Born: March 2, 1942; John Cale, Born: March 9, 1942; Nico (Christa Paffgen), Born: October 16, 1938, Died: July 18, 1988; Sterling Morrison; and Maureen "Moe" Tucker*

*Nico departed in 1967. Cale left in 1968 and Doug Yule was added on bass. Tucker and Reed left in 1970 and Billy Yule and Walter Powers joined the band. Morrison left in 1971 and Willie Alexander was added. Group disbanded in 1972. Group re-formed in 1993: Cale, Reed, Morrison, and Tucker. Morrison died on August 30, 1995.

Reed met the well-schooled musician John Cale at a party, and the two decided to form a band. Reed recruited Sterling Morrison, whom he met while studying creative writing at Syracuse University, while Cale hooked his neighbor Angus MacLise. Whenever and wherever possible they played, often under a variety of names including the Primitives, which actually recorded a few singles for Pickwick Records. MacLise, deep in thought, chose the name the Velvet Underground from a pornographic paperback.

The bulk of 1965 was spent refining skills and recording demos at Cales' apartment (56 Ludlow

Street, NY, NY). They hook up with pop artist and soup can painter Andy Warhol, who following a gig at Greenwich Village's Cafe Bizzare, decided to become their manager. It was pop disciple Warhol who decided that Nico (Christa Paffgen), who sang at a local lounge, should join the band. Although perplexed by the decision, the band, with the exception of MacLise, welcomed her. MacLise instead opted to head to Nepal, where he died of malnutrition fourteen years later. Maureen Tucker replaced him in the band. On November 11, 1965, the band played its first gig at a high school dance in Summit, New Jersey.

In 1966, the Velvet Underground continued its residency at the Cafe Bizzare, which was now becoming more of an eclectic gig, because cult followers began to emerge from various New York enclaves. In 1967, now signed to MGM's Verve label, the group released the debut The Velvet Underground and Nico (#171, 1967). The avant-garde Warhol created a distinctive peelable banana that was featured on the sleeve. The album highlighted the apocalyptic lyrics of Reed combined with the mystic gothic vocal style of Nico. Classic cuts like "Heroin" and "Venus in Furs" are now revered, as is the album, however, at the time of the record's release, little attention was paid to it. Following the release Reed assumed control of the band when Nico left and Warhol's services came to an end.

White Light, White Heat (#199, 1968) was released amongst tension in the band that eventually led to Cale's departure. Without Warhol's name, and his knack for publicity, it didn't take long for the band to fade from public attention. Bassist Doug Yule replaced Cale. The Velvet Underground (1969) followed, as Atlantic Records inked the band to a contract. The band returned to New York in June 1970 to begin a month residency at Max's Kansas City club and to rekindle interest in the band, much of what was lost with the softer-sounding last release. During this period Loaded was released, and included the classics "Sweet Jane" and "Rock and Roll." The band then toured the East Coast under various personnel changes.

On August 23, 1970, Lou Reed played his last gig with the band at Max's and then headed home to Long Island, where he worked in his father's office as a typist. In 1971, Squeeze was released only in the U.K., and for all intents and purposes, only included Yule. He did manage to keep the name, however, until 1973. In 1972, Atlantic released Live at Max's Kansas City, taken from a low-grade cassette recording of a fan, and in 1974, 1969 Live was released by Mercury.

Because a new wave of followers began covering the group's music, the Velvet Underground generated more interest a decade after its existence. In 1989 Cale and Reed did several performances of a song cycle they composed in memory of Andy Warhol, who

died in 1988. The songs were contained on the 1990 *Songs for Drella*. On June 15, 1990, the original group, minus Nico who died in an accident in 1988, performed together for the first time since 1969, while attending a Warhol retrospective at Jouy en Joas, outside of Paris, France.

In 1991, the original Velvets also recorded together on Maureen Tucker's *I Spent a Week There the Other Night*. The group then re-formed to perform live in Europe and released *Live MCMXCIII* (#180, 1993), but soon after, they split once again. The band made attempts to re-form, and occasionally did minus a member, like at the Andy Warhol Museum in Pittsburgh on November 18, 1994.

On January 17, 1996, the Velvet Underground was inducted into the Rock and Roll Hall of Fame and sang a new composition, "Last Night I Said Goodbye to My Friend," written for Morrison who died a few months earlier.

AUTOGRAPHS

A CD, LP, magazine cover, ad, photo, or card signed by the group: $200-$450*
*Original lineup

OFTEN OVERLOOKED MEMORABILIA

Movie memorabilia from *Hedy the Shoplifter* (1966); Loop, magazine box set, 1966, the disc comes with 12 pop art paintings, writings by Lou Reed, a newspaper, and other goodies

REFERENCES/BOOKS

Numerous resources exist. Serious collectors and fans should purchase *The Velvet Underground Handbook* by M.C. Kostek and *Nico: The Life & Lies of an Icon* by Richard Witts

The Ventures

Formed 1959

Bob Bogle, Born: January 16, 1937; Don Wilson, Born: February 10, 1937; Nokie Edwards, Born: May 9, 1939; and Howie Johnston*

* Johnston left in 1961 and Mel Taylor was added. Edwards left in 1967 and Jerry McGee joined the band. Johnny Durrill was added on keyboards in 1969. McGee left in 1970 and Edwards rejoined band. Edwards left again in 1985.

Often thought of as a surf-rock band, the Ventures actually pre-dated that wave and lasted much longer. This instrumental guitar-based combo scored hits with "Walk Don't Run," "Ghost Riders in the Sky," "Perifia," "Lullaby of the Leaves," "Diamond Head," "2,000 Pound Bee," "Lonely Bull," "I Walk the Line" and the theme to the television show *Hawaii Five-O* (#4, 1981)

AUTOGRAPHS

A CD, LP, magazine cover, ad, photo, or card signed by the group: $20-$45

The Village People

Formed 1977

Victor Willis, David Hodo, Felipe Rose, Randy Jones, Glenn Hughes, and Alex Briley*

*Willis left in 1979 and Ray Simpson was added. Simpson left in 1982. Numerous personnel changes in the band from 1982.

The group was conceived and formed by Jacques Morali, a French producer who, after seeing young men dressed in costumes at a New York disco, decided to bring the idea to reality. He started by recruiting Rose, then Willis, followed by Hodo, Jones, Hughes, and Briley to form the Village People. Morali signed the group to Casablanca Records in the U.S. and Mercury/Phonogram for the rest of the world. Their debut album *Village People* (#54, 1977) included the group's first disco hit "San Francisco (You've Got Me) (#45, U.K., 1977).

Macho Man (#24, 1978) was the group's sophomore effort and contained the hit title cut, which reached Number Twenty-five on the U.S. singles chart. *Crusin'* (#3, 1979), their third album, contained the smash hit "Y.M.C.A." (#3, 1979). *Go West* (#8, 1979) quickly followed and scored a big hit with extracted single "In the Navy" (#3, 1979), however, the title cut, which was also released as a single, only went as high as Number Forty-five on the U.S. charts. Their final album of the year was *Live and Sleazy* (#32, 1979), which was both a live and studio release. During this time, Willis left and was replaced by Ray Simpson.

Can't Stop the Music (#47, 1980), a soundtrack album for the film by the same name, was released as the Village People had a chance to see themselves in the movie. The group then moved to RCA Records, and in a bold move, tried to change its image with *Renaissance* (#138, 1981), however, the concept failed.

In 1982, Simpson left and was replaced by Miles Jaye. As the disco fad began to fade away, the group's commercial music appeal left, but the band, which underwent numerous personnel changes, continued to be a strong live act for the rest of the decade. The group still resurfaces occasionally when music covers or imagery evoke its past success. Remember, it Takes a Village, People!

AUTOGRAPHS

A CD, LP, magazine cover, ad, photo, or card signed by the group: $20-$50*
*Original lineup

TOUR BOOKS/PROGRAMS/PASSES

Tour Books:

Village People on Tour, Spring 1979- $35

Backstage Passes:

Cloth: $5-$8; Laminated: $8-$10 (1980-Present)
Cloth: $10-$15; Laminated: $15-$25 (1977-79)

POSTERS/PRESS KITS

Promotional Posters:

Casablanca: $10-$35
RCA: $5-$15

Press Kits:

Casablanca: $15-$50
RCA: $8-$15

OFTEN OVERLOOKED MEMORABILIA

Movie memorabilia from *Thank God It's Friday* (1978) and *Can't Stop the Music* (1980); jigsaw puzzle (APC) - $50; View-Master (GAF) - $12; buttons - $3-$7; bumper stickers - $6-$10

Vincent, Gene

(Eugene Vincent Craddock)
Born: February 11, 1935, Died: October 12, 1971

At a time when every label was on the lookout for another Elvis Presley, Vincent entered Capitol Records' "Elvis Soundalike Sweepstakes" and was signed to the company. In May 1956, Ken Nelson of Capitol Records arranged a recording session for Vincent, who recorded with a backup band now known as the Blue Caps. In June, "Woman Love/Be-Bop-A-Lula" was released and by July 28, 1956, the group was performing on NBC-TV's *Perry Como Show*. The first week of August saw "Be-Bop-A-Lula" (#7, 1956) rise into the Top Ten on the U.S. singles chart, creating a strong demand for live performances by Vincent.

A poster for a Gene Vincent Manhattan, KS, show from Sept. 26, 1958. This poster is one of only three U.S. Vincent posters known (all three are different). It is valued at $2,000. From the collection of Hank Thompson.

Blue Jean Bop (#16, 1956), Vincent's debut album, was his only chart entry. "Race with the Devil" (#96, 1956) and "Blue Jean Bop" (#49, 1956) climbed the chart as the band headed to Holly-wood to film a slot in an upcoming movie. By the end of the year, the Blue Caps had lost Willie Williams and Cliff Gallup (numerous personnel changes followed).

In 1957 Vincent went to the hospital for treatment to his injured leg—caused by a 1955 Navy motorcycle accident. He was fitted with a metal brace, and the Blue Caps resumed touring. As "Lotta Lovin'"/"Wear My Ring" (#13, 1957) climbed the U.S. singles chart, the group joined Eddie Cochran and Little Richard for a tour of Australia.

"Dance to the Bop" (#23, 1958) climbed the chart after being featured live on *The Ed Sullivan Show*. The group then took on a torrid touring and production pace, that ended up wearing down the musicians and taking a toll on Vincent. With no big hits in over a year, and small live fees, Vincent relinquishes the band in mid-tour because he couldn't pay them. The Blue Caps split, and Vincent, now without a union card, headed northwest to play in impromptu bands.

In June 1959, with guitarist Jerry Merritt, Vincent and his new band toured Japan, where they were met with open arms. After that time, Vincent headed to L.A. to record "Crazy Times," which failed commercially. Vincent then went to Europe, where despite the lack of recent hits, he was still very popular. During this time he also agreed to appear on the U.K. TV rock show *Boy Meets Girl*.

In 1960, buddy Eddie Cochran flew to the U.K. to join Vincent on tour, and both even made television appearances together. On April 17, 1960, the car taking Vincent and Cochran to the London Airport at the end of their current U.K. tour crashed, killing Cochran. Vincent, who suffered numerous serious injuries, managed to survive, although he was emotionally scarred forever by the death of his closest professional friend. Later that year, backed by a different band, he cut "Pistol Packin' Mama" (#15, U.K., 1960) before returning to the U.S.

"She She Little Sheila" (#22, U.K., 1961) and "I'm Going Home" (#36, U.K., 1961) became his last two major U.K. singles. Although he continued to record and tour, often to rave reviews, it was clear that his time had passed. The lack of success marred his personal life, causing him to miss gigs, drink heavily, and lose his fourth wife. On September 12, 1970, he died in a California hospital from a bleeding ulcer at the age of 36.

AUTOGRAPHS

An LP, magazine cover, ad, photo, or card signed by the artist: $200-$350

OFTEN OVERLOOKED MEMORABILIA

Movie memorabilia from *The Girl Can't Help It* (1956) and *Hot Rod Gang* (U.S.)/*Fury Unleashed* (U.K.) (1958); a copy of the 1969 BBC-TV documentary *The Rock 'n' Roll Singer*; memorabilia from many individual tribute recordings

REFERENCES/BOOKS

A few resources exist. *Gene Vincent: A Discography* by Derek Henderson is a MUST read

****

"On The Edge"

Violent Femmes

Collectors can begin and end with *Violent Femmes* (Slash/Warner Bros., 1983), now an artifact of the 1980s, you can pass it down to your children's children who won't have the foggiest idea what to do with it.

Promotional posters, obviously ineffective, can be picked up for around $10. Example: Add It Up, band's silhouettes, (18" x 24") - $10. Pre-1990 concert posters run about $15-$20, while post 1990 can be picked up for $10-$15.

****

Vixen

Formed 1980

Janet Gardner, Jan Kuehnemund, Share Pedersen, and Roxy Petrucci

Vixen is best known as the all-female group that worked with the 1980s "hair bands," i.e. Bon Jovi/Warrant. The band was founded by drummer Roxy Petrucci in the early '80s. The group hit the club circuit strong, and even endured after numerous personnel changes.

Vixen (#41, 1988), the group's debut offering, featured the hit extracts "Cryin'" (#22, 1989) and "Edge of a Broken Heart" (#26, 1988). The follow-up *Rev It Up* (#52, 1990) also scored with the single "How Much Love" (#44, 1990).

Guitar pick from Vixen

When EMI dropped the band, the members disappeared from public, although bassist Share Pederson reappears periodically.

AUTOGRAPHS

A CD, LP, magazine cover, ad, photo, or card signed by the group: $20-$25

USED CLOTHING/EQUIPMENT

Guitar Pick: $5

Wailer, Bunny

(Neville O'Reilly Livingstone)
Born: April 10, 1947

Forever known now as the last surviving member of the original Wailers, Bunny Livingstone actually left the band before the band ever toured the U.S. Although he loved the band, he deplored traveling, and it wasn't until 1986 that he kicked off a large U.S. and European tour. Trademark Bunny Wailer tunes include "Let Him Go," "Who Feels It," "Pass It On," and "Jail House."

Before quitting the Wailers he tried his luck at a solo career, using his own Solomonic label, for releases such as "Life Line," "Bide Up," and " Arab Oil Weapon." Following his departure from the Wailers, he retired from music until 1976. *Blackheart Man* (1976, Island) marked his return to music, and even included the services of his former bandmates. He followed with *Protest* (1977) and *Struggle* (1979). Both were rougher edged than expected and, as such, were less well received.

Bunny Wailer Sings the Wailers (1980) brought him back to basics and received higher regard by critics than its predecessors. By 1981 it was clear that he was back, because he scored Jamaican hits with "Ballroom Floor," "Galong So," and "Collie Man." The following year "Cool Runnings" and "Rock and Groove" continued his success.

In 1990 his tribute to bandmate Bob Marley, *Time Will Tell*, won a Grammy for Best Raggae recording, a feat he repeated in 1994 with *Crucial!*.

AUTOGRAPHS

A CD, LP, magazine cover, ad, photo, or card signed by the artist: $30-$100*

*Wailers related item

OFTEN OVERLOOKED MEMORABILIA

Movie memorabilia from *Jazz Odyssey* (1972)

Wainwright III, Loudon

Born: September 5, 1946

Having grown up on both coasts, Wainwright attended St. Andrews school in Delaware, where he developed an interest in folk music. He then attended Carnegie Mellon Institute and studied drama, before eventually dropping out. Wainwright then began playing the club and college circuit and developed his witty stage presence. *Album I* (1970), appropriately titled, was his debut album on Atlantic Records.

His first two efforts went relatively unnoticed, because his satirical approach to his trade was not yet acceptable. With *Album III* (1972) he toned down his image, but improved his slapstick approach, best exemplified in his Top Twenty single "Dead Skunk." *Attempted Mustache* (1973) followed with little accolades, but by *Unrequited* (1975) it was clear he had headed down a better path. For his next two offerings, *T Shirt* (1976) and *Final Exam* (1978), he was backed by a five-piece rock band named Slow Train, giving him a more distinctive sound.

During the '80s, Wainwright primarily concentrated on his acting ability, which included a variety of media. He moved to the U.K. and teamed with Richard Thompson for *I'm Alright* (1985). He didn't really surface again until 1994 when he contributed "Man Who Couldn't Cry" to the Johnny Cash album *American Recordings*.

AUTOGRAPHS
A CD, LP, magazine cover, ad, photo, or card signed by the artist: $10-$15

USED CLOTHING/EQUIPMENT
Guitar Pick: $10-$12

OFTEN OVERLOOKED MEMORABILIA
A Broadway playbill from *Pump Boys and Dinettes* (1982) - $10; copies of *M.A.S.H.* television episodes he appeared in; movie memorabilia from *The Slugger's Wife* (1985) and *Jacknife* (1989); television episodes of the BBC series *The Jasper Carrott Show*

Waits, Tom

Born: December 7, 1949

After dropping out of high school, Waits sang and played professionally in his late teens and early twenties. Like many teenagers of the era, he grew fascinated with the beat scene, in particular poet Jack Kerouac. Successfully covering the Southern California bar circuit—by living in his car—his rock and blues sound soon developed a solid cult following, leading to many support opportunities for much bigger acts.

In 1972, Waits signed to Elecktra/Asylum to work with ex-Lovin' Spoonful and now producer Jerry Yester on his debut *Closing Time* (1973). When it was met with little success, he went out on tour in 1973, even surviving opening a number of nights for Frank Zappa and the Mothers. *The Heart of Saturday Night* (1974), his sophomore release, also failed to generate any interest, but during the same year the Eagles covered his composition "Ol' 55."

In 1975, in an attempt to get something started, he expanded his touring. The result was a much better reaction to his third album *Nighthawks at the Diner* (#164, 1975). The touring/release recipe continued with albums *Small Change* (#89, 1976), *Foreign Affairs* (#113, 1977), and *Blue Valentine* (#181, 1978), the latter of which included a picture of Rickie Lee Jones on the back cover, whom he had been romantically linked with—all met with modest commercial appeal.

The next decade saw him concentrate on both his acting and musical contributions to the world of film. From playing a honky-tonk pianist, to singing Academy Award nominated soundtrack tunes, Waits found a new home. Up until *Heartattack and Vine* (#96, 1980), music had taken a backseat to celluloid. *Swordfishtrombones* (#167, 1983) was an eclectic mix of bizarre instrumentation that lent itself more to Captain Beefheart than to Waits. It was followed by *Rain Dogs* (1985), which was similar in sound and met with similar success.

Franks Wild Years was a diversion into a musical play written with the woman he would marry, playwright Kathleen Brennan. The album *Bone Machine* (1992) won a Grammy Award for Best Alternative Music in 1992—his first. He next dips his hand into theater, along with cohorts Robert Wise and William Burroughs, to produce a short lived theatrical opera, " The Black River," which is based on her album of the same name.

Known more as a song writer than a singer, Rod Stewart took his "Downtown Train" straight up the charts. Now widely covered by a variety of musicians, Waits seems satisfied to occasionally kick out an album in between his numerous movie and theater projects. Anyway you look at his legacy, his songwriting will always shine brightly. Like many of music's key contributors, he was often ahead of his time.

AUTOGRAPHS
A CD, LP, magazine cover, ad, photo, or card signed by the artist: $20-$30

POSTERS/PRESS KITS
Promotional Posters: $10-$25
Press Kits: $15-$25

USED CLOTHING/EQUIPMENT
Guitar Pick: $15-$35

OFFEN OVERLOOKED MEMORABILIA

Movie memorabilia from *Paradise Alley* (1979), *On the Nickel* (1980), *Night on Earth* (1992), *One from the Heart* (1982), *12 Monkeys* and *Dead Man Walking* (1996) and movie memorabilia from his acting contributions in *Rumble Fish*, *The Cotton Club*, *The Outsiders*, *Bram Stoker's Dracula*, *Down by Law*, *Ironweed*, *Short Cuts*, and *Smoke* (1995); a copy of the Seattle documentary *Streetwise* (1985); memorabilia from his self-produced documentary *Big Time* (1988)

REFERENCES/BOOKS

Limited resources exist. *Small Change: A life of Tom Waits* by Patrick Humphries is a MUST for fans! There are no dedicated collector books.

Waldman, Wendy

Born c. 1951

Waldman was one of many female would-be pop singers to emerge out of the plethora of musicians staking claim on the West Coast. She began performing in L.A. as a teenager, and in 1969, landed with Karla Bonoff and Andrew Gold to form the folk-rock unit Bryndle. The group split a year later, but the friendship endured, and all members chose alternative music routes.

Love Has Got Me (1973) was the artist's debut album. The method of contributing material to other artists' albums found Waldman, Linda Ronstadt, Emmylou Harris, and Maria Muldaur exchanging songs like recipes over the years that followed. Although she continued to release some quality albums, she was having difficulty breaking out on her own.

The Nitty Gritty Dirt Band struck gold with her "Fishin' in the Dark " (#1, C&W, 1987) while Waldman continued to write for other musicians including Rita Coolidge, Kenny Rogers, and Johnny Mathis. Waldman scored a big hit by penning "Save the Best for Last," the 1993 hit for Vanessa Williams. She also produced the singer's album, "The Comfort Zone"— which extracted the single, in a recording niche where she was becoming increasingly comfortable. She managed to reunite with Bryndle in 1995, which released a self-titled album.

AUTOGRAPHS

A CD, LP, magazine cover, ad, photo, or card signed by the artist: $10-$15

OFTEN OVERLOOKED MEMORABILIA

Her collaborations, and contributions, with and to other artists

The Walker Brothers

Formed 1964

John Maus, Born: November 12, 1943; Scott Engel, Born: January 9, 1944; and Gary Leeds, Born: September 3, 1944*

*Numerous personnel changes

Better known in the U.K., where the members were teen sensations, than the States, the Walker Brothers are best remembered for the singles "Make It Easy on Yourself" (1965) and "The Sun Ain't Gonna Shine (Anymore)." They later scored a hit with "No Regrets" (1975) before fading from the music scene.

AUTOGRAPHS

A CD, LP, magazine cover, ad, photo, or card signed by the group: $15-$20

Walker, Jerry Jeff

(Ronald Clyde Crosby)
Born: March 16, 1942

Another "cosmic cowboy" and former member of Circus Maximus ("The Wind"), Jerry Jeff Walker is commonly associated with his penned classic "Mr. Bojangles."

AUTOGRAPHS

A CD, LP, magazine cover, ad, photo, or card signed by the artist: $5-$20

OFTEN OVERLOOKED MEMORABILIA

Videotapes of the television program *The Texas Connection* (TNN), which Walker hosts

Walker, Jr. and the All Stars

Formed 1961

Jr. Walker (Autry Waliker), Vic Thomas, Willie Woods, and James Graves

A gifted musician, with his trademark sandpaper voice, Jr. Walker and his All Stars landed numerous classic upbeat hits including "Shotgun" (#4, 1965), "Do the Boomerang" (#10, R&B, 1965), "Shake and Fingerpop" (#7, R&B, 1965), "How Sweet It Is (to Be Loved By You)" (#18, 1967), "I'm a Road Runner" (#20, 1966), "Pucker Up Buttercup" (#3, 1967), and "Come See About Me" (#24, 1967).

The group had hits with softer numbers including "What Does It Take (to Win Your Love)" (#4, 1969), "These Eyes" (#16, 1969), "Gotta Hold on to This Feeling" (#21, 1970), "Do You See My Love (for You Growing)" (#32, 1970), and "Walk in the Night" (#46, 1972)

The eighties found Jr. Walker less active, although he contributed a memorable sax solo on Foreigner's single "Urgent" in 1981 and released the album Blow The House Down in 1983. The artist succumbed to cancer and died on November 23, 1995.

AUTOGRAPHS

A CD, LP, magazine cover, ad, photo, or card signed by the group: $20-$45

Walker, T-Bone

(Aaron Walker)
Born: May 28, 1910 Died: March 16, 1975

Aaron Thibeaux Walker moved to Dallas, TX, at an early age, where he became interested in music through the influence of the church and his stepfather. He acquired his nickname early in his life, a derivative of sorts from "T-bow" which was short for Thibeaux. By the time he was in his teens he had already played around town accompanying his stepfather at soft drink stands. His abilities soon landed him with the legendary Blind Lemon Jefferson, one of the pivotal bluesman of the 1920s.

Both Jefferson and Walker stuck together until late in 1923, when Walker was getting itchy for a change. He toured Texas with Dr. Breeding's Big B Tonic road show, followed by a stint with singer Ida Cox's road show (1925). He returned to Dallas in 1929 and began recording as Oak Cliff T-Bone, before heading back out on the road. Walker then landed on the West Coast in 1934, got married, and hooked up with a variety of talents that kept him busy in the decade that followed. He picked up the notion of playing the primitive early models of electric guitars in the mid-30s. Walker used a sprung-rhythm, single-string lead style that he had picked up from Blind Lemon Jefferson's acoustic playing.

By the early '40s, he was already quite proficient at his new found craft, and was evolving the technique with each passing year. "Call It Stormy Monday" (1943) was one of his biggest hits, and now considered a classic.

He spent the better part of the next two decades touring and recording with a variety of groups. He became a staple at many jazz and blues festivals throughout the world, including both Monterey and Montreaux. Walker also picked a Grammy for Best Ethnic/Traditional Recording in 1972, with Good Feelin'.

AUTOGRAPHS

A CD, LP, magazine cover, ad, or photo signed by the artist: $100-$150
Signature only: $30-$40

OFTEN OVERLOOKED MEMORABILIA

Movie memorabilia from Jazz Odyssey (1972)

Walsh, Joe

Born: November 20, 1947

Walsh, who at an early age learned clarinet and guitar, was raised in New Jersey and played in bands such as the G-Clefs and the Nomads, before he headed west to attend classes at Kent State University. While there he played in the popular campus band the Measles and when it split, he had an opportunity to join the Cleveland, Ohio, based band the James Gang. In 1969 the group, comprised of Walsh, Tom Kriss (who was replaced the following year by Dale Peters), and Jim Fox, charted with Yer' Album (#83, 1969).

In a big break, the James Gang, which had opened up for the Who the previous year (1969), was asked to join the band on its European tour. In September 1970, single "Funk #49" (#59, 1970) peaked as the group's album The James Gang Rides Again (#20, 1970) sold a gold. Thirds (#51, 1971) earned another gold disc, and single "Walk Away" (#51, 1971) nearly broke into the Top Fifty. In fall of 1971, The James Gang Live in Concert (#24, 1971) was warmly welcomed on the album charts, although "Midnight Man" (#80, 1971) failed to make any real significant damage on the singles chart.

In January 1972, Walsh quit the James Gang and headed west to the mountains and fresh air of Boulder, CO. There he entered Caribou Studios and churned out Barnstorm (#79, 1972), backed by Kenny Passarelli and Joe Vitale. He later added keyboardist Rocke Grace to support him on a major U.S. tour supporting Stephen Stills.

Nineteen Seventy-three started out with The Best of the James Gang Featuring Joe Walsh (#79, 1973), which climbed up the album charts, and Walsh heading even further west to L.A. In June he released The Smoker You Drink, The Player You Get (#6, 1973), which included the hit single "Rocky Mountain Way" (#23, 1973). The popular live number was very reminiscent of the James Gang sound only with a clever "talk box" added. By the end of the year, however, Barnstorm, although publicly always viewed as a back-up band, split.

Walsh watched the single "Meadows" (#89, 1974) climb the chart, and he worked as a session musician and during his free time concentrated on his next solo release So What (#11, 1975). On December 20, 1975 he joined his friends as a member of the Eagles, replacing Bernie Leadon. The addition of Walsh to the Eagles added a more dynamic guitar range and crisper sound, immediately evident on songs such as "Hotel California."

In another wise move, Walsh, although a fully participating member of the Eagles, did not abandon his successful solo career, and released You Can't Argue

with a Sick Man (#20, 1976). Whether it was the creative environment, or the security blanket the Eagles provided Walsh, the recipe seemed to revitalize the artist who released *But Seriously, Folks...* (#8, 1978) with extracted single "Life's Been Good" (#12, 1978).

Walsh, who is prolific, talented, and very humorous, is often viewed as the "Buffalo Bill" of rock 'n' roll, simply taking life with a grain of salt—certainly evident by his album titles. With the Eagles inactive he released *There Goes the Neighborhood* (#20, 1981), which included the single "A Life of Illusion" (#34, 1981). It was followed by *You Bought It—You Name It* (#48, 1983), *The Confessor* (#65, 1985), and *Got Any Gum?* (#113, 1987), a succession of gradually less commercial albums.

Ordinary Average Guy (1991) was released amid a variety of projects Walsh was working on, from benefit concerts to session work. He later reunited with the Eagles for their succesful mid-90s tour.

AUTOGRAPHS

A CD, LP, magazine cover, ad, photo, or card signed by the artist: $40-$50

POSTERS/PRESS KITS

Promotional Posters:
(1972-1975): $15-$35
(1975-1981): $10-$25
(1981-Present): $8- $12

Press Kits:
(1972-1975): $15-$30
(1975-1981): $10-$15
(1981-Present): $10

USED CLOTHING/EQUIPMENT

Guitar Pick: $40-$50

OFTEN OVERLOOKED MEMORABILIA

Movie memorabilia from *Urban Cowboy* (1980); all items associated with the release of *The Simpsons Sing the Blues* (1990) (Walsh played guitar on "School Days"); a copy of "The Class of 1970" Cleveland television special featuring the reunited James Gang (1990)

REFERENCES/BOOKS

The Story of The Eagles, The Long Run, by Marc Shapiro

War

Formed 1969

Harold Brown, Born: March 17, 1946; Papa Dee Allen (Thomas Allen), Born: July 19, 1931, Died: August 30, 1988; B.B. Dickerson, Born: August 3, 1949; Leroy "Lonnie" Jordan, Born: November 21, 1948; Charles Miller, (1939-1980); Lee Oskar, Born: March 24, 1948; and Howard Scott, Born: March 15, 1946*

*Numerous personnel changes

A talented group of musicians, War's distinctive funk kept them on the charts throughout the '70s.

They had two distinctive phases, the first as Eric Burden and War (1969-1971), where they scored hits such as "Spill the Wine" (#3, 1970) and "They Can't Take Away Our Music" (#50, 1971), and the second more fruitful period without Burden that included hits such as "All Day Music" (#35, 1971), "Slippin' into Darkness" (#16, 1972), "The World Is a Ghetto" (#7, 1972), "The Cisco Kid" (#2, 1973), "Gypsy Man" (#8, 1973), "Me and Big Brother" (#15, 1973), "Low Rider" (#7, 1975), "Why Can't We Be Friends?" (#6, 1975), and "Summer" (#7, 1976). The group slipped following the departure of Dickerson in 1979. In 1980 Miller was the victim of a robbery, during which he was murdered. Personnel changes plagued the band during the '80s, a decade which also saw more tragedy for the band, as Allen later died while on stage performing in 1988.

AUTOGRAPHS

A CD, LP, magazine cover, ad, photo, or card signed by the group: $25-$75

POSTERS/PRESS KITS

Promotional Posters: $10-$45
Press Kits: $10-$50

OFTEN OVERLOOKED MEMORABILIA

Movie memorabilia from *Youngblood* (1978) and *The River Niger*

Ward, Billy and His Dominoes

Formed 1950

Billy Ward, Born: September 19, 1921; Clyde McPhatter (Clyde Ward), Born: November 15, 1931, Died: June 13, 1972; Charlie Ward; Joe Lamont; and Billy Brown*

*Numerous personnel changes. Members have included: James Van Loan; David McNeil; Jackie Wilson, Born: June 9, 1934, Died: January 21, 1984; Cliff Givens; Milton Merle; Eugene Mumford; and Monroe Powell

A pivotal '50s R&B vocal group, Billy Ward and the Dominoes are not only known for their songs, but also for their personnel, which included Clyde McPhatter, Jackie Wilson, and later Eugene Mumford.

With McPhatter the band scored three Top Ten R&B hits with "Do Something for Me" (#6, 1951), "I Am With You" (#8, 1951) and "Sixty-Minute Man" (#17, 1951), which is typically referred to as the first R&B record by a black group to make the pop charts. The following year the band also scored R&B hits with "Have Mercy Baby" (#1), "The Bells" (#3), "I'd Be Satisfied" (#8), and "These Foolish Things Remind Me of You" (#5), McPhatter's last single with the group before he departed and formed the Drifters.

Jackie Wilson then took over and sang lead on "Rags to Riches" (#2, R&B, 1953) and "St. Therese of the Roses" (#13, 1956), before going solo. Eugene Mumford then took over and delivered "Star Dust"

(#12, 1957), "Deep Purple" (#20, 1957), and their last charting record "Jennie Lee" (1960). Mumford also pursued a solo career at this point and later joined various groups including the Ink Spots.

Billy Ward and His Dominoes have secured their position in rock history and should collectors be fortune enough to find a piece of their memorabilia, they would be crazy to pass it by.

AUTOGRAPHS

An LP, magazine cover, ad, photo, or card signed by the band: $480-$1,200*

*Original band on vintage piece of memorabilia

Individual

Clyde McPhatter: $400-$1,000
Jackie Wilson: $20-$45

Warnes, Jennifer

Born: March 3, 1947

Warnes, billed as Jennifer Waren, made the first of many regular appearances on *The Smothers Brothers Comedy Hour* in November of 1968 (CBS-TV). Mason Williams, one of the show's writers, even invited her to duet with him on a song for his album *The Mason Williams Ear Show. I Can Remember Everything* and *See Me, Feel Me, Heal Me!* were her first two album releases appearing on Decca Records imprint Parrot. She soon became a veteran in the L.A. folk scene, noted most for her interpretations of the poems of Leonard Cohen.

In 1972 she signed with Reprise Records and released *Jennifer*, and despite all-star guest appearances, failed to garner any new attention. Unwavering, she signed with Arista Records in 1977 and released *Jennifer Warnes* (#43,1977), which included extracted hit singles "Right Time of the Night" (#6, 1977) and "I'm Dreaming" (#50, 1977).

Shot Through the Heart (#94, 1979), her next offering, included singles "I Know a Heartache When I See One" (#19, 1979), "Don't Make Me Over" (#67, 1980), and "When the Feeling Comes Around" (#45, 1980). *The Best of Jennifer Warnes* (#47, 1982), a retrospective, was released, but she longed to work on movie soundtracks. This passion later yielded her excellent results, including two Academy Awards and two Grammy Awards.

In 1987, newly signed to the Cypress label, she recorded the highly praised and successful album *Famous Blue Raincoat* (#72, 1987), which featured only Leonard Cohen songs. A key release, it sold more than a million copies worldwide. On November 28, 1987, she topped the U.S. chart with "(I've Had) The Time of My Life," a duet with Bill Medley.

For Our Children (#31, 1991), *Just Jennifer* (1992), and *The Hunter* (1992) followed with moderate sales success.

AUTOGRAPHS

A CD, LP, magazine cover, ad, photo, or card signed by the artist: $20

POSTERS/PRESS KITS

Promotional Posters: $10-$25*
*Academy and Grammy Award related
Press Kits: $10

OFTEN OVERLOOKED MEMORABILIA

A playbill from *Hair* (11/22/68) that opened with Warnes as Sheila - $20; movie memorabilia from *Norma Rae* (1980) ("It Goes Like It Goes"), *Ragtime* (1982) (One More Hour"), *An Officer and a Gentleman* (1982) ("Up Where We Belong" with Joe Cocker"), *All the Right Moves* (1983), *Blind Date* (1987) ("Simply Meant to Be"), and *Dirty Dancing* (1987) ("(I've Had) The Time of My Life")

Warrant

Formed 1984

Joey Allen, Jerry Dixon, Jani Lane, Steven Sweet, and Erik Turner

Turner teamed with Dixon to formed Warrant in L.A., first adding vocalist Adam Shore, who was replaced by Jani Lane and Steven Sweet, who had played together in Plain Jane. The last to be recruited, Joey Allen was a former bandmate of Turner in Rebellious Youth. Already fairly well-known individually, the group took little time to build a following. In 1988, they were signed to CBS/Columbia Records and released the album *Dirty Rotten Filthy Stinking Rich* (#10, 1989). The smash debut was driven by extracted singles "Down Boys" (#27, 1989), "Heaven" (#2, 1989), "Big Talk" (#93, 1989), and "Sometimes She Cries" (#20, 1990). Warrant then supported Mötley Crüe during a U.S. tour preaching their gospel through glamour anthems and sexual hooks that appealed to the " Lost Eighties" generation. Labeled everything from "glitz rock" to "glam rock," to simply just another "hair band," the group enjoyed success before controversy erupted over their next release.

Cherry Pie (#7, 1990), with its self-titled extracted single (#10, 1990), was harshly criticized for its overtly sexual connotations, which was enhanced by MTV's heavy rotation of the companion video. The band toured extensively in support of the record, drawing sellout crowds in many arenas. "I Saw Red" (#10, 1991), "Uncle Tom's Cabin" (#78, 1991), "Blind Faith" (#88, 1991), and "We Will Rock You" (#83, 1992) made up the band's last string of singles, and *Dog Eat Dog* (#25, 1992) was their last album.

By 1993, grunge was in and glitz and glam were out. The "hair bands," led by Warrant, eventually retired their blow dryers.

AUTOGRAPHS

A CD, LP, magazine cover, ad, photo, or card signed by the group: $30-$40*

*Original members

TOUR BOOKS/PROGRAMS/PASSES

Backstage Passes:

Cloth: $5-$8;
Laminated: $10-$15

POSTERS/PRESS KITS

Promotional Posters:
$8-$25
Press Kits: $10-$20

USED CLOTHING/EQUIPMENT

Guitar Picks:

Joey Allen: $5-$10
Jerry Dixon: $5
Jani Lane: $5
Erik Turner: $5-$20*
*Cherry Pie picks
**Look for some creative pick quotes such as "Pie Slice" or "Ultranaked Tour c-ya" and others!

Drum Stick:

Steven Sweet: $10

A guitar pick from Warrant

OFTEN OVERLOOKED MEMORABILIA

Movie memorabilia from the *Game of War* (1984) and *High Strung* (1991); promotional Cherry Pie golf ball - $25; promotional Cherry Pie hair spray (withdrawn)

Warwick, Dionne

(Marie Warwick)
Born: December 12, 1940

Successful '60s pop singer Dionne Warwick is best known for her interpretations of songs written by Burt Bacharach and Hal David, many of which she placed high on both the R&B and pop charts. "Don't Make Me Over" (#21, 1962) was the first of these songs for her, followed by "Anyone Who Had a Heart" (#8, 1963), "Walk On By" (#6, 1964), "Message to Michael" (#8, 1966), "I Say a Little Prayer" (#4, 1967), and "Alfie" (#18, 1967). She followed these with the "(Theme from) Valley of the Dolls" (#2, 1968) (not a Bacharach-David song), "Do You Know the Way to San Jose" (#10, 1968), "This Girl's in Love with You" (#7, 1969), and "I'll Never Fall in Love Again" (#6, 1970).

She scored ten more Top Forty songs before her 1971 move to Warner Brothers, which in retrospect depleted much of her career momentum. She did score with her 1974 "Then Came You" (#1) with the Spinners, but it seemed to be a confusing era for the artist. Warwick returned in 1979 with "I'll Never Love This Way Again" (#5) and "Deja VU" (#15) and later with "Heartbreaker" (#10, 1982).

During the '80s, she turned to duets, the biggest hits being "Love Power" (#12, 1987) with Jeffrey Osborne and "That's What Friends Are For" (#1, 1985) with Elton John, Stevie Wonder and Gladys Knight. She reunited with Bacharach and David again for "Sunny Weather Lover" off of her 1993 album *Friends Can Be Lovers*, which also included a duet with her cousin Whitney Houston, "Love Will Find a Way." She has since focused much of her interest on humanitarian causes and her numerous businesses.

AUTOGRAPHS

A CD, LP, magazine cover, ad, photo, or card signed by the artist: $10-$20

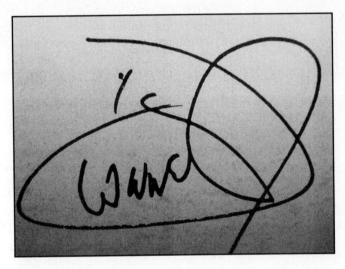

Dionne Warwick's signature

OFTEN OVERLOOKED MEMORABILIA

Pamphlets and brochures from her interior design firm; a bottle of her perfume Dionne; a bill from the Psychic Friends Network; movie memorabilia from *Valley of the Dolls*; artifacts from the musical *Promises, Promises*

REFERENCES/BOOKS

Limited resources exist. There are no dedicated collector books. Serious collectors should opt for a Fan Club: Dionne Warwick Fan Club, P. O. Box 343, Wind Gap, PA 18091

Washington, Dinah

(Ruth Jones)
Born: August 29, 1924, Died: December 14, 1963

A talented, versatile, and popular singer, Dinah Washington is often remembered for her rich, but raspy voice on R&B classic such as "Baby Get Lost" (#1, 1949), "Trouble in Mind" (#4, 1952), and "This Bitter Earth" (#1, 1960). She also sang with Lionel Hampton from 1943 to 1946, scored numerous other R&B hits, and helped refine the intricate New York blues sound.

Dinah Washington was inducted into the Rock and Roll Hall of Fame in 1993.

AUTOGRAPHS

An LP, magazine cover, ad, photo, or card signed by the artist: $125-$250

OFTEN OVERLOOKED MEMORABILIA

A sheet of her commemorative postage stamps (1993); her work with Lionel Hampton

Washington Jr., Grover

Born: December 12, 1943

A talented multi-instrumentalist whose jazz fusion melded with a pop structure defined his successful sound over the '70s and '80s, Grover Washington, Jr. landed first with his album *Mister Magic* (#1, 1975), the first of seven jazz chart toppers. Often associated with his *Winelight* hit extract "Just the Two of Us" (1980) featuring Bill Withers and his television theme songs, Washington also topped the chart in 1992 with *Next Exit*, which included the Grammy nominated song "Summer Chill" cowritten with his son.

AUTOGRAPHS

A CD, LP, magazine cover, ad, photo, or card signed by the artist: $10-$30

Was (Not Was)/Don Was

Formed 1981

Don Was (Donald Fagenson), Born: September 13, 1952; David Was (David Weiss), Born: October 26, 1952; Sweet Pea Atkinson; Sir Harry Bowens; and Donald Ray Mitchell

Don and David Was are students of popular music. Best known now for their production, they also gained moderate success with their eclectic albums *What Up, Dog?* (#43, 1988), which included the hit "Walk the Dinosaur" (#7, 1989), and *Are You Okay* (#99, 1990). Their noted production has included Bonnie Raitt's *Nick of Time* (1989) and her follow-up efforts, and works for Iggy Pop, David Crosby, Paula Abdul, Willie Nelson, Waylon Jennings, and Bob Dylan. While winning the 1994 Grammy for Producer of the Year certainly wasn't needed to enhance his demand, it was well deserved and long overdue.

AUTOGRAPHS

A CD, LP, magazine cover, ad, photo, or card signed by the artist: $20-$30

OFTEN OVERLOOKED MEMORABILIA

Associated artifacts from their production work

W.A.S.P.

Formed 1984

Blackie Lawless (Steve Duren), Born: September 4, 1954; Chris Holmes; Johnny Rod; Randy Piper; and Tony Richards*

*Richards departed in 1986 and Steve Riley was added. Riley left in 1987 and Glen Soderling joined the band. Soderling left in 1989 and Frank Banali and Ken Hensley were added. Numerous personnel changes followed.

Decadent and revolting, W.A.S.P. is best known as the band cited during the 1985 Senate Commerce Committee Hearings as the prime purveyor of indecency in rock and roll. Lawless' buzz-saw crotch photo was an instant collectible, as were the band's albums *The Last Command* and *The Headless Children*, both of which sold into the Top Fifty.

AUTOGRAPHS

A CD, LP, magazine cover, ad, photo, or card signed by the group: $20-$40*

*A provocative piece signed by the band

OFTEN OVERLOOKED MEMORABILIA

A copy of the 1985 Senate Commerce Committee Hearings

The Waterboys

Formed 1981

Mike Scott, Anthony Thistlethwaite, and Kevin Wilkinson*

*Karl Wallinger and Roddy Lorimer were added in 1983. Numerous personnel changes followed.

The foundation of the Waterboys is singer/songwriter Mike Scott, who has been the common denominator of this English group. The Waterboys as an entity, however, have been far from consistent, delving into brassy rhythms, Irish folk, and even pop rock. Their success, primarily in the U.K., has been attributed to Scott's shrewd lyrics that are almost always tainted with a bit of dynamic lure.

Growing up on the coast of Scotland, he started a music magazine called *Jungleland*, and began playing similar music. Following a stint at Edinburgh University, he moved to London, playing first in Another Pretty Face, followed by the Waterboys. At that time he was fortunate enough to recruit the talented Anthony Thistlethwaite, who along with Scott, handled most of the instruments on their debut *The Waterboys* (1983). They were then joined by keyboardist Karl Wallinger for their next two releases, *A Pagan Place* (#100, U.K., 1984) and *This Is the Sea* (#37, U.K., 1985), which yielding the hit single "The Whole of the Moon" (#26, U.K., 1985; #3, U.K., 1991). It was during this period that the media coined their sound "big music." Wallinger then left to start World

Party, while Scott headed briefly to Ireland mainly to develop a more traditional sound, before moving to London.

Fisherman's Blues (#13, U.K., 1988) and *Room to Roam* (#5, U.K., 1990) gave Scott the sound he was looking for, however, by this time it was now the electric guitar that he most sought. Leaving his Irish bandmates behind, he headed to New York, recruited a batch of session musicians, and released *Dream Harder* (#5, U.K., 1993). When he failed to recruit new band members, he left New York. He eventually relocated in London and signed a record deal with Chrysalis and released *Bring 'Em All In* (#23, U.K., 1995).

AUTOGRAPHS

Group:
A CD, LP, magazine cover, ad, photo, or card signed by the group: $20-$45*
*Lineup that includes Wallinger

Individual
Mike Scott: $10-$15

TOUR BOOKS/PROGRAMS/PASSES

Backstage Passes:
Cloth: $10; Laminated: $10-$20

POSTERS/PRESS KITS

Promotional Posters: $10-$20
Press Kits: $10-$25

USED CLOTHING/EQUIPMENT

Guitar Picks: $10-$15

OFTEN OVERLOOKED MEMORABILIA

A videotape from their television debut on BBC2-TV's *The Old Grey Whistle Test* (5/83); a videotape from the TV documentary *Bringing It All Back Home* (1991)

Waters, Muddy

(McKinley Morganfield)
Born: April 4, 1915, Died: April 30, 1983

Given his nickname while being raised on the Mississippi Delta, Muddy Waters took up the harmonica at the age of eight before moving on to the guitar in his teens. Influenced by the music of Robert Johnson and Son House, he recorded his first two songs, "I Be's Troubled" and "Country Blues," in 1941 for a now classic folk/blues anthology being produced by a Library of Congress archivist Alan Lomax. Waters then headed to Chicago where he was introduced to the South Side blues scene by blues-man Big Bill Broonzy. Backing acts such as Sonny Boy William-

son, he quickly polished his skills as and delighted his audiences.

He recorded for Columbia Record's Okeh imprint in 1946, but the tapes didn't surface until decades later. Leonard and Phil Chess signed Waters to their Aristocrat Records label in 1946, where he filled in on sessions for Sunnyland Slim and Big Crawford, a bass player, who teamed up with Waters on his first solo material in 1948 "I Can't Be Satisfied/(I Feel Like) Going Home" (#11, 1948), his chart debut. His riveting electric guitar meshed with thick Delta blues soon became his hallmark. Both "Screamin' and Cryin'" and "Rollin' and Tumblin'" were released the following year, but it was not until 1950 when he released "Rollin Stone," his first Chess (Aristocrat) single, that the recipe sounded complete. Waters had teamed with Little Walter, Otis Spann, and Jimmy Rogers, later adding Willie Dixon and Elgin Evans on the much fuller sounding single.

In 1951, "Louisiana Blues" (#10, R&B, 1951) became his second national hit, in a string that included "Long Distance Call," "Honey Bee," "Still a Fool" (1951), "She Moves Me" (1952), "Mad Love" (1953), "I'm Your Hoochie Coochie Man," "Just Make Love to Me," "I'm Ready" (1954), the classic "Manish Boy," "Sugar Sweet" (1955), "Trouble No More," "Forty Days & Forty Nights," and "Don't Go No Farther" (1956). Producing a string of the finest blues recordings ever made, Muddy Waters was revered for this work throughout his entire lifetime.

"Close to You," released in 1958, was his last R&B hit. That same year Chess released his first album *The Best of Muddy Waters*. During his first U.K. tour, his presence was acknowledged as inspirational to many of the early architects of British rock and roll, including Alexis Korner. Although the blues audience dissipated in America, thankfully future Waters' releases followed including *Muddy Waters Folk Singer* (1964), *The Real Folk Blues* (1966), *More Real Folk Blues* (1967), and *Muddy, Brass and the Blues* (1967). Two then controversial releases follow, *The Super Blues Band* (1968) and *Electric Mud* (#127, 1968), recorded with Bo Diddley and Howlin' Wolf—they were deemed "psychedelic," while the public was still trying to understand the '60s.

After the Rain (1968), *Fathers and Sons* (#70, 1969) (with Paul Butterfield and Mike Bloomfield), and *They Call Me Muddy Waters* (1972), which was recognized as Best Ethnic or Traditional Recording at the 14th Annual Grammy Awards, followed, and *The London Muddy Waters Sessions* (1972) picked up the identical award the following year. A serious car accident then sent the musician into seclusion for two years. He emerged with *The Muddy Waters Woodstock Album* (1976), which again garnered him a Grammy Award, an award he won three more times (1978, 1979, 1980).

Hard Again (#143, 1977), *I'm Ready* (#157, 1978), *Muddy Mississippi Waters Live* (1979), and *King Bee*

(1981), all produced by musician Johnny Winter and partner Steve Paul for their Blue Sky label, were praised by critics and highly acknowledged for their contribution to the genre.

Muddy Waters died on April 30, 1983, leaving behind a legacy that will be researched, studied, and emulated for generations.

AUTOGRAPHS

An LP, magazine cover, ad, photo, or card signed by the artist - $50-$150

OFTEN OVERLOOKED MEMORABILIA

Copies of the Levi's 501 jeans TV commercial featuring Mannish Boy (1988)

Watley, Jody

Born: January 30, 1959

Attractive and talented, Jody Watley struck pay dirt with her eponymous debut (#10, 1987) and its hit extracts "Looking For a New Love" (#2, 1987), "Don't You Want Me" (#6, 1987), and "Some Kind of Lover" (#10, 1988). She followed with her album *Larger Than Life* (1989), which spun off the hits "Real Love" (#2, 1989), "Everything" (#4, 1989), and "Friends" (#9, 1989).

AUTOGRAPHS

A CD, LP, magazine cover, ad, photo, or card signed by the artist: $10-$15

POSTERS/PRESS KITS

Promotional Posters: $10
Press Kits: $10-$15

OFTEN OVERLOOKED MEMORABILIA

Videotapes of her dancing on television's *Soul Train*; all of her associated artifacts from when she was with Shalamaar; all Band Aid (1984) memorabilia

Watson, Johnny "Guitar"

Born: February 3, 1935, Died: May 17, 1996

This talented guitarist is known for his late '50s and early '60s hits which included "Three Hours Past Midnight," "Those Lonely, Lonely, Nights," "Cuttin' In," and "Space Guitar," one of the first reverb and feedback tunes, along with his career re-birth hits in the '70s, "A Real Mother For Ya" (#41, 1977), "I Don't Wanna Be a Long Ranger," and "It's Too Late."

AUTOGRAPHS

A CD, LP, magazine cover, ad, photo, or card signed by the artist: $12-$25

Weather Girls

Formed 1982

Martha Wash and Izora Armstead

Rooted in Gospel and largely talented, Weather Girls, also known as Two Tons of Fun, are best known for the single "It's Raining Men" (#46, 1983). Wash's work has also included sessions with Black Box, C+C Music Factory, and Luther Vandross, as well as a successful debut solo effort that included the dance hits "Carry On" and "Give It to You."

AUTOGRAPHS

A CD, LP, magazine cover, ad, photo, or card signed by duo: $8-$20

POSTERS/PRESS KITS

Promotional Posters: $10
Press Kits: $10

OFTEN OVERLOOKED MEMORABILIA

The duo's contributions to other musical efforts

Weather Report

Formed 1970

Josef Zawinul, Wayne Shorter, Miroslav Vitous, Alphonse Mouzon, and Arito Moreira*

*Numerous personnel changes. Members have included: Eric Gravatt, Dom Um Romao, Ishmael Wilburn, Alphonso Johnson, Alyrio Lima, Ndugu (Leon Chancler), Chester Thompson, Jaco (John) Pastorius, Alejandro Neciosup Acuna, Manola Badrena, Peter Erskine, Victor Bailey, Jose Rossy, and Omar Hakim.

Best known as a creative and successful electronic jazz ensemble, Weather Report, despite the numerous personnel changes, has had two key members, Josef Zawinul and Wayne Shorter. The band was founded in the fusion of the late '60s and is best known for its most commercial album *Heavy Weather*, which included the Zawinul penned "Birdland." The band's prestigious musicians contributions alone could fill a book, with a few going on to nearly legendary status, such as Pastorious.

It's revolving door philosophy toward members has been critical in the development of its music and jazz in general.

AUTOGRAPHS

A CD, LP, magazine cover, ad, photo, or card signed by the group: $25-$40*

*Original band; add additional value for other key members such as Pastorious

The Weavers

Formed 1949

Original lineup: Pete Seeger, Born: May 3, 1919; Ronnie Gilbert; Fred Hellerman; and Lee Hays (1914-1981)*

*Additional musicians have included: Erik Darling, Frank Hamilton, and Bernie Krause. Group disbanded in 1963. Group re-formed in 1980.

The foundation for the early American folk revivalists, as well as one of the most successful, the Weavers are best known for their early hits "Tzena, Tzena, Tzena" (#2, 1950), "Goodnight Irene" (#1, 1950), "So Long (It's Been Good To Know You)," and "On Top of Old Smokey." During the early '60s their songs were covered by numerous musicians, many of which became hits including "Kisses Sweeter Than Wine," "Wimoweh (The Lion Sleeps Tonight)," "If I Had a Hammer," "Guantanamera," and "Turn!, Turn!, Turn!."

AUTOGRAPHS

A CD, LP, magazine cover, ad, photo, or card signed by the group: $45-$150*
*Original band members

REFERENCES/BOOKS

Limited resources exist. *Lonesome Traveler* by Doris Willens is a MUST for fans! There are no dedicated collector books.

Webb, Jimmy

Born: August 15, 1946

A gifted composer, his songs have included "By The Time I Get to Phoenix," "Up, Up and Away," "Whichita Lineman," "MacArthur Park, "Galveston, "The Moon Is a Harsh Mistress," and "All I Know." Webb has also written numerous popular jingles, and has scored films and television shows, but has never been able to garner commercial success with his solo albums— perhaps a mute point considering such an enormous talent.

AUTOGRAPHS

A CD, LP, magazine cover, ad, photo, or card signed by the artist: $20-$65

OFTEN OVERLOOKED MEMORABILIA

Movie memorabilia from *Doc* and *The Last Unicorn*; videotapes of television shows that have used his themes including *Amazing Stories*, *Tales from the Crypt*, and *Faerie Tale Theater*; also videotapes of his popular television commercials that use his jingles such as Chevrolet and Doritos tortilla chips; associated memorabilia from other musicians covers of his work

Wells, Junior

(Amos Blackmore)
Born: December 9, 1934

This legendary Chicago blues singer and harmonica player is best remembered for his hits "Hoodoo Man" and "Messin' with the Kid," along with his long partnership with musician Buddy Guy.

AUTOGRAPHS

A CD, LP, magazine cover, ad, photo, or card signed by the artist: $10-$20

Wells, Mary

Born: May 13, 1943 Died July 26, 1992

Wells is best known as Motown's initial attraction and for her collaborations with Smokey Robinson on numbers such as "The One Who Really Loves You" (#8, 1962), "You Beat Me to the Punch" (#9, 1962), "Two Lovers" (#7, 1962), "Laughing Boy" (#15, 1963), "Your Old Stand By" (#40, 1963), and her biggest hit "My Guy" (#1, 1964). Her succinct delivery and glamorous style, accompanied by Robinson's strong arrangements, became her trademark. She duetted with Marvin Gaye on "What's the Matter With You Baby" (#17, 1964) and "Once Upon a Time" (#19, 1964). She then sued Motown, the first to do so, and despite proving her case, the whole incident marred her career.

"Dream Lover" (#51, 1965) scored for her new label Atco, but that was about it for the artist, who then turned her interest to her family. She later was stricken by cancer and the incident devastated her both personally and financially. It later claimed her life.

AUTOGRAPHS

A CD, LP, magazine cover, ad, photo, or card signed by the artist: $25-$45

Wendy and Lisa

Wendy Melvoin and Lisa Coleman

Best known as former Prince protégée, Wendy and Lisa have reached some level of success with their eponymous debut album (#88, 1987) and their sophomore offering *Fruit at the Bottom* (#119, 1989), but both failed to spin off any hit singles.

AUTOGRAPHS

A CD, LP, magazine cover, ad, photo, or card signed by the group: $8-$10

Wham!

Formed 1982

George Michael (Georgios Panayiotou), Born: June 25, 1963; and Andrew Ridgeley, Born: January 26, 1963

Michael met Ridgeley on the very first day of class at Bushy Meads Comprehensive School in 1975. They formed the Executives with Ridgeley's brother Paul, David Austin, and Andrew Leaver, and played the local scene for about a year and a half before disbanding. Michael and Ridgeley continued to work together on songwriting while preparing numerous demo tapes, one of which contained "Wham Rap!," "Come On!," "Club Tropicana," and "Careless Whisper." Ignored by numerous companies, the act signed with small dance-based label Innervision in 1982. "Young Guns (Go For It)" (#3, U.K., 1982) slowly charted, pushed primarily through a television appearance on *Top of the Pops* (BBC-1TV).

Both "Wham Rap!" (#8, U.K., 1983) and "Bad Boys" (#2, U.K., 1983) charted, but the group began to have problems with its label. The debut album *Fantastic* (#1, U.K., 1983) entered the chart at the top, while its fourth single "Club Tropicana" (#4, U.K., 1983) sustained the streak of successful extracts. During the summer the band announced its first concert tour, as the weakly marketed extract "Bad Boys" (#60, 1983) failed to enter the U.S. Top Forty. By this time the band was nearing the end of its relationship with Innervisions, as legal sides were fortified.

Having signed with Epic Records in March 1984, the band released "Wake Me Up Before You Go Go" (#1, U.K., 1984), a smash hit that topped both the British and American singles charts. The ballad "Careless Whisper" repeated the feat as the group's enormous success catapulted it into the spotlight. *Make It Big* (#1, 1985), the band's second effort, was also a smash. The band's fame landed it an invitation to perform live in China, the first western pop group to have such an honor. "Everything She Wants" (#1, 1985) topped the singles charts as Michael's independence was becoming increasingly recognized by the public. "Freedom" (#3, 1985) followed but didn't climb into the Number One singles slot. "I'm Your Man" (#1, U.K., 1985) sat atop the charts as privately the duo agreed to split the following year.

Amidst numerous honors and solo projects, the duo released its final Wham! single in the form of a four-track EP. "The Edge of Heaven/Where Did Your Heart Go" (#1, 1986) topped the chart the same week as the duo's farewell. "The Final," a farewell concert took place at Wembley Stadium during the summer of 1986. *Music from the Edge of Heaven* (#10, 1986), *Wham!*, a hits compilation followed as Michael pur-

sued a solo career and Ridgeley focused on racing and acting.

The band did reunite briefly for a few numbers at Rock in Rio in January 1991. The duo's mark in music history is often scoffed at by critics due to its overt commercial appeal, however, by all accounts it was an integral part of George Michael's career and as such deserves inclusion in music history books.

AUTOGRAPHS

Group:

A CD, LP, magazine cover, ad, photo, or card signed by the group- $45-$175

Individual

George Michael (Georgios Panayiotou): see individual entry

TOUR BOOKS/PROGRAMS/PASSES

Tour Books:

Whamamercial Tour, 1985: $25

Backstage Passes:

Cloth: $10-$15; Laminated: $15-$25

POSTERS/PRESS KITS

Promotional Posters: $15-$25
Press Kits: $15-$25

OFTEN OVERLOOKED MEMORABILIA

Fila sportswear memorabilia associated with the band's first tour (1983); fan club items; a re-marketed *The Final*, a boxed set, included a pencil, paper pad, and poster; videotapes of the duo's numerous television appearances including *Top of the Pops* (10/82); artifacts from the 30th annual Ivor Novello Awards (Michael was the recipient); all items from the group's historic visit to China (1985)

REFERENCES/BOOKS

Numerous resources exist, but none do justice to the group in my opinion. There are no dedicated collector books.

The Whispers

Formed 1962

Walter Scott, Born: September 3, 1943; Wallace Scott, Born: September 3, 1943; Nicholas Caldwell; Marcus Hutson; and Gordy Harmon

Slow to ignite, this talented group of musicians put together a series of successful minor R&B hits during the late '60s and '70s, but didn't really break through until the '80s when "Rock Steady" (#7, 1987) catapulted the band into stardom. Other popular but lesser known hits included "And the Beat Goes On" (#19, 1980), "Lady" (#28, 1980), and "It's a Love Thing" (#28, 1981).

AUTOGRAPHS

A CD, LP, magazine cover, ad, photo, or card signed by the group: $25-$40

Whitcomb, Ian

Born: July 10, 1941

A multitalented individual, who is perhaps best known for his 1965 hit "You Turn Me On," Whitcomb has worked as a producer, disc jockey, and has even scored films.

AUTOGRAPHS

A CD, LP, magazine cover, ad, photo, or card signed by the artist: $5-$15

OFTEN OVERLOOKED MEMORABILIA

Associated memorabilia from his numerous side projects, production work, etc.

REFERENCES/BOOKS

After the Ball—Pop Music from Rag to Rock (1972) by Ian Whitcomb; *The Beckoning Fairground: Note of a British Exile in Lotus Land* by Ian Whitcomb (1994)

White, Barry

Born: September 12, 1944

With a voice as distinctive as James Earl Jones', Barry White's seductive musical arrangements melt his listener's hearts in seconds. He became a sex symbol in the '70s and a pioneering producer during the disco movement. Often adding orchestras to his lavish compositions, nearly all of his songs focused on the topic of love.

He began singing in his Galvaston church choir at an early age and worked his way up to playing organ and eventually he became the part-time choir director. He joined an L.A. R&B quintet, the Upfronts, and added his voice on their second single for Lummtone Records in 1960.

He tackled session work when available and formed the Atlantics in 1963, followed by the Majestics with Carl Carlton. He added his arrangement assistance to a Bob and Earl release "The Harlem Shuffle," which charted into the Top Fifty. His honed production and writing skills eventually landed him a job at Mustang Records. There he discovered the female vocal trio Love Unlimited (sisters Glodean and Linda James and Diane Taylor), and was so impressed that he became their manager and producer— he even eventually married Glodean. In 1972 he produced their hit single "Walking in the Rain with the One I Love" (#14, 1972).

Now under his own name, Barry White scores hits with "I'm Gonna Love You Just a Little More Baby" (#3, 1973), "Never, Never, Gonna Give Ya Up" (#7, 1973), and "I've Got So Much to Give" (#32, 1973). He also penned the orchestral disco hit and art room favorite "Love's Theme" (#1, 1973) for the Love Unlim-

ited Orchestra (LUO), in a year where everything White touched turned to Gold or Platinum. His succesful works included *Rhapsody in White* by LUO (#8, 1974), *Can't Get Enough* (#1, 1974), "Can't Get Enough of Your Love, Babe" (#1, 1974), "You're the First, the Last, My Everything" (#2, 1974), *Just Another Way to Say I Love You* (#17, 1975), and *Barry White's Greatest Hits* (#23, 1975). Later, *Barry White Sings for Someone You Love* (#8, 1977) went platinum, as "It's Ecstasy When You Lay Down Next to Me" (#4, 1977) became his fifth and final solo gold single. The following year he added "Playing Your Game Baby" (#8, R&B, 1978) and "Your Sweetness Is My Weakness" (#2, R&B, 1978) to his hit resume.

By the late '70s, White's seduction appeal was wearing thin, no thanks at that time to his link with the disco movement. In 1979 he had moderate success covering some Billy Joel tunes, and *The Man* (#46, U.K., 1979) slowly climbed the British album chart. He then moved to his own Unlimited Gold label with "The Message Is Love" (#67, 1979). He and his wife Glodean did land two minor R&B chart singles with "Didn't We Make It Happen Baby" (#78, R&B, 1981) and "I Want You" (#79, R&B, 1981), while later in the decade he resurfaced with "Sho' You Right" (#17, R&B, 1987), "For Your Love (I'll Do Most Anything)" (#27, R&B, 1987), and the R&B chart topper "The Secret Garden (Sweet Seduction Suite)" (#31, 1990) featuring Al B. Sure.

The '90s saw White evolve with "I Wanna Do It Good to You" (#26, R&B, 1990), "When Will I See You Again" (#2, R&B, 1990), and "Put Me in Your Mix" (#2, R&B, 1991). In 1994 White even landed a chart topper with "Practice What You Preach" (#1, R&B, 1994) from his very successful *The Icon Is Love* (#20, 1994). In June 1995 he embarked on a U.S. tour, his first in many years. Just when you think there is no love left, Barry White will prove you wrong!

AUTOGRAPHS

A CD, LP, magazine cover, ad, photo, or card signed by the artist: $20-$30

TOUR BOOKS/ PROGRAMS/PASSES

Backstage Passes:
Cloth: $8-$10;
Laminated: $10-$12 *

POSTERS/ PRESS KITS

Promotional Posters:
20th Century-Fox (1973-1978): $15-$30
Unlimited Gold (1979-1983): $10-$20
A&M (1987-1992): $5-$8
Mercury (1994): $5-$7

A Barry White backstage pass

Press Kits:
20th Century-Fox (1973-1978): $15-$30
Unlimited Gold (1979-1983): $10-$15
A&M (1987-1992): $10
Mercury (1994): $7

OFTEN OVERLOOKED MEMORABILIA

Movie memorabilia from *Together Brothers* (1974) (LUO soundtrack); videotapes of his numerous television appearances including *Late Night With David Letterman* (5/24/83, 5/18/90), *The Arsenio Hall Show* (11/8/91), *The Simpsons* (4/29/93), *The Late Show With David Letterman* (11/7/94), *The Tonight Show* (1/9/95); NBC-TV 1995 Valentine's Day promotional clips

White, Bukka

(Booker T. Washington White)
Born: November 12, 1906, Died: February 26, 1977

A legendary Delta bluesman, cousin of blues guitarist B.B. King, Bukka White began recording in Memphis in 1930 and had his first hit seven years later with "Shake 'Em On Down." He was later recorded for the Library of Congress and fell into obscurity until 1963, when John Fahey tracked him down to record on his Takoma label. His career then enjoyed a brief revival of sorts before he later fell prey to cancer.

AUTOGRAPHS

An LP, magazine cover, ad, photo, or card signed by the artist: $20-$45

White, Karyn

Born: October 14, 1965

A talented singer with a polished delivery, Karyn White, who had fronted the L.A. group Legacy and backed up numerous R&B musicians, released her eponymous debut album (#19) in 1988. It included the hits "The Way You Love Me" (#7, 1988), "Superwoman" (#8, 1989), and "Secret Rendezvous" (#6, 1989). She followed with her sophomore effort *Ritual of Love*, which spun off hits "Romantic" (#1,1991) and "The Way I Feel About You" (#12, 1991). The singer, who is married to the very talented producer Terry Lewis (Terry Lewis & Jimmy Jam), released *Make Him Do Right* in 1994, which sold well in R&B circles.

AUTOGRAPHS

A CD, LP, magazine cover, ad, photo, or card signed by the artist: $10-$25

White, Tony Joe

Born: July 23, 1943

Tony Joe White is a heartfelt Louisiana swamp rocker, who sold better in Europe than the U.S. He's best known in the States for "whomper stomper" guitar playing and bayou classic "Polk Salad Annie." His songs have been covered by numerous artists including Elvis Presley, but most notable is Brook Benton's version of "A Rainy Night in Georgia."

AUTOGRAPHS

A CD, LP, magazine cover, ad, photo, or card signed by the artist: $8-$15

OFTEN OVERLOOKED MEMORABILIA

Videotapes of his commercial work including McDonald's and Levi's

White Lion

Formed 1983

Vito Bratta, Dave Capozzi, Felix Robinson, and Mike Tramp*

*Robinson and Capozzi left in 1987 and James Lomenzo and Greg D'Angelo were added. Both Lomenzo and D'Angelo left in 1991 and Tommy Caradonna and Jimmy DeGrasso joined the band.

This '80s metal hair act's debut album *Pride* (#11, 1987) sold extremely well and yielded two hit singles, "Wait" (#8, 1987) and "When the Children Cry" (#3, 1988). Other albums followed, but contained no hit singles, and the lion no longer roared.

AUTOGRAPHS

A CD, LP, magazine cover, ad, photo, or card signed by the artist: $8-$15

Whitesnake

Formed 1978

Original lineup: David Coverdale, Born: September 22, 1949; Mickey Moody; Bernie Marsden; Brian Johnston; Neil Murray; and David Dowle*

*Numerous personnel changes. Musicians have included: Jon Lord, Ian Paice, Mel Galley, Colin Hodgkinson, Cozy Powell, John Sykes, Richard Bailey, Don Airey, Aynsley Dunbar, Adrian Vandenburg, Vivian Campbell, Rudy Sarzo, Tommy Aldridge, and Steve Vai.

Prompted by a disappointing U.K. tour , the latest lineup of super group Deep Purple dissolved, leaving vocalist David Coverdale without a band, yet still covered under contractual ties. The vocalist moved

to West Germany to begin writing new material, all while Deep Purple's legal problems were sorted out. His solo debut *Whitesnake* (1977) was released to little acclaim, and he finally returned to Britain to form a band to promote his second solo effort, *Northwinds* (1978). Recruiting some of the finest session musicians he could entice, David Coverdale's Whitesnake began its debut U.K. tour on February 23, 1978.

In June 1978 the band released a four-track EP, *Snake Bite* (#61, U.K., 1978), which became its first chart success. Meanwhile, personnel changes continued and ex-Deep Purple colleague Jon Lord was added at keyboards. *Trouble* (#50, U.K., 1978) was the first full-group album and was followed by *Love Hunter* (#29, U.K., 1979).

The band's breakthrough year was 1980, as "Fool for Your Loving" (#13, U.K., 1980) became the band's first legitimate hit single. "Ready An' Willing (Sweet Satisfaction)" (#43, U.K., 1980), "Fool for Your Loving" (#53, 1980), and "Ain't No Love in the Heart of the City" (#51, U.K., 1980) quickly followed . Album production included *Live at Hammersmith*, *Ready An' Willing* (#6, U.K., 1980), and *Live in the Heart of the City* (#5, U.K., 1980).

Come An' Get It (#151, 1981) featured the two extracts "Break My Heart Again" (#17, U.K., 1981) and "Would I Lie to You" (#7, U.K., 1981). Following the Monsters of Rock festival and a tour of West Germany, friction developed in the band, causing it to be put on indefinite hold. In 1982, Coverdale re-assembled the band with a new lineup and resurrected some previously recorded tracks, which were modified and completed as *Saints 'n' Sinners* (#9, U.K., 1982). The following year the band was put into a tail spin as Coverdale fired his producer, collapsed from exhaustion, and watched as more personnel left.

"Give Me More Time" (#29, U.K., 1984), "Standing in the Shadow" (#62, U.K., 1984), and "Love Ain't No Stranger" (#44, U.K., 1985) were all extracted from *Slide It In* (#9, U.K.; #40, U.S., 1984), while a resurrected band performed in West Germany, Japan, the U.S., and at Rock in Rio. A breakthrough came with the release of the Coverdale & Sykes penned *Whitesnake 1987* (#2, 1987), which was supported by the latest lineup: Coverdale, Vandenburg, Campbell, Sarzo, and Aldridge. Extracted singles "Still of the Night" (#79, 1987) and "Is This Love" (#9, U.K.; #2, U.S., 1987) helped push album sales. The band also re-cut "Here I Go Again" (#9, U.K., 1987), which re-charted.

"Give Me All Your Love" (#48, 1988) was re-recorded and released as single. Late in 1988, a very unproductive year for the band, Campbell left the group. Guitar jockey Steve Vai replaced him. *Slip of the Tongue* (#10, 1989) with single "Fool for Your Loving" (#37, 1989) was released to strong sales that pushed it to the platinum level.

"The Deeper the Love" (#28, 1990) and "Now You're Gone" (#96, 1990) charted in 1990, while the band played at a variety of one-off gigs. By September it was becoming increasingly clear that Coverdale had dissolved the group, a fact that was later confirmed. *Coverdale / Page* (#5, 1993) a collaboration between Coverdale and Jimmy Page, included the singles "Take Me for a Little While" (#20, U.K., 1993) and "Take a Look at Yourself" (#43, U.K., 1993).

Whitesnake's Greatest Hits (#161, 1994) saw Coverdale resurrect a lineup that included Vandenburg, Sarzo, Warren DiMartini, and Denny Carmassi, for a European tour. As for Whitesnake, where Coverdale goes, so does the band!

AUTOGRAPHS
A CD, LP, magazine cover, ad, photo, or card signed by the group: $40-$75*
*Original members

TOUR BOOKS/ PROGRAMS/PASSES
Tour Books:
Tour '87-'88: $10
Backstage Passes:
Cloth: $10; Laminated: $10-$20

POSTERS/PRESS KITS
Promotional Posters:
$8-$25, Examples:
"Greatest Hits"
(20" x 30") - $10,
Press Kits: $10-$25

USED CLOTHING/ EQUIPMENT
Guitar Picks: $10-$25

OFTEN OVERLOOKED MEMORABILIA
Old logo die-cut (23") long - $7-$10; Now You're Gone - counter display (13") - $15; Glands Across America tour crew itinerary - $40; all memorabilia associated with the controversial "Love Hunter" cover; movie memorabilia from *Days of Thunder* (1990); *Shake With the Snake* promo black panties w/logo- $6

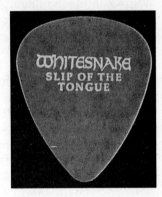

A Whitesnake guitar pick

White Zombie

Formed 1985

Rob Zombie (Robert Straker), Sean Yseult, Ivan dePrume, and John Ricci*

*Ricci left in 1989 and Jay "J." Yuenger was added. dePrume left in 1993 and Phil "Philo" Buerstatte joined the band. Buerstatte left in 1995 and John Tempesta was added on drums.

Comic collector and unacknowledged super hero Zombie recruited de Prume, Tom Guay, and female bassist Yseult to form the heavy metal influenced White Zombie. *Psycho Head Blowout*, an EP, was the band's first release on its own label Silent Explosion in 1987. It was followed by the 1988 album debut *Soul*

Crusher. During this period guitarist John Ricci replaced Guay, while the band prepared for the release of *Make Them Die Slowly* (Caroline Records, 1992), which was followed by an EP that featured the band's interpretation of the Kiss classic "God of Thunder." Cultivating a strong underground following, and having added "J" to replace Ricci, the band signed with Geffen Records in 1991.

La Sexorcisto: Devil Music Vol. 1 (#26, 1993) was their fiendish first Geffen release and featured the ghoulish ranting of lead vocalist Zombie. Its lengthy chart climb was attributable to the band's highly theatric, extensive touring. Later in the year, *The Beavis & Butt-head Experience* (#6, 1993) album climbed into the Top Ten and contained the group's "I Am Hell." The MTV cartoon duo responded favorably to White Zombie inclusion, but denied the invitation to be added to the band's road crew, opting instead for a movie career.

Meanwhile, the band continued to be plagued by drummer problems—in 1994 the third skin beater, John Tempesta, was added. *Astro Creep: 2,000 Songs of Love, Destruction and Other Synthetic Delusions of the Electric Head* (#6, 1995) was released and climbed into the Top Ten on the U.S. album chart, while extracted single "More Human Than Human" (#51, U.K., 1995) drew attention to the project.

On July 14, 1995, the band appeared on CBS-TV's *Late Show With David Letterman*, whose host said that he once felt like a Zombie.

White Zombie collected the Best Hard Rock Video trophy for "More Than Human," on September 7, 1995 at the 12th Annual MTV Video Music Awards. The following year the band released *Electric Head Pt.2* (The Ecstacy) (#31, U.K., 1996) prior to beginning a two-month U.S. tour.

AUTOGRAPHS
Group:
A CD, LP, magazine cover, ad, photo, or card signed by the group: $30-$40
Individual
Rob Zombie: $10-$20

Guitar pick from White Zombie

TOUR BOOKS/ PROGRAMS/PASSES
Backstage Passes:
Cloth: $8-$12; Laminated: $12-$20

POSTERS/PRESS KITS
Promotional Posters: $10-$15
Press Kits: $10-$15

USED CLOTHING/ EQUIPMENT
Guitar Picks: $10
Drum Sticks: $10-$12

REFERENCES/BOOKS
Limited resources exist. There are no dedicated collector books. Serious collectors should opt for a Fan Club: Psychoholics Anonymous, P.O. Box 885343, San Francisco, CA 94188

The Who

Formed 1964

Peter Townshend, Born: May 19, 1945; Roger Daltry, Born: March 1, 1944; John Entwistle, Born: October 9, 1944; and Keith Moon, Born: August 23, 1947, Died: September 7, 1978*

*Following Moon's death, Kenny Jones, Born: September 16, 1948, was added.

Townshend, Entwistle, and Phil Rhodes formed the Confederates (the Aristocrats/the Scorpions) while at grammar school. Townshend, who hailed from a musical background and fancied the guitar, was determined at an early age to become a rock star. Entwistle, an artisan in his own right, played in his school's orchestra before seeking his first career as a civil servant. Townshend headed to art college, where most '60s British rock and rollers were weaned, just look at the Rolling Stones.

Roger Daltry, the former schoolmate of both Townshend and Entwistle, asked both to join his band. Rounded out by drummer Doug Sandom, the first formation of the band took place in 1962. They honed their skills the following year supporting artists such as the Rolling Stones, while tackling classic R&B covers mixed with original material.

In 1964, they met publicist Pete Meadon who turned them on to the burgeoning new London "mod" scene. Packaging them into the mod element, Meadon begins his marketing of the band. Sandom then departed; various drummers filled in for him. While playing a gig in London's Oldfield pub, a drunken patron dressed like a UPS driver decided to exhibit his uncharacteristic banging on the old skins. A bit cocky, Keith Moon was nevertheless accepted into the band permanently as the drummer. The new foursome became the High Numbers and secured a one-off single deal with Fontana Records.

In July 1964, "I'm The Face" was released by Fontana with little accolades. In September director Kit Lambert and his partner Chip Stamp took over the group's management. Playing at its regular venue the Railway Hotel in Harrow, Middx., a place noted for its low vertical clearance, Townshend accidentally put part of his guitar through the ceiling, causing a chain reaction of equipment destruction that became a normal part of the group's stage show. Lambert changed the group's name back to a former moniker, the Who.

"I Can't Explain" (#93, 1965) was the group's first single release by Brunswick, which the group se-

cured a record deal with. Produced by Shel Talmy, it also included guitar licks by Jimmy Page. It was followed by "Anyway Anyhow Anywhere" (#10, U.K., 1965), which was adopted by ITV's *Ready Steady Go!* as its theme song, and then "My Generation" (#2, U.K., 1965), which was the title of the Who's debut album (#5, 1965) and an anthem of sorts. By this time the group's unique image was well solidified.

Talmy was replaced by Lambert as producer following the band's fourth single "Substitute" (#5, U.K., 1966). The incident prompted a legal battle, and Talmy eventually gained future royalties. *A Quick One / Happy Jack* (U.S.) (#67, 1967) was the band's sophomore effort and featured the single "Happy Jack" (#24, 1967) and a mini-opera called "A Quick One While He's Away." The band's management was then being handled by Allen Klein and Andrew Oldham.

The Who Sell Out (#48, 1967), with tracks linked by commercial radio advertisements, contained another min-rock opera, "Rael," a prelude of what was to come, and the smash hit "I Can See for Miles" (#9, 1967). Later that year *Magic Bus* (#39, 1968), a compilation of singles and B sides, was released to allow Townshend time enough to finish his quest, a rock opera.

"Pinball Wizard" (#19, 1969) was released as a prelude to the album *Tommy* (#4, 1969), the story of a deaf, dumb, and blind boy who turns to pinball for his satisfaction, later to become a champion/prophet who is adored by his following. The album became the first successful rock opera and laid the foundation for future concept albums. Following its initial release, it was performed in its entirety, a situation that would recur periodically during the groups existence. Excerpts such as "See Me, Feel Me" and "Pinball Wizard" were integrated into the group's alternate tours, while a controversial 1975 version of *Tommy* saw film, and Broadway in 1993.

Live at Leeds (#4, 1970) was followed by another Who landmark, *Who's Next* (#4, 1971), which contained "Won't Get Fooled Again" (#15, 1971), an FM and rock classic. The album also marked Townshend's first use of synthesizers, most notably on "Baba O'Riley." *Meaty Beaty Big and Bouncy* (#11, 1971) was a greatest hits release and peaked around the same time as single "Behind Blue Eyes" (#34, 1971). The year also saw John Entwistle earn some solo success with his album *Smash Your Head Against the Wall* (#126, 1971) the first band member to releases an independent venture.

Quadrophenia (#2, 1973), an introspective look into the mods, was the Who's second double-album rock opera. It also saw film in 1979, and was performed in its entirety as late as 1996/1997 by the band. The album also seemed to mark a mid-life crisis of sorts for the group, which saw its audience changing and reacting differently to its music. *Odds and Sods* (#15, 1974), a compilation of outtakes, pre-

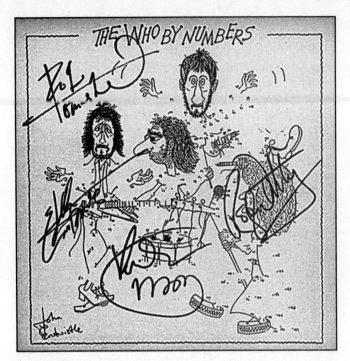

The Who By Numbers signed on the front cover by Keith, Pete, Roger, and John. Courtesy Phillips Son & Neale.

ceded *The Who By Numbers* (#8, 1975), which yielded the hit single "Squeeze Box" (#16, 1975). Following the album, it was clear that individual efforts were beginning to dominate the band members.

On September 8, 1978, Keith Moon died from an overdose of Heminevrin, a drug used to combat alcoholism. Ironically, the incident took place in the same London apartment Mama Cass died in four years earlier. The tragedy overshadowed the successful rise of the next album *Who Are You* (#2, 1978); its self-titled release landed in the Top Fifteen on the singles chart. The record was the last and highest charting album by the original band and, for all intents and purposes, the real end of the band.

The Kids Are Alright (#8, 1979) was the soundtrack to the documentary of the band's formative years. The group also produced a soundtrack to the film *Quadrophenia* (#46, 1979). Immersed in nostalgia, Kenny Jones (Small Faces) was asked to replace Moon and session keyboardist John Bundrick was also recruited for the road. On May 2, 1979, the new Who made its debut at the Rainbow Theatre to begin a tour. It too, however, could not circumvent tragedy. On December 3, 1979, eleven members of the audience at the Cincinnati concert audience were trampled to death.

Face Dances (#4, 1981) was the first release by the new line-up, and although it sold well and contained the singles "You Better You Bet" (#18, 1981) and "Don't Let Go the Coat" (#84, 1981), Townshend later stated it was a disappointment. *It's Hard* (#8, 1982), the group's next and possibly last studio offering, climbed into the Top Ten on the album charts, as the band embarked on its final North American tour. The

Who's final show on December 17, 1982, was filmed for television, a month before "Eminence Front" (#68, 1983), its last official single, reached its chart peak. On December 16, 1983, the Who officially split.

The Who brought rock and roll a foundation, a framework, and a finished product. Built to perfection, under the highest tolerances imaginable, it performed like a Rolls Royce and curved your appetite like good caviar. The music speaks to its time, but is timeless. As apostles to their art, they were never an apostasy.

Long Live Rock!

AUTOGRAPHS

Group:

A CD, LP, magazine cover, ad, photo, or card signed by the entire band: $1,000-$1,500*

*High-end reflects vintage signed memorabilia of original lineup

Individual

Peter Townshend: $75-$125	Roger Daltry: $50-$75
John Entwistle: $35-$60	Keith Moon: $200-$250
Kenny Jones: $30-$40	

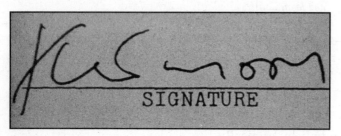

SIGNATURE

Keith Moon's autograph

TOUR BOOKS/ PROGRAMS/PASSES

Tour Books:

The Who 1981: $10-$15
The Who, Official Program (1982): $10-$12
Tommy, N.Y. & L.A. Show Program (1989): $10

THE WHO 1981

Tour book from the Who's 1981 tour (Designed by Richard Evans)

THE WHO
OFFICIAL PROGRAM

The Official Program (Design by David Costa)

RADIO CITY MUSIC HALL   UNIVERSAL AMPHITHEATER
NEW YORK CITY   LOS ANGELES
TUESDAY 27 JUNE 1989   THURSDAY 24 AUGUST 1989

Program for Tommy (N.Y. and L.A.) (Designed by Icon)

Backstage Passes:

Cloth: $8-$15; Laminated: $15-$30 (Post-1980)

POSTERS/PRESS KITS

Press Kits:

Thirty Years: $15

USED CLOTHING/EQUIPMENT

Guitar Picks:

Pete Townshend: $75-$125
Roger Daltry: $50-$75
John Entwistle: $50-$80

Drum Sticks:

Keith Moon: $75-$150*
Kenny Jones: $35

*scarce and difficult to authenticate

OFTEN OVERLOOKED MEMORABILIA

Track promotional toy London Transport double-decker bus, 1968; Sounds Like the Who By Numbers, Polydor promotional cardboard headband, 1975; Who Are You, Polydor promotional track suit; The Who, Track promotional pillow; CD-ROM, *Pete Townshend Presents Tommy: The Interactive Adventure* (1996); playbill from Daltry's performance as the Tin Man in *The Wizard of Oz* in New York's Avery Fisher Hall, (1995) - $10; award ceremony memorabilia; Rock and Roll Hall of Fame associated memorabilia especially 1990; *Tommy* playbills and memorabilia especially the Broadway performance (1993) playbill, which commands about $10-$12; videotapes from Daltry's television movies such as *Forgotten Prisoners: The Amnesty Files* (1990); movie memorabilia from *The Threepenny Opera* (1989) (Daltry), *McVicar* (1980), *Quadrophenia* (1979), *The Legacy* (1979), *The Kids Are Alright* (1979), *Lisztomania* (1975), *Tommy* (1975), *Stardust* (1975) (Moon), *200 Motels* (1972) (Moon), and *The Rolling Stones Rock and Roll Circus* (1968/96); all fan club trinkets; SONY advertising campaign memorabilia that stated "It's like having Keith Moon in the room. Only Safer" (1976); copies of *The Guiness Book of Records* (c. 1976) listing the Who as loudest performance (120 decibels) - $10-$15; newspaper clipping from hotel wrecking exploits, Montreal, 1973 - $3-$10; advertising from The U.S. Council for World Affairs using the theme "Join Together" (1972); *The Observer* color supplement (3/19/72) - $20-$25; all Woodstock

memorabilia (8/16/69); American Cancer Society items associated with "Little Billy" jingle (1968); buttons - $3-$25; Chicago Farewell Performance (12/8/92) unused ticket - $15

Albums:

Quadrophenia: Track proof copy cover with alternate artwork including a book and a square cube (5") U.K., 1973

Tommy: cassette given to those attending the L.A. performance of *Tommy*. It came in a silk screen waist bag with a party pass and sunglasses, U.S., 1989

REFERENCES/BOOKS

Numerous resources exist, so take your pick. There are no dedicated collector books.

THE WHO REUNITED

Selected Dates 1983-1997

July 13, 1985: Live Aid benefit concert at Wembley Stadium

February 8, 1988: BRIT Awards, London's Royal Albert Hall

June 1989: The Kids Are Alright Tour: 1964-1989, North American Tour

January 17, 1990: Induction Into Rock & Roll Hall of Fame

February 23-24, 1994: Daltry Sings Townshend, Daltry's 50th birthday

Summer 1996/97: Quadrophenia, selected performances

Williams, Deniece

Born: June 3, 1951

Williams is a former member of Stevie Wonder's Wonderlove vocal group. Her debut *This Is Niecy* included the hit extract "Free" (#25, 1977). The following year she dueted with Johnny Mathis on "Too Much, Too Little, Too Late" (#1, 1978) and later landed another hit with "It's Gonna Take a Miracle" (#10, 1982). "Let's Hear It For the Boy" (#1, 1984) was her last major pop hit. Then the artist shifted to gospel albums during the latter half of the '80s, experienced enormous success, and landed a few Grammys along the way.

AUTOGRAPHS

A CD, LP, magazine cover, ad, photo, or card signed by the artist: $10-$20

Williams, Hank

(Hiram Williams)
Born: September 17, 1923, Died: January 1, 1953

Country & Western music's most influential artist, Hank Williams had thirty-six Top Ten C&W hits including the chart toppers "Lovesick Blues," "Why Don't You Love Me," "Long Gone Lonesome Blues," "Moanin' the Blues," "Cold, Cold Heart," Hey, Good Lookin'," "Jambalya (On the Bayou)," and "I'll Never Get Out of the World Alive." This extraordinary performer also had three posthumous Number One C&W hits: "Kaw-Liga," "Your Cheatin' Heart," and "Take These Chains From My Heart."

His tender and emotional songwriting went on to inspire generations, while his versatility was crucial to the development of future C&W offshoots such as rockabilliy. His early link with producer/arranger Fred Rose, of Acuff-Rose fame, also helped solidify his song production over the years that followed. His exposure increased during the summer of 1948, when Williams joined the popular KWKH country music radio program Louisiana Hayride in Shreveport. From there it was off to the Grand Ole Opry, where he debuted on June 11, 1949. The rest was history from this point on. Unfortunately Williams never saw his thirtieth birthday—he died in the back of his car from a heart attack en route to a show.

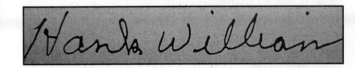

A scarce example of Hank Williams' signature

AUTOGRAPHS

An LP, magazine cover, ad, photo, or card signed by the artist: $800-$1,400

REFERENCES/BOOKS

Numerous resources exist. *Hank Williams: A Bio-Bibliography* by George William Koon is a MUST purchase for fans and collectors!

Williams Jr., Hank

(Randall Hank Williams)
Born: May 26, 1949

Perhaps it was inevitable that young Hank follow in papa's footsteps. What was unexpected was just how talented and determined "Jr." was to carve out his own legacy, which he certainly has. He cut his first record at fourteen and made his debut performance at the Grand Ole Opry in 1960. By sixteen he had already received a BMI citation and by 1966 had a Number Five C&W hit with "Standing in the Shadows."

He became disillusioned with the business during the '70s and left Nashville. On August 8, 1975, he suffered a near fatal 490 foot fall while mountain climbing. Lucky even to be alive, he was hospitalized for an extended period of time in which he underwent numerous reconstruction surgeries. He emerged a year and a half later with more of an "outlaw" attitude toward his music and performing. The result seemed to work as the hits just flowed, including "All My Rowdy Friends (Have Settled Down)" (#1, C&W, 1981), "Honky Tonkin'" (#1, C&W, 1982), "Man of Steel" (#3, C&W, 1984), "I'm for Love" (#1, C&W, 1985), "Ain't Misbehavin'" (#1, C&W, 1986), "Country State of Mind" (#2, C&W, 1986), "Mind Your Own Business" (#1, C&W, 1986), "Born to Boogie" (#1, C&W, 1987), "Young Country" (#2, 1988), and "There's a Tear in My Beer" (#7, C&W, 1989).

Many were introduced to Williams' work through his theme to Monday Night Football, which has become a staple among sports enthusiasts, who now find it a tradition similar to the national anthem. With well over fifty albums to choose from, it's hard to say just where to begin your collecting!

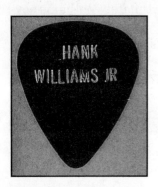

A guitar pick from Hank Williams, Jr.

AUTOGRAPHS
A CD, LP, magazine cover, ad, photo, or card signed by the artist: $20-$40

OFTEN OVERLOOKED MEMORABILIA
Movie memorabilia from *Time to Sing* and *Kelly's Heroes*; a copy of the made for television film *Living Proof: The Hank Williams Jr. Story* (1983); videotapes of his various opening sequences for Monday Night Football.

USED CLOTHING/EQUIPMENT
Guitar Picks: $10-$15

REFERENCES/BOOKS
Living Proof by Hank Williams, Jr. (1979)

Williams, Larry

Born: May 10, 1935, Died: January 2, 1980

The alliterative Larry Williams, a poor man's Little Richard, or Jerry Lee Lewis is best remembered for his hit song flurry which included "Short Fat Fanny" (#5), "Bonie Moronie" (#14), and "Dizzy Miss Liz-

zy" (#69, 1958). When his brief streak stalled, Williams pondered production before teaming up with Johnny "Guitar" Watson and laying down a few R&B hits. Haunted by a record of narcotics trafficking, he committed suicide in 1980.

AUTOGRAPHS
An LP, magazine cover, ad, photo, or card signed by the artist: $15-$35

Williams, Lucinda

Born: January 26, 1953

A talented songwriter, Lucinda Williams is best known for her songs "The Night's Too Long," covered by Patty Loveless, and "Passionate Kisses," winner of a Grammy for Mary Chapin Carpenter.

AUTOGRAPHS
An LP, magazine cover, ad, photo, or card signed by the artist: $8-$12

Williams, Maurice and the Zodiacs

Formed 1959

Maurice Williams, Born: April 26, 1938; Henry Gaston; Wiley Bennett; Charles Thomas; Little Willie Morrow; and Albert Hill

Beach Music Hall of Famers the Zodiacs are best remembered for the shortest Number One in rock and roll history, "Stay." While it was short in length, it was long on the charts where it stayed in the Top Forty for three months in 1960. Williams had previously also recorded "Little Darlin'," later a hit for the Diamonds.

AUTOGRAPHS
An LP, magazine cover, ad, photo, or card signed by the group: $15-$40

Williams, Otis and His Charms

Formed 1954

Original lineup: Otis Williams, Born: June 2, 1936; Rolland Bradley; Joe Penn; Richard Parker; and Donald Peak

Best known for their R&B hits "Hearts of Stone" (#15, 1955), "Ling, Ting, Tong" (#26, 1955), and "Two Hearts" (#9, R&B, 1955), Otis Williams and His Charms also later scored with "Ivory Tower" (#11, 1956).

AUTOGRAPHS
An LP, magazine cover, ad, photo, or card signed by the artist: $10-$25

Williams, Paul

Born: September 19, 1940

Actor, singer, and songwriter Williams teamed up with Roger Nichols in 1967 and wrote "We've Only Just Begun," "Rainy Days and Mondays," "You and Me Against the World," "Old Fashioned Love Song," and "Out in the Country."

Williams then turned to singing his own songs and playing the Vegas circuit before focusing more on his film scoring. "Evergreen," his collaboration with Barbra Striesand from her film remake *A Star Is Born*, won them both an Oscar, while plunging Williams further into the spotlight. The success led to other film scores and an opportunity to even get in front of the cameras in flicks such as the *Smokey and the Bandit* series.

AUTOGRAPHS

An LP, magazine cover, ad, photo, or card signed by the artist: $5-$25

OFTEN OVERLOOKED MEMORABILIA

Movie memorabilia from *Phantom of Paradise* (1976), *Bugsy Malone* (1977), *A Star Is Born* (1976), *The End* (1978), *The Muppet Movie* (1979), *The Secret of NIMH* (1982), *Rocky IV* (1984), *Ishtar* (1987), *The Muppet Christmas Carol* (1992), *Smokey and the Bandit* series (1977-83), *The Doors* (1991), *A Million to Juan* (1994), *Headless Body in a Topless Bar* (1995), *The Loved One* (1964), and *The Chase* (1965); videotapes form his numerous television appearances including *Picket Fences* and the miniseries *People Like Us*; associated memorabilia from other musicians' covers of his work

The Tony Williams Lifetime

Formed 1969

Tony Williams, Born: December 12, 1945; John McLaughlin, Born: January 4, 1942; and Larry Young*

*Jack Bruce, Born: May 14, 1943 was added in 1969. McLaughlin and Bruce left in 1971 and Ted Dunbar, Warren Smith, Don Alias, and Juni Booth were added. Numerous personnel changes followed.

Best known for helping define the music as a member of the Miles Davis Quintet of the '60s, Williams later left to form one of the first jazz-rock fusion bands.

AUTOGRAPHS

An LP, magazine cover, ad, photo, or card signed by the artist: $15-$25

Williams, Vanessa

Born: March 18, 1963

When it appeared as if all odds were against her success, Vanessa Williams persevered to become an outstanding singer and actress. While attending Syracuse University, she entered the Miss America pageant and won, becoming the first African American winner in history. Not long after her victory *Penthouse* magazine published provocative photographs of her taken during a modeling session as a teenager. The scandal rocked the tabloids and the pageant, forcing her to relinquish her crown.

Miraculously, she later reappeared did some commercials, and went on to some acting roles. In 1987 she then inked a deal with PolyGram's Wing Records, where she released her debut album *The Right Stuff* (#38, 1988). The album spun off the successful extract "Dreamin'" (#8, 1989) and was followed by her sophomore album *The Comfort Zone* (#17, 1991). "Work to Do," "Running Back to You," and "Save the Best for Last" (#1, 1991) were all Top Five singles—the latter was even a Grammy nominee.

Her career now ignited, she landed on the charts again dueting with Brian McKnight on "Love Is" (#3, 1993), hosted *The Soul of VH-1*, and was involved with numerous other efforts before releasing her next album, *The Sweetest Days* (#57, 1994). While the title track of her latest album was climbing the singles charts, she turned her attention to Broadway and appeared in *Kiss of the Spider Woman*. "Colors of the Wind," from the Disney animated film feature *Pocahontas* was her next chart success, while she also appeared with Arnold Schwarzennegger in the film *Eraser*. In 1997, Williams co-starred with Lawrence Fishburne in the movie *Hoodlums* and toured in the fall with Luther Vandross. Her album *Next*, released on August 26, 1997 continued to show her dynamic vocal evolution, while tackling familiar emotional themes.

AUTOGRAPHS

A CD, LP, magazine cover, ad, photo, or card signed by the artist: $20-$55

OFTEN OVERLOOKED MEMORABILIA

All associated Miss America related items, including tabloids and periodicals; *Penthouse* (7/84) magazine; movie memorabilia from *Pocahontas* (1995) and *Eraser* (1996); videotapes of her appearances on *The Soul of VH-1*; memorabilia from the television soundtrack to *Beverly Hills 90210*; all theatre memorabilia from her performance in *Kiss of the Spider Woman*

Willis, Chuck

Born: January 31, 1928, Died: April 10, 1958

Known as "The King of Stroll," Chuck Willis is best remembered for his hit "C.C. Rider" (#12, 1957), along with "What Am I Living For?" (#9, 1958), "Hang Up My Rock and Roll Shoes," "It's Too Late," and "I Feel So Bad."

AUTOGRAPHS

An LP, magazine cover, ad, photo, or card signed by the artist: $75-$200

Willis, Bob and His Texas Playboys

Formed 1935

Bob Willis, Born: March 6, 1905, Died: May 10, 1975

Best known as a Western swing band, which merged big-band elements with pop, blues, and country, Bob Willis and His Texas Playboys introduced horns, drums, and even electric guitars to their genre. The band changed the course of country and pop music in the '30s and beyond with hits such as "San Antonio Rose" (#11, 1944), "Smoke on the Water" (1945), "Stars and Stripes of Iwo Jima" (1945), "Silver Dew on the Blue Grass Tonight" (1945), "White Cross on Okinawa" (#1945), "New Spanish Two Step" (1946), and "Sugar Moon" (1947). Other familiar group tunes followed, including "Faded Love," "Cotton Eyed Joe," "Take Me Back to Tulsa," and "Time Changes Everything" before the '60s started to take a toll on Willis' health. He suffered a stroke in 1973 that eventually led to his death in 1975.

AUTOGRAPHS

An LP, magazine cover, ad, photo, or card signed by the artist: $40-$125

Wilson, Jackie

Born: June 9, 1934, Died: January 21, 1984

Exquisite is the first adjective that comes to mind when speaking about one of the top vocalists and performers of the late '50s and the '60s, Jackie Wilson. Often referred to as a combination of James Brown and Sam Cooke, Wilson could ignite a crowd faster than the nearest pyromaniac. He was smooth, pro-

vocative, and sexy and when he delivered such songs as "To Be Loved" (#22, 1958), "Lonely Teardrops" (#7, 1958), "That's Why (I Love you So)"(#13, 1959), and "I'll Be Satisfied" (#20, 1959), he had the crowd in a frenzy—so crazy in fact that a fan shot and seriously wounded the singer in 1961. His hits continued into the '60s and included "Baby Workout" (#5, 1963), "Whispers" (#11, 1966), and "(Your Love Keeps Lifting Me) Higher and Higher" (#6, 1966), before tailing off. He died in 1984 and was inducted into the Rock and Roll Hall of Fame in 1987.

AUTOGRAPHS

An LP, magazine cover, ad, photo, or card signed by the artist: $25-$65

OFTEN OVERLOOKED MEMORABILIA

His work with Billy Ward and The Dominoes

Wilson Phillips

Formed 1989

Chynna Phillips, Born: February 12, 1968; Carnie Wilson, Born: April 29, 1968; and Wendy Wilson, Born: October 16, 1969

Typically first associated with their rock and roll fathers, Phillips, the daughter of John and Michelle Phillips (Mamas and the Papas) and the Wilson sisters, daughters of Beach Boy surf guru Brian Wilson, they caught a wave with their self-titled debut (#2, 1990) that spun off the successful singles "Hold On" (#1, 1990), "Release Me" (#1, 1990), You're in Love" (#1, 1990), and later "Impulsive" (#4, 1990). But in stark contrast, *Shadows and Light* was released when the tide was out, and it yielded no hit singles and perhaps even depressed a few fans along the way. The group was even forced to cancel a 1992 summer tour due to poor ticket sales.

AUTOGRAPHS

A CD, LP, magazine cover, ad, photo, or card signed by the group: $15-$35

Winger

Formed 1986

Kip Winger, Reb Beach, Paul Taylor, and Rod Morganstein*

*Taylor departed in 1990 and was replaced by John Roth.

A popular light metal "hair act," led by singer Kip Winger, the band had a successful debut album (#21,

1988) that spun off the hit extracts "Seventeen" (#26, 1989) and "Headed for a Heartbreak" (#19, 1989). Winger's sophomore effort *In the Heart of the Young* (#15, 1990) included the extracts "Can't Get Enuff" (#42, 1990), "Miles Away" (#12, 1991), and "Easy Come Easy Go" (#41, 1990). As the band's appeal waned, the members went their separate ways.

A guitar pick from Winger

AUTOGRAPHS

A CD, LP, magazine cover, ad, photo, or card signed by the group: $15-$25

USED CLOTHING/EQUIPMENT

Guitar Picks: $5

Winter, Edgar

Born: December 28, 1946

Multi-talented musician and younger brother of Johnny Winter, Edgar Winter broke first as a concert attraction with White Trash in the early '70s before forming the experimental, yet commercially successful, hard rock foursome the Edgar Winter Group. The group became well known for the hits "Frankenstein" (#1, 1972) and "Free Ride" (#14, 1973), as well as for being an energetic live attraction. The band showcased other talented musicians including Dan Hartman, Ronnie Montrose, and Rick Derringer, all of whom had success as solo artists or with other projects.

AUTOGRAPHS

A CD, LP, magazine cover, ad, photo, or card signed by the artist: $15-$40

OFTEN OVERLOOKED MEMORABILIA

Movie memorabilia from *My Cousin Vinny*

Winter, Johnny

Born: February 23, 1944

Widely popular in the '70s, during a decade that welcomed the white guitarist, Johnny Winter dug deep into his blues roots to "rough em' up" with a rock edge sound. His debut on Columbia sold well, and by the end of the '60s, he garnered a significant reputation while playing at the Scene in New York. He then restructured his band to include his brother Edgar, Rick Derringer, Randy Hobbs, and drummer Randy Zehringer, and released *Johnny Winter And*, along with a live album that then included Bobby Caldwell, who had replaced Zehringer. Both albums, accompanied by his extensive touring schedule, bolstered his growing following that became immediately evident with the sales of his albums *Still Alive and Well* (#22, 1973) and *Saint and Sinners* (#42, 1974). In 1976 Johnny worked with his brother Edgar, whose popularity now eclipsed Johnny's, on *Together* (#89, 1976). From this point on he played in Muddy Waters' backing band, toured a bit, and has occasionally resurfaced, always to critical acclaim and in reverence to one of rock's preeminent white bluesman.

AUTOGRAPHS

A CD, LP, magazine cover, ad, photo, or card signed by the artist: $15-$40

Winwood, Steve

Born: May 12, 1948

When you think of the many creative and talented rock musicians who have truly left an indelible mark in music history, Steve Winwood is not the first name that comes to mind, but little time will pass before he is mentioned. Over three decades worth of musical innovation, from child prodigy to accomplished solo artist, he has played with some of the biggest names in the business including Spencer Davis, Dave Mason, Jim Capaldi, Eric Clapton, and Ginger Baker.

His early interest in music was cultivated by his parents, whose appreciation for the art form influenced both Steve and his older brother Muff. Both brothers were soon playing in their father's combo while continuing their music education in school. Steve studied guitar and piano and eventually joined his brother in the Muff Winwood Jazz Band. In 1963, while playing in Birmingham on a bill with guitarist Spencer Davis, both forces, who shared a common direction, decided to merge their talents.

At the young age of fifteen, Steve Winwood became a member of the Spencer Davis Group. A strong live reputation, which often included support for many blues giants, soon established a base following for the band. A hit single became the next stepping stone, and it arrived with "Keep On Running" (#1, 1966). Winwood's confidence grew, and it wasn't long before "Gimme Some Lovin" and "I'm a Man" delivered the Spencer Davis Group to a different level.

At the age of eighteen he soon caught the attention of many of his peers including Eric Clapton. Together both enjoyed some brief studio work with a band called Powerhouse. Clapton then went on to work with Cream and, having left the Spencer Davis Group in early 1967, Winwood formed Traffic. Traffic was an ongoing outlet for Winwood (1967-74), who when bored would venture into other projects including Blind Faith and Ginger Baker's Air Force.

Traffic delivered some outstanding works including *Mr. Fantasy*, *John Barleycorn Must Die*, *The Low Spark of High Heeled Boys*, and *When the Eagle Flies*. The group's success cemented Winwood in rock's history, but he still desired one other element—a solo career. It began in 1971 with *Winwood* (United Artists), a modest success, but bloomed with *Arc of a Diver* (#3, 1981). "While You See A Chance" (#7, 1981) became Winwood's first solo hit single, before "Still In The Game," "Higher Love" (#1, 1986), "Freedom Overspill" (#20, 1986), "The Finer Things" (#8, 1987), "Back In The High Life Again" (#13, 1987), "Valerie" (#9, 1987), and "Roll With It" (#1, 1988) confirm his status as a bona fide hit maker. "Assisted by its inclusion in a Michelob Beer television commercial, "Don't You Know What the Night Can Do?" (#6, 1988) crept into the Top Ten on the singles charts. "Holding On" (#11, 1989) and "Hearts On Fire" (#53, 1989) rounded out his single production for the remainder of the decade.

An established Steve Winwood entered the '90s confident in style, but a bit less ambitious than the previous decade. *Refugees of the Heart* (#27, 1990) spun off extract "One and Only Man" (#18, 1990), as the artist saw far less album production in the years that followed. Perhaps a bit nostalgic, he reunited with Traffic for the album *Far from Home* before supporting the release with a 1994 fall tour. In the works at this time is a four-CD set retrospective, *The Finer Things*, which chronicles the many facets of this extraordinary musician's career. With his position in rock history solidified, and clearly with little to prove to any critic, Winwood can now just sit back and "Roll With It"!

AUTOGRAPHS

A CD, LP, magazine cover, ad, photo, or card signed by the artist: $15-$25

TOUR BOOKS/ PROGRAMS/PASSES

Tour Books:
Roll With It Tour of the World, 1988: $12-$15

A Steve Winwood tour program valued at $12-$15 (1988 F.S. Ltd.)

OFTEN OVERLOOKED MEMORABILIA

Roll With It, Virgin Records promotional dice, 1988; a handbill from his performance in *Tommy* (8/24/89); videotapes from his television appearances including *Late Night With David Letterman* (4/12/91)

REFERENCES/BOOKS

Limited resources exist, but none do justice to the singer in my opinion. There are no dedicated collector books.

Wire

Formed 1976

Colin Newman, Bruce Gilbert, Graham Lewis, and Robert Gotobed (Mark Field)

Wire was an avant-garde punk band whose art school approach and back to basics foundation during the late '70s were an inspiration to many acts that followed, including R.E.M. and the Cure. The band split up in 1980, but got together years later for no particular reason or result.

AUTOGRAPHS

An LP, magazine cover, ad, photo, or card signed by the group: $8-$25*
*On vintage pre-1980 memorabilia only!

Withers, Bill

Born: July 4, 1938

Talented singer/songwriter in both R&B and pop, Bill Withers is commonly associated with his hits "Lean On Me" (#1, 1972), "Ain't No Sunshine" (#3, 1971), "Use Me" (#2, 1972), and as co-author of "Just the Two of Us" (#2, 1980), although he has delivered numerous successful R&B offerings.

AUTOGRAPHS

A CD, LP, magazine cover, ad, photo, or card signed by the artist: $5-$15

OFTEN OVERLOOKED MEMORABILIA

Memorabilia associated with other musicians who have covered his work

---

Womack, Bobby

Born: March 4, 1944

Gifted writer, performer, and guitarist Bobby Womack has forged a legacy for himself in both rock

and soul, penning standards such as "It's All Over Now" and "Lookin' for a Love." He sat in on sessions with Aretha Franklin, Ray Charles, and King Curtis, and wrote and played guitar on Janis Joplin's "Trust Me" and George Benson's "Breezin'." Womack also landed solo hits with "That's the Way I Feel About 'Cha" (#27, 1971), "Woman's Got to Have It" (#1, R&B, 1972), and "Daylight" (#5, 1976). He resurfaces periodically on a variety of projects, and has been active in numerous humanitarian efforts.

AUTOGRAPHS
A CD, LP, magazine cover, ad, photo, or card signed by the artist: $8-$30

OFTEN OVERLOOKED MEMORABILIA
Memorabilia associated with other musicians who have covered his work

Wonder, Stevie

(Steveland Morris)
Born: May 13, 1950

Blind since birth, and inspired by the golden voice of Ray Charles, by the age of seven Stevie Wonder was already fairly proficient on a variety of instruments. He formed a duo with John Glover, whose cousin Gerald White was a brother of Miracles member Ronnie White. Through White, Wonder was introduced to Motown Records' legend Berry Gordy and producer Brian Holland. Impressed by Wonder's ability, the ten year old was signed to a long-term contract.

On August 16, 1962, his first single was released, "I Call It Pretty Music (But the Old People Call It the Blues)," featuring drummer Marvin Gaye. He then briefly honed his live act before being added to a two-month Motown Records package tour that also featured Marvin Gaye, the Miracles, the Supremes, and Mary Wells (1962).

Recorded Live—The 12 Year Old Genius, topped the U.S. charts on August 24, 1963,—the first live record to do so—as "Workout Stevie, Workout" (#33, 1963) began an upward singles climb. "Castles in the Sand" (#52, 1964) and "Hey Harmonica Man" (#29, 1964) were his next singles and as the moniker " Little" was no longer appropriate, it was deleted from his name. In 1965, the Motown review, with Wonder, opened a 21-date U.K. package tour in March, before "High Heel Sneakers" (#59, 1965) became the next Wonder single.

"Uptight (Everything's Alright)" (#3, 1966) catapulted the artist's status as a performer and topped the R&B charts. He followed it with single "Nothing's Too Good for My Baby" (#20, 1966), while the album *Up Tight Everything's Alright* (#33, 1966) entered

the Top Forty. Follow-up hit singles "Blowin' in the Wind" (#9, 1966) and "A Place in the Sun" (#20, 1967), preceded the release of his next album, *Down to Earth* (#92, 1967). "Travelin' Man" (#32, 1967) and "Hey Love" (#90, 1967) then landed on the singles chart, before his next album *I Was Made to Love Her* (#45, 1967) emerged, with the extracted title cut (#5, 1967).

Greatest Hits (#37, 1968) was released while "Shoo-Be-Doo-Be-Doo-Da-Day" (#9, 1968) began its rise up the singles chart, followed by "You Met Your Match" (#35, 1968). "For Once in My Life" (#2, 1968), his next smash single, drove sales of the identically titled parent album (#50, 1969). "I Don't Know Why" (#39, 1969) and "My Cherie Amour/I Don't Know Why" (#4, 1969) continued his streak of Top Four Hits, before "Yester-me, Yester-you, Yesterday" (#7, 1969) closed out his singles releases for the year.

"Never Had a Dream Come True" (#26, 1970) was his first hit of the year, to be followed by "Signed, Sealed, Delivered I'm Yours" (#3, 1970) and "Heaven Help Us" (#9,1970). His album production for the year included *Stevie Wonder Live* (#81, 1970) and *Signed, Sealed, Delivered* (#25, 1970). On September 14, 1970, he married Syreeta Wright, a former Motown Records secretary. The following year's singles included "We Can Work It Out" (#13, 1971) (a Beatles cover), "Never Dreamed You'd Leave in Summer" (#78, 1971), "If You Really Love Me" (#8, 1971), while albums included *Where I'm Coming From* (#62, 1971) and *Greatest Hits, Vol.2* (#69, 1971).

Beginning with *Music of My Mind* (#21, 1972), Wonder began his transition into becoming a more introspective musician. As he supported the Rolling Stones 1972 50-date North American journey, "Superwoman (Where were You When I Needed You)" (#33, 1972) and "Keep On Running" (#90, 1972) were released as singles. Pivotal album *Talking Book* (#3, 1972) was released in the fall as "Superstition" (#1, 1973) topped the U.S. singles chart a few months later. "You Are the Sunshine of My Life" (#1, 1973) gave the artist his second straight Number One hit, and solidified his position as a hitmaker.

As Rufus released "Tell Me Something Good" (#3, 1973), penned by Wonder, the artist was seriously injured in an automobile accident. He recovered, although he did suffer some ramifications. *Innervisions* (#4, 1973), a complete Wonder package, climbed into the Top Five on the album chart, while singles "Higher Ground" (#4, 1973) and "Living for the City" (#8, 1974) sustained his name atop the singles listing. The album garnered the artist numerous honors including Album of the Year, at the 16th annual Grammys.

Fulfillingness' First Finale (#1, 1974) topped the U.S. album chart in September 1974, while singles "Don't You Worry 'Bout a Thing" (#16, 1974), "You Haven't Done Nothin'"(#1, 1974), and "Boogie On Reggae Woman" (#3, 1975) added to the artist's long

run of successful hits. As Wonder continued to be flooded with another round of awards for his latest Number One album, he watched his penned "Lovin' You" top the singles chart for Minnie Ripperton.

In 1976 Wonder released the masterful *Songs in the Key of Life* (#1, 1976). The double album, which also included an EP, was lauded as not only the artist's finest, but certainly one of the most outstanding works in recorded history. "I Wish" (#1, 1977) and "Sir Duke" (#1, 1977) were two more chart toppers for Wonder, who again added more Grammy Awards to his showcase, including Album of the Year.

Journey Through the Secret Life of Plants (#4, 1979), which took three years to make, was a soundtrack to a documentary film and a precursor to the more reflective *Hotter Than July* (#3, 1980). "Master Blaster (Jammin')" (#5, 1980), "That Girl" (#4, 1982), "Do I Do" (#13), and "Ebony and Ivory" (#1, 1982) with Paul McCartney maintained the artist's singles chart presence.

The Stevie Wonder of the '80s slowed a bit in studio work, but continued to tour and contribute his efforts to many humanitarian causes including Peace Sunday, AIDS Awareness, and anti-apartheid efforts. "I Just Called to Say I Love You" (#1, 1984), extracted from the soundtrack *The Woman in Red* (#4, 1984), won that year's Oscar for Best Song. *In Square Circle* (#5, 1986) included the hit single "Part-Time Lover" (#1, 1985), while the artist also landed a hit with the collaboration "That's What Friends Are For" (#1, 1986). Neither *Characters* (#17, 1987) or *Jungle Fever* (#24, 1991) (a soundtrack) lived up to expectations. He returned in 1994 with *Conversation Peace* (#16, 1995), which was praised by the critics and included duets with Michael Jackson and Julio Iglesias.

As one of rock and roll's most successful artists of all-time, he has transcended numerous musical boundaries, through both innovation and creativity. As a lifelong advocate of nonviolent political change, he has been a hallmark for many who followed. In my opinion, he is not only one of the most outstanding musicians of this decade, but one of the finest humanitarians of our time.

AUTOGRAPHS

A CD, LP, magazine cover, ad, photo, or card signed by the artist: $20-$45

TOUR BOOKS/PROGRAMS/PASSES

Tour Books:
Wonder... In Square Circle, 1986: $25

Backstage Passes:
Cloth/Paper: $12-$20; Laminated: $15-$35

POSTERS/PRESS KITS

Promotional Posters: $10-$45
Press Kits: $20-$50

OFTEN OVERLOOKED MEMORABILIA

Movie memorabilia from *Bikini Beach* (1964), *Muscle Beach Party* (1964), *The Woman in Red* (#1984), and *Jungle Fever* (1991); any items related to Eivets Rednow, a moniker he has used in the past; programs from the numerous shows where he has collected awards; all items associated with his efforts to have the birth date of Martin Luther King celebrated as a U.S. national holiday; any items associated with his numerous charity ventures; videotapes form his numerous television appearances; *Ebony* magazine (October 1991)

REFERENCES/BOOKS

Limited resources exist, but none do justice to the singer in my opinion. There are no dedicated collector books.

World Party

Formed 1986

Karl Wallinger

A veteran of bands Zero Zero, Invisible Body Club, and Out, Wallinger answered an ad placed by the Waterboy's Mike Scott, who was looking for a guitarist. In 1966 Wallinger left the band after two albums, primarily out of frustration, and formed World Party. The band, essentially Wallinger only, added guests on an "as needed" basis. His ecologically theme driven debut record *Private Revolution* (#39, 1987) was aided by heavy college airplay, extensive touring, and the extracted single "Ship of Fools" (#27, 1987). Album guests included Waterboys Steve Wickham and Anthony Thistlewaite, along with Sinead O'Connor.

Goodbye Jumbo (#36, 1990), another environmentally focused release, slowly climbed the charts as World Party supported the release through touring and the sales of single "Message in the Box" (#39, U.K., 1990). Wallinger then once again retreated to the comfort of his home studio, only to resurface during special events or projects.

Bang! (#2, U.K.; #126, U.S., 1993), the group's third album, sold strong in Britain and made strides in the U.S. Single success was limited to the U.K. as "Give It All Away" (#43, U.K., 1993) and "All I Gave" (#37, U.K., 1993) gave the band more exposure.

AUTOGRAPHS

A CD, LP, magazine cover, ad, photo, or card signed by the artist - $20-$40

TOUR BOOKS/PROGRAMS/PASSES

Backstage Passes:
Cloth: $8-$12; Laminated: $12-$20

OFTEN OVERLOOKED MEMORABILIA

A copy of the *Sounds* advertisement placed by Mike Scott looking for a guitarist; artifacts from the numerous causes Wallinger has been active supporting; videotapes of the

group's numerous television appearances including *Late Night With David Letterman* (5/17/90) and *Saturday Night Live* (11/10/90); associated festival memorabilia; movie memorabilia from *Reality Bites* (1994)

Wray, Link

Born: May 2, 1935

This fuzz-toned '50s rock guitarist is best known for his 1954 hit "Rumble" and his 1959 instrumental "Raw-Hide" (#23, 1959).

AUTOGRAPHS

A CD, LP, magazine cover, ad, photo, or card signed by the artist: $5-$25

OFTEN OVERLOOKED MEMORABILIA

Memorabilia associated with other musicians who have covered his work

Wreckx-N-Effect

Formed 1987

Miggady-Mark (Markell Riley), A Plus (Aquil Davidson), Brandon Mitchell, and Keith KC

Wreckx-N-Effect is best known for the album *Hard or Smooth* (#9, 1992) and extract "Rump Shaker" with its controversial promotional video.

AUTOGRAPHS

A CD, LP, magazine cover, ad, photo, or card signed by the group: $5-$10

Wright, Betty

Born: December 21, 1953

Wright came out of the '70s music scene in Miami to make a presence on the R&B charts throughout the '80s with songs such as "Clean Up Woman" (#6, 1971), "Baby Sitter" (#46, 1972), and "Let Me Be Your Lovemaker" (#10, R&B, 1975).

AUTOGRAPHS

A CD, LP, magazine cover, ad, photo, or card signed by the artist: $5-$10

Wright, Gary

Born: April 26, 1943

This ex-Spooky Tooth member is best known for his late-70s solo singles "Dream Weaver" (#2, 1975) and "Love Is Alive" (#2, 1975).

AUTOGRAPHS

A CD, LP, magazine cover, ad, photo, or card signed by the artist: $3-$12

OFTEN OVERLOOKED MEMORABILIA

Memorabilia associated with other musicians who have covered his work; *Waynes World* memorabilia

Wright, O.V.

(Overton Wright)
Born: October 9, 1939, Died: November 16, 1980

Wright, a talented R&B soul singer, cowrote "That's How Strong My Love Is" and landed R&B hits with "You're Gonna Make Me Cry' (#6, R&B, 1965), "Eight Men, Four Women" (#4, R&B, 1967), and "Ace of Spade" (#11, R&B, 1970).

AUTOGRAPHS

An LP, magazine cover, ad, photo, or card signed by the artist: $5-$15

Wright, Syreeta

Performer and songwriter Syreeta Wright, formerly Mrs. Stevie Wonder, is best known for her duet with Billy Preston on "With You I'm Born Again" (#4, 1980) and for the songs she cowrote with Wonder including "Signed, Sealed, Delivered" and "If You Really Love Me." The two were married on September 14, 1970, and divorced eighteen months later.

AUTOGRAPHS

A CD, LP, magazine cover, ad, photo, or card signed by the artist: $5-$20*
*Wonder-related key memorabilia

Wynette, Tammy

(Virginia Wynette)
Born: May 5, 1942

A talented country singer who placed nearly thirty Top Tens on the country charts between 1967 and 1979, seventeen of which landed atop the chart including "My Elusive Dreams," "I Don't Want to Play House," "D-I-V-O-R-C-E," and "Stand By Your Man," Wynette's tumultuous personal life has been heavily

chronicled. A victim of five marriages, Wynette has often used her songs to vent her frustrations. Her work with George Jones was more successful than the couple's marriage—they did, however, reunite for her album *One* in 1995.

X

Formed 1977

John Doe, Exene (Christine) Cervenka, Billy Zoom, and Don J. Bonebrake*

*Zoom left in 1985 and was replaced by Tony Gilkyson.

A consumate player in the maturing Southern California punk movement, X began in 1977 when John Doe and Billy Zoom hooked up through a L.A. advertisement. Zoom brought with him some experience, having played with Gene Vincent for awhile in the '70s. Cervenka had migrated from Florida and met Doe at a poetry workshop in Venice, California. Both became not only bandmates, but eventually husband and wife. The group began playing at the Masque, Hollywood's noted punk porthole, with added drummer Don Bonebrake. After seeing the band play at the Whiskey, former Door keyboardist Ray Manzarek became their producer.

The group's debut release *Los Angeles* (1980) sold extremely well for an indie release. It was followed by *Wild Gift* (1981), which also sold very well. Cervenka and Doe gelled well, both vocally and as co-writers. Critics praised both albums, and not a single underground rag sheet could be found that didn't evoke the band's name in reverence.

The attention also found its way to major record labels and in 1981 the band signed with Elektra. The band's third album *Under the Black Sun* was in great contrast to *Wild Gift*, but at least it was on a big label. *Ain't Love Grand* (1985) followed and included "Burning House of Love," the crossover hit that wasn't. Billy Zoom split when it appeared as if nothing was really going to happen—he was right!. Blaster Dave Alvin, who was a member of the one-off Knitters, filled in. *See How We Are*, which wasn't much better than it predecessor, included new guitarist Tony Gilkyson. The album noticeably lacked Gloom's high level energy, with the exception of "4th of July" contributed by Alvin.

While the band was unraveling, so was Cervenka and Doe's marriage. *Live at the Whiskey A Go-Go on the Fabulous Sunset Strip* (1988) proved that the only thing fabulous with this record was the title. The band then retreated to solo efforts before finally regrouping in 1990 for *Hey Zeus!*. Heavily supported and well received, the record enjoyed mediocre success. *Unclogged* (1995), a name too cute to be a real X title, featured live acoustic versions from the group's catalog, but also failed to gain any significant recognition.

Gone are the catchy phrases that hung on you like skin affixed to a vinyl chair, the torrid guitar discharges of thunder guitar guru Billy Zoom, and the adrenal rushes from songs like "Johnny Hit and Run Pauline" and "Los Angeles" that made you think that your arteries would explode just prior to a major seizure. *Wild Gift* (Slash, 1991) and any associated pieces of memorabilia from its release are musts for any X collector and/or music historian.

REFERENCES/BOOKS

Adventures Anonymous by Exene Cervenka and Lydia
Lunch

X-Ray Spex

Formed 1977

Poly Styrene (Marion Elliot), Lora Logic (Susan Whitby),
Jak Airport (Jack Stafford), Paul Dean, and Chris Chrysler*

*Logic left in 1978 and was replaced briefly by Rudy
Thompson (Steven Rudan), then Glyn Johns.

X-Ray Spex flashed with its first hit with "Oh
Bondage Up Yours!" in 1977, featuring the ever seductive Poly Styrene panting out that, you know,
that seen not heard line. It was easy to get passed
her brace-infested smile, but those exotic outfits, oh
well. Subsequent singles included "The Day the
World Turned Dayglo" and "Identity." The group,
whose only album was *Germ Free Adolescents*, broke
up two months after the debut album offering. "Highly Inflammable" was a posthumous release, as Poly,
now suffering a nervous breakdown from a UFO
sighting, flocked to join the Krishna Consciousness
movement.

Marion Elliot returned in 1980—no doubt rejuvenated by the sabbatical—to release a solo album,
Translucence, followed by the EP *Gods and Goddess-
es* (1986). The band did reunite in 1991 for a "punk
nostalgia night"—aren't you glad you lived long
enough to see such an event!

AUTOGRAPHS

A CD, LP, magazine cover, ad, photo, or card signed by the
group: $10-$20

XTC

Formed 1977

Andrew Partridge, Colin Moulding, Terry Chambers, and
John Perkins*

*Perkins departed in 1977 and was replaced by Barrry
Andrews. Andrews left in 1978 and Dave Gregory was
added. Chambers left in 1982.

Partridge, Moulding, and Chambers, all ex-mem-
bers of Star Park/Helium Kidz were joined by Barry
Andrews (King Crimson). Playing the London club
circuit, the four began to establish a strong following.
Signed to Virgin Records, they released their debut
EP, *3-D* (1977). The band's first album, *White Music*
(#38, U.K., 1978), sold well, and the band was quickly
added to a new wave roster. *Go 2* (#21, U.K., 1978)
the next album, was driven by extracted single "Are
You Receiving Me?."

In January 1979, Andrews quit and later teamed
up with Robert Fripp to form League of Gentlemen;
he was replaced by Dave Gregory. *Drums and Wires*
(#94, U.K., 1979) became the band's third offering
and included the single "Making Plans for Nigel"
(#17, U.K.; #176, U.S., 1979). The double A-side "Gen-
erals and Majors/Don't Lose Your Temper" (#32,
U.K., 1980) climbed the charts as the band released
Black Sea (#16, U.K., 1980). The band then elicited
comparisons to the nostalgic British invasion acts for
its pop hooks and shattering rhythms. "Black Sea"
(#41, 1980-1981) was pushed by extracts "Towers of
London" (#31, U.K., 1980) and "Sgt. Rock (Is Going
to Help Me)" (#16, U.K., 1981).

"Senses Working Overtime" (#10, U.K., 1982), the
group's biggest success, climbed the singles chart as
English Settlement (#5, U.K., 1982) was praised by
critics. Touring in support of the album, Partridge
collapsed twice from health problems, causing the
tour to be canceled. Drummer Chambers then departed, only months before it was announced that the
band would no longer play live. Compilation *Wax-
works: Some Singles (1977-1982)* (#54, 1982), which
is initially released with a free companion B-sides
collection called *Beeswax*, finished out a tough year
for the band.

Mummer (#51, U.K., 1983), Partridge's convalescence project, was released, but when the band refused to tour in its support it caused friction with the
group's label. It was followed by *The Big Express*
(#178, 1984), which was well received in the U.K., the
group's stronghold of support. The group then rotat-
ed its identity and recorded the mini-album *The
Dukes of Stratosphear: 25 O'Clock* under the name
Dukes of Stratosphear— you know, the " Johanson
to Poindexter" transition. More than a year later Virgin released *The Compact XTC*, an 18-track retrospective. The band then turned to the U.S. to record
Skylarking (#70, 1986). The album, produced by
Todd Rundgren, caught the eyes of many in a country
that had yet to really discover the band. It was followed by another strong release, *Oranges & Lemons*
(#44, 1989), the group's strongest U.S. album to date,
and continuation of its mnovement up the charts.

Nonsuch (#97, 1992), XTC's first album of the '90s,
featured a greater emphasis on orchestration and
keyboards. In 1994 the band contributed a song to
Carmen Sandiego: Out of This World, its first recording in two years. It is followed by the archive release
*Drums and Wireless: BBC Radio Sessions: 1977-
1989.*

AUTOGRAPHS

A CD, LP, magazine cover, ad, photo, or card signed by the
group: $20-$45

TOUR BOOKS/PROGRAMS/PASSES

Backstage Passes:
Cloth: $10-$15; Laminated: $15-$25

POSTERS/PRESS KITS

Promotional Posters: $10-$35
Press Kits: $25-$50 (1976-present)

OFTEN OVERLOOKED MEMORABILIA

Movie memorabilia from *Time Square* (1980); artifiacts from the group's numerous aliases, such as the Virgin promo pack for "Psonic Psunspots" that came with an embroidered bag that included badges, a ball, rolling papers and oil.

REFERENCES/BOOKS

Chalkhills and Children by Chris Towmey - $20

Yankovic, "Weird Al"

Born: October 23, 1959

"The potent prince of parody," Weird Al is to music what Max Patkin was to baseball. Constantly adding his profound lyrics to current hit songs, he drives the sales of his records through slapstick video parodies of those created by the original artists. Therefore, "Smells Like Teen Spirit" by Nirvana can be creatively Yankovized into "Smells Like Nirvana" (#35, 1992). You've got the picture!

Alfred Matthew Yankovic got his first big break after mailing a tape to syndicated radio show host Dr. Demento. He recorded a parody of the Knack's "My Sharona," "My Bologna," in a bathroom. It became so popular with Demento's audience that Capitol released it as a single. His follow-up "Another One Rides the Bus, based on the Queen hit "Another One Bites the Dust," became one of Demento's all-time most requested songs.

Yankovic eventually signed on with Rock 'n' Roll Records (a CBS subsidiary) and released his self-titled debut in 1983. His first hit video parodied Toni Basil's "Mickey" by adding a twist from TV's classic *I Love Lucy*. "Ricky" (#63, 1983) was followed by "I Lost on Jeopardy (#81, 1984) and "Like a Surgeon" (#47, 1985).

When music-infused *Polka Party* (#177, 1986) bombed, he returned back to his rock roots with *Even Worse* (#27,1988), which included the Michael Jackson parody "Fat." *Alapalooza* (#46, 1993) mocked the traveling summer tour Lollapalooza, and just when you thought he couldn't go any farther, or find anyone else to pick on, Yankovic turned to the Amish. *Bad Hair Day*, with the extract "Amish Paradise," landed in the Top Fifty albums of 1996.

AUTOGRAPHS

A CD, LP, magazine cover, ad, photo, or card signed by the artist: $10-$20

POSTERS/PRESS KITS

Promotional Posters: $10-$25

OFTEN OVERLOOKED MEMORABILIA

Movie memorabilia from *UHF*; a copy of the video *The Compleat Al* (1985)

The Yardbirds

Formed 1963

Keith Relf, Born: March 22, 1943, Died: May 14, 1976; Chris Dreja, Born: November 11, 1946; Jim McCarty, Born: July 25, 1943; Paul Samwell-Smith, Born: May 8, 1943; and Anthony "Top" Topham*

*Topham left in 1963 and was replaced by Eric Clapton, Born: March 30, 1945. Clapton left in 1965 and was replaced by Jeff Beck, Born: June 24, 1944. Samwell-Smith departed in 1966 and Jimmy Page, Born: January 9, 1944, was added. Beck also left in 1966. The group disbanded in 1968.

Relf, Samwell-Smith (Country Gentleman), McCarty (Country Gentleman), and Tony Topham joined forces at the Kingston Art School, Kingston, Surrey, as the Metropolitan Blues Quartet. The group began by playing small venues before crafting its trade and moving on to London, including Studio 51, before taking over the residency at Giorgio Gomelsky's Crawdday club, left vacant by the extremely popular Rolling Stones. When Topham left to return to college, he was replaced by Eric Clapton, Relf's art school friend. While reading through a Jack Kerouac book, Relf stumbled upon the name Yardbirds and applied it to the group.

The group then signed to EMI's Columbia label and cut three songs in its first recording session in February 1964. *Five Little Yardbirds* was released in December 1964 and began moving up the charts as the band opened The Beatles Christmas Show at London's Hammersmith Odeon on Christmas Eve.

"For Your Love" (#5, U.K., 1965) became the group's first major hit, as bandmate Eric Clapton departed from the band to join John Mayall's Bluesbreakers; he was replaced by Jeff Beck, formerly of the Tridents.

In April 1965 the group undertook a 21-date U.K. package tour supporting the Kinks, as "Heart of Soul" (#2, U.K., 1965) climbed the British charts. By the summer, "For Your Love" (#6, 1965) had climbed the U.S. charts while the album of the same name jumped into the Top One Hundred. The group finally began a short ten-day U.S. Tour in Chicago, IL, on September 18, 1965. While single "Heart Full of Soul" (#9, 1965) ascended on the U.S. charts, the band performed the song on the ABC television show *Shindig* (9/23/65). In November the band began a 16-date U.K. tour as "I'm a Man" (#17, 1965) climbed the U.S. singles chart.

In January of the following year (1966), *The Yardbirds with Sonny Boy Williamson*, recorded in December 1963, was released by Fontana, and "Shape of Things" (#3, U.K.; #11, U.S., 1966) peaked in March. On May 1, 1966, the Yardbirds took part in the annual New Musical Express Poll Winners Concert at the Empire Pool, Wembley, U.K. A month later Samwell-Smith decided to leave the band, opting for a career as a producer. Dreja then moved to bass, and session guitarist Jimmy Page joined the band. He made his debut with the band on June 21, 1966, at the Marquee in London.

As "Over Under Sideways Down" (#10, U.K.; #11, U.S.,1966) moved up the charts, the group joined Dick Clark's Caravan of Stars U.S. tour from August 5 to September 4, 1966. For a short time during this tour both Page and Beck shared lead guitar, until Beck fell prey to illness. *Yardbirds* (#20, U.K., 1966) and *Over Under Sideways Down* (#52, U.S., 1966) maintained the band's presence on major album charts and continued to be supported by the band including the 12-date Rolling Stones '66 tour. On October 23, 1966, the band played at the Fillmore Auditorium in San Francisco, just five days before embarking on another Dick Clark Tour. Beck, increasingly uncomfortable with his situation, quit the tour.

Now a four piece band, it began the year with a Far East tour, then an appearance at the Cannes Film Festival (5/8/67) to coincide with their appearance in the film *Blow Up*. Meanwhile *The Yardbirds Greatest Hits* (#28, 1967) and *Little Games* (#80, 1967) attacked the charts. "Ten Little Indians" (#96, 1967), penned by Harry Nilsson, peaked in November as the band begins an altercation with their record company over distribution and release.

In January 1968 the band entered the studio for their final record "Goodnight Sweet Josephine." The band then went on tour in the U.S. from March 22 to April 28, 1967, before a short visit to Japan. On July 7, 1968, the band split following its final gig in Luton, Beds., U.K. Relf and McCarty formed Together, which would eventually become Renaissance, while Page and Dreja formed the New Yardbirds, primarily to fulfill contractual obligations. Dreja eventually left to pursue a successful career in commercial photography. He was replaced by John Paul Jones, who joined Page, vocalist Robert Plant, and drummer John Bonham in a lineup that soon became known as Led Zeppelin.

Dreja, McCarty, and Samwell-Smith eventually even reunited for gigs in June 1983 at the Marquee Club—augmented by a lead vocalist. *The Yardbirds Featuring Performances by Jeff Beck, Eric Clapton, Jimmy Page* (#155, 1970) was one of the band's final compilations to hit the album charts. On January 15, 1992, the band was inducted into the Rock and Roll Hall of Fame, its place in music history now firmly entrenched.

AUTOGRAPHS

Group:

A CD, LP, magazine cover, ad, photo, or card signed by the entire band: $500-$750

Page, Relf, McCarty, Dreja, and Beck: $700-$750

Individual

Keith Relf: $40-$55

Jim McCarty: $20-$35

Tony Topham: $10-$15

Jeff Beck: (See Entry)

Chris Dreja: $15-$20

Paul Samwell-Smith: $10-$15

Eric Clapton: (See Entry)

Jimmy Page: (See Entry)

USED CLOTHING/EQUIPMENT

Guitar Picks:

See individual or associated band entries.

OFTEN OVERLOOKED MEMORABILIA

Memorabilia from the first Rhythm & Blues Festival (2/28/64) (Yardbirds performed), and the National Jazz & Blues Festival (86/65) at the Athletic Club, Richmond, U.K.; memorabilia from Michelangelo Antonioni's film *Blow Up* (the band appeared in sequence); any items relating to the one week release of *Live Yardbirds Featuring Jimmy Page*, Epic, 1971, which Page managed to block via legal threats

REFERENCES/BOOKS

Limited resources exist, but none do justice to the group in my opinion. There are no dedicated collector books.

Yearwood, Trisha

Born: September 19, 1964

Trisha Yearwood packed her bags and headed to Nashville in 1985. Like all seeking fame and fortune, she made as many connections as possible and recorded demo tapes. It wasn't long before she caught the eye of Garth Brooks, who was so impressed he enlisted her to tour with him. It was Brooks who began to open a few doors for the young singer, one of which led to producer Garth Fundis. Upon hearing the singer, Fundis jumped at the opportunity to record Yearwood. Her debut record *Trisha Yearwood* (#2, C&W, 1991) was met with overwhelming enthusiasm, while extracted hit single "She's in Love with the Boy" (#1, C&W, 1991) kept driving the album up the charts. "Like We Never Had a Broken Heart" (#4, C&W, 1991) and "That's What I Like About You" (#8, C&W, 1992) also climbed the singles chart, as Yearwood was recognized as Top New Female Vocalist by the Academy of Country Music in 1992.

Hearts in Armor (#46, 1992) was her welcomed sophomore effort and included country hits "Wrong Side of Memphis" (#5, C&W, 1992), "The Woman Before Me" (#4, C&W, 1992), and "Walkaway Joe" (#2, C&W, 1993), a powerful duet with Eagle Don Henley.

The Song Remembers When (#40, 1993) was her third album and included the singles "You Say You Will" (#12, C&W, 1993), "Down on My Knees" (#19, C&W, 1993), and the title track (#2, C&W, 1993). Yearwood also found time to contribute "New Kid in Town" to the Eagles tribute album *Common Thread*.

In 1994 Yearwood hooked up with Aaron Neville to duet on the Patsy Cline favorite "I Fall to Pieces," for the anthology *Rhythm, Country and Blues*. *Thinkin' About You* (#3, 1995), her fourth album, exhibited much of the maturity one would expect from Yearwood. "Everybody Knows" finished at #63 for the year 1996, while single "Believe Me Baby (I Lied)" finished at #22.

A great subject to collect, Yearwood only entices collectors by being so nice to her fans. Begin your collecting with promotional items from her MCA debut release while you can still find some things!

AUTOGRAPHS

A CD, LP, magazine cover, ad, photo, or card signed by the artist: $15-$25

TOUR BOOKS/PROGRAMS/PASSES

Backstage Passes:
Cloth: $8-$10; Laminated: $10-$12

POSTERS/PRESS KITS

Press Kits: $10-$25,
Example: Trisha Yearwood - $25,
Hearts In Armor - $15-$17,
Everybody Knows - $15

OFTEN OVERLOOKED MEMORABILIA

Memorabilia from the movie Honeymoon in Vegas (1992) (she contributed "You're The Devil in Disguise") and *This Thing Called Love*; all associated Revlon Wild Heart perfume promotional items, posters, samples, etc.

REFERENCES/BOOKS

Get Hot or Go Home—Trisha Yearwood: The Making of a Nashville Star by Lisa Gubernick

Yes

Formed 1968

Jon Anderson, Born: October 25, 1944; Peter Banks; Tony Kaye, Born: January 11, 1945; Chris Squire, Born: March 4, 1948; and Bill Bruford, Born: May 17, 1949*

*Banks left in 1971 and Steve Howe, Born: April 8, 1947, was added. Kaye also left the same year and was replaced by Rick Wakeman, Born: May 18, 1949. Bruford departed in 1972 and Alan White, Born: June 14, 1949, was added on drums. Wakeman left in 1974 and was replaced by Patrick Moraz. Moraz left in 1976 and Wakeman returned. Anderson and Wakeman both left in 1980 and were replaced by Trevor Horn and Geoffrey Downes. The group re-formed in 1983: Anderson, Kaye, Squire, White, and Trevor Rabin. Anderson left again in 1990. Anderson, Bruford, Wakeman, and Howe was formed in 1991. The group re-formed in 1993.

A chance meeting in a Soho night club between Jon Anderson and Chris Squire led to the formation of Yes. Adding Peter Banks, Tony Kaye, and Bill Bru-

ford to the duo, and taking advantage of Anderson's industry contacts proved to be an invaluable start for Yes. The band even was fortunate enough to open Cream's farewell concert at London's Royal Albert Hall on November 26, 1968. The gig led to a steady run at the Marquee club in London. The group also opened for Janis Joplin at the Royal Albert Hall on April 21, 1969. Just before signing with Atlantic Records the band had a chance to perform at the Montreux TV Festival in Switzerland on April 25-26, 1969, which they took full advantage of.

The band's self-titled debut album was released in November 1969; by then the band had won nearly instant critical acclaim for its live performances. Like any band, changes were inevitable. Peter Banks, formerly with bands such as Savoy Brown, was the first casualty. He was replaced by Steve Howe (formerly the Syndicate and Tomorrow), who made his first London appearance with the band on March 21, 1970, at Queen Elizabeth Hall. Howe's influence was immediately evident during the recording of *The Yes Album* (#40, 1971), the group's first commercial breakthrough release. By now critics were panning the band as a leader in the burgeoning progressive classical rock field.

Tony Kaye then departed in August 1971 to form Badger. Replacing him was ex-Strawbs showman, keyboardist Rick Wakeman. On September 30, 1971, the group, with the new keyboardist, set out on a 23-date U.K. tour in Leicester, U.K. Because this was the group's first major tour, it marked a good place for Yes collectors to begin their pursuit of memorabilia.

Fragile (#4, 1972) unified the group's now distinct sound and was the first release to feature the cover artwork of Roger Dean. It was Dean who designed the group's logo and was responsible for the futuristic artwork that became a hallmark of the band. The album yielded the edited single "Roundabout" (#13, 1972), a song that became a live favorite with Yes fans. *Close to the Edge* (#3, 1972) followed the success of its predecessor, allowing the group to take greater freedom with song arrangements and their length. It spun off the lengthy single "And You and I (Part II)" that made it into the Top Fifty in the U.S. The band's next casualty was drummer Bill Bruford, who quit to join King Crimson; ex-Plastic Ono band member Alan White replaced him.

The band's success led to Wakeman's solo offering *The Six Wives of Henry VIII* (#30, 1973) and the ambitious *Yessongs* (#12, 1972), a three-album live performance release. To compliment its work, the band also premiered a movie with the identical title the following year. The band's next studio release was the aggressive two-album set *Tales from Topographic Oceans* (#6, 1974), which quickly sold gold. Following the success of its latest release, the group announced plans for each member to release a solo

album. Unfortunately Rick Wakeman had other plans and announced he was leaving the band. He was replaced by ex-Refugee member Patrick Moraz on August 18, 1974.

Relayer (#5, 1974) followed and was extremely similar in format to *Close to the Edge*. It featured "The Gates of Delirium," based on Tolstoy's novel *War and Peace*. *Yesterdays* (#17, 1975) was a compilation release that even included tracks form the group's first two albums. The release gave the band members time to pursue individual projects. The solo efforts that followed included Howe's *Beginnings* (#63, 1975), Squire's *Fish Out of Water* (#69, 1975), Moraz's *Patrick Moraz* (#132, 1976), and Anderson's *Olias of Sunhollow* (#47, 1976). Following Anderson's release, it became clear that the whole was far greater than the sum of its parts. On December 3, 1976, Wakeman rejoined the band, replacing Moraz who eventually found himself in the Moody Blues. Yes then returned with *Going for the One* (#8, 1977), followed by *Tormato* (#10, 1978). The compressed, yet commercially appealing song structures provided a nice transition for the band, and were well accepted by fans.

In March 1980, following an unsuccessful attempt to record a new album, both Anderson and Wakeman left the band. On May 18, 1980, it was announced that two members of the Buggles, Trevor Horn and Geoff Downes, had joined the band. In August of the same year, Yes released *Drama* (#18, 1980), of which not much was included. To no one's surprise, the group's rumored break-up was confirmed on April 18, 1981. The family tree then grew an unexpected off-shoot when Squire and White joined forces with ex-Led Zeppelin members Robert Plant and Jimmy Page to form an anticipated supergroup although nothing ever came about. Downes and Howe then moved to Asia, and released an impressive debut album. Meanwhile, Anderson, who teamed up with Vangelis, was enjoying enormous success—selling out Madison Square Garden three straight nights! Squire and White planned to start a band called Cinema, only to find themselves in mid-1983 with Anderson, Kaye, and Trevor Rabin in a re-formed YES.

90125 (#5, 1983), ignited by "Owner of a Lonely Heart" (#1, 1983), was the band's next release and triumphant return. The band's new style was fresh and very well received by the public. Some claimed it was due to producer Trevor Horn, while others insisted that the band finally found the right recipe. By *Big Generator* (#15, 1987), Rabin's songwriting was noticeably dominating the band, a situation that no doubt led to Anderson's departure. The end of the decade found the members involved in legal battles over the group's name. When they finally put the issue behind them, all eight members reconciled for *Union* (#15, 1991).

Talk (#33, 1994) reunited Anderson, Rabin, Squire, Kaye, and White and was supported by a U.S. tour from June 2 to September 10, 1994.

AUTOGRAPHS

Group:
A CD, LP, magazine cover, ad, photo, or card signed by the entire band: $150-$300*
*High-end reflects vintage signed memorabilia or the lineup of Bruford, Anderson, Squire, Howe, Wakeman (8/71-7/72)

Individual:

Jon Anderson: $35-$45	Peter Banks: $25-$35
Tony Kaye: $20-$30	Chris Squire: $35-$45
Bill Bruford: $30-$40	Steve Howe: $35-$45
Rick Wakeman: $30-$40	Alan White: $25-$35
Patrick Moraz: $10-$15	Trevor Horne: $5-$15
Geoffrey Downes: $10	Trevor Rabin: $10

TOUR BOOKS/PROGRAMS/PASSES

Tour Books:
1975, U.S. Tour: $40
Yesshows World Tour
1977: $40
1979, U.S. Tour: $75
Tormato Tour: $75
Yesshows 1979/80 U.K., scarce: $75
World Tour 1984: $25
Union Tour: $40

Backstage Passes:
Cloth: $8-$15; Laminated: $15-$25 (Post-1980)

A Yes backstage pass

POSTERS/PRESS KITS
Promotional posters: $10-$75, For example, Yesyears promotional poster two-sided (24" x 36") - $30
Press Kits: $20-$80

USED CLOTHING/EQUIPMENT

Guitar Picks:

Peter Banks: $40-$50*	Chris Squire: $45-$75
Steve Howe: $45-$100	Trevor Rabin: $15-$30

*scarce and difficult to authenticate

Drum Sticks:
Bill Bruford: $25-$40
Alan White: $20-$35

OFTEN OVERLOOKED MEMORABILIA

A *Relayer* numbered limited edition (9800), (34" x 21.5") - $100; Press release announcing the band's new lineup included in *Into the Lens*, Atlantic one-sided promotional album; Owner of a Lonely Heart black football - $8-$10; Compton's New media CD-ROM Yes: Active; movie memorabilia from the 1925 movie classic *Phantom of the Opera* (Wakeman wrote score for reissued film (1991)); movie memorabilia associated with the official FIFA 1982 World Cup film *Goal!*; all associated memorabilia from members' solo releases, "Tormato" display - $80

```
***********************
```

Yo La Tengo

Notable Yo La Tengo efforts include *President Yo La Tengo* (Coyote, 1989) and *Painful* (Matador, 1993). Collectors can begin here and just wait, wait for Yo La Tengo to sort out the sounds that seem to be trapped within their heads.

```
***********************
```

Dwight Yoakam. Photo by Steve Jennings. Courtesy Reprise Records.

Yoakam, Dwight

Born: October 23, 1956

Honky-tonk to the heart, Yoakam was raised on classic country music (Hank Williams, Bill Monroe, etc,) as a child in southern Ohio. By the time he was in high school had his own rockabilly band. He attended Ohio University to study history and philosophy, but his calling to Nashville seemed to out weight the significance of everything else in his life, so he traveled to the capital of country music in the mid-70s. When he failed to get anyone to recognize his potential in Tennessee, he relocated to L.A. and quickly began to establish some roots by playing in local clubs and opening for a variety of acts including Los Lobos.

To supplement his income he worked days as a truck driver and at various other odd jobs. He managed to score brief recording stints first with Oak Records, followed by Enigma, but little attention was paid to the releases. In 1986, now signed to resurrected Reprise Records, he entered the country charts with a Johnny Horton cover called "Honky Tonk Man" (#3, C&W,1986). The following month his debut album release *Guitars, Cadillacs, Etc., Etc.* (#61, 1986) showcased his California honky tonk sound, along with a good bit of his songwriting. Stetson-fitted Yoakam initially appealed to a non-country base and even attracted a strong yet unanticipated U.K. audience.

Hillbilly Deluxe (#55, 1987), recorded in L.A., quickly became an impressive sophomore offering for the artist who, along with other "newcomers" like Randy Travis, were being labeled as part of the "new country" scene. *Buenas Noches from a Lonely Room* (#68, 1988) topped out in September 1988, and fizzled faster than a beer on a night stand. While the following month Yoakam received his first Country chart-topper "Streets of Bakersfield", a duet with his childhood idol Buck Owens. By then Yoakam had es-

tablished a reputation for snubbing the country scene in Nashville, and his California-themed single certainly didn't help relations. Although Yoakam continued to produce, his efforts, unlike peers such as Randy Travis, were often overlooked by the Nashville-based country media. "I Sang Dixie" (#1, C&W, 1989), also extracted from his third album, became his eighth Top Ten on the country charts. *Just Lookin' for a Hit* (#68, 1989) was followed by *If There Was a Way* (#96, 1990) and the emotional *This Time* (#25, 1993), which included the hit "Ain't That Lonely Yet" (#2, C&W, 1993). *Dwight Live* (#56,1995) was released in the summer of 1995, followed by the November release *Gone* (#30, 1995).

AUTOGRAPHS

A CD, LP, magazine cover, ad, photo, or card signed by the artist: $25-$40

TOUR BOOKS/PROGRAMS/PASSES

Backstage Passes:
Cloth: $10-$12; Laminated: $12-$15

POSTERS/PRESS KITS

Promotional Posters:
$10-$25, Example: This Time - $10
Press Kits: $20-$35, Example: This Time - $30

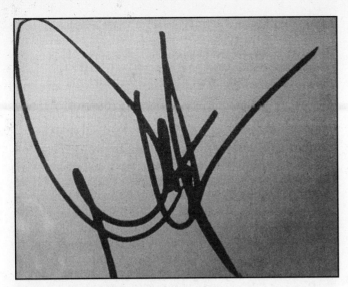

The signature of Dwight Yoakam

USED CLOTHING/EQUIPMENT
Guitar Picks: $25-$40

OFTEN OVERLOOKED MEMORABILIA
Memorabilia from the movies *Red Rock West*, *White Sands* (soundtrack), and *Honeymoon in Vegas* (contributed "Suspicious Minds" (#35, C&W, 1992)); playbill from his acting debut in *Southern Rapture* at the Met Theater in L.A. (1993); any memorabilia associated with his contribution of "Truckin'" that appeared on *Dedicated*; videotapes from his appearances on the *Late Show With David Letterman* (2/1/95), *Saturday Night Live* (4/9/94), *Late Night With David Letterman* (5/13/93 and 11/30/90), *The Tonight Show* (3/26/93), "Hats Off to Minnie—America Honors Minnie Pearl" (10/26/92), and *P.S. I Love You* (12/14/91)

****

"On The Edge"

Young Marble Giants

Collectors can grab what they can from *Colossal Youth* (1980; Crepuscule, 1994). Both the band and album became just more forgotten fossils looking for a museum home following a key archeological dig.

****

Young, Neil

Born: November 12, 1945

Young grew up in Winnipeg, Canada. His interest in music found him playing in several high school bands including the Esquires, the Stardusters, and the Squires. While playing and enjoying the local folk clubs, he met Stephen Stills and Joni Mitchell. In the mid-60s he moved to Toronto, where he first performed solo and then joined the Mynah Birds. When this venture failed, he and bandmate Bruce Palmer headed to L.A. in Young's very conspicuous Pontiac hearse. When they arrived on the West Coast, they crossed paths with Stills and another mutual friend, Ritchie Furay. With Dewey Martin, they all decided to form Buffalo Springfield in March 1966.

Buffalo Springfield played its last gig on May 5, 1968, in Long Beach, CA, after which Young went on to pursue a solo career. He recorded debut *Neil Young* on Reprise Records and released it in January 1969, but it was not until his sophomore effort was released a few months later that anyone really took notice. *Everybody Knows This Is Nowhere* (#34, 1969) was supported by the hastily formed backing band Crazy Horse. The record included three Young to-be classics: "Cinnamon Girl," "Down by the River," and "Cowgirl in the Sand." Young later claimed all three were written in one day while he was sick.

During this period Young decided to split his time between Crazy Horse and Crosby, Stills and Nash. On July 25, 1969, he played his first gig with the latter at the Fillmore East, N.Y. Although asked only to join for live work, he recorded with the group during the next two decades. *Deja Vu*, the group's debut release, quickly became the year's best selling album, thrusting each member into the spotlight as a rock superstar. In the wake of the popularity,

Neil Young. Photo by Mike Hashimoto. Courtesy Reprise Records.

Young's "Cinnamon Girl" (#55, 1970) was extracted from his second album. Although still with CSN&Y, Young released his solo offering *After the Goldrush* (#8, 1970) and finished the year watching "Only Love Can Break Your Heart" (#33, 1971) climb the singles chart.

In March, Young's groundbreaking fourth solo album *Harvest* (#1, 1972) hit the top of the charts. Extracted singles "Heart of Gold" (#1, 1972) and "Old Man" (#31, 1972) proved to be FM favorites for years, while album sales exceed three million in the U.S. *Journey Through the Past* (#45, 1972) chronicled Young's career in a double album set, and later a film, but added only one new song, "Soldier." *Time Fades Away* (#22, 1973) featured further collaborations with David Crosby and Graham Nash, while Young toured the U.K. with the Eagles. The Crazy Horse lineup had been altered following the death of guitarist Danny Whitten in 1972. Its members were now Ralph Molina, Billy Talbot, Nils Lofgren, and Ben Keith.

Young reunited with CS&N as *On the Beach* (#16, 1974) featuring the unforgettable single "Walk On" (#69, 1974) climbed the chart under mixed reviews. *Tonight's the Night* (#25, 1975), dedicated to Whitten and a former roadie Bruce Berry, featured live tracks with no overdubbing — unheard of for this era. Young followed it with *Zuma* (#25, 1975), an album that contained one CSN&Y song, "Through My Sails."

Long May You Run (#26, 1976) featured Stills and Young and was release prior to the Young's attendance at "The Last Waltz" on November 25, 1976. *American Stars 'n' Bars* (#21, 1977) featured the artist back on his own, with guest vocal spots by Linda Ronstadt, Emmylou Harris, and Nicolette Larson. In ever prolific Young fashion, *Decade*, a three-disc retrospective, was released as a historical chronicle. The platinum record, which is rare for a package marketed in this format, bought the artist some time to concentrate on his next work.

Comes a Time (#7, 1978), primarily an acoustic effort, was very well received as Young departed on the Rust Never Sleeps Tour. The tour produced both a concert film and an album (#8, 1979) by the same name. *Live Rust* (#18, 1979) soon followed — Young's obsession with the reddish-brown coating formed on iron or steel continued.

Hawks and Doves (#30, 1980) was his first release of the new decade, now without Crazy Horse and featuring Levon Helm. It was followed by the R&B influenced *Re•ac•tor* (#27, 1981), his last record for Reprise. Possibly influenced by his work with Devo on his *Human Highway* film, Young released the techno-tinged *Trans* (#19, 1983, Geffen), followed by *Everybody's Rockin'* (#46, 1983). Country flavored *Old Ways* (#75, 1985) sounded forced, possibly due to a lawsuit with Geffen Records claiming that Young was delivering an unsuccessful or an inferior prod-

uct. In an interesting dichotomy of sorts, Young's next release *Landing on Water* (#46, 1986) was very hard edged in contrast to its predecessor. He continued to try to recapture his sound with *Life* (#75, 1987), but when it didn't happen, Geffen dropped him.

In 1988 Young returned to Reprise and delivered *This Note's for You* (#61, 1988), a satirical attack on corporate sponsorship in music. In what most considered to be an excellent move, he returned to CS&N to record *American Dream* (#16, 1988), a well received album that seemed to bolster his confidence. He followed up the effort with *Freedom* (#35, 1989), which found Young back at home in the Top Forty on the U.S. album chart. The album was chosen by *Rolling Stone* as the 1989 Critic's Choice for Best Album.

Ragged Glory (#31, 1990) found Young back with Crazy Horse, churning out a heavier sound. In an unexpected move, he supported the album with a tour featuring Sonic Youth and Social Distortion as opening acts. Just when it appeared that he had found his groove, he released the catastrophic *Weld* (#154, 1991), a three-disc set that failed to put anything together. It was his first album in twenty-two years that didn't enter the U.S. Top One Hundred.

In another extraordinary move, Young released the sequel to *Harvest, Harvest Moon* (#16, 1992). Similar in format and style, the release was praised and secured Young's reputation once again. During the summer, *Unplugged* (#23, 1993) was released and contained some outstanding and emotion renditions to some of the artist's classic works.

In a tribute to his strength as an artist, *Sleeps with Angels* (#9, 1994) debuted in the Top Ten, despite no promotion or touring. The album's title cut was about the death of Nirvana lead singer Kurt Cobain, who left a suicide note that contained a quote from a Young song. Young then hooked up with Pearl Jam, an association that began when Eddie Vedder inducted the artist into the Rock and Roll Hall of Fame on January 12, 1995. The group backed him on *Mirror Ball* (#5, 1995).

Highly creative, albeit a bit off the wall at times, Neil Young is a visionary, an eloquent singer/songwriter who has endured because he has never forgotten that music is a dynamic entity. He is one of the few artists who can feel comfortable playing an acoustic ballad alone, or cutting some heavy guitar riffs with Pearl Jam. Highly prolific, my guess is that he still has albums worth of material in cans lining the vaults at Reprise, although Geffen probably found better uses for its items. As he will endure, now is the time to grab as much memorabilia as you can — while you can still find some.

AUTOGRAPHS

A CD, LP, magazine cover, ad, photo, or card signed by the artist: $50-$100*

*High-end reflects vintage signed memorabilia

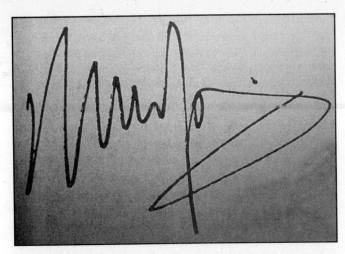

Neil Young's signature

TOUR BOOKS/PROGRAMS/PASSES
Tour Books:
North America 1987: $15
Backstage Passes:
Cloth: $8-$12; Laminated: $12-$20 (post 1990)

A Neil Young back-
stage pass

POSTERS/PRESS KITS
Promotional Posters:
$10-$50 (1976 - present)
Examples: Mirror Ball - $25,
Rust Never Sleeps
(24" x 36") cartoon drawing - $25
Press Kits: $15-$40 (1976-present),
Examples: General 1981 - $17,
Mirror Ball - $20, Broken Arrow- $15

USED CLOTHING/EQUIPMENT
Guitar Picks: $30-$60

OFTEN OVERLOOKED MEMORABILIA
Movie memorabilia from *Landlord* (soundtrack), *Journey Through the Past* (1973), *Rust Never Sleeps* (1979), *Human Highway* (1982), *Philadelphia* (1994), and *Dead Man Walking* (1996); Lionel Train items (Young owns 30% interest in Linotech); Sleeps with Angels - display - $15; Rockin' in the Free World - counter display - $20; Broken Arrow promo metal, arrow shaped like desk display - $75, - life size "Harvest" stand-up display - $300

REFERENCES/BOOKS
Neil Young, The Visual Documentary by John Robertson (1994) - $20; *Complete Guide to the Music Of* by Rogan - $8. There are no dedicated collector books.

Young, Paul

Born: January 17, 1956

Young was enticed at an early age to pursue piano, and by age fourteen, he had even tried his hand at the bass. Having already played in the local outfit Kat Kool & the Kool Kats, he formed the rock group Streetband, which signed to Logo Records. Following the release of two albums and the novelty U.K. hit "Toast" (1978), the Streetband split. Young took John Gifford and Mick Pearl on to form the eight-piece Q Tips.

The group signed to Chrysalis and released the self-titled *Q Tips* (#50, U.K., 1980). It was the group's only release and, despite extensive touring, the band's only chart appearance. Following the release of *Live at Last* the band split up. Young went on to sign a solo deal with CBS/Columbia; he released his debut single "Iron Out the Rough Spots." But it was not until "Wherever I Lay My Hat (That's My Home)" (#1, U.K., 1983), the popular Marvin Gaye cover, was released that the artist had a hit single. The singles were included on his debut album *No Parlez* (#79, 1984), which was supported by a tour with his backup band the Royal Family band and backup singers the Fabulous Wealthy Tarts. When Young's voice failed him during the tour, he was forced to convalesce. As "Come Back and Stay (#22, 1984) and "Love of the Common People" (#45, 1984) climbed the chart, his backup band split to forge its own path.

A new singing trio was added and a healthy Young went back on the road in support of singles "I'm Gonna Tear Your Playhouse Down" (#9, U.K.; 1984, #13, U.S.) and "Everything Must Change" (#9, U.K., 1984). It would be the single "Everytime You Go Away" (#1, 1985), a Daryl Hall cover, that would really bring Young into the spotlight. As his new band gelled, they watched his sophomore album release *The Secret of Association* (#19, 1985) sell into the Top Twenty. Numerous invitations were then extended to him to participate in festivals and benefits including Live Aid (7/13/85) and the Prince's Trust Rock Gala (6/20/86).

Between Two Fires (#77, 1986) sold well and included singles "Some People" (#65, 1986) and "Why Does a Man Have to Be Strong" (#63, 1987). It preceded an eighteen month period of inactivity for the artist who focused on his family life. *Other Voices* (#142, 1990), his fourth solo album, gained modest sales, as single "Oh Girl" (#8,1990), a revival of the 1972 classic Chi-Lites tune, landed him in the Top Ten on the U.S. singles chart.

From Time to Time/The Singles Collection (#1, U.K., 1991) was a CBS hit retrospective that gave Young time to concentrate on his U.K. only effort *The Crossing* (#23,1993). He contributed "I'm Your Pup-

pet" to Elton John's *Duets* album. "It Will Be You" (#34, U.K., 1996) climbed the U.K. charts in the spring while Young prepared for the soul release *Reflections* (#64, U.K., 1994).

Young is a good example of an artist who is easier to collect in the U.K. than in the U.S. Before choosing him as a collectable subject, be aware of the limitations you may face in acquiring some of his materials.

AUTOGRAPHS

A CD, LP, magazine cover, ad, photo, or card signed by the artist: $20-$30*

*Higher in the U.K.

TOUR BOOKS/PROGRAMS/PASSES

Tour Books:
World Tour 1983: $10
World Tour 1987: $10

Backstage Passes:
Cloth: $8-$10; Laminated: $10-$12

POSTERS/PRESS KITS

Promotional Posters: $15-$25*

*Not particularly easy to find in the U.S.

Press Kits: $15-$25

OFTEN OVERLOOKED MEMORABILIA

Movie memorabilia from *Switch* (1991)

The Youngbloods/Jesse Colin Young

Formed 1965

Jesse Colin Young (Perry Miller), Jerry Corbitt, Joe Bauer, and Banana (Lowell Levinger)*

*Corbitt left in 1969 and Michael Kane was added in 1971. Bauer died in 1988.

Young, while working as a folk singer in New York, met Bobby Scott, who helped him land a single release solo deal with Capital Records, *The Soul of a City Boy*. He then moved to Boston to play the clubs and released his follow-up album *Youngblood* on Mercury Records. He then teamed up with Jerry Corbitt to form the Youngbloods, which released "My Babe" before Joe Bauer and Banana (Lowell Levinger) were added.

The Youngbloods (#131, 1967), the group's RCA debut, included singles "Grizzly Bear" (#52, 1967) and the hallmark "Get Together" (#62, 1967). *Earth Music* quickly followed, and Corbitt left to pursue a solo career. The following year found the band playing several stints at the Avalon Ballroom in San Francisco and at festivals including the Sky River Rock Festival and Lighter-than-air Fair.

"Get Together" (#5, 1969) was rejuvenated through its promotional use in an ad campaign, while *Elephant Mountain* (#118, 1969) was released. Extracted single "Darkness Darkness" (#86, 1970) scored moderate success as the group signed a new record deal with Warner Brothers. *The Beast of the*

Youngbloods (#144, 1970), an RCA release, came before the group's new label (Racoon) release *Rock Festival* (#80, 1970). The following year three album releases maintained the group's exposure: *Ride the Wind* (#157, 1971), *Sunlight* (#186, 1971) (another RCA compilation), and *Good 'n' Dusty* (#160, 1971).

In 1972 the group began to pursue solo avenues: Young released *Together* (#157, 1972), Banana had *Mid Mountain Ranch*, and Bauer experimented with *Moonset*. The final group album was *High on a Ridgetop* (#185, 1972).

In 1973 Young began what eventually became a very successful solo career, issuing periodic hit albums *Song For Juli* (#51, 1973), *The Soul of a City Boy* (reissue) (#172, 1974), *Light Shine* (#37, 1974), *Songbird* (#26, 1975), *On the Road* (#34, 1976), *Love on the Wing* (#64, 1977), and *American Dreams* (#165, 1978).

AUTOGRAPHS

Group:
A CD, LP, magazine cover, ad, photo, or card signed by the group: $55*

*High-end reflects vintage signed memorabilia

Individual:
Jesse Colin Young: $20-$25

POSTERS/PRESS KITS

Promotional Posters: $10-$30
Press Kits: $15-$35

USED CLOTHING/EQUIPMENT

Guitar Picks: $15-$20

Young MC

(Marvin Young)
Born: May 10, 1967

Young MC moved to Hollis, Queens, when he was just a few years old. At an early age he began writing songs and poetry, based on the many tales he heard as a child. He started his rap career in high school. While at the University of Southern California, he met Michael Ross and Matt Dike, producers and co-owners of the Delicious Vinyl label. Young recorded "I Let 'Em Know" for the label, which garnered some success.

In 1989, linked with Tone-Loc, contributing to the pop hit "Wild Thing" (#2, 1989) and its follow-up success "Funky Cold Medina." While still in school he released his debut as Young MC, *Stone Cold Rhymin'* (#9, 1989), with extracted hits "Principal's Office" (#33, 1989) and "Bust a Move" (#7, 1989), which won a 1989 Grammy for Best Rap Performance.

Contract problems then erupted between him and Delicious Vinyl, precluding him from some outstanding projects. The whole mess was finally settled out of court in 1991. Young MC then released *Brainstorm*

(#66, 1991, Capitol), with extracted minor hit "That's the Way Love Goes" (#54, 1991). His next effort *What's the Flavor?* left a bad taste in everyone's mouth and failed commercially.

AUTOGRAPHS

A CD, LP, magazine cover, ad, photo, or card signed by the artist: $10-$15

TOUR BOOKS/PROGRAMS/PASSES

Backstage Passes:

Cloth: $8-$12; Laminated: $12-$20

Zapp/Roger

Formed 1975

Roger "Zapp" Troutman, Lester Troutman, Terry Troutman, and Larry Troutman

In 1975, Roger Troutman and his three brothers formed Roger and the Human Body. Growing up in Hamilton, Ohio, the brothers often turned to music for solace, and often experimented with the medium in search of a distinctive sound. The group recorded an independent record that found its way to George Clinton (Parliament/Funkadelic), who helped the band, now called Zapp, secure a recording contract with Warner Brothers Records.

Zapp (#19, 1980), the group's impressive debut, included the extracted singles "More Bounce to the Ounce" and "Be Alright" (#26, R&B, 1980). *Zapp II* (#25, 1982) followed and contained the hits "Doo Wah Ditty (Blow That Thing)" (#10, R&B, 1983) and "Dance Floor (Part I)" (#1, R&B, 1982). With the group's robotic funk firmly taking hold, *Zapp III* (#39, 1983), although charting lower that its predecessors, spun off singles "I Can Make You Dance (Part I)" (#4, R&B, 1983) and "Heartbreaker" (#15, R&B, 1983).

A two year delay followed before the release of *The New Zapp IV U*, with its hit single "Computer Love (Part I)" (#8, R&B, 1986). The influx of rap by the release of *Zapp V* (#156, 1989) seemed to obscure the artist's work. Roger Troutman countered with several solo albums in the '80s and '90s, one yielded hit single "I Wanna Be Your Man" (#3 pop, #1 R&B).

In 1993, now Zapp & Roger, the group released *All the Greatest Hits* (#39, 1993), which included singles "Slow and Easy" (#43, 1993) and "Meg Medley" (#54, 1993). Meanwhile Roger, who also produced, continued to pursue his solo career.

AUTOGRAPHS

A CD, LP, magazine cover, ad, photo, or card signed by the group: $15-$20

Zappa, Frank/Mothers of Invention

Born: December 21, 1940, Died: December 4, 1993

Mothers of Invention formed 1964

Musicians have included: Ray Collins, Dave Coronada, Roy Estrada, Jimmy Black, Elliot Ingber, Bunk Gradner, Jim Sherwood, Don Preston, Billy Mundi, Lowell George, Art Tripp, Ian Underwood, Howard Kaylan, Mark Volman, Jim Pons, George Duke, and Aynsley Dunbar

A prolific artist, composer, and musician, whose talents seem to transcend all boundaries, "The Master of Pop Idioms," gained notoriety through his controversial musical satires. This characteristic followed him throughout his career and even to the floor of Congress to fight against censorship. Zappa's musical intellect went with him in the studio, where he became a master in recording technology. Forever innovative, each release had to cross a new musical border, but always with a message—often political.

He began to write songs and play various instruments while attending high school in California. It was there that he met Don Van Vliet (Captain Beefheart) and they formed the Blackouts. Following graduation he penned a couple of B-movie soundtracks (*The World's Greatest Sinner* and *Run Home Slow*), which enabled him to finance the purchase of his own studio. Studio Z in Cucamonga, CA, with its modern equipment, soon became a one-off singles production facility.

In 1964 the studio was shut down after Zappa produced a mock-pornographic tape for a vice squad officer posing as a used car salesman. The $100 event cost him a ten-day sentence in jail and a three-year probation. He then moved to L.A. to form the Muthers with the remains of an earlier band (the Soul Giants). In 1965, the Muthers changed to the Mothers, were offered a management contract, and became the "ad hoc house band" at the Whiskey A-Go-Go club.

In 1966 the group, now the Mothers of Invention, was signed to MGM/Verve and recorded *Freak Out!*. Associated memorabilia from the release is now highly prized by collectors, including bumper stickers, promotional puzzle (from the album cover), and buttons. "Suzie Creamcheese" became a household word. Key gig memorabilia during this period includes tickets and programs from the Fillmore Auditorium (5/28-29), Garrick Theater, NYC (11/26), and The Trip, L.A. (5/3-29).

Absolutely Free (5/26/67) was the band's next venture. Often overlooked collectibles from this album are the song lyrics, copies of which could be obtained directly from Zappa—the record company thought they were too obscene to reproduce with the release. *Lumpy Gravy* was also released during this period.

It included a 50-piece orchestra and some of the Mothers.

We're Only in It for the Money (9/68) found the band in New York City. It was followed by *Cruising with Ruben and the Jets* (11/68), which was recorded simultaneously with *Uncle Meat*, a double album soundtrack for a never completed movie. It was during this period that his trademark complex-metering really enveloped his music. Following *Uncle Meat* he moved the band back to L.A. and married his second wife, Gail.

Zappa also started his own record company, Straight and Bizarre labels (Warner/Reprise) in 1968. The first two releases on Bizarre were *Lenny Bruce: The Berkeley Concert* and *An Evening with Wild Man Fischer (with Wild Man Fischer)*. Worth collecting in 1968 are relics from the Fillmore Auditorium (March), Fillmore East (Mother's Day Concert), and The Shrine Exposition Hall, L.A. (12/6-7) (also on the bill the GTOs, Alice Cooper, and Wild Man Fischer!).

The Mothers temporarily disbanded in October 1969—Zappa cited overwhelming expenses and public apathy. Members Lowell George and Roy Estrada founded Little Feat and Art Tripp hooked up with Beefheart. Zappa began the *200 Motels* (10/71) soundtrack and recorded his first solo album, *Hot Rats* (10/10/69). The key ticket then, and certainly collectible now, is the 1970 (5/15) performance with Zubin Mehta and the Los Angeles Philharmonic performing the score to *200 Motels* conducted by Frank Zappa. It was during the summer of 1970 that Zappa re-formed the Mothers, and recorded *Live at the Fillmore East* (8/71) and *Just Another Band from L.A.* with the band (5/72), and *Waka Jawaka* (7/5/72) and *Chunga's Revenge* (10/23/70) alone.

The band headed to Europe in 1971, and while playing The Casino in Montreux, Switzerland (12/4), the building caught fire, gutting it and destroying all of Zappa's equipment. The gig was forever immortalized *in Smoke on the Water* by Deep Purple, the opening act that evening. With just ten gigs left, the band decided to continue despite adversity. On December 10, while playing an encore at The Rainbow Theatre in London, a member of the audience (Trevor Charles Howell) ran on stage and pushed Zappa off the platform, plunging the artist ten feet into the orchestra pit. Zappa sustained multiple injuries including a broken leg. He spent most of the first half of 1972 recuperating at home. Relics from both these shows are highly sought by Zappa collectors, as is memorabilia from the 1971 Fillmore East shows (6/5 and 6/6)—John Lennon and Yoko Ono recorded with Zappa on the 6th, eventually becoming Side 4 of *Sometime in New York City*.

The Grand Wazzoo (12/72) was followed by *Over Nite Sensation* (6/73), and *Apostrophe* (4/22/74), which yielded "Don't Eat the Yellow Snow" (#86). *Bongo Fury* reunited Zappa with Beefheart, who had

disconnected himself with the artist after appearing on the cover of *Trout Mask* (1969). *Sheik Yerbouti* (#21, 3/3/79) was the first release on Zappa Records following his departure from Warner Brothers. The album lampooned the disco crowd and spun off the single "Dancin' Fool" (#45, 1979). *Joe's Garage, Act I*, Zappa's *Tommy*, was the first release of a three-act rock opera. "Catholic Girls," the third track on the album, created another characteristic controversy. During this time he also released the film *Baby Snakes*, which contained footage of the band, both on and off the stage along with clay-figure animation.

After Mercury failed to release a controversial single, Zappa started his own Barking Pumpkin label. On April 17, 1981, he hosted "A Tribute to Edgard Varese" at The Palladium in New York City. The first album Zappa ever owned was by Varese, who inspired him throughout his life. The album *Ionizations* by Varese and memorabilia from this tribute are musts for Zappaholics. In a new twist, Zappa also released a limited-edition, mail-order only three-album series, *Shut Up 'n Play Yer Guitar*.

Ship Arriving Too Late to Save a Drowning Witch was released in May 1982. The album spun off the single "Valley Girl" (#32, 1982), which parodied the spoiled daughters of San Bernardino Valley. Zappa's 1982 European Tour was tarnished during various stops. A few German gigs were canceled after the band was pummeled with objects while on stage in Kiel (5/23). A similar incident also happened in Geneva, Switzerland, on June 30. On July 14 the show was stopped in Palermo when a riot broke out, inciting Zappa to claim that it was his last European Tour.

The end of the '80s found Zappa focusing on his business affairs, advocating free-speech, and campaigning for voter registration. Zappa's merchandising end was called Barfko-Swill. In addition to the products it offered, relics from the artists non-musical endeavors are also worth picking up.

In 1988, Zappa set out on an East Coast and European tour which was documented on *Broadway the Hard Way*. It was also the year he won a Grammy for Best Rock Instrumental Performance for *Jazz from Hell* (11/15/86), a synthesizer extravaganza. He also concentrated a significant amount of his energy converting his work to the now popular compact disc format. In 1991, on the eve of a tribute concert "Zappa's Universe," his son and daughter revealed that he had been diagnosed with prostate cancer. He died on December 4, 1993, at his home in L.A.

AUTOGRAPHS

Zappa had always been fairly accessible to his fans. He typically signed "F. Zappa" or "Frank Z.," seldom choosing to sign his entire name. Full signatures can command higher prices; add another $100-$150 for these examples.

A CD, LP, magazine cover, ad, photo, or card signed by Zappa: $200-$325*

*High end reflects vintage signed memorabilia

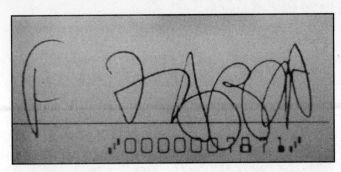

The signature of Frank Zappa

TOUR BOOKS/ PROGRAMS/PASSES

The early Fillmore programs will cost you some money, that is of course if you can find them ($75-$125). The easiest of all Zappa programs to find is from the Fall 1980 Tour, leading me to believe it that it was overproduced, or widely counterfeited.

Backstage passes remain tough to find, even counterfeit ones!

1980 Frank Zappa tour program (1980 Frank Zappa)

POSTERS/PRESS KITS

Promotional posters, primarily pre-1975, are sought by America collectors. Although not particularly easy to find, they are also not usually expensive upon discovery: $10-$50

USED CLOTHING/EQUIPMENT

Guitar Picks: $275-$300

OFTEN OVERLOOKED MEMORABILIA

Album inserts, stickers, and buttons; movie memorabilia from *The World's Greatest Sinner* (1960), *Run Home Slow*, *200 Motels*, and *Baby Snakes*; artifacts from his Studio Z in Cucamonga, CA; any items related to his "Pigs, Ponies and Rock 'n' Roll" 1969 lecture tour; videotapes of his numerous television appearances including *Late Night With David Letterman* (10/31/83), *Miami Vice* (3/86), and *Frank Zappa's Wild Wild East* talk show (2/26-28/90); a copy of his autobiography *The Real Frank Zappa Book* (1989)

Zebra

Formed 1975

Guy Gelso, Felix Haneman, and Randy Jackson

Centered around flex guitarist Randy Jackson (Shepard's Bush), Zebra scored big with its self-titled debut (#29, 1983). Jackson, who had played with Haneman (Shepard's Bush), hooked with Gus Gelso (Maelstrom) to form Zebra in 1975. Moving to Long Island, New York, in 1977, they thundered through the island's club scene, and developed a strong East Coast following.

With the band now signed to Atlantic, *Zebra* was released to accolades and strong sales, but *No Tellin' Lies* just didn't have the strength to follow the band's initial success. By the release of *V.3* (1987), and despite adding famed saxophonist Stan Bronstein (Elephant's Memory), the stripes were fading. Following the release of *Live* (1990) and seeing the writing on the wall, Jackson recorded his technologically influenced *China Rain*, his first solo album. In Rungrenesque fashion, Jackson now tours accompanied by his computer or with a band.

AUTOGRAPHS

Group:
A CD, LP, magazine cover, ad, photo, or card signed by the band: $10-$20*

Individual:
Randy Jackson: $10-$15

POSTERS/PRESS KITS

Promotional Posters: $5-$10
Press Kits: $10

USED CLOTHING/EQUIPMENT

Guitar Picks:
Randy Jackson: $10

Zevon, Warren

Born: January 24, 1947

Warren Zevon, the son of Russian immigrants, grew up in the southwest, where he taught himself to play guitar and wrote his own material. Bored with playing the local club circuit, he headed to San Francisco, via New York. His debut *Wanted—Dead or Alive* on Imperial showcased both his songwriting ability and his unique sense of humor. When the album failed, he continued writing jingles to pay the bills and working with his friends the Everly Brothers.

In 1976 "Hasten Down the Wind" was covered by Linda Ronstadt, who was at a pinnacle of popularity. The exposure drew attention to Zevon's work, which was solidified when Ronstadt also covered "Carmelita" and "Poor Poor Pitiful Me" on her *Simple Dreams* album. Jackson Browne then persuaded Zevon, who was living in Spain, to return to the U.S. and record an album. *Warren Zevon* (1976), produced by Browne, was praised by critics. The artist followed it with breakthrough album *Excitable Boy*, which included the hit single "Werewolves of London" (#21, 1978).

Zevon, who had established himself as a unique songwriter, also became known for his erratic behavior. Often referred to as the Martin Scorsese of the pop world, Zevon didn't record for two years due to

a variety of problems. *Bad Luck Street in Dancing School* and *Stand in the Fire* were both released in 1980 and marked a comeback of sorts. While his music was appreciated by the connoisseurs of pop, his satirical spin was less appreciated by the general public.

Sentimental Hygiene (1987), with backing by members of R.E.M., *Transverse City* (1989), and *Mr. Bad Example* (1991) all followed to far less commercial success. Although *Learning to Flinch* (1993), his second live album, clearly exhibited that the artist "still had it" musically, but it also showed that he "didn't still have it" commercially.

Perhaps his satires had run their course, "send lawyers guns and money" used to be cute when you heard it the first time; nowadays it seems too valid to be a satire. Whatever the problem is, Zevon still retains a bundle of creativity. Finding someone strong enough to contain it, patient enough to record it, and willing enough to package it properly seems to be the solution. Something tells me the "Boys from Athens" might be able to pull this off, but we'll see. In 1997, Zevon filled in for band leader, Paul Schaffer on CBS' *Late Show With David Letterman* for a two week stint.

Zevon is far from a boring subject to collect. In the '90s he has concentrated on writing television theme songs—he wrote scores for *Tales From The Crypt* (1992) and *Route 66* (1993)—making this another media form to collect. Memorabilia associated with his first three Asylum offerings is an excellent place to begin.

AUTOGRAPHS

A CD, LP, magazine cover, ad, photo, or card signed by the artist: $15-$20

POSTERS/PRESS KITS

Promotional Posters: $10-$30

The Zombies

Formed 1963

Colin Blunstone, Born: June 24, 1945; Paul Atkinson, Born: March 19, 1946; Rod Argent, Born: June 14, 1945; Hugh Grundy; and Paul Arnold*

*Arnold was replaced by Chris White in 1964

The Zombies were formed while Argent, Blunstone, Grundy, and Atkinson were in St. Albans Grammar School. Chris White replaced original bass player Paul Arnold in September 1963. While the band rehearsed and wrote material together, gigs at local clubs and colleges funded its new passion. In June 1964 the band, having won the a local newspaper music competition, auditioned, then signed with Decca Records.

In July 1964, the members left school and turned professional, and the debut single "She's Not There" (#12, U.K., 1964) was released. By December "She's Not There" (#2, U.S.) had sold more than a million copies in America. Amidst immigration issues, the group traveled to the U.S. in December 1964 and performed a ten day stint as part of Murray The K's Christmas Show.

"Tell Her No" (#6, 1965) was the next hit single from the debut album *The Zombies* (#39, 1965). A short U.K. tour proceeded the group's first American tour, which was a 34-date journey as part of the Dick Clark Caravan of Stars. The tour was used to support the album and the new single "She's Coming Home" (#58, 1965), which was followed by "I Want You Back Again" (#95, 1965).

"Indication" (1966) and cover "Goin' Out of My Head" (1967) were the group's final single offerings on Decca Records, which the band had been growing increasingly disenchanted with. In June 1967 the band signed with CBS/Columbia and released concept album *Odyssey and Oracle* (#95, 1969). "Friends of Mine," "Care of Cell 44," and "Time of the Season" generated interest in the recording, but by December 1967 the band had split, prior to the album's U.S. release.

In March 1969, "Time of the Season" (#3, 1969) nearly topped the charts on the way to becoming the group's second million seller. While lucrative offers to re-group were issued from the U.S., the offer was relatively ignored by former members. Meanwhile, Rod Argent began assembling members for his new band Argent, as bogus groups begin touring the U.S. as the Zombies.

AUTOGRAPHS

A CD, LP, magazine cover, ad, photo, or card signed by the artist: $25-$65*

*High end for autographed first album or sleeve to "She's Not There"

OFTEN OVERLOOKED MEMORABILIA

Movie memorabilia from *Bunny Lake Is Missing* (1966) (the group made a cameo appearance) and *Awakenings* (1991) ("Time of the Season" included on soundtrack)

Zorn, John

Born: September 2, 1953

Emerging from New York's Downtown avant-garde scene of the '80s, composer, instrumentalist, and jazz connoisseur John Zorn, who had already developed his own style, cut his first record, *The Big Gundown* (1986), on the Elektra Nonesuch label. The record was a tribute to cult spaghetti film composer Ennio Morricone.

Pooling his talents with other avant-garde innovators of his era, Zorn's music created a cult following of sorts around albums such as *Spillane* (1987), *Spy Vs. Spy: The Music of Ornette Coleman* (1989), and *Naked City* (1990). He later formed Naked City with Fred Frith, Bill Frisell, and Joey Baron. He was so well respected that when he turned forty in 1993, the Knitting Factory—NY's premier "new movement" music club—presented him for the entire month. He is well worth a listen, and probably worth setting aside some memorabilia from.

AUTOGRAPHS

A CD, LP, magazine cover, ad, photo, or card signed by the artist: $10-$20

ZZ TOP

Formed 1970

Billy Gibbons, Dusty Hill, and Frank Beard

Billy Gibbons (formerly with the Saints, the Coachmen, and the Ten Blue Flames) formed the Moving Sidewalks, a psychedelic band, in the late '60s with Lanier Gregg and Dan Mitchell. The group had a series of local hits before releasing *Flash* (Wand). The group even opened up for the Jimi Hendrix Experience in June 1968.

Meanwhile Dusty Hill, along with his older brother, formed the Warlocks, and released some local (Dallas, TX) singles and eventually recruited drummer Frank Beard. The Warlocks, with a heavy blues sound, changed its name to American Blues in 1968 and released two albums, *The American Blues Is Here on Karma* and *The American Blues Do Their Thing* (Uni Records, 1968).

As fate might have it, both groups disbanded in 1969 and Gibbons began auditions for a new Texas-Style rock band called Z.Z. Top. Through various channels, Beard and Hill joined Gibbons and released a debut single, "Salt Lick" (1969, Scat). The group then played its first ever gig in Beaumont, TX (2/10/70), while London Records inked a U.S.-only

Billy Gibbons autographed this guitar (Hard Rock Café, Key West)

deal with the band. Z.Z.Top's *First Album* spun off a locally accepted single, "Shakin' Your Tree," but it failed to sell beyond Texas. The group then took to the road for a grueling and lengthy series of concert dates, which found it opening for a wide variety of established acts.

In May 1972 the group was added as support act for the Rolling Stones' U.S. tour. The increased exposure helped push the group's next album *Rio Grande Mud* (#104, 1972) to a charting position. The group's popularity was well entrenched in Texas, where it attracted 80,000 to Z.Z. Top's First Annual Texas Size Rompin' Stompin' Barndance Bar-B-Q at the University of Texas in Austin.

Tres Hombres (#8, 1973) ignited the band's following beyond the Southern Midwest. The group embarked on a 17-date U.S. tour on August 10, 1973, in support of both the album an its hit single "La Grange" (#41, 1974). Now sporting a heavier sound, the group released *Fandango!* (#10, 1975), which yielded the now classic single "Tush" (#20, 1975). The group's expanded following even broke many attendance records in both major and minor markets.

In 1976 the sidewinders from Texas decided to take their barbecue on the road in the fashion of Z.Z.Top's Worldwide Texas Tour. Complete with 75 tons of equipment, which included nearly $150,000 worth of livestock, the tour set out to complete one hundred U.S. dates. Plans for the group's first concerts in Australia, Japan, and Europe were planned, although the later leg was canceled.

Exhausted by the lengthy tour, the band released *Tejas* (#17) in February 1977, before commencing a two year vacation. During this period London Records kicked out *The Best of Z.Z. Top* (#94), while the band began developing a new image that would carry it through the next decade. Now with Warner Brothers Records, the group reemerged, sporting lengthy beards and a new album, *Deguello* (#24, 1979). Serious touring resumed in 1980 and supported two new singles, "I Thank You" (#34) and "Cheap Sunglasses" (#89).

El Loco (#17) was released in August 1981, but the band struck pay dirt in 1983 with the release of *Eliminator* (#9, 1983). Its success attributed to brilliant marketing and creative video clips, the band enjoyed a new round of success with the MTV generation. Its Texas miner, rather than musician, image was enhanced by the appearance of a Gibbons-restored cherry red 1933 Ford coupe, which soon became part of the band's hallmark. *Eliminator* spent three and a half years on the chart and yielded the hit singles "Gimme All Your Lovin'" (#37, 1983), "Sharp Dressed Man" (#56, 1983), "Legs" (#8, 1983), and "TV Dinners." "Legs," which was eventually used in a Legg's pantyhose TV commercial, took the honors for Best Group Video during the 1984 MTV Music Video Awards. The 1984 worldwide Eliminator tour soon became a sellout.

In December 1985, the group's Afterburner Tour opened in Toronto, Ontario, Canada, the first of 212 grueling dates, in support of the new album *Afterburner* (#4, 1985). The commercially successful album included the hits "Rough Boy" (#22, 1985), "Sleeping Bag" (#8, 1985), "Velcro Fly" (#35, 1986), and "Stages" (#21, 1986). The awards continued: "Rough Boy" picked up an MTV Video Music Award for art direction, the band became official Texas Heroes, and the members were even named Texas county deputies. The Afterburner Tour finally came to a conclusion on March 21, 1987, in Honolulu, HI.

In 1988 Z.Z. Top spearheaded a drive to raise $1 million for a permanent Muddy Waters exhibit at the Delta Blues Museum in Clarksdale, MS. The band released *Recycler* (#6, 1990) and began a supporting tour on October 2, 1990, at PNE Pacific Coliseum, Vancouver, BC, Canada. The album sold far less than its predecessors and yielded only the minor hits "Doubleback" (#50, 1990) and "Give It Up" (#79, 1990). Following the Warner Brothers release of *Greatest Hits* (#9, 1992), the band left the label in favor of RCA.

Antenna (#14, 1994) was the band's debut RCA release. The band had time to appear on the *Late Show With David Letterman* CBS-TV on March 4, 1994, before supporting their new album with a U.S. Tour beginning on April 30, 1994. *One Foot in the Blues*, a two-decade collection of the band's blues treatments, was issued on November 22, 1994.

On February 15, 1996, the band conducted its first Internet chat on America On Line. Listeners were asked to bring their own barbecue sauce!

AUTOGRAPHS

ZZ Top can be elusive, yet obliging to autograph requests. I once followed their limousine to a health food store to get an autograph. The guys are big motor vehicle fans—catch them at the Z.Z./Pro Technik Racing Team gathering during the Rolex 24 Hour race in Daytona, FL or possibly at a Harley Davidson company anniversary event. Frank lives on a ranch in Fort Bend County near Houston, called Top Forty Ranch. Dusty likes sports, old Elvis movies, and the club scene and lives in Houston, TX. Billy fancies old cars, odd guitars, and even gets involved with various activities—he is a board member of the Contemporary Arts Museum in Houston.

Group:

A CD, LP, magazine cover, ad, photo, or card signed by the entire band: $65-$180

*High end reflects vintage signed memorabilia

Individual:

Billy Gibbons: $25-$50
Dusty Hill: $25-$50
Frank Beard: $20-$45

TOUR BOOKS/PROGRAMS/PASSES

Tour Books:

1981 World Tour: $20-$23
Worldwide Texas Tour: $15-$20
Donington Park, 8/17/85, U.K.: $25

ZZ Top backstage pass (Printed by Perri Ent. Services Inc.)

Backstage Passes:

Cloth: $10-$20;
Laminated: $20-$30
Examples: Afterburner Tour, "Aftershow" (cloth): $10, "Artist" (laminated) : $20

POSTERS/PRESS KITS

Promotional Posters:

$10-$25,
For example,
Antenna (40" x 60")
U.K. promo poster - $22
Press Kits: $15-$25

USED CLOTHING/EQUIPMENT

Guitar Picks:

Billy Gibbons: $15-$25
Dusty Hill: $15-$25
Drum Stick:
Frank Beard: $30-$35

A nice grouping of ZZ Top guitar picks

OFTEN OVERLOOKED MEMORABILIA

A ZZ Topper mattress (subject of a lawsuit) - $100-$125; promo Afterburner golf shirt - $50; Antenna promo sticker - $3; Recycler Tour, 1991, European Tour Scarf - $10; bumper stickers - $3-$5; The Year of the Beard Promo, 1983 — beard w/keychain - $50

REFERENCES/BOOKS

Numerous resources exist, but none do justice to the band in my opinion. There are no dedicated collector books. Serious collectors should opt for a Fan Club: ZZ Top International Fan Club, P.O. Box 19744, Houston, TX 77224 ($15 fee)

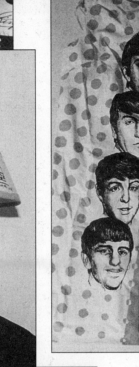

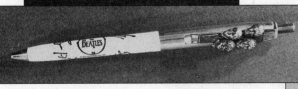

Top L to R: Miscellaneous Beatles memorabilia including a pennant (most pennants are worth between $20 and $55), a record player, and Yellow Submarine hangers (valued at $45 to $90 for the set of four); Beatles dolls from Remco (1965). The dolls are worth $40 to $80 (add 25% for John); Middle L to R: A Beatles lamp valued at $550; Beatles dress is worth about $300; Beatles Colorforms kit, a soap box, and an alarm clock and box. The Colorforms are worth $300 to $550, the soap box has an offer for inflatable dolls and contains four different colored soaps ($135 to $250), and the alarm clock with its box is worth between $400 and $700; Bottom L to R: Beatles pen. Authentic Beatles pen are worth anywhere from $40 to $100; The "Authentic Beatle Wig" manufactured by Lowell; Paul McCartney "Personality Bath" bottle in its original package (1965). It is valued at between $50 and $175.

Top L to R: The Kiss "On Tour Game"; a Kiss radio; Middle L to R: Gene Simmons doll in its original box (manufactured by Mego). It is valued at around $100; Kiss steel lunch box (worth $85), 1977, and King Seeley thermos; Bottom L to R: Kiss comics. The one at left claims it was "printed in real KISS blood," and the one at right contains a bonus pull-out poster. Kiss comics range in value from $32 (#1) to $3; Paul Stanley doll with its original box (manufactured by Mego). Notice the box was signed by Stanley. The doll with its box is valued at around $100 alone.

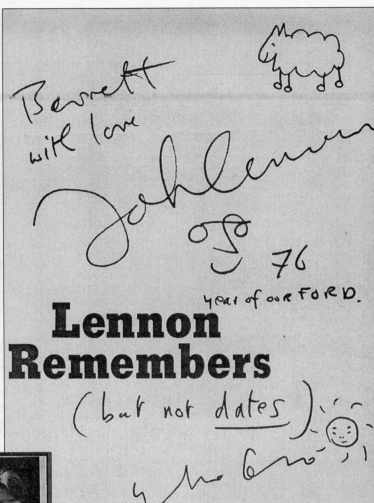

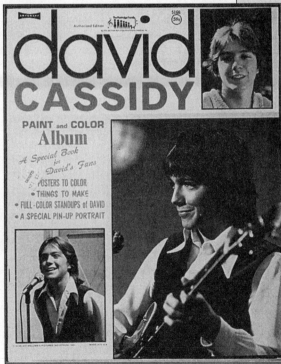

Clockwise from Top Left: Movie poster for the Beatles A Hard Day's Night; a great example of John Lennon's signature accompanied by a couple of drawings. His signature alone can fetch $700; a nice autographed Kiss concert poster. Items autographed by the members of Kiss can range in value from $175 to $275 (high end reflects vintage signed memorabilia); David Cassidy paint and color album valued at $30.

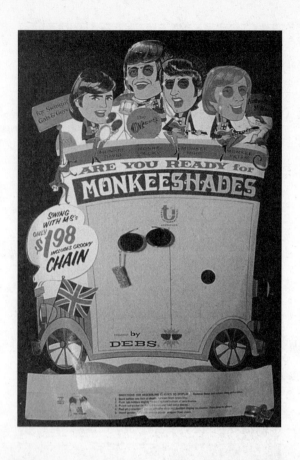

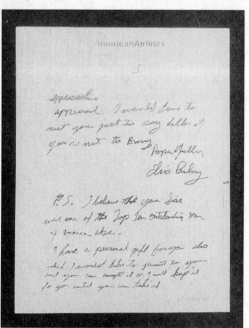

*Clockwise from Top Left: A store display for Monkees
sunglasses; RIAA gold award for Elvis Presley's Roustabout; a
piece of paper alone signed by Elvis is worth between $450 and
$550. Authentication is difficult; RIAA platinum award for
Elvis Presley's Elvis' Golden Records.*

Bibliography and Recommended Reading

Books*

ASCAP Biographical Dictionary, 4th Ed. New York: R.R. Bowker, 1980.

Augsburger, Jeff, Marty Eck, and Rick Rann. *The Beatles Memorabilia Price Guide*. Radnor, PA: Wallace Homestead Book Company, 1993.

Azerrad, Michael. *Come as You Are, The Story of Nirvana*. New York: Main Street Books, 1994.

Banasiewicz, Bill. *Rush Visions, The Official Biography*. London: Omnibus Press, 1988.

The Billboard Book of Number One Hits, 3rd. Fred Bronson, editor. New York: Billboard, 1992.

Bessman, Jim. *The Ramones, An American Band*. New York: St. Martin's Press, 1993.

Blake, Benjamin, Jack Rubeck, and Allan Shaw. *The Kingston Trio on Record*. Naperville, IL: Kingston Korner Inc., 1986.

Doughton, K.J. *Metallica Unbound, The Unofficial Biography*. New York: Warner Books Inc, 1993.

Giuliano, Geoffrey. *The Beatles: A Celebration*. London: Something Fishy Productions, Ltd, 1995.

Giuliano, Geoffrey. *The Rolling Stones Album*. New York: Viking Studio Books, 1993.

Glebbek, Caesar and Douglas Noble. *Jimi Hendrix, The Man, The Music, The Memorabilia*. New York: Thunder's Mouth Press, 1996.

Goldmine 1996 Annual. Iola, WI: Krause Publications, 1996.

Grant, Adrian. *Michael Jackson, The Visual Documentary*. London, England: Omnibus Press, 1994.

The Guitar Players. James Sallis, editor. Lincoln, Nebraska: University of Nebraska Press, 1994.

The Harmony Illustrated Encyclopedia of Rock, 7th Ed. Mike Clifford, editor. New York: Crown Publishers, 1992.

Henkel, David K. *The Official Identification and Price Guide to Rock and Roll*. New York: House of Collectibles, 1992.

Heylin, Clinton. *A Life in Stolen Moments, Day by Day: 1941-1995*. New York: Schirmer Books, 1996.

Hoover, Will. *Picks! The Colorful Saga of Vintage Celluloid Guitar Plectrums*. San Francisco: Miller Freeman Books, 1995.

Industrial Plastics: Theory and Application, 2nd ed. Terry L. Richardson, editor. Albany, New York: Delmar Publishers, Inc. 1989.

Jal de la Parra, Primm. *U2 Live: A Concert Documentary*. London: Omnibus Press, 1994.

Kay, Hilary. *Rock & Roll Memorabilia: A History of Rock Momentos*. New York: A Fireside Book, 1992.

King, Eric. *The Collector's Guide to Psychedelic Rock Concert Posters, Postcards and Handbills, 1965-1973*. Svaha Press, 1996.

Mabbett, Miles & Andy. *Pink Floyd, The Visual Documentary*. London: Omnibus Press, 1994.

Maycocl, Stephen. *Miller's Rock and Pop Memorabilia*. London: Miller's, 1994.

McDermott, John, Billy Cox, and Eddie Kramer. *Jimi Hendrix Sessions*. New York: Little, Brown and Company, 1995.

McWilliams, Courtney. *The Beatles: A Collectors Guide to Beatle Memorabilia, Yesterday & Tomorrow*. Atglen, PA: Schiffer Publsihing, Ltd., 1997.

Moody, Pau1. *Oasis, Lost Paradise*. London: UFO Music Ltd, 1996.

Morse, Greg. *A Price Guide to Rock & Roll Collectibles*. Aumsville, OR: Greg Morse, 1993.

Neely, Tim. *Goldmine Price Guide to Alternative Records*. Iola, WI: Krause Publications, 1996.

Nilsen, Per. *Prince, A Documentary*. London: Omnibus Press, 1993.

Nolan, A.M. *Rock 'n' Roll Road Trip*. New York: Pahros Books, 1992.

Osborne, Jerry. *The Official Price Guide to Elvis Presley Records and Memorabilia*. New York: House of Collectibles, 1994.

Rees, Dafydd and Luke Crampton. *Encyclopedia of Rock Stars*. New York: DK Publishing Inc., 1996.

Rees, Tony. *The VOX Record Hunter: Collector's Guide to Rock and Pop*. London: Boxtree Ltd., 1995.

Rettenmund, Matthew. *Encyclopedia Madonnica*. New York: St. Martin's Press, 1995.

Rogan, Johnny. *Crosby, Stills, Nash & Young, The Visual Documentary*. London: Omnibus Press, 1996.

Rohers, Kalen. *Tori Amos, All These Years*. London: Omnisbus Press, 1994.

The Rolling Stone Encyclopedia of Rock & Roll. New York: Rolling Stone Press, 1995.

Templeton, Steve. *Elvis! An Illustrated Guide to New and Vintage Collectibles*. Philadelphia: Courage Books, 1996.

Umphred, Neal. *Goldmine Price Guide to Collectible Record Albums*. Iola, WI: Krause Publications, 1996.

Williams, Fred. *The 1996 Rock Poster Price Guide*. Salt Lake City: Dallas Design Group, 1995.

*In addition to those referenced in the text

Periodicals

Autograph Collector, Odyssey Publications, Inc., 510-A South Corona Mall, Corona, CA 91719

Autograph Times, 1125 W. Baseline Rd. #2-153, Mesa, AZ 85210

Backstreets, Backstreets Publishing Inc., P.O. Box 51225, Seattle, WA 98115

Billboard, 1515 Broadway, New York, N.Y. 10036

Circus Magazine, 6 West 18 Street, New York, N.Y. 10011

Goldmine, Krause Publications, 700 E. State St., Iola, WI 54990

Grateful Dead Almanac, P.O. Box X, Novato, CA 94948

Guitar World, 1115 Broadway, New York, NY 10010

Hit Parader, Hit Parader Publications, Inc., 40 Violet Ave., Poughkeepsie, NY 12601

Homespun, Friends of Live, P.O. Box 20266, Lehigh Valley, PA 18002

Q Magazine/Select/MOJO, Mappin House, 4 Winsley Street, London W1N 7AR

Record Collector, 43/45 St. Mary's Road, Ealing, London W5 5RQ

Relix Mgazine, Inc., P.O. Box 94, Brooklyn, N.Y. 11229

U2 - Propaganda, P.O. Box 5406, London, W7 1ZU, England

About the Author

Mark Allen Baker is a respected author and historian, whose work has appeared in more than fifty periodicals. He is the author of numerous books, including the *Baseball Autograph Handbook, Team Baseballs, All Sport Autograph Guide, Auto Racing Memorabilia and Price Guide,* and the *Collector's Guide to Celebrity Autographs.* His work has been both referenced and featured in numerous major publications including *Sports Illustrated* and *USA Today*. Mr. Baker also acts as the historian for the International Boxing Hall of Fame in Canstota, New York. A graduate of the State University of New York, Baker has also worked in a variety of finance, marketing, sales, and executive management positions for the General Electric Corporation, Genigraphics Corporation, and Pansophic Systems, Incorporated. Additional biographical data can be found in numerous professional directories including *Who's Who in the East, Who's Who in Entertainment,* and *Who's Who in America.*

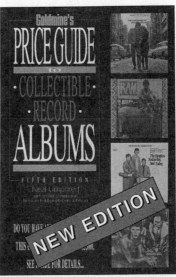